P9-DXI-536

For Reference

DISCARD

Not to be taken from this room

The
Oxford History
of the
Classical World

The
Oxford History
of the
Classical World

EDITED BY

JOHN BOARDMAN

JASPER GRIFFIN

OSWYN MURRAY

LCCC LIBRARY

DISCARD

Oxford   New York

OXFORD UNIVERSITY PRESS

1986

8-6-86 P0304&73&T

Oxford University Press, Walton Street, Oxford OX2 6DP

Oxford New York Toronto
Delhi Bombay Calcutta Madras Karachi
Kuala Lumpur Singapore Hong Kong Tokyo
Nairobi Dar es Salaam Cape Town
Melbourne Auckland

and associated companies in
Beirut Berlin Ibadan Nicosia

Oxford is a trade mark of Oxford University Press

© Oxford University Press 1986

All rights reserved. No part of this publication may be reproduced,
stored in a retrieval system, or transmitted, in any form or by any means,
electronic, mechanical, photocopying, recording, or otherwise, without
the prior permission of Oxford University Press

British Library Cataloguing in Publication Data
The Oxford history of the Classical World.
1. History, Ancient
I. Boardman, John   II. Griffin, Jasper
III. Murray, Oswyn
938   DE86

ISBN 0-19-872112-9

Library of Congress Cataloging in Publication Data

Main entry under title:
The Oxford history of the classical world.
Bibliography: p.
Includes index.
1. Civilization, Classical.   I. Boardman, John,
1927-   . II. Griffin, Jasper.   III. Murray, Oswyn.
DE59.094 1986   938   85-21774

ISBN 0-19-872112-9

Set and printed in Great Britain by
Butler & Tanner Ltd.
Frome, Somerset

REF DE59.094 1986

615980

CONTENTS

GREECE AND ROME

ROME

LIST OF COLOUR PLATES

LIST OF MAPS

ACKNOWLEDGEMENTS

THE editors wish to express their thanks to the many institutions and individuals named in the List of Illustrations for provision of photographs and drawings, and permission to use them; and to Philippa Lewis who did the picture research. A special debt of gratitude is owed to Roger Ling who undertook the main responsibility for the choice of illustrations and the writing of captions from Chapter 13 onwards. The pictures and captions of earlier chapters were chosen and written by John Boardman. Oswyn Murray compiled the Chronological Charts. The index was compiled by Peter Tickler. Many members of the Press have devoted their skills to the creation of this volume, but our principal debt must be to the authors for their patient co-operation.

Introduction

❦

JASPER GRIFFIN

THE subject of this book is enormous. In time it covers a period of well over a thousand years, from the poems of Homer to the end of pagan religion and the fall of the Roman Empire in the West. In geographical extension it begins in Greece with small communities emerging from a dark age of conquest and destruction, and with Bronze Age villages on the hills of Rome; it ends with an Empire which unified the Mediterranean world and a great deal besides, from Northumberland to Algeria, from Portugal to Syria, from the Rhine to the Nile. The fall of Rome was further removed in time from Homer than we are from the Norman Conquest; as for political scale, the Roman Empire comprised the whole or part of the territory of what are now thirty sovereign states, and it was not until 1870 that Italy, for instance, achieved again the unity which Rome had imposed before the birth of Christ.

That world is given the title 'classical'. The word carries the implication that the works of art and literature produced in Graeco-Roman antiquity possess an absolute value, that they form the standard by which all others are to be judged. In the Renaissance and even after it that was indeed what many people thought; Swift's *Battle of the Books* expresses the idea with wit and brilliance, and in painting such works as Raphael's *Parnassus* in the Vatican, showing Apollo and the Muses with the great poets of Greece and Rome, or the ineffably academic *Apotheosis of Homer* by Ingres, give it visual form. The time is past when it could make sense to think of the ancient world as passing judgment on its successors. On the one hand, the technical advances of the last five generations have transformed life in too many respects for such a comparison to make sense; on the other, interest in other early cultures outside the classical framework has shown that Greece and Rome were less unique than our ancestors supposed.

Yet while we can no longer allow to classical antiquity the exclusive dominance which its study once enjoyed in the schools and universities of Europe, it must retain a special interest for the western world. The art of Michelangelo and Rubens, the poetry of Milton and Keats, the architecture of our cities, with their domes and triumphal arches deriving from Rome and their pillared porticoes deriving from Greece, are only a few examples of the pervasive presence of the ancient world in the modern. No less important has been Greek mythology: Helen, Oedipus, Narcissus, the Minotaur in the labyrinth. Other myths have been no less haunting: Athenian democracy, Spartan austerity, the stern virtue of the Roman Republic, the luxury and order of her Empire. And that world presents, as no other can, the prospect of a society which, though distant, was not merely barbaric, but which attained high sophistication and produced great works of art, and which is in addition directly linked by history with that of the modern West, as the societies of ancient China and Peru, for instance, are not. Western civilization grew out of the classical world, and it never lost the knowledge that a high culture had preceded it, whose legacy was there to be emulated and exploited. The study of that distant but not completely alien world can allow us to understand that there are alternatives to our own ways and assumptions, and so it can help to liberate us from the tyranny of the present.

The story is a long one, the setting is wide and varied. Many varieties of human society are to be found in it: primitive villages, fiercely independent city-states, great kingdoms, even federal leagues. Democracy was invented, practised, lost. Tyrants seized power; aristocrats fought to retain it; philosophers argued and speculated on the origins of society, the nature of justice, the duties of the citizen. In the beginning there was verse and song, and with time prose literature can be seen coming into being, with philosophy and history and fiction. Rational thought struggles out of the mythical and poetic mode. We see the interaction of Greek intellectual supremacy and the irresistible military might of Rome, in many ways a tragic story, and one which is full of significance for our own time. Not less resonant for us is the twofold breach of continuity at beginning and end of our work. The polished society which produced the palaces of Minoan Crete was destroyed, and the splendours of Mycenaean Greece, the imposing citadels, the ivory and the gold, found no successors in the next three hundred years of low artistic standards, depopulation, and poverty. The fall of Rome was followed by an age of barbarian invasions, universal insecurity, destruction of cities and works of art. High civilization, once achieved, can be lost: that is among the reflections suggested by the study of the classical world.

The ancestors of the Greeks, like those of the Romans, belonged to the great Indo-European family of peoples, which spread in the course of many centuries from an original home somewhere near the Caucasus into India, Iran, and Europe. They began to enter Greece from the north about 1900 BC. From the great steppes they entered a world in which the sea was of primary importance for communications; the land of Greece is mountainous, broken up into a multitude of separate small plains, river valleys, and islands. The fierce particularity of classical Greece, in which every city as a matter of course had its own coinage and even its own calendar, with jealous hostility and intermittent war the rule between neighbouring cities, is clearly connected with the terrain. Italy, too, is

A RIVER VALLEY IN ARCADIA, east of Olympia. Rivers in such a landscape are treacherous in flood, though commonly dry in midsummer, and have carried away much cultivable soil even since antiquity when the land may have been better wooded.

not a country of great navigable rivers: the Romans were astonished by the broad and equable rivers of Gaul. The climate of Greece is temperate, although the Aegean Sea is notorious for sudden storms, and a man needed little—by the standards of the wet and chilly North—for reasonable comfort. Open-air gatherings and a life largely lived out of doors came naturally in such surroundings. However spectacular the public buildings on the Acropolis, the life-style of a classical Athenian was very modest. The Greeks themselves said that poverty was their great instructor in hardihood and self-reliance.

Mycenaean Greece was culturally dependent on the sophisticated arts of the Minoans, the non-Indo-European people flourishing on Crete and some of the Aegean islands. It was in contact also with other ancient cultures of the Near East: Hittites, Egyptians, Syrians. The sea made it natural for Greeks to turn to neighbouring maritime peoples rather than to the hill-dwellers who lived on the European mainland. Egypt and Asia Minor were more interesting than Macedonia or Illyria. From those already ancient cultures these early Greeks learned many things: the names of exotic gods and goddesses such as Hera and Athena, who became fully naturalized, part of the classic pantheon; luxury arts; music and poetry. When all the other arts were temporarily lost in the dark age which followed the fall of the Mycenaean citadels about 1150 BC, poetry and song survived and kept alive the memory of an age of great kings and heroes, of Mycenae, not an abandoned ruin but rich in gold, the seat of Agamemnon king of men. The Bronze Age Mycenaean culture was the setting of the myths, whose importance for classical Greece cannot be exaggerated. In the dark age which followed its fall the complex inheritance from the earlier centuries was digested and organized. At its end the pantheon is virtually complete, and religion has taken its lasting form; contact with the East is restored; and the *polis*, the independent city-state, is settling into its classic shape.

It is a revealing piece of evidence for the importance of the surrounding cultures that in Greek most names of musical instruments, and even those of many poetical forms, such as elegy, hymn, iambus, are loan-words from languages which were not Indo-European. Poetry and literature always remained the supreme arts in Greece, both in social prestige and in impact; and their forms, like their mythical content, went ultimately back to a time when the ancestors of the Greeks found themselves arriving in a world of settled dwellings, palaces, frescoes, music. That early contact must be a great part of the explanation for the Greek achievement. Their distant kinsmen who invaded the Indus valley found there cities and temples, which gave a flying start to Aryan culture in India; the first Greeks, similarly, were helped by contact with sophisticated societies to develop along lines very different from the Germans and the Celts, wandering in the northern forests, who remained for centuries in something far more like the original tribal society.

The Greeks themselves were aware of their debt to Phoenicia for the origin of their alphabet, to Egypt for their early style of sculpture, to Babylon for mathe-

THE LION GATE AT MYCENAE. This monumental gateway to the citadel at Mycenae was built in the mid thirteenth century BC and was never lost to view. It, and the massive walls, thought by classical Greeks to have been built by giants, were a reminder to them of the achievements of their Age of Heroes, the period about which Homer sang. It is shown in this old photograph as it may have appeared to the Greeks themselves.

matics. In Greece all these things developed in a particular and characteristic way, sculpture, for instance, achieving a realism and also a range quite different from Egyptian art, while in mathematics a keen and novel interest arose in questions of proof and the basing of the whole system on axiomatic foundations. The alphabet was perfected into a script which in its Roman form has satisfied the western world ever since. Above all, the human scale, both in art and in society, characterized Greece. The independent city-state, in which alone a man could develop to the full as a citizen, is the central Greek achievement. It was possible because the great kingdoms of the East, which were close enough to give seminal inspiration, were not close enough to subjugate Greece: when Xerxes finally tried, it was too late.

Greek culture was competitive. Each successive historian and philosopher made a point of showing how he improved on his predecessor; the great Panhellenic occasions, at Olympia and Delphi, centred on athletic competitions; when tragedies or comedies were put on in Athens, it seemed natural that they should be ranged in order by a panel of judges. It was also a culture which raised in acute

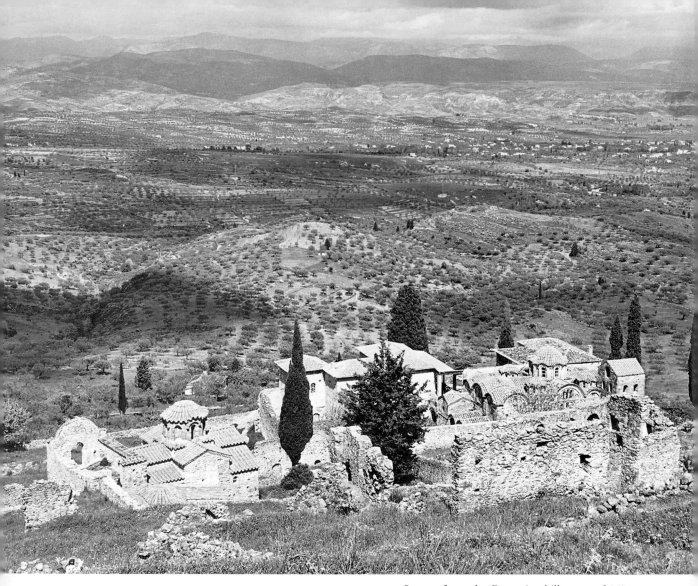

A VIEW EAST ACROSS THE EUROTAS VALLEY, near Sparta, from the Byzantine hill-town of Mistra. This is one of the broader, fertile valleys of south Greece, some 5 km across and with easy access to the sea at the south: an easier landscape than most in the Peloponnese but dominated by the massif of Mount Taygetus on the east.

form all the basic questions about human life: Is slavery wrong ('against nature')? What is the ultimate source of law, human or divine? Should the family be abolished? (Plato abolished it in theory, and Sparta went a long way towards abolishing it in fact.) Is civil disobedience sometimes right? How can the rule of law be established over blood-feud and family loyalties? What justifies a state in ruling other states? What is the ideal size for a community? What is the role of heredity and what of education in the formation of character?

It was marked in all its aspects by an extraordinarily strong feeling for form. That was what gave Greek art and literature their immense impact on the other societies with whom they came into contact. The formal perfection of Greek architecture and town planning, the self-conscious precision of the statues, the strict and exacting requirements which were felt to be appropriate to each genre of literature: all these trained in the audience a demanding and knowledgeable taste. Those who acquired that taste—Etruscans, Lydians, Lycians, Sicels, Messapians—found their own native productions by contrast embarrassingly crude and provincial. Only works in the Greek style would do, and literature in the Greek language. The other languages failed to produce literature and (with the exception of Hebrew) were marked for disappearance. Only in Rome was the heroic decision taken to avoid the easy option of writing in Greek, and to embark on the enormous task of creating in Latin a literature which could be judged by the most exacting Greek standards. This aesthetic precision must also explain in large part the failure of the Greeks to achieve more technical progress. Even such simple devices as the windmill and the screw were invented late and exploited little by a people ingenious enough to devise machines powered by steam. The existence of slavery does not account for this: slaves were a small part of the work-force in Greece. There was a general preference for aesthetic perfection rather than innovation—a thought-provoking contrast with our own age. We could take as symbolic the riders on the Parthenon frieze, controlling their mounts without stirrups: their beauty is marvellous, and the absence of gear increases it, but the early mediaeval invention of the stirrup would transform the power of cavalry.

In Rome, too, the Indo-European inheritance was strongly modified. The influence of the Etruscans was great enough to leave Rome, for instance, with a triad of gods worshipped on the Capitol—Jupiter, Juno, and Minerva—which makes sense only in Etruscan terms, and with elaborate systems for discovering the divine purposes by omens, which were officially practised by Roman magistrates. Even their own names came to follow an alien pattern, the Indo-European single name (Menelaus, Siegfried) giving place to a complex style (Marcus Tullius Cicero). Etruria also transmitted the influence of Greece, especially in the visual arts.

Early Rome was characterized by a powerful public opinion, a strong public spirit, and a marked distaste for eccentricity and individualism. The 'way of the ancestors' (*mos maiorum*) possessed a great moral force, and within the family the father enjoyed a degree of power over his sons, even when they were grown men, which astonished the Greeks, and which is reflected in many stories of fathers who put their own sons to death and were admired for doing so. It is not difficult to imagine the stress produced in Romans by such pressures, and it is tempting to connect with it the double Roman obsession, on the one hand with parricide, and on the other hand with *pietas*, dutiful behaviour to parents, the archetype of which was the figure of Aeneas, founder of Rome, carrying his old father on his shoulders out of burning Troy. The anxiety engendered by such conflicts within the psyche, issuing in restless energy, might be part of the explanation for that astonishing fact, which seemed to the Romans themselves to be explicable only by constant divine favour: the fact that this city, not particularly well sited or obviously well endowed, conquered the world.

Roman art and literature alike present the men of the Republic as tight-lipped, tight-fisted, and resolute. Such qualities as *parsimonia, severitas, frugalitas, simplicitas*, constantly praised, tell their own story; as does the moral ascendancy of a man like Cato, the quintessential peasant farmer magnified into a senator and consul. The names of many Roman grandees poignantly reveal their peasant origin. Cincinnatus and Calvus ('Curly' and 'Baldy'), Capito and Naso ('Bighead' and 'Nosey'), Crassus and Macer ('Fatty' and 'Skinny'), Flaccus and Bibulus ('Floppy' and 'The Drinker'), are the names of Roman consuls and poets, the inheritors of Etruscan kingly regalia and Greek aesthetic refinement.

Our richest and clearest evidence is for the late Republic, when the system was visibly breaking down, and when the old safeguards could no longer restrain the magnates from looting the provinces and even marching with armies on Rome in pursuit of their own aggrandisement. It is tempting to suppose that the reality had always been as venal and as ruthless. Yet it is clear that there had really been a change. When for twenty years Hannibal led an invincible army about Italy urging Rome's Italian allies to revolt, the great majority of them stood firm; not much more than a hundred years later their grievances drove them to make war on Rome themselves. Roman justice and self-restraint, the public spirit which impressed Greeks when they met it in the second century BC, were not a myth.

Archaic and classical Greece, the truly creative period of antiquity, involve a comparatively small area of the eastern Mediterranean. The conquests of Alexander spread the language, architecture and art of Greece as far to the East as India; the rise of Rome led eventually to the whole Mediterranean world, and its 'fringe' as far as Britain, Romania, Iraq, sharing in one recognizable culture with two great languages, Greek and Latin. Anything like modern nationalism was strikingly ineffective, and the Empire was not held down by force: for most of the first century AD, for instance, there was only one legion stationed in north Africa, and none at all in Spain. The same books were studied by schoolboys all over that huge world, and whether in Provence or in Turkey or in north Africa cities arose whose lay-out and temples and public buildings shared the same repertory of forms and decorations. The silver on the table, the mosaics on the floor, the under-floor heating: a uniformity of style existed which is only now returning to our world.

That style was not, of course, all inclusive. It was the creation of a leisured class, and Berber tribesmen or Illyrian goatherds doubtless felt little sympathy with it. The Empire must have depended on unfree labour to a much greater extent than Greece; and the slums of Rome show that many of the free urban poor lived lives of great poverty. Yet Rome was extraordinary among slave-owning societies in that slaves were constantly freed in great numbers, and that the moment they were freed they became citizens. More than half of the thousands of epitaphs extant from imperial Rome are of freedmen and freedwomen. The poor citizen had the great public baths and public squares and parks and forums, in which he reckoned to spend far more time out of his house than is normal in the modern north.

Still darker aspects are not to be glossed over: the slave trade, infanticide, the gladiatorial shows, absolute power which could be in the hands of irresponsible or unbalanced men. Caligula and Nero, the spectacle of bloodshed and the sinister opulence of the orgy, have haunted the imagination of Europe. One of the ways in which the Roman Empire is interesting is that it shows certain sides of human nature developed to their fullest extent: 'Remember', Caligula used to say to

THE APPROACH TO DELPHI FROM THE EAST, through the foothills of Mount Parnassus. Land communications in Greece were not easy, and often circuitous: one reason for preferring coastwise traffic by water where possible. These lower slopes may have been better wooded in antiquity, but limited farming has always been possible between the rocky outcrops, and there are good upland pastures.

people, 'that I can do anything to anybody.' The past is the laboratory in which human nature can be studied with security, perhaps the only way it can really be studied at all.

The ancients believed in the power and significance of great individuals. The daemonic Alcibiades, the imperturbable and ironic Socrates, the vehement Alexander: these stand beside such Romans as the all-conquering Caesar, the gallant but profligate Mark Antony, the demented aesthete Nero. The will to power incarnated in great individuals, the qualities of resolution, magnanimity, pride: the ancients saw events very much in such terms. Such qualities as pride and magnanimity are essentially un-Christian. In the Middle Ages and still more in the Renaissance such pagan virtues, which Christian Europe had in reality by no means renounced, could be glorified in the persons and stories of the ancient world. The Trojan War and the Quest for the Golden Fleece, for instance, were good pretexts for the glorification of purely pagan chivalry and passion. Important human qualities which Christianity seemed to leave out, or which it rejected, could be depicted with sympathy in Achilles or Caesar, Helen or Cleopatra; in the rational suicide of Seneca or the passionate suicide of Dido.

The incompatibility of some pagan virtues with Christianity draws attention to an important aspect of the scope of this book. Jews and Christians are in principle not included—the *Envoi* looks forward to Christian Europe. The Jews and the Greeks do not mention each other at all until a surprisingly late period, and when they did meet neither side was very favourably impressed with the other. In the early second century BC there was a time when it seemed possible that Judaea would become altogether Hellenized: there was a high priest named Menelaus, a gymnasium was constructed near the Temple, and young men started to wear the Greek dress. The nationalistic rising of the Maccabees put a stop to this. At the time of St Paul there were plenty of Hellenized Jews in the Mediterranean world, but the chance that Judaism would peter out had vanished.

Judaism and Christianity do not belong in a History of the Classical World because they were too separate, too unclassical. The presuppositions of Jewish literature were essentially different from those of Greece and Rome, and so were its characteristic forms. Rome could come to terms with Judaism, an ancestral cult, at least, if a bizarre one, more easily than with Christianity, which was not even respectably ancient, and which in vital respects contradicted the fundamental nature of the pagan state. Other-worldliness, celibacy, refusal to take an oath or offer the regular sacrifices—all this was more than official Rome could stomach, while the uncouth literary form of Christian writings and their outlandish message repelled the educated class: to the Greeks it seemed foolishness, St Paul admits of the Gospel. Yet there was a perspective in which, at least later, the classical world could be seen as necessary for the universal acceptance of the Christian revelation. The glorification of Socrates' condemnation and death as being a martyrdom, a triumph, which was proclaimed with all the literary genius of Plato and accepted by the educated of Greece and Rome alike, prepared the way for the understanding of the Passion of Christ. The Roman Empire had pacified and united the world in time for the Gospel to be proclaimed everywhere. Rome the Imperial City became Rome the Holy City, and her bishops took the old Roman title of Supreme Pontiff. The universal claims of Rome assumed a sacerdotal form, but the continuity is obvious.

The classical tradition, a large fraction of the history of the West, is too vast a theme to be more than glanced at here. Greece and Rome provided the languages of the Western and Eastern Churches, when the unity imposed on the Mediterranean world finally broke in half with Rome's fall, and they continued to be the vehicle of intellectual communication for many centuries. The Eastern Empire continued to call itself 'Roman' to the end, in 1453, but it did so in Greek. Some of ancient literature survived, including many masterpieces, although much more was lost. It proved to be highly important that in later antiquity so much scholarly work had been done, establishing texts, commenting on them, compiling grammars and dictionaries. They helped to make the texts intelligible. By contrast a literature like Old Irish, where there was very little scholarly apparatus of this kind, is full of words whose meaning is now quite lost. After great struggles and doubts on the part of Fathers of the Church it was widely, though never universally, accepted that the pagan classics could be read and taught by Christians. Virgil and Terence continued for a thousand years to be fundamental texts at school in the West.

The idea of Rome haunted the imagination of Europe; Charlemagne went to the inconvenient Italian city to be crowned Emperor, and the struggle for and against a Roman Empire with universal claims dominated the history of Italy and Germany for hundreds of years. Napoleon revived it again, and Mussolini claimed to have 'restored the fasces' (whence 'fascists') and reconstituted an Empire for Rome. Shakespeare explored the dilemmas of power more deeply in his Roman tragedies than in his English history plays; Kipling, in some of his best poems and stories, took the Roman Empire as a paradigm of the British Raj. In the sphere of political reality the same idea can be seen. The trial of Warren Hastings for oppression and extortion in India was felt by all the participants to be an echo of the celebrated trials of Roman governors like Verres, denounced by Cicero. The word 'proconsul' was unselfconsciously applied to British colonial administrators.

The founders of new constitutions often took Roman models: thus there are Senates in France, Ireland, Italy, and the United States. The radical political wing could also find Roman models. French Revolutionaries took names like Gracchus and claimed the inheritance of the tyrannicide Brutus and the Roman Republic. A German revolutionary movement named itself after the rebellious slave Spartacus; a left-wing magazine in Britain is still called *Tribune*. The Roman Church, of course, re-enacted the claims of the Empire on a different plane.

In the period of Charlemagne the study of the ancient texts aimed to produce churchmen and state servants who could write intelligible Latin. Later in the Middle Ages those texts were devoured as the best books available on logic, or architecture, or medicine. The Renaissance found their literary form, its shapeliness and concision, a delightful relief from mediaeval formlessness; and many tried to emulate the lofty spirit, magnanimous and pagan, which they depicted in ancient men. The Augustans of the eighteenth century were impressed by the urbanity and correctness of Horace and Cicero. Romantic poets, such as Keats and Shelley and Hölderlin, turned from Latin literature to Greek: 'We are all Greeks,' said the painter Delacroix. The last hundred years have seen a great anthropological interest in antiquity, from Frazer and Jane Harrison to Louis Gernet and Jean-Paul Vernant, and impassioned performances of Attic tragedies. This brief and exaggeratedly pointed survey brings out the Protean character of the ancient world, which in every period has had different things to offer, and which has been exploited with extraordinary thoroughness over the centuries.

For the arts the influence of antiquity had three aspects: subject matter, form, and spirit. The myths of Greece were the other great subject of Renaissance art, along with Christian themes; the myths of Ovid were painted by Titian and Correggio, Rubens and Poussin; Mantegna and Piranesi and David created visual images of Rome; Michelangelo began his career as a sculptor by creating works so closely modelled on ancient models that they passed as genuine antiques. The genres of ancient literature, too, lived on. Pastorals and epics, elegies and satires sprang up in every European language; the Italian musicians and patrons who created the first operas were trying to reconstruct the musical drama of antiquity; before Greek tragedy was understood, the rhetorical melodramas of Seneca were a formative influence on the tragedy which blossomed with Marlowe and Shakespeare. In another art the triumphal arch, the Doric and Ionic and Corinthian capitals, the fountains with marble nymphs and river gods, the ornamental urns, all proliferated through the cities. The spirit is even more pervasive. David's Marat stabbed in his bath recalls the philosophical suicides of Rome; the grand manner of Raphael and Milton is inseparable from their classical studies; Dante claimed Virgil as his master, and for all the enormous difference of their styles the claim clearly expresses an important truth.

The philosophical legacy is also vast and various. Greek thought penetrated Christian doctrine from the first: 'In the beginning was the Word' is intelligible only in the light of Greek theories of the Logos. St Augustine was much influenced by Plato, and many theologians attempted to reconcile Platonism and Christianity, both in the Middle Ages and, like Sir Thomas More, in the Renaissance. Aristotelian logic laid the basis of scholasticism and was finally reconciled with orthodox belief by Aquinas. The brilliant guess of the atomic theory was remembered in the Renaissance, when also the proud virtue of the Stoics provided a model for generals and dynasts. Platonism, increasingly freed from Christian colouring, was the dominant school of philosophy in England in the nineteenth century.

The idea of a university goes back to Plato's school at Athens, which lasted for nearly a thousand years. From Greece it passed to Europe by way of the Arabs, like the text of Aristotle; Universities spread north from Salerno, where contact with the Muslim East had planted the seed. Textual criticism began with the study of corrupt texts of classical authors. Such words as 'museum', 'inspiration', 'poet laureate', reveal their ancient connections: a temple of the Muses, the 'breathing into' a poet of his inexplicably splendid verse by some supernatural force, the crowning of a successful poet with laurel. The modern cult of athletics and the revival of the Olympic games are of course strongly Greek.

The English language itself is distinguished from its cousins in the Germanic branch of the Indo-European family by the very large number of words which have come into it from Latin and, to a lesser extent, from Greek; some directly, others through French or Italian. People sometimes talk as if such words were always massive and abstruse, like 'psychiatry' or 'prelapsarian', and indeed the vocabulary of abstract thought, of science and culture, is especially full of such words. But the following sample of twenty-five may remind the reader that many short and basic words have the same source; act, art, beauty, colour, crime, fact, fate, fork, hour, human, idea, justice, language, law, matter, music, nature, number, place, reason, school, sense, sex, space, time.

Every generation approaches classical antiquity in a different way, draws different lessons from it, finds different things about it interesting. It is hoped that this book will help contemporary readers to understand something of its continuing significance and fascination.

GREECE

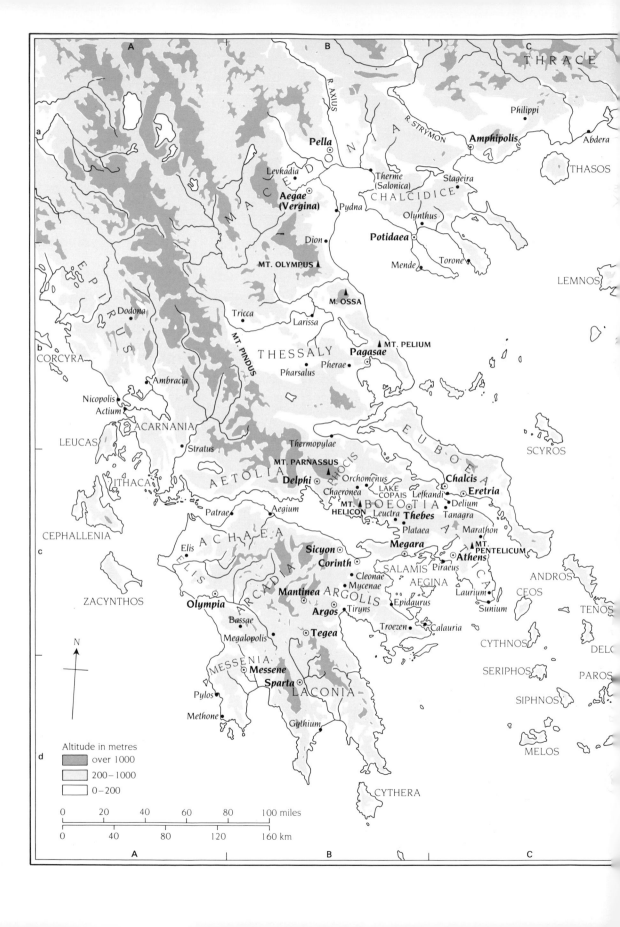

THRACE

Philippi

R. AXIUS

R. STRYMON

Amphipolis

Abdera

Pella

THASOS

Levkadia

Therme
(Salonica)

Stageira

CHALCIDICE

Aegae
(Vergina)

Pydna

Olynthus

LEMNOS

Dion

Potidaea

MT. OLYMPUS

Mende

Torone

Dodona

Tricca

M. OSSA

EPIRUS

Larissa

MT. PELIUM

CORCYRA

THESSALY

Pagasae

MT. PINDUS

Pherae

Ambracia

Pharsalus

Nicopolis

Actium

LEUCAS

ACARNANIA

Stratus

Thermopylae

EUBOEA

SCYROS

MT. PARNASSUS

PHOCIS

Delphi

Orchomenus

Chalcis

ITHACA

AETOLIA

LAKE
COPAIS

Lefkandi

Eretria

Chaeronea

Delium

Patrae

Aegium

MT.
HELICON

BOEOTIA

Leuctra

Thebes

Tanagra

CEPHALLENIA

ACHAEA

Plataea

Marathon

ATTICA

MT.
PENTELICUM

Sicyon

Megara

Athens

Elis

ELIS

Corinth

Cleonae

SALAMIS

Piraeus

ANDROS

ZACYNTHOS

ARCADIA

Mantinea

Mycenae

AEGINA

CEOS

Olympia

ARGOLIS

Epidaurus

Laurium

TENOS

Bassae

Argos

Tiryns

Sunium

CYTHNOS

DEL

Megalopolis

Tegea

Troezen

Calauria

MESSENIA

SERIPHOS

PAROS

Messene

Sparta

LACONIA

SIPHNOS

Pylos

Methone

Gythium

MELOS

N

CYTHERA

Altitude in metres

over 1000

200–1000

0–200

0   20   40   60   80   100 miles

0   40   80   120   160 km

A   B   C

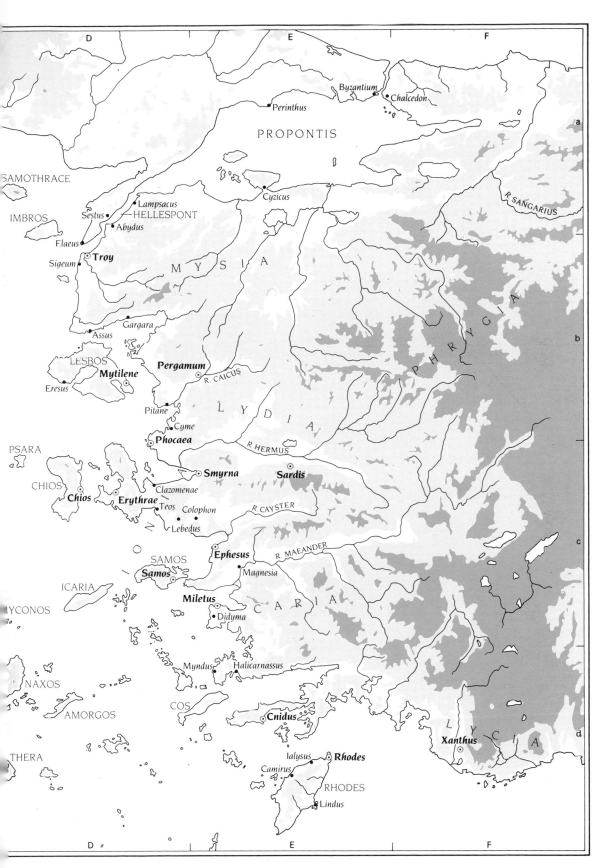

MAP I. GREECE AND THE AEGEAN WORLD

I

Greece: The History of the Archaic Period

GEORGE FORREST

The Emergence of the Polis

FOR most historians the characteristic and peculiar element in Greek political life has been the *pólis*, the city-state, an institution of which any precise definition obscures the variety in size or shape or social and political organization. Very roughly, it was a community of citizens (adult males), citizens without political rights (women and children), and non-citizens (resident foreigners and slaves), a defined body, occupying a defined area, living under a defined or definable constitution, independent of outside authority to an extent that allowed enough of its members to feel that they were independent. The land at large may have been virtually empty of residents or occupied by farmhouses or villages or even small towns, but there had to be one focal point, religious, political, administrative, around which usually grew up (Sparta was a notable exception) a city, the *polis* proper, usually fortified, always offering a market (an *agora*), a place of assembly (often the *agora* itself), a seat of justice and of government, executive and deliberative, in the early period monarchic or aristocratic in type, later usually oligarchic or democratic.

The physical base was almost essential, but even more so was the sense of community. 'We Athenians have a city so long as we have our ships', Themistocles was to say at Salamis (below, p. 45). So too the notion of independence. Some part of it could be shed involuntarily, by acceptance of tribute-paying to a stronger power, or voluntarily, by joining an alliance or even a federation (the Thessalian or Boeotian, for instance), but a sense of 'autonomy' had to be there. This institution at its best, the ancient theorists argued, should be neither too large nor too small, neither too self-sufficient nor too dependent, neither too oligarchic nor too democratic. Certainly, for the archaic and classical periods, most historians have been right to regard the *polis* as the characteristic form of political organization; certainly, too, many *poleis* approached somewhere near the happy norm. But recent enquiries have drawn attention to two other factors which in earlier years will somehow have influenced the origins of the city and may have continued for some time to colour its development.

The first of these is the repopulation of large tracts of the Greek countryside after the collapse of Mycenaean society. The immediate consequence of this collapse was a long period of chaotic tribal wandering which by about 1000 BC had set the pattern for the future: Dorians, newcomers from the north, in most of the Peloponnese, Crete, south-west Asia Minor and its offshore islands; Ionians in Attica, Euboea, most of the Aegean islands, and on the central coast of Asia Minor; in the north, in Lesbos, and north-west Asia Minor a mixture which we may roughly call Aeolian. But at the start most of the settlements were small nuclei with much land around them left to occupy.

The second factor is the appearance of associations of communities, clearly linked with, but not necessarily in all respects coterminous with, this repopulation. Greek tradition hands on several examples of such associations, some mere hazy recollections, some surviving as more or less empty religious institutions, some few surfacing occasionally in later political life. The six Dorian cities of south-west Asia Minor; the twelve Ionian states to the north, capable once of concerted action in the 'Meliac' war, too far away in time to be properly recalled; the amphictyony (a league of neighbours) of Anthela at Thermopylae which owed survival and prosperity to its association with the sanctuary of Apollo at Delphi. Except in the last case, however, vagueness of information has tended to divert attention to more solid things, to Athens, Sparta, Corinth, to real city-states.

But excavations of the last decade or so awaken interest and prompt a new perception. There existed archaeologically in central Greece an area of common culture: southern Thessaly, Boeotia, Euboea, and the islands around its eastern coast, an area which has been given new focus by the discovery of a major settlement at Lefkandi on the west coast of Euboea, half-way between what have hitherto been regarded as the island's two main cities, Chalcis and Eretria. Stunningly prosperous (by contemporary standards) throughout the Dark Age, say 1100 to 750, it appears to have reached a height of wealth in the late ninth century, but more than a century earlier it could offer the tomb of a hero, buried with his consort and with his horses, of unparalleled grandeur and wealth. On available archaeological evidence Lefkandi was the core of the wider community. Was it also the religious core? It is tempting to say that it was not, to think rather of Thermopylae some 60 miles to the north across the narrow water, the site of the amphictyony which, it was said, originally included precisely those same peoples, Thessalians, Boeotians, the smaller tribes between them and the Ionians, no doubt the Ionians of Euboea. Did it, or Thermopylae, provide any kind of political core? Who knows? But stories or hints of early collaboration, commercial and military, between various parts of the area, read against the firm archaeological background and with the likelihood of some religious association, argue for some much greater degree of cohesion than has previously been countenanced.

LEFKANDI. The site lies on the shore of the Straits of Euboea, between Chalcis and Eretria, and must have been the focus of the early dispute between these cities, as well as a prime source for early Greek exploration and colonization. British excavations there have dramatically changed our view of the so-called Dark Ages of Greece, in the tenth and ninth centuries BC.

THE BURIAL OF A WOMAN AT LEFKANDI. She wore gold jewellery and an unusual gold brassière. Near her was the cremation burial of a warrior, his ashes wrapped in a cloak. Both were found in a great apsidal building over 45 metres long, with an external wooden colonnade. This is a striking demonstration of Lefkandi's wealth and industry, and a surprising discovery for a period in which Greece offers no other notable architecture. The burial, of the tenth century BC, is truly heroic, and seems to suggest a rich, dynastic society, with overseas connections.

Greater cohesion here encourages belief in greater cohesion elsewhere and poses questions about the political unification of Attica under Athens, about the relationship between Sparta and other communities in Laconia in the first two centuries or so after its Dorian foundation in the late ninth century, about the Theban expansion in Boeotia in the sixth century, and so on. Answers would be premature, but the questions are there.

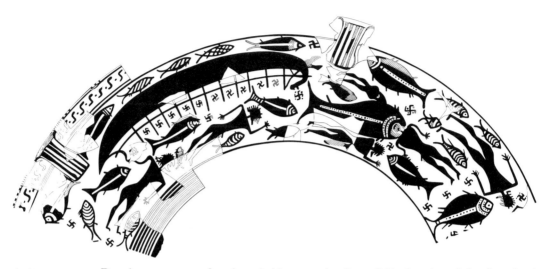

A SHIPWRECK. Drawing on a vase found on Ischia, near the Bay of Naples, site of the first Greek settlement in the west. It shows an upturned ship and men thrown into the sea—one being eaten by a fish; the record, it may be, of a disaster in waters far from the homeland. The style is Euboean (Ischia was settled by Euboeans), but made locally in the later eighth century BC.

More immediately relevant is the disintegration of the Euboean 'organization' in the late eighth century. By 800 some Greeks had begun to wander abroad, in the main, we suppose, in search of metal, and some even settled where they could find it, on the north-Syrian coast (before 800); in Italy a little later; perhaps on the south coast of the Black Sea. The chief operators were the Euboeans, still acting in concert; one of the chief profit-makers was Lefkandi. But about 730 Chalcis and Eretria quarrelled and started the so-called Lelantine War which, Thucydides said, ranged 'the rest of the Greek world in alliance with either side'. Historians have been puzzled. Why should old friends quarrel? Why should 'the rest' join in? What can be meant in such early times by 'alliance'? The puzzles remain real. But comparatively large-scale associations lead more readily to contacts, to friendships and enmities at a distance than do little city-like units; international interests can more readily cement or break such friendships or enmities. In the world sketched above, the hypothesis that some distant outbreak of trouble (say between Phrygia and Assyria, at war with each other about 720-710) raised tensions among interested Greeks, principally Euboeans; that one city broke with existing friends but kept or found others elsewhere, so that the 'rest of the Greek world' became involved—that hypothesis begins to make sense. Be that as it may, the war ended in Eretrian defeat, Lefkandi (which had probably been the site of early Eretria) was abandoned, the community had crumbled. The strains of war brought other readjustments elsewhere, and something more like the city-state structure of later centuries began to appear.

It would not be absurd to see these same strains as in some measure an explanation of the other phenomenon of the late eighth century, a second and much greater wave of emigration, from the mainland, from Ionia and the islands. The earlier adventurers will have brought home news of opportunities abroad that could tempt the less timid or the more desperate, in trade, in military service with foreign powers, above all in agriculture. If the war did not wipe out timidity, it must at least have increased desperation among the defeated or disrupted.

Already, as the war was beginning, Corinth had established a settlement on Corcyra, on the route to the riches of the West, and, in the midst of those riches, Sicilian Syracuse (733 BC); somewhat earlier still Euboeans were developing sites on the north-west coast of the Aegean. Thereafter, throughout the war and the century that followed, what we rather misleadingly call colonization went on in earnest—misleadingly because a 'colony', though a state-organized enterprise, often sent in a direction that would further the state's interests, became an independent unit, normally keeping no more than sentimental and religious ties with its mother city; colonists remembered more vividly and with more gratitude their founder, the man who had led them out, than their foundress city. Overpopulation, an occasional famine, political trouble, any of these could persuade a government to unload some of its unwanted and send them off, with of course its religious blessing, into the known or the unknown. Just as mixed were the motives for going; compulsion, desperation, ambition; to farm, to trade, to take a chance.

It is mistaken to draw too clear distinctions, between trade and agriculture for example. What part did trade play in Greek politics in general? With some few exceptions, the Greek trader was not a powerful man; respectable Greeks grew things rather than sold them; on the land, not in the market-place, were found Greeks who formed governments. But the Greek who grew things had to sell them or persuade traders to sell them for him. The element cannot be ignored, but we do not need to start talking of 'a powerful merchant class'. For instance, the founding fathers of Syracuse were farmers from an inland village near Corinth, scarcely entrepreneurial material. But they were led by a member of Corinth's ruling family—was he sent on a government-inspired mission or was he merely unpopular with his kinsmen? They settled at Syracuse, rich land, but with the finest harbour in eastern Sicily. Did they settle to survive or to sell? Whatever it was, there is no sign of any very significant relationship with the folks back home. Contrast contemporary Corcyra, surely strategic in intent and to acquire even more strategic importance when it found itself astride the route

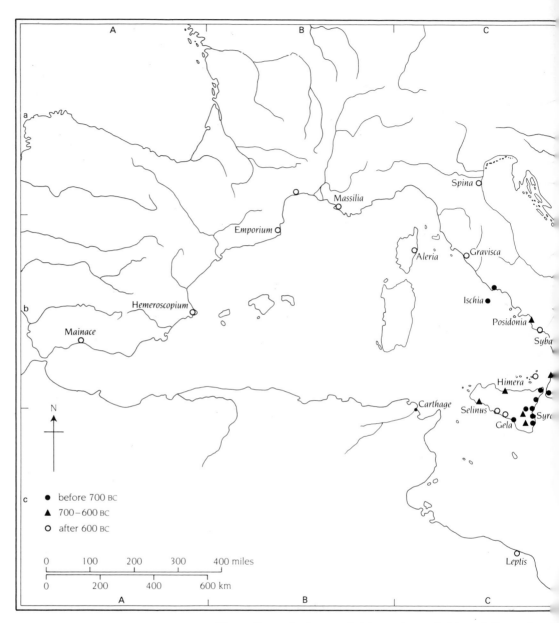

MAP 2. GREEK COLONIZATION. The earliest colonies were led by trade—to Ischia and Cumae in central Italy, close to Etruria. Consolidation soon followed in the agriculturally more promising areas of South Italy and Sicily. The Adriatic approaches were also explored, and the north coast of the Aegean (neighbouring the Thracians) from the later eighth century on. Early exploration of the Black Sea took Greeks to its farther shores, first (Olbia) where there was river-access to the hinterland, with later consolidation which gave access to the Caucasus (Phasis) and the corn-rich lands of the Danube valley (Istrus). The approach to the Black Sea was at the same time secured with cities on the Hellespont and Bosporus. On the east and south shores of the Mediterranean expansion was contained by the strengths of local kingdoms, but the south coast of Asia Minor was explored and Al Mina in Syria

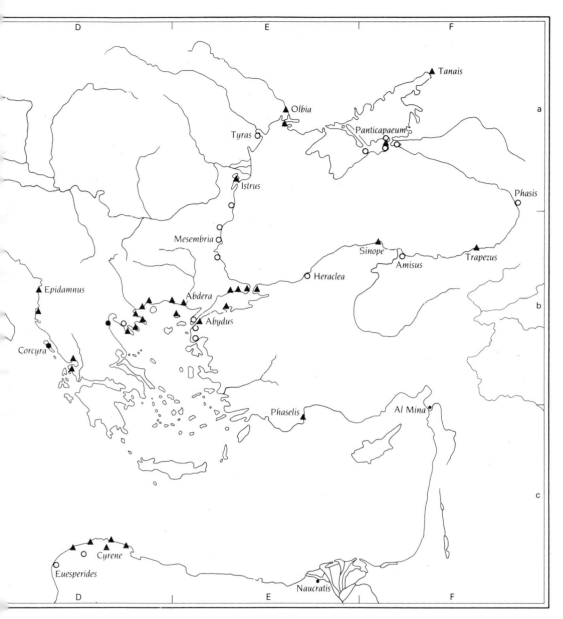

had served as a trading port for Greeks, apparently with Greek residents, from before 800 BC. Naucratis in Egypt served a similar function from the later seventh century on. Cyprus admitted substantial Phoenician (ninth-century) and Greek (eighth- to sixth-century) settlements, the latter becoming mainly Greek cities in later years. Most of the Libyan cities were settled by 600 BC, but further expansion to the west was contained by Phoenicians (in Carthage, Sardinia, and Spain), although in Sicily they had been confined by Greeks to the western end of the island. In Italy Spina and Gravisca were Greek settlements beside Etruscan towns. The principal colonizing cities were, in the eighth century, the Euboean Eretria and Chalcis (who had also opened trade through Al Mina), followed by Corinth in Sicily and North Greece (with Megara and Achaea), and Miletus and the Ionian cities in the Black Sea.

to Adriatic silver as well as western grain. There the story is one of repeated conflict between the 'maternal' interests of Corinth and the legitimate Corcyrean feeling that they had come of age. Contrast again Cyrene, established with no maternal guidance from drought-stricken Thera about 630 BC. The settlers were conscripted and warned clearly that their return would not be welcome.

These examples show how foolish it is to generalize about colonization. We must argue for confusion, a confusion which by about 600 BC found Greeks established in southern France, northern Africa, Egypt, the Black Sea and the entrance thereto, along the north coast of the Aegean, above all in Sicily and southern Italy. Similar confusion upset the established order at home and produced the political revolution to which we must now turn.

The Invention of Politics

Throughout the Mediterranean, eighth-century Greeks had absorbed new experiences: in Egypt wealth and civilization at a level they could not have imagined; in the Near East power and organization, in the west barbarism and potential wealth, in the north a mixture. Being Greeks, they exploited all to their profit and their progress. Artists were captivated by oriental motifs, arms makers by oriental weaponry, traders by hauls of metal, timber or grain, poor farmers by the chance to emigrate, richer farmers by the chance to grow crops that would sell abroad (wine and oil), the sophisticated by different kinds of political life, poets and thinkers and businessmen by the alphabet—above all, everyone by the dawning of the idea that other places existed and might have something to contribute, material or mental. In the late eighth century a peevish Boeotian poet and farmer, Hesiod (below, pp. 88 ff.) was making discontented, but unsatisfiable, noises about the narrow aristocratic society in which he lived, a society pictured, a few years before, from within by the first and greatest epic poet known to us, Homer (below, Ch. 2). The epic does not grasp a particular moment in history though it claims to describe one. It grows with the society for which it is performed, and we cannot now separate the stages of growth. But Homer's heroes at the siege of Troy in his *Iliad*, proud, brave, honourable, touchy, vengeful, were understood by his aristocratic audience, and their values cannot have been wholly dissimilar, nor can their total disregard for men like Hesiod be unreal. But by the early seventh century Hesiod's peers were claiming regard.

It is vital to insist that this opening of the Greek mind is much more important than the particular forms of government which were produced by the opening. Here there was 'tyranny'; there 'oligarchy'; here 'a constitution'; there 'anarchy'. Common to all of the more flexible societies is turmoil, and common to all is the achievement in the end of some sort of what we are prepared to describe as the constitutional government of the city-state.

But the routes were indeed diverse. In Sparta in the early seventh century a great lawgiver, Lycurgus, it was said, laid down the rules for a system of military training (one could hardly call it education) which turned Sparta into the most efficient military power in Greece, helping it to hold ruthless mastery over the southern half of the Peloponnese, and by stages to acquire a more subtle control over the rest of the peninsula. At the same time he formalized and thus reformed Sparta's social structure and produced a constitution which guaranteed to all Spartans some form of political equality the like of which had not been imagined by Hesiod and was not to be realized elsewhere for many a day.

Sparta's position as mistress of vast tracts of conquered territory and vast numbers of subjects, compared with her own population (the notional figure was 9,000 adult males, outnumbered seven to one), was rare, but not unparalleled; her solution was to expropriate the bulk of the territory for state-controlled, but privately managed, exploitation and enslave, but not quite enslave, the subjects. Again, the state 'owned' the slaves (called 'helots'), but the individual Spartan took half the production. The numbers of the breed and its real or imagined racial coherence established helot discontent, the danger of helot revolt, as the key to much of Spartan behaviour for centuries. At the same time a fair number of more significant communities in the subjected area were given special treatment and recognized as having some independence in their own domestic affairs. These were the *perioikoi*, the neighbours, who had much less to complain about than the helots, but were not always as docile as a Spartan might like.

It is against this background that we must see the development and, after Lycurgus, the freezing of Spartan institutions. If her position was rare, her solutions made her unique. Most Greeks retained some traces of a state-imposed military training for the young; in Crete, for example, many close similarities to Spartan customs can be seen. But only in Sparta, so far as we know, was a child completely robbed of home and family between the ages of five and thirty and even thereafter compelled to devote his days to military training and his evenings to the company of his messmates. Most Greeks entered the archaic age with aristocratic attitudes, and in most some faint elements of these attitudes long survived. But of the states that mattered it was only in Sparta that these were captured and preserved so early and with so little chance of change in the composition or the interests of the aristocracy. And there was the compounding factor that Sparta retained its hereditary kingship, no mere titular kingship, when others had or were in the process of losing theirs. More oddly still there were two kings, drawn from two great houses, who by their friendships or rivalries could only emphasize the basic aristocratic principle of dependence of the small on the great.

In its constitution Sparta also stood apart, but here in a different way. The kings were the military commanders; with the aristocratic council, the Gerousia, they initiated most political and took most judicial decisions. But there was also an assembly of all Spartan citizens which met at fixed times and passed final judgements on most things that mattered—all Spartan citizens, that is, as defined by the great Lycurgus, all who had survived their training, who had been allotted state land in the conquered territory with helots to work it, and who continued to obey the rules. They called themselves *homoioi*, equals, and by doing so not only registered discontent with their earlier status, whatever it may have been, but justify the use a few lines ago of the word 'citizens'. Equality was more a statement of a basic minimum than of any absolute standard, but it does not matter much that some Spartans were rich (private as opposed to state-allotted land existed), others comparatively poor; it does not matter that some Spartans were of noble birth, others ordinary people; it does not matter that in a militarily based society political independence is not encouraged or even tolerated. What does matter is that, by the assertion of the basic minimum, Spartans were beginning to grope towards a definition of the citizen as a member of a society who was automatically entitled to certain rights (however small), who had a sense of community (however much it was merely the product of a shared fear of helots or a shared desire to exploit those helots for their own profit).

To the mechanics of the Spartan revolution we shall return. Spartan aristocrats did not cede 'equality' with good grace, but they used little violence. Elsewhere the process was different. In Corinth, for example, control of the state and of the wealth that could be gained thereby had lain with one aristocratic clan, the Bacchiadae. In 657 a half-member of the clan, Cypselus, collected sufficient support to kill or expel them and to take over as what later Greeks call 'tyrant'. Of the nature of Cypselus' government nothing is known except that enough of his support came from people experienced and competent enough to provide the city with uninterrupted, indeed increasing, prosperity. Nor can we tell what Cypselus had promised to them except a share in government, or to the wider circle who followed, except that his propaganda used a word, *dikaiōsei*, which can mean anything between 'put [Corinth] to rights' through 'give [Corinth] a set of rules' to 'give Corinth justice'. Whatever the precise meaning, there is more than a hint here of that same desire for 'equality' which had excited Spartans, even if that equality was limited to equality before the law and, paradoxically, was to be won under that most unequal of regimes, 'tyranny'.

No doubt Corinthians had other reasons for supporting Cypselus, at the lowest level a simple desire to beat up the Bacchiads; and in other cities of which we know less, where tyrants appeared or tried to appear, their supporters will have had their private reasons. But a widespread phenomenon invites some general explanation, and the theme of justice in some form or other is alluded to often enough in the seventh century to suggest that it was the first constituent in the Greeks' slow and uneven expansion of the idea of what it was to be a *polītes*, a full member of a *polis*. It was the arbitrariness of what passed for justice that had irked Hesiod; 'Justice done and seen to be done' (in Sparta) won confident praise from the seventh-century poet, Terpander of Lesbos.

But what had happened to turn despair into confidence, to produce this first crack in the aristocratic fabric? And what tools were used to produce it? The answer to the second question has been thought to lie, and probably does lie, in the murky area of military history. The basic unit of an early Greek army was the aristocrat and his entourage, collectively a 'phratry', members of his family, lesser dependent nobles, richer farmers, and so down through the social scale. The spearhead, literally, of this unit was the aristocrat, well armed, well trained, standing out in front of the rest, which was itself protected as its affluence permitted, or unarmed as poverty dictated, giving its moral or physical support by whatever methods or with whatever weapons came to hand. The developed army, on the other hand, while it might still contain some elements of cavalry and more of light-armed troops, depended for its effect on some thousands of heavily, and more or less uniformly, equipped infantry called hoplites. The hoplites were still often brigaded by phratry, though there was a shift in some places towards more firmly defined geographical units; but success required cohesion of the whole force, a line usually eight deep, helmeted, corsleted, greaved, presenting a solid front of round shields and thrusting, no longer throwing, spears, winning by co-operative weight. As the mid-seventh-century Spartan poet, Tyrtaeus (below, p. 102), put it: 'Stand near and take the enemy, strike with long spear or sword, set foot by foot, lean shield on shield, crest upon crest, helmet on helmet . . . .'

This is hoplite fighting in spirit, but how sophisticated in form? Here we appear to be faced with a paradox. Some random elements of hoplite equipment were being fashioned as early as the eighth century, but the earliest representations

RANKS OF HOPLITE SOLDIERS depicted on a Corinthian vase of about 650–640 BC. They advance on each other, with a piper to help keep the step. This style of warfare replaced the Homeric duels of leaders supported by light-armed rabble, and was generally adopted in Greece during the seventh century BC. The men are well armoured, with helmets, shield clamped on to the left arm by two grips, corselet and greaves. The main weapon is a thrusting spear, and victory lay with the ranks that kept their order, were not outflanked, and did not break.

of an organized phalanx in vase-painting do not antedate by much the middle of the seventh century. Yet an individual hoplite is a curious object to imagine in aristocratic battle, while the creation of the phalanx with its practised cohesion surely demands one moment of decision. But the puzzle is not, perhaps, too real. It is the result of too easy a slide from thoughts of the single champion to pictures of the massed infantry of later years; of failure to recognize that an easier supply of metal and more wealth to make use of it could gradually lead to a multiplication of 'champions'; of collaboration between small numbers of them; of not asking what minimum number might be needed to form an effective unit of hoplite type (surely some hundreds, not thousands). The change could well be in train and even far advanced in the first half of the century, years before the painters appreciated it or mastered the technique of depicting a hoplite army on a pot.

If this is so, it becomes easier to answer the more important question. What, if anything, did military innovation have to do with political revolution? In Corinth in 657 Cypselus had the army behind him; he expelled the Bacchiads by force and did not need a bodyguard. Earlier, in Sparta, the army and its structure was at the heart of the Lycurgan revolution. To put it crudely, if there were 300 Bacchiads armed as hoplites, it needed only 301 other Corinthians similarly clad and with the added weapon of revolutionary fervour to overthrow them. The much larger numbers involved in Sparta need not yet have acquired even the measure of cohesion that Tyrtaeus implies, so long as they had enough to make themselves felt.

But military change was in the main only one factor in the mechanics of revolution. It will have affected its course but not its substance. It guided, but it did not generate, except in so far as new conditions would, of course, help to create a sense of common situation, to bolster confidence; and the newer the conditions the greater would be the effect. The origins of the move against aristocratic monopoly lie further back, in the consequences of eighth-century adventure and expansion. Economic expansion, even if only agricultural, as in Sparta, relief of population pressure, the experience of different worlds (the word *tyrannos* was of eastern origin), these did not create a new 'middle class' of well-fed farmers, still less a party of rich merchants. But they did produce tensions, between aristocrat and aristocrat, lesser aristocrat and greater, with the odd successful trader or pirate thrown in to complicate things still further. The old rules were not flexible enough, or later clearly enough defined, to cope.

Some states tried a third route to the new world, constitutional, like that of the Spartans, but less idiosyncratic, very much more humane. The setting up of a colony invited, if it did not demand, some conscious thought about the character of the new settlement, some element of self-consciousness even where the desire may only have been to reproduce what had been left at home (a desire that cannot have been profound, since most colonists left home because they did not like what they had experienced there). Thus a new need was added to the new instinct for change, or at least dissatisfaction with the existing order, the need to formulate; and (yet again) eastern experience will have shown that formulation was possible. It is thus no surprise that Crete, a natural link with the East, should have become for Greeks the home of lawgiving, that Crete (according to one story) should have inspired Sparta, that a Cretan should have taught the earliest named colonial legislator, Zaleucus of Italian Locri (c.670), and that other Italian and Sicilian colonies should have become a lawgiver's paradise.

But this is all shadow. It is only in mainland Attica that the translation of the desire and the idea into fact can be followed. Attica had survived post-Mycenaean turmoil better than most, but here too there had been economic collapse and only gradual redevelopment. When things settled down the city of Athens was at the head of whatever association Attica may once have been, not, like Sparta, a city of 'equals' surrounded by *perioikoi* or helots, but the centre of an Attica riddled throughout with inequalities. There were aristocrats, free men, and dependents in and around the city as there were in Eleusis, Marathon, or Sunium. It is not the least of Athenian achievements that she contrived to diminish or delete the distinctions across the country while building up the city as acknowledged capital, preserving at once local pride, national identity and individual dignity.

Around 630 there was an attempt at tyranny; around 620 the response was a law-code, the work of Draco, of which we know virtually nothing beyond its severity. But to insist on the severity is to ignore the point that by the mere fact of definition it invited criticism and change, and that Athenians went on to accept the invitation. Zaleucus' code was also said to have been severe, but the Locrians too ultimately made changes. It is the sad thing about Spartans that what had been 'good enough for grandfather' remained 'good enough for me'.

In Athens the first changes came after some twenty-five years. There arrived a moment of crisis, or near-revolution, when it was decided to appoint an arbitrator to produce a second, very different definition. Out of the background of discontent with Draco and the aristocratic in-fighting it had generated came the choice of one revolutionary leader, Solon, who, fortunately for us, was not only a politician, but a poet, albeit a somewhat self-centred, self-righteous, and just a trifle pompous one.

Solon, elected chief magistrate for 594, had one weakness. He did not like killing people. He could have made himself tyrant, but, as he wrote, 'Tyranny is a very pretty position. The trouble is that there's no way out of it.' Given this fastidiousness, he had to persuade two sides, 'the people' and 'those who had power', to ignore 'those who were in the game for plunder' and agree on a Spartan-type equality which satisfied both. It was not an easy job. 'Those who had power' had exercised it socially through an Athenian version of the widespread share-cropping system, in which a large number of Athenians paid one-sixth of their produce to a superior individual, not to the state, in return for freedom to work their land, a system which grew around or upon the phratry system of dependence described above (p. 29). Politically they had exercised it by an automatic consequence of this; a monopoly of the important magistracies and of the council, the Areopagus, recruited from ex-magistrates, the only deliberative body in the state. There was a citizen assembly, but it is not likely to have played much part except in moments of crisis when public opinion had to be tested or in annual magisterial elections where at most it might occasionally be allowed to show preference for the candidates of one noble faction against another. The Areopagus and the magistrates, indistinguishable in class or interest, ran Athens.

Much of what Solon did, like much of what Draco had done, was merely to codify existing practice, but in his search for something that he could present as a fair compromise he made some astute moves. 'Those who had power' kept their property, much of their position and, more seductive still, their lives. In exchange 'the people' were given 'the dignity that was their due'.

How? All debts had been secured upon the person of the borrower, and so a defaulting share-cropper became a defaulting debtor. Now existing debts were cancelled and personal security was forbidden. Share-cropping ceased to exist ('I freed the soil of Attica that had once been enslaved') and no Athenian could henceforth suffer the indignity of enslavement for debt. The political propagandist added a nice touch: 'I brought back home many who had been sold abroad. . . . who had even forgotten how to speak their native tongue.' One wonders how many he could find.

Politically too some element of equality was sought. The assembly won new authority, perhaps in some ways of which we know nothing (regularity of meeting, possibly? definition of proper business or method of voting?) but certainly by the acquisition of a new directing body, a rival council to the Areopagus, a 'second anchor for the city'. It does not matter how this council was constituted or what wider powers of administration it may have had. It prepared the assembly's programme, oversaw the exercise of any further popular say in elections to office, and was a buffer against Areopagite interference. Such things make a difference. So too did Solon's assertion that the assembly was to be the ultimate court of law. An Athenian could appeal to the assembly or a committee of it against a magistrate's verdict in his court. In the first decades not many will have had the courage to appeal, but the right was there, and was to be exploited.

To each according to his deserts. All Athenians deserved freedom from the threat of slavery, a guarantee against legal oppression, some voice in the direction of the city. But some Athenians, chief among them Solon's supporters, deserved more in the way of real political power. Solon, no less than Cypselus, had had some big men behind him, and they wanted a reward. The solution was simple, but very radical. Access to major political and military office, the archonship, previously restricted by convention to a limited group of families, the Eupatridae (the 'well born'), was to be determined by wealth in land. All Athenians were divided into four classes. To the top class or classes went the top offices, to the lowest, the *thētes*, only membership of the assembly, with consequent judicial influence. So far as can be judged the potential number of 'those with power' was doubled—no mean change.

If there is a note of cynicism in this account of Solon, it is introduced only to remind that Solon was, and had to be, a practising politician, that he was not a sage of moderation called down from Olympus to settle Athens' ills, but a shrewd operator and a radical thinker, a very good and brave man who gave Athenians a chance of peaceful change which, as we shall see, they did not immediately take.

Revolution is rarely in itself a pleasant thing. Even without violence some nice people and nice things tend to get upset. It is comforting that Greek revolutions on the whole led to pleasant things. Under Cypselus and his son Periander Corinth extended and tightened her colonial enterprise, while Corinthian potters and painters made very pretty pots; in Athens a later awakening produced a more startling wakefulness (again reflected for us mainly in the arts) while the liberated share-cropper made the most of his 16-per-cent relief; even in Sparta an imported poet, Alcman (below, pp. 107 f.), talked happily of days, and nights, of pleasure by the banks of the river Eurotas. The distasteful martial spirit of Tyrtaeus was forgotten when Alcman wrote of food, admittedly not elegant food, of wines, and of girls who 'cast glances that are more melting than sleep or death'.

But, as Greeks were fond of saying, though they said it more gracefully, one can have too much of a good thing. Corinthians who had followed Cypselus could not see why they should follow his son or his descendants. Periander's successor was expelled, and Corinth lapsed into an undistinguished oligarchy. Spartans were so pleased with themselves that they turned to further expansion. Some leisure and some freedom made Athenians lust for more of both. The results were gradual decline for Corinth (very gradual—she was always there to be reckoned with), a chequered domination for Sparta, and ultimately democracy in Athens.

Ultimate democracy; first there was a half-century of intermittent tyranny. Solon had refused the role of tyrant and had hoped to inoculate Athenian society against the disease; a young supporter, worse still a relative, proved to be infected and after two trial runs put himself firmly in charge in 546, to be succeeded by his sons after his death in 528. It is not easy to say why Pisistratus was able to establish himself with popular goodwill. Attica had been divided between those who lived around the coast, land that might be generating new wealth in the shape of olive oil, and the outback, rich enough, but far from the centre of things. Pisistratus, though as blue-blooded as any, came from and led the outback. What made it possible? Were his clients in the plain of Marathon producing better oil? Were some of them beginning to exploit the rich silver deposits at Attica's south-east corner? Was there, as a result of economic development or just for its own sake, a feeling that further parts might reach for the centre?

However it came about, it is arguable that a generation of tyranny did more to encourage Athenians towards the three goals mentioned above, national unity, local pride, and individual dignity, than would a continuing adherence to Solonian constitutionalism. Attention was attracted to the city of Athens, not only by the fact that power now rested there, but by public works, temples, fountain-houses, even drains, which made it seem a worthy seat of power, by fostering the cult of the goddess Athena, patroness of Athens and (Pisistratus liked to claim) of Pisistratus himself, by the encouragement or creation of national festivals and games: the Panathenaea, at which (shrewd advertising) the prizes were jars of Attic olive oil; the Dionysia, where first moves were made towards one of Athens' greatest creations, the drama.

Local pride needed no encouragement, but at least the central authority could show that it cared: a panel of itinerant judges was established to settle local disputes, previously in the hands, no doubt, of the local aristocrat. And it is in and around the standing of these aristocrats that lies the solution of the paradox that an autocrat, a tyrant, could, in fact, promote individual freedom and individual dignity.

Solon had opened government to new men, but had done nothing positive to diminish the aristocrat at local level, beyond robbing him of legalized mastery over the poorer around him. Now he had either died in the last battle against Pisistratus or thought it prudent to go into exile or, even if he stayed, knew that he had to acknowledge the existence of someone more powerful than himself.

THE ASSASSINATION OF THE ATHENIAN TYRANT HIPPARCHUS IN 514 BC BY HARMODIUS AND ARISTOGEITON. This event was celebrated by the new democratic regime (after 510 BC) with a statue group which was stolen by the Persians in 480 BC. The group was replaced, and is known to us from copies of the Roman period. Soon afterwards (c.470–460 BC) an Athenian artist offered this version of the event with figures which are inspired by the statues of the replacement group without copying them, but he added the victim.

Thus the rest either lost their master or realized that he did not matter so much as before. To change allegiance from one master to another may not seem to us a momentous step, but it is the first step towards a sense of being one's own master.

Thus, when Pisistratus' sons were expelled in 510 by a combination of exile, intrigue, and Spartan arms (below, p. 36) and the old guard thought that they could resume old-style politics, they found that the audience had changed. One of them, Cleisthenes, head of the great noble house that had supported Solon, the Alcmeonidae, sensed this change sooner than his rivals and, in Herodotus' words, 'added the people to his faction, the people who had previously been ignored, now by offering them a share in everything . . .' Cleisthenes' own motives may have been selfish; some of the things he did may have been designed to secure his own or his family's political future. That is no matter. He offered and with popular support gave Attica a new socio-political structure which served it well for some 200 years.

The essence of the new system was the recognition that small local units, country villages or townlets, wards of the city, should control their own affairs independently of the local aristocrat. Each chose its mayor and its council, and minded its own business. Then, for state purposes, these 'demes' as they were called, were grouped into larger more or less coherent geographical blocks (there are some signs of gerrymandering here) and from these blocks were constructed ten new tribes, each with one block from what were called the 'Plain', the 'Coast', and the 'City'. Upon the tribes were then based not only the army, but other parts of the administrative system, above all the Solonian council, now fifty from each tribe, each contingent serving as a standing committee of the whole council for one-tenth of the year.

In this way an Athenian in his village could make use of whatever self-confidence he may have had; at the same time, at state level, he could develop that sense of nationality which the tyranny had begun to encourage. It is never easy to judge how far legislation promotes a change of attitude, how far it merely recognizes one. Of Athens we can only say that Cleisthenes' legislation came in time to avoid trouble and that it was enough in accord with what was wanted to allow Athenians to do what later they did. He did not tamper with existing social groups, with their cherished cults, or with their prestige. He had no need to: he merely created a new structure and gave it the authority.

The Leadership of Sparta

One thing Athenians did was to fight against the Persian invasions, and morally theirs was the credit for Greek victory. But technically it was taken for granted by the Greeks who chose to resist that Sparta should be their leader. Why? Thanks to the Lycurgan rules Sparta had the only professional army in Greece. She could field 5,000 or so hoplites of her own, backed by a similar number of adequately trained *perioikoi* and many more thousands of lightly armed helots. But this army had no great record of success in the sixth century, and it was as much or more due to diplomacy, given weight by the threat of that army, that she held the respect that she did.

Herodotus says that, thanks to Lycurgus, the Spartans, 'their soil being good and the population numerous . . . sprang up rapidly to power and became a flourishing people. In consequence they soon ceased to be satisfied and to stay quiet . . .' In other words, they were not content to enjoy the relaxed pleasures of Alcman but chose to try to extend their domination into northern Peloponnese. They were opposed by one major city, Argos, and a number of lesser cities, settlements, or tribal agglomerations. Against Argos they won, though in no decisive fashion; against the rest they failed. But failure taught them the lesson that expansion by annexation and enslavement could not work, that to subdue an immediate circle of hostile neighbours would only create a more distant circle of hostile neighbours. A wise Spartan (some Spartans were wise) saw that expansion by diplomacy could be cheaper and more effective.

This sage was Chilon who, in 556 BC, held the office of ephor, an office which had been created in the turmoil of the Lycurgan period for purposes which we cannot now descry, but basically to give the Spartan 'Equals' a chance through an annual election to have their immediate favourites in a position to assert themselves against kings or Gerousia, or to side with one against the other. Chilon is the earliest ephor upon whom we can focus and it is clear that, with the 'Equals' behind him, he transformed Spartan thinking.

The problem was racial as well as military. Out of the confusion of the post-Mycenaean world came a Greece divided between Dorians, Ionians, and others. All were Greeks, all spoke Greek, but very different forms of Greek, all accepted that the Dorians were intruders, though perhaps a rather superior kind of intruder. It is hard to judge what these distinctions meant in day-to-day practice, but they did mean something, and it was Chilon's genius to see that playing down Sparta's Dorianism could cajole hostile non-Dorian neighbours into alliance, with no less profit in the end for Sparta.

So treaties were made city by city, with Corinth, with Sicyon, with the communities of Arcadia, indeed with almost all except the old rival for Dorian hegemony, Argos. In some cases, to fix the alliance, Sparta had to take a hand in the internal affairs of the future ally, and in some cases, in Sicyon for example, this interference led to the expulsion of a tyrant, thus giving a start to Sparta's later reputation as an opponent of tyranny as such. Spartans were not opposed to tyranny as such, except in Sparta, but her expansionism in the next half-century or so (Chilon had changed Spartan methods but had not quenched Spartan ambition) brought her up against various powers which were under tyrants and for differing reasons these had to be removed, chief among them being the sons of Pisistratus in Athens whom, in 510, Sparta successfully attacked with the encouragement and support of Athenian aristocrats in exile.

CORINTH. The city site is in the foreground, dominated by the remains of the sixth-century BC Temple of Apollo. In the distance to the south rises the citadel, Acrocorinth, linked by long walls to the city in the fourth century BC. It is the most impressive of the *acropoleis* of mainland Greece.

Differing reasons. Some tyrants (the Athenian among them) had been friends of Argos, some had established links with a new factor in Aegean politics, the expanding Persian Empire. About 546 the Persians, having absorbed the greater part of the Middle East and Asia Minor, appeared among the Greeks of the Aegean's eastern coastline, who had previously enjoyed a comparatively unoppressive dependence on the non-Greek powers of the hinterland, especially Lydia, under its amiable King Croesus (c.560–546). The Persians believed in tighter control, and compliant tyrants were installed or supported in the Greek cities. In 525 the Persians took over Egypt and then moved along the coast of north Africa; in 514 they crossed into Europe and, in spite of a disastrous foray into southern Russia, maintained a presence in Thrace and influence as far as Macedon. Thus the Greek mainland and the islands were beset to north, south, and east, while even in the west another alien power, Carthage, was pressing on the opulent outposts of Hellenism, the cities of Sicily and southern Italy, which from their poor colonial beginnings were now often as rich and as sophisticated as any in the homeland. The Persians may not have had any immediate ambition to occupy Greece, but they were there and had to be reckoned with. All Greek states we know of were divided about their response. In some the majority, in power if not in numbers, felt that an offer of compliance or even subservience was the more profitable course; others thought that they should fight; in every case there was domestic disagreement, and in every case it was easy for domestic disagreements on other issues to become entangled with the Persian question. A political loser might look to Persia for support, even a political winner could feel more secure with Persian favour. So the surviving exiled son of Pisistratus found sanctuary in Persian territory, and the most powerful family in northern Thessaly, the Aleuadae, lent towards collaboration. It was no different in Sparta. Although for long aware of the problem she resolutely and consistently refused to become involved, but in the end even there a quarrel between the two kings in the late 490s drove one of the disputants, Demaratus, to the Persian court.

Demaratus' opponent, Cleomenes, was clever, over-clever. He was also devious, unscrupulous, ambitious, cruel, and, it was believed, mad. There is no reason to think that this belief was wrong. At any rate, forceful though he was, ingenious though he was, most of Cleomenes' schemes turned sour (in a fit of ultimate despair and lunacy he committed suicide). Yet, paradoxically, his failures strengthened Sparta.

The alliances we have mentioned were between city and city, but the standard formula of a Greek alliance, 'to have the same friends and the same enemies', raised a problem; who was to decide who was whose friend, who was whose enemy? Between Sparta and a tiny community in Arcadia the question was academic; between Sparta and a state such as Corinth it was more delicate; between Sparta and the host of entities large and small to whom she was now allied it was unanswerable. Consequently the system of separate associations, one with one, had to be modified. Gradually or suddenly the idea of a league of states was created or recreated. Sparta was the military commander and effective mistress, but others had a voice. Perhaps they looked back to those other associations we have mentioned. In what must have been a very hazy process one moment stands out. In about 506 Demaratus, supported by the Corinthians and other allies, refused to follow Cleomenes in an attack on Athens (his first interventions had not gone well). Thereafter the 'Peloponnesian League' met in congress and acted only after debate and vote. Sparta provided the military expertise; the rest gave support. And so was created the military organization on which was based the Greek resistance to Persia when in the end Persia decided to invade.

The Persian Wars

In about 500 BC Sparta was the recognized leader of an alliance which embraced virtually all states of the Peloponnese except Argos; neither she nor her allies had shown any commitment on the Persian issue, though she had inadvertently acted against some who found Persians sympathetic. Athens was free of her tyrants, and Athenians were slowly growing to appreciate the 'democratic' constitution that Cleisthenes had invented (it is to be remembered that the word 'democracy' itself had not yet been invented). They had no unanimous view on Persia. Other states were similarly divided, and Herodotus sums it up, cynically but effectively, when he says of the decision of the men of Phocis, a small community in central Greece, to fight: 'My guess is that they did so because they hated the Thessalians. If the Thessalians had chosen to resist the Persians, the Phocians, I think, would have collaborated.'

The first serious trouble showed itself in Asia Minor. There, in the city of Miletus, a Persian-installed tyrant, Histiaeus, who had been adopted as political adviser at the Persian court, and his deputy, Aristagoras, whom he had left behind to look after affairs in Miletus, found themselves at loggerheads with the official Persian authorities. They had believed that they could insinuate themselves into a role of authority; they were wrong, and their machinations produced what later historians have described as a great patriotic outburst, Greek against barbarian, what Herodotus more soberly calls 'the beginning of troubles'. In 499 some (not all) of the Ionian cities, some (not all) of the Aeolian states to the north, perhaps some of the Dorian cities to the south disposed of their tyrants and began open revolt against the Persians. Sparta refused to help. Athens chose—hesitantly, but with irrevocable results—to support the rebels.

So Athens was to be punished, and in 490, after the Ionians and their friends had been squashed in 494, a Persian fleet crossed the Aegean to land on Attic soil at Marathon. Their number is not known, but it was vastly larger than the 10,000 hoplites that Athens and one small friend, Plataea, could put into the field against them. Persians, it is to be remembered, were good soldiers and were commanded

BRONZE HELMET DEDICATED AT OLYMPIA BY MILTIADES in the early fifth century BC. The dedicator's name appears incised along the lower rim—'Miltiades dedicated to Zeus'. It is difficult not to identify this Miltiades as the victor of Marathon. It was customary to dedicate spoils of the defeated (there is a Persian helmet dedicated at Olympia by the Athenians) so this is perhaps not from Marathon, but from some other encounter, with Greeks.

THE PLAIN AT MARATHON. In the decisive battle in 490 BC, in which the Athenians repelled the Persian invasion, the Greeks formed up in the foothills and the flow of the battle was, in this picture, from left to right. The tumulus covering the Athenian dead appears at the centre. This fertile coastal plain is typical of the shore line of central Greece.

by able generals. Yet, miraculously, the Athenians won. More than 6,000 Persians died; some 200 Greeks. The results were many. We note three.

Greeks had distinguished between themselves and 'those who spoke other languages'; other civilized societies had done the same. Now two notions were added to the factual description. One of hostility, the other of superiority. There was something indecent in the idea that a Greek should work on equal terms with a 'barbarian' (one who spoke another language). Practical Greeks did not allow the idea to affect their behaviour. But many exploited it in immediate propaganda, and in the end it was only one who had exploited it to the utmost, Alexander the Great, who began dimly to see that it was absurd.

But the military superiority was real. In some extraordinary way 10,000 or so Greek hoplites had routed a great mass of Persians. It did not need a sophisticated military mind to draw the conclusion that a hoplite phalanx, even if only moderately well trained, could win against cavalry, archery, or any other sort of infantry however armed or brigaded. Spartans were brought up to believe that they were the finest soldiers in the world, but even Spartans must have been encouraged by the Athenian success.

The third result was even more important. Cleisthenes had recognized a change in Athenian attitudes and exploited it against other aristocrats by devising a social and political system which, either by accident or Cleisthenic design, gave scope for further enormous changes of mood. But traditional habits of thought do not die ovenight; in 507 most aristocrats will still have been behaving as they had always behaved. More importantly, most ordinary Athenians will in many respects have continued to behave as they always had. Some few aristocrats and rather more ordinary folk felt otherwise. By 480 the army was still commanded and the city administered by the old ruling class, but its absolute control over Athenian minds was beginning—we stress 'beginning'—to be blunted. Such movements are subtle and hard to plot even when evidence is abundant; they are not only gradual, they are irregular. When evidence is sparse and the atmosphere at start and finish impossible to catch with any precision, when men do not talk explicitly about shifts of this kind, we can only register the fact and look for any clues there are. Aristotle, with characteristic shrewdness, remarks that victory at Marathon gave the Athenian people political confidence. His illustration is the fact that in the decade after Marathon the Athenians first made use of a curious institution, ostracism, another Cleisthenic invention, which allowed the assembly to decide every year to send, should it wish, one of its political figures into temporary ten-year exile without loss of property. The explicit reason for the first three ostracisms was suspicion of treachery in 490, but Aristotle is surely right to think that courage to exercise power is as significant as the occasion for its exercise.

Whether this same surge towards democracy lay behind another constitutional change of these years we cannot say. In 487 direct election to the archonship was replaced by a system which combined election with the use of lot. Was this a conscious 'democratic' move? (Lot was a great feature of the developed democracy.) In the long run the ten generals (normally elected one from each tribe) came to replace the archons as the chief officers of state: desire for elected efficiency overcame principle. But long-term results are frequently not foreseen. We can only note the coincidence of time. The issues are obscure, as are those of the following years, and not only in domestic politics. It would be wrong to assume that, as they saw the tail of the Persian fleet scurrying home in 490, all, or even many, Athenians concentrated on the likelihood that the Persians would return.

Boeotia, increasingly united under its leading city, Thebes, posed no problem. Persuaded by King Cleomenes to share in his unhappy campaign against Athens in about 506, the Boeotians had been soundly thrashed. Nor any longer did Sparta itself. During the nineties her preoccupation was with the Peloponnese, with Argos, on which Cleomenes inflicted a terrible defeat at Sepeia about 494, nearer home with her own helots, who attempted a revolt (of uncertain date and duration), and nearer still with the quarrel between her kings, which led to

Demaratus' withdrawal to Persia. Moreover, at some point she committed herself in principle to the anti-Persian cause and even sent out her army to Marathon—though it arrived only in time to congratulate the Athenians on their success.

But there was another enemy. The rich, commercial island of Aegina, its triangular peak clearly visible some 20 miles from Athens' harbour at Phaleron, was a hostile rival as soon as Athens turned her attention seriously to the sea. There had been one early war. Now, about 500, began a period of conflict or threats of conflict which lasted through the eighties. How many Athenians felt in 489 that Persian flight had left them free to deal with a more immediate enemy?

There is an interesting clue. In 482 an exceptionally rich vein of silver was discovered in the Attic mines at Laurium. There was debate on the use of the profits. One side, led very probably by Aristides, nicknamed 'the Just', a hero of Marathon (he was elected archon in 489), later to distinguish himself in the crisis of 480/79 and to organize the Delian League in 478, argued for a simple distribution among the citizens. Others, whose spokesman was Themistocles, felt otherwise. Themistocles was renowned for his cleverness (some did not use the word in a friendly sense) and foresight. Foresight he had certainly shown when as archon in 493 he had begun to fortify a new and safer harbour at Piraeus, and would show afterwards when he tried to warn and literally fortify Athens against the threat of Spartan jealousy. In 482 he argued that the windfall should be used, not for largesse but for the building of a fleet, 200 warships ('triremes'), which would, as it turned out, be the backbone of Greek resistance to the Persian navy. But that was not his point at the time. He urged instead that a fleet was needed against Aegina, a point which at least reveals the priorities among his audience. Was this deception, or may even his foresight have been a bit blunted by what Pericles later described as 'the eyesore of the Piraeus'—Themistocles' new Piraeus?

The Persians felt no need of foresight, only determination to get their revenge. The Great King, Darius, was fond of Greeks (witness Histiaeus; above, p. 39) but not of Greeks who defeated him, and immediately after Marathon he began to prepare for a greater onslaught. But the plans were thwarted by a revolt in Egypt (487) and Darius' death soon after. Revenge was left to his son, Xerxes. Egypt was brought to order in 485, and the great scheme could be resumed.

Let us remember the situation. Persia held North Africa as far as Cyrenaica, while beyond that was the friendly Phoenician colony of Carthage, itself pressing on the Greeks of Sicily. Persia held the north coast of the Aegean as far as Macedon. Persia held Asia Minor and the offshore islands of the Aegean. Mainland Greece was a very small nut between the teeth of a mighty nutcracker. It never ceases to amaze that it should have been thought to merit the attention it was given. Darius' pride had been injured (but it had already suffered once in southern Russia without similar reaction); his queen, Atossa, was said to have coveted the services of Greek handmaidens; Xerxes may have been touched with megalomania, but none of these things seems to justify the effort—or the risk.

The nut itself was not wholly sound. Greek attempts, once the imminence of

THE ATHENIAN TREASURY AT DELPHI. The Greek states dedicated treasuries at the major national sanctuaries, to house rich offerings and display their own wealth and piety. This stands just below the temple terrace at Delphi beside the Sacred Way, and was dedicated by the Athenians to commemorate their victory at Marathon (490 BC). It was rebuilt at the beginning of this century. It is a small Doric building, of Athenian marble, with sculptural decoration in the metopes, showing the exploits of Heracles and Theseus.

danger had been realized in 481, to find help at any distance, from Crete, Corcyra, and Syracuse, were refused or turned aside with equivocation. North of the
Isthmus of Corinth only Athens and one or two small states, Phocis, Plataea,
Thespiae, were prepared to fight; but neither Thessaly nor Boeotia had much
enthusiasm for the cause. Inside the Peloponnese Argos was neutral. At the heart
of Greek sentiment, Apollo's oracle at Delphi was counselling what at the most
generous can only be called prudence.

When what Herodotus calls 'the Greeks who had the best thoughts for Greece'
met at Sparta in 481 and then at Corinth in spring 480, they resolved to forget
their differences (chiefly those between Aegina and Athens) and gave Sparta the
command on land and, with no material but some diplomatic justification, at sea
(though the voice of the new Themistoclean navy could never be ignored). The
Spartan kings could muster some 40,000 hoplites and substantially more light-
armed troops; the Spartan admiral (the kings rarely took to sea) something over
350 ships—fine forces in Greek terms, but puny in the face of the army which
Xerxes had collected from all his empire and which was on its way towards the
Hellespont and Europe as the Greeks were talking at Corinth, or in the face of
the navy, drawn principally from Phoenicia and the subject Greek states of Asia
Minor, which was to accompany that army along the coast of Thrace while it
looked for a river that it would not drink dry. It is impossible to fix even
approximate figures. Herodotus' 1,750,000 for the army is absurd; 200,000 might
be nearer the mark. His 1,200 ships owes less to fantasy; let us say about 1,000.
No matter—the Greeks should have been overwhelmed.

The only answer was to find a position to defend where Persian numbers
would be of less account and which could not readily be turned by the Persian
fleet (though many throughout seem to have been less aware of this than they
should have been). The first choice was the Gorge of Tempe where the coast
road to the south turns into north-western Thessaly, and a force of 10,000 was
sent to hold it. But closer inspection either confirmed fear of Thessalian irreso-
lution (one of Thessaly's leading families, the Aleuadae, was said to have been
among the foremost in urging Xerxes to invade), or exposed geographical vul-
nerability (there were other routes from the north; naval landings were possible
in the south). The Greeks retired south, and northern Greece was left to the
Persian.

Two defensive lines remained, at the narrow coastal pass of Thermopylae
where the fleet could block the adjacent north-Euboean strait, or at the Isthmus
itself with the fleet a little to the north at Salamis. Against the latter was the
abandonment of Attica, against the former a natural Peloponnesian reluctance to
fight for anything but their own. There are signs of some indecision, but the
choice fell on Thermopylae. Leonidas, who had succeeded to the Spartan throne
after his brother Cleomenes' suicide, moved north with a small Peloponnesian
force, including 300 Spartan 'Equals', and with a hollow promise of full reinforcement, collected willing contingents from some neighbouring states, with 400

Thebans more as hostages than troops, and occupied the narrow pass. The fleet settled off the coast by Artemisium.

Herodotus does not integrate the operations on land and sea that followed when the Persian arms arrived; nor, therefore, can we. But they were interdependent. The fleet, primarily Athenian, was there only to protect the army and, perhaps, to test its new ships against what its commanders must have known were the faster vessels and better seamanship of the Phoenicians and the other Asiatics. With some confusion, some panic, and much help from (it was believed) 'God', it achieved both aims. The serious naval engagements were indecisive, but even that was encouraging. Meanwhile storm had already wrecked many Persians on their way south and now wrecked as many more when Xerxes sent a squadron of 200 to encircle Euboea and catch the Greeks in the rear, 'God' thus doing his best, Herodotus says, to equalize the opposing forces.

In the pass Leonidas' men held out magnificently for two days against the best that Xerxes could send at them. But on the third the Persians found an ill-guarded mountain track and moved round on Leonidas' rear. Most of the Greeks were sent home, but Leonidas, his famed 300, and the men of Thespiae, who merit equal fame, remained; the Thebans stayed too—but not because they wanted to. All but the Thebans, who surrendered, fought and died. It was almost a victory.

Two lessons had been learnt, that Greek ships and sailors were adequate and that the Greek hoplite was supreme. The problem now was to apply those lessons. The second did not immediately arise. When Xerxes occupied an evacuated Attica, his first concern was, very properly, with the sea. It is a pity for him that he was not in a position to concern himself with one seaman, Themistocles, in command of the Athenian navy which he had created. It was he who saw that the only hope lay in battle not anywhere in the open sea, further south at the Isthmus of Corinth or elsewhere, but in the narrow strait between Salamis, to which the fleet had withdrawn, and the mainland where Persian numbers would not count, indeed would count against them. His problems were to persuade his allies that this was what they had to do, and persuade the Persians that that was what they wanted to do. A mixture of diplomacy and blackmail ('either you stay or we go and found a new city in the west') solved the former; a ruse, a secret message to the Persians, solved the latter. Early one morning the Persians rowed into the confusion of the narrows; by afternoon the survivors were struggling out again. The bravery of the Greeks, foremost the Aeginetans and Athenians but Corinthians and the rest as well, and the skill of Themistocles had broken Xerxes' fleet and his nerve. The fleet was sent home, and Xerxes with the bulk of his army painfully retraced the confident steps of a few months before.

There will have been some celebration on Salamis that night. There was cause for celebration in Sicily as well. Some said on the very day of Salamis, the Syracusans had crushed the Carthaginian advance at Himera. In east and west the pressure was off, or so it must have seemed.

THE SITE OF THE BATTLE OF SALAMIS (479 BC) seen from the Island of Salamis facing east across to the Attic mainland and Mount Aegaleus (on the sky line) where the Persian King Xerxes sat to watch his fleet. The Greek ships formed up just beyond the small island (Psyttaleia) and the Persians approached from the open sea, top right. They outnumbered the Greeks by three to one, but once they were drawn into the narrows, they were readily confounded by the greater manoeuvrability and enterprise of their opponents.

FOUR EARLY GREEK COINS (*facing page*). (a) is of electrum, a metal alloy of gold and silver readily obtainable in western Asia Minor where (in Lydia) coinage traditionally started. The dump of metal is struck into the decorated die by a broken metal bar, leaving the rough incuse square sinkings on the back. The example shown carries a stag and the name Phanes, perhaps a ruler or moneyer, and may have been struck in Ephesus in 600 BC. In the Greek homeland the first coinage is struck in silver, on Aegina, probably by the mid sixth century. The device (b) is a turtle and the markings on the punch at the back show that the pattern of the broken metal bar had been stylized into quarterings. Athens soon followed Aegina's lead and her early coins (e.g. c: second half of the sixth century) have heraldic devices—here a Gorgon head and, in the punch mark on the back, a lion's head and paws. From now on a reverse type such as this is a regular feature of Greek coins. Among the western Greeks a flatter coin was developed in the late Archaic Period, with the reverse bearing a hollowed and simplified version of the obverse type. The example from Caulonia (d), of about 510 BC, shows Apollo carrying a branch and a small running figure, with a stag before him. The top two coins are shown at three times actual size, the bottom two at twice.

(a) × 3

(a) × 3

(b) × 3

(b) × 3

(c) × 3

(c) × 2

(d) × 2

(d) × 2

But Xerxes had left behind his general, Mardonius, with a large force of his best soldiers, far more than the 35,000 or so that the Greeks could muster. In face of this the unity of Salamis began to look a little hollow. Quite simply, the Athenians wanted their homes back in security; the Peloponnesians felt happier behind the Isthmus wall. One wanted offensive war, the other did not. There was a winter of bitter argument before Athenian threats were again effective (Themistocles does not now appear by name; instead Aristides edges forward) and the Spartan Pausanias, regent for Leonidas' son, came out to face Mardonius at Plataea on Boeotia's southern border.

The battle, when it came, was more typical of battles in general than Salamis had been—it was a chaotic affair. Neither side, the Greek especially, knew what it was doing, but the Greek hoplites, primarily the Spartans, pushed their way out of the mess to complete victory. On the same day, it was said, the fleet, which had ventured hesitantly across the Aegean, landed on the Ionian coast at Mycale, routed the Persians who opposed them, destroyed much of what was left of their ships, and so cleared the Aegean and began the liberation of the Asiatic Greeks.

There is no one explanation of the outcome. That the hoplite phalanx was a superior military machine; that the Persians made more mistakes than the Greeks (not many); that the Persians were far from home while the Greeks were at home and fighting for their home; that those who fought willingly as free men, 'fearing the laws more than your [Xerxes'] subjects fear you', as the exile Demaratus had once boldly said to the King—all these things counted, and so did luck, or 'God'.

The results can be more clearly seen. The distinction between Greek and barbarian (foreigner) became one between Greek and Barbarian (national enemy), 'appeasement' became 'treachery'. Sparta had won on land, Athens at sea; were these two supremacies to continue, were they to merge or clash? Athens had won as a budding democracy, Sparta as a monarchic oligarchy; would the difference divide not only them, but other Greeks? So the pattern was set.

Further Reading

A. Andrewes, *Greek Society* (Harmondsworth, 1975) is the best general introduction to Greek history; O. Murray, *Early Greece* (London, 1980) is a good modern account of the period. A more detailed account will be found in the second edition of the *Cambridge Ancient History;* with vol. iii 3 (1982) it has reached *The Expansion of the Greek World, Eighth to Sixth Centuries BC.* C. W. Fornara, *Archaic Times to the End of the Peloponnesian War* (Cambridge, 1983) is a useful collection of sources in translation.

For dark age Greece see A. M. Snodgrass, *The Dark Age of Greece* (Edinburgh, 1971); V. R. D'A. Desborough, *The Greek Dark Ages* (London, 1972); J. N. Coldstream, *Geometric Greece* (London, 1979). For the historical value of Homer, discussion starts from M. I. Finley, *The World of Odysseus* (Cambridge, 1954). The hero's tomb at Lefkandi (Euboea) discovered in 1980 is described by M. R. Popham, E. Touloupa, and L. H. Sackett in *Antiquity* 56 (1982), 169-74.

For archaic Greece see W. G. Forrest, *The Emergence of Greek Democracy* (London, 1966); L. H.

Jeffery, *Archaic Greece* (London, 1976); A. M. Snodgrass, *Archaic Greece* (London, 1980). Two books by A. R. Burn offer an excellent longer account: *The Lyric Age of Greece* (London, 1960); *Persia and the Greeks* (London, 1962; 2nd edn., with an appendix by D. M. Lewis, 1984). Important works on individual topics are J. Boardman, *The Greeks Overseas* (3rd edn., London, 1980); A. Andrewes, *The Greek Tyrants* (London, 1956); C. M. Kraay, *Archaic and Classical Greek Coins* (London, 1976); H. W. Parke, *Greek Oracles* (London, 1967); W. G. Forrest, *A History of Sparta* (2nd edn. London, 1980); P. A. Cartledge, *Sparta and Laconia* (London, 1979); J. B. Salmon, *Wealthy Corinth* (Oxford, 1984); R. A. Tomlinson, *Argos and the Argolid* (London, 1972); T. J. Dunbabin, *The Western Greeks* (Oxford, 1948).

2

Homer

OLIVER TAPLIN

Preamble

THE early Greeks envisaged the world as encircled by the mighty freshwater river of Ocean, and held that all springs and streams derived from him. Ocean became their image for Homer: all poetry and eloquence derived from him as he surrounded and encompassed their thought-world. (Among the literary papyri found in Egypt those of The Poet, as he was known, outnumber all the other authors put together.) Alexander Pope, Homer's greatest translator into English, found a different image: 'our author's work . . . is like a copious nursery, which contains the seeds and first productions of every kind, out of which those who followed him have but selected some particular plants . . .' Like all really great literature, it is fecund and inexhaustible, generous to all comers, and it may be cultivated in apparently limitless ways.

There is, in my view, no point in searching for 'Homer' by the marshlight of a pocket biography of the author. Even if this were a good way of approaching literature in general, we simply do not have the material. The many ancient accounts of his life ('. . . mother's name . . . Chios . . . blind . . . died, etc.') are largely, if not entirely, demonstrable fictions: he was given suitable lives, not a true one. The firm conclusions of modern research are meagre, and even then are disputed. Date—somewhere in the area of 750–650 BC; place—the northern-Aegean coast of Asia Minor in the Smyrna area; poetic art learned from other bards in a tradition of performed poetry. It will not do to try to fit these mighty poems to the little we know of the poet. Even if 'Homer' is taken less as a person than as a historical context for the poems, there is little to be gained: we have no firm external evidence of Homer's audience or circumstances of performance. It is inside out to speculate and build up an *external* mould or framework called 'Homer' and then to try to fit the poems to it. The poems themselves are our firm evidence and they contain everything worth knowing about 'Homer'. The poet and his audience must be reconstructed to fit around them. This *internal* approach from within the poems follows the motto of some ancient scholars,

Homēron ex Homērou saphēnizein, 'you should elucidate Homer by the light of Homer.'

'Homer' is, then, for our purposes, the *Iliad* and the *Odyssey*. And what are they? They are narrative poems; they 'tell a story'. But the interest lies not in the story, but in the telling, the way it is turned into literature. Rather than summarize the plot of the *Iliad*, I shall attempt some account of its thematic shape, of some of the fundamental concerns beneath the narrative, such as life and death, victory and defeat, glory and ignominy, war and peace. It is for these that the *Iliad* has won its fundamental place in European literature.

A further reason for not attempting to give yet another brief summary of the plots is that both poems are extremely long—several hundreds of pages of long lines, which would each take about twenty-four hours to read at conversation speed. Each of them is arranged in twenty-four books. While convenient and sensitively done, the division does not go back to the poet. (There is one book for each letter of the later Greek alphabet, and it is unlikely that Homer knew any alphabet, let alone one with twenty-four letters.) It goes against the very nature of the poems to be summarized. Yet this lengthiness is not the result of telling a long and eventful saga from beginning to end: on the contrary, both poems are highly selective. In fact there is reason to think that other epic poets composed poems which were shorter and yet which told of many more events in a much more summary way. While this would be in keeping with the performance of the bards whom we see in the *Odyssey*, the more direct evidence concerns other early epic poems which were around in antiquity, though they are now all but lost. These were known as the 'Cycle' and told other legends such as those of Thebes as well as stories connected with Troy, from the Apple of Discord right through to the death of Odysseus at the hands of Telegonus, his son by Circe. The 'Cycle' known to antiquity was clearly a response to the stature of the *Iliad* and *Odyssey*, since its poems were constructed around them.

One of the most famous poems of the cycle was the *Cypria*. It was apparently longer than most, yet rather less than half as long as *Iliad* or *Odyssey*. So the scant summary we have of its contents is revealing: 'Rivalry at the marriage of Peleus and Thetis . . . . the judgement of Paris on Mount Ida . . . Paris visits Sparta . . . elopes with Helen . . . sacks Sidon . . . Meanwhile Castor and Pollux . . . next Menelaus consults Nestor . . . the expedition is summoned . . . Odysseus feigns madness . . . At Aulis . . . Achilles on Scyros . . . Telephus at Argos . . . back at Aulis the sacrifice of Iphigenia . . . Philoctetes . . . Protesilaus . . .'—and there is still quite a lot to come.

The contrast between this skimming saga and the *Iliad* and *Odyssey* is the subject of some observations made by Aristotle which are extremely enlightening.

[Epic should be] about one whole or complete action with a beginning, middle parts, and end, so that it produces its proper pleasure like a single whole living creature. Its plots should not be like histories; for in histories it is necessary to give a report of a single period, not of a unified action, that is, one must say whatever was the case in that period about one man or more; and each of these things may have a quite casual interrelation. . . . Most epic poets do make plots like histories. So in this respect too Homer is marvellous in that he did not undertake to make a whole poem of the war, even though it had a beginning and an end. For the plot would have been too large and not easy to see as a whole, or if it had been kept to a moderate length it would have been tangled because of the variety of events. As it is he takes one part and uses many others as episodes, for example, the catalogue of the ships and the other episodes with which he breaks the uniformity of his poem. But the rest make a poem about one man or one period of time, like the poet of the *Cypria* or the *Little Iliad*. That is why the *Iliad* and *Odyssey* have matter only for one tragedy or only for two, whereas there is matter for many in the *Cypria*, and in the *Little Iliad* for more than eight . . . (*Poetics* 1459, trans. M. E. Hubbard)

The Iliad

This prompts me to approach the *Iliad* by considering its shaping of time and place. It is not my purpose to make great claims for these frameworks as such, but rather to use them to bring out something of the thematic moulding of the *Iliad*, its underlying geology. I shall try to give some idea how this has a large-scale artistry and coherence, whatever the problems, most of them trivial, of the narrative surface.

The *Iliad* picks a few days only out of the whole story: not the most obvious days (which might be the arrival of the Achaeans, or the wooden horse and sack of Troy), but almost the only days during the ten years when the Trojans had the better of the fighting. It does not matter exactly how many days pass during the poem; what matters is that about twenty-one days pass in the opening scenes and another twenty-one in the closing scenes, thus separating the core from the years that stretch on either side. A very short time passes in between. In fact almost everything from Book 2 all the way to Book 23 takes place during only four days and two nights. Within this very economical time-scheme there is a tight grip on the dramatic calendar.

Take, for example, the great central day which dawns with the first line of Book 11 and sets at 18. 239–40 (almost exactly one-third of the length of the entire *Iliad*). It is tensely awaited during the previous night in the last part of Book 8 and throughout Book 9. When the day comes it is Hector's: despite setbacks he storms the ditch and wall, reaches the ships, kills and strips Patroclus. Zeus explicitly lets him know: 'I guarantee power to Hector to kill until he comes to the benched vessels, until the sun goes down and blessed darkness comes over' (lines 192–4 = 207–9). Hector refers to this message when he rejects the cautious advice of the seer Polydamas (12. 235–6), and when he calls for fire by the ships—'now Zeus has given us a day worth all the rest of them' (15. 719). Zeus himself repeats the terms of his undertaking as he pities Achilles' immortal horses: he will let Hector kill 'until the sun goes and blessed darkness comes over' (17. 453–5). Surely we are to have this in mind when the sun does eventually go

THE MISSION TO ACHILLES, to persuade him to return to the battlefield, was described in *Iliad* 9. The scene becomes popular on Athenian vases in the early fifth century, when the story was also treated on the stage by Aeschylus. On the vases the heroes involved and Achilles' mood do not closely mirror Homer's treatment. On this vase Odysseus is seated arguing with the disconsolate Achilles. At the left is an old man, Phoenix (Achilles' mentor) and at the right Patroclus. The artist (the Cleophrades Painter) is particularly fond of Trojan scenes: the date is about 485–475 BC.

ACHILLES FIGHTS MEMNON, on a vase by the Berlin Painter of about 490 BC. At the left Achilles is encouraged by his mother Thetis, and at the right a distressed Eos (Dawn), mother of Memnon, gesticulates towards her doomed son. The duel did not appear in the *Iliad*, but is popular with artists. It was preceded by a weighing of the souls of the heroes before Zeus (*psychostasia*) such as was performed for Achilles and Hector in *Iliad* 22, and it was attended by their mothers, which is why they are often also shown attending the fight. Memnon was an Ethiopian prince, the most handsome man at Troy.

down in Book 18. Immediately after that Polydamas advises the Trojans to retreat inside the walls; and it is the subtle control of the time-scheme which give the point to Hector's deluded reply;

> But now, when the son of devious-devising Kronos has given
> me the winning of glory by the ships, to pin the Achaians
> on the sea, why, fool, no longer show these thoughts to our people.
>
> (18. 293-5)

'Now' is wrong: Hector's day is over, and the next will be his last.

But while the action itself is so tightly bound in a few days, the *Iliad* makes us feel the pressure of the time that has gone before and will come after. Much of the long span between the quarrels on earth and Olympus in Book 1 and the first full-scale battle well on in Book 4 is taken up in giving us some sense of the previous nine years. Agamemnon himself admits

> And now nine years of mighty Zeus have gone by, and the timbers
> of our ships have rotted away and the cables are broken,
> and far away our wives and our young children
> are sitting within our halls and wait for us, while still our work here
> stays forever unfinished . . .
>
> (2. 134-8)

The frustration weighs heavy, and Odysseus has to remind the Greeks of Chalcas' interpretation of the omen at Aulis, that they would take Troy only in the tenth year (2. 299 ff.). Then we have the marshalling of the Achaeans, the catalogues of Greeks and Trojans, and the advance of the two armies. In Book 3 we have Helen of Troy, the view from the walls which further introduces the Greek leaders, the attempt at negotiations, the single combat of Paris and Menelaus, and the repetition of the fatal coupling of Paris and Helen. In Book 4 the treachery of Pandarus re-enacts the guilt of Troy; and then at last battle is joined. The past of the war has passed fleetingly before our eyes.

The future is almost all concentrated into two momentous events of destruction: the death of Achilles and the sack of Troy. Though they will happen months after the end of the poem, both are made the inevitable consequence of events within it. The death of Patroclus means the return of Achilles to battle; that means the death of Achilles himself and the death of Hector; and that means the sack of Troy. We are made to anticipate and envisage these future events so that imaginatively they are part of the *Iliad*. Of the many previsions two of the most vivid come close to the very death of Hector. With his last words he warns Achilles of the threat of his doom, but Achilles knows it well already and replies: 'Die: and I will take my own death at whatever time Zeus and the rest of the immortal gods choose to accomplish it' (22. 365-6). And as Hector's corpse is dragged in the dust the lamentation goes through Troy—'It was most like what would have happened, if all lowering Ilion had been burning top to bottom in fire' (22. 410-11).

The poem is rounded off by the meeting of Priam and Achilles which leads to the burial of Hector 'and on the twelfth day we shall fight again, if so we must do' (24.667). The poem is opened by the visit to the Greek camp of another old man who comes to ransom his child; and the speculation that Chryses was invented to counterbalance Priam is hard to resist. The few days in between are in no way a snippet from the Trojan saga, but stand for the whole war from the crime of Paris to the ashes of Troy.

There is a comparable economy of place. In fact nearly all the *Iliad* is set in one of four places, distinct in topography and significance: the city of Troy, the Greek camp, the plain in between, and Olympus. The city is ringed by its great walls and gates. Within it has broad streets and fine houses built of ashlar blocks, dominated by the mighty palace of Priam (described at 6.242ff.). These houses contain fine furniture, clothing, treasures; but above all they contain the Trojans' old people, wives, and children. It is no doubt significant that the first Trojan home we are taken inside is the childless one of Helen and Paris; but when Hector comes back to Troy in Book 6:

> all the wives of the Trojans and their daughters came running about him
> to ask after their sons, after their brothers and neighbours,
> their husbands . . .   (283ff.)

In peacetime, before the Achaeans came, Troy had been a prosperous city ornamented with all the features of a civilized society. The standard epithets of Troy ('with broad streets', 'horse-pasturing', etc.) act as a constant reminder, almost subliminal in effect, of the constriction of the siege.

For all its fine stonework Troy is vulnerable and may be burned. This is even more true of the Achaean camp, which consists of wooden ships and shelters. So far the Greeks have felt so secure that they have not even built defences. At 7.436ff. they build a wall and ditch in one day, and this is fought over and breached in Books 11–15. Unlike Troy, this temporary camp has no past; it had been mere beach, and it will in time disappear again (7.446ff.; 12.1ff.). Over the years the shelters have grown quite substantial, and Homer seems to have a clear 'map' of the different bivouacs along the beach, with Achilles at one end and Ajax at the other. They contain possessions and women taken from neighbouring cities, but they are not homes. The Greeks have left their wives and children and parents at home. Phrases about 'the ships' are everywhere throughout the *Iliad*. They are the 'subliminal' reminder that the Greeks are away from home in a setting which is not household or city.

For both sides there are turning-points in past and future connected in time and place. For the Trojans the crucial day was the day the ships arrived on the beach; in the future it will be either the day they depart or the day that the city is burned. For the Greeks the crucial past event was the day each left his home—an event often recalled; in the future it will be death or return to parents, wife, and children. This may help us see why Homer devotes so much trouble to the

THE DRAGGING OF HECTOR'S BODY BY ACHILLES. On this late-sixth-century Athenian vase the artist expresses several different aspects of the story. The hero leaps on to his chariot to which Hector's corpse is already attached. At the left Hector's parents (Priam and Hecuba) mourn in a setting which represents the Trojan palace. At the right the white mound is the tomb of Patroclus whose shade (the little winged warrior above it) is to be appeased by this act. The winged woman in the foreground is not easily identified, but may be Iris, who was sent by Zeus (in *Iliad* 24) to tell Priam to ransom his son's body (see next illustration).

delightful journey to the city of Chryse in Book 1 (430–80): it helps to establish the framework of time and place for both sides still at Troy.

The plain which lies between the two sides is much less specific in topography and in human associations. For much of the war it has been an empty no-man's-land, or it has been occupied by the armies in the morning and emptied again in the evening. After their victory in Book 8 it is the first time in nine years that the Trojans have even contemplated camping out in the plain; the next night in Book 18 is the second and last time. In peacetime the plain may have been the deep tilth and horse pasture of Troy's traditional epithets, but in the *Iliad* it is dusty and almost barren. It is simply the place where warriors win glory and get killed.

During the *Iliad* the gods travel far and wide, but they always converge on Mount Olympus. There they have their homes each built by Hephaestus, though they usually meet to feast and converse in the great palace of Zeus. It is an immortal world of feasting and splendour. The gods are deeply involved in the Trojan war and are not untouched by the sufferings of city, camp and plain below; but the contrast is still extreme. For the gods there are no crucial turning-points in past or future; their life is diluted by immortality.

Homer is abundant, and there are many aspects which I have scarcely touched on yet. The most pressing is perhaps the *Iliad's* creation of memorable and persuasive human portraits. Quite apart from the scores of minor figures, there is a spread of some two dozen finely individualized major characters. I shall select only the two most important, Achilles and Hector. It would be too simple to claim Achilles as *the* hero (as was seen by whoever it was who early on titled the poem *Iliad—The Poem of Troy*). Achilles occupies the second half of the first line, but Hector occupies the same place in the last. The balance and contrast between these two connect revealingly with the underlying themes already sketched.

Thus Achilles is a young adventurer away from home, out to win loot and glory. His closest bond (apart from his parents) is with Patroclus, his fellow warrior who looks after his horses. Achilles sleeps with captured women—though there is a poignancy in the hints that had he returned home he would have properly married Briseis. Achilles' loyalties and responsibilities are only to those friendships and relationships which he chooses to stand by, and to himself.

Hector, on the other hand, is the greatest of Priam's sons—'but one was left me who guarded my city and people' (24.499). He fights before the eyes of his parents, brothers, and whole family. His fellow citizens depend on him: if he falls, they all fall. As he makes clear in Book 6 (440ff.) and again in 22 (99ff.), it is his sense of responsibility for them that keeps him in the front line and in the end sends him to his death:

> Now, since by my own recklessness I have ruined my people,
> I feel shame before the Trojans and the Trojan Women . . .
>
> (22.104–5)

His closest relationship is not with another man, but with his wife Andromache (she even looks after his horses—see 8.185-90). Their meeting in Book 6, one of the great scenes, must also serve as their farewell, since they do not meet again in the poem. Their small son is the bond between them and their reason to look to the future; and yet he epitomizes the 'heroic paradox'. Hector prays for him:

> Zeus, and you other immortals, grant that this boy, who is my son,
> may be as I am, pre-eminent among the Trojans . .
>   . . . and let him kill his enemy
> and bring home the bloodied spoils, and delight the heart of his mother.
>
>   (6.476-81)

The urge to gain heroic glory kills both Hector and his son, for it demands a loser as well as a winner. The *Iliad* never shirks this two-sidedness.

Near the end of the poem Hera compares the two men:

> Hector was mortal, and suckled at the breast of a woman,
> while Achilles is the child of a goddess . . . you all
> went, you gods, to the wedding . . .   (24.55 ff.)

Hector is a great man; Achilles is mortal as other men, but there are ways in which he is close to the divine. He has possessions which were presents from the gods—his spear, his horses, the great shield and armour which Hephaestus makes for him in Book 18. His mother Thetis, caught between the two worlds, can tell him more than other men know, and can give him special help. She can even gain him special favours from Zeus, as is shown in the first book. Even so Achilles is a man and cannot see everything that this means. Only too late can he see:

> My mother, all these things the Olympian has brought to accomplishment.
> But what pleasure is this to me, since my dear companion has perished . . .
>
>   (18.78 ff.)

There is one thing, however, which Thetis can tell Achilles for certain, while for all other men it remains the great unknown. He has a choice of long life or young death, which is also a choice between uneventful obscurity and eternal glory (9.410-16).

So when Achilles decides, without hesitation ('then let me die soon', 18.98), that he must return to the fight for vengeance on Hector, he does so without any doubt that his own death will follow soon after. Hector, on the other hand, must, like everyone else, hope against hope for a long and prosperous life. Even when the dying Patroclus prophesies his death (16.843 ff.), Hector retorts:

> Patroclus, what is this prophecy of my headlong destruction?
> Who knows if even Achilles, son of lovely-haired Thetis,
> might before this be struck by my spear, and his own life perish?

Even when he faces Achilles he maintains that the battle is not a foregone conclusion; and it is only at the last minute that he realizes that this is indeed the

THE RANSOM OF HECTOR. From the left Priam approaches with attendants bearing rich gifts. Achilles, at ease on his dining couch beneath which lies Hector's corpse, turns away to tell a cup-boy to bring more wine (the boy carries sieve and dipper). The mood is one of supplication to an arrogant hero rather than the more sympathetic one of Homer (*Iliad* 24), but was long preferred in Greek art. This Athenian cup is by the Brygos Painter, of about 490–480 BC.

end (22. 296ff.). But it is then, when he knows he has lost and when he has no aid from god or man, that Hector shows his finest heroism:

> Let me at least not die without a struggle, inglorious,
> but do some big thing first, that men to come shall know of it.

> (22. 304–5)

Hector loses, and yet he still wins immortal fame. He wins it because of the quality of his life and of his death. The *Iliad* is not so much concerned with what people do, as with the way they do it, above all the way they face suffering and death.

Achilles is the greatest warrior, the greatest looter and killer of all. But what makes him great is not that, but the uniquely penetrating way in which he thinks matters through. He sees and expresses the human condition without evasion or periphrasis. We feel this quality when he refuses compromise in Books 1 and 9, and when he shows no mercy to Lycaon in 21 (34 ff.) nor to Hector in 22.

> For as I detest the doorways of death, I detest that man, who
> holds one thing in the depths of his heart, and speaks forth another.
>
> (9. 312–13)

But it is this same quality that leads to his treatment of Priam in Book 24, when, as Alfred Heubeck has put it, 'the image of the great man replaces that of the great hero.' Achilles sees, and brings the old father Priam to see, that it is the human lot to be bereaved, to endure—and as tokens of this to eat, drink, make love, and sleep. These things transcend the barriers which break men up into individuals and nations.

So Homer wins immortal glory in rather the same way as his finest characters, by going beyond the mere narrative achievements of killing and derring-do. He sets mighty deeds in a context of defeat as well as victory, woman as well as man, peace as well as war, doubt as well as confidence, feeling as well as action.

The Odyssey

Whether the *Iliad* and the *Odyssey* are by one and the same poet is one of the great unanswered questions of literary history. We should concentrate, without attempting here any answer, on the ways in which the two poems complement each other, helping to define each other's qualities. The obvious analogy—and one which is indeed directly related—is the complementary natures of tragedy and comedy. In the *Iliad* noble heroes move inexorably, by way of a combination of choice and of forces beyond their control, towards destruction and dissolution. We are left with mourning, honour, endurance, and pity. In the *Odyssey* a somewhat dubiously heroic hero wins his way through various fantastical hazards by means of trickery and ingenuity. The *Odyssey* is not exclusive; it has room for travel, for rustics and servants, for low life, and for dastardly villains. Its overall movement is away from war and from barbarity towards prosperity and peace, centred on the wife and a happy domestic scene. We are left with celebration and poetic justice, with loyalty and perseverance and intelligence rewarded. The beggar has turned out to be Odysseus in disguise, home at last. The tragedy-comedy dichotomy should not, however, be pushed too far. The *Iliad* has its humour especially, but by no means exclusively, at the funeral games in Book 23. The *Odyssey* contributes much to the future of tragedy: one only has to think of the recognition scenes, of the scenes of foreboding, and the tense planning of revenge.

The frameworks of time and place may again prove a way of bringing out some of the 'thematic geology'. The handling of the time-scheme is rather similar to that of the *Iliad*. Odysseus was ten years returning from Troy, but the poem picks up only the last forty days or so, and one-third of the poem (Books 16–23) takes only two days. Care is taken in the opening 100 lines of the poem to associate the taking up of the stories of both Odysseus and his son Telemachus, though they are worlds apart on anarchic Ithaca and the unreal island of Calypso. The number of days between then and their reunion in time and place at the shepherd's farmstead in Book 16 is carefully limited, though not precisely plotted. Odysseus' time on Phaeacia, however, is made to fit into three days (the middle one including the tales of his wanderings stretches from 8. 1 to 13. 17).

There is a certain symmetry to the two climactic days on Ithaca. At 16. 1 dawns the day which sees Odysseus enter his palace and endure maltreatment at the hands of the suitors and their minions. At the end of 18 the suitors go to their own homes for the night; but we are made to wait before Odysseus sleeps. First there is his long interview with Penelope, which is itself held in suspense when the aged nurse Eurycleia finds her master's old scar. Eventually Odysseus beds down in the opening lines of Book 20, only to hear his maidservants giggling on their way to join the suitors:

> He struck himself on the chest and spoke to his heart and scolded it:
> 'Bear up, my heart. You have had worse to endure before this,
> on that day when the irresistible Cyclops ate up
> my strong companions, but you endured it until intelligence
> got you out of the cave . . .'

The next day, however, gets off to a good start. Zeus thunders, and Odysseus overhears an old woman who is grinding corn:

> Father Zeus. . . . you show this forth, a portent for someone.
> grant now also for wretched me this prayer that I make you.
> On this day let the suitors take, for the last and latest
> time, their desirable feasting in the halls of Odysseus.
>
> (20. 91–121)

This is the day set for the contest of the bow and axes. It does not come to an end until Odysseus and Penelope have gone to bed, have made love, and have talked. (The strange episodes of Book 24 take one further day.)

Within these few days, however, the *Odyssey* knows scarcely any limits in place. This is very different from the *Iliad*. The *Iliad* looked outward from a narrow focus at Troy: in the *Odyssey* the journeys are converging, and converging from various places. It is a poem of the sea as well as of land, it reaches to the verges of the known world, and beyond into the realms of fable, and even ventures to the underworld of the dead (briefly in Book 24, as well as in Book 11). The opening lines of the entire poem prepare us for this broad geography:

> Tell me, Muse, of the man of many ways, who was driven
> far journeys, after he had sacked Troy's sacred citadel.
> Many were they whose cities he saw, whose minds he learned of,
> many the pains he suffered in his spirit on the wide sea,
> struggling for his own life and the homecoming of his companions.

It was a master stroke to devote the opening books of the poem not to Odysseus but to Telemachus. This gives us at the start a picture of the masterless palace on Ithaca and the unruly suitors who disrupt it. We then follow Telemachus on the relatively limited journeys he makes to Pylos and Sparta, to enquire after news of his father, journeys which are vital to his developing realization of what it means to be the son of Odysseus. He is also given the chance to see what stable and civilized households are like and to appreciate the worth of proper hospitality.

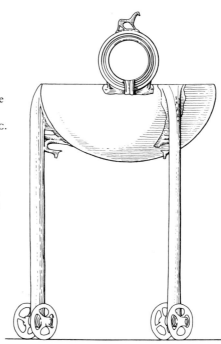

WHEELED BRONZE TRIPOD, found in a sea-shore cave at Polis on the island of Ithaca. Late eighth century BC. The cave appears to have housed a cult of Odysseus, which must have been inspired by the story of the hero's return home as told in the *Odyssey*, where he brings thirteen tripods (at least twelve were found) from Phaeacia and hides them in a cave near his landing place.

We first find Odysseus in Book 5 'suffering' the hospitality of the mysterious island-nymph Calypso. She has kept him as her lover for all the years since he lost his ships and men. Her island is paradisiacal (see the description at 5.55–74) but it does not satisfy Odysseus: he is a man and longs for a proper home among men, and he longs for his mortal wife. After a vast and terrifying journey alone across the sea, Odysseus makes his vital landfall on Phaeacia. He kisses the soil and beds down under cover of a thicket of wild and cultivated olive (5.463, 476ff.) Phaeacia is a land which is in several ways half-way between the real world and 'fairyland'. Demodocus, the bard at the court of King Alcinous, sings of one end of that world, the great deeds at Troy. Troy is Odysseus' departure point when he himself tells of his travels, and he is almost home (9.79) when he is driven away into the world of the 'traveller's tales'—the wanderings which may have made the word 'Odyssey' part of our everyday vocabulary. The lotus-eaters, the Cyclops, Circe, the Sirens, Scylla and Charybdis, and finally the cattle of the Sun—these are the archetypal adventures of the European consciousness, material for the imaginations of poets, painters, and children ever since.

By the time Odysseus leaves Phaeacia the *Odyssey* is just over half-way through, and Odysseus is about half-way from the fringe world of Polyphemus and Circe towards a homecoming. While he makes this last marine transition he sleeps (13. 78–80):

> They bent to their rowing, and with their oars tossed up the sea spray,
> and upon the eyes of Odysseus there fell a sleep, gentle,
> the sweetest kind of sleep with no awakening, most like death . . .

On land Odysseus sleeps by an olive tree with his treasures, and when he realizes that this is Ithaca he kisses its soil (13. 102ff., 120ff., 354). So the threads of the vast journey of Odysseus and the lesser apprentice voyage of Telemachus (with a last view of Sparta and Pylos at 15. 1–300) are drawn together at the remote, yet very real, farmstead of the loyal swineherd Eumaeus, a straightforward dwelling free from strangeness, danger, and deceit.

The time comes for Odysseus to make his way from this outpost to his own palace in the town. It is a significant journey which culminates with the recognition by the old dog Argus (17. 182–327).

> The doom of dark death now closed over the dog, Argus,
> when, after nineteen years had gone by, he had seen Odysseus.

The palace is the setting of the next six-and-a-half books, and attention is lavished on this setting, its rooms, corridors, stairways, and courtyards. But two rooms are given special significance: the great hall, which is the battlefield where the suitors feast and where they spill their blood in recompense; and the marital bedroom which Odysseus himself made immovable around the stock of a mighty olive. 'They then gladly went together to bed, and their old ritual' (23. 296). The poem ends at the farm of Laertes, Odysseus' father, in the Ithacan countryside near by.

The first word of the *Odyssey* is *andra*, 'the man', and that man is far more directly the core of the poem than 'the wrath of Achilles' is of the *Iliad*. The first four books, the 'Telemachy', is the only substantial part in which Odysseus is not involved; and even that is very clear preparation for him. Telemachus finds out the nature of a properly civilized society, the sort worthy of that great friend and fellow fighter of Nestor and Menelaus, Odysseus.

Odysseus left Troy a great hero. We hear from Demodocus of his finest hour at the sack. But as his travels go on he loses his treasure and his companions. To escape the Cyclops he even toys with losing his name. As part of his plot to escape he gives his name as 'Noman'. Once at sea Odysseus cannot resist revealing his real name. Though this gives the Cyclops a name to curse, it also salvages Odysseus' heroic identity. But after many years of slothful obscurity with

Calypso (whose name is close to the Greek word for to 'conceal') what is there left of the celebrated Odysseus? On his journey to Phaeacia he loses even his clothes. He has no possessions at all, and to approach Nausicaa he has to hold a branch in front of his nakedness. Only his wits are left to him, and these he puts to good use.

It is not until he has proved himself in Phaeacia that he is ready to proclaim himself. Despite the urgent curiosity of his hosts, the moment is held back until Book 9 (19-28):

> I am Odysseus son of Laertes, known before all men
> for the study of crafty designs, and my fame goes up to the heavens.
> I am at home in sunny Ithaca . . .
> a rugged place, but a good nurse of men; for my part
> I cannot think of any place sweeter to look at.

To win on Ithaca he has to disguise himself and reveal his identity to as few as possible. But when the vital moment comes, there is no need for Odysseus to declare his name, and he identifies himself with great dramatic understatement:

> You dogs, you never thought I would any more come back
> from the land of Troy, and because of that you despoiled my household . . .

> (22.35ff.)

The *Odyssey* is not, then, only a journey of physical endurance for Odysseus; the survival of his heroic stature and his reputation are put to the test. He has to come back from the very verges of civilization and of humanity; and to do so he has to show patience as well as cunning. He must never give himself away until he is sure of the other party; and so again and again there are scenes of testing— Odysseus even tests his old father after the danger is past. He always keeps his guard up. The only time it fails is when his wife out-tests him with the secret of the construction of their bed: Penelope shows herself worthy of Odysseus (Book 23).

But it is not only loyalty which is tested in the *Odyssey*. It is an overtly moral poem in which villainy meets its just deserts. The villains are those who do not care for a secure and prosperous world; and it is especially by the testing of hospitality and inhospitality that the various societies visited by Odysseus are distinguished. It is, of course, the suitors above all who abuse all the rules of civilized behaviour. They ransack another man's property, try to murder his son, importune his wife, sleep with his servants, and use his house for their riotous living. Their insolence towards all comers is illustrated in such profusion that we hardly need the explicit moralizing of 22.373-4:

> '. . . so you may know in your heart, and say to another,
> that good dealing is better by far than evil dealing.'

This clear pattern of crime and punishment is quite different from the tragic inscrutability of the *Iliad*. This is reflected on a divine plane also. The suitors offend the divine laws no less than the human—

'. . . fearing neither the immortal gods who hold wide heaven
nor any resentment sprung from men to be yours in future.'

(22.39-40)

Odysseus is not only a man reclaiming his own, he is an agent of divine punishment. The way that he comes in disguise to test people, and then rewards or punishes their reception of him, draws on the perennial 'story-pattern' of the god or angel or fairy who visits earth in humble disguise. It is not only Odysseus' homecoming which is at stake, but our whole sense of whether the gods care about right and wrong in this world. As long as the suitors flourish, this remains in doubt. The delight we take in the outcome is voiced by the ancient Laertes when he exclaims

'Father Zeus, there are gods indeed upon tall Olympus,
if truly the suitors have had to pay for their reckless violence.'

(24.351-2)

The pleasure we take in the *Iliad* is the pleasure proper to tragedy, the salvage of humanity amid destruction: the *Odyssey* indulges our optimism, our hopes that all will turn out to be well, that the strange beggar will set all to rights.

The Tradition

I have presented the *Iliad* and *Odyssey* as coherent works of art, held together on many levels by organic links both sweeping and intricate, 'like a single whole living creature', as Aristotle put it. But this view has been by no means an orthodoxy. I have up till now scarcely touched on the questions which dominated Homeric studies from 1795 for the next 140 years or more: the dispute between so-called 'analysts' and 'unitarians'. In 1795 F.A. Wolf published, with considerable misgivings, the first serious case for holding that the *Iliad* and *Odyssey* as we have them are compilations put together from the works of many poets.

Once the notion was established, scholars devoted themselves to analysing the poems into their constituent contributors, and to isolating the 'real' Homer among them. However much aesthetic intuition might feel the poems to be unities, the experts insisted that reason and science showed them on analysis to be many poems more or less incompetently combined. My own view is that, subject to some relatively minor reservations, the poems are in a better form as they are than they can have been at any earlier stage of development. Whoever put them in their present form was, that is to say, so much the best of the poets who contributed to them that he is The Poet.

In any case the great bulk of the arguments which the analysts brought to bear have been invalidated by the recognition in the last fifty years of the relation of Homer to his tradition, to the poets before him. We have come to see that there are ways in which many poets may have contributed to the *Iliad* and *Odyssey* other than by the editorial combination of separate and separable parts. Much analytic work was based on the unravelling of elements, often inconsistent with each other, which were claimed to come from different periods of history; these included linguistic as well as material and cultural elements. Most analysts also took verbal repetitions as evidence for their theories: only one occurrence was the 'original', and all others were later and derivative additions. All of this collapses once it is seen that the poetic tradition which Homer inherited would by its very nature have incorporated elements from different periods and even different cultures, regardless of technical consistency; and that it would have positively depended on verbal repetition. While this discovery did not come out of nowhere, the credit for its synthesis goes to the Californian Milman Parry (who died at the age of thirty-three in 1936).

Every work of art comes out of a unique interaction between tradition and the individual talent. But Homer's debt to his tradition is different, in both quality and quantity, from any kind familiar in the rest of European literary history. The key to this difference is that Homer learned to compose poetry *aurally*, by listening to more experienced bards. Whether he could himself write or whether he composed *orally* remains controversial. But the case—as near to 'proof' as can be expected—has been made that he is the beneficiary of a tradition passed orally from generation to generation.

ODYSSEUS AND CIRCE. Greek artists, like the playwrights of comedy, could take a relaxed view of mythical occasions. This cup is of a class well represented in the fourth century at the Sanctuary of the Cabiri near Thebes. It shows a puzzled, but determined, Odysseus with drawn sword, threatening Circe, who has left her loom to mix him the potion by which she hopes to turn him into an animal, as she had already his companions. The *Odyssey* enjoyed the attention of classical artists less than the *Iliad*, but there are some favoured scenes.

THE CYCLOPS' CAVE. A unique scene, on an Athenian vase of about 480 BC showing the giant Cyclops (Polyphemus) blinded by Odysseus, blocking the exit from his cave while his flock pass by him with Odysseus and his companions clinging on beneath their bellies—the story of *Odyssey* 9. About 480 BC by an artist who also left us a good study of Odysseus with the Sirens.

Parry worked from the ubiquitous verbal repetitions. The fixed epithets are the most obvious, with both proper names and ordinary nouns—'much-enduring Odysseus', 'wine-dark sea'—but there are also whole lines and even blocks of lines which come again and again. Virgil's 'pius Aeneas', like Tennyson's 'And answer made the bold Sir Bedivere', imitates this pervasive characteristic. Parry made the crucial connection between this 'formulaic' diction and the possibility, long speculated on, that Homer was an oral bard rather than a literate writer. He started from proper names and their epithets, and demonstrated how these constitute a remarkable system within the technically demanding epic metre, the dactylic hexameter. (Which like all Greek metres is based on certain combinations of long ($-$) and short ($\cup$) syllables.) By means of this system Homer had at his disposal a noun-epithet combination to fit all forms of the names of all his main characters (as e.g. nominative *Hēctōr*, accusative *Hēctŏră*). What is more, he had a different noun-epithet combination to go in each of the main sections into which the line might be divided. For example, the last six or seven syllables of the line, $\underline{\cup\cup} - \cup\cup - \underline{\cup}$, often form a section after a verb (such as the very common *prŏsĕphē*, 'he/she said') which needs to be filled with a noun–epithet combination. On the other hand, while Homer has a formula ready for all these standard eventualities, he has by and large one, and only one, for each eventuality. Thus after *prŏsĕphē* Hector is *always kŏrўthāiŏlŏs Hēctōr*, 'of the shining helmet'. The remarkable thoroughness of this system of 'extension' and 'economy', as Parry called them, must have been the product of an inherited tradition. The concomitant processes of enlargement and refinement must have taken generations, and must have been the product of composition by oral improvisation. The development of the diction, passed from master to apprentice over generations, was practical as well as aesthetic.

Once we have in mind this process of an oral tradition constantly acquiring attractive and useful new material and casting off outmoded or unpleasing or superfluous material, it may be extended beyond names and nouns to verbs and phrases and whole lines. For example, in the part of the line before the verb *prŏsĕphē* there is a whole range of formulae, mostly using participles, which give a tone or attitude to 'he said'—'in reply', 'standing near', 'greatly troubled', 'looking darkly', etc. It is rather like a system of chemical elements which can combine in all sorts of different ways to make up different molecules. There has been a tendency, however—partly due perhaps to the molecular or 'building-block' analogy—to reckon the range of combinations and possibilities of expression to be far more limited than they are. Parry and his successors may also have based too much on the analogy of still surviving traditions of oral verse-making, especially in Croatia; these have comparable formulaic systems, but they are far more limited and crude than those at Homer's disposal. The possibilities of his diction are amazingly rich, with an abundance of variation and flexibility and a huge range of subtly differentiated vocabulary and formulaic phrases. Homer never seems at a loss or stuck in a corner for the right means of expression. His formulaic diction increases rather than limits his poetic inventiveness.

But while the range and fecundity of the traditional oral language should not be underestimated, neither should its pervasiveness in the making of Homeric poetry. The inheritance of ready-made elements extends beyond phrases and lines to whole scenes. This is clearest in the scenes such as serving a meal or launching a ship, 'typical' scenes as they have come to be known, where whole blocks of lines are completely or nearly repeated verbatim. But the traditional 'formulaic' scene-shape can often be seen in sequences where there is little actual verbal repetition. This has been amply demonstrated by Bernard Fenik for the mass of battle scenes in the *Iliad*, material which one would expect to be highly traditional. But the same inherited shaping may be seen in recurrent sequences in the *Odyssey*. For example, the hero arrives in a strange place and is at a loss; he is met by a noble stranger who helps him and directs him to the royal palace. The outline provides a set of directions for the oral poet to work within.

Once more we should not assume that the traditional pattern is restrictive or inflexible. It creates expectations which as well as being satisfied may on occasion be varied or contradicted. Take, for example, the slight variation on the usual scene-sequence of the arrival of a stranger at a hospitable house, which we have when Telemachus arrives at Sparta at the beginning of *Odyssey* 4. Usually the host himself takes charge of the guest at once; but here there is a wedding feast in progress and Telemachus is met by Menelaus' henchman, who is not sure what to do and consults Menelaus while Telemachus waits outside. Menelaus is angry at this and insists that the strangers should be treated properly whatever the circumstances. The variation in the pattern shows the example of really noble hospitality. The pattern of a 'typical sequence' can also be carefully adhered to and thus create a sense of order and orthodoxy. A remarkable use of this possibility comes in the last book of the *Iliad*. Feasting in Homer, and no doubt in epic bards before him, is narrated with a set of procedures which include many recurrent formulaic lines. A sense of ceremony and normality is thus imparted to this daily social occasion which ratifies a communal bond. In *Iliad* 24.621 ff., however, these regular procedures, told in the familiar way, take on a special colour and significance since the two parties are Achilles and Priam. The uniqueness of the occasion, and its boldness, gain greater depth from its typicality.

Parry's discoveries have, then, opened up new explanations and significances for the 'repetitiousness' of Homer. They also account for the strange linguistic phenomena of Homeric diction. His language is evidently nothing like the Greek that any native speaker ever spoke. Most of the word-forms are variants drawn from the dialects of different places and periods, but never spoken together in any one time or place. Some of the forms are even, it seems, completely artificial, the word-forging of poets, especially under metrical pressure. Philologists are largely agreed that, while the basic dialect of Homeric Greek is that of Ionia in the archaic period, there are many features quite foreign to that time and place. The most interesting is perhaps the occurrence of outcrops of so-called 'Arcado-Cypriot'. The evidence of Linear B tablets confirms that this is the Greek of the Mycenaeans some 500 years before Homer and on the mainland of Greece. The oral tradition can accommodate all this: travelling bards will over the years have picked up some phrases and discarded others according to their tastes and needs. Gradually a language comes into being which is special to epic poetry. Some phrases go back hundreds of years; others are recent acquisitions; others are new on the very day of performance. In this sense hundreds of anonymous bards may well have contributed to the *Iliad* and *Odyssey*, in that they will have contributed phrases, lines, or scene-sequences which became part of the tradition.

This 'artificiality' of epic language does not mean that it was precious or outlandish. Although it contained words and forms that the audience will never have heard outside poetry, it will have been a language made familiar by poetry and proper to it. It makes for pace and assurance infused with an epic and high colour. These qualities were well seen by Matthew Arnold: 'He is eminently rapid; he is eminently plain and direct both in the evolution of his thought and in the expression of it . . . he is eminently noble.' Colin Macleod has brought out the insights underlying these epithets: 'Arnold saw, with the acumen of the critic, that what is artificial in origin need not be artificial in effect ("rapid . . . plain . . .") and that judgements of poetic quality are vacuous if they take no account of moral quality ("simple . . . noble . . .").'

The idea that dozens of nameless bards have made their contribution to Homer is an attractive one. The poems become the achievement of a group or guild. But Milman Parry and some of his successors have been carried away by this 'folkist' romance, and have become so set on the notion of traditional poetry that they have denied all individuality to the bard within it, adding that such a tradition has no place or value for originality. For them 'Homer' is the tradition, handed down over the centuries. This runs into problems, if only because the tradition must somehow have developed and grown; it cannot have instantaneously sprung into mature existence. And, unless it is maintained that all of Homer's rivals, earlier or contemporary, all produced poetry just as good as his— in fact indistinguishable from it—then there must have been ways in which Homer was better. The ways in which he was better than the others constitute his originality. So, however much he was within his tradition, he must also have improved on it.

The question now is, how far was Homer the servant of his tradition, how much its master? Must he have worked entirely with it and within it, or might he have worked against it also? It is still an open question, indeed, whether very long epics were a centuries-old norm or an invention of Homer; whether or not something very like the *Iliad* or the *Odyssey* could have been heard generations before Homer.

We have not got any of the poetry of Homer's predecessors or rivals, and so nothing much can be said with confidence; that this or that was innovative or anti-traditional on the part of Homer must remain a speculation. There are those, for instance, who have claimed that Patroclus is a Homeric invention, and Eumaeus, and the pastoral element in the *Odyssey*. The hope for progress on such issues is one of the great challenges facing Homeric scholarship.

It seems to me more than plausible that Homer was doubly original, that he worked against the tradition as well as within it. Take as a test case the attitude of the *Iliad* towards Troy. The tradition seems to have been partisan in favour of the Greeks and to have supplied Homer with much more material for telling of Greek victories than of reverses. Although the Trojans generally have the better of Books 8 to 17, more Trojans are killed than Greeks, and there are constant Greek revivals, and—a telling detail—the left and right of the battlefield are always viewed from the Greek perspective. In creating a epic where the Trojans have the better of the battle for much of the time, and where the battle is in poetic terms seen from their side no less than from the Greeks', it looks as if Homer must have gone against his tradition. The challenge of doing so seems indeed to have been an essential poetic catalyst.

Long similes are one of the special glories of Homer and one of his distinctive
contributions to the whole future of European poetry. They may be another
example of an innovation or late development in tension with the tradition. It is
widely supposed that long similes are a product of long epic, and that 'monumental' compositions like the *Iliad* and the *Odyssey* are a late development. On
the other hand it would be no surprise to find the standard long similes of beasts
of prey, especially lions, well back in the tradition of heroic epic. The philologists
say that the language of the similes is notably non-formulaic and late: but this
seems largely explicable by the non-heroic subject-matter of many similes. What
seems to me most unlikely to be traditional about Homeric similes is the wide
variety of relationships between the similes and their surrounding contexts. Each
seems to set the audience a challenge in working out the connection. Some work
by similarity, some by contrast, some concentrate on a physical comparison,
others on comparison of tone or emotion.

An example from each poem will have to suffice. At *Iliad* 21. 342 ff. Hephaestus,
helping Achilles against the river Scamander, burns the vegetation and corpses
on the banks of the river:

> As when the north wind of autumn suddenly makes dry
> a garden freshly watered and makes glad the man who is tending it,
> so the entire flat land was dried up with Hephaestus burning . . .

Hephaestus and Achilles rejoice in the drying blast: on the other hand it is the
river which keeps fertile the vegetation of Troy and which supplies irrigation for
the gardens. The simile draws attention to the destructive reversal of nature when
fire burns water. At *Odyssey* 5. 388 ff. Odysseus is lifted on a wave and sees the
coast of Phaeacia in the distance:

> And as welcome as the show of life again in a father
> is to his children, when he has lain sick, suffering strong pains,
> and wasting long away, and the hateful death spirit has brushed him,
> but then, and it is welcome, the gods set him free of his sickness,
> so welcome appeared land and forest now to Odysseus . . .

This is indeed the first moment at which there is hope that Odysseus will survive
after all, and will eventually live to see his family. When he is at last safe in the
arms of Penelope it is a simile which reminds us of the feats of endurance that
Odysseus has had to go through:

> And as when the land appears welcome to men who are swimming,
> after Poseidon has smashed their strong-built ship on the open
> water, pounding it with the weight of wind and the heavy
> seas, and only a few escape the grey water landward
> by swimming, with a thick scurf of salt coated upon them,
> and gladly they set foot on the shore, escaping the evil;
> so welcome was her husband to her as she looked upon him . . .
>
> (23. 233 ff.)

To regard the thematic interaction of these two similes as coincidence seems absurd; to attribute it to tradition seem scarcely less implausible.

In recent years there has been something of a reaction against Milman Parry and the approach to Homer through tradition that he opened up. There has been a feeling that this approach has failed to deliver the great insights it claimed it would reveal. It is true that it cannot resolve the sort of large questions about Homer's place within and against the tradition which I have been raising; it is still very important, however, and especially on the level of the formulaic phrase, the basic unit from which Parry started. The reason is not just that the exigencies and pressures of oral composition help to explain away the infelicities and inconsistencies that so exercise the analysts; this is a petty gain, merely making excuses. There are much more important insights to be won. The whole inimitable rapidity and directness of Homeric poetry may be seen as the benefit of the oral tradition. In a writing poet 'pius Aeneas' or 'bold Sir Bedivere' are in danger of becoming precious, but in Homer the unobtrusive reiteration of such characteristics seems perfectly natural. Thanks to the repeated phrases and scene-sequences we are in a familiar world where things have their known places. It is a world which is solid and known, and yet at the same time coloured by the special diction with an epic nobility. Robes, beds, sheep, springs, mountains—their constancy is conveyed by the traditional language. The sun rises each day in familiar terms; Achilles remains swift however inactive he may be. Set against this formulaic backcloth are the unique, terrible events. The sun sets as ever, but Hector is dead. In Homer we have a supremely pervasive counterpoint of static and dynamic, the constant and the ephemeral. This owes much to the essential style of the poetry.

Homer and History

The old question of whether Homer was one poet or many has, then, been largely displaced by the new question of Homer's relation to his tradition. The other great Homeric controversy, which goes back to even earlier than Wolf, is still as lively as ever, and has in fact captured more widespread interest than the scholars' obsession with multiple authorship. How 'true' is Homer? What is the relation of the *Iliad* and *Odyssey* to any historical reality? Was there ever a Greek siege of Troy? Did the Phaeacians exist, and if so where?, etc., etc. The issue of the 'truth' of Homer has often been connected with the question—in most respects a very different one—of the historicity of the Old Testament. This should sound the warning that we must ask questions appropriate to the work. Inappropriate questions will lead to false answers.

While there have always been a few who are happy to regard the events of the poems as fiction set in a world which is largely the creation of poetic fantasy, there have been many more who have passionately believed that Homer is, more or less, history. They seized on Robert Wood's reports in the eighteenth century that the topography and natural history of Turkey corroborated Homer's accuracy. They drew more comfort from the archaeological discovery in the late nineteenth century that there really had been a great Mycenaean civilization. The romantic fabrications of Heinrich Schliemann clearly satisfied a popular desire by 'verifying' Homer.

Most vindications of Homer's historicity have claimed him as an accurate record of the Mycenaean Age of about 1400-1100 BC. A few, however, have claimed him as a record of his own contemporary world (say ninth or eighth century). But, against this latter, it seems inevitable that a distant world of heroes calls for a way of life different from that of the audience (they eat roast meat every day, for example); and that it has to be free from blatant 'anachronisms' known to be recent innovations—hence, for example, the absence of literacy from the poems. The most influential modern claim for this historicity of Homer, M.I. Finley's *World of Odysseus*, looks neither to the Mycenaean past nor Homer's present, but the 'Dark-Age' Greece of about 1050-900 BC. He claims that Homer accurately records that world in such anthropological aspects as social and kinship structures, moral and political values, and general world-view.

Although archaeologists continue to dispute, it is now generally agreed that various elements of the material world of Homer are derived from different periods. Fighting weapons and armour, for instance, are all bronze, while iron is a rare metal: this preserves the metallurgy of the Mycenaean (Bronze) Age. On the other hand, the dead are cremated rather than buried, and this is a post-Mycenaean Iron Age practice. In some places the heroes carry huge Mycenaean shields, in others the smaller 'modern' sort. The material world seems to come from different times, spread over many centuries, and as likely as not from different places also. In this respect it is very like the language of the poems and the explanation must surely be the same. The oral poetic tradition has created, by a long process of addition and rejection, an amalgam. In matters of armour, burial, and so forth this amalgam, while historically impossible, is aesthetically coherent and convincing. What mattered to the poet was not that he should be accurate—why should that matter?—but that he should be plausible and enthralling, that he should create a past that was solidly imaginable and yet suitable for heroes.

Just as Homeric language included an element of poetic diction which no one had ever spoken, so there was surely a considerable made-up element in the world of Achilles or Odysseus. The twin springs of the river Scamander in *Iliad* 22. 145-56 provide a good illustration since much of the topographical search for a real setting for the *Iliad* and the Trojan war has concentrated on them. There are two springs, one icy cold, the other steaming hot, and close by them are the stone-washing troughs where the Trojan women used to do their laundry. It is by them that Hector, after being chased three times round Troy, takes his final stand against Achilles. Needless to say, no explorer has managed to find such a hydrological curiosity outside the walls of any ancient city, though apparently there are springs of varying temperatures somewhere in the mountains of north-west Turkey. The springs are not there for the sake of descriptive accuracy, but for their dramatic and poetic topicality. Not long before, in Book 21, Hephaestus and Achilles defeated the Scamander, the river of Troy; now Hector, the protector of Troy, runs for his life past the springs of Scamander. The washing troughs stand for Troy's former delight and prosperity. Troy will never know that peace again, once Achilles has caught Hector. Its fine clothes will be taken as booty, and its women will labour at far-distant springs.

Could it be that, even if Homer's material world is mixed from different periods with a strong leavening of invention, its social structures and values are still drawn from the real world, indeed from a particular historical reality? Finley's case is that Homer is consistent and anthropologically plausible on such matters as Agamemnon's constitutional position, the inheritance customs on Ithaca, the status of wives and monogamy, the legal and social treatment of murderers, to give four examples. I would maintain that in all four cases the poems are in fact inconsistent, treating the issue differently in different contexts. There is no need, for instance, for the Achaeans to have a consistent constitutional procedure or a defined hierarchy of kings, elders, assemblies, etc., as long as their debates and deliberations convince the poet's audience on each particular occasion. It is, in fact, important for the *Iliad* that Agamemnon should not have a definite constitutional position.

When it comes to morality and values, it is also widely claimed that these are consistent and furthermore simple. The 'Heroic Code' consists of precepts such as that you must strive to be first, you must kill and humiliate your enemies, and you must preserve your honour, which is measurable in material goods. But much of the *Iliad* is spent in disputing and debating about these very precepts, and many others. One of the reasons why so much of the poem consists of direct speech is that so much of it is spent in argument about values. If the 'Heroic Code' were agreed and beyond dispute, there would be no real conflict. In fact the criteria for approval and disapproval are open for consideration; and much of the power of the *Iliad* comes from its lack of moral simplicity and consistency.

Scholars have been even more determined to impose a religious 'reality' on Homer (and here the Old Testament analogy may have been particularly influential). Out of all the variety of manifestations of the divine, they have laboured to produce theological consistency and system, the actual religion of an actual historical moment. Here again, in my view, they produce their theologies as the answer to questions of a sort which it is not appropriate to ask of a work of literature. They ask, for example, what kind of god is Fate (*Moira*), and is Fate more powerful than Zeus? When Athena intervenes in *Iliad* 1. 193 ff. is she merely a poetic personification of Achilles' better judgement? What is the function and power of non-Olympian powers such as Ocean, Sun, Scamander?

One illustration will have to suffice to suggest how the gods in Homer do not have a theological existence independent of particular poetic context. In *Iliad* 22 Achilles is pursuing Hector round Troy:

> But when for the fourth time they had come around to the well springs
> then the Father balanced his golden scales, and in them
> he set two fateful portions of death, which lays men prostrate,
> one for Achilles, and one for Hector, breaker of horses,
> and balanced it by the middle; and Hector's death-day was heavier
> and dragged downward toward death, and Phoebus Apollo forsook him.
>
> (22. 208–133)

It seems to me simple-minded to conclude from this that Fate is superior to Zeus because Fate must tip the scales. In the context it is clear that the scales do not determine who will win, but when Achilles will win. The outcome of the battle is already put beyond doubt by many other factors, human, divine, and poetic: the scales mark a dramatic turning-point. It is at this point that Apollo leaves Hector and Athena joins Achilles. But it would again be a theological over-simplification to conclude that the battle is merely divine puppetry without any place for human achievement. The gods do not change the outcome of the battle. Nor do they diminish the victory or the defeat; on the contrary their interest and participation elevate them. Great heroic deeds are marked by the attention of the gods. So the golden scales are neither a real theological belief nor mere picturesque ornament; they are the elevation of a turning-point.

The conclusion that the Homeric world is through and through on every level a poetic amalgam is in no way inconsistent with its having exerted a powerful influence on the real life of the Greeks over the next 1,000 years after its creation. Homer provided one persuasive, universally known, and inspiring model of heroism, nobility, the good life, the gods. Homer affected history. But it is not by being a faithful representation of history that his world-picture has captured the imagination of so many people for so long. It is much more memorable and universal than that.

There does remain, however, one time and place in history which Homer tells us about, though indirectly. There must have been an occasion for the creation of the *Iliad* and *Odyssey*. The very fact that they came into existence says a lot about the concerns and sensibilities of Homer's own audience. For I take it as axiomatic that these great works of art would never have come into existence without an audience. There must have been people who were willing to pay attention to these poems, to make the trouble worth Homer's while by listening to them properly—and quite likely by supplying his livelihood also. They must have been able to appreciate Homer: otherwise he would never have made the poems. And if the *Iliad* and *Odyssey* are the kind of works which I have argued for in this chapter then that is an important thing to know about some Greeks in the general area of Ionia around the date of 700 BC.

Further Reading

TRANSLATIONS

The translation of Homer into English, since the first by Chapman, epitomizes the development of national taste and letters. (It is no chance that Matthew Arnold made it the subject of one of the classics of literary criticism.) The greatest is surely that of Pope, which has laboured too long under the vacuous reproof of Richard Bentley—'a very pretty poem, Mr. Pope, but you must not call it Homer.' William Cowper's translation into Miltonic blank verse has been unjustly neglected. Among modern translation it is unfortunate that neither the Loeb nor the Penguin series does even remote justice to Homer's poetry and power. There are, however, two good versions, both by Americans. Preferences will vary between the tough shorter lines of Robert Fitzgerald (New York, 1961, 1974; Oxford, 1984), and the more literary, close and slow-pace six-stress metre of Richmond Lattimore (Chicago, 1951, 1965)—the source of most of the translated passages in this chapter. There is also a fine *Odyssey* in high prose by Walter Shewring (Oxford, 1980).

INTRODUCTIONS

There is a variety of introductions to be recommended. Chapter 3 of A. Lesky's *History of Greek Literature* (translated by J. Willis and C. de Heer, London, 1966) is admirably catholic. Adam Parry's long Introduction to his father's work *The Making of Homeric Verse: The Collected Papers of Milman Parry* (Oxford, 1970) is an important evaluation of the achievements and shortcomings of the approach through the oral tradition. W. A. Camps, *An Introduction to Homer* (Oxford, 1980), is rich in detail, but somewhat simple and pedagogic in approach. J. Griffin's *Homer* (Oxford, 1980) in the 'Past Masters' series aims to bring out the quality of Homer's thought and imagination. The Introduction to C. W. Macleod's text and commentary on *Iliad*, Book 24 (Cambridge, 1982) is far more than is usually expected of that genre: it is a tragic, yet humane, interpretation of the *Iliad* of the kind intuitively glimpsed by Simone Weil (*L'Iliade ou le poème de la force*, trans. M. McCarthy, New York, 1940); and it is explored on the level of detailed phrasing as well as larger structure.

THE ILIAD

Among the more specialist works on the *Iliad* B. Fenik's *Typical Battle Scenes in the Iliad* (Wiesbaden, 1968) demonstrates how the oral tradition works on the scale of whole scenes. C. Segal, *The Theme of the Mutilation of the Corpse in the Iliad* (Leiden, 1971), traces the cumulative sequence of an important motif. J. M. Redfield, *Nature and Culture in the Iliad* (Chicago, 1975), while 'anthropological' in mode, makes many sensitive observations on the human stuff of the poem. J. Griffin's *Homer on Life and Death* (Oxford, 1980) is more perceptive about Homer's gods in the course of showing that the poem's fundamental 'subject' is mankind's state of mortality.

THE ODYSSEY

B. Fenik's *Studies in the Odyssey* (Wiesbaden, 1974) goes much further than his *Iliad* book in showing how typical scenes contribute to the character of the whole poem. N. Austin's collection of essays *Archery at the Dark of the Moon* (Berkeley, 1975), while fanciful in places, is also a serious attempt to capture the *Odyssey*'s elusive allure. W. B. Stanford's *The Ulysses Theme* (2nd edn., Oxford, 1958) is a classic study of the archetypal character of Odysseus in the *Odyssey* and later literature.

BACKGROUND AND HISTORY

It may be noticed that nearly all the books mentioned so far have been published since 1965. Most of the work in English for thirty years and more after Milman Parry's discoveries was on the background to Homer rather than the poems themselves. These studies concentrated on the development of the oral tradition and the relation of Homer to the Mycenaean age. They culminated in two wide-ranging books, *A Companion to Homer* (London, 1962), made up of chapters by many scholars edited by A. J. B. Wace and F. H. Stubbings; and G. S. Kirk's *The Songs of Homer* (Cambridge, 1962, also in a shortened version, *Homer and the Epic*, Cambridge, 1965).

The modern classic on Homer and history is M. I. Finley's *The World of Odysseus* (2nd edn., London, 1977), but this is an attempt to illuminate history by means of Homer, not the other way round. Homer's integrity as a creative artist is better respected by O. Murray, *Early Greece* (London, 1980), chs. 3–4, and A. M. Snodgrass, *Archaic Greece* (London, 1980), ch. 2.

3
Greek Myth and Hesiod

❦

JASPER GRIFFIN

Myth

EVERYONE is familiar with some Greek myths: that Oedipus solved the riddle of the Sphinx and married his mother, that the Argonauts sailed away in search of the Golden Fleece. Many people know that there is a large modern literature about mythology, from Sir James Frazer's *Golden Bough* and Robert Graves's *Greek Myths* to the dense and complex accounts given by Claude Lévi-Strauss and the Structuralists. Myth is a very attractive subject, but the immense disagreements of the experts show that it is also a very difficult one. It was a brilliant stroke of George Eliot to show the learned Mr. Casaubon, in *Middlemarch*, struggling to write a *Key to all Mythologies*, swamped and overwhelmed by masses of material on which he could not impose any intelligible order.

Even to define myth is extraordinarily difficult, if it is to be marked off from legend, folk-tale, and other relatives. It will perhaps be best to settle provisionally for something like the modest definition of G. S. Kirk, 'A special sort of traditional tale', to suspend the search for a single source, and to offer, instead, a couple of examples of the typically mythical mode of thought, in contrast with something recognizably different.

In the fifth century, Greeks were struck by the fact that whereas their own rivers tended to flood in winter and dry up in summer, the Nile flooded in the summer and not in winter. Pindar, in a lost poem, told of a 'guardian daemon' a hundred fathoms tall, who caused the flood by the movement of his feet. Herodotus, by contrast, considers three theories (including the correct one of melted snow in the distant mountains), but settles for a theory of his own about the movement of the sun, which 'behaves as it normally does in summer', but is subject to deflection by storms at a certain time of year. He is anxious, that is, to give an explanation in terms of familiar natural laws, not fantastic personalities. Again, the old story explained why the Greek chiefs followed Agamemnon to Troy by saying that Helen's father made all her suitors swear in advance to come to the aid of her chosen husband, if her beauty should lead to her abduction. Thucydides rejects this story, replacing it with an explanation in terms of eco-

nomic power: Agamemnon was the most powerful man in Greece as the heir of
the wealthy immigrant Pelops, and he had 'courted the favour of the populace';
the chiefs followed him 'from fear rather than goodwill'. In these examples we
see an older sort of explanation in terms of the free acts of striking individuals,
succeeded by one in terms of rationalistic physical speculation, or of reflection on
the real nature of political power. It is no accident that Thucydides' Agamemnon,
wealthy, democratic, and master of a fleet, is so reminiscent of the Athens of the
Peloponnesian War.

Until this century 'myth' virtually meant 'Greek myth', but now anthropologists and others have collected immense stores of myths from all over the world.
It soon becomes clear that those of the Greeks are unusual in important ways.
The great majority of Greek myths are concerned with heroes and heroines: that
is, with men and women of a definite period in the past, who had greater powers
and were more interesting than modern people, but who were not gods. The
mythologies of Egypt and Mesopotamia are not much concerned with heroes.
Very rare in Greek myths are talking animals; and in general, although there are
many exceptions, the events of the myths are an exaggeration or heightening of
ordinary life rather than the wholly bizarre and dream-like sequences found in
so many of the world's traditional tales. This special character of Greek myth has
proved a considerable stumbling-block to modern general theories of mythology.

Another way in which Greek mythology is a special case is its pervasiveness
and importance, in a society more advanced than most of those in which modern
missionaries and travellers have been able to interview native speakers. From
Homer to Attic tragedy, it is in terms of the myths that poets work out their
deepest thoughts; both history and philosophy emerge from mythical thought,
and both poetry and the visual arts remained always attached to mythical
subjects.

Greece did, of course, have its cosmogonies, myths which told of the creation
of the world, and other stories which took place on the purely divine level.
Hesiod, as we shall see, told in his *Theogony* of the coming into existence of Earth
(Gaia) and her son-partner Heaven (Uranus), and how they were separated, and
how Zeus came to be the ruler of the gods. That story has been heavily influenced
by eastern sources, and it has little connection with real Greek cult or Greek
religion. Another tale which is clearly early is that of the abduction of Persephone
(or *Korē*, 'the Maiden', as she is more usually called) by the Lord of the Underworld. In anger and grief her mother Demeter made the whole world barren,
and in the end Kore was restored to her for two-thirds of the year, but had to
spend one-third of it under the earth. It is natural to connect her absence with
the 'dead' time when the corn is in the earth, before it comes up.

One striking omission in the *Theogony* of Hesiod is any account of the origin
of mankind; and early Greek thought had in fact no agreed account of it.
Sometimes men are said to come from ash trees, or to be made from clay by
Prometheus, or to have emerged from stones; in some sense Zeus is the 'father'

of all men. The omission seems strange to readers of the Bible, which opens so memorably with Adam and Eve; but it is interesting that after the Book of Genesis Adam is never named again in the Old Testament, in which 'in the beginning' is normally expressed by reference either to Abraham or to Moses. Early man is not as constantly aware of his ultimate origins as those who are brought up on the theory of evolution.

Another point worth making at the outset is that there was no standard or orthodox version of a myth. The fact that a story was told in one way in Homer did not prevent later poets from telling it very differently. To give a striking instance, the lyric poet Stesichorus, in the early sixth century, produced a celebrated poem denying that Helen ever went to Troy at all—which of course made nonsense of the Trojan War. Euripides exploited the ironic potential of that subversive tale in his *Helen*, and Herodotus, with delightful rationalism, says that it must be true, as otherwise the Trojans would obviously have given her up long before the destruction of their city. 'And I think Homer knew this story,' he adds, 'but because it was not so appealing a subject for poetry, he preferred the other': a good example of the judgement passed by fifth-century enlightenment on the historical value of the poets and their myths. Certainly we hear, from the beginning of Greek literature, protests at the mendacity of poets. 'We know how to tell many lies that look like truth,' say the Muses to Hesiod, 'but we know how to tell the truth when we choose'; and Solon, himself a poet, said (in verse), 'Poets tell many lies'. Each new poet had the right to interpret the tradition in his own way, and the audience did not feel committed to accepting what he said, however fascinating, as necessarily true.

Some myths are closely related to a ritual: for instance, the myth of Kore. When she disappeared, her mother wandered barefoot seeking her over the world, fasting; at Eleusis she was persuaded to smile, and to partake of a special barley drink, by the obscene jesting of a woman called *Iambē* (evidently a name related to the iambic metre often used for coarse personal attacks); she regained her daughter, and she gave blessings to men. All this was acted out by those who flocked to be initiated into the great Eleusinian mysteries. Fasting and abstaining from drink, they made their way in long procession from Athens to Eleusis. At a certain point on the pilgrimage obscenities were shouted. Initiates drank the *kykeōn*, the special barley drink, to break their fast. And the change of the goddess from gloom to gladness was echoed by the sudden blaze of light from darkness in the hall of the mysteries, followed by rejoicing. It is evident here that the worshipper is acting out the sufferings of the goddess—a comparison with the Stations of the Cross is not unnatural—and that myth and ritual are, on different levels, the same.

But the myth does more than that. The anger of Demeter plunged the world into an abnormal and horrible state, in which the earth's fertility failed, and it seemed that mankind would die out and the gods would cease to receive their cult and their honours. The idea that normal life might fail serves to add value to its continued existence; and the anxiety which naturally arises in the mind when the seed is sown in the earth—suppose it fails to grow?—is given form, removed to the past, and provided with a satisfying conclusion. There is another level, too. The seed dying and being reborn suggests the idea of rebirth and immortality: 'Except a corn of wheat fall into the ground and die, it abideth alone; but if it die, it bringeth forth much fruit' (John 12:24). The seed is sown, it disappears in the darkness, and yet it lives and will rise again; Kore was snatched away to the Underworld, and yet she comes back; and the initiates at Eleusis were promised a happier and more glorious life after death.

Some myths, like that of Kore, relate not only to ritual, but also to ideas of the reversal of ordinary civilized life. On the island of Lemnos once a year all fires were extinguished for nine days; family life ceased, and an atmosphere of grimness prevailed, as the women separated themselves from the men, who lay low. Then new fire was fetched from Delos, and new purified fires were kindled; there was a great festival of rejoicing, with laughter and sexual intercourse. The mythical counterpart of all this is the story that the women of Lemnos were once afflicted by Aphrodite with an evil smell, so that their husbands rejected their embraces; they then murdered all the men, and there were only women on the island until suddenly the Argonauts arrived. The women welcomed them, games and festivities were held, and the island was repopulated, Jason begetting twins on the queen Hypsipyle (the twins then had an eventful mythical career . . .). No doubt the women of Lemnos, in reality, ate garlic in the period of separation, as we know that the women of Athens did at the festivals of the Scira and the Thesmophoria, to mark their withdrawal from sexual activity. The nine days are a time of reversal: women are in the ascendant, unattractive and unapproachable; there is no cooking and no sacrificial ritual. Then normality is restored with exultation. Again we see the reinforcement of the value of ordinary civilization; and again we see a release of anxiety, this time the tension natural between the sexes. At regular intervals the women were violently released from their normal domestic round; and the men had their most horrid secret fears about the evil potentialities of their wives and womenfolk brought out into the open and, perhaps, disarmed.

Myths in which women reject their ordinary feminine role are numerous. Their natural role, their *telos*, was marriage. Those who reject marriage become, in the myths, hunters and outdoor girls—the outdoors belonging, in the normal way, to men. Girls such as Atalanta and Callisto chose that life, only to be overcome in the end and brought back to marriage. Others behave in an irregular manner within marriage. Fears about a wife naturally focused on sexual misconduct and disloyalty, and we find bad wives like Phaedra making advances to young men. The seer Amphiaraus knew that if he joined the doomed expedition of the Seven against Thebes, he would not return: his wife was bribed to make him go to his death. Agamemnon's wife Clytemnestra took a lover in his absence and murdered her husband on his return. Evil deeds or rejection of their role on the part of mythical women are a way of defining and endorsing that role. We shall find that the potential of men, too, is limited and clarified in myth in a similar way, when we turn to the aspirations of the hero.

A myth can have a political function ('charter myth'). In Cyrene a historian told the story that once the local Africans were plagued by a monstrous lion. In desperation their king proclaimed that whoever destroyed it should be his heir. The nymph Cyrene killed the lion, and her descendants, the Cyreneans, inherited after her. This tale legitimizes the Greek colony: not just invaders, the settlers inherited the land from a heroine who earned it as reward for a memorable action. Again, the Athenians got control of the island of Salamis in the sixth century. Not only did they make Ajax, the great Salaminian hero, the eponym and theoretically the ancestor of one of the ten tribes of Attica: they also, so other Greeks alleged, introduced a spurious line into the text of the *Iliad* to support the assertion that Salamis and Attica went together in the heroic period (*Iliad* 2.558). The Dorians, too, had an elaborate myth which presented their invasion of the Peloponnese, in which they were the last Greeks to arrive, as being in reality a return, to claim an inheritance which was their due: the children of Heracles, their ancestor, having been driven out and coming back several generations later. In the modern world we think of the many myths of nationalism, or of the importance to modern Israel of the possession of its land by distant ancestors.

The myths were all that later Greeks knew about their own early history, apart from a few striking remains such as the 'Cyclopean' walls of Tiryns and the citadel of Mycenae. Systematic excavation was neither a practical possibility nor an ideal. In the middle of the nineteenth century there was a fashion for saying that apparently historical myths contained no truth at all, being in reality disguised or allegorical statements about natural phenomena such as the sunrise or the coming of winter. Schliemann's discoveries at Troy and Mycenae, and those of Evans in Crete, showed that such radical scepticism was mistaken: Mycenae had been 'rich in gold', as Homer said, and at Cnossus there had been a great and complex building and some strange sport involving bulls—the originals of the Labyrinth and the Minotaur. Already in the fifth century the two possible ways of treating myth for the purposes of history were both understood. Thucydides, in the opening chapters of the first book of his *History*, gives a brilliant sketch of early Greece, reinterpreting the myths in the light of modern rationalism, with a heavy emphasis on economic factors. We have seen how he dealt with Agamemnon (above, pp. 78 f.). For Thucydides, King Minos of Crete was 'the first man we hear of to have a fleet'; ruler of much of the Aegean, he 'put down piracy, it is reasonable to suppose, so that his revenues would come in' (l. 4). No mention, needless to say, of the Minotaur. Herodotus, on the other hand, at one moment at least envisages rejecting the myths completely, as being just different from history. He says of the sixth-century tyrant Polycrates that 'He is the first man we know of who set himself to rule the sea, except indeed

GOLDEN MASK FROM A TOMB AT MYCENAE. When Schliemann excavated this he declared it the 'Mask of Agamemnon'—a claim which would no doubt have been echoed by any Classical Greek who had come upon it. Although much older than the assumed period of Agamemnon and the Trojan War it is an example of a type of Bronze Age artefact which, with the great fortified citadels themselves, demonstrated to Classical Greeks the wealth and power of their heroic forefathers, the kings of Mycenae 'rich in gold', as Homer described it.

for Minos and anyone there may have been before him who did it; of what is called human lineage, Polycrates was the first' (3. 122).

Myth could preserve certain things from the past: names, great events, historical places. Of course it transformed and distorted them. Troy was once taken by storm, and there was a great king in Mycenae; but we cannot know how much truth there is in the story of a great expedition against Troy, and Achilles in his origins is clearly more akin to a saga-figure such as Siegfried than to a historical person such as Augustus. But another sort of survival in the myths is no less interesting: that of customs, and indeed of a picture of a society as a whole. As an example of the preservation in myth of an archaic custom, we can take the story of the adoption of Heracles by Hera. After his apotheosis,

Zeus persuaded Hera to adopt him as her son and henceforth for all time to cherish him with a mother's love. The adoption is said to have taken place in the following way: Hera reclined on a bed, drew Heracles towards her, and let him fall through her clothes to the ground, acting out what happens in real childbirth. This is what non-Greeks do to this day, when they carry out an adoption. (Diodorus Siculus 4. 39. 2)

It is clear that what is described is an archaic and rather naïve procedure: a child cannot be adopted without being, symbolically, born of his adoptive mother. The Greeks observed that many things which among them happened only in myths were regular in the society of contemporary 'barbarians'.

Myth could preserve features of archaic life and society. But it could also transform quite recent history for spectacular exotic potentates: Cyrus the Mede and Croesus of Lydia, historic personalities of the mid sixth century, were given in the fifth century strong mythical features. Cyrus was exposed at birth and brought up by an animal, like Romulus or Aegisthus; Croesus was carried off from death by Apollo and given eternal happiness among the Hyperboreans, because of his great offerings at Delphi.

That children exposed at birth might survive was a natural wish in a society in which such exposures were not uncommon, and in myth, as in comedy and in the novels, we find many examples. That a world-conqueror such as Cyrus, or a great figure such as Oedipus, should have risen to the zenith of prosperity from the desperate position of an exposed infant had the added appeal of a superlative 'log-cabin to White House' story. It is another sort of fantasy when, as in the myth of Anchises and Aphrodite, a beautiful girl drops from the sky to seduce a young man minding his flocks on the hills. Darker fantasies found cathartic expression in myth: every variety of incest, murder of kindred, cannibalism, sexual union with animals. The speculative imagination combined various creatures into compound monsters: man–horse centaurs, man–bull river gods, woman–bird harpies, the woman–lion sphinx, the winged horse Pegasus. Here the visual arts led the way for literature. Fantastic changes of scale produced giants and pygmies. The dog Cerberus had three heads, Geryon had three bodies; Argus had a hundred eyes, Briareus and his brothers a hundred hands. The whole natural world could be peopled with Pan and the satyrs, with Artemis and her retinue, and with nymphs in the trees, the streams, and the mountains.

We have seen (above, p. 81) how the myths helped to define the nature and position of women in relation to men. They also were the framework within which men were defined not only in relation to women, but also in relation to gods. The mythical period in Greece is not like the 'Dreamtime' of Australian aborigines, a remote and dateless past. It consisted of two or three generations, the time of the Theban and Trojan wars; and it could be dated and fitted in with history. Hellenistic scholars calculated that Troy fell in 1184 BC. What happened after that period was different: tragedies, for example, were not written about the colonizing period or about the tyrants, although some of the stories in Herodotus about Periander of Corinth might seem suitable material for one. No doubt this is due, at least in part, to the incalculable impact of the Homeric poems. The epic showed the heroic age as one in which gods intervened openly in human life, in a way in which later they did not. That in turn implied two things: both that the gods took the events of that age very seriously, and also that the events are transparent, allowing the hearer to discern through them the will and working of the gods, as he cannot in ordinary life. The few known historical tragedies, such as the *Persae* of Aeschylus, dealt with the Persian conquest and disasters, events on so vast a scale that they seemed to reveal the working of the divine in human history, and so to resemble myths. A final consideration is that everybody was familiar with the persons and stories which figured in the epic.

The total effect of all these considerations was to make the heroic period the natural setting for serious poetry. The Homeric epic handled the myths in one way, smoothing away the bizarre, the monstrous, the horrible; incest, killing of kindred, human sacrifice, are all reduced to a minimum or excluded altogether—Homer does not mention the sacrifice of Iphigenia, and though the *Odyssey* repeatedly dwells on Orestes' killing of Aegisthus, it never says that he killed his mother Clytemnestra. Homosexual love is also excluded from the epics. They do, however, deal with the position of men in the world, aspiring to be 'god-like', struck down by the gods when they attempt to go too far, and doomed in the end to die. The lyric tradition of Stesichorus was more picturesque, less tragic, sometimes pathetic. Pindar sheds radiance on his athletic victors by juxtaposing their triumph with some story from the career of a hero; the achievement of victory raises the athlete for a moment to a stature and significance which puts him beside the heroes, humdrum ordinary existence transfigured with the timeless splendour of the mythical world. Aeschylus is able to express his most profound broodings on the true nature of war in the odes in the *Agamemnon* about the fall of Troy, and Sophocles finds in the story of Oedipus a vehicle to represent a view of human life which is at once both bleak and terrifying, and also, as we experience the courage and resolution of the hero, and his capacity for suffering, strangely exhilarating. Epic had tended to purify the myth of precisely the things which tragedy emphasized in it, and almost every possible variety of incest, killing of kindred, and human sacrifice, is presented in the tragedies known to us. The dark colouring of tragedy as a form, with its ritual lamentations and masks of woe, explains this in part; but no doubt it is right to see also a new attitude, questioning and exploring, and delighting in extreme actions and painful conflicts.

In the myths men and gods were close. Heroes were sons of gods, greater than modern men, aspiring to fight with the gods themselves: Achilles says to Apollo in the *Iliad* 'How I would pay you out for this, if only I had the power', and both Diomede and Patroclus attack gods and are sharply called to order by Apollo: 'Remember what you are! Gods and men can never be equal' (*Iliad*, 21. 20, 5. 440, 16. 705).

In the myths we constantly see men tempted to go beyond mortal limits: we feel pleasure as they enlarge our conception of human powers, and then a different pleasure at their inevitable defeat or destruction. Agamemnon walking on the precious tapestries, Ajax telling Athena he has no need of her, Hippolytus defying Aphrodite, the Greek commanders in the *Troades* behaving with arrogant cruelty in ignorance of the ruin the gods have planned for them, Achilles at the end of the *Iliad* forced to come to terms with the mortality which links him with his enemies—all these and many more are examples of a use of myth which became central to Greek culture. The same idea of human limitation is expressed in a less tragic way in the myths which say that life could indeed be what we wish it to be—peaceful, beautiful, eternal—only it must be somewhere cut off from us in time (the Golden Age), or in place (the Hyperboreans at the back of the North Wind; the Ethiopians where the sun rises and sets). The existence of such images is like the existence of the blessed gods: it defines by contrast the real lot of man.

Two outstanding questions remain. The first is that of the fate of myth in Greece after the rise of technical philosophy and history, prose and rationalism, in the late fifth century. The mythical genealogies gave place to a conception of history which tried to exclude the supernatural: Thucydides himself says, rather grimly, that 'the absence of the mythical element' may make his *History* less immediately enjoyable, but that it will be the more instructive. The cosmic speculations of myth gave place to philosophy, and the Presocratics, whose minds still naturally worked in a quasi-mythical way, are rejected for that very reason. Aristotle can say coolly that 'Hesiod and the theological writers were concerned only with what seemed plausible to themselves, and had no respect for us... But it is not worth taking seriously writers who show off in the mythical style; as for those who do proceed by proving their assertions, we must cross-examine them...' (*Metaphysics*, 2. 1000^{a}9). When we add to this the moral criticism of the content of the myths, which had been vocal for at least a century, and which led Plato to demand that the myths be radically censored, it is clear that time had run out for myth as the vehicle of serious thought. *Mythos* now becomes opposed to *logos*: a 'story', an 'old wives' tale', as opposed to a 'rational account', 'a definition'.

Plato invented his own myths. Some of them are indeed memorable, but they are radically different from the old ones, and carefully scrutinized by their inventor for impropriety or pessimism. The old myths were kept alive in local cults; they continued to haunt poetry, from the *Hymns* of Callimachus to the *Dionysiaca* of Nonnus in the fifth century AD, and to form the main subject matter of painting and sculpture; in Latin poetry, too, the Greek myths had a great future, from the frivolity of Ovid to the seriousness of the *Aeneid*. But the natural medium of serious argument is now prose; and mythology, and poetry with it, was more and more an ornament—admittedly a beloved and indispensable one— rather than the serious thing which it had been before 400 BC.

The second of our outstanding questions is that of the analysis of the myths. This chapter has been suggesting that myths are of different kinds and various origins, and that they did not all serve one purpose; that there is, in fact, no Key

HERACLES LEADS CERBERUS to the terrified king Eurystheus, on a vase by a Caeretan painter—an immigrant Ionian working in Etruria in the later sixth century BC.

FLORAL FANTASY with ostrich-riders, wildlife, and a Triton on the neck of the vase, made by an immigrant Ionian in Etruria in about 540 BC.

to all Mythologies. It still remains possible that some myths may be deciphered, analysed, and (in the structuralist phrase) 'decoded'. If we renounce the idea of one key to all myths, is it true that each individual myth can be definitively analysed?

The myth of Adonis will serve as a sobering example. His mother Myrrha fell in love with her own father and conceived a child by him. She was metamorphosed into the incense tree. The baby was very beautiful from birth, and Aphrodite herself fell in love with him. She gave him to Persephone in a chest, but Persephone too became enamoured of his beauty; the goddesses had to divide his favours. He was killed by a boar while hunting, and every year he is lamented by women. Such in outline is the myth. For Frazer, Adonis was a divinity of vegetation and fertility, dying every year and returning to life with the new crops; but it was pointed out that virtually no ancient source ever mentions a resurrection of Adonis. Recently, two interesting attempts have been made to unriddle the myth.

A structuralist analysis is given by M. Detienne. For him the myth is concerned with marriage, and with excess and mediation. Adonis, irregularly conceived, is precociously attractive and dies in adolescence. The 'gardens of Adonis' which were planted in his honour consisted of shallowly rooted plants which similarly were quick growing and sterile, soon withering. As his sexual career was opposed to the fruitful norm of marriage, so his gardens were the opposite of true agriculture. His festival was held in the sultry and sensuous Dogdays. The perfumed spices associated with his mother mediate between gods and men, in sacrifice-ritual; and also play a part in attraction between the sexes, which in marriage can be good, but which can also threaten to turn into mere sensuality. And incense is the food of the gods, on which men cannot subsist: the Phoenix is the creature associated with them, and it is solitary and sexless. Detienne finds four 'codes' in the story: botanical, zoological, alimentary, and astronomical. The whole account, to which so short a summary cannot do justice, is worked out with great brilliance.

W. Burkert has also analysed the Adonis myth. He begins, 'If we take the "Adonis myth" to be the story about his death by the boar . . .' This story is descended from a myth of the ancient Sumerians, about a hunter named Dumuzi. The contest between Aphrodite and Persephone for the boy is a conflict between love and death; Adonis is a hunter, and the mourning for him is in reality a means by which hunters work off their feelings of guilt and anxiety about killing animals.

We look at these two able and learned accounts of the same myth, and we see that they have nothing in common. They seem to be explaining two different stories, and to start from totally different positions, which reflect the interests of the two scholars. It is impossible to imagine a process of argument which would make one prevail over the other. That, of course, raises the question of the logical status of this sort of theory. What *are* these accounts of Adonis, if they are not really susceptible to argument? The answer, I think, must be that what we have here is two more myths. Frazer's Dying God had a great vogue in poetry and novels; although now despised and rejected by anthropologists, he was a powerful myth for modern men. Few scholars write as well as Frazer, but the mythopoeic faculty does live in some of them. Some myths are, I have suggested, simple to analyse; but others are elusive, complex, many-faceted. Different minds see different patterns in them, as they do in the interpretation of dreams. In antiquity itself the myths were often reinterpreted. For many myths we may indeed find suggestive and even poetical flashes of insight; but to grasp for 'the' meaning may be as hopeless as to grasp the evanescent shadows of the dead.

Hesiod

The first author of a systematic mythology is also the first personality in Greek literature, the poet Hesiod. It is likely that he was composing his poems about 700 BC. The impersonal manner of the Homeric epic admitted no personal revelations at all by the poet, but Hesiod goes out of his way to tell us a number of facts: that his father came from Cyme (on the coast of Asia Minor, slightly south of Lesbos), leaving home—

> Not running away from prosperity, nor from wealth and ease,
> But from the ills of poverty, which Zeus gives if he please.
> Near Helicon he stopped, in a poor place, the best he could:
> In Ascra, bad in winter, worse in summer, never good.
>
> (*Works and Days*, 637–40)

Ascra is in Boeotia, and Hesiod's father had settled far from home. Hesiod also tells us that he was made a singer when he met the Muses under Mount Helicon and they gave him a staff and breathed song into him; that he went to the funeral celebrations of one Amphidamas of Chalcis, on Euboea across the strait, and in the singing competition won a prize, a tripod, which he dedicated to the Muses; and that he had a brother named Perses. Perses, however, is a problem, and we shall have to come back to him. In addition to giving us these facts, Hesiod has a strong personality, which also marks off his work from the epic. In place of aristocratic withdrawal we find a speaker who is argumentative, suspicious, ironically humorous, frugal, fond of proverbs, wary of women.

His two poems, *Theogony* and *Works and Days*, are traditionally classed as didactic. They are in hexameters, like Homer, and Hesiod describes himself as a singer; it is natural to suppose that these poems, too, develop out of an oral tradition. Some think that Hesiod himself was the first to write his songs down. They contain highly poetical passages, but in general M. L. West's phrase 'Hesiod's hobnailed hexameters' is pretty fair. The *Theogony* was composed first. At the beginning Hesiod presents his credentials, telling how the Muses inspired him and told him to 'sing of the blessed deathless gods, and first and last to sing of themselves'. Hesiod fulfils this instruction by starting at the very beginning, with Chaos (something like 'Yawning Space', not 'Disorder)'), then Gaia/Earth, the broad seat of gods and men, and Tartara beneath the earth, and Love. Gaia/Earth gives birth to Uranus/Heaven—the double names are an attempt to convey the double aspect of these beings, who are both the natural objects and also anthropomorphic personalities. Thus Uranus is 'starry', but also he begot children on Gaia and then 'hid them away at their birth in a cleft of Earth and would not let them into the light; and he exulted in his evil-doing'.

The beginning of the gods is the beginning of the world, and theogony includes cosmogony. Earth is the first requisite, since everything else is placed by reference to it, either on it or under it. Heaven, as we have seen, is secondary to Earth, but is a good partner, being of comparable size; and since Earth, out of which things come to birth, is obviously a mother, Uranus/Heaven must be a father. The world is then built up and furnished by a series of sexual unions which produce offspring. That incidentally explains why Love is given such a very early position. Love has no children of his own, but he is the principle of procreation which is to create the world. The idea is a simple one, but we can see Hesiod developing it: one thing can be the 'offspring' of another in several different senses.

The children of Night will serve as an example. Night gave birth to black Doom and Death, and to Misery and Retribution and Strife (and other disagreeables), and to Sleep and the tribe of Dreams, and to Deceit and Affection, and to Day and Ether, and to the Hesperides. Death is dark and inactive, *like* night; misery and retribution are dark and deadly; sleep happens *in* the night; deceit perhaps started out as simply one of the unpleasantnesses, but suggested seduction—and love-play happens at night; day comes to birth, visibly, *from* night, and Ether is the sky left bright by night's departure; the Hesperides simply live in the west, where the sun goes down. Much of this, no doubt, is Hesiod's own invention. The purely mythological conception of genealogy has been half changed into an intellectual device to impose a different sort of order on the world.

The story opens with Gaia and Uranus. Zeus is not yet on the scene; in fact he is the grandson of Uranus/Heaven, and his father Cronos of the crooked counsels was supreme between them. Hesiod tells the story, known to Homer, of the succession of sky gods. First Uranus was supreme, but he suppressed his children, and Gaia encouraged his son Cronos to castrate him. Cronos in turn devoured his own children, until his wife Rhea gave him a stone to eat in place of Zeus; the child Zeus was brought up in Crete, compelled his father to disgorge his siblings, and with them and other aid defeated Cronos and his Titans and cast them down into Tartarus. This barbaric tale was always an oddity. Zeus' own name (akin to the Latin *dies*, 'day') meant 'sky', though classical Greeks had forgotten that; and it was strange that he should have a grandfather whose transparent name is the ordinary Greek word for 'sky'. Moreover, both Uranus and Cronos hardly existed as realities in cult. In this century the decipherment of a number of ancient Near Eastern languages has shown that the story is a version of a very archaic one, known to the Hittites by 1200 BC, to the Hurrians and the Phoenicians, and recited at Babylon annually in the poem known as *Enuma Elish* perhaps as much as 600 years earlier. Its ultimate origin seems to have been Sumerian. In these eastern stories we find a succession of gods, and the motifs of castration, of swallowing, and of a stone recur in ways which, though varying, show that the resemblance with Hesiod is no coincidence. And we see that while the predecessors of Zeus are shadows whose existence is virtually limited to this myth, in Mesopotamia one city did indeed rise and oust another from supreme power, and in turn give its own god the supreme position in Heaven: so Marduk of Babylon replaced Enlil of Nippur. The myth made sense on a Mesopotamian background as it did not in Greece.

ZEUS BLITZES A GIANT OR TITAN. From the corner of the pediment of the Temple of Artemis on Corcyra (Corfu), early sixth century BC. Apotropaic monsters such as the Gorgon (which figures at the centre of this pediment) or violent scenes of Olympian power such as this, are favourite themes for the decoration of early temples. Later the scenes are more closely related to local cult or history. The giant is here wholly human, Zeus naked as is common with gods and heroes, displaying their power and reflecting Greek acceptance of and pride in nudity.

ZEUS BLITZES A MONSTER. This vase, made in a Chalcidian colony in South Italy in about 550–525 BC, shows Zeus attacking with thunderbolt a male monster with wings and snake-legs. Its identity is not certain, but it may be Typhon. In Hesiod this monster has a hundred serpent heads but artists seldom follow literary prescriptions for such creatures, and compound them from various sources, sometimes Near Eastern. Giants are often given snake-legs in later art but seldom wings.

Oriental influence, then, is certain for an important myth in Hesiod. That raises the question of the character of his poems as a whole; for both cosmogonical and what may be called 'wisdom' literature was widespread in the Near East. Apart from Mesopotamia, we find it in Egypt, among the Phoenicians and Canaanites, and of course among the Hebrews. Striking parallels to lines in the *Works and Days* can be found in the Book of Proverbs; Genesis opens with the creation of the world before going on to human genealogies and the origins of the different nations. The early Greeks found themselves in a world which contained ancient and impressive civilizations, which they were not yet ready to dismiss as 'barbarians'. Oriental influence, since the story of Zeus' succession is so firmly embedded in Homer and Hesiod, may well go back to the Mycenaean period.

The *Theogony* does not give any account of the creation of man. It does, however, like Genesis and other legends, imagine that there was a time when man existed, but woman did not. The creation of woman came about in the following way, as a consequence of the peculiarities of Greek sacrificial ritual. Once upon a time the clever Prometheus (a god, not a man: but his actions involve men for ever) tricked Zeus by cunning division of a slaughtered ox. In one pile he put the flesh, making it look meagre and unattractive in the animal's paunch: in the other he put the bones, covering them with a toothsome layer of fat. Zeus, remarking on the unequal division, seized the fat and bones; and that is why, ever since, bones and fat are what the gods get, while men feast on the meat. The original sense of the ritual of sacrifice was not of feeding the gods at all, but of offering them back the bones which are the basic structure of the animal, probably as a magical device to ensure that they in turn would not withhold animals in future from the hunters. Later, an explanation was felt to be necessary for a custom which gave the worshipper all the good bits. The explanation is older than Hesiod, who says:

> Zeus in eternal wisdom knew the trick, was not deceived,
> But planned for men disasters which should never be relieved.
> He seized the white fat with two hands: his wrath was very great
> To see the white bones underneath, Prometheus' clever cheat.
>
> (*Theog.* 550-5)

We see the attempt, quite in Hesiod's manner, to preserve the omniscience of Zeus, although the story clearly assumes that the god was really taken in.

Hesiod develops his story to deal with two other great features of the world: fire and women. In anger at his deception Zeus deprived men of fire, but Prometheus brought it back in a hollow tube. Angered still more, Zeus devised the first woman, the mother of the disastrous race of women, who live with men like drones with bees, parasitic and profligate; yet necessary, if a man is not to be without children to care for his old age. We see the contrast between this peasant misogyny and the tragic clear-sightedness of the *Iliad*, when we compare Achilles' description to Priam of the two jars of good and evil from which Zeus gives to mankind either a mixture of both or unmixed evil: 'So did the gods deal with my father Peleus . . . and you too, old man, we hear were happy once, before the Achaeans came . . .' (*Iliad* 24. 534 ff.), with Hesiod saying that if a man gets a good wife, then he has something to offset the bad; but with a bad one life is unbearable (*Theog.* 607 ff.).

The poem establishes Zeus as ruler, and runs out (the original end is lost) in a catalogue of the offspring of divine and human amours. In the fifth century Herodotus could say of Hesiod and Homer (in that order), 'They it was who composed the theogony for the Greeks, giving the gods their titles and assigning them their honours and their occupations.' To some extent Hesiod was an authority for later Greeks in such matters, but there was no question of universal acceptance. His count of nine Muses did not prevent different people from talking of them as three, four, five, seven, or eight in number; the Hecate of Hesiod is quite different from the goddess we find elsewhere.

The *Works and Days* is evidently a later work. In the *Theogony* Hesiod listed Strife as one of the horrid children of Night; but in the *Works* he has thought further, and now he finds that after all there are two kinds of Strife. One is bad, but a second, characteristically called 'the elder', meaning 'the better', is a healthy spirit of competitiveness, which makes men work. For brother Perses has been

BRONZE WARRIOR FIGHTING A CENTAUR, BOTH
HELMETED. Geometric style of the later eighth
century BC. The centaur need not be the creature
fought by a Heracles or Theseus in later scenes, but a
generalized monster of the wild, possibly a giant or
Titan. Identities in this early period are not assured.

RELIEF VASE FROM BOEOTIA, of a type made
both in Boeotia and the Greek islands in the mid
seventh century. PERSEUS BEHEADS THE GORGON
MEDUSA. Perseus wears his cap of darkness and magic
boots, and carries a small bag in which to carry the
head. He looks away since the head literally petrifies.
The Gorgon has a horse body because her father was
Poseidon, god of horses, and she will give birth to
the winged horse Pegasus in her death throes. Later
artists do not generally give her a horse's body, but a
human one with wings, and a different lion-mask
face.

THE DECORATION OF A HANDLE OF
THE FRANÇOIS VASE, a large Athenian
mixing-bowl (crater), 66 cm high, found in
Etruria at Chiusi. It is one of the earliest
Athenian vases devoted completely to
figure decoration—270 human and animal
figures with 121 inscriptions, painted about
570 BC. Artemis is shown here in her early
guise as a mistress of animals, and winged,
a form which may owe much to the Near
East: later her relationship with the animals
changes and she is a huntress. The warrior
carried from the field of battle is a stock
group, with the figures here identified as
Ajax with Achilles, as commonly, but not
exclusively, on other works.

behaving badly, demanding more than his share of the inheritance and bribing
the local 'kings' to adjudge it to him. Instead of that sort of wickedness, he
should work:

> Work, Perses, my fine gentleman, that Hunger may keep clear,
> But fair Demeter love you well and fill your barn with cheer.
>
> (299–300)

The poem opens with moral remonstrances, hammered home in every way
that Hesiod can think of; it turns into a more or less systematic account of the
farmer's year, as far as agriculture and vines go, with miscellaneous precepts and
a long excursus on sailing. 'If you are taken by desire for uncomfortable seafaring', says the poet characteristically, '. . . I will tell you the ways of the sea',

> Not as a seasoned mariner: I've never been on ship,
> Except indeed from Aulis to Euboea's nearest tip
>
> (649–50)

—a distance of perhaps 100 yards. Thoughts of morality, of right and wrong ways of getting a livelihood, and of the land of which Perses has robbed the poet, gradually crystallize into an account of the farmer's year; which was not what we expected at the beginning.

Perses, the bad brother, appears initially to have cheated Hesiod and to be living on the fat of the land: 'Let us settle the case afresh, with an upright decision' (35). But later on it appears that he is impoverished and scrounging on Hesiod. Strip to sow and strip to plough, says the poet, lest you be forced to go a-begging, 'as now you come to me: but I will give you nothing more' (396). The discrepancy has led some to think that Perses is a fiction, a mere peg to hang the poem on. It is indeed quite regular for works of moral instruction to have a narrative framework. The Book of Ecclesiastes is put into the mouth of a disillusioned old king of Israel; and in other Near Eastern literatures we find a Sumerian work in the form of a father's remonstrance with his prodigal son, Egyptian wisdom texts spoken by viziers or unfairly disgraced priests, and so on. The narrative is evidently meant to catch the reader's attention for the instructions.

But it is not easy to imagine that Hesiod could have travelled the countryside singing a song which accused the local magnates at Ascra of 'devouring bribes' and incurring the vengeance of heaven on the whole community, if everybody knew the case was a fiction. The details about the father, too, seem to be truthful: it is hard to see why Hesiod should have invented that sort of background for himself. So the explanation is probably twofold: the song went on forming and enlarging itself in his mind, so that the situation of Hesiod and his brother could develop and change; and also the changing focus and emphasis of the poem led the poet to make his brother, at moments, fit in with the things he wanted to say.

THE CALYDONIAN BOAR HUNT on the neck of the François Vase (see illustration on p. 94). An epic occasion introducing many important heroic figures. Atalanta (white-skinned, to the left) struck the first blow but Meleager, before the boar, kills it. The Dioscuri, behind it, share a spear.

Another thing Hesiod has continued to think about is the Prometheus myth. In the *Works* he wants a general explanation for the hardness of life and the necessity of work: that, too, is given by the same myth. This time the mood is even gloomier: the Father of gods and men 'laughed aloud' as he promised condign punishment for men (59), and the woman—Pandora is now her name—is not just a calamity in herself, concealing beneath her seductive appearance 'the mind of a bitch and a heart of deceit' (67); she takes the lid off a great jar in which diseases and ills of every sort had hitherto been locked away. So now the world is full of them. 'You cannot make a fool of Zeus' (105). We think of Eve, also saddled with the responsibility for all that is unsatisfactory in the world.

That story, though elliptically told at some points, goes with a swing. It is typical of Hesiod that at the end of it he is temporarily stuck for a way to go on with his poem, and can only say 'Now if you like I'll tell you another story', this time a version of the decline from the Golden Age of lost Paradise, by way of increasingly inferior Silver and Bronze Ages, to the awful Iron Age in which we have the misfortune to live. This is another eastern idea: Hesiod has rudely adapted it to Greek notions about the past by inserting the age of heroes, who could not be left out, between the Bronze Age and our own. The heroes are, as they have to be, 'better and more virtuous' than the berserkers of the Bronze Age, and that spoils the elegant shape of the tale; but Hesiod, we feel, finds it hard to force his thoughts into shape, and he has to accept such inconcinnities.

Also typical of Hesiod is the way in which, in the opening 300 lines of the *Works*, he wavers between addressing Perses and addressing the 'kings'. He has things to say to both. 'I will tell a fable to the kings', says he, and tells of the hawk who caught the nightingale.

> The nightingale wept piteously, but harsh was the reply:
> 'You fool, a stronger has you now; no use to wail and cry.
> You'll come where I shall carry you, for all you sing so sweet;
> And as I choose I'll let you go, or have you for my meat.'
>
> (205 ff.)

Having reached this point, Hesiod tells his brother 'Don't you try to behave violently: a small man can't get away with it'. That suggests the perils of wrong-doing in general, which extend to the whole community; so he addresses the kings, urging them to turn to justice (248 ff.); the eye of Zeus sees everything; then back to Perses—he should forget violence and be mindful of justice. 'For Zeus made it right for fishes and beasts and *birds who fly* to eat each other, for they have no justice; but to men he has given justice . . .' That, as the emphasis on the birds helps to show, is the moral of the fable: the kings have treated me as animals treat each other, without thought of right and wrong. But with the difficulty of managing both his targets, it is Perses in the end who gets the moral meant for the kings.

Some parts of the poem are more closely organized than others. There are passages in which Hesiod slides from thought to thought. 'Be pious and offer sacrifice—invite neighbours to eat of the meat—neighbours are important—invite those who invite you—give to those who give to you—giving is good, violent taking is bad—even in small things—small acquisitions do add up—it's good to build up stores—think ahead—but misplaced economy can be mean—don't stint on wages; trust and mistrust can each be fatal—don't trust a woman—as for having children, one son is best—but Zeus may provide for several and still make you rich—if you want to be rich, here is the Farmer's Year.' That would be a rough summary of the connections of thought from line 336 to line 383. They are there, but you can miss them.

Other passages are poetical in a more ambitious sense. The Prometheus stories in both poems are well told. The battle of gods and Titans, and Zeus' fight with the monster Typhoeus (*Theog.* 674-712, 820-68), aim at the grandiose; more attractive to most readers will be the description of winter (*Works* 504-35), with the wild animals cowering, the old man bent like a hoop by the wind, the young girl staying at home and protecting her beauty, and 'the boneless one gnawing his foot in his fireless house and gloomy lair' (a riddling allusion to the octopus); and of summer, when 'women are lewdest and men are feeblest', but one can enjoy a picnic in the shade of a rock (*Works* 482-96).

The poems are by their nature rather formless, and the end was especially vulnerable to addition. The *Works* peters out into a rather random list of taboos (724-59), then a list of lucky and unlucky days of the month (765-828), after which in antiquity there followed a treatment of bird-omens. It is hard to know how much of this is by Hesiod. The *Theogony* as we have it leads directly into the most important of the other works sometimes ascribed to Hesiod, the long *Catalogue of Women* or *Ehoiae*. We now have very considerable fragments of this poem, which organized the heroic Greek genealogies back to Deucalion and the Flood. It cannot be by Hesiod; for example, it includes the story of Cyrene, but Cyrene was not founded until 630 or so. Some passages are quite picturesque, but as mythical narrative it is no rival to Homer. Its subject-matter was in the fifth century turned into prose by mythical historians like Acusilaus and Phere-cydes. A short epic called the *Shield of Heracles* survives under Hesiod's name; it is a rather lurid production. Of the ten other poems ascribed to Hesiod by one ancient writer or another, none of them perhaps on any substantial grounds, we know too little to say anything significant.

Further Reading

MYTH

H. J. Rose, *A Handbook of Greek Mythology* (London, 1928: 6th edn., paperback, 1958) gives a reliable account of the main mythological stories. The Loeb edition by J. G. Frazer of the ancient mythological compilation known as Apollodorus' *Library* (2 vols., 1921) contains a mass of detailed information about them. A more amusing way of making the acquaintance of these myths is by reading the *Metamorphoses* of Ovid.

G. S. Kirk discusses the particular character of Greek mythology in *The Nature of Greek Myths* (Harmondsworth, 1974); his book *Myth: Its Meaning and Functions in Ancient and Other Cultures* (California, 1970: paperback) deals with the role of myths in different societies and with modern theories on the subject. Both books show a certain dissatisfaction with the 'rational' atmosphere of most Greek myths. M. P. Nilsson showed that many of the myths go back to the Mycenaean period: *The Mycenaean Origin of Greek Mythology* (California, 1932: paperback). C. Lévi-Strauss, in *Anthropologie structurale* (Paris 1958, 1973) and *Mythologiques* (4 vols.: Paris, 1964–71)—available in English as *Structural Anthropology* (Paris, 1972) and *Introduction to a Science of Mythology* (4 vols.; London, 1964–81)—applied a radical structuralist analysis to mythology, primarily that of South America. Structuralist works on Greek myth include M. Detienne, *Les Jardins d'Adonis* (Paris, 1972) (in English, trans. J. Lloyd, *The Gardens of Adonis*, Hassocks, 1977), and *Myth, Religion and Society*, Structuralist Essays edited by R. L. Gordon (Cambridge, 1981: paperback). W. Burkert, *Structure and History in Greek Mythology and Ritual* (California, 1979: paperback) criticizes such views from a standpoint closer to that of the zoological researches of Konrad Lorenz and the new science of ethology.

On the moral implications of myth, see H. Lloyd-Jones, *The Justice of Zeus* (California, 2nd edn. 1984: paperback). Bruno Snell, *The Discovery of the Mind* (Harvard, 1953: paperback), gives an idea of the uses of myth in literature—see especially chs. 2, 4, 5, 12. K. Schefold, *Myth and Legend in Early Greek Art* (London, 1966) discusses the visual arts; J. Seznec, *The Survival of the Pagan Gods* (New York, 1961: paperback) traces the myths through the Middle Ages to the Renaissance.

HESIOD

There is an English translation in the Loeb Classical Library volume (with the Homeric Hymns). Modern text and commentary of great learning and interest are in the editions by M. L. West of the *Theogony* (Oxford, 1966) and *Works and Days* (Oxford, 1978). The oriental material is discussed in these two books; much of it is conveniently assembled by J. B. Pritchard (editor), *Ancient Near Eastern Texts Relating to the Old Testament* (Princeton: 3rd edn. 1968). A. R. Burn, *The World of Hesiod* (London, 1936), puts the poet in his historical setting. The third chapter of H. Fränkel, *Early Greek Poetry and Philosophy* (Oxford, 1975), is a valuable discussion of Hesiod.

4
Lyric and Elegiac Poetry

EWEN BOWIE

ONLY of hexameter poetry have we examples earlier than 700 BC. But many genres first known to us from the seventh century were certainly thriving long before—that century gives us our first elegiac, iambic, and melic poetry because by then writing was spreading, so that the works of celebrated poets could be recorded as those of their predecessors could not. Of our genres only elegiac significantly exploited those formulaic phrases which both aided the composition and recitation of epic and contributed to its oral preservation. Furthermore much of our poetry was composed with particular audiences and occasions in view, so that incentives to preserve it orally were fewer.

Also different from epic is the prominence given to the personality of the poet or singer. The first person becomes the focus of attention, and 'I' (occasionally 'we') tell of 'my' loves, griefs, hates, and adventures. This has sometimes misled scholars into seeing the seventh century as an efflorescence of individualism. Not only, however, did such poetry exist earlier, but the 'I' of a poem cannot unquestioningly be referred to the person of the singer or poet. As traditional folk-songs and modern popular songs show, 'I'-songs can be sung with feeling by many other than their composers. Rarely do we take such statements as autobiographical; sometimes indeed no composer is known. Hence we should hesitate to use fragments of such poets as Archilochus to ascribe strident self-assertion or to reconstruct biography.

Three more preliminaries. First, although what survives is ascribed to a few dozen figures, the genres exemplified, and many conventional themes and approaches, will have been attempted by hundreds over the Greek world. Most of our poetry was not, like epic, the virtuoso's preserve, but was designed for occasions where amateurs contributed. This is clearest in the tradition about after-dinner singing at Athens: a myrtle branch circulated, and with it the obligation to sing. The songs, Attic *skolia*, were short and simple; and some drew a distinction between these and songs sung by the 'more talented'. This relates to only one city, but much early poetry is designed for similar occasions, and we should not imagine *soirées* at which only one virtuoso sang while other people listened or chatted.

Second, relative importance of text and accompaniment. Melic and elegiac poetry was sung, usually accompanied respectively on the lyre and the *aulos* (an oboe-like wind instrument). For no song can we reconstruct the vocal or instrumental line, and indeed we have only a rudimentary understanding of what it might have been like. In many songs music may have contributed more to initial impact than text, in many more it was an integral part of the effect. Doubtless the texts selected for copying and transmission were those whose words were of greater moment than music: but never forget that, even reading these poems aloud, we gain access only to part of their intended effect, and before impugning deficiency of thought or skill, ponder whether modern song-writers would gladly be judged on 'lyrics' alone.

Third, the work of almost all these poets has survived only in shattered fragments, preserved by later quotation or on papyri recovered from Graeco-Roman Egypt. We have a few dozen elegiac poems arguably complete, but of melic poets other than Pindar and Bacchylides only half a dozen complete songs remain.

Some poets composed in several genres. Since many composed both elegiac and iambic poetry, I treat these genres together. They share numerous themes and stances and were probably intended for similar occasions. They also exhibit clear differences. Elegiac poetry alternates the dactylic hexameter (used line after line for epic) with a 'pentameter' built up from the same metrical unit, the *hemiepes*, giving

$$- \cup\cup - \cup\cup - \cup\cup - \cup\cup - \cup\cup - - \text{ (hexameter).}$$
$$- \cup\cup - \cup\cup - \| - \cup\cup - \cup\cup - - \text{ (pentameter).}$$

Like epic, elegiac couplets were sung to an accompaniment, in elegy's case the *aulos*: being a wind instrument, this must have been played by someone other than the singer. Doubtless this relatively formal presentation and a metre accommodating to epic vocabulary invited a certain dignity of tone—neither theme nor language descends to the depths plumbed by iambic poetry. This seems to have been recited, not sung, and its rhythms (commonest the iambic trimeter) readily accepted everyday speech. Occasionally poets combine dactylic and iambic rhythms in a form often (confusingly) called 'epode'.

Archilochus (*c.*650 BC) used all these metres. Traditionally he was the son, albeit bastard, of the leader of the Parian colony to Thasos, and a high place in society is corroborated by some poems' address to Glaucus, also distinguished in Thasos' early history. His elegies were probably sung at *symposia*, post-prandial drinking parties which only wealthier male citizens are likely to have attended. Such men were also in the front line when Thasians fought Thracians or other Greeks, and the treatment of these struggles in some long iambic fragments suggests that Archilochus took them seriously. Serious, too, is a reflective elegy

on friends lost at sea and man's need to endure what gods dispose (fr. 13). But
he also played on the contrast between war and singing (fr. 1), and a song
imitated by Alcaeus, Anacreon, and Horace shows how conviviality encouraged
suspension or mockery of normal values:

> My shield delights some Thracian, for I dropped
>   the blameless gear, unwilling, in a wood—
> but saved my skin: what is that shield to me?
>   Stuff it! I'll get another just as good.

The pithiness and balance of this, perhaps complete, song foreshadow the
elegiac metre's later use for epigrams. Some iambic poems were much longer.
Themes of fighting and shipwreck may reflect Archilochus' own life, but in fr.
19, opening with a high-minded rejection of kingly wealth and power, the
speaker emerges as not Archilochus, but a carpenter, Charon, and in another (fr.
122) a father commenting on his daughter's conduct. Both situations may be
invented, but fr. 122 is often linked with Archilochus' supposed affair with
Neobule, inferred in antiquity from his poems: when her father Lycambes ended
it Archilochus' embittered iambics allegedly drove him and his daughters to
suicide. Historical or invented, they figure in several poems, notably a fragmentary epode where the fable of the fox and the eagle warns Lycambes that betrayal
doesn't pay. In another, discovered almost complete in 1973, Archilochus tells a
male friend of his passion for Neobule's younger sister and how he seduced her
in a flowery meadow. His 'reported' words criticize Neobule savagely:

> Let me tell you this. Neobule
>   let another man have:
> ah! *she*'s gone off—she's twice your age
> and all her young girl's bloom has flowed away
>   and the charm she once had.
>   (fr. 196A. 24–8)

But her sister's conquest is narrated tenderly and without coarseness:

> These were my words: and 'mid the blooming flowers
>   I embraced the young girl
>   and laid her down, and with a soft
> cloak covered her, her head clasped in my arms.
>   a-trembling with fear
>   just like a fawn [   ]
> and gently stroked my hands across her b[   ]s.
>   (ibid. 42–8: square brackets mark gaps)

The poem extends Archilochus' known range of themes and tones. The scanty
fragments of his near-contemporaries, Tyrtaeus, Callinus, and Mimnermus, who
also composed poetry for the *symposion,* hardly suggest similar versatility, but
their range may be inadequately reflected in what survives. Our only substantial

elegy of Callinus of Ephesus exhorts young men to fight for their country; so too Tyrtaeus' elegies for Sparta, sung (according to fourth-century sources) at banquets during campaigns. Mimnermus of Colophon also sang martial exhortations (fr. 14), but it was songs on love, youth, and age that immortalized him. Tyrtaeus urged a warrior to

> hold his shield fast
> making his own life his enemy, and the black spirits
> of Death as dear to him as the rays of the sun.
>
> (fr. 11. 6–8)

Mimnermus turned this image to praise of youth and abhorrence of age:

> But we, like the blooms that blossom in the season of many flowers,
>   Spring, when they suddenly shoot, caught by the sun's bright rays—
> like these, for a cubit's length of time the flowers of youth
>   we enjoy, at the hands of the gods knowing not evil days
> nor good. But beside us there stand the black spirits of Death,
>   one of them holding an end in age with its dreadful pain
> and the other in death: but of youth only a short time lives
>   the fruit—for as long as the sun spreads itself over the plain.
>
> (fr. 2. 1–8)

Such themes suited *symposia*, but disclose little about Mimnermus' society at large. Even in warlike Sparta, after all, where Tyrtaeus demonstrates elegy's popularity, elegies praised drinking; and the Athenian lawgiver Solon's songs enthused over love and the good life (frs. 23, 25, 26). However, Solon's poems also exemplify lengthy treatment of political issues—doubtless common topics in after-dinner conversation, and so not surprising candidates for song in the same setting. A fanciful anecdote has Solon recite in the *agora* a 100-line elegy urging the Athenians to recapture Salamis; but, like other political fragments, this song is simply a particular form of elegy's reflective and exhortatory mode. Another (fr. 13) is our longest early elegy to survive. In its seventy-six lines (probably a complete poem) Solon prays for wealth—but justly acquired, for Zeus punishes evil—shifts to the emptiness of man's hopes, slides into a catalogue of different human activities, then returns to actions' uncertain outcome—uncertain save that greed attracts god-sent ruin. Despite loose construction the poem has power, momentum, and several striking images. Solon's iambics, apparently all political, exploit less poetic vocabulary, but here too is a moving personification of 'Black Earth, greatest mother of the Olympian gods' (fr. 36. 5–6), called to witness how Solon freed her, the soil of Attica, by abolishing serfdom. Note too that in such poems (fr. 33) Solon, like Archilochus, made others speak.

Alone of early elegiac and melic poets Theognis of Megara (*c.*540 BC) has had some poetry transmitted in a continuous manuscript tradition. Less fortunately for him, the 1,400 or so lines there ascribed to him are a mixture of his and

‍

others' elegies; and snippets, as naturally in an anthology, outnumber complete songs. Nevertheless the collection is priceless. First, much of Theognis' work is identifiable by being addressed to his boy-friend Cyrnus: we hear a sententious oligarch, bitter at his class's loss of power and distrusting all about him. Some songs are distinguished, notably 237–54 (probably complete), confidently promising Cyrnus poetic immortality, only to conclude:

> And yet I receive from you not even a little respect.
> But, as if I were a small boy, you deceive me with tales.

Secondly, that Theognis' platitudes on friendship, wine, or wealth became the core of a song-book exposes the general level of singing and the preferred themes of *symposia* c. 500 BC. Finally, several passages overlap quotations elsewhere from other elegists, augmenting their known work.

Although some fifth-century pieces survive, by then elegy, like aristocratic *symposia*, is in decline; by the fourth century it is dead. Iambic poetry also disappears, its metres annexed by Attic drama. Even for its acme iambic fragments are too sparse to allow confident reconstruction of the genre. Some poets other than Archilochus and Solon stand out. Semonides, who led a Samian colony to Amorgos c.630 BC, composed a witty male-chauvinist piece whose 118 lines compare women unflatteringly with various animals (fr. 7). Bitter invective marks one iambic fragment of Anacreon (fr. 318); another (fr. 335), addressing a reluctant girl as an unbroken filly in an extended *double-entendre*, exhibits the wit that dominates his melic poetry (below, p. 106). But the most colourful exploiter of autobiography and invective was Hipponax of Ephesus (c.540 BC). Prayers to Hermes, god of thieves, and sordid orgies with the mistress of the sculptor Bupalus, take us lower in society than Hipponax probably lived. Perhaps he carried Archilochus' mixture of fantasy and reality one stage further, and complete poems might show us an interesting coda to the iambic tradition.

Alongside iambic recitation and *aulos*-accompanied elegy, both composed for individual performance, there flourished singing to the lyre, 'melic' poetry. This was sometimes sung by individuals (like the songs of Sappho and Alcaeus) and sometimes by choirs (like those of Alcman and Pindar). Whereas elegy originated in Ionia and retained features of the Ionic dialect even in Dorian Megara and Sparta, melic poetry was at home everywhere. When individuals sang to the lyre, therefore, their vernacular was used, which aided the directness often praised in archaic monody. Apart from some work-songs, most monody seems, like elegy, to be intended for *symposia* or comparable female gatherings. Such gatherings existed, at least in Lesbos, since it is from Sappho of Lesbos (c.600 BC) that some of our masterpieces come.

Sappho's poetic personality is as clear as her life is obscure. The singer is forever in love: Aphrodite's patronage helps her win girls who reject her (fr. 1); for her the love-object outshines anything else mankind admires (fr. 16); desire precipitates complete physical collapse (fr. 31). Love is not simply the centre of Sappho's universe, it *is* her universe. When not creating song around 'her own' feelings she presents herself consoling a girl-friend leaving her in tears:

'and honestly I want to die'
—so sobbing, many times, she left me

and she said this [to me]
'My god! what awful things are happening to us:
Sappho, I swear I am leaving you against my will.'

And I replied to her in these words:
'Go with a light heart, and with memories
of me, for you know how we cherished you.

And if not, then I want to
remind you [   ]
[   ] and we had good times

For ma[ny garland]s of violets
and roses [   ] together
and [   ] you put on beside me

And many garlands
woven from flowers about your soft neck
[   ] fashioned

And with m[uch] myrrh
from rich flowers [   ]
and royal you rubbed your skin

And on soft beds
tender [   ]
you would satisfy desire [   ]

And there was no [   ] nothing
holy nor [   ]
from which [we] kept away

No grove [   ]
[   ] sound
[   ]'   (fr. 94)

These lines well illustrate Sappho's simple language and presentation. Recollections of shared pleasures demonstrate that, whatever roles (e.g. music teacher) are alleged on the scanty evidence of certain poems, she claimed that of lover of girls unashamedly and openly. Presumably audiences knew, and might include, her current flame, though in two songs (frs. 1, certainly complete, and 31) Sappho, in declaring love, names no beloved. Girls are named when Sappho's interest is less immediate: Anactoria, whose absence provokes the love-object's exaltation in fr. 16, or Atthis, recalled as a past flame in fr. 49. Atthis' part is different in fr. 96, consoling her for the departure of *her* lover. Solace is drawn from memory of mutual fondness (cf. fr. 94), but also from the lover's beauty:

> now she shines out among the women of Lydia
> as sometimes, when the sun has set,
> the rosy-fingered moon
>
> outshines all the stars: and its light
> spreads over the salt sea
> and alike over the many-flowered fields
>
> and the dew falls fair, and in full
> bloom are the roses ...   (fr. 96. 6–13)

Despite the image's ambiguous relation to the girl it evocatively conveys her beauty: with Sappho's rococo scene of Aphrodite's descent from Olympus (fr. 1) it attests her skill in vivid depiction. Of more formal poetry we have but scraps of wedding songs and thirty-five lines describing Hector and Andromache's wedding (fr. 44)—here myth is narrated not as illustration, but for its own sake.

Alcaeus, her contemporary from Mytilene, deploys the same language and metres on similar themes. Myth figures in hymns, and in two poems is narrated for its own sake. Like most personal poets, Alcaeus sang of love, but the songs most read later are political—one-sided views of aristocratic power-struggles in Mytilene *c.*600 BC. For Alcaeus success—such as one tyrant's overthrow, which evoked 'Now we must get drunk, since Myrsilus is dead' (fr. 332)—was rare and brief. Pittacus, once Alcaeus' ally, himself became tyrant, and his 'betrayal' of Alcaeus prompted his most vigorous poetry. One fragment (129) recalls oaths sworn together and calls upon Zeus, Hera, and Dionysus to succour Alcaeus and his exiled friends while an avenging Erinys pursues Pittacus. Another (130) voices despair at exclusion from the political life enjoyed by his ancestors. Elsewhere he suppresses his political message until another theme has captivated his listeners. Thus a long fragment (298 *Suppl.*) blames Ajax's rape of Cassandra in Athena's temple for the Achaeans' troubles returning from Troy: the rape fills four stanzas, then a storm punishes Ajax with death. This, we now discover, illustrates a community's need to destroy its sinners before gods act, a message presented as relevant to the Mytileneans harbouring the 'sinner' Pittacus. Two other vivid storm scenes, perhaps allegorical (frs. 6, 326), also have political contexts.

Many songs, like that on Myrsilus, take their cue from the drinking central to *symposia*. Like love, this theme can be given many twists. So, trite but apt, fr. 335:

> We should not abandon our hearts to our woes
> for we gain not a whit by our moping;
> but, Bycchis, the medicine best for our case
> is to pour out the wine and start toping.

More ingenuity goes into fr. 338 (imitated by Horace) where drink is invoked to combat wintry weather. Naturally summer heatwaves allow the same conclusion (fr. 347).

Wine and love were handled very differently by two poets whose careers crossed about 530 BC at the Samian court of Polycrates. Ibycus of Rhegium presumably became known in Italy and Sicily before attracting Polycrates' hospitality. Anacreon was from nearby Teos, and when Polycrates was murdered he moved to Pisistratid Athens, probably staying on after Hippias' expulsion. Both resort frequently to provocative imagery, often symbolic. But Ibycus' aim in accumulating images of passions seems to be to saturate one's mind by their intense lushness:

> In spring the Cydonian quinces bloom,
> watered from the rivers' streams,
> where lies the maidens' unplucked garden,
> and the vine-blossoms
> thrive, taking their strength
> beneath the vine's shady shoots:
> but my Love rests at no season;
> [but like] the Thracian North Wind
> blazing with lightning
> it darts from the Cyprian goddess
> with wasting frenzies
> dark and fearless
> and all-powerfully shakes
> my heart from its very roots.   (fr. 286)

Anacreon, by contrast, unfolds scenes swiftly, image by image, suddenly imposing a surprising and witty perspective by twists at the end. Thus fr. 358, probably complete:

> Once again his crimson ball
> Love, golden-locked, throws my way
> challenging me to play
> to a gaudy-sandalled lass's call:
>
> But she—from an isle with a touch of class,
> Lesbos—my hair (now turned
> white) has spurned
> and makes eyes at another lass.

Anacreon's songs also differ from Ibycus' in scale. Several of around eight lines look complete, a length typical also of his Hellenistic imitators. Ibycus is more problematic: fr. 286 and another about love could come from short poems, but quotations of mythological details suggest heroic narrative unattested for Anacreon. It may, of course, have served as illustration. Certainly in one forty-five-line fragment (282) Ibycus catalogues Trojan-war episodes and figures he will *not* sing of, using them as a foil to his concluding praise of Polycrates' renown, boldly linked to his own. Often he recalls Stesichorus in metre and language, and clearly stands close to that tradition of heroic narrative which Stesichorus alone represents.

Much about Stesichorus (*c.*560 BC) has become clearer from recent discoveries. His treatment was so expansive that Alexandrian editors gave songs individual papyrus rolls and titles. Thus *Geryoneis*, telling of Heracles' fight with three-bodied Geryon, exceeded 1,800 lines. *Oresteia* in two books must have been longer still. Other features too explain the ancient assessment of Stesichorus as 'most Homeric'. Many phrases evoke, without duplicating, Homeric formulae, and *Geryoneis* shows how Homeric motifs were transposed. At *Iliad* 12. 322 ff. Sarpedon urged Glaucus to fight, since even survivors of the battle would one day die. Geryon adapts this to answer a long speech counselling him not to face Heracles. 'If I am immortal it would be better to [   ]. But if I must grow old among mortals, far nobler now to face my destiny' (*Suppl.* 11). Later, when a poisoned arrow has cleft the last of Geryon's three heads, Stesichorus creates sympathy by developing an Iliadic simile (8. 306–8):

> and then Geryon's neck leaned over
>   to one side, as when a poppy
> disfiguring its soft body
>   suddenly casts away its leaves
>   (*Suppl.* 15 col. ii, 14–17)

Stesichorus' metre, although dactylic, like Homer's, is different in important ways. Units of varying length form a strophe: this is repeated (antistrophe), then follows a shorter system (epode) giving a triadic structure (in *Geryoneis* twenty-six lines) repeated throughout the song. Ancients credited Stesichorus with this structure's invention and classed his songs as choral. This classification has been challenged, and it is disputed whether his songs were sung by choirs or, like Homeric epic, by the poet himself.

Before considering poets whose songs were certainly choral, we note another point that groups Stesichorus with them and not with Homer. Whereas Homer suppresses his personality, choral songs regularly highlight poets' views of life and their creative role. Thus Stesichorus' second *Helen*: his first told the *fable convenue*, but, doubtless eager to exploit a box-office success, he completely changed the story in the second, sending Helen to Egypt and only a phantom to Troy, and explicitly criticized Homer and Hesiod for their mistakes, claiming that his own information came from Helen's angry appearance to him in a dream (frs. 192–3).

Assertion of moral outlook and mythological variants becomes most prominent in Pindar. But already about 600 BC Alcman deployed maxims to point up narration of myth by his chorus of Spartan girls: 'Let none from mankind fly up to heaven' (fr. 1. 16) and, rounding off his myth, 'There is some punishment from gods: but blessed is he who in good heart weaves his day tearless' (fr. 1. 36-9). Fr. 1, once probably 140 lines, is Alcman's only substantial monument. Of its first part only scraps of thirty-five lines surrvive, glimpses of a myth involving sexual violence. The second, largely complete, turns abruptly to praise two girls, apparently chorus leaders: 'but I sing of the light of Agido: I see her like the sun, whom Agido calls to shine as our witness' (fr. 1. 39-43). Brilliant light yields to racehorses as the image compared, then returns with Hagesichora's golden hair and silver face. There follows praise of eight other singers, some merely named, all set clearly below the leaders. The last two systems of the poem, even if complete, would still leave puzzlement about the local deities alluded to and the ceremony being performed (simply a *rite de passage*?) in which girls sing of gods, heroes, and themselves. Puzzling too are innuendos of sexual attraction towards their leaders: 'Nor will you say "May I get Astaphis, and may Philylla look upon me, and Damareta, and desirable Wianthemis"—but it is Hagesichora who wastes me away' (fr. 1. 74-7). These go even further in another choral song enthusiastically praising Astymeloisa's charms (fr. 3).

Songs for girl choruses were still composed by Pindar. But the form which dominates his and Bacchylides' remains is the victory song, commissioned to celebrate competitors' successes at the great Panhellenic festivals. About the lesser poet, Bacchylides of Ceos (active *c*.485-450 BC), we knew little until in 1892 a papyrus yielded twenty poems, many almost complete. Its fourteen victory songs can be confronted with those of Pindar (active *c*.500-446 BC) to reveal common elements of the genre and each poet's individuality. Praise of the patron is naturally prominent—not only his recent victory, but other marks of excellence, including the now enhanced distinction of family and city. Equally mandatory was a myth, found in all but the shortest songs. Its bearing upon the victory varies: it brings victor and audience into the world of gods and heroes, but it can also underline man's limitations and constant risk of grief and pain. To emphasize such messages the poet plays the moral teacher, studding his composition with maxims, and since their worth and that of the whole song depends upon the poet's own distinction, he highlights his part in its creation and his poetic superiority.

In Bacchylides the relation between these elements is clearer and narrative of myth more straightforward than in Pindar. Language flows lucidly, metre is simpler. Aspects of the difference emerge from two songs for the victory of Hiero, tyrant of Syracuse, in the horse race at Olympia in 476 BC.

Bacchylides' *Ode* 5 opens with an address to Hiero, complimenting his literary taste and stating the poet's wish to praise him (1-16). An eagle, unfettered by 'the peaks of the mighty earth or the craggy waves of the tireless sea' (16-30) stands for the poet who has countless ways to praise Hiero (31-6). The horse Pherenicus has won, at Olympia as at Delphi—never yet, the poet swears, has he been defeated. Then a maxim: 'Blessed he to whom god has given a share of fine things, and to live a life of wealth with enviable fortune: for no one among earth-dwellers has been happy in all things' (50-5, cf. Alcman, quoted above). Now the myth: unconquered Heracles, braving the underworld to fetch Cerberus, 'encountered the souls of wretched mortals ... like the leaves that the clear-blowing wind ripples on the sheep-grazed ridges of Ida'. Amazed by Meleager's might, Heracles asks how he died: Meleager tells how the Achaeans at last vanquished the boar sent by a wrathful Artemis to ravage Calydon of the fair choruses, but how then he, embattled over the spoils with his mother's kin, died when she burned the magic log embodying his life (56-154). Then only Heracles wept, saying 'Best for mortals not to be born, nor to see the light of the sun; but since nothing is achieved by lamenting this tale, have you a sister alive whom I might wed?' Meleager names Deianeira; there Bacchylides leaves his myth (175) and we understand that Heracles (to be killed unintentionally by over-loving Deianeira) exemplifies, like Meleager, an unhappy end. Briefly Bacchylides hymns Zeus and Olympia, and, quoting Hesiod, defends unenvious praise of success (176-200).

Pindar opens *Olympian* 1 more obliquely. 'Best is water, and gold shines out like a blazing fire in the night beyond any proud wealth: and if you wish to sing of prizes, dear heart, seek no other bright star that is hotter in the day than the sun in the empty sky, nor shall we name a contest better than Olympia.' Thus Pindar introduces praise of Olympian Zeus for Hiero who 'picking the crown of all the virtues' glories in music (1-17). Pherenicus' renown in the Peloponnese leads to the myth—Poseidon's love for Pelops. Disparaging false tales and insisting that a mortal utter fair things about the gods, Pindar explains Pelops' disappearance as a Ganymede-like visit to an immortal lover, and tales of Tantalus stewing and serving him to the gods as a jealous neighbour's invention (18-51). 'But for me there is no way I could call any of the blessed ones belly-mad. I recoil. Loss has time and again been the portion of ill-speakers' (52-3). Tantalus, however, honoured by the gods, 'could not digest his great prosperity' and blindly stole divine food and drink to entertain his friends: 'if any man hopes to do something without god's notice, he is wrong' (54-64). Pelops, sent back to earth, obtained Poseidon's help in defeating Oenomaus, king at Olympia, in the chariot race required of his daughter's suitors (with certain death if they lost). Here again Pindar silently rejects discreditable stories of sabotage, giving Pelops a noble appeal to Poseidon: 'but for those who must die—who would simmer in vain an inglorious old age sitting in darkness with no portion of all that is fair?' (82-4). By Pelops' marriage, progeny, and tomb Pindar brings us back to Olympia, its contests, victory's lifelong reward, his own song and Hiero's pre-eminent taste and power (90-105). God cares for Hiero, and Pindar expects to praise even sweeter successes. But 'Peer no more into the distance. On this day may you step high, and may I have this commerce with victors, conspicuous for my skill among Greeks worldwide' (114-16).

Although the ingredients, and some images, recur in Pindar's forty-four other victory songs, each is rewardingly diverse, carefully matched to a different patron. Substantial fragments of his *Paeans* (hymns, especially to Apollo) and some of his *Dithyrambs* (associated with Dionysus) show similar complexity of thought and language: we glimpse what we have lost because these genres lack what illuminates victory songs, Pindar's continuous manuscript tradition and Bacchylides' long papyrus. That papyrus indeed contains six 'Dithyrambs'. *Ode* 17, more properly a Paean, narrates Theseus' quarrel with Minos: as in *Ode* 3, direct speech is prominent. *Ode* 18, probably for an Athenian festival, focuses upon Theseus' return to Athens. Its dramatic form is unique: four metrical systems are sung alternately by an unnamed questioner and by Theseus' father, Aegeus.

Transmission has been less generous to Bacchylides' uncle, Simonides of Ceos (active *c.*520–468 BC). Simonides composed in all the genres just mentioned, and probably even pioneered the victory song, yet of his melic poetry we have little. Tradition associated him with Hipparchus in Athens, the Scopads of Thessaly, and the Sicilian tyrants, making him the first to write for money and imputing avarice. In our longest fragment (542) Simonides addressed Scopas, arguing from maxim to maxim with un-Pindaric patience: only god, not man, can achieve a state of virtue; man can only *act* well, when circumstances permit—'I proclaim to you what I have discovered; and I praise and love all those who willingly do nothing shameful; but against necessity not even gods struggle' (26–30). As often, we can only guess at the song's genre and context. Simplicity could also mark his treatment of myth, as emerges from the narrative of Danae and Perseus drifting in their castaway chest: 'If for you the fearful had been fearful', she says to Perseus, 'then indeed to my words would you have turned your tiny ear. But I bid you sleep, my babe, may the sea sleep, and may our boundless trouble sleep; and may some change of heart come from you, father Zeus' (fr. 543. 18–23).

Antiquity admired Simonides' evocation of pathos. This was probably due less to such pieces as fr. 543 or his encomium of Leonidas and the Spartan dead at Thermopylae (fr. 531), than to his epigrams. The poetry hitherto considered was composed for singing or recitation, and certainly to be heard, not read. But from the seventh century dactylic verse—initially hexameters, then hexameters or elegiac couplets—was also used for inscribed dedications and epitaphs. The earliest distinguished poet known to have written these was Simonides. Because his epigrams became famous, many were later ascribed to him that cannot be his: of those that can only a few certainly are, like that on his friend Megistias, vouched for by Herodotus (vii. 228):

> Here famed Megistias is laid, whom once the Mede
> slew at the crossing of Spercheius' flood:
> this prophet clearly saw the Fates' attacking wings
> but did not stoop to leave the Spartan kings.
>
> (*Epigr. gr.* 6)

Possibly Simonidean is a couplet from a statue group commemorating the Athenian tyrannicides:

> Harmodius and Aristogeiton slew
> Hipparchus, and brought Athens light anew.
>
> (*Epigr. gr.* 1)

But the puzzles that confront scholars in studying archaic literature are epitomized by this couplet's doubtful attribution, and by the fact that an inscribed version from the Athenian *agora* shows that there, at least, another couplet followed this one (previously known from quotation).

A great poet's attention to a written genre heralds a new literary epoch in which prose and poetry were composed to be read, not heard. Religious songs were still composed, although no great names succeed Pindar and Bacchylides. But by the beginning of the fifth century, secular, informal monody was in decline, and by its close the songs sung at *symposia* to *aulos* or lyre were not new compositions, but the heritage of archaic poetry already becoming classics.

Further Reading

Greek texts of the poets discussed in this chapter will be found in the following editions (whose numeration is used in references within the chapter). The elegiac and iambic poets in *Iambi et Elegi Graeci*, ed. M. L. West (Oxford, 1971-2), and in his OCT (which contains all fragments of importance and alone has the new Archilochus, 196A) *Delectus ex Iambis et Elegis Graecis* (1980). The melic poets in *Poetarum Lesbiorum Fragmenta*, edd. E. Lobel and D. L. Page (Oxford, 1955) for Sappho and Alcaeus, and *Poetae Melici Graeci*, ed. D. L. Page (Oxford, 1968) for the remainder—a selection containing all fragments of importance from both editions appears in the OCT *Lyrica Graeca Selecta*, ed. D. L. Page (1968), and more recent fragments in *Supplementum Lyricis Graecis*, ed. D. L. Page (Oxford, 1974). Epigrams in the OCT *Epigrammata Graeca*, ed. D. L. Page (1975).

Greek texts with facing page translations into English are available in the Loeb Classical Library *Greek Lyric*, ed. D. A. Campbell, vol. i *Sappho and Alcaeus* (1981, others forthcoming); this replaces the three-volume *Lyra Graeca*, ed. J. M. Edmonds (Cambridge, Mass./London, 1922-7), which is unreliable as well as outdated, but at present the only edition with translation of early melic poets other than the Lesbians; the iambic and elegiac poets are to be found in J. M. Edmonds's Loeb, *Greek Elegy and Iambus* (Cambridge, Mass./London, 1931). Selections of Greek texts with translation will be found in the *Penguin Book of Greek Verse*, ed. C. A. Trypanis (Harmondsworth, 1971) and in the separate volumes of the *Oxford Book of Greek Verse*, ed. C. M. Bowra (1930) and the *Oxford Book of Greek Verse in Translation*, edd. T. F. Higham and C. M. Bowra (1938).

The best commentary on the poets up to and including Bacchylides is that of D. A. Campbell in his selection *Greek Lyric Poetry* (London, 1967; 2nd edn. Bristol, 1981). For Bacchylides there is now a full commentary in German in the edition by H. Maehler (with German translation, Leiden, 1982); English translation by R. Fagles (New Haven, 1961). Useful, but very dated, literary discussion can be found in C. M. Bowra, *Early Greek Elegists* (Cambridge, Mass., 1935); id., *Greek Lyric Poetry*[2] (Oxford, 1961); G. M. Kirkwood, *Early Greek Monody* (Cornell, 1974); H. Fränkel, *Early Greek Poetry and Philosophy* (Oxford, 1975); and for a more recent conspectus see A. J. Podlecki, *The Early Greek Poets and their Themes* (Vancouver, 1984). Fundamental points of text, language, genre, and interpretation of the elegiac and iambic poets are discussed by M. L.

West, *Studies in Greek Elegy and Iambus* (Berlin, 1974). The most interesting assessment in English of Archilochus is that of A. P. Burnett, *Three Archaic poets. Archilochus, Alcaeus and Sappho* (London, 1983). For the Lesbians D. L. Page's *Sappho and Alcaeus* (Oxford, 1955) remains fundamental, but valuable perspectives can be obtained from Burnett, op. cit., and from the essay by R. H. A. Jenkyns in *Three Classical Poets* (London, 1982; also paperback). For epigrams see the commentary by D. L. Page in *Further Greek Epigrams* (Cambridge, 1981), esp. pp. 186–302 (on Simonides and *Simonidea*).

Pindar is much better served. The best text is the Teubner, edd. B. Snell and H. Maehler, 2 vols. (1971–5); OCT² (1947) by C. M. Bowra. Text with facing English translation in Loeb Classical Library, 2nd edn., ed. J. E. Sandys (Cambridge, Mass./London, 1919). Commentaries on Olympian and Pythian Odes by B. L. Gildersleeve (New York, 1890); on Isthmians by J. B. Bury (London, 1892); on all (with transl.) by L. R. Farnell, 3 vols. (London, 1930–2). Fundamental work for understanding the genre by E. L. Bundy, *Studia Pindarica* i–ii (Berkeley, 1962). A useful introduction to the epinician genre in M. R. Lefkowitz, *The Victory Ode* (Park Ridge, NJ, 1976) and H. Lloyd-Jones, 'Modern Interpretation of Pindar', in *Journ. Hell. Stud.* xciii (1973), 109–37. C. M. Bowra, *Pindar* (Oxford, 1964) is still usable with caution. English translation by F. J. Nisetich (Baltimore, 1980).

5

Early Greek Philosophy

MARTIN WEST

In the eighth and seventh centuries BC the Greeks appear as a lively and talented people, active in trade and exploration, endowed with no little skill and individuality in the visual arts, rich in heroic legend, and above all remarkable for a poetry in which a wide range of human experience and feeling was given highly articulate expression. If they had achieved nothing more than that, they would still claim our attention as the most interesting and sympathetic of ancient peoples. In fact they went on to add immensely to that claim. They added to it in many fields: art, literature, mathematics, astronomy, medicine, government, to name half a dozen. But the most significant single addition was perhaps philosophy. Its origins and development make an essential strand in the cultural history of the sixth and fifth centuries.

As in dealing with other aspects of archaic and classical Greek culture, it is important to remember that different towns and regions had their own traditions, and that initiatives taken in one did not necessarily affect others quickly or at all. We must not assume that each philosopher's pronouncements were public knowledge, from one end of the Greek world to the other, as soon as he made them, or that divergent pronouncements by subsequent philosophers were necessarily made in reaction or modification. Early Greek philosophy was not a single vessel which a succession of pilots briefly commanded and tried to steer towards an agreed destination, one tacking one way, the next altering course in the light of his own perceptions. It was more like a flotilla of small craft whose navigators did not all start from the same point or at the same time, nor all aim for the same goal; some went in groups, some were influenced by the movements of others, some travelled out of sight of each other. We run them together as 'philosophers', but they had no generic name for themselves. Philosophy is of course a Greek word—it meant originally something like 'devotion to uncommon knowledge'—but it did not acquire a specialized sense or wide currency until the time of Plato. It is not easy to draw a line between 'philosophers' and others. There were some for whom a philosophical theory, original or borrowed, served as a basis or buttress for something else—a religious or moral diatribe, a dissertation on some aspect of medicine, or an essay on the development of civilization. Some such writers are traditionally included among the philosophers while others are excluded. There were others again, especially poets, who made use of philosophical arguments or theses on occasion but in whose work this was no more than a minor element.

Some examples will help to make clear the variety of the subject. The first 'school' that we can identify is constituted by three sixth-century thinkers from Miletus, one of the principal Ionian towns on the coast of Asia Minor: Thales, Anaximander, and Anaximenes. Thales left no writings to posterity, though Aristotle, who regarded him as the first real philosopher, knew of certain doctrines which were ascribed to him. Presumably he expounded his ideas orally to those of his fellow citizens who were interested in hearing them, and certain of them were recorded as his by some early Ionian writer. In subsequent decades Anaximander and Anaximenes likewise gave discourses (Anaximander is said to have worn splendid clothes, as did later sophists and rhapsodes), and their books, which were among the earliest works written in Greek prose, were the record of their discourses. This Milesian phenomenon of the philosopher who discoursed before an audience and also issued a written account of his opinions presently became a wider Ionian phenomenon. But it may have been some while before readers outnumbered listeners. Heraclitus, about the beginning of the fifth century, refers to people hearing his discourse; and in alluding to other philosophers he does not say 'all those whose books I have read' but 'all those whose discourses I have heard'.

This, then, was one mode of philosophical expression. Less direct ones were employed by Pythagoras of Samos, who seems to have been part philosopher, part priest, and part conjuror. He too is said to have worn imposing costume, to wit a gold coronet, a white robe, and trousers. Instead of discoursing in reasoned prose he appealed to the authority of poems under the name of Orpheus, which he was suspected of having composed or at least doctored. He also bequeathed to his disciples in south Italy a quantity of brief maxims, catechisms, and enigmatic sayings, some expressing old religious taboos, others cosmological or eschatological dogmas. Some of his followers added to these, or composed new Orphic poems embodying a picturesque metaphysics. Others, taking their inspiration from Pythagoras' (probably mystical) interest in number and music, developed the study of mathematics and harmony in a more scientific spirit. 'Pythagoreanism' thus came to cover a strange gamut of different phenomena, and it became difficult to disentangle the master's own ideas and achievements from those of his successors.

There were others in the early fifth century, especially in the western colonies, who regarded poetry as a suitable medium for reasoned argument: Xenophanes, who, like Pythagoras, migrated from Ionia to the west; Parmenides of Elea; Empedocles of Acragas. Empedocles was another who dressed to attract attention, and besides expounding the nature of the world he claimed to impart cures for sickness or old age, and the ability to control wind and rain or raise men from the dead. People followed him in droves, he tells us, adorning him with ribbons and garlands, and asking for oracles and remedies.

Clearly the identification of 'philosophy' is a delicate task. Our primary concern is with the development in Greece of critical and constructive thought about the physical world, the place of gods and souls in it, the relationship between reality and appearance, the origins and nature of human society, and the principles which ought to govern it. But this process was concurrent with, and to some extent implicated in, the spread of untraditional doctrines derived not from pure reason but from oriental myth. The mind that was willing to question conventional assumptions was receptive to novel ideas from abroad; or perhaps the mind that was aware of alternative accounts of things was stimulated to think.

Thales taught that everything is derived from water and that the earth rests on water. Perhaps he was attracted to these tenets, as Aristotle conjectures, 'from seeing that the nutriment of all things contains moisture, and that heat itself comes from this and is sustained by it; and because the seeds of all things have a moist nature, and water is the basis of moisture'. At the same time it is hard to separate Thales' world picture from Egyptian and Semitic creation stories in which the initial state is a waste of waters, now covered over by the earth.

Anaximander taught that the world, and countless other worlds beyond our ken, came into being out of the Boundless and will eventually be absorbed back into it. He gave a detailed account of the stages by which the parts of the cosmos were differentiated, and of their shape and arrangement. What we see as the sun, moon, and stars are really, according to him, great rings of fire, respectively twenty-seven, eighteen, and nine times the diameter of the earth, and encircling it, but each concealed in a tube of mist except for certain holes through which the fire shines out. The earth, a drum-shaped body with its depth a third of its diameter, floats in the middle. The cosmos's existence is an imbalance in the Boundless, an 'injustice', which must in due course be corrected in accordance with an ordinance of Time. All cosmic change, in other words, has its appointed season. The Boundless itself is everlasting and inexhaustible, encompassing and directing all things. Now we may admire the grandeur of this system, and allow that it is in some sense philosophical. Anaximander attempts to explain the visible world as the product of orderly, universal processes, which, he infers, must continually be producing other worlds elsewhere. (As Metrodorus of Chios later remarked, you do not get only one ear of corn growing in a field.) But the system is only to a limited extent deduced from the visible world. Much is postulated that can have no basis in rational inference, and some of it is undoubtedly inspired by Iranian cosmology. The sequence earth–stars–moon–sun is distinctively Iranian, not Greek, and the Boundless that lies beyond the sun corresponds to the Beginningless Lights which are the abode of Ohrmazd and the highest paradise for the Zoroastrian. Ohrmazd created this world with the blessing of the unaging god Time, and a finite duration of 12,000 years has been appointed for it. Thus the 'ordinance of Time' in Anaximander's system was not a creation of his intellect but can be traced to barbarian theology. There, however, it is a single, non-recurrent act of will; Anaximander made it into something resembling a law of nature. This illustrates an important feature of the Greek philosophers' approach. They sought to eliminate the arbitrary events characteristic of mythical narratives; but this did not by any means incline them to eliminate divinity from the world. They preferred to depersonalize their gods and identify them with the unchanging forces that govern the working of the universe.

The third of the Milesians, Anaximenes, goes further in the direction of extrapolating from the visible world to what lies outside it. He holds that it is encompassed not by an undefined Boundless but by air, to which he gives the qualities of Anaximander's Boundless: infinite extent, immortality, and perpetual motion leading to the formation of worlds. Air surrounds and contains the world just as the soul, which also consists of air, holds the body together. All other substances are derived from air by condensation or rarefaction. The earth is flat and thin like a table and supported by air, as in Thales it was supported by water. Vapours rising from it become rarefied and form fiery discs which also float on the air, like leaves, and are the sun, moon, and stars. Among them, invisible to us, move certain solid bodies, probably intended to account for eclipses. It is difficult not to find Anaximenes' system somewhat crude after Anaximander's. Anaximander had made a tremendous imaginative leap forward by reducing the earth to a small body in relation to the cosmos and by dispensing with a material support for it; he apparently thought that equipoise was enough. Anaximenes reverted to more conventional presuppositions. At the same time his is a more economical construct. Nature does not change into something unimaginable at the edge of his cosmos. Everything, inside and outside the cosmos, is based on something we have experience of, air and its transformations. It is in a sense a materialistic cosmology. But Anaximenes does not conceive of his air as an inert substance which needs something else to set it in motion. He regards movement as an intrinsic property of air. It is, as it were, a *live* substance, and the parallel he draws between the cosmic air and the human soul implies an assumption that certainly became general in the fifth century, namely that the soul is not something apart from the material world but a natural part of it. It is tempting to see here an affinity with the Upanishadic doctrine of a universal wind or breath with which both the unchanging life-soul of the world and the individual self are identical, by which living things and worlds are held together, and which the whole universe obeys. Two details in Anaximenes' system which do not suit it very well, the dark bodies that cause eclipses and the notion that the heavenly luminaries circle round a great mountain in the north, seem to be of Iranian provenance.

The Milesians were unable completely to free themselves from the preconceptions of the myth-makers of the pre-philosophical age. Like them, they assumed that something so complex as the present world must have originated from something simple; that the earth is finite in extent and more or less circular, with something different underneath it; that the sky is a physical entity at a definite distance from the earth; that there are immortal sources of energy which are the moving or directing forces in the universe. Their new, philosophical assumptions were that these forces operate in a perfectly consistent way that can be observed in everyday phenomena; that everything can thus be explained from the working of a few universal processes in a single original continuum; and that there is no such thing as creation from nothing or decay to nothing, only change of substance. They tried to account systematically for all the most notable features of the world about us: the movements of the heavenly bodies, phases of the moon, eclipses; lightning, thunder, rain, snow, hail, rainbows, earthquakes, the annual inundation of the Nile.

One thinker who did succeed in breaking right away from conventional world models was Xenophanes. His independence of mind took him in a direction so contrary to the truth that he gets little but derision from modern writers; yet no one else so ruthlessly followed the rule of measuring the unseen by the seen. What he saw was earth stretching in all directions, with empty air above it. He accordingly declared that the earth was of infinite length, breadth, and depth, and that the air extended infinitely upwards. The disappearance of the sun and other luminaries beyond the western horizon he explained as an optical illusion: they were really continuing in a straight line, just getting further away. The sun that arrives in the east the next morning is a different one. There are, moreover, other suns and moons moving on parallel tracks over other regions of the earth, because the rising vapours form clouds which become incandescent, and this happens with strict regularity.

His theology also was radical, without being so eccentric. He was certainly not the first to reject the idea of gods having human shape or behaving as immorally as they do in Homer, but it was he who pointed out that the Thracians represent the gods as like Thracians, the Negroes as negroid, and if cows and horses had hands they would no doubt depict their gods as cows and horses. The late sixth to the early fifth century was a time when the Greeks were developing a particular interest in the beliefs and customs of other nations. As Xenophanes' argument illustrates, the effect was to make them aware how much their own beliefs and customs were based on mere convention, which might profitably be challenged. Xenophanes' god is equally suitable for Thracians or cows. He does not have eyes or ears: every part of him is sentient. He does not go about from place to place but stays still, effortlessly moving everything else by the power of his thought.

Heraclitus, who wrote in a particularly haughty and oracular manner, and was unusual among the early philosophers in criticizing others by name, castigated Xenophanes as one of several notable men to whom learning had not taught sense. Yet he shared some concepts with him, including that of a unique divine intelligence which governs everything. Both men accepted the existence of other gods, but looked for an overriding master purpose. Heraclitus said that the Intelligence 'does and does not want to be called Zeus'. This, he is saying, is what your 'Zeus' really is, but it is an inadequate name. He also speaks of the thunderbolt, Zeus' traditional weapon, as directing all things. He holds the cosmos to have always existed, and to be a fire which is never extinguished, though not all parts of it are alight at once. The parts that are not alight exist as other substances, convertible with fire at a measured rate, as goods are for money. So he finds unity in the apparent diversity of the world by regarding everything as participating in one great continuous process—a conception which a few centuries later was to form the basis of Stoic cosmology. This process is controlled by divine agents of justice, and perhaps given direction and momentum by the thunderbolt. It is characterized as 'strife' or 'war', because Heraclitus sees the continuance of the cosmos as dependent upon the sustained differentiation of opposites. But because of the underlying unity, apparent opposites are really aspects of the same thing. Heraclitus collected many quite dissimilar examples to illustrate this paradox. Hot and cold, wet and dry, living and dead, are not irreconcilable opposites, since things pass from one state to the other. The road up is the same as the road down. Sea water is simultaneously drinkable (for fish) and undrinkable (for men). A monkey may be at once handsome (by monkey standards) and ugly. In one extraordinary fragment Heraclitus identifies day and night, summer and winter, war and peace, famine and abundance, as different manifestations of God.

He did not offer answers to all the cosmological questions which exercised the Milesians—he had nothing to say, for example, about the shape or support of the earth, or what there was outside the cosmos—and there is reason to think that what lay at the centre of his interest was rather religion, morality, and the destiny of the soul. The cosmic stock exchange, however, is the setting in which this is seen. Souls die by turning into water, which dies in its turn by becoming earth; they thus participate in the cyclic transformation of elements which, starting from fire, continues throughout the world. To preserve one's soul one must keep it dry, especially by avoiding alcoholic and sexual indulgence. At death, according to a plausible reconstruction of Heraclitus' theory, souls rise into the air, the damper ones to the level of the moon, where they contribute to winter, night, and rain, drier ones to the purer region of the sun and stars; some particularly favoured ones become the watchers of living and dead that men call heroes. The cosmos is crowded with spirits. There is, moreover, a Great Year of 360 human generations in which the balance swings between the dominance of damp and bright—a concept which was to be developed further by Plato and the Stoics.

Heraclitus could not have arrived at such a system by pure reason, and it has many points of contact with Zoroastrianism and with the Upanishads. In the latter, souls which fail to pass the moon return to earth as rain and are reincarnated in whatever animal form is appropriate to their conduct in their last life.

AN OIL VASE (*lekythos*) made for an Athenian burial by the Achilles Painter in about 450–440 BC, showing a muse on Mount Helicon. The figures on these vases must resemble those of contemporary and earlier (Polygnotan) wall-paintings.

STATUE OF A GIRL (*korē*) dedicated on the Athenian Acropolis about 520–510 BC. Probably Ionian (Chian) work.

The doctrine of reincarnation is not attested for Heraclitus, but it had gained a foothold in Greece in the mid sixth century, a century or so later than in India. Pythagoras believed in it, and it was taken up by Empedocles, who denounced the killing and eating of animals as murder and cannibalism, and implored men to abandon it.

Like Heraclitus, Empedocles endeavoured to integrate his teaching about the fortunes of the soul in a general theory of cosmology involving cyclical changes over vast periods of time. Everything in the world is produced by the mixture and separation of four elements, earth, air, fire, and water, which Empedocles identifies with certain of the traditional gods. Xenophanes, as we saw, rejected Homer's gods, so much prey to love and strife. At about the same period one Theagenes from Rhegium developed a line of defence that was to remain popular into the Middle Ages, interpreting the Homeric deities as allegories of the physical world. What Empedocles is doing is akin to this. He elevates the gods' love and strife into a pair of supreme powers who rule in regular alternation by the terms of a treaty. When Love's power is absolute, the divine elements are completely blended into a featureless, homogeneous sphere. As Strife gradually makes its way in, they begin to separate and form a cosmos. Eventually they will be four separate masses, a ball of pure earth in the centre with successive spheres of water, fire, and air surrounding it. We can see that the universe is on the way towards that state. Subsequently the reverse process will operate until the cycle is completed. Empedocles went into much ingenious detail in explaining astronomical and meteorological phenomena and the evolution and physiology of living creatures. He apparently found room for gods within the cosmos other than the elements themselves. They are presumably entities of a fiery nature. When one of them yields to the influence of Strife, he is torn away from the company of his fellows and forced to consort with the other elements for myriads of years, a soul going through countless animal and plant lives.

Empedocles has turned away from the idea held by some Ionians that one original substance can change into others. To account for the diversity of substances in the world he finds it necessary to postulate a set of contrasted primary elements which can be combined in countless ways. This pluralist approach was taken to an extreme by Anaxagoras, an Ionian who taught at Athens for many years in the mid fifth century. Like Empedocles, only without his cyclicalism, Anaxagoras begins his cosmogony from a state of perfect mixture which is then unbalanced by the operation of a divine force. But there is no limit to the number of ingredients in the mixture, and the separation process is never absolute. There always remains a proportion of every substance in everything; we name each thing according to what predominates in it, as if it were composed purely of that substance. This is why whatever Miss T. eats turns into Miss T. It always contained flesh (even the vegetables), and when she eats it a material rearrangement takes place making flesh the dominant constituent. The only thing not mixed with everything else, and therefore able to control everything else, is the finest and purest of all: Mind. This is the divine force that gives the cosmos its initial impulse and supervises the whole process of creative separation.

Socrates, according to Plato, read Anaxagoras' book and was disappointed that he still made so much use of mechanistic explanations instead of making Mind shape each detail of the world for an intelligent reason. Anaxagoras seems here to have fallen between two stools: the Milesian desire to explain the world as the natural product of certain given processes, and a new inclination (perhaps implicit in Xenophanes and Heraclitus) to see it as planned. Diogenes of Apollonia, a somewhat younger man who began his book on human physiology with a cosmology, argues explicitly that the balanced arrangement of the seasons, among other things, must be the work of intelligence. He identifies this divine intelligence with the material element air, which, like Anaximenes, he regards as the single substance from which all others are derived. Everything that breathes air partakes of intelligence.

A sense of proportionate arrangement, whether imposed by a divine Mind or resulting automatically from natural processes, had been a feature of cosmological thought since Anaximander. The discovery that simple mathematical ratios underlie the fundamental musical concords led some Pythagoreans to focus on number as the essence of the universe. One of them (perhaps Philolaus) formulated a theory according to which numbers are generated from an initial One as it 'breathes in' a portion of the adjacent infinity; this portion becomes finite and at the same time divides the one into two. The evolution of the cosmos from a primordial unity is simply an example of this process. Things are numbers, and their relationships (justice, for instance) are mathematical relationships. Aristotle's allusions to the theory hardly allow us to grasp its meaning, and he was doubtless justified in complaining that it left all sorts of questions unanswered. But it is regrettable that we do not understand more about a doctrine which threw the universe into such a novel perspective.

The thinkers so far discussed accepted that the material world is on the whole (allowing for certain misinterpretations on our part) as our senses represent it to us. Meanwhile Parmenides, at the beginning of the fifth century, had struck out along a path of logical reasoning about Being which threatened to undermine that assumption. To put the argument in a nutshell: only Being can exist; there can be no coming-to-be or passing-away, because they imply non-being; no gap or discontinuity in Being; no movement, for lack of space (=non-being); not even any qualitative change, for that would mean the not-being of what had been. *Ergo*, reality consists simply of indivisible, changeless, featureless, motionless, rock-solid Being. The whole phenomenal world with its colour, movement and impermanence must be a sham. It is of course a sham with a pattern, and Parmenides feels obliged to offer an account of it, while emphasizing that he is analysing an illusion or *fable convenue*. He reduces its diversity to a basic duality of light and dark, each of which subsumes a range of other qualities. He claims that this is the best analysis attainable by man, but, being unable to reconcile it with his account of the nature of Being, he has to say that it is ultimately false.

Parmenides' reasoning, though brilliant, is at the same time so artificial that we may suspect his conclusion of being preconceived, particularly as his vision of Being shows resemblances to a certain type of mystical experience in which space and time seem to lose all significance and there is an acute sense of the unbroken unity of all things with each other and with the self. He actually presents his philosophy as derived from a private divine revelation. But nothing is more significant of the intellectual climate in which he lives than the fact that he does not say 'the goddess showed me, and I saw', but 'the goddess proved it with the following arguments'. He is concerned to rationalize his vision.

Parmenides had two followers. Zeno also came from Elea, Melissus from Samos; by convention the three are collectively called the Eleatics. Zeno re-inforced the case against plurality and motion with arguments and paradoxes of a mathematical nature, including the famous paradox of Achilles and the tortoise: Achilles can never overtake the tortoise because every time he reaches the point where it was, it has moved on. Melissus went beyond Parmenides in arguing that Being is infinite in extent (Parmenides had made it finite and spherical) and that it is incorporeal, because otherwise it would have parts, implying plurality. The divorce between the philosopher's 'reality' and the world of experience could not be made more complete.

Eleaticism was in one sense a dead end. But the concept of an unchanging reality beyond the material world endured in, and because of, Plato; and a passage in which Melissus argues that if there were after all a plurality of things, they would all have to be as unchanging as his One, points the way to the greatest inspiration of ancient physical theory, the atomism of Leucippus of Miletus. Leucippus follows the Ionian tradition for the general shape of his cosmos, and contradicts the central axiom of the Eleatics by asserting that Non-being (empty space) exists just as much as Being. But he reduces matter to minute particles which resemble the Eleatic One in being indivisible (*atoma*), indestructible, and qualitatively neutral; they differ from one another only in shape and orientation. Different rearrangements of them produce the effect of changeable qualities such as colour, heat, hardness, etc. There is no guiding intelligence, just the blind mechanical interplay of flying and colliding atoms.

The atomist system was appropriated by the prolific writer Democritus, per-haps to serve as the background to his account of the origin and development of civilization. This became a popular subject of theorizing in the mid fifth century. It quickly came to be common ground that primitive man was merely an animal, sheltering in caves and eating whatever grew wild, until gradually he developed his skills, built houses and cities, tamed animals, invented language, and so on. Socrates' teacher Archelaus gave an account (prefaced by a cosmology on An-axagorean lines) designed to bring out the conventional nature of law and justice. The most influential of these reconstructions of prehistory may have been due to Protagoras, whose several visits to Athens (like Democritus, he was a native of

Abdera) attracted much attention. Protagoras stands at the head of that series of intellectuals whose discourses on a range of philosophical and technical subjects seemed so instructive that they were able to charge attendance fees, and who are called Sophists. They offered, among other things, stimulating reflections on the theme of nature versus custom, the bases of morality, the power of education; scientific treatment of subjects like grammar, metre, music; not least, displays of the adaptability of argument to support any conclusion, or either of two opposite conclusions. At this point we can no longer take it for granted that what appears to be a philosophical argument is meant seriously. Gorgias, an orator and essayist from Sicily notorious for his euphuistic style, published a lengthy proof that nothing exists. He was, no doubt, simply enjoying himself, as when he devoted another work to the defence of the infamous Helen of Troy, describing it as 'an encomium for Helen and amusement for me'. Socrates had some of this playfulness.

The early philosophers were aware that they were seeking answers to questions that lay beyond the bounds of possible human knowledge. 'No one has ever known or ever will know for sure,' says Xenophanes, 'for even if what he says is exactly right, he does not *know* it is—it is all a matter of opinion.' It was something of a commonplace that our senses are weak and easily misled, but that we must extrapolate from the observed to the unobservable. The Greeks were not as quick as they might have been to draw the inference that an accumulation of systematic scientific observation is desirable, though we do see something of the sort in the fifth century in the field of medicine. Some real ground was gained, though gradually, by astronomy. About 500 BC it was realized that the moon shines by reflected light, while by 400 the view that the earth is spherical was gaining adherents, and the planets had perhaps all been identified. In other areas unverifiability precluded consolidation. Atomism remained one theory among many. There was no agreement on which facts to extrapolate from. One seized on one physical phenomenon or logical formula as the key to the universe, another on another. What provokes admiration is the mental vigour and independence with which these people sought after coherent systems and did not shrink from following their lines of thought to astonishing conclusions. It may well be that contact with oriental cosmology and theology helped to liberate their imagination; it certainly gave them many suggestive ideas. But they taught themselves to reason. Philosophy as we understand it is a Greek creation.

Further Reading

The best introduction is E. Hussey, *The Presocratics* (London, 1972); while assuming no knowledge of Greek, it maintains close contact with the primary sources. A. Wedberg, *A History of Philosophy*, I *Antiquity and the Middle Ages* (Oxford, 1982), is very concise but lucid and well judged. G. S. Kirk and J. E. Raven, *The Presocratic Philosophers* (2nd edn. with M. Schofield, Cambridge, 1983), give a good selection of texts with translations and critical discussion. Translations are also available in J. Burnet, *Early Greek Philosophy* (4th edn, London, 1930) and in Kathleen Freeman's *Ancilla to the Presocratic Philosophers* (Oxford, 1948).

On an ampler scale are W. K. C. Guthrie, *A History of Greek Philosophy* (Cambridge, 1962-81; the first three of the six volumes cover the pre-Platonic period), and J. Barnes, *The Presocratic Philosophers* (London, 1979, 2 vols.). Guthrie is comprehensive and safe; Barnes is dense and dazzling, concentrating on philosophical interpretation.

The following are concerned with particular aspects of the subject: G. E. R. Lloyd, *Polarity and Analogy* (Cambridge, 1966: discusses in depth two of the main types of argument and explanation used by early Greek thinkers); W. Jaeger, *The Theology of the Early Greek Philosophers* (Oxford, 1947); D. R. Dicks, *Early Greek Astronomy to Aristotle* (London, 1970). Knowledge of Greek is required for C. H. Kahn, *Anaximander and the Origins of Greek Cosmology* (New York, 1960: wider in scope than its title suggests), and M. L. West, *Early Greek Philosophy and the Orient* (Oxford, 1971).

Useful collections of important, mostly rather specialized articles have been published in book form by D. J. Furley and R. E. Allen, *Studies in Presocratic Philosophy* (London, 1970-5, 2 vols.), and by A. P. D. Mourelatos, *The Pre-Socratics* (New York, 1974).

6

Greece: The History of the Classical Period

꙲Ꙏ꙳

SIMON HORNBLOWER

Outline of Events (479–431)

THE Athenians founded a naval empire in 478, thus replacing the Spartans as leaders of Greece. Their power expanded in the 470s and 460s, as they took the offensive against the Persians, the recent invaders of Greece. The climax of this offensive was reached in the early 460s when the Athenian commander Cimon won a battle in Pamphylia in southern Asia Minor, the battle of the Eurymedon. The suppression of a revolt from Athens by the northern Aegean island of Thasos in the mid 460s was another landmark: it led to a deterioration in relations with Sparta and her league, the Peloponnesian League. From *c.*460 to 446 a war, the so-called First Peloponnesian War, was fought between Athens and the Peloponnesian League; in the early phases of this war Corinth, not Sparta, was more obviously to the front in the fighting, though the Spartans did invade Attica in the last year of the war. Corinth's uncharacteristic hostility towards Athens was the result of the adhesion to Athens of Megara, the small state which separated Athens from Corinth geographically, but hatred of which had united Athens and Corinth politically up to now. In the 450s Athens, despite the warfare on her hands in Greece, fought in support of anti-Persian rebels in Egypt (a revolt which failed disastrously and cost many Athenian lives) and opened diplomacy with communities in Sicily. Formal hostilities with Persia ended in about 449 with the Peace of Callias. The settlement in 446 of the First Peloponnesian War recognized the existence of the Athenian Naval Empire and was thus a victory for Athens, although she had to abandon the mainland Greek territories which she had acquired in fighting, notably Boeotia. Athens was now free to expand to the north, where in 437 she fulfilled an old dream by establishing a settlement at the timber-rich site of Amphipolis; to the east, where she imposed her authority more firmly on Samos, which had revolted unsuccessfully in 440/39; and to the west, where she made a series of alliances, perhaps hoping for uninterrupted

THE ERECHTHEUM ON THE ACROPOLIS AT ATHENS. An unusual, asymmetrical building of the Ionic order, which housed the cults which were once served in the Archaic Temple of Athena. This had been burned by the Persians in 480 BC: its foundations lie in the foreground and were perhaps left exposed as a memorial to the Persian attack. The Caryatid porch, with statues of girls supporting the roof, overlaps these foundations; the porch itself is accessible only from within the building. The Erechtheum was built just after the Parthenon, and completed in the last years of the Peloponnesian War. It is the most sophisticated application of the Ionic order to any Classical building and elements of it—the Caryatid porch and the columns of the north porch—were often copied in antiquity and in nineteenth-century Europe.

supplies of the timber which she needed for her navy. This western and northern expansion, combined with renewed aggression against Megara, reawakened the suspicions of Corinth in the 430s, for Corinth had traditional ties with her colonies in Northern Greece and in Sicily. The result was the Second or Great Peloponnesian War of 431–404, which Athens lost.

The historian of this war, Thucydides of Athens, makes the great leader Pericles say that Athens will be remembered for having ruled more Greeks than any

THE ENTRANCE TO THE ACROPOLIS AT ATHENS SEEN FROM THE HILL OF THE AREOPAGUS. The small, late-fifth-century BC Temple of Athena Nike (Athena Victory) stands clear on a bastion beside the entrance, to the right. The dominant outline is of the Classical entrance-way, the Propylaea, which housed a picture gallery; but from this view the bulk and sheer sides of the rock demonstrate well the Acropolis' original role as a citadel.

other Greek state. Thucydides (or Pericles) was wrong; it is only specialist ancient historians who know about Athenian imperialism, but everybody has heard of the Parthenon, and of Greek tragedy. We ought rather to say Athenian tragedy, because Aeschylus, Sophocles, and Euripides were all Athenians. Specifically, the treatment by those tragedians of a handful of myths continues to provide the direct inspiration for modern thinkers (such as Freud), dramatists (Brecht, Anouilh), and novelists (Thomas Mann's *Death in Venice* is a variant on Euripides' *Bacchae*). These are the achievements which justify the intensive study to which ancient Greek culture, and especially its literature, have been exposed since the Renaissance. Thucydides was not alone in the lopsidedness of his judgement: Aeschylus wrote his own verse epitaph, boasting of his military service in the Persian Wars, and neglecting to mention that he was a playwright; Socrates, the great teacher and philosopher, features in the contemporary histories only for the stand he took over a piece of purely political injustice. It is even possible that Sophocles' Oedipus, a legendary king of Thebes, is meant as a portrait of imperial Athens: quickwitted, meddlesome, and doomed because of those precise elements in his greatness. An audacious anachronism.

But we should not be lopsided in the other direction, and neglect the military and political successes which underwrote fifth-century culture. First, it was the

THE TEMPLE OF HEPHAESTUS IN ATHENS, SEEN FROM THE SOUTH-WEST. This is the best preserved of all Doric temples of mainland Greece; it owes its survival to its conversion to a Christian church. It was completed while the Parthenon was being built, in the third quarter of the fifth century BC, and dedicated to Hephaestus with Athena, as joint patrons of crafts in Athens. It overlooks the Agora, which lies to its south-east.

Persian Wars which, by worsening the political atmosphere in Ionia, filled Athens with a diaspora of intellectuals such as Hippodamus of Miletus who replanned the Piraeus, the harbour town of Athens; and Anaxagoras, the philosopher friend of Pericles. But above all, aristocrats such as Cimon and Pericles, by their political and military leadership, brought in the public wealth which subsidized the buildings and sculptures of Phidias, Ictinus, and Mnesicles on the Acropolis; and, by making available their private wealth for public purposes, they financed the festivals and dramatic productions which gave classical Athens its attractive power. (This was the liturgy system, a tax on the rich which conferred prestige when taken beyond what was obligatory.) Pericles' first known act was to pay for Aeschylus' great historical opera, the *Persae*. We know this not from Thucydides, who idealized Pericles, but from a list carved on stone. Such lists are the raw material of the present chapter, which is political and military. We should not forget that such evidence can help the literary student.

Empire: Athens and the Alternatives

'Shared blood, shared language, shared religion, and shared customs.' These, according to Herodotus, were the ingredients of *to hellēnikon*, 'Greekness'. This definition of nationality, which would not disgrace a modern anthropologist, proves that by the middle of the fifth century some Greeks recognized what they had in common. That common feeling had been most strengthened by the menace of the common enemy, Persia, in the wars of 499–479. However, the Greeks of the classical period never managed to translate their psychological awareness of their 'Greekness' into political unity. The history of the classical Greek city-states is a history of failure to achieve unity: Sparta would not, and Athens could not, impose it indefinitely by force as Macedon and Rome were to do. There is a way of achieving unity without force, namely by federalism, and this method was experimented with in the fourth century by a third great Greek power, Boeotian Thebes, which in the time of Epaminondas (below, pp. 149 f.) exported federalism beyond the frontiers of Boeotia (but not without a compulsion which was fatal to Theban popularity). The classical Greek cities valued their independent traditions too highly to be prepared to subordinate themselves to a system in which their vote would be one among several. (The Athenians and Spartans both found ways of controlling decision-making within their leagues so effectively that they might better not be called leagues at all.) We call this attitude 'valuing independence'; a candid Greek might have called it *phthonos*, envy. It is above all the *phthonos* felt by Sparta for Athens which determines the course of fifth-century Greek history. Unwilling, for reasons we shall discuss, to lead the Greek world herself, Sparta (or rather, some Spartans, some of the time) could not bear to see Athens do the job instead: the 'dog in the manger' is in origin a Greek story, one of the fables of Aesop. As Arrian makes the Spartans say at the beginning of Alexander the Great's reign, Sparta traditionally leads, she does not follow.

Greece, and especially the east-Greek islands still threatened by the Persians, needed a leader in 478. There were not many candidates. Sparta was the most obvious, because in the recent fighting she had led the Greek League against Persia, a temporary coalition distinct from any so far mentioned. Sparta was certainly unwilling to let Athens lead: the rebuilding of Athens' walls—a precondition of any active foreign policy—drew a protest from Sparta in the form of a delegation, which was nullified only by the wit of Themistocles. More positively, Sparta can be detected in pursuit of expansionist goals in the period after 479, but by land (in central Greece) rather than at sea, an element on which she had little experience. Thus her king Leotychidas intervened in Thessaly, resuming a line of policy begun, perhaps, by King Cleomenes I in the late sixth century. This interest in Thessaly on the part of Sparta and her rivals, including fourth-century Thebes and Macedon, will run right through our period; and it is worth noticing here what Thessaly had to offer. Thessaly was agriculturally rich and thus able to support horses on a scale well beyond what most Greek states could afford. So cavalry was the first of Thessaly's advantages. The second was her advantage of position, athwart the main land route to Macedon and Thrace, places to which Greeks looked for grain and ship-building timber; a stranglehold on eastern Thrace and the Hellespontine region would have an additional economic attraction: control of the Hellespont meant control of grain shipments from another main source of supply, namely south Russia (via the Black Sea). It was important for Athens to keep this supply line open, as it was for her enemies to close it. The third advantage of Thessaly was its excellent harbour at Pagasae (modern Volos), the best in central Greece. Finally, Thessaly controlled a majority of votes in, and traditionally supplied the president of, the Delphic amphictyony, the international panel which controlled the affairs of the shrine of Apollo at Delphi, seat of the most famous oracle in the ancient world. It was the amphictyony that declared the 'Sacred Wars', which throughout Greek history—there were no less than four between 600 and 336—were a device for mobilizing Greek opinion and Greek military forces against some real or alleged sinner. Control of the amphictyony thus had enormous propaganda and political value. Spartan interest in the amphictyony is specifically attested for the 470s, when she tried to get Persian sympathizers voted off the panel, thus strengthening her own hold; as with the attempt to prevent the rebuilding of Athens' walls, it was Themistocles who stopped this.

Nevertheless Sparta did pass up the hegemony after 478 and for the next fifty odd years (in Greek the *pentekontaëtia* of 479-431) was content, or obliged, to let Athenian power grow. Only on three occasions did Sparta stir against Athens: in 465 she promised, but in the event failed, to invade Attica as a way of relieving the pressure which Athens was applying to the wealthy island of Thasos; in 446, near the end of the First Peloponnesian War, the Spartan king Pleistoanax did invade Attica, but then withdrew; and in 440 Sparta voted to go to war with Athens who was disciplining another powerful subject ally, Samos. But again this did not come to anything because Sparta allowed herself to be outvoted by her allies at a second meeting, of her whole league. These three occasions have a common feature: Sparta ultimately draws back, just as she had drawn back after 478. If Sparta was an imperialist she was a singularly reluctant one.

The reasons for this reluctance lie in her domestic difficulties. Like all Greek states, Sparta had a population of slaves, but her slave problem was unique both because of the sheer numbers involved and because most of them, the helots, who approximated more closely to medieval serfs than to chattel slaves of an ordinary Greek type, were of one single nationality, Messenians. Because these Messenian helots all spoke Greek (unlike, for instance, Athens' slaves who were a wide racial mix and had no common language in which to articulate discontent), and had a national self-consciousness, they posed special problems of security for their Spartan masters, whose own numbers were constantly on the decline. Apart from the helots, a second set of domestic difficulties faced Sparta after 478, difficulties which had to do with the Peloponnesian League. There is evidence of serious unrest in one area in particular during the 470s and 460s, namely Arcadia, north of Sparta. There were several reasons for this. First, the Peloponnesian League had been called into existence in the first place by fear of

Argos; but Argos was now in low water as a result of her defeat by Cleomenes of Sparta in 494. The Arcadians may thus have felt that the league now lacked a justification. Second, Cleomenes' own suppression by the Spartan authorities may have caused disaffection among the Arcadians, whom he seems to have singled out with promises of a personal relationship with himself, perhaps involving lighter control. Third, there is the unsettling effect of Athenian democracy, which had, in the years after its establishment by Cleisthenes in 507, shown itself to be militarily capable as well as politically attractive: it was now no longer necessary for the Greek cities of the second rank to choose between tyranny on the one hand and Spartan-sponsored oligarchy on the other. A third possibility now existed, namely imitation of, or affiliation to, democratic Athens. It is likely that this possibility was made concrete by the presence in the Peloponnese of Themistocles in the late 470s and early in the 460s. Though he had fallen from favour in Athens, he continued to oppose Spartan interests on Sparta's own doorstep, by encouraging democrats in Arcadia and Argos.

So much for Sparta, and the domestic reasons which ruled her out as permanent leader. An additional worry, which may have been felt by her or her would-be supporters, was perhaps the thought that Sparta had little experience of naval warfare, or of overseas empire.

In this she was unlike Corinth. Corinth did have a naval tradition, and she had experience of administering distant colonial possessions, places like her colonies in north-west Greece, for instance Ambracia or in the northern Aegean, but Corinth had been too close to Sparta for too long to be able to contemplate defying or superseding her; and from the point of view of the other Greek states she lacked the ideological magnetism exerted by Athens or by Sparta, whose *agōgē* (military training and discipline) was not just an effective repressive device, but was thought of in many quarters as somehow admirable in a positive way.

That left only Athens; for the other main classical Greek states, Thebes and Argos, had disqualified themselves for the moment, as had Thessaly, by taking the Persian side in the Wars ('Medism'). Argos was in any case, as we have seen, in poor shape in the early fifth century. She was indeed to make a short-lived bid for power during a lull in the Great Peloponnesian War (the so-called Peace of Nicias of 421), when she attempted to revive the old Argive greatness of the heroic age: such nostalgic, but altogether sincere, attempts to capitalize on traditional or mythical periods of supremacy are characteristic of Greek politics and poetry. As for Thebes, her bid for hegemony was to be postponed still later, until the 360s; even Thessaly, so often the object of the avarice of other states, had a brief fling on her own account in the 370s, under Jason of Pherae who, like the Argives after 421, defined his aims in very ancient terms, levying the 'tribute of Scopas', and modelling his military reorganization on the army of Aleuas the Red. Scopas and Aleuas were figures of the dim past of Thessaly.

Athens in 478 had all the advantages, and none of the disadvantages, of the other claimants we have considered. She had no helots or discontented Arcadians to stab her in the back. She had (unlike Corinth) positive incentives to offer, in her democracy and her *paideia* (culture): thanks to the artistic and literary patronage of the sixth-century Pisistratid tyrants she was already a strong cultural magnet, to which many dispossessed Ionian intellectuals were drawn after 480. As for the claims of history, memory, and myth, Argos may have had her ancient kings, and Thessaly her Aleuas and Scopas; but Athens produced some of the ablest propagandists ever to advertise on behalf of an imperial power. Cimon was to justify coercion of the island of Scyros, in the early days of the Athenian empire, by discovering there the bones of Theseus, mythical king of Athens. The image of Athens as universal benefactor of mankind (and hence morally justified in her suzerainty) was propagated by means of the myth of Demeter and her gift of corn to man. This cult was centred on Eleusis, a great religious focus—but also a constituent village of Attica and so in the territory of Athens. The great Athenian leader Pericles, and his successors, took a leaf out of Pisistratus' book when they placed this emphasis on Eleusis; and there is a further explicitly Pisistratid reminiscence in the 'purification' of Apollo's sanctuary of Delos carried out in 426. The central-Aegean island of Delos was the spiritual heart of the Athenian Empire (and incidentally acted as the imperial bank where monetary tribute from the allies was stored until 454). That empire was, in racial terms, largely 'Ionian', and it was another brilliant coup of fifth-century Athenian propaganda to exploit and magnify, for imperial purposes, an undoubted historical fact: the part played by Athens in the colonization of Ionia in the Dark Ages. By posing as the 'mother-city' of all her subject allies, irrespective of the often hazy reality in particular instances, Athens could demand the religious homage which, according to Greek notions, a daughter city owed to the place which had founded her. Finally, the Athenians had—unlike the medizers of Argos, Thebes, and Thessaly—performed noble service to Greece in the most recent historical past, sacrificing their physical city to Xerxes. Athenian orators were still reminding each other of this well into the fourth century. And the theme was stressed in fifth-century architecture: the 192 figures in the cavalcade on the Parthenon frieze have been ingeniously interpreted as an attempt to represent the dead heroes of Marathon. The victory at Marathon was certainly in the mind of the architect of the mid-fifth-century temple of *Nemesis* (i.e. divine punishment of the Persians) at Rhamnous near Marathon. In fairness, not all this religious glorification of Athens was of her own manufacture: the oracle of Apollo at Delphi, which was to side with Sparta in the Great Peloponnesian War, nevertheless called fifth-century Athens an 'eagle in the clouds for all time'.

Above all, Athens had, like Corinth, a formidable fleet (above, p. 42). And Athens, like Corinth, had already had the beginnings of an overseas empire by the late archaic period; apart from her emotional and religious links with Ionia, there were her settlements at Sigeum near Troy, at the mouth of Hellespont, at the Chersonese and (nearer home) on the islands of Salamis and Euboea. One chief reason for this early transmarine activity is food: archaic and classical Athens needed the south-Russian grain which, as we have seen, came through the Hellespont. This gave Athens a special motive for responding to the appeal of the east-Greek islanders in the early 470s: economic necessity. To say, with one modern Marxist (de Ste. Croix), that fifth-century Athens 'pursued a policy of naval imperialism, but for this there were very special reasons', namely economic reasons, is therefore correct, but we need not follow this writer when he goes on to minimize the element of what he calls 'naked aggressiveness and greediness'. We shall see that individual Athenians, and not just hungry members of the poorer classes, stood to make economic gains from the empire which went well beyond the filling of their stomachs. As for aggression, many Athenian manifestations of it are remote from any immediate anxieties about the corn supply. We should at least expand the economic argument so as to include desire for precious metal for coinage (a supplement to the Laurium output), which goes far to explain the attack on Thasos in 465; and desire for ship-timber, which is relevant to Amphipolis in 437 and perhaps to the colony sent to Thurii in 443. Thurii is near the Sila forests in Bruttium (South Italy), and Thurian timbers are listed in Attic accounts in 407.

All that was in the future in 478; and even the wish for Black Sea grain is not formulated as a motive by Thucydides when he describes Athens' assumption of the leadership. Rather, the talk is of revenge and booty to be extracted from Persia, though in speeches we do hear of more high-minded motives of liberation.

SILVER COIN (TETRADRACHM) OF ATHENS, 440–430 BC. The types for Athenian coins, with Athena's head and the owl with olive twig, change only in style from the end of the sixth century through the Hellenistic period. Athens enjoyed her own supply of silver from the mines at Laurium and attempted to monopolize the coining of silver throughout her empire in the fifth century. The coin is shown at three times actual size.

'Revenge' is, however, stated to be a 'pretext' (rather than the whole story), and scholars have legitimately wondered what Thucydides took the whole story to be. Perhaps he meant that continued mobilization against Persia was a front for enmity directed against Sparta; or more likely he was thinking of the developed empire, whose activities were directed against the Greek world at large.

That the fifth-century Athenian Empire (despite the protection which it offered to the more uncomfortably placed Greeks against Persia and, we should add, pirates) was, or became, an oppressive instrument should not be disputed. The strongest argument, against desperate efforts to see it as a benevolent and generally popular institution, is to be found in an important inscription of the year 377, which sets out the terms and aims of a second Athenian naval confederacy and explicitly repudiates for the future a number of fifth-century practices—tribute, territorial encroachments, garrisons, governors, and so forth—which were clearly felt in retrospect to have been abuses. The only real argument is not over the adjective 'oppressive', but over the appropriate verb, 'was' or 'became'. That is, was the empire (always), or did it (gradually) become, oppressive? There is very little detailed evidence of any kind about the Athenian Empire before about 450, so that the appearance of qualitative change after that date may be a delusion. Nevertheless formulas do get more candidly imperialistic even in the period for which inscriptions survive in numbers, and from the Tribute Lists it is plausible to reconstruct a period of crisis after the Peace of Callias in 449. Late payment and non-payment of tribute in those years suggest disaffection due to a feeling that the originally anti-Persian organization had lost its justification. But whatever is taken to be the point of change, it is sure that there was one: the remark made in 411 by a speaker in the pages of Thucydides, that what the 'allies' really wanted was freedom from both Spartan-sponsored oligarchs and Athenian-supported democrats, could not have been made in the euphoric atmosphere of 478.

What forms, then, did Athenian interference and control, or (less neutrally) oppression, take? First, economic: obedient to the economic compulsion which we have noticed already, Athens used imperial institutions to make sure of her own corn-supply. We hear of 'guards of the Hellespont', who determined how much grain was permitted to consumers other than Athens; of 10-per-cent taxes levied on shipping there (grain bound for Athens herself was presumably exempt); and, in the fourth century at any rate, of laws restricting commercial transactions involving grain bound elsewhere than for Athens. More generally we have already noticed that desire for precious metal and ship-timber was part of the explanation for aggression against, and settlements at, Thasos, Thurii, and Amphipolis. Above all there was tribute, in ships or money (increasingly the second was preferred by all parties).

Second, administrative and military garrisons and garrison-commanders are amply attested, by no means all of them to be explained as present by invitation, like Russian tanks rolling into 'fraternal' Prague or Kabul. And the greatest weapon of all was the fleet.

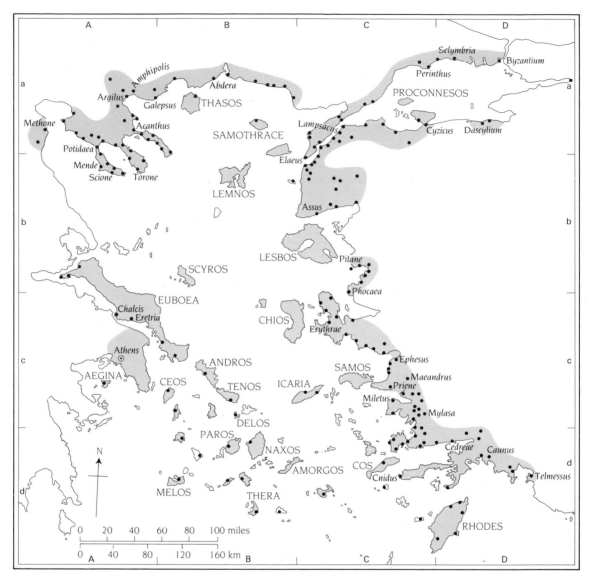

MAP 3. THE ATHENIAN EMPIRE. The shaded area on the map shows the maximum extent of the Athenian Empire: 'the cities which the Athenians rule' is how the Athenians themselves would have put it; alternatively, 'the islanders'. This map shows why the second description was appropriate. It should be remembered that some places in Asia Minor probably paid tribute to Persia as well as to Athens; that some strategically important and financially valuable possessions (such as Amphipolis in the north) did not pay tribute in a way which caused them to be entered on the so-called Tribute Lists at all; and that the Athenian Empire was not exclusively, though it was primarily, an 'Aegean', i.e., east Mediterranean affair. For instance, payments from some Italian and Sicilian communities in about 415 were handled by the *Hellenotamiai*, the imperial treasurers; and it has been suggested that Orchomenus in land-locked Boeotia paid tribute in the mid-century. The 'Tribute Lists', from which we learn details of the payments, were great marble stelae set up on the Acropolis which recorded that one-sixtieth of the tribute which was due to Athena; substantial fragments survive.

Third, judicial. Inscriptions show that serious cases were concentrated in Athens. Literary sources allege, no doubt truly, that the popular lawcourts (below, p. 136) were used for the persecution of anti-Athenian elements, a category which overlaps, but is not necessarily identical with, oligarchs. A final judicial shortcoming: Athenian law never anticipated Roman in developing a separate category of 'extortion' offences, specifically framed to protect oppressed provincials from the rapacity of governors.

Fourth, religious. Doctrinaire imposition of religious views was generally alien to Greek and Roman thinking, but we have noticed already the way in which Athens, the self-proclaimed metropolis of Ionia, exploited religious propaganda as a way of asserting her authority over her allies. A more concrete abuse of religion was the territorial encroachment on allied territory by the 'goddess Athena' herself, whose precincts were delimited by a number of surviving boundary-stones. Since this land might then be leased out to individual Athenians, this is really a subclass of our next category of interference.

Fifth, territorial. Settlements on allied or conquered territory brought obvious and immediate benefits to the lower classes; but recent work has rightly insisted that there were ways for the upper classes to profit too, and profit prodigiously. The chief evidence lies in the inscribed lists of the property of some Athenian aristocrats confiscated and sold as the result of an internal Athenian scandal half-way through the Great Peloponnesian War. These lists show that wealthy Athenian individuals owned holdings of land in allied territory, sometimes very large and valuable, in defiance of local rules about land-tenure (most Greek states confined land-tenure to their own nationals). This land-grabbing, which helps to explain why we hear so few voices raised against the morality of the empire by the representatives of any social class at Athens, was the major positive benefit which the rich derived from the empire. Their other chief benefit was negative: without a tributary empire the rich would have had to pay for the fleet themselves, as they had to do in the fourth century—with resultant class tensions absent in the fifth.

Sixth, social. A law of the year 451 restricted citizenship and thus its benefits—which, as the above discussion shows, were increasingly worth having as the century went on—to persons of citizen descent on both sides. It is surely not fortuitous that the law coincides with the planting of the first fifth-century settlements in allied territory. Athenian (and Spartan) stinginess with the citizenship was singled out by panegyrists of Rome as the chief cause of the brevity of their empires. Grants of privilege to isolated communities (Plataea in Boeotia, Euboea, Samos in 404) were made, but they were too late and too few to bridge the psychological gap between rulers and ruled.

Seventh and finally, political interference. The crucially important truth that Athens generally supported democrats against oligarchs was taken for granted in antiquity, but her occasional support of oligarchs was also noticed. She was not doctrinaire in her support of democratic factions, so long as the money flowed in. Even on the strategically and politically important island of Samos our two main literary sources disagree about whether the settlement imposed after the revolt of 440/39 took an oligarchic or a democratic form, and the text of a relevant inscription can be restored so as to yield either sense.

When Sparta, in 431, responding to pressure from Corinth, agreed to liberate Greece, we are told that the goodwill of the Greek world inclined to the Spartan side. The tight methods of control enumerated above show that there were indeed grounds for resentment of Athenian power.

Democracy

The connection between the empire and democracy was close, in that Athens usually supported democracies abroad. There was another connection, this time internal, between the democracy and the empire. It was the revenue from the empire, greatly increased as a result of Cimon's operations in the early 460s, which made possible the democratic changes at Athens of 462, associated with the names of Ephialtes and Pericles. These reforms increased the power of the popular assembly (*ekklēsia*). Solon at the beginning, and Cleisthenes at the end, of the sixth century had left Athens still in many respects an aristocratic state. In particular the introduction of 'appeal to the people', which the fourth-century thinker Aristotle regarded as one of the most 'democratic' things that Solon did, remained only potentially democratic until the introduction of jury pay in the 460s meant that large popular juries (*dikastēria* of hundreds or even thousands) could attend frequently without loss of income to the jurymen. Other kinds of democratic pay—pay for attendance at the council of 500 members which prepared the *ekklēsia's* business (the *boulē*), and at the city's festivals—were introduced over the next decades, and to this extent it is undeniable that the Athenian democracy was paid for by the allies. Attempts have been made to deny this, by arguing that after Athens was defeated in 404 and her empire brought to an end, fourth-century Athens went on distributing pay (and indeed she introduced a major new category of pay after 404, pay for attending the *ekklēsia*). Therefore (it is said) there was no necessary connection between democratic pay and the empire. The argument is politically naïve: once a vote-catching measure has been introduced—such as a new bank holiday in modern times—it takes a courageous politician to stand up and urge its abolition, at least in the kind of democracy which reserves to itself the right to sack its leaders instantly (Athens had nothing like the modern British notion of a five-year parliamentary term).

Democracy at Athens was both more and less democratic than in modern Britain or the United States; more, for the reason just given: the *ekklēsia* enjoyed more immediate power than a modern electorate, partly because the number of voters was so much smaller in ancient Athens; and less, for a reason also concerned with the number of voters: whole groups—slaves; women; the subject allies, whose lives were affected by many of the *ekklēsia's* decisions—were excluded from

FRAGMENT OF THE TRIBUTE LIST FOR THE YEAR 440–39 BC, recording 1/60 of the sums paid to Athens by contributing states of the Athenian League. The main headings here are for the Hellespontine District and the Thraceward District. The sums are in drachmae, written in Attic alphabetic numerals. The lists of payments were exhibited on the Acropolis.

the franchise. This left some 40,000 adult males who were eligible to vote. Of these perhaps as many as 6,000 (which is nearly the maximum seating capacity of the Pnyx, the *ekklēsia*'s meeting place, and was the quorum required for certain kinds of decision) may have attended for important debates.

The theory was that the *ekklēsia* was sovereign in Athenian political life, though it is hard to find a clear statement of this principle anywhere: the cry that 'it would be shameful if the people were not allowed to do what it wishes' is once raised—but to justify a piece of gross illegality. Aristotle perhaps puts it best when he says that the people would like to be sovereign. Actual popular sovereignty is best illustrated by the power which the people retained—and used—to depose and punish its servants, among whom the ten generals were conspicuous: they held the most important classical Athenian office to which appointment was by election, not by lot.

But there were various ways in which the sovereignty and importance of the *ekklēsia* were eroded in practice. The first limit on its importance was the vigour of deme life. The demes (there were 139 of them) were the constituent villages of Attica; each deme supplied a given number of councillors to the *boulē*, the numbers varying in proportion to the population of the deme. But that was far from being the only thing that demes did: like the democratization of Attica, the sixth-century centralization of Attica was a very partial affair, in that the city of Athens never absorbed all the political energies of the citizens of Attica; instead Attica was a kind of federal state in which local and national loyalties coexisted. Deme decrees, which survive on stone, are the best proof of this: they begin with formulas which closely echo the language of 'national' decrees ('it seemed good to the demesmen of . . .', corresponding to 'it seemed good to the Council and People' of Athens), and cover such topics as the lending out of deme money, the leasing of a deme theatre, the construction of a deme 'civic centre' (*agora*), and the conferring of honours on men from other demes, and even on foreigners. The mention of theatres and *agora* (whose existence has occasionally been confirmed by archaeology) is itself suggestive: these buildings were characteristic of a developed *polis* and the Attic demes have been described in modern times as 'city-states in miniature'. A further proof of this is the intense religious life at deme level, which inscriptions attest, including long and complex cultic calendars (one inscription even shows an admittedly large and prestigious deme consulting the oracle at Delphi on its own initiative). Religion was central to the life of the *polis*, as to the deme. Naturally there were limits to the autonomy of demes: they had no 'foreign policy' beyond the right to honour foreigners, and in some respects their finances were subordinate to those of the city of Athens; for instance, the fortifications of militarily exposed demes were a state responsibility. But the absence of deme inscriptions after about 300 BC sadly illustrates the decline of one highly characteristic aspect of classical Athenian *polis* life, although, centuries after 300, Athenians still identified themselves by the old double system of father's name and deme.

The second limit on the *ekklēsia* was the *boulē* of 500 members, whose main function was to consider in advance everything which came before the *ekklēsia*. Like the Attic demes, the *boulē* has been described—this time by an ancient author—as a microcosm (*mikra polis*) of Athens, and the traditional view that the *boulē* was merely the agent and servant of the *ekklēsia* largely depends on this assumption that the *boulē* was socially representative and a 'cross-section' of the people. The assumption is not well founded. The *boulē* was elected and unpaid when Cleisthenes devised it in 507, and the first evidence for appointment of councillors (*bouleutai*) by lot from demesmen is about 450, and for pay no earlier than 411. That is not to say that these were the dates when those institutions were actually introduced (in both cases it is tempting to associate them with Ephialtes and the changes of 462), but it is important to remember that the change from an aristocratic to a democratic *boulē* was a gradual one. Actual evidence that the *boulē* was socially unrepresentative, in that wealthy and influential citizens preponderated, is harder to assess. There is practically no literary evidence; but by examining surviving lists of councillors, which begin in the fifth century, and checking them against independent evidence of wealth, we can see that membership of the *boulē* was associated with higher social rank than we should have expected had the system been really random. There are also allegations, in the writings of Athenian orators, that so-and-so wangled his way on to the *boulē* in a given year, and there are some striking coincidences—father–son or brother–brother teams serving together, or famous politicians who sit on the *boulē* in particularly exciting years for foreign policy—which all suggest that there were ways of circumventing the lot (which was supposed to ensure that *bouleutai* were supplied by demes in a random way). The most obvious method of circumvention was simple willingness to sacrifice time and therefore money when one's fellow demesmen were unwilling, but the 'wangling' allegations may imply that more positive pressures were applied by the ambitious, who could for instance have bribed fellow demesmen not to put their names forward at deme level. All this means that the *boulē*, as a collection of influential and self-confident semi-professionals, might be expected to lead the *ekklēsia*, not just to follow, and we do indeed find the *boulē* engaging in diplomacy which (judging from the formulas of the relevant inscriptions) was never ratified by the *ekklēsia*; moreover there is undeniable evidence of diplomacy being conducted, on occasion, in secret from the *ekklēsia*. There were of course limits to the *boulē*'s authority; for instance, membership lasted only a year, and nobody could serve more than twice (provisions which prevented the *boulē* from acquiring the hereditary prestige enjoyed by councils in some ancient states); but even this should not be exaggerated: a particular political group would surely take steps to see that it always had a representative, in an informal sense of that word, on the *boulē*. Mention of the formal rules about service in the *boulē* raises a fundamental question: were the lowest property group, the *thētes*, eligible for service? If not, that would be highly relevant to what was said above about the élite character of the *boulē*. But the evidence is unclear and the answer disputed.

Third, the generals. We have noticed that generals could be deposed, as even Pericles was, shortly before his death in 429. But common sense suggests that in ordinary conditions, and especially in wartime, the generals must have had great executive latitude: for instance, security considerations, although admittedly never a strong point with Greeks, must have made it undesirable to discuss detailed strategy in the full *ekklēsia*. And because it was an elected office, with no limit on re-election, the generalship enjoyed unusual respect.

Fourth, the 'demagogues', the popular leaders, such as Cleon in the 420s and Hyperbolus after him, who without necessarily holding any particular office nevertheless exercised great power by oratorical and persuasive skills. Vilified by the literary sources, men like Cleon can be partly rehabilitated by the help of inscriptions, which have shown not only that their social origins were not nearly so obscure as comic playwrights like Aristophanes say, but also that a Hyperbolus

THE FURNITURE OF DEMOCRACY, fifth to fourth century BC. The bronze wheels are public ballots: Aristotle tells us that those with solid axles were for acquittal, the hollow for condemnation, and the voter could conceal his vote by holding the axle between his fingertips. These were found in a building at the north-east corner of the Agora in Athens, near a clay bin, which might be a ballot box, and a water-clock (*klepsydra*) for timing speakers in the law court. The fragmentary inscribed plaque is an identity card for a juror; the bronze ball for use in a machine by which jurors were alloted at random to serve in different courts.

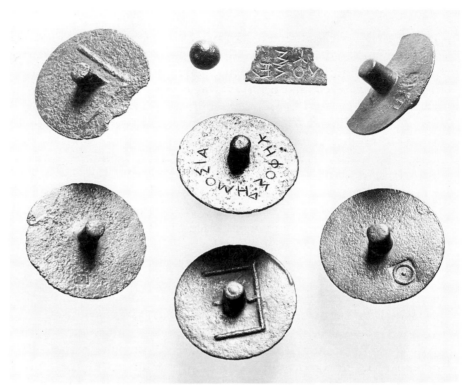

OSTRACA FOUND IN THE ATHENIAN AGORA. These are votes cast to choose a victim for ostracism—banishment from Athens for ten years. They are scratched on potsherds and the examples shown name four prominent politicians of fifth-century Athens—Aristides, Themistocles, Cimon, Pericles.

was capable of thinking out complex and sensible legislation. In fact the demagogues (and Pericles was himself only a grander kind of demagogue) owed their positions of influence to a structural gap in the democracy: imperial administration meant an ever-increasing volume of work, and the Athenians, lacking a civil service of a modern type, allowed such work to be done by politicians who made detailed knowledge their business: knowledge was power. The sanction against a Hyperbolus was ostracism, a way of exiling a man for ten years by a kind of popular referendum (the word comes from the potsherds, *ostraka*, used in the 'polling' process). In the fourth century there was a more sinister development: specialist politicians got a firmer grip on power by being elected, for instance, to control state funds, jobs from which it was harder to unseat them.

Fifth and finally, there were features of the *ekklēsia*'s own procedure and psychology which reduced its democratic effectiveness and independence. It met much less often than the *boulē*, and infrequent meetings do not make for informed debate. Its votes were not counted; opinion was manifested by show of hands and this was then gauged impressionistically, as at a modern trade-union mass meeting. And even as late as the end of the fifth century, the age of the demagogues, there is evidence that the democratic Athenian voter 'loved a lord': the young aristocrat Alcibiades in 415 could still demand a high office of state on the grounds that his racehorses had won at the recent Olympic Games. Such claims show the enduring power of wealth, especially inherited wealth, which inevitably militates against democracy. Despite all the blemishes and shortcomings of Athenian democracy, its long arm did act as a protector against arbitrary treatment of the poorer classes by oligarchs throughout the fifth-century Aegean world, and from the point of view of those classes it was a tragedy that that world gradually lost faith in its protector.

War

The democracy just described was called 'generally acknowledged folly' by Alcibiades; but we have seen that Alcibiades and his class stood to gain from the combination of democracy and empire: magistracies and military commands were conferred on them through the deference of their political 'masters' in the *ekklēsia*, and the empire brought them territorial and other material benefits. They were therefore ready to fight to preserve the 'acknowledged folly' when the Great Peloponnesian War broke out in 431. But that war was to break the power and influence of the Alcibiades class; virtually no Athenians entered chariot teams at Olympia in the three generations after 400 (as opposed to twelve in the single generation 433–400), and when the empire itself disappeared in 404 there disappeared also the motive for upper-class co-operation with what one oligarch's epitaph called, with engaging frankness, the 'accursed people'; so that the rich no longer splashed out on civic expenditure at home with their old panache. The greatest change effected by the Peloponnesian War was an increase in professionalism generally, and naturally this was most conspicuous in the military sphere. Politician and general are henceforth separate callings in Athens, a development foreshadowed in the career of Pericles himself, whose first known activities (in the 460s) are purely political; only later came the great military commands. This professionalism meant that Alcibiades' horses, even supposing that the accursed *dēmos* had let him keep them in the more vindictive atmosphere of the fourth century, would not have sufficed to guarantee him political or military success. Such professionalism affected more than the officer class. The fourth century has been called the age of mercenary soldiers, but the change begins in the last decades of the fifth century: when in 400 the Athenian Xenophon helped to lead a paid army of 10,000 Greeks eastwards in support of a Persian pretender, Cyrus, the financial terms of mercenary service are already fixed and taken for granted. Persian satraps (provincial governors), and even the Athenians themselves, had been using mercenaries for two or three decades before 400.

The Peloponnesian War also brought changes in the methods of fighting. The traditional Greek infantry technique was hoplite fighting, which required heavy and relatively expensive armour, but during the Peloponnesian War we hear for the first time of experiments with lighter-armed troops (peltasts, named from their shields); they became fashionable partly because of their greater flexibility and partly because a peltast cost less to kit out. Although the peltast never replaced the hoplite in classical Greek warfare (most of the great set battles of the fourth century were hoplite affairs), the combination of heavy and light armed was specially formidable. The social effects of a diminished dependence on hoplites, who had tended to be citizens of the states they were fighting for, and of the increased use of peltasts and mercenaries, was to weaken the link between the *polis* and the men who fought to defend it. The numbers, and potential for damage, of the rootless 'men without a city' may have been exaggerated by the fourth-century writer Isocrates, who is a spokesman for the propertied class; but the problem certainly got worse as a result of the Peloponnesian War, if only because after 404 there was no single leading power to impose its own political order as Sparta and Athens had done at different times. This led to a general increase in political instability with violence. Hence the exiles of whom Isocrates complained.

Sea warfare and siege techniques also developed more quickly after 431. By contrasting the accounts of Athenian naval techniques in Books 1 and 2 of Thucydides we see that in just a year or so the Athenians under Phormio have acquired the courage and skill to manœuvre in the open sea. In siege warfare, the agent of change in the late fifth century was not the Peloponnesian War, but the contemporaneous warfare in Sicily against the Carthaginians: this led to the invention of non-torsion catapults about 400 BC (to be followed by torsion cata-pults, perfected—apparently in Thessaly—about 350). Though the defenders of cities were quick to adapt, with new kinds of wall circuit and more effective fortifications, it was now possible to take fortified cities by storm. Alexander in

DEPARTURE SCENE on an Athenian vase of about 450 BC. A hoplite warrior clasps the hand of his father, while his wife or mother stands with a jug and *phiale* cup for the ritual libation of farewell. These poignant scenes are characteristic of Classical art and a similar mood is expressed on the later grave reliefs.

the 330s succeeded in Western Asia, where the Spartan king Agesilaus in the 390s had failed, largely because of the presence in the Macedonian army of Thessalian siege engineers recruited by Alexander's father Philip.

Strategic thinking was the slowest department of classical Greek warfare to change, even under the strain of the Great Peloponnesian War. In tactics, the generals of most Greek states continued to be the servants of the political assemblies, who were reluctant to grant them more than the minimum of formal powers. But there were changes even here: at the battle of Delium in 424 we hear for the first time of a deepened file of troops on the Theban side: these extra troops are a kind of tactical reserve, of a kind later perfected by the Theban Epaminondas in the fourth century. Henceforth more was to depend on the judgement and timing of the general who had to decide when and where to deploy the reserve. Handbooks about, and the oral teaching of, tactics (both of which we hear of first in the late fifth century) announce the change of intellectual attitudes: if warfare is to be scientific it can be taught like any other science.

But strategy, in the sense of grand strategy—the achieving of political results by the best military means—was cautious to a degree in the early phases of the Peloponnesian War. The best strategy which the Spartans could think of at the beginning of the war was to invade the territory of Attica every year in the hope of making the Athenians submit. This was bound to fail because Pericles' strategy for Athens was to abandon the territory of Attica and concentrate the population within the walls of the city and its harbour town Piraeus 9 kilometres away (Athens was joined to Piraeus by a line of parallel walls, the 'Long Walls', so that the two places formed a defensible unit). Access to Piraeus meant access to the food and commodities which Athens' imperial possessions could provide. All Athens needed to do to win the war was to survive it: Thucydides uses the same Greek word for 'survive' and 'win'. She had the financial resources of the empire, capital accumulated over many years, to pay for any disciplining of her allies which might be necessary to ensure that essential supplies kept coming through.

Sparta's position was less easy: she had no reserves or tribute and so had to satisfy the military and political wishes of her allies, on whose human resources she was dependent for her levies. But those wishes included, above all, the 'liberation' which we saw the Greek world expected of her in 431, and liberation meant taking the initiative, taking positive steps to dismantle the Athenian Empire. But, for that purpose, Sparta needed extra manpower, which her social system was ill equipped to provide, and above all the money to pay for more audacious campaigning, possibly by sea (which would mean building a fleet, a costly business). There was one way out: to apply to the richest non-Greek power in the offing, namely Persia; but here the Spartan dilemma became acute because the 'liberation' of Greece from Athens, which Sparta's allies required of her, logically implied as the next step liberation of the east Greeks of Asia Minor from Persia—a point which Alcibiades makes to a Persian satrap in the final phase of the war. Before paying for the Spartan war effort, Persia would require guarantees about Spartan intentions in the east Aegean, guarantees which Sparta's obligations to her own League allies made it impossible for her to give. Nor did Persia have any special motive for disturbing the satisfactory relationship with Athens created by the Peace of Callias.

So Sparta must think of some way of striking a positive blow at Athens and her empire; and that blow must be struck without help from Persia—that is, without a fleet. The answer she hit on in 426 was the resumption of her old central-Greek aspirations. Much of Thucydides' account of the fighting in the middle years of the so-called Archidamian Wars of 431-421 is concerned with the northern activities of the Spartan commander Brasidas. But it is important to notice that the first step, the founding of a large-scale military colony at Heraclea-in-Trachis at the southern approach to Thessaly, was taken in 426, before Brasidas moved with his army to the north. So some Spartans other than the unusually energetic Brasidas were after all forcing themselves to think about grand strategy. It was, however, Brasidas' successful operations against Athens' Thracian and northern possessions (including Amphipolis, which he captured in 424), which made Athens happy to make peace by the end of the 420s; Sparta was equally ready to cease hostilities because Cleon, partly by chance and partly by a skill with which Thucydides does not credit him, had taken prisoner several hundred full Spartan citizens at Pylos in the western Peloponnese. Full Spartan citizens in these numbers could not be spared; the result was that Brasidas' successes were cancelled politically by Cleon's, and the Peace of Nicias was made (421–415). Athens had kept her empire and won the Archidamian War.

Thucydides calls this peace a 'festering peace', and it is true that though there were no formal hostilities Athens, prompted by Alcibiades and perhaps by Hyperbolus, was energetic in stirring up anti-Spartan elements within the Peloponnese. This came to nothing because in 418 Sparta defeated a coalition of her enemies at Mantinea. But a far more important development than all this inconsequential diplomacy was a catastrophic error made by Athens at some point in the years of peace; she supported two Persian satraps in western Anatolia, Pissouthnes and then his son Amorges, who were in rebellion against the Persian King. It was this which gave the Persian King the motive for helping Sparta against Athens, which in the Archidamian War he had lacked. Hence when Athens sent a fleet against Sicily in 415, and this fleet was annihilated at Syracuse (413), with a consequent shaking of confidence in Athens within her empire, Persia at last seemed in a position to win the war for Sparta.

But, despite Sicily and despite a short-lived oligarchic revolution in 411 in the aftermath of Sicily, Athens fought on for a further nine years. Indeed as early as 410 she had scored one major naval success, the battle of Cyzicus, which actually caused the Spartans to sue for peace. Only when Persian money, supplied through the King's son Cyrus, began to pour in without stint, after 407, did Sparta under Lysander force Athens to capitulate, after the battle of Aegospotami (405)—and even then it was not the battle, but the subsequent blockade of the Hellespont, which was decisive. The war was lost; the empire was dissolved; the eagle had been shot down from the clouds.

Hegemony: The Fourth-Century Struggles

'Freedom, or rule over others' is a phrase which Thucydides puts into the mouth of one of his speakers. The equation is instructive about Greek attitudes: freedom to oppress others was valued at least as much as freedom from oppression. Sparta's behaviour, after she had finally 'liberated' Greece from the Athenian Empire, was to illustrate the positive, sinister side to the notion of liberation. A few years after 404 Sparta was to be engaged in war in Greece, the Corinthian War (395–386) against a coalition of Greek states: Boeotia, Corinth, Argos, and, remarkably, a revived Athens which had got rid of the oligarchic junta briefly imposed by Sparta after the Peloponnesian War. At the same time (400–390) Sparta was fighting in Asia against Persia. Alcibiades had been right: liberation of mainland Greece by Sparta did lead to her attempted liberation from Persia of the Greeks of Asia Minor.

How had this warfare come about? Spartan expansionism in this period is the answer, an unqualified expansionism to all points of the compass, which has to be connected with the personality of Lysander. But in some respects Lysander was only resuming in a more single-minded way Sparta's traditional, but intermittently pursued, policies, just as the Spartans who planned Heraclea in 426 were resuming the central-Greek policies of Leotychidas and Cleomenes I.

We may start with Heraclea and central Greece, for the renewal of Spartan aims here posed grave threats to Boeotia and Corinth—the risk of encirclement. Shortly after the end of the war Sparta reasserted her authority in Heraclea, which in the years since its foundation had oscillated between Spartan and Boeotian control. Moreover Sparta seems, on the evidence of an intriguing speech delivered by a Thessalian politician in 404, to have interfered in the politics of Thessaly proper, and she certainly threw a garrison into the Thessalian city of Pharsalus. This interference threatened to bring her into collision with the dynamic Macedonian king Archelaus (413–399), who also had Thessalian ambitions. The presence of Lysander in north and central Greece at the appropriate times is securely enough attested for us to associate him with these policies.

So much for the north. Then there is the west: in Sicilian Syracuse, at about the time that the Peloponnesian War was ending in Greece, the tyrant Dionysius I established himself in power—with Spartan help. Again we may suspect the hand of Lysander, who, according to an early chapter of his biography by Plutarch, paid a visit as ambassador to Dionysius. Here were grounds for unease in Syracuse's mother city of Corinth, especially since the help given by Sparta to the tyrant included the assassination of a Corinthian mysteriously described as a 'leader' of the Syracusans.

Then there is the south. Another of Lysander's attested visits was to the Egyptian oracle of Ammon at Siwah; and since Lysander's brother was called Libys ('the Libyan') this may indicate family links. Now Egypt, since 404, had been in revolt from Persia under a rebel native Pharaoh, and it is possible that Lysander was playing the same game in Egypt as at Syracuse—backing, and thus placing under obligation, a newly emergent power. Certainly both Dionysius and the new Pharaoh repaid the debt with concrete naval help to Sparta in the Corinthian War.

Finally and most important—since it concerned Persia directly—the east. Spartan involvement in Asia Minor after 404 begins surreptitiously, with the help to Cyrus, now in revolt against his brother the new King, given by Xenophon's 10,000 (above, p. 142): this force had official backing from the Spartan state, but that is an aspect which the pro-Spartan Xenophon is at pains to suppress in his account of the expedition, his *Anabasis*. Sparta acted more openly in Asia against Persia when appealed to directly by some Ionian cities: a series of expeditions sent between 400 and 396, the last of them actually led by a Spartan king, the newly acceded Agesilaus, crossed to Anatolia and campaigned there till recalled by the outbreak of the Corinthian War (395). But even a defeat (Cnidus, 394) at sea by a Persian fleet commanded by the Athenian admiral Conon was not enough to cause Sparta to renounce her Asiatic ambitions. That was only achieved (in 392) by the ravaging of the Spartan coast-line by Conon and a Persian satrap, for this raised the old possibility of revolt by helots who would be encouraged to see Spartan enemies so close. The result, after a few years more of desultory fighting, was the King's Peace (387/6), which finally settled that Asia Minor should be Persian and that the Greeks should be 'autonomous'. The delay between 392 and 387/6 was due partly to the need to starve Athens into submissiveness, but largely to the Persian King's hostility towards Sparta because of her help to Cyrus in 400.

IMPRESSION FROM AN ENGRAVED CHALCEDONY GEMSTONE FOUND AT BOLSENA IN ITALY. A Persian horseman attacks a Greek soldier. The style is 'Greco-Persian', current in the southern states of Asia Minor in the later fifth and fourth centuries BC, and serving Persian or Persian-dominated courts. The style and spirit of the subject matter, however, owe much to Greek art.

The 'autonomy' provision of the King's Peace was greatly to Sparta's advantage, for she could use it as a pretext to dismantle those of her enemies whose organization could be held to be a violation of internal 'autonomy': thus Mantinea, in Arcadia, a unified and democratic *polis* since Themistocles' day, was broken up into its constituent villages. It is doubtful, however, whether Sparta relied on legal technicalities about autonomy to intervene in Mantinea; the fact was that her prestige as a result of the King's Peace, of which she was appointed by Persia to be in some sense the guarantor, gave her the power to do what she liked. This was especially true since two of her main enemies, Thebes and Athens, were caught by the 'autonomy' clause: Thebes had to renounce her position of dominance over the Boeotian League, and Athens had to abandon for the moment her hopes of a revival of her old empire. There is no doubt that those hopes had revived, very soon after 404: an Athenian orator in 392 refers to the desire to recover the overseas possessions which Athens had lost by the war, and in the period after the battle of Cnidus Athens had revived the old 10-per-cent tax at the Hellespont. This hankering after empire on fifth-century lines, and especially the desire to recover another northern possession, Amphipolis, determined the course of Athenian foreign policy down to the age of Philip.

The King's Peace left Sparta free, not merely to coerce immediate neighbours such as Mantinea, but to go north again: in 383 she attacked Olynthus, in the Chalcidice. But *en route* for the north the Spartan commander Phoebidas was invited into Thebes by a pro-Spartan faction, and seized the Theban citadel, the Cadmeia. This blatant aggression was viewed by the pious Xenophon, for all his Spartan sympathies, as a piece of divinely sent madness, and certainly it created a mood of violent antipathy to Sparta in the Greek world at large, so that when some Theban exiles liberated their city in 379 they were able to call in help from Athens. Capitalizing on the anti-Spartan atmosphere, and perhaps fearful of Spartan reprisals for their part in the recent events at Thebes, the Athenians now (378) gathered together an alliance, the second Athenian Naval Confederacy, with Thebes as the most noteworthy ally. As we have already remarked, the new alliance was careful to abjure the most hated of the fifth-century imperial practices (tribute, garrisons, cleruchies); even so there was no immediate rush to join. Only when the new confederacy showed its effectiveness in practice by a naval defeat of Sparta off Naxos in the Aegean (376) did adherents flock in. Athens' new position was recognized in a renewal of the King's Peace in 375. The Athenian

THE ATTIC FORT AT PHYLE ON MOUNT PARNES. It was built in the early fourth century BC and guards the most direct route from Athens to Thebes.

eagle had taken wing again, though it was altogether a less plump and formidable bird. Despite the promises of 377 (above, p. 133), the energetic naval campaigning of the decade had to be paid for, and by 373 we hear for the first time of financial 'contributions'—the old fifth-century tribute under another name. And in the same year there is evidence of the first Athenian garrison, on the island of Cephallenia off the west of Greece.

Not only did Athens begin thus early to break her negative pledges; more important, the ideological justification of the new league—originally, a democratic freedom-fight against Sparta, with Athens and Thebes as joint leaders—was called into question by Thebes' own behaviour in the 370s. Soon after the liberation of the Cadmeia Thebes reclaimed her position within Boeotia, reviving the Boeotian League under Theban leadership. The recalcitrants among the smaller Boeotian cities were bullied and some even destroyed. At next-door Athens all this was watched with alarm. When at the battle of Leuctra in 371 the Thebans confronted Sparta and—to the amazement of Greek opinion, accustomed for generations to the idea of Spartan invincibility—defeated her, Athens received the herald who announced the Theban victory with arctic incivility, and henceforth moved closer to Sparta diplomatically, a shift which dismayed the other allies of Athens. The decade of Theban hegemony had begun.

Leuctra was a defeat for Sparta, but its most important consequence for her was the Theban refoundation of Messenia as an independent state after many centuries of helotage (369). Sparta now, deprived of the economic means to pursue the old *agōgē* on which her supremacy had rested, and which required the leisure which only massive dependent labour could bring, sank to second-class rank among the Greek powers.

This allowed Thebes and Athens to pursue their rivalry in the vacuum created by Sparta's disappearance. In Thessaly a third power whom we have already met, Jason of Pherae, destroyed the walls of Heraclea to prevent any enemy coming that way again. That was the end of Sparta's central-Greek ambitions. But Jason was assassinated, and Thessaly became once again, as the 360s opened, a passive object of the covetousness of others. Thessaly and Macedon, the latter at this time tormented by dynastic disputes, are the first main theatre of Theban activity in the 360s: it was the Theban Pelopidas who led this diplomatic and military penetration into Macedon and Thessaly. Here Theban interests clashed with Athenian, for one result of Leuctra was to reawaken serious hope at Athens for the recovery of Amphipolis and the Chersonese. All that either side was able to achieve in the north, however, was to prevent the other being successful without qualification, thus making easier the eventual task of Philip II of Macedon. Thebes did however gain one positive advantage; control via Thessalian votes of an outright majority on the Delphic amphictyony.

The second main area of Theban activity was the Peloponnese, where Epaminondas, the victor of Leuctra, followed the refoundation of Messenia with the creation of a new federal Arcadian state with a capital Megalopolis, the 'Great

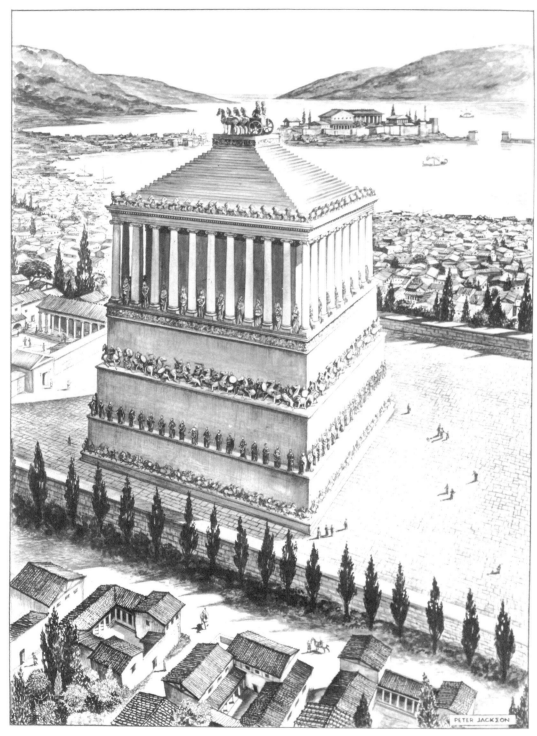

THE MAUSOLEUM AT HALICARNASSUS. Reconstruction by Peter Jackson. One of the Seven Wonders of the World, it was built in the mid fourth century for King Mausolus of Caria by his wife Artemisia, who was said to have employed the leading Greek sculptors of the day. The building is described by Pliny, but the site has been excavated and many pieces of the sculpture decoration recovered (see next illustration), mainly from their re-use in the castle of St Peter, built by the Knights of St John, overlooking the harbour of the modern town (Bodrum).

City'. Such foundations, like the export of federalism to Aetolia and the creation of a new Boeotian federation (distinct from the Boeotian League—which continued in being—and modelled on the Second Athenian Confederacy), represent Thebes' main legacy to Hellenistic Greece.

The third and final area of Theban expansion was by sea in the Aegean. Here again the enemy was Athens, who in 365 had overstepped herself in the eyes of her allies by sending a settlement to Samos, thus breaching another confederacy pledge. The breach was moral rather than formal since, first, Samos was not a confederacy member, and, second, the Athenian action was provoked by a Persian garrison, in violation of the King's Peace, which had granted Asia (but not offshore islands like Samos) to Persia. The violation was flagrant, and Athens was entitled, in view of the strategic strength of Samos, to react as she did. But her action, the installation of the settlement, was deeply and (as pro-Samian inscriptions show) widely resented. This resentment enabled Thebes to seduce some of Athens' most valuable allies out of the confederacy, notably Byzantium on the Hellespontine corn-route (also, temporarily, Rhodes). Epaminondas is in this respect the forerunner of Mausolus, the Persian satrap who further exploited allied grievances against Athens in the 350s, taking Rhodes and other places finally out of the Athenian camp in the Social War. This satrapal infiltration of the islands, which took an oligarchic form, starts as early as the 360s in some places (notably Cos). It did much to settle the 'class struggle' in the Aegean world between oligarch and democrat, tilting the balance against the democrats; but we

RELIEF SLAB FROM THE TOMB OF MAUSOLUS AT HALICARNASSUS (see last illustration). It shows Greeks fighting Amazons, who were skilful archers and riders (note the figure at the left, shooting from the saddleless horse).

IVORY HEAD, probably a portrait of Philip II of Macedon. Part of the relief decoration of a wooden couch found in the tomb of Philip II at Vergina, with other ivory heads, apparently portraits of other members of the royal family.

should remember that it was Athenian selfishness—the pursuit of private goals like Amphipolis—which led democrats such as the Rhodians to prefer even Mausolus to their fellow democrats at Athens.

When the 360s ended, feeling against Athens was running strong inside her own confederacy, Thebes was generally unloved, and Sparta broken. So when Philip II, whom a contemporary historian described with justification as 'the greatest man Europe had ever produced', succeeded to a debilitated Macedonian kingdom in 359, he was fortunate above all in the weakness of the states who should have been making it their business to confront him; otherwise that personal greatness would have remained merely potential. We can add that the Syracusan tyranny had ended after the second generation, true in this respect as in others to the pattern of the old archaic tyrannies of the Greek mainland; and that mid-fourth-century Sicily, anarchic and economically battered, was in no position to intervene against the new king in Macedon. A Corinthian called Timoleon was to restore and revive Sicily in the 340s, but it was not till the Hellenistic age had begun that a Sicilian ruler would again play a part in world politics. The problems of Athens, Sparta, and Thebes got worse in the course of the 350s: Athens' confederacy, as we have seen, was torn apart in the Social War of 357–355; Sparta's efforts to recover Messenia were futile, but consumed all her energies; Thebes picked a quarrel with neighbouring Phocis in the early 350s and induced her stooges on the Delphic amphictyony to declare Sacred War on Phocis. But the Phocians seized the Delphic temple treasures, hired mercenaries, and made such a good showing against Thebes that the war was ended in 346 only by Philip's intervention. The importance of the Sacred War, in thus bringing Philip into the heart of Greece, can hardly be exaggerated. But, to return to the 350s, Philip had been taking advantage of the disunity and the private preoccupations of the Greek states to seize a string of northern places, including Amphipolis, and to acquire control of Thessaly with all its assets. Olynthus succumbed in 348, unaided by Athens, despite the oratory of her great patriot Demosthenes, who in the late 350s had been slow to identify Philip (rather than Persia or Sparta) as Athens' real enemy, but rarely faltered after 349. By 346 Athens' military struggle against Philip had achieved so little that formal diplomacy was substituted, the so-called Peace of Philocrates, whose most important single clause

PORTRAIT HEAD OF DEMOSTHENES. Copy of a portrait made by Polyeuctus, forty-three years after Demosthenes' death in 322 BC. The original bronze stood in the *agora* at Athens and was a whole figure, dressed, with hands clasped before him.

from Athens' point of view was her acquiescence in the loss of Amphipolis. From Philip's point of view it may have mattered more that he had not only a peace but an alliance with Athens, since there is reason to think that he was already contemplating the war against Persia which his son Alexander the Great carried through: for that purpose he would need Athens' navy or at least her neutrality. The peace of 346 was, however, impermanent, and it is a question whether it was Philip or the endlessly provocative Demosthenes who willed that it should be so. Philip used the later 340s to strengthen his hold over Thessaly and Thrace, and to install (or perhaps merely encourage) his partisans elsewhere, for instance on Euboea. By Demosthenes the interval was spent rallying Greek opinion against 'the barbarian', as he unjustly and inaccurately called the Macedonian (the near-Greekness of whose culture is now revealed in a clearer light by such archaeological finds as the painted frescoes at Vergina, uncovered in 1977). That Demosthenes' propagandist and political efforts almost succeeded is shown by the closeness of Philip's final victory on the field at Chaeronea (338). The result of Chaeronea was diplomacy of a new kind: a settlement (the 'League of Corinth', which had little to do with classical ideas of federalism), with a king as its centre, and relying for its maintenance on the goodwill of the possessing classes whom it entrenched in power. They were never, either under Macedon or Rome, to lose that position of power; the classical class struggle had been decided: democracy and Athens had lost, as a result of Athens' own folly. Imperialism had after all proved incompatible with democracy.

Further Reading

The ancient sources for the period from the Persian to the Peloponnesian wars were collected in G. F. Hill, *Sources for Greek History 478-431 B.C.* (revised edn. Oxford, 1951 by R. Meiggs and A. Andrewes). The indexes are specially useful because they set out the ancient references under geographical and chronological headings. The fifth-century part of Fornara (above, p. 48) translates many of the items, literary and epigraphic, in Hill. The later part of the period is covered by P. Harding, *From the end of the Peloponnesian War to the battle of Ipsus* (Cambridge, 1985). There are good revised Penguin translations of Thucydides (revised by M. I. Finley) and Xenophon (revised by G. L. Cawkwell), *The Persian Expedition* and *A History of My Times*.

There are two recent histories of classical Greece: J. K. Davies, *Democracy and Classical Greece* (London, 1978), the subject-matter of which is broader than the title implies: this is a stimulating general history of the period; S. Hornblower, *The Greek World, 479-323 B.C.* (London, 1983), which gives fuller bibliographies than is possible in the present work.

On the Athenian Empire the major works of modern times are B. Meritt, H. T. Wade-Gery, and M. F. McGregor, *The Athenian Tribute Lists* III (Harvard, 1950) and R. Meiggs, *The Athenian Empire* (Oxford, 1972, with paperback reissue in 1979). (The same author's *Trees and Timber in the Ancient Mediterranean World* (Oxford, 1982) brings out the importance to imperial Athens of sources of timber supply.) An excellent brief survey is P. J. Rhodes, *The Athenian Empire* (*Greece & Rome New Surveys in the Classics* xvii, 1985). The relevant source-material is translated and commented on in M. Greenstock and S. Hornblower, *The Athenian Empire* (LACTOR I[3], 1983).

On Athenian democracy, much work and rethinking has been done since C. Hignett's conservative and sceptical *History of the Athenian Constitution* (Oxford, 1952) and A. H. M. Jones's still invaluable *Athenian Democracy* (Oxford, 1957). The most important books (though many of the major new theses have been advanced in articles) are W. R. Connor, *The New Politicians of Fifth-Century Athens* (Princeton, 1971); P. J. Rhodes, *The Athenian Boule* (Oxford, 1972) and the same author's magnificent *Commentary on the Aristotelian Athenaion Politeia* (Oxford, 1981); M. H. Hansen, *The Athenian Ecclesia: a collection of articles, 1976-1983* (Copenhagen, 1983); M. I. Finley, *Politics in the Ancient World* (Cambridge, 1983); and J. K. Davies, *Wealth and the Power of Wealth in Classical Athens* (New York, 1981: a supplement to his *Athenian Propertied Families*, Oxford, 1971).

On the Peloponnesian War, A. W. Gomme's *Historical Commentary on Thucydides*, completed after Gomme's death by A. Andrewes and K. J. Dover (Oxford, 5 vols. 1945-80) is fundamental. G. E. M. de Ste. Croix, *The Origins of the Peloponnesian War* (London, 1972, paperback 1982) is rich in discussions which go beyond the scope of the title; he returns to some relevant themes of classical Greek history in ch. 5 of his *Class Struggle in the Ancient Greek World* (London, 1981, paperback, 1982). On the final phase of the war, D. M. Lewis, *Sparta and Persia* (1977) ch. 4 and 5 are crucial.

The fourth century has been worked on more in articles than books until recently; but T. T. B. Ryder's *Koine Eirene* (Oxford, 1965) is useful on the complicated diplomatic history (especially relations with Persia) in the period. The second Athenian confederacy is re-examined with perhaps too kindly an eye in J. Cargill, *The Second Athenian League, Empire or Free Alliance* (California, 1981); J. Buckler, *The Theban Hegemony 371-362 B.C.* (Harvard, 1980) has much chronological and political detail; but it is still necessary to consult works like J. A. O. Larsen, *Greek Federal States* (Oxford, 1968) for the importance of federal developments in the 360s. For Thessaly, H. D. Westlake, *Thessaly in the Fourth Century B.C.* (London, 1935) is good and has not yet been surpassed. S. Hornblower, *Mausolus* (Oxford, 1982) discusses, in ch. 7, the Athenian and Persian aspects to the 370s and 360s and treats the Social War and (in ch. 6) the Satraps' Revolt in detail.

Philip II has been well served recently in monographs; the best is probably G. L. Cawkwell, *Philip of Macedon* (Faber, 1978); more detailed discussion of modern views in G. T. Griffith's contribution to N. G. L. Hammond and G. T. Griffith, *History of Macedonia* ii (Oxford, 1979).

Finally, a book which contains contributions of importance on several themes covered in this chapter: P. Garnsey and C. Whittaker, (edd.), *Imperialism in the Ancient World* (Cambridge, 1978); see especially Andrewes on Sparta, Finley on the fifth-century Athenian Empire (this is reprinted in his *Economy and Society in Ancient Greece*: London, 1981; Pelican edn., 1983), and Griffith on the second Athenian League.

7

Greek Drama

❧❧❧

PETER LEVI

Introduction

THERE is plenty of drama in everyday life, and the experience of life is the source of everything that succeeds in the theatre. Almost every human society has formal drama of one kind or another, if we define the word loosely. We know the Greeks sat on theatre benches to watch sacred rituals. The ceremonies of state and of religion, and the moments of birth, death, marriage, harvest, and so on, have a great deal in common with theatrical drama, but we recognize drama strictly speaking because it uses actors, takes place in something like a theatre, an area defined by an audience, and probably has a plot, and more importantly an inner form, that we have learnt to expect. Once there is a theatre, there will be many other conventions: applause, competition, a style of speech, maybe the mask and the dance.

These conventions were not invented, though the Greeks believed that some of them were, but inherited and modified from social and religious ceremonies in which the drama began before it became theatrical. The obvious direct ancestor of theatrical choral lyrics is the dithyramb, which was a processional and choral lyric performance with narrative themes. When did the first actors step out from the chorus line? The history of the theatre, like all social history, is always the history of change; conventions may alter and then recur, but the inner form of theatrical performance, the skeleton of what is expected, becomes utterly transformed in time; this transformation is irreversible.

Then what about the origins, the very earliest adaptations? First one, then two, then three actors, always with the same choral background, though the chorus could be used in quite different ways.

Three kinds of plays—tragedy, comedy, and plays in which the chorus was the satyrs who belong to Dionysus. Music, with a history of its own. It is apparent that in the course of the fifth century BC, Athenian plays tended roughly to become more human and realistic, rather more secular and less religious, more fictional and less mythical, although none of these changes ever reached its final stage even in the fourth century, and tragedy with invented plots, as opposed to the wild and original adaptations of Euripides, was an innovation that had no future for many centuries. It was made late in the day by the sophisticated young poet Agathon who figures in Plato's *Symposium*; we know little about it.

The origins of Athenian tragedy are almost equally obscure. There is no doubt that dancers in animal masks performed in the sixth century in various parts of Greece. The origins of tragedy are certainly ritual and religious. The first tragedies in Athens were performed around a cart in the *agora*, which was mostly an open space. The actors probably came in from the country, perhaps from the sanctuary of Dionysus at Icaria or from Eleutherae. The fact that they spoke in verse should not surprise us: impromptu dialogue in verse between actors and audience could be heard at the Zacynthus carnival until the other day.

But beyond this we are in an area where the findings of modern folklore studies and social anthropology must be called in to cast their flickering and often misleading light. Occasionally, in a play we have, one seems to catch a whiff of origins, of a dying god or the rituals of initiation or the animal dancers, but these sensations are insecure, and the romantic arguments and general theories they have sometimes given rise to have been unsatisfactory. All the same, the English miracle plays, mystery plays, and mummers' plays, the goat dancers of Scyros, and the *commedia dell'arte* do throw some light on the nature of drama itself, and on the peculiar mixture of its origins.

The most important feature of early Greek tragedy that we should notice, apart from its extreme formality in performance and its slow, controlled progression like that of music (and determined in fact by music and ritual dancing) is that tragedy was a substitute for Homer. It was from Homer that tragedy took many of its themes, its irony, its preoccupation with justice, and the inner form of tragedy itself: the destruction of a hero or a superman: Homer is already tragic, and in everything but theatrical convention Homer in the first book of the *Iliad* is already the greatest tragic dramatist. Aeschylus was right to say 'We are all eating crumbs from the great table of Homer.' The influence of epic poetry on fifth-century Athenian theatre is vast and pervasive. Aeschylus in the *Oresteia* consumes some two-thirds of the *Agamemnon* in setting history in the context of epic. Even the fact that we are never given the precise origin of the curse on the house of Atreus can be seen as epic convention. True epic poetry is always an episode, the origins belong to another genre, to poems like Hesiod's *Theogony*, and even they are full of unexplained episodes.

Let us descend from these cloudy observations to what we know more exactly. The inscribed list of winners in Athenian dramatic festivals seems to have been begun or reorganized by the newborn democracy; they were festivals of the whole people. But the chief, and in the early fifth century the only, tragic festival was the Great Dionysia in spring, which was probably organized originally by the tyrant Pisistratus and remodelled by Cleisthenes. Clearly enough, the popularity of the tragic performances produced the development of the form and the extension of the set days. At first three poets presented three tragedies each, and one

FIGURE OF AN ACTOR on a fragment of a vase from Tarentum, painted about 340 BC. He is shown holding a mask, as for a king, carries a sword, and wears elaborate stage buskins.

satyr play. For most of the fifth century, the staging of plays was very simple, even to naïvety, with two or three actors and a chorus of twelve or later fifteen.

In 488/7, comedies began to be organized at the Dionysia. Until then comedy was in the hands of 'volunteers'. It was a wilder growth, and it existed elsewhere in Greece; Epicharmus was composing comedies in Sicily in the early fifth century. At Athens, by 440 BC, comedy had spread to the Lenaea, a winter festival of the same god at which the weather cannot always have been clement (about 2 February). Tragedy spread to that festival about 432 BC: usually two poets with two tragedies each, it seems. Comedies were more numerous, five at each festival, except during wartime when the number was three. Were tragedies more expensive and grander? Or was comedy more popular? They were both popular, since in the fourth century they both spread through villages of the Athenian country-side at the Country Dionysia in autumn. As time went on they spread all over the Greek world, and travelling groups of players must have had trouble, as athletes did, in keeping their numerous appointments. The Athenian drama was never quite isolated: Aeschylus wrote plays in Sicily, and Euripides and Agathon were lured to Macedonia. At the Athenian Lenaea resident aliens were permitted to perform, though there is no doubt that both the tragedies and the comedies were great state occasions and popular national events. Phrynichus in his *Phoenissae* and *Fall of Miletus*, his slightly younger rival Aeschylus in the *Persae*, and also much later writers dared to treat contemporary political themes directly in the theatre. Many other tragedies touched on the real world in a few verses or less directly. The *Oedipus at Colonus*, the last masterpiece of Sophocles, cannot be fully understood without the force of its real context, its first production as the city of Athens toppled to its fall.

AESCHYLUS

We have seven complete plays by Aeschylus, unless we accept the opinion recently accepted by many scholars that *Prometheus* is not his. But it is worth while noting at once that wonderful as the texts are that came down to us, they are a pitiful remnant of what once existed; their isolation from a huge context of similar works has surely distorted our judgement of them in many ways. The fragments we have of the lost plays of Aeschylus extend his range as poet and dramatist, and some of them are surprising. Who for example would have predicted his humorous touch and gentle handling in satyr plays? But he was champion of that genre. And who would have supposed that Aeschylus would present Achilles and Patroclus as full homosexual lovers? The fragments of religious sublimity are less unexpected, yet every new fragment of Aeschylus on papyrus as it turns up is always a surprise.

Only from Aeschylus have we a complete trilogy: that is, on at least one occasion his three tragedies were a coherent series, a continuous story. This is the Oresteia, of which the first play, the *Agamemnon*, has the most powerful impact of any ancient tragedy, grander and more thrilling even than the *Oedipus* of Sophocles, which Aristotle took to be *the* classic tragedy. The resolution of the *Oresteia* in the *Eumenides*, its third play, remains strangely moving to this day, and perhaps as close as we can come to intellectual understanding of the problems and solutions of the late archaic Greek world. It is a world utterly remote from ours, but the further one enters into it the more surely one realizes that we cannot afford to neglect it. Aeschylus is Blake-like, but without the obscurities or the divided mind of Blake. He is Shakespearean, but with a terrible concentration. His theatre is a circle of dead silence, and he used the form of his plays to the marrow of their bones.

Agamemnon begins quietly, with the Watcher on the roof. The chorus of old men is to come; this is the moment before daybreak, the opening of the theatre festival in 458, when Aeschylus was about sixty-seven. He had two more years to live.

> I ask the gods for relief of these labours,
> this watch from year's end to year's end, crouched
> on the roof of the Atreidae like a dog.
> I know the assembly of night stars
> the bright lords glittering in upper air
> that bring winter and summer to mankind.
> I attend for the signal light to burn
> and for the flame to blaze the news of Troy,
> the city fallen. We are mastered here
> by a woman's man-minded all-hoping heart.
> While my night-restless bed wettens with dew
> and no dreams ever watch over my sleep,
> because I must not shut my eyes and sleep,
> pounding out song for a drug against sleep,
> then I weep for the miseries of this house
> that lacks the good management of the past.
> O for lucky relief of these labours
> and the fire of good news in the darkness!
>
> O Hail bright shiner, daylight at midnight,
> beginning of dancing in all Argos!
> Yooo! Yooo!
> I signal clear to Agamemnon's wife
> to come quickly from bed and raise her cry
> in thanksgiving and welcome to this light,
> because the city of Troy has fallen,
> so says the messenger of fire at night.

It will be seen at once, even through the smoky medium of a modern translation, that this is a poet of brilliant and yet simple strokes. His images are very simple, his observation is acute, and he tells us far more than he says. His language has a stately formality but it moves swiftly and vividly. This is cumulative poetry; it builds on itself as music does. It is intensely dramatic. The special interest of this particular piece is that it begins from nothing, and from a minor character. But it leads into a magnificent set-piece, a long, very lively account of the chain of signal-fires on every mountain top and headland from Troy to Argos; spanning the whole of eastern Greece. It is curious and characteristic of Aeschylus, that he often highlights long geographical catalogues, real or half imaginary, and that this taste goes back to Homer and can be found after Homer, and (interesting to note) in each of the three long Homeric hymns, to Demeter, to Apollo, and to Hermes. It expressed one of the ancient purposes of poetry. Ancient Irish poetry has it; so has ancient French poetry.

Some scholars have spent time recently in tracing particular images through whole works of Aeschylus. I doubt whether those complex patterns have great significance. He works cumulatively, but quite simply. His thoughts are not hidden in the imagery, but stated in so many words, or stated and contradicted, as must happen in dramatic poetry. His mightiest strokes are often simply to turn a homely and familiar image inside out and make it terrifying: the friendly *kōmos*, for instance, which is a controlled alcoholic riot, and the visit from relatives, and the friendly dog a word or two turns sinister. In such simple terms Cassandra tells her vision of Agamemnon's house.

> I shall not speak in riddles anymore.
> Be witness that I smell out swiftly
> the tracks of evils that have long been done.
> There is a choir that never leaves this roof,
> unmusical, in concert, unholy.
> And it has grown drunken and overbold
> on human blood, it riots through the house,
> unriddable, blood-cousins, the Furies.

Most of what Aeschylus has to teach is dark, though the sublimity (simple once again) of his view of Zeus constantly bursts out, with the same naïvety as the psalms of David have, and a poetry perhaps nearer to our own expectations of poets. The force of the *Oresteia* is dramatic; the same lines would work much less well in an anthology, or if they were fragments. There is an important sense in which all this wonderful language is about the murder of Agamemnon by his wife. The scene of his death, which happens like nearly all horrors in the Greek theatre off stage, is well prepared at a conscious and an unconscious level; when it comes, the thud is terrible. What Aeschylus has done is to present a squalid and bloody killing, quite unacceptable in principle to Greek feelings about women, in such a way that one is awestruck rather than horrified by the character of Clytemnestra. Everything in the play, even Agamemnon's power and magnificence, is tailored to her appalling greatness. For her lover Aegisthus Aeschylus has nothing but scorn. The *Agamemnon* belongs to the theatre, though not alas in the hands of most modern directors. It is simple, bare, and forceful, and its pace is slow, its gestures slower than most dancing.

In the second play we have implicit compassion, ruthless action, and a long anguish with formal prayers. The queen and her lover are killed at last by Orestes, Agamemnon's son. Orestes is pursued by the Furies which rise from a mother's spilt blood. This is not really what Elizabethan scholars call a revenge tragedy; it is cumulative, but in its slow balance it says something dreadful about the justice of Zeus and the nature of the gods. The third play, which, most unusually, has a change of scene to accommodate Apollo at Delphi in a story which Aeschylus firmly transfers for its conclusion to Athens, brings good out of evil. The most venerable Athenian lawcourt is instituted by Athena and, by the reversal of what we know as a traditional cursing formula of great antiquity, the

Furies become the guardian spirits of Athens—Eumenides, the kindly ones. There are some lines that indicate a political message, not very clear to us, but the chief point that Aeschylus is making is a blessing on Athens that has the weight of the *Oresteia* behind it.

The *Persians* (472 BC) is based on an interesting device. The tragic hero has to be the Persian King, because there is no other way of showing the Athenian victory in the sea-battle at Salamis in a tragic form. Only losers can be heroes. Homer demands our sympathy for Troy partly because he has to make the Trojans talk like Greeks, but the lamentation for Hector is convincing because epic poetry was very closely bound up with lamentation. Aeschylus makes us feel, as Homer does, that war is terrible, and in his description of the battle of Salamis, of which he was very likely an eyewitness, nothing is spared. He sees it certainly as a great and inspiring Greek victory, but the battle is described by a loser; it is terrible, and the massacre in which it ends appalling. The whole action of this play is fascinating, but the battle scene stands alone. It does in verse what prose would take a long time to learn to do half as well. That is not only a technical device of tragedy. One must add that Aeschylus wrote his own epitaph, from which it appears he wanted to be remembered only as one who had fought in the infantry at Marathon.

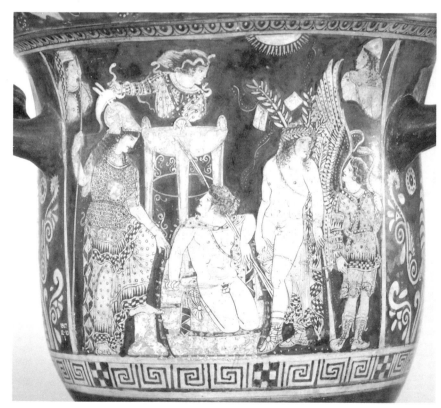

THE *EUMENIDES* BY AESCHYLUS. Scene on a vase made in Paestum by the artist Python, about 350–340 BC. The fourth-century Greek vases of Italy often display scenes which seem to be inspired by stage presentations of tragedies by Athenian poets. Here Athena (at left) comforts Orestes who has taken refuge before the tripod and *omphalos* (navel-stone of the earth) at Delphi. Apollo stands at the right beside a snake-trimmed Fury (there is another over the tripod) waiting to wreak vengeance on Orestes for the murder of his mother. Apollo will purify Orestes, and Athena eventually rescue him while the Furies become the Kindly Ones (*Eumenides*).

SOPHOCLES

Sophocles used to be thought of as the most truly classic of the three great poets, the incarnation of tragic wisdom, a poet poised by a kind of controlled passion between the untrimmed grandeur of Aeschylus and the literary inventiveness of Euripides. That is probably because Aristotle took *King Oedipus* as the perfect example of tragedy. In Sophocles he thought the art of tragic poetry had 'attained its nature' and ceased to be capable of genuine development. Aristotle was looking back over many years, and in view of the extravagance of later productions and compositions it is not surprising that the clarity and austerity of structure of Sophocles' plays attracted him by comparison. The structure of *King Oedipus* in particular is as lucid as the skeleton of a fish; indeed its lucid structure contributes to its force. But the structures of the seven plays of Sophocles we have differ remarkably, the verse style of Sophocles is mannered in iambic passages and in choral lyrics often compressed and exotic.

Sophocles lived from about 496 to 406 BC, that is, nearly all the years of the fifth century. At the age of about twenty-eight he won a festival competition against Aeschylus, in 468. In the year of his own death he paraded his chorus in mourning for the death of Euripides. He was comparatively rich and several times took part in public life. He treated the gods with respect, and several kinds of pain, affliction, and horror with extraordinary directness. It is therefore all the more interesting that in real life he played an important part in the introduction of Asclepius to Athens, which effectively means the founding of the first public hospital. In the theatre he was particularly interested in consequences, and in the fulfilment of prophecy. The common ending of Athenian children's stories or folk-tales was apparently 'and so the story came true.' With his vigorous and memorable poetry one must beware of identifying what the chorus chants or what is spoken in passionate irony or grief with the wisdom of the poet himself.

The momentum of any tragedy leads to the end of the action. In Sophocles' *Women of Trachis* this is five minutes after the end of the play, when Heracles will be consumed by fire and rise out of it unconsumed to be a god. In the *Philoctetes* the end of the action is rather far in the future and involves the fall of Troy. Reconciliation is to come; the audience need not think much about it; the pain of the hero's wound is an unforgettable impression. In the Ajax the suicide of the hero is in a sense the end of the action, and it comes early, but the force of the play is in the consequences and in his burial. The *Electra* of Sophocles, which corresponds to the second play of the *Oresteia*, is like a frame with action at the start and finish, but its centre and substance is a play about women to which the thought of action gives great tension. The greatest set-piece in it is a long, thrilling story about a death, which the audience knows is a lie, a deceiving fabrication.

> Look, here Orestes is, who by device
> was dead, and by device was saved alive.

What all these varied structures have in common is their restrained clarity of line; the clarity in turn permits a quantity of formal embroidery in speech. In the *Antigone*:

> She howls in the sharp
> tongue of that bitter bird which sees the void
> bed of its marriage emptied of all young.

And again in the same play:

> we were two sisters of two brothers robbed
> killed on one day each by the other's hand.

There is a certain strength in these verses that flows into them from the very marrow of tragic form, the marrow of folk-tales. Their likeness to Elizabethan verse, which I do not think I have exaggerated in translation, is striking and may derive from the same cause. Sophocles is also capable of great and moving simplicity, yet again for a similar reason. Here, for instance, in a prayer, a lyric chant from the *Electra*:

> O Furies, dreadful children of the gods,
> who see all murders of the unjustly dead
> and see all beds of marriage that are robbed,
> come now, help now, avenge our father killed.
> Send me my brother home. I can no longer
> carry the weight of grief I am to bear.

For two plays by Sophocles we have the admirable translations of W. B. Yeats, with some interesting music he commissioned for the choral lyrics. They are the two Oedipus plays, which with the *Antigone* are probably the greatest and to most people the most living of Sophocles' works. *King Oedipus* is an expression of such passionate rage and grief that in modern production control of pace becomes a problem, and usually Oedipus rants. *Oedipus at Colonus*, the death of the old man, goes to the heart of that mystery by which, in Greek subconscious belief, punishment, affliction, plague, blindness, and madness are intimately linked to the special protection and the dreadful blessing of the gods for victims: that is, to what becomes, by the degree of its affliction and degradation, taboo and then holy, sacred, a source of benefits. This is a mystery without mechanical solutions, but one on which social anthropology can cast much light.

> Make way for Oedipus. All people said
> 'That is a fortunate man';
> And now what storms are beating on his head?
> Call no man fortunate that is not dead.
> The dead are free from pain.

That is how *King Oedipus* ends, with that slow drumbeat. In another final chorus Yeats makes the same point even more generally. Rather interestingly it was perhaps not really written by Sophocles; it looks like a distillation of many dark sayings from here and there in the play, strung together as the conclusion of a late production. By that time, if not earlier, the audience expected a message, almost a sermon of tragic wisdom. It is almost equally interesting that Yeats, who was not to know the technical arguments against the authenticity of these lines, later adapted and re-used them as tragic wisdom of his own, as the end of a sequence of lyrics called 'A man young and old'. They are worth quoting here as among the most Sophoclean lines ever written in English, in spite of pedantic arguments. Some very great scholars have believed they are genuine.

Endure what life God gives and ask no longer span;
Cease to remember the delights of youth, travel-wearied aged man;
Delight becomes death-longing if all longing else be vain.

Even from that delight memory treasures so,
Death, despair, division of families, all entanglements of mankind grow,
As that old wandering beggar and these God-hated children know.

In the long echoing street the laughing dancers throng,
The bride is carried to the bridegroom's chamber through torch-light and tumultuous
    song;
I celebrate the silent kiss that ends short life or long.

Never to have lived is best, ancient writers say;
Never to have drawn the breath of life—never to have looked into the eye of day;
The second best's a gay good night and quickly turn away.

Sophocles would not have given his thoughts the romantic touches that Yeats gives to these lines. If there is a perfect Greek tragic line in English it is probably one by Webster: 'the friendless bodies of unburied men'. Yeats is at his best in the play *Oedipus at Colonus*, but that is a strange and wonderful place. The play centres on a holy wood near Colonus, where Sophocles was born. In that wood the gods grant Oedipus his death; beyond it he vanishes. Theseus, who accepted him, tells us that the grave where Oedipus is buried, in a place no man knows, will have an infallible protective power between Athens and its borders. A great deal is made of the trees themselves, the wood is almost a character.

Come praise Colonus' horses, and come praise
The wine-dark of the wood's intricacies,
The nightingale that deafens daylight there,
If daylight ever visit where,
Unvisited by tempest or by sun,
Immortal ladies tread the ground
Dizzy with harmonious sound,
Semele's lad a gay companion.

Yeats has transformed his original, but not without tact, and much less wildly than most translations. His trees are splendid.

> . . . The self-sown, self-begotten shape that gives
> Athenian intellect its mastery,
> Even the grey-leaved olive tree
> Miracle-bred out of the living stone;
> Nor accident of peace nor war
> Shall wither that old marvel, for
> The great grey-eyed Athene stares thereon.

What Sophocles stresses, and what means less to a modern audience, is that Athenian olive trees have no rival in Asia or in southern Greece, and that no enemy can destroy them. But when this play was produced the Spartans and their allies were all round the walls of Athens; they were visible, very close to the sacred wood of Colonus. Sophocles was dead by then, the play was posthumous. And of course the trees were cut down in the end.

He is supposed to have written about forty-one series of three plays, won competitions twenty-four times, and never come lower than second place. He said of himself that his early style was full of Aeschylean grandeur, his second period developed a style of his own, which he came to feel was artificial and without sweetness, but his last period was suppler, better fitted to individual characters. No plays of his first twenty-five years in the theatre survived; in the *Ajax*, and a few years later in the *Antigone* (probably 441 BC), he was already moving into his final mastery.

In a way the *Antigone* is also the tragedy of Creon. Because Antigone insists after the Theban civil war on more than one attempt to bury her brother, which in Greek feeling and in the speeches that Sophocles provides was her absolute natural duty, the tyrant Creon condemns her to death. His own destruction begins from that moment, and the end of the play is like an avalanche. It is not that we underestimate Creon; the thrilling figure of Antigone belongs to a world of absolutes and consequences no political man could be at home in; Sophocles had little sympathy with any other. If there was one supreme hour in the fifth century BC, perhaps it was that of the *Antigone* of Sophocles, which was composed while the Parthenon was being built.

EURIPIDES

Euripides was country-born as Aeschylus was, quite early in the fifth century, in about 485 BC; that means he was no more than ten years younger than Sophocles, and was eighty when he died in 406. It is tempting to think of his work as a third chapter, a new generation, and it is true that he entered the theatre when Aeschylus was already dead; his first success was in 441 BC, when he was forty-four. We have seventeen complete tragedies by him, one satyr play, which is worth a separate discussion, and one, the *Rhesus*, wrongly attributed to him. It is as well to remember that this comparatively huge mass of poetry represents his popularity among poets, professional scholars, and teachers of the late Greek world, long after the collapse of Athens. He wrote something like ninety-two plays, but in his lifetime he won only four theatrical competitions. All the same, he is wonderful as a dramatist, full of originality at every stage of his development. His plays are remarkable for their range of tones and the gleeful inventiveness, which morose critics call cynical artificiality, of their construction. He is the master of the unexpected, and the building-blocks he uses are not so much characters as set scenes like the recognition scene, the scene of self-sacrifice, the furious quarrel, and so on. In his last plays the surprises are often hectic and elaborate, although the greatest of all his plays, the *Bacchae*, is the last or one of the last he ever wrote, and its construction is bold and simple, its colouring here and there Aeschylean.

The *Hippolytus* (428 BC) is dramatically exciting, very beautiful and harmonious, and tragical. It is one of his most satisfying plays, and one of his few successful ones with the contemporary audience. The hero is acceptably naïve.

> O Goddess, I bring you what I have made:
> a twisted wreath picked from pure meadow ground,
> where no shepherd ever pastures his flock,
> no steel has come, only the bee in spring
> passes across the untrodden meadows,
> Virginity keeps them with sprinkling streams.

The last of these lines I find untranslatable in verse. It means really that Shame, or Respect, the personified quality of youthful respect and restraint, which carries strong implications of virginity, is the gardener of the meadow, sprinkling it with the dew of rivers or streams. Maybe the lack of a precise English equivalent for the Greek *Aidōs* debars us from the world of Hippolytus. Here he is paying his tribute to virginal Artemis, and neglecting Aphrodite, who contrives his downfall through the hot passion of his stepmother, and then his death through his father's curse. In its terrible and effective alterations of tone, this play remains in tension with itself until the final scenes, one between Artemis and Hippolytus, in which the goddess speaks for the first time, and then a death scene which occurs uniquely in Greek tragedy on the stage.

> I shall be firm, I am dying, father,
> Cover my face up swiftly in your robe.

Euripides' other great masterwork about women's passion is his *Medea*, a tragedy so terrible that it can end only with the famous sorceress flying away in a chariot drawn by dragons. She has murdered her children out of a passionate hatred which is the dark side of rejected love, and out of insulted honour. The verses of this play are so convincing that it becomes easy to enter into these scenes even today; for whatever reason, the murderess and sorceress is more alive than the unhappy male characters in the play. Some of her speeches have that curious ring of modernity with which Euripides is sometimes rather mistakenly

THE *IPHIGENIA IN TAURIS* BY EURIPIDES. Scene from a vase made in Campania, about 330–320 BC. The stage building is shown with projecting wings, architecturally elaborated. The one at the left serves as the temple of Artemis, in which her statue is seen; the one at the right, the house of the priestess Iphigenia who emerges to speak to her brother Orestes and his companion Pylades who have come to steal the statue.

credited. It is only an uninhibited and passionate reasoning, but the passion, not the argument, is fundamental. Euripides picks the arguments and the point of view of each character with cool deliberation, and carries them through with great dramatic power. The theatre demands freshness; old stories demand intellectual versatility. But a passionate coherence and a passionate understanding of life underlie *Medea*.

In 415, the year of the expedition against Syracuse, the high tide of Athenian power-hunger and also a time of increasing superstitious fear, Euripides produced three tragedies on the Trojan war. The first showed the youth of Paris and the seed of destruction, the second dealt with Palamedes, the inventive Greek, but we know little of its plot. The third is the *Trojan Women*, a succession of tragic episodes under the walls of fallen Troy. In verse that differs with brilliant technical effect from one episode to another, Euripides delivers a series of hammer blows. They are linked only by black lamentation, with a faint spark of human compassion from the Greek herald, and a few strangely nostalgic lines about the holy land of Greece. Sometimes the magnificence of language puts fire and brimstone into the air, sometimes the formal clang of verses lends a sharpness, sometimes rhetorical patterns overspill like waterfalls.

> O throne of Earth and thou whose seat is earth
> hard to be known whatever thou mayest be,
> necessity of nature, mind of man,
> Zeus I pray to thee, who doest lead mankind
> in justice by a road not to be blamed . . .
>
> O mortal fool who will pull cities down,
> temples and holy places of the dead,
> and make all those a desert, and then die . . .
>
> To bring her where she shall be put on board . . .
>
> Lead me, who walked soft-footed once in Troy,
> lead me a slave where earth fails sheer away
> by rocky edges, let me drop and die
> withered away with tears. Never say now
> that happy was happy until we die.

The cumulative effect of the *Trojan Women* is strong. This is not the formalized story of a legendary prince, it is more like history, more like the experience of life.

The *Bacchae*, the punishment of King Pentheus by Dionysus disguised as his own priest and then terribly revealed, may possibly be an adaptation from a lost work of Aeschylus. It is the most unforgettable play Euripides wrote, its poetry is towering; unlike the *Trojan Women*, if it had not been written it would have been unimaginable.

> I bring you him who put to ridicule
> me and my mysteries. Take your vengeance.
> And as he spoke one flash of dreadful light
> struck at the earth and struck against heaven.
> The air was silent. The wooded ravine
> held all its leaves silent. No creature called.

This language, which occurs just in the moment before the awful climax of the play, when Pentheus will be torn to pieces by his own mother and the other women, is nothing if not dramatic. The most dramatic verses and the most effective set-pieces in Greek tragedy are spoken by messengers; they describe action elsewhere. Tragic poetry is in this also an extension of Homeric poetry.

Tragic Poetry (Conclusion)

In the *Bacchae* of Euripides the chorus hardly speaks at all; it virtually confines its expressions to song. Is that a modern, that is, a late Euripidean device? Is it because he can no longer bear the intrusions of the chorus? In the earliest tragedies and in all Aeschylus, the chorus had an all-important function. It was as if the first actors had only just stepped out of its ranks, and lacked confidence. Even where the usual characterization of the chorus as old citizens, full of their proverbial wisdom and hopelessness, serves a purpose of mere contrast or transition between speeches, as similar utterances sometimes do in the choral lyric poetry of Pindar, their presence was significant to the unfolding of the plot. They are like those black-dressed women near a small harbour or those black-dressed peasants around a market square, who give sudden murder or the vengeance of the gods its social meaning. The tragic action fixes them like a photographer's flashlight.

> Many the transformations of the gods:
> and many things they judge as we do not:
> and what appeared was not what was fulfilled;
> the god found a way through the unlikely.
> And that was how this matter concluded.

These lines occur as conclusion of a number of Euripidean tragedies, including his *Alcestis*, and they do represent the stupefied, reverent, and somewhat dark attitudes of the chorus to events. One should be careful not to identify any chorus with the tragic poet, although there are times, for instance late on in *King Oedipus*, when they certainly speak for the audience. But the chorus can have many different functions. Sophocles varies the use of his chorus as he does the construction of his plays. In the *Prometheus* the chorus are Airs, Winds, divine beings. At the end of the *Agamemnon* they threaten violence. In another play they are *Suppliant Women*. Euripidean choral lyrics are often exotic and simple at the same time. Their geography and some of their other allusions are bizarre. Aeschylus is a great lyric poet in a more authoritative sense; he is Pindar's contemporary. But throughout its development the Greek tragic chorus was most austerely restrained, compared to later interpretations and revivals. It can never now be recreated. Even if all its conventions were rediscovered and re-enacted, they would not be conventional to us.

The text of tragedies was fixed by being written down and learnt by heart, though actors' interpolations do exist in tragedies, and much worse producers' interpolations. A stage direction survives from a late production of the *Agamemnon*: 'Enter the chariots, the army, and the spoils of Troy'. That is not the style of Greek tragic poetry, which was lavish only in messenger speeches, in conjuring the imagination of an audience, and in certain choral lyrics. The plots were given a new direction, a new meaning, quite boldly by every new treatment, and as much by Aeschylus and Sophocles as by Euripides.

The bones of the verses are what today we call rhetoric. Whenever we read the dialogue of tragedy, with its line-for-line correspondence and apparently artificial figures of speech, we should remember that this imitates a reality. Properly read aloud, it ought to sound like a quarrel between fishwives: I suppose I mean Greek fishwives. Both the continuity of the underlying rhythm and the sharp breaks, the mutual parodies and ironies, are precisely real. The fact that later teachers offered to classify every syntactic figure and every device of argument or persuasion should not affect our views. But ancient tragic poetry is rhetorical only in a subtle sense, and each of the great poets is his own rhetorician. The day of common rhetorical rules mechanically applied began in the fourth century BC, with its dead characters, its foolish plots, and its wooden tragic poetry.

A few marginal elements in tragic production in the fifth century are still important enough to merit some notice. One which is quickly disposed of has to do with the theatre of Dionysus at Athens. Leaving aside all the arguments about the raised stage and the stone house for actors and the high places where gods appeared, all of which are much later than people used to believe, we should consider a great rock that stuck out into the acting space until it was in the end removed on architectural grounds. How could the Athenians have permitted it? They accepted it tranquilly, they adapted it, and used it. It became the rock of Prometheus and other famous crags. They used it because it was to hand, just as their fathers would have done, acting round a cart in the *agora*. Of the original stones of the theatre of Aeschylus' time at Athens there are fewer than seven that still survive. They are hard to find and hard to recognize; only their simplicity makes them moving.

But in the course of the fifth century at Athens there arose an art of scene-painting which two or three centuries later, and perhaps elsewhere, was to produce elaborate perspective painting. It spread to the walls of houses, the house of Alcibiades first, and, like Oxford ragwort, which died out in the gardens, but was found flourishing centuries later in the walls, this new art of scene-painting survived a long time. Its theatrical origin explains the continual theatrical allusions in the wall-paintings of Pompeii, where fully developed perspective painting was several times imitated.

Satyr Plays

It is tempting to call the satyr plays simply pastoral plays, but they are not about nymphs and shepherds in idyllic countryside. They are usually set in wild countryside, with wild satyrs for a chorus, amoral, humorous, and pathetic creatures with human weaknesses for drink, sex, and the safety of their own skins. The chorus leader seems to be their father, but they are always lost, always in search of their master Dionysus. Otherwise there seem to be no rules about the plot. They receive the stolen fire from Prometheus, or they greet the infant Perseus, born in a chest floating out to sea, or the Cyclops has them as servants in the cave where he entertains Odysseus. The verse is somewhere between tragic and comic; it has a comic enchantment without being as boisterous as Aristophanes. The custom was to present one satyr play with three tragedies, and it is

SCENE FROM A SATYR PLAY, on an Athenian vase of about 470–460 BC. That these are not real satyrs is shown by the loin-cloth to which are fastened their tails and phalli, and the piper and bystander at the right indicate that this illustrates a stage production. The satyrs are carrying pieces of a throne which they are assembling, and we have the title of a satyr play by Aeschylus called *Thalamopoioi*, which might be roughly translated 'The Interior Decorators'.

very likely that they preserve something of the origins of Greek dramatic performance. Tragic solemnity could hardly have coexisted with an animal chorus.

The only complete satyr play we have is the *Cyclops* of Euripides, which is an interlude half the length of a tragedy, with tragic, comic, obscene, and religious elements curiously combined.

> I on the prow held a great fitted beam,
> while my sons were labouring at the oars
> whitening grey sea-water into foam:
> and all this in search of you my lord.
> We had sailed close in to the South Cape
> when a wind out of the sun's eye hit the beam
> and threw us up on the Etnaean rock
> among the one-eyed sons of the sea-god
> the murderous Cyclopes of desert rocks.

It is obvious at once that this kind of verse is intended as simple entertainment. If one spotted a *double entendre* in this or some other passage, one would not feel ashamed of oneself. Later, Euripides shows a flair for comedy of character at the same time. The Cyclops defends his cannibalism and his way of life.

Wealth, little man, is the god of the wise.
The rest is fine words and pretentiousness.
I bid my father's headlands of the sea
go fly away. Why should I pretend?
I don't fear Zeus' thunderbolt, my friend,
I don't see Zeus is stronger than I am.
That's all I care about; you want to know why?
Then listen. When he pours the rain down
I have a dry shelter under this rock.
I dine on a roast calf, I dine on game,
I lie back and I wet my belly well,
drink milk by the bucket, screw my cloak,
and make thunder as Zeus makes thunder.
And when the Thracian wind comes with the snow
I wrap my body up in pelts of beasts,
and make my fire up, snow doesn't worry me.
Earth produces grass by necessity
whether it likes or not, and fattens my flock.
I sacrifice to no god but myself
and to my belly here, to this great god.

The Cyclops is preposterous, and meets an unhappy end, of course, but the poet does feel some sympathy. At least he gives the Cyclops some good lines and some interesting arguments. It may be that the sudden excitement of the sophistic movement, the professional arguers and perverse philosophers who arrived in Athens during Euripides' lifetime, is nicely caught in this spirited composition. Plato is full of jokes and parodies; I do not think we are a thousand miles here from the kind of argument he deals with.

It is a pity we have no complete satyr play by Aeschylus. The fragments of his *Net-Fishers*, in which the satyrs fish up Danae and the baby Perseus, are very promising. It is hard to reconstruct the plot, but the characters include a king's brother called Net, and an old man of the island, possibly a god, just possibly the old Silenus, father of the satyrs. who will have owned the physical net and claimed what it netted. The island is Seriphos, and the character called Net is a traditional element in the story, which originally had no satyrs in it. He was the fisherman, and Aeschylus adopted him. The pleasantest surviving passage is a lyric fragment where the satyrs entice the child: 'Come along darling' (they use a Doric diminutive). There follows a whole line of that 'popopopo' noise which is still part of the Greek repertory of sounds. 'Come along quick to the children. Come nicely to my nursing hands, my dear. You will have weasels to play with and fawns and baby hedgehogs, and sleep in the same bed as your mother and father.' These words are not as innocent as they appear: Silenus appoints himself as father without consulting Danae. We know from another line that the baby was amazed by the erection which was part of a satyr's stage dress. 'What a cocklover the little fellow is', says the satyr. Unfortunately there is little more to be done with the fragments of this play; we must just hope that one day the goddess of papyri is merciful and we get the rest of it.

Comedy

INTRODUCTION

The main surviving mass of ancient Greek comedy begins only with Aristophanes, who was born within a few years of the mid fifth century, long after the great tragedians and too late to tell us much about the riotous early days of the comic chorus, before the state took it over. The consolation of this is the youth and zest of his work in the twenties of the century, and the fact that he worked on with great originality until 388 BC. In the early plays of Aristophanes, traditional Athenian comedy, the Old Style, as it came to be called, had already reached its full development; it has, as Aristotle remarked of tragedy, 'attained its nature'. The chorus was all-important, and the revelation of its dress and dances and music as the *Wasps* or the *Wine-bottles* or the *Clouds* or the *Caterpillars* was central to the competition. Not all the choruses were animal or even precisely humorous. The *Knights* and the *Towns of Attica* will not have been played entirely for laughs.

The comic theatre in the fifth century was directly political in a way that tragedy was not; its jokes had a bite and were often meant to be taken seriously. Aristophanes used his chorus at a certain moment in the play to address the audience directly; sometimes the chorus itself, the Birds or Clouds or Wasps or Frogs or whatever, seems to be speaking to us, sometimes the poet himself speaks through them. The connection of the Athenian political theatre with direct democracy is obvious. Its imaginative devices are bold and its characters are very plain-spoken. The Aristophanes who speaks in Plato's *Symposium* is surely very close to the real man, but the same cannot be said for the Socrates in Aristophanes' *Clouds*. The style of parody of individuals in the theatre is simple, vivid, and full of glee. It is not naturalistic.

All the same, real Athenians could be parodied by name or mostly thinly disguised, and plays could even be named after them. We know that the politicians resented this, which is hardly surprising, but there is no evidence that they ever managed to stamp it out under the fifth-century democracy. Maybe laughter really is like the crackling of thorns under a pot: hard to stamp out, and kicking only scatters it. Aristophanes attacks with joyful accuracy anyone and anything that strikes his fancy. As for his own political views, clearly enough they were democratic and patriotic. He was devoted to the Athenian democracy, and even more so to the comic theatre, perhaps the most characteristic of all its institutions. It was never a 'theatre of the common man'; it was nothing so safe. It was alive, part of a real democracy.

Comedy had its solemn as well as its political side. The plots were topsy-turvy. Right deserted to the side of Wrong, you could fly to heaven on a beetle, but

CLAY FIGURES OF COMIC ACTORS, both masked, and the one on the right wearing the characteristic short padded dress with phallus attached. Fourth century BC. These are from Attica, which is the principal source, but the types are met all over the Greek world and the masks shown on these and later figures can often be matched closely with those defined by the second-century AD writer Pollux for use on the Attic stage.

the bawdy irreverence with which gods and men were treated was somehow set in a frame, it was 'only a joke'. Serious things like peace, the city of Athens and her goddess and her physical beauty, were handled gently and beautifully. It is the few nostalgic verses, and those haunting lyrics in which poetry is suddenly set free from the comic action, which one never forgets. Aristophanes intended to give pleasure in as many ways as possible, and he still does so. Some of his allusive jokes that were meant to go fast raise only a gentle smile on the tired faces of scholars. Some of the puns and obscenities are only as memorable as their modern equivalent, for better and worse. But Aristophanes probably intended only his lyrics to be learnt by heart in Athens. Unfortunately they have never been successfully translated; almost no Aristophanes has been.

The greatest comic poet we know much about before Aristophanes is Cratinus. They overlapped; young Aristophanes attacked old Cratinus as a drunk who had given up poetry. Cratinus replied the next year, 423 BC, with a play in which the poet deserts his wife Comedy to go whoring after boys called Wine-bottles and a slut called Drunkenness. In that year's competition, Cratinus came first, and the

Clouds of Aristophanes came second. Since it was in the *Clouds* that Aristophanes attacked Socrates, one may hope that Socrates took it in the same spirit as Cratinus. We are told that the basic conception of plays was Cratinus' strong point. There is little to add except his vigorous obscenity, compared to which Aristophanes was a pale writer, and his uninhibited attacks on Pericles and his mistress Aspasia. It is probably true that vigour and obscenity and personal invective declined as the century wore out, though we shall see there are some exceptions.

The nearest contemporaries to Aristophanes in his working lifetime were Eupolis, who started producing comedies in 429 BC and died young in the course of the war, by drowning at sea, and a comic poet called Plato, younger than either of them, at work from about 410 to some time after 390. Eupolis presented Dionysus in the armed forces, subject to tough discipline, and in the *Towns of Attica* a scheme that was both solemn and humorous, and had a huge influence on Aristophanes' *Frogs*. In the competitive theatre of those years, it was inevitable that each year's plays, thirsting for an original idea, should often find it in last year's successes. Aristophanes and Eupolis shared some targets, and Aristophanes had already denounced Eupolis for plagiarism. In the *Towns of Attica* dead Athenians in the underworld argue about who should be sent back from the dead to put Athens in order; the Towns of Attica seem to be the chorus. In the *Frogs* the dispute is only over putting the tragic theatre in order.

The *Frogs* embodies a feature of comedy that is somewhat hard to explain: its parodying of tragedies, sometimes too self-consciously, as if comedy has to be a poor cousin of tragedy. Well, perhaps it was so. It is also true that the audience was the same for both, and the festivals came to be the same. Comedy was founded on mockery, and the stage mocked itself. But of all the elements in comic verse that meant most to an ancient audience, the one that most seldom amuses us now is the parody of tragedy—with the shining exception of the *Frogs*, which can be very funny indeed.

ARISTOPHANES

In the course of his career, Aristophanes spans the first two of the three phases or styles of Greek comedy. We must leave Epicharmus in Sicily out of account; Sicily and Athens in his day were separate planets. But starting in the twenties with vigorous and farcical burlesque, intermingled with savage onslaughts on politicians, he moved through the sadder, and in places more solemn, schemes of comedies such as the *Frogs* (405 BC) to the revival of comedy after the fall of Athens. If we believe that tragedy never did flower again, that may be because the fall of the city coincided with the deaths of Euripides and Sophocles, at about eighty and ninety years old. Comedy did reflower, perhaps because Aristophanes and the comic poet Plato survived.

Of the plays we have, the very first is like a bucket of cold water in the face.

It not only sounds, it trumpets the great themes of comic poetry: sex, life on the farm, the good old days, the nightmare of politics, the oddities of religion, the strange manners of the town. It is called the *Acharnians* (425 BC). The *Knights*, in the next year, adds to the old mixture some stern moralizing, some furious invective, and some lyrical patriotic politics. The quarrel with Cleon had begun earlier, in a severe onslaught in 426, in the *Babylonians*, Aristophanes' second play, which alas has not survived. Cleon was the leader of those who had wanted a year earlier to massacre the people of Mytilene, and he nearly brought that off. Aristophanes in the *Babylonians* showed cities of the Athenian League as slaves grinding at the mill.

We cannot avoid taking an interest in Aristophanes' attitude to slavery. Laughter without pity probably does not exist, but Aristophanes certainly introduces comic slaves. Yet racial comedy is not involved, because anyone could get enslaved, and it is noticeable that he shows his slaves with humanity, and with no more indignity than other characters. What he really hates, apart from such scum of the earth as Cleon, is charlatans and pretentiousness and pseudo-reform. But he differs from modern satiric writers in having a strong and passionately held moral standard, rooted in a society that he profoundly loves. Also, of course, in being a poet, perhaps a great poet, with a mind as open as daylight. Combine all these contradictions together and add a comic genius, and you will have Aristophanes, but only in the fifth century. What went to produce him is so many elements, so highly specific, they can never again be repeated. The most important is direct democracy in a traditional society.

His early comedies were political, his latest began to be social. In the second phase of Athenian comedy, to which Aristophanes is virtually our only witness, the chorus withered away to some musical interludes, plot knitted together into coherence, and a kind of realism took over. The early plots had been as wild as English pantomimes used to be. They were terribly spirited. The society they showed was diverse and in numerous ways eccentric: the overlap of generations, given the speed of change at that time, and the intermingling of types when Athens was under siege, produced plenty of paradoxes and comic fireworks. But in the fourth century something smoother, more like a bourgeoisie, began to emerge. It was mirrored, not very kindly, in the comic theatre. It was bourgeois in its morality, in its limited views of things, in its tastes and ambitions. No doubt such people can be justified by history. Aristophanes would not have liked them, nor would his Acharnian peasant. His *Wealth* (388 BC) reflects only the transition. What was coming was comedy as the modern world has known it, beginning with Menander.

As an imaginative artist, Aristophanes was fully developed by the end of the twenties, and already in *Peace* (421) he was driven to wild fantasies to express his longing for war to end. In 414 the heroes of the *Birds* are two Athenians who despair of the city altogether. He makes the point lightly, but make it he does.

> We're flying away from home with both our feet,
> not that we hate that city, not at all,
> that great city happy by nature
> and general provider for all men.
> But the crickets sit singing on the branches
> for one or two months; Athens does it for ever,
> singing away their lives in the lawcourts.

Life at Athens being no longer worth living, they go to consult a mythical hero who was turned into a bird. The plot of the play is the building of the city of the birds. One of its chief pleasures is a very long aria, a long lyric poem in a series of attractive metres sung by one character, the hoopoe, who calls the other birds with some bird-mimicry such as possibly a bird-snarer might use. Apart from the *Wasps*, who are melodious in Vaughan Williams but less so in Aristophanes, this is the first animal chorus we have from Aristophanes. The bird mimicry is remarkable. It is untranslatable, of course, because a lot of it depends on onomatopoeic words in Greek. For gaiety and lightness of touch, Aristophanes perhaps never outdid that scene.

The birds set up a blockade to cut off sacrifices from earth to the gods. The play ends as comedies were supposed to end, with a celebration. The gods make peace with the birds and mankind, and we have a marriage hymn with prayers to Zeus, shouts of victory, and the play disappearing in a shower of fireworks. At the festival of that year, the winning play was called the *Revellers*, this was second, and the third was called the *Solitary*; it was another escapist play. The *Birds* is crammed with comic inventions, including Prometheus hiding under an umbrella from the other gods, Iris captured in mid air by the birds, a Thracian god of extreme barbarity, and a poet who wants to be turned into a nightingale.

For a really funny play by modern standards we can turn to 411 BC, to the *Lysistrata*. By this time Aristophanes' despair about altering the course of events seems to have set hard. What he proposes is a conspiracy of women to refuse sex with their men until the men agree to make peace. This has to be world-wide within the Greek world, and the priestess of Athena, who seems to be based on someone real, has organized it. The characterization of women from all over Greece is hilariously funny, and so are the details of the plot as it unfolds. It is one of the few ancient comedies that entrances modern audiences. It is also the earliest in which one may suspect a touch of compassion in the rather vigorous treatment handed out to people. When the old men are grovelling, there is one case where one is almost sorry for the poor beast. Aristophanic comedy usually has a string or two strings of episodes in which various characters get attacked or seen off; one is not usually sorry for them. Maybe *Lysistrata* is close to the beginning of a new sense of laughing through tears, which made Menander possible and the old style impossible. We need not necessarily see this as a change for the better.

If we do not, we can be pleased that most of *Lysistrata* is splendidly heartless.

It is not Aristophanes' only women's play, but the only one in which they are really heroes. The other two are the *Thesmophoriazousae*, from the same year as *Lysistrata*, which is almost entirely based on jokes about Euripides, and *Women in Parliament*, an extravaganza of 392 BC, the year of an alliance between Athens and Sparta. Women take over the state in it and announce communism. The plot is incoherent because it lacks political drive: Aristophanes does no more than toy with his themes, and the political humour which once generated such alarming fantasies has sunk to a whimsical level. The *Lysistrata* is stronger because it deals with impossibilities as if they were real; it belongs to a year in which something was still possible, maybe everything.

The *Frogs*, in 405 BC, is in one way the saddest play of Aristophanes that we still have, because the only thing it puts right is the theatre. But there is no lack of brilliance in its verbal texture, and no weakness of construction. It does raise problems, since unless there were two choruses, which would be unique in our experience, then either the Frogs themselves or the choirs of the Blest never appear. The essential plot of the *Frogs* is the descent of Dionysus, a god with many human weaknesses, to the underworld, mocked by the Frogs as he learns to row in Charon's boat; he is searching for a great tragic poet, and chooses between Aeschylus and Euripides by a contest in which they destroy one another's lines with parody and mockery. This process is for once extremely funny, and (even more unusually) instructive, since it tells us something about the texture and technique of tragic verse. Still, the tendency of mockery is to suppress extremes, and the view of poetry that Aristophanes takes is too safe to be sound.

He does take his own calling as a poet most seriously, in a way unfamiliar in our times, but as a comic poet in the theatre of Athens his responsibility is greater than that of modern writers. He says 'We must indeed say things that are good, because to little children it is the schoolmaster who speaks, but to those past puberty it is poets'. From his very first play, which was about modern versus old-fashioned education, at least down to the *Frogs*, which contains strong moral views thinly disguised, Aristophanes writes as if the lines I have quoted here are important to him. Aeschylus wins the contest in the underworld, Sophocles being too peaceable to take part. At the very end we suddenly have these words:

> The graceful thing
> is not to sit
> by Socrates and talk
> and cast aside the Muse
> and all the great matter
> of the tragic art.

He wants more poetry and fewer philosophers; particularly he wants more Aeschylus. Dare one say he was wrong? Would Socrates say so?

His last surviving play, *Wealth*, was produced in 388 BC. Wealth is notoriously blind, and gives his benefits to the wrong people, so Apollo shows him how blindness can be cured by Asclepius at Athens. Wealth does recover his eyesight, but the resulting redistribution of money produces comic confusion. The old rich woman loses her gigolo, because now he has enough without her; Hermes reports chaos among the gods; Wealth gets enthroned in his home of the good old days, the national treasury inside the west end of the Parthenon. This play has no choral lyrics and hardly any chorus, its arguments are in social and philosophic, not in political terms, the humour is more often low than obscene, and even the most farcical episodes begin to be handled more gently.

MENANDER

Comedy never seems to have hardened or died on its feet as tragedy did, but the next substantial glimpse that we get of Athenian comedy in good health is many years after the deaths of Aristophanes and the comic poet Plato. A generation had passed, and few alive had any serious recollection of the fifth century, when Menander was born in 342 BC. He lived through the reign of Alexander and its aftermath. He was a baby when the freedom of Greece was lost, and by the time he was twenty Alexander was dead. His Athens was cosmopolitan, crowded, full of foreign business. But it could not take its fate into its own hands or alter its future. Even in private life fate was something that was done to you; it was what happened more than what you did. Great cities had their Lady Luck as well as individuals; in a world in which everything was uncertain, people concentrated on their private lives. Philosophy was some consolation; it implied an order of a kind.

This state of things produced a comedy of manners, with social targets and an action of limited consequences. It depended on surprise piled on surprise by the turning wheel of fortune, and the guiding genius of the comic poet came to include some of the skills of the modern thriller-writer. Writing for the theatre became a sophisticated, technical matter. It was no longer a mystery or a matter of genius. And yet what was produced is astonishing. The numerous papyrus texts of Menander recovered in the last hundred, even in the last thirty, years, have heavily reinforced his reputation. He is funnier, faster, and stronger altogether than scholars used to expect. It is much better to emphasize heavily the intervening darkness between him and Aristophanes, to forget regret, and to see Menander's theatrical poetry as a new-created world. His work has not been successfully translated. He was a poet after all, and his subtly modulated verse demands more understanding of poetry than it has been offered.

One could hardly go beyond the mythic hero and the comic type after all, in a theatre in which masks were still worn, though the masks were more realistic now, and so were the clothes and settings. Still, it is surprising how much can be done with type-cast characters. One may question whether Agatha Christie in our own times ever used anything else, though she was no poet, and not so great an artist as Menander.

His world is one in which soldiers thought to be killed in some Asian battle turn out to be 'living and saved as never before', thus confusing people's hopes to inherit. A chest is fished out of the sea, the shipwrecked come to land, or a treasure gets dug up in a field. Intrigues between lovers and confidential slaves produce intricate crossed lines. Slaves turn out to be free-born, kidnapped in childhood. Families are reunited, and improper marriages become suddenly possible. The love interest is not dominant, though; it is largely secondary to the relationships and fortunes of the inner family, and a young man may as easily

THE NEW COMEDY POET MENANDER (who died about 292 BC). Mosaic portrait found in a Roman villa of the fourth century AD near the main town on the island of Lesbos (Mytilene). Other panels showed figures from the poet's plays, similar to that found at Pompeii and illustrated on p. 440. These may derive from illustrations to manuscripts, possibly of Hellenistic date.

fall for a whore as for a character capable of a permanent romantic link. This is one inherited convention among others.

In the *Shield* Fortune herself appears after the first scenes to explain to the audience what really is going on. This too is a convention simply accepted and objectively treated. Choice between the delights of foreseeing and those of surprise seems to have been a consuming problem in Menander's theatre. At any rate the end of every play could be foreseen: it would be happy. It might recall ancient comedy by being a mildly riotous celebration. The *Difficult Man* ends with dancing to flute music at a picnic near the cave of Pan, who in that play represents the contriving and benevolent divine powers. In fact this pleasant ending, after which there is only an invitation to applause, is the most memorable feature of the *Difficult Man*. If one wants to laugh aloud one would do better to delve among the fragments for a scene of divine possession, possibly false, observed by two terrified Greeks. The play is *Theophoroumenē*, 'The Possessed Woman'.

Some of the plots are elaborately complicated; it would be hard to recount them in less length than that of the plays. They are like dances, with contrasted couples, ill suited and well suited, and a variety of interlocking opposites. The conclusions are also dance-like, shadow-footed, magical in a sense in which Aristophanes was not. Everything mysteriously falls out just right, at the very last moment and in spite of numerous unlucky strokes and incompetent intrigues.

All the same, the harmonious confusion and the mild violence within the magic circle of Menander's theatrical effects are meant to keep out the black outside world, just as the philosophers of escape tried to keep it out. It is even probable that Menander and Epicurus, who were exactly the same age, had done their Athenian military training together. There are touches of Epicurean pleasure and gentleness here and there in Menander. As for the outer world, we have very few dates for individual works of Menander, so it is hard to trace any development in his poetry or his invention, or any more precise relation with the events of history. His poetry is just a patch of sunlight moving over the grass. The famous humanity was only one of his qualities, but the more detail of plots and counterplots we recover, the more meaning his urbane and somewhat sweet-tasting philosophic remarks take on.

One very odd element in Menander's plots is moral reformation. Of course he inherits a morality from fifth-century comedy, in which characters get taught a lesson or won round by comic means. But he wants to philosophize and moralize these conversions, although at the same time he wants to characterize his people more fully and realistically. The result is a character like the Difficult Man, beautifully observed, perfectly convincing, who suddenly sprouts a lot of noble philosophic thoughts. The robust action is not enough: the old gentleman has just fallen down a well after all, and being rescued is what converted him. He still has to reason it out in noble sentiments. One is tempted to say that in the world of Menander poetry belongs to children; for those past puberty it is the moral philosopher who speaks.

In another play a shepherd and a charcoal-burner quarrel over a baby they find lying about abandoned with its few little treasures; they go to an old man for decision, but little does he know the baby is his grandchild; his daughter got into trouble at a night festival and threw away the resulting baby for shame. This is only one tiny area of an unbelievable web of intrigues; in the end the man who fathered the baby at the night festival turns out to be the girl's husband. One can sympathize with the German nineteenth-century scholar who remarked that the most immoral feature of such immoral plays as this was their happy endings. The Lord of Misrule had not lost all influence over the Greek comic theatre; the absurdity of the story-line of these plays, as well as their elegance of construction, was intended to give delight, and so it does.

A COMIC PRODUCTION WITH *PHLYAX* ACTORS (probably so-called for their padded costumes), on a vase made in Apulia about 375 BC. They resemble Athenian comic actors in their dress, masks, and prominent phalli. They do not act in a formal theatre but on a low wooden stage, with lean-to roof and steps up from the auditorium, seen here in profile. To judge from the vases the subjects were comic versions of Greek myth and some everyday situations recalling Athenian Middle and New Comedy. Here the old centaur Chiron (but shown as human) is helped on to the stage by Xanthias. Comic nymphs watch (top right), and standing at the right is a 'normal' youth, perhaps the stage-manager. This is a theatrical genre peculiar to South Italy in the fourth century BC. See also p. 443.

The Results of Comedy

Without comedy, without the long development and the transformations of comedy at Athens, there would have been no invention of pastoral poetry or the fishermen's poetry that corresponds to it. The romance, and the novel that arose in the end from plays and romances, have their taproot in the comic theatre. They derive from Euripides as well, but only because comedy had shown how Euripides could be adapted and travestied. The oddest of all the survivals of Greek comedy was through its offshoot as Latin comedy, in the revived Latin and vernacular comedy of the renaissance. That line of descent is much more direct and easier to trace than the rediscovery of tragedy, which happened at many removes, partly through the blood-soaked exaggerations of Seneca, exaggerated still further in translation by Jasper Heywood, who became a Jesuit, was arrested, and died mad.

There is a sense in which Menander's comedies, filtered as they were through

Plautus and Terence, gave us our fundamental ideas about what human beings are like: not only through the refined and noble sentiments which spread like bindweed through the whole literate world, in books of sayings and copybooks of every kind, but our idea of urban man, and civilized man, and his limitations. That is surely because of Menander's apparent interest in individuals and his real handling of types. As the life of individuals and the ambition of families became newly interesting to the literate classes in the late Middle Ages, it was natural that ancient comedy should be their model. Menander was part of the culture of St Paul; his unassuming nobility, his humanist maxims, above all his universality and vague compassion had melted into the moral atmosphere. The urbanity and the liberty turn out to be inseparable. Medieval and Byzantine satire are the steam screaming out of an engine. Horatian satire is quiet and deadly; it derives from Athens, and runs through Voltaire and Diderot, nearly down to our own times. In Byzantium, what comedy could there be? Only a venomous courtly hissing, or a popular comedy so low it would escape notice: something like the shadow-theatre of Karaghiozis. Admirable as that is, it belongs to the comedies of the 'volunteers', before comic poetry became an art. One of the bravest, most inspired steps the Athenian democracy ever took was to make comedy a state event: for that to happen comedy had to exist already, and its audience had to exist.

Further Reading

Albin Lesky's *History of Greek Literature* (London, 1966) discusses all the Greek theatrical writers and the general problems that they raise. He is useful even when one disagrees with him. His *Greek Tragic Poetry* (Yale, 1983) goes into considerable detail about every play. More challenging is Brian Vickers, *Towards Greek Tragedy* (London, 1973), which uses both anthropological and Shakespearean material to illustrate the nature of myth and of suffering in tragedy.

A. D. Trendall and T. B. L. Webster, *Illustrations of Greek Drama* (London, 1971), has replaced all earlier works of this kind and presents the evidence of visual art extremely clearly. A. W. Pickard-Cambridge, *The Dramatic Festivals of Athens*, (2nd edn., revised by J. Gould and D. M. Lewis, Oxford, 1968) is a reliable guide to its subject.

O. Taplin, in *The Stagecraft of Aeschylus* (Oxford, 1977), has opened a new and much clearer way of reading and understanding Aeschylus; his *Greek Tragedy in Action* (London, 1978) effectively brings out the significance of performance and spectacle in Attic tragedy. There are particularly good books on Sophocles: Karl Reinhardt's *Sophocles* (English trans., Oxford Blackwell, 1978); *Sophocles: an Interpretation* by R. P. Winnington-Ingram (Cambridge, 1980) and B. M. W. Knox's *The Heroic Temper: Studies in Sophoclean Tragedy* (California, 1966). These works bring out well the nature of Sophocles' world and the stature and situation of his central characters. Gilbert Murray's classic *Euripides and his Age* (1913, Oxford; paperback 1965) is still worth reading. An excellent book in French: J. de Romilly, *L'évolution du pathétique d'Eschyle à Euripide* (Paris, 2nd edn. 1980). There is a paperback *Oxford Readings in Greek Tragedy* (1983) edited by E. Segal, which reprints many interesting papers, some of them translated from other languages.

Richmond Lattimore, in *The Poetry of Greek Tragedy* (Baltimore, 1958) and *Story Patterns in Greek Tragedy* (London, 1964), both brief books, does more than many longer ones to make plain the things we most want to know about the subject.

Hugh Lloyd-Jones in *The Justice of Zeus* (California, 2nd edn. 1984) and E. R. Dodds, in *The Greeks and the Irrational* (California, 1951) constantly discuss tragedy, and their work is an indispensable introduction to this as to other matters.

T. B. L. Webster's *Introduction to Menander* (London, 1974) makes many useful observations and is sound and thorough, though F. H. Sandbach's general book, *The Comic Theatre of Greece and Rome* (London, 1977), is more intuitive; sounder still, and easy to read, which Webster is not, K. J. Dover's reliable *Aristophanic Comedy* (London, 1972) is an admirably precise, if sometimes laconic, treatment. Kenneth McLeish's *Theatre of Aristophanes* (London, 1980), on the other hand, is a very lively book, brimming over with ideas and full of insights. It is appealingly unsober and romantic.

Hugh Lloyd-Jones's translation of the *Oresteia* (London, 1979) with new introductions to the three plays in this edition, is the best English version and literary interpretation that we have for any Greek play. The most successful versions by poets are the Oedipus plays by W. B. Yeats and the *Women of Trachis*, eccentric but brilliant, by Ezra Pound. No wholly satisfactory translations of most tragedies or any comedies exist in English, though Dudley Fitts has produced actable adaptations of Aristophanes of great interest, and the Penguin translations of Aristophanes have great merits (by D. Barrett and A. H. Sommerstein).

Impressive versions of tragedies by Louis MacNeice and Rex Warner can still be found in second hand bookshops.

8
Greek Historians

OSWYN MURRAY

The Origins of History

M ANY societies possess professional remembrancers, priests or officials, whose duty it is to record those traditions thought necessary for the continuity of social values; many societies also possess priestly or official records, designed to help regulate and placate the worlds of gods and men, but capable of being converted by modern scholars into history. Yet the actual writing of history as a distinct cultural activity seems in origin independent of these natural social attitudes, and is a rare phenomenon: it has in fact developed independently only in three very different societies: Judaea, Greece, and China. The characteristics of history in each case are distinct: history is not a science, but an art form serving the needs of society and therefore conditioned by its origin.

The Greek tradition of history writing is our tradition, and we can best see its peculiarities by comparing it with that other tradition which has so strongly influenced us, the Jewish historical writings preserved in the Old Testament. Greeks and Jews came to history independently, but at roughly the same time and in response to the same pressures, the need to establish and sustain a national identity in the face of the vast empires of the Middle East: just as the struggles with Assyria, the exile in Babylon, and the return to the promised land created Jewish historical writing, so the sense of national identity resulting from the defeat of Persia created Greek historical writing. But the presuppositions and the materials with which the two historical traditions worked are very different. For the Jews history was the record of God's covenant with His chosen people, its successes and disasters conditioned by their willingness to obey His commands. History was therefore a single story, belonging to God: the different elements and individual authors are moulded (not always successfully) into a continuous account. Greek history, while it could recognize a moral pattern in human affairs, regarded these affairs as in the control of man: history was the record, not of the mercy or wrath of God, but of the great deeds of men. Among those deeds was the writing of history itself: so a Greek historian is an individual who 'signs' his work in its first sentence—'Herodotus of Halicarnassus, his researches ...', 'Thucydides of Athens wrote the history of the war ...' The great exception to this rule serves to confirm it: those who, like Xenophon, sought to continue the unfinished work of Thucydides, chose not to reveal their identity: Xenophon begins his work, 'Some days later ...', and nowhere mentions his own name, although he is far freer than Thucydides with opinions delivered in the first person. We do not even know the name of the author of another (and better) continuation of Thucydides, partly preserved on papyrus, the 'Oxyrhynchus historian' (so called from the village in Egypt where the copy of his text was found). Later Christian generations in fact tried to transform this individualistic group of historical writings into a tradition of the Old Testament type, and succeeded through instinct or economy of effort in selecting a 'chain of histories', so that only one historical account now survives for each period, and these accounts give a relatively continuous narrative history of the ancient world. A proper history of Greek history writing must take due notice of what has been lost as well as of what survives.

A second difference between Jewish and Greek historical writing is in their sources and attitudes to the sources. The Jewish historical account is built on a multiplicity of evidences which would do credit to a modern historian, and are of three basic types—acts (customs, taboos, rituals, and their explanations), the spoken tradition (hymns, poetry, prophecy, myths, folk-tales), and the written tradition (laws, official documents, royal and priestly chronicles, biographies); it is prone to quote proofs and evidence such as documents. The source material used by Greek historians is initially far simpler and more rudimentary, and the Greeks were always more concerned with the literary, rather than the evidential, aspects of history; they therefore seldom quote documents. Paradoxically the Greek tradition remains superior to the Jewish in its ability to distinguish fact from fiction: God can falsify history far more effectively than the individual historian with his mere mortal bias. The Greeks indeed taught the West how to create and write history without God.

Both peoples learned the alphabet from the same source, the Phoenicians who invented it; writing came to Greece in the eighth-century BC, yet Greece long remained an oral culture in which men spoke in prose, but composed in verse. The distinction between poetry and prose was later a mark of the difference between myth and history, but the earliest known prose literary work was philosophical rather than historical, and related to the need to formulate and convey thoughts in a precise and accurate form; about 550 BC the philosopher Anaximander of Miletus wrote a book *On Nature*, which discussed both the basic structure of the physical world and its visible forms: it contained the first maps and descriptions of both earth and the heavens. Some fifty years later Hecataeus of Miletus similarly wrote a *Description of the Earth* accompanied by a map: it was divided into two books, one for Europe and one for Asia, and recorded the information he had gathered from his own and others' travels. Geography and ethnography are important components in the Greek view of history.

Another work of Hecataeus called *Genealogies* has often been thought to be the first to exhibit that spirit of critical enquiry which is characteristic of western history writing, for it began: 'Hecataeus the Milesian speaks thus: I write these things as they seem true to me; for the stories told by the Greeks are various and in my opinion absurd' (*FGH* 1, F.1). The book actually seems to have been a collection of heroic myths and genealogies of heroes, designed to reduce them into a pseudo-historical account by rationalizing them; it is a curious false start to history, on the one hand recognizing the need to understand the past in rational terms, but on the other hand using the fundamentally unsuitable material of myth. It shows both a desire to liberate history from myth, and an inability to distinguish between the two.

Herodotus

From time to time critics have tried to discover lost historians in the generation after Hecataeus to help explain the next development in the writing of history; but such theories are based on shaky evidence and a mistaken belief that local history or the monograph must come before general history with a grand theme. Herodotus of Halicarnassus in fact deserves his ancient title of 'father of history'. His work is the earliest Greek book in prose to have survived intact; it is some 600 pages or nine 'books' long. Its theme is presented in the first sentence: 'This is the account of the investigation of Herodotus of Halicarnassus, undertaken so that the achievements of men should not be obliterated by time and the great and marvellous works of both Greeks and barbarians should not be without fame, and not least the reason why they fought one another.'

The ultimate justification of the work is the account of the conflict between Greece and Persia, culminating in the Great Expedition of Xerxes to Greece in 480 BC described in the last three books: it is the story of how an army of (allegedly) one and three-quarter million men and a navy of 1,200 ships was defeated by the fragmented forces of the Greeks, who in no battle could muster more than 40,000 men and 378 ships; we may doubt the Persian numbers, but the strategy shows that we cannot doubt the fact that the Greeks were heavily outnumbered on each occasion (above pp. 44 ff.) A fleet from Herodotus' city had fought on the Persian side, and one of his earliest memories was perhaps of the setting out and return of that fateful expedition; he grew up in an Ionia suffering the joys and pains of its liberation and then subjection by the victorious Athenian navy (above, pp. 133 ff.) For the generation of Herodotus the epic achievements of their fathers had created the world in which they lived, as the return of the exiles from Babylon had created the world of Ezra. In his last books Herodotus sought to raise a fitting monument to the new race of heroes, using all the literary skills at his command, 'so that the achievements of men should not be obliterated by time'.

The central theme of this conflict requires Herodotus to go back to its origins:

'who was the first in actual fact to harm the Greeks'. So the work begins with the earlier struggles between the Ionian Greeks and the kingdom of Lydia, before passing on to the origins of Persian power and the story of Cyrus the Great, and then the further conquests of the Persians, in Egypt and north Africa, and around the Black Sea, until we see that the conflict was inevitable.

But this central theme is merely one aspect of the work; there is another, at least as important—'the account of the investigation' or 'researches' of Herodotus (this is in fact the original meaning and the first recorded use of the word *historiē*). Like Hecataeus, Herodotus was a traveller: in the first four books and often thereafter the theme of the conflict is subordinate, a thread on which to hang a series of accounts or stories gathered from different places. These range from individual stories about famous figures (the mythical poet Arion or the Persian court doctor Democedes of Croton, for instance) to substantial histories of the rise and fall of cities (Athens, Sparta, Naucratis in Egypt) and finally to full-scale geographical and ethnographic accounts of civilizations, the most extended of which, on Egypt, occupies the whole of Book 2.

The result is far more than an account of the causes and events of a mere conflict. It is rather a total picture of the known world, in which the geography, customs, beliefs, and monuments of each people are at least as important as their often tenuous relationship to the war. It is this which gives added depth to Herodotus' account, and makes it both a great work of art and a convincing history of a conflict not just between two peoples but between two types of society, the Mediterranean egalitarian city-state and the oriental despotisms of the Middle East. It also makes Herodotus more modern than any other ancient historian in his approach to the ideal of total history.

Herodotus' openness to other cultures indeed caused him to be called a 'barbarophile'. It reflects in part an older Ionian view from an age of exploration, reinforced perhaps by the traditions of Herodotus' own community of Halicarnassus, which was a mixed Greek and Carian city. But these attitudes have been systematized under the influence of the new sophistic interest in the relationship between culture and nature, *nomos* and *physis*; 'For if anyone, no matter who, were given the opportunity of choosing from amongst all the nations of the world the set of beliefs which he thought best, he would inevitably, after careful consideration of their relative merits, choose those of his own country.' Herodotus illustrates the point with a story of the confrontation between Greeks and Indians arranged by King Darius; the Indians were disgusted to hear that the Greeks burned the corpses of their dead parents, the Greeks appalled that the Indians ate theirs: 'One can see from this what custom can do, and Pindar, in my opinion, was right when he called it "king of all"' (3. 38).

The two aspects of the work in one sense reflect the two main literary influences on it, Homer and the world of war and conflict, Hecataeus and the world of peace and understanding. They also probably reflect a chronological progression in the development of Herodotus' book. He seems to have begun as an expert on foreign cultures, a travelling sophist who lectured on the marvels of the world; only later did he arrange his researches around a unifying theme. Despite much modern controversy, that still seems the most satisfactory account of the various peculiarities in the book.

How did Herodotus acquire his information? Some information may have come from previous literary works; but Hecataeus is the only such author Herodotus mentions, and no convincing traces of the use of earlier written narratives have been detected. Herodotus can quote poetry and oracles, and occasionally gives information ultimately based on eastern documentary sources; but it is clear that he did not regard written documents as an important source of information, indeed that he knew no language but Greek. Herodotus' own characterization of his sources is always the same, and is consistent with the types of information he gives. He claims to practise that most modern of historical disciplines, oral history, the collection and interpretation of the living spoken tradition of a people: his sources are 'sight and hearing', what he has seen and what he has been told; the two of course interrelate, since monuments and natural phenomena preserve and call forth verbal explanations. His travels included Egypt and Cyrene in north Africa, Tyre in Phoenicia, Mesopotamia as far as Babylon, the Black Sea and the Crimea, and the north Aegean, apart from the main cities of Asia Minor and Greece, and ultimately (though this has left little if any trace in the *Histories*) south Italy where he settled. In each place he seems to have sought out 'men with traditions', particular groups, interpreters, priests, or leading citizens, and to have recorded a single version of the oral tradition available, a version which may of course often have been partial, biased or merely frivolous; he compares different versions only if they come from different places. The difficulties of writing oral history are well recognized today; yet on the main cultures such as Egypt and Persia, where Herodotus can be checked he is revealed to be remarkably well informed for someone working from such oral sources.

It is in his Greek history that Herodotus reveals the most important aspect of his artistic personality. For mainland Greece his information seems to come from the leading political groups in the cities. For Sparta he gives an official line, for Athens a version based at least in part on particular aristocratic traditions; the narrative is concerned with events and wars, rational in tone, without moral or religious colouring, and designed to enhance or justify the status of particular groups. At Delphi a different type of tradition was available, a series of stories told by the priests and related to the monuments and offerings at the shrine. These stories contain many folk-tale motifs and have a strong moral tone: the hero moves from prosperity to misfortune as a victim of divine envy—the ethical teaching is not aristocratic, but belongs to the shrine of a god whose temple carried the mottoes, 'Know yourself', and 'Nothing too much'. The same types of story pattern are dominant in Ionia: Herodotus' history of his home area is far less 'historical' and far less political than his account of mainland Greece. He is, for instance, often thought to have had particularly good sources for the history of Samos, where he spent much of his youth, yet his account of the tyrant Polycrates only two generations earlier has already turned into a folk-tale.

This characteristic of his Ionian sources suggests a popular, non-aristocratic tradition of story-telling which is directly related to Herodotus' achievement. For the overall shape of his history shows the same moral patterning as his Ionian and Delphic stories: the story of the Persian Wars is a story of how 'the god strikes with his thunderbolt the tall, and will not allow them to display themselves, while small beings do not vex him; you see how the lightning throws down always the greatest buildings and the finest trees' (7. 10). The message is created through a series of devices derived from the art of the folk-tale: the warning dream, the figure of the wise counsellor disregarded, the recurrent story pattern. Just as behind Homer there lies a long tradition of oral poetry sung by professional bards, so behind Herodotus there lies an Ionian tradition of story-telling of which he himself was the last and greatest master.

Thus Herodotus' collecting of information was not guided by any spirit of systematic enquiry, neither was it the product of random curiosity. It was informed from the start with the principle of the *logos*. Herodotus uses the word *logos* to refer to the whole of his work, to its major sections (the Egyptian or the Lydian *logos*), and to the individual stories within it: he surely regarded himself as a *logos*-maker in the same way as he regarded both Hecataeus the mythographer and Aesop the creator of animal fables; Thucydides indeed dismisses him as a '*logos*-writer'. The word *logos* in this context may very often seem to mean little more than the English 'story', as long as we remember that a story has a shape, a purpose: it is not an isolated fact preserved for its own sake; it may be true, but it must be interesting. The achievement of Herodotus was to harness the skills of the *logos*-maker to the description of human societies in peace and war.

From the evidence for his friendship with the poet Sophocles, Herodotus was already active as a lecturer in the late forties of the fifth century; the final version of his history was published shortly before 425 BC, when Aristophanes parodied his account of the causes of the Persian Wars in his comedy, *The Acharnians*. Already Herodotus seemed old-fashioned, for the wider Ionian responsiveness to the interplay of civilizations had been replaced by a narrower concern with the Greek city-state and its interests; history became the history of the *polis*, and took new directions.

Local History and Chronography

The first of these consisted in a fragmentation of the synoptic view of Herodotus into the systematic exploitation of local traditions, and more importantly local archives. These local or ethnic histories satisfied the interests of a local audience for the history of their particular city, and continued to be written throughout antiquity as long as the *polis* survived; all are now lost, but the Augustan critic Dionysius of Halicarnassus describes their general characteristics:

These men made similar choices about the selection of their subjects, and their powers were not so very different from one another, some of them writing histories about the Greeks and some about the barbarians, and not linking all these to one another, but dividing them according to peoples and cities, and writing about them separately, all keeping to one and the same aim: whatever oral traditions were preserved locally among peoples or cities, and whatever documents were stored in holy places or archives, to bring these to the common notice of everyone just as they were received, neither adding to them nor subtracting from them. (*On Thucydides* 5)

This movement for the first time in Greece set the written archive alongside oral tradition as a source for history; two figures from its earliest stages will illustrate its character. About the end of the fifth century Hippias of Elis, travelling sophist and lecturer on antiquities of cities, published the victor list of the Olympic Games, which took chronology back in a four-year cycle to 776 BC; this became the basis for Greek time-reckoning, just as the Romans counted from the foundation of their city, the early Christians from the birth of Abraham, and ourselves from the birth of Christ. Chronology, the dating and ordering of human events, is the basic grammar of history: Hippias began a tradition which continued through the Hellenistic period, to produce in late antiquity the surviving chronological tables of sacred and profane history compiled by the Christian writers Eusebius and Saint Jerome.

Hellanicus of Lesbos in the last third of the fifth century similarly published a whole series of local histories and chronographies (at least twenty-eight), based at least in part on archival research. Among these was the first history of Athens; and the discovery in Egypt of a papyrus of Aristotle's lost work on the *Constitution of Athens* (written in the late fourth century) enables us to reconstruct the development of one city history in some detail. The *Atthis* (or history of Athens) began with Hellanicus, a non-Athenian working in a wider tradition; later authors were mainly Athenian, often from priestly families (Cleidemus) or politicians (Androtion, the author on whom Aristotle largely relied) or both (Philochorus). Their works were characterized from the start on the one hand by a strong interest in local myth, on the other by the possession of a firm chronology: events were arranged (perhaps somewhat arbitrarily) in accordance with the Athenian list of their annual chief magistrate or *archon*. Fragments of such a list inscribed on stone and dating from the 420s BC have in fact been found in the Athenian *agora*: the public record is almost certainly evidence of state interest in the discoveries of Hellanicus, which stimulated the Athenians to set their archives in order. This is a good illustration of the interplay between civic pride and the writing of history; not surprisingly such a tradition is dominated by the interests of the *polis*, its local cults and its politics.

Thucydides

Thucydides too is a product of the world of the developed city-state, and belongs to roughly the same generation as the first local historians; but he proclaims himself a conscious rival of Herodotus in his first sentence:

Thucydides of Athens wrote the history of the war between the Peloponnesians and the Athenians, beginning it as soon as war broke out and believing that it would be a great war and more worthy of record than any preceding one, on the evidence that both sides went into it at the height of preparedness, and seeing the rest of the Greek world taking one side or the other, either immediately or after consideration.

The main themes emerge at once: the explicit rivalry with Herodotus in the description of a great war, the claim to contemporaneous recording, the emphasis on proving his views, the self-conscious assertion of being a writer not a performer in an oral tradition, all expressed in a prose of extraordinary density and sophistication. The war that Thucydides describes is the Great Peloponnesian War between Athens and Sparta, which lasted for a whole generation from 431 to 404 BC with only a short interlude of official, but broken, peace from 421 to 416, and ended with the defeat of Athens and the collapse of her empire. Thucydides did not live to complete his work; Book 8 breaks off in mid sentence in 411; and whereas Books 6 and 7 on the Athenian expedition to Sicily seem to be a polished work of art, there are signs of lack of finish in Books 5 and 8. Thucydides' own activities in the war are best described by himself:

I lived through the whole of the war, being of an age to comprehend events, and giving my attention to them in order to know the exact truth about them. It was also my fate to be an exile from my country for twenty years after my command at Amphipolis [in 424 he had failed to save the city from a surprise attack]; and being present with both parties, and more especially with the Peloponnesians by reason of my exile, I had considerable leisure to observe affairs. (5. 26)

Thucydides is first of all a historian's historian: he is obsessed with methodology. He sets out to prove the greatness of his war by a long excursus on earlier history designed to show the comparative insignificance of earlier wars and the poverty of earlier generations; and at the same time he offers a devastating critique of the standards of evidence employed by Herodotus. He establishes with precision the starting-point and the end of his war, and argues carefully that the so-called period of peace was really part of a single war. Like his contemporaries he is fascinated by chronology, but he rejects their lists of magistrates as unsuitable for military history; instead he dates by campaigning seasons, 'by summers and winters'. He attacks the lack of care others take in ascertaining facts, and asserts that he was not satisfied with any one eyewitness account, but took great pains to correlate and judge between the often differing accounts of different participants. Even for the speeches in his work, he claims in a famous problematical passage to give 'whatever seemed most appropriate to me for each speaker to say in the particular circumstances, keeping as closely as possible to the general sense of what was actually said'. These principles he recognizes will detract from the literary charm of his work: no matter, for its aim is scientific, to be 'a possession for all time, not a display piece for instant listening' (1. 22). In such attitudes we recognize the first critical historian, the founder of the western tradition. It is perhaps curious that we do so, for Thucydides is not of course a historian at all. He claimed that it was impossible to write accurately about the past; his methods and his standards of proof are applicable only to the present. He is a social scientist, a student of the contemporary world, not a historian. It was not until the nineteenth century that the discovery of archives and the invention of the techniques of source criticism allowed historians of the past to believe that they could meet the standards demanded by Thucydides. And it was not until this century that these standards could even begin to be applied to the study of Greek history, with the publication by F. Jacoby of the fragments of the lost Greek historians.

One area illustrates well Thucydides' advance on Herodotus: his account of the causes of the war. Contemporaries found Herodotus' frivolous mythology of rape and counter-rape, from Io to Helen of Troy, hilarious, and failed to note the problem that a clash of cultures ultimately leads to a war whose causes are incapable of being isolated, inherent in the nature of the societies in question. In the case of Greek city-states, however, there were established rules of international relations: an act of aggression or the refusal of a just request were causes of war which had an overt political nature. It is to Thucydides' credit that he does not remain on this level of claim and counter-claim. Instead he argues in detail for two episodes as the generally accepted grievances which led to war, and for a 'truest cause seldom mentioned explicitly'. The two episodes were military adventures involving a clash of interests and of military forces between Athens and Sparta's leading ally, Corinth. The nature of 'the truest cause' is harder to define, and it is indeed described as a personal opinion—'the Athenians becoming great and provoking fear in the Spartans compelled them to fight' (1. 23). Is this a statement about social psychology, or an assertion of inevitability? How unmentioned was it, and where does it leave responsibility for the war? These questions have been endlessly debated; here we need only note the sophistication of a view which goes behind the diplomacy, and asserts two types of forces at work, two levels indeed of causation. It is this abandonment of the obvious, and of the idea of a single cause or type of cause, which is the decisive step in our understanding of the idea of causation in human affairs.

Where did Thucydides learn his method? The theory of politics and society was still in its infancy, and there is nothing of comparable depth in any contemporary sophist. The medical writers operated with ideas of underlying disposition to illness, and active cause for it, not unlike those of Thucydides, and they had developed a science combining theory with practical insight which was analogous to his. But we have only to read Thucydides' account of the Great Plague at

Athens in Book 2 to see his superiority even in describing a medical phenomenon: no contemporary medical writer has his clear description of the two central medical concepts in disease of contagion and immunity. In fact we may say with confidence that Thucydides' conception of social and historical method is his own creation. The problem of Thucydides is essentially his isolation.

This conclusion is reinforced by consideration of Thucydides' literary style. It derives ultimately from the antithetic periods of contemporary sophistic orators; but these have been twisted to present a succession of broken opposites and ill-matched pairs, where no one word is the obvious word and each phrase is unexpected. Its vice is that the simple becomes tortuous, the complex incomprehensible; its virtue is not in its precision (for the precision is a false one), but in the way that it forces the reader—even the contemporary Greek reader—to consider the exact significance and placing of every word. No other Greek ever wrote or thought like Thucydides.

The result is, of course, that he has his limitations. The silences of Colonel Thucydides are impenetrable for us; we have no means of knowing why he does not mention what he does not mention, or how much he does not mention. We cannot construct history from him, we can only accept or reject his conclusions. This would not matter if he were as perfect a historian as some have believed. But there is good reason to suspect that he was sometimes swayed by personal bias: his account of Pericles is surely too favourable, his account of Cleon omits a number of vital facts. Again what ultimately do the speeches represent, if no one ever spoke like that, and word and thought are so closely connected? Where does this leave his account of decision-making? Moreover the very power of Thucydides' illumination throws into prominence the darkness around it: he systematically ignores the significance of Persia—the war is a war of Greek states. Would he ever have faced the fact that ultimately it was Persian gold which defeated the Athenians?

Many of these limitations reflect the aims of his work: 'it will be enough if it is considered useful by those who wish to judge clearly both what has happened and what will come about again in the future, in the same or similar fashion, given the nature of man' (1.22). Thucydides here asserts no crude theory of repetition, but merely the usefulness of the study of human society in action. But what sort of society? Obviously not Persian, yet equally perhaps not merely Greek—rather the self-conscious political society in which decisions are taken by rational and open discussion and in accordance with rational principles. That is why political scientists from Machiavelli onwards have taken Thucydides as their ideal historian: Thomas Hobbes called him 'the most politick historiographer that ever writ'.

The influence of the sophists on Thucydides' theory of politics is clear. Thucydides seems to accept as a general fact about human society that 'might is right'—societies are in fact organized in terms of self-interest, and states act in accordance with self-interest: appeals to sentiment are seldom made in his work, and when made are unsuccessful. Athens holds her empire as a tyranny 'which it may have been wrong to acquire, but is dangerous to surrender' (speech of Pericles, 2.63). The philosophical expression of such views is given most clearly by the sophist Thrasymachus in the first book of Plato's *Republic*. So in terms of social morality no one is ever in the right or the wrong: once Sparta's fear of Athens has been isolated, it is clear that the war is 'in accordance with nature'. We know that this view of society was not a universal view in the fifth century, and very probably not a majority view; nevertheless it was clearly an influential one, and Thucydides cannot be accused of solipsism or completely falsifying the nature of political debates. That he has not given a full account of the decision-making procedure is already obvious from the way that the speeches are offered as antithetical pairs, not as part of a general debate. Many of the speeches in fact serve more as a vehicle for exploring the consequences of the Thucydidean view of politics than as an accurate account of what was actually said. On the two occasions when Thucydides himself offers sustained political analysis he is less successful: the account of the development of political leadership at Athens after the death of Pericles (2.65) and the discussion of the nature of political revolution during the war in relation to the example of Corcyra (3.82-4) are both unsatisfactory in their attempt to impose a linear progression on complex phenomena.

Despite his acceptance of this type of social theory, Thucydides is deeply concerned with its consequences, and especially with the resulting problems of morality; he seems particularly interested in the effects of such theories on internal politics. The famous funeral oration of Pericles over the Athenian dead in Book 2 portrays a society without conflict or tension, united in pursuit of an ideal, in contrast to the pathological state of a city like Corcyra, torn apart by civil strife. In general he highlights the occasions which raise such questions in their most crucial form. In Book 3, for instance, there are three great set episodes, the question of how Athens should punish the Mytileneans for their revolt, the question of how Sparta should deal with the captured Plataeans, and the story of the revolution at Corcyra. In the first, the new morality of empire leads to the conclusion that it is more advantageous to rule by kindness than by terror. In the second, the representatives of the old morality reject an appeal to sentiment, and destroy the sacred city of the Persian Wars: they decide to liberate the Greeks through terror. In the third, Thucydides explores the breakdown of trust and social order when a society is entirely ruled by the new morality, and the only madness is to be a moderate.

Book 3 is the centre of the original history of Thucydides, which described the first part of the war and ended at 5.24. Already he has shown himself ambivalent about the desirability of the world he portrays as reality. In the second half of his work this unease, this sense of an 'anti-Thucydides in Thucydides', is magnified. The reason lies in the logic of events: if the laws of politics which Thucydides has accepted are laws of nature, then their full horror will be brought home in the greatest tragedy of all, the destruction of Thucydides' own city of

Athens; and the pessimism of the historian concerning human nature will be finally justified in that fall. There are strong signs that Thucydides began to articulate the second half of his history around the conception of a tragedy. In Book 5 the Athenians make an unprovoked attack on the small island of Melos, and the Melians challenge the morality of their action in a passage cast in dialogue form: the Athenians respond with the arrogance of a tyrannical city. The episode in Thucydides is deeply influenced by the literary forms of Greek tragedy, and it also embodies that deed of pride on the part of Athens which will lead to calamity in the Great Sicilian Expedition of Books 6 and 7; the story of that expedition itself is told with a passion and an artistry which show Thucydides' belief that it is the turning-point of the war: his own involvement in the telling of it is all the more effective for being disguised. We do not know how Thucydides would have ended his story; in particular we do not know how he would have explained why Sparta did not destroy Athens completely, as she should surely have done on his theory: the problem for the historian is that history is not capable of being an artistic unity, it is always being falsified by events. Thucydides' history demonstrates on the one hand the moral development of an author experiencing the events he describes as a contemporary, and on the other hand the impossibility of scientific history.

Thucydides' view of history was dominant in antiquity, as it is today. Each society gets the sort of history it deserves. Machiavellism or *Realpolitik* is still seen as the only rational response in politics, even when it leads to self-destruction. That is natural once Thucydides' characterization of history is accepted, as being the realm of politics and war. The lesson is already there in Thucydides himself, that a society which lives solely by such criteria will inevitably destroy itself.

Xenophon

History continues, and so must historians: that was the problem of the fourth century. The fact that Thucydides was unfinished at first made it easier, as the examples of his continuators showed: one could simply begin 'Some days later', at least attempting to reach the same standards of dispassionate accuracy. The Oxyrhynchus historian achieves this, Xenophon almost does in the first two books of his *Hellenica* or Greek History, which carry the story of the Peloponnesian War down to its end in 404 BC. But when later in life he came to continue the story to the battle of Mantinea in 362, covering the period of the Spartan leadership in Greece, its collapse, and the short-lived Theban leadership, he produced an account so careless, so lop-sided, and so prejudiced that it would not be taken seriously if it were not the only surviving contemporary account: even the claim that he was writing memoirs, not history, fails to excuse a work whose omissions are more interesting than its contents. The sadness is that Xenophon did fulfil the Thucydidean criterion of being an eyewitness and participant in these events, and yet missed completely the tragic theme of the failure of the

Spartan way of life which he was so well qualified to interpret. Nevertheless Xenophon's fresh and easy style, his simple view of virtue and vice, and his unqualified admiration for Sparta make a pleasant change from the rigours of his predecessor.

Style and a moral content suitable for schoolchildren made Xenophon popular throughout antiquity and ensured the survival of all his works. Many of these are on the fringes of history. The *Anabasis* is a boy's own adventure story of the march of 10,000 Greek brigands through the heart of the Persian Empire, told by one of its leaders; the *Agesilaus* is an obituary piece praising the record of Xenophon's lifelong friend and protector, Agesilaus, king of Sparta; the *Memoirs of Socrates* presents an intimate portrait of a famous man whom Xenophon probably never met, in the tradition of literary memoirs going back to the fifth century. Another work of Xenophon's, the *Cyropaedia*, can claim to be the first historical novel: it is a very long and completely fictitious account of the education and exploits of the founder of the Persian Empire, Cyrus the Great; its usefulness as a mirror for princes and its emphasis on moral leadership made it one of Europe's most popular books until kings went out of fashion. In antiquity it was responsible for a number of semi-historical accounts of the education of the hero from Alexander the Great onwards. But the East had more claim to be exotic than moral; and Ctesias of Cnidus, court doctor of Artaxerxes II in the early fourth century (who had actually been present at the same battle of Cunaxa as the Xenophon of the *Anabasis*, but on the other side) wrote an enormously popular and wildly fanciful (lost) history of Persia, which gave inside authority to a view of Persia 'breathing seraglio and eunuch perfumes, mixed with the foul stench of blood' (Eduard Meyer). Never trust a doctor: such writing derives from Ionian popular story-telling, and has its proper continuation in the romantic novels of the Hellenistic period.

Hellenica

The mainstream of Greek history-writing remained the Thucydidean history of city-states in conflict, but now standardized in a series of connecting and competing *Hellenica* or histories of Greece. Among the lost historians of the fourth century two stand out. Ephorus of Cyme wrote a Greek history in thirty books, which sought to replace all rivals by beginning at the beginning with the return of the sons of Heracles and ending in 341 BC. He is interesting for his attempt to delimit the sphere of history from that of myth, and for the way he justified his wider approach in a series of prefaces to individual sections which asserted the unity of history. As a pupil of Isocrates (below, p. 230), he began the dangerous relationship between rhetoric and history, with its tendency to sacrifice truth to effect. He also had other vices: he had a sharp eye for the use of poetry as evidence for history, but little judgement in exploiting it; and he sought to disguise his dependence on earlier historians by 'modernizing' facts and figures, and where necessary inventing circumstantial detail. His style and completeness unfortunately made him rather popular, but at least he stands out as one who had thought about the purposes that history should serve, and got them wrong.

To the modern eye another pupil of Isocrates, Theopompus of Chios is more attractive; he wrote a *Hellenica*, a continuation of Thucydides, and then a work which suggests by its title the new direction that history was taking, a *Philippica*, or history with Philip, king of Macedon, at its centre. These works gaily exposed both the deviousness and corruption of Athenian politicians at all periods and the drunken barbarism of the new Macedonian ruler of Greece. Anti-history, the exposure of vice and incompetence, is always fun, and Theopompus wrote to puncture the pretensions of the great. But he also foresaw the need for a new type of history, as the title of his *Philippica* shows—history for (or against) a world ruled by kings.

History for Kings

Alexander the Great was the first serious challenge, and, being a man who knew that he was making history, he was careful to take a historian along to record it. His choice was unfortunate; Callisthenes, Aristotle's nephew, after displaying a mixture of sycophancy and sullenness, began tampering with the Royal Pages and had to be disposed of. The actual Alexander historians are a motley crew, to judge from their fragments—for ironically no continuous account of this great event, the conquest of the world, survives from before the Roman imperial period. Our standard history, written more than four centuries later by Arrian, a Roman official, chose to use two eyewitness narratives which were certainly competent, one by Aristobulus, an architect, and one by Ptolemy, a junior commander who later became founder of the Egyptian successor kingdom. Other accounts such as that of Diodorus use a popular romantic version written by Cleitarchus, a shadowy figure of uncertain date and not necessarily a participant. Many who went on the expedition wrote their memoirs in different literary styles. The most genial is Nearchus, Alexander's admiral, who explored the Indus valley, the Punjab, and the desolate Makran coast to the mouth of the Tigris in 326–324, and wrote a Herodotean account of it which is an important source for Arrian's description of the Indian expedition. But the most lasting consequence of the career of Alexander the Great was the tradition of the Alexander Romance, perhaps the most popular book in world literature, compiled in late antiquity from various Hellenistic strands such as a fanciful biography and collections of forged letters and treatises: the result is sheer fairy-tale, with Euphrates and Tigris flowing into the Nile and Alexander born of an Egyptian snake, visiting men without heads and Indian brahmins (the last a true episode), descending to the seabed in a diving bell, and flying in a basket powered by griffins.

The Hellenistic Age

The challenge of the historical Alexander was therefore refused, and it is worth asking why neither the age of Alexander nor the period of the Hellenistic kingdoms produced a new form of political history, why no tradition of biographies of kings or dynastic histories emerged to cope with the great empires and kingdoms. One reason was the strength of the tradition of history-writing created by the city-state; another was the lack of a real biographical tradition in Greece. For such reasons it was left to the Romans to discover the fascinations of imperial history and of political biography; the most successful political historians in the Hellenistic age continued to write *Hellenica*, usually chronicles of their own day, merely incorporating the new Hellenistic kingdoms into the old framework.

The best of these histories was that which lies behind Books 18-20 of Diodorus, by Hieronymus of Cardia, an administrator of public affairs in various kingdoms, whose adult life covered three generations from Alexander to about 260 BC, when he died in full possession of his faculties at the age of 104; not surprisingly his history was so long that 'no one could read it through to the end', But it was also clearly a marvellously accurate and balanced account of an age when politics and war spanned the world from the Indus to the Nile and the Danube; in particular these books of Diodorus offer a version of military history better even than that in Thucydides. The lesson that Hieronymus learned from the dismemberment of Alexander's empire and the creation of the great successor kingdoms was perhaps that most important of all truths in history, that it is chance, not human skill, that rules human affairs. The goddess Tyche presides over his history and over that of his successors down to Polybius—chance both blind and yet capable of being used by those who understand her ways: 'there is a tide in the affairs of men'.

The other main development in political history is known largely through the polemics of Polybius against his predecessors: it is aptly named the 'pathetic school of history', in which rhetoric and history join hands, to recreate through pathos the sensations of the past. Whether this school, which only too easily sacrificed truth to effect, had a basis in an Aristotelian theory of 'tragic history' is disputed; the claims of these historians do, however, foreshadow some aspects of the theory of Benedetto Croce, that all history is contemporary history, the re-enactment of past experience relevant to the present.

The early Hellenistic period also saw the renewal of the Herodotean tradition. Already writers such as Nearchus had recognized the relevance of Herodotus to their experience; when the new kingdoms began to consider their native subjects, they felt the need to understand these alien customs, and to create some sort of identity for their kingdoms. The result was a revival of the Herodotean *logos* in a systematic form as scientific ethnography, often patronized by kings and written by experts who might be non-Greek, resting on records and inside knowledge, and arranged in a standard form—myth and religion, geography and natural history, political history, social customs. The earliest of these authors, Hecataeus of Abdera, wrote for Ptolemy I of Egypt, and is the source for Diodorus Book 1; in the next generation he was followed by the Egyptian priest Manetho, whose chronology is still the basis of Egyptian history. In the Seleucid kingdom, Berossus, a bilingual priest of Baal, wrote a Babylonian history, and Megasthenes, ambassador of Seleucus to the court of Chandragupta in India, wrote an impressive survey of the beginnings of the Mauryan empire. This renewal of the relation between history and geography in ethnography was undoubtedly the most important cultural result of Alexander's conquests. For a brief period once again the Greeks were able to stand outside themselves and their city-states, and wonder at the world around them.

The city-state rapidly reasserted itself and drove ethnography into the area of utopian philosophical romance, with the imaginary worlds of Euhemerus and Iamblichus. There continued to be good geographers like Eratosthenes and Strabo (whose work survives), and from time to time a figure of interest emerged to unite the main strands of history. The most important of these was Posidonius, philosopher and polymath, whose lost history continued Polybius and recorded the harsh realities of Roman imperialism in the late Republic. But it is Polybius who represents the way forward, as the emergence of Rome on the Mediterranean scene gave a new unity and direction to political history in the tradition of Thucydides. So the culmination of this tradition in Greek historical writing was in a history of Rome, whose importance must be explored in Chapter 25.

Towards the end of the millennium that encyclopedic tendency emerged which heralds the closing of a cultural tradition; for us the importance of the tendency is that many of these bulky works survived to drive out their predecessors, but also to offer the evidence for reconstructing the historical tradition. The late Hellenistic world is a world of big books and small men with big pretensions. Dionysius of Halicarnassus in his *Roman Antiquities* provided Rome with a respectable local history like a proper Greek city; in the same age the *Historical Library* of Diodorus is important, both for its attempt to improve on Ephorus by including all civilizations (not just all Greece) in the realm of history, and as a quarry for lost historians—for the work is genuinely a library, a succession of abbreviations of other people's books.

In the course of 350 years the Greek tradition of history-writing had invented most of the styles of history that we still practise, and tried to analyse most of the political and social problems that we still face. It had established standards of accuracy and a variety of approaches which make it clearly superior to any other historical tradition. If it had one defect, it was a defect we share, the inability to cope with the power of God in history; happy the age that can afford to ignore God. The end of the Hellenistic period saw the beginnings of a new religion, and the flowing together of the traditions of Greece and Judaea into a new form of history, the working out of God's salvation on earth. The Books of Maccabees and the works of Josephus are products of this fusion of cultural traditions which survive, to point the way forward to the *Church History* of Eusebius and the Christian world of Byzantium.

Further Reading

I

Of the main extant works, Herodotus, Thucydides, Xenophon's *Hellenica* and *Anabasis*, Aristotle's *Constitution of Athens* and Arrian's *History of Alexander* are available in good Penguin translations, with introductions by leading modern scholars; the best translation of Thucydides is however still that of R. Crawley (1876, often reprinted in Everyman's Library, London and New York). The lesser works of Xenophon and other authors (Diodorus, Dionysius of Halicarnassus, Josephus) are most easily found in the Loeb Classical Library, with facing text and translation; special mention should also be made of the new two-volume Loeb Arrian, with important introduction, notes and appendices by P. A. Brunt (Harvard 1976, 1983). *Aristotle's Constitution of Athens and Related Texts*, translated and with commentary by K. von Fritz and E. Kapp (New York, 1950) is excellent.

The fragments of the lost Greek historians have been collected by Felix Jacoby, who devoted his life to the task; his monumental *Die Fragmente der griechischen Historiker* (Leiden, 1923–58) in fourteen volumes is the most important work on Greek history of this century. Jacoby died before he could finish it; it is arranged according to types of history, and the main areas which remain to be covered are geography, and literary and philosophical history and biography. The work consists of the evidence for the life of each historian, the fragments of his works, and an often extensive commentary in either German or English. There is no translation.

II

The most illuminating modern work on Greek history-writing is that of A. Momigliano; his more important essays are collected in two volumes, *Studies in Historiography* (London, 1966), and *Essays in Ancient and Modern Historiography* (Oxford, 1977). For the relations between Greek and other historical traditions there is much of interest in Herbert Butterfield's unfinished *The Origins of History* (London, 1981). See also the survey of the Mediterranean and the Middle East in J. Van Seters, *In Search of History* (Yale, 1983), which is primarily focused on the Jewish tradition. The beginnings of Greek historical writing are surveyed by L. Pearson, *Early Ionian Historians* (Oxford, 1939, repr. Connecticut, 1975), and R. Drews, *The Greek Accounts of Eastern History* (Harvard, 1973, to be treated with caution). For the problems faced by Herodotus the best introduction is the general work by the anthropologist Jan Vansina, *Oral Tradition* (Harmondsworth, 1973); see also A. Momigliano, *Studies* chs. 8 and 11. The best recent general book is J. A. S. Evans, *Herodotus* (Boston, Mass., 1982); other books offer more partial insights.

The development of local history is discussed by Momigliano, *Studies*, ch. 1; for the local Athenian historians there is the masterly book of Jacoby, *Atthis* (Oxford, 1949), and his commentary in English on them in *FGH* III b Supplement; see also P. J. Rhodes, *A Commentary on the Aristotelian Athenaion Politeia* (Oxford, 1981). Three books on Thucydides stand out for their different strengths: F. M. Cornford, *Thucydides Mythistoricus* (London, 1907), J. De Romilly, *Thucydides and Athenian Imperialism* (Oxford, 1963), and G. E. M. de Sainte Croix, *The Origins of the Peloponnesian War* (London, 1972). Thucydides is also the subject of a great commentary in five volumes (Oxford, 1945–81), begun and planned by A. W. Gomme, and finished by A. Andrewes and K. J. Dover.

For Xenophon see J. K. Anderson, *Xenophon* (London, 1974), and the introductions by G. L. Cawkwell to the two Penguin volumes. For Ephorus see G. L. Barber, *The Historian Ephorus* (London, 1935); for Theopompus, Gilbert Murray, *Greek Studies* (Oxford, 1946), ch. 8, and

W. R. Connor, *Theopompus and Fifth Century Athens* (Washington, DC, 1968). All studies of Alexander the Great devote much time to the historical sources for his career; the most complete survey is L. Pearson, *The Lost Histories of Alexander the Great* (New York, 1960); the studies by W. W. Tarn, *Alexander the Great* Volume II: *Sources and Studies* (Cambridge, 1950), are controversial. For Arrian, see Brunt's Loeb (above); P. A. Stadter, *Arrian of Nicomedia* (North Carolina, 1980); A. B. Bosworth, *A Historical Commentary on Arrian's History of Alexander*, vol. I (Oxford, 1980).

Jane Hornblower, *Hieronymus of Cardia* (Oxford, 1981) is a brilliant recreation of that lost masterpiece, and the best general account of the working methods of Diodorus. For other early Hellenistic historians in the ethnographic tradition, see O. Murray, 'Herodotus and Hellenistic Culture', *Classical Quarterly* 22 (1972), 207 ff. For Josephus see T. Rajak, *Josephus* (London, 1983).

9

Life and Society in Classical Greece

OSWYN MURRAY

Society

By the classical period of the fifth and fourth centuries BC there were hundreds of communities of Greeks living scattered around the shores of the Mediterranean 'like frogs around a pond', as Plato put it. From the central sea of the Aegean, with its island communities, and the coastal towns of Turkey and eastern and southern Greece, they had spread to north Greece, the Black Sea coast and southern Russia, to Sicily and south Italy, and as far as Provence, Spain, and north Africa. These communities regarded themselves as basically similar, as living in a *polis*, the only form of truly civilized life. Of course many aspects of their social and economic life were different: some cities possessed large agricultural territories or serf populations, others were heavily engaged in trade in raw materials such as corn, olive oil, dried fish, wine, metals, timber, slaves, or in manufactured goods, whether made on the spot or imported from eastern and other cultures; there was also a huge outflow of Greek goods in certain areas, and of skilled labour such as doctors, stonemasons, and professional mercenaries. The economy of the cities varied enormously, and so did their functions: some were essentially fortresses, others based on a religious shrine; but most had ports, and all had some land and constituted an administrative centre. In principle it should be possible to reconstruct the social and economic life of a typical Greek city, much as Plato in the *Laws* and Aristotle in the last two books of the *Politics* believed it possible to discover an ideal city behind the unsatisfactory multifariousness of real cities.

The reason that we cannot do this satisfactorily is not so much the absence of evidence as its concentration on two unrepresentative examples. Only Athens offers a sufficient variety of material for us to be able to understand in detail the way people lived; and from that evidence we see that Athens was fundamentally untypical, in being more varied, and yet more systematic in its interrelations, in fact more advanced than most, if not all other, Greek cities. In contrast Sparta is described for us by Athenian writers as the opposite of Athens, so that we see only those parts of it which are different from Athenian institutions. Order and obedience are contrasted with anarchy and freedom, the agricultural economy with trade and manufacture, the freedom of women with Athenian restrictions. Where there is no opposition the sources fall silent: our main writer, Xenophon, in his little book on Sparta, forgets to mention the Spartan helot serfs, because slavery was universal; and we hear nothing of the massive armaments industry which must have provided the standardized weapons of the Spartan military caste. Outside these two cities we have only scattered information or chance finds, such as the great law-code of the small city of Gortyn in inland Crete.

So Athens must be the focus, in the knowledge that we are describing life in other cities only in so far as they resembled Athens, and in the belief that at least the basic social and economic relationships of Greek cities are more similar to each other than to the tribal and non-Greek areas which surrounded them. Yet even for a single society we must recognize that there is no one viewpoint: each individual witness will describe his world differently. Plato's dialogues portray Athens in vivid detail, as a world of young and godlike intellectuals meeting in private houses for conversation or social drinking, strolling in suburban parks or walking down to the Piraeus for a festival, listening to famous visitors skilled in rhetoric or philosophy from all over Greece. Even when Socrates is in prison under sentence of execution, the authorities allow large groups of his friends to visit him and discuss with him such questions as whether he should escape, and the nature of life after death. Finally Socrates drinks the hemlock, and his limbs slowly lose sensation as he converses peacefully and rationally.

Yet for most of the time which Plato describes, Athens was fighting a long and bloody war in which at least half the population died, many of them from a particularly horrifying plague which scarred even those who survived it, and which was partly the consequence of the unsanitary conditions in which vast numbers of citizens were camped, at first in the heat of the summer, and later all year, on every available space of open or sacred land within the city walls. In reality travel was dangerous and very much restricted; and the way down to the Piraeus must have been as filthy, as stinking, and as crowded as the slums of Calcutta. Nor were Athenian prison conditions as humane or as clean as Plato suggests; and the medical effects of hemlock are not mere numbness of the limbs—they include choking, slurring of speech, convulsions, and uncontrollable vomiting.

Plato's Athens is an ideal vision which reflects reality as much as the naked figures of the Parthenon reflect the pock-marked and poorly dressed peasants who stared up at them; yet we need to know the ideals which a society sets for itself. Attic comedy for its own purposes seized on certain aspects of daily life, to exaggerate them for comic effect; yet once again we may wonder whether the obscenities and the constant references to bodily functions are typical of a society

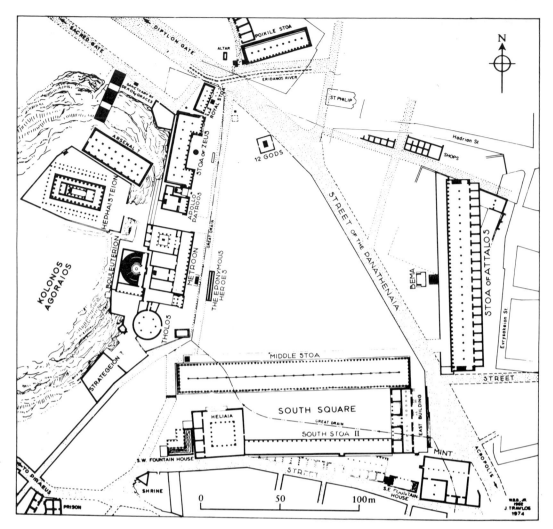

PLAN OF THE *AGORA* (MARKET-PLACE) IN ATHENS IN THE HELLENISTIC PERIOD. The square had been cleared early in the sixth century, then supplied with public buildings along its west side, behind which there later stood the temple of Hephaestus. Among the early buildings are the Royal Stoa, office of the royal archon (*archon basileus*) who saw to religious matters. There was also a council house (*bouleutērion*), archive (in the *metrōon*), and magistrate's club house (*tholos*), shown here in their Classical form. The Painted Stoa at the north held the early Classical paintings of Polygnotus and Micon. Across the square ran the Panathenaic Way which passed from a city gate (Dipylon Gate) to the Acropolis. At the south are sixth-century fountain houses and the state mint. The stoae—shops and offices—which close the square are comparatively late additions, the Stoa of Attalus, a gift of the Pergamene king, being now rebuilt to serve as museum and workrooms for the Agora excavations.

which kept its women in strict seclusion, rather than a form of ritual release reserved for the theatre: how regular was father-bashing or female drunkenness off the stage? Did women ever really dream of taking over the state? Again law-codes tell us only of the boundary areas where crime and punishment are thinkable, not of what is either normal or tabu. Then the speeches of Athenian lawyers concern a special group of the rich, and situations where there is an inherit-

MODEL OF THE WEST SIDE OF THE ATHENIAN AGORA IN THE LATE CLASSICAL PERIOD, seen from the south. Compare the plan, opposite.

ance to be disputed or a business interest to conflict; hidden behind them is a world of normal activity. For all the vividness of our evidence we are dealing with a set of stereotypes and partial views which inform us only indirectly of what it was like to be an Athenian.

The *polis* was essentially a male association: citizens who were men joined together in making and carrying out decisions affecting the community. The origin of this activity doubtless lay in the military sphere and the right of warriors to approve or reject the decisions of their leaders; the development of the *polis* is the extension of this practice to all aspects of social life, with the partial exception of religion. Politics, direct participation in the making of rational choices after discussion, was therefore central to all Greek cities. In Athens and Sparta all male citizens participated at least in principle equally; elsewhere particular rights could be confined to certain groups, richer or better born, thereby necessarily creating conflicts and a hierarchy of rights within the citizen body. Nevertheless the forms of political life, mass citizen assembly, smaller council, and annual executive magistrates were general, though the powers and attributes of the different elements varied widely.

It is already obvious that such a developed type of organization must relate itself to other more 'natural' and presumably earlier forms of association, of the kind generally described by modern anthropologists as kinship groups. Most Greek cities divided their citizens into hereditary 'tribes': Dorian cities traditionally possessed three, Ionian cities four, but political reformers were given to tampering with the organization, and Cleisthenes at Athens had changed the number there from four to ten (about 507 BC; above, p. 35). The lack of any organic connection between these city tribes and a real tribal past is shown by the fact that they only existed as social divisions in the *polis* communities, and are absent from the genuinely tribal areas of north Greece; they were in fact ways of dividing the citizen body for military and political purposes, sanctioned by tradition and reinforced by specially organized state religious cults.

In Athens the reforms of Cleisthenes had also reorganized the associations based on locality. The village or deme had become an administrative unit, with a local official and a local assembly to control all aspects of local government, and most importantly to maintain the citizen lists; there was a complex procedure for ensuring enrolment on the citizen list, and a legal machinery for appeal in the case of exclusion. Because of this connection with citizenship, membership of the deme remained hereditary, regardless of actual domicile, and every Athenian citizen was required to state his deme in any official transaction: so Socrates' official designation was 'Socrates son of Sophroniscus of the deme of Alopeke'. But however great the population movements, the deme remained a geographical focus for most Athenians because they lived there. Even more important to the ordinary Athenian than these central and local government organizations was the phratry (*phratria*), the group of *phrateres*. This is the sole context in Greek of the important linguistic root common to most Indo-European languages, found for instance in the Celtic *brathir*, German *Bruder*, English *brother*, Latin *frater*, or French *frère*; in Greek it designates the non-familial type of 'brotherhood' (there was a quite different word for the blood relationship of brother). These brotherhoods were originally perhaps aristocratic warrior bands, but once again the democratic state had reorganized them to make them open to all: every male Athenian belonged to a phratry, and it was his phratry which dominated his social life. Each phratry worshipped a male and a female god, Zeus Phratrios and Athena Phratria, at a general annual festival held in traditional localities and under local phratry control: the mixture of uniformity with a spurious diversity suggests strongly a remoulding of older institutions at a particular date. The various rites of passage of the young male Athenian were connected with this festival. At an early age he was presented to the *phrateres* by his father and relatives at the altar of his Zeus Phratrios, and the acceptance of his first sacrifice signified his acceptance into the community. In adolescence he was again presented and dedicated to the god his shorn hair; the *phrateres* then voted to admit him as a phratry member and inscribed his name on the phratry list. It was also the *phrateres* who witnessed the solemn betrothal ceremony which was the central public act of the Athenian marriage, and who celebrated with a feast paid for by the bridegroom its final consummation. Thus the phratry was involved in all the main stages of a man's life and was the focus of his social and religious activity; when in difficulties, for instance needing witnesses at law, he turned first to his *phrateres*. The only area in which the Athenian phratry was not concerned was death, though elsewhere this too was part of their functions.

This type of association was common in the Greek world, and had developed for different ends in different cities. Sparta is the most striking example: the male citizen body was divided into *syssitia* or mess groups on which the entire social and military organization of the state depended. Here the normal practices of the Greek world had been transformed to create a military élite. From the age of seven, boys were given a state-organized upbringing, and brigaded into age groups. They lived communally from the age of twelve, taught all sorts of skills useful to self-reliance and survival, and provided with inadequate clothing and food to toughen them. At twenty they joined the *syssitia* where they must live until the age of thirty, and even thereafter they were required to eat daily those common meals to which they had to contribute from the land allotted to them and farmed by state-owned slaves, who were in fact the enslaved descendants of neighbouring communities, constantly rebelling and requiring suppression. The theoretical elegance of this solution (soldiers make slaves, slaves make soldiers, slaves need soldiers to suppress them), and the way it built on traditional Greek social customs, much impressed ancient political thinkers, and offered a counter-ideal to the Athenian democracy. The two examples show how differently similar institutions could develop in different states, and produce societies with utterly opposed characteristics.

The need to belong remains, and in an open society like Athens it led to a multiplicity of social groups more or less integrated into the state. There were aristocratic religious groups called *gennētai* who claimed descent from a common ancestor and monopolized the priesthoods of the more important city cults. Lower down the social scale there were other religious groups centred on the worship of lesser gods and heroes, but with a strong social purpose in feasting and mutual help. There were aristocratic drinking groups, which might even on occasion be mobilized for political ends, but which were more often to be found indulging in mindless post-prandial destruction and the molesting of innocent passers-by; in the daytime the same young men would be found in other but overlapping groups associated with the various sporting complexes or *gymnasia* of the city. There were benefit clubs and burial clubs, and clubs associated with individual trades and activities. There were religious or mystical sects, and intellectual organizations such as the philosophical schools of Plato and Aristotle. Characteristic of these organizations are a cult focus, the ownership of property for the common benefit, the existence of a formal constitution with officers and a means of taking formal decisions, often recorded on stone, and a strong element of common feasting and drinking; characteristic too is the fact that these are all-male groups engaging in all-male activities. Occasionally we hear of equally exclusive female organizations, usually connected with specific cults confined to women, but these tend to be or to be seen as mere extensions of the male world. The range of such associations is shown by the Athenian law relating to them; 'If a deme or *phrateres* or worshippers of heroes or *gennētai* or drinking groups or funerary clubs or religious guilds or pirates or traders make rules amongst themselves, these shall be valid unless they are in conflict with public law.'

The developed Greek city was a network of associations: as Aristotle saw, it was such associations which created the sense of community, of belonging, which was an essential feature of the *polis*: the ties of kinship by blood were matched with multiple forms of political and religious and social groupings, and of companionship for a purpose, whether it be voyaging or drinking or burial. This conception of citizenship could even be invoked in time of civil war: when the democrats and the oligarchs of Athens were fighting in 404 BC, a priest of the Eleusinian mysteries, a man of noble family on the democratic side, made this appeal:

Fellow citizens, why are you driving us out of the city? Why do you want to kill us? We have never done you any harm. We have shared with you in the most holy rites, in sacrifices, and in splendid festivals; we have danced in choruses with you and gone to school with you and fought in the army with you, braving together with you the dangers of land and sea in defence of our common safety and freedom. In the name of the gods of our fathers and mothers, of the bonds of kinship and marriage and companionship, which are shared by so many of us on either side, I beg you to feel shame before gods and men and cease to harm our fatherland. (Xenophon, *Hell.* 2. 4. 20–2)

In such a world it might be argued that multiple ties limited the freedom of the individual, and there is certainly an important sense in which the conception of the autonomy of the individual apart from the community is absent from Greek thought: the freedom of the Greeks is public, externalized in speech and action. This freedom derives precisely from the fact that the same man belongs to a deme, a phratry, a family, a group of relatives, a religious association; and, living in this complex world of conflicting groups and social duties, he possesses the freedom to choose between their demands, and so to escape any particular dominant form of social patterning. It is this which explains the coexistence of the group mentality with the amazing creativity and freedom of thought of classical Athens: the freedom which results from belonging in many places is no less a freedom than that which results from belonging nowhere, and which creates a society united only in its neuroses.

Family

The Greek family was monogamous and nuclear, being composed in essence of husband and wife with their children; but Greek writers tend to equate it with the household as an economic unit, and therefore to regard other dependent relatives and slaves as part of it. The family fulfilled a number of social functions apart from the economic. It was the source of new citizens; in the classical period the state intervened to establish increasingly stringent rules for citizenship and so for legitimacy: ultimately a citizen must be the offspring of a legally recognized marriage between two Athenian citizens, whose parents must also be citizens; this increasingly sharp definition tended to exclude the more flexible unions of an earlier period. It became impossible for an Athenian to marry a foreigner or to obtain recognition for the children of any other type of liaison: the development is essentially democratic, the imposition of the social norms of the peasant majority on an aristocracy which had previously behaved very differently; for the aristocracy had often married outside the community and thereby determined its own criteria for legitimacy. Indeed Pericles, the author of the first of these

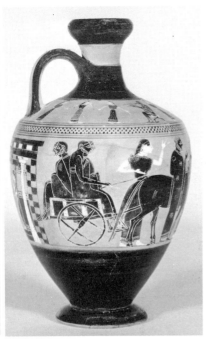

WEDDING PROCESSION on an Athenian vase by the Amasis Painter, about 540 BC. Bride and groom sit in a mule cart, accompanied by relatives and guests, on their way to their new home. The bride's mother leads them carrying torches, and in the house the groom's mother is also seen with a torch. The preparation of the bride, the procession, and special occasions for the receiving of gifts, were the main ceremonies of a Greek wedding, apart from the contract about property.

citizenship laws, demonstrates the painfulness of the process of adaptation; for, when his legitimate children died of the plague, he was forced to seek from the assembly permission for his children by Aspasia, his Milesian mistress, to be declared legitimate Athenian citizens. Other individuals, often of aristocratic birth, found themselves reclassified in this process as bastards, without either citizenship or rights of inheritance.

For a second function of the family, intimately connected with citizenship, was the inheritance of property. Greek society in general did not practise primogeniture, the right of the eldest son to inherit; rather the property was divided equally by lot between all surviving sons, so that the traditional word for an inheritance was a man's *klēros* or lot. This is one important reason for the instability of the Athenian family, for each family survived only as long as its head, and its property was redistributed on his death. There were of course countervailing tendencies. The common practice of burial in family plots gave a focus for a group of families over several generations, at least among those able to afford the considerable expense of the land and the impressive monuments which were a feature of these group burials: the phenomenon is perhaps a case of the wealthier citizens imitating aristocratic practices. Marriage, even at the highest levels, was endogamous, within a close circle of relatives, in order to preserve family property from fragmentation. More generally, for the same reason, it was common to limit family size; and that could often lead to the absence of male heirs through death, and the redistribution of the property among the wider group of relatives, who also had duties to prosecute a man's murderer. But in general there is little evidence for extended family groups being important in the classical age.

Another function of the family raises one of the central problems in our understanding of Athenian social values: the family clearly served as the means of protecting and enclosing women. Women were citizens, with certain cults reserved to them and not allowed to foreign women, and they were citizens for the purposes of marriage and procreation; but otherwise they lacked all independent status. They could not enter into any transaction worth more than one *medimnos* of barley; they could not own any property, with the conventional exception of their clothes, their personal jewellery and personal slaves. At all times they had to be under the protection of a *kyrios*, a guardian; if they were unmarried, their father or closest male relative, if they were married their husband, if widowed their son or other male relative by marriage or birth. At all times the woman belonged to a family and was under the legal protection of its head.

The two types of occasion when a woman could be involved in property transactions illustrate the nature of this protection. The first concerns the dowry: it was the duty of a *kyrios* to provide a dowry for all women in his family: the lack of a dowry demonstrated extreme poverty, and might even lead people to suspect that no legal marriage had in fact taken place. The formula in the betrothal ceremony was:

> I give this woman for the procreation of legitimate children.
> I accept.
> And (e. g.) 3 talents dowry.
> I am content.

Marriage was deemed to have taken place on receipt of the dowry. The dowry accompanied the woman, but did not belong to her: it was in the complete control of her husband; but in the case of divorce or the death of the husband it could be reclaimed along with the woman, and was only really transferred once the woman had a male heir to inherit, and to be her *kyrios*.

A woman could also be the carrier of property in the absence of a will and of male heirs in the appropriate degree. In this case the woman became an *epiklēros*, or heiress: her name was publicly proclaimed in the assembly, and she and the property were adjudged to the closest male relative of the deceased who was prepared to marry her, often her paternal uncle. This was a well-established procedure: soldiers were given special leave to press their claims; a claimant was entitled to divorce his wife in order to marry the heiress, and could even take the heiress from her husband if she were already married, provided the marriage was childless: 'many who were married have had their wives taken from them', says one orator in a speech in which he explains that his father did not claim an inheritance belonging to his mother, for fear that one of her relatives would then seize her in marriage.

A system of law and private property reflects the prejudices of the society which creates it; the Athenian system was unusual in ancient Greece merely in being more systematic; but it was possible for other cities to develop differently. In Sparta, for instance, the freedom of women was notorious, and much disapproved of by those very philosophers who idealized Sparta otherwise; in Sparta too women could inherit land in their own right, until by the third century the fact that two-fifths of the land was in their hands provoked a political revolution. The status of women in Athens does perhaps require explanation.

CLAY FIGURES OF A WOMAN KNEADING BREAD AND A COOK WORKING AT A GRILL. Fifth century BC. There are several of these Classical studies of work in the kitchen, mainly from Boeotia.

There are two different strands in the Athenian attitude to women. The first is the effect of democracy on the status of women. Aristocratic women at least had been freer in earlier times, but the coming of democracy meant the imposition of the social norms of the majority. Many peasant societies combine a high value placed on women with mistrust of them. Semonides of Amorgos in the sixth century described the appalling varieties of women that the gods had made to be a burden on men, in terms of their animal characteristics; only one type is any good, and she is like the bee: 'She causes his property to grow and increase, and she grows old with a husband whom she loves and who loves her, the mother of a handsome and reputable family. She stands out among all women, and a godlike beauty plays around her. She takes no pleasure in sitting among

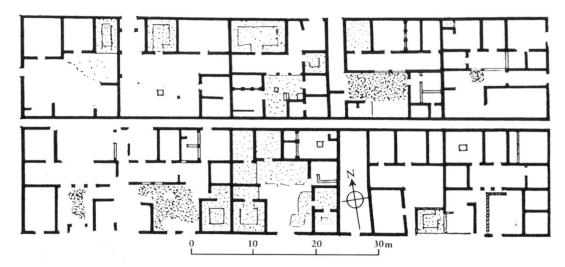

A STREET 'BLOCK' OF FOURTH-CENTURY BC HOUSES AT OLYNTHUS IN NORTH GREECE. There is some variety in the basic scheme of entrance to a courtyard from which there is direct access to living rooms, bedrooms (upstairs), and the men's dining room (*andrōn*). Compare the more elegant villa at Olynthus shown in the next illustration.

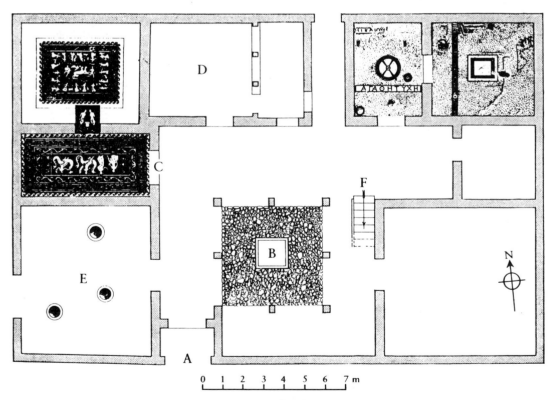

THE VILLA OF GOOD FORTUNE AT OLYNTHUS, fourth century BC. The main entrance (A) is into a verandahed courtyard with a central altar (B). The men's dining room (*andrōn*) is reached from it through an anteroom (C), both with mosaic floors. The kitchen is adjacent (D) and the sunken store-room (E) can also be reached from a side street. At the east are workrooms and the stairs (F) to the upper floor (bedrooms and women's rooms). This area also has access from a back door, while the main door leads directly to the dining room, leaving the women's quarters separate, though not secluded.

woman in places where they tell stories about love' (83–93). Such attitudes compound fear of the irrational and passionate nature of women with an exaggerated belief in their value and the importance of protecting them from the public eye. In agrarian societies these attitudes are held in check by the need for women's labour in the fields; with the advent of urban life the woman is confined to the house, and increased wealth brings with it aspirations to liberate her even from domestic duties. In a dialogue of Xenophon, Socrates confronts the problem of a friend who, because of the political turmoil, finds himself with fourteen female relatives living in his house, all well brought up and therefore unused to any form of work: Socrates persuades him that he should nevertheless provide them with suitable work such as spinning; their tempers are much improved, and the only problem is that they now complain of the idleness of their protector—but, says Socrates, his duty is to protect, as the sheepdog cares for the sheep (Xenophon, *Memorabilia* 2.7).

At a quite different level similar attitudes emerge among intellectuals. Philosophers (with the honourable exception of Plato) agreed that women are less endowed with reason than men—as Aristotle put it, 'the deliberative faculty is not present at all in the slave, in the female it is inoperative, in the child undeveloped'; the family is a natural relationship involving ruler and ruled and 'as regards male and female this relationship of superior and inferior is permanent'. Tragedians and comic poets may portray women with greater vividness and character than men: the most powerful figures in Greek tragedy are women. But the reason for this is precisely that women are believed to be more liable to extremes of emotion and to consequent violent actions. The tragedians show great insight into the predicament of women:

> But now outside my father's house I am nothing; yes, often I have looked on the nature of women thus, that we are nothing. Young girls, in my opinion have the sweetest existence known to mortals in their fathers' homes, for innocence keeps children safe and happy always. But when we reach puberty and understanding, we are thrust out and sold away from our ancestral gods and from our parents. Some go to strangers' homes, others to foreigners', some to joyless houses, some to hostile. And all this, once the first night has yoked us to our husband, we are forced to praise and say that all is well. (Sophocles, *Tereus*, fr. 583)

But these very insights are embedded in stories of appalling violence: in this lost play of Sophocles, Procne is preparing to kill her son in revenge for her husband's seduction of her sister. In the religious sphere, too, women were seen as different from men in their suitability for the blacker, less rational, more orgiastic aspects of belief and ritual. Despite the many signs of empathy with the female condition, the result was a reinforcing of social attitudes that women needed protection from themselves and from the outside world.

Such attitudes relate only to Athenian women:

> For this is what having a woman as a wife means, to have children by her and to introduce the sons to members of the phratry and the deme, and to betroth the daughters

to husbands as one's own. Call-girls (*hetairai*) we have for the sake of pleasure, mistresses for the daily refreshment of our bodies, but wives to bear us legitimate children and to look after the house faithfully.

Thus did an Athenian speaker appeal to an Athenian jury to remember the distinction between Athenian women and others.

It is an outrage if a stranger enters a house where women are or may be present, unless invited by the master. The layout of Athenian houses in fact suggests even within the house a strict segregation between women's quarters and the public rooms for men: in larger houses the women's quarters are situated away from the street entrance which is well guarded by a slave porter. In the country the characteristic shape of the farmhouse is a courtyard where the women and children live during the day, surrounded by single storey rooms; in one corner stands a strong storage tower, into the upper floors of which the women retreat if strangers come. In smaller city houses the men's quarters are on the ground floor, the women's on the upper: in a famous murder trial the defendant claims that his young wife persuaded him to swap sleeping quarters so that she would be near the well to wash the baby—and so that her lover could visit her. But how had this lover even made contact with a married woman? He had noticed her at a funeral, he had bribed her slave-girl to run messages, he had met her under cover of the women's festival of the Thesmophoria: only on such occasions would she have left the house. It was of course legal for the husband with a gang of neighbours to kill the lover caught in the act: the prosecution could only claim that the murder was planned beforehand for other reasons. Women normally left the house accompanied; and the fact that a woman worked in public was either a sign of extreme poverty or evidence that she was not a citizen.

It is not easy to come to terms with such attitudes, however common they may be in peasant societies, if only because we idealize the Greeks as the originators of western civilization. But we should remember that (polygamy apart) the position of Athenian women was in most important respects the same as that of the 200,000,000 women who today live under Islam, and that in the history of the world only communism and the advanced capitalist societies have made any pretence of treating men and women equally.

The consequence of these attitudes in Athens, combined with the importance placed on male social groupings, was to establish public life as the centre of the *polis*: the balance in ancient Athens was shifted away from the family and towards the community: hence the magnificent festivals and displays, the great public buildings for religious and political purposes. It was surrounded by these buildings, in the *agora*, that the Athenian male spent his time. In contrast his home was mean and unimpressive: it was not safe in a democracy to display a lifestyle different from that of other citizens, and anyway a man's life was lived in public not in private. Here lies a fundamental reason for the achievement of Athens in exemplifying the ideal type of the ancient city; the erosion of the family was the price to be paid for her success in escaping from the ties of tribalism and kinship to create a new type of social and political organization.

Economy

It is all too easy to compare and contrast ancient economies with modern ones, and fall into the trap of believing that the ancient economy was primitive and agrarian, as if agrarian economies are naturally simple. The example of Athens is a useful corrective. The land of Attica is fundamentally unsuited to a simple economy: it consists of about a thousand square miles of mountain, upland forest and grazing, with only small pockets of cultivable land, most of that suitable only for olives; such geographical constraints imply a number of quite different and highly specialized agricultural activities, co-ordinated by a central settlement for exchange. One of the curious consequences of recent study of the political system established by Cleisthenes at the end of the sixth century is our ability to plot the population distribution in Attica at the start of the classical period, since each deme provided a number of city councillors proportionate to its population. The richest lands were the plain of Eleusis, the valley of the Cephissus river, and the plain of Marathon: here arable farming and viticulture must have been dominant; the next most fertile area of the Mesogeia is still the centre for *retsina* production. Not surprisingly these areas account for about two-fifths of the population. The city itself, where manufacture, trade, and service activities will have been concentrated, comprises a further fifth. What is perhaps remarkable is the evidence for large settlements in the uplands, and in the rocky Laurium peninsula: here the main activities will have been olive-growing where possible, but otherwise pastoral, centred on sheep and goats for wool and milk products (meat at all times in the Greek world being reserved for festival occasions and the eating of the sacrifice), and also forestry: even today Attica is still heavily wooded. As a result, although the overall population density is naturally lower in these areas, they contain many of the largest individual settlements; the largest of all, with roughly double the representation of other comparable demes and more than half that of the city of Athens itself, is Acharnae, famous for its charcoal industry: charcoal was, before coal, the main domestic and industrial fuel, required in huge quantities for smelting metal, and for cooking and heating under urban conditions. Nor should such activities as fishing in the coastal areas be forgotten.

There is no such comparable evidence for the classical period; but already, before the full development of urbanization in Attica, a complex and diversified agricultural economy existed. It is also clear that the conurbation of Athens required from a very early date the importation of cereals in large quantities; evidence of serious interest in corn imports goes back to the late seventh century, and the protection of the corn routes, especially from the Black Sea, was a major

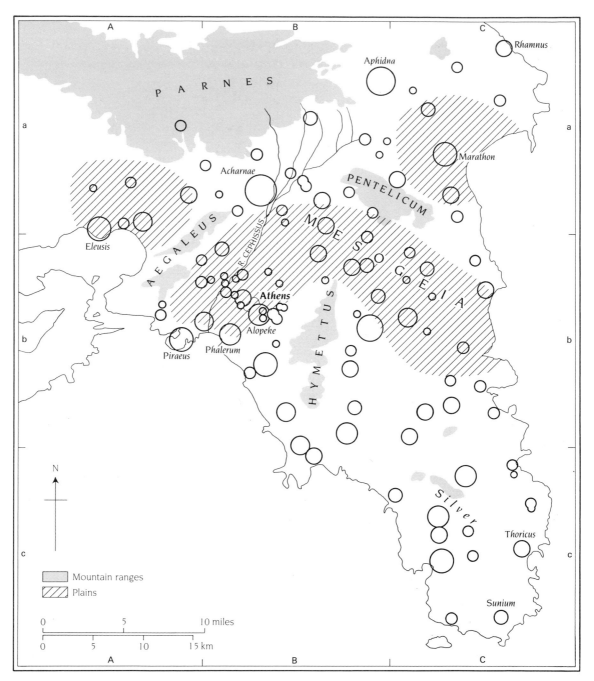

MAP 4. ATTICA. Attica, the territory of the city of Athens, comprises about 1,000 square miles, and is one of the largest city territories. The fertile agricultural areas are in the Cephissus valley and the Mesogeia, together with the plains of Eleusis and Marathon. Upland pastures and woodland cover the rest of the area, together with the bare mountain ranges of Hymettus, Pentelicum, and Parnes. This map shows the population distribution at the start of the Classical period (509 BC): the circles are graded according to the population of the settlements. Note how in the lowlands the villages are often located just off the plains, and also the evidence for large centres of population in the uplands.

determinant of Athenian public policy throughout the classical period. The adult male citizen population rose from about 30,000 to about 40,000 in the fifth century, and then dropped to the 21,000 shown in a census of 317 BC, largely during the Peloponnesian War; the same census reveals 10,000 resident foreigners. These figures may very approximately be multiplied by four to account for freeborn dependents, and we should add around 100,000 slaves. Figures available for the corn yield of Attica in the fourth century suggest that in order to feed this population at least half and probably nearer 80 per cent of corn, the staple food, had to be imported. Trade was therefore a vital component in the Athenian economy. The corn trade was strictly regulated: it was forbidden for Athenian residents to ship corn except to the Piraeus; there were laws preventing the re-export or stockpiling of corn, and special officials to regulate the market. The system of mixed loan, profit sharing and insurance, by which individuals lent capital at a very high rate of interest to shipowners for particular voyages, the loan to be repayable only if the voyage was successfully completed, seems to have been primarily designed for the corn trade. But Athens encouraged the development of other areas of trade by quick and easy access to her courts, fair treatment of foreigners, and encouraging foreigners to settle in Athens (below p. 222). The basis for the trading supremacy of Athens was laid by Themistocles in the early fifth century with the fortification of the Piraeus and the establishment of a proper port; and the unification of the old city and the port was completed in 457 BC by the building of the Long Walls between them. By the end of the century Athens was the leading trade centre in Greece; her position was scarcely affected by her defeat in war and the collapse of her empire, and she began to lose it only with the shift of economic focus as a result of the conquests of Alexander and the unification of the eastern Mediterranean with the Middle East around the new Hellenistic city foundations.

A second type of economic activity in Athens resulted from the public works programme initiated by Pericles in the mid fifth century (below, pp. 298 f.). The records of accounts that survive relate to the later stages of building, the finishing work and the activities of skilled craftsmen on the sculptural decoration: it emerges that the labour force is mixed Athenian and foreign, free and slave, and that the wages for each type of work are identical regardless of social category. Earlier there must have been a large demand for unskilled labour in the digging of foundations, levelling of sites and the main stages of the building; equally the building programme itself used for the first time on a large scale the marble quarries of Mount Pentelicum, and created a great demand for labour both there and in the transport of stone to Athens (always the costliest part of an ancient or medieval building operation). In the absence of large gangs of slave labour it is virtually certain that the poor citizen population benefited most from this work. There is a well-established continuity between the public sculpture of the fifth century and the private grave monuments of the fourth century: when temple building stopped, sculptors moved either elsewhere in Greece or into the private

WORK IN THE CLAY PIT. A small clay plaque, one of hundreds dedicated at a shrine near the potters' quarter at Corinth in the sixth century BC. Many bear scenes of the potters at work, this one the quarrying for clay with refreshment being lowered to the workmen in the pit.

sector. Similarly with unskilled labour: it is noticeable that the democratic state at Athens at all times, except during war and periods of financial crisis, supported a major public works programme; the great frontier forts and the building programme of Lycurgus in the fourth century are the direct continuation of a policy of providing state employment on public works, which had begun as early as the sixth century under the Athenian tyrants.

Other economic activities rested mainly on craft skills, and did not therefore employ large numbers; nevertheless in total they were of considerable importance in creating a lively and varied market. Athens had become the main centre for high-grade painted pottery in Greece in the fifth century, and she remained dominant until the late fourth century, when the increased availability of precious metals from Alexander's conquests removed the need for art pottery. A famous part of the city was known as the *Kerameikos*, the Potters' Quarter. It has been calculated that the number of actual master vase-painters working at Athens at any one time was no more than a hundred, and some at least of these were also potters; nevertheless, taking into account every stage of the process, from the clay digging and fuel suppliers to the workshop staff, and finally the network of merchants who distributed the results as far away as Etruria and Spain, it is clear that this was a major economic activity.

Other crafts had developed beyond the workshop stage towards the factory, largely through the use of slave labour: the father of the politician Demosthenes owned two manufactories, one making swords with over thirty slaves, the other making couches with twenty; the shield factory of Lysias (below, pp. 222 f.) is the largest establishment known, with 120 slaves. A number of prominent politicians of the classical age seem to have drawn considerable revenues from such enterprises, to judge from remarks made in the comic poets about their professions (to the comic poets the wealthy Cleon, for instance, was a tanner); the development is to be explained in part by the existence of government contracts, espe-

THE SILVER MINES AT LAURIUM IN ATTICA. A view looking east over part of a fourth-century industrial complex at Agrileza, including a washery for silver ores uncovered in recent British excavations.

cially in the armaments sector, and in part more generally by the needs of a large city.

A final source of wealth must be mentioned, the mining of silver. In the early fifth century a new deep vein of silver was discovered in the Laurium hills, and silver mining continued intensively, with intermissions in times of disturbance, throughout the classical period. Concessions were leased by the state to Athenian entrepreneurs and syndicates, who worked them with slave gangs. The profits were enormous; the total state revenue was of the same order as the total cost of the corn trade, and individual concessions could make as much as 100 talents over three years. The fifth-century politician Nicias profited in a different way, by supplying the labour: he had a gang of 1,000 slaves whom he let out for work in the mines, drawing an income of 10 talents a year, a return of 33 per cent on his capital. Plato's *Protagoras* and Xenophon's *Symposium* are set in the house of the aristocratic Callias, who belonged to one of the most prominent political families of the fifth century, whose immense wealth was largely derived from the silver mines.

The rich have always preferred to live off rents and profits rather than engaging in direct economic activity; but it is only the prejudices of ancient philosophers which deceive us into thinking that the ownership of land was the only respectable source of wealth. The declarations for tax and inheritance purposes demonstrate a variety of sources; the categories are listed in a standard form: agricultural property, town property let out, manufactories and craft workshops owned, private possessions, money in hand, money deposited or out on loan. Those declarations known to us list capital and income in all or most of these categories.

Among ordinary Athenians, it is true that those who had land were primarily engaged in agriculture; but there were many at all levels of prosperity whose livelihood depended on other activities, and there is little evidence for social barriers: some of the most prominent dedications on the archaic Acropolis were those of craftsmen; potters and sculptors especially had a high social status. One prejudice did however exist: with the exception of state employment, wage labour was despised, and only under exceptional circumstances or in extreme necessity would Athenians work for others on a permanent basis. This was perhaps the chief consequence of the existence of slavery, that no man would willingly work for a master, since to do so was to put himself in the position of a slave; thus slavery both caused and filled a gap in the labour market.

One-third of the free population was non-citizen. The resident foreigner was called a metic (*metoikos*). At Athens he must find a citizen protector and register with the authorities, paying a small annual tax; in return he acquired effectively full protection at law and most of the duties of a citizen, such as contributing to public funds and financing expenses at festivals as well as military service: he was merely not allowed to marry a citizen or to own landed property in Attica. The boundary between citizen and metic was crossed only under exceptional circumstances, and later writers often contrasted the exclusiveness of Greek cities with Roman liberality, claiming that this was why Greek empires were so short lived and unpopular. However in practice, throughout the classical period, the metic population in Athens was large and prosperous, loyal to the city, and proud of its status; it was concentrated in the Piraeus, and its members were naturally especially prominent in the non-agricultural sectors, in manufacture, skilled crafts, trade, and commercial enterprises such as banking. One example will show how integrated the metic could become. Cephalus the Syracusan was invited to Athens by Pericles: he owned a large shield factory clearly fulfilling government contracts; his house in the Piraeus is the scene of Plato's *Republic*, and the dialogue begins with a discussion between him and Socrates on his attitude to his enormous wealth. His sons Polemarchus and Lysias were strong supporters of the radical democracy; Polemarchus was executed and they lost their property under the pro-Spartan oligarchy of 404 BC. Lysias fled into exile, and on his return was rewarded with citizenship for his loyalty, though the grant was soon annulled on legal grounds. Lysias then became the leading composer of legal speeches until his death about 380 BC; the fact that as a non-citizen he could not speak in court mattered little, since all litigants had to speak for themselves, and employed professionals merely to write the speeches. It is clear that Cephalus and his family mixed freely with the aristocratic and intellectual élite of Athens; they were themselves leading members of Athenian society and unswervingly loyal to it, even if they did not possess citizenship.

Unlike wage labour, slavery was a natural form of exploitation in the ancient Mediterranean; and, though we have no precise figures, it is likely that the number of slaves in Attica was roughly equal to the number of free inhabitants, or around 100,000. Slavery as a social status is unproblematic: the slave is in Aristotle's phrase 'a living tool' whom the master can treat as he wishes, though only a fool would maltreat his tools; damage to a slave by others involved compensation to the owner. It was, however, a rule of Athenian law that a slave's evidence was only admissible if procured under torture, for the obvious reason that, in order to liberate a slave from fear of his master, one must substitute a greater fear.

To begin with numbers, there is ample evidence that, while the very poor possessed no slave, this was considered a grave misfortune, and all aspired to own at least one slave: one might compare the modern European's attitude to owning a car. However, as with other consumer durables, possession increases the need up to the limit of what one can afford. Every soldier on campaign was accompanied by a slave, which would normally imply others left at home. Towards the top end of the scale a really rich man might own more than fifty slaves, and employ them in manufactories, as well as possessing household slaves. Larger numbers were exceptional outside the special case of the silver mining gangs. The evidence of the titles of the different jobs we find slaves performing (porter, nurse, tutor, maid, cook, and so on) suggests a comparison with the numbers of servants in Victorian households of various social classes. Agricultural slavery was limited by economic considerations: it is unlikely that the average peasant working his own land with his family could support more than one or two slaves; but those with enough land to choose to live without working would immediately require a slave overseer and a minimum of four or five farmhands, perhaps as many as fifteen.

The question of numbers is important, because it serves to demonstrate how, in most areas of the economy, slave and free worked alongside each other and under the same conditions: indeed one category of slaves actually worked independently as craftsmen, paying a part of their earnings to their owner. This working relationship explains why in many respects, while Athenian society was definitely a slave-owning society, it lacked the characteristics of a slave economy, in that special modes of exploitation had not evolved: in a real sense slavery was a substitute for wage labour, implying the same sort of social conditions. The situation is caricatured by a reactionary Athenian critic:

Now as for the slaves and metics in Athens, they live a most undisciplined life; one is not permitted to strike them there, and a slave will not stand out of the way for you.

Let me explain why. If the law permitted a free man to strike a slave or a metic or a freedman, he would often find that he had mistaken an Athenian for a slave and struck him, for, so far as clothing and general appearance are concerned, the common people look just the same as the slaves and metics. (Pseudo-Xenophon, *On Athens* 1. 10)

In only one area had a true slave economy developed: the silver mining gangs were organized to obviate the need for free labour in conditions which no free man would tolerate. The slave-owner's contract protected him against loss by insisting on the replacement of all slaves who died, but this scarcely offered much protection to the slave, for the owner's profit was such that he could afford a new slave after three years. The skeletons and evidence of living 300 feet underground in tunnels fed with air through downdrafts created by fires halfway up the shafts, the niche for the guard at the mine entrance, and the fact that the tunnels were so small that the face workers must have crawled and knelt at their work while all porterage was carried out by pre-adolescent children, reveal the truth. Few Athenians cared to visit their investments in the Laurium mines, and special overseers were employed; even on the surface miners were kept chained. It is indeed an appalling indictment of Athenian indifference that Nicias, whose money was made from child labour of this sort, could widely be regarded as the most moral and religious man of his generation.

Culture

Culture requires leisure and occasion: leisure is not usually a problem in the pre-industrial world, or where one works for oneself rather than another. There were two main types of occasion in the classical world, private and public, the *symposion* and the festival.

The *symposion* or male drinking group belongs to the world of social groups already described, and embodies essentially an aristocratic form of culture still practised in the classical age, but no longer dominant. Earlier much of Greek poetry, Greek music, and Greek pottery had been created for such groups, whose character was remarkably uniform across the Greek world; if artistic creativity had diminished, the *symposion* was still a main focus of social life. The *symposion* took place in a room called 'the men's room' (*andrōn*), often specially designed, with the door off-centre to accommodate the couches on which the participants lay, one or two to a couch, propped on their left arm. Before them were light snacks on low tables. The size of the rooms varied from three to twelve or more couches, so the groups were relatively small. In the room stood a large *kratēr* or mixing bowl, in which the wine was mixed with water in proportions usually of two or three of water to one of wine: the alcoholic content was therefore less than that of modern beer; the wine-pourers were young male or female slaves, often chosen for their beauty. The participants drank occasionally out of metal, but more often out of the fine painted pottery which was an Athenian speciality,

SYMPOSION, on an Athenian cup by the Brygos Painter of about 490–480 BC. Reclining at a feast—an eastern habit—was adopted by Greeks before 600 BC. The furniture is as that for the bedroom, but often more elaborate, and the couches determined the size of the room in the house (the *andrōn*) set aside for banquet and *symposion*. Women attend only to entertain, boys to provide music or bring wine. The artists dwell on the lighter-hearted aspects of the *symposion*, but it could serve more serious social and even political purposes as a private gathering of men from different families—like a club.

and followed complex social customs in their behaviour, under the direction of a leader. Poetry continued to be performed; although there are no great names like Anacreon or Alcaeus, and those anonymous drinking rounds (*skolia*) which can be dated are mostly earlier, the collection of short elegiac poems attributed to Theognis seems to go back to sympotic song-books of this period. There were games (*kottabos*, flicking wine at a target, was one of the most developed), and increasingly professional entertainments performed by slave girls and boys. Our literary evocations of the classical *Symposium* by Plato and Xenophon illustrate two basic features. The first is the element of order and succession: the speaking, like the drinking, is ordered—each man talks in turn on a chosen theme. The second is the importance of love and sex: excluded from the family setting, these natural emotions found their place in the drinking group. Here is the main reason for the importance of homosexuality in ancient Greece; for the *symposion* provided the focus for liaisons of both 'earthly' and 'spiritual' type, whether in relation to fellow drinkers or the slave boys: the idealization of these emotions inspired some of the highest expressions of love in European literature. Athenian women never attended the *symposion*; but 'call-girls' or *hetairai* were common, slaves often owned by one or more men and accompanying them as part of the entertainment: 'the defendant Neaera drank and dined with them in the presence of many men, as an *hetaira* would do'—therefore she cannot be an Athenian citizen. Vase-painting illustrates most clearly the range of behaviour which resulted; in literature Xenophon is the best guide, with his informal account of conversations about love, of Callias' infatuation with the son of one of his guests, and of the entertainment provided by two professional slave performers, both acrobatic and erotic. After the evening was over, the party often ended with a drunken riot through the streets, in which innocent bystanders might get beaten up, or sinister events might occur, such as the smashing of the herms outside the doors of Athenian citizens one dark night in May 415 BC. It was even alleged that the Eleusinian Mysteries had been deliberately profaned behind closed doors at a number of parties.

These activities were aristocratic: the social gap is exemplified in the scene in Aristophanes' *Wasps* where 'aristocratic' son tries to teach his 'working-class' father how to behave:

> Come and lie down, and learn how to behave at *symposia* and parties.
>   How do I do it then? Come on, tell me.
> Elegantly.
> You mean like this?
> Oh *no*.
> How then?
> Straighten your knees and pour yourself over the cushions, flowing like an athlete.
> Then praise one of the bronzes, inspect the ceiling, admire the hangings in the hall.

Needless to say, the old man ends up behaving disgracefully, stealing one of the flute-girls and pursued by outraged citizens threatening writs for assault.

The *symposion* was part of a youth culture which also found its expression in the *gymnasion*. Greek society was the first known to us to take sport seriously. The circuit of international festivals where top athletes competed (the Olympic Games being only the most famous) was set up in the sixth century; and athletes were famous figures in their own cities, feasted and celebrated in victory odes by men such as Pindar: rather surprisingly, given the importance of the group in these and so many other activities, team sports did not exist. Young men spent much of their day at the *gymnasion* where they exercised naked, pursued their loved ones, or passed the time in conversation. It is no accident that two famous *gymnasia*, the Academy and the Lyceum, gave their names to two famous schools of philosophy, those of Plato and Aristotle; for these philosophers had established their activities deliberately in proximity to the exercising grounds.

Festivals were the focus of democratic culture, where the people could enjoy displays which were a combination of public feast, religious experience and great art. Other chapters explore the theatrical (Ch. 7) and religious (Ch. 11) aspects of the festival; here it is enough to remember that the different aspects cannot be separated. At the Great Dionysia the theatrical performances were preceded by a day in which perhaps as many as 240 bulls might be ritually slaughtered and eaten, there was drunken revelry, and many people spent the night sleeping in the streets: part of the experience of the tragic audience must have been the reek of dried blood and a monumental hangover. In cultural terms the important aspect is the shift in patronage that public festivals imply. It is no longer the tyrant or the aristocrat who commissions great art, but the *dēmos* as a whole. The art produced responds to the demands for a more public, more colourful display: building on the traditions of choral dance appropriate to religious festivals, it creates a truly public art. But there was still a place for that close relationship between artist and patron which seems essential to great art, for the people 'realize that, where it is a matter of providing choral or dramatic festivals or athletic contests or of equipping a naval trireme, it is the rich who put up the money, while the common people enjoy their festivals and contests and are provided with their triremes.' The rich were in fact required by law to undertake these public 'liturgies', and competed to display their generosity before the people.

Education

The Greek alphabet, which is essentially our alphabet, was adopted from the Phoenicians in the eighth century, and created the preconditions for widespread literacy. By the fifth century the ability of male citizens to read and write is taken for granted, which makes it difficult for us to determine how widespread literacy actually was. But certain facts are clear. Literacy in Greece was never a

A READING LESSON. On the interior of an Athenian cup of about 430–420 BC. The boy stands reading a folding wooden tablet, the leaves of which would have been waxed, while the man reads from a scroll. The scene is contemporary Athenian, but the figures are given mythical identities with the names Musaeus and Linus, a poet and a teacher of the Heroic Age.

craft skill, possessed only by experts; from the start writing was used for a great range of activities, from composing poetry to cursing enemies, from displaying laws to voting, from inscribing tombstones or dedications to writing shopping lists. To be completely illiterate was to be ignorant, uncultured; but our evidence shows that there existed all levels of skill in writing, spelling, and grammar: only a society in which literacy is widespread can offer such a range of evidence from semi-literacy to illiteracy. There is of course no sign that women were expected or encouraged to read, though many of them could. To be cautious, we may say that in a city like Athens well over half the male population could read and write, and that levels of literacy in the Greek cities of the classical and Hellenistic periods were higher than at any period in western culture before this century. Yet it is important to remember that for many purposes Greek culture remained an oral culture, in which the preferred forms and means of communication were oral not written.

Widespread literacy implies widespread schooling: organized schools are first heard of at the end of the sixth century. Education had to be paid for, but the cost was low, since schoolteachers were generally despised. Athenian law laid down the hours of opening and closing of schools, the numbers of boys permitted and their ages, and established state supervision of teachers, apparently in the interests of the moral protection of the children from their teachers; those who could afford it were accompanied to school by a slave. Schooling began at the age of seven, and doubtless for many did not continue beyond the three or four years necessary to learn the basic skills. But the next stage in life was thought of as starting about eighteen, so we must assume that many had as much as ten years of schooling. Education was traditionally divided into three areas, under three different types of teacher: literature, physical education, and music. Literature began with reading and writing, grammar and language work, and included learning poetry by heart (especially Homer), imbibing its moral content, and discussing a limited range of literary and other questions raised by the authors; there was a great deal of emphasis on mechanical exercises and rote learning, and teachers made up for their low social status by imposing discipline through corporal punishment. Prose authors were not studied, nor were mathematics or any technical subject: the general Greek view of the usefulness of the poets for practical instruction and their moral value reflects their educational practice. Physical education was carried out at the *palaistra*, some at least of which were public, under special teachers, and included the basic sports practised in Greece, which were again individual rather than team sports. Music seems to have been losing ground in the classical period; it included choral dancing as well as performing on instruments.

It is easy to see that this education is essentially aristocratic in origin, providing the basic cultural and physical skills needed to shine in the *gymnasion* and the *symposion*; but in classical Athens there are signs that it was being made available to a far wider group, which may explain some of the tension between styles of education evident in Aristophanes' *Clouds*. Towards the end of the fourth century the Athenian system was sufficiently standard and universal to be completed by a state system of youth training, in which all young men from the age of eighteen spent two years in the *gymnasion* and in military training under specially appointed officials: this institution, called the *ephēbeia*, became in the Hellenistic period the mark of a Greek city, and the chief distinction between citizen and non-citizen.

The main point of Aristophanes' *Clouds* is, however, a different conflict, that between lower and higher education. By the 420s, when that play was written, there was becoming available a systematic form of higher education intended to train young men for public life. The travelling lecturer, displaying his knowledge of esoteric subjects such as antiquities, anthropology, mathematics, or linguistics, and more especially his skill at public speaking, was an established part of fifth-century life, reflecting ease of communication and a premium on intellectual showmanship; the development of Athens caused these lecturers to converge on the city, and Plato captures well the excitement caused by the visits of mcn such as Gorgias of Leontini, Protagoras of Abdera, Prodicus of Ceos, Anaxagoras of Lampsacus, Hippias of Elis, or (we may add) Herodotus of Halicarnassus. Plato also sets up an antithesis between these figures, the so-called 'sophists', and Socrates the Athenian: they profess knowledge of all sorts, he professes ignorance; they parade skill in public speaking, he can only ask questions, and rejects the elegant prepared answer; they offer to teach, to make men better, he merely offers to confirm man's ignorance; they charge high fees, his teaching is free. But the great confrontations in such dialogues as the *Protagoras* or the *Gorgias* do not reflect contemporary opinion, which did not distinguish the activities of Socrates from those of the sophists. Sophistic ideas are discussed elsewhere (below, p. 236); but to Aristophanes, reflecting the prejudices of the ordinary Athenian, these men were all pretty similar in their scepticism and moral relativism, their love of money and pretentious intellectual claims: they made people question the basic values of society like the existence of the gods and the duty to obey the laws; some of them even seemed to encourage their pupils to think that the political constitution was a matter of indifference. If they taught anything useful, it was 'the ability to make the worse seem the better cause': skill in public speaking implied the development of a rudimentary theory of argument and an understanding of the psychological springs of persuasion, together with a will-ingness to regard the art of rhetoric as separable from belief in truth. The results of this set of techniques might seem mildly useful, as for instance the lists of arguments and counter-arguments in the anonymous late-fifth-century text called the *Dissoi Logoi* (Opposite Arguments), or Antiphon's *Tetralogies*, pairs of speeches on opposite sides of imaginary murder trials; but if a man learned to argue both sides of a case, how would he know which was right?

The impact of the sophists on the aristocratic youth of the late fifth century was enormous: a whole new generation of politicians emerged, more sophisticated and more cynical, to counter the plebeian attitudes of the demagogues; their involvement in the various oligarchic coups of the period discredited the attempt to claim politics as an art, at least in the practical world. But the sophistic educational system developed in two directions, notably under the two great fourth-century educators, Plato and Isocrates. Behind the informal fifth-century world of Plato's dialogues lies an increasingly efficient fourth-century educational establishment attempting to create leaders for a new philosophical age, and studying more or less systematically the various branches of what we know as philosophy, from mathematics to metaphysics. Isocrates was a born educationalist, the most tedious writer Athens ever produced, who unfortunately lived to the age of ninety-eight. He took the sophistic movement forward to offer a training in technique without content: rhetoric became a universal art, suitable for all verbal occasions, not just public speaking. He also offered an education in general culture, and numbers of competent speakers and literary figures are said to have studied under him; but his theories lacked any incentive to serious thought. They were therefore eminently suited to become the standard pattern for organized higher education. This conflict between Plato and Isocrates developed the systematic theories of logic and of rhetoric which we find in Aristotle; it also developed a polarity between philosophy and rhetoric as two forms of mental activity suited to the adult mind, which was to dominate culture for the rest of the ancient world.

The development of the profession of medicine is a phenomenon parallel to the development of rhetoric and philosophy, and subject to many of the same tendencies. Greek doctors were already famous for their skills in the sixth century, and could command high salaries at the courts of Greek tyrants or the Persian king, or significantly as publicly paid city doctors; their scientific theory was drawn from the Ionian philosophers, their skills were acquired by apprenticeship, heredity, and practice. In the fifth century more stable identifiable groups begin to emerge, in south Italy, and in the two Ionian cities of Cos and Cnidus; by the end of the fourth century these last two had become established medical schools with specific traditions: the parallel with the contemporary development from itinerant sophist to philosophical and rhetorical school is plain. The process can be followed in the so-called *Hippocratic Corpus*, a collection of medical treatises attributed to Hippocrates of Cos, contemporary of Socrates, and mostly belonging to the period 430 to 330 BC. These works reveal already an established body of empirical data on most aspects of medicine—anatomy, physiology, gynaecology, pathology, epidemiology, and surgery; most of the observations are related to general physical theories such as that of the four humours. There is a lot of emphasis on diet and regimen, not surprising in a science where pharmacology and surgery necessarily played a smaller role. Many of the early treatises show attempts by doctors to distinguish their profession from the activities of natural philosophers, sophists, and 'irrational medicine'—magicians, sorcerers, and quacks; although they regarded themselves as a guild under the protection of

AN EAST GREEK GRAVESTONE FOR A DOCTOR, about 500 BC. Two metal 'cups' hang in the background. Heated and applied to the flesh, they drew evil humours and pains from the body: a commonly applied remedy in antiquity and not forgotten to the present day.

Asclepius, there is virtually no recourse to divine explanations for illness or cure, and one is left puzzled about the relationship between the medical profession and the various healing cults (involving incubation, dream therapy, incantation, prayer, holy water, and various non-rational types of cure), which are usually associated with Asclepius or other healing gods: perhaps the two attitudes to medicine coexisted in much the same way as orthodox medicine and homeopathy today—the more rationally, since it is surprising that scientific medicine could survive at all in a world where it must have seemed so much less effective than belief.

The Hippocratic Oath embodies the principles of that new medicine, and reveals its organization:

I will pay the same respect to my master in the Science as to my parents and share my life with him and pay all my debts to him. I will regard his sons as my brothers and teach them the Science, if they desire to learn it, without fee or contract. I will hand on precepts, lectures, and all other learning to my sons, to those of my master, and to those pupils duly apprenticed and sworn, and to none other. . . .

The conception of medicine as a craft to be learned by apprenticeship or heredity has fused with the conception of medicine as a body of scientific knowledge and as a moral way of life; it is not surprising that this oath and the attitudes it enshrines have remained central to the practice of medicine down to our own day.

Society is composed of interrelating phenomena, and there is a fascination in seeing how they fit together; perhaps that aim is sufficient justification for this chapter. But social history may also be seen as the background against which man creates his art, his literature, and his systems of thought; it is essential to understanding them, and yet it does not explain them. What is unique about the classical Greek world is its cultural achievements. If we may pause to ask how these came to be, I would suggest that there was, at least in the case of Athens, a crucial conflict between a traditional society and the complexities of its public and private life, which can be traced in the social, economic and cultural developments of the classical age; these complexities liberated the individual from the constraints of tradition without causing him to lose his social identity. The conflict is potentially present in the Greek city-state, and actualized in the case of Athens: Athens is the paradigm of the latent forces of the *polis*.

Further Reading

The various authors mentioned are available in the Loeb Classical Library; the most interesting individual texts are Xenophon's *Symposium* and *Oeconomicus*, the first book of Aristotle's *Politics*, the murder trial in Lysias, *Oration 1*, and Demosthenes, *Oration 59* (against Neaera). The Gortyn Law-code is discussed in R. F. Willetts, *Aristocratic Society in Ancient Crete* (London, 1955). For the evidence of Aristophanes see V. Ehrenberg, *The People of Aristophanes* (2nd edn. London, 1951). The death of Socrates and the evidence for the effects of hemlock are discussed in C. J. Gill, 'The death of Socrates', *Classical Quarterly* 23 (1973), 25–8.

There is a lively general account of *Athenian Culture and Society* (London, 1973) by T. B. L. Webster. For Spartan society the best discussion is W. Den Boer, *Laconian Studies* (Amsterdam, 1954), part III; see also E. Rawson, *The Spartan Tradition in European Thought* (Oxford, 1969).

H. W. Parke, *Festivals of the Athenians* (London, 1977), describes the Athenian religious year; D. M. Macdowell, *The Law of Classical Athens* (London, 1978), is the best introduction to the complexities of Athenian law. Athenian social values are described in K. J. Dover, *Greek Popular Morality in the time of Plato and Aristotle* (Oxford, Blackwell, 1974). On kinship, women, and the family see W. K. Lacey, *The Family in Classical Greece* (London, 1968); S. C. Humphreys, *The Family, Women and Death* (London, 1983). On women the best general book is Sarah B. Pomeroy, *Goddesses, Whores, Wives and Slaves* (New York, 1975); see also *Images of Women in Antiquity*, ed. A. Cameron and A. Kuhrt (London, 1983: essays by Ruth Padel and Susan Walker); David M. Schaps, *Economic Rights of Women in Ancient Greece* (Edinburgh, 1979).

On the economy of Athens the best general account is S. Isager and M. H. Hansen, *Aspects of Athenian Society in the Fourth Century B.C.* (Odense, 1975); for a very different account, see M. I.

Finley, *The Ancient Economy* (London, 1973). On special topics see A. Burford, *Craftsmen in Greek and Roman Society* (London, 1972); J. S. Boersma, *Athenian Building Policy from 561/0 to 405/4 B.C.* (Groningen, 1970); C. Conophagos, *Le Laurium antique* (Athens, 1980; an excellent account by a professional mining engineer who has also excavated); D. Whitehead, *The Ideology of the Athenian Metic* (Cambridge, 1977). For slavery the only up-to-date general account is in French, Y. Garlan, *Les Esclaves en Grèce ancienne* (Paris, 1982); there are excellent essays in *Slavery in Classical Antiquity* ed. M. I. Finley (Cambridge, 1960), and in his own collection on the history of modern scholarship, *Ancient Slavery and Modern Ideology* (London, 1980).

For sport see H. A. Harris, *Greek Athletes and Athletics* (London, 1964), and the same author's *Sport in Greece and Rome* (London, 1972). There is an interesting lecture by Michael Vickers on *Greek Symposia*, published by the Joint Association of Classical Teachers, London, no date. Homosexuality is discussed by K. J. Dover, *Greek Homosexuality* (London, 1978). On education see H. I. Marrou, *History of Education in Antiquity* (English trans. New York, 1956); G. B. Kerferd, *The Sophistic Movement* (Cambridge, 1981). The extent of literacy in Athens is discussed in an important article by F. D. Harvey, 'Literacy in the Athenian Democracy', *Revue des Études Grecques* 79 (1966), 585–635. For the consequences of the change from oral to literate culture, see J. Goody (ed.), *Literacy in Traditional Societies* (Cambridge, 1968); E. A. Havelock, *The Literate Revolution in Greece and its Cultural Consequences* (Princeton, 1982). There is an excellent collection of the *Hippocratic Writings* (Penguin, London, 1978), ed. G. E. R. Lloyd; see also his essays, *Magic, Reason and Experience* (Cambridge, 1979); E. D. Phillips, *Greek Medicine* (London, 1973).

Any discussion of the fundamental questions of freedom of thought and religious belief in ancient Greece begins from the work of E. R. Dodds, notably *The Greeks and the Irrational* (Berkeley, 1951), chs. VI and VII; *The Ancient Concept of Progress and other Essays* (Oxford, 1973).

10

Classical Greek Philosophy

❧❧

JULIA ANNAS

Background: Philosophy in the Fifth Century

WHEN Plato began to write, philosophy in Greece already had a long and striking history—a history against which Plato himself in his early dialogues rebels. It is tempting for us to take Plato as marking a fresh start in philosophy, and we are encouraged in this by the fact that his are the first complete works that we can discuss philosophically without the preliminary labour of piecing out fragments and disentangling later reports. But Plato's work as a whole is best seen against the background of the philosophical tradition that he found; and this is even more true of Aristotle, who indeed largely charts that tradition for us, and whose work is deeply marked by his continued engagement with, and responses to, previous thinkers.

Plato's dialogues, written in the fourth century, are for the most part set dramatically in the fifth. Socrates, whom they depict, was then doing philosophy in Athens, at the time when it had become the intellectual centre of the Greek world, and philosophical activity had become exciting and diverse.

Philosophy in Greece had begun as cosmology, explanation of the universe in terms of unifying and simplifying principles which render intelligible a wide variety of phenomena. By the fifth century we find that this activity continues, but its status has changed. There are figures such as Diogenes of Apollonia and Archelaus of Athens, who produce traditional cosmology after giving perfunctory attention to newer metaphysical concerns; but they now represent only one option, one way of doing philosophy in a world conscious of alternatives. The explanation of nature is on its way to becoming only one part of philosophy.

We can see from Plato's *Theaetetus* 179d–180c that in the fifth century philosophers were aware of another tradition of philosophy also, a quite different one going back to Heraclitus. In that passage Heraclitus' followers are berated as arrogant, unco-operative individualists: a recognition, though a hostile one, of a tradition exalting self-understanding and the importance of turning inwards to seek it, something each of us can only do in our own case. Heraclitus despises conventional ways of looking for truth, including cosmology as done by others;

by his pronouncements and his enigmatic style he tries to prod each of us into a personal search for inner enlightenment, a search that will also lead to the excellence (or 'virtue', *aretē*) of *sōphrosynē* or soundness of mind, the state of the person whose clarity about himself leads him to act appropriately towards others. According to Plato, Heraclitus' followers degenerated into pretentious would-be gurus; none the less by Socrates' time thinkers had been introduced to the idea that human excellence, intellectual and other, lies not in curious exploration of the world around us but in a right use and ordering of our own rational faculties.

More striking and widespread than the effects of Heraclitus, in fifth-century philosophizing, were the effects of the arguments propounded by the Eleatic thinkers Parmenides and Melissus. They proved, by an argument that nobody could fault, a conclusion that nobody could believe: that although it appears to us that we refer to a plurality of qualified and changing objects, in reality there is only one thing to be referred to, and to conceive of this as qualified, divided, or pluralized in any way is to imply absurdities. Until Plato and Aristotle nobody challenged the actual arguments, but the conflict they forced between the results of reasoning and the assumptions of experience was taken to heart in two ways. First, traditional philosophizing, mainly occupied with explanation of the world, was jolted into self-consciousness about the issues of reality and appearance and, relatedly, of reasoning and experience. Fifth-century cosmologies show continued confidence in our reasonings about explanation and the ultimate constituents of things; but confidence in the phenomena to be explained has gone. In deference to the Eleatic arguments the world of our experience is thought of as mere appearance, and theories become, for the first time, reductive: they tell us what is really there (atoms and void, for example) and the world of our experience is consigned, mysteriously, to mere convention. Anaxagoras criticizes as wrong the common-sense belief that things come into being and perish; the truth is no longer available to us without philosophers' theories, and it comes to be taken for granted that philosophical thinking reveals a contrast between reality, displayed by theory, and the world as it appears to us, which we pre-reflectively accept. But we find a record of puzzles on this topic rather than solutions; it is not a primary interest for any thinker until Plato.

The outrageousness of the conclusions of Eleatic argument produced another striking development: a new awareness of argument itself, and its use and abuse. It was a novelty when Zeno of Elea, in defence of Parmenides, produced a whole book consisting solely of arguments. It was even more of a novelty when Gorgias of Leontini (*c.*485–*c.*380) produced a book proving by argument that there is nothing, that if there were we couldn't understand it, and if we could we couldn't communicate it. We admire the ingenuity of Gorgian argument while remaining unsure of his commitment either to its validity or to the truth of the conclusion.

At a time when such detachment was new, this could easily strike people, and did, as disturbing and irresponsible. By the time of Aristophanes' *Clouds* cleverness in argument is feared, but it is perceived as a dubious talent, likely to go with indifference to the truth of what is in dispute. This was a sad state of affairs, largely due to confusions about the nature of argument which were not definitively cleared up till Aristotle. But that the suspicions were often deserved can be seen from such a text as the fifth-century *Dissoi Logoi* or 'Double Arguments'. In it arguments are listed pro and con a number of theses; interesting arguments and feeble fallacies are indifferently lumped together; and there is no attempt to understand the grounds or point or mutual relations of any of the theses.

Gorgias was one of the first of the 'sophists', teachers who went round various cities offering, for a fee, the only available 'higher education'. Other famous sophists were Protagoras (*c*.490–421), Prodicus (*c*.460–390s), Hippias (roughly contemporary with Prodicus), Antiphon and Thrasymachus (both difficult to date but active in the late fifth century), Alcidamas and Lycophron (late fifth century, the former a pupil of Gorgias). As well as further instruction in subjects like mathematics, the sophists taught 'rhetoric', the art of arguing convincingly, irrespective of subject-matter. Their services were welcome because the art of arguing other people down was useful in the highly public arena of city politics; thus they tended to pride themselves on skill in arguing, without being clear what in this was due to rhetorical tricks and what to serious philosophical points. Plato depicts them as pretentious, but with little understanding of the techniques and arguments they manipulated; and although we are at a disadvantage because of our dependence on the indirect tradition, we certainly get the impression that they enjoyed the sheer exercise of raising logical puzzles and paradoxical statements without any strong drive to get systematic understanding of them.

Their contribution was not all negative, however; they developed what had hitherto been marginal in philosophy: the study of ethics and politics. People making their livings by teaching the means of success in a number of places were bound to pay attention to the differences between the political institutions and ethical codes of various cities. Protagoras was most famous for drawing relativistic conclusions from this; Plato in the *Theaetetus* presents the relativism of 'Protagoras' as undifferentiated and confused, but we have no way of knowing how fair this is. It became also more and more fashionable to claim that human institutions are a matter of *nomos* (law, rule, interpreted increasingly as arbitrary convention) and not of *physis* (nature). The general idea is clear: human institutions, unlike the laws of nature, can be changed to serve different purposes. But so many different notions were brought under the alluringly vague contrast that it came to bring more confusion than illumination. Callicles in Plato's *Gorgias* is put forward as an example of someone who parades the contrast without meaning anything clear by it. Callicles illustrates also the widespread tendency to draw (largely unjustified) amoralistic conclusions about *nomos* from its vaguely specified contrast with *physis*, and to reject not only inherited customs but any kind of laws or norms as being merely arbitrary and deserving no respect.

Socrates was thus aware of a philosophical tradition that had already become diverse and pluralist. Traditional cosmology continued alongside the newer developments of ethics and the art of reasoning, with some interest in metaphysics and the theory of knowledge. And, especially at Athens, personal certainties had been shaken: not so much by awareness of alternative ways of life, which was hardly new, but by a growing feeling that inarticulate tradition now needed reasoned defence. Respect for the powers of argument created a demand that what was valued be argued for; but the respect was indiscriminate, the nature of argument ill understood, and the result often confusion. Such was the state of philosophy when it was, for a time, revolutionized by a powerful personality.

Socrates

Socrates (470–399) was an ordinary Athenian citizen belonging to no philosophical school; he may have had an early interest in cosmology, but if so, he abandoned it. He wrote nothing, and our reports of him come from sources (Plato, Xenophon, Aristophanes) that give widely divergent pictures. If our interest is philosophical, however, we have no choice but to follow Plato; and although we have always to remember that the Platonic Socrates is Plato's creation, we can form some idea of what it was about the historical Socrates that led Plato to use him as the main spokesman for Platonic ideas. The most important facts about Socrates were that he lived, uncompromisingly, for philosophy; and that he was put to death on anti-intellectual grounds, the charges being that he introduced new divinities and corrupted the youth. It is plausible that behind this lay unspoken political motives, since Socrates had associated with many of the aristocrats who had overthrown the democracy, but the dislike was in part genuinely anti-philosophical. Socrates remained for Plato the prototype of the person unconditionally committed to philosophy; his conception of philosophy changed, but never his conviction of the importance of Socrates' example.

The later cliché about Socrates was that he turned philosophy from science to ethics; but there had already been plenty of ethical and political enquiry. What he did was to make philosophy personal again. He ignored Protagoras' theories about society as much as Anaxagoras' theories about matter, and instead went around picking on individuals and addressing to each of them the disconcerting and unpopular question, 'Do *you* understand what you are talking about?' This naïvely direct refusal to take at face value claims to philosophical and other expertise marks a return to Heraclitus' kind of concern: scientific and sociological enquiries are rejected until we have the self-knowledge to understand the proper use to make of the results. Until we do, the most urgent task for each person is to turn inwards rather than outwards; and in keeping with this Socrates refused to write down any teachings or speechify in any way. Whereas Heraclitus did think he had access to the truth, Socrates represents himself as ignorant, superior only in argumentative technique and self-awareness; he is, he says, merely the gadfly that stings people out of their complacency. But he has a much more intellectual conception of understanding and its requirements than Heraclitus. He argues people into realizing what an undefended mess their views are. He insists that his questioning will only be halted by a rational defence of the interlocutor's views, when he can 'give an account' of them. Indeed, we can see a tendency on Socrates' part to demand a more intellectual articulation than is actually appropriate in the case of the ethical and practical matters on which his interest centres. He demands that practical capacities, including the virtues, be utterly transparent to the agent in a rationally articulated form which he can produce and defend, and this seems a dubious demand. The biographical tradition reinforces our unease by depicting Socrates as in many ways a weird and inhuman person making excessive demands on human nature in both himself and others. (But we have little chance of finding out what, if any, historical reality lies behind these stories.)

Plato

Plato (*c*.427–*c*.347) was an aristocratic Athenian who followed Socrates' example in devoting his life to philosophy, but did not follow him in his rejection of the permanent written word in favour of personal encounter. However, although he did write, a great deal, he retained some Socratic suspicion of writing: *Phaedrus* 274 b–277 a is a famous passage where he warns us that written words are dead and cannot answer back, whereas true philosophy is always a live activity and interchange of thought. Plato's early writings are designed to avoid these dangers; he rejects the established media of prose (or verse) exposition for what must have seemed at the time an amazing choice—the dialogue, which had hitherto been used only for fairly low-grade entertainment. Some of Socrates' other followers, such as Antisthenes and Aeschines of Sphettus, wrote Socratic dialogues, but only with Plato can we see the form put to philosophical use. He employs it to present philosophical arguments in a way that ensures that the listener is stimulated to participate and continue, rather than passively learning off doctrines. Plato never speaks in his own person, and this makes a certain detachment inevitable; we have to make what we can of the picture of Socrates arguing. No message is forced on us, but we are made aware of a problem, and of the need for argument and thought to get further with it.

The dialogues that have these characteristics, and are traditionally accepted as early, are: *Apology* (a monologue), *Crito, Euthyphro, Ion, Lesser Hippias, Greater Hippias, Laches, Lysis, Menexenus, Protagoras, Euthydemus, Charmides, Lovers, Hipparchus, First Alcibiades.* (The last three have been excluded from the Platonic 'canon' since the nineteenth century, but for no good reason; so have a number of others whose authenticity is more doubtful.)

Usually grouped as 'middle' dialogues are *Gorgias, Meno, Phaedo, Symposium, Republic, Phaedrus, Cratylus.* With these some would put *Timaeus* with *Critias*; others would place these with the dialogues usually grouped as 'late': *Theaetetus, Parmenides, Sophist, Statesman, Philebus, Laws.* The dialogues are often 'placed' chronologically by the prominence of certain stylistic features, such as the avoid-ance of hiatus; but this is a very fragile aid in the case of a conscious literary artist who revised his works. In any case we do not yet possess an adequate statistical analysis of Plato's style. But a rough grouping of the dialogues forces itself on us: the middle and late dialogues are radically different from the early ones. They are much longer, mostly undramatic, especially in their use of Socrates, and above all are didactic. The stylistic changes reflect a shift away from the personal urgency of Socratic enquiry: from the middle dialogues on, we are in no doubt that Plato does have views of his own which the figure of Socrates serves merely to present. When he gives us a theory of society (in the *Republic*) or a cosmology (in the *Timaeus*) or a long set of arguments about the Eleatic One (in the *Parmenides*) the dialogue form is serving merely to make the argument more accessible. Often it does not succeed in this; and sometimes it produces an un-suitably casual drift in the argument or exposition. The dialogue form, and the use of Socrates, become strained to breaking-point as Plato becomes ever more engaged in straightforward philosophical debate, often with contemporary posi-tions. All the same, Plato never wholly abandoned dialogue, and clearly contin-ued to value its detachment, and the avoidance it necessitates of more than a mild degree of technicality and systematization of different positions.

His followers and interpreters (with a few exceptions such as the sceptical New Academy) have mostly displayed a different spirit. The dialogue form has usually been taken as a way of communicating different parts of a single system of ideas, a purely literary device which philosophers can safely ignore. Such an approach is unsubtle and risks insensitivity to differences between different dialogues each of which is self-contained. We can readily find in Plato continuing preoccupation with certain themes; but to build a system of Platonic doctrines is to do what he never did. He never commits himself *in propria persona* to any of the doctrines commonly thought of as Platonic; still less does he tell us which of the ideas he discusses are most basic for him and what their relationships are. There are dangers also in trying to go behind the elusive dialogue form to a supposedly more solid historical development of Plato's thought and personality. The 'bio-graphical' tradition is untrustworthy, going back to later interpretations of the dialogues. There are several 'Letters' purporting to be by Plato, of which the Seventh is often claimed as genuine. But forgery of 'letters' was quite standard with famous figures; the 'Seventh Letter' is so peculiar philosophically that it would be perverse to use it as a basis for interpreting the philosophy in the dialogues; and it is as a whole such an unconvincing production that its acceptance by many scholars is best seen as indicating the strength of their desire to find, behind the detachment of the dialogues, something, no matter what, to which Plato is straightforwardly committed. Plato himself thought it important to frustrate just this desire.

A search for the factor, whatever it is, that distinguishes *knowing* from other states, has preoccupied many philosophers, and preoccupies Plato, in changing form. In the early dialogues his concern is the individual agent's understanding of what he is doing. Socrates picks on people whose reasons for acting are second hand, picked up in an unreflective manner, who do not realize that tradition (even a good one) if followed passively will leave one acting in a way which one does not oneself fully understand and cannot defend. Ion, a famous performer of Homer, Laches, a brave general, Euthyphro, a religious expert, and many others are brought to see that they do not really have any idea of why they act as they do. The early dialogues are in this respect variations on a single theme, and leave many dissatisfied, since we get little indication as to what further we are to do. But possibly Plato thought that beyond this there was nothing general to say, that once shorn of pretensions each person must achieve understanding for and by himself. This fits well with a cryptic insistence in some early dialogues on the importance of coming to know oneself. In the *First Alcibiades* the stage after the victim's conviction of his own lack of knowledge is followed (132 ff.) by an exhortation to look at his own inner self, his soul, to find understanding there. It is assumed without argument (in a way recalling Heraclitus) that each person must achieve self-knowledge in his own case, that this self-knowledge amounts to the virtue of *sōphrosynē*, and that having this soundness of mind ensures that one will have a proper appreciation of one's relations to others (indeed in the *Lovers* (138 b) it is identified with the virtue of justice).

The emphasis on self-knowledge as the basis of one's understanding of others is suggestive, but not followed through. One reason can be found in the *Charmides*, where discussion of self-knowledge peters out because no coherent sense can be made of it. The problems seem to lie in the assumption that knowledge must have an independent object, which 'self-knowledge', however interpreted, is unable to provide; and the appearance of this assumption is of great importance. Concentration on individuals' self-understanding turns out to have been a false start, and the model of attaining knowledge comes to be quite different: a grasp of a systematic body of truths which is objective, independent of the individual agent, and capable of being imparted.

In a famous passage in the *Meno* (82 b–86 c) Socrates takes a slave boy ignorant of geometry through a proof, in such a way that he becomes able to see what the right answer is; he has become able to work out for himself why the result must be the way it is. Socrates draws from this the optimistic conclusion that knowledge is really 'recollection' of what our souls know already (hence, knew before our present embodiment). Here we see clearly that knowledge involves having rational grounds in argument and proof (so that it becomes unclear how we can have knowledge of something we simply find out from experience, such as the road to Larissa). Plato has no doubt that such reasoning is objective; it reveals what is really there, just as a geometrical proof does. And our reasoning capacity, identified with the soul, is sharply separated from our empirical means of cognition. The *Phaedo* develops this conception in two ways. The soul, the reasoning ability which grasps reality, is even more drastically separated from the body, understood as everything in us that is not pure reasoning. And Plato is more aware of the need to systematize reasoning, making suggestive, but obscure, remarks about the organization and testing of arguments (100 a, 101 d–e.)

In the central books of the *Republic* this model of knowledge, which clearly owes much to mathematics, is fully displayed. Now knowledge is acquired only after years of preliminary training in mathematical disciplines (inculcating the need to rely on argument rather than experience) and in 'dialectic' or philosophical reasoning, in which 'hypotheses' about the nature of reality are put forward and exhaustively tested by questioning until they can be fully and explicitly defended. Knowledge is systematic and hierarchical: one's beliefs are understood only when one comes to see where they belong in a system of truths where some are basic and some derived. Knowledge so conceived has two further features: it can be imparted, and it requires time and effort, being achieved only by those who have actually come to understand in context what others appreciate only in unintegrated fragments. Unsurprisingly, knowledge will be something only few can attain, and most people's beliefs, however individually well qualified, will not count. It does not follow from such a view that we cannot have systematic understanding of the physical world we experience, but (with a few lapses) Plato's stress on pure reasoning leaves no room for this.

The more emphasis is put on knowledge as grasp of an objective, shared, impartible system of hierarchically ordered truths, the more we wonder what has happened to Plato's original concern to wake each of us up to personal understanding as the basis of our actions. In the *Republic* Plato still insists on the importance of the individual's own insight, and also insists that knowledge culminates in and flows from the Good, and thus has practical import; but most readers are rightly not satisfied that Plato has retained good grounds for this insistence. The original problems about knowledge that come alive in the context of Socratic refutation have got lost.

In the later dialogues we find that, although Plato continues to assert that knowledge requires a rational basis, he seems to have lost confidence in the middle-dialogues model. It is never explicitly argued against or replaced, but it is not put to any use either, and Plato's last thoughts on knowledge are inconclusive ones—the brilliant dialogue *Theaetetus*, where instead of giving us a model for knowledge Plato turns at last to asking what knowledge actually is, and finds the answers, as many have since, persistently elusive.

But the *Republic* model remains pervasive in interpretations of Plato, partly because it is impressive, though vague and never given precise application, partly because it goes naturally with a similarly impressive though vague conception of the reality that corresponds to knowledge.

The knowledge that interlocutors in the early dialogues lack is a grasp of the basis of whatever virtue is in question. They cannot 'give an account' of it which will define the real nature which underlies its various manifestations, and which explains and corrects our ordinary beliefs. What marks off the person with understanding is grasp of what there is real and objective to know about bravery or beauty or justice, or whatever is in dispute. This is what Plato calls (untechnically and with a variety of vocabulary) the Form, the real basis of qualities like the virtues, which can be grasped only by people who have thought and reasoned and is not accessible to those who wrangle blindly about their experience without reflecting on it. Corresponding to the way that knowledge comes to be seen more and more as systematized pure reasoning, the Forms come to be conceived of as objects of pure thinking, cut off in a mysterious way from our experience.

It is often said that Plato has a 'Theory' of Forms and even that it dominates his entire work. In fact Forms appear rarely and are always discussed untechnically; they answer to a variety of needs which are never systematically brought together; and they are prominent only in the early to middle dialogues, which progress towards an ever more grandiose and all-embracing conception of them. They are objects of pure thinking, and thus separate from our experience; yet in a strange fashion they motivate us to grasp them in a way that lifts us out of our everyday individual concerns. In the *Phaedo, Symposium, Republic*, and *Phaedrus* Plato gives famous poetic expression to the thought that the reasoning part of us is drawn to the Forms in a way that is both rigorously argued and a kind of mystical communion; and that by comparison the rest of our life is worthless and a mere distraction.

If we ask 'What are Forms?' we find a variety of answers. They are objects of knowledge (and hence, as we have seen, of reasoning). A central thought is that the Form *F* is what has the quality *F* essentially; this is the heart of the most extended argument for Forms, which recurs in different guises (*Phaedo* 74–6, *Republic* 475–80, 523–5). When we say of things in our experience that they are just, or equal, we can equally well ascribe to them the opposite of that quality, for a variety of reasons, such as applying a different standard. This possibility, it is claimed, shows that in our experience there are no beautiful things that are not also ugly, no just actions that are not also unjust. So (unless we are to infer, which Plato never does, that the use of these terms is always relative to some standard) they cannot be applied without the possibility of the opposite also applying within our experience, but only to the Form, the Form of *F* which is essentially *F* and never not-*F*, and which the *F* things and actions in our experience 'partake of' (in so far as we can correctly call them *F*) but also 'fall short of' (in so far as we can also say of them that they are not *F*). This argument applies only to terms that have opposites, and so, while it will serve for terms that exercise Plato in the early dialogues, such as *just, beautiful*, and *equal*, it will not show that there are Forms of Square or Triangle, or of substances such as men or artefacts such as tables. It is disputed whether Plato ever seriously wanted there to be Forms for these cases, and, if so, what his motivation could have been. In *Republic* 10 we find the notorious Forms of Bed and Table, but at *Parmenides* 130 b–d young Socrates is made to say that he is unsure whether there are Forms even for substance terms. Plato never gets to the root of another problem, either: why, given the argument, he concludes that they are Forms for the good opposites only and not for *ugly*, *unjust*, and so on. Mostly he ignores these, though in one passage (*Theaetetus* 176–7) he allows that there are evil and negative Forms, which the evil and ignorant person comes to resemble.

The role of Forms as essential bearers of qualities which in our experience always turn up contaminated by the possible application of their opposites explains some of the uses to which they are put: for example, in the *Phaedo* (100 ff.) they figure as preferred explanations for why things in our experience have the qualities they do. But some of the Forms' roles are less clearly motivated; sometimes, for example, they are taken to be stable and unchanging objects as opposed to the changing objects in our experience; occasionally we find Forms to be models for artefacts. Most centrally, Forms are contrasted with the supposedly defective way in which particular objects have certain qualities: but sometimes it is types of object or action that provide the contrast. However, sometimes they are contrasted with particular objects themselves, whose supposed fault is that they change, or even that there are many of them and not one. Because of the dialogue form, Plato never has to say which of his arguments for Forms is fundamental, and what their relations are; and because the arguments and contexts of discussion differ so widely in point and result, it is never made clear what the basic motivation for Forms is, nor what the range of Forms is, nor what it is (particulars, types, instantiation of qualities) that they are primarily opposed to. The 'Theory' of Forms is not a theory at all, but an imaginative holding together of different ideas which we glimpse in different contexts, without getting the chance to demand answers to questions about the overall structure of the ideas. The 'Theory' appeals to those who can enter imaginatively into the spirit of it without worrying too much about these questions. It has also been found fascinating precisely by those who want to press these questions and see whether a single coherent theory survives when they are made rigorous. The first of these is Aristotle, who in a work *On the Forms* distinguishes different arguments for Forms and their implications, and concludes that Plato has no single coherent theory of Forms (though he finds them compelling enough to develop his own theory of form).

One of the most disputed questions in recent Platonic scholarship has been whether Plato himself came later to criticize his earlier indiscriminate acceptance of Forms. In the first part of the *Parmenides* young Socrates puts forward what looks like the middle dialogues' conception of Forms, only to have it torn to shreds by the unhistoric, but symbolic, figures of Parmenides and Zeno. And in other late dialogues there are many arguments which do in fact undermine some of Plato's earlier uses of Forms. This certainly looks like self-criticism; but Plato draws no explicit morals. The ideas which for a time he held together in passionate conviction are quietly allowed to fall apart again, and in the late dialogues he pursues different interests for their own sake without over-ambitious synthesis.

The late dialogues are a disparate collection of often unattractively written works. In them we no longer find powerful overall ideas such as Forms or the middle dialogues' model of knowledge; what we do find are detailed and rich investigations of particular themes, which do not lend themselves to synthesis, or to individual summary. These dialogues have always been found most rewarding by philosophers, and this is surely largely due to the fact that in them we find Plato returning to traditional philosophical concerns which he had earlier impatiently rejected. (It is as true now as when they were written that the early dialogues appeal to non-philosophers, whereas only a philosopher will get through the *Parmenides* and the *Sophist*.) Not only is Plato taking traditional philosophical questions more seriously, it is probable that these dialogues were written at a time when Plato had founded a philosophical school, the 'Academy', and come to accept the idea of philosophy as something that could be imparted, as a co-operative and developing endeavour rather than a matter of intense personal insight. As Plato engages more and more in the tradition of cosmology, study of society, and investigation of argument, particularly Eleatic argument, Socrates becomes an increasingly inappropriate and anachronistic representative of his views.

Repeatedly in these dialogues we find that earlier intransigent attitudes have become modified, and that Plato is more willing to discuss and take seriously others' philosophical views. Socrates in the *Phaedo* sees cosmology merely as a mistake, but in the *Timaeus* Plato accepts that it is a legitimate part of philosophy and produces his own (very bizarre) explanation of the physical universe. In the *Gorgias* rhetoric is angrily rejected; in the *Phaedrus* it is an area where superior philosophical understanding can be advantageously applied. In the *Parmenides* and *Sophist* Plato gives careful attention to the structure and sources of the Eleatic problems which he had hitherto tried to solve by his ambitious theory of reality. In the *Cratylus* (which shares many characteristics with the late dialogues) he discusses current theories of language and word-meaning. Most strikingly, perhaps, the nature of his interest in ethics and politics changes considerably. In the early dialogues he is concerned with the personal achievement of virtue, and this is still the theme of his most famous middle dialogue, the *Republic*. In that dialogue his interest has spread sufficiently to society for the account of the just person to be placed against a background of the just society; but it is made clear that this is a society which is *ideally* just, an ideal which has no practicable political application. However, in the late dialogues we find Plato returning at length and several times to ethical and political questions from a changed perspective, one that has much in common with the formerly despised approach of Protagoras and the other sophists. In the *Statesman*, the *Critias*, and the *Laws* he returns to fifth-century questions about the origins of society, takes history and prehistory seriously, and investigates from several angles the issue of what social arrangements actually work and produce a stably functioning real society. The study of ethics and politics is no longer seen from the viewpoint of the individual concerned to become just, but is carried out from the external viewpoint of the investigator, impersonally and historically. (As we would expect, the result is much duller, though more solid and doubtless more useful.)

The late dialogues show a fairly comprehensive reversion to traditional issues which Socrates had swept aside: cosmology; concern with the Eleatic arguments; interest in reasoning and in rhetoric; and the historical and political study of society. Further, the late dialogues are the product, most probably, of teaching and discussion with pupils, in the established forum of the philosophical school. We even hear that Plato came to propound 'unwritten doctrines' of a Pythagorean-sounding kind, a bizarre mathematical metaphysics in which the contents of the universe were 'derived' from the One and the Indefinite Two. (The chief interest of this lies in Aristotle's criticisms of it in *Metaphysics M* and *N*.) Plato has travelled a long way back from Socrates to rejoin the tradition.

It would be wrong, however, to see this as a failure of nerve, or of originality. Plato's ambivalent relation to philosophy as he found it brought it about that he enriched and transformed the tradition to which he returned. Like his ambivalent relation to writing, it produced a corpus of work unparalleled for its variety of appeal, and one in which discussions of contemporary issues are never conventional or derivative. Plato would not have been the great philosopher he is if Socrates had not influenced him, or if he had influenced him more consistently.

Aristotle

Aristotle (384-322) was a product of the Academy; he came there when he was eighteen and stayed there till Plato's death. He came from Stagira in the north of Greece, from a medical family with connections at court in the increasingly powerful state of Macedonia. After he left the Academy he spent some time at the court of Assus in Asia Minor, and then acted as a tutor to Alexander the Great—an episode that made remarkably little impact on either of them. About 335 he returned to Athens and set up his own philosophical school, the Lyceum. In 323 he fled to escape the hostility to pro-Macedonians that was set free by Alexander's death, and he died in Euboea the following year. We know as little about him personally as we do about Plato, and in his case the 'biographical' tradition is even more untrustworthy; it has been infiltrated by hostile and interested sources. We do get the impression of an attractive personality from his will, preserved in the *Life* by Diogenes Laertius.

Aristotle wrote a great deal, and like Plato produced many works in dialogue form for the general public. These survive only in fragments, and what we read as the 'Corpus Aristotelicum' consists of lectures and notes on courses within his school. Later these were grouped by an editor into the books we now read as the *Metaphysics*, *Physics*, *Organon*, and so on; but there are many signs that these unities are factitious. We find different treatments of the same issues; puzzling cross-references; later insertions; and a very uneven level of stylistic finish. The argument is usually very dense, and was clearly used as a basis for discussion; the reader can seldom coast along, and has to pause and work slowly through the thought. Aristotle has been found defeating by those who look for purely literary appeal; but he is an exciting and rewarding author if one has the right expectations of hard work and co-operation.

Unlike Plato, Aristotle never leaves the tradition in which study of the natural world, and its systematic explanation, are normal philosophical tasks. The *Physics*, the *De generatione et corruptione* and the *De caelo* explain natural events in terms of highly theoretical principles, and give an account of the structure and physical constitution of the universe. But Aristotle's energetic appetite for explanation does not stop there; it comes down to more mundane levels. In the *Meteorologica*, for example, he produces an (understandably primitive) geology, meteorology, and chemistry: in the *De sensu*, ch. 3, we find a theory about colours. But it is living things that absorb Aristotle's interest to the greatest extent. The *De anima* and *Parva naturalia*, essays which create the science of the psychology of living things, are followed by massive studies of various aspects of the animals (including humans): the *De generatione animalium* discusses their reproduction, the *De motu* and *De incessu animalium* their modes of movement, the *De partibus animalium* their parts and structure. The *Historia animalium* is a record of animals' behaviour and habits, a record that must have been compiled in collaboration with others and that, although often wrong and sometimes credulous, is a famous historical monument of empirical science. Aristotle was the first biologist and is still respected by biologists. Instead of haphazardly using available reports, he made great efforts to observe many creatures for himself, seeking data and observations relevant to his enquiries. It is characteristic of Aristotle to devote energy both to theoretical physics and to empirical biology, valuing both with a width of vision impossible to recapture today.

Of all beings naturally composed, some are ungenerated and imperishable for the whole of eternity, but others are subject to coming-to-be and perishing. It has come about that in relation to the former, which possess value—indeed divinity—the studies we can make are less, because both the starting-points of the inquiry and the things we long to know about present extremely few appearances to observation. We are better equipped to acquire knowledge about the perishable plants and animals because they grow beside us ... Both studies have their attractions. Though we grasp only a little of the former, we gain more pleasure than from everything around us ... (but because the latter) are closer to us and belong more to our nature, they have their own compensations in comparison with the philosophy concerned with the divine things ... Even in the study of animals unattractive to the senses, the nature that fashioned them offers immeasurable pleasures ... to those who can learn the causes and are naturally lovers of wisdom ... For in all natural things there is something wonderful. (*De partibus animalium* 1. 5, Balme translation)

Aristotle's methods are, of course, unlike any in modern science (for which he has received rather disproportionate criticism). Although interested philosophically in mathematics he does not apply it systematically to the study of physical

BRONZE WARRIOR, found in the sea off Riace in south Italy. About 450 BC.

IRON CORSELET with gold attachments from the tomb of Philip II of Macedon (died 336 BC) at Vergina (ancient Aegae).

reality; qualitative change is basic in his physics and he makes no attempt to give a more basic quantitative analysis of it. But he had no good reason for so doing; the mathematical models of physics that he knew, from Plato and the Pythagoreans, were fanciful and unrealistic. He does in fact apply mathematical models, especially geometrical ones, in particular areas where this can illuminate; to analyse the colour spectrum or to reduce to essentials the patterns of animal movement. Another frequent charge is that he does not employ experiment; certainly he shows no interest in systematically varying the conditions under which a phenomenon is studied. But this is surely due to an assumption not queried until fairly recently: that items display their real natures in their customary environments in the actual world, not in artificially created ones. In fields such as physics and chemistry, where this assumption has been found unfruitful, Aristotle's work has only museum status; but it retains real interest in areas such as zoology and ethology, where a modern scientist still thinks that lions reveal the nature of the species better in their natural habitat than in laboratories or zoos.

Aristotle is a collector of facts; but he is far from being just that. In all his major works his treatment of the facts is informed by consciousness of philosophical issues, and it is here that he is most aware of belonging to a long tradition of philosophy and developing it further. He collected books and read them thoroughly and repeatedly; he worked in close familiarity with the works of his predecessors (including Plato) and usually this resulted in close criticism. Often he will illuminate and expand a discussion by referring to some treatment of it from the history of philosophy; and it is standard for him to begin a discussion by running through previous positions, and pointing out what in them is systematically promising or mistaken. He has been attacked as though this were arrogant cannibalizing of previous philosophy in the interests of his own ideas, but this is mistaken. His attitude in fact shows profound intellectual humility:

No-one is able to attain the truth adequately, while, on the other hand, we do not collectively fail, but everyone says something true about the nature of things, and while individually we contribute little or nothing to the truth, by the union of all a considerable amount is amassed. (*Met.* 993ª31–ᵇ4, Ross translation)

Aristotle never tries to make a radical break either in style or in aim with the cumulative and developing body of philosophical thought available to him (indeed, his treatment of Plato is often insensitive to the extent to which Plato begins by making such a break). He sees himself as a partner in a joint enterprise, able to advance as he does thanks to the spade-work of others. Original achievement consists not in pushing forward unaided but in making intelligent use of what others have provided:

We must first consider what is said by others, so that, if there is anything which they say wrongly, we may not be liable to the same objections, while, if there is any opinion common to them and us, we shall have no private grievance against ourselves on that account, for one must be content to state some points better than one's predecessors and others no worse. (*Met.* 1076ª12–16, Ross translation)

Aristotle's philosophical methodology is subtle and avoids the trap of applying in one area an approach suitable only in others. ('It is the mark of an educated mind to look for precision in each class of things just so far as the nature of the subject admits' (*Nic. Ethics* 1094^b 23–5).)

In both the *Physics* and the *Ethics* he is explicit that a good treatment of an issue will do justice to the appearances or 'phenomena', where these cover both 'the facts', the way the world appears to us, and the observations and explanations that it prompts us to. He does not have uncritical respect for the phenomena, but he feels no urge to find theories that explain them away: long familiarity with the history of philosophy shows that such theories are likely to lead to dead ends. He begins by laying out various views that recommend themselves to us about time, say, or space, or weakness of will; then he analyses problems and conflicts that these produce. His own answer tries to understand and rationalize this material, showing why we are inclined to certain views, or why we tend to go wrong in accepting others. This does not mean that his own answers will be conservatively respectful of common sense: often they are highly technical and imply that our beliefs are largely mistaken. (We are, for example, tempted to the belief that there is such a thing as 'void' or empty space, but Aristotle's analysis shows us, surprisingly, that there cannot be, and that our concept of it is radically confused.) What is important is that his analysis should explain the phenomena: he aims to show us not just what the right answer is, but why we make both the advances and the mistakes that we characteristically do.

Aristotle's works are characterized by the kind of answers this methodology produces. He is subtle and nuanced, often introducing technical terms to gain precision. The course of his thought may be difficult to follow because he prefers inconclusive discussion of problems to the manufacture of speciously clear solutions. All his writing is marked by a balance between doing justice to observed complexity and bringing to our puzzlement the clarity of philosophical explanation. He strives always for the appropriate level of generality which will illuminate without over-simplifying.

The *Physics*, one of his most attractive works, displays this concern perfectly. It is not 'physics' in the modern sense. Rather it is the book where he argues for, and refines, the analytical concepts with which we understand the physical world, notably time, space, infinity, process, activity, change. Pre-reflectively, for example, we find it unproblematic that things change; but making philosophical sense of change runs up against what seem to be impossible philosophical difficulties. Aristotle analyses the sources of difficulty and shows them to be uncompelling in the light of his analysis of change, which focuses on the central case of an object coming to have a property that it formerly lacked. Arguably his paradigm is too restricted and blinds him to the importance of other kinds of changes, where we cannot plausibly find an object with properties. But is is an analysis that gives us a deepened view of what we naturally perceive as basic examples of change; it gives us theoretically grounded insight into the reason why we were right to find the world intelligible that way.

Equally characteristic is his analysis of explanation itself (the so-called doctrine of 'four causes'). Where Plato, in the *Phaedo*, impatiently rejected all other kinds of explanation (*aitia*) for Forms, Aristotle, in *Physics* 2, gives a careful analysis of four mutually irreducible types of explanation: 'form' or defining characteristics; 'matter' or constituents; source of movement (the nearest to our 'cause'); and end or aim (teleological explanation). The history of philosophy is full of (failed) attempts to reduce all kinds of explanation to one favoured kind; Aristotle is notable in his firm refusal to over-simplify and to rush to elegant, but falsifying, unification of phenomena which remain stubbornly complex. There are many kinds and levels of explanation, and they do not exclude one another. Aristotle can be systematic. His most systematic work is the *Posterior Analytics*, an ambitious classificatory structuring of the different branches of knowledge into what seems like a Platonic hierarchy, in which from basic truths are derived ever more specialized truths in various fields. But Aristotle's system is more realistic. The sciences each have their own basic axioms and are not derived from a single source; and the system itself serves as a regulative ideal, a representation of the ordered state of completed science, which we do not, of course, possess now.

Aristotle's 'metaphysics' is in many ways a continuation of his 'physics'. He develops his concepts of form and matter, actuality and potentiality, substance and attribute, as tools of explanation, used very much like those of process and change. He does believe that some items are metaphysically fundamental, independent of, and basic to, an explanation of the rest; and his views on this undergo change. In the *Categories*, usually accepted as an early work, concrete individuals such as Socrates and Coriscus fill this bill, and are called 'first substances'. In the *Metaphysics*, especially the difficult central books, substance appears to be not the individual but its form, and difficulties arise which are not clearly solved, given some of the other metaphysical roles that form plays. Aristotle's views here have been very variously interpreted and estimated; and it is more obvious here than in other parts of his work that what matters for him is getting properly to the roots of a difficulty rather than coming up with simple answers to the problem as originally posed. On one point he never wavers: hostility to Plato's Forms (or numbers or other abstract objects) conceived of as separate from the world we experience, existing independently of it. It is crucial that we do have understanding of the world; a theory must be wrong that cuts us off from what is supposed to make the world intelligible.

A most striking advance on his philosophical inheritance, and the only case where Aristotle consciously claims to innovate, is his great clarification of the nature of argument. The *Topics* and *Sophistical Refutations* are early records of his study of 'how to argue effectively'; but his real breakthrough is marked by the *Prior Analytics*, the first work of formal logic, where by the use of schematic letters he first isolates the notion of logical form and systematically classifies the forms of valid argument. Having made it possible for the first time to distinguish the soundness of an argument from its power to persuade Aristotle also, in the *Rhetoric*, performs the complementary task of classifying the various sources of persuasion in argument. To sort out so rigorously and definitively the various aspects of the 'art of argument' from its muddled state in the fifth century, and even in Plato, was an amazing achievement, displaying both the powers of Aristotle's intellect and his concern not to lose any aspect of the subject he is analysing. The logical and rhetorical works remained more prominent in estimations of Aristotle until the twentieth century; new developments in logic have shown the limitations of Aristotelian logic rather strikingly, and rhetoric is no longer a serious study. As a result it is easy for us to undervalue what appeared to Aristotle's contemporaries (and rightly to Aristotle himself) as an unparalleled achievement.

Aristotle devotes a large proportion of his philosophical energy to the study of people in society and to various phenomena of social life. Sometimes these are activities which Plato had attacked, such as drama and the arts, and Aristotle's subtle and complex theory of various literary genres in the *Poetics* can be seen as rescuing them from Plato's needlessly intemperate attacks. But mostly Aristotle carries on from Plato fairly directly; one such area is that of the monumental studies of society in the late dialogues. We have a number of works now grouped as the *Politics*, and three works on ethics; the *Nicomachean* and *Eudemian Ethics*, and the *Magna Moralia*. (The relation of the first two is very disputed, and so is the authenticity of the third.) Aristotle also deepens and carries further Plato's later interest in history as casting light on present political arrangements: he organizes research into the histories of the institutions of a large number of Greek states (one of these, the *Constitution of Athens*, survives) and makes chronological improvements to the important public records of athletic victors. The distribution of his interests reflects closely what we find in the physical works: thorough research is vital, but it is guided always by a concern for theoretical clarity. (Historians' appreciation of his work has thus varied a great deal, depending on how theoretical their own conception of their subject has been.) Aristotle is not philosophically interested in history for its own sake, as we can see from a famous aside in the *Poetics*: poetry is 'more philosophic and of graver import' than history since it is not concerned with mere brute facts. But history, and other forms of human practical activity, contingent and particular though they are, can still be usefully clarified and analysed by the philosopher. The *Nicomachean Ethics* in particular has deservedly attracted lasting detailed concern because in it the concerns of practical life—excellence, the best life, practical reasoning—are analysed with a beautifully appropriate degree of rigour and abstraction. The theory that 'virtue lies in a mean', for example, shows us the structure of our dispositions to action, and clarifies them to us without forcing them into over-simple, artificial moulds. On practical reasoning, a topic on which few philosophers have said anything both true and illuminating, Aristotle's account is still arguably the best in the field, showing us the structure in what looks like the chaos of everyday deliberations without implausibly reducing all our reasonings about action to a single form of calculation about how to achieve a single fixed end. The project of explaining rather than rejecting the appearances appears here in its most accessible and still relevant form. The ethical works display in a particularly happy way Aristotle's talent for applying the appropriate method, for producing the explanation which clarifies the subject, but clarifies it in such a way that we do not lose touch with our original view of the subject-matter and the difficulties it gives rise to.

Aristotle has throughout appeared as belonging to the more outward-turning philosophical tradition focused on explanation of the physical world and human society from the observer's viewpoint. It may seem that he lacks Plato's, and Heraclitus', concern for the inner, the search in philosophy for personal enlightenment. In fact it is easy to overdraw this contrast; there is in Aristotle a strong mystical streak. But it finds expressions that are impersonal. In short, difficult, and undeveloped passages in *De anima* 3 and *Nic. eth.* 10 he presents the peak of human achievement as abstract thinking which is a unity with its object. And the first mover of Aristotle's universe, established through remorselessly technical argument in *Physics* 7 and 8, is in *Metaphysics* 12 identified with god, and, in difficult and intense passages, with thinking of this abstract kind, which is, in the case of god, 'thinking of thinking', a thinking that escapes the mundane limitations of our cognitive activities, which always require a distinct object. It is clear that these short and cryptic passages contain ideas of considerable importance to Aristotle, but he presents them with no personal urgency, and, perhaps because he suspects it, none of Plato's appeal to the reader's imagination.

It soon became standard to contrast Plato and Aristotle and to claim that their 'systems' were opposed in every way. (A minority tradition claimed that they merely had different approaches to the same truths.) There are obvious contrasts between them, beginning with their styles, but these are not easy to characterize in general terms, if we give due attention to Plato's late dialogues and bear in mind the long period of their common philosophizing in the Academy. Plato was always to have the wider appeal throughout antiquity, partly because of his literary skill, partly because in the middle dialogues he attracts the part of us that loves exciting generalizations. Despite Plato's more vivid depictions, it is Aristotle who is concerned not to lose the complexity and delicacy of everyday experience; but this can be done only at the cost of hard and detailed work not lending itself to popularization or literary glamour. Typically, Aristotle's discussion of the soul or *psychē*, in the *De anima* and other works, is both careful in its study of human and other animal physiology, and suggestive in its theorizing; philosophers find it exciting but it is too difficult to have wider appeal. Plato writes about the soul in a way that is lofty and inspiring, and has appealed to poets and religious thinkers and many people not otherwise interested in philosophy; but philosophers have found it less satisfying, and have often been frustrated by the way Plato fails to distinguish importantly different ideas in his contrast of body and soul.

'Platonism' as a set of doctrines extracted from the dialogues had much wider appeal than Aristotle's ideas. Plato's school was luckier also, though partly by historical accident. The Academy and the Lyceum both became respected educational institutions. But whereas the Academy, under Plato's successors Speusippus and Xenocrates, concentrated on mathematical metaphysics, and later, under Crates, Crantor, and Polemo, on ethical instruction, the Lyceum had made a commitment to scientific research, and it suffered both from a narrowing of interests and from war damage to its records, equipment, and buildings, which were more exposed than the Academy's. The Academy continued, to be rejuvenated as the New Academy; but Aristotle's school, as the active and developing philosophical community he represented in spirit, soon petered out. His successor Theophrastus produced distinguished work in many fields, and his successor Strato was well known for his scientific enquiries; but after that the headship of the Lyceum passes to a string of unoriginal nonentities. Interest in Aristotle's ideas survived, but more and more in the unhelpful form of finding in him a set of doctrines to be mechanically applied. In this form 'Aristotelianism' was to have a long life, but of a kind most inappropriate to Aristotle.

Further Reading

THE SOPHISTS AND THE BACKGROUND

A good full account: W. K. C. Guthrie, *History of Greek Philosophy*, vol. III (Cambridge, 1971): available in two paperback volumes as *The Sophists* and *Socrates*. G. B. Kerferd, *The Sophistic Movement* (Cambridge, 1981) is less massive.

The Greek texts and translations are printed, with a helpful commentary, in G. S. Kirk and J. E. Raven, *The Presocratic Philosophers*, 2nd edn, by M. Schofield (Cambridge, 1984): available in paperback.

PLATO

A large volume, *The Collected Dialogues of Plato*, ed. E. Hamilton and H. Cairns, Bollingen Series 71 (Princeton, 1973) contains almost all the dialogues in good translations. The dubious works which it omits are included in the volume in the Loeb series which contains also the *Charmides*, *Minos*, and *Epinomis* (ed. W. Lamb, London and Cambridge, Mass., 1964).

Secondary literature on Plato is enormous. The following works will guide the reader to particular areas of it: I. Crombie, *An Examination of Plato's Doctrines*, 2 vols. (London, 1963); G. Vlastos, *Platonic Studies*, 2nd edn. (Princeton, 1981).

There are some good collections of articles: R. G. Allen (ed.), *Studies in Plato's Metaphysics* (London, 1965); G. Vlastos (ed.), *Plato* I (articles on Metaphysics and Epistemology) II (on Ethics, Politics, Philosophy of Art, Religion) (London, 1972).

The fourth and fifth volumes of Guthrie's *History of Greek Philosophy* deal with Plato and the Early Academy in detail.

ARISTOTLE

The Oxford Translation of Aristotle, revised by J. Barnes, 2 vols. (Princeton, 1984), contains translations of all the complete extant works and some of the fragments of lost ones.

J. Barnes, *Aristotle* (Oxford, 1982: in the Past Masters series) concentrates on the scientific and logical works. G. E. R. Lloyd, *Aristotle: The Growth and Structure of His Thought* (Cambridge, 1968: paperback) reconstructs Aristotle's intellectual development. On the ethics: A. Rorty, *Essays on Aristotle's Ethics* (California, 1980).

There is a good set of collections of articles: J. Barnes, M. Schofield, R. Sorabji (eds.), *Articles on Aristotle* (London, 1975–9): 1. Science; 2. Ethics; 3. Metaphysics; 4. Psychology and Aesthetics.

The sixth volume of Guthrie's *History of Greek Philosophy* (the last to be completed) deals with Aristotle.

II

Greek Religion

❧

ROBERT PARKER

Gods and Men

GREEK religion belongs to the class of ancient polytheisms: one can in very general terms compare the religions of Rome, of Egypt, of the ancient Indo-Iranians, and most of the religions of the ancient Near East. The gods of such a polytheism have each a defined sphere of influence. The balanced worshipper does not pick and choose between them but pays some respect to them all. To neglect one god (Aphrodite, for instance) is to reject an area of human experience. Individual Greek communities paid special honour to particular gods (put the other way, gods 'took most delight' in particular sanctuaries), but not to the exclusion of others. Athena, for instance, was the divine patroness of Athens, and Hera that of Samos; an Athenian decree of 405 BC which celebrates Athenian-Samian co-operation is topped by a relief showing the two goddesses clasping hands; but Hera was also an honoured goddess in Athens, and vice versa.

The number of principal gods was always quite restricted. Homer shows ten important gods in action (Zeus, Hera, Athena, Apollo, Artemis, Poseidon, Aphrodite, Hermes, Hephaestus, and Ares) and these, together with Demeter and Dionysus, made up the 'twelve gods', the conventional total recognized from the fifth century onwards. Alongside them, there were innumerable lesser figures, some quite obscure, but others, such as Pan and the Nymphs, just as important in cult as the junior partners among the twelve, Hephaestus and Ares. Genealogies varied, but the twelve were all often said to be either siblings or children of Zeus, 'the father of gods and men'. Most of them could be conceived as living, a sprawling family, in Zeus' palace on the heavenly mountain Olympus. (At other times they were imagined as dwelling in their favoured cities.) They were thus the Olympians. Contrasted to them was a less clearly defined group of chthonians (from *chthōn*, earth), gods of the earth and the underworld, grouped around Hades, the god of death, and his luckless spouse Persephone. Since crops spring from the earth, the chthonians were not merely a negative counterpoise to the gods of heaven, and even the lord of the Olympians had also, as 'Zeus under the earth', a chthonic aspect.

This restricted cast of principal gods could be made to play an almost infinite number of roles in cult practice by the addition of specifying epithets. A single cult calendar from Attica prescribes offerings on different days for Zeus as 'Zeus of the city', 'kindly Zeus', 'Zeus who looks over men', 'Zeus of fulfilment', 'Zeus of boundaries', and 'Zeus of mountain tops'. He had, in fact, several hundred such epithets. The epithet sometimes indicated the power in virtue of which the worshipper was appealing to the god: Zeus 'the general' evidently did not have in his gift the same benefits as Zeus 'of property'. Sometimes it seems that the epithet's main function was merely to introduce local discriminations within the pantheon common to all Greece. Villagers no doubt took pleasure in knowing that their Zeus or Athena was not quite the same as the one worshipped in the next village over the hill.

'There is never equality between the race of deathless gods and that of men who walk the earth', says Apollo in Homer. The gods had human form; they were born, and they might have sexual contacts, but they did not eat human food, and they would not age or die. Pindar tells how the two races both spring from Mother Earth but 'are kept apart by a difference of power in everything: the one is nothing, but for the other the brazen heaven is a fixed habitation for ever.'

ATHENA SHAKES HANDS WITH HERA. The goddesses symbolize the states of Athens and Samos. The relief crowns an inscription which records Athens' gratitude to Samos for loyalty even after the defeat at Aegospotami in 405 BC. The decree begins with the name of the officiating registrar, then an address 'to those Samians who stood with the Athenian people'. The *stele* was found on the Acropolis at Athens.

The gods were 'blessed', 'best in strength and honour'; men were 'wretched', 'powerless', 'creatures of a day'. In the golden age, men had dined with gods, but the two races were later 'divided'; this division occurred at the time of the first sacrifice, and each subsequent sacrifice was a reminder to man that he no longer dined with the gods but made offerings to them from a distance. Again, it was (with very rare exceptions) only in a greater and more glorious time that gods had visited mortal women to sire godlike sons.

Alongside men and gods there was a third estate, that of heroes. The term 'hero' had a technical sense in Greek religion: a hero was a figure less powerful than a god, to whom cult was paid. He was normally conceived as a mortal who had died, and the typical site of such a cult was a tomb. But various kinds of minor supernatural figure came to be assimilated to the class and, as in the case of Heracles, the distinction between a hero and a god could be uncertain. From Attica alone several hundred heroes are known; some have names and even legends, while others are identified merely as 'the hero beside the salt-pit' or the like. (In such a case it was presumably the existence of a conspicuous tomb that evoked the cult.) These heroes of cult were not identical with the heroes (this is Homer's word) of epic poetry, Achilles, Odysseus, and the rest, but the classes were not altogether distinct. Many of the poetic heroes did receive cult, and one reason for worshipping heroes must surely have been the feeling that they had been beings such as Homer described, stronger and altogether more splendid than the men of today. Large Mycenaean tombs, visible tokens of an ampler past, were often centres of hero-cult. Even historical individuals who displayed out-standing powers—warriors, athletes, founders of colonies—could become heroes. Above all, perhaps, it was the restricted and local scope of the heroes that made them popular. The hero retained the limited and partisan interests of his mortal life. He would help those who lived in the vicinity of his tomb or who belonged to the tribe of which he himself was the founder. Gods had to be shared with the world, but a village or a kinship group could have exclusive rights in a hero. (Heracles with his Panhellenic scope was a rare exception.) Thus hero-cults were the best focus for particular loyalties; and heroes were in general the great local helpers, particularly in battle, their natural sphere.

Greek religion had no single origin. The Greeks were an Indo-European people who settled in the non-Indo-European Aegean basin; they thus came into contact with the many advanced civilizations of the ancient Near East. Elements from all these sources contributed to the amalgam. Only one god bears a name that can be interpreted with certainty: Zeus *patēr* ('father') is the equivalent of Roman *Diespiter* (*Juppiter*) and Indian *Dyaus pitar*, all descended from the Indo-European god of heaven. Similarities, not of name, but of attribute, suggest the Indo-European origin of certain lesser figures, Sun, Dawn, and above all the Dioscuri, Castor and Pollux, who strikingly recall another pair of heavenly twins parti-cularly associated with horsemanship, the Asvin of early Indian poetry. The closest equivalents to Aphrodite, on the other hand, are found in the love god-

THE TEMPLE OF APOLLO AT DELPHI, showing the foundations and restored columns and looking south-east over the lower sanctuary terrace (Marmaria), with a Temple of Athena, and to the pass leading east to Boeotia. The other approach led up from the Gulf of Corinth, at Itea, from the south west. The dramatic sanctuary site is built on a steep slope beneath the gleaming cliffs (Phaedriades) on the flanks of Mount Parnassus. At the left is the gully with the sacred spring of Castalia.

desses of the Near East, the Sumerian Inanna and the Semitic Astarte/Ishtar. This may mean, though, that Aphrodite has acquired oriental traits rather than that she is wholly oriental by origin: the individual gods often appear to be composite no less than the pantheon as a whole. Artemis too belongs in part to a near eastern type, that of the 'Mistress of Animals', while there are non-Indo-European traits in Apollo and Hephaestus. And the 'Kingship in Heaven' myth told by Hesiod is a particularly clear case of borrowing from the Near East in mythology (above, pp. 89 f.).

Thanks to the decipherment of the Linear B script in 1952, we can give some

MODEL OF THE SANCTUARY AT OLYMPIA. At the centre is the temple of Zeus and to its right the ash altar and the smaller, older temple of Hera. The small buildings at the right are treasuries dedicated by Greek states, beside the tunnel leading to the stadium, bottom right. The area before the temple was closed by a stoa. At the left are administrative buildings and beyond a big guesthouse and exercise areas. The columnless gabled building is Phidias' workshop in which the gold-and-ivory Zeus was made.

account of the state of Greek religion in the period 1400–1200 BC. The Linear B tablets reveal that the pantheon of this Minoan–Mycenaean civilization was already to a large extent that of classical Greece. Of great gods, Zeus, Hera, and Poseidon are certainly attested, and also, with varying degrees of probability, Artemis, Hermes, Ares, and Dionysus. A 'Lady of Athana' is doubtless a precursor of Athena, and several lesser figures appear—Eileithyia, the goddess of birth, Enyalios, a god of war who declined into an epithet of Ares, and Paiaon, a healer who was similarly absorbed by Apollo. Aphrodite, Apollo, and (except very questionably) Demeter are so far unattested, but they were not necessarily unknown. There is also, certainly, much that is unfamiliar, both among the gods (who is 'Drimios son of Zeus'?) and in cult practice and organization. The impression that the art of the period conveys, of a religion still dominated by pre-Greek goddesses of nature, is perhaps partly confirmed by a series of anonymous divine 'Ladies' who appear in the texts; but in general the Minoan–Mycenaean divine world now seems much more Greek than it did when only the artistic evidence was available.

With the fall of the Mycenaean civilization around 1200, Greece relapsed into illiteracy. When writing revived with the introduction of the Phoenician script in the ninth or eighth century, the crucial transition from Mycenaean to Greek religion had already occurred. The new script was used to record the poems of Homer and Hesiod, the earliest documents of true Greek religion, but for the preceding centuries we have only the fragmentary and ambiguous evidence of archaeology. Very few Mycenaean holy places continued to be used for cult throughout the Dark Ages. There is a growing body of evidence for oriental influence during the period, perhaps transmitted first through Cyprus and later through the trading post of Al Mina in Syria. From the eighth century, for instance, a typical religious site consisted of a free-standing temple, a cult image inside it, and a fire-altar in front of it; there are Near Eastern, but not, it seems, Mycenaean, antecedents for such a complex. Apollo and Zeus could be portrayed in the eighth century in the guise of the Hittite-Syrian war god. It was perhaps not until early in the Dark Ages that the cult of Aphrodite was introduced from the East (or took on eastern characteristics) and not till the end of them that the Kingship in Heaven myth was translated into Greek. It was almost certainly in this period that two foreign gods won a place on the fringe of Greek religion, Adonis the lover of Aphrodite (compare the Semitic word *adon*, 'lord') and the mountain mother *Kybelē/Kybēbē* (*Kubaba* is known as an Anatolian goddess). There is also a striking 'hymn to Hecate' in Hesiod's *Theogony*. Hecate seems to be a goddess of Asia Minor by origin, and Hesiod's hymn perhaps reflects the propaganda of a cult that was newly entering Greece. (Greek religion never lost this openness to foreign gods: at the end of the fifth century, for instance, two new gods arrived in Athens, Sabazius from Phrygia and Bendis from Thrace, and, though the cult of Sabazius was confined to private associations, Bendis found a place in public religion.) On the more important theme of religion's internal development in the period in response to social change we can say little. The cult of heroes seems to have had its origin in these centuries, beginning possibly in the tenth century and becoming more widely diffused (perhaps under the influence of epic poetry) in the eighth. To judge from epic, communities of this period were heavily dependent for their defence on individual warriors such as Homer's Hector, who 'alone kept Troy safe'. This prominence of the aristocratic champion in life may well have helped to foster the cult of heroes who continued to guard their people from the grave. But the archaeological evidence alters at the moment from year to year, and theories to explain the innovation (if such indeed it was) proliferate.

To understand the place of religion in Greek society we must think away the central religious institution of our own experience, the Church. In Greece power in religious matters lay with those who had secular power: in the household with the father, in early communities with the king, in developed city-states with the magistrates or even with the citizen assembly. At Athens it was a magistrate who impersonated the god Dionysus in an important ritual of 'sacred marriage', and decisions about the use of sacred moneys or land were taken by the democratic assembly. (As a result the gods found themselves willy-nilly financing Athenian efforts in the Peloponnesian War.) Individual gods had their priests, but to hold a priesthood was a part-time activity which normally required no special quali-fication or training. There was no institutional framework to unite the priests into a class with interests of its own. The only true religious professionals in Greece were the seers. They were important figures, because omens were taken before many public activities, such as dispatching a colony, beginning a military campaign, or joining battle. As interpreters of the divine will, seers could come into conflict with generals and politicians and their secular plans. There are several reflections in literature of this tense relationship (Hector and Poulydamas, Aga-memnon and Calchas in the *Iliad*; Teiresias and various kings in tragedy). These were not, however, disputes about the rival claims of piety and patriotism, since there could be no conflict of interest between the good of the city and of the 'city-keeping' gods, but about the best means to secure the agreed end of the city's welfare. And such turbulent seers had no actual powers behind which to take their stand. In high literature the seer is always right (for 'the mind of Zeus is ever superior to that of men'), but the theme has tragic potential precisely because he cannot enforce his view. The seer knows, but the ruler decides. In life a layman could even challenge and defeat the experts on their own ground. When the Delphic oracle in 480 BC advised the Athenians to 'put trust in their wooden walls' against the Persian threat, the professional interpreters understood this as a warning to remain within the city walls. The politician Themistocles argued against them that the god was referring to the fleet. Themistocles' inter-pretation prevailed because the final decision lay not with the seers, but with the citizen assembly.

There was, therefore, no religious organization that could spread moral teach-ing, develop doctrine, or impose an orthodoxy. In such a context a creed would have been unthinkable. In a famous passage Herodotus casts two poets as the theologians of Greece:

Not till the day before yesterday, so to speak, did the Greeks know the origin of each of the gods, or whether they had all existed always, and what they were like in appear-ance. . . . It was Homer and Hesiod who created a theogony for the Greeks, gave the gods their epithets, divided out offices and functions among them, and described their appearance. (2.53)

It is, no doubt, true that the prestige of Homer's and Hesiod's poetry did much to stabilize the Greeks' conceptions of their gods. But everyone knew that the Muses who inspired epic poets told lies as well as truth, and in many details of divine genealogy Homer's and Hesiod's accounts were in fact contradictory. Such discrepancies caused no anxiety, and there was no need to question one's con-science before doubting or disputing a traditional myth. There were no heretics because there was no Church. The only religious crimes were acts or attitudes that caused general public resentment. The most obvious was sacrilege in all its forms (including, for instance, the profanation of Mysteries). Another was the crime that Socrates was charged with, 'not recognizing the gods that the city recognizes'. This was to put oneself outside the norms of society in a way that might be found intolerable. Both the flexibility and the sticking-point can be seen in Euripides' *Bacchae*. King Pentheus is here urged by his advisers to recognize Dionysus, and they offer the god to him in a variety of guises: if Pentheus doesn't believe the myths about Dionysus, can't he think of him as the divine principle in wine? And if not that, wouldn't he at least like people to believe that his aunt Semele had given birth to a god? But Pentheus refuses accommodation on any terms, and so he is destroyed by the god.

Cult

'Recognizing the gods' was principally a matter of observing their cult. Piety was expressed in behaviour, in acts of respect towards the gods. (A sociologist would be liable to say that the Greeks valued 'orthopraxy', right doing, rather than 'orthodoxy'.) Religion was not a matter of innerness or intense private communion with the god. This does not mean that strong feelings of loyalty, dependence, and even affection were impossible. Zeus was a 'father' as well as a 'king'; appeals to 'dear' gods are commonplace, and in literature we often find close and relaxed relationships between men and particular gods (Odysseus and Athena in the *Odyssey*, Sappho and Aphrodite, Ion and Apollo in Euripides' *Ion*, Hippolytus and Artemis in Euripides' *Hippolytus*). But piety (*eusebeia*) was literally a matter of 'respect', not love, and even the warmest relationship would quickly have turned sour without observance of the cult. Religion was never personal in the sense of a means for the individual to express his unique identity. No Greek would ever have thought of keeping a spiritual diary. Indeed many classes of person had much of their religion done for them by others: the father sacrificed and besought blessings 'on behalf of' the household, while the magistrates and priests did the same for 'the people' ('and its wives and children', the Athenians eventually added). In all of this religion reflected and supported the general ethos of Greek culture. It discouraged individualism, a preoccupation with inner states and the belief that intentions matter more than actions; it emphasized the sense of belonging to a community and the need for due observance of social forms.

What, then, of right conduct? To those used to Christianity Greek religion often seems a strangely amoral affair. Man was not for Greeks a sinful being in need of redemption; piety was not a matter of perpetual moral endeavour under the watchful guidance of conscience. The gods excelled in strength and skill more obviously than in the quieter virtues. Indeed their behaviour in myth was often scandalous:

> There might you see the gods in sundry shapes
> Committing heady riots, incest, rapes.

But even these easy-going rulers insisted (Zeus in particular) on certain standards of behaviour without which life would have dissolved into barbarism. They punished offences against parents, guests/hosts, suppliants, and the dead. They

SACRIFICE TO APOLLO, on an Athenian vase of about 440 BC. The statue of the god, holding bow and laurel branch, and laurel-crowned like his worshippers, stands on a pillar at the right behind the bloodstained altar. The priest is offering on it the offal and bones due to the gods. The edible meat from the sacrificed animal has already been cut up and wound on to the spits carried by the boy behind the priest, to be cooked.

particularly abhorred oath-breakers, destroying them 'with their whole stock'; such a man might seem to have escaped, but never did—his children would suffer, or he himself in the Underworld. Since oaths accompanied almost all of life's most important transactions (contracts, marriages, and peace-treaties, for instance), Zeus of Oaths was also inevitably a guardian of social morality. Zeus was in fact often said to care for justice in general, and it was a basic presumption of popular belief that, at bottom, the gods were on the side of good men. 'The gods exist', the simple Greek exclaimed when a villain came to a bad end. The Greek was not in danger of slipping inadvertently into sin, as the rules of conduct were clear. But if he broke these rules he forfeited 'good hopes' for the future.

All this, however, was a prerequisite for winning divine favour by ritual, not a substitute for it. Formal cult remained essential. Its most important form was the sacrifice. The typical victim was an animal, but there were also 'bloodless' or 'pure' sacrifices of corn, cakes, fruit, and the like, sometimes offered in addition to animals and sometimes in place of them. A Greek religious calendar was a list of sacrifices; several such survive, indicating what god or hero was to receive what offering on what day. In the commonest form, the thigh-bones of the slaughtered animal, wrapped in fat, were burnt on a raised altar for the gods; the meat was then cooked and eaten by the human participants. Such a sacrifice was a 'gift to the gods'. The gods had to receive their share of all human goods— first-fruits of harvest, libations at drinking parties, tithes of hunting catches, of spoils of war, and the like. In this case it was rather a meagre share, since they were given only the inedible portions of the carcase. Comic poets joked about this unequal division, and it was already a puzzle to Hesiod, who tells a myth to explain it: when gods and men first divided out the sacrificial portions, man's helper, Prometheus, tricked Zeus into taking the wrong share. None the less, by a convenient fiction, these useless parts were deemed an acceptable gift for the gods. Thus a basic form of human festivity, the communal banquet, was sanctified and became a means of approach to the gods.

Sacrifice was a theme on which subtle and expressive variations could be played. Sex, age, and colour of the victim varied with the god or festival concerned; there were rules governing who might participate and what portion of the meat fell to each. In an important alternative form the animal was held close to the ground while its throat was cut, so that the blood would drip into the earth. The carcase was then, it seems, normally burnt whole close to the ground. This ritual was used in particular in the cult of heroes and of powers of the earth (though they also received sacrifices of the other form); it probably derived from the cult of the dead. The antithesis between Olympian sacrifice and this earth-bound form was marked in various ways: on the one side a high altar, smoke rising to heaven, light-coloured victims, libations of wine (the drink of normal civilized life), sociable sharing of meat; on the other a low altar or pit, blood dripping down to 'glut' the powers below, dark victims, wineless libations, destruction of the victim uneaten. (Such wanton annihilation is a funerary practice, seen, for instance, at Patroclus' funeral in the *Iliad*.) And because the killing of animals was the central religious act, there were further rituals that exploited this source of power even though they were not sacrifices to any god: to purify a murderer, for instance, to solemnize an oath, or to take the omens before battle, the parts of slaughtered animals were manipulated in various symbolic ways. Human sacrifice, by contrast, was unknown in the historical period. It is common in mythology, but that is not good evidence even for prehistory, since the horrors that stories postulate to thrill us need not ever have occurred. They may have done, however; what had been the fate of a woman who was recently discovered, laid out with a sacrificial knife beside her head, in a warrior's tomb of the tenth century at Lefkandi in Euboea (above, p. 21)?

One should not be misled by the goriness of the ritual and the savagery of certain myths into thinking that this was a religion of horrors, of self-torment, and of perpetual confrontation with the unspeakable. Certainly, a few rituals were deliberately uncanny; a few festivals or parts of them had a gloomy or penitential tone. An Athenian festival of Zeus, the Diasia, was performed 'with a certain gloominess', and the Panhellenic women's festival of the Thesmophoria involved a day of fasting. There was even in many Ionian cities a ritual expulsion (though not killing) of human scapegoats that must have involved real cruelty. But the dominant tone of Greek ritual was one of festivity and celebration. Herodotus expresses this when he speaks of a group who spent their days 'sacrificing and having a good time'. Processions were very common, ranging from those of a single household (there is one in Aristophanes' *Acharnians*) to those such as the Panathenaic procession that involved the whole city. We can see from the Parthenon frieze or the end of Aeschylus' *Eumenides* what splendid occasions these were. The gods loved beauty: one dedicated to them the loveliest objects that one could, and the word for cult-image, *agalma*, means 'thing to take delight in'. The gods were happy too to see performed in their honour many of the activities that humans most relished. Singing and dancing in a chorus was one basic form of worship, and competing at athletics was another. The great Panhellenic games and the great Athenian dramatic festivals had moved far from their origins, but remained religious ceremonies. One had to put on a good show for the god. When the Thracian goddess Bendis was received in Athens late in the fifth century, she was honoured not by a relay race of torch-bearers on foot (old hat by now), but by a special torch relay on horseback. It never occurred to anyone to object, as did Newman of the Neapolitan carnival, that 'Religion is turned into a mere occasion of worldly gaiety'. At the festivals of country gods such as Demeter and Dionysus the fun did not even have to be kept clean. There were obscene jokes, gestures, and objects (although not normally acts)—the whole range of what scholars term 'ritual obscenity' (as if that made it less fun). The gods were lustrous, graceful, carefree beings, and a shoddy or joyless performance would not fulfil a festival's proper function of 'delighting' them.

Ritual was accompanied by prayer. It was unusual to pray seriously without making an offering of some kind (a sacrifice, a dedication, or at least a libation) or promising to make one should the prayer be fulfilled. By his gift the worshipper established a claim to the counter-gift that he requested, according to the notorious principle of 'do ut des', 'I give so that you will give.' In their prayers Greeks often alluded explicitly to this nexus of mutual benefit and obligation between man and god:

If ever I burnt the rich thighs of bulls and goats in your honour, grant me this prayer.

Maiden [Athena], Telesinos dedicated this image to you on the acropolis. May you take delight in it, and allow him to dedicate another [by preserving his life and wealth].

Protect our city. I believe that what I say is in our common interest. For a flourishing city honours the gods.

Mistress [Athena], Menandros dedicated this offering to you in gratitude, in fulfilment of a vow. Protect him, daughter of Zeus, in gratitude for this.

The gods were thus brought within a comprehensible pattern of social relations. As an old tag said, 'Gifts persuade the gods, gifts reverend kings'; gift-giving was

A RUSTIC PROCESSION FOR DIONYSUS, on an Athenian cup of about 550 BC. The image of a large, hairy satyr holding a massive phallus erect, is carried by a group of village boys, one of whom has climbed on to the satyr's back. Ivy tendrils and ribbons add a festive air to what was probably a ribald occasion celebrating the god of wine and fertility. The satyr, attendant of the god, is a fine creation of the Greek artist's imagination, horse-tailed and horse-eared, often depicted as a randy coward, but here in effigy on a mortal occasion of worship.

perhaps the most important mechanism of social relationships in Homeric society. It might seem to follow that the richest men could secure the most divine favour, and that punishment for crime could be bought off by gifts. The rich and the villainous were certainly free to nourish such hopes. Their subjects and their victims, though, might take a different view. There were always those who insisted that the gods 'rejected the sacrifices' of oath-breakers, and that the modest offerings of the innocent were more acceptable than hecatombs slaughtered by the lawless rich. One offered what one could from what one had. A Greek was not ashamed to mention to the gods that if he were a little richer (wealth being a gift of the gods) he could bring larger offerings. The real psychological significance of 'do ut des' was not the hope of bribery, but the fact that it allowed the worshipper to feel that he had established an ordered, continuing, two-sided relation with the god.

Religion and Society

Economic historians have found that the modern notion of an autonomous 'economy' is inapplicable to ancient societies, where economic activity was influenced by innumerable social constraints. To describe ancient conditions they have developed the concept of the 'embedded' economy. We need for the Greeks a similar concept of embedded religion. It was a social, practical, everyday thing. Every formal social grouping was also a religious grouping, from the smallest to the largest: a household was a set of people who worshipped (in the Athenian case) at the same shrine of Zeus of the Courtyard, while the Greeks as a nation were those who honoured the same gods at the Panhellenic sanctuaries and festivals. To belong to a group was to 'share in the lustral water' (used for purification before sacrifice). The Panhellenic sanctuaries were the great meeting-places, where one could swagger before an audience from all Greece. Perhaps the most important was Delphi, perched above a majestic valley on the slopes of Mount Parnassus in central Greece; it owed its original fame to the oracular shrine of Apollo, already mentioned by Homer, but also became the site of a great athletic festival. Its rival in importance, Olympia in the territory of Elis in the Peloponnese, sacred to Zeus, was home of the original and always most prestigious games, the Olympics.

Since religion was thus embedded, social and religious history are virtually inseparable. At Athens, for instance, the growth of the democracy involved a transformation of the forms of religious life. Cults that had been controlled by aristocratic families were absorbed into the public calendar of the city; new public cults were established, free from aristocratic influence; alongside the traditional groupings, based on kinship, the local group of the deme or village gained importance in religion just as it was doing in politics. Even associations that one entered by choice (the clubs of the Hellenistic period, philosophical schools) were normally dedicated to the cult of particular gods. Since slaves, by contrast, had no social identity as a group there was no distinctive slave religion. Such as it was, their religious life was conducted as humble participants in the cults of their masters' household and in a few public festivals that derived from household cult.

The goals of religion were practical and this-worldly. One important function was of course to steer the individual with appropriate rites of passage through the great transitions of birth, puberty, marriage, and death. Many public festivals throughout Greece had to do with preparing boys to be warriors, girls to be mothers. Another numerous class, including most of the many festivals of

THE ORACLE AT DODONA. After Olympia Dodona was the principal shrine of Zeus, where he gave oracles through the rustling of leaves of his sacred oaks, or the booming of his bronze cauldrons. These needed interpretation by priests. A more direct approach was to write a question on a lead tablet, such as the one shown, and receive the answer inscribed on the back—often just a 'yes' or 'no'. On this sixth-century example the writing is *boustrophēdon* ('as the ox ploughs'), running in lines alternately to left and right. Hermon asks which god he should approach in order to beget useful children by his wife Cretaea.

Demeter, goddess of corn, and Dionysus, god of wine, related to the events of the agricultural year. Others celebrated the political order; so, for instance, the Panathenaea (the 'all-Athenians' festival) and the Synoecia (the festival of synoecism, political unification as a single city) at Athens. Dangerous activities such as seafaring and warfare required especial protection from the gods; there were clusters of rituals associated with them, and even in the historical period gods or heroes were often thought to have intervened to save a ship or support a hard-pressed army. Craftsmen appealed to their divine patrons, and it was a common event in social, judicial, and even commercial life to summon the gods, by sacrificial ritual, to witness an oath. There were above all two practical goods that every Greek desired from the gods, prophetic advice and healing. Prophecy was obtained from oracular shrines, such as Apollo's at Delphi, from wandering oracle-mongers with their books of prophecies, or from seers who drew omens from the entrails of sacrificial animals and the flight of birds. It had, as we saw above, an important role even in public life. For the kind of enquiry that a private individual might make we have good evidence from the oracle of Zeus at Dodona, since some of the lead question-tablets survive:

Heracleidas asks the god whether he will have offspring from the wife he has now.

Lysanias asks Zeus Naios and Dione [Zeus' consort at Dodona] whether the child Annyla is pregnant with is his [often it was the obscurity of the present rather than the future that the god was asked to illumine].

Cleotas asks whether it would be beneficial and advantageous for him to keep sheep.

As for healing, there were healing gods and heroes throughout Greece, their shrines bedecked, like those of Catholic saints, with the votive offerings of grateful patients (often clay images of the affected organ). The commonest technique of healing was by incubation: the patient spent a night in the temple, and the god appeared to him in a dream to perform a miraculous cure, or at least to prescribe a treatment. The most successful such cult was that of Asclepius at Epidaurus, from which there survives an inscription recording miraculous cures. A typical specimen runs:

A man came to the god as a suppliant who was so blind in one eye that he only had the eyelids left and there was nothing between them, but they were wholly empty. Some of the people in the shrine made fun of his folly in thinking that he could see when he had no trace of an eye but only the place for it. He went to sleep in the shrine and a vision appeared to him. It seemed to him that the god boiled up a drug, drew apart his eyelids, and poured it in. When day came he went away, able to see with both eyes.

All this was practical religion. There were few expressions of unpractical religion, of concern for a world other than this. After death, according to Homer, a kind of wraith of the dead man vanished to the underworld, there to lead a joyless, eventless, meaningless shadow existence. (Bliss and punishment were re-

DIVINE HEALING. A relief dedicated about 370 BC by Aeschinus to the hero healer Amphiaraus. The relief is in the form of a building, with the god's all-seeing eyes shown on the roof. At the right the patient sleeps in the sanctuary and is visited by the divine snake which licks his wounded shoulder. At the left the god himself operates. Incubation in the sanctuary brought psychologically reassuring dreams of healing, and this, with more practical assistance, may sometimes have effected cures.

served for a few select heroes.) Nothing therefore of any value persisted beyond the funeral pyre. In classical times it was normal to bring offerings of food and drink to the dead (indeed at Athens this was a condition of inheritance; when an inheritance was disputed, unseemly competitions in mourning took place), but there was no clear theory about the afterlife to justify them and no substantial hopes were based upon them. We often find in Athenian orators the cautious formula, 'The dead, if they have any perception, will think ...' Stories about punishment and reward in the underworld were in circulation, but were only half believed. The whole question was an open one, as Socrates' remarks in Plato's *Apology* (41) show. Firmer claims were made in connection with certain 'mysteries' or secret rites, entry to which was by 'initiation' (not an ordeal, but a spectacular and moving ritual lasting several days). The most important mysteries were those of Demeter and Persephone at Eleusis near Athens, which promised a better lot in the afterlife (eternal feasting perhaps), while for non-initiates 'everything there would be bad' (by the fifth century specific torments had been devised for them). The Eleusinian cult was famed throughout the Greek world, and it is spoken of with a reverence, tinged with moral awe, which shows that initiation was somehow much more than a technique for purchasing such felicity as might be available in the afterlife. But Greeks did not allow such an experience to inspire them with more than, at most, 'good hopes'. Even though many Athenians had been initiated, the normal attitude to the afterlife at Athens remained, as we have seen, one of uncertainty.

The Eleusinian cult was incorporated into the public religion of the Athenian state. Other more radical religious movements of the archaic age defied assimilation. Late in the sixth century Pythagoras taught that souls migrated after death into other bodies, both human and animal. Meat-eating was therefore an abomination, a form of cannibalism. As vegetarians, his followers were excluded from the principal institutions of social life; they lived in closed communities of their own, subject to strict rules of conduct. Probably in the same period poems began to be composed that bore the name of Orpheus, the mythical singer. 'Orpheus' taught that man was a guilty and polluted being. The human race as a whole was descended from 'unjust ancestors', the wicked Titans who dismembered and ate the young god Dionysus. For Orphism, as for Pythagoreanism, meat-eating was a further pollution, repeated day by day. The soul required 'purification' from these taints, or it would pay the penalty in the next incarnation or the next world. In these two interconnected movements (best illustrated for us by Empedocles' poem *Purifications*) we find a series of phenomena untypical of Greek religion: asceticism, preoccupation with the afterlife, rejection of profane society, the concept of a special religious way of life, doctrines of guilt and salvation. Herodotus believed that Pythagoras had imported his doctrines from Egypt, and external influence is not to be excluded; another important factor was doubtless the growing individualism of archaic Greek society, which loosened the traditional ties of kinship and encouraged the quest for individual salvation. Some of these ideas seem to have affected the Eleusinian cult, and there was an important Pythagorean influence on Plato. But it was on the outskirts of the Greek world, particularly in Italy and Sicily, that such movements had most adherents, and they remained marginal phenomena.

An abnormal approach not to the next life but to this one was offered, in particular to women, by certain forms of the cult of Dionysus (best illustrated by Euripides' *Bacchae*). In myth and literature Dionysus is represented as an outsider, a stranger from Lydia, and scholars used to believe that his cult had indeed been introduced to Greece at some date within folk memory. The decipherment of Linear B showed that he was almost certainly already known in Mycenaean times, and it now seems that the myth of Dionysus' arrival is not a reminiscence of historical fact but a way of saying something about his nature. Dionysus Bacchius had to be a stranger because the ecstatic irresponsibility that he offered to women was unique in Greek religion. All women's festivals were a release from domestic confinement, and most of them entailed a kind of temporary repudiation of male authority (the fantasy of Aristophanes' *Women at the Thesmophoria* has a real basis); but their content was often austere, and they normally related in some way to woman's proper function as a fertile being (which allowed her to promote the fertility of crops too, by sympathy). The votaries of Dionysus Bacchius, by contrast, laid down their weaving and abandoned their children to follow the handsome god to the mountains. There as 'maenads' they would dance, revel, and even (so it was said) tear apart live animals and eat them raw. Even in Greek states where such a flight to the mountains was not practised, some form of ecstatic dancing by women in honour of Dionysus certainly took place. But if this was a liberation it was only a temporary one, and indeed in an important sense it tightened the chains, since it confirmed the belief that woman was a volatile and irrational being in need of close control. Maenadism could thus be readily accommodated within public religion. Male bacchic ecstasy, on the other hand, seems to have been long confined to disreputable private associations. (It was in time taken up by Orphism, another fringe movement, and given a novel eschatological meaning.)

It is hard to summarize Greek attitudes to their gods. Much depends on the kind of evidence that one selects. The high literary genres tend to offer a pessimistic view. They often stress the unbridgeable gulf between blessed gods and

DANCING FOR DIONYSUS, on an Athenian cup by the painter Macron, of about 490 BC. The god is worshipped as a pillar, dressed, with a head carved atop and sprouting vines with odd globes attached. The women perform the ecstatic dance of maenads—one on the right holding the thyrsus wand of fennel with ivy leaves wrapped around its tip.

A HERM FROM SIPHNOS, of the later sixth century BC. Herms are stone pillars, topped with the head of the god Hermes and commonly with an erect phallus carved on the front. On the block-shoulders wreaths or clothes could hang. They were set up by roads, at street corners and in other prominent public places to solicit worship from, and offer protection to passers-by. The type of mount is later used for other deities (Heracles, Dionysus, Pan) and in the Roman period for portrait busts.

puny, doomed, suffering man. The gods' concern for mortals, creatures of a day, is necessarily limited, and they rule the universe for their own convenience, not for ours. Sufferings come even to the strongest, wisest, and most pious of men; one scarcely knows why, but 'nothing of this is not Zeus'. Poets who wrote so were not trying to do down the gods but to describe what, at the limits, human life is like. The gods can appear comfortless beings because life itself is brutal, and there was for the Greeks no power distinct from the gods, no devil, to be blamed for the wrongness of things. But since not everyone cared to look into life's worst possibilities so closely there was always room for a more optimistic view. According to Zeus in the *Odyssey*, men are responsible for their own misfortunes; far from hurting them the gods do what they can to save them from themselves. This comfortable doctrine was taken up by the Athenian statesman-poet Solon and became a keynote of Athenian civic religion. Whatever he might hear in the tragic theatre, the Athenian in daily life did not normally doubt that the gods were on his side. For their own Athena the Athenians clearly often felt a genuinely warm affection. Comic poets could even make good-humoured fun of certain gods. How indeed could one help being amused by Hermes, in myth a merry thieving rogue, in image little more than a huge erect phallus? There was nothing irreligious about such laughter, the expression of a relaxed and unthreatened piety. As we have seen, the mood of cult was normally one of festivity, and dedications express gratitude and faith: one of the seventh century, for instance, from the precinct of Hera on Samos was set up 'in return for great kindness'. The divine lustre, which is emphasized in high literature to bring out by contrast the murkiness of man, was also available to be admired in itself. It is clear from art and poetry (particularly the *Homeric Hymns*) that Greeks rejoiced in the grace and radiance of the immortals. They were marvellous figures; their deeds and their loves were as fascinating as those of film stars. Tragic literature was not, therefore, a simple expression of a generally shared tragic world view. (And there is, of course, much variety of attitude even within tragedy.) On the contrary, it often gained its effects by putting optimistic popular beliefs, such as that in the justice of the gods, to the test of extreme cases. The chorus in Euripides' *Hippolytus* comments, when faced by the downfall of a most virtuous man: 'To think of the gods' care for men is a great relief to me from pain. Deep within me I have hopes of understanding; but when I look around at what men do and how they fare I cannot understand.'

Traditional, local, mythological religions such as that of Greece are thought to have little power of survival. The proselytizing international religions based on books and doctrines mop them up. Greek religion, however, lasted for more than a thousand years, and it was able to do so largely because of its very lack of doctrinal precision. Criticism had begun in the sixth century with Xenophanes, who said that 'Homer and Hesiod ascribed to the gods everything that among men is a shame and disgrace: theft, adultery, and deceiving one another.' But it was easy to counter the objection, by rewriting embarrassing myths (as Pindar did in *Olympian* 1), interpreting them allegorically, or simply refusing to believe them (so Plato). Xenophanes went on to criticize anthropomorphic conceptions of deity: Ethiopians made their gods black and snub-nosed like themselves, and if cows had hands they would represent the gods as cows. He declared that god was in truth a single disembodied mind. Other pre-Socratic philosophers had already by implication banished anthropomorphic gods—for them the divine was some first force or principle of the world—and were ready to explain all observable phenomena in terms of natural laws: thus Zeus was robbed of his thunderbolt. No philosopher henceforth seems to have believed in the literal reality of deities such as those of Homer, human in form and erratic in conduct. There is, however, no evidence that, when first advanced, such ideas caused scandal. But late in the fifth century there was a kind of religious crisis at Athens. Protagoras the sophist announced: 'About the gods I cannot declare whether they exist or not'; other sophists speculated about why men had ever come to believe in deity, and it is possible that Anaxagoras, the leading scientist of the day, was an atheist. Men began to notice the moral implications of the scientists' physical explanations of the world, which left the gods powerless to intervene in defence of their ordinances. It is clear from Aristophanes' *Clouds* that traditional religion was felt to be under threat, and with it, crucially, traditional social morality. Late sources tell of a persecution of intellectuals at this time; details are very uncertain, but it is symptomatic that one of the charges brought against Socrates was that of 'not recognizing the gods that the city recognizes'.

But—we do not quite know how—the crisis was surmounted. Explicit atheism remained virtually unknown. Scientific enquiry ceased to be seen as threatening: even if Zeus did not hurl the thunderbolt with his own hand, might he not be working through the mechanisms postulated by the physicists? Philosophers could not accept the riotous Olympians of mythology, since it was now axiomatic that any god must be wholly wise and good, but they had no wish (least of all the influential and conservative Plato) to dispense with the divine. A compromise was therefore possible. One might not believe in the traditional gods exactly as they were described and portrayed, but one believed in the divine and in piety, and there was no reason not to pay homage to the divine principle through the forms of worship sanctified by tradition. Many philosophers even came to terms with a traditional belief as problematic as that in divination.

The institution of ruler-cult has often been seen as a symptom of a religion in decay. It was first paid, to our knowledge, to the Spartan general Lysander by the Samians late in the fifth century, and subsequently to Alexander and many Hellenistic kings. This was certainly a radical change, but the real precondition for it was a loss not of faith but of political freedom. In an autonomous democracy or even oligarchy there had been no room for men-gods. The divine kings did not supplant the old gods but took their place alongside them; they had little in common with, say, Asclepius, but were not so different from Zeus the King or Zeus the Saviour. The gods lived on. The traditional religion could still in the second century AD win the earnest devotion of a man as cultivated as Plutarch. It was still the old religion that was vanquished in the end by Christianity.

Further Reading

Fortunately the whole subject has recently been treated in a masterpiece of lively learning, W. Burkert, *Griechische Religion der archaischen und klassischen Epoche* (Stuttgart, 1977; English translation, Oxford, 1985). This is much the best starting-point on almost all the topics discussed here. A shorter general study is W. K. C. Guthrie, *The Greeks and their Gods* (London, 1950); there are concise introductions to particular aspects in M. P. Nilsson, *Greek Popular Religion*

(Columbia, 1940: issued in paperback as *Greek Folk Religion*); H. W. Parke, *Greek Oracles* (London, 1967).

Source books: J. Ferguson, *Greek and Roman Religion: a Source Book* (New Jersey, 1980), contains some classical material, but intermingled with much else; F. C. Grant (ed.), *Hellenistic Religions* (Indianapolis, 1953), is excellent for post-classical evidence. Two important texts, Hesiod's *Theogony* and the *Homeric Hymns*, are available in prose translation in H. G. Evelyn-White, *Hesiod, the Homeric Hymns and Homerica*, Loeb Classical Library (Harvard, 1914, and many reprints).

Some works that are especially provocative in approach or perspective are: W. Burkert, *Structure and History in Greek Mythology and Ritual* (Berkeley, 1979) on the psychodynamics of ritual, seeking parallels with animal rituals; E. R. Dodds, *The Greeks and the Irrational* (Berkeley, 1951) is wide-ranging; a classic; P. Friedrich, *The Meaning of Aphrodite* (Chicago, 1978); J. Griffin, *Homer on Life and Death* (Oxford, 1980), chs. 1, 5, 6; H. Lloyd-Jones, *The Justice of Zeus* (Berkeley, 2nd edn., 1984); W. F. Otto, *The Homeric Gods*, trans. M. Hadas (London, 1955), a vigorous assertion of the truth and value of Greek religion; and a collection (ed. R. L. Gordon), *Myth, Religion and Society: Structuralist Essays* (Cambridge, 1981) and other works of the same school listed there. E. Rohde, *Psyche*, trans. W. B. Hillis (London, 1925) on the soul, immortality, Dionysus, is now largely outdated in theory, but unsurpassed in learning and vigour. Two recent works valuable for full and alert descriptions are J. D. Mikalson, *Athenian Popular Religion* (North Carolina, 1983), on attitudes rather than acts, and W. K. Pritchett, *The Greek State at War*, Part iii, *Religion* (Berkeley, 1979). The best introduction to attitudes to divination is A. D. Nock, 'Religious Attitudes of the Ancient Greeks' in his *Essays on Religion and the Ancient World*, ed. Z. Stewart (Oxford, 1972). On science and religion there is a brilliant study by G. E. R. Lloyd, *Magic, Reason and Experience* (Cambridge, 1979). B. F. Meyer and E. P. Sanders (eds.), *Jewish and Christian Self-Definition* iii: *Self-Definition in the Greco-Roman World* (London, 1982), contains expert essays on the Orphic/Pythagorean movement and on Dionysiac cult.

On particular topics there are:

J. Bremmer, *The Early Greek Concept of the Soul* (Princeton, 1983).

W. Burkert, *Homo Necans*, trans. P. Bing (Berkeley, 1983), on sacrifice.

E. R. Dodds, edn. of Euripides, *Bacchae* (Oxford, 1960^2) (on Dionysus).

E. J. and L. Edelstein, *Asclepius* (Baltimore, 1945).

L. R. Farnell, *The Cults of the Greek States*, 5 vols. (Oxford, 1896–1909), and *Greek Hero Cults and Ideas of Immortality* (Oxford, 1921) are still valuable works of reference.

A.-J. Festugière, *Personal Religion among the Greeks* (Berkeley, 1954).

W. K. C. Guthrie, *Orpheus and Greek Religion* (London, 1935).

D. C. Kurtz and J. Boardman, *Greek Burial Customs* (London, 1971).

I. M. Linforth, *The Arts of Orpheus* (Berkeley, 1941).

G. E. Mylonas, *Eleusis and the Eleusinian Mysteries* (Princeton, 1961).

M. P. Nilsson, *The Minoan–Mycenaean Religion* (Lund, 1951^2), is comprehensive, but prior to the decipherment of Linear B.

M. P. Nilsson, *Cults, Myths, Oracles and Politics in Ancient Greece* (Lund, 1951).

H. W. Parke and D. E. W. Wormell, *The Delphic Oracle* (Oxford, 1956^2).

H. W. Parke, *Festivals of the Athenians* (London, 1977).

Robert Parker, *Miasma: Pollution and Purification in Early Greek Religion* (Oxford, 1983).

H. S. Versnel (ed.), *Faith, Hope and Worship. Aspects of Religious Mentality in the Ancient World* (Leiden, 1981), includes essays on prayer and votive offerings.

G. Zuntz, *Persephone* (Oxford, 1971), on eschatological beliefs of Greek Italy and Sicily.

Le Sacrifice dans l'antiquité, *Entretiens sur l'antiquité classique*, xxvii, Fondation Hardt (Geneva, 1981); several essays in English.

12

Greek Art and Architecture

❧❧

JOHN BOARDMAN

Introduction: Greekness

THE arts of the western world have been dominated by the art of the Greeks. Even the alternative arts of Celtic Europe or the Asian steppes were infiltrated by classical imagery. Although this record makes it easy for us to isolate those characteristics which distinguish Greek art from the arts of other cultures, contemporary or later, it has probably also made it the more difficult to assess on its own terms, to judge its role and the response of those for whom it was practised, and to value justly its profound innovations. And the attempt to define its characteristics may also do less than justice to that other remarkable phenomenon, the rapidity of its evolution from virtual abstraction to realism; while if its history *is* defined in such bald terms we may also miss other fundamental qualities—its unusual (for antiquity) subject-matter and its preoccupation with form and proportion.

The subject-matter of Greek art was essentially man (and to a lesser degree woman). Even when he worked in near-abstract, geometricized forms the artist's prime subjects were human, and this remains true when his skills allowed him to imitate closely, or even to improve upon, nature. Man's actions and aspirations are performed in Greek art by the figures of gods or heroes more often than of mortals, and often in settings, which, though dressed and furnished by their own world, belonged to their heroic past. The gods and heroes were their ancestors; they looked like men and behaved like men. A picture of heroic myth carried a simple message of narrative, but might equally reflect mortal and contemporary problems or successes, as surely as the Attic playwrights explored problems of contemporary society through their dramatized versions of tales of Troy or the heroes. A god in Greek art had the body and carriage of a perfect mortal athlete: a goddess, that of a beautiful, or at least a determined, maternal and wise woman. Supernatural features—breathing fire, multi-limbed, hybrid—are generally abjured except in stories and depictions of what is virtually timeless folk tale. Monsters are remarkably plausible: we can believe in centaurs. And, however horrific, they are there to be beaten, rather than to threaten or terrify. The petrifying Gorgon head evolves from an eastern lion mask to the head of a beautiful woman with snake locks, no less deadly. Animals are subordinate, decorative, or at best an expression of man's dependence on the fertility of his beasts, or they are used in parables for mortal behaviour—the concept of Achilles as a lion and of Aesop's talking creatures is as familiar in art as in literature, though less readily recognized. In such an art landscape is no more important than furniture. Set all this beside the art of Egypt and the Near East, obsessed with the demonic or the ritual of court, temple, or tomb, and judge the difference.

By about 500 BC, in little over 200 years, the Greek artist's presentation of man had progressed from a composition of geometricized parts to an image as detailed and plausible as any in Egypt or the Near East. To this image he added life, and the image based on pattern and on what he knew or had been taught about the representation of man was transformed by what he now looked at and deliberately sought to copy. The art that had offered symbols of the natural world, now by choice imitated it. Illusion began to replace the conventional symbol: the artist began to create replicas of man as skilfully as the poet explored his fears and hopes—to the distress of some philosophers who detected a desire to deceive.

The images were of man, the male body, and generally naked. In classical Greece athletes exercised naked, warriors could fight near-naked, and in everyday life the bared young male must have been a fairly common sight. Artists did not need to look for naked models of their idealized athlete figures; they had grown up in a society in which male nudity was commonplace and a well developed body was admired. The foreigner found this behaviour disgusting, and the foreign artist depicted nudity mainly for religious, erotic, or pathetic appeal. The Greek artist's interest in the naked male may have exaggerated what he saw in life, but it was not to him a conscious aesthetic device. The image of the 'heroic nude' may stem from classical Greece, but the concept does not. Later Greeks, and Romans, used Greek nude types for heroized or deified mortals, and the genre is familiar enough to us since the Neo-classical Revival, in subjects which range from Voltaire to Napoleon, from Beethoven to Mussolini. For us it is unnatural in life, but we have learnt to accept it in art. In classical Greece it was not unnatural in life, and in art it required neither excuse nor explanation.

We measure the world around us, ourselves included, in feet. The human body is the natural, common reference point for measurement, and the non-Greek world had devised complicated systems of measurement interrelating width of finger, of palm, length of forearm (cubit), foot, and so on in proportion and multiples that approximated to nature. Before life became the model, if an artist wished to draw a human figure at any scale, preparing to sculpt it, for example, he would have recourse to the hierarchy of measure, and in Egypt this was rationalized into a simple grid on which the human body could be drawn in a plausible form. This appealed to the Greeks, but they were soon concerned less with absolute ideal measurement than with proportion, and sought to express a

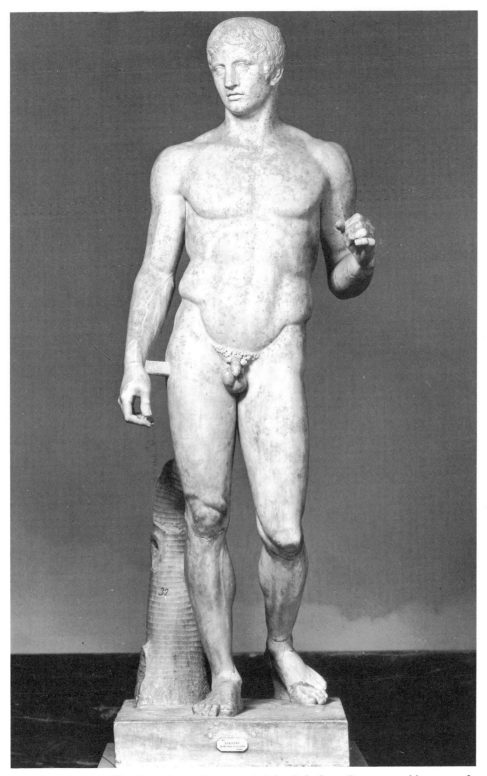

THE IDEAL MAN. The Doryphorus (spear-carrier) by Polyclitus. Roman marble copy of a Greek bronze original of about 440 BC. The original was known as the 'Canon' and had been used by the artist to display his views about the ideal proportions for the human figure. The type differs from the Phidian (as on the Parthenon) and was on the whole more influential in antiquity. The tree trunk and struts are the copyist's additions.

theorctical basis for this ideal. Polyclitus, the fifth-century sculptor, wrote a book on the subject which he illustrated by a statue (his Doryphorus or Canon—'rule'). It expressed his views on *symmetria*, the commensurability of parts of the body. The notion seems mechanical, but his figures, known to us only in copies, were clearly no less life-like than those of his contemporaries. This controlling principle in Greek art appears with no less subtlety in architecture. It is demonstrated by the shapes of vases, by the articulation of the decoration upon them, by the suiting of a subject's size and pose to its field. It determined the shape and decoration of an eighth-century Geometric vase no less than it did the Parthenon pediments. The challenge in Greek art which guaranteed movement and progress was the desire to reconcile what might seem uncompromising opposites, the instinctive sense of pattern and proportion, and the growing awareness of what might be expressed through a more accurate representation of natural forms.

Stimuli and Origins

The greatest stimulus to progress and belief in a future is knowledge and understanding of a past. The Greek of the ninth century BC, living in a sparsely populated country, in a manner seldom rising above the austere, had around him the evidence of the civilization of his predecessors, the Bronze Age Mycenaeans and Minoans. The massive stones of their citadels were built by giants. The gold and ivory on their deserted sites and cemeteries showed where gods had walked with men, and where gods should, therefore, still be worshipped. The techniques of the past were lost when the Bronze Age palace societies crumbled. There was physical survival, and some cultural survival, notably in areas less disturbed by the break-up of the old world, as in Crete, but on the whole this evidence of their past stood more as a challenge than as a model to be copied, and although we may discern in the Mycenaean something of those qualities which later distinguish Greek art, physically there is virtually a new start, a renaissance. It was bred on formal patterns which mainly derived from the older repertory, but were executed with a new discipline and balance. Greek art had been given a false start in the Bronze Age by the dominant modes of the non-Greek Minoans. Fortunately, the new Geometric arts of Greece could respond differently and profitably to foreign inspiration.

The style is best expressed on painted vases, but can be seen on metal-work as well. Proto-Geometric artists (mainly of the tenth century) had subjected the free curvilinear patterns of the past to the authority of the compass. Rectilinear patterns—the meander, zig-zag, swastika—provided the main themes in Geometric art (ninth to eighth centuries) and beside them crept in simple figure subjects—a mourner on a grave vase, the prestigious symbol of a horse, pattern bands of animal bodies. After barely a generation of experiment with scenes of human figures, some in action, the Athenian Dipylon Master was able to offer on his vases the classic statement of Geometric art, panels of pattern which are

THE ATHENIAN ACROPOLIS (*above*); THE FOURTH-CENTURY THEATRE AT EPIDAURUS (*below*).

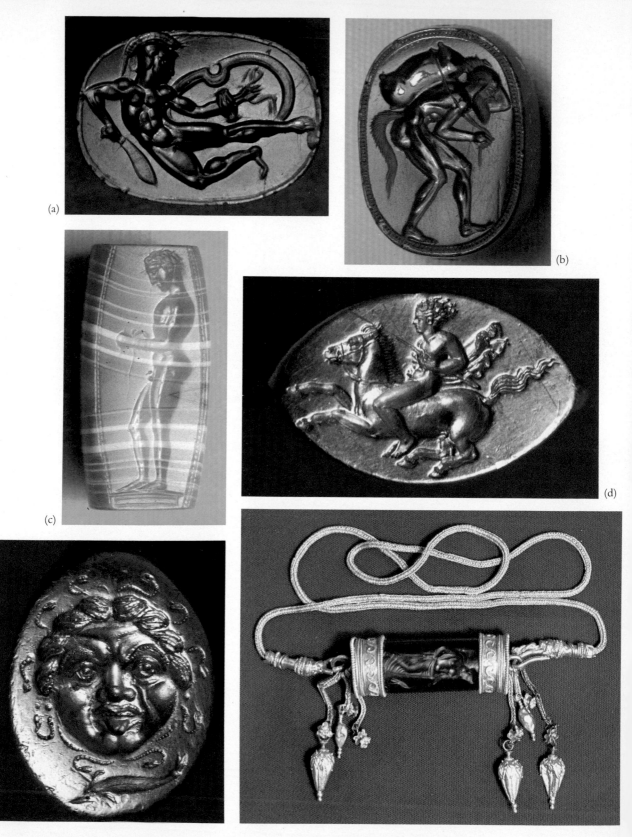

ENGRAVED GEMS, FINGER RINGS, AND JEWELLERY: (a) and (b) are of around 500 and 470 BC; (c) and (d) are Classical; (e) and (f) are of the fourth century BC.

PROCESSION TO THE TOMB, drawn on an Athenian Geometric vase of about 740 BC. With the simplest conventions of drawing the artist conveys a complicated scene of women mourners (below the handle and behind the cart), males and a child above, with the chequered shroud raised over the dead man on his funeral bed which rests on the cart for its journey to the grave. In front of the horses are warriors. This was a grand funeral, and it decorates a large vase (in all 123 cm high) which served as a grave marker.

resolved into figures of mourners and the dead in the ritual of laying out (*prothesis*) and burial. The scenes are not demonstrably other than of contemporary practice. The silhouette figures, composed of geometric patterns, can step beyond being symbols for man to some expression of his behaviour, by nuances of gesture or drawing, but something more was needed to translate this art into a medium for greater narrative expression.

Contact with the eastern shores of the Mediterranean had never, perhaps, quite been broken. The Cyprus–Crete route seemed well established, and via Cyprus, no doubt, the Levantine prospectors brought the exotica which began to appear even in Proto-Geometric Greece. In the ninth century the Phoenicians founded their city on Cyprus, Citium, but it seems to have been left to the Greeks, from Euboea and the islands, to guarantee trade with the Aegean by planting their own emporium at the mouth of the Orontes in Syria (Al Mina) by the end of the century. This model for trade they followed in succeeding centuries on Ischia in Italy and at Naucratis in Egypt.

Eastern goods and eastern craftsmen (for sophisticated techniques cannot be learnt by mere observation of their products) brought to Greece foreign styles and long-lost techniques of handling precious and foreign materials like ivory. Through the eighth century the orientalizing crafts in Greece, notably in Athens and Crete, were practised alongside the native Geometric, with little cross-fertilization. But gradually the orientalizing bronze shields made for the Idaean Cave in Crete admitted Greek motifs; gradually the jewellery of Attica and Crete geometricized its shapes and patterns; gradually eastern techniques and patterns were admitted to native forms, while eastern subjects were Hellenized, like the naked ivory goddess (Astarte) who in Attica acquired a meander-patterned cap and a trim Greek physique.

The gifts of the East to the Greek artist were manifold. The mere example of an art devoted to figure and animal decoration may have encouraged him to develop figure decoration in his native, Geometric idiom, though even these angular forms were by no means alien to eastern arts. The incised eastern bronzes and ivories showed how detail could be added to silhouette figures, bringing the possibility of closer definition of dress and action, and eventually differentiation of the figures which went beyond differentiation of sex. In vase-painting this produced the incising miniaturist black-figure technique of Corinth by the end of the eighth century, but some studios, in Attica and the islands, clung to larger outline-drawn figures with linear details, products mainly of the seventh century.

The animals and animal-frieze decoration of the easterners were not unfamiliar to the Greeks, and in some centres they became dominant at the expense of human figure or abstract decoration. Animal friezes long remained a hallmark of the orientalizing style, even long after their source was forgotten. The creatures patrol Corinthian, later Attic, and east-Greek vases well into the sixth century. The wildlife was not unfamiliar, either, but some had slipped from the repertory since the Bronze Age. Lions were not to be seen in mainland Greece, except perhaps in the very north, and could be treated as monsters, like sphinxes or griffins, both well known to Bronze Age Greek artists. A Greek hybrid too, the centaur, could be added, and new monsters for myth created from eastern models—the chimaera, the Gorgon—to depict creatures of sung story who had no image.

Where the Greek preferred Geometric friezes or panels the East had curvilinear or floral patterns. This new, rank growth never quite ousted the Geometric, and was itself subjected to Greek discipline through the seventh century until the friezes of lotus and palmette, overlapping leaves (becoming egg and dart) and cable, became an integral part of Greek Classical design at any scale, from jewellery to temple architecture. More importantly, new techniques allowed action scenes of narrative to be created which could depict more than mortal rituals or adventures, and they opened the way to pictorial narrative of myth.

Orientalizing stimuli continued with distinctive, if diminishing, effect through the seventh and sixth centuries, the role of the Phoenicians and what they carried from further east being taken over by the example of Egyptian, Assyrian, Babylonian, and Persian arts. They sometimes led nowhere or served to stereotype rather than quicken new forms, but they were more than mere catalysts, and in this formative period the coherent and natural characteristics of Greek art are demonstrated most clearly by what their artists chose and what they rejected in the many new models, techniques, and materials with which they became familiar.

The Archaic Style

Archaism in Greek art ran to the early fifth century. Down to that time its course was swift but, except in some exploitation of unusual media, such as vase-painting and architectural sculpture, it was not very dissimilar to that of other cultures, and it held little obvious promise of what was to follow. With hindsight we may try to claim the inevitability of the revolution which the fifth century ushered in. The seeds were there, but so were they in the arts of the Assyrians and Egyptians. In other arts the Greeks had already explored new fields in narrative and lyric. The artist, it may be, lagged behind the poet and philosopher, but was inspired by the same spirit of enquiry, and whether his dismantling of Archaic convention was inevitable or accidental, it was clearly something that is less surprising in Greece than it would have been elsewhere in the ancient world.

Archaic Greek art was highly conventionalized, and most of its conventions depended in varying degrees on foreign arts. It is generally in these strictly orientalizing essays that progress was slowest and the incentive to change least urgent. One example is metal-work: the type of full-rounded Eastern cauldron, with cast animal attachments, had a longer vogue than its Geometric predecessors, the big tripod cauldrons (yet it was the Geometric shape that survived in Greece for prestigious votive offerings or prizes). The griffin heads that decorated many of the cauldrons, which became favourite dedications at Greek sanctuaries, may have acquired a new serpentine elegance in Greek hands, but they are still recognizably the creatures introduced from the East at the end of the eighth century. These vessels, however, had encouraged Greek artists to develop other types of cast attachment for vases and utensils, and although these too owe something to the foreigner, this was a genre with greater possibilities.

A sculptural type, characterized by frontal features and wig-like hair, misleadingly called Daedalic by modern scholarship, also derives from the East. With it was introduced the use of the mould for mass production of figurines and plaques, another instrument inimical to change. Even so, it was a style which the Greeks exercised with imagination in different media—usually clay, for figurines, plaques, or on vases, but also up to lifesize in limestone, and in miniature in gold or ivory.

The third gift from the East, incising on silhouette figures, was practised on pottery (as it had not been in the East) as well as on metal-work. Black-figure

THE AUXERRE STATUETTE (*left*). Seventh-century sculpture is four-square, with emphatic, angular forms. Only in the second half of the century was marble used, and on life-size or colossal figures. This is one of the latest (about 625 BC) of the smaller (65 cm high) figures in the 'Daedalic' syle, cut in soft limestone. The cast shown here has been painted with what is believed to be the original colouring. There must have been much wooden sculpture of this style in this period.

A *KOUROS* (*right*)—grave-marker of about 530 BC from Keos. The *kouroi*, and their lady counterparts, the *korai*, could serve as grave-markers or votive offerings. The boldly patterned anatomy recalls nature without copying it and the figure stands squarely balanced, one foot before the other.

vases began to be made in Corinth in the seventh century, and at the end of the century the technique was adopted in Athens. Other Greek studios followed their lead in the sixth century. There is something uncompromising about silhouette, especially when executed in brilliant black gloss on a pale clay (buff in Corinth, orange in Attica), and the incised line which reveals the clay through the black is crisp but generally unsubtle. Colour additions are no more than dabs of white and red—real polychromy was for the early Archaic Island schools, and rare in black-figure, being technically difficult, although artists brought up in areas where panel- or wall-painting (commoner than the scant surviving examples would lead us to believe) was practised were bolder: for instance, the east-Greek painters who emigrated to Etruria in the sixth century. The Eastern animal-frieze style too long obsessed the painter, but later some artists were able to rise above the limitations of their technique and produce works whose quality of mass, line, and mood anticipate the Classical. Here Athens leads.

In sculpture it was a different overseas source that inspired change, replacing one convention for another, but offering new possibilities for progress. In Egypt Greeks of the mid seventh century and later saw colossal works of hard stone, learnt the techniques of laying out figures at such a scale (the tools they had already: better than the Egyptians who used no iron) and returned to exploit the fine, hard white marble of their island quarries on Naxos, and then Paros. In later Greek art the truly colossal was generally reserved for cult statues, but in the early years the new marble workshops produced massive works which served as dedications and grave markers. The standing naked male, the *kouros*, was the most important of the new types to emerge. At first the figures are carefully, but rather dully, cut four-square, with a pattern of surface detail for anatomy. Experiment, and a natural selection of the more lifelike forms, led the artist, by the end of the Archaic, to figures which are superficially realistic, though still the slaves of pattern in faces, hair, muscles, pose. The addition of colour, now lost, would not have made them much more real, but they were proud, imperishable statements of man's place in the world—not kings, priests or viziers, but citizens serving a god or commemorating the dead.

Their female counterparts, the *korai*, were dressed, and the pattern of their dress exercised the artist as did the anatomy of their brothers. Again, interest in pattern defied reality and dress-making. If we replace the lost colour, we see them as rather garish compositions of line, fold, and zig-zag. The *korai* serve sanctuaries rather than graves.

Egypt also taught the Greeks about the use of stone for columns and architectural ornaments. Until the later seventh century the Greeks built in brick, wood, and mainly undressed stone. Only in the seventh century had fired clay tiles begun to replace thatch or mud for roofs, and the only major buildings were temples, *oikoi* (houses) for the god's image. The need to create an image for a god had slight effect on the early development of sculpture, but the requirements of his house dictated the development of architecture, and only in the sixth

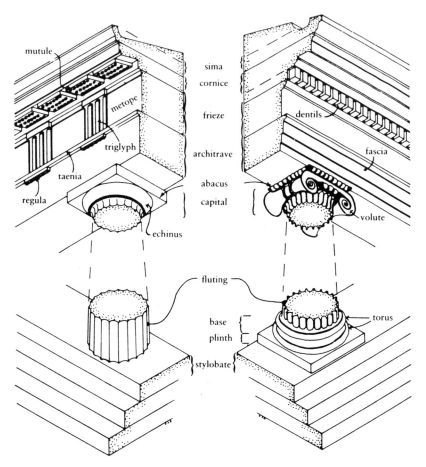

THE ELEMENTS OF THE CANONIC CLASSICAL DORIC (*left*) AND IONIC (*right*) ORDERS OF ARCHI-
TECTURE.

century did other public buildings begin to attract the architectural elaboration
otherwise reserved for temples. The Greek response to the use of dressed and
carved stone was, predictably, the establishment of new conventions. In plan this
meant the regularizing of the earlier, basic type of deep hall and porch, which
had already in places been provided with encircling colonnades. In elevation it
meant the creation of decorative schemes for these colonnades and the upperworks of the buildings. By the end of the seventh century the Doric order
emerged in mainland Greece, its intricate but austere patterns based on the tim-
bering of earlier structures. Soon afterwards the east-Greek world contributed
the Ionic order, based on orientalizing patterns of flower and scroll. As in sculpture, the colossal was not shunned, and some of the largest temples of the Greek
world, double-colonnaded, were planned in the sixth century by Ionian tyrants,
in Samos, Ephesus, Miletus, Didyma. In both orders development was slow, and
it is in some respects easier to judge the date of a building by the proportions of

its overall plan and elevation, of its columns and friezes, than from the detail of its mouldings and capitals. For decoration the temples were provided with sculpture: *akrotēria* for their roofs; relief or figures in the round for the low Doric gables—a dire challenge to the artist's skills in space-filling; reliefs in the Doric metope panels, or on Ionic friezes. These proved important fields for the display of religious and state propaganda, as had the very differently disposed, wall-covering reliefs and paintings of Near Eastern palaces and temples.

The intractable character of black-figure for vase-painting was resolved in about 530 by the invention in Athens of a new technique, red-figure. The

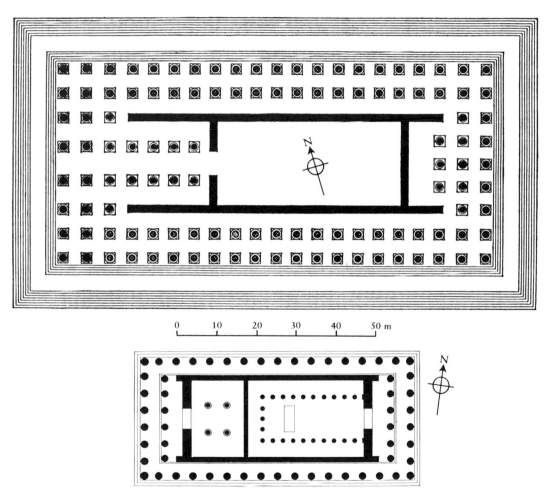

THE FOURTH-CENTURY TEMPLE OF ARTEMIS AT EPHESUS (*top*), AND THE FIFTH-CENTURY PARTHENON AT ATHENS (*bottom*). Plans to scale. The gigantic Ionic temples, like the Ephesian, with their forest of columns, were no smaller even in the sixth century (this plan is of the replacement of the burnt Archaic temple). They dwarf even the Parthenon, the largest Doric temple of the Greek mainland of its day (exceeded only by temples built for Sicilian tyrants). Ephesus, like most Greek temples, had open porches. The Parthenon has shallow porches and a closed back room which was the Treasury. (For a reconstruction of its interior see illustration on p. 305.)

drawing was now done in outline, the background blacked in and the figures reserved in the clay ground with detail painted on where before it had been incised. Replacing the graver with the brush gave the artist a subtler line and a new range of linear expression. There was soon to be less colour, and the old sex differentiation of white = woman, black = man was lost, but by the end of the century the Pioneer Group of painters was experimenting with a rendering of anatomy which the sculptor was only later to emulate in three dimensions. The style was certainly closer to that of painting on wall or panel, but this seems not to become a major art form until the fifth century.

Athens figures large in this account of the Archaic, but it was a period in which virtually every major city in Greece had its own studios for most media. Regional styles are most readily distinguished on vases, but in sculpture too east Greece had its own way both in patterning the *korai* and in giving *kouroi* a fuller, fleshier physique, or even dressing them. Colonial Greece played its part too. The West had no white marble but developed skills in terracotta statuary or made do with limestone. Styles could travel with their artists. Persian pressure on east

HERACLES WRESTLES WITH THE LIBYAN GIANT ANTAEUS, on a vase by the Athenian red-figure Pioneer Euphronios about 510 BC. A fine display of precise anatomical detail. The kempt Greek hero with his curls rendered in low relief, is contrasted with the wild hair, beard and appearance of the giant, which closely resembles some representations of Libyans in Egyptian art. Notice the giant's grimace of pain and limp hand.

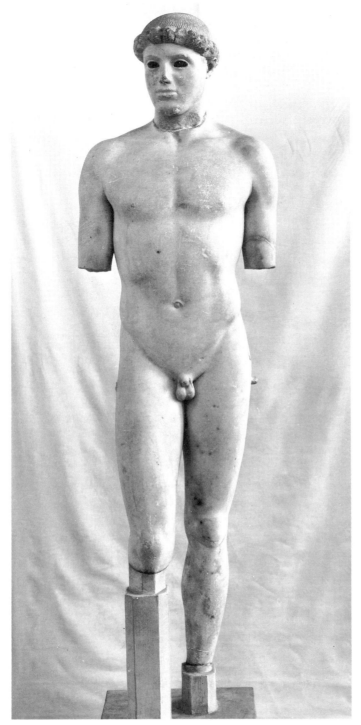

THE 'CRITIAN BOY'. Marble statue (height 85 cm) found on the Athenian Acropolis with debris from the Persian attack of 480/79 BC. The earliest near-complete example surviving of the new style which breaks with the rigidity of the Archaic *kouroi* and shows the weight of the body shifted on to one leg, with the corresponding adjustment of hips and shoulders—trivial features, but a landmark in the history of western art.

Greece in the mid-sixth century led to a diaspora of artists which brought Ionian styles to Attica, and to Etruria where they determined the course of late Archaic Etruscan art.

Athens was the home of the best black-figure, and the inventor of red-figure, vase-painting. Its sculpture was of high quality and more familiar to us through the Attic practice of using *kouroi* and relief gravestones in their cemeteries, and through their burial of the overthrown marble monuments of the Acropolis after the Persian sacks of 480/79. Among these sculptures is one which vividly demonstrates the sculptural revolution which had already taken place and which the vase-painters had presaged. The 'Kritian boy' has abandoned the four-square stance of a *kouros*. He stands in a natural, relaxed posture, weight mainly on one leg, his hips, trunk, and shoulders shifting to adjust to the stance. This is a vital novelty in the history of ancient art—life deliberately observed, understood, and copied. After him all becomes possible.

The Classical Style

The sculptor's new understanding of what he could achieve once he had decided to *look*, continued to be expressed in the standing male, and the succession is clear, from the early Classical Apollos, to Polyclitus' Doryphorus, and, in the fourth century, Lysippus' athlete Apoxyomenus. These were still commemorative statues, not (as the Archaic *kouroi* had been) to mark a tomb or serve a sanctuary, but more explicitly of individuals—athletes or warriors—to be dedicated for success in games or under arms, or more self-consciously (as by Polyclitus) to demonstrate proportions and technique. Progress was slow but certain in rendering the effect on the body of a shift in its weight and balance, or of partly resting on a separate support. This may seem little enough, but it was novel and could have appeared grotesquely inadequate in the hands of the incompetent or imperceptive. Fighting or exercising figures are often less subtle but no less accurate in the observation of life which they display, but there is an age of experience between Myron's discus-thrower who is virtually a freestanding relief, and Lysippus' who seems to pull the viewer round to admire him from any angle. Frontality came naturally to an Archaic artist and was encouraged by architectural sculpture and the setting of most statues. The abandonment of the implied frame or backdrop in statuary was answered in painting by a new sense of space which had also to be balanced in the composition.

Sculpture remains the senior art. Our knowledge of it is poor. Few of the finest works, generally bronzes, survive, and little architectural sculpture (but, luckily, that of the Parthenon) is of prime quality. Other original works are decorative or commemorative, like the grave reliefs, and seldom of high quality. And we have Roman-period copies of Classical works, identified for us with their artists from the texts of later writers. These may reveal little more than

IAMOS, from the east pediment of the Temple of Zeus at Olympia, completed in 546 BC. The artist has carefully observed the flaccid, ageing body, and in the gesture and features he expresses the old seer's anticipation of disaster.

subject and general appearance, and we rely on them for what we think we know of the style of a Myron, Polyclitus, or Lysippus. But when original works of the first rank do appear, like the Riace bronzes from a shipwreck off Italy (plate facing p. 246) we begin to sense how much we are missing, how less than perfect such familiar masterpieces as the Delphi charioteer may be.

Many think that the Riace bronzes are from a dedication set at Delphi in the mid-century by the Athenians to celebrate their success at Marathon. We can read what we will into the extrovert young male and his quieter more mature companion (and there must have been more to the group). Apart from such works, an Athens which had stopped decorating its tombs around 500 and had decided not to rebuild the temples destroyed by the Persians, offers us little for some fifty years. But at Olympia a new temple of Zeus was being built, and a sculptor imposed a style on his team which typifies for us the early Classical of roughly the second quarter of the fifth century (the temple was dedicated in 456). Of the two pediments the western offers Archaic vigour (the centaur fight), the

BRONZE ZEUS FROM ARTEMISIUM, recovered from an ancient shipwreck, no doubt en route to Italy. Made about 460–450 BC. A prime example of an early Classical bronze (as the Delphi charioteer, or the slightly later Riace bronze—plate facing p. 246). He held a thunderbolt (some have thought him Poseidon with a trident; far less probable).

GODS FROM THE EAST FRIEZE OF THE PARTHENON. Hephaestus, Apollo, and Artemis are seated with their fellow Olympians, awaiting the procession of the Panathenaic festival, which occupies most of the 160-metre-long frieze, in honour of Athena (who sits with them).

eastern Classical calm which is also a pregnant silence of reflection and foreboding. While the masons had yet much to learn of anatomy or the proper lie of dress, they succeeded in rendering nuances of age and mood with a subtlety far removed from the rather theatrical conventions of the Archaic.

Their successors include in the Peloponnese Polyclitus, with his essays in human proportions and, in an Athens which under Pericles had decided to revoke its decision not to rebuild its temples, Phidias. The Phidian school we judge from its architectural sculpture for Athens and Attica. It did not pursue the nuances of expression of the Olympia Master. Without the obsessions of a Polyclitus, it evolved a pure Classical style which idealized rather than individualized. At no time in the history of Greek art was the image of the divine so human, the human so divine. The placidity of the figures, even when represented in acts of vigour or high emotion, is not empty-headed, but other-worldly. As the body was understood so too was dress, and it can play its part in conveying the forms of the figure beneath, its action or inaction. Indeed, towards the end of the century there was a fashion for wind-blown or 'wet' dress, pressed against the body and contrasting with the deep shadows of the free-hanging or flying folds. With its 'Classic' style the Phidian studio became more than the school of Greece, since it was the style against which later sculptors' work was ever judged, and which was consciously recaptured by the artists of early Rome.

In the other arts vase-painting began its decline into fussiness or banality, but still attracted some fine draughtsmen, and the Attic red-figure style, transplanted to the Greek colonies of south Italy, enjoyed an Indian summer. Wall-painting of the early Classical period we have to judge from descriptions. On the walls of public buildings at Delphi and Athens Polygnotus painted great friezes with figures set up and down the field, though without perspective, and presented epic scenes of Troy and the underworld, and Micon the more recent, but heroically conceived, struggle for freedom at Marathon. The manner must have been sub-Archaic and, though much admired in later centuries, it was not copied. Their successors experimented at last with perspective and, more importantly, with realistic shading and coloration, and preferred the smaller panel to the great wall compositions which were the closest Greeks had come to the treatment of eastern or Egyptian walls. The anecdotes told about the realistic work of a Zeuxis or Apelles—the birds that pecked at the painted grapes, the painted curtain which could not be pulled—show that this is where the true tradition of western painting begins. It is the style copied on Roman walls, and the few original examples

ARTEMIS AND APOLLO SHOOT DOWN THE CHILDREN OF NIOBE, on an Athenian vase by the Niobid Painter of about 460 BC. The way in which the figures are set up and down the field, and not on a single ground-line, must be inspired by the new wall-painting compositions by Polygnotus which were appearing on public buildings in Athens.

HADES CARRYING OFF PERSEPHONE IN HIS CHARIOT. Painting of the second half of fourth century BC, on the wall of the small tomb within the great tumulus at Vergina (the Macedonian Aegae), which also covered the famous tomb of Philip II, discovered in 1977. The colours are red, yellow, violet, brown, orange (in Hades' hair). A very rare example of original Classical painting of high quality.

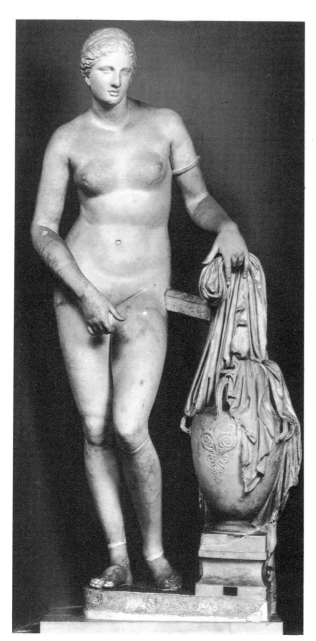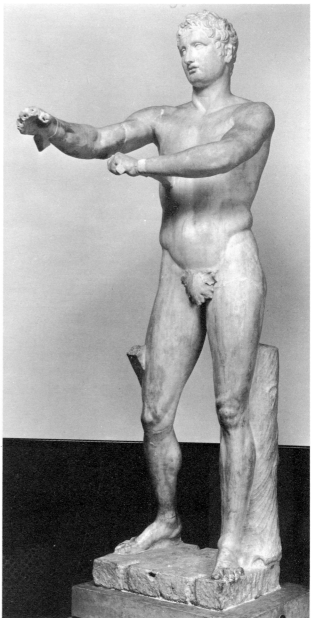

THE APHRODITE OF PRAXITELES (*left*). Roman copy of a marble original of about 340 BC. It was displayed in a temple at Cnidus in virtually peep-show conditions and widely held to be the greatest statue of antiquity. It is also one of the earliest female nudes in which the flesh-like qualities of marble must have been well exploited by the sculptor (earlier, major free-standing figures were usually of bronze). The type was endlessly copied, at various scales, in antiquity, and still is. No copy does more than hint at what must have been the quality of the original.

THE APOXYOMENUS (SCRAPER) OF LYSIPPUS (*right*). Roman marble copy of a bronze original of about 325 BC. The figure is of a young athlete scraping his forearm after bathing. The more relaxed, twisting pose offers a figure which claims no single optimum viewpoint, unlike Polyclitus' Doryphorus (illustration on p. 277). This is a new trait in sculpture, and Lysippus introduces also new ideal proportions, with a relatively smaller head.

which we have from the end of our period bear an uncanny likeness to styles of the Italian renaissance.

In the fourth century, until the patronage and aspirations of Hellenistic kings changed the focus of Greek life, thought, and art, the sculptors modestly explored beyond Phidian or Polyclitan Classicism. Praxiteles perfected the more feminine line of sinuous grace, and the female nude at last enters the history of western art. The louring brows of Scopas' heads marked a clear step towards the exaggerated expressionism of the Hellenistic. Lysippus had new views on ideal human proportions and could conceive and execute his figures in a fully three-dimensional manner, which must have revolutionized the setting of figures as well as the reaction and behaviour of viewers. All this amounts to further exploration of the possibility of realism, *pari passu* with the painters and, inevitably, of the realistic presentation not merely of specific types or age or mood, but of named individuals. Earlier commemorative statues of athletes or generals normally presented them in an idealized form with minimal personal traits. It is perhaps surprising that it took so long for observation and expression of the type to turn to observation and expression of the individual, especially since dedicatory practice and Greek personal pride gave every opportunity and encouragement. There must have been latent inhibitions about imposing personal features on generalized or idealized figures which were models for both men and gods. But the Greeks were becoming more aware of the divine in man, heroizing their dead and soon to declare divinity in certain favoured or powerful living. Thus, true portraiture of the contemporary, rather than idealized character studies of the dead, was another gift of the fourth century to western art.

Praxiteles was an Athenian, but Scopas was of Paros, the marble island, and Lysippus of Sicyon. Greece no longer had a dominant school or showplace. The masterpieces of the fourth-century artists are lost to us, and even the Praxitelean Hermes at Olympia no better than an excellent copy. We have to judge minor arts (minor in size only), or works commissioned for the barbarians such as the tomb of Mausolus in Caria with its colossal figures and relief friezes, or in areas where conditions of burial have ensured survival, as in Philip II's tomb at Vergina in Macedonia. The last provides the clue to the new patronage which dictated the future of Greek art.

Patronage, Private and Public

In Egypt and the East most works of art were commissioned for temples, palaces, or royal tombs. Decorative arts for the pleasure of most of the populace were thinly spread, though there was some elegant furnishing in the Levant, and engraved seals or scarabs and similar trinkets were fairly common (plate facing p. 279). In Greece there was no palace society in our period, but there were many state or religious projects to occupy the artist. A very high proportion of what survives was designed for the use of a wide spectrum of society. Many

GRAVESTONE FOR A YOUNG MAN, from near the River Ilissus, Athens. He is characterized as an athlete, accompanied by a weary child, his dog, and a pensive old man, perhaps his father. About 340 BC. The youth's proportions are Lysippan (see illustration on p. 294 right). The Classical gravestones of Athens commonly carry quiet contemplative groups of this type, recalling the dead in life. Few, however, are of this exceptional quality.

NIKE (VICTORY) BUILDS A TROPHY. Blue chalcedony gemstone, carved in intaglio, shown here at three times actual size. Victory, like Aphrodite, invites nude statues from the fourth century on. These hard-stone gems offer masterpieces of miniaturist art and must have been cut by major artists of their day. A big fourth-century stone such as this would have been set on a pendant since the practice of setting such stones in finger rings was still quite rare.

painted vases served the *symposion*, the drinking-party feast which played as important a social role as it did an entertaining or nourishing one. Others were used in ritual, often domestic, or were destined for dedication or grave furnishing. Most, in fact, survive thanks to the brisk export trade to Etruria and to Etruscan burial customs which guaranteed the preservation of so many intact. A private person could commission a dedication, paying for it with a tithe from some successful transaction or as a thanks-offering for some benefits thought to be divinely bestowed. If not a painted vase, there could be a bronze vessel of types which also served as prizes and might be dedicated after success in games or in the theatre. For poorer folk clay or wooden figures sufficed. At best a statue or group might be commissioned, like the athlete statues at Olympia, and a statue or relief for a grave monument.

Wealth acquired in the form of precious metal might be converted into jewellery for wear or silver plate for use, but in temple inventories the value of such dedications is reckoned as bullion without regard to the added value of workmanship. Greek jewellery was generally plain in colour and seldom even juxtaposed gold and silver, but it was technically perfect, and not the least of the peculiarities of Greek art is its display of both brilliant miniaturism (jewellery, engraved gems) and sheer monumentality.

State patronage was concerned principally with public buildings and their decoration, with commemorative dedications, usually at the major national sanctuaries such as Olympia and Delphi which thus became showcases of Greek art, and with coinage. A classical democracy could prove no less ambitious in promotion of its image at home and elsewhere than an archaic tyrant. Sources of funds were roughly similar—booty, taxes, ownership of mines—and the line was thinly drawn between expenditure on public works, even fleets and armies, and religious ones. Indeed the resources, including works of art, of the latter, could be called upon by the state to finance the former in times of crisis.

Temples were the prime demonstration of state wealth, to say nothing of piety (the backroom of the Parthenon was the treasury). They were also, in their way, the first museums, being display places for precious booty and for interesting bygones (Heracles' cup, the Amazon queen's belt, and so on). The tyrants of archaic Ionia went for sheer size with no little element of competition in overall dimensions (the late Archaic Artemisium at Ephesus measured 115.14 × 55.10 m.). This was a tradition sustained by the nouveaux riches tyrants of the western colonies as at Syracuse or Acragas, but the Parthenon shows that a democracy too could aim to impress by bulk (69.50 × 30.88 m.). The logistics of these undertakings probably presented more problems of personnel than of finance. Slaves might be hired for haulage, but for the finer work Pericles had to drain Greece of masons to rebuild Athens, though there seems to have been a remarkable reservoir of citizen talent.

Even with a democracy it was open to prominent private citizens to promote building. After the Persian invasion Cimon and his kin in Athens appear to have been responsible for the creation of a shrine for Theseus (which he endowed with a prize exhibit, the bones of the hero himself) and of the gallery which became known as the Painted Stoa for its panel paintings, which combined mythological narrative with state propaganda.

Pericles' decision to use League funds, contributed for the war against Persia, for the rebuilding of Athens (above p. 219) heralded the most important programme of state patronage to have been seen in Greece, only to be rivalled later in the capitals of the Hellenistic kings. Work was not completed until the end of the century, the last phase being undertaken despite the distractions of a crippling and unsuccessful war. But even these latest additions can be seen as necessary parts of the overall programme. The Acropolis was to have a new, or rather redesigned, temple to replace the incomplete one overthrown by the Persians. The Parthenon was less a cult place than a war memorial, dedicated as much to the glory of Athens and Athenians as to the city goddess Athena. While it was building other temples were planned and under construction in Athens and in the Attic countryside, some not to be completed until later in the century, when also the Acropolis received its new monumental gateway (Propylaea, in the 430s) and the Erechtheum (mainly 421–406), to house its oldest cults. The architects, Ictinus, Mnesicles, and whoever planned most of the countryside temples (with the Hephaesteum in Athens) refined principles of proportion and detail for the Doric order, introducing new subtleties of line to distract the eye from the possible deadening effect which the comparatively primitive engineering of the structures could induce. The highest standards of design and execution were applied at every stage, from overall plan to the detail of a ceiling coffer. An infinite ability to take pains has not always been a characteristic of major art, and in some arts it proves positively hostile, but it is part of the essence of Greek art and architecture, an enhancement not a distraction.

The state too took a hand in the construction of other public buildings, the colonnaded stoas which served administration or commerce, council halls, theatres whose function was social as well as religious. Away from home a tyranny or state advertised itself by expensive dedications in the national sanctuaries. In the Archaic period these might take the form of treasuries, elaborate architectural and sculptural pavilions. At Delphi we should single out that of Siphnos (about 525 BC) with its proliferation of sculptural ornament, a tithe from a lucky strike of gold and silver in the island; and at Olympia the series of treasuries dedicated by prosperous colonies in south Italy and Sicily. At Delphi Athens set the bronze group which celebrated the victory at Marathon, but many a state dedication was for success over other Greeks, and the sanctuaries commemorated inter-state conflict far more often than any co-operative efforts against foreign aggressors.

Coinage from the start generally carried a state blazon for identification and as guarantee. Once devices were set also on the reverses of coins they could carry

SILVER COIN (DECADRACHM) OF SYRACUSE (*left*), of about 395–380 BC, showing the head of the local nymph Arethusa, and signed by the artist Euainetus. One of the largest and finest of Greek coins. Three times actual size. SILVER COIN OF ELIS (*right*), of about 350 BC, showing the head of Zeus. These fine issues were probably associated with Olympic festivals, controlled by Elis. Three times actual size

other emblems of political or religious importance, and once the coins were in common inter-state use rather than for local exchange (for services, fines, taxes, etc.) they became as much ambassadors of the issuing city as its dedications might seem to be at Olympia or Delphi, and dies were commissioned from artists of quality, some of whom even signed their work.

Much of Greek art was, in the broadest sense, functional. Artists were commissioned for works which had a fairly clearly defined purpose, so it is important to understand the motives and resources of those who stimulated production of the objects and buildings which we tend to view and judge in a far more disinterested manner.

Narrative in Art

The art historian's view of Greek mythology is subtly different from that of the student of Greek literature. Most of the mythological scenes which have survived, and they are myriad, appear on objects of ordinary use, or at least not of extraordinary use like temple sculptures. Most Greeks learnt their myth-history from a rich and infinitely varied oral tradition. Our classical studies start from texts: theirs did not, and we exaggerate their literacy (there are more outward signs of literacy in the Indian subcontinent today than there were in ancient Greece, yet well over 70 per cent of the population cannot read or write). Most of the artist's stories were closest to those understood by everyman, often just as illogical, contradictory, and distorted or improved in the telling through generations. The poet's stories were more consciously adapted to the context of his poem or play, to the patron or society for which he was writing or for the moral he wished to draw from his use of myth as parable. Sometimes art follows texts, sometimes texts follow art: there are some scenes of our period which deliberately follow texts, though probably fewer than is generally thought. The artist had the same freedom as a writer to adjust his story, but he was more restricted even in the content of what he portrayed by the formulae of his craft. He could not, for instance, offer continuous narrative and there was a limit to what could be explained by inscription. He was also in many respects more conservative than the poet. He was not in our period guided by pattern books, but clear conventions for particular subjects and for generic scenes were established. Nevertheless, all but the veriest hacks avoided repeating themselves line for line, not deliberately, but because there was no need or compulsion to do so.

The earliest pictures are symbols for contemporary events, of burial or battle, and the example of the East led the artist to an idiom in which more specific detail of a historical (to us, mythical) story could be expressed. The first myth-scenes are prompted by formulae suggested by orientalizing arts. They have virtually nothing in common with the rich visual imagery of Homer, least of all in his Ionian homeland, beyond sharing the same traditional oral sources and, more tentatively than he, employing the same language of metaphor.

Abjuring the strip-cartoon system of narration the Greek artist was obliged to encapsulate the narrative and message of a story in a single scene. The Archaic artist generally chose a moment of maximum action: the Classical, relying on his viewer's knowledge of the story, could sometimes dwell on proem or aftermath, which might be psychologically or dramatically more telling. Both relied for the identification of their figures on conventional dress, attributes, and poses. Few scenes are helped by inscriptions, and figures are more often allowed interjections than conversations. Reliance on detail of pose or attribute also enabled the artist to introduce an element of continuous narrative by allusion to past and future. Latter-day theorists devise imposing names for this process, as though it was a deliberate invention and not inescapable in a period in which the 'camera-still' was unknown and the media offered single panel or frieze compositions, not acres of temple and palace walls as in Egypt and the Near East.

THE DEPARTURE OF AMPHIARAUS FOR THEBES. Drawing from a Corinthian vase of about 560 BC (see text for description and commentary).

A classic example is the Corinthian crater of about 560, showing Amphiaraus departing for his doomed expedition (with the Seven) against Thebes. His wife Eriphyle stands off to the left, holding prominently the necklace with which she had been bribed to persuade the King to go to war. Behind him is his son Alcmaeon who will avenge him. To the right his seer whose gesture shows his foreknowledge of the outcome of the expedition. And there is a plentiful animal presence, no doubt omens. More subtly, in the east pediment at Olympia, the remorseless vengeance of Zeus on oath-breakers, which pursued the house of Atreus, is recalled not by any major episode of action but at the moment of the oath-taking, before the race between Pelops and Oinomaos. Juxtaposition of scenes involving the same figure, though not in episodes of the same story, seems to have been introduced with the new Theseus cycle in Athens at the end of the sixth century, and is taken up to better effect for the series of Heracles' Labours.

In the popular arts such as vase-painting the choice of subject seems generally

THE DEEDS OF THESEUS, on the interior of an Athenian cup of about 430 BC. It is unusual in being decorated around its central medallion with a frieze (which is repeated on the outside of the cup). In the centre Theseus pulls the dead Minotaur from the Labyrinth. In the frieze are six of Theseus' exploits on the road from Troezen to Athens, and his subsequent encounter with the Marathonian bull. Episodes of this type from a single cycle are run together on painted vases, kept discrete on temple metopes.

that of the artist who, of course, knew his market, and specially commissioned pieces for dedication or other occasions can generally be identified in an artist's work by their (for him) uncharacteristic subjects. He was influenced in his choice mainly by tradition. In some periods, as in fourth-century south Italy, stage subjects seem deliberately sought, and there is sometimes the echo of the stage on fifth-century Athenian vases. New stories, such as the Theseus cycle, or an emphasis on certain myths which answered state propaganda, were quickly mirrored in the popular arts. Theseus' role in the new Athenian democracy is clear enough in literature as in art. Before him it is in art that we most clearly observe a new treatment of Heracles with his patron Athena as symbol of the Athenian state and especially of its tyrant family. New cults too—Athens' adoption of Eleusis or the arrival of an Asclepius—are reflected in the popular arts. Certain almost ritualized aspects of everyday life, presumably of a significance which goes beyond mundane interest in the world around them, also occupied artists and were blessed with their own iconographic conventions, like myths: the symposium, courting of youths, athletics, wedding preparations.

In the major arts, wall-painting and temple sculpture, there were other considerations, not least the fact that they were for public display, not ephemeral consumption, and that these expensive and lengthy projects were not appropriate fields for experiments. The Parthenon is unusual in having its sculptural themes all closely related to Athena, Athens, its glorious past, both mythical and recent, and Athenians. On other temples the relevance of the subject is sometimes less apparent, and we may imagine that the decisions were those of a committee of magistrates and priests rather than of the artists. Many demands, of patronage, politics, and religion might need to be answered.

While individual figures of myth, monsters or heroes, may seem to serve mainly decorative functions, generally Greek art is telling a story or setting a scene. The student of style may find the subject-matter irrelevant, and the mythographer may discount the power of tradition or of what, in terms of technique and convention, was possible in the representation of myth. But a study of Greek art can no more ignore its subjects than its style or purpose.

Religious Art

Most of Egyptian or Indian art and a large proportion of the arts of Mesopotamia were religious: that is to say, they were designed to attract or appease a deity, to inspire or intimidate worshippers, to guarantee a life beyond the grave. Hardly any of this is true of Greek art, which may reflect upon man's relationship to his gods but is seldom dictated by exclusively religious requirements. At a fairly low level some degree of near-magical use of art is seen in the apotropaic devices, usually animals or monsters, sometimes the human eye or male genitals, on various objects, but Greek art was not dominated by such crude symbolism. The sphinxes or lions on grave monuments no doubt did guard the grave, just as the Gorgon head in early pediments guarded the temple (but from what?). There must have been no less of the irrational in the thought of ancient Greece than in that of other cultures, but it was expressed in literature, and hardly at all in art, where even the monsters and demons have a stunning plausibility.

The artist was virtually never called upon to exercise his skills on objects destined only for the grave. The oil flasks (white-ground *lekythoi*) made for some two generations in Athens deliberately as grave furniture were placed on as well as in tombs. The Archaic grave monuments idealized the dead in an anonymous way, and the Classical ones expressed no more than a calm confrontation of the live and the dead, as if both were alive: no demons, no gods of the Underworld, no threats, no violent grief, more expressions of human dignity or even pride than of desolation or dumb acceptance. The idealizing qualities of Greek art abet these attitudes magnificently.

Dedications could flatter a deity with his image or a portrayal of his power in scenes of action, but they were as often images of mortal attendants for the god (the Archaic *korai* and *kouroi*), and if they portrayed the dedicator himself it is not in a servile manner, but in the pride of his profession—soldier, athlete, or citizen. Remarkably, it became possible for a votive relief to depict the worshipper and his family in the presence of the deity, with only their smaller size to indicate the profound difference in status.

Scenes of cult and sacrifice were simple statements of the act, and the deity was often shown virtually as a mortal onlooker. The orgiastic rites of Dionysus, on which ancient literature is reticent, were ritualized into dance and myth by the artist. The god himself was wrested from his role of rustic fertility spirit into joining the Olympian family where his appearance and behaviour were made by the artist to conform with his new setting. But he rubbed shoulders with humanity more than most, mainly through his gift of wine, and this was well expressed on the clay vases, many of which were designed for the symposium. On them his maenad-nymphs impersonate his ecstatic mortal followers, while the satyrs, nature demons recruited into his troupe, act out mortal aspirations which wine, women, and song can promote, and become one of the most engaging creations of the Greek artist. Other mystic religions or beliefs, the Pythagorean or Orphic, found as little response in Greek art as did Hellenized foreign goblins such as Lamia.

Cult statues had a more clearly defined religious purpose, as symbols of the god's presence in his house. The earliest acquired their sacred power from their antiquity ('fallen from heaven' or the like), not their appearance, and were sometimes barely shaped logs which could be decked out on festive occasions with dress or weapons. When the old images had to be replaced or supplemented by new ones, the artist could have sought through his art to express something of the same magic power. But apart from attributes or dress or sheer size the cult statues are indistinguishable in appearance from statues of mortals. With the fifth century they sought to impress more through size—the Zeus at Olympia would have gone through the roof if he stood up—and material, the chryselephantine with beaten gold dress and ivory flesh. The setting, in the columned interior of a temple and barely lit from the doors or windows before them and, at Olympia and in the Parthenon, by the light reflected up from a broad shallow pool before them on the floor, will have enhanced their appearance. It was for much later writers to dwell on the spiritual aspects of Phidias' Zeus at Olympia. In its day his Athena Parthenos seems to have excited more concern over the accounting for her materials, and Pericles could point out to the Athenians that her gold was removeable and could help pay for war. Experience of the theatre, and of art for the theatre, may have had its effect on the artist's designs and settings for his works, but he made no special provisions for imbuing them with the numinous.

Even in his execution of religious subjects the Greek artist worked within the confines of his training, but could exercise imaginative invention to the full. The restraint was technical rather than psychological, and his choice of image did not depend, as in other periods and places, on prayer or meditation. Poets, actors, musicians, dancers, even historians had their Muse, but not artists.

RECONSTRUCTION IN THE ROYAL ONTARIO MUSEUM, TORONTO, OF THE INTERIOR OF THE PARTHENON, WITH THE GOLD AND IVORY STATUE OF ATHENA PARTHENOS BY PHIDIAS. The architectural setting is certain and the statue can be restored from numerous reduced copies. A shallow pool of water before her reflected light on to the statue (and kept the atmosphere humid for the ivory). She stood some 40 feet tall.

Decoration in Art

Nothing, except perhaps the heroic nude, provokes recognition of Greekness more readily than ornaments such as meander, egg-and-dart, palmette friezes. Subsidiary ornament was subjected to the same discipline as major designs, and in some periods and media we find objects devoted wholly to pattern. The need to articulate and frame friezes or panels allowed the development of orientalizing florals which adopted the rows of palmettes and lotuses of eastern art, created new and less botanically correct patterns, and established a decorative scheme that only in the fifth century gave way to more realistic florals with some observation of live forms, and the evolution of leafy, but strictly controlled, arabesques. Many patterns belong to woodwork, but have become more familiar translated and enlarged on to stone architecture. Care was taken to see that the profile of a moulding and its decoration were matched. The Eastern volute-trees could become adjusted in scale or use to Ionic columns or to decorative details of furniture or utensils.

Many arts have sought to animate objects by introducing human or animal features to otherwise functional forms. The Greeks were not obsessive about this, nor did they let it dominate what they made, and there are a few Archaic vessels in the shape of whole animal or human figures. But handles could be created from the curving body of an athlete or a leaping lion, human heads could spring from handle attachments, feet become lion paws. Curly extremities grew snake heads: Athena's aegis, Hermes' caduceus, the Chimaera's tail. The Greeks spoke of parts of the vase as parts of the human body, just as we do (lip, neck, shoulder, foot, ears = handles) and, mainly in the Archaic period, allowed this conceit expression by painted or moulded additions—eyes under arched handles, or on eye-cups where, with the ear-handles and trumpet foot (like a mouth), the whole vessel can look like a mask when raised to the drinker's lips.

The question of colour in Greek art is a difficult one. Architecture under a Mediterranean sun tends to simple, clear, bright forms, with colour in detail, not mass. On Greek architecture the colouring of details in the upperworks of buildings could have done little more than help articulate the sharply carved forms. Only in the clay revetments of Archaic roofs does there seem to have been a positive riot of colour. On sculpture it seems that colour was used to lend verisimilitude, but we know too little about how intense the colours were when applied. Neo-classical versions of Greek statues, with colour supplied, are disturbing, and we have become so used to judging form without colour that it is distracting. The few coloured marbles left from antiquity, as at Pompeii, look like rather crude dolls. There seems no indication of coloured outer walls for buildings, and for any painting on interior walls, figural or decorative, we have no evidence. New discoveries could dramatically change our view. Scraps of painted plaster show that the seventh-century temple of Poseidon at Isthmia near Corinth had somewhere upon it large (though not life-size) figures of animals.

We may, then, underestimate the value of colour in Greek art, but in their language they are strangely vague in defining colours, their jewellery long abjured settings of coloured stones, and the modest use of dark stone in architecture is in marked contrast with Rome's addiction to variegated marbles. Their vase-painting evolved from four-colour black-figure to two-colour red-figure, while their most famous Classical painters were said (as seems true, to judge from near-contemporary mosaics) to have worked in four colours only.

If not in colour, in form at least there was a tendency to what we would regard as the over-ornate. When execution and design is perfect a degree of elaboration is acceptable—I think of the finely chased and cast bronze and silver

BRONZE CRATER (MIXING BOWL), from Derveni, near Salonica, found in 1962. Late fourth century BC. The most elaborate of its type preserved (most must have been claimed by the melting pot in antiquity), with Dionysiac relief scenes on the body and figures in the round seated on its shoulders. It stands 90.5 cm high and had served as a funerary urn.

vessels of the later Classical period; where workmanship is poorer, or the medium less inspiring, it would become difficult to admit the products to one's drawing room—I think of the large, over-decorated, clay vases of south Italy in the fourth century. Knowing where to stop is the hallmark of the great artist. Not all Greek artists were sublime, nor their customers always impeccable in their taste.

The Artists

Greek art was not the big business in antiquity that it is today. Some portable works, jewellery and plate, were expensive, and it is notable that we have learned most about these from finds made outside the Greek world, where they appear as gifts or booty in native kingdoms, or as court furniture, from the Seine to Persepolis. Even the finer red-figure vases passed for hardly more than a worker's day wage. Some potters, especially in sixth-century Athens, observed the export market to Etruria closely enough to specialize in export models designed to attract by their familiar shapes or acceptable styles of decoration: the so-called Tyrrhenian amphorae and the products of Nicosthenes' workshop. The returns were no doubt gratifying, and some potters or pottery-owners could afford sculptural dedications on the Acropolis. In the Classical period the big names in sculpture and wall-painting could command high fees and provoke competition for their services, but these were men who travelled freely and worked wherever employment was offered. Only in the Athenian pottery trade and probably in metal workshops elsewhere (Corinth, Sparta) do there seem to have been industries which came to serve more than the local market. Specialized local industries for the national or international market were uncommon in Greece, and artists were in no different position in this regard from shoemakers or carpenters. Indeed, no distinction was drawn in antiquity in favour of those whom we designate artists—it was all craft (*technē*). Only with Phidias, and then increasingly with his successors, did any special social status appear to have been accorded to successful artists, although they had been housed at the courts of the Archaic tyrants, like musicians, entertainers, and doctors.

There was a tendency for crafts to be practised in families: a master's natural apprentice would have been his own son. There is evidence for this in pottery and in sculpture, but there was versatility too. Some of the finest vase-painters, known to us from only one or two vases, may also have been panel-painters. A sculptor might prefer modelled bronze to carved marble, but most could work in either and at any scale. He might also be an architect (Scopas) or painter (Euphranor). Some crafts were easily mobile—the jeweller, die-engraver, indeed even the sculptor who had to travel from home to quarry to finishing workshop on the site of his commission. While the family businesses helped to establish local styles and traditions, mobility meant rapid dissemination of new ideas and techniques, and the major sanctuaries served as galleries for both masterpieces of the past and novelties.

More than half the sculptors named in the Erechtheum accounts were Athenian citizens, but in earlier years the potter and painter signatures on Athenian vases reveal a high proportion of non-Athenian, or even non-Greek names, or nicknames which conceal nationality. In simpler crafts the immigrant Greek (metic) or non-Greek no doubt played an important role in the workshops and in a state like Sparta his role must have been a major one, but this did nothing to weaken the strong local character of Spartan art in the Archaic period. In Athens Solon is said to have encouraged the immigration of artists in the early sixth century and this, followed by the patronage of a tyrant court, may do much to explain Athens' busy record in the arts thereafter.

The number of artists' signatures from the Archaic and Classical periods is another peculiarity of Greek art. They appeared by around 700 and were by no means confined to major works or major artists. The desire of the vase-painter to sign his work might seem unusual, and the practice was fairly haphazard: for some we have only one extant signature on some fifty vases, and for most none at all. As advertisement it could have done little, and simple pride was probably the motive. The signature was often discreet, but not always: on Archaic grave monuments the artist's name may be as prominent as the deceased's. On late sixth-century Athenian red-figure vases the so-called Pioneers are free with challenges to their fellows' work or mottoes naming them. From their vases and inscriptions alone we can reconstruct a lively and very self-conscious artistic community. It was unusually literate too and may have had social pretensions, although inscribing references to handsome well-born youths of the day (the *kalos* inscriptions; irrelevant to the scenes they accompany) need not always imply close familiarity, and was as much practised by lesser artists on poorer works. The competitive spirit between artists seems also to have been exploited by patrons, but our record of these competitions, like that for the Amazons at Ephesus where each artist put his own work first and the prize went to the agreed second, Polyclitus, may have been distorted by the promotional tales of local guides who tend to be free in their use of great names and good stories.

The singular physical character of Greek art, when compared with those of other ancient cultures, was remarked at the beginning of this chapter. Its preoccupation with the human and with the gods' proper place in the world of men (rather than vice versa) was also the concern of Greek writers. The Greek artist served the society in which he lived by answering the requirements of a far wider range of the community than its priests and governors, and he demonstrated for the first time in the history of man the potential of a truly popular art in reaching beyond the demands of magic or display of status. In such service the concept of art for art's sake was unknown and unnecessary.

Further Reading

A comprehensive and well-documented account of Greek Art from Bronze Age to Hellenistic is M. Robertson, *A History of Greek Art* (Cambridge, 1975), with his *Shorter History of Greek Art*

(Cambridge, 1981). Shorter handbooks arc G. M. A. Richter, *Handbook of Greek Art* (London, 1974) by subject, and J. Boardman, *Greek Art* (London, 1985) by period.

For period studies there are J. N. Coldstream, *Geometric Greece* (London, 1977); J. Boardman, *Greeks Overseas* (London, 1980), and *Preclassical Style and Civilization* (Harmondsworth, 1967); J. Charbonneaux, R. Martin, and F. Villard, *Archaic Greek Art* and *Classical Greek Art* (London, 1971, 1973).

Sculpture. G. M. A. Richter, *Sculpture and Sculptors of the Greeks* (Oxford, 1971) for a detailed survey, and her comprehensive *Portraits of the Greeks* (Oxford, 1984). B. Ashmole, *Architect and Sculptor in Ancient Greece* (London, 1972) for important essays on Olympia, the Parthenon, and the Mausoleum, and *Olympia* (with N. Yalouris; London, 1967). J. Boardman, *Greek Sculpture: Archaic Period* and *Greek Sculpture: Classical Period* (London, 1978, 1985), heavily illustrated handbooks. F. Brommer, *The Sculptures of the Parthenon* (London, 1979). R. Lullies and M. Hirmer, *Greek Sculpture* (London, 1960) with fine pictures. C. Rolley, *Greek Bronzes* (forthcoming).

Architecture. There is no modern handbook, but W. B. Dinsmoor, *The Architecture of Ancient Greece* (London, 1952), is still useful, if taken with A. W. Lawrence, *Greek Architecture* (Harmondsworth, 1957). For other aspects, J. J. Coulton, *Greek Architects at Work* (London, 1977); R. E. Wycherley, *How the Greeks built Cities* (London, 1962) and A. W. Lawrence, *Greek Aims in Fortification* (Oxford, 1979).

Vase-painting. R. M. Cook, *Greek Painted Pottery* (London, 1972), a basic handbook. For pictures, P. Arias, M. Hirmer, and B. B. Shefton, *History of Greek Vases* (London, 1961). Period studies with full illustration are J. N. Coldstream, *Greek Geometric Pottery* (London, 1968); J. Boardman, *Athenian Black Figure Vases* and *Athenian Red Figure Vases: Archaic Period* (London, 1974, 1975). A. D. Trendall, *South Italian Vase-painting* (London, 1966), is a valuable brief survey.

Other Arts. R. A. Higgins, *Greek Terracottas* and *Greek and Roman Jewellery* (London, 1963, 1961); J. Boardman, *Greek Gems and Finger Rings* (London, 1971); D. Strong, *Greek and Roman Gold and Silver Plate* (London, 1966); C. M. Kraay and M. Hirmer, *Greek Coins* (London, 1966).

Many of the works named here relate also to the Hellenistic period, and some to the Roman.

GREECE AND ROME

A

B

C

a

ILLYRIA

GETAE

R. HYPANIS

R. BORYSTHENES

Olbia

Tyras

MAEOTIS

R. DANUBE

Istrus

Panticapaeum

Théodosia

Tomis
Callatis

BLACK · SEA

Odessus

Mesembria
Apollonia

b

MACEDONIA

R. AXIUS

Pella *Therme*

Aegae

CORCYRA

THRACE

THASOS

Byzantium

Nicomedia

BITHYNIA

PAPHLAGONIA

Sinope

Heraclea

Amisos

Demetrias

EUBOEA

LESBOS

Amphipolis

Cyzicus *Nicaea*
Prusa

R. SANGARIUS

Ancyra

R. HALYS

MYSIA
ATTALIDS

Pergamum

PHRYGIA

GALATIA

Gordium

CAPPADOCIA

Thebes

Athens

Corinth

CHIOS

LYDIA

Smyrna *Sardis*

Ephesus

Apamea
Antioch

Iconium

Tyana

Sparta

SAMOS

Miletus *Aphrodisias*

CARIA

LYCAONIA

Lystra

Cnidus

LYCIA

Rhodes *Xanthus*

PISIDIA

Perge

Eurymedon *Side*

ISAURIA

CILICIA

Tarsus

Issus

S E

Nagidus

Al Mina

Thap

Cydonia

Cnossus

RHODES

ANTIOCH

Antioch

c

Gortyn

CRETE

Salamis

Citium

CYPRUS

Paphos

SYRIA

Apamea

Palm

R. ORONTES

Byblus

Sidon

Damascu

Apollonia

Cyrene

Tyre

PHOENICIA

CYRENAICA

Gadara

Gerasa

Jerusalem

Ascalon

Gaza *Marissa*

Alexandria

Naucratis

Pelusium

d

Altitude in metres

Over 1000

200 – 1000

0 – 200

N

P T O L E M I E S

Memphis

Petra

E G Y P T

FAYUM

R. NILE

0   100   200   300 miles

Oxyrhynchus

0   100   200   300   400   500 km

RED
SEA

A

B

C

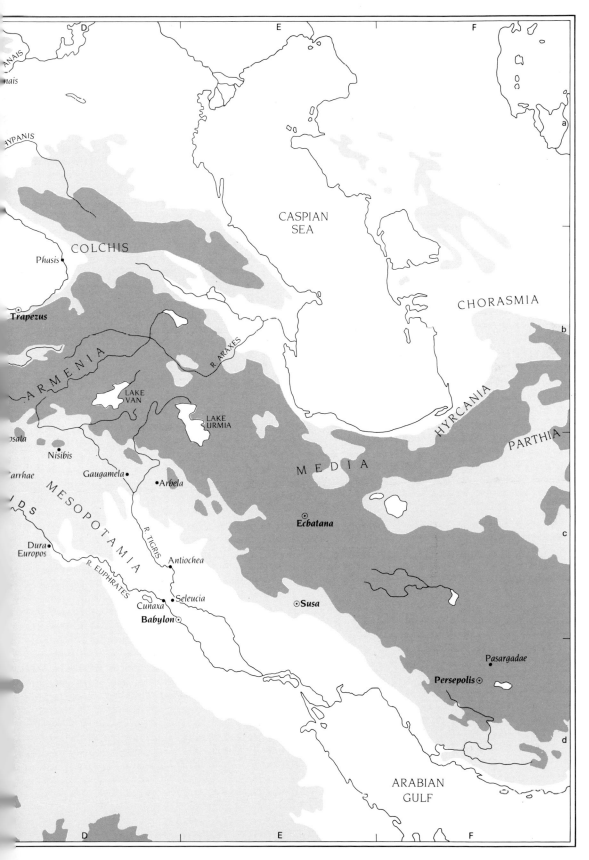

CASPIAN
SEA

COLCHIS

Phasis

⊙ **Trapezus**

CHORASMIA

A R M E N I A

R. ARAXES

LAKE
VAN

LAKE
URMIA

HYRCANIA

PARTHIA

...*sata*

Nisibis

M E D I A

...*arrhae*

Gaugamela •

Arbela

..DS

M E S O P O T A M I A

R. TIGRIS

⊙ **Ecbatana**

Dura
Europos •

R. EUPHRATES

Antiochea

c

Cunaxa

• *Seleucia*

⊙ **Susa**

Babylon ⊙

Pasargadae
•

Persepolis ⊙

ARABIAN
GULF

d

MAP 5. THE HELLENISTIC WORLD

13

The History of the Hellenistic Period

❦

SIMON PRICE

THE Hellenistic period, the 300 years between the reigns of Alexander the Great of Macedon (336–323 BC) and Augustus, the first Roman Emperor (31 BC–AD 14), is often seen as an uninteresting and incoherent part of Greek history. Falling between the two 'central' periods of classical Athens and Ciceronian or Augustan Rome, the period seems to be merely the melancholy story of the decline of the Greek city, subjected first to Alexander and his successors and then to the Romans.

In fact the period has both internal coherence and topical interest. Its central feature is the establishment of Greek monarchies by Alexander and his successors which together controlled the area from Greece to Afghanistan. The impact of these monarchies on the Greek world is the theme of this chapter. I shall start by outlining briefly the reign of Alexander and the history of the four main Hellenistic kingdoms. In the wake of Alexander's conquests the new kingdoms consolidated the expansion of the Greek world: the kings founded new cities which ensured the dominance of Greek over native cultures. The connection visible here between political power and cultural dominance has an interesting analogy in the spread of European culture to our colonies. The needs of the competing kingdoms led to important administrative and military developments, which underpinned royal power. The kings ruled over numerous Greek cities, but what sort of impact did they make on them? What was it like to be subordinate to a superpower? Finally, within the cities themselves, civic life changed as a result of the growth of monarchy.

The Hellenistic Kingdoms

Alexander the Great is one of the archetypally romantic figures, as is shown by the vitality of the Alexander legend from antiquity to Mary Renault. Emulating the Homeric Achilles, he won a reputation for military genius and personal

BUST OF ALEXANDER THE GREAT, the so-called 'Azara herm': a Roman copy thought to be based on a bronze statue, possibly showing the king in heroic nudity holding a lance, by the court-sculptor Lysippus (*c*.330–320 BC). The tilt of the head and the mane-like hair were standard features of Alexander's portraits.

prowess. To him were attributed extraordinary tales: for example, Callisthenes, one of his court historians, recounted how once the sea had retreated from Alexander's path and bowed in homage before him. Though many of the stories, like this one, are at best dubious, their circulation as early as the lifetime of Alexander reflects his almost unthinkable achievements.

When Alexander succeeded to the throne of Macedon after the murder of his father Philip, he inherited a kingdom which had just come to dominate the affairs of mainland Greece. With enormous energy Alexander launched a crusade, long called for by Greek propagandists and indeed planned by Philip, to punish the Persians for Xerxes' invasion of Greece, almost 150 years earlier. Within a year Alexander had won control of the Greek cities of western Turkey, and he pressed east to Gordium. Here story told of an oracle that the person who loosed the knot that tied the yoke to the chariot of the ancient king of Gordium would become master of Asia: Alexander cut the knot. A romantic tale and possibly true. Only a month or two later he defeated Darius the Persian King at Issus (333 BC). Darius escaped, but Alexander was able to turn south and take control of Phoenicia and Egypt. From there he made an extraordinary expedition out west through the desert to the oracle of Zeus Ammon. No strategic purpose was served by this long march, but Alexander had a question to put to the god. We know neither the question nor the answer, but he was greeted at the oracle as 'son of Ammon', one of many intimations of his divine status. Thus encouraged, he marched north and east into Mesopotamia, where at Gaugamela (331 BC) he defeated Darius again, this time decisively). The Persian Empire, which had been a threat to the Greeks for more than 200 years, was now in the hands of Alexander.

Alexander did more than simply take over the Persian Empire. He continued his campaigns into the eastern part of it, putting down revolts and founding cities. In the far north-east, in Sogdiana, resistance was fierce, but Alexander captured the final stronghold, and an unbelievably beautiful woman, Roxane. He fell in love and married her. There was also other business in hand. He crossed from Afghanistan into the Punjab where he defeated the Indian king. Only a revolt of his troops prevented him from going further east, and he returned west via Baluchistan, a disastrous journey reminiscent of Napoleon's retreat from Moscow. Two years later, in 323, he died at Babylon, aged only thirty-two.

Alexander left behind not only conquests, but also monarchy. Monarchy, a traditional part of the Macedonian state, had been peripheral to the Greek world until the reign of Philip. Alexander succeeded in making it central. He provided a model for the series of Hellenistic kings that followed. The diadem, the plain headband worn by Alexander, became the standard symbol of monarchy; the title 'king', which Alexander had probably begun to use when addressing the Greeks, was employed by all the Hellenistic rulers and, as we shall see, there were generally accepted conditions for the assumption of the title. Stories about Alexander no doubt established the expectation that kings should have a striking personal appearance and a dignified bearing, or, less favourably, that they had arrogant pretensions and an offensive and haughty manner of dealing with visitors. Like it or not, the model of kingship was established.

Alexander's followers aspired not only to his ideals but also to his lands. The twenty years following his death saw tortuous struggles between his kin and his generals as each attempted to establish himself as his sole successor. The attempts failed, and by about 275 BC there had emerged the three kingdoms which were to dominate the eastern Mediterranean until the Romans came. First, Egypt. Ptolemy, who was granted Egypt at the death of Alexander, succeeded in founding a dynasty which ruled the country until his most famous descendant, Cleopatra, was defeated by Augustus (31 BC). The Ptolemies also at various times controlled lands outside Egypt: Libya, southern Syria, Cyprus, parts of southern Turkey, and the Aegean islands.

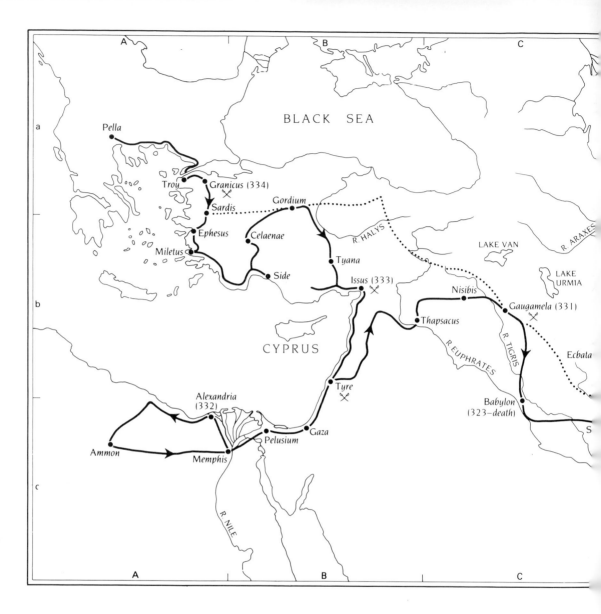

Secondly, the eastern conquests of Alexander. The capture of Babylon in 312 by Seleucus marked the foundation of the Seleucid dynasty. Seleucid territory at its greatest extent was by far the largest of any of the Hellenistic kingdoms; with its centre in Syria, it ranged from western Turkey through to Afghanistan. But it lost territory, both in the East and in the West. In the East there were two problems. The mountainous province of Bactria (Afghanistan) was turned into an independent Greek kingdom (256 BC), and there also emerged the non-Greek kingdom of Parthia (c.238) which effectively blocked the Seleucids from the east.

In the West the Seleucids also lost ground. A new Greek kingdom of the Attalids with its capital at Pergamum was carved out of Seleucid territory in western Turkey. Though the first two Attalids (283-241) had been only partially

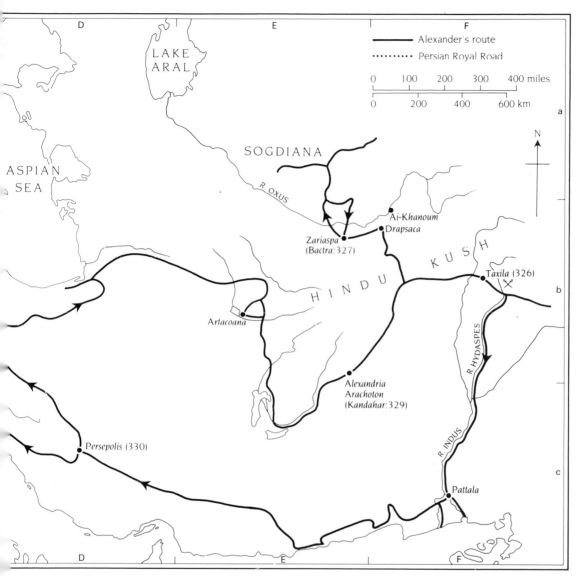

MAP 6. ALEXANDER'S JOURNEYS

independent of the Seleucids, the victory of Attalus I over the Galatians (*c.*238) allowed him to assume the title of king. In the second century Attalid power was further increased by Rome, to whom the kingdom was bequeathed by the last king (133). The Seleucid kingdom itself by the first century BC had been reduced (partly because of internal dissension) to a small area of northern Syria, and it finally fell into the hands of Rome (64 BC).

Thirdly, Macedon. The ancient dynasty from which Alexander himself came was exterminated, and possession of the land was fiercely contested, no doubt partly because it was Alexander's country, until in 276 Antigonus Gonatas succeeded in establishing himself securely in power. His heirs, the Antigonid dynasty, ruled the country until it was conquered by Rome in 168 BC.

STATUE OF A GAULISH CHIEFTAIN, the so-called Ludovisi Gaul, thought to be a copy of a bronze original which formed part of a monument set up in Pergamum in the late third century BC to commemorate Attalus I's victory over the Galatians. Various elements, including the arms of the warrior and the left arm of his dead wife, are modern restorations.

The Limits of Hellenism

Within the boundaries established by the conquests of Alexander there were dramatic cultural changes as Hellenization spread thousands of miles over the whole of the Middle East. This process used to be seen through rose-tinted spectacles as the innocent gift of civilization to the benighted barbarians; after all the British were doing precisely the same thing in their empire. No doubt the Greeks themselves saw matters in this way. But our own post-colonial age is more aware that culture is intimately bound up with politics: we can see that Greek culture dominated other, ancient cultures, and that this process of Hellenization was in part a product of the power of the kings.

The creation of new Greek cities was fundamental to the process of Hellenization (for their design see below, p. 501). Alexander himself was reported to have founded over seventy cities (the actual figure may be half that), while the Seleucids created over sixty new settlements in the area from western Turkey to Iran. Some of these 'new' cities were in fact old settlements with a new, dynastic name and a Greek constitution. Others were in areas previously not highly urbanized. For example, the second Seleucid king founded a new city on the

AERIAL VIEW OF ANTIOCH ON THE ORONTES (modern Antakya, in south-eastern Turkey). Founded by Seleucus I in 300 BC and named after his son Antiochus, this new city became the capital of the Seleucid Empire. It shows the typical gridiron plan of the Seleucid foundations, with five avenues running south-west to north-east and at least twenty streets running cross-wise.

Persian Gulf, naming it Antioch after himself, and later took steps to increase its population by 'inviting' Magnesia on the Maeander, an old city in western Turkey, to send out colonists. New cities were founded even where there were perfectly adequate existing settlements. Thus in Egypt two Greek cities were founded, of which one, Alexandria, replaced the old Pharaonic city of Memphis as the Ptolemaic capital; while the ancient city of Babylon was superseded by the new Seleucid capital Seleucia on the Tigris, some 50 kilometres away. There could be no clearer illustration than these two cities of the dominance which the Greeks were to exercise over the non-Greek populations.

The new settlements varied enormously in size and status. First, there were the military colonies founded by the Seleucids in various parts of their kingdom, from western Turkey to (it seems) Kurdestan. These settlements might be small, with only a few hundred men, and they had few autonomous institutions and little independence from the king. Their purpose was to act as a safeguard against disaffection and their inhabitants were obliged to serve in the king's army (below, p. 327). Secondly, there were the new, independent cities with populations of several thousands, ranging up to Alexandria, a great cultural centre, which in the first century BC was reckoned to be the largest city in the (Mediterranean) world.

The culture of these cities was strongly Greek. At the most obvious level there developed a new Greek language, the *koinē* or common language, which transcended the divisions of the old Greek dialects (Dorian, Ionic, and so on). There is generally nothing in the language or the script of a document to indicate from which part of the Greek world it comes. In addition, the political institutions of the cities were closely modelled on traditional Greek practices. Susa, for example, one of the four Persian royal centres, was refounded in the late fourth century as Seleucia on the Eulaeus. Over 300 years later the city, by then in the Parthian Empire, still had a constitution which would have been familiar to a Greek of the classical period; the council proposed and scrutinized candidates for public office, who were then elected by the full body of the citizens. There was a treasurer and a college of magistrates, of whom two gave their name to the year. Seleucia illustrates both the 'exporting' of Greek constitutions and the tenacity with which they were maintained in an alien world.

One of the key institutions which supported the Greek culture of the cities was the *gymnasion* (above, p. 226). This was not just a place for a casual work-out; it was an educational institution promoting both physical and intellectual culture. The building itself was often centrally placed and at Alexandria, for instance, was reckoned to be the most beautiful building in the city. More importantly, all full members of the city were expected to belong to the *gymnasion*. Strict rules governed eligibility for admission. In mainland Greece we hear of the exclusion of (among others) slaves, freedmen, their sons, and those practising vulgar trades. It is likely that in the new foundations such rules effectively excluded those who were deemed not to be Greek. But those natives who did succeed in proving their eligibility had to exercise in the *gymnasion* naked—an abomination to non-Greeks. Stripping naked marked their alienation from their native background and their incorporation into the Greek world.

The remarkable cultural achievements of the Greeks must not blind us to their exclusivity against indigenous cultures. For example, the population of Seleucia on the Eulaeus remained exclusively Greek. Even 300 years after its foundation there is no known case where a person with a Greek name did not have a father with a Greek name. That is, there was no Hellenization of the native population, which remained excluded from the civic institutions. Similarly in Egypt there was a sharp divide between Greek and native culture. The Egyptians continued to build temples on the traditional model and to produce a lively and diverse literature of their own (there are as many Hellenistic papyri in demotic Egyptian as in Greek). But the Greeks commissioned sculpture which shows no points of contact with Egyptian art and resolutely read literature of the classical period. In the field of law too, there were separate Greek and Egyptian courts administering different law-codes, while the law of Alexandria itself was modelled in part on that of Athens.

The continuing coexistence of cultures is not an indication of liberal pluralism. Greek culture was dominant, even if kings did sometimes show respect for native cultures and were happy for their rule to be honoured in native contexts (the Ptolemies, for example, were depicted like the Pharaoh in Egyptian temples). The only way to gain entry to the new system of power lay in the adoption of Greek culture. One of the key strategies was to claim ancestral Greek connections. Thus about 200 BC a leading citizen of Sidon, an ancient Phoenician city, was able to compete in (and win) one of the 'Panhellenic' competitions in mainland Greece open only to Greeks; his eligibility was proved by the 'fact' that Thebes in Boeotia was founded by the son of the first ruler of Sidon. When it was convenient the Greeks themselves employed the same strategy to integrate outsiders into the Greek world. The city of Lampsacus in north-west Turkey appealed to the Romans for their help against the Seleucid king Antiochus III on the ground that they were kinsmen: Lampsacus was near the site of Troy, the home of Aeneas the founder of Rome. Lampsacus could not foresee how momentous the subsequent involvement of Rome would be for the history of the Greek world.

Conflict over non-Greek communities' adoption of foreign ways did sometimes arise; the interaction of Judaism and Hellenism in the second century BC is the best-documented example. The leader of one faction of Jews in Jerusalem succeeded in becoming High Priest with the backing of the Seleucid king Antiochus IV and immediately set up a *gymnasion* (174-171). To the horror of the rest of the Jews, the priests ceased to show any interest in the divine services and hurried off to take part in the unlawful exercises on the training ground at the earliest opportunities. Some even gave up circumcision. Though the subsequent events are obscure (we are dependent almost entirely on 'orthodox' Jewish sources, especially the first two Books of the Maccabees), opposition both to the Hellenizing party and to their backer Antiochus grew. This reached crisis point

HEAD OF A PTOLEMY IN THE GUISE OF
AN EGYPTIAN PHARAOH. The dichotomy
in style between the official portraits of the
Ptolemies, produced by Greek artists, and their
portraits in Egyptian contexts, which
continued the Pharaonic tradition, reflects the
dichotomy between Greek and native cultures
in Hellenistic Egypt.

when Antiochus stripped the Temple of its treasures and ordered the Jews to give up their distinctive ways, replacing Jewish with pagan cults. Open insurrection followed, which soon led to the restoration of Temple cult, but the conflict between the Jews and the Seleucids continued until the Jews gained their independence in 141 BC.

This affair illuminates the relationship between Hellenism and the power of the kings. The Greeks believed in their cultural superiority over 'barbarians', and for them this belief justified political dominance. We, however, need to look further at the political function of Hellenism. The populations of the new cities were, at least initially, drawn largely from the old Greek world, and the culture of the cities remained resolutely Greek. The Greek inhabitants of a new city on the shores of the Persian Gulf were tied to their king by both culture and self-interest, needing support from the king in an alien world. Through the cities the kings could control their territories without the need for a substantial royal bureaucracy. Antiochus IV would naturally help the Hellenizing party in Jerusalem, especially as it probably intended to transform Jerusalem into a Greek city named after him. Active resistance to Hellenism was strong only in three areas, Egypt, Persia, and Judaea; all three had firm traditions of indigenous monarchy, and all three formulated their resistance in religious terms. The Book of Daniel, composed at the time of Antiochus IV, foresaw the further extension of his rule:

Yet he will come to his end—there will be no help for him. At that time Michael will stand up, the great prince who mounts guard over your people. There is going to be a time of great distress, unparalleled since nations first came into existence. When that time comes, your own people will be spared, all those whose names are found written in the Book. (12:1)

Courtiers and Soldiers

The king was the key figure in the royal administration. To him were addressed petitions by individuals and communities, and all major decisions were represented as emanating from the king himself. Not that the king stood alone. The Seleucid king had an official in charge of the royal finances and also one general aide 'in charge of affairs'. To return to the Second Book of the Maccabees, the successor of Antiochus IV decided to reverse his father's policy of forcible Hellenization of the Jews and wrote to 'his brother Lysias' to that effect. Lysias was not in fact the king's brother, but his assistant, holding various titles: 'brother', 'cousin', and 'in charge of affairs'.

Outside the court the king could act through a hierarchy of officials. The Seleucid kingdom was divided into a number of provinces (seventy-two in the time of Seleucus I), each under a governor; Lysias, for example, was governor of southern Syria and Phoenicia when Antiochus IV died. Through the governors the king could carry out plans, specific or general. Antiochus III was responsible for initiating a cult of himself and his ancestors throughout his kingdom; he later wrote to the governors of each province, informing them of the appointment of high priestesses of the queen in each province and instructing them to make the necessary arrangements. (There happen to survive three copies of Antiochus' letter, from western Turkey and Iran. For the very different royal cults organized by cities see below, p. 336.) The governors then issued instructions to their deputies to carry out the royal provisions.

In Egypt the royal administration was larger and more elaborate; the Ptolemies, in contrast to the Seleucids, had only three Greek cities in Egypt to provide a basic administrative framework. They therefore adopted the Pharaonic organization of the country: Egypt was divided into about forty 'districts', each subdivided into 'areas' and 'villages'; each unit of each tier was the responsibility of a specific official. The Ptolemies added to this Pharaonic system a new military organization with soldiers stationed throughout Egypt and a more complex taxation system.

The administration of both the Ptolemies and the Seleucids was staffed largely by Greeks, not by natives. The Seleucid ruling class completely excluded subject populations for about two generations; even after that it never included more than about 2.5 per cent of non-Greeks. One exception shows how non-Greeks might be admitted in peculiar circumstances. The First Book of the Maccabees recounts how two rivals for the Seleucid throne (Demetrius I and Alexander

Balas) contended for the support of Jonathan, the Jewish leader. Alexander gave Jonathan a whole series of titles normally accorded only to Greeks—'friend of the king', 'brother', 'first friend'—and finally a gold brooch 'of the kind customarily presented to the cousins of the king'. Jonathan thus reached the highest grade of court dignitaries, and for a time he did indeed support Alexander Balas. Similarly in Egypt the forms and language of the administration became Greek, and Egyptians were employed only so long as they learned Greek. The systems of royal administration thus served to reinforce both the dominance of Greek culture and the power of the king. But courtiers and administrators stood on the backs of the soldiers.

Warfare was basic to the Hellenistic world, in two ways. First, the legitimacy of the Hellenistic king rested in part on his military prestige (contrast the individual city-state where authority rested on tradition). The king, like Alexander and the Homeric heroes, was expected to take part in the hardships of campaigns and even in the dangers of combat. On one occasion the appearance of the king in battle inspired his men with courage and struck terror into the enemy. Victory also justified the assumption of the title of king, as we have already observed. A successful military expedition to the East even allowed the Seleucid Antiochus III to be called 'the Great King'.

Secondly, the scope of warfare was enlarged. When conflict was simply between two neighbouring cities over disputed territory the implications of warfare were limited; by contrast, in the Hellenistic period there was everything to fight for. Huge areas of land were regularly in dispute, even if the heartlands of each of the kingdoms remained secure throughout the period. The whole of mainland Greece, the Aegean islands, western Turkey, and southern Syria were fought over by various kings. The greater scale of the prizes, in comparison with the classical period, was responsible for an increased brutality. The total destruction of cities and the enslavement of their citizens by the kings became more common; the scale of Roman brutality towards Greece was even greater. The actual size of battles also increased. Whereas the decisive battle of Philip of Macedon against the Greeks at Chaeronea saw forces on each side of about 30,000, the Hellenistic kings could range 60,000 to 80,000 troops against each other. This was the maximum size of army thought possible as late as the eighteenth century.

The fundamental importance of warfare for the kings entailed major changes in military organization. Even those features of warfare that went back into the fourth century were given a new importance. (See above, pp. 142f. for the earlier developments.) Heavy-armed infantry (hoplites) had long been the basic fighting force of Greece; Philip's reorganization of the Macedonian army created an improved heavy-armed infantry (the phalanx) which differed from the old primarily in replacing the short throwing spear with a long pike (about 5.5 m. in the time of Alexander; about 6.5 m. a century later). This type of force, along with an important cavalry arm, formed the core of the Hellenistic armies.

The kings also made novel arrangements to ensure an adequate supply of men

ALEXANDER IN THE VAN OF BATTLE, detail of a figured frieze on a sarcophagus from the royal cemetery at Sidon (Phoenicia) (*c*.325–300 BC). The great king's exploits in battle cost him several wounds but set an example for his successors to imitate. On horseback at the left, he is shown wearing the heroic lion's-scalp helmet which likens him to Heracles.

for their forces. Ordinary cities seem to have supplied few men for the royal armies; special arrangements had to be made. The Seleucids, as we have already seen, established numerous military colonies, whose landholders were obliged to serve in the army; their sons had the option of forming the Guard, another part of the regular army. The Ptolemies followed a slightly different policy of granting scattered landholdings which were in principle revocable. In contrast to fifth-century Athens, where war orphans were given public financial support until they came of age, in Egypt one official could write to another: 'the cavalry men listed below have died; therefore take back their holdings for the crown.' This is the world of professional, not citizen, soldiers.

The kings supplemented their basic fighting force by employing mercenaries. Mercenaries were not new in this period (above, p. 142), but their importance increased greatly. Alexander had tens of thousands in his service and they formed an important element in the Hellenistic armies, sometimes in the phalanx, but more often as light-armed troops. Mercenaries generally have a bad reputation (down to Shakespeare's braggart soldier and beyond), but this is largely unjustified. As professional soldiers, they were concerned about their pay, and on one occasion they abandoned a defeated king and went over to the other side. But mercenaries did not betray their king for gold. After some difficulties with one of the Attalid kings, his mercenaries even took a solemn oath of obedience to him and his descendants. The king did not have the unquestioned allegiance which a general of the classical period could assume from his own citizens, but equally disloyalty was rare.

The techniques of combat of these armies, despite the continuing reliance on heavy-armed troops, became more sophisticated. The most extravagant novelty was elephants. Five hundred were given by the Indian king to Seleucus I in 302 in return for a cessation of hostilities. Four hundred of them were able to fight on his side and played an important part in securing him a crucial victory the following year.

Many of these elephants continued in Seleucid service, and, despite attempts to breed elephants in Syria, fresh supplies were called for occasionally; an astronomical tablet in cuneiform records the sending from Babylon to Syria of twenty elephants which had been delivered by the governor of Afghanistan. The Ptolemies also had war elephants; the first Ptolemy had a force of Indian elephants, but the Seleucid kingdom later cut off the supply from India and the Ptolemies had to use the smaller African variety ('forest' elephants), which they went to considerable lengths to capture. Unfortunately elephants were cumbersome— soldiers learned to sidestep their attacks and then stab the elephants' flanks or even to hamstring them—and they did not transform the patterns of warfare.

A comparable phenomenon is the competition between the major kingdoms in building ever more elaborate and impressive ships of war. Down to the time of Alexander the standard Greek warship was the trireme, a ship whose design

TERRACOTTA STATUETTE FROM MYRINA, showing an Indian war-elephant crushing a Celt, perhaps a reference to Antiochus I's victory over the Galatians about 272 BC. Elephants, often described as the tanks of ancient warfare, were an important element in the armies of Hellenistic times, notably in the Seleucid army, which secured them from India, and that of the Ptolemies, which got them from north Africa.

ROUNDED TOWER IN THE WALLS OF ASSUS (north-western Turkey). Built in ashlar masonry in the Pergamene style of the second century BC, this tower bears witness to Hellenistic developments in siege warfare—slit windows for bolt-projecting catapults are set half-way up, and broader openings for stone-projectors at the top.

is much disputed (it either had three banks of oars or three men to an oar). From the end of the fourth century onwards the standard warship was the quinquireme, rowed with five men to an oar. There were also prestige ships which reached fantastic sizes in the third century: we hear of a 'seven', 'eleven', 'thirteen', 'sixteen', 'twenty', 'thirty', and even a 'forty'. It is not clear how these ships actually worked, and their limited usefulness is indicated by the fact that the Romans never found it necessary to employ such showy vessels. But this ancient naval arms race, along with the trouble taken to maintain a supply of elephants, are vivid tokens of the dependence of the kings on military prestige.

Changes in siege techniques were of greater importance militarily. In the classical period good walls had been impregnable; the Spartans never even thrcatened the Long Walls which connected Athens to the sea. However, the development of the torsion catapult, probably by Philip, tilted the balance decisively away from the besieged in favour of the besieger. Alexander's use of the catapult and of siege towers enabled him to capture every city he assaulted. In response walls were made more sturdy, but further improvements were made in catapults. The patronage of Ptolemy II resulted in the discovery of formulas which enabled a precise calibration of the weight of missile against desired range. Some cities did still make successful resistance, but by now no individual city could feel secure when faced with an assault by a king. This crucial fact underlies the dominance of kings over cities.

The Kings and the Cities

Reconciling the power of the kings with the traditions of the cities was a recurrent problem of the Hellenistic period. The kings had overwhelming superiority over almost all individual cities, while the cities possessed the ideal of political independence. In the face of this contradiction, how could the kings wield their power and the cities maintain their dignity?

The problem was eased because the kings did not set out to impose positive policies on the cities. Like the early Roman Emperors, they were an essentially passive force, interested primarily in hegemony. They did not on the whole issue direct instructions to their subject cities. There were, however, ways of ensuring that the royal will was followed. For example, Alexander wanted to have exiles restored to their cities, but he had no need to issue orders directly to the cities. He had a letter read out at the Olympic games informing the assembled exiles that he would ensure their return. The operative legislation was carried out by the cities themselves. A decree of Mytilene which was probably passed after this announcement happens to survive in part; it makes detailed arrangements for the restoration of exiles, but merely refers to 'the settlements which the king [Alexander] has determined' and establishes a celebration of the king's birthday.

Without making crude interventions in cities, the kings infringed the freedom of cities both externally and internally. Externally they constrained the scope of a city's foreign policy, without having to direct it explicitly. Thus Antioch on the Persian Gulf agreed to participate in the new games of Magnesia on the Maeander (a non–political act), but carefully avoided a direct response to Magnesia's request for special diplomatic status ('holy and inviolate'). Despite its gratitude to Magnesia for having provided colonists, Antioch knew that this was a matter for the Seleucid king to decide.

Internally, the kings infringed civic freedom by raising large amounts of money from the cities. In principle all cities subject to particular kings were liable to pay them tribute, though the picture is obscure and we cannot quantify total royal revenues. But the imposition of tribute on individual cities might be a heavy burden. Miletus, for example, once had to borrow money from another city in order to pay its annual tribute of 25 talents. The scale of the tribute is clear not only from Miletus' difficulties but also from a comparison with the fifth century when the maximum Miletus is known to have paid Athens was only 10 talents. The kings also made special levies in case of war and controlled certain local taxes.

Some cities were able to gain exemptions from these royal controls. Politically the king could permit a city 'freedom and autonomy', that is, the ability to determine its policies both internally and externally. 'Freedom and autonomy' was a privilege, which the king could always rescind, but it should not therefore be seen as meaningless. The slogan, proclaimed by the immediate successors of Alexander, remained a potent political ideal, and cities treated it very seriously. Indeed one city (Colophon), when given its freedom at the end of the fourth century, decided to build itself fortifications, a vivid token of independence within the framework laid down by the kings.

Exemptions from financial obligations were also made. Tribute was the most resented royal imposition on the cities, as it had been in the fifth-century Athenian Empire, and some cities were fortunate enough to gain remission. Miletus, when it passed into the Ptolemaic sphere of influence, was able to gain the remission of 'harsh and oppressive taxes and tolls which certain of the kings had imposed'. While some remissions were made by the kings as a matter of principle, often they occurred in order to alleviate particular distress. Thus when the Seleucid king Antiochus III took over Teos in Ionia from the Attalid kingdom (in the words of a Tean decree), 'he saw that we were exhausted both in our public and in our private affairs because of the continual wars and the great burden of contributions we were bearing ... He therefore granted to our city and territory to be holy, inviolate and free from tribute, and undertook to free us himself from the other contributions we were paying to King Attalus [I].'

Subtle forms of indirect control over the cities also existed which helped to ensure peace and public order. First, in regulating the relations between two cities the kings adopted the traditional practice of appointing a third city as an arbitrator. For example, when Antigonus wanted to ensure peaceful relations between two cities (Teos and Lebedus) which he wished to unite into one city, he appointed a third city (Mytilene) to settle any disputed lawsuits between the members of the two cities.

Secondly, the kings or their officials used indirect means of ensuring harmony within cities. The judicial apparatus of individual cities often broke down because of internal political tensions; the problem was not new, but there developed in the early Hellenistic age the practice of requesting another city to provide an impartial panel of judges. Such requests, particularly in the early part of the period, often originated with the king or one of his agents; for example, a Ptolemaic official 'wishing the city [of Samos] to be in a state of concord, wrote a letter requesting the people of Myndus to send a panel of judges to settle the contracts in suspense.' The growth of this practice is probably due to the concern of the kings that their cities be docile. Both practices, that of arbitration and that of foreign judges, were convenient devices enabling the kings to secure harmony between and within cities without involving invidious direct interventions.

Civic Life Transformed

Royal control, even if mediated indirectly, had important implications for the internal politics of the subject cities. It underlies the paradox that, while democracy was accepted by all as the ideal civic constitution, in practice real popular participation in government declined in the Hellenistic age and dominance by the wealthy increased.

Democracy was espoused by the kings from Alexander onwards. Alexander himself established democracies in place of tyrannies and oligarchies in the Greek cities of Asia Minor which he freed from Persian rule; this gross interference with their internal affairs was presumably a popular move. His successors on the whole pursued the same policy. Thus the new cities established by Hellenistic kings were all, it seems, based upon democratic principles; all had magistrates, a council, and a popular assembly. The old cities also continually asserted the desirability of democracy against oligarchy or tyranny. Citizens newly incorporated into the city of Cos had to swear the following oath:

I will abide by the established democracy . . . and the ancestral laws of Cos . . . I will also abide by the friendship and alliance with King Ptolemy and the treaties ratified by the people with the allies; I will never set up under any pretext an oligarchy or a tyranny or any other constitution apart from democracy, and if anyone else establishes such a regime I will not obey, but will prevent him as far as possible . . . (Austin, no. 133).

Such measures helped to ensure that actual oligarchies were confined to the fringes of the Greek world. Tyrannies did sometimes arise, but the real danger lay in the informal monopolization of power by the wealthy. The kings could pose as democrats while being indirectly responsible for the growing power of the rich.

In the Athenian democracy of the fifth and fourth centuries a delicate balance had been established between the power of the people and the power of the rich. The rich served the community by paying for religious festivals and for the maintenance of the fleet, and in return gained great prestige. But the people did not allow individuals to gain too much honour; they turned down the offer made by Pericles and his sons to pay for some building works, in favour of expenditure from the tribute money. But by the end of the fourth century the balance between the power of rich and poor had shifted in favour of the rich. Cities became dependent on the rich for their very survival.

Wealthy individuals now played a crucial role in mediating between their city and the king, thus gaining power over the city. One rich Athenian, the comic poet Philippides, over a twenty-year period (301–283/2 BC) was able to confer great benefactions on his city. Being at the court of King Lysimachus, he could gain from the king gifts of wheat, money, and other supplies; he buried Athenians who had died in battle, and gained the release of others who had been taken prisoner. In the past officially appointed civic ambassadors, rather than informal 'friends' of the king, had performed the task of diplomacy; the cities had not needed to depend on their own citizens for favours. The danger which the cities felt about the new situation is captured by one phrase in the decree honouring Philippides: 'and he has never said or done anything contrary to the democracy'. It might have been otherwise.

The wealthy also now began to deploy their wealth within the city in a more blatant manner, and gained overwhelming prestige. Though in many places the change from the classical system was gradual, as the cities became accustomed to dependence, in Athens a specific reform was carried out by a tyrant backed by Macedon. The new system, which gave the rich much greater prominence within the city, is well illustrated by Philippides.

When he was appointed agonothete [in charge of the city's competitions, in 284/3 BC] he complied with the will of the people voluntarily from his own funds, offered the ancestral sacrifices to the gods on behalf of the people, gave to all the Athenians (presents) at all the contests and was the first to provide an additional contest for Demeter and Kore [Persephone] as a memorial of the people's liberty, and augmented the other contests and sacrifices on behalf of the city and for all this he spent much money from his own personal resources and rendered his accounts according to the laws. (Austin, no. 43).

The cities devised a whole new series of honours designed to recompense the rich for their services. Thus the Athenians voted Philippides a gold crown and a bronze statue in the theatre and for him and his descendants free public meals and a seat of honour at all the contests organized by the city. Honours, rather than laws, now formed the framework which defined the relationship of wealthy and city, and honours inevitably left the power with the rich.

This transformation of the relationship between rich and poor is linked to a decline in real democracy, that is, genuine popular control over political life. Popular assemblies continued to meet and to pass decrees, but the power of magistrates and council over them was greater than in the radical Athenian democracy. Magistracies themselves became the preserve of the rich, in part because of the growing expectation of considerable private expenditure from them. Aristotle in his *Politics* had already offered advice to oligarchs on how to control a state which prefigures Hellenistic practice: 'Those who enter into office may also be reasonably expected to offer magnificent sacrifices and to erect some public building, so that the common people, participating in the feasts and seeing their city embellished with offerings and buildings, may readily tolerate a continuation of this constitution [oligarchy]' (*Politics* 6.1321ᵃ).

In addition to the *de facto* restriction of office-holding to the wealthy, the popular courts, which had underpinned the Athenian democracy, also fell into their hands. In early-third-century Ptolemaic Egypt an uproar in council and assembly was quelled by the magistrates, who 'then voted that the council and the lawcourts should be recruited from pre-selected men.' Preselection would help to end uproar, that is, popular participation. Local courts were also circumvented by the use of judges from other cities for particularly sensitive cases, who were all well-to-do. Rome then consolidated the *de facto* power of the wealthy by instituting technical wealth qualifications for office-holding. But the assemblies continued to be open to all citizens, and so the constitutions were still 'democracies'. The political cant of the period strikes a curiously modern note. Today too we are all 'democrats': the western democracies, the Union of Soviet Socialist Republics, the People's Republic of China, and Democratic Kampuchea alike.

The decline in popular power was not, however, a peaceful process. There was always the danger of revolutionary activity. The citizens of one place in Crete were obliged in the third century BC to swear an oath of loyalty to the city, which included the following revealing clause: 'and I will not initiate a redistribution of land or of houses or of dwelling-sites or a cancellation of debts.' The fear of the two revolutionary demands, the redistribution of land and the cancellation of debts, does not often come to the surface of Hellenistic history. But it helps to explain, for example, an otherwise peculiar clause in a loan contract between Praxicles, an individual from Naxos, and the city of Arcesine on Amorgos at the turn of the fourth and third centuries: if the city did not repay the money, Praxicles was entitled to exact it by any means he chose from both the public and the private property of the Arcesineans and those living in Arcesine. Such a clause was the only protection for Praxicles against a legal cancellation of debts by the city.

The tensions between rich and poor were aggravated by the advent of Rome, and there was popular agitation, which the Romans naturally portrayed in the worst possible light. A Roman governor at the end of the second century BC sentenced to death those responsible for the burning and destruction of the town hall and the public records and the drafting of laws contrary to the (oligarchic) constitution given by the Romans to the Achaeans: 'those who carried out these things were to my mind manifestly laying the foundations of the worst state of affairs and of disorder for all Greeks—for not only are these things in keeping with a state of mutual disaffection and cancellation of debts, but they are also at odds with the freedom returned in common to all the Greeks and with our policy.' Roman freedom did not include the freedom to re-establish true democracies.

As these 'disturbances' indicate, the Greek city was far from dead in the Hellenistic period. There is no sign that people in general began to feel lost in the new world or to retreat towards quietism (below, p. 371). The cities, rather than the Hellenistic kingdoms, continued to provide the basic focus of attachment for their inhabitants and to have much vitality; in illustration of this point, I close by considering two types of civic response to royal power.

First, leagues of cities, which were a feature of mainland Greece in the Hellenistic period. In contrast to the classical leagues dominated by a single city (Athens or Sparta) these new leagues were an attempt by a number of small cities to group themselves in the face of the threat of royal power. The Achaean League, centred in the northern Peloponnese, is our best example. By the early part of the third century this ancient league had fallen into disarray; some of the cities had garrisons imposed on them by the Macedonians, others tyrannies. In the 280s and 270s some seven small cities came together to form the new Achaean League, expelling their tyrants and garrisons. Under the leadership of their great statesman Aratus, the league continued to pursue a single goal, 'the expulsion of the Macedonians from the Peloponnese, the overthrow of tyrannies, and the guarantee for each city of their common, ancestral freedom'. The institutions of the league—a primary assembly, a council and elected magistrates—formed, in theory, a democratic constitution which enshrined the equality of the member states. The competence of the league was limited to foreign policy; it, like the kings, passed a decree recognizing the special diplomatic status requested by Magnesia on the Maeander. There was no intervention in the internal running of the cities. Until Aratus turned to the Macedonian king to save the league from Sparta and perhaps also to ward off popular revolution in the Peloponnese (227–224), the league succeeded in preserving civic independence from royal power.

COINS OF THE ACHAEAN LEAGUE (after 280 BC). The idea of confederacy is emphasized by the silver coinage, which employs a common obverse type, the laureate head of Zeus, but varies the details of the reverse according to the city of issue. Within a wreath, tied either above or below, is set the Achaean League monogram (based on the Greek letters A and CH) and different letters and symbols, here a flying dove for Sicyon (*left*) and a winged horse for Corinth (*above*).

Secondly, civic cults of kings. It is a striking feature of the Hellenistic (and Roman) cities that they established cults of their rulers. Some see these cults simply as political honours, which are a mark of the decline of the traditional civic cults. I suggest on the contrary that cults of the gods were not in decline in the Hellenistic period (the special diplomatic status which Magnesia on the Maeander sought was because of her cult of Artemis), and that the royal cults were an attempt to relate king and city by incorporating the king within the main symbolic system of the city.

The cult of Antiochus III at Teos offers a good illustration. Teos had been captured by Antiochus from the Attalids and gained certain privileges (*c*.204), as we have seen (above, p. 331). In return the city established a cult which related Antiochus and his wife to Dionysus, the chief god of the city. Cult statues of the king and queen were dedicated beside the cult statue of Dionysus in his temple. There was also a cult statue of the king in the council house, and each year an offering of the first fruits was placed before this cult statue, which was also crowned with the produce of the seasons. The king, like Dionysus, is associated with the fertility of the crops; in particular, the Teans explained, his benefactions to the city had made agriculture more profitable. The cult of Antiochus allowed the citizens to represent the power of the king to themselves in a comprehensible and acceptable form. But Antiochus was shortly afterwards defeated by Rome. Perhaps only a decade or two after the cult of Antiochus was established, the neighbouring island of Chios established a cult of Roma, the personification of the power of Rome. There was a festival with a procession, a sacrifice, competitions, and a dedication probably showing the wolf suckling Romulus and Remus. With that the Greek cities entered a new period of their history.

Further Reading

The best general accounts of the period are F. W. Walbank, *The Hellenistic World* (London, 1981), with a good bibliography, and S. M. Sherwin-White, *The Hellenistic World 323–31 B.C.* (London and New York, forthcoming). See also W. W. Tarn and G. T. Griffith, *Hellenistic Civilisation*[3] (London, 1952); P. Grimal *et al.*, *Hellenism and the Rise of Rome* (London, 1968); C. B. Welles, *Alexander and the Hellenistic World* (Toronto, 1970). For more detail see the classic work of M. I. Rostovtzeff, *The Social and Economic History of the Hellenistic World*, 3 vols. (Oxford, 1941), M. Cary, *A History of the Greek World from 323 to 146 B.C.*[2] (London, 1963), and the new edition (forthcoming) of the *Cambridge Ancient History*, VI–IX. The key sources, including most of those that I discuss, are translated in M. M. Austin, *The Hellenistic World from Alexander to the Roman Conquest* (Cambridge, 1981), with a useful supplement in R. S. Bagnall and P. Derow, *Greek Historical Documents: the Hellenistic Period* (California, 1981). For the historians see Ch. 8.

Alexander has found numerous biographers. R. Lane Fox, *Alexander the Great* (London, 1973) is lively, J. R. Hamilton, *Alexander the Great* (London, 1973) more balanced; R. Lane Fox, *The Search for Alexander* (London, 1980) includes excellent photographs. The political histories of the individual kingdoms are listed by Walbank (above). G. J. D. Aalders, *Political Thought in Hellenistic Times* (Amsterdam, 1975) includes kingship theory, and some texts on this subject are translated by J. F. Gardner, *Leadership and the Cult of the Personality* (London and Toronto, 1974).

On the Greeks in India see R. Thapar, *A History of India*, I (Harmondsworth, 1966), V. Dehejia, *Early Buddhist Rock Temples* (London, 1972), J. W. Sedlar, *India and the Greek World: A Study in the Transmission of Culture* (Totowa, 1980). For Afghanistan see F. R. Allchin and N. Hammond (eds.), *The Archaeology of Afghanistan from the Earliest Times to the Timurid Period* (London, New York, and San Francisco, 1978), which includes Ai Khanoum, and J. M. Rosen-field, *The Dynastic Arts of the Kushans* (Berkeley, 1967). For the Parthians see M. A. R. Colledge, *Parthian Art* (London, 1977), and G. Herrmann, *The Iranian Revival* (Oxford, 1977), both well illustrated. For the limits of Hellenism see S. K. Eddy, *The King is Dead: Studies in the Near Eastern Resistance to Hellenism 334-31 B.C.* (Lincoln, Nebraska, 1961), M. Hengel, *Judaism and Hellenism* (London and Philadelphia, 1974) and A. D. Momigliano, *Alien Wisdom* (Cambridge, 1975).

W. W. Tarn, *Hellenistic Military and Naval Developments* (Cambridge, 1930), G. T. Griffith, *Mercenaries of the Hellenistic World* (Cambridge, 1935), and B. Bar-Kochva, *The Seleucid Army* (Cambridge, 1976), survey different aspects of the military history.

A. H. M. Jones, *The Greek City from Alexander to Justinian* (Oxford, 1940), is basic to this and the next section. See also V. Ehrenberg, *The Greek State*² (London, 1969), P. M. Fraser, *Ptolemaic Alexandria* (Oxford, 1972).

A. R. Hands, *Charities and Social Aid in Greece and Rome* (London, 1968), discusses civic benefactors, and includes a dossier of texts in translation. G. E. M. de Ste Croix, *The Class Struggle in the Ancient Greek World* (London, 1981), documents the decline of democracy. S. R. F. Price, *Rituals and Power: The Roman Imperial Cult in Asia Minor* (Cambridge, 1984), includes Hellenistic ruler cults. Religious history may be approached through A. D. Nock, *Conversion* (Oxford, 1933), or H. I. Bell, *Cults and Creeds in Graeco-Roman Egypt* (Liverpool, 1953); sources are translated in F. C. Grant, *Hellenistic Religions, the Age of Syncretism* (New York, 1953).

14

Hellenistic Culture and Literature

❧

ROBIN LANE FOX

Introduction: The World after Alexander

AFTER Alexander the horizons of the Greek world extended as far as India. Even Alexander had been surprised by the size of it all: he wondered if the Caspian Sea was the outer ocean of the world, and in India he began by thinking that the River Indus ran cosily round into Egypt's Nile. The new horizons were not altogether lost on those whom the Greeks bordered. Around 260 BC the Indian king Asoka dispatched an edict for inscription throughout his realm which referred to the 'world my children'. It listed exactly the Hellenistic kings from his Asian border through Egypt and Macedon to Cyrene in north Africa. A copy stood in Greek near the Greek and Macedonian settlement at Kandahar.

In the West, meanwhile, intriguing discoveries had been made by Pytheas, a ship's captain from Marseilles who sailed north past Scotland in, or shortly after, the age of Alexander. Noting the midnight sun, he continued north 'until there was no proper sea, land, or air, but a sort of mixture of all three like a jelly-fish, in which one can neither walk nor sail ...': anyone who has sailed in the Arctic will recognize the clamminess of the northern fog-bank. Afterwards, the best Greek geographers never made sense of Europe above and along the line of the Danube. The Celts were indiscriminate barbarians, and nobody bothered with inland Spain until the Roman conquests.

In the East, were the new settlers equally uninfluenced by their findings? At a great banquet Alexander had prayed for 'partnership' in rule between Macedonians and Persians: his partnership, however, required its orientals to speak and learn Greek. In a good story, he is said to have arranged Greek lessons for the captive women of the Persian King's family. In the East Greeks kept on exercising in Greek *gymnasia* from the Oxus to the Persian Gulf and explaining the peoples around them by their own culture's myths: the Armenians, they thought, descended from Jason, while 'Bouddhas' had followed their own Dionysus. In a world where it became usual to be bilingual, Greeks spoke and read Greek only. They imported vines into Egypt and Babylonia: wherever possible, they grew their olives. For most of them culture and politics still centred on the 'city' or *polis*, and on the disruptive power of kings who took Greece and the Aegean very seriously. The court and the city, not Persia or India, were the setting for Hellenistic culture and literature.

At the major courts the kings and their top friends had the money to be spectacular in open defiance of reason. The difference in style between a major and minor court was that the major had a bigger store of precious metal. On one winter's day in Alexandria during the 270s Ptolemy II staged a grand procession whose central section honoured Dionysus. Mechanical statues processed on huge floats; wine ran freely over the streets from vast pitchers; sweet refreshments were given out to the spectators. Actors and masses of women joined officials who had dressed as satyrs in a show which included scenes of Dionysus' drunken return from India, the figure of Alexander, and an enormous gold phallus, 180 feet long, covered with ribbons and tipped with a large gold star. The Morning Star led the way; the Evening Star brought up the rear. Between marched 2,000 oxen smothered in gold, 2,400 dogs, some giraffes, antelopes, Indian parrots, elephants, a gnu (or a hartebeest), ostriches pulling carts, and a 'white she-bear' which was not, alas, from the Arctic. The figure of 'Corinth' led a parade of women named after the cities of Ionia and the islands; she was a clear allusion to

INSCRIPTION OF ASOKA FROM KANDAHAR (Afghanistan). The great Mauryan king Asoka (*c*.268–232 BC), ruler of an empire covering much of the subcontinent of India, was converted to Buddhism about 257 and set up a number of inscriptions exhorting his subjects to lead lives of tolerance and self-sacrifice. Most were written in the native Prakrit, but in the north-west some were in Aramaic and/or (as here) in Greek.

EXEDRA IN THE *GYMNASION* AT AÏ KHANOUM, Afghanistan (late second century BC). Such recesses, equipped with benches against the walls, served as meeting-places where philosophers and other teachers gave instruction to the young men who frequented Greek *gymnasia*. The presence of a *gymnasion* at Aï Khanoum is a vivid testimony to the spread of Greek culture to the remote corners of the Hellenistic world.

the League of Corinth and the Ptolemies' concern for Greek freedom. Slaves dragged the carts and the military processed in thousands.

This extraordinary show combined artistry and free drink, the wonders of the world and a mobile zoo, the political themes of the dynasty's care for Greece and the power of a modern march-past. The elements differed in degree, not in kind, from the style of a royal wonderland which attaches to so much of the court culture in this period. It is matched by the taste for books on unscientific marvels among the literary scholars. It also shows in the royal mania for books themselves.

All the courts had libraries, even on the Black Sea, but Alexandria's are the most famous. Followers of Aristotle had settled in that city with memories of their master's learned society and great collection of books. Probably they suggested the ideas of a royal museum and library to the first Ptolemy. The royal library was probably attached to the colonnades and common room of the museum and served more as a vast arsenal of books than as a separate set of reading rooms. Nearly half a million book-rolls are alleged to have been stored inside, while another 42,000 are said to have lived in a second library attached to the temple of Serapis. Texts became hot royal property. When ships landed in Alexandria they were searched for books. Any found on board had to be surrendered for royal copying in scrolls stamped with the words 'from the ships'. The 'borrowing' of the master-scrolls of the great tragedians from the Athenians was one of the sharpest coups of Ptolemaic diplomacy. Pirating, in our modern sense, was a Hellenistic invention. As demand was insatiable, supply rose to meet it, aided by plausible forgery. Texts were faked and 'flogged' to the kings, until Aristotle had been credited with all sorts of interesting, if little-known, titles.

Why did the kings bother? As the Aristotelians had no doubt explained to a willing Ptolemy I, libraries and scholarly studies kept a king abreast of man's understanding of the world. The Ptolemies had had good tutors and they did not lose interest in learning. Ptolemy IV built a temple to Homer and wrote a tragedy on which a courtier politely wrote a commentary; rancorous Ptolemy VIII argued that the flowers in Calypso's garden were water parsnips, not violets. One of the last Seleucids wrote on snake-bites in verse. Royal extravagance inflated these tastes, and when others entered the race, book-collecting became a mad competition. To hinder the Attalid kings in Pergamum, the Ptolemies are said to have cut off the export of Egypt's papyrus. Thereupon, the Attalids pioneered parchment, or 'pergamene skins'. It is a good story, but fine parchment already existed.

Competition promised well for literary culture. In a court epigram Ptolemy

MAIN HALL IN THE LIBRARY AT PERGAMUM. Founded by Attalus I (241–197 BC), the library has been identified in a group of first-floor rooms behind the north portico of the sanctuary of Athena. It has been suggested that the line of holes visible in the walls may have helped to support book-cases, but the room was probably surrounded by statues of poets and historians.

III was honoured as a man 'good at battle and the Muses'. It was important to be both, for the kings were also competing for a pool of talent from the older Greek cities. Many of these men were exiles who found a better home as advisers and men of letters at the new courts. Museums and libraries were unquestioned goods to a Ptolemaic agent like Zeno. From his papyri we know this estate manager as the probable owner of a lovely, early text of Euripides' *Hippolytus*, the patron of epigrams for his hunting dogs, and the orderer of books and speeches on embassies which were to be sent from Alexandria to his brother, no doubt to polish him up. The ethical ideals of school philosophy were urged on the kings and repeated in the praises and edicts of their officials and agents. Like books, they made the kings more attractive.

Through these migrant courtiers the kings kept contact with the culture and education of older Greek cities. There was a reverse traffic, too, as part of their covert political publicity. They sent royal architects to the cities, encouraged participation in royal festivals, gave generous buildings, including libraries, and paid big sums for the education of the cities' youth: in the late 220s, Athens received a 'Ptolemaeum', a *gymnasion* for her young citizens which also housed books and hosted lectures. These gifts were apt attempts to influence and impress, for the grossness of the royal wonderland did not stifle keen, civic education. In Greek cities children now began to learn at the age of seven in privately funded schools, assisted sometimes by an individual's benefaction. They learnt to read and they practised writing in sentences, some of which, as known on papyrus, have an extreme anti-feminine and anti-barbarian content. Discipline was maintained by flogging. Aged fourteen, they passed on to a secondary stage which

DETAIL OF A SCHOOLTEACHER'S MANUAL from the Fayûm in Egypt. Dated to the last quarter of the third century BC, this papyrus scroll gives an idea of the somewhat artificial nature of many aspects of Hellenistic education. It begins by listing notional monosyllables and obscure, tongue-twisting words, then proceeds (here) to names from geography and mythology.

was dominated by literary exercises, the names of Greek rivers, and quizzes on Homer's Trojans. The old gap before the 'ephebe' stage, at the age of eighteen, was filled for many Hellenistic men with studies of the classics, including older poetry, and school composition. Then future citizens passed to the *gymnasion*, which was funded under civic control by a rich official. The hard core of its training was sport, but some *gymnasia* had libraries and held lectures too. Richer young men aspired further, to a private teacher in rhetoric or philosophy. The rhetorical training was very mechanical. By the later second century BC there are signs that more and more formal grammar was being taught in the earlier stages and that, overall, the studies were becoming ever more literary. There had never been lessons in law, while mathematics, for most men, was alarmingly elementary. As music became specialized, it withdrew from general schooling.

In every city the culture of the ephebes continued to be valued highly. Fathers troubled to put their sons down for a good *gymnasion*, and in later life the *gymnasia* looked to their 'old boys' for financial support. By the later second century BC Athens, the smartest centre of all, was admitting rich foreigners among her ephebes. In turn, they helped to keep up the idealization of the city. What, though, was the social value of all this Homer and arduous listing of Spartan rivers? It has been explained as a 'culture of reinforcement' to keep up Greek morale abroad and to keep out barbarians. That purpose is not convincing: the same studies flourished in old Greece where nobody risked being swamped. More relevantly, it marked social divisions between Greeks themselves. Vulgar people could not enter *gymnasia*. The parents were usually rich: in later third-century Athens there were scarcely forty new ephebes each year. This exclusiveness worked wonders for the city's international image. In the mid second century a recently found decree from a Macedonian city excluded slaves and freedmen, their children, those who had not attended wrestling school, anyone who had practised a trade in the *agora*, anyone who was drunk or mad. It also banned paederasts. *Gymnasia* were scenes of the golden years of romances between young men, but they were for 'amateurs' only.

Extravagant royal culture, therefore, was only the icing on a dry and well-established cake. Financed by their richer citizens, the cities set men's cultural horizons. Their speakers and antiquarians were not 'irrelevant'. They served on the vital embassies, while historians and local experts played a fascinating part in local boundary disputes and the many boards of arbitration. History had urgent public uses. At their own level cities also remained lively centres of shows and recitals, games and drama. They were served by wandering poets and musicians and the troupes of professional actors who were declared 'inviolable' on their travels through warring Hellenistic kingdoms.

A huge theatre has been unearthed at Alï Khanoum beside the Oxus river, and it is possible that the forms of Greek drama influenced the emergent theatrical art of India. The Hellenistic age also saw the flowering of many small societies in which members used to dine and patronize recitals. Non-citizens in places such as Rhodes or Delos found a focus for their loyalties in these groups, which were often organized with titles from civic life. By 300 BC they were joined by the foundations set up to honour a dead man's memory. Below the city's public patronage these groups all multiplied the centres of local cultural life.

Across such an area, how far was there a single culture? In the cities there was no common calendar and no common body of law. But there were broad similarities in civic life and the many sets of athletic games. At court, the kings used the 'common Greek' prose, or *koinē*, which developed from Attic origins and gradually pushed the older dialects in Greece itself into retreat. A measure of linguistic unity thus emerged around official, Hellenistic Greek. A common feeling was also aroused by the threat of barbarians, best seen in the sigh of Hellenic relief which followed the repulse of the Gauls from Greece and Delphi in 279 BC. Culturally, the kings all respected Athens' legacy. She had invented the theatre which every good city now imitated. Her fourth-century prose and her past record against Asian barbarians combined with the prestige of her former philosophers and dramatists. Together they kept up her appeal.

If there was a measure of common culture, how did it differ in the cities from fourth-century culture, except that we happen to know more about it? The differences were more of degree than of kind, and they are best brought out by some Hellenistic improvements. Closer contact with eastern spices transformed the industry of female scents and soaps. Make-up is thought to have been improved by Near Eastern skills, not least in the art of eye-shadow. There had never been such prostitutes as the great Attic mistresses of the Macedonian generals: the loose women of Alexandria were famous. The game parks and wild animals of Asia made the old Greek hare-chasing seem as tame as beagling. Indian blood bred newer and better hounds for spectacular hunting across Asia. The cooking, surely, improved: Alexandrian sauces for fish and gourds passed into Roman cook-books; the best banquets were spectacular, and although one of the Ptolemies kept pheasants without eating one, he crossed them with guinea-fowl and ate the result instead. Egypt's cabbage was so bitter that seed was imported from Rhodes to combat it. For one happy year it worked, but then the old bitterness emerged again. Greeks introduced chick-peas from Byzantium into Egypt, and a better wheat almost drove out the old, husked grain. An experiment was made with palm-trees in Greece, and estate owners in the Near East struggled to produce frankincense. We know too little about royal gardening, but there is an ominous hint in a letter from a Ptolemaic minister to his agent, telling him to plant 300 fir trees in the park on his estate, not just for ship-timber but for the 'tree's striking appearance': did other Greeks spatter Egypt with conifers? In places they greatly extended the area and yield of cultivable land. In Egypt's Fayum basin they are thought to have trebled it; the plain behind their city on the Oxus was never better irrigated or more densely worked. At Olympia we find baths with under-floor heating in the early second century, surely before any Roman influence. The Hellenistic *gymnasia* invented the detailed health exercises

REMAINS OF HYPOCAUST IN THE GREEK BATHS AT OLYMPIA. This underfloor heating system, dated about 100 BC, foreshadows the subsequent developments of thermal architecture in Roman Italy. The flue in the foreground leads into the heated room at the rear, with its floor supported on brick pillars.

which passed into the handbooks of the second century AD. Distinct from mere sport, they were planned as a 'work-out': jogging was said to be good for sexual diseases.

Most of this cultural life was restricted to the very few who could afford it. On the reverse side of Alexandrian elegance lay a battery of royal taxes and dependent workers and the appalling inhumanity of gold-mines. By the 150s they were manned by political prisoners and their innocent families. When Alexander founded cities beyond the Oxus he gave a horde of rebellious Asiatics to one of them, presumably as slaves. The huge benefactions of a rich citizen in a late-third-century city on the Black Sea have been shrewdly related to profits in the local slave trade. In the ancient economy people lived well only at the glaring expense of others.

To participate in cultural life natives had to Hellenize, and in a fascinating aspect of the period we see them doing just that. The kings settled colonies of native soldiers who spoke Greek in royal service and thus left signs of their Hellenization at unlikely spots in Asia. At Marissa, scarcely 30 miles across the

Jordan from Jerusalem, the burial ground produced handsome tombs and paintings in a Greek style. One of them had a frieze of wild animals, matching the African species known in the orbit of the Ptolemaic court. On its wall a Greek poem was beautifully inscribed, telling how a woman took temporary leave of one of her two lovers. At Marissa the Ptolemies had settled troops from Sidon: in the poem the woman keeps her lover's coat as a pledge, a theme which has been traced to old Semitic culture.

Greek culture was not always imposed: it could exert its own fascination. Among the Jews we know of voluntary Hellenizers who wished to go over to Greek ways and religion. They were only stopped after a bitter war, and Jewish culture emerged into the Maccabean age (175–63 BC), essentially resistant to the hard core of Hellenism. The Romans were far more flexible, and the Parthians, too, picked up the fashion: at their early capital instructions have been found for making a Greek actor's mask. Greek culture was so lively and such fun. It had

THE STADIUM AT PERGE IN SOUTHERN TURKEY. Though the present seating is Roman, the stadium was certainly laid out in Hellenistic times. Such stadia, designed to accommodate the running and field events of a local athletics festival, are one of the hallmarks of the Greek way of life which was carried into the newly conquered regions of the Hellenistic world.

PAINTED ANIMALS IN A TOMB AT MARISSA (Marêshah) in Jordan (second half of the third century BC), The creatures represented were all native to north Africa or believed to be such; here we see an elephant and a rhinoceros, both identified by tiny labels. The larger letters painted over the frieze refer to a subsequent burial.

theatres and athletics, some fascinating books, and a refined style of dining, the symposium. In response to it, a mid-second-century Jew turned the story of the Exodus into a Greek tragedy. By comparison it must have been rather dull to be a Jew in the evenings before the Greeks came. In their trading and art, their warfare and intellectuality, their literature and culture, the Greeks towered over their Asian subjects. In reaction, only Jews wrote anything literary, but it was minor stuff, largely taking refuge in divine revelation and sacred 'wisdom'. It is surely only a second-century-BC legend that Ptolemy II patronized the literal, clumsy Greek translation of Jewish Scripture, the Septuagint. Although some believe this story, it was probably attached to the translation later to give it prestige.

What, in return, of the Greeks? Like Alexander, the vast majority were not bilingual, and their schooling still absorbed them. Beside the Oxus, the wall which appears to divide the Hellenistic city has been proposed as a wall to divide the Greeks from the natives, as in old Massilia (Marseilles). But there is more to be said here. The rulers were often more open in their patronage than the cities: court Jews and a few Egyptians served several of the early Ptolemies. Alexander's associates did not at once forget his ambition; the army needed good men, especially Iranian horsemen; Ptolemy invented a new god, Serapis, which was indeed a fusion of Greek and native forms. True, the Attalid kings at Pergamum celebrated themselves as the defenders of Greek culture from the raids of barbarian Gauls. In Egypt, however, the earlier Ptolemies set Greek culture beside and above the customs of their new kingdom. A man such as Eratosthenes, the polymath, had an openness to people of all native origins, underpinned by his general theory of climatic 'zones' and geography. Clearchus, who walked to the

HEAD OF SERAPIS IN GREEN BASALT, now in the Villa Albani in Rome. This Roman copy probably reflects the cult-statue made (third century BC) by Bryaxis for the temple of Ptolemy I's new god in Alexandria. Serapis was created by grafting Greek elements on to the old Egyptian god Osor-Apis; but this image is very much in the Greek style, with a head closely related to depictions of the Greek gods Zeus and Asklepios. The corn-measure (*modius*) on the head is a symbol of fertility.

Oxus river from Delphi, also compared the wisdom of the Jews, the Brahmins, and the Magi. A Seleucid envoy to India, Megasthenes, left a fascinating mixture of observation and venial misunderstanding from his journey to the Indian court of the Maurya king on the Ganges. Greek education and theory did not entirely distort the value of the lively account of the Red Sea tribes which was written by a secretary to an official of the later Ptolemies, the appealing Agatharchides (flor. 170–145).

On one cardinal point, Greek observers of foreign peoples were more sharp-eyed than a whole generation of their modern historians. Intelligent men were quick to spot the lethal designs of Roman power, the 'cloud in the West' which menaced their freedom. Certainly the war with Hannibal was not far gone before mainland Greeks saw that Rome, not Carthage, was the threat, exemplified already in Sicily. They had not learned Latin, but they were already more perceptive than scholars who have learnt it since. By 146 Corinth was sacked and Agatharchides was remarking how the remote Sabaean Arabs owed their luxurious survival 'until our time' to their distance from 'people who turn their powers against every place'. He was referring, surely, to the Romans.

Literature and Patronage

Between 300 and 145 BC, how does the best Hellenistic literature fit into this context of lavish kings and a tenacious city culture? We have lost so much, especially in prose, that judgements are all provisional; might there be a master to our taste among the 130-odd names who wrote Hellenistic tragedy? It was an exciting time to be a man of talent, for new forms emerged from the old conventions in prose and verse. Every author of high quality came into contact with the patronage of kings of royal cities. Do the kings, then, take the credit for this new liveliness?

Only an exile, a gaolbird, or a starving man, said a character in late fourth-century comedy, would bother to resort to a king. Authors saw their chance. They were always claiming to be hungry and often they took up writing when exiled from their homes. Although Menander refused to leave Athens, subsequent literary men headed freely for the royal cities. At the courts, literary life was not too awkward. There are no stories of official works which the poets were asked to write, but refused. There was no need for a tactful intermediary to guide relations between the kings and their authors. The Attalids received their celebratory prose, the Seleucids their verse epics, but these works were not the sum of their authors' interests. In Alexandria poetic compliments to the dynasty were often paid in a witty and oblique style, and the best of them attached to the queens, not to the kings. At Pella, too, there are hints of give-and-take.

What studies, however, did the kings patronize with any permanency, beyond the occasional hand-out for good verses? We know most about patronage in Alexandria, where the Ptolemies' record was limited: the literature they patronized did not produce major talents in history and philosophy. They had an alphabetical list of pensions, a museum, and two libraries. They had a serious need for a royal tutor to teach the little princes and a royal librarian to preside over the growing arsenals of books. Long-term patronage was for useful industry: tutoring, science, the library, and textual scholarship. At first the tutors and librarians included men who also wrote excellent poetry. In the second century BC they were critical literary scholars, not original authors.

Poetry, except drama, was incidental to their patronage. Poets moved freely from king to king, whereas textual scholars were less mobile. The poetry which we still have and admire was not popular. Major Hellenistic poetry survives on only two papyri before about 100 BC. One was probably a manual for school-teachers; the other included a paraphrase in prose of the many verses which were too difficult. On prose, too (except history), the kings' persons weighed less than heavily. Just as the development of monarchy in twelfth-century Europe encouraged a better fund of royal stories, so the new age of kings and courtiers developed into a golden age of recorded gossip. Some of the best attached to the kings themselves: in his memoirs, even Ptolemy VIII ran through the fascinating list of Ptolemy II's mistresses a century or so earlier. An upper class reveals itself by its gossip, and to judge from theirs, the Hellenistic courts were elegant, ironic, and not overawed by royalty. Gossip crossed the literary boundaries: in Alexandria Machon, the comic poet, published witty verses on the dealings of great men and prostitutes, while later in Pergamum good anecdotes seem to have been a mainstay of Carystius' *Historical Notes* in prose. High society liked to read how the tireless Hippe called Ptolemy II 'Daddy' in private, and how King Demetrius the Besieger did and said the crudest things while asking Lamia ('Vampire') to choose from an array of scents and ointments. In Antioch the popular nicknames of the later Seleucids were bestowed in a similar irreverent spirit.

The libraries proved more of a dead weight. Scholarship had been the invention of fourth-century authors, and royal patronage merely gave it its head. Literature was prized for being antiquarian, and in royal circles its scope (excepting history) bears a striking resemblance to titles produced later by the scholars and courtiers in the equally polished society of ninth- and tenth-century Muslim rulers. It extended to brief biographical dictionaries, lists and catalogues, lively works on natural curiosities, and a long chain of titles on the wonders and marvels of the world. Like the Muslim courtiers, Hellenistic authors had an encyclopedic range and an interest in the fabulous and the exotic, which made better reading than a brilliant scientific tract by Archimedes in 'peculiarly rusty Doric'. These books were works to dip into, in search of something odder than Aristotle knew. They were totally unscientific, but they made for good conversation, like the popular lists of the world's biggest rivers and most impressive sights. We should remember this saving grace. Very little survives from the laborious volumes in which prose authors showed off so cheerfully, but the titles tell their own story, none more clearly than the works of Callimachus. His *Table of the Rare Words and Compositions of Democritus* was for enthusiasts only, but readers may have found more in his *Customs of Barbarians*, his *Collection of Wonders of the World*, and his books *On the Rivers of Europe, On Birds, On Winds*—but perhaps not so much in his monograph *On Changes of Names in Fish*.

The most punishing endeavour of Hellenistic learning was better directed. The first librarians in Alexandria were scholar poets, and from this combination grew the science of specialized scholarship which was at its peak from the 220s onwards. The poet's role in its origins is explicable. Prose used the common Attic dialect of the courts and did not react against its growing colloquialism until the classical revival of the first century BC. All Hellenistic poets, however, ignored the spoken dialects and looked back to the language and metre of the old classics. Difficult metres were revived or applied to unlikely subjects: Callimachus added a new one, by copying the hardest of all forms, the staccato galliambics which were used in one type of cult-hymn. Scholar poets set out to enrich the language by their own researches. In our own age W.H. Auden allotted poets the duty of legislating for language and guarding its purity. Hellenistic poets laid down the law too, but on dead, literary words. Much of their poetry is very difficult to translate, as it is packed with their sub-Homeric coinages, puns and glosses on obscure phrases in the classics, and an extravagant love of synonyms. On a mid-third-century papyrus we have a piece of a poetic 'vocabulary' which lists rare compound words. When searching for the *mot juste*, lesser poets could look at these handy catalogues. By the early second century, Aristophanes, the librarian in Alexandria, had compiled a big work called *Words*, perhaps the same as his *On Words Suspected of Not Being Used by The Early Writers*. By 200, literary scholarship had its own specialists who were no longer poets.

In the service of Philip and Alexander, the royal tutor Aristotle and his kinsman Callisthenes had worked on the text of Homer, whom their great pupil loved. In Alexandria scholarship became a science, spearheaded by the royal librarians from about 201 to 145 BC. Callimachus had already published a famous catalogue in 120 books, the *Tables of Persons Conspicuous in Every Branch of Learning and a List of Their Compositions*. Future scholars did more to swell libraries than reduce them. No critical work on forgeries is attested, and as scholars declared the old texts to be unsatisfactory, kings had to acquire their works and the new texts too. The master of the art was Aristarchus (*c*.215-143). Both tutor and librarian, he taught the best critics of the next generation and was distinguished by his flashes of historical sense, his caution, and his sane theory of regularity in grammar. The conjectures and deletions which these critics proposed have had less influence than their arrangement of the texts we now read.

The great age of scholarship ran from the later third century to the mid second, and afterwards, like philosophy, it lapsed into the industrious synthesis of rival views. As in philosophy, so in criticism: this synthesis followed an age of fierce dispute between sects, the second-century 'analogists' of Alexandria and the 'anomalists' at Pergamum. These subjects were best learnt by personal contact and thus among grammarians the ties of master and pupil were drawn very tightly. What exactly had Aristarchus said? There were no mass copies of his teaching, and a familiar industry developed in the circulation of first-hand lecture notes. Inevitably scholarship began to be practised on the scholars' works themselves. Ammonius, librarian and pupil of Aristarchus, wrote that jewel of Hellenistic piety, *On The Fact That There Were Not More Than Two Editions Of Aristarchus's Recension Of The Iliad*.

Royal men of letters did not only have to live with their texts. They had to live with each other. How did a man prove himself more learned than some wretched contemporary, except by compiling more information and attacking other men's views? An apt legend later credited the Alexandrian scholar Didymus with 3,500 books, justifying his nickname 'Brass Guts'. The remarkable

Eratosthenes spanned a range which few have matched since, writing well on geography, chronology, astronomy, on *Good and Bad Qualities*, and adding some notable poetry, including a brilliant epigram on the method of doubling a cube. A host of lesser minds ranged almost as widely and at similar length.

The quarrels, at first sight, are more depressing. The Museum was once described as the 'bird-cage of the Muses', and its subjects saw some spectacular cock-fights. They were led by Callimachus' attacks on poets and critics who did not share his taste and aims. On the topic of textual scholarship, Alexandria and Pergamum staged their own minor Hellenistic war. Literary critics throve on attacks: Aristarchus attacked Zenodotus, Demetrius and Crates attacked Aristarchus, Polemo attacked Eratosthenes, and so forth. One-upmanship made a man's name: Aristophanes even wrote a book *Against Callimachus' Library Lists*. Yet it is a dead subject which does not cause scholarly dispute. The personal tone was frightful, but on inspection these quarrels were not mere fights for promotion or the savage reaction of the old to the young. The competitors believed that principles were at stake. Callimachus, not unjustly, thought one wing of poetic taste entirely misguided. In scholarship it mattered greatly if a man was sensible and an analogist, or irresponsible and an anomalist, with a faith in allegory as a device to make the poets 'mean' things quite remote from their manifest meaning. Through the grammarians' invention, the worst-attested personal quarrel has become the most notorious. The two Alexandrian poets, Callimachus and Apollonius, were later alleged to have fought bitterly, perhaps because Callimachus' pugnacity was well known and, as master and supposed pupil, the two seemed inevitable enemies to later scholars who cast them in their own image. Modern scholars have given the legend a new twist, alleging that Callimachus abused his pupil for taking his material without acknowledgement. That is an amusing comment on scholars, but not on poets, who are happy to be imitated. The 'quarrel' lacks any good evidence.

In this atmosphere of industry and competition, where is good, readable writing still to be found? In the little which we still know of prose, new forms and a new emphasis show through, but they owe nothing directly to royal patrons. The earlier forms of biography blossomed in this age of individuals and educated interest in great men of the past. It was feeble, however, because it lacked a sense of social and psychological context and tended to be static and anecdotal. The germs of romantic fiction also hatched generously. The Alexander Romance excelled them all, beginning within a decade of the great man's death. Popular novels were matched by a new form of popular moralizing, cast in prose as the 'diatribe' and attached to the name of the itinerant Bion. The scholar Eratosthenes dismissed him as a fraud decked out in the flowery dress of a harlot. We know too little to decide, but there was some originality in the satirical mixtures of prose and verse invented by his near-contemporary Menippus. These pieces made fun of philosophers and their double standards, and later they interested Roman satirists. The best may have come from that sympathetic figure, Timon. One-eyed, he was remembered for many virtues, his love of gardens, his skill at avoiding pupils, and his hatred of interruptions from dogs and servants. In satirical sketches he took off the philosophers and made fun of contemporary geographers. He called the inmates of the Museum 'cloistered book-worms' and deflated the literary scholars, saying that the best texts of Homer were the old ones, before the poems had been altered out of recognition. It would be good to know more of this man who began by earning his living as a dancer.

Less attractively, the decade after Alexander's death saw the extension of school declamation with its mock speeches on particular dilemmas and legal decisions: we first hear of them in the early years of the New Comedy which shared something of their spirit. We also know of a taste for rhythmical, inflated rhetoric which became known as the Asianic style. Critics in the Augustan age gave Romans the credit for ending this extravagance and returning prose to a sober classicism by their steadying, moral influence. This view is questionable. Oratory had not declined into bombast, for it remained central to the cities' endless embassies to the kings and, later, to Rome. We have lost this practical oratory, and already in the 140s the master of 'Asianism' was being criticized by Agatharchides, whose own prose style earned high praise later for its dignity and nobility, its clarity and artistry with words.

Hellenistic Poetry

Poetry, however, is the form in which surviving Hellenistic literature excels. Of the classic styles of poetry, lyric was the obvious candidate in the wake of Aristotle and Alexander. The days when an aristocrat could advise or abuse his fellow citizens on politics were gone, but men still died and fell in love, wined and dined and pursued their ever-elusive boys. The traditional drinking party, or *symposion*, flourished among citizens and courtiers and remained a natural setting for polished poetry. Without any royal encouragement, the first Hellenistic poets saw their chance and returned to the themes, metre, and manner of older lyric masters. Like the early poets, they also attended to lower, popular songs. They twisted these themes to suit new settings and added the learning, wit, and urbanity which befitted true 'old boys' of a civic education.

We know so little of poetry in the fourth century that we may miss the roots of lyric's rediscovery. For us its impact is plainest in the epigram, which enjoyed a golden age between about 300 and 240 BC. Its masters filled it with their personality and literary tastes, capping one another's poems and contriving *doubles entendres* so neat that they are still being unravelled with pleasure. In Alexandria, especially, the epigrams convey the impression of a coterie of intimate and free-living friends, revelling in the polish of their new device. They give us more poems with point and dialogue, and they cast them in enigmatic settings. They convince us of their self-awareness and their life among wine and women, *symposia* and fickle boys.

The earliest master was Asclepiades from Samos, a respected poet who survives for us largely in his love poems. There is point and a genial self-awareness in his poems on favoured courtesans and on themes made familiar in the setting of the *symposion*. The relations of love and wine are his main subjects, with an awareness that if one love fails there is always another for another day. Posidippus covers similar ground and has also left us some pleasant epigrams on major buildings in the city. Scholars found it hard to separate Asclepiades' poems from those of a fellow Samian, Hedylus, and perhaps they were close companions. Hedylus' epigrams survive as poems against gluttons and gross banquets; they remind us that a good *symposion* was an expression of taste and civility. This trio were followed by the ornate and appealing Dioscorides, who takes us out of this small urban world in his epitaphs for a Persian and for settlers in the Egyptian country-side. A series of poems on past and present dramatists raise tantalizing problems of literary history, while his florid phrasing sits well round the pudgy, hospitable figure of Doris, his bed-fellow.

The master of the epigram was Callimachus, the royal tutor. He knew the others' work and attacked them for their taste in longer poems. In return, they took one of his best lines and reset it in an obscene context. If Callimachus' epigrams were all we had of his work, how differently we would picture him. In them his language is clear and fluent, while his grasp of the verse form remains the envy of all composers of Greek elegiacs. In his epigrams we meet Callimachus, the unhappy lover of boys, prey to passions which he cannot control and others will not oblige. He is Callimachus who 'knew how to have fun while the wine passed round', Callimachus who can chide the judgement of the gods. Nothing defies his art. He can construct good puns on a salt-cellar or defend his own refined literary tastes. The self-awareness is sharper, the emotions deeper than the themes to which our poems of Asclepiades are now limited. The royal tutor and cataloguer could also be playful. He addressed a perfect set of verses to his friend Philippus the doctor, to assure him that while poetry was one cure for the love of boys, hunger could prove as effective: the poet and his friend can defy love, as they possess both remedies. The reference to poetry possibly alluded to a poem by the great Theocritus. The epigram's language had a medical tone which suited a doctor.

More profoundly, Callimachus has left us a group of the best epitaphs in Greek. These themes were traditional for the epigram, and flowered again for several lost friends, among them poor, talented Heraclitus who 'tired the sun with talking' and left us one subtle funerary poem as his memento. These are great poems: simple, well angled, and profoundly moving. Epigrams, however, were incidental to Callimachus' patronage. No king gave long-term support to the other masters as poets only. Their debt was to the wonders of the city and the court society on which they touched. Two of the major poets came and went from Alexandria, while other good epigrams were written away from kings altogether. They lacked, however, the tone of the big city.

From Tarentum in the Greek west came Leonidas, whose major gifts lay with the scenes and objects of rural life and verses on his own simple, impoverished existence. In a similar style, we hear from two talented women, Nossis of Locri and her poems on female domestic life, and Anyte from little Tegea, whose charming poetry conveys a strong sense of a pastoral setting. To Anyte we owe the first known epitaphs for favourite animals, a genre which quickly extended to poems on the dogs of Ptolemaic 'top people' and on animals killed more nobly in hunts in Egypt or Afghanistan. The tone of these 'western' epigrams is lost by translations which turn them into rhyme. Generally, they die away, ending 'not with the thud of the hammer on the anvil, but the dying notes of a guitar'. This mood of a serene and wistful still-life has to struggle with elaborate language and the lack of perfect metrical polish, but at times it wins the battle.

By the 240s, the first age of invention and rivalry was fading. The style was imitated sweetly, and its centre shifted from Alexandria to the Syrian cities. The Syrian Meleager included the work of some fifty epigrammatists in his great anthology, the *Garland* (*c.*100 BC). In its first flush the epigram takes us to the frontiers of the new poetry. Its poets drew the new contemporary interests into their polished elegiacs: the mime and the pastoral, the enlarged iambic, and the taste for wit and pathos. Faced by a classic tradition, the early Hellenistic masters did not rebel against form and rules. There were no Vorticists and Imagists. Instead, they perfected form and multiplied metrical rules and archaism. Greek artists were particularly effective when particularly constrained by their own limits.

Dioscorides' epigrams honour the new dramatists, but nothing survives by which to judge them. At a lower level, however, there was a sudden new interest in the mime. This coarse, popular sketch had flourished in Doric prose, and its Sicilian master, Sophron, had once impressed Plato. Characteristically, it was given a literary twist and polish by the Hellenistic poets, Herodas and Theocritus. Herodas' talent has been underestimated. His poetry only reappeared on a papyrus in 1891, and it was wrongly identified with the contemporary style of 'realism'. Critics mistook his form and language. He revived the limping iambic metre and the old Ionic dialect of sixth-century-BC poetry, and attached this learning to the lowly mime. His surviving sketches are lively and give a wicked glimpse of social history. The best concern women, though seldom in a favourable light. One woman attempts to persuade another whose husband is away in Egypt that she must follow her instincts and have an affair. A cross mother takes her dissolute son to his schoolmaster for a thrashing: best of all, a woman who has been making love to her slave decides to have him flogged for his infidelities, then moderates her rage at the plea of a fellow servant. There is no reason why a good actor could not have performed these sketches on the stage. Herodas had his critics, and there is a strong case for connecting one of his sketches with the island of Cos, bringing him within the Ptolemies' inner political orbit, and attaching him to high literary culture. Certainly he left one of the most mischievous Hellenistic jokes: when one of his women sings the praises of a dildo which she has found in her friend's house, she is told that it once belonged to 'Nossis and Erinna'. These two names refer to famous poetesses. Herodas is surely having fun with two staid ladies of the literary world.

Our other mime-poems, written by Theocritus, are equally learned in tone and language. He cast them in hexameters, a grand metre for a low subject, producing a calculated incongruity. The best tells of the visit of two Syracusan ladies to a royal festival in Alexandria. The dialect, the irony, and the sense of simple visitors' wonder as they struggle through the crowds, are a brilliant sketch of the big city. A drama of magic and teenage first love is nearly as good, while a dialogue between two poor fishermen should be better known, whether or not Theocritus wrote it. He is the one consistently fine poet of this period. He was born in Sicily, probably in Syracuse. In the 270s he flattered Ptolemy II and then, or later, King Hiero in his own war-torn Sicily. Once he alludes to the Alexandrian·masters, and two of his best poems are set in Alexandria's orbit, one in the city, one on the island of Cos. There is a slight bias towards the flora of the east Aegean, not Sicily, in the many plants he mentions. Otherwise, he is a mystery to us, although a good short epic-sketch in a hymn to Pollux shows that he understood boxing. Here he excelled the contemporary librarian in Alexandria.

Theocritus' good poems are varied, but his fame rests on his invention of pastoral poetry. From his example began the tradition which has given us Virgil's *Eclogues*, Spenser's shepherds, Handel's *Acis and Galatea*, and Shakespeare's *Winter's Tale*. He is the one Hellenistic poet to have been translated internationally: he even left· a direct influence on nineteenth-century Russian poetry. The ancients themselves were puzzled where pastoral had come from. They guessed, probably wrongly, that it arose from choir-songs at various festivals of Artemis. A better guess may be the shepherd-songs of herdsmen with time enough to while away. In many cultures shepherds are associated with song.

Readers have long been bothered by widely differing aspects of his pastoral form: that point, said Sir Philip Sidney, 'where the hedge of poetry is lowest'. Some have regretted his realism, others his artifice. How could shepherds talk like that? Equally, how could Theocritus make his shepherds quite so coarse? Eighteenth-century pastoral preferred Virgil. 'I do not look on Theocritus as a romantic writer', Lady Mary Wortley Montagu told Alexander Pope, himself a pastoral poet in his youth; 'he has only given a plain image of the way of life among the peasants of his country . . . I do not doubt, had he been a Briton, that his *Idylliums* had been filled with descriptions of threshing and churning . . .'

In fact, the charm of Theocritus is that he keeps a foot in both camps. His shepherds still abuse each other with coarse jokes and hiss at their flocks. The feel of the Greek seasons and insects is still there, along with an eye for plants so precise that one critic has argued he studied botany with the doctors on Cos. At the same time he teases us with his urbanity and his uses of the set themes of early lyric poetry. Theocritus' shepherds meet, then challenge each other to sing.

PAINTING OF POLYPHEMUS AND GALATEA from the villa of Agrippa Postumus at Boscotrecase, near Pompeii (*c.*10 BC). The whimsical tale of the brutish Cyclops who fell in love with a
sea-nymph inspired two of Theocritus' *Idylls* and appealed to the educated taste of the Roman
nobility of the early Empire.

Their songs enchant us with their refrains and repetitions, a style which may derive from real songs in the hills. But they also weave together the themes of excluded lovers and revellers, poems for departing and returning travellers, which we find so often in past elegy and lyric. There is wit in the ugliness of the characters who love, the 'urban' laments of a Cyclops by the seaside, and the playfulness of the girl whom he woos among barking dogs and armfuls of apples. In one of its forms, the elegy, pastoral poetry has pleased almost every taste. In Theocritus' hands it gained form and pathos. All nature joined in the lament for a dying shepherd-poet, echoed by a polished use of the refrain. The pastoral elegy for the shepherd Daphnis developed into elegies for a dead poetic friend or master. In the touching lament for Bion it gave us the finest Greek poem to survive from the years around 100 BC. Writing in Italy, its unknown author contrasted the yearly renewal of nature and the death of man for ever. Directly from these elegies we derive three great poems, Milton's *Lycidas* (for his undergraduate friend Edward King), Arnold's *Thyrsis* (for the poet Clough), and the *Adonais*, or lament for Keats, which was the triumph of Shelley. His friend, Leigh Hunt, had introduced him to Hellenistic pastoral in autumn, 1816: 'like the odour of the tuberose,' he later wrote, 'it overcomes and sickens the spirit with excess of sweetness.'

The birth of pastoral has been misunderstood against the rise of the Hellenistic city. There is a pleasant story that Ptolemy II, when suffering from gout, once looked out of his palace window and envied the lives of simple Egyptians, seen picnicking on the banks of the Nile. That feeling was not the origin of pastoral. It took no interest in the foreign inhabitants of the new cities' territories. Theocritus' pastoral poems are not demonstrably linked to Alexandria, and in all but this huge city men walked easily into the fields near by, like the characters on Cos in his seventh *Idyll*. Town and country ran into each other everywhere, and nobody suffered from urban suffocation. The division, rather, was cultural. Pastoral transposed extreme urban wit and refinement on to those who owed least to urban values. Pastoral has always flourished in periods of an exquisite, urban culture, Spenser's England or Watteau's France. In Greece it arose from the same values of polish and technique and the reflective study of a classic tradition. These tastes had been bred by civic culture of the later fourth century BC, not by early Hellenistic 'urbanism' or by royalty.

Like the literary mimes and the epigrams, the pastoral combined learned language and metre with urbanity. Urbanity won, helped by the example of earlier lyric. In Alexandria the same values were pursued in bolder forms by the two top scholars in residence, the royal tutor and the royal librarian.

The librarian, Apollonius, was the younger, and his one known poem was audacious. He attempted an epic on the much studied adventures of the Argonauts, in an age when the social context and oral culture of the great epics had long since vanished. The ancients alleged that Apollonius wrote the poem as a young man, retired to Rhodes after a poor first reception, and then returned with a revised version. This 'second edition' seems correct, but the range of reading behind it suggests that the lure of the royal library came into the story, whether before or after Apollonius' appointment. The ancient commentators were stretched to the limit by his learning. Behind his language we can suspect the arguments of contemporary Alexandrian scholars on the precise meaning of particular words. Behind his content, prose-works on local antiquities kept company with subtle Homeric word-play and allusions to more recent poets. Among the full range of his references, the obvious allusions and debt to Callimachus have been greatly exaggerated. There is no reason, either, why the librarian and the tutor could not have read similar books on this familiar subject independently.

The poem's weaknesses are obvious. It has no balance, and it ends with a bump. One moment we are meeting Circe in the west, beset by her dreams of foreboding. 200 lines later we are sweltering on the sands of Libya while Medea's maids sing their swan-song, fearing death. From our point of view some of his learned passages have rather the air of versified footnotes, and the treasures of the royal library were a constant temptation to the poet. The story itself is intrinsically episodic—a long journey to Colchis (Books 1–2), events at Colchis (Book 3), a long return home (Book 4). Apollonius has not overcome this unsatisfactory structure, and in some ways his four books are less an epic than an intermittent display of gifts common in the best Hellenistic poets. In spirit, if not in form, he is often Theocritean.

At his best Apollonius can be excellent. His most famous scene is the epic's third book, which develops the love of the young Medea for Jason. Aphrodite inspires this passion by the arts of her mischievous child, Cupid, but we see it through Medea's own thoughts and emotions: how could she prefer a stranger to her parents? why should her parents come first? She longs to see him; when she does, she blushes and can hardly speak. They face each other like oaks or pines, silent till the breeze stirs them. This book is the Greeks' most brilliant portrayal of a girl falling passionately in love. Throughout the poem Apollonius placed Homeric similes, seventy-six in all, which developed odd perceptions or scenes from daily life. For Medea, his comparisons hit the mark. Her heart melts like 'the dew round roses warmed by the morning light'; her mind wavers like sunlight reflected on the wall of a house from a freshly-poured pail of water. Virgil, a careful reader of Apollonius, was quick to see the charm of this episode and take it as his starting-point for his deeper and more mature meeting of Aeneas and Dido.

The episode of Jason and Medea had already been foreshadowed by the excellent encounter of Jason with Queen Hypsipyle in Book 1, a scene worth reading for the same qualities. It was not lost on Virgil, either, as he brought his Trojans to the Queen of Carthage. Yet Apollonius retains a certain detachment from the adventures he relates. He is witty and ironic. He has the light touch and pictorial gift of a Sebastiano Ricci, and when he tells how the sea-nymphs tossed the good ship Argo to and fro for a whole day, like girls playing ball on the beach with

EUROPA AND THE BULL, Pompeian painting from the House of Jason, or of the Fatal Loves (first quarter of first century AD). This genteel version of one of Zeus' best known zoomorphic seductions nicely catches the romantic spirit of Hellenistic poetry, as represented by Moschus' *Europa*.

their skirts tucked up, we can see him smiling at his own rococo imagination. Over the sands of Libya the good ship Argo is led by the prow like a trusting horse in a head-collar. Apollonius loves the witty reversal: at heart he is an early Hellenistic master, as we begin to see the type.

His epic was not, then, such an anachronism. It veered between the two extremes of Hellenistic culture, and it shone wherever it escaped the one and approached the other. It almost avoided the dry learning of lesser authors in the 'didactic' style, poems like Aratus' on the stars, whose 'Hesiodic' quality and 'sleepless' effort were admired by Callimachus. These poets wrote a mass of versified learning on topics from cooking to farming. What survives is hard to admire: Nicander wrote a poem on *Antidotes to the Bites of Wild Creatures* which is as deadly as the hazard he professed to cure.

Conversely, Apollonius came very close to the charming epic sketches which focused on a lesser figure, often a female, and an unfamiliar incident in myth. These shorter poems were composed independently, as 'tiny epics' or *epyllia*. Court scholars such as Callimachus and Eratosthenes wrote them too, and we have a splendid example from Moschus (a pupil of Aristarchus) on the topic of Europa, crossing the sea on the back of Zeus as a bull. They are witty and often romantic, and their high colours conjure up a fine Tiepolo fresco. It took Virgil to tease and transform the grimmer, didactic poets and pass on their genre, through his *Georgics*, to its golden age among the Augustan poets of Georgian England. But the epyllion was transferred, not transformed. It passed first to Rome, then to Elizabethan poets, its aptest heirs at a moment when learning competed once more with playfulness. Though directly inspired by Ovid, Marlowe's sensuous *Hero and Leander* is in many ways a Hellenistic pearl.

Could a royal tutor escape the faults of a royal librarian? Like Apollonius, whom he may have taught, Callimachus could write fine, uncluttered verse. His epigrams were exquisite. He had thought seriously about poetry's options and asserted his choice against what he calls the 'envy' of his critics in epigrams, iambics, and a famous 'second Prologue' to a late, collected edition of his more experimental work. He exalted 'technique' and 'skill', the 'slender' Muse, the 'untravelled road', the waters from pure, unvisited fountains. Hesiod was a possible model, Homer an irrecoverable genius. He refused to write a long, continuous poem of epic proportions on a single subject of myth or ancient history. 'A big book', he wrote, 'is a big pest.' If he differed from Apollonius, it must have been on this point. In his forceful iambic pieces he defended his own versatility and his readiness to range between different genres, metres and dialects. With the help of ancient commentators we can put names to his dislikes. His bugbear was 'the fat woman', a long poem by Antimachus, the *Lyde*, which the great epigrammatists had admired, incurring his attack. He also opposed a critic who was probably Aristotelian. The issue, perhaps, was Callimachus' dislike of 'continuous' plot.

To Roman poets no name was weightier to drop than that of Callimachus, and Virgil made famous use of his Prologues in a poem on poetry's predicaments. Talk of 'new' poetry strikes home to readers in the wake of Pound and Eliot. Callimachus' learning and range were powerful, but what of their results?

Unfortunately, his most original works are known only in fragments; new ones are still being discovered, and a major new piece was published from papyrus in 1977. His iambics widen the range of the metre's subjects, but the surviving pieces are very difficult, written in a style which is oblique and highly erudite. Posterity respected his four books *On Origins* (*Aetia*) but they are an odd collection. In the first two books Callimachus asks puzzling questions, usually of the Muses, once of a stranger whom he had met and befriended at a coarse symposium which is described in a flash of oblique liveliness. Here is the 'new' poetry, the 'untravelled way': questions on why the people of Paros do not use flutes at sacrifices, or why the Icians are connected with Thessaly. The origin of a noble family on Ceos is the peg on which he hangs a witty and allusive account of a mythical wooing (Acontius and Cydippe, frs. 67–75): he explores local cults whose origins were linked with the Argonauts, handling prose sources which he and Apollonius could both read, but using them more tersely and subtly. The virtues of this poetry defy translation. Callimachus found much of his material in scholarly prose works, and strung it together with an abruptness which tested his readers. His vocabulary was very recherché indeed. In the poem's last two books Callimachus seems to have worked in witty praises of Queen Berenice, her chariot-victory in Greece, and her lock of hair, set among the stars as the *Coma Berenices* (the 'Lock of Berenice').

Like other Hellenistic poets, Callimachus ranged between the different genres, and some of his most appealing work belongs in forms which he shared with contemporaries. Like them, he tried a 'little epic', the *Hecale*. Its occasion was a heroic exploit of the young Theseus, but typically the poem dwelt on accompanying scenes, on Theseus' reception, the night before his ordeal, by the poor, but hospitable, old woman Hecale; on her simple entertainment, her reminiscences, even a dialogue between a pair of birds.

Of his six Hymns, which survive complete, the best three are set in the cities of Cos, Argos, and Cyrene. They combine the spectators' vivid sense of the gods' presence at their festivals with a playful excursus on relevant myths of their encounters with men. Are they proof of Callimachus's own sincere piety? Rather, the poet amuses himself and us by playing with the simple faith of the uneducated, in a style which presupposes high sophistication.

Born in Cyrene, Callimachus had taught as a school-master before coming to the Alexandrian court. Like many lyric poets and most Greek historians, he was an exile. In his surviving love poems he writes wittily of his loves for boys, but never of women. However, this taste was common among his contemporaries. His exile and his homosexuality have been curiously emphasized as forming his horizon, but his most obvious debt is to his days as a schoolteacher. He recalls the strengths and vices of the literary education of his age: the Homeric quizzes, the antiquarian catechisms, the sexual crushes, and the concern for rare words. Like so many schoolmasters, Callimachus was most successful when most conventional, in his funerary epigrams and classic hymns.

On one point Callimachus was proved right. His *Origins* and *Iambics* claimed to be poems for the refined few. The new papyrus of his *Origins'* third book was handsomely copied within a generation of the poet's death. Already it needed a literal prose paraphrase for many of its lines. In the Roman age Callimachus' 'new path' became an acknowledged model for the great Augustan poets. It is not altogether clear how much they read of it. Callimachus' poems survived to the end of antiquity, the delight of scholars and *érudits manqués*: we know of a tax clerk in Egypt in the 170s AD who amused himself by translating the name of an Egyptian on his register by Callimachus' rare word for 'mousetrap'.

Like Apollonius, Callimachus had enjoyed the direct patronage of kings and access to the great royal libraries. Like Apollonius, he had a playful, Hellenistic talent, immortalized in his epigrams and hymns, but he dressed it in learning and rare language. The library, one feels, was at times his worst enemy. Between 300 and 240 BC the most fruitful impulse for poetry belonged elsewhere, in the use of archaic lyric. So far as patronage helped, it was as a source of leisure and as the setting for secure life in a great capital city. To that degree, there is a connection between literature and the political fate of the monarchies. Stable kingdoms meant stable cities, in which poets could mature and practise, and court societies in which they could experiment and come and go. The earliest Hellenistic poets grew up in the city-states before Alexander and moved into the range of the kings while their courts were still young. By the 270s the new monarchies seemed settled: these are the years in which poets write of the 'calm weather' of the Alexandrian court. That serenity was never repeated. Failures abroad, internal squabbles, the rise of the new barbarians, Rome and Parthia, and the savagery of the Egyptian crowds whom Alexandria had simply excluded and exploited: the Hellenistic poets did not have the talent to make art from anarchy, and by the 240s the best was done. After the 240s the new excitement of Alexandria wore off, and poets were left to imitate the previous age's inventions. Scholarship emerged as a specialized art, and poetry, by the second century BC, relapsed into provincial sweetness. In 145 Ptolemy VIII drove the scholars and intellectuals out of Alexandria and scattered them like sparks across the Aegean. Writers of pretty Greek verses reached Roman patrons in the first century BC, but Catullus, Horace, and Virgil were right to look back and pick their models with such taste.

The great poetry had been wholly divorced from politics. It was witty and ironic, urbane and perceptive, yet aware of the sadness in life. It delighted in scenes of emotion which it found in odd episodes of myth, in the child and the old, the housewife as well as the heroine. Like much poetry of seventeenth-century Europe it drew an image or two, no more, from the sudden horizons of new science and travel. It preferred rococo wit and colour and the world of the older Greek city. We might long to tug Callimachus east to look for Zoroastrians or hear the minstrels of east-Iranian nobles. But he and his contemporaries had the polish of excellent 'old boys', brought up in a school and a civic culture which no eastern peoples matched. A host of unacknowledged schoolmasters had done far more for this last age of poetry than any well-intentioned king.

Between us and their playful urbanity lies the barrier of Romantic taste. The contrast brings out the best in these first, Hellenistic minds. In his fine *Sonnets on the River Dudden*, Wordsworth used an art which Callimachus would have applauded. The poems were short and their topic was a river and its origins. They were abrupt in their changes of tone and subject and were packed with learning and local legend. As the river ran into the sea, Wordsworth turned to Hellenistic pastoral:

> We, the brave, the mighty and the wise,
> We men, who in our morn of youth defied
> The elements, must vanish: be it so!

The lines were based on the Lament for Bion. But, he concluded,

> "enough . . . if, as toward the silent tomb we go,
> Through love, through hope, and faith's transcendent dower
> We feel that we are greater than we know".

In the wake of Aristotle, the best Hellenistic minds had had no room for such feelings. From Egypt to India, Greek culture made sense of human life; the marvels of the world made excellent reading, but its elements ran by natural rules; and third-century men of taste, through their schooling and philosophies, were neither less nor greater than wit and reason knew.

Further Reading

There are full, international bibliographies of Hellenistic culture in C. Préaux, *Le Monde hellénistique* (Paris, 1978), and C. Schneider, *Kulturgeschichte des Hellenismus* (Munich 1967), while P. M. Fraser, *Ptolemaic Alexandria* (Oxford, 1972) is a fundamental collection and discussion of evidence. H. I. Marrou, *History of Education in Antiquity* (London, 1956) is a classic study, although the English translation is erratic. A. Momigliano, *Alien Wisdom* (Cambridge, 1975), R. Pfeiffer, *A History of Classical Scholarship*, vol. I (Oxford, 1968), W. S. Ferguson, *Hellenistic Athens* (London, 1911), and M. Hengel, *Hellenism and Judaism* (London, 1978) are also indispensable. The range of M. I. Rostovtzeff's *Social and Economic History of the Hellenistic World* (Oxford, 1941) has not been surpassed. On the geographers, M. Cary and E. H. Warmington, *The Ancient Explorers* (London, 1963) give a lively introduction. P. M. Fraser, 'Eratosthenes of Cyrene', *Proceedings of the British Academy*, lvi (1970), 175–209, is a vivid portrait. Robin Lane Fox, *Alexander the Great* (London, 1973) and *The Search for Alexander* (Boston, Mass., 1980) describe and illustrate the first conquests and their impact. Hellenistic literature is surveyed by A. Lesky, *A History of Greek Literature* (London, 1966), pp. 642–806. P. M. Fraser's *Ptolemaic Alexandria* (Oxford, 1972) discusses the Alexandrians' literary achievement, and more particularly, a view of Callimachus. A selection of epigrams are translated in *The Greek Anthology*, ed. Peter Jay (London, 1973); Herodas was translated by his editor, W. Headlam (Cambridge, 1922); Apollonius is translated in the Penguin Classics series, by E. V. Rieu (Harmondsworth, 1958).

15

Hellenistic Philosophy and Science

❧❧

JONATHAN BARNES

GREEK philosophy has a continuous history. The death of Alexander the Great heralded no intellectual revolution, and the Hellenistic thinkers placed themselves in the tradition of Thales and of Socrates. But after Aristotle the emphasis changed: Hellenistic philosophy—in its scope, its aim, its self-understanding—differed somewhat from the discipline practised in earlier centuries.

Philosophy became an Art of Living. The pursuit of scientific knowledge ceased to be the defining mark of the philosopher. Rather, a man's philosophy was something that he lived by, and a philosopher's task was to discover the 'best life', to teach it, and to live it. Ethics, or practical philosophy, emerged as the regent part of the subject.

Practical utility determined the philosophical curriculum. As ethics rose, so metaphysics descended. More significantly, science divorced itself from philosophy and became the pursuit of professionals. The divorce was confirmed by geographical dislocation: Athens remained the chief centre of philosophy, but science migrated to Egyptian Alexandria and the financial subventions of the Ptolemies. Philosophy retained indeed a part called 'physics', and the general understanding of natural science never lost its importance; but Hellenistic philosophers did not care to describe the organs of the octopus or to chronicle the movements of the stars.

On the other hand, the Hellenistic period was marked by a passionate concern with the theory of knowledge. The art of living must rest upon a firm knowledge of the nature of things, and the foundations of knowledge must be philosophically secure. The challenge of scepticism was accepted by the Hellenistic thinkers: some of the subtlest work of the age was provoked by the debate over doubt and dogmatism.

For the Hellenistic philosophers wrote against one another. Philosophy became sectarian, and the sects squabbled. There was, to be sure, dispute within the

IMPRINT OF A GREEK PAPYRUS found in the palace at Aï Khanoum, Afghanistan. The papyrus has perished, leaving only the traces of ink preserved in reverse on the fine earth formed by decomposed mud bricks where they had fallen on the floor. Certain words which can be deciphered suggest that the text belonged to a dialogue of philosophical, and more specifically Aristotelian, character.

schools: thought did not ossify into doctrinal inflexibility. But variation was held within limits. A man would be characterized as a Stoic or an Epicurean or an Academic: he would be thought of primarily as a member of a school, devoted to its theories and to the art of living which those theories supported; only secondarily might he be regarded as an ingenuous seeker after truth.

The sects did not form exclusive or esoteric clubs. Men might study under several masters and migrate from school to school. Philosophy was both esteemed and popular. The Hellenistic monarchs solicited the presence of philosophers at their court. The city of Athens voted public honours to the Stoic Zeno. Nor was the subject limited to a rich or intellectual clique: Theophrastus attracted as many as 2,000 students to his lectures, and when Stilpo visited Athens men left their workshops and ran to see him. Far from Athens, in a remote garrison town in Afghanistan, archaeologists have recovered evidence of an interest in Aristotelian philosophy.

To those generalizations let there be added a puff. Scholars sometimes dismiss the Hellenistic philosophers as *epigoni*, men of a silver age whose lustre could not match the golden gleam of Plato and Aristotle. That is mistaken. The gleam did not fade; in some parts it glowed more brightly than before. The period produced work of the utmost brilliance.

After Plato's death in 347 the Academic coterie continued to philosophize, under the successive guidance of Speusippus (d. 339), Xenocrates (d. 314) and Polemo (d. *c.* 276). Aristotle's school likewise survived: Theophrastus (d. *c.* 287) carried on his work, and Theophrastus was followed by Strato of Lampsacus. But on Strato's death (c. 269) the school ran out of power, and for most of the Hellenistic period Aristotelian philosophy was a thing of the past—a thing of influence, but devoid of life.

Platonism too died. The Academy lasted as a school until the first century BC, but the Hellenistic Academicians, although they claimed to be the true heirs of Socrates and Plato, maintained none of the doctrines which we take to be constitutive of Platonism. When Arcesilaus of Pitane (d. *c.* 242) became head of the school in about 270 he converted the Academy to scepticism. The New Academy was a new school. Under its two greatest leaders, Arcesilaus and Carneades of Cyrene (*c.* 219–129), it developed a wholly negative and critical mode of philosophizing.

Constructive philosophy in the Hellenistic age was located neither in the Lyceum nor in the Academy but at two new sites, the Garden of the Epicureans and the Porch of the Stoics.

Epicurus was born of Athenian parents on the island of Samos in 341. He eventually settled in Athens in 307, where he taught until his death in 271. The philosophy to which he gave his name can be summarized thus: in ethics, hedonism—pleasure is the sole good; in physics, atomism—the universe consists of minute corpuscles moving in empty space; in logic, empiricism—all our knowledge is grounded ultimately on experience and perception.

Epicureans were notoriously conservative: they did not slavishly repeat their master's words, yet they refrained from doctrinal innovation. In the first century BC the Roman poet Lucretius (below, pp. 479 ff.) composed his *De rerum natura*, an exposition of Epicurean thought. In his eyes Epicurus was 'the father, the discoverer of things', and his poem follows Epicurus with fidelity. Lucretius was not resuscitating a superannuated philosophy: the system he admired and delineated was still vividly alive.

The Porch, like the Garden, was at Athens, but none of its major figures was Athenian. Zeno (*c.* 333–262), the founder of the school, hailed from Cyprus. He came to Athens in *c.* 310, where he established a school in the *Stoa Poikilē*—the 'Porch'. His mantle was assumed, and his views were developed, by Cleanthes of Assus (d. *c.* 232); and Cleanthes' successor Chrysippus (d. *c.* 206), who also came to Athens from Asia Minor, transmuted Stoicism into a comprehensive and systematic philosophy—it was said that 'if Chrysippus had not existed, the Stoa would not have existed either'.

PORTRAIT OF EPICURUS (341–270 BC), based on a commemorative statue of the mid third century BC. The founder of the Epicurean school of philosophy taught that pleasure (that is, freedom from pain and peace of mind) was the goal of life. His 'atomic' theory of the universe inspired Lucretius' great poem *De rerum natura* in the first century BC.

The Stoics were not traditionalists. The school's long history divides into three phases, Old, Middle, and Late. The Middle Stoa, whose chief ornaments were Panaetius of Rhodes (*c.* 185–109) and Posidonius of Apamea (135–51), substantially altered the emphasis of the school. So, too, did the Late Stoa, which is represented for us by Seneca (below, pp. 663 f.), Epictetus (pp. 708 ff.), and Marcus Aurelius (pp. 711 ff.) from the first two centuries AD. Nor was the Old Stoa marked by doctrinal uniformity. There were renegades, of whom the most important was Ariston of Chios. He limited his concerns to ethics, rejecting physics and maintaining that 'dialectical reasonings are like spiders' webs—they seem to display some artistry but are in fact useless'. Chrysippus himself 'differed on many points from Zeno and also from Cleanthes, to whom he would often say that he only needed to be taught the theories and would discover the proofs for himself'.

None the less, the central tenets of the Old Stoics remained firm. In ethics they rejected hedonism and counselled a life of 'virtue'; in physics they accepted a form of materialism but denied atomism; in logic they were empiricists, but they assigned a major role to reason in the development of knowledge.

Philosophy was pursued outside the main schools. Pyrrho of Elis (*c.* 365–*c.* 270) adopted an extreme scepticism, holding that our senses are unreliable, that we should commit ourselves to no judgements—and that tranquillity of mind will

THE STOIC PHILOSOPHER CHRYSIPPUS (d. between 208 and 204 BC): a seated statue reconstructed with the aid of a body in the Louvre and a cast of a head in the British Museum. It may be based on a statue in Athens mentioned by Cicero which showed the philosopher sitting with hand extended (a typical gesture of philosophical disputation).

supervene upon such a practice. Pyrrho was perhaps influenced by the Indian ascetics whom he encountered as a member of Alexander's expedition to the East. In his turn he influenced the Academic scepticism of Arcesilaus. The Cyrenaic sect, founded by Aristippus (*c.* 430–*c.* 350), was also of a sceptical inclination: 'they abstained from physics, because its subject-matter was evidently unknowable; but they studied logic because of its utility'. Their chief doctrine, however, was ethical: they maintained a radical hedonism, according to which bodily pleasure was the supreme good. The affinities between Aristippus and Epicurus were often remarked upon.

Aristippus was a pupil of Socrates. So too was Euclides of Megara (*c.* 435–*c.* 365). Euclides and his followers, of whom the most eminent was Stilpo (d. *c.* 300), were celebrated in their day. They had views on ethics and on various topics in logic, but little is now known about them. Allied to the Megarians was a group called the Dialecticians, whose interest centred upon logical paradoxes. Diodorus Cronus (d. *c.* 284), the leading Dialectician, had an importance we can only dimly discern.

Antisthenes (*c.* 450–*c.* 350) was another pupil of Socrates. He and his follower Diogenes of Sinope (d. 323) were the founders of Cynicism. Cynicism was a way of life rather than a theoretical philosophy. Cynics proclaimed the supreme importance of individual freedom and self-sufficiency; they preached the 'natural' life and rejected with contempt the customs and conventions of society, thinking

DIOGENES IN HIS STORAGE JAR, as depicted on an engraved gem-stone of the Roman age. The story that the Cynic philosopher (414–323 BC) lived in a jar reflects the ascetic manner of life which he and his followers favoured. He is shown with the stick and dog of a beggar, debating with a seated disciple who holds a scroll.

nothing of wealth, position, or reputation. They also affected to despise pleasure ('I would rather go mad than enjoy myself', said Antisthenes). Their ostentatious asceticism was a common spectacle, admired or ridiculed according to the spectator's taste.

Arcesilaus and Carneades wrote nothing, but their thoughts were recorded by their disciples. Epicurus wrote at huge length, and so did the Old Stoics. Of that massive volume little has survived. Epicurus has come off best: three introductory essays, in the form of letters, are preserved, substantial fragments have been recovered from the ruins of Herculaneum, and in addition we have Lucretius. For the Old Stoa and the New Academy we are obliged to rely almost entirely on second-hand sources—on quotations, paraphrases and allusions in later writers. Much of the testimony comes from hostile or tendentious witnesses. The difficulty of assessing such reports exacerbates the problem of piecing together a coherent system from scattered and fragmentary evidence.

Ethics

Philosophy was customarily divided into three parts: logic, physics, and ethics. Hellenistic ethics, like the ethics of Aristotle, turns on the notion of *eudaimonia*— of well-being, welfare, flourishing. The task of ethics is to analyse human welfare and to determine the conditions under which it may be attained. There was some measure of agreement among the schools at the most general level. According to Epicurus, we should 'refer all choice and avoidance to health of the body and tranquillity of the soul, since that is the goal of a happy life'. Tranquillity or *ataraxia* ('untroubledness') had been similarly exalted in the old Academy of Xenocrates, and it was to become the watchword of the Pyrrhonian sceptics. The Stoics, too, acknowledged the same ideal; for 'they expel from mankind all the passions by which the mind is disturbed—desire and delight, fear and grief'.

In order to achieve tranquillity and to calm what Epicurus called 'the storm of the soul', we need only take thought. It is an assumption implicit in Epicureanism that fears will dissipate once the beliefs on which they are grounded are shown by philosophy to be false. Chrysippus explicitly contended that the passions were themselves beliefs of a sort, and hence subject to rational control. Such optimistic rationalization is no less foreign to the philosophy of Aristotle than the ethical quietism which it subserves.

That quietism is sometimes represented as a disengagement from social and political life, and it is interpreted as a reaction to the tumultuous and troubled world of Hellenistic Greece. The interpretation is implausible: life in Hellenistic Greece was no more upsetting, no more at the mercy of fickle fortune or malign foes, than it had been in an earlier era. Nor does *ataraxia* imply a withdrawal into the self or an obsessive individualism. Epicurus abjured the political life ('You must free yourself from the prison of politics and the daily round'), but he placed happiness in friendship and society—and an Epicurean 'will cultivate a king when it is opportune'. The Stoics valued social life, and they urged an involvement in politics. According to Chrysippus, a wise man 'will willingly assume a kingship and make money from it—and if he cannot be king himself he will live with a king and accompany a king to war'. *Ataraxia* was not to be achieved by shunning the world.

Within that broad area of agreement, Epicurean and Stoic ethics are regularly presented as antithetical: if both sects sought contentment, they sought it in contrary directions. For Epicurus, the direction was determined by nature:

You need only possess perception and be made of flesh, and you will see that pleasure is good.

I summon you [he wrote to Anaxarchus] to continuous pleasures—and not to virtues which are empty and vain and which hold out troubling expectations of rewards.

We say that pleasure is the beginning and end of a happy life; for we recognize it as a primary and innate good, and from it we begin all choice and avoidance, and to it we return, judging every good thing by the standard of that feeling.

In his own lifetime Epicurus was vilified as a crude and unlettered sybarite. But although he held that 'the beginning and root of every good thing is the pleasure of the belly', his hedonism is not an excuse for sensual indulgence. First, Epicurean pleasures are rationally selected, and the Epicurean is aware that today's delights will be paid for by the misery of the morrow. That is why 'sometimes we pass over many pleasures when greater discomfort follows for us as a result of them'. In fact, calculation reveals that 'the pleasant life is produced not by a string of drinking-bouts and revelries, nor by the enjoyment of boys and women, nor by fish and the other items on an expensive menu, but by sober reasoning'. Secondly, Epicurus has an idiosyncratic account of the nature of pleasure. 'When we say that pleasure is the goal, we mean ... being neither pained in the body nor troubled in the soul.' Pleasure is construed negatively, as the absence of pain, and 'the limit to the magnitude of pleasures is the removal of everything that pains us'. Thus the pleasures of a sensualist are inferior to those of a sober reasoner: the sensualist's pleasures are followed by pain, and in any case the sensualist can never achieve more than that total freedom from pain which is equally within the grasp of the reasoner. 'True pleasure is a serious business', as the Stoic Seneca put it.

An Epicurean hedonist is virtuous as well as sober. For 'it is not possible to live pleasurably without living sensibly and nobly and justly'. 'A just man', for example, 'is least troubled but an unjust man is loaded with troubles', for 'up to the time of his death it is not known if he will go undetected'. Epicurus' invitation to Anaxarchus was disingenuous: an Epicurean will pursue virtue, and he 'revels in the pleasure of the body—on a diet of bread and water'.

Nature led Epicurus to pleasure, the Stoics to virtue. According to the Old Stoa, 'the goal is to live in agreement with nature—which is the same as to live in accordance with virtue, since it is virtue to which nature leads us'. But the road along which nature directs us is long and difficult to follow.

We are led first to ourselves. Chrysippus insists that 'the first thing congenial to any animal is its own constitution and its awareness of that'. But an initial egocentricity naturally develops into altruism: as a later writer puts it, man 'is a social animal and requires others. That is why we live in cities; for every man is part of a city. Again, we readily form friendships ...' Thus we come to do what is 'appropriate' for us (*kathēkon*). 'An appropriate act is one which, being consistent with the agent's mode of life, can be reasonably defended.' The reference to reason is not casual: indeed, it can be said that 'appropriate acts are those which reason selects—for example, honouring parents, brothers, country; consorting with friends'.

The performance of appropriate acts is a sign of progress, but it is not a mark of success. According to Chrysippus, 'a man who is progressing to the summit certainly performs all appropriate acts and omits none; but his life is not yet a flourishing one'. For he has not yet achieved virtue, and 'a flourishing life is found only in a life in accordance with virtue'. Virtues are mental states or dispositions—indeed, they are cognitive states. The 'perfect' virtues (i.e. the four 'primary' virtues of good sense, justice, courage, and temperance, together with the virtues subordinate to them) are forms of knowledge and 'consist of theorems'. An appropriate act, when it is performed virtuously, is perfect; and perfect acts are 'successes' (*katorthōmata*). The good life, according to the Stoics, is a sequence of successes, of appropriate acts virtuously performed, of acts in conformity to nature performed in full knowledge of their conformity.

Stoic ethics forms a rich and complex system. It is sometimes decried as being paradoxical and grim. That it was paradoxical the Stoics themselves allowed, and they revelled in remarking that 'all mistakes are equally bad' or 'only a wise man is rich'. Yet on inspection the paradoxes turn out to be verbal rather than real. As for grimness, the Stoics certainly deny that pleasure is a good thing; but they give a welcome to what they call joy: 'they say that joy is the contrary of pleasure, being rational elation'. In fact, we are told that a Stoic will like horses and hunting, that he will go to parties, that he will fall in love with beautiful young men; and 'what adornment', the Stoics asked, 'can a household enjoy to compare with the companionship of a man and his wife?' A Stoic is not debarred from the pleasures of life: he may enjoy them all—provided that he does so virtuously.

Nor is the Stoic maxim that 'virtue alone is good' a confession of moral severity. Its force is best shown by reference to the Stoic account of 'indifferents' or things neither good nor bad. 'Of indifferents they say that some are promoted, some demoted, some neither promoted nor demoted'. Things are said to be promoted 'not because they contribute and work towards welfare but because we should choose them rather than what is demoted'. Health is thus promoted, for plainly we should prefer it to illness; but health is not good -for 'what can be used both well and badly is neither good nor bad, and all foolish men use wealth and health and bodily strength badly'. Health is not good in itself; but health well used is good: health—and everything else—is advantageous only when it 'participates in virtue' or is wisely used. That is the sense in which virtue is the sole good.

There are differences, both theoretical and practical, between Epicurean and Stoic ethics. But the popular picture of a sybaritic Epicurean confronting a puritanical Stoic is a caricature: to an external observer there would in truth be little difference between members of the two sects.

Physics

Physics is subordinate to ethics. According to Chrysippus, 'the study of nature is to be undertaken for no other end than the discrimination of good things and bad'. Epicurus asserted that 'you must first realize that knowledge of celestial matters, like other branches of study, has no other goal but tranquillity and firm conviction'; and 'if we were not at all disturbed by our apprehensions concerning celestial phenomena and death ... and by our failure to understand the limits of pains and of desires, we should have no further need of natural science'.

The first theorem of Epicurean physics maintains that 'the nature of things consists of bodies and void.' Epicurus commends the theorem by urging that 'perception in itself universally testifies that there are bodies ... and if place, which we call void or space or intangible substance, did not exist, then bodies would have nowhere to be and nothing through which to move'. Bodies are either composite or simple. The simple bodies are atoms: indivisible, changeless, microscopic; infinite in number and roaming in infinite space; possessing size, shape, weight, mobility, but devoid of colour, taste, smell, and the like. The moving atoms sometimes collide. As the hooks of one atom chance to catch the eyes of another, macroscopic bodies are formed: the furnishings of the world— sheep, horses, chariots, and the souls of men—are congeries of atoms, their sensible forms and qualities determined by their corpuscular structures. Atomism is thoroughly mechanistic. Everything is explained by the laws of atomic motion. Lucretius instructs us to 'avoid the error of thinking that the bright orbs of the eyes were made in order that we might be able to see', or that any natural phenomena are amenable to teleological explanation in terms of goals or purposes.

Atomism has two profound implications. First, the heavenly bodies are not divine intelligences: according to Epicurus, 'since they are aggregates of fire, we should not suppose them to possess happiness and pursue their courses voluntarily'. There are indeed gods in the Epicurean universe, admirable beings who live a life of tranquillity far off in intergalactic space. But those gods are not to be feared. 'What is happy and indestructible neither is troubled itself nor causes trouble to others—hence it is moved neither by anger nor by gratitude.' Thus the heavenly rumblings at which the superstitious quake are purely material events, and the real gods have no interest at all in life on earth.

Secondly, 'those who say that the soul is incorporeal are foolish; for if it were it could neither act nor be acted upon—but in fact both those properties are plainly observed to belong to the soul'. The soul is a body within the body, 'composed of fine particles spread all through the structure, most like wind with an admixture of heat'. Thus 'when the whole structure is dissolved, the soul is dispersed and no longer retains its powers'. It follows that 'death is nothing to us; for what is dissolved has no perception, and what has no perception is nothing to us'. It is as absurd to fear the time after death as it would be to fear the time before birth. Lucretius makes the point vividly:

Just as in time past we felt no disquiet when the Carthaginians arose on all sides in conflict and all was shaken by the fearful tumult of war ... so when we shall no longer exist, when the body and soul from which we are compounded shall have separated, then nothing at all can happen to us, who then shall no longer exist; nothing will stir our senses, though the earth mingle with the sea and the sea with the heavens.

True physics dispels both the grosser fears of Hell and the more sophisticated inquietude aroused by the anticipation of future non-existence.

If we are fearless of the gods and of death, may we not still be troubled by pain and by the desolation of frustrated desires? Epicurean physics includes a psychological analysis of human desire. 'Of desires, some are natural, others empty; and of natural desires, some are necessary, others merely natural.' Non-natural desires—such as the desire to be honoured or to be commemorated—'depend upon an empty opinion' and depart once the opinion is seen to be false. Similarly, 'those natural desires which bring no pain if they are not satisfied [a desire for roast beef, say, or for claret] ... depend upon an empty opinion'. There remain natural and necessary desires, such as the desire for food or for drink. Those desires cannot be eliminated, for the opinions on which they rest are true; yet they are also easily satisfied. As for pain, Epicurus is brusque: 'All pain is to be despised; for pains which hurt sharply remain briefly and those which endure in the flesh are blunt.' Moreover, pain is counterbalanced by pleasure. Epicurus himself, dying of strangury and dysentery, wrote 'on this happy day' to his friend Idomeneus that all his agonies were 'balanced by the joy in my soul as I recollect the conversations we have had together'.

Physics produces tranquillity by proving our fears to be groundless. To achieve that end, Epicurus believes that he must establish the fundamental truths of atomism. But he does not think it necessary to provide detailed explanations of natural phenomena—'the investigation of risings and settings and solstices and eclipses makes no contribution to happiness'. Indeed, such knowledge is unattainable: in the case of the first principle of physics, 'there is only one explanation which harmonizes with the phenomena, but that is not so in celestial matters: they admit more than one explanation of their happening and more than one account of their nature which harmonizes with perception'. Epicurus' scepticism is amateur, and the truth is that he does not care to know. 'If we recognize that an event can happen for a variety of reasons, we shall be as tranquil as if we knew that it happened in precisely *this* way.' At bottom one thing matters: 'only let superstition be absent'.

The Stoics, like the Epicureans, were cavalier about particular scientific theories but intensely concerned with the foundations of physics. 'They hold that the first principles of things are two in number: what acts, and what is acted upon. What is acted upon is qualityless substance, which is matter; what acts is reason in matter, which is god.' Since 'Zeno thought that nothing could in any way be caused by anything incorporeal', the active principle is itself material, and the Stoic universe is as thoroughly corporeal as the Epicurean. But the Stoics admit no empty space into the world, and do not suppose that matter comes in atomic parcels. Rather, the world is a continuous mass of stuff, gapless and infinitely divisible; it is a blend of the two principles, 'the mixtures of which' according to Chrysippus, 'are through and through ... and do not occur by way of circum-location or juxtaposition'.

The active principle, sometimes characterized as fire or 'breath', fashions the world, first creating the four elements of fire, air, water, and earth, and thence forming the structures of the cosmos. The universe 'is governed by reason and providence', for the active principle 'is an immortal living thing, rational, perfect in felicity, admitting no evil, providing for the world and the things in the world'—and it is called Zeus and Hera and Athena and the like. The world is not a machine, unthinking and purposeless: it is imbued with intelligence, and any explanation of its functionings must be primarily teleological.

We are little parts of the cosmic animal, having a proper place in its natural economy. Like Epicurean souls, Stoic souls are corporeal. They are fragments of the active principle, and a later writer explains that the soul 'is not contained in the body as in a vessel—like liquid in a cask—but is wonderfully blended and mixed throughout the whole of it, so that not even the smallest part of the mixture fails to have a share of each constituent'. Chrysippus agrees with Epicurus that the soul does not survive the dissolution of the body, but he can offer us a sort of spasmodic immortality: 'after our deaths, at a certain period of time we shall again come to be in the state in which we now are'. For the cosmos enjoys a cyclical history. At fixed intervals, the world is consumed by fire: after the conflagration, a new world, just like its predecessor, is formed, itself doomed to fiery destruction. Each world contains us: we shall live again, infinitely often—and we have already enjoyed infinitely many lives, each identical in its biography.

But man's place in the world is in one respect problematical, both for Chrysippus and for Epicurus. For men can act freely, and free action is not easily contained in a rule-governed universe.

Epicurus' world, though mechanistic, was not determined by iron necessity.

The atoms sometimes deviate from their normal trajectories by a minute amount: and the deviation, or swerve, has no cause. 'If the atoms do not swerve and thereby produce a sort of beginning of motion which breaks the bonds of fate so that cause does not follow cause everlastingly, what is the source of the free will which living things possess throughout the world?' Freedom implies the absence of external necessitation, and the postulated swerves ensure that necessity is not ubiquitous. Free actions are determined by the agent's will. And the will, thanks to an uncaused deviation in the atoms of the soul, is not wholly dependent on external events.

The Stoics thought little of that device to save free will: 'they do not allow Epicurus to swerve his atoms a jot, for he thereby introduces an uncaused motion', Chrysippus insisted that, 'since universal nature extends to everything, it will be necessary for everything whatever to occur in accordance with nature and with its rational principle, in due order and ineluctably'. Fate is the name the Stoics gave to the chain of causes and effects which binds the universe together: 'everything happens in accordance with fate'.

The Sceptical Academy launched a major attack against this Stoic position. One of their arguments—the 'Lazy Argument', probably formulated by Arcesilaus—ran as follows: 'If it is fated for you to recover from this illness, you will recover whether you call a doctor or not; again, if it is fated for you not to recover from this illness, you will not recover whether you call a doctor or not; but one or the other is fated: therefore it is pointless to call a doctor.' Carneades produced a different line of thought: 'If everything comes about by antecedent causes, everything comes about in a web or net of natural interconnections; if that is so, necessity causes everything; if that is true, nothing is in our power.'

The debate between the Academy and the Stoa was long and intricate. Chrysippus had a subtle reply to the Lazy Argument, but his most interesting manoeuvre depended on a distinction among types of cause. 'Some causes are perfect and principal, others auxiliary and proximate. Thus when we say that everything happens by fate in virtue of antecedent causes, we wish to be understood to mean not perfect and principal but auxiliary and proximate causes.' An example makes the point clear. A man places a cylinder on a flat surface and gives it a push: it rolls. 'Just as the man who pushed the cylinder gave a start to its motion but did not make it such as to roll, so an object that appears to us will impress us and as it were seal its form in our mind, but assent will be in our power; and, as we said in the case of the cylinder, assent, though pushed externally, will for the rest move by its own force and nature'. The antecedent cause—the man's push—makes the cylinder move; but it does not determine the cylinder to roll rather than to slide. That the cylinder rolls is due to its own nature, not to external circumstances. Similarly, Chrysippus urges, the antecedent cause—the impression of an external object—causes the mind to move; but it does not determine the direction of the movement. That the mind assents to or dissents from the impression is due to its own nature—it is something within our power.

That ingenious comparison did not end the debate. Chrysippus' successors elaborated his classification of causes, and the attempt to reconcile freedom and fatalism exercised the Stoa for the whole of its history. Whether or not the attempt succeeded, it inspired the subtlest analysis of the notion of causation in the history of philosophy.

Logic

Physics will succour ethics only if it is grounded in firm knowledge. Here the logical part of philosophy enters; for, according to the Stoics, 'everything is discerned by way of logical study—both what falls within the province of physics and what falls within the province of ethics'. Now things are either 'evident' or 'unclear'. If evident, they are grasped 'immediately' or 'directly'; if unclear, they are grasped indirectly and by the mediation of other things. Thus logic will have two main aspects: it will provide a 'criterion of truth', as the Hellenistic philosophers called it, by which we may judge what is evident; and it will offer a theory of inference, by which we may attain knowledge of what is unclear.

The Stoic theory of inference—Stoic logic in the narrow sense of the term—rests upon a detailed theory of language. It begins with the conception of an *axiōma* or proposition, 'something which in itself denies or asserts something—e.g. "It is day", "Dion is walking"'. Propositions are either simple or non-simple, the non-simple being 'those consisting of a repeated proposition or of several propositions' joined by a connecting particle. (Stoic theory concentrated on three connectives: 'if', 'and', 'or'.) An argument is 'a system of premises and a conclusion', where premises and conclusion are all propositions, simple or complex.

Like Aristotle, the Stoics recognized that a logician's business is with forms of argument rather than with particular inferences; and like Aristotle they achieved the generality which the business requires by the use of schemata. Again like Aristotle, the Stoics were systematic: 'there are certain arguments which are non-demonstrable (for they do not need to be demonstrated)'—Chrysippus lists five such arguments, others list others; and every argument is constructed by way of those. The five 'indemonstrables' play in the Stoic system the part played in Aristotle's syllogistic by 'perfect' syllogisms: they are basic, and other argument forms are derivable from them.

In content, Stoic logic is very different from Peripatetic. It corresponds roughly to what modern logicians call propositional or sentential logic. The foundation of Chrysippus' system consists of the following argument-schemata, the five indemonstrables: (i) If 1, then 2; but 1: therefore, 2. (ii) If 1, then 2; but not 2: therefore, not 1. (iii) Not both 1 and 2; but 1: therefore, not 2. (iv) Either 1 or 2; but 1: therefore, not 2. (v) Either 1 or 2; but not 1: therefore, 2. The logic which Chrysippus erected on that modest base was powerful and sophisticated.

Logic is the servant of knowledge, and its service consists in the provision and ratification of proofs. Not all arguments are proofs. Rather, 'a proof is an argument which, by way of agreed premisses, reveals by deduction an unclear conclusion'. The notion of 'revelation'—of uncovering or explaining—is crucial to the closely connected concept of a 'sign'. The world is full of signs—clouds signify future rain, scars are signs of past wounds—and signs are appropriately expressed by way of conditional propositions; indeed, a sign was loosely described as 'an antecedent proposition in a sound conditional which reveals the consequent'. Consider, then, a standard example of a proof: 'If sweat permeates the skin, the skin has imperceptible pores; but sweat permeates the skin: therefore the skin has imperceptible pores.' The argument has the form of the first indemonstrable; both its premisses are true or 'agreed'; its conditional premiss expresses the fact that perspiration is a sign of perforation; its conclusion is 'unclear' (the pores are not available to direct inspection). Thus by virtue of inference we advance from evident facts to a knowledge of what is unclear.

'Many people believe that if the gods studied logic it would be the logic of Chrysippus.' The Epicureans dissented—indeed, 'they reject dialectic as redundant' and they preferred to call the third part of philosophy 'canonics' or the theory of judgement. But they still required some account of how we might come to know 'unclear' facts. The later Epicureans, whose arguments are preserved in Philodemus' treatise *On Signs*, disputed the Stoic theory of signs and substituted an account of their own. Epicurus himself spoke not of proof and signs but of 'confirmation' and 'disconfirmation': 'if judgements are not confirmed or are disconfirmed, falsity arises; if they are confirmed or not disconfirmed, truth'. A later author illustrates the notion: 'when Plato is approaching from far off, I conjecture and judge because of the distance that it is Plato; after he has approached and the distance is reduced, it is testified and confirmed by direct evidence that it is Plato'. The ideas of confirmation and disconfirmation are relatively plain, but non-confirmation and non-disconfirmation produce puzzles: those puzzles may have spurred Epicurus' successors to develop their own theory of signs.

What, next, of the 'criterion of truth' by which we judge what is 'evident'? In general, 'the old philosophers say that there are two kinds of evident things, those which are discerned by one of the senses ... and those which strike the mind with a primary and non-demonstrable impression'. According to Epicurus, all objects are continuously emitting effluences of various kinds. When the effluences strike an appropriate part of a sensitive body—the ears or the nose, say—their parent object is perceived. The effluences which affect the eyes and cause the parent object to be seen are *simulacra* or replicas—thin skins which preserve the contours of the object as they speed through space. Thought is analogous: Lucretius states that 'the mind is moved by replicas of lions and of everything else it grasps in just the same way as the eyes are—except that it perceives more flimsy replicas'.

Such effluences supply us with the concepts we employ and form the basis of our knowledge. Moreover, the impressions they make on us are in some way infallible: 'whatever impression we grasp directly by the mind or by the sense-organs, whether of shape or of other properties—*that* is the shape of the concrete body ... Falsity and error always depend on a superadded opinion.'

The Stoics agreed that our conceptual resources and our knowledge are founded upon direct impressions from external objects. They differed over the physics and physiology of cognition. But their most important difference from the Epicureans lies in their assessment of the impressions themselves. For the Stoics held that our knowledge rests upon one special type of impression. These 'apprehensive impressions' were defined as impressions 'deriving from an existing object, signed and sealed on the mind in conformity with the existing object itself, of a sort which could not derive from anything other than the existing object.' The impressions of a madman may be mere figments, deriving from no existent object; an impression may derive from a real object and yet misrepresent it; an impression may represent an object correctly, yet fail to record its peculiar individuality. No such impression is apprehensive. 'For they require that apprehensive impressions genuinely grasp their objects and imprint exactly all their individual characteristics.'

Epicurean impressions are all true: falsity enters only when we misinterpret our data. The Stoics allow that the data themselves are often distorted: in order to avoid falsity we must scrutinize and select. But both schools insisted that we do obtain knowledge from our impressions, and each faced challenge from the sceptics of the Academy.

The Epicurean dogma appeared easy to attack: there are familiar perceptual illusions, and the senses sometimes offer conflicting testimony—how, then, can all impressions be true? The Epicureans were well aware of the phenomenon of illusion, for which they offered physical explanations. Lucretius knows that a square tower when seen from a distance may be judged round. The replicas which leave the tower have sharp edges, but 'as they travel through a large space of air, the air by frequent collisions blunts them' and they become rounded. Even so, the tower does not *look* round: 'the stone structures look as though they had been turned on a lathe—yet they do *not* look like stones which are nearby and genuinely round, but seem to be, as it were, sketchy likenesses of them'. Again, 'Timagoras the Epicurean denied that when he pressed his eye he ever seemed to *see* two little flames in the lamp—the falsity belongs to opinion, not to the eyes.' Careful attention to the exact content of our impressions will show that illusions are due to the mind's misreading, not to the eye's misleading.

As for conflicting perceptions, each is true—but true of only a part of the object perceived. 'Since everything is mixed and compounded, and different things naturally fit different people ... people encounter only those parts with which their senses are commensurate.' The water feels cold to me, warm to you. We are both right, or partly right; for the water contains cold elements and warm elements, the former affecting me and the latter you. Perception does not err.

The Epicurean defence of impressions was not mere quixotry. Epicurus asserted that 'if you reject absolutely any perception ... you will confound your remaining perceptions too with that empty belief, so that you will reject every criterion'. If any perception fails, all fail—and knowledge is lost. The Academics were not satisfied, but they were more interested in the Stoics than in the Epicureans.

The focus of the dispute was the final clause in the Stoic definition of apprehensive impression: the impression must be 'of a sort which could not derive from any other existing object'.

There are four points which imply that there is nothing that can be known, grasped or apprehended ... First, some impressions are false; secondly, they cannot be apprehended; thirdly, if there is no difference between two impressions it cannot be that one of them can be apprehended but the other not; fourthly, for any true impression derived from the senses there is another adjacent impression which does not differ from it at all and which cannot be apprehended.

If Chrysippus claims to possess a true impression, the Academics will offer him another impression which is false but which Chrysippus cannot distinguish from the impression he claims to be true. Hence his impression is not apprehensive; for it could have derived from something else, namely from the object from which the indistinguishable false impression derives. The Academics produced pairs of eggs, identical twins, real and wax apples, in an attempt to substantiate their claim that for every true impression there was an adjacent false impression indistinguishable from it. The Stoics made defensive manoeuvres. They claimed distinctions where the Academy saw none, they added an extra clause to their definition of apprehensive impression.

Moreover, they took the battle into the Academic camp. Without belief, life is impossible; for we lose all reason for action. The Epicureans made the same point. According to Lucretius, 'life itself is immediately ruined if you are not prepared to believe your senses—and to avoid precipices'.

Science

Even if scepticism does not subvert life, surely it will subvert science? The Hellenistic period was the golden age of Greek science, and it is natural to wonder whether the scientists noticed the concerns and perplexities of their philosophical contemporaries.

Euclid's *Elements* are perhaps the most celebrated product of the period. Euclid (*fl. c.* 300) 'composed his *Elements* by systematizing much of the work of Eudoxus and completing much of that of Theaetetus, putting into irrefutable demonstrative form propositions which had been somewhat loosely proved by his predecessors'. Euclid's achievement lay in form rather than in content: he insisted on a rigorous and systematic presentation of mathematical theorems. Archimedes of Syracuse (287–212) and Apollonius of Perge (*fl. c.* 200) opened up new areas of mathematical knowledge. 'His contemporaries called Apollonius a great geometer because of the remarkable features of the theorems on cones which he proved,' and modern scholars judge his work on conic sections one of the masterpieces of Greek geometry. Archimedes' was a more universal talent: he did original work in astronomy and engineering as well as in mathematics. Within mathematics he excelled in geometry (where he calculated the approximate value of pi), in mechanics (where he developed statics and invented hydrostatics), in arithmetic (where he discovered ways of calculating with very large numbers).

Astronomy is a mathematical science, and both Archimedes and Apollonius were astronomers. Early in the third century Aristarchus of Samos (*fl. c.* 275) 'hypothesized that the fixed stars and the sun stay motionless, and that the earth moves in a circle about the sun which lies at the centre of its orbit.' But Aristarchus' innovative hypotheses were not developed by his successors, who returned—in part for good scientific reasons—to a geocentric model of the universe. Apollonius was the first to devise a system of epicycles and eccentric orbits: the system was elaborated by Hipparchus of Nicaea (*fl. c.* 135), the second astronomer of the age, and it reached its zenith of sophistication in the work of Ptolemy

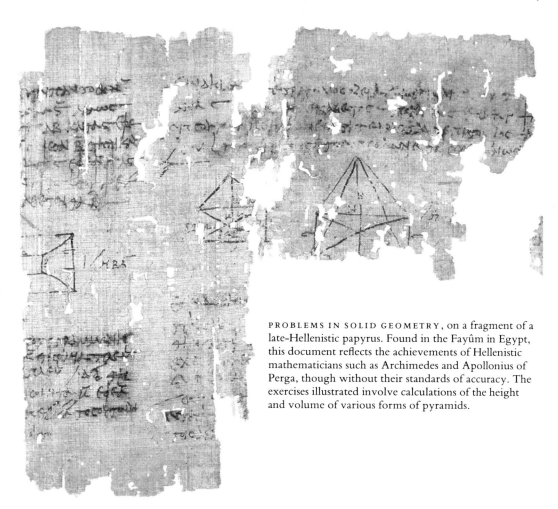

PROBLEMS IN SOLID GEOMETRY, on a fragment of a late-Hellenistic papyrus. Found in the Fayûm in Egypt, this document reflects the achievements of Hellenistic mathematicians such as Archimedes and Apollonius of Perga, though without their standards of accuracy. The exercises illustrated involve calculations of the height and volume of various forms of pyramids.

some three centuries later. Hipparchus was also an empirical astronomer: he invented or improved various optical aids; he produced a star-map; he discovered the precession of the equinoxes. Beside Hipparchus, the polymath Eratosthenes of Cyrene (*fl. c.* 225) cuts a small figure—indeed, 'because he was second best in every branch of study ... he was nicknamed Beta'. But he merits mention here for his calculation of the circumference of the earth: his method was sound, and his result was astonishingly accurate.

Eratosthenes had studied under Zeno and Arcesilaus, and the scientists doubtless knew, or knew of, the philosophers. Equally, some of the philosophers were aware of scientific speculations; thus 'Cleanthes thought that the Greeks should indict Aristarchus of Samos for impiety, inasmuch as he set the hearth of the world in motion'. But there is little evidence of any interdisciplinary influence or understanding. Problems of perception engaged the philosophers, and observational difficulties troubled the astronomers: the two areas did not overlap. The scientists discussed questions of method, and the philosophers speculated on the foundations of knowledge: the two enquiries were separately conducted. Astrology has been thought to link science and philosophy inasmuch as the astronomers may have regarded their science as a servant of astrology while the Stoics' fatalism made them likely to succumb to that occult science. But the link is tenuous. Hipparchus is said 'to have shown that we are related to the stars and that our souls are a part of the heavens', but that report is vague, and it is unlikely that the Hellenistic astronomers anticipated Ptolemy's addiction to astrology. Moreover, there is little evidence for any interest in astrology on the part of the Old Stoa.

In truth, the philosophers did not care for mathematical arcana, and the mathematical scientists ignored philosophy—they were more interested in the technological applications of their studies than in any theoretical speculations. Thus engineers such as Ctesibius of Alexandria (*fl. c.* 270), Philo of Byzantium (*fl. c.* 200), Hero of Alexandria (*fl. c.* 60), and Archimedes amused themselves and diverted their masters by inventing new machinery—water-clocks and mechanical puppets, fire-pumps and steam-toys, and many engines of war.

Hellenistic astronomy was rivalled only by Hellenistic medicine, the protagonists of which were Herophilus of Chalcedon (*fl. c.* 270) and Erasistratus of Ceos (*fl. c.* 260). Both men were practical physicians. Herophilus had an interest in new drugs, and he also developed a diagnostic technique which relied upon distinguishing different types of pulse. Both men were also interested in the theoretical aspects of medicine. Herophilus was the first scientist to describe the structure and function of the duodenum, an organ which is still known by the name Herophilus gave it. He also examined the brain. Erasistratus developed a physiological theory which rested on mechanical principles. The theories had an empirical base:

Herophilus and Erasistratus ... were given criminals from the prison by the kings <of Egypt> and dissected them alive; while they were still breathing they observed parts

MECHANICAL GADGETS described by Hero of Alexandria (first century AD) in his *Pneumatica* and *Auto-matapoeica*. (*Left*) Steam from a cauldron of boiling water is forced into a hollow sphere from which its only escape is via two small hooked pipes placed opposite each other; the result is that the sphere rotates. (*Right*) An automatic libation. The heat of the altar-fire forces hot air down into a tank of oil contained in the platform; the oil in turn is forced up through tubes within the bodies of the two statuettes and drips out from vessels held in their hands.

which nature had formerly concealed, and examined their position, colour, shape, size, arrangement, hardness, softness, smoothness, connection . . .

Nor is it cruel, as most people allege, by causing pain to guilty men—and only a few at that—to seek out remedies for innocent people of every age.

Such bloody researches may seem far removed from the contemplative arm-chair of the philosopher. But Greek medicine had a long association with philos-ophy, and the philosophical interests of the Hippocratic writers of the fifth and fourth centuries were inherited by their Hellenistic successors. Erasistratus was said by his followers 'to have associated with the Peripatetic philosophers', and his physiological theory betrays the influence of Epicurus and of the Stoa. He wrote a work *On Causes* which appears to have been primarily philosophical in tone. Herophilus too was exercised by the notion of causation: he 'cast doubt on all causes by many powerful arguments', and came to a sceptical conclusion: 'whether or not there are causes is by nature undiscoverable, but in opinion I hold that I am made hot and cold, and am filled by food and drink'. Herophilus was the first of a long line of medical sceptics which culminated in the second century AD in the figure of Sextus Empiricus, physician and Pyrrhonist.

Epilogue

To some degree the doctors preserved the Aristotelian ideal which the Hellenistic philosophers had generally discarded: science and philosophy, for them, were complementary aspects of a unified search for understanding. At the end of the Hellenistic age that ideal was briefly revived by an eminent philosopher.

Posidonius was an admired figure in his day, a friend of Cicero and of Pompey. In philosophy he was a Stoic, and though he was no blind follower of Chrysippus his Stoicism was hetcrodox only on the periphery. What was unorthodox about Posidonius was his voracious appetite for learning of every kind. He was a voluminous historian, who undertook a continuation of the work of Polybius; an original ethnographer, who described the manners and *mores* of the Celts; a travelled geographer, who propounded a theory of the Atlantic tides; a student of logic and mathematics, of botany and zoology, of seismology, geology, and mineralogy. In sum, as one ancient admirer put it, 'he Aristotelizes'. But Posidonius was a giant apart. He had no followers. Polymathy was outmoded, Aristotelian man extinct.

The river of philosophy ran a clear course for some two centuries, its two main channels, the Stoic and the Epicurean, being clearly marked. In the first century BC the waters became turbid. The Middle Stoa relaxed the canons of Chrysippus and advanced a more eclectic philosophy. The New Academy passed out of existence when the last proponent of scepticism, Antiochus of Ascalon (*fl. c.* 85), became a Stoic in all but name (below, p. 703). Even Epicureanism altered, as the writings of Philodemus of Gadara (*fl. c.* 55) demonstrate. Pyrrhonian scepticism was rekindled by Aenesidemus (*fl. c.* 90). Platonism received fresh attention and attracted new followers. The edition of Aristotle's treatises by Andronicus of Rhodes (*fl. c.* 50) revived interest in the philosophical parts of the Peripatetic system.

The face of philosophy changed, but the Hellenistic age had left its mark. The systems of the Porch and the Garden never lacked adherents, and modern philosophy has been influenced as much by them as by the Lyceum or the Old Academy. Moreover, the conception of philosophy—of its scope, its subject-matter, its methods—which we have inherited from Greece is not the generously ambitious ideal of Aristotle but the narrower and more introspective notion of the Hellenistic schools.

Further Reading

Systematic accounts of Stoicism and Epicureanism can be found in Books 7 and 10 of Diogenes Laertius' *Lives of the Philosophers* (Book 10 includes the three *Letters* of Epicurus). For the New Academy the most useful single text is Cicero's *Academica*. The works of Sextus Empiricus—*Outlines of Pyrrhonism* and *Against the Mathematicians*—contain a mass of further material. All those texts are available in English translation in the Loeb Classical Library. Much of our information, however, comes in fragments. For Epicurus the indispensable aids are: G. Arrighetti (ed.), *Epicuro—Opere* (Turin, 1973²); H. Usener (ed.), *Epicurea* (Leipzig, 1887). The fundamental work for Stoicism is H. von Arnim (ed.) *Stoicorum Veterum Fragmenta* (Leipzig, 1903–24). There is nothing comparable for the New Academy.

The best English introduction to the subject is A. A. Long, *Hellenistic Philosophy* (London, 1974). Modern research can be approached by way of two collections of papers: M. Schofield, M. F. Burnyeat, J. Barnes (eds.): *Doubt and Dogmatism* (Oxford, 1980); J. Barnes, J. Brunschwig, M. F. Burnyeat, M. Schofield (eds.): *Science and Speculation* (Cambridge, 1982).

A · · · · · · · · B · · · · · · · · C

• Virunum

TRANSPADANA

Mediolanum

a

VENETIA

Aquileia

• Tergeste

PANNONIA

Sirmio ⊙ **Verona** ⊙
Cremona · **Patavium**

Mantua

HISTRIA

Bedriacum

Placentia ⊙
· Parma

R. PADUS

Pola •

DALMATIA

· Genua

AEMILIA

Ravenna ⊙

R. DANUBE

Carrara ·

R. RUBICON
· Ariminum

Salonae (Split)

Pisa ·
Faesulae ·

R. ARNUS
Florentia ·

UMBRIA

Ancona ⊙

Volterra ·

Arretium ⊙

Cortona ·
· Iguvium

b

Populonia ⊘
Vetulonia ·
Clusium ·
· Perusia

PICENUM

b

ETRURIA

Volsinii ⊙
Asculum •

SABINES

Aleria •

CORSICA

Volci ·
Cosa ·
Falerii ·

R. TIBER
Tarquinii
Veii ·
Rome ⊙

Spoletium ·
Alba
Fucens ·
R. Liris
Corfinium •

SAMNIUM

LATIUM

Praeneste ·

APULIA

Ostia ·

Luceria •
Sipontum •

Velitrae ·
Antium •

CAMPANIA
Arpinum ·
Fregellae ·
Cales ·

Cannae •
Barium •

Minturnae •
Capua ·
Beneventum •

c

Olbia •

Cumae ⊙
ISCHIA
Puteoli ⊙
Neapolis ·
· Nola
MT. VESUVIUS ▲
Pompeii ·

Tarentum

CALABRIA

Brundisium •

c

SARDINIA

Paestum •

Metapontum •

Heraclea •

Velia
(Elea) •

LUCANIA

Laus •
Thurii •

Caralis •

Croton •

Terina •

N

Hipponium •

BRUTTIUM

Lipara •
Medma •

Messana ⊙

d

Panormus •

Tyndaris ·
Rhegium ⊙
Locri •

d

Segesta •
Himera •

MT. ETNA ▲
Taurominium •

Altitude in metres

Lilybaeum •

SICILY
Centuripae ·
Enna •

Over 1000

Selinus ⊙

Catana •

200–1000

Agrigentum ⊙
Leontini •
Syracuse ⊙

0–200

Utica ·
Carthage

Gela ⊙

0   25   50   75   100 miles

Camarina •

0   50   100   150 km

A · · · · · · · · B · · · · · · · · C

MAP 7. ITALY

16

Early Rome and Italy

MICHAEL CRAWFORD

THE central theme of this chapter is the Italian element in Roman history. Already under her early kings, before 509 BC, Rome was beginning to expand at the expense of her immediate neighbours. This process continued under the Republic, so that by the early third century Rome had no serious rivals south of the Po valley, where the Gauls remained an active threat. But Rome had not simply conquered Italy, she had also forced its different peoples to fight for her when required. The military manpower thus acquired was used first to defeat an invader from the east, then to win two wars against Carthage, then to conquer the whole of the Mediterranean basin.

The great wars of conquest after 200 BC form one of the themes of Chapter 17. But the relationship of Rome with Italy remained till the age of Augustus one of the determining factors in her history. The conquest of the Mediterranean basin led to changes in the economy of Italy, which from the end of the second century onwards generated a series of political crises, some of which form the theme of Chapter 19, but some of which are considered here, since they concern the relationship between Rome and Italy. At one level, these crises were resolved by the emergence of Augustus as Emperor; at another level, their resolution involved the final stages of the Romanization of Italy and the Italianization of Rome.

The Peoples of Italy

In attempting to write of the early history of Rome, one is confronted at once by the fact that no account written earlier than the late third century ever existed and that no continuous account written earlier than the age of Augustus now survives. (The Roman tradition of historical writing is discussed in Chapter 26.) Perhaps the gravest weakness in the literary tradition on early Rome, however, is its ruthlessly Romanocentric character. Before Polybius, Greek writers such as Aristotle occasionally became conscious of the existence of Rome, and some of this material is preserved, either directly or as used by later writers. But the

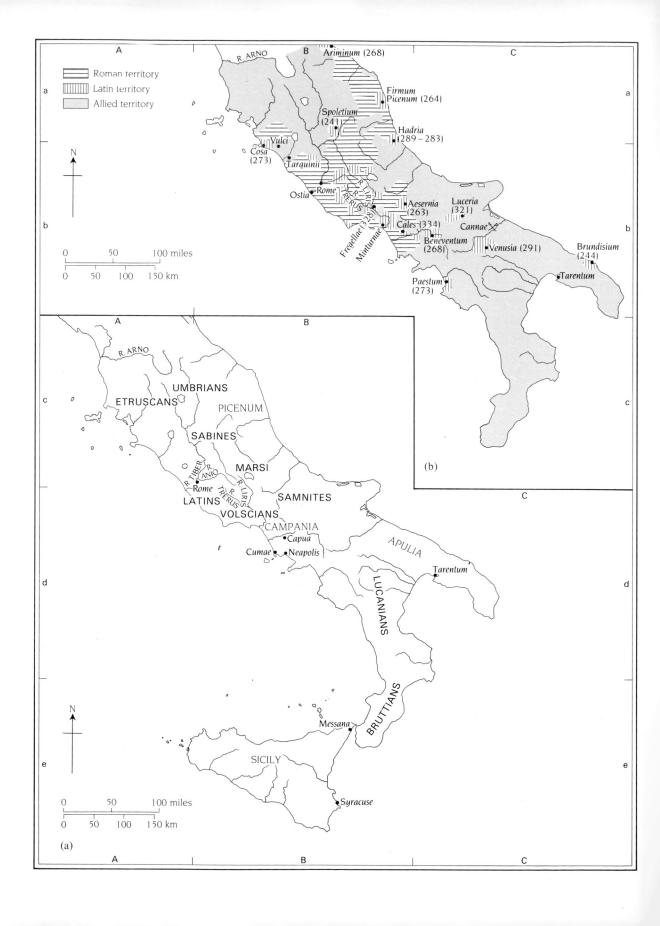

Roman territory
Latin territory
Allied territory

N

0   50   100 miles
0   50   100   150 km

R. ARNO

Ariminum (268)
Firmum Picenum (264)
Spoletium (241)
Hadria (289–283)
Vulci
Cosa (273)
Tarquinii
Ostia
Rome
R. LIRIS
R. TRERUS
Aesernia (263)
Luceria (321)
Cales (334)
Cannae ✕
Fregellae (328)
Minturnae
Beneventum (268)
Venusia (291)
Brundisium (244)
Paestum (273)
Tarentum

(b)

N

0   50   100 miles
0   50   100   150 km

R. ARNO

UMBRIANS
ETRUSCANS
PICENUM
SABINES
MARSI
R. TIBER
R. ANIO
Rome
R. LIRIS
R. TRERUS
SAMNITES
LATINS
VOLSCIANS
CAMPANIA
Capua
Cumae   Neapolis
APULIA
Tarentum
LUCANIANS
BRUTTIANS
Messana
SICILY
Syracuse

(a)

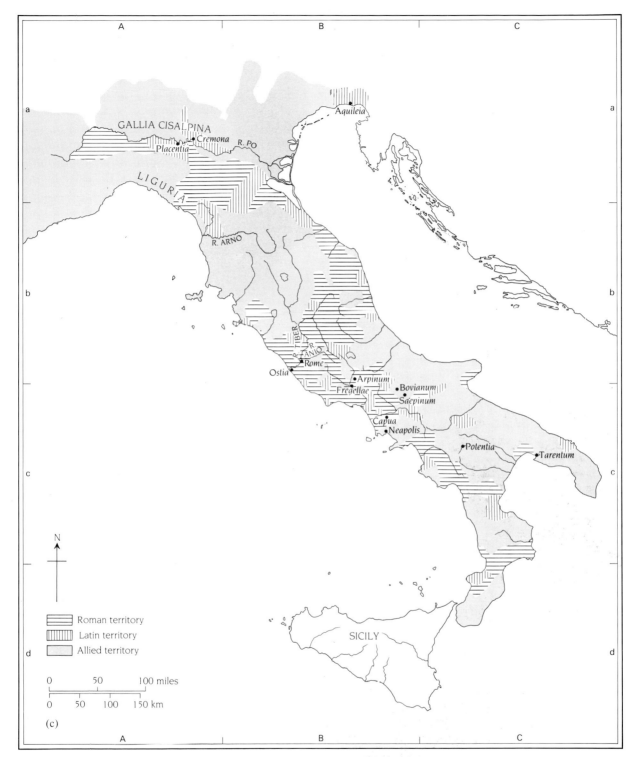

A   B   C

a

Aquileia

GALLIA CISALPINA

Cremona
Placentia   R. PO

L I G U R I A

R. ARNO

b

R. TIBER

R. ANIO

Rome
Ostia

Arpinum
Fredellae   *Bovianum*
Saepinum

Capua
Neapolis

Potentia
Tarentum

c

N

Roman territory
Latin territory
Allied territory

0   50   100 miles

0   50   100   150 km

SICILY

d

(c)

A   B   C

MAP 8. THE GROWTH OF ROME IN ITALY (*Facing bottom*): In the early period of her history, Rome was no more than one city among many in Italy, her territory restricted to the area immediately outside her wall, the Latins one tribe among others competing for mastery. (*Facing top*): By 241 BC not only did Roman territory spread south into Campania and south-east to the Adriatic, but a far-flung network of Latin colonies controlled much of the rest of Italy. (*Above*) By the time of the outbreak of the Social War, Roman and Latin territory had penetrated and isolated allied territory throughout Italy; the rebels of 91 were essentially the inhabitants of the last great block of allied territory in the central and southern Apennines.

ARCHITECTURAL TERRACOTTAS FROM CAPUA. The two antefixes (eaves ornaments) are both datable to the second half of the sixth century BC and illustrate the strong Greek influence at Capua during the period of Etruscan rule. Both the female bust and the gorgon's head with its frame of radiating tongues are related to work in the coastal cities of Cumae and Pithecusae.

histories written by Etruscans and other local traditions have disappeared almost without trace. It is thus extraordinarily hard to grasp the enormous diversity in ethnic formation, social and economic structure, political organization, religion, language, and material culture of the different peoples of Italy. Rome succeeded in conquering and assimilating not only peoples like the neighbouring and related Latins, but peoples who were as like to herself as chalk to cheese.

The most distinctive group within Italy is formed by the Greek colonies of the south, strung out along the coast from Cumae to Tarentum. Founded as self-contained cities from the eighth century onwards, they ensured that territories which they controlled became in every essential respect part of the Greek world. From the fifth century onwards, however, these territories became increasingly subject to attack and conquest by the peoples of the mountainous interior. Bruttians in the toe, Lucanians in the instep, Samnites further north, a variety of small tribes including the Marsi to the east of Rome, were all anxious to control the fertile lands and established wealth of the coast. The consequence, however, was sometimes very far from being a process of take-over and barbarization.

These peoples of the mountainous interior spoke similar languages (labelled as 'Italic' by scholars) and certainly in historical times regarded themselves as related to each other. Further north, the Latins on the coast and the Sabines and Umbrians in the interior spoke languages belonging to the same 'Italic' group, but had a rather different history from the peoples further south. Legend regarded both Sabines and Latins as playing a part in the formation of the Roman state, and the history of the two peoples was always very closely intertwined. But the crucial influence both on Rome and on Umbria was Etruria. Here, from the eighth century onwards, there developed by a combination of internal evolution and outside, largely Greek, influence (the Etruscan language is neither Greek nor Italic) an advanced urban civilization; this civilization was essentially homogeneous, although the different Etruscan cities remained separate political entities.

Umbrian civilization in the early period was on the whole a pale imitation of Etruscan, and the Etruscan script was used to write the Umbrian language; but at Rome something rather different happened. The villages on the hills around what became the Forum linked up into a single city in the course of the sixth century; a similar process probably occurred at about the same time in the case of other Latin communities, such as Gabii or Praeneste. The material culture of archaic Latium has much in common with Etruscan; but Rome never became either culturally or politically a mere Etruscan dependency.

The story of Campania is even more complex. Here the Greek cities of the coast, principally Cumae and Neapolis, coexisted in the late archaic and classical period with an Etruscan principality based at Capua. The arrival of the Samnites in the fifth century did not lead to the destruction of the civilization which had emerged in Campania, although no Etruscan city survived as such and only Neapolis survived as a Greek city. Rather the Samnites became the new ruling class. The incorporation of this area by Rome in the fourth century was probably the most important formative experience in the history of the republic.

The contrast between Latium and Campania on the one hand and Picenum and Apulia on the other hand is instructive. In both areas a population which seems to have had little in common with the group of peoples extending from the Umbrians to the Bruttians underwent a certain development as a result of contact with the Greek world, in the case of Picenum passing Greek traders, in the case of Apulia the Greek city of Tarentum. But Picenum remained materially backward, barely literate, and hardly urbanized; and although Apulia came to possess a number of cities of native origin, the area seems to have run out of steam, culturally and politically, at the same time as did the Greek cities of the south, between the fourth and the third centuries.

Cutting across the ethnic differences there were important differences in economic and social structures. The Greek colonies were of course fully fledged *poleis*, and it is clear that places such as Etruscan Veii or Capua, Latin Rome or Praeneste, were in many respects similar. But much of central Italy remained without cities down to the age of Cicero. Here the pattern was of scattered villages and farmsteads, often within reach of a fortified hill-top, where it was possible to take refuge in time of war, but which was never built up or lived in, indeed which did not even fulfil the political or religious functions of a city. A clear example of this pattern of settlement is provided by Pietrabbondante, where the greatest of the Samnite sanctuaries, which served also as a meeting place, lay on the open hillside below a hill-top fort, both sanctuary and fort being completely detached from any trace of settlement.

One should not suppose, however, that the absence of cities meant the absence of settled agriculture. Naturally, the Greek *poleis* recruited their armies from the free peasant element of their populations, and the same was true of Rome. It must have been true also of the other communities of early Italy. For the Roman conquest of Italy involved a sequence of battles between the Roman heavy-armed infantry and that of their enemies; and the existence of heavy-armed infantry implies the existence of free peasants. This must be true for Etruria, although what our sources talk about is the serf element of the population (one thinks

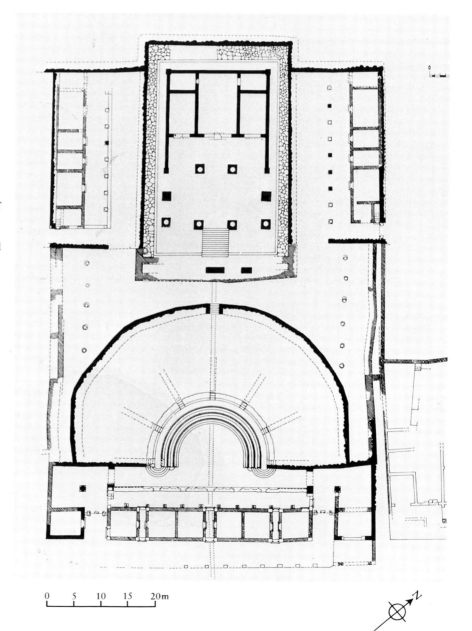

PLAN OF THE SANCTUARY
AT PIETRABBONDANTE
(*c*.100–91 BC). The grandest of
the Samnite religious centres
of the Republican period
testifies to the wealth achieved
by Italian merchants and
bankers shortly before the
Social War. The arrangement
of a temple axially placed
behind and overlooking a
theatre is typical of central-
Italian sanctuaries at this time.

0   5   10   15   20m

of Sparta where the helots supported a hoplite, not an aristocratic society); it must be true of Samnium, although our sources often give the impression that the population consisted of shepherds. And in fact, if one travels in Italy, as opposed to merely looking at a map, one comes time and again on pockets of good land, often at a great height, where arable farming is possible and was certainly practised in antiquity.

That is not to say that there were no shepherds. And the combination of the Italian climate—hot dry summers and cold wet winters—with Italian geography—river and coastal plains and high mountains—meant that sheep farming took on a characteristic form found elsewhere in the Mediterranean. This involved pasture in the lowlands, often on farmland where grain had been harvested, from late summer till spring, and in the high mountains on grassland watered by melting snow for the hot season. Such a system, known as transhumance, might simply involve moving flocks up and down the side of a single valley; or it might involve movement over long distances, from winter pasture in Apulia, for instance, to summer pasture in the central Appennine mountains, when political conditions made this possible.

Early Rome

The city of Rome was formed by the linking of a number of villages; the consequence was that the Forum ceased to be used for burials and became the public open space of the new city. It is interesting that the great Etruscan city of Veii, which was for many years the principal rival of Rome, consisted of a plateau also originally occupied by separate villages. The comparison with Veii is interesting in another respect also; for Rome and Veii were not simply bigger, but orders of magnitude bigger, than any other community in the lower Tiber valley.

Certainly, Rome was a prize worth having, and Roman tradition was unanimous in holding that Rome was originally ruled by kings, and that two of the last three successors of Romulus, eponymous founder of the city and first king, were Etruscan adventurers, Tarquinius Priscus and Tarquinius Superbus. Their arrival in and seizure of power at Rome illustrates an important aspect of archaic society in central Italy as a whole, namely its openness to horizontal penetration. Just as in archaic Greece, tyrants and aristocrats of one *polis* intermarried with those of another, so in archaic Italy there was no rigid conception of citizenship to tie a man to the community of his birth. What is more, openness to horizontal penetration seems to have been true of all social levels; for in the years immediately after the fall of the monarchy at Rome, the Sabine aristocrat Appius Claudius and his retainers were admitted to membership of the community, he at the social level appropriate to his existing standing, they at the level appropriate to theirs. And when from the fourth century we can make reliable inferences about the nature of the relationship between Rome and other Latin communities, we can observe that an essential element of the relationship is freedom of movement between one community and another. It does not much matter whether this element of the relationship is a survival of a period when the Latins were a tribal community or whether it is the product of the diplomatic history of the sixth and fifth centuries. What matters is that it seemed acceptable in the context of archaic central Italian society.

In talking of the social level appropriate to the retainers of Appius Claudius, I have so far left on one side one of the crucial problems of early Roman history. Roman tradition is unanimous in holding that there existed already under the monarchy a group of families known as patricians which succeeded in the early years of the Republic in acquiring both a monopoly of secular and sacred office and almost complete control of the economic resources of the community. Those who were not patricians are presented by our sources as plebeians; this is the system they knew in their own day, but it is likely that the early community of the Romans included social groups which were neither patrician nor plebeian. What is clear is that there emerged with great rapidity a plebeian movement, which created an organization parallel to, and alternative to, that of the patrician state, in the course of what is known to scholars as the struggle of the orders. The plebeian organization set out to break the patrician monopoly of secular and sacred office in the Roman state and to reduce the extent of economic exploitation of the poor by the rich. In the pursuit of its first objective, the plebeian movement was wholly successful; and in the second century Cato could assume that there were no *formal* barriers in the way of any Roman citizen achieving the highest office of the state. We shall see shortly how plebeian economic aspirations were fulfilled.

I have used the term 'Roman citizen'; and the unitary concept of Roman citizenship is the result of the process I have been describing, at the end of which, if one was domiciled at Rome, one was either free and a Roman citizen or a slave. It cannot be too strongly emphasized that the openness of Roman society to plebeian mobility which is the corollary of this fact is *as far as we know* a feature unique to Rome; though it may have applied to other Latin communities, it probably did not apply to Etruscan communities, which continued to display, like some Greek communities, a range of statuses between slave and free.

But there is more. To the astonishment of Greek observers, a slave freed by a Roman citizen became a Roman citizen. And, as we shall see, Roman citizenship came to be available in due course not simply to members of Latin communities, but also to entire Italian peoples. Given the fact that by the time this occurred Rome was the dominant power in central Italy, this too is to be seen as involving the openness of Roman society to penetration from below.

I have talked in general terms of secular and sacred office in early Rome and of the creation of a plebeian organization parallel to that of the Roman state. Under the monarchy, presumably, the kings were in the habit of consulting a body of advisers, the institution which became in due course the Senate of the

Republic. At the end of the sixth century the king holding office for life was replaced by two consuls holding office for one year at a time. There appear in addition in our sources for the early years of the Republic specialist financial officials (quaestors) and a variety of military offices. Probably the sources had no accurate information; but the supposition that there existed already under the monarchy a differentiated administrative structure is entirely reasonable; the method of appointment presumably changed from nomination to election with the arrival of the Republic. There also existed already under the monarchy two different ways in which the Roman people was organized as an assembly, the Comitia Curiata, the people organized in kin groups, and the Comitia Centuriata, the people organized in army units. The growth of the plebeian organization involved the creation of plebeian officials, of whom the most important were the tribunes of the plebs, and of another assembly, the Concilium Plebis or Comitia Tributa, the people organized by *tribus*, areas of domicile.

As the plebs achieved its aim of equality of political and religious rights with the patricians its organization was simply grafted on to that of the Roman state. The tribunes became for all practical purposes officials of the Roman state, the Concilium Plebis became with the name Comitia Tributa one of its assemblies. The plebeian organization, in creating its assembly, also preserved one of the most curious features of existing Roman assemblies, namely voting by groups. No Roman assembly ever reached a decision by a simple majority of those present and voting; each group, however defined, reached a decision in this way and the decision of the assembly was the decision of a majority of the groups.

In the case of the Comitia Centuriata, whose functions included the election of the consuls, the groups were organized in such a way as to facilitate the dominance of the rich. For, at any rate in its developed form in the middle Republic (the fourth and third centuries BC), the Comitia Centuriata contained a number of groups of men who were wealthy enough to serve as cavalrymen, a number of groups with a slightly lower property qualification, and so on. The richer the group, broadly speaking, the fewer men it contained; as a result their influence in the assembly was disproportionately large. Under the monarchy and in the early Republic the system was certainly less complicated, but the underlying principle is likely to have been the same. Of course this principle was not consciously formulated until much later, but its effect was that the wealthy, who paid more in taxes and on whom a greater burden fell in the defence of the community, had a greater say in the making of policy. It must be said, however, that the rich determined the outcome of a vote only if they were united—probably a rare occurrence. Obviously the nature and aims of the plebeian assembly were reflected in the fact that in it no advantage was conferred on the rich in the way in which the groups were formed.

Rome under the monarchy had a relatively differentiated administrative structure, and here too there is continuity of development from the earliest times onwards, as there was in the evolution of the different Roman assemblies.

Throughout their history the Romans showed remarkable willingness to create new offices to take over specific functions from the consuls; thus the praetors came in due course to take over the specialized function of the administration of justice, the censors that of listing roughly every five years the members of the citizen body and the amount of their property liable to taxation, and of renewing the prayers of the Roman people for the favour of the gods. Throughout the Republic, indeed, until the anarchy of its last years, the census was the process whereby men were assigned their place in the community, as soldiers, taxpayers, and voters.

The Roman community did not consist simply of the citizens who belonged to it, together with their female, young, and slave dependents. It also included the gods, and Roman religious structures and history form in a number of very striking ways the mirror image of secular structures and developments.

In the first place, the relative complexity of the administrative structures of the early Republic is paralleled by the diversity of its priesthoods. There were from the start two major colleges, the *pontifices,* with the *pontifex maximus* at their head (and the Vestal Virgins under his general control), and the *augures;* the former were concerned in general terms with sacrifices to the gods (the Vestal Virgins with the sacred hearth of the community), the latter with ascertaining the will of the gods, for instance by observing the flight of birds. And just as the state created new secular offices to meet new needs, so too in the field of religion new priesthoods were created from time to time. Moreover the priesthoods of the Republic were often held by men who also held secular office, with the difference that a priesthood was for life, a consulship for a year at a time. For at Rome religion and politics were not two worlds, but inseparable parts of the same world. One must not suppose that there was something 'wrong' with Roman religion because the world of the gods was involved in the world of political dispute.

Second, the plebeian organization, which developed in parallel to that of the Roman state, created also its own apparatus of cult, centring on the Aventine hill, outside the original boundary of the city of Rome, and involving the cult of Ceres, Liber, and Libera.

Finally, the readiness to innovate in the sphere of religion, which we have observed in the creation of new priesthoods and of a plebeian religious structure, operated also in a much wider context. Perhaps the most conspicuous feature of the religious history of the Republic is the steady importation of new deities, from Etruria, from elsewhere in Italy, or from overseas. The practice is not an indication of dissatisfaction with existing gods, but rather the reverse. Just as her citizens gave Rome her military strength, and Rome sought for most of her history constantly to increase their number, so also, as the gods helped Rome to win battles, the more gods one worshipped the better.

Apart from the creation of the militarily successful patrician–plebeian state, one other consequence of the struggle of the orders requires mention. Among the demands of the lower orders was the demand that the provisions of the Roman civil law be codified and recorded, in order that their interpretation should not be at the fancy of patrician office-holders. The result was the so-called Twelve Tables (traditionally *c.*450 BC), whose provisions still formed the basis of the Roman civil law in the age of Cicero. As a result of citations by writers of this and later periods, we have a fair idea of the original contents of the Twelve Tables; they reveal a society which is still that of a small agricultural community, but one in which the importance of the kin-group is already diminishing and in which there are already substantial numbers of slaves.

The Early Republic

The early years of the Republic were marked by an attempt on the part of the patrician families to achieve a monopoly of secular and sacred office. The fall of the monarchy also meant the partial loss of the superiority which Rome had achieved *vis-à-vis* her immediate neighbours. Furthermore, in the fifth century the Volscians emerged from the upper Liris valley and conquered most of the Trera valley and the coastal plain south of Rome. The first century and a half of the Republic saw first the reassertion of Roman leadership of the other Latin communities and then a long sequence of wars against the southern Etruscan cities, principally Veii (captured and destroyed in 396), and against the Volscians to the south. In the latter struggles Rome and the Latins could usually rely on the Hernicans, who had also suffered from Volscian expansion.

It was undoubtedly a period of economic difficulties which weighed heavily on the lower orders and exacerbated their resentment at patrician exclusiveness. At the same time the fact that some of the lower orders (not the very poor) contributed the manpower on which Roman military success depended conferred bargaining power which they were not slow to use. The erosion of patrician privileges went hand in hand with the steady acquisition of land by conquest, which was used to satisfy the economic aspirations of the lower orders. Such land either formed the territory of a new community, or *colonia*, possessing local self-government, or provided isolated plots of land for settlers not organized as a group. The Gallic sack of Rome in 390, traumatic though it must have been at the time, had little effect either on internal developments at Rome or on the process of conquest. The land acquired as a result of the capture of Veii was distributed to the poor at Rome, resulting in the creation of an enormous new reserve of peasant soldiers. By the middle of the fourth century Rome dominated south Etruria, no longer had anything to fear from incursions by tribes in the upper Anio valley, and was poised on the northern edge of Campania.

The crucial moment in the history of the Roman conquest of Italy came in 338. Most of the Latin communities around Rome, viewing her growing preponderance with alarm, attempted to reassert their independence. They were rapidly defeated and all, except the largest and most distant, incorporated in the

Roman citizen body. From this time on, the original cities of Latium and the *coloniae* founded by them in association with Rome ceased individually or as a group to have any destiny separate from that of Rome. But Rome made the momentous decision to continue to found new communities with the status of Latin cities. Certainly later, and probably by now, Latin status *vis-à-vis* Rome and other Latin communities was defined essentially as involving rights of intermarriage, the enforceability of contractual obligations, and the right to change domicile, with the acquisition of the citizenship appropriate to the new domicile. The first of the Latin *coloniae* founded after 338 was Cales in northern Campania, founded in 334. The primary function of this and later *coloniae* was defensive, to hold down conquered territory or guard Roman territory against invasion. The foundation of a *colonia* was one way in which land acquired by conquest was used to relieve the poverty of the lower orders in Roman (and Latin) society; but *coloniae* of Latin status were also powerful factors making for the Romanization of Italy. They possessed from the outset constitutions modelled on that of Rome, and by their mere presence in an area previously without significant contact with Rome served to spread the Roman model of government. Recent archaeological evidence from Cosa (founded 273) suggests very strongly that Rome exported to the Latin *coloniae* her peculiar practice of voting in groups. But there is an even more important side to the foundation of Latin *coloniae*; it seems that membership was not limited to those who were already citizens of Rome or a Latin community, but that any Italian ally was eligible. The Latin *coloniae* thus served to elevate large numbers of Italians to a status close to that of Roman citizenship. Neither this fact, however, nor the fact that Latin *coloniae* provided a context in which land was assigned to the poor meant that the *coloniae* were egalitarian or democratic foundations. A significant part of the population of Latin *coloniae* was more richly endowed with land than the rest, to provide a social élite and a governing class.

Both before and after 338 Rome also founded a number of *coloniae*, the members of which possessed Roman citizenship. These *coloniae* tended when founded to be smaller than *coloniae* of Latin status and to have guard duties of a very limited and precise nature, for instance at Ostia at the mouth of the Tiber or at Minturnae at the mouth of the Liris. But those possessed of Roman or Latin citizenship were eligible to take part in the settlements and Roman *coloniae* provided an avenue, even if not a very important one, whereby men whose families were of Italian origin could achieve Roman citizenship without moving to Rome.

Far more important as a means of creating new Roman citizens was the incorporation of entire Italian communities as citizens without the vote. Such communities possessed all the other rights of Roman citizens, primarily legal and social, and were also bound to perform all the duties of citizens, to pay taxes, and to fight. We do not know whether the act of conferring citizenship without the vote (perhaps sometimes withheld for reasons of distance or linguistic incompatibility) was intended as a reward or as a means of subjection, and perhaps it does not much matter. Large parts of Italy *became* Roman in this way, however, conspicuously the great Graeco-Etrusean-Samnite city of Capua, and also Arpinum, later the birthplace of C. Marius and of Cicero. The details of the process whereby Capua and indeed much of Campania were in the middle of the fourth century incorporated in the Roman state are obscure and controversial. What matters is that what was by then the richest and most developed area of Italy entered the Roman sphere (below, pp. 402 f.).

The Unification of Italy

We have seen that there were a number of ways in which men belonging to different Italian communities, whether conquered or not, might come to acquire Roman citizenship or Latin status. But there are other aspects of the process whereby Rome succeeded not simply in conquering Italy, but also in moulding it into a single world. In the foundation of Latin *coloniae* Rome exported her own hierarchical pattern for the organization of society. The same general approach was extended to her dealings with the Italian allies. Systematically Rome sought out and privileged their upper classes; she supported them in a crisis, if they were faced with catastrophe from without or revolution from within; in normal times relations between Rome and any Italian community were conducted by means of the personal links between the upper orders of the two cities, based on a close community of interest and involving frequent contact, including intermarriage.

Given this network of personal relationships, it is not surprising that Rome found little difficulty in seeing that the principal demand she made on the communities of Italy was fulfilled. The demand was for troops, a fact which sets Rome apart from most other ancient empires and helps to explain the nature of Roman imperialism.

Most ancient empires demanded tribute from their subjects; superiority was symbolized by the demand, and its fulfilment provided tangible material rewards for having achieved rule over others. Rome, clearly at a very early stage, simply extended to other Italian peoples the demand for manpower which she made on her own citizen body. The result was that the only way in which she could symbolize the power she had over the Volscians or the Etruscans was by demanding troops and the only way in which she could derive any benefit was by using the troops to acquire booty, land, and yet more power. It should not be supposed, however, that the demand for troops necessarily fell on unwilling ears. For although Rome was less generous in distributing booty or land to her allies than she was to her own citizens, she did share some of the ever increasing rewards of victory with them.

The Roman conquest of Italy was also accompanied by a striking physical expression of the fact of a Roman presence. Prior to its distribution, whether as

CENTURIATION IN THE PO VALLEY. The modern road and field system in this air photograph taken in 1945 clearly reveals its origins in the Roman land-divisions of the second century BC. Large squares with sides of 20 *actus* (2,400 Roman feet=710 metres) and an area of 200 *jugera* are subdivided into narrow strip-fields.

isolated lots or in the territory of a *colonia*, conquered land was at any rate from the late fourth century onwards measured and marked out by an elaborate process eventually known as *centuriatio*. Initially, perhaps from 334 onwards, land was divided into strips 10 *actus* wide (1 actus = *c.* 35.5 m.); the lines of division were known as *decumani*. In due course a full rectangular grid was marked out; the transverse lines of division were known as *kardines*. Just as in the simpler system the *decumani* were sometimes more or less than 10 *actus* apart, so in the developed system a grid of 20 x 20 *actus* was the norm, but not universal. When such a grid was used, the result was 100 *jugera*, or a *centuria*, within each square.

But this elaborate process was not used merely for measuring the land; the lines of the grid were marked out by roads and ditches which left an indelible mark on the countryside; they patterned and structured its use for centuries, if not millennia, and survive in many areas to this day, despite industrial development and mechanized farming.

On one hand, then, there was an almost violent expression of Roman control of the land; but on the other hand, the pattern of Roman-organized colonization in Italy facilitated the acquisition of Latin, or eventually Roman, citizenship by Italians; it also permitted the presence and assimilation of existing ethnic elements. Thus the foundation of the Latin colony of Ariminum (in 268) in what had been Umbrian territory did not have an adverse effect on the major pre-Roman sanctuary of the area, outside the walls of the *colonia*; rather, as the offerings show, the sanctuary continued to be central to the life of the *colonia*, as it had been to that of the area before its foundation. At the other end of Italy, early inscriptions of the colony of Luceria (founded 314), on the borders of Samnite, Lucanian, and Apulian territory, show a mixed Latin-based dialect, which presupposes a mixed population.

A second-century inscription from Aesernia in Samnium (founded 263) shows a group of 'Samnites incolae', resident Samnites, clearly not citizens, but harmoniously established, going about their business and with their own form of corporate organization. And we know from literary sources that a large number of Samnites and Paelignians migrated to Fregellae in the early second century; we have no idea whether they became citizens, but their presence was clearly acceptable.

INSCRIPTION FROM AESERNIA (ISERNIA) (second century BC): dedication of a statuette to Venus by the *Samnites inquolae* (resident Samnites), evidently a corporate organization of the native Samnite population within this Latin colony. Four *magistri* (officers) of the body are named. The statuette-base (front at the left, back at the right) has been reconstructed on the basis of a pre-war drawing.

These examples of coexistence and assimilation come from those parts of Italy where the population may be defined as Italic, in general terms ethnically and linguistically close to the Latins. There were two areas of Italy where the story was rather different, Etruria and Gallia Cisalpina. In each case, a distinctive and remarkable culture was eventually submerged without trace, though for rather different reasons. In the case of Gallia Cisalpina, memories of the Gallic sack of Rome in 390 and the role played by his Gallic allies in Hannibal's invasion of Italy largely explain the brutality of the Roman conquest of the area. The first steps were taken already in the third century with the virtual destruction of the Senones, and the policy continued in the second century (below, pp. 408 f.). In Etruria the effect of the early wars in the fifth and fourth centuries had been to create a solid swathe of Roman or Latin territory in the south, leaving a few barely viable Etruscan enclaves, such as Tarquinii or Vulci. In the north, Etruscan territory and culture remained intact, but in an increasingly isolated backwater.

Rome and the Greek Cities

In the sixth century, Greek culture had been mediated to Rome by Etruria. In the fourth century, with the absorption of Campania, Rome entered into close and direct contact with the Greek world, contact that was to increase in intensity and significance over the next three centuries. The Roman link with Campania

STONE SARCOPHAGUS OF L. CORNELIUS SCIPIO BARBATUS (consul in 298 BC). The Scipios, unlike most republican families, favoured inhumation rather than cremation, and a series of inscribed sarcophagi was found in their family tomb on the Via Appia outside Rome. This is the earliest and the best preserved, remarkable for its hellenizing architectural decoration.

DISH IN GENUCILIA WARE, Rome's answer to Greek-style painted pottery (fourth century BC). Both the female head wearing a diadem and the wave pattern round the rim are favourite motifs of the Genucilia potters.

was both symbolized and strengthened by the building of the Via Appia from Rome to Capua in 312, by Ap. Claudius Caecus as censor. It is likely that it was in this context that the first Roman silver coinage was produced, on the Greek model. The late fourth and early third centuries, indeed, saw the beginning of the rapid Hellenization of Rome. It was in this period that Rome absorbed from the Greek world an interest in the expression of the ideology of victory, a phenomenon which was not the least of the legacies of Alexander the Great. The consequence at Rome was the introduction of new cults of gods of war, gods of victory, Victory herself. It was in this period also that the cult of Hercules, heavily dependent on Greek models, became widespread in the Roman world, evidenced both by the institution by the state of new cults and by the upsurge in humble offerings to the new hero. At the same time a Greek influence on the material culture of the republic became even more apparent. At one level there is the sarcophagus of L. Cornelius Scipio Barbatus, found in the tomb of the Scipios on the Via Appia, which used Greek architectural motifs in its decoration.

At another level, Rome began to produce around 380 her own local pottery, imitated from South-Italian or Etruscan red-figure pottery, known as Genucilia ware, and then in the early third century a fine black-slip pottery, imitative of Greek metal ware.

The late fourth century saw also the development by Rome of increasingly complex administrative structures, going beyond the simple adoption of coinage on the Greek model. It was certainly in this period that there evolved the developed structure of five census classes, each with different fiscal and military responsibilities.

The Defence of Italy and the First War against Carthage

The last serious wars fought by Rome against an Italian people were the wars against the Samnites. These were effectively over by 295, when the Samnites were defeated at Sentinum in northern Italy, along with Umbrian, Etruscan, and Gallic allies; for the Umbrian and Etruscan cities which remained independent had decided to make one last attempt to assert their freedom, while some of the Gallic tribes of the Po valley had decided to attempt to repeat the success of 390.

Fifteen years later the Romans met their first invasion from overseas. We have already seen that the Greek cities of the south were faced from the fifth century onwards by the territorial and political ambitions of their 'barbaric' neighbours (above, pp. 390 f.). Tarentum declined to compromise, as did Cumae or Posidonia, which had accepted the presence of a partially Samnite or Lucanian élite. Instead, she called to her aid a succession of Greek mercenary commanders. The last of

ROMAN SILVER COIN (DIDRACHM) OF THE PYRRHIC WAR (275–270 BC). On the obverse the head of Apollo wearing a laurel-wreath; on the reverse a horse galloping to the right beneath a sixteen-pointed star. By the depiction of Apollo, the Greek god who had lately repulsed the Gauls from Delphi, Rome promotes itself as the champion of civilization against the forces of barbarism.

these was Pyrrhus, king of Epirus, who was summoned in 280 to deal not with Tarentum's Lucanian neighbours, but with the Romans, who were now the principal threat to the independence of Tarentum.

It should be remarked that Tarentine opposition to Rome was by no means typical of the reaction of the Greek *poleis* of the south. Many welcomed the protection and alliance of Rome, both now and later. The obverse type of the issue of silver coins which Rome struck during the war against Pyrrhus should be seen as quite deliberately placing Rome on the side of civilization in the fight against barbarism. The type in question is a head of Apollo, the god who had become in 279 the symbol throughout the Greek world of the victory of the civilized over the barbarous, by reason of his defence of Delphi against a band of marauding Gauls. Rome too, as we have seen, had defeated a similar band, in 295, along with her other enemies.

Pyrrhus succeeded initially in winning a number of costly victories over the armies of Rome (hence the phrase 'Pyrrhic victory'). But he was in due course defeated at Beneventum and returned across the Adriatic. It was undoubtedly his defeat at the hands of Rome that caused the Greek historian, Timaeus of Tauromenium, writing in exile at Athens, to take notice of the new power in the West.

Shortly afterwards, this new power found itself at war with the other power in the West, Carthage, longer established as such and much better known in the Greek world as a result of the long series of bloody wars which she had fought with the Greeks in Sicily.

The earlier relations of Carthage with Rome had been pacific, and the two states had indeed made three treaties with each other, agreeing not to interfere in their respective spheres of interest. The treaties are preserved by Polybius. The earliest, belonging to the first year of the Republic, is the earliest Roman document known in something like its entirety.

In addition to the factors making for Roman expansion which we have already considered, others are evidenced by the outbreak of the First Punic War. Polybius reports that the Senate did not vote for action, but that the assembly did, and there is no doubt that sheer greed played a large part in swaying opinion. The action that led to war was to send an army to protect Messana, in the hands of a band of Italian mercenaries, against Hiero of Syracuse, despite the fact that the protection of Carthage had already been invoked. The action was in character; neither the Roman aristocracy nor the Roman state as a whole could ever resist the temptation to intervene when the chance arose.

The war lasted from 264 to 241 and was in effect a war for the control of Sicily, since Hiero of Syracuse decided at an early stage in the proceedings to throw in his lot with the Romans. Roman persistence won through, and Roman chicanery added Sardinia to the prize. Much is obscure about the way in which Rome set about organizing her new acquisitions, but two points are worth making. In the first place, it is clear that the Italian model of a treaty which imposed on the defeated community the obligation to provide manpower at the behest of Rome was not applied; both Sicily and Sardinia were regarded as territories to be ruled and taxed. In the second place, a group of recently discovered inscriptions from Entella in western Sicily reveal at least one Italian in a semi-official position of influence under Roman auspices during the First Punic War, and probably profiting from the position.

Politics in the Middle Republic

Leadership in the wars that Rome fought in the fourth and third centuries was provided by the mixed patrician–plebeian nobility which had emerged as a result of the resolution of the struggle of the orders. Holders of the consulship or other high office and their descendants came to be regarded as forming the nobility under the new dispensation. It was this group that constituted the Senate in the traditional age of senatorial domination.

It must be said that our ignorance of how politics worked in this society is almost total. The problem arises at at least two levels, within the senatorial élite and between the élite and the population as a whole. Although what our sources tell us about this period, the period of the middle Republic, is no doubt heavily tinged with romanticism, it seems reasonable to suppose that both the élite and society as a whole were united to an extent that was clearly not true in the age of Cicero.

Obviously there was competition within the élite for office, power, and influence. We possess from the third century one early grave monument, that of L. Cornelius Scipio Barbatus (above, p. 402; the inscription is later than the sarcophagus) and part of the *elogium* pronounced at the death of L. Caecilius Metellus, consul in 251. Neither the inscription of Barbatus nor the *elogium* on Metellus makes sense except in the context of a competitive aristocracy. Clearly there were moments of tension, as when an ancestor of Sulla (below, pp. 413 f., 459 ff.) was expelled from the Senate for excessive display of wealth. But it is wildly unlikely that the fourth and third centuries were characterized by the bitterness and the unscrupulousness which marked political conflict in the age of Cicero. The consul of 251 was described as possessing great wealth, honourably acquired. Only the first part of this description could have been applied to Caesar.

When there was disagreement within the élite over policy, we simply do not know how it was resolved. It is, however, worth remarking that one modern theory, according to which entire *gentes* such as the Cornelii or the Caecilii operated as single entities, building stable alliances with other *gentes*, is almost certainly fantasy. The theory does not work for any period where we have first-hand evidence, and it is paradoxical to apply it when there is no such evidence; and men such as Barbatus and Metellus emerge as larger-than-life *individuals*, whose ambitions sometimes actually played a part in pushing Rome into war.

We are even more in the dark when it comes to understanding the nature of the relationship between the élite and the population as a whole. Again, of course, there was controversy, over matters which were to be characteristic causes of controversy in the second and first centuries; thus there was argument in 290 over the relative balance to be achieved in the use of conquered land in Sabinum between its distribution to the poor and its sale to the rich; and Polybius records a controversy aroused in 232 by the proposal to distribute land in Picenum and the south-east of the Po valley. But Roman history in the fourth and third centuries is incomprehensible except on the assumption that the lower orders were largely satisfied with the leadership of the nobility and with the rewards to be won under their command.

Conventionally *clientela*, a traditional, often inherited relationship of dependence of one man on another, is regarded as the principal integrating factor in Roman society of the middle Republic. But other factors were surely at work. Although Rome, as we shall see in a moment, was already in the third century large in comparison with most ancient states, it was probably still a society where contact between different social levels was relatively easy; the number of enterprises, such as war and colonization, in which élite and people shared, ensured that the two remained relatively closely integrated. And now, as later, the élite could and did justify its actions to the population as a whole in terms of shared values; these values involved, among other things, the belief that the approval of the gods was necessary and that with it Rome could not fail.

The third century was not only, as Polybius observed, the high point in the development of the Roman body politic; it also marked the acme of the system of Italian alliances which Rome had built up, before the strains began to show. The last great Gallic invasion which Italy had to face was that of 225, and it is in the context of the preparations against it that Polybius describes the manpower resources available to Rome. To do so he drew on the account given by the first Roman historian, Q. Fabius Pictor, himself a witness of the events of 225. Although the list in Polybius contains some obscurities in detail, it fits with what else is known of Roman citizen numbers in this period and suggests that the Roman and Italian pool of men on which Rome could draw was of the order of 6–7 million.

Hannibal's Invasion: The Second Punic War

The existence of such a reserve enabled Rome to withstand the shock of Hannibal's invasion of Italy in 218. This invasion, the resources for which were provided by the Carthaginian acquisition of an empire in Spain, was a deliberate attempt to reverse the verdict of the First Punic War. Between 218 and 216, Hannibal, a brilliant general, was able to inflict a series of crushing and bloody defeats on the Roman armies sent to face him, culminating in the battle of Cannae in 216, and was able to detach a number of Rome's allies, notably Capua;

at the same time, Carthage attempted to recover Sicily and in due course brought Syracuse over to her side.

But Rome was always able to field new armies to replace those which were lost, and most of her Italian allies never regarded Italy without Rome or Italy under Carthage as serious alternatives to the system with which they had become familiar. Rome first succeeded in confining Hannibal to Bruttium, while simultaneously recovering Sicily, seizing Spain, and fighting against Macedonia, which had allied with Carthage in 215 after the battle of Cannae. In due course the war was carried over to Africa; Hannibal was recalled from Italy in 203, to be defeated at the battle of Zama in 202; Carthage sued for peace and the attempt to dispute Roman hegemony in the western Mediterranean was over.

Hannibal's Legacy

What were the effects on Italy of fifteen years of warfare on Italian soil? It has been argued that the devastation of much of Italy by Hannibal led to the deracination of many Roman and Italian peasant soldiers and a shift to large farming enterprises owned by the élite and run by slave labour; whence the problems which Ti. Gracchus set out to resolve two generations later (below, pp. 411 f.). The argument is hard to maintain. Rome not only continued to field large armies of peasant soldiers throughout the Second Punic War, but undertook after it was over both the final conquest of the Po valley and a series of wars overseas (below, ch. 17).

For those Italian communities that had allied with Hannibal, however, the consequences of his defeat were grave. The Bruttii were deprived of any form of communal institutions and were not even allowed a role in the armies levied by Rome, except as servants. They and many other communities lost land, a fact which lies behind some of the economic developments of the second century. Those communities which continued to provide troops for Rome were forced to provide disproportionately large contingents. In effect, if not in theory, second-century Italy was a single state ruled by Rome, with local government in the hands of its scattered communities, not a mosaic of independent states bound together by a network of alliances.

The principal Roman military effort in Italy after 201 was directed to the definitive conquest of the Po valley. The process had begun after the defeat of the Gallic invasion of Italy in 225, with the foundation in 218 of the *coloniae* of Cremona and Placentia. Rome picked up after the Second Punic War where she had left off, and the next generation saw both the military subjugation of the area and the settlement, either in *coloniae* or in scattered plots, of tens of thousands of Romans and Italians, from Placentia in the west to Aquileia in the east. Of the different Gallic peoples, the Boii simply ceased to exist, as had the Senones earlier. The Cenomani and Insubres survived, albeit with their freedom gone.

Both the nature of the landscape and the unfolding of the Roman conquest help to explain why Gallia Cisalpina is the area characterized more than any other by Roman centuriation (above, p. 400). As they moved across the largest plain in Italy, the Romans felt themselves bound by no existing political, social, economic, or even geographical pattern. A *tabula rasa*, the Po valley was imprinted for ever with the marks of the Roman presence, and absorbed over a whole generation much of the military and colonizing energy of the Roman people, energy which appears undiminished by the experience of the Second Punic War.

Meanwhile, however, the overseas wars which followed the Second Punic War were transforming the social and economic fabric of Italy. These wars had two consequences which concern us here. They led on the one hand to a steady professionalization of the Roman and Italian soldier. Strictly speaking, it is inappropriate to talk of such a thing as the Roman army at this date, quite apart from the fact that an army levied to fight for Rome consisted of a large number of notionally independent contingents. But whereas down to 201 it had been normal for a man to fight in the spare time left over from farming, it became increasingly common after 200 for men to serve abroad for years on end.

At the same time, the wealth of the Mediterranean was pouring into Italy, partly in the form of booty, partly in the form of payments exacted from defeated enemies. Some of this wealth was distributed to the lower orders on the occasion of the triumph celebrated at the conclusion of a successful campaign, but much ended up in the hands of the élite. Further wealth was acquired in the course of the administration of overseas territories or by lending money at exorbitant rates of interest to foreign communities.

What happened to all this money? Some of it, both that which remained under the control of the community and that which had passed into private hands, was expended on the erection of public, as well as private, buildings in Rome and Italy. Rome showed the way, with projects such as the linking of the temples (still visible) in the Largo Argentina into a single monumental complex. Similar projects, on a scale hitherto undreamt of, were carried out elsewhere in Italy. Thus the Latin *colonia* of Fregellae possessed before its revolt and destruction in 125–124 a gigantic sanctuary of Aesculapius—temple, portico on three sides, stone treasure chest, altar, water-supply, monumental access ramp.

Obviously, in so far as free labour was used in the execution of such projects, the lower orders benefited economically. And indeed the emergence of urban markets with considerable spending power is a necessary hypothesis to explain another important second-century development. For it seems clear that much of the new wealth of the Roman and Italian élite was invested in land, in large farming enterprises run by slave labour. These were essentially of two types, market gardens, olive groves, or vineyards on the one hand, transhumant sheep farming on the other. Both types of enterprise created a demand for land in central Italy, to the detriment of the peasant farmer, whose plot might be requested in purchase or sometimes even seized and whose access to common land

REMAINS OF REPUBLICAN TEMPLES IN LARGO ARGENTINA in Rome. Temple C (entrance stairway in the left foreground) is the earliest, probably going back to the early third century BC and dedicated to the Italic deity Feronia. Temple A (standing columns at the rear) is the next oldest, probably dedicated to Juturna in 241 BC. The circular temple B, in the middle, is thought to be that of Fortuna Huiusce Diei (Fortune of the Present Day), inaugurated in 101 BC soon after the unification of the temples into a single monumental complex.

on which he depended might be rendered more difficult. In concentrating central-Italian land in its hands, the Roman and Italian élite was to a certain extent acting against its own interests, since it needed to ensure a steady supply of men for the legions in order to organize its wars of conquest overseas. But men do not always act wholly rationally.

The Age of the Gracchi

A pattern seems to have emerged in the second century whereby peasant soldiers in central Italy surrendered their land and their rights to common land, from which they had in any case become detached in the course of long service overseas, and went to settle in the Po valley; their sons provided the next generation of soldiers. But with the pacification of that area, the great days of colonization came to an end, and there seems to have followed in the generation before 133 a steady build up of men without land of their own and without hope of land to go to. What Ti. Gracchus attempted to do was to reverse the trend in central Italy and increase the number of peasants at the expense of large-scale farming enterprises.

Elected tribune for 133 BC, he introduced a land bill limiting the size of holdings of public land, and redistributing the surplus to the people. The Senate retaliated by putting up another tribune, M. Octavius, to veto the proposal, and Tiberius was finally forced to procure his fellow tribune's deposition from the people. He further antagonized the Senate by seeking to interfere in the arrangements for the kingdom of Pergamum, left by will to the Roman people: the administration of foreign affairs was traditionally a prerogative of the Senate. Finally, in the disturbances caused by his attempt to secure re-election to the tribunate for a second term, he was murdered together with 300 of his supporters.

Perhaps the principal consequence of the attempts at reform in this period was the inextricable entangling of Italian with Roman politics. But there is a further process which must be considered before we can turn to this particular problem, the progressive Romanization of Italy. The golden age of Roman road-building is the generation or so before Ti. Gracchus; as a result the whole of Italy became linked together, both actually and symbolically, to a far greater extent than ever before.

Italy also became in the years after the Second Punic War a monetary and economic unity. Down to the end of that war there circulated in the different areas large numbers of coins produced by Italian communities other than Rome; after the end of the war few communities felt themselves sufficiently independent of Rome to produce coinage for themselves, and earlier issues rapidly disappeared from circulation. It was soldiers returning from service with the armies of Rome who carried Roman coinage into the remote backwaters of the Appennines. And it was the developing market economy of Italy in response to the wealth flowing in from the East that took the monetary and economic unity of Italy a stage further. Down to the middle of the second century there were some inequalities in the pattern of circulation of Roman coins in Italy, both in terms of types and in terms of quantity. These inequalities then disappeared, clearly a sign of the developing process of exchange of money for goods.

The armies of Rome were important in another respect also, as a powerful factor for linguistic unity. During and after the Second Punic War men were away from home for much longer than before, in an essentially Latin-speaking environment. Etruscan survived, as did the languages of Samnium and Lucania, but the rest were in the process of disappearing in the period before Ti. Gracchus.

The principal problem to be faced in dealing with Gracchus' legislation is that we simply do not know whether, let alone to what extent, it was intended to revive peasant farming, not only in Roman, but also in Italian communities in central Italy, although it must be the case that these were suffering from the same developments.

What is clear, however, is that Ti. Gracchus' attempt to resume public land in the hands of the rich in order to distribute it to the poor adversely affected the interests of Italian élites as well as those of the Roman élite. It was not long before the idea was floated of giving Roman citizenship to some or all Italians, partly to compensate them for reduced access to Roman public land, partly to give them a say in the making of policy in this sphere. Once floated, the idea would not go away, though it was not till 91 that the Italian demand for Roman citizenship exploded into war.

Meanwhile politics at Rome between 133 and 91 were marked by a series of attempts, analogous to that of Ti. Gracchus, to win for the Roman poor a larger share in the rewards of the Empire which as soldiers they had helped to win, whether those rewards were in the form of land or subsidized corn. The attempts often ended, as had that of Ti. Gracchus, in the violent death of their authors. Two must be mentioned specifically, the programme devised by Tiberius' brother C. Gracchus, in 123–122, which aimed not simply to improve the material lot of the poor, but also to shift the balance of power within the Roman state; and the career of L. Appuleius Saturninus, who in 103 and 100 set out, in alliance with the conqueror of Jugurtha of Numidia and of the Cimbri and the Teutones, C. Marius, to provide for the need of his veterans for land. The alliance between tribune of the plebs and general was one fraught with danger for the future.

The Division of the Spoils

One reason why the political argument at Rome over the division of the spoils of empire became so bitter in the last generation of the second century was precisely because these were becoming ever richer. In 133 the last king of Pergamum had actually left his kingdom to the Romans; the Roman acquisition of what became the province of Asia falls in the middle of the second great period of Roman acquisition of territory (not to be confused with acquisition of power), between Africa and Achaea in 146 and Provence in 121. The result was a rapid rise in the numbers of Romans and Italians living overseas, as tax-collectors, money-lenders, and slave-traders. Their activities happen to be principally documented in the East, and the greatest wealth was no doubt to be acquired there; but the process clearly went on in the West as well. What is important in this context is that Italians abroad were treated as equals with Romans by the people with whom they dealt; the lack of Roman citizenship was no doubt felt ever more acutely.

Other factors deserve a mention. There certainly took place in this period some genuine urbanization, as opposed to the embellishment of existing centres. For instance, at Bovianum and Saepinum, in central Samnium, where previously there had been scattered villages or farms and hill-forts as places of refuge, urban growth began on the plains below the hill-forts. At Monte Vairano, the hill-fort itself began to be permanently occupied. The Roman urban model of society was spreading. All these developments certainly made Italian communities feel even more acutely their formal inferiority and their lack of control over Roman policy. Romans sometimes behaved high-handedly to members of local élites. And the career of C. Marius—six times consul between 107 and 100, victor over Jugurtha, saviour of Rome from the Cimbri and Teutones—showed what could be achieved by an aristocrat from an Italian community which had been enfranchised.

At the same time, it is certain that the actual grievances of the allies were increasing, as Rome sought to avoid the consequences of her own lack of peasant soldiers by shifting ever more of the military burden on to her Italian allies. It is remarkable in these years how difficult Rome found it to defeat the relatively minor figure of Jugurtha of Numidia and how vulnerable she was to the Cimbri and Teutones. It was luck that brought them no nearer Rome than the Po valley. And one may wonder whether either Jugurtha or they would have been defeated without the skill of C. Marius.

Citizenship for Italy

By 91, it was no longer possible to evade the issue of granting Roman citizenship to the Italians, and when M. Livius Drusus' proposal to do so failed, half of Italy rose in revolt (the so-called Social War). Rome disarmed the revolt by agreeing to grant what she had at first refused and was able with the help of those who remained loyal to subdue the rebels who held out (for what, it is not clear).

The result was that the whole of peninsular Italy together with existing *coloniae* in the Po valley was organized into communities of Roman citizens. We are ignorant of the details of the process, but it was largely complete by 83. For it was in that year that L. Cornelius Sulla, who had in 88 fought a brief civil war in order to secure the command of the Roman armies in the East, returned to

Italy. He was ruthless with particular communities or peoples which opposed him, but made no attempt to undo the enfranchisement or organization of Italy as a whole. In 89 the Po valley had been placed on the road to assimilation with peninsular Italy; Cn. Pompeius Strabo, the father of Magnus, gave the status of a Latin *colonia* to those communities in the Po valley and Liguria which were not already either Roman or Latin. Full Roman citizenship was delayed for more than a generation, but was granted by Caesar.

I have already drawn attention to the spread of the urban model in Italy. But what happened after the enfranchisement of Italy was of a rather different kind. Amidst all our ignorance, it is clear that new Roman communities were equipped with relatively homogeneous constitutions, appropriate to urban societies. Rome in fact found it difficult to think other than in terms of urban centres when dealing with other communities. The enfranchisement of Italy thus provided, with the creation of new Roman communities, a powerful spur to the development of urban centres. This in itself is likely to have been in turn a factor making for the Romanization of Italy.

There are at least two levels at which the phenomenon of Romanization needs to be considered. It is probably easiest to begin with the level of the élite. The Roman system had always been characterized by a relatively high degree of élite mobility. It was naturally rare for a man, none of whose family had ever held office, to reach the consulship, as did C. Marius and Cicero. But the ascent of a family to the consulship over several generations was a common enough phenomenon; and a man who ennobled himself and his descendants by being the first of his family to achieve the consulship or other high office was known as a *novus homo*, new man. Families from newly enfranchised communities, throughout the history of the republic, waited perhaps for a generation and could then begin their ascent to high office. The story was no different with the mass enfranchisement of Italy after 91–89; by the time of Augustus, the Roman Senate was full of members of the élites of recently enfranchised communities, many of whose descendants went on to hold the consulship. The avenues of advancement were those which had always applied, friendship with those already in positions of power, wealth, oratorical skill, military expertise (see Ch. 20 for Italian authors of the late Republic).

Much more difficult to assess is the Romanization of the population of Italy as a whole; we must admit that we can know nothing of the culture of an illiterate farm labourer, too poor even to be drafted into the armies of Rome. All our knowledge relates, if not to the élite, at least to those close to it. Given this limitation, there are four indicators worth considering of the survival or submergence of distinctive local cultures in Italy: language, religious practices, family structures, and funeral rites. The last, if valid, is particularly useful, since there is substantial archaeological evidence.

The evidence of language is striking. Northern Etruria remained substantially untouched by Roman influence down to 91. It is also an area where inscriptions in Latin down to the same date are conspicuous by their absence. In the generation after Sulla, however, bilingual inscriptions make their appearance, and within the lifetime of Cicero Etruscan had virtually disappeared. The case of Samnium is harder to assess, since the destruction wrought by Sulla in 82–81 means that there was little in the way of urban life till Caesar. Inscriptions in the local language, one of the varieties of what is known to modern scholars as Oscan, certainly disappear; but the argument from silence is dangerous. Further south in Lucania, however, the same pattern occurs, without any reason to suppose that Sulla was responsible; and indeed inscriptions in Oscan are here replaced by inscriptions in Latin. It is worth citing the evidence provided by the recent excavations at Rossano di Vaglio; here a rural Lucanian sanctuary was absorbed after Sulla into the administrative structures of the near-by city of Potentia.

The evidence for religious practices and family structures is exiguous; what there is suggests that during the lifetime of Cicero traces of religious diversity, such as different local calendars, disappeared and rules governing marriage and inheritance became steadily more uniform. The evidence relating to funerary practices is substantial, and is spread throughout Italy; it consistently portrays the replacement of distinctive local practices, often of great antiquity, by a relatively uniform set of customs. There remained, of course, enormous variety according to the wealth of the deceased, but that is another matter.

TOMBSTONE FROM S. ANGELO IN FORMIS, near Capua (first half of first century BC), a good example of funerary sculpture in late-Republican Italy. The general type of the commemorative relief has Greek antecedents, but the style of the figures is Italic, and the motif of full-length portraits within a deep-sunk field particularly associated with the Capua region. In the panel below is a scene interpreted as the sale of a slave. The inscription records that the stone was set up by the freedman M. Publilius Satyr for himself and for his own freedman Stepanus.

If it is true that the period between Sulla and Augustus saw an enormous advance in the level of Romanization achieved, it remains to ask why. The principal reason is to be sought in the process of veteran settlement between 59 and the early 20s BC. Beginning in 59 with the veterans from the eastern wars of Cn. Pompeius Magnus, enormous numbers of men, uprooted from their homes, serving together for long periods, were settled in groups far from their place of birth. The consequence for the next generation was the shattering of the existing social fabric both in the places of origin and in the communities where these men were settled. The Italian society of the early Empire which resulted was perhaps the most important and the most lasting consequence of the Roman revolution.

Further Reading

M. Beard and M.H. Crawford, *Rome in the Late Republic* (London, 1984), as well as providing a critical account of the main problems, contains a full account of the available translations of the ancient sources for Republican history as a whole and a full bibliography for the end of the Republic.

T. Cornell and J. Matthews, *Atlas of the Roman World* (Oxford, 1982) contains a good general account of Roman history and an excellent selection of maps and pictures.

Among histories of Rome, note R. M. Ogilvie, *Early Rome and the Etruscans* (London, 1976) and M. H. Crawford, *The Roman Republic* (London, 1978); H. H. Scullard, *History of the Roman World 753-146 BC*, 4th edn. (London, 1981), and *From the Gracchi to Nero,* 4th edn. (London, 1976); P.A. Brunt, *Social Conflicts in the Roman Republic* (London. 1971).

T. R. S. Broughton, *Magistrates of the Roman Republic* (New York, 1960), provides a year by year list of magistrates, with references to the sources and modern discussions.

For an analysis of recent work in the area, see M.H. Crawford, 'Rome and Italy', in *Journal of Roman Studies* 71 (1981), 153-60. Important books are E. T. Salmon, *Roman Colonisation* (London, 1969); *The Making of Roman Italy* (London, 1983), despite its narrowly political focus; A. N. Sherwin-White, *The Roman Citizenship*, 2nd. edn. (Oxford, 1973); E. Badian, *Foreign Clientelae* (Oxford, 1958); P. A. Brunt, *Italian Manpower* (Oxford, 1971); E. Gabba, *Republican Rome, the Army and the Allies* (Oxford, 1976); T. P. Wiseman, *New Men in the Roman Senate* (Oxford, 1971); E. T. Salmon, *Samnium and the Samnites* (Cambridge, 1967).

For the Roman political system, see H. F. Jolowicz and B. Nicholas, *Historical Introduction to Roman Law* (Cambridge, 1972); E. S. Staveley, *Greek and Roman Voting and Elections* (London, 1972).

For Roman religion, see the seminal article by J. A. North, 'Conservatism and change in Roman religion', in *Papers of the British School at Rome* 44 (1976), 1-12; also J. H. W. G. Liebeschuetz, *Continuity and Change in Roman Religion* (Oxford, 1979).

On the working of Roman politics, see M. Gelzer, *The Roman Nobility* (Oxford, 1969); P. A. Brunt, '*Nobilitas* and *Novitas*', in *Journal of Roman Studies* 72 (1982), 1-17; K. Hopkins, *Death and Renewal* (Cambridge, 1983), ch. 2.

On Rome and the outside world, see K. Hopkins, *Conquerors and Slaves* (Cambridge, 1978), ch. 1; W. V. Harris, *War and Imperialism in Republican Rome, 327-70 B.C.* (Oxford, 1979); J. A. North, 'The Development of Roman Imperialism', in *Journal of Roman Studies* 71 (1981), 1-9; A. D. Momigliano, *Alien Wisdom* (London, 1975); W. V. Harris (ed.), *The Imperialism of the Roman Republic* (Rome, 1984).

For the transformation of Italy in the age of revolution, see L. Keppie, *Colonisation and Veteran Settlement in Italy 47-14 B.C.* (London, 1983).

17

The Expansion of Rome

ELIZABETH RAWSON

The Conquests of Rome

POLYBIUS thought that no one could be so worthless or indolent as not to wish to know how, and under what sort of government, the Romans had succeeded in less than fifty-three years in subjecting almost the whole inhabited world to their rule (below, pp. 639 ff.). We are now to consider Rome's expansion abroad from the beginning of the Punic Wars: but we will carry on the story after Polybius' death to the end of the Republic.

In 264 BC Rome controlled the whole of the Italian peninsula, except the Po valley ('Cisalpine Gaul'), and her defeat of Pyrrhus (above, p. 405) had attracted Greek interest. In that year a Roman army crossed to Sicily, partly to prevent the Carthaginians taking Messana and dominating the straits, and after twenty years' fighting, during which Rome turned herself into a naval power, she expelled the Carthaginians from the island. Part of it was left to friendly Syracuse and other Greek cities; for part Rome seems to have taken responsibility. In 237 she seized (on a poor excuse, but the islands were strategically vital now that Rome and Carthage were foes) Sardinia and Corsica, previously controlled by Carthage. In 227 two new magistrates were elected, for the 'jobs', *prouinciae*, of Sicily and Sardinia. Rome had also just intervened against the newly expansive and piratical Illyrians across the Adriatic, where a protectorate, including some Greek states, was established along the coast. When another and desperate clash with Carthage occurred (the Second Punic War) and Hannibal invaded Italy in 218, Roman forces were sent against his base in Spain, which they were not to leave again, though the peninsula was not wholly pacified till Augustus' day. Finally Hannibal was penned into the toe of Italy, and Scipio, who had fought with success in Spain and won over many tribes, moved the war to Africa itself, to which Hannibal was recalled only to be defeated at Zama in 202. Carthage lost territory to Roman allies in Africa and became another client state. On the other hand, the whole of Sicily became a province, for Syracuse had proved disloyal.

Hannibal's alliance with Philip V of Macedon had also led to Roman troops being deployed across the Adriatic, and finally to the Second Macedonian War, in which the King was defeated by T. Flamininus, though the kingdom was allowed to survive, and Greece proper was declared 'free' in 196; Roman influence in the whole area was, however, now paramount. Thus integrated into the world of the great Hellenistic powers, Rome involved herself in a victorious struggle, led by Scipio and his brother, against Antiochus III of Syria; again, though Rome annexed no territory, she cut down the power of Syria and arranged the affairs of the eastern Mediterranean as she pleased, to the advantage of her friends, the kingdom of Pergamum and the island republic of Rhodes.

The Romans after a time accused King Perseus, Philip's son, of disloyalty; he was crushed in 167 by Aemilius Paullus at the battle of Pydna, and Macedon was split into four tributary republics ('First', 'Second', and so on). There was no war with Egypt, the third of the great kingdoms that had emerged after Alexander's

GOLD COIN (STATER) OF T. QUINCTIUS FLAMININUS, issued after the Roman general had defeated Philip V of Macedon at Cynoscephalae in 197 BC. On the obverse the head of Flamininus, rendered in romantic Hellenistic manner; on the reverse a figure of Victory. The occasion of the issue was probably the famous proclamation of 'freedom' for Greece in 196.

death, but she too almost became a protectorate, as was dramatically shown when a Roman envoy drew a circle with his staff around the person of the invading Antiochus IV and told him to order retreat before he stepped out of it. It is up to this point, from 220 BC, that Polybius' fifty-three years run. The fact that Rome had annexed little territory did not make him doubt that she had an Empire; the Greeks were used to seeing these based on alliances or leagues.

Polybius lived on to recount the anti-Roman movements in Macedon and Greece in 148, which were brutally put down, the city of Corinth being utterly destroyed. Macedon became a province and its governor was made responsible for Greece. Almost simultaneously Carthage, harassed by Rome's ally the King of Numidia, revolted, and was wiped from the face of the earth by the younger Scipio; her territory became the province of Africa. In 133 the last king of Pergamum died without a legitimate heir, leaving his kingdom to Rome (his motives are to some extent disputed), and part of it became the province of Asia. The need to safeguard the route to Spain, and obligations to Rome's old ally Massilia, led to fighting in Transalpine Gaul, and finally the establishment of a province in the area still called Provence.

However, towards the end of the second century Rome met with a number of defeats at the hands of barbarian enemies, notably Jugurtha in Africa and the northern Cimbri and Teutones who had invaded Italy (both wars were in the end successfully concluded by C. Marius). She was also preoccupied by internal problems brought to a head by the brothers Gracchi (above, pp. 411 f.), and from 91 with the 'Social' War against the Italian allies (above, pp. 413 f.). Upon this followed the first real civil war, leading to Sulla's brief dictatorship and his restoration of senatorial government. Understandably only small gains were made abroad in this period. Neglect of the East, which had allowed the rise of Mithridates of Pontus, who seized all Asia Minor, exploiting anti-Roman sentiment, and whose forces even invaded Greece, was ultimately remedied. The Roman general Pompey (below, pp. 463 ff.) decided that more direct rule was needed. He set up provinces in Syria (where the Seleucid kingdom had been in decline since its original defeat by Rome, with resulting disorder) and in Bithynia–Pontus in northern Asia Minor; he enlarged the 'province' of Cilicia, where Rome had for some time been trying to deal with pirates based on the wild coast. The rest of the East was put under selected kings and dynasts, at least some of whom paid tribute to Rome. The Empire had now reached the Euphrates, and Rome was in direct touch with Armenia and Parthia beyond it, kingdoms where the Greek cultural influence predominant in most of the Near East began to wear very thin.

Only a few years later, in 58 BC, C. Julius Caesar (below, pp. 467 f.) became governor of southern Gaul and embarked on a war of conquest in the centre and north which even took him across the Rhine and the English Channel. He failed to make Britain tributary, but Gaul was organized as a province. This was the first of Rome's conquests remote from the Mediterranean or its extension the Black Sea, and led on to the successful Alpine and Balkan, and unsuccessful German, campaigns of Augustus. However the attempt by M. Crassus, the third member of the so-called First Triumvirate (below, pp. 469 ff.), to invade Parthia was a disaster, and the next major annexation completed the circuit of the Mediterranean: Cleopatra was encouraged by her Roman lover, Antony, to rebuild Egypt's power in the eastern Mediterranean, but they were defeated by Antony's rival for supremacy at Rome, the future Emperor Augustus.

The Evidence

No one disputes that the consequences for Rome of these conquests were vast, economically, socially, culturally, and politically. But to particularize raises hotly debated issues. The difficulties are due partly to the shortcomings of our sources. Polybius wrote a full and pretty reliable account of most of Rome's wars from

SHIPWRECK AT LA MADRAGUE DE GIENS, off the south coast of France, near Toulon (first century BC). The wreck is shown in the course of excavation, and most of the cargo of amphorae and Campanian pottery has been removed, exposing the timbers of the hull. The amphorae are of Italian origin, and the majority bear the stamps of a producer based near the Lake of Fondi, home of the famous Caecuban vintage.

264 to 146, but his later books survive only in fragments and for the earlier ones he depended on previous writers whom he knew to be biased. Some of the missing parts of Polybius can be reconstructed from Livy, who sensibly used him for Rome's relations with the East; but Livy, who is again incompletely preserved (only in epitomes and derivatives after 167) also used the so-called annalistic tradition of his Latin-writing predecessors. Its reliability, and the extent to which it draws on documentary evidence, is disputed, but it certainly often distorts events for patriotic or dramatic ends (the desire of most historians to provide moral *exempla*, and their training in rhetoric, must be borne in mind). Of authors later than the Augustan Livy, the Greek historian Appian, who recounts many

of Rome's wars, is notable, as is Plutarch, though the main interest of his *Lives* is in individual character. For Caesar's campaigns we have his own *Commentaries*, often disingenuous; and Cicero's speeches and letters throw much light on his own period, and incidentally on earlier ones. (A fuller account of the Roman historians is given in Ch. 26 below.)

To some extent the literary sources can be supplemented, especially in the Greek world, where there was a tradition of recording documents on stone (in the West bronze was often used for the less common inscriptions, and might be melted down for re-use). In all areas what survives does so by chance, often in fragments; but recent discoveries have changed our ideas in many respects. Archaeology proper shows us how in some parts of Italy in the second century subsistence agriculture gave way to larger slave-run estates producing for a market, and documents the growth of overseas trade with these more developed

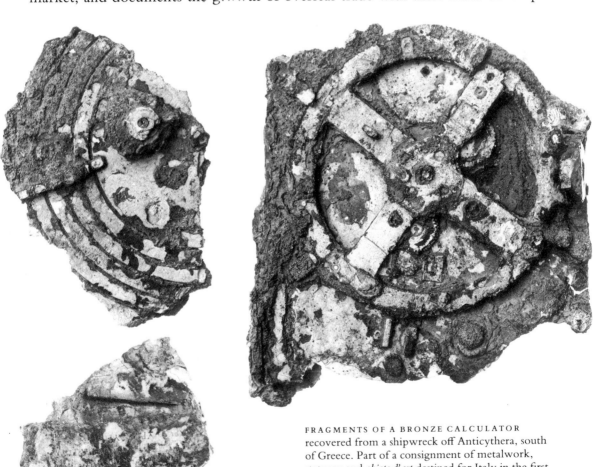

FRAGMENTS OF A BRONZE CALCULATOR recovered from a shipwreck off Anticythera, south of Greece. Part of a consignment of metalwork, statuary and *objets d'art* destined for Italy in the first half of the first century BC, the mechanism employed a highly elaborate system of inter-meshing gears to operate a series of rotating dials which indicated the conjunctions of various calendars and astronomical phenomena. It was probably operated by hand.

areas. But not all Italy has been, or can be, surveyed; and outside it most of the work has been concentrated in, this time, the western Mediterranean. And much trade leaves no trace; pottery and marble may survive, but what of slaves, corn, dried fish, spices? Still, we know that black-glazed table ware was exported from the western coast of central Italy to Gaul and Spain from the earlier second century, with an increasing number of the amphoras or wine-jars, of which it has been estimated that perhaps 40,000,000 were imported into Gaul between 150 BC and the end of the Republic. Wrecks of ships on their way to Rome from the East have also been found; works of art old and new (statues, that is; paintings would perish) have been recovered, with in one case such curiosities as old Greek inscriptions and a complex astronomical device. Finally numismatics, as coin hoards and other discoveries gradually fix the date of Greek and Roman issues, can tell us something of economic changes. But controversy still rages, for example about why, on several crucial occasions, Rome went to war.

Roman Imperialism

The central debate turns on the question: in what sense was Rome imperialist? It was once thought that Rome was not an aggressive power; that she had few contacts with the Greek world in the third century, apart from the old alliance with isolated Massilia, and was uninterested in the East: during the Hannibalic War her treaty with the Aetolians in northern Greece claimed only the movable booty from joint operations, the real estate being left to the Aetolians, and she campaigned without energy, making few, if any, other formal alliances. She was slow to annex, for example setting up in 167 four artificial 'independent' republics in Macedon. She sometimes refused lands bequeathed by will—notably Egypt in the early first century BC—while it took her twenty years to get round to organizing Cyrenaica, left to her in 96. It was further argued that the historians always showed Rome to have declared war for defensive reasons, or to assist allies to whom she had obligations and a reputation for *fides* (good faith) to keep up. For the idea of the *bellum iustum*, 'just war', undertaken in self-defence or to aid allies, obsessed her. Rome perhaps sometimes believed wrongly that she was under threat; there has been argument over whether there was, or Rome thought there was, a secret pact between Philip and Antiochus III in 200, and whether Perseus was really preparing war in the 170s. But if Rome's fears were mistaken, this showed her ignorance of the outside world. Polybius' belief that Rome aimed at world dominion was dismissed as the opinion of a Greek theorist, influenced by Thucydides on Athenian imperialism or by the career of Alexander; his own narrative refuted his general interpretation.

It was also argued that Rome rarely acted from economic motives. Policy was made by senators, and they were forbidden by the Lex Claudia of 218 to own ships over a certain size, and barred from the lucrative public contracts which included supplying the armies and in time collecting provincial taxes. (Anyway such activities were thought low.) There soon came to be tension between the Senate and the contractors, *publicani*, who were mostly of the wealthy class later known as *equites* or knights, whose interests the Senate would oppose; some of the mincs of Macedon were shut after 167 to prevent exploitation by the *publicani*. In addition, many of the *negotiatores* ('men of affairs'), engaged in money-lending, banking, trade, and even agriculture, whom we know from literary and epigraphic sources to have settled all over the Mediterranean world in the second century, were mostly, so it was held, until the Social War not citizens, but Italian allies, for whom Rome felt little responsibility. The names indeed of many are not Latin, and point to Oscan-speaking southern Italy, especially Campania (for instance, Stlaccius, found on the island mart of Delos). It has even been argued that most of what trade there was (it is still often minimized) was designed to supply Roman armies and Roman settlers, not to make a profit from the natives, though it had to be admitted that in the first century generals and *publicani* influenced policy, and Roman rule was detested for its greed.

This picture will not altogether do. Rome was in touch with the Greek world from an early date. And Roman society was militaristic. Polybius paints the Romans as above all soldiers of great discipline and ferocity: sacking a city, they even kill the animals. The Senate liked to keep the army in training. Young aristocrats were expected in Polybius' time to serve ten campaigns before standing for office; the top offices were basically military ones. Military prowess was valued above all things—*uirtus* meant primarily valour. The highest ambition was for a triumph, the pompous celebration of a major victory by a grand procession exhibiting the spoils of war, in which the victor was for a day almost equated with a god. (Triumphs proliferated in the second century and had to be regulated.) Only less regarded was the thanksgiving to the gods decreed by the Senate in the name of a victorious commander. Campaigns provoked by generals to earn a triumph undoubtedly occurred, even before the first century when the Senate lost control. A correspondent wished the unwarlike Cicero, then governor of Cilicia, 'enough fighting for a triumph', and he was himself shamefacedly eager for one. Admittedly, generals were often also anxious to end a war and take the troops home to grace the event.

If enough members of the oligarchy were to have a chance of distinction—and there was great pressure on the sons of aristocrats to emulate their ancestors—wars had to be almost continuous. There was resentment against men who, like Scipio, hogged big commands for years, and there was jockeying for appointment if a good war was in prospect. There might be disagreement about where to fight, but not about fighting somewhere. Roman aristocratic tradition was reinforced by Greek influence. Scipio already perhaps modelled himself on Alexander; Pompey notoriously did, adopting his hair-style and letting panegyrists exaggerate his youth at the time of his eastern conquests; Caesar is said to have wept in youth at the thought of the Macedonian, who had conquered the world at an age when he himself had done nothing. But there is public as well as personal glory; first-century Romans were intensely proud of their world Empire and set the globe on their coins.

The Economic Motive

All booty was legally at the general's disposal, though he was expected to give some to the Treasury and use some himself on public works, notably temples vowed in battle. Such buildings, apart from providing employment (to men who would support their employer at elections) kept a man's name, often emblazoned on the façade, before the public. And, as the standard of luxury—and later of electoral bribery—rose, spoil provided the quickest way to the wealth needed by the competitive upper class.

It was also the quickest way to wealth for the troops, to whom the general distributed part of the official booty—there was doubtless unofficial booty too, in spite of the rules. Although the really poor were not eligible for the army till the late second century, the (probably increasingly small) small-holders serving were often in debt to richer neighbours, and doubtless anyway eager to make their fortunes. Later, in a letter of 43 BC, D. Brutus tells Cicero that he has led his men against some Alpine tribes to meet their wishes. During the Italian wars victory had often led to conquered land being parcelled out among poor citizens. This happened much less after wars overseas, though the state acquired some land to rent out, to foreigners or citizens; but a few veterans were placed in the second century in Spain and the Balearics, and there was much settlement in Cisalpine Gaul. Gaius Gracchus, however, who, like his brother Tiberius, had a new vision of how the Empire could be used to support the poor of Rome, proposed colonies abroad; Saturninus, another demagogic tribune at the end of the second century, had a broad plan of transmarine settlement for both veterans, now including many landless, and the urban *plebs*. But in practice Caesar was the first to plant both classes abroad on any large scale.

It has also been suggested that, till the Social War, Rome's only way to profit from her alliances in Italy, since the allies paid no taxes, was to call them out to fight. Most Italian peoples had their own military tradition, and if at times they found Rome's demands oppressive, they took pride in their share in her victories, which many came to feel earned them a right to political equality and Roman citizenship. They did not always get an equal share of booty, but the grand buildings set up at some Italian shrines shortly before the Social War may show its deployment by local magnates; equally, the *negotiatores* hailing from Campania and elsewhere may have sometimes begun operations abroad by investing the profits of war. Pompeii documents the prosperity of Campania, partly the result of such *negotia*.

Booty included slaves—either those already such, or prisoners of war (the Romans perhaps rarely allowed ransom). Marxists, exaggerating the admittedly great importance of slavery in ancient society, have supposed that Roman conquests were fuelled by the need for slaves. No ancient source hints at this, but the sources are coy about the slave trade. Masses of slaves did result from Rome's wars; Aemilius Paullus, the victor of Pydna, is said to have sold 150,000 inhabitants of Epirus in northern Greece, on the Senate's order to deal harshly with the area; it became a virtual desert. Slaves were also acquired by trade; we are told that some Gallic chiefs were so fond of Italian wine they would give a slave for a single jar, and there is literary evidence for Gallic slaves in Italy. The geographer Strabo says that at the height of its prosperity about 100 BC Delos could handle 10,000 slaves a day (some originally kidnapped by pirates or slave-dealers, some foundlings or enslaved for debt, many bought from barbarian tribes in Thrace and elsewhere). It is not strange that servile revolts broke out in Italy and Sicily

REVERSE OF SILVER COIN (DENARIUS) STRUCK BY CN. LENTULUS (76-75 BC). The symbols denote Rome's world power by land and by sea: a sceptre with wreath, a globe, and a rudder. The obverse shows a male bust representing the Spirit of the Roman People (Genius Populi Romani).

in the late second and early first centuries. Though the great expansion in the use of slaves in Italy on the land and on a smaller scale for skilled jobs, including teaching (these were mostly easterners) seems a result, rather than a cause, of the first transmarine conquests, it is likely that later the makers of Roman policy gave some thought to the supply; landowners needed slaves more than anyone, though they were used in every type of enterprise and small men too would profit from low prices.

The growing evidence for commerce after the Hannibalic War also makes it unlikely that senators were totally uninterested in trade. Italian exports were largely in agricultural produce, wine, and to some extent oil; great landowners may have traded in the name of freedmen, who could legally own big ships and were still bound to assist their masters, or sold their produce, sometimes still on the tree, to a merchant, as the elder Cato's agricultural treatise indicates. A gentlemanly distance was thus combined with profit. Even before Sulla enlarged the Senate (below, p. 462) there was intermarriage with rich non-senatorial families; and it has been shown that many of the far-flung *negotiatores* did come from parts of Italy given Roman citizenship well before the Social War. Certainly after Sulla many new senators had close relatives involved in business matters, while some probably refused to drop their own old interests; Cicero tells us in

426 The Expansion of Rome

70 that the Lex Claudia and similar measures were disobeyed, though Caesar may have reasserted them in 59. The rich also depended on luxuries from the East to sustain an increasingly sumptuous way of life; works of fine and applied art, rare foods and wines, skilled slaves, spices transmitted from distant climes.

Senators might lend money at interest; Cato, in the mid second century, did so through a freedman to finance trading voyages, and later senators made a corner in lending to ambassadors at Rome. It seems also that in the first century they could or did take shares in the great companies of *publicani* now farming some provincial taxes. Finally, in spite of friction between the classes, the system of patronage will always have meant that many business men could put pressure on individual senators to support their interests. It is thus hard to maintain that the Senate almost never had an eye to commercial interest, let alone other types of economic advantage.

Cicero indeed claims that Rome often went to war for her merchants. This is partly true, for example, of the First Illyrian War, though at that time and place they will in truth have been mostly Italians (trade in this region is not yet well documented archaeologically); but there was also mistreatment of envoys to avenge and perhaps appeals to answer. In 187 Rome laid down that Romans and Latins (and possibly Italians) should be exempt from harbour dues at Ambracia, and this may not have been the isolated action our sources suggest. The making of Delos a free port in 167 weakened Rhodes and benefited Roman and Italian traders. And Cicero indicates that some time before 129 Rome forbade Trans-alpine peoples (in southern Gaul; attempts to explain the notice away are perverse) to plant vines and olives, perhaps to protect her own trade in wine and oil. Admittedly this seems a unique measure; and Rome did not, for example, impose a common coinage over her sphere of influence, unlike Athens.

The one form of trade in which the state took a direct interest was that in corn. The urban *plebs* must not starve, the armies must be provisioned. With the increase in population at Rome corn (mainly wheat) from abroad had to be provided regularly, not just in crises (the rest of Italy still fed itself or even sent grain to Rome). Sicily annually gave up a tithe of its harvest as tax (and had from 73 to sell another to Rome at a fixed price if needed). After 146 the corn of Africa became vital. We now know that on one occasion in the second century a Roman magistrate got the Thessalians, in northern Greece, to bring corn to Rome; however, till the city became dependent on Egypt in the imperial age, the East was not often drawn on. Private merchants were responsible for the transfer of corn to Rome, but the Senate must have kept an eye on the situation. Most other basic raw materials, such as wood, were available in Italy, though the mines of Spain were important, and those of Macedon were soon reopened.

The Treasury became increasingly dependent on foreign revenues. At first Rome did not, it seems, always impose taxes, but just demanded reparations, or large sums for which no special justification was claimed; Antiochus III was mulcted of 1,500 talents. In civilized Sicily Rome took over the tax system

AGORA OF THE ITALIANS ON DELOS. Built with endowments from several private benefactors in the late second century BC, this building served as the social and business centre of the Italian community in the Aegean's greatest slave-market. In the foreground, two columns of the portico which surrounded the central court have been reconstructed; behind lies part of an entablature inscribed with the names of the original sponsors.

existing under Syracuse, but it was perhaps gradually that proper taxes were imposed in Spain and the mines let. Contractors' fees, 'indemnities', taxes, and booty became so valuable that direct tax on citizens was abolished after Pydna, even though the armies, now serving all year round, were increasingly expensive to maintain. Taxes were sometimes lowered when an area was reorganized, but new customs dues, for example, were also imposed. Later, particularly after the Social War and Sulla's dictatorship, the state, with heavy wars on hand, faced severe financial problems; it now had to pay for the large part of the army previously financed by the Italian allies, and soon C. Gracchus' corn subsidies in Rome, abolished by Sulla, were reintroduced. Cicero claimed in 66 that the only province to provide a surplus after defence and administration was Asia. But Plutarch says the tax income was doubled by Pompey's new arrangements. Gaul was also to contribute, and Egypt even more.

Finally, many senators made private fortunes from the Empire. Polybius believed that until his time Roman magistrates were remarkable for probity. Cato certainly reiterated that he had not made a sesterce from his service abroad. But Cicero's speeches illustrate the behaviour too common in his day, though we need not think that every governor was a Verres, emulated in rapacity by all his staff. Cicero himself was honest enough, and says in a letter from Cilicia that the other governors then in the East were all decent (though his own predecessor, Ap. Pulcher, was 'not a man, but some sort of wild beast'). The *Verrine Orations* detail every possible abuse, from conniving with pirates to stealing statues on such a scale that the Sicilian tourist trade was ruined. From the second century governors could be prosecuted for extortion, but it was hard for provincials to organize a trial at Rome, or to secure conviction, even at periods when it was the *equites*, not the senators, who formed, or formed a majority on, the jury.

The Reluctance to Annex

If senators and *equites*, private soldiers and the public Treasury, even the urban *plebs*, all profited from Rome's expansion, why was she so slow to annex territories that fell into her lap? Occasionally moral reluctance might be mooted: Flamininus refused to abolish the kingdom of Macedon at the Aetolians' demand, saying that it was unRoman to annihilate an enemy. There was hesitation about the final razing of Carthage, which was felt hard to justify to public, especially Greek, opinion; and the idea that states need an external threat to prevent corruption and decline was perhaps put forward. Not that the Romans doubted the morality of ruling an Empire as such; when the provocative Greek philosopher Carneades, in a lecture at Rome in 155, suggested that justice would demand that they should give up their conquests and return to shepherds' huts, there was outrage. At most, individual wars might be attacked as inspired by one's opponents' greed: thus Cato opposed a project of war with Rhodes in 167, and many objected to Crassus' Parthian campaign.

But it is significant that many people did just as well where annexation had not taken place. 'Kings, nations, and cities', even if technically 'free', were an integral part of the Empire. Some kings already claimed in the second century to be mere agents of Rome. Free states could be expected, or bound by treaty, to send aid in war; an increasing proportion of Rome's forces, especially in ships and cavalry, were 'auxiliary'. Where individuals are concerned, Verres carried off treasures from 'free' as well as from 'stipendiary' cities. Great Romans were patrons of dynasts and communities outside, as well as inside, the provinces, thus gaining power, prestige, and even profit—the line between gift and bribe was fine, as the friends of King Jugurtha of Numidia found. We can see how the Claudii, over two and a half centuries, extended their *clientela* in Greek-speaking lands, or how the Domitii Ahenobarbi, with an ancestor who had fought in southern Gaul and estates on the west coast of Italy, built up influence in the western Mediterranean. (A patron might be able to protect his clients from mistreatment; if he mistreated them himself it was hard for others to intervene.)

Trade and money-lending could be carried on almost better where there was no Roman governor for oppressed natives to appeal to, and where any action against *negotiatores* could be represented as anti-Roman. The wine trade stretched up into central Gaul well before Caesar's time, and when Cicero was in the East the unfortunate young King Ariobarzanes of Cappadocia ('Pious' and 'Pro-Roman' by style) was deep in debt to Roman moneylenders, including M. Brutus, that 'honourable man', and Pompey, a flock of whose agents were dunning him for interest. There is no sign that *negotiatores* wanted annexation; Marius, a friend of the *equites*, did not extend the province of Africa. But Rome's power was there to protect or at least avenge them; Jugurtha's massacre of the hated *Italici* had been one of the causes of the war, and it is significant that if they called themselves *Italici*, the Greeks called them all *Rhōmaioi*, Romans.

Roman conservatism is also relevant. Rome had stretched the idea of the city-state to its limit, but not abandoned it; citizens had to vote in person, and not too many of the upper class at least should be on business abroad. The Senate, until Sulla, consisted of about 300 men, in practice all ex-magistrates; more provinces meant more offices. And the oligarchy, though continually replenished from wealthy outsiders—Marius was one—would not wish the process to be too rapid. It also feared individuals acquiring *regnum*, quasi-monarchic power, for which prolonged absence in a distant province could provide the base—though so might a war not ending in annexation. Sulla attempted to control ambitious governors by a law (flouted by Caesar in Gaul) forbidding among other things leaving one's province with an army without senatorial permission. The Senate set its face against annexing Egypt in the earlier first century partly because the untrustworthy and greedy Crassus wanted to be involved in it.

Furthermore, in the third and second centuries the army was not a standing one, but in theory raised annually, chiefly from the peasantry. Long and hard campaigns were unpopular with the troops, especially in Spain, not an area as rich in booty as the East. Cato said in 167 that Macedonia could not be annexed, because it could not be defended (in part from barbarians on its frontiers). The Romans indeed became anxious at this time about a decline in military quality, partly due to the decline, in some areas, of the peasant class; this was followed by a period, already mentioned, of military disasters, and that, as also noted, by one of financial stringency. No wonder many places were left to defend and police themselves.

Some peoples, too, were attached to their native rulers and better left to them. And where the Greek cities were concerned, Rome discovered that 'liberation' was the best policy—perhaps already in Sicily and on the Adriatic coast, certainly when Flamininus, after defeating Philip of Macedon, declared Greece free at the Isthmian Games of 196, to frantic enthusiasm, and evacuated it completely. Some Greek cities had treaties with Rome (how many is disputed), which left them internal autonomy but bound them to give help in war (only treaties not described as equal bound them to respect the *maiestas* of the Roman People in all ways). Others were simply declared free unilaterally by Rome, a status which, it was in time discovered, she was ready unilaterally to revoke. The desire of Rhodes for a formal alliance in 167 shows this was felt to be some kind of safeguard; but in the end Rome refused to be shackled even by her treaties.

The policy of freedom for Greeks was not inspired by sentimental philhellenism, though Rome had more respect for Greek public opinion than she did for barbarian tribes, against whom her record was undoubtedly worse; rather its purpose was to reduce the power of Macedon and Syria. Rome did not apply it when it did not suit her: for example, she handed over various cities to her friends Pergamum and Rhodes. Under the Roman moral system, by which every *beneficium* had to be repaid by *officium* (act or sense of duty), the 'free' states were expected to conform to Rome's wishes. They did not always grasp this, a fact which contributed to the souring of Rome's relations with the various squabbling Greek states in the first half of the second century, until some of her generals began to behave to the Greeks, shortly before the war with Perseus, with brutality and contempt; this *noua sapientia*, as Livy called it, or new wisdom, was disapproved of by some prominent Romans, in vain.

The Protection of the Propertied Classes

In fact, even where the 'stipendiary' or tribute-paying inhabitants of a province were concerned, much responsibility was left to local communities, especially Greek cities. The Roman governor's duties were chiefly defence (hence the first of the great Roman roads outside Italy) and the administration of justice to Roman citizens; he could take cases between natives, but clearly not all of these, and Cicero says his (not unique) proclamation that he would take none was popular. The Romans made no attempt to impose uniformity; in some provinces a magistrate, the quaestor, was responsible for the collection of direct taxes, but probably only by overseeing local officials. In others both direct and indirect taxes were collected by tax-farmers, sometimes not even Roman, and these might have large staffs; even so, in some cases the cities did the basic work. These cities carried on their political life largely unhampered; when Pompey wanted to annex part of Pontus, he felt it best to found a group of Greek-style cities, if with larger territories than usual. As a result of this system the Romans, in spite of severe friction at times, developed a partnership with the upper classes who did much of the administration for them, and whom they defended against the cry of the poor for the division of land and abolition of debts that was sometimes heard.

Flamininus had left the cities of Greece in the hands of the well-off. Perseus appealed to the poor, though not only to them, for support; and anti-Roman feeling was often based on hostility to the rich—though it would be voiced by well-off leaders, jealous of whatever pro-Roman clique was in power, or genuinely idealistic or nationalistic. It is uncertain how far Rome intervened to make constitutions more oligarchic, as they tended to become; but we have on stone a letter from a governor of Macedon to a Peloponnesian city, of the late second century, which reveals that he has taken steps to crush social unrest there. Polybius, who came of a distinguished political family, thought a newly slavish adherence to Rome deplorable, but realized that dignified independence was only possible

INSCRIPTION RECORDING A LETTER FROM THE ROMAN GOVERNOR OF MACEDONIA. Addressed to the magistrates and council of the Achaean city of Dyme, the letter records measures taken by the proconsul Q. Fabius to deal with the ringleaders of a revolutionary movement: two of them have been condemned to death and a third sent to stand trial in Rome.

within narrow limits. He believed, however, that in spite of recent abuses and the new harshness Rome had given the Greek cities great benefits, and that the revolts of 148 were insane folly (these were again partly inspired by the poor, who would be less aware than the upper classes that Rome was too strong to resist).

Certainly Greek communities, from whatever motives, paid Rome every sort of honour. In early years her *fides*, the good faith to which communities were to entrust themselves, was much celebrated. From the early second century cults were founded to the goddess Roma (*Rhōmē* in Greek significantly means power); the poetess Melinno's hymn to Rome perhaps dates from this period. Cults were also set up to individuals, starting with Flamininus; Plutarch describes the ceremonies in his name still carried out in Euboea in his own day. The honour was gradually devalued: even Cicero was voted temples, which he refused in an attempt to keep the cities' expenditure within bounds. No wonder Roman statesmen began to feel themselves the equals of Hellenistic kings. Lesser honours—titles, statues—abounded, even for prominent *negotiatores*, such as the Cloatii who lent to and protected—or ran—the little town of Gytheum near Sparta in the early first century.

Even in the dark days of the Mithridatic War, when many places slaughtered the blood-sucking *negotiatores*, a few cities of Greece and Asia stayed loyal, if sometimes from traditional enmity to rebellious neighbours. Thus the Assembly at Aphrodisias in Asia Minor, where Rome honoured the shrine of Aphrodite, voted to go with every available man to help a Roman general, for 'without the protection of the Romans we do not even wish to live'. But the first century was a terrible time for many Greek cities. They suffered in the fighting against Mithridates, and Sulla exacted large sums to punish disloyalty and finance civil war. Piracy got out of hand, till Pompey suppressed it; so it seems did the *publicani*, till Caesar restricted their powers in Asia at least. Communities, like individuals, fell hopelessly in debt to Roman money-lenders. Cicero says in a speech of 66 (of course with an ulterior motive) 'it is hard to express, citizens, how loathed we are by foreign nations.' It was greed he blamed. The poverty of many cities is visible archaeologically; there was little new building. The East had not fully recovered when renewed civil wars broke out. Pompey and Caesar, Brutus and Cassius, Antony and Octavian, all financed their campaigns from Rome's subjects. When Judaea could not pay what Cassius demanded, he sold four towns and many officials into slavery; as Antony observed, this was unauthorised by the laws of war. Cassius also besieged the free city of Rhodes, so long a friend of Rome, and carried off all its wealth except the chariot of its patron god the Sun. An even older friend of Rome's, Massilia, had been taken by Caesar, for supporting Pompey.

And yet, through it all, many members of the upper class saw private and public advantage in—or no alternative to—supporting Rome. They cultivated ties with important Romans, whether in Rome themselves as ambassadors (a second-century inscription thanks a group of these for going round to the morning receptions of great nobles) or when putting up Roman governors on their way to, or on circuit in, the provinces. By the end of the Republic foreign *amici* had even begun to wield power in Rome as advisers to the great dynasts; Theophanes of Mytilene was an intimate of Pompey's, and L. Cornelius Balbus of Gades was Caesar's trusted agent. Though it had for long occasionally been granted as a reward for service in war, citizenship was first given on a larger scale by Caesar, in whose time the rule that Roman citizenship could not be combined with that of another state seems to have lapsed. The way was open for the gradual extension of privilege, ultimately even of senatorial rank, which was to hold the Empire together in succeeding centuries.

Hellenism at Rome

Co-operation between the Greek and Roman élites was possible because the Roman upper class, though loyal to much of its own tradition, became very Hellenized. Indeed, there were attempts to prove that the Romans *were* Greeks, descended not only from Trojan Aeneas, but from Evander the Arcadian (familiar from the *Aeneid*), or from Hercules, and their followers. Some scholars held that Latin was a dialect of Greek. The attitude of many Romans to Greeks and Greek culture was, it is true, ambiguous; they believed in their own superiority in war and statecraft (and Cicero said other systems of civil law were puerile). Many people suspected customs that seemed softening or apt to distract from serious matters. Close and often unhappy experience of second-century Greeks led to these being characterized as effeminate, time-serving, politically inept (a useful justification of Empire), loquacious, and prone to abstract argument at the wrong time. Perhaps they had degenerated; there *are* some men worthy of ancient Greece, concedes Cicero (more philhellene than most), warning his brother to be wary of intimacies in his province. And the inhabitants of the now Greek-speaking cities of the East might be thought inferior to 'real Greeks'. But in Athens itself, which, like Delphi, Rome had treated with respect, Cicero expressed dismay at the arrogant treatment of the locals by his (strictly upright) suite.

Few well-off Romans, however, could resist the attractions of civilized Greek life, and some realized that it was only from the Greeks that they could learn much that the rulers of the world needed to know. Rome had perhaps never been wholly out of touch with the Greek world. Many of her gods had been identified with Greek ones, her art derived from Greek art; some Romans must always have known some Greek, and even perhaps read some Greek books. But a new epoch dawned in the mid third century, with the first plays on the Greek model in Latin (below, pp. 438 ff.), and (it seems) more formal schooling, in both tongues. In the Hannibalic War new Greek cults (and even the Great Mother from Asia) were introduced, to protect the city. The sack of Syracuse in 212 marked for Polybius the start of a taste for Greek art (a pity, he thought; states should stick to their own traditions); certainly innumerable statues and paintings were to be carried off to Rome in the next centuries. The physical face of the city was transformed as it became a great capital, though Polybius shows that its rustic air was mocked by cosmopolitan visitors in his day, and a truly Greek architectural style came a little later; marble was not much used for building purposes till later still.

But the upper classes' way of life was soon transformed. Historians tended to see Roman history in terms of moral decline, especially into avarice and luxury, and liked to mark its stages; some thought the booty brought back from Asia in 190, including handsome furniture, initiated the process. Polybius stressed the defeat of Macedon at Pydna and the wealth it brought: the young went mad for the worst aspects of Greek manners, pederasty, banquets to the sound of music,

ROUND TEMPLE BY THE TIBER, probably to be identified as the temple of Hercules Victor: one of the rare examples of a Greek-style marble building in Rome before Augustan times. Sponsored in the late second century BC by the rich merchant M. Octavius Herrenus, it lacks the emphatic entrance and high podium of Roman Italic temples. The entablature is missing and the present roof is modern.

and so on. Cato had tried to outlaw, and then to tax prohibitively, various forms of luxury, and continued to inveigh against spending on handsome slaves or imported food, and adorning one's house with statues of the gods 'as though they were furniture'. But even Cato, as his buildings while censor and his own writings show, could not turn the clock back.

The crux of the matter was education, for to the Greeks their *paideia* was their culture. By tradition the upper-class Roman boy absorbed political and legal experience from his father's friends, and spent the campaigning season, from the age of seventeen, with the army. But the Greeks had developed a pattern of formal study, first of literature (primarily Homer), and then rhetoric and, for some, philosophy. Aemilius Paullus provided his sons with a bevy of Greek masters, even in music and hunting, and a philosopher doubling as drawing master. He also brought the royal library of Macedon to Rome, the first great Greek library to reach it. Polybius attests that there were now many Greek teachers there. Distinguished savants began to arrive, at first as envoys; the serious study of *grammatikē* was dated to the embassy of Crates of Pergamum, who broke his leg in an open sewer and lectured while immobilized. And in 155 Athens sent the heads of three philosophical schools, whose lectures caused a sudden rage for philosophy—though Cato, who thought philosophy 'mere gibberish', pressed the Senate to conclude their business quickly so that the young could return to learning from 'the laws and the magistrates'.

One must not exaggerate the depth of Greek influence at this period. There is evidence that Greek medicine was regarded with suspicion still, and in general the Romans were intellectually, as also artistically, clumsy and immature. Poetry was more developed than prose, though even poetry was crude, as Horace complained. Cicero thought that it was only towards the end of the century that orators really profited from the study of rhetoric, which taught one how to organize and argue, as well as ornament, a speech. What we know of prose literature suggests that the Romans, like many primitive peoples, found generalization and abstraction hard. It was only from about 100 BC, too, that they began to use traditional Greek logical structure in treatises, with explicit definitions of the subject and all key concepts, and careful division of the material into parts or aspects, instead of piling up information hugger-mugger like Cato in his agricultural treatise. And it was in the first century that Latin was refined into the splendid vehicle it was to be for prose as well as poetry, and that Latin authors colonized many new prose genres, including the philosophic treatise.

It was only now too that it became common for young gentlemen to study rhetoric or philosophy at Athens or Rhodes (more independent Alexandria seems to have been out of bounds), though sons of *negotiatores* were often educated in the East, and might go through a city's *ephēbeia*, a state-run training course now more cultural than military. The Mithridatic wars swept Greek refugees and captives to Rome, both classes including learned men; also great libraries. And they detained many Romans long years in the East. (The historian Sallust dated

Rome's collapse into luxury from Sulla's campaigns in Asia.) Afterwards, Rome was equal to Alexandria as a magnet for Greek artists and intellectuals; there was patronage to be found almost nowhere else. And the Romans felt that they were, in one field after another, catching up with the Greeks. Cicero and his friend Atticus, admittedly exceptional men, must have met their Greek *amici* on fully equal terms.

In the West Rome felt she had little to learn, though an isolated work on agriculture was translated by official order from Punic. But the very fact that Romans rarely bothered to learn western languages helped to prepare for an extension of privilege here too; for the native élites gradually took on the colours of what seemed a superior, if at first often a hated, civilization. Trade and the influx of settlers helped to Romanize. Rome rarely consciously forwarded the process, though there was some encouragement in Spain of agriculture and urban settlement in the valleys, to replace less controllable pastoral communities. Though there was cultural prejudice against barbarians, there was little racial prejudice. If barbarians gave up their ways (beastly, like the habit of some Spanish tribes of washing their teeth in urine, or less so, like those of the Gauls, whom Caesar found intelligent and courageous, if unsteady), they could rise above the status of barbarians; the geographer Strabo's description of southern Spain in the time of Augustus is illuminating here. In fact, Balbus and his nephew from Gades (admittedly an ancient and civilized Punic city) entered the Senate—though the very idea shocked Cicero—before the son of Pompey's friend Theophanes of Mytilene did so; and the Balbi were soon followed by a few Gallic nobles who, or whose fathers, owed the citizenship to Caesar or Augustus. The lineaments of the Roman Empire in its maturity were taking shape.

Further Reading

A translation of Polybius is most easily available in the Loeb edition; there is a Penguin volume of selections, and F. W. Walbank's *Polybius* (California 1972) provides a good discussion of his work. Books of Livy are also available in the Penguin Classics, and there are Loebs of his entire work and those of the other authors mentioned. For Cicero see pp. 477 f.

The *Cambridge Ancient History* vol. viii (cf. also ix) gives a classic account, in the chapters by M. Holleaux, of the older view of Roman expansion; it is soon to be replaced by a new edition. For a more modern approach, see W. V. Harris, *War and Imperialism in Republican Rome 372–70 B.C.* (Oxford, 1979), with P. A. Brunt's chapter in *Imperialism in the Ancient World*, ed. P. D. A. Garnsey and C. R. Whittaker, (Cambridge, 1978) and J. A. North, 'The Development of Roman Imperialism' in *Journal of Roman Studies*, 1981. There is a good general account in C. Nicolet, *Rome et la conquête du monde méditerranéen*, ii: *Genèse d'un empire* (Paris, 1978); cf. also R. M. Errington, *The Dawn of Empire: Rome's Rise to World Power* (Ithaca, NY, 1972).

E. Badian has followed up his important *Foreign Clientelae* (Oxford, 1958), with *Roman Imperialism in the Late Republic* (Oxford, 1968) and *Publicans and Sinners* (Oxford, 1972). The first two sections of K. Hopkins, *Conquerors and Slaves* (Cambridge, 1978) deal with the transformation of Italian agriculture and economic life as a result of expansion; for *negotiatores* abroad, see A. J. N. Wilson, *Emigration from Italy in the Republican Age of Rome* (Manchester, 1966), less readable than

J. Hatzfeld, *Les Trafiquants italiens dans l'orient hellénique* (Paris, 1919). See also J. H. D'Arms, *Commerce and Social Standing in Ancient Rome*, (Cambridge, Mass. 1981); and M. H. Crawford, 'Rome and the Greek World: Economic Relations', *Econ. Hist. Review*, 1977; for the trade in corn, the first two chapters of G. Rickman, *The Corn Supply of Ancient Rome* (Oxford, 1980).

For study of individual figures, see F. W. Walbank, *Philip V of Macedon* (1940, repr. Hamden, Conn., 1967); R. M. Errington, *Philopoemen* (Oxford, 1969—Philopoemen was a leading figure in the Achaean League, admired by Polybius for his attitude to Rome); A. E. Astin, *Scipio Aemilianus* (Oxford, 1967) and *Cato the Censor*, (Oxford, 1978).

For the East, see A. H. M. Jones, *The Greek City from Alexander to Justinian* (Oxford, 1966) and D. Magie's massive *Roman Rule in Asia Minor* (Princeton, 1950), also D. C. Braund, *Rome and the Friendly King* (London, 1984) and R. Mellor, *Thea Rhômé: The Worship of the Goddess Roma in the Greek World* (1975), also, now A. N. Sherwin-White, *Roman Foreign Policy in the Greek East* (London 1984) and E. S. Gruen, *The Hellenistic World and the Coming of Rome* (California 1984), neither available when this chapter was written.

For Roman attitudes to foreigners, J. P. V. D. Balsdon's *Romans and Aliens* (London, 1979).

18

The First Roman Literature

❧❧

PETER BROWN

Plautus

LATIN literature begins with a bang, with a dazzling display of virtuoso verbal fireworks in twenty comedies written by Plautus between about 205 and 184 BC. The start of Latin literature is conventionally dated to the performance of a play by Livius Andronicus at Rome in 240 BC, but these comedies by Plautus are the earliest works to have survived complete. They are modelled on Greek comedies, nearly all of them 'New Comedies' written by Menander and his contemporaries about 100 years before Plautus. Like the Greek comedies, they are written in verse. Greek comedies were written for performance in a permanent theatre at Athens, as central elements in a religious festival. Roman comedies were also performed at religious festivals, but they were one source of entertainment among many, and they were performed on a temporary stage erected for the occasion. Romans of all classes came to watch. We cannot tell to what extent Plautus adapted his style to the taste of his audience and to what extent he helped to form that taste; but he has imported into his plays a boisterousness and a broadness of comic effect which remind us more of Aristophanes (though there is much less obscenity) than of Menander.

The Greek originals of Plautus' plays have not survived, though a tattered papyrus published in 1968 contains the lines on which *Bacchides* ('The Bacchis Sisters') 494–561 are based and enables us to study Plautus' techniques of adaptation at first hand for this stretch of the play. Plautus has preserved the basic plot and sequence of scenes, but he has cut two scenes altogether, and at one point he reverses the order of entry of two characters so as to eliminate a pause in the action where there was an act-break in the original (Roman comedy was usually written for continuous performance, and the act- and scene-divisions found in modern editions do not go back to the authors). The tormented monologue of a young man in love has had some jokes added to it. Passages which would have been spoken without musical accompaniment in the original Greek are turned into passages in longer lines to be accompanied on a reed-pipe. Plautus' play is still set in Athens, and his characters have Greek-sounding names; but he

DETAIL OF THE ALEXANDER MOSAIC (2nd century BC). The Persian king Darius, in his chariot, looks back in consternation as the onslaught of the Macedonians forces his charioteer to turn in flight.

HELLENISTIC EARRINGS. The smaller example (second or first century BC) is decorated with a cock coated with enamel; the larger one from Cyme (third century BC) carries a series of half-open buds suspended from chains.

INTERIOR OF THE TAZZA FARNESE (first century BC). This dish, carved from sardonyx, and possibly commissioned by Cleopatra, presents an allegory of the fertility of Egypt under the protection of Isis, Horus, and Osiris–Sarapis.

has changed most of them from the original, most significantly that of the scheming slave who dominates the action: Plautus calls him Chrysalus (Goldfinger) and adds some colour to his part by punning on this name (240 'Goldfinger's got to get his fingers on some gold', 361–2 'He'll change my name from Goldfinger to Gallowsbird', etc.). The papyrus shows that this character in the original had the less striking name of Syrus (The Syrian), which adds spice to Chrysalus' boast at 649 that he is superior to run-of-the-mill slaves with names like Parmeno and Syrus—though the joke would doubtless have been lost on most of Plautus' audience.

The plots of the plays show considerable variety. In *Amphitruo*, Jupiter descends to earth disguised as Amphitruo in order to seduce the latter's wife Alcumena; when Amphitruo himself arrives home from a military expedition the next day, he is dismayed to discover from his wife's reception of him that she believes him to have spent the previous night with her. *Mercator* ('The Businessman') shows father and son in love with the same girl, as does *Casina* (named after the girl)

BRONZE BUST OF MENANDER (*c*.342– 292 BC), the most famous exponent of the 'New' Comedy which inspired the Latin playwrights Plautus and Terence. In contrast to the rumbustious burlesque of Aristophanes and his contemporaries, Menander wrote situation comedies involving such stock characters as the stern father, profligate son, scheming slave, and good-hearted prostitute.

MOSAIC PANEL FROM POMPEII (second or first century BC) showing a scene from the beginning of Menander's play, the *Synaristosai* ('Breakfasting Women'). Only fragments of the original play survive, but a version by Plautus remains complete (the *Mostellaria*).

MARBLE RELIEF ILLUSTRATING A SCENE FROM NEW COMEDY (first century AD?). The situation is typical of Menander and his Roman imitators: an angry father emerges to chastise his drunken son but is restrained by a neighbour, while the son is egged on by a wily slave. The characters are clearly labelled by the form of the masks worn by the actors.

THEATRE AT POMPEII: Initially constructed during the second century BC, it is the earliest surviving theatre in Italy outside the Greek colonies; auditoria like this might have housed the first performances of plays by Plautus and Terence. Its present form, however, is the result of extensive modernization in the time of Augustus.

in which one of the tricks used to thwart the father is the impersonation of Casina in the bedroom by a male slave. *Rudens* ('The Rope') is set on the coast of north Africa near Cyrene: a slave-dealer is shipwrecked there in a storm, and one of the girls in his possession turns out to be the long-lost daughter of a man living there in exile from Athens. But beneath the surface variety of the plays the basic structure of the plot (preserved from the Greek original) nearly always concerns the removal or overcoming of some apparent obstacle to the course of true love.

But Plautus' main interest was not so much in reproducing dramatic structures as in using them as an opportunity for virtuoso display. We have seen from *Bacchides* that he wrote a creative adaptation rather than a slavish translation of Menander's text. In many respects he can be said to have changed radically the type of comedy which the plays contain. Consistency of characterization and plot development are cheerfully sacrificed for the sake of an immediate effect. The humour resides less in the irony of the situation than in the cracking of jokes and the perpetration of puns. Instead of characters in a dramatic context we sometimes see comedians going through a routine. Three things in particular stand out: the glorification of the scheming slave, the musical element, and the creation of an imaginary world which is set in Greece but includes many Italian features.

Plautus did not invent the scheming slave: the Greek original of *Bacchides* was called *The Double Deceiver*, and the part played in it by Syrus must have been similar at least in outline to the part played by Chrysalus in Plautus' play. But Chrysalus dominates *Bacchides* not simply by his scheming (which is not particularly ingenious) but by his boasting. His plan to trick his master out of money is seen as a military campaign, and his description of it is embroidered at some points with triumph imagery which is peculiarly Roman. Chrysalus has an extended monologue in which he compares his campaign with that of the Greeks in the Trojan War (925 ff.):

They say the two brothers, the sons of Atreus, did a great deed when with their weapons and their horses, with their army and outstanding warriors, and with their thousand ships they overcame after ten years Priam's town of Troy, its fortifications built by the hands of gods. But that was less than a blister on the foot in comparison with the way I'm going to conquer my master without fleet, without army, without that great number of troops

—and so on for fifty lines, with a succession of fantastic and mutually contradictory parallels between the plot of the play and the events of the Trojan War. When he has completed his deception he boasts (1068 ff.):

That's the way to carry out your projects properly. Now I can triumph in style, laden with booty. Safe and sound, the city captured by a trick, I now lead my whole army home intact. But, spectators, don't be surprised that I'm not actually celebrating a triumph: everyone does that, I can't be bothered with it. All the same, my troops will be treated to a tipple. Now I shall take all this booty straight to the quaestor.

ZEUS VISITS ALCMENE: *phlyax* vase painted by Asteas (third quarter of fourth century BC). The *phlyakes* were actors in a popular form of south-Italian farce whose subjects included parodies of Greek myths. This particular subject recurs in Plautus' *Amphitruo*, his only known play with a mythological theme, perhaps based on a 'hilarious tragedy' by the Syracusan playwright Rhinthon (*c.* 300 BC). See also p. 183.

The effect of such passages is to focus our attention on Chrysalus' trickery as an achievement on its own account rather than as a necessary device to secure a sum of money to help a young man in love. The Plautine slave enjoys scheming for the sake of scheming and scarcely requires any further motivation for his actions.

Chrysalus' monologue on the Trojan War was written to be accompanied on a pipe, and we saw earlier that Plautus had increased the musical element in the passage of *Bacchides* which we can compare with its Greek original. In fact substantial portions of his plays would have been accompanied, a considerably larger part of them than of their originals. The effect of the music is entirely lost to us. But we can see that Plautus' language often becomes more colourful for these accompanied passages, and the music perhaps did no more than reinforce the effect of the words. Most striking are the so-called *cantica*, operatic arias and duets written in a variety of metres and displaying many features of high flown style. They normally do little or nothing to further the action, and we know of nothing like them in Greek New Comedy. Chrysalus' 50-line monologue (his 'Troy-*canticum*') may have been expanded from a far briefer monologue in the original or it may have been spun altogether out of Plautus' head. A favourite type of *canticum* comes in the mouth of a slave who rushes on to the stage in great excitement to deliver an important piece of news. He is in a hurry but takes time to utter a lengthy monologue on entry. Thus the slave Acanthio at *Mercator* 111 ff.:

Strive with all your strength, struggle with might and main, to save your young master by your efforts. Come on, Acanthio, drive away your tiredness, don't indulge in idleness. I'm plagued by panting, I die for want of wind. What's more, the pavements are packed with people in my way: drive them off, knock them over, push them into the road! What dreadful manners people have here! When a man's in a tearing hurry, not one of them sees fit to make way for him. So you have three things to do at once, when you've begun to do one: dash, bash and brawl in the street!

Plautus is prodigal of his stylistic resources in the *cantica*, and it is presumably no accident that a *canticum* often comes near the beginning of a play where it is important to catch the audience's attention.

We saw that Chrysalus' boasts at *Bacchides* 1068 ff. contained references to the Roman institution of the triumph and to the quaestor, who was a Roman official. There is also a contemporary Roman reference in his remark about the frequency of triumphs (whether this is taken as referring to the celebration of triumphs by generals in real life or by slaves on the stage). There is no attempt to sustain the illusion that we are watching Greek characters in a Greek setting; and the dramatic illusion is further broken by Chrysalus' explicit address of the audience. This is altogether typical of Plautus. Sometimes he goes out of his way to remind the audience that his play is set in Greece, as at *Stichus* 446-8 (where once again the audience is addressed): 'Don't be surprised that mere slaves can drink, make love and accept invitations to dinner: we're allowed to do these things at Athens.' But when his characters talk of a dissolute life-style they speak of 'going Greek' (*pergraecari* or *congraecari*)—a Roman and not a Greek way of putting it. There are many allusions to Roman practices and Roman officials; and when the pimp Ballio addresses the members of his establishment at *Pseudolus* 143 and 172 he speaks as a Roman magistrate issuing an official edict. In the *canticum* at *Menaechmi* 571 ff. Menaechmus of Epidamnus complains that he has wasted his day acting as *patronus* (protector) on behalf of a *cliens* (dependant) in a lawsuit. He begins with a general complaint:

What a completely crazy custom this is of ours, a terribly troublesome one! It's above all the top people who have this habit: everyone wants to have lots of clients; they don't ask whether they're good or bad. They ask more about the reputation of their clients' wealth than of their honesty. If a man's poor and not bad, he's regarded as worthless; if he's rich and bad, he's thought to be a worthy client.

As he proceeds to describe the duties of a patron, he mentions a number of Roman legal technicalities. The entire passage has to do with social practices at Rome in Plautus' day. In effect, the play is set simultaneously in Epidamnus and in Rome.

The element of social comment in this last passage is not typical. Plautus was above all an entertainer and a poet. He uses colloquial speech, but Romans presumably did not often speak in the alliterative style with which this passage opens: 'Ut hoc utimur maxime more moro molestoque multum!' He abounds in wordplay and puns (at *Rudens* 102 a roof whose tiles have been blown off in a storm lets the daylight through 'quam cribrum crebrius': it is 'more perforated than a percolator'), in startling personifications (*Rudens* 626 'twist the neck of wrongdoing'), and in riddling expressions (*Mercator* 361 'My father's a fly: you can't keep anything secret from him, he's always buzzing around'). It is the sheer enjoyment in playing with words that is the hallmark of Plautus' genius.

Terence

The next Latin works to have survived are six comedies written by Terence in the 160s BC. These too are based on Greek New Comedies and written in verse. But there is a world of difference between Terence and Plautus. We do not have any substantial portions of the Greek originals of Terence's plays; but (although we know him to have changed some things) he seems to have preserved far more carefully than Plautus the ethos and general construction of the Greek plays. Roman technical language is occasionally used, but not as obtrusively as by Plautus. There is a considerable musical element, but hardly anything as extensive or as exotic metrically as a Plautine *canticum*. Above all, the comedy remains essentially situation comedy, in which consistency of characterization and clarity of plot construction are of vital importance.

The plots are once again concerned with love affairs and with the misunderstandings which arise from ignorance. In *Andria* ('The Woman from Andros') Simo wants his son Pamphilus to marry the daughter of Chremes, a respectable Athenian citizen; but Pamphilus is in love with a girl from Andros (Glycerium) who appears to be far less respectable. Intrigues and counter-intrigues lead to a number of emotional complications, which are resolved by the discovery that Glycerium is herself a daughter of Chremes. In *Hecyra* ('The Mother-in-Law') a young man (another Pamphilus) has married a woman already pregnant (though he does not know this) as the result of being raped. When she gives birth to a child of which there is every reason to suppose that he is not the father, their marriage appears to be at an end. In the course of the play his wife's attempt to conceal her condition gives rise to various misunderstandings: in particular, we see her mother-in-law being blamed by her father-in-law for the breakdown of the marriage. But all ends happily when it is discovered that it was Pamphilus himself who had raped her one night when drunk in the street. (It seems that the

Greek society portrayed in these plays was prepared to take a tolerant attitude to rape, as being a natural result of youthful drunkenness or high spirits. The girls in question led secluded lives, and young men had few opportunities to strike up acquaintance with them in a more leisurely way. Also, a citizen girl who had succumbed before marriage to a sustained campaign of seduction would have made a less sympathetic heroine than one who had been overcome by force. But the playwrights are not insensitive to the predicament of the victims of rape.) In *Eunuchus* ('The Eunuch') young Chaerea disguises himself as a eunuch in order to gain access to the bedroom of the girl with whom he is infatuated and there rapes her. The girl turns out to be the daughter of respectable Athenian parents, and Chaerea's father agrees to his marrying her. At the centre of the action is the prostitute Thais, who has taken the girl under her wing and is determined to help her find her parents. The picture of Thais is thrown into sharper relief by the fact that other characters in the play entertain quite unjustified suspicions of her behaviour.

These plots are less varied than those of Plautus, but their basic structure is not very different. The main difference between the two playwrights lies in the use which they make of their plots. Terence does not treat them as a springboard for extraneous jokes but preserves from the Greek originals the more elusive and ironic humour which arises out of a carefully constructed dramatic situation. We are told that Greek influence at Rome had increased considerably in the 160s, and Terence's plays have been taken as evidence that Greek refinement was now more widely appreciated than it had been by Plautus' less cultured audience. But there is a danger of exaggerating this difference. Some of the changes which Terence made to his Greek originals suggest that he was still aiming to appeal to a fairly unsophisticated kind of Roman. In adapting Menander's *Eunuchus* Terence has added from another play by Menander the characters of the boastful soldier and his fawning parasite, who bring with them some broad comic effects; and to Menander's *Adelphoe* ('The Brothers') he has added from a play by a different Greek author a scene of movement and violence in which a slave-dealer fails to prevent a young man from abducting one of the prostitutes he owns. Terence tells us of these additions in the prologues which he wrote to be delivered before the start of the plays themselves; and one of his prologues tells us something of the conditions in which his plays were performed. This is the prologue he wrote for the third performance of *Hecyra*, describing how two previous attempts to stage it had been failures:

The first time I began to perform this play, there was talk of a boxing match, and there were also rumours that a tight-rope walker was going to perform. Slaves were arriving, there was a din, women were shouting; and the result was that I had to give up before the end. ... I put it on again: the first act went down well, but then word got around that a gladiatorial show was going to be given. People flew together, there was an uproar, they were shouting and fighting for somewhere to sit. It was impossible for me to hold my own against that.

Hecyra is the only play of Terence which we know to have had difficulties with the public. His more boisterous *Eunuchus* was an unprecedented success.

Terences's prologues are quite unlike anything we know of in New Comedy or in Plautus. He uses them to conduct feuds with his literary rivals and defend himself against criticisms which they have made of him. They give us an exceptional glimpse of the literary world in which he worked, though they do only give his side of the arguments. If we can trust them, he was criticized (among other things) for feebleness of style, for plagiarism, and for combining more than one Greek original to construct a single Latin play ('contamination', as his critics called it). Although more faithful than Plautus to his originals, he seems not to have been faithful enough for some of his contemporaries. We learn of other innovations made by Terence from a commentary on his plays written in the fourth century AD by the famous grammarian Donatus. We can deduce, for instance, from what Donatus tells us, that Terence has spun the first twenty lines of his first play, *Andria*, entirely out of his own head. And one major change which he has made to the openings of his plays is that his prologues do not give the background to the plot (as those of Menander and Plautus do). Perhaps he regarded that as an artificial device, preferring to convey what information he could more naturalistically in the mouths of his characters in the course of the play. The result is that some opportunities for irony are missed, since the audience do not always learn all that there is to learn until a late stage of the play.

Terence is thus a more enigmatic figure than Plautus. He chose to adapt Greek plays whose appreciation often demands some moral and emotional involvement, and he was faithful most of the time in reproducing their essential qualities; but he did not do so slavishly, and he added some scenes with a cruder comic effect. It was no doubt the liveliness of his *Eunuchus* that ensured its success in his lifetime; but it is the quieter elements in Terence's plays that have most impressed his readers in subsequent generations: his sympathetic portrayal of the problems and predicaments of individuals, and his concern for the serious issues underlying the comedy of his plays. These elements ensure that his plays repay thoughtful study more than those of Plautus can ever do. But they are probably reproduced from the original Greek plays; and there is room to doubt whether Terence himself always cared about the refinements he has reproduced, as we shall see in the case of *Adelphoe*.

One thing which was undoubtedly Terence's own achievement was the creation of a Latin literary style quite unlike that of Plautus or of any other previous writer. Although criticized for its feebleness in Terence's own life, it has since then been more generally admired for its elegance and clarity. Terence was the first Latin writer to reproduce the elliptical style of natural conversation. It is not a low colloquial style, but its clipped constructions have a realistic ring which is generally absent from Plautus.

Within a century of his death, Terence's plays had become school texts; and they have continued to be so for as long as we know Latin to have been studied

CIE abſquiuiſ homine cum eſt opuſ beneficium accipere gaudeaſ. uerum enim uero iddemū
iuuat. ſiquem aequum eſt bene facere. iſ benefacit. o frater frater. quid ego tenunc lau
dem ſatiſ certo ſcio. numquam ttamagnifice quicquā dicam id uirtuſ quin ſuperet tua.
itaq; unam hanc rem me habere praeter aliaſ praecipuam arbitror. fratrem homini
neminem eſſe primarium artium magiſ principem. SYR o cteſipho. CIE o fr̄re aeſchi
nuſ ubi eſt. SYR ellū te exſpectat domi. CIE hem. SYR quid eſt. CIE quid ſtilluſ
opera fr̄re nunc uiuo feſtiuum caput quin omnia ſibi poſt putaritteeſſe p meo cōmodo.
maledicta famam meum amore & peccatū inſe tranſtulit nihil ſupra poteſt. quiſnā
foreſ crepuit. SYR mane mane ipſe & it foraſ.

AESCHINUS   CIESI PHO II SYRUS   SERUUS SAN NIO II
ADULES
CENS

AES ubi eſt ille ſacrileguſ. SAN men quaerit nū quid ham offert occidi nihil uideo.
AES ehem opportune te ipſū quer̄to. quid fit cteſipho intuto eſt omniſ reſ. omitte uero triſti
tiam tuā. CIE ego illā facile uero omitto. qui quidem te habeam fratre omr̄ aeſchine
omiger mane. aduereor cōra in oſ te laudare ampliuſ. ne id ad ſen tandi magiſ quā qd̄
habeam gratum facere & iſfames. AES age in epte. quaſi nunc non noſ imuſ noſ internoſ.
cteſipho ſed hoc mihi dolet noſ paene ſero ſciſſe & paene meū locū rediſſe ut ſi omneſ
cuperent tibi nihil poſſent auxiliarier. CIE pudebat. AES aha ſtultitia eſt iſtaec
non pudor. tam ob paruolā rem paene & patria turpe dictum. deoſ quaeſo ut iſtec phibeant.
CIE peccaui. AES quid ait tandē nobiſ ſannio. SYR iam mitiſ eſt. AES ego ad forum ibo
ut hunc abſoluam. tu intro ad illā cteſipho. SAN fr̄re infta. SYR eamuſ nāq; hic p
petat inirptum. SAN ne tā quidem quā uiſ & iā maneo otioſuſ hic. SYR reddetur
netime. SAN at ut omne reddat. SYR omne reddet tace modo ac ſequere hac.
SAN ſequor. CIE heuſ. heuſ fr̄re. SYR hem. quid eſt. CIE obſecro hercle te hominem iſtū

in Europe, holding a central place in the school curriculum until the nineteenth century. He has been admired for his style and for his moral sentiments, which can be made to sound more uplifting than Terence intended by being quoted out of context: the most famous of all, 'Homo sum: humani nil a me alienum puto' ('I am a man: I regard all that concerns men as concerning me') comes in the mouth of a tedious old busybody who has been asked why he is poking his nose into his neighbour's affairs. Its effect in context is to make him look pompous and ridiculous. But Terence has not been much praised for his humour, partly no doubt because it depends for its effect on the context created by the plot of the play. In the following passage from *Adelphoe* (413 ff.) the old man Demea boasts to the slave Syrus (who has just returned from buying fish in the market) about the method he has used in bringing up his son to be well behaved. Demea believes his method to have been effective, whereas Syrus and the audience know that the son (now an adolescent) is living a much wilder life than Demea imagines. It is clear that Syrus is mocking Demea in the second half of the passage, but the absurdity of Demea's boasting is much more comic if we bear in mind how wrong he is about the effectiveness of his method of upbringing:

D. I take a lot of trouble over it; I don't let anything slip; I train him. In fact I tell him to look into the lives of others, as into a mirror, and to learn from their example. 'Do this', I say.
S. Quite right!
D. 'Don't do that.'
S. Clever!
D. 'This is praiseworthy.'
S. Just the thing!
D. 'This is blameworthy.'
S. Excellent!
D. Furthermore —
S. Well, look, I really haven't got time to listen now. I've got the fish I wanted; I must make sure nothing goes wrong with them. ... To the best of my ability I give instructions to my fellow slaves just like the instructions you give: 'This is over-salted; this is burnt; this one hasn't been properly washed. That one's right: remember to do it like that next time.' I take a lot of trouble to teach them as well as my wits allow. In fact I tell them to look into the dishes, Demea, as if into a mirror, and I tell them what needs to be done.

Adelphoe is Terence's masterpiece. It was his last play and is the one that provokes most thought about a subject of perennial importance. But there is reason to think that he has distorted the balance of the play by striving for comic effect in its closing scenes. The thought-provoking theme is the question of what the relationship should be between a father and his adolescent son. We have just seen Demea being mocked for his misplaced confidence in a strict, didactic method of upbringing. His views are contrasted with those of his brother Micio, who believes that adolescent sons should be handled with openness and tolerance.

Micio's method seems to be presented for most of the play as the more humane and sympathetic one, and also the more successful. Demea's blind confidence makes him an appropriate comic butt, and Micio seems much more in control of events. But towards the end of the play there is a startling reversal: Demea starts to dominate at the expense of Micio, forcing him to agree to a number of unwelcome proposals (not least that he should marry a 'decrepit old woman'); and it looks as if the final judgement of the play is that Micio's approach was over-indulgent and excessively easy-going. This is very hard to reconcile with the rest of the play. Demea turns the tables on Micio and makes us laugh; but we are left uncertain where our sympathies should lie. Many scholars feel that Menander would not have written an ending so much at odds with the bulk of the play and that it is Terence who has sacrificed consistency to a desire to entertain or satisfy his Roman audience. But *Adelphoe* is not only about tolerance and strictness; it is also concerned with love between father and son and with lack of self-knowledge. Its handling of these themes combines comedy with telling characterization. It is precisely because the play is otherwise so successful that the ending has been found a puzzle; and the merits of the ending have long been hotly debated and will long continue to be so.

Plautus and Terence have survived; and they have influenced the European dramatic tradition. *Ralph Roister Doister* makes use of Plautus' *Miles Gloriosus* and Terence's *Eunuchus; The Comedy of Errors* is based on Plautus' *Menaechmi* and *Amphitruo*. Molière is one of many playwrights to have adapted the latter play, and he also followed Plautus' *Aulularia* (in *L'Avare*) and Terence's *Adelphoe* (in *L'École des maris*) and *Phormio* (in *Les Fourberies de Scapin*). Boastful soldiers, rediscovered foundlings, and scheming servants have long been standard ingredients of comic writing, not only for the stage: although P. G. Wodehouse told me (when I wrote to ask him) that he had not read Plautus or Terence, his Jeeves is clearly heir to the tradition of the scheming servant.

Ennius

One author who has not survived except in fragments must be mentioned because of his importance in the development of Latin literature. This is Ennius (239–169 BC). We have more certain information about his life than about those of Plautus and Terence: born in Calabria, he was brought to Rome in 204 or 203 by M. Porcius Cato and gave lectures on poetry. He accompanied M. Fulvius Nobilior on his Aetolian campaign in 189 and wrote in praise of his patron's achievements. His name is also linked with those of other prominent Romans. One benefit which he derived from such patronage was the Roman citizenship, conferred on him in 184 (by Nobilior's son, according to the traditional but unreliable account).

Ennius was a more versatile writer than Plautus or Terence, composing tragedies, comedies, satires, and a number of minor works in addition to his epic

BRONZE BUST OF A POET, from the Villa of the Papyri at Herculaneum. Long identified as Seneca, it is now generally regarded as an imaginary portrait of Hesiod; but a recent theory sees it as Ennius (239–169 BC), the first great epic poet in Latin. The statue on which it is based evidently belonged to the second century BC.

Annals; but it was this last work that represented his greatest contribution to Latin literature. Covering in eighteen books the history of Rome from Aeneas' flight from Troy down to Ennius' own day, it was written during the last fifteen years or so of his life. We now have about 600 lines, many of them single lines and not all of them complete, from a work which may originally have had 20,000 or more. The lines which have survived have done so because they were quoted by later authors, often to illustrate a linguistic point or an Ennian reminiscence in Virgil. We do not always know their context, and it is often only in the barest outline that we can hope to reconstruct the sequence of events in a book of the *Annals*. But enough survives to make us regret keenly the loss of the rest. Ennius set the tone for Latin hexameter writing in the high style for the next century and a half. Lucretius and Virgil were considerably influenced by him, and if we had more of his work we should understand more of theirs.

Ennius' most important contribution was perhaps the hexameter itself, the traditional metre of Greek epic. He was not the first to write an epic in Latin: Livius Andronicus had written a translation of the *Odyssey*, and Naevius had written an epic about the First Punic War towards the end of the third century. But these authors both wrote in the jerky Saturnian metre. Ennius introduced the more smoothly flowing hexameter into Latin epic, and to go with the new metre he moulded a poetic diction which served as the basis for the style of his successors.

At the beginning of the *Annals* Ennius claimed to be a reincarnation of Homer: the ghost of Homer had revealed this to him in a dream. Many features of his epic were Homeric: a Council of the Gods, battle descriptions, and similes. But there is much which strikes a different note, not least the discussion of his own poetic activity at the beginning of the work. Another autobiographical passage opened Book vii, where Ennius contrasted his own craftsmanship with the crude composition of his predecessors. His self-conscious proclamation of his stylistic skill reminds us more of Callimachus than of Homer. His own style came to seem crude by later canons of taste; but it is clear that he devoted some care to it in full awareness of his rôle as a pioneer. There is also a moralizing streak which must have helped in the establishment of Ennius as a central author in the school curriculum until the time of Virgil. Over half the work was devoted to events of Ennius' lifetime, the Second Punic War and the subsequent remarkable expansion of Roman power. Ennius glorifies the military achievements of the Roman nobility and supports traditional Roman morality. Individual virtue is praised, as in the famous lines about Q. Fabius Maximus Cunctator:

> One man by his delays restored our nation.
> Our weal he put before his reputation.
> Thus now his glory shines more brightly yet
> In later years . . .

('Unus homo nobis cunctando restituit rem . . .'). Such glorification of an individual was perhaps not in the best Roman traditions; but the heroes of the *Annals* displayed virtues which were very much admired by Romans. And other passages combined profound reflection with stylistic vigour in a memorable way, for instance the following on the disruptive effects of war:

> Wisdom is driven out: violence holds sway.
> Sound speakers scorned, rough soldiers have their day.
> No longer with abuse or skilful speech
> Do men express their hatred, each to each.
> But now with weapons, not with writs, they fight;
> They strive to rule, press on with massive might.

Further Reading

There is an excellent survey of Early Latin Literature by A. S. Gratwick in *The Cambridge History of Classical Literature*, II, *Latin Literature* (1982), 60–171 (this survey forms the bulk of the first volume of the paperback edition of the Cambridge History, 'Part I: The Early Republic').

The Loeb Classical Library includes complete texts with translations of Plautus (in five volumes) and Terence (in two volumes); the fragments of Ennius are included in the volume *Remains of Old Latin*, I. In the Penguin Classics series nine plays of Plautus have been translated by E. F. Watling and all the plays of Terence by Betty Radice. There are also lively translations of selected plays of Plautus by Erich Segal (*Miles Gloriosus, Menaechmi, Mostellaria*: London, 1969), Christopher Stace (*Rudens, Curculio, Casina*: Cambridge, 1981) and James Tatum (*Bacchides, Casina, Truculentus*: Baltimore, 1983). The plays of Terence have been translated by Frank O. Copley, The Library of Liberal Arts (Indianapolis, 1967) and by P. Bovie and others (New Brunswick, NJ, 1974).

The standard books in English on Roman Comedy are George E. Duckworth, *The Nature of Roman Comedy* (Princeton, 1952) and W. Beare. *The Roman Stage* (3rd edn., London, 1964), both reprinted in paperback. Much of what they say about Greek New Comedy has been rendered obsolete by the discovery of substantial portions of plays by Menander since 1958. For a briefer but more up-to-date account see F. H. Sandbach, *The Comic Theatre of Greece and Rome* (London, 1977: available in paperback).

The most important book on Plautus this century has been the book in German by Eduard Fraenkel, *Plautinisches im Plautus* (Berlin, 1922), which was reissued in an Italian translation with additional notes as *Elementi Plautini in Plauto* (Florence, 1960). Fraenkel was concerned to identify and evaluate the original features in Plautus' adaptations of Greek comedies. Erich Segal's book *Roman Laughter: The Comedy of Plautus* (Harvard, 1968) is an entertaining and enthusiastic account of the 'festival' elements in Plautus' plays, the ways in which they invert everyday Roman values and behaviour.

There is no recent book in English on Terence. Gilbert Norwood, *The Art of Terence* (Oxford, 1923; repr. New York, 1965), though outdated in some important respects, provides a very sympathetic appreciation of Terence.

The fragments of Ennius' *Annals* have been edited by O. Skutsch, *The Annals of Q. Ennius* (Oxford, 1985).

19

Cicero and Rome

❧

MIRIAM GRIFFIN

THIS chapter is devoted to the period which opens with the dictatorship of Sulla in 82 BC and closes with that of Caesar in 44 BC. It is concerned with the political life and death of the later Roman Republic.

Cicero

If we know more about these years than about any other period of Roman history, it is due principally to one man, Marcus Tullius Cicero. We have an abundance of speeches and letters written when he was deeply involved in day-to-day politics, either holding the highest offices of state or in contact with the men who were settling the future of the Mediterranean world. But it is not only political history that his works illuminate so brilliantly. When not at the centre of the stage, Cicero turned to literature of a more reflective sort and composed a corpus of theoretical works on philosophy and rhetoric richly adorned with contemporary examples and redolent of contemporary attitudes. Precisely because he was not an original thinker, Cicero helps us to recapture the intellectual habits of his generation. ·

The voluminous correspondence which Cicero maintained throughout all the vicissitudes of his adult life remains, however, his most valuable legacy to the historian. Some letters were private and not intended for publication; others were clearly written with a wider circulation in mind. Over 900 in number, they concern personal and cultural matters, as well as providing official and unofficial, public and private, views of the most important political events of the day. Of Cicero's most candid letters, those to his intimate friend Atticus, a younger contemporary was to write: 'Whoever reads the eleven books of the correspondence hardly feels the need of an organized history of the time.'

There is a dark side, however, to this picture. Cicero was an intelligent observer, but he was not detached; he was perceptive, but mercurial in mood and outlook; he was interested in other people, but, above all, obsessed with his own reputation. Moreover, his contemporaries have left little to serve as a corrective to his version of things. Their speeches, their works on philosophy and rhetoric

M. TULLIUS CICERO, the great Roman orator and statesman, whose speeches and letters are such a valuable source of information for the high society and politics of his time. Born in a well-to-do family at Arpinum in southern Italy in 106 BC, he rose to be leader of the Roman bar in 70, consul in 63, and a prominent figure in the political intrigues of the 50s; he died in the proscriptions of 43 BC.

have not survived intact, and much of what we know of them comes from Cicero. Over seventy letters from friends and acquaintances are preserved with Cicero's, but as they are mostly letters to him, they throw little light on matters outside his concerns. If it were not for Caesar's account of the Gallic and Civil Wars, Varro's antiquarian and agricultural writings, and some Roman legal documents preserved on stone or bronze, we might almost believe that the life of late-republican Rome, as we conceive it, was a creation of Cicero's fertile imagination.

We need, therefore, to ascertain how great is the distortion which the inevitable prominence of Cicero lends to our conception of the last and greatest phase of the Roman Republic. As regards Latin prose, we can rest easy. However regrettable the loss of works by other authors, either for their intrinsic merits or their value as evidence, Cicero rightly dominates the scene. There is copious testimony to the fact that the survival of so many of his works corresponds to their superiority in the eyes of the Romans themselves. After Cicero, no one could compose a speech in Latin, or a letter of any literary pretensions, or a work on philosophy or rhetoric, without author and audience being acutely conscious of the great exemplar. His works survived as textbooks in the grammar schools and models in the rhetorical schools. He was savagely criticized and passionately defended. Only his poetry was consistently and, as the remains show, justly ignored.

For the critic Quintilian (below, p. 657), Cicero was 'the name, not of a man, but of eloquence itself'. In what did the literary significance of Cicero consist? In oratory first of all, the indispensable accomplishment of an ancient politician. Cicero excelled in all three branches, deliberative, epideictic (display speeches), and forensic. His speeches before the Senate and people show us how he could present issues differently to different audiences, almost always with success. As consul he could turn the Roman populace against measures of debt relief and land distribution, though there were genuine shortages of currency and corn. At the end of his life he was able to persuade the Senate to vote official powers to Octavian, a revolutionary with a private army, in the name of the Republic. Epideictic oratory was less important as a genre at Rome, but it contributed vital ingredients, invective and eulogy, to different kinds of speech: if Cicero's praise of Pompey's achievements and Caesar's conquests moves us less than it did his contemporaries, we still find his absurd portrait of the ex-consul Piso in the speech *In Pisonem*, with his tame Epicurean philosopher and his mobile eyebrows, or his caricatures of the stern Stoic Cato and the pedantic jurist Sulpicius Rufus in the *Pro Murena*, hard to resist.

The most taxing and the most esteemed type of oratory at Rome was forensic. For at least twenty years, until his death in 43 BC, Cicero dominated the Roman courts, where arguments derived from law and fact counted for less than appeals to passion and prejudice. Though he boasted of being able to 'throw dust in the eyes of the jury', alleging in one case that there had been bribery in a *cause célèbre* and denying it in another four years later (and winning both cases), he was particularly famed for his ability to arouse and calm the emotions of jurors and spectators. He was for that reason regularly asked to give the concluding speech in defence.

The periodic style that Cicero developed, with its elaborately balanced clauses and careful rhythmic cadences, was less florid than that of Hortensius, the great rival of his youth, but by the end of his career it was becoming too ornate for the taste of the younger generation. Hence there is an apologetic element in his major works on rhetoric, which draw on Greek theory and on his own experience in order to present a picture of the perfect orator. In the *Brutus*, a history of Roman oratory written in 46 BC and ostensibly inspired by the death of Hortensius four years earlier, Cicero's own achievement is coyly represented as the climax of Roman eloquence. Here, as in the earlier *De Oratore* and the later *Orator*, Cicero lays great stress on the proper training for an orator, which he believed should not be just a matter of mastering techniques but of acquiring a broad education based on Greek culture. Cicero's hero, L. Licinius Crassus, to whom he had attached himself as an 'apprentice', had, as censor in 92, opposed the opening of schools to give rhetorical instruction in Latin alone: Greek was a richer language with an established tradition of great oratory that had to be mastered.

Though he regarded history and law as essential parts of the orator's education, it is Greek philosophy that Cicero recommends most strongly in these works: first because it imparts wisdom which the statesman needs to combine with eloquence, but also because it offers training in argument. These motives for interest in philosophy help to explain Cicero's choice of philosophical sect. Though he exposed himself to all the major schools, Epicureanism, which preached abstention from public life and had little interest in fine words, he gladly left to his friend Atticus. A Stoic philosopher named Diodotus lived in his house while he was still a boy and eventually died there: with him Cicero studied dialectic. His preference went to the teachers of the New Academy, the name given to a sceptical phase in the history of Plato's school, who taught that certain knowledge was not to be had, but that probability was an intellectually respectable basis for practical life. They were naturally committed to the Academic tradition of arguing both sides of a question, which gave excellent practice in speaking. Their beliefs also gave Cicero the freedom to choose what philosophical view he found most convincing on particular issues. For example, he was able without inconsistency to favour Stoic views on divine providence and on fundamental morality, while rejecting their view that oratory should be unemotional.

Though Cicero always maintained that public service should take precedence over study and writing, philosophy remained his favourite leisure activity. But it really came into its own when the political scene ceased to be hospitable to his talents. Given his priorities, it is not surprising that the first theoretical works he produced were the treatises on rhetoric we have mentioned and two works of political philosophy, *De re publica* and *De Legibus* ('On the State' and 'On the Laws'). But already in 46, two minor works gave the sign of things to come. *The Paradoxes of the Stoics* is a rhetorical *tour de force* in which Cicero defends these extreme formulations of Stoic doctrine, for instance, that virtue is the only good, and that all bad deeds are equally wicked. The work is dedicated to Cato's nephew Brutus and opens with praise of Cato for his ability to make his philosophy acceptable to the general public. Cato was then leading the Republican forces in Africa, which no doubt explains why Cicero wished to make amends for the ridicule he had heaped on his Stoicism some seventeen years earlier. Later in the year, after Cato's suicide, Cicero was to produce a moving eulogy of him.

By the next year he had embarked on a grand plan 'to provide for my fellow citizens a path through the noblest form of learning'. In the next two years he produced a dozen works, mostly in the dialogue form that Plato and Aristotle had invented, covering the three branches of ancient philosophy. The series began with the *Hortensius*, an exhortation to the study of philosophy now lost but whose impact can be judged from the words of St Augustine: 'That book changed my character and directed my prayers to you, Lord.' To the logical branch of philosophy, he devoted only one work, the *Academica*, which presented the sceptical standpoint of the New Academy. In the other two branches, he started with an 'academic' exposition of the views of the different schools on the most basic and general philosophical questions and then proceeded to defend his preferred doctrine on the more specific and practical questions. Thus in natural philosophy, the dialogue *On the Nature of the Gods* was followed by works *On Divination* and *On Fate*, and in moral philosophy the dialogue *On Ends*, discussing the goal of life as advocated by the different dogmatic schools, was followed by the *Tusculan Disputations* and *On Moral Obligations*, which defend the Stoic view of happiness and of duty.

Yet Cicero's purpose was not to preach particular philosophical doctrines. Indeed, even in his more dogmatic works, he asserts that there is no certain truth and defends his right to find different views more convincing according to the argumentation used on each occasion. His desire was to do the state some service and, in the process, to earn glory for himself when other avenues were closed. He made no claim to original philosophical ideas. What he had to contribute was his ability to reproduce Greek philosophy in eloquent Latin, to create a philosophical literature for Rome that could rival that of Greece, as Roman oratory already did. The eloquent orator would repay his debt to his education. Serious philosophical discourse had up to now been written in Greek: even Lucretius seems to have been regarded as a poet rather than as a philosopher. Cicero did not altogether reverse the pattern; but he had a firm follower in Seneca (below, pp. 663 f.), and his ultimate heirs were the Latin Church Fathers. 'Latin philosophy, which before him was rough and ready, he polished by his eloquence', wrote a contemporary. He himself, in explaining how he could write so many books so quickly, says to Atticus: 'They are only copies and involve little effort; only the words are mine, of which I have a copious store.' There were Epicureans and Stoics who wrote in Latin before him, but they themselves, he says, made no pretension to stylistic elegance or even definition and arrangement. Though Cicero here exaggerates his role as a mere translator, which he elsewhere denies, there is no doubt that most of the evidence for his taking pains concerns not the meaning of the Greek doctrines but the choice of interlocutors and the problems of vocabulary. It was Cicero who fixed the correlation between Greek technical terms and the Latin word or words used to render them, because he was more interested in instructing all educated readers than in preaching to the converted. Not only does he often give the Greek original: he often discusses alternative translations and changes his mind in later works.

Before and after Cicero, it was common to complain of the deficiencies of Latin as a philosophical language. Cicero protested, with some justice, that new subjects in any language require the creation of new words, and that Greek philosophers too had resorted to neologisms. He himself introduced, for example, *qualitas*, *moralis*, and *beatitudo*, for 'quality', 'moral', and 'happiness' (it is suggestive that Rome, left to herself, needed no word for happiness). But though he patriotically maintained that Latin was potentially richer than Greek, it had certain fundamental limitations that were particularly serious for philosophical exposition: Latin was inhospitable to compound words, and it lacked the definite article. As Seneca was to complain, '"Quod est" is a feeble substitute for Plato's *to on*,' ('that which exists'). Cicero often resorted to periphrasis, especially as he was aiming for eloquence, which meant respecting the genius of the language. 'We do not need to translate word for word, as unstylish translators do', he writes. The same consideration lead to the more irritating habit of translating Greek technical terms differently in different places, or by pairs of words, in accordance with his normal style. Nonetheless, his achievement was immense. His greatest pagan successor, Seneca, though he added many new terms of his own to the Latin philosophical vocabulary, almost never rejected one of Cicero's translations: they permanently enlarged the resources of Latin.

That such a self-conscious stylist should also leave behind the most spontaneous personal letters may at first seem paradoxical. But it was part of Cicero's consummate talent for finding the right style for each occasion. The letters include official dispatches to the Senate on military affairs in his province which are quite different, in their formal simplicity, from the witty and entertaining picture of his duties that he gives his young friend Caelius, or the irritable coldness with which he addresses his inconsiderate predecessor Appius Claudius, or the bitter and anxious confidences he makes to his friend Atticus. The letters not only show us Cicero's literary versatility and the intricacies of Roman politics: they give us a glimpse of cultivated and sophisticated society—marriages and dowries, divorce and bereavement, property and investment, patronage and promotion, declamation and dinner parties. Above all, they furnish us with a more candid and intimate picture of an individual than we shall meet again until Marcus Aurelius and St Augustine.

Cicero's place in the political, military, and social history of Rome is not as secure as his place in cultural history. It is true that he held the major magistracies, that he suppressed a serious social revolt in his consulship, and that he governed a distant province for a year and might even have attained a triumph for his military achievements in the Taurus mountains, had the civil war not intervened. On the other hand, he can claim no part in the constitutional reforms or extensive conquests of his generation.

Sulla and his Legacy

The closest approximation to a historical account of Cicero's time written by a contemporary was eventually provided by Sallust (below, pp. 642 ff.). His monograph on the conspiracy of Catiline, the chief episode of Cicero's consulship, demonstrates to the full how difficult it was even for a contemporary witness of events to escape from Cicero's interpretation of them. Yet at the same time, the work exposes the misleading character of Cicero's version. For Sallust affords glimpses of the economic and social problems that afflicted the Italian peninsula and led to the unrest represented by Cicero as the work of a few aristocratic reprobates.

Sallust is valuable in another respect: he furnishes us with a starting point for the period of the late Republic, namely, the dictatorship of L. Cornelius Sulla. He singled out the return of Sulla's booty-laden legions from the East, their seizure of the city by force, and the vindictiveness of Sulla's victory as the final turning-point in Roman conduct. Decline, he held, had set in when the destruction of Rome's mighty enemy Carthage left her without an incentive to self-discipline. Now personal greed and ambition came to dominate Roman political life. The historical perspective of Sallust, if not his diagnosis of the Republic's demise, can stand: it is not difficult to show that the age of Cicero was, in many respects, the legacy of Sulla.

Not only Catiline, whom Sallust specifically described as the product of the corrupt Sullan era, not only Crassus and Pompey, who were active partisans of Sulla, but Cicero, born in 106, Caesar, born in 100, and the younger Cato, born in 94, could remember the first armed conquest of Rome by a Roman, the proscriptions in which men all over Italy lost their property and their lives, and finally the astonishing abdication in 80 BC.

Though related by marriage to Sulla's enemy Marius, Cicero and his family, like many others, kept a low profile during the fighting and stayed in Rome when Sulla was away fighting Mithridates. Until 84, when Sulla's return was imminent, things were peaceful under the regime of Cinna and Marius; but the state was, as Cicero later described it, 'without law, without any semblance of authority'. As a result of the 'total dearth of orators', the young Hortensius Hortalus, only eight years older than Cicero, gained the limelight, and it was he whom Cicero opposed when he pleaded his first case after Sulla's return to Rome. Cicero's next two cases brought him face to face with the hardship inflicted on Italy by Sulla. The speech in defence of Roscius of Ameria in Umbria, delivered in 80, revealed the corrupt way in which Sulla's minions exploited the proscriptions and local feuds in the Italian towns for their own profit. In the second, delivered after Sulla had retired into private life, Cicero defended the rights of a woman of Arretium, one of the towns in Etruria from which Sulla had attempted to remove the rights of citizenship.

Cicero's attitude was not out of tune with the times. Many of Sulla's own allies had soon realized that the ruthlessness with which he destroyed his enemies and rewarded his friends could, in the long run, jeopardize his constitutional arrangements. To deflect the antagonism generated by his methods from the nobility that Sulla had left in charge, stories were circulated to the effect that this or that prominent supporter had queried the extent of the proscriptions, asking 'With whom shall we conquer?' The Metelli, the family of Sulla's wife, turned out in force to demonstrate sympathy with Roscius. Pompey, always adept at seeing how the wind was blowing, made a marriage alliance with them and

REMAINS OF THE TABULARIUM IN ROME, the building which housed the state archives. It was commissioned by one of Sulla's lieutenants, Q. Lutatius Catulus, and designed by the architect L. Cornelius in 78 BC. Only the high podium and a gallery at first-floor level survive; the upper storey has been replaced by the medieval Senatorial Palace.

successfully supported for the consulship of 78 a man no longer favoured by Sulla. This was Marcus Aemilius Lepidus, who was eventually to side with the dispossessed of Etruria when they attacked the Sullan colonists planted like garrisons on their land.

If Sulla had hoped that his confiscations would make his veterans prosperous and Italy secure, he was mistaken. The land allotted was often not of the best, while the forces that had been driving the small farmer off the land for a century—extended military service and capitalist farming by the rich—continued to operate. Some of the confiscated land had not actually been allocated and was held either by the original Marian partisans or by Sullan squatters. Threatened by every agrarian proposal, these men remained insecure in their tenure and hence ripe for revolution for the duration of the Republic.

Sulla's methods also left moral scars. The richest prizes had been used to keep and buy the loyalty of the upper orders. Leading men of the late Republic were known to be enjoying ill-gotten gains, and few consciences were absolutely clear. It is not surprising that in the seventies and sixties there were repeated attempts to revoke Sulla's exemptions and reclaim for the state treasury the price of proscribed property and the rewards given to agents of the proscriptions. One of Caesar's early claims to political notoriety was his willingness, as president of the murder court in 64, to accept charges against those who had killed for Sulla. Cicero was only too willing to exploit in his campaign for the consulship that year the threat this posed to his competitor L. Sergius Catilina whom men could still remember carrying the head of one of Marius' kinsmen through the streets of Rome to present it, still 'full of life and breath', to the dictator himself. Once elected, however, Cicero opposed a move to restore political rights to the sons of the proscribed, for, he argued, 'nothing could be crueller than to exclude men of such excellent families from political life, but the cohesion of the state is so dependent on Sulla's laws that it cannot survive their dissolution'.

Public Life at Rome

Most of Sulla's constitutional and legal arrangements survived to determine the character of political life throughout the late Republic. The dictator had laid down rules for the senatorial career, the *cursus honorum*, which were designed to ensure that men who finally found themselves, after holding the top magistracies, in command of armies and provinces would already have sat in the Senate for twenty years, absorbing its traditions and learning to set a high value on oligarchic cohesiveness. Holders of the quaestorship, the lowest office to carry senatorial rank, were now to number twenty a year, instead of eight, in order to maintain a Senate of 600. For the old council of 300 was inadequate to provide juries for all of Sulla's reorganized statutory courts where senators, as before C. Gracchus, were to be tried for public crimes by their peers. The number of officials required to administer Rome and its ten provinces was ensured, without damage to the prestige of the highest offices, by retaining two as the number of annual consuls and increasing the number of praetors from six to eight. Savage competition was built into the system, for every year saw twenty men spurred by initial success to hope for high office, fewer than half of whom would ever be elected praetor. It is therefore not surprising to find an increased emphasis on legislation against electoral corruption in the late Republic. Sulla's *lex de ambitu* carried the penalty of ten years' disqualification from public office; Cicero's *lex Tullia*, passed in his consulship, imposed ten years of exile.

Cicero's speeches give a vivid picture of a highly organized system for distributing largesse to the voters in various forms, from free seats at the games to outright bribes. In his indictment of C. Verres, who was on trial in 70 for extortionate practices as governor of Sicily, Cicero recounts how Verres tried to use his illicit gains to prevent Cicero's election to the aedileship in that year. One effect of the increased competition resulting from Sulla's measures was to make it even more difficult than before for a man of non-senatorial background to reach the higher offices, and Cicero wanted the aedileship, an optional office between quaestorship and praetorship, because it offered an opportunity to give games and win popularity. Despite Verres he was successful, but in that very year the electoral situation was made still more complex by the activity of the censors.

The year 70 was altogether momentous. For it was then, in the consulship of Cn. Pompeius Magnus and M. Licinius Crassus, outstanding partisans of Sulla, that the dictator's restrictions on the legislative and judicial powers of the tribunes of the *plebs* were removed, after nearly a decade of popular agitation. After his election, Pompey had made a speech combining this promise with an attack on the corruption of provincial governors and the senatorial juries who failed to punish them. A decade of expensive and prolonged war with accompanying food shortages had made the senatorial government vulnerable to criticism. Scandals involving marked ballots and lavish bribery had rendered the senatorial courts, despite the conviction of Verres, indefensible. If Sulla's senators were, as he probably hoped, less liable than their predecessors to acquit their peers, since most of them would never enjoy the same opportunities, they were more vulnerable to bribes, since the new men among them found maintaining a senatorial life-style a strain and could not borrow easily in the expectation of later provincial profits. Though Pompey does not seem to have specified how the judiciary was to be straightened out, he did not oppose the passage of the *lex Aurelia* which gave the *equites* two-thirds of the seats on the juries.

The censors of the year, friends of Pompey, ejected from the Senate sixty-four members, mostly men who had proved themselves corrupt in the provinces or the courts. Their struggles to recover senatorial rank by being elected to office again compounded electoral competition in the sixties, while other action by the censors introduced a further element of uncertainty into the electoral game. The Italians, who had gained the franchise at the end of the Social War (above, pp. 413 f.) were at last enrolled in the thirty-five Roman tribes. Henceforth candidates for office had to consider a wider electorate, of whom at least the more prosperous members might actually find it worth while to come to Rome and vote. Thus when Cicero was planning his consular campaign, he included in his schedule a visit to the governor of Cisalpine Gaul (the Po valley) for 'the district is likely to count heavily in the voting'.

Optimates and Populares

Sulla's legislation and the struggles that led to its modification also had a profound effect on terminology and habits of thought.

It was in this period that the ideology or, on a cynical view, the propaganda familiar to us from the works of Cicero and Caesar became defined. The habit of mapping out the political scene in terms of a Right and a Left by the words 'Optimates' and 'Populares' could in fact be older than the days of Sulla, for the programmes and methods of the Gracchi gave shape to such a division. But it was Sulla's legislation that made explicit the dominance of the Senate that had developed in the third and second centuries BC and started to be seriously challenged in the middle of the second. It was, in essence, Sulla's view of the proper balance of the constitution that became the bulwark of the Optimates. And it was the struggle over the modification of his laws, principally in 70, that gave definition to the *popularis ratio*.

In speaking of Optimates and Populares we are speaking of ideological labels, not of organized political parties. Indeed 'popularis', as applied to people, normally refers to leading politicians with a certain political style, not to leaders and followers, and usually to a succession of such leaders, not a group working together. A *popularis* was a politician who used and defended the powers of the popular assemblies and the popular office of tribune as a counterweight to senatorial authority and/or championed such economic measures as land distribution, debt cancellation, and subsidized corn.

In the years immediately following the resurrection of the tribunate some ambitious men held the office and sponsored legislation that the establishment regarded as a threat. Gabinius even threatened to re-enact the most notorious act of Tiberius Gracchus (above, pp. 411 f.) and depose his colleague from office rather than accept his veto. The kind of left-wing image affected by the tribune Rullus in 63 who, according to Cicero, grew his hair long and took to wearing dirty old clothes and a farouche expression; the self-advertisement of his colleague Labienus who put a statue of his uncle, the martyred tribune Saturninus, on the rostra—these were only to be expected of young men on the make; they might yet end as stalwart supporters of the Senate. For there is no warrant to assume sincerity, or even consistency, in the conduct of Roman politicians. Indeed the prime example of ambiguity and opportunism was the restorer of the tribunate himself.

Pompey

Though he had inherited from his father some connection with Marius' ally Cinna, Pompey raised an army of his father's clients in Picenum and joined Sulla on his return from the East. For his ruthlessness in destroying Sulla's enemies in Sicily and Africa he acquired the nickname 'teenage butcher'; for his selfish ambition he earned the distrust of his own side. From the dictator, who had treated him as an exception to his own rules and allowed him to command legions when he had not held public office, Pompey extorted a triumph. After being cut out of Sulla's will for supporting Lepidus, he then suppressed Lepidus' rebellion and used his troops to extort the Spanish command from the Senate. In Spain he managed to steal the limelight from Metellus Pius, who was already making headway against the rebel general Sertorius, and then returned to Italy to do the same to Crassus. After dealing with some fugitives from the rising led by the gladiator Spartacus, Pompey wrote to the Senate that Crassus had conquered the slaves, but that he himself had extirpated the war.

Pompey had nothing to lose by a shake-up of the Sullan system. He had made too many enemies to fit comfortably into Optimate politics: only the presence of his army in Italy had secured him senatorial dispensation to stand for the consulship without having held the lower offices. Now, after the popular measures of his consulship, enthusiastic tribunes secured for him from the people first, in 67, sweeping powers to clear the Mediterranean of pirates and then, in the next year, the command of the war against Mithridates, in which, true to form, he replaced Sulla's trusty officer L. Licinius Lucullus, who had been appointed some years ago by the Senate.

In Pompey's absence, Rome speculated on the manner of his return. Would the great man come home in a conservative or a radical mood? In the end he tried to manoeuvre a return in the company of his troops as in the past, but a

HEAD OF POMPEY (CN. POMPEIUS MAGNUS), the most powerful Roman general of the 70s and 60s BC and chief architect of the downfall of Sulla's political system. During the 50s he lost ground to his fellow triumvir, Julius Caesar, and was assassinated in the course of the civil wars of 49–45. The romantic Alexander-inspired hairstyle sits oddly on the realistic facial features— furrowed brow, large nose, small piggy eyes, double chin.

move to recall him to suppress Catiline's forces was thwarted by the consul's decisiveness and the Optimates' determination. Eventually, towards the close of 62, Pompey dismissed his army at Brundisium and returned to confront the Senate of Sulla making its last stand.

Cicero, Pompey's exact contemporary, presents a similarly complex, if less sinister, political image. By conviction he was a conservative, by temperament a moderate, while his municipal equestrian background gave him a certain perspective on the Roman scene. To enhance the favour his forensic work could bring him, Cicero identified himself with the rising star, prosecuting in 70 the man who had mistreated Pompey's Sicilian clients and going on to support the proposal to give Pompey the Mithridatic command. In the first he castigated the corruption of senatorial juries; in the second he lamented the sufferings of the Asian *publicani*. These were themes to attract the *equites*, but in 65 he defended Pompey's ex-quaestor Cornelius and the radical activities of his tribunate, with moving appeals to the ancient struggles of the *plebs*. His famous doctrine of the *concordia ordinum* (harmony of the orders) was more in line with Sulla, who had himself broadened the composition of the Senate: the upper orders, senators and *equites*, were to fulfil their different public obligations and co-operate against revolutionary movements. But when Cicero opposed a whole series of tribunician proposals which appealed to the rural and urban poor, he said, and no doubt partly believed, that he was a *popularis consul* safeguarding the true interests of the people.

Cicero believed that in 63 he had actually achieved the *concordia ordinum* and indeed a wider 'consensus of right-thinking men' against the subversive movement of Catiline. The Senate, too, was in elated mood and, led by a young man who succeeded by force of personality in persuading his peers that he embodied old republican morality, faced the demands of the triumphant Pompey in an uncompromising spirit. Pompey wanted a marriage alliance with Cato, but, to the disappointment of the women of his family, Cato said 'No'. Pompey wanted the Senate to ratify his eastern arrangements, which reversed many decisions of Lucullus, immediately and *en bloc*; Cato, a relative of Lucullus, and others said 'No'. Pompey wanted to distribute to his veterans and needy citizens Italian land, including the *ager Campanus* which even the Gracchi had spared; here even Cicero said 'No', for the rents from the Campanian land provided the closest, and hence the most reliable, source of public revenue.

Cato had the bit between his teeth. One of the effects of the civil wars of Sulla and Marius had been to deprive Rome of the men who should have been her senior statesmen. Those that were left were often too inclined, Cicero thought, to withdraw to their luxurious villas and fishponds and lead a life of cultured ease. Hence there was room for a strong character such as M. Porcius Cato to become a leader of the Senate before he had held the praetorship. Pompey was not his only target. Cato offended the *equites* by threatening the long-standing immunity from prosecution for bribery that equestrian jurors enjoyed. In addition he opposed making any concession to the *publicani* who had overbid for the tax-contract in Asia in the expectation that the province would quickly return to normal after the Mithridatic War. Here Cicero parted company with him. Cato was destroying the *concordia ordinum*: he behaved 'as if he were living in Plato's Republic and not in the cesspool of Romulus'.

Crassus

In the course of his crusade, Cato alienated not only Pompey but Crassus who had urged the tax-farmers to ask for a remission of their contract. The importance of Marcus Crassus is easier to demonstrate than to explain. He was a decent orator, but easily surpassed by Cicero; he was a talented general, but outclassed by Pompey and Caesar; he was rich, but hardly more so than Pompey when he returned home with his eastern booty. Like Pompey, Crassus had raised an army and joined Sulla on his return to Italy; unlike Pompey, he was a notorious profiteer in the proscriptions. What ancient writers liked to emphasize was his avarice and the political ambition he made it serve. He was said to have augmented his property by taking advantage of the frequent fires in Rome and the lack of a regular fire brigade: owners of burning buildings would sell them for a song, and Crassus, with his team of trained slaves, would repair and rebuild them for profit. A much quoted remark of his was, 'No man is rich who cannot support an army': the fact that Crassus could may help to explain how he obtained the command against Spartacus at a time of financial stress.

  Less dramatic uses of his wealth included lending money to political associates free of interest, and providing lavish hospitality. The result, we are told, is that Crassus had considerable influence with the Senate. It is likely that he was one of the first to take the measure of the changed political conditions brought about by Sulla's doubling of the Senate's membership. The new men often needed money to maintain their new station, and they would relish invitations to dine with a noble of ancient family. But Crassus was not content to be a conservative politician. Shady and unorthodox himself, he liked to support black sheep and sponsor radical causes. Though resentful of Pompey's successes, he joined him as consul in 70 in restoring the rights of tribunes, and in successive years he supported several tribunes on trial. He also lent money to young aristocrats such as Caesar, or funded their electoral campaigns, as in the case of Catiline. Some of his more daring political initiatives were often unsuccessful: both of his projects as censor, to enfranchise the communities of Cisalpine Gaul and to exploit the will of the Egyptian king who left his country to Rome, were baulked by his colleague.

Caesar

While Cato preached and Pompey and Crassus fumed, an abler politician than any of them was planning how to exploit the situation. 'Caesar, from the outset

C. JULIUS CAESAR, the conqueror of Gaul and dictator of 48–44 BC. He rose to power as a politician 'of the left', but achieved his ultimate triumph through brilliant generalship. Subsequently, however, his accumulation of powers and honours alarmed even his own supporters, and he was assassinated in the famous Ides of March conspiracy.

and as it were by hereditary right the head of the popular party, had for thirty years borne aloft its banner without ever changing or even so much as concealing its colours.' So Mommsen wrote of the murdered dictator, 'the sole creative genius ever produced by Rome'. C. Iulius Caesar has been appreciably cut down to size in the past century, but it remains hard to deny that he was the most consistent politician of the late Republic.

Related by marriage to Marius and Cinna, he had escaped the proscriptions because of family connections on the other side. But tradition credited Sulla with the prediction that he would eventually destroy the Optimates for 'he harbours in him many a Marius.' In 70 he supported the restoration of the tribunes' powers and the amnesty granted to the followers of Lepidus, one of whom was his wife's brother. In youth Caesar had refused Sulla's request to divorce Cornelia, who was Cinna's daughter; when she died in 67 he delivered a public eulogy of her. In the same year, at the funeral of his aunt Julia, he displayed the images of her husband Marius, not seen since the days of Sulla. Then, as aedile in 65, Caesar restored to public view the trophies that Marius had brought back from his victories, and in 64 he countenanced the prosecution of Sulla's agents.

To the development of his *popularis* image Caesar brought all his considerable talent for publicity. In 63 he prosecuted Rabirius, first by an obsolete procedure dating from the time of the kings, then by trial before the popular assembly. Through this attempted vindication of the murdered tribune Saturninus, Caesar demonstrated not only his belief in the Gracchan principle that no citizen could be put to death without a trial authorized by the people, but also his grasp of ancient tradition and religious lore. For Caesar was aiming to be elected *pontifex maximus*, the head of the state religion. A similar combination of political principle and personal ambition had led him to support the bills granting Pompey his great commands. Then, in the last phase of the Catilinarian affair, he nearly succeeded in swaying senatorial opinion against the execution of the captured conspirators without trial, and he made clear his support for the recall of Pompey to deal with the rebel forces.

Caesar had become a much hated man in some quarters. When he returned from governing Spain early in 60, Cato led the Senate in blocking his request to be allowed to stand for the consulship in absence. Caesar wished to remain outside the sacred boundary of the city which he would then cross as part of his triumph, a privilege which the Senate had already granted him. The Senate further showed its reluctance to have him as consul by allocating as the consular provinces for that year the task of clearing out the woods and cattle-runs of Italy: there lurked the remnants of the bands of Spartacus and Catiline, the latter, as some alleged, Caesar's own supporters.

The 'First Triumvirate'

Caesar gave up his triumph and retaliated by soliciting the support of those other victims of Cato's righteousness, Pompey and Crassus. Once elected consul for 59 BC, he reconciled the two rivals and set out to fulfil the promises he had made to them. Cato was therefore largely responsible for the formation of the so-called 'first triumvirate', and that moment, he later said, was the real beginning of the end for the Republic.

It is tempting to conjecture what might have happened had Caesar not been denied his triumph and the expectation of an important province after his consulship. Caesar was no radical fanatic: he had performed the requisite military service under two Sullan generals and not felt tempted to join the Marians under Lepidus and Sertorius. He was ultimately to say that his honour had always come before anything else; he held it dearer than his life. If he had not felt humiliated by the Senate, might he have proved a decorous consul, a rebel who had 'come round', as Cicero always hoped he would? Perhaps the answer does not matter so very much. Perhaps the same can be said even of that more obvious, but related, question: might civil war have been averted in 49? The interesting question for the historian is not whether any particular event is inevitable, but whether it is explicable. Why the fall of the Republic occurred exactly when and how it did is, after all, secondary to the main question: why did leading members of the Roman governing class, who themselves had most to gain from the existence of the Republic, destroy it, thereby committing political suicide?

The Romans, as we have said, thought of the issue in terms of moral degeneration. They believed that, whereas their ancestors had aspired to glory through service to the state, their contemporaries had come to put their own ambitions above the public welfare. The catalyst in the decline of traditional morality they felt to be the increase in Rome's power and wealth. The enormous opportunities for ruthless self-aggrandizement by individuals threatened the state in two directions. If her subjects were exploited, Rome might lose her Empire, for she had not the men or money to control such a vast area by brute force: an element of consensus in her rule was essential. Again, if some members of the governing class became a great deal more powerful than others, the essentially oligarchic system of the Republic would be replaced by one less beneficial to the governing class as a whole. Roman thinking ran on patriotic self-control where we might stress the need for institutional checks on the power of individuals. In fact some of the legislation they traditionally saw as encouraging the first can be interpreted as steps towards the second: sumptuary laws to limit conspicuous consumption and largesse, extortion laws to check greed and related abuses by Roman officials, canvassing laws to prevent men from buying their way into office on the profits of Empire. But certain changes, such as making generals strictly accountable for their booty, or taxing citizens enough so that the state could itself provide for discharged veterans, or creating a police force that could control political violence, were not in keeping with the closely guarded tradition of aristocratic independence. It was easier for the Senate to forgo a rich and strategic province such as Egypt, which might give excessive scope to one of its members, than to make the great generals, who behaved like kings abroad, toe the line when they returned home.

The standards for success were rising as the Empire grew. After the military triumphs of Marius in the West and Sulla in the East, Pompey would not have been satisfied with the normal one-year governorship after his consulship. Caesar, too, would be thinking of prolonged and extraordinary commands. Eventually Pompey could not bear an equal nor Caesar a superior. But the Republic was incompatible with the ascendancy of one or two. It was also incompatible with

PAINTING OF A FRIGHTENED GIRL: detail of a mural frieze at Pompeii (c.60–50 BC). This famous composition, consisting of twenty-eight or more figures, is the finest surviving specimen of the grand figure-painting of the so-called Second Style.

TABLINUM OF THE HOUSE OF M. LUCRETIUS FRONTO, at Pompeii (*c*.AD 40–50). The rich but delicate wall-decoration marks the break-up of the Third Style of Pompeian painting. In place of restrained elegance and restful colouring we find a more complex colour-scheme, with more elaborate painted detail, and hints of the reappearance of architectural perspective.

the notion that great deeds exempt one from the legal restraints placed on one's peers, an idea Caesar is said to have voiced as he surveyed the enemy dead after Pompey's defeat: 'They would have it so. Even I, Gaius Caesar, *after my great achievements*, would have been convicted in the courts, had I not sought help from my army.' Socrates knew that the laws must be obeyed even when they led to an unjust decision. By the start of the Civil War in 49 the laws of Rome had been bent and ignored by powerful individuals too often to seem worthy of obedience.

The expediency of conciliating Rome's subjects, however, had been grasped by intelligent men of differing political complexion, such as the Gracchi, Sulla, Pompey, Cicero, and Cato. Even Caesar, who was to treat the conquered Gauls with great brutality, tightened up the extortion law. A more difficult issue was how far to share the profits of empire with the whole citizen body, for there was no conception of an impersonal 'government' that bestowed specific benefits. The established tradition of aristocratic largesse made it easy for men who legislated for the distribution of land or money to gain the same credit and popularity as those whose generosity came from their own pockets. Thus *popularis* moves to increase the welfare or power of the *equites* or the *plebs* looked like threatening bids for individual power. It was bad enough when a tribune of the *plebs* made himself a nuisance in this way; still worse when the tribune was in league with a senior magistrate. The year 59 presented the spectacle of a consul who himself behaved like a tribune and had the support, not only of a tribune, but of a general whose veterans were on the scene. It is not surprising that on the brink of civil war there were Optimates who feared nothing so much as the thought of Caesar holding that office again.

Caesar's First Consulship

Caesar began, however, by attempting to secure a smooth passage for his legislation through tact and diplomacy. The settlement of Pompey's veterans had top priority, and in December of 60 Caesar solicited the support, or at least the silence, of the best orator in Rome, who had already sabotaged two previous attempts. Cicero was flattered, but decided to remain independent: he valued the opinion of Cato and others who had called him 'Father of his Country' after his consulship. In March Cicero confirmed Caesar's worst fears by indulging in critical remarks about the state of public affairs. Caesar, with the co-operation of Pompey (both in their priestly capacities), retaliated by carrying out a highly questionable adoption of Cicero's personal enemy, Clodius, into a plebeian family so that he could be elected tribune that summer. They no doubt hoped to lure Cicero, this time by fear, into collaboration, but, if that failed, Clodius would remove the nuisance. Cicero refused invitations from Caesar to serve on his agrarian commission or accompany him to his province (where he would have provided excellent company in the long evenings). Cicero paid for his refusal by being sent into exile in 58 for his execution of the conspirators five years earlier. When he was recalled through Pompey's good offices over a year later, he was easy to divert from further moves towards independence.

It is important to realize that our best informant was not only hostile to the coalition, but did not enjoy the confidence of its members. Though Caesar's invitations amply demonstrate that Cicero's political importance was not a figment of his own vanity, he can offer us only his own intelligent speculations on the motives and plans of those who came to control the destiny of Rome.

Casesar's other attempt to employ diplomatic methods was also unsuccessful. He carefully omitted from the agrarian proposal itself all the most controversial features of the earlier bills, excluding the Campanian land from distribution, using only Pompey's new revenues for purchase of land, and relying on voluntary sale. He brought the proposal to the Senate and, only after meeting with total and unreasoned opposition, put it to the Assembly without senatorial sanction. Caesar's colleague in office was Cato's son-in-law, M. Calpurnius Bibulus, whose obstruction Caesar no doubt hoped to avert by impressing the body of the Senate with his sweet reasonableness. From now on, however, he showed how little he could be deflected from his course by shame or the pressure of public opinion. He affixed to the bill a clause, associated with Saturninus, that required the senators to swear individually to uphold it. Pompey and Crassus were induced to speak openly in its support and to promise to meet force with force. Against Optimate tribunes and his consular colleague, Caesar invoked the violence of the mob and Pompey's veterans. After the bill was passed, Caesar took all of his subsequent proposals directly to the people. His other bills ratifying Pompey's eastern settlement, granting a concession to the tax-farmers, recognizing the Egyptian king (who paid handsomely for the privilege), were passed without regard to opposition. Bibulus had resort to religious obstruction of an unorthodox kind and on an unprecedented scale: from his house he observed bad omens every day.

The intense opposition Caesar faced in passing measures that were addressed to real problems arose from fear of the political power he would thereby acquire with the *plebs*, with the veterans, with the *equites*, and with foreign potentates. Worse was still to come. The tribune Vatinius secured for him from the people a five-year command in Cisalpine Gaul and Illyricum: the first would enable him to keep a threatening eye on Rome when not on campaign, while the second offered him the opportunity for glory in forging the land route through the Balkans that Pompey's expansion of the eastern Empire now made imperative. In the end, politics interfered with the rational expansion of Rome, and Caesar extended the Empire north to the Channel and beyond. For his legislation, including the *lex Vatinia*, was vulnerable to subsequent attack because of the way it had been passed, and Caesar was therefore eager to gain the additional province of Gaul from the Senate. This he achieved through Pompey, whose continued loyalty he had secured through a marriage alliance.

Caesar was well aware, however, that Pompey was an unreliable ally. Dependence on a junior, though it had achieved its end, seemed to Pompey a humiliating position, which the scurrilous edicts of Bibulus and the growing unpopularity of the three only aggravated. As time rendered less vulnerable what he had gained from Caesar, his hankering for respectability, already demonstrated in 62, would reassert itself. But for a while the malice of his enemies made him cling to the alliance which was, in fact, renewed in 56, just as Cato's brother-in-law was about to stand for the consulship. The presence of Caesar's troops on leave in Rome ensured the election of Pompey and Crassus instead, and they promptly renewed Caesar's command in both Gauls and secured for themselves the control of Spain and Syria for five years.

Crassus left for Syria and was killed a year later fighting the Parthians. Caesar was tied up in Gaul and unable to cross the Alps until the winter of 53/2. But Pompey, who chose to govern Spain through legates and remain in the vicinity of Rome, was in a position to exploit political developments. Electoral chaos and gang violence eventually played into his hands since, as proconsul with the power

MODEL OF THEATRE AND PORTICOES OF POMPEY IN ROME. Pompey inaugurated the first permanent stone theatre in Rome in 55 BC, perpetuating a time-honoured tradition of self-advertising munificence on the part of leading politicians during the Republic. The adjacent Porticoes of Pompey contained trees and fountains, and acted as a kind of public art-gallery for paintings and sculptures.

to command and levy troops, he was the obvious person to restore order. When Clodius was murdered at the start of 52, the Senate had him elected sole consul. The death of Caesar's daughter Julia in 54 had already ended Caesar's family connection with him, and Pompey now seemed within reach of recognition as leader of the traditional government. But, to keep his options open, he supported a tribunician bill which granted Caesar the right to stand for a second consulship in absence: he would be eligible for election in 49 after the requisite ten-year interval had elapsed.

Civil War

Meanwhile a change in the method of appointing provincial governors not only resulted in the dispatch of the reluctant Cicero to govern Cilicia, but introduced complications into Caesar's length of tenure in Gaul. Behind the legal question, however, lay constitutional questions, and behind them lay a struggle for power more complex than the rivalry of Pompey and Caesar.

Cato's antagonism had removed any temptation Caesar may have felt to sacrifice his *popularis* image to his ambition. Instead, he remained true to the first as long as there was any risk to the second. Caesar now took his stand on the fact that the people had granted his command and the right to stand for the consulship in absence, which, he claimed, implied that he would still be in his province in the summer of 49. The Optimates had always disapproved of provincial commands granted by the people: they believed that the Senate should retain over foreign affairs the control it had acquired *de facto* as the only organ of government with a continuous existence and membership. Though sovereignty lay with the people, they did not agree with those Populares who held that the people could properly legislate on any matter, even without senatorial guidance. Had not the Republic long been thought of as 'the Senate and People of Rome'?

Marcus Marcellus, the consul of 51, tried to force the issue and recall Caesar a year early. Pompey tried to arrange a compromise, while nevertheless agreeing that the Senate ought to be obeyed. In 50 and early 49 Caesar had recourse to conciliatory offers, reinforced by the vetoes of friendly tribunes: when the diehards ignored them, he crossed the Rubicon, the river that marked the boundary of his province, in defence of their sacred rights—and of his honour.

Pompey went east to gather his forces, saying 'Sulla did it: why not I?' But the only resemblance lay in his threat of reprisals against his enemies. Speed and organization belonged to Caesar, and his policy of clemency captured public opinion.

Cicero, an honourable man trying to choose the side of the Republic, lamented that neither Pompey nor Caesar had any aim but *dominatio*. He could not do other than attribute blame to the protagonists, including the enemies of peace in the Senate, because he believed that the political system itself was blameless. If Cato spoke as if living in Plato's Republic, Cicero had written that the Roman

Republic surpassed even that utopia. In the late fifties, when chaos and violence had become the order of the day, he was moved to write two works of political philosophy based, in title and in content, on Plato's *Republic* and *Laws*. In the first he explained that Roman tradition had evolved a mixed constitution, which was the most balanced and stable kind. The laws he presented in the second work were designed for a future citizen body trained to virtue and resembled closely existing law and practice. What innovations there are in the part of the treatise that survives are designed to increase the power and authority of the Senate and senior magistrates.

Both *De re publica* and the roughly contemporary *De oratore* are set in the past when public affairs were in the hands of Scipio and Laelius or Lucius Crassus and Marcus Antonius. Cicero's answer to the problems of the Republic was the existence of statesmen or a statesman of their calibre who could serve as a model of conduct to others. He had never entertained such hopes of Pompey and Caesar, though he had once offered to play Laelius to Pompey's Scipio and was to offer advice to Caesar as dictator.

The Dictatorship

Caesar's victory destroyed the system within which he had wanted primacy. There is little sign that he enjoyed the task of reconstruction. Perhaps the only thing that rings true in Cicero's fawning speech *Pro Marcello*, delivered in 46, is his picture of the arbiter of men's destinies as weary of life. Until the spring of 45 Caesar could turn his attention to Rome's problems only in the intervals of fighting the civil war all over the Mediterranean. By March of 44, when he was killed, he was planning to leave Rome to fight the Parthians. Cicero was baffled. What of the programme he had outlined for him: the reorganization of the courts, the restoration of financial credit, the passing of moral legislation, the reform of political life? Caesar had in fact taken steps to ease the burden of debt. He had legislated against luxury and in favour of increasing the birth-rate. But Cicero could not grasp the difficulty of reforming Roman politics any more than he could appreciate Caesar's concern for Italy and the provinces.

In the short time he had, Caesar achieved enough to show how widely his mind ranged. The settlement of his veterans was to contribute to the restoration of Italian agriculture and manpower, for they were to be scattered up and down the peninsula, not planted like garrisons in the Sullan mode. Some of the administrative anomalies neglected since Italian towns became Roman *municipia* after the Social War were sorted out. The number of magistrates was increased to allow for the expanding number of provinces, and the unsatisfactory system of tax-collection by *publicani* based in Rome was discontinued, at least in Asia. Most important of all was the enfranchisement of Cisalpine Gaul and the settlement of veterans and poor citizens in colonies abroad. The immediate effect of the colonies would be to cut down the urban population and, with it, public disorder and the

SHOPS IN THE FORUM JULIUM, Caesar's answer to Pompey's theatre and porticoes. Begun in 51 BC to provide a much-needed enlargement to the old Roman Forum, this complex introduced the formula adopted by the subsequent imperial *fora*, i.e. a colonnaded piazza dominated at the rear, directly opposite the main entrance, by a grand temple (here that of Venus Genetrix, the alleged ancestress of the Julian family).

cost of the corn dole. But in the long run the colonial policy, combined with Caesar's generosity in granting citizenship to individuals and communities, was to rejuvenate both the Roman legions and the Roman governing class. Caesar, who included some provincial aristocrats in his enlarged Senate, was perfectly aware of what he was doing.

The reform of Roman government was a different story. It was hard for a man of fifty to think afresh about the system that had so far determined his life: Caesar applied some traditional remedies, such as the abolition of certain urban clubs, the revision of criminal statutes, the restriction of the tenure of provincial commands. Accustomed to working at top speed in Gaul—he dictated letters to two secretaries while on horseback—Caesar had lost patience with the niceties of political life: Cicero complained that his own name was attached to senatorial decrees passed in his absence. Worse still, Caesar was about to leave for an indefinite period, having been made *dictator perpetuus* ('dictator without term'): perhaps he wanted to preclude any wrangles this time over his tenure of command, but it looked as if he had lost the will to restore the Republic. As dictator, he had shown no sign of relinquishing his stranglehold on the political machinery, designating governors, appointing many of the magistrates, and exercising personal jurisdiction. Hence the Ides of March.

After Caesar's death one of his intimates, Gaius Matius, was to lament: 'If he, for all his genius, could not find a way out, who is going to find one now?' Caesar knew that his peers disliked being kept waiting in his antechamber while he monopolized affairs. Yet what solution would they accept to the political chaos and armed conflicts he had brought to an end? Augustus was to avoid many of Caesar's mistakes, including the celebrated clemency which left his most determined opponents alive. Yet Augustus' solution was not so different, though he was more creative in adapting traditional language to describe his paralysis of the constitution. The greatest difference lay in the attitude of others. Another round of civil war had by then made peace in any form seem acceptable to those who survived. Augustus was young and had time to evolve a solution. The Catos and the Ciceros were gone. Who was there left who had seen the Republic?

Further Reading

PRINCIPAL ANCIENT SOURCES

The works of Cicero are readily available in translation. The Loeb Classical Library offers the complete works translated by different hands with facing Latin text. The Penguin Classical Series includes volumes of selected speeches in translation and, particularly worthy of note, a rendering of the letters by D. R. Shackleton-Bailey. This is a byproduct of his great edition and commentary, published by the Cambridge University Press, of which only the volumes of the *Letters to Atticus* contain a translation.

Other ancient works which contribute to our knowledge of the period can also be consulted in English. Sallust's monograph on the Conspiracy of Catiline appears in the Loeb and in the Penguin *Sallust*. One volume in each of these series is devoted to Caesar's accounts of his campaigns in Gaul and in the Civil War. The *Life* of Atticus by Cornelius Nepos can be found in the Loeb volume containing Florus. Plutarch's *Lives* of Sulla, Crassus, Pompey, Caesar, and Cicero feature in the Penguin *Plutarch: Fall of the Roman Republic*. They can also be found, with other relevant biographies, in the eleven Loeb volumes containing all of Plutarch's *Lives*. Suetonius' biography of Caesar is available in the Penguin volume *Suetonius: the Twelve Caesars* and in the first volume of the Loeb *Suetonius*.

MODERN WORKS

There are many modern accounts of this, the most richly documented period of the Roman Republic. They vary greatly in scope, emphasis, and level of detail.

Brief accounts in a long perspective can be found in the works of H. H. Scullard, P. A. Brunt, and M. Crawford, mentioned on p. 416.

For more detailed narrative, older works such as volume iv of the Everyman Edition of T. Mommsen's *History of Rome* (Engl. trans. 1880) and T. Rice Holmes, *The Roman Republic*, 3 vols. (Oxford, 1923), are still worth reading. The relevant chapters of the *Cambridge Ancient History*, vol. ix (1932), are still useful, though soon to be superseded by a new edition.

The great modern work on the fall of the Republic is Sir Ronald Syme's *The Roman Revolution* (Oxford, 1939), which concentrates especially on the later part of this period. A more recent analysis of political activity in the late Republic, combined with a penetrating, but controversial, diagnosis of the fall of the Republic, is contained in E. S. Gruen's *The Last Generation of the Roman Republic* (Berkeley, 1974). For a lively account of the working of Roman politics and of the mechanics and setting, see Lily Ross Taylor's *Party Politics in the Age of Caesar* (Berkeley, 1949) and *Roman Voting Assemblies* (Ann Arbor, 1966).

Much of the up-to-date and detailed analysis of the politics of the period is, however, contained in biographies of the leading figures. Most notable are those by M. Gelzer, of which only *Caesar, Politician and Statesman* (Oxford, 1968) is available in English. J. P. V. D. Balsdon's *Julius Caesar and Rome* (Harmondsworth, 1967) is brief and readable; Z. Yavetz, *Julius Caesar and his Public Image* (London, 1983), concentrates on his dictatorship. Several biographies of Pompey have appeared recently, by J. Leach (1978), R. Seager (1979), and P. Greenhalgh (1980–1), of which Seager's is the most detailed on politics at Rome. The unrewarding task of constructing a biography of Crassus has been attempted by B. Marshall (1976) and A. Ward (1977).

Cicero, the most feasible subject for a biography, has been well served in English. D. L. Stockton's *Cicero, a Political Biography* (Oxford, 1971) provides a useful account of his work as a statesman; D. R. Shackleton Bailey in *Cicero* (London, 1971) makes good use of his work on the letters in evoking Cicero the man; E. D. Rawson offers a sympathetic and well-rounded study in *Cicero, a Portrait* (London, 1975; repr. Bristol, 1983). Different aspects of Cicero's life and work are illuminated in a collection of essays edited by T. A. Dorey (London, 1965).

Finally, it may be useful to list a few books that help to put the political life of the late Republic in a broader social context: C. Nicolet, *The World of the Citizen in Republican Rome* (London, 1980); J. Crook, *Law and Life in Rome* (London, 1977); W. Liebeschuetz, *Continuity and Change in Roman Religion* (Oxford, 1979); K. Hopkins, *Conquerors and Slaves* (Cambridge, 1978); *Death and Renewal* (Cambridge, 1983); C. Wirszubski, *Libertas as a Political Idea at Rome* (Cambridge, 1960).

20

The Poets of the Late Republic

❧❧

ROBIN NISBET

Lucretius

EARLY in 54 BC Cicero ended a letter to his brother with a note on his recent reading. 'Lucretius' poetry is just as you say; many brilliances of natural genius, all the same much technique; but more anon. If you read Sallustius' *Empedoclea* I'll think you a man, but I'll not think you a human being' (*QF* 2. 10. 3). Here we glimpse a society where some public men find time for new literature, and comment on it without affectation. Both the works mentioned are philosophical and scientific, reflecting the intellectual curiosity of a small Hellenized élite, an enlightenment that Cicero was to transmit but did not originate. The didactic poem was a familiar form that continued the Alexandrian tradition of versified scholarship; Cicero himself in his youth had produced a translation, innovating for its day, of the astronomical *Phaenomena* of Aratus. Such works were more noted for technique than genius, but Lucretius in his six books *De rerum natura* found a theme to engage both the reason and the imagination, the now fashionable Epicurean explanation of the universe. The poet himself is a shadowy figure, no doubt comfortably born, certainly well educated, perhaps recently dead; his poem will speak for him.

'Aeneadum genetrix, hominum diuumque uoluptas,/alma Venus', 'Mother of Aeneas' race, pleasure of men and gods, life-giving Venus' (1. 1 f.): already in the resounding invocation we find the complexity of reference that was thereafter to characterize much of the greatest Roman poetry. Venus is the mythical and literary goddess of Love, the ancestress of the Roman People, the protecting deity of Memmius, the ambitious politician for whom the work is nominally written, but at a deeper level she personifies the creative forces in the world, and in particular *uoluptas* or pleasure, the prime impulse and supreme good of the Epicurean moral system. The poet tells how at the goddess's epiphany the inventive earth sends up fragrant flowers, and beasts bound through the lush pastures: the universality of the divine influence is described in conventional religious patterns, but the comprehensive sympathy suits a philosophy that sees man as part of nature. Then, as is appropriate in prayer, the suppliant relates Venus' powers to his own needs: 'forasmuch as without thee nothing rises to the radiant shores of light, nor does anything joyful or lovable begin ... grant, goddess, to my precepts a charm everlasting' (28 'aeternum da dictis, diua, leporem'); the archaic alliteration suits the solemnities of old Roman poetry, but 'charm' (here paradoxically combined with 'everlasting') suggests a more up-to-date awareness of beauty. Finally Lucretius prays that Venus may bring peace on earth by making love to the war-god Mars; once again he astonishes us by blending traditional religious diction with a sensuousness of description associated with the poetic movements of his own day (35 f. 'leaning back his shapely neck, and gasping at thee, goddess, he feeds his greedy gaze with love'). He conflates scandalous Homeric story-telling with a more sophisticated hint of Harmonia, the daughter of Mars and Venus; at the same time he includes a reference to the political anxieties of 60–55 BC, when Caesar was already subverting the Republic.

Lucretius next turns to a panegyric of Epicurus, who like Hercules ridding the world of monsters liberated oppressed mankind from the lowering menace of religion. In a typically Roman metaphor we are told how the philosopher's mind sallied forth through the walls of the world, and after scouring the universe like a reconnoitring raiding party, brought back 'a knowledge of what can be and what cannot': 'quare religio pedibus subiecta uicissim/obteritur, nos exaequat uictoria caelo' (78 f. 'and so religion in turn is crushed underfoot and victory raises *us* to heaven'). These fighting words are at odds with the mild piety of Epicurus, who recommended the observance of one's local form of worship, and Lucretius recognizes that his line of argument may be thought wicked; but he reflects that the true impiety is religion's. With suitably epic, or rather tragic, diction he pictures the fate of Iphigeneia, whose significance is of course symbolic rather than literally relevant to Roman cult: 95 ff. 'lifted by the hands of men she was escorted trembling to the altar, so that pure impurely, at the very time for her to marry, she might fall a sorrowing victim, slaughtered by her sire.' And so to the scathing summing up, not easily paralleled in antiquity, 'tantum religio potuit suadere malorum' (101 'so much evil could religion recommend').

The first two books are devoted to the atomic theory of Epicurus (above pp. 374 f.), which was itself derived from Leucippus and Democritus (above, p. 121). Lucretius copes skilfully with his technical problems, the poverty of his ancestral tongue ('patrii sermonis egestas') at least before Cicero standardized an abstract vocabulary, the clumsiness of Latin compared with Greek as a vehicle for subtle disputation, the constraints of the metre (for the hexameter was not indigenous in Rome and still could prove a recalcitrant medium). The theme required argumentation of a kind unusual in poetry, at least since the fifth-century Empedocles, and as suits a rationalist, there is an abundance of prosaic, logical words like 'for', 'whereas', 'nevertheless', 'moreover', 'finally', 'therefore'. Each book is ordered into self-contained sections, which ram home a point by repetition as well as deduction, often ending with a triumphant restatement of the propositions with which they began (for the procedures are more polemical than those of a technical philosopher); and as in the physical system that is being described, these sections interlock in larger structures. It would be quite wrong to suppose that the work consists of purple passages of eloquence stitched to a monotonous scientific fabric: when Lucretius talks of 'smearing honey on the medicine cup' (1.936 ff.), he is referring not to the set-pieces, but to the poetic form itself, which must have startled more professional Epicureans (their founder had rejected the arts as not conducive to happiness). But while some of the poet's qualities can be demonstrated, the grasp of reality, the passionate faith in reason, the actuality of the supporting illustration, no anthology can do justice to the interdependence and cumulative persuasiveness of the system as a whole.

The second book opens with an exposition of Epicurean ethics, for which the physical theory was simply the foundation. 'suaue, mari magno turbantibus aequora uentis, / e terra magnum alterius spectare laborem' (2.1 f. ''tis sweet, when the winds disturb the calm of the great sea, to look from land at the great tribulation of another'): here we have the Epicurean ideal of *ataraxia* (freedom from turmoil) expressed with the self-centredness of ancient moral philosophy. 'Sweet' is not just a conventional poeticism, but alludes to Epicurus' theory of pleasure, not the excited pleasure that he disapproved of, but the static sort which arises from the absence of pain and anxiety. To know the true pleasures of the body, men do not need a house shimmering with gold and silver, or panelled ceilings echoing to the lute, as they can enjoy themselves by lying on the soft grass, beside a stream of water, under the branches of a tall tree (29 f. 'prostrati in gramine molli / propter aquae riuum sub ramis arboris altae'); such passages show how far Epicurus was from the popular misconception of the epicure (above, p. 372). Fame and riches do no more for the mind than for the body: you may see your legions swarming over the plain, and still be obsessed by religious scruples and the terror of death (40 ff.). Men are like children fearing phantoms in the dark: 'hunc igitur terrorem animi tenebrasque necessest / non radii solis neque lucida tela diei / discutiant, sed naturae species ratioque' (59 ff. 'this terror and darkness of the mind must be dispelled not by the rays of the sun or the shining shafts of day but by the outward appearance and inner rationale of nature').

Lucretius then reverts to his atoms, whose unseen collisions and reboundings he illustrates by characteristically memorable analogies: they manœuvre and fight like specks of dust seen in a sunbeam in a darkened room (114 ff.), but their motion is no more visible to the senses than that of sheep crawling on a far-off hill (317 ff.). They move in the first place because they have weight and fall; but if they fall in parallel lines, that does not explain the collisions that produce aggregations of matter (the poet is unaware of the possibilities of attraction). They cannot catch up with one another by falling at different speeds, for as they fall in a void they must all fall at the same speed (225 ff.). Lucretius is thus led to the theory of the *clinamen* or swerve which was Epicurus' most important contribution to atomic physics: 'at times quite undetermined and undetermined places they veer a little from their track, with the smallest possible change of course' (218 ff.). Cicero thought that nothing was as disgraceful for a scientist as to say that something happens without a cause, but modern physicists can understand an appeal to indeterminacy; they will be more shocked by Epicurus' ethical intention, a desire to exempt human volition from the shackles of determinism, (above, pp. 376 ff.).

The third book expounds the structure of the soul, and its mortality. Lucretius tells how Epicurus banished the fear of death: it is this that muddies the waters of life, clouding them with darkness, and leaving no pleasure clear and unpolluted. Men profess a disbelief in survival, but in adversity the mask is torn off, and they revert to their old superstitions (55 f.). Such remarks reflect a traditional preoccupation of the Epicureans, and Philodemus himself, the most distinguished contemporary member of the school, wrote a treatise *On Death*. Nor should one underestimate the credulity about an after-life in the poet's own society; it is true that Cicero mocks the Epicurean obsession ('what old woman is crazy enough to be afraid of such things?'), but he confines the issue to the fables of mythology, and his rational scepticism was untypical even of the governing class. Some have thought that Lucretius protests too much, but for a poet he seems remarkably clear-headed: St Jerome's story of his madness can be explained by the incomprehension of the Church.

Lucretius naturally rejects the mind–body dualism that has haunted the history of thought for so long; as Epicurus had uncompromisingly put it, 'soul is body'. He also opposes the more plausible view that the soul is simply a condition of the body, or *harmonia* as it was called ('attunement' gives the idea); he derisively comments that the *organici* or instrumentalists are welcome to keep the word (131 f.). Following the psychology of his master he distinguishes the *anima*, the vital principle that is common to all living creatures, from the governing *animus* or mind, that is found only in man; but as both are equally mortal, he does not always use his terms precisely. The soul can influence the body, and the body the soul; this can only be effected by physical contact, and touch is a property of body (161 ff.). The atoms of the mind are exceptionally small and smooth, as is shown by the speed with which volition can be translated into action; in the same way a puff of breath can scatter a heap of poppy seeds, while corn-ears are too big and spiky (196 ff.).

Lucretius now accumulates some thirty arguments to show that the soul cannot survive the body. As it consists of small atoms of exceptional mobility, when its vessel is shattered it must dissipate like smoke (425 ff.). The mind keeps in step with the body in its birth, development, and decay, as can be seen from children and old men; therefore it dies with the body (445 ff.). The body and mind are affected together by drunkenness (476 ff.) and epilepsy (487 ff.); the fact that the mind can be cured, i.e. changed, by medicine is itself an indication of its mortality (510 ff.). Sufferers from creeping paralysis lose sensation first in the toes and the feet, 'and then through the other limbs go haltingly the steps of cold death'

(529 f.); as the soul cannot be concentrated in the sound part of the body (which does not acquire extra sensation), it must be mortal. The mind cannot originate in the head or the feet (Lucretius put it in the breast), but has a fixed place appointed for it where alone it can exist (615 ff.). If the soul is to have sensation when separated from the body it must be endowed with five senses, as poets and painters have portrayed the dead in the Underworld; but in isolation from the body it cannot have eyes or nostrils or hand or tongue or ears (624 ff.). When you cut through a snake, the severed part twitches, and similar things can be seen in chariot battles (a very Roman illustration); but if the soul can be severed it cannot be immortal (634 ff.). Plato and others had argued that the soul had a previous existence, but if it has forgotten its past, that is virtually equivalent to death (670 ff.); for the ancients the notions of pre-existence and after-life were closely connected, as they reasonably thought it implausible that what is born should be eternal. The different species of animals inherit temperamental as well as physical characteristics (741 ff.); this shows that the soul and body grow up together. It is ridiculous to suppose that at the moment of conception immortal souls are queueing up for a body to occupy (776 ff.).

Lucretius sums up the conclusion of his argument with an aphorism of Epicurus, 'nil igitur mors est ad nos' (830, 'therefore death is nothing to us'). If anyone takes it amiss that his body will rot in the grave or be consumed in the pyre, he must have some lingering belief in survival after death. And so to the mourners' memorable lament, which is meant to sound over-emotional and cliché ridden, even if humanity seems to break in:

> Iam iam non domus accipiet te laeta neque uxor
> optima, nec dulces occurrent oscula nati
> praeripere et tacita pectus dulcedine tangent . . .
> $$(894 \text{ ff.})$$

Now no more will your household greet you joyfully, nor your best of wives, nor will your dear children race to snatch first kiss and touch your heart with a silent sweetness . . .

Epicurus had urged a serious and rational enjoyment of the present ('life is whittled away in thinking of the morrow, and each of us dies before he has time to relax'). His sentiments are here echoed in a remonstrance from a personified Nature, who speaks with the derisive vigour of popular philosophy (931 ff.):

Away with your tears, you rascal, and muzzle your moans . . . Because you always long for what you don't have and disregard what you have, your life has slipped away from you unfulfilled and unenjoyed . . . Now give up things unsuited to your years and make way for younger men; for there is no escape.

(Lucretius emphasizes, as elsewhere, the natural cycles of growth and decay.) Then with a characteristic rationalization of myth he explains that the fabled punishments of the underworld represent the self-inflicted torments of life (978 ff.): the overhanging rock of Tantalus stands for the oppressive terrors of religion, the vultures that tear at Tityos are the desires of the flesh, Sisyphus pushing the stone up hill is the ambitious politician (what did Memmius make of that?). The sermon then turns to the staple of consolation through the ages, 'You are not the first'. Good King Ancus died, and Scipio, the terror of Carthage, and Epicurus himself, who dimmed the light of all men as the sun blots out the stars (1042 ff.). We spend our lives running away from ourselves, without understanding the cause of our discontent; peace of mind can only be attained when we accept that death is eternal.

The fourth book first defends the Epicurean theory of perception, by which objects give off a thin film of atoms, (above, pp. 379 f.), like heat from the sun or exhalations from the sea. Lucretius is at his vivid best in describing distortions of perception, the motion of hills when seen from a passing ship (389 f.), the continued rotation of hall pillars when children have stopped spinning (400 ff.), the bending of oars as they pass beneath the surface of the sea (440 'refracta uidentur'). 'A gathering of water no deeper than a finger's breadth, standing between the stones on the paved street, provides a view beneath the earth with a reach as far as the chasm of the sky stretches on high above the earth' (414 ff.): the image shows the child-like clarity of the poet's vision, and his ability to use minute observation to achieve immense perspectives. Yet in spite of strange cases Lucretius insists that knowledge depends on the senses, which are irrefutable. In yet another section he denies that the eyes were created to give us sight, a teleological explanation that is literally preposterous, as it confuses cause and effect: 'nothing grew in the body in order that we could use it, but what has grown generates a use' (834 f.). Here he is reacting against Aristotle and the Stoics, with an approach that went back to Empedocles and Democritus: Bacon and Darwin understood.

The latter part of the book provides a mechanical explanation of sex that is extended to the emotional concomitants; here Epicurean non-involvement is expressed with a cynicism that counters the growing romanticism of the poets.

Fathers' hard-won earnings turn into ribbons and head-scarves, ... yet from the very fountain of enchantment a bitterness wells up ('surgit amari aliquid'), to bring anguish amid the blossoms, when the lover's mind is gnawed by the awareness that he is passing his life in idleness and going to ruin in brothels, or because she has left unclarified a word she has let fly that sticks fast in his passionate heart and ignites like a flame, or because he thinks she flaunts her eyes too freely or gazes at another, and he sees in her face the traces of a smile. (1129 ff.)

This leads to a satirical account of lovers' euphemistic endearments, which are expressed in the affected Greek of the girls concerned: 'the black is "honey-gold", the filthy and smelly "unadorned"' (1160 'nigra melichrus est, immunda et fetida acosmos'). Yet the poet concedes that even an unattractive woman may persuade you to live with her by her trimness and obliging ways; even without divine assistance habit can make you love her, like water dripping on a stone (1278 ff.). This cool conclusion may have encouraged the story, familiar from Tennyson's poem, that Lucretius was driven mad by an aphrodisiac administered by his wife.

The fifth book turns to the cosmos, which originated from the concourse of atoms and will one day disintegrate. The gods had no part in creating it, and no reason to think of such a thing (165 ff.): serene and immortal beings could not be dissatisfied with their previous condition. (Epicureans were not atheists, but their gods were indifferent to the world of men.) The natural order was not made for us: there is too much wrong with it (199). Much of the earth has been denied to man by mountains, forests, and the sea, as well as the extremes of cold and heat; and hard-won cultivation may be blighted by sun, frost, or wind.

Furthermore a baby, like a seafarer cast up by the cruel waves, lies naked on the ground, speechless and lacking all vital support, when once nature has ejected him on the shores of light by travail from his mother's womb, and he fills the place with woeful wailing, as is right for one who is destined in life to pass through so many troubles. But the different flocks and herds and wild beasts thrive without need of rattles, and none has to be treated to soothing lisps by a cherishing foster-mother (222 ff.)

Though Lucretius is far from idealizing the animals, he sees like others before him the particular helplessness of the human child.

The latter part of the book gives a non-theological explanation of the origin of life and the development of civilization. Grass and shrubs came first (783 ff.), and then animals, which grew up in wombs rooted in the soil (a curiosity derived from Epicurus himself). The poet more plausibly emphasizes the warmth, moisture, and fertility of the primeval world, which nowadays is like a woman past the age of child-bearing. Many individual monstrosities were produced (837 ff.), but if they could not find food or reproduce, they died out; Lucretius is using an idea of Empedocles, but rejects his fantastic belief in hybrids of men and beasts. The species that have survived have been preserved by cunning, courage, or speed (857 ff.), or, like dogs and sheep, by the protection of man. But in spite of the notion of natural selection, Lucretius has no idea of evolution: though the species were originally produced by chance, they remain for him distinct and immutable.

Primitive men had no agriculture or navigation, but lived in woods and caves off acorns and berries. They must often have been mangled horribly by wild animals (a good instance of the poet's constructive imagination), but thousands were never slaughtered in a single day's battle (999 ff.): Lucretius has no illusions that our first ancestors can have been anything but brutish, but he is also aware that technical innovation need not be accompanied by moral development. In due course men acquired huts and skins and fire, which was produced in the forest by lightning or friction. They were softened by family life (in his grim chronicle Lucretius finds a place for the Epicurean virtues of friendship and affection), and formal compacts for mutual support; these must have been kept for the most part (1025 ff.), otherwise the human race would not have been preserved (a sometimes forgotten aspect of the 'survival of the fittest'). Language was not arbitrarily invented but grew out of natural cries, as can be seen from the variety of sounds made by dogs:

> when they set about licking their puppies fondly with their tongues or throw them about with their paws and as they go for them with bites put on a show of soft gobbling without using their teeth, they nuzzle up to them with eager moans that are very different from their baying when left alone in the house or their whimpers when with cringing body they shrink from a beating. (1067 ff.)

Here we have a poet who loves words and dogs and ideas all at once.

Towns were built and lands distributed, and men competed for wealth in a self-defeating search for security (1120 ff.). Kings rose, and were toppled by envy, and violence gave way to law. Men saw gods in visions and dreams, and falsely assumed that natural phenomena were devised by them (1183 ff.); that is why they still spatter altars with blood, and shiver at thunder, and pray in storms at sea. Metals were discovered in forest fires (1241 ff.), and then mined in the earth (first bronze, then iron). Horses were tamed for war (1297 ff.), and less successfully bulls and lions. Plaiting came before weaving, as looms need metal parts (1350 ff.); men worked wool before women, as they are the more ingenious sex. Then as things became easier, music was made in imitation of birds and the wind (1379 ff.); by Epicurean doctrine the inventiveness that was first prompted by necessity was extended to add the graces of life. Lucretius has no nineteenth-century belief in ever-continuing improvement, but following ideas current in the Hellenistic world he recognizes that progress has historically occurred: 'usus et impigrae simul experientia mentis / paulatim docuit pedetemptim progredientis' (1452 f. 'practice and with it the experimentation of the active mind taught men gradually as they felt their way forward').

After a eulogy of Epicurus and Athenian civilization, which serves as a climax to what has preceded, the sixth book expounds irregular natural phenomena, thunder and lightning, waterspouts and rain, earthquakes and volcanoes. Lucretius wishes to show that his system can provide rational explanations for these traditional puzzles, some of which were responsible for the terror and superstition that the Epicureans were so concerned to avert; if some of his details were now out of date, that simply underlines that he was a moralist and a poet rather than a scientist. Finally he turns to epidemics with a description of the plague at Athens four centuries before (1138 ff.); his treatment is less objective than that of Thucydides, on whom he depends, but he is not so concerned with a clinical scrutiny of the physical symptoms as with a rhetorical presentation of human nature under stress. The end of the work is gruesome and abrupt, with mourners fighting to lay their dead on other people's pyres, and some have suspected that the poet was interrupted by terminal illness; yet the passage implies a plan, as it sets off not only the panegyric of Athens at the beginning of the book but the joyous hymn to Venus at the beginning of the poem. Familiar themes recur, the mechanical causation of the calamity, man's social and self-seeking propensities, the terror of death, the uselessness of religion. If we are not explicitly offered the consolations of philosophy, that is not just because the plague came before Epicurus. Better simply to describe things as they are, and the limits of human capacity.

Catullus

There is much about humanity in Lucretius, but no people. The balance is redressed by his young contemporary Catullus, the second-greatest poet of the Republic.

> Marrucine Asini, manu sinistra
> non belle uteris: in ioco atque uino
> tollis lintea neglegentiorum.
> hoc salsum esse putas? fugit te, inepte:
> quamuis sordida res et inuenusta est . . .
> (12. 1 ff.)

Asinius from the Abruzzi, that's not a nice thing to do with your left hand: in the middle of fun and wine you nick the napkins of the inattentive. So you think it's smart? You're making a big mistake, you clown: it's as nasty and unattractive a thing as you can think of.

Asinius has gone off with a table-napkin belonging to Catullus, who pretends to believe that he has stolen it deliberately. Episodes as personal and particular are uncharacteristic of Hellenistic epigram, but a new generation of Roman poets had the individuality to make everyday occurrences a subject for verse. Such poems were too slight to be categorized as lyrics; for the graceful metre with its eleven syllables ('hendecasyllables') one may refer to Tennyson's imitation, 'Oh you chorus of indolent reviewers'. The sometimes mannered vogue-words commend an informal elegance and wit, both in life and in poetry, and show a corresponding distaste for rusticity and ineptitude. Friends are treated as unique and precious individuals: the shift from teasing mockery of Asinius to over-exquisite affection for others is typical of this self-regarding coterie. The poem catches a society in transition as well as a literature: we are meeting here for the most part not the old Roman aristocracy but rich young men from Italy who are very conscious of their newly acquired metropolitan sophistication. Catullus himself, like other poets of the 'Neoteric' movement, (below, pp. 593 f.) came from beyond the Po (Cisalpine Gaul, as it was then called); his father was a leading citizen of Verona, with an estate at Sirmione on the Lago di Garda. Asinius may be derided as a countrified boor (1, 'Marrucine'), but his grandfather had led Italy against Rome in the Social War; his smart young brother Pollio was to become a tragedian, patron of Virgil, consul, *triumphator*, and historian.

Catullus provides a sketch-book of incidents and people that can be paralleled in antiquity only in Cicero. Among many vivid characters we meet the polished

Suffenus, who yet writes poetry like a *caprimulgus* or goat-milker (22), Egnatius with the silly grin, who cleans his teeth in the Spanish manner (39), Sestius whose frigid oratory gave the poet a bad cold (44), Arrius who has trouble with his aspirates, and says 'hinsidiae' or 'hambushes' (84). Catullus tells how he boasted to a girl that he had acquired eight litter-bearers in Bithynia, only to be found out when she asked for a lift (10. 33 f. 'you're a tactless, tiresome creature, not to let a fellow be careless'). He recalls to his brother-poet Calvus a competition of the previous evening (50. 4 ff. 'the two of us played at writing verselets, now in one metre, now in another, tit for tat amid laughing and drinking'); the very fact that he explains the details shows that he is building up the occasion for a wider public. With the verbal and political licence of his day he directs ribald fantasies at his enemies, even Julius Caesar and his chief-of-staff: 57. 6 ff. 'morbosi pariter gemelli utrique, / uno in lecticulo erudituli ambo, / non hic quam ille magis uorax adulter, / riuales socii puellularum' ('a couple of queers, both identical, two *cognoscenti* in one snug sofa, each an equally avid adulterer, partners in competing with the girlies of the town'). Caesar was not amused but knew the rules of the genre, and on receiving an apology asked the poet to dinner.

Catullus did not address all his poems to men. Of the dozen pieces on the lady he called Lesbia we may begin with one that is written without disillusionment:

> Quaeris, quot mihi basiationes
> tuae, Lesbia, sint satis superque.
> quam magnus numerus Libyssae harenae
> lasarpiciferis iacet Cyrenis
> oraclum Iouis inter aestuosi
> et Batti ueteris sacrum sepulcrum;
> aut quam sidera multa, cum tacet nox,
> furtiuos hominum uident amores:
> tam te basia multa basiare
> uesano satis et super Catullo est,
> quae nec pernumerare curiosi
> possint nec mala fascinare lingua. (7)

You ask, Lesbia, how many kissings of you are for me enough and to spare. As many as the grains of the Libyan sand that stretch in silphium-bearing Cyrenaica between the oracle of sweltering Jove and the hallowed tomb of old Battus, or as many as the stars that when night is hushed look on the stealthy loves of mortals: so many kisses are enough and to spare for crazed Catullus to kiss you with, so that busybodies cannot count them up or an evil tongue cast a spell on them.

At a formal level this belongs to the same category as the poem to Asinius: *basia* is a colloquial word for kisses, unsuited to serious literature; the repeated 'enough and to spare' keeps up the informal tone; the pedantic formation *basiationes* and the mock-conventional 'silphium-bearing' or 'asafoetidiferous' are humorously pretentious; though the poet claims to be crazed, he has not lost his sense of proportion. But there is also a more serious note that raises the poem far above the level it professes. Sand and stars are the tritest of models for the innumerable, but here they evoke an atmosphere that is more important than the literal comparison: the ancient shrine in the desert heat and the dispassionate witnesses in the silent night suggest the tranquillity that envelops the lover's passion. The last couplet adds a typically wry assertion of self-sufficiency: if the kisses are too many to count, the gossiping tongue, like the evil eye, will lose its power to blight. The poem has an emotional range that belies its informal manner, but unlike the critics who write about him Catullus is content with fifty-seven words.

Love-poetry of this sort has no precedent in Greek literature, and was conditioned by a novel combination of social circumstances. The Lesbia of Catullus was really Clodia, one of the spectacular sisters of the aristocratic demagogue Clodius, and probably the wife of Metellus Celer, the consul of 60 BC. Upper-class women had achieved greater emancipation than at any time in the ancient world, and Clodia had not only the style to inspire sophisticated poetry but the education to understand it. If she showed a conspicuous disregard for the ancestral proprieties, her lover could woo her with a sense of adventure and write about her with a lack of reticence impossible within the context of marriage. It is true that some Greek courtesans had been cultured and intelligent, but new elements were the Roman interest in the individual (witness Lucilius and Cicero's letters) and the outspoken independence of a privileged class. When Meleager writes elegant epigrams to his Zenophila or Heliodora, nobody cares whether they ever existed, but Catullus can build up a convincing series of poems about a real relationship in all its vicissitudes. Nothing like that had ever been done before.

Most of the Lesbia cycle is in fact poetry of disillusionment. What gives it its characteristic tone is not just the piquant blend of apparently incompatible emotions but the persistence of the rational voice: here we find subsisting together rueful self-examination, resolute self-exhortation, reasoned reproaches, and virulent hate. Catullus may start at the traditional level of epigram, but he ends by adding a new element to literature.

What a woman says to her eager lover should be written in wind and in swirling water (70. 3 f.)

I hate and yet love. You may wonder how I manage it. I don't know, but feel it happen, and am in torment. (85)

I loved you then not just as the world loves its girl but as a father his sons and sons-in-law (72. 3 f.)

Poor Catullus, you must stop being silly and cut your losses (8. 1 f.)

It's hard suddenly to put aside a long love; it's hard, but somehow you must accomplish it. This is the only way out, this fight you've got to win, this you must do whether it's possible or impossible (76. 13 ff.)

Let her go and get on with it with those lechers of hers whom she clasps in her embrace, three hundred at once, loving none really but repeatedly bursting the loins of all of them, and let her not this time count on my love which has collapsed through her fault like a flower on the field's edge when touched by a passing ploughshare (11. 17 ff.)

The modern world tends to regard such personal pieces as the poet's most significant achievement, but ancient critics would have set a higher value on his more elaborate artefacts. Catullus was a member of the so-called 'Neoteric' movement, which with its precision and preciosity suddenly made traditional narrative poetry seem old-fashioned; though there was an overlap with the writers of occasional short poems, the two trends were distinct in origin. The new movement, which had its roots in Callimachus, was stimulated by the Greek poet and mythographer Parthenius, who was brought to Rome as a prize of war about 65 BC; his captor Cinna has been identified with the Cisalpine poet of that name, who will be familiar to readers of Shakespeare's *Julius Caesar* ('tear him for his bad verses'). The young officer found Parthenian poetics so seductive that he spent nine years composing a short and obscure mythological poem on Zmyrna's passion for her father, and an admiring epigram by Catullus brings to life what the Neoterics were about (95):

My Cinna's *Zmyrna* has been published at last nine summers and nine winters after it was begun, when meanwhile Hortensius(?) has written half a million lines in a single month. *Zmyrna* will be sent as far as her waters of Satrachus [a river of Cyprus which figured in the poem], *Zmyrna* will long be read through by the white-haired centuries. But the *Annals* of Volusius [a conventional narrative poet] will expire at the mouth of the Po [where their author belonged], and will provide lots of loose wrappers for mackerel [i.e. to fry them in]. Dear to me be the small-scale memorials of *my* favourite writer, but the vulgar can rejoice in their bloated Antimachus [a verbose poet derided by Callimachus].

The Neoteric influence on Catullus may be seen at its simplest in a harmonious wedding-poem whose symbolism goes back to Sappho: 'ut flos in saeptis secretus nascitur hortis / ignotus pecori, nullo conuolsus aratro, / quem mulcent aurae, firmat sol, educat imber' (62. 39 ff. 'as a bloom grows secluded in a walled garden, unfamiliar to the herd, plucked by no ploughshare, that the breezes fondle, the sunshine builds up, the shower brings on'). A more fantastic specimen of the movement's tastes is a bizarre *tour de force* on the self-castration of Attis, which with its syncopated rhythms and accumulation of short syllables evokes the orgiastic music of Cybele's eunuch-priests:

> Where the cymbals' voice is sounding, and the tambourines re-echoing,
> And the Phrygian piper blaring with a curved pipe's cacophony,
> Where the ivy-wearing Maenads toss heads energetically
> And with shrilling ululations celebrate rites inviolable,
> Where is wont to come cavorting Cybele's vagrant retinue,
> It befits us there to hasten with accelerated three-step.   (63.21–6)

In a more profound poem that was to become the prototype of Roman elegy Catullus relates the sorrows of his life to the paradigms of myth. Just as Laodamia's passionate marriage was unhallowed from the beginning, so Lesbia came to him with an omen of doom: 'my radiant goddess entered with dainty steps, and planting her gleaming foot on the worn threshold, halted there with a click of her slipper' (68. 70 ff.). In the same way an anguished couplet on his brother's death near Troy recalls the sufferings of the *Iliad*: 'Troia—nefas—commune sepulcrum Asiae Europaeque / Troia uirum et uirtutum omnium acerba cinis' (68. 89 f. 'Troy, oh horror, the common burial-ground of Asia and Europe, Troy the untimely dust of all true men and manhood'). Greek elegiac poetry was never as personal or as deeply felt.

Catullus' most ambitious work is the 'Wedding of Peleus and Thetis' (64), a poem in the hexameters of epic, but in accordance with neoteric principles lasting only for 400 lines. He begins with the wondrous voyage of the first ship Argo 'Phasidos ad fluctus et fines Aeeteos' (2 'to the floods of Phasis and the realm of Aeetes'); the exotic proper names and the slow quadrisyllabic line-ending already suggest the poem's languorous beauty. 'As soon as the ship ploughed the windy plain with her beak and churned by the oars the wave whitened with spume, there emerged strange faces from the shining deep, the Nereids of Ocean marvelling at the apparition. In that and no other dawn mortals saw with their own eyes nymphs with bared bodies protruding to their breasts from the white deep' (64. 12 ff.). Such was the first encounter of the mortal Argonaut Peleus with the divine sea-nymph Thetis, and the rest of the poem depicts the celebration of their wedding. Pindar says that Peleus then achieved the highest happiness known to mortals, but even he was doomed to sorrow: the child of the marriage, Achilles, was to die young at Troy. Catullus' poem cannot be understood unless we remember both the supreme felicity of the occasion and the implicit undercurrent of sadness.

After recording the arrival of the guests, Catullus turns to the splendours of the scene, in particular a tapestry on the bed that depicted the story of Theseus and Ariadne (50 ff.). First we see a windswept heroine on the shore of Naxos as she gazes out to sea at her departing lover. Then a flashback describes how she had first met Theseus and how he had slain the Minotaur. Then we return to Naxos and hear an emotional soliloquy from Ariadne on her lover's forgetfulness. Next comes a projection of Theseus' return to Athens: he had forgotten to signal his victory by hoisting white sails, an arrangement expounded in another flashback, so his father Aegeus jumped over a cliff. Then back to Naxos again, where Bacchus approaches Ariadne with his outlandish revellers. The happy ending is hinted at rather than stated: every literate person knew that the god would marry the heroine and translate her to the sky.

The presentation of this digression illustrates important characteristics of the Neoteric poets and their Hellenistic predecessors. The dislocations of chronological order show a lack of interest in story-telling for its own sake: organic unity of action now matters less than the effects of diversity and surprise, and the aesthetic balance of the composition as a whole. The significant moments are caught in a series of colourful tableaux which suggest the influence of a pictorial art that was romantic in conception and ultra-realistic in execution. The love interest is neither Homeric nor traditionally Roman but derives from the psychologizing of some Hellenistic poets, especially Apollonius in his *Argonautica*: so too the attempt of a male-dominated world to enter into a rejected woman's feelings, an approach that went back to the *Medea* of Euripides and was to influence Virgil's portrayal of Dido. The sheer length of the episode may seem curious (it takes up more than half the piece), but such digressions were regular in poems of this type. Nor need we speak of irrelevance unless we apply inappropriate criteria: in ancient poetry descriptions of works of art often include elements that foreshadow something in the main action, and Ariadne's change from misery to happiness, while it reverses the movement of the poem as a whole, underlines the vicissitudes of human experience.

The action resumes with the departure of the wedding guests, which is described in a simile which no earlier Roman poet could have written:

> hic, qualis flatu placidum mare matutino
> horrificans Zephyrus procliuas incitat undas,
> Aurora exoriente, uagi sub limina Solis,
> quae tarde primum clementi flamine pulsae
> procedunt, leuiterque sonant plangore cachinni,
> post uento crescente magis magis increbescunt,
> purpureaque procul nantes ab luce refulgent.
>
> (269–75)

Then just as the West Wind ruffles the calm sea with morning breath, and sets the waves rolling, as dawn rises, towards the portals of the roving sun, and driven by the gentle breeze they proceed slowly at first, and their ripples sound with a soft plash; then, as the wind freshens, they crowd thicker and faster, and as they float along, shimmer afar with the purple light.

The comparison primarily illustrates how a trickle of departing guests develops into a flood, and nobody who has taken in the poet's words will forget them on such occasions. But there are other points of correspondence: 'cachinni' suggests the guests' merry babble, 'purpurea' their fine clothes, 'nantes' their undulating movement. The luminosity of the passage is typical of the poem as a whole: Catullus has imitated the more glittering aspect of Hellenistic poetry and given it a delightfully new colour and freshness.

As the poem draws towards its close it appropriately includes an epithalamium, which is sung not by a choir of young girls (the usual practice), or by the Muses (as in Pindar's account of this particular wedding), but by those grisly spinstresses, the Fates. Their chant begins normally enough with a mention of the Evening Star, a commendation of wedded bliss, and an annunciation of the child of the marriage. But the prophecy of Achilles gradually assumes a sinister note: 'his surpassing merits and glorious deeds mothers will often acknowledge at the funerals of their sons, when they let fall dishevelled hair from grey heads and bruise withered breasts with palsied palms. Run, drawing the threads, run, spindles' (348 ff.). And to remove all doubt about the poet's stance, they predict that Achilles' tomb will be honoured by the sacrifice of a girl. The poet's revulsion at these barbaric deeds is all the more effective for the matter-of-fact way in which they are presented. The poem's limpid beauty, which suited so well the lost age of innocence, now takes on a characteristically ironic note: just as in some of the love poems, the subject-matter and the style have begun to pull in opposite directions.

In spite of their very different subjects, Lucretius and Catullus have much in common. Both are recognizably poets of the Republic, and can describe intellectual or emotional adventures with a candour difficult in later periods. Both write Latin with an elegant propriety that is sometimes lost in the subtleties of the Augustans. Both observe the world with an uncluttered directness that had been unknown for centuries, and was never quite recovered in antiquity. Lucretius' awareness of beauty shows the influence of the new poetry, and some of Catullus' descriptions are modelled on Lucretius. But though the Neoteric movement refined techniques and enlarged sensibilities, its effect on literature was not all good. When art is pursued for art's sake, there is a danger of forgetting the nature of things.

Further Reading

LUCRETIUS

The best way of finding what Lucretius was like is to buy M. F. Smith's revision (Cambridge, Mass., 1975), including text and translation, of W. H. D. Rouse's Loeb edition. The standard commentary is by C. Bailey (3 vols., Oxford, 1947, including text and translation); this is particularly informative on the Epicurean background, but is long for non-specialists. There is a good short commentary on Book III by E. J. Kenney (Cambridge, 1971).

E. J. Kenney has summarized the issues in a very useful pamphlet (*Lucretius*. Greece & Rome New Surveys in the Classics, no. 11, Oxford, 1977). D. West, *The Imagery and Poetry of Lucretius* (Edinburgh, 1969) encourages the reader to look closely at the Latin, and should be compulsory reading for all who wish to understand any Roman poetry. D. R. Dudley, *Lucretius* (London, 1965), includes articles of varying interest by different hands. P. Boyancé, *Lucrèce et l'épicurisme* (Paris, 1963), is a specialized account of the philosophy of the poem.

CATULLUS

The best introduction is G. P. Goold, *Catullus* (London, 1983); this contains a text that is more radical than most, and a facing translation that is both literal and literary. The best English commentary is by C. J. Fordyce (Oxford, 1961, revised 1973); this includes Mynors's Oxford text except for a number of poems that have been expurgated. The commentary by K. Quinn (London, 1970), which contains all the poems, is better on bibliography but less good on Latin.

A. L. Wheeler, *Catullus and the Traditions of Ancient Poetry* (Berkeley and Los Angeles, 1934) is full and informative, but old-fashioned in manner and some of its matter. K. Quinn, *The Catullan Revolution* (Melbourne, 1959; Cambridge, 1969) covers less ground but will appeal more to the literary reader. Perceptive criticism may be found in the relevant chapters of R. O. A. M. Lyne, *The Latin Love Poets from Catullus to Horace* (Oxford, 1980) and R. Jenkyns, *Three Classical Poets/Sappho, Catullus and Juvenal* (London, 1983); the latter helps the reader to appreciate the beauty of the poet's words.

21

Hellenistic and Graeco-Roman Art

❧❦❧

ROGER LING

Introduction

HELLENISTIC art is an unfashionable field. To the *aficionados* of the Archaic and Classical periods it seems a bewildering farrago of divergent styles, at one extreme bloated and showy, at the other flaccid and derivative: it is almost as though Greek art, hitherto carried forward in a relatively comprehensible and consistent pattern of development, loses its way and threshes around without a sense of purpose. To the students of Roman art, with its clearer chronological framework and (in the mainstream at least) its firm political thrust, the Hellenistic age is the shadowy and half-understood background out of which emerge the technical know-how and many of the stylistic features which go into the making of the Roman state tradition. These attitudes of course do scant justice to the achievements of Hellenistic art. The period 323–31 BC saw the creation of some of the greatest of Greek masterpieces—masterpieces which have exercised considerable influence on the artists and art critics of recent centuries, especially the seventeenth and eighteenth.

The main reason why Hellenistic art has been neglected, if not denigrated, is the difficulty of studying it. The new political situation, in which Greek culture was brought into contact with various alien traditions and at the same time diffused over areas too vast for effective communications to be maintained, inevitably led to regional variations: there is no single current that can be traced. More serious are the problems of dating and attribution, due chiefly to the shortage of written evidence. After the comparative abundance of literary and epigraphic testimonia for the Classical period, our sources for Hellenistic art are exiguous. The Elder Pliny, previously our main support, provides no more than a few scattered and barely datable references for the 150 years between the early third and mid second centuries BC; and fragments of Hellenistic authors quoted by Athenaeus in his *Deipnosophistae* (*c.*AD 200), together with isolated snippets of information in the architectural treatise of Vitruvius and in the histories of Diodorus and Valerius Maximus, do very little to fill the gap. Archaeological associations are also less helpful for dating than in the previous period. The works of art which can be connected with precise historical events are few and far between: the Romans left very little behind when they destroyed Corinth in 146, and it is not always clear whether the abandonment of buildings on Delos is to be attributed to the sack by Mithridates in 88, to the pirate raid of 69, or to a later turn of events. There are in addition relatively few Hellenistic buildings which are closely dated by inscriptions. Nor do any classes of Hellenistic ceramics supply dating evidence comparable to that offered for previous centuries by Athenian black-figure and red-figure: only lately have more rigorous pottery studies sharpened the cutting edge of this particular chronological tool.

All this has contributed to an inextricable confusion surrounding Hellenistic art; but nonetheless certain generalizations can be made. First, the artistic centre of gravity in the Greek world shifted eastwards. While Athens remained an important focus of patronage and production, the great centres of Hellenistic times were in Asia Minor and the eastern Mediterranean: Pergamum, Rhodes, Antioch, Alexandria. Secondly, the type of patronage changed. Whereas in Classical times Greek artists had worked primarily for cities and private citizens, now they found themselves receiving commissions from all-powerful kings and their ministers; and the old ideals of civic pride and religious reverence which had inspired the great works of the Classical period gave way to the personal whims and propaganda of the new ruling classes. These circumstances, combined with the development of science and humanism, account for several aspects of Hellenistic art which will be illustrated below: the broadened range of subjects, a trend towards the secularization of art, the emergence of academic and ostentatious work, generally the tendency of art to entertain rather than to elevate the viewer. Ultimately, with the encroachment of Roman power upon the Greek stage, the focus of attention moved westwards and new patrons appeared: the merchants, magistrates, and military potentates of Rome. This ushered in a new phase of classicism and eclecticism and began the process whereby Greek artists were schooled to interpret the imperialist ideologies of the new world-power.

Architecture

In architecture the Hellenistic age saw an increased loosening of the rules which had governed Classical design, a fuller and more flamboyant use of surface decoration, often at variance with the interior structure, a gradual development of new structural forms and techniques, and the creation of the first truly homogeneous planned complexes in which each individual building was designed to fit in the ensemble.

The rules of Classical design had centred upon the two architectural orders, Doric and Ionic. In Hellenistic times not only were the rules of each order relaxed, but we find the two orders more freely combined within one building, for example in the superimposed storeys of a portico (*stoa*), or even elements of the one grafted on to the other to form a kind of hybrid order. In Doric there was a tendency for columns to become slimmer and more widely spaced, with three or four metopes and triglyphs per intercolumniation in place of the 'canonical' two. The lighter, more spacious effect was more in harmony with the aesthetic of Hellenistic times, which found traditional Doric too severe and heavy. At the same time the Doric triglyph frieze could be inserted in an Ionic order, as in the Sanctuary of Athena at Pergamum, and conversely the dentils of Ionic could be combined with Doric columns and entablature, as in the north *stoa* of the *agora* at Priene. A certain amount of mixing had taken place especially in the western colonies as early as the Archaic period, but the thoroughgoing hybridization of Hellenistic times betokens a new attitude in which the traditional orders lost much of their independence and became a common repertory of ornament to be dipped into almost at will.

This new flexibility is symbolized by the progress of the Corinthian order. Used in the fourth century for interior columns in such buildings as the temple

PORTICO OF THE SANCTUARY OF ATHENA AT PERGAMUM, built by Eumenes II (197–159 BC). Characteristic of the Hellenistic age are the combination of a Doric colonnade in the lower storey with an Ionic in the upper, and the relaxation of the rules governing the syntax of the orders (including the insertion of a Doric frieze within an Ionic entablature).

COLUMNS OF THE OLYMPIEUM IN ATHENS. Begun by Pisistratus in the sixth century BC probably as an Ionic temple, this most ambitious of all religious buildings in European Greece was resumed by the Seleucid King Antiochus IV (176-165 BC) in the Corinthian order. It was not completed until the time of the Roman Emperor Hadrian (AD 117-38).

of Athena at Tegea and the *tholoi* (rotundas) at Delphi and Epidaurus, this ornate subform of Ionic had hitherto seemed too avant-garde for exteriors except those of baroque follies such as the monument of Lysicrates in Athens. But the rich taste of Hellenistic times and the greater adaptability of the Corinthian capital, which, unlike the Ionic, can be viewed to good effect from all angles, led to increasing popularity during the third and second centuries, culminating in the adoption of Corinthian capitals for the main order of one of the most prestigious of all building projects, Antiochus IV's revival of work on the temple of Olympian Zeus in Athens.

The Corinthian style may have enjoyed particular favour in the Seleucid area, but florid decoration, in which relatively naturalistic vegetal forms played an important role, occurs widely in the Hellenistic world. Good examples can be seen in the massive new temple of Apollo at Didyma, begun about 300 BC and still incomplete 700 years later; a beautiful frieze of foliate scrolls and heraldic pairs of griffins which ran round the interior court is dated to the first half of the second century BC. Foliate decoration was especially popular in Pergamum, from where it was carried to Rome during the late second and first centuries.

This sort of surface decoration fits within the confines of columnar construction, but another Hellenistic trend sees the columnar orders themselves used increasingly in a decorative fashion, applied in a non-structural role to walls and façades. The exterior wall of the *bouleutērion* (council-house) at Miletus, built between 175 and 164 BC, was divided into two storeys, of which the lower was treated as a plain podium, while the upper was decorated with engaged columns. Here at least the horizontal moulding dividing the two storeys corresponded to a structural division in the interior, namely the top of the semicircular auditorium; but elsewhere the articulation of exterior walls responded to no internal logic. For example, the façade of the Great Tomb at Levkadia (*c.*300 BC) is decorated with an engaged Doric order surmounted by a continuous frieze of stucco reliefs, surmounted in turn by a small Ionic order carrying a pediment; but behind this pseudo-structural screen is a plain vaulted antechamber rising to full height: apart from the spring of the vault there are no internal caesuras to justify the external show. Such display architecture is epitomized by the mausoleum at Belevi, near Ephesus, perhaps intended as the tomb of Lysimachus, where the monumental masonry and elaborately carved mouldings of the great cube containing the burial chamber are merely a surface dressing for a massive outcrop of living rock. The divorce between structure and decoration is one of the important Hellenistic legacies to the Roman age.

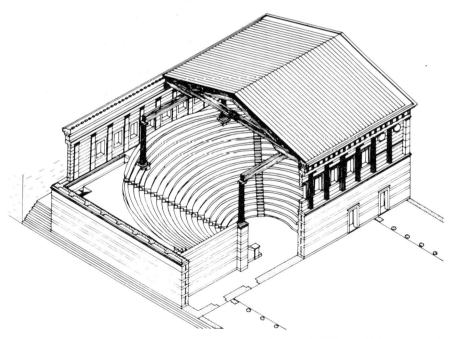

COUNCIL CHAMBER AT MILETUS (*c.*170 BC). A new type of public building which emerged during the fourth and third centuries BC was the concert or assembly chamber with a semi-circular auditorium like that of Greek theatres set within a great rectangular hall. Here an additional feature of interest is the use of engaged semi-columns as a purely decorative device on the exterior.

CRYPT OF THE SO-CALLED ORACLE OF THE DEAD AT EPHYRA, in western Greece (third century BC). It is typical of Greek architecture that the vault is used in an underground structure. The principle of the arch and vault was known to Democritus in the fifth century BC, but surviving examples date to the second half of the fourth century or later.

New structural forms and techniques did not make enormous headway east of the Adriatic. Post-and-lintel construction remained the basis of architectural form, and dressed stone, timber, and mud brick the staple constructive materials. In the time of Alexander, however, perhaps as a result of experience gained by his engineers in the East, vaults and arches became more common in the Greek world. Vaults were used to span the tomb-chambers of Macedonian nobles, and isolated examples are found in later buildings, generally in an inconspicuous or subordinate role. Sloping vaults covered the narrow passages leading to the interior court of the temple at Didyma, and barrel-vaults met at right angles in various Pergamene buildings. Elsewhere arches were used in subterranean structures to support stone paving above or (in the crypt of the third-century Nekromanteion at Ephyra) to bear the weight of a barrel-vault. In all cases the construction was carried out in stone, even though this might lead to structural weakness, especially where vaults intersected. The octagonal Tower of the Winds in Athens, an elaborate water-clock and planetarium built by Andronicus of Cyrrhus in the mid first century BC, was roofed by a series of long wedge-shaped blocks bearing upon a central keystone. Only with the development of concrete construction in

Italy (below, pp. 516 ff.) did vaulting become a fundamental component of architecture, destined to open up undreamt-of possibilities in the expansion and manipulation of interior space.

One final general aspect of Hellenistic architecture is the composition of ensembles which were visually unified, whether by the use of recurrent motifs or by the setting of one building as a foil to another. The urban foundations which Alexander and his successors planted in the newly conquered areas were a good testing ground for the planners. Most of them were laid out in accordance with the traditional Hippodamian, rectilinear grid, and, though development could be piecemeal and incoherent, as it had often been in the past, there was increasing concern to relate buildings to one another and to frame and define space by means of the ubiquitous *stoa*. The best-known examples are the monumental piazzas of Miletus and Priene, both pre-Hellenistic chequerboard cities which experienced major programmes of building during the third and second centuries BC. Even the chaotic sprawl of the *agora* in Athens had some order imposed upon it at this time with the construction, at right angles to each other, of the Middle Stoa along the south side and the Stoa of Attalus on the east. In another pre-Hellenistic city, Rhodes, unknown planners stacked buildings on the acropolis in a masterful exercise in giving architectonic shape to a sloping terrain. It was from beginnings such as these that the great terraced complexes at Lindus and Cos, with their broadly axial layouts and monumental stairways, evolved. But the finest architectural composition of the age dispensed altogether with orthogonal patterns. The upper city of Pergamum (first half of the second century) grew organically out of the landscape in a series of terraces climbing fan-like up a crescent-shaped hill in which the auditorium of a steep theatre formed a kind of valve. At the foot of the theatre, providing a firm visual basis for the great ensemble, ran a horizontal esplanade supported by a high retaining wall whose massive buttresses took root in the lower slopes. Throughout the composition Doric stoas acted as a leitmotif, both defining and unifying the different spaces. They also masked changes of level, being two-storeyed on one side and single-storeyed on the other.

Among individual building types in Hellenistic architecture most had existed before, but many now assumed more monumental form. Great altars with colonnaded enclosures approached by broad stairways were built at Magnesia, Pergamum, and Priene; in each of them sculpture played an integral part in the overall effect, statues being set between the columns at Magnesia and Priene, and high reliefs taking over the podium at Pergamum (below, pp. 509 f.). The huge *tholos* of Arsinoe at Samothrace dispensed with internal and external colonnades but incorporated an open gallery at the top of the wall. Stone theatres became a characteristic feature of Hellenistic cities and were now endowed as a matter of course with architectural stage-houses, including a high proscenium which encroached upon the circular space formerly allotted to the orchestra. In utilitarian building an important step was the introduction of heated baths: simple hypocaust

MODEL OF THE ACROPOLIS AT PERGAMUM, a *tour de force* in the adaptation of urban planning to the configuration of the land. At the bottom, the Theatre Terrace leading (at the left) to the small temple of Dionysus; above this, the fan-like auditorium of the theatre; round the theatre, from right to left, the court of the Great Altar (*c*.166 BC), the sanctuary of Athena (late third to early second century BC); and the second-century AD temple of Trajan.

systems are attested at Piraeus, at Gela in Sicily, at Gortys in Arcadia, and about 100 BC in the small Greek bath-suite at Olympia. Residential buildings too began to acquire some architectural pretensions, as the rise of officials in the new kingdoms and the emergence of wealthy merchant classes in the commercial cities created a demand for better-quality housing. Focused upon a small court, the typical middle-class house in cities such as Priene and Delos boasted at least one large reception room, frequently opening from the north side of a peristyle or a two-columned antechamber to catch the sun in winter; its interior surfaces were protected and enhanced by mosaic pavements and painted stucco wall-decorations; and quite often there were statues or marble furnishings set in the colonnades. A fine example is the House of the Hermes on Delos, terraced into a hillside on four levels, with a peristyle court rising through three of them.

Sculpture

For free-standing statuary there is a rather better survival rate in Hellenistic times than in the preceding period. This is partly because the major artists, following the lead given by Praxiteles, were less disdainful of marble as a sculptural material than had been Lysippus and, before him, many of the great fifth-century sculptors, whose massive output of works in bronze finished up in the melting-pots of the Middle Ages; and partly because several of the principal centres of patron-

PERISTYLE COURT IN THE HOUSE OF THE DIONYSUS ON DELOS (late second century BC). Such courts were the normal focus of the well-to-do houses in the Athenian colony of the second century BC. One portico was often deeper, and sometimes taller, than the others, in order to protect and enhance the entrance to a large reception room (here at the rear). A well-head (here in the right foreground) covers the opening to the cistern which provided the Delian house with its water-supply.

age now lay east of the Aegean and in the Levant and were not subjected to the wholesale plunder suffered by Corinth and other cities of European Greece in the wake of the Roman conquest. At a minor level there are large series of terracotta figurines, produced in factories such as those of Taranto, Tanagra in Boeotia (demure ladies in their Sunday best), Myrina in Asia Minor (characters from New Comedy), and Alexandria (ethnic and genre types).

Despite this relative abundance of evidence the problems of dating already mentioned make it well-nigh impossible to establish any sort of stylistic framework for the period. The most widely accepted schema is that of the German art historian Gerhard Krahmer, who postulated three main phases: a severe style distinguished by 'closed form', that is, by statues or statue-groups whose structure leads the eye into an inner focus (*c.*300–*c.*240 BC); the High Hellenistic phase, characterized by grandeur and pathos (*c.*240–*c.*150 BC); and the Late Hellenistic phase, in which open form and one-sided compositions reminiscent of earlier styles prevailed (*c.*150–*c.*100 BC). This and similar systems are however dependent upon a few datable works, chiefly from one or two main centres, and make too many presumptions about works for which the dating evidence is slim or non-existent; so they can at best be regarded as no more than a broad guide. It remains safer and more satisfactory to review the achievements of Hellenistic sculpture in general terms, category by category.

One category in which distinctive trends were developed was the draped figure. Alongside the high-waisted, narrow-shouldered look of the Tanagra ladies and many full-size statues, a look which was a condition of contemporary *haute mode* as much as of sculptural style, there are works which show a conscious virtuosity on the part of the sculptor. A favourite device was the stretching of

NIKE (VICTORY) FROM SAMOTHRACE (*c.*200 BC), a statue set up in the sanctuary of the Great Gods in commemoration of a naval victory, perhaps by the Rhodians. The goddess is shown alighting on the prow of a ship, which was originally set in a rock-filled pool—the kind of landscape composition which seems to have been especially popular in Hellenistic Rhodes. She probably held a bronze victory-wreath in her right hand.

TERRACOTTA FIGURINE OF LADY WITH DOVE from Tanagra (late fourth or third century BC). Wrapped in a voluminous cloak (*himation*), with a fan in her left hand, and her hair centrally parted and gathered in a chignon at the back of her head, she is the height of early Hellenistic fashion. Such figurines were highly popular trinkets at the time.

the drapery across the body to create a pattern of taut and loose folds almost independent of the form beneath: good examples are provided by the statue of Tyche of Antioch (soon after 300 BC), known only from Roman copies, and a bronze statuette of a veiled dancer in the Metropolitan Museum of Art, New York. Another device, cultivated especially in the cities of western Asia Minor during the last two centuries BC, was the exploitation of different textures, and especially the rendering of the mantle to produce the effect of a silken shawl, through which the folds of the dress are clearly visible. But the finest of Hellenistic draped statues, the Nike (Victory) of Samothrace, employed a more traditional style, contrasting clinging folds over the breasts, abdomen, and left leg with deep-cut swathes in other areas. Here, however, the contrasts are more exaggerated than they had been in fifth-century Athenian sculptures, and the folds over the advanced right leg are used in an impressionistic manner, swinging this way and that without rhyme or reason to suggest the force of the wind as the winged goddess comes in to land. It is characteristic of the Hellenistic age that the Nike served a semi-decorative role as the crowning ornament of a triumphal ship-monument and that this monument was merely the centrepiece of a landscaped composition of rocks and water: more varied functions and more pictorial settings were one result of the new kinds of patronage.

Another important category of statue was the female nude. Praxiteles' much admired Aphrodite of Cnidus (above, p. 294) was the forerunner of a long series of Hellenistic Aphrodites, including a beautiful statue from Cyrene and the self-conscious *poseuse* commemorated in the Capitoline Venus. An interesting variant is the crouching goddess attributed by some to a Bithynian sculptor of the third century: the thrusting knees, the raised right and lowered left arm, the sharply turned head, and the torsion about the waist, accentuated by unflattering folds of flesh, produce an effect of tension and imminent movement which would have been inconceivable in any statue before the time of Lysippus. Equally restless, but much more subtle, is the majestic Aphrodite from Melos (Venus de Milo), a late-second-century work. Here the slightly twisting torso and the broad mass of drapery clinging precariously to the hips and sweeping over the raised and advanced left thigh were merely part of the complex composition: one has also to imagine the missing arms, which must have been extended to the side, perhaps holding a bronze shield in which the goddess admired her reflection.

A whole range of themes which would have been considered undignified or demeaning in the art of previous centuries now entered the repertory of sculptors: sleeping figures, drunks, cupids, old hags, thugs, hermaphrodites. Some of the more playful subjects, such as the delightful sleeping cherub in New York, the famous boy-and-goose composition of Boethus, and the various tussles between nymphs and satyrs, have reminded commentators of the rococo of the eighteenth century; and they indeed betoken the same sort of light-hearted, almost frivolous taste. Many must have been designed for the amusement of wealthy private collectors. So too may some of the more ugly and horrific subjects. They tend

APHRODITE FROM MELOS (VENUS DE MILO), the finest of all surviving nude female statues (late second century BC). It is normally argued that she held her drape with the right hand and rested the left on a pillar at her side; but the old view that she was looking at her reflection in a shield (like her prototype, the so-called Capua Aphrodite) is still attractive.

to be characterized as examples of Hellenistic 'realism'; but a glance at the bronze boxer in the Terme Museum in Rome, with his ostentatious wounds, exaggerated musculature, yet artistically ordered hair, will show that even now Greek sculptors were more concerned with types than with real appearances.

One area where types were less important was portraiture. Here, partly inspired by the activity of Lysippus and his school, including his brother Lysistratus who is said to have invented the practice of taking casts from the human face, sculptors broke new ground in the characterization of the individual. A fine example is the statue of the orator and statesman Demosthenes set up in Athens about 280 BC and known to us from copies (above, p. 153). The severe expression, furrowed brow, and stooping shoulders correspond well enough to the description given in Plutarch's biography, and the eloquent gesture of the clasped hands expresses something of the tragedy of Demosthenes' hopeless struggle against Macedonian imperialism. Replicas of other fine portrait-statues include the seated philosopher Chrysippus reconstructed in the Louvre (above, p. 369). But most

STATUE OF A CHILD PLAYING WITH A GOOSE, a Roman copy of a Hellenistic composition dated to the third century BC. A passage in Pliny's *Natural History* refers to a work by one Boethus which showed an infant strangling a goose (perhaps 'by embracing it', but the reading is uncertain); it may be the source of this type.

noteworthy were the long series of royal portraits running from the romantic Lysippan Alexander (above, p. 316), with tilted head, upturned eyes, and flowing hair, to the nice blend of realism and idealization found in heads of the Bactrian and Indian kings, known chiefly from their coins. As in earlier times, the Greek portraitist felt that the whole figure was essential to convey the character of the sitter, and therefore sculptured portraits were always full statues; but as time went on there was an increasing emphasis upon the expressive quality of the face and an increasing readiness to show wrinkles, creases, and other features which artists of the fifth and fourth centuries would have glossed over.

COIN PORTRAITS OF BACTRIAN KINGS: (*Left*) Antimachus (*c*.185 BC), (*right*) Eucratides I (*c*.165–150 BC). The portraits of this remarkable dynasty on the far-eastern fringe of the Hellenistic world show a degree of individuality never matched by the often bland depictions of their royal contemporaries further west. Eucratides is helmeted; Antimachus wears the Macedonian royal beret, or *causia*.

Another sculptural genre which owed much to the influence of Lysippus was the figure-group. Lysippus' exploitation of the third dimension, and no doubt the famous multi-figure compositions in bronze with which he and collaborators had commemorated the exploits of Alexander, paved the way for a whole range of virtuoso statue-groups, in which two, three, or more figures were arranged in complex relationships which required a new attitude on the part of the viewer. The wrestlers in Florence, the Ludovisi Gaul in the Terme Museum (above, p. 320), and the elaborate Rhodian composition showing the punishment of Dirce, reflected in a Roman copy in Naples, cannot be fully appreciated from any one viewpoint, but demand to be studied from all angles. The Ludovisi Gaul, whose prototype, together with that of the dying Gaul in the Capitoline Museum, formed part of a larger aggregation of bronze statues set up in Pergamum to commemorate the victories of Kings Attalus and Eumenes, also illustrates further facets of Hellenistic group composition, in particular its love of drama and of studied contrasts. The act of the Gaulish chieftain who has killed his wife and plunged the sword in his own breast rather than surrender might have seemed theatrical were it not for the impressive nobility of the warrior's face and figure. At the same time the artist makes great play of the contrast between the vigorous action of the Gaul and the limpness of the dead wife, between the muscularity of his virtually naked body and the lifeless fall of her drapery. Yet the two figures are artistically united in a favourite pyramidal structure by the left arm of the warrior supporting his wife's collapsing form. It is significant that this Hellenistic victory-monument expressed its message in more human terms than its great Classical predecessors: not only were the actual Gaulish foes of Pergamum represented where Classical sculptors would have chosen some remote mythological allegory, but they were also rendered with sympathy both for their distinctive physiognomy (broad cheeks, chunky hair, the man's moustache) and for their great courage and dignity. Other groups showed an increased emphasis on horror. For example, the old myth of Marsyas, hitherto represented in its earlier, milder stages, the discovery of the flutes and the musical contest between the satyr and Apollo, now moved on to its gruesome climax: a number of copies attest the existence of a group, again probably Pergamene, consisting of the terrified Marsyas strung up on a tree, a brutal, balding Scythian slave sharpening the knife with which he is to be flayed alive, and (no doubt) a pitiless seated Apollo.

In relief sculpture the Alexander sarcophagus (above, p. 327), apparently carved for Alexander's client king in Sidon, reveals a number of important developments of the early Hellenistic period. The representation of actual events involving living or recently dead personages (hunting scenes and episodes from Alexander's battles) and the portrayal of precise details of national costume and armour look forward to the Pergamene Gauls and ultimately to the historical reliefs of imperial Rome; while the complexity and interlocking of the main battle relief mark a complete break from the well-spaced duels which prevailed in fifth- and fourth-century sculpture. One effect here was a diminution in importance of the background, which had always been the essential foil to reliefs of the Classical period. This development reached a climax in the sculptures of the Great Altar at Pergamum (second quarter of the second century BC). The larger frieze, situated on the exterior of the podium, depicted the time-honoured subject of the battle of gods and giants, but did so with a bravado and grandiloquence never equalled in ancient art. Almost every inch of the available surface was covered with a writhing mass of bodies, wings, drapery, coiling snakes, and animal forms, all rendered with a loving attention to texture which can distinguish, for example, between the nap and plain surfaces of the same piece of cloth. The effect was to destroy the visual function of the podium and to leave the superstructure of the altar floating, as it were, above the cosmic tumult of the sculptures. A particularly good example of the ambivalent relation between architecture and decoration was the group of giants which rested hands, knees, and snake-coils directly on the steps of the monumental entrance stairway, as if trying to crawl out of the frieze. Along with the technical brilliance went a typically Hellenistic academi-

DETAIL OF THE BATTLE OF GODS AND GIANTS: frieze of the Altar of Zeus and Athena at Pergamum (*c*.166–159 BC). Athena seizes the giant Alcyoneus by the hair and wrenches him away from his mother Ge (Earth), while Victory flies in to place a wreath on Athena's head. A good example of the bombast and virtuosity of this most extravagant of ancient sculptural creations.

cism: in addition to the twelve Olympian gods, the artists had introduced about seventy-five lesser deities and personifications, all of whom, like the giants, were labelled with inscriptions for the benefit of passers-by. It is difficult to remember that all this, like most Greek sculpture in stone, must originally have been coloured.

While the great frieze denied the existence of the background, the smaller frieze of the interior court turned it into real space. This frieze, which told the story of Pergamum's legendary founder Telephus, a romantic tale of a type much favoured among Hellenistic court poets, employed a continuous narrative technique in which the same characters appeared again and again at different moments of time. Each episode ran on from the previous one without a break, but the shifting setting was indicated by landscape elements: the sacred laurel tree of Delphi, hangings in Aleos' palace, the oak forest in which Heracles seduced Auge. More striking, the figures occupied only two-thirds of the height of the frieze, so that the upper third was available for rocks, foliage, architectural members, and so forth, or could alternatively be left free to suggest sky. Sometimes a hint of perspective was conveyed by the placing of certain figures above those in the foreground: that they were not merely conceived as at a higher level is indicated by their slightly smaller scale. This 'activation' of the background, which surely owed much to the influence of painting, was echoed, in more tentative fashion, on a number of minor Hellenistic reliefs but was to be more fully exploited only in Roman times.

Painting and the Other Arts

Pictorial reliefs bring us naturally to painting. Here, however, much less can be said, because there is almost no direct evidence apart from funerary paintings in one or two Macedonian chamber tombs and on gravestones from Alexandria and Demetrias in Thessaly.

Major paintings probably continued to be carried out mainly on wooden panels. Alexander's reign was evidently a highpoint in the history of pictorial art, to judge from the literary references to the work of his court painter Apelles, at least three of whose famous masterpieces were later displayed in Rome. This golden age of painting continued at the courts of the Successors, who commissioned various works to commemorate the achievements of the great Macedonian. We hear of at least two multi-figure paintings of Alexander's battles (by Philoxenus of Eretria and a Graeco-Egyptian paintress Helen) and get hints of others. If, as seems likely, one of them was reproduced three centuries later in the famous mosaic pavement from the House of the Faun at Pompeii (photo facing p. 438), the artists of this time were capable of highly complex compositions with a full mastery of foreshortening and of modelling by means of deep shadows and strong highlights: see especially the horse shown in back view in the foreground. They also conveyed a degree of emotion in the faces of the figures: Alexander's grim determination is contrasted with the alarmed expressions of Darius and the other Persians. In colour, though obviously the mosaicist was to some extent restricted by his materials, the copy seems to reflect a deliberate limitation of the painter's palette to red, yellow, black, white, and tones available from combinations of these, an aesthetic device whose popularity in the works of Apelles and his contemporaries is recorded by Pliny. Blue is absent and green confined to inconspicuous details.

The action of the Alexander mosaic takes place on a shallow stage between a brown foreground and a white sky, the effect of space being achieved principally by spears on the skyline. The only true landscape element, forming a counterbalance to the prominent figure of Darius in his chariot, is a dead tree. It has often been claimed that landscape was used sparingly in Hellenistic painting and always in a subsidiary role to human figures, much as it appears in the Telephus frieze. But a painted frieze above the entrance of a recently excavated tomb at Vergina dated as early as the fourth century shows a hunt scene in which landscape plays a larger role; the mounted huntsmen move in and out among trees as in a real environment. How far landscape settings had developed by late Hellenistic times is shown by the *Odyssey* paintings from a first-century house on the Esquiline hill in Rome, almost certainly adapted from a Greek frieze of the previous century. Here the story of Odysseus' adventures was told with small figures set within a vast unfolding scenario of trees, cliffs and water. Even so there is no evidence that landscape as a subject in its own right, that is, with the figured element reduced to staffage, was developed before the Roman period.

Among the other funerary paintings some interest attaches to the figures on the façade of the Great Tomb at Levkadia, representing a soldier, Hermes the guide of souls, and two judges of the dead, and to the interior scheme of the tomb chamber of Lyson and Callicles, also at Levkadia, which already in the second century offers a foretaste of the *trompe l'oeil* architecture to come in mural painting, albeit in a very simple form (shaded pilasters linked by hanging festoons). The painted gravestones are of limited interest, for they show mostly simple one- or two-figure commemorative subjects, like their Classical predecessors; only the *stēlē* of Hediste from Demetrias (third century) gives an indication of the kind of elaborate architectural interiors which may have occurred as backdrops in more monumental art. Otherwise our knowledge of Hellenistic painting is confined to little more than literary references (mainly lists of artists'

PAINTING OF ODYSSEUS IN THE LAND OF THE LAESTRYGONIANS, part of a frieze depicting scenes from Homer's *Odyssey* found in a house on the Esquiline Hill, Rome (*c*.50–40 BC). Such friezes, as Vitruvius tells us, were a popular feature of Roman wall-decorations in the first century BC. Some of the figures are labelled with their names in Greek.

DETAIL OF A PEBBLE MOSAIC AT
PELLA in Macedonia (*c.*300 BC). The
mosaic, which formed the centrepiece of a
floor in a grand town-house, depicted a
lion-hunt, a subject which became popular
in the arts following Alexander's conquest
of the Persian kingdom. The figures were
carried out in natural pebbles of various
colours; salient details were outlined with
thin strips of terracotta or lead.

names) and tantalizing echoes. We know from Pliny that the period saw the
emergence of new genres, such as caricature, everyday life, and still life, but there
are no surviving examples before Roman times. The mythological scenes in
Pompeian wall-decoration may in many instances go back to 'old masters' of the
Hellenistic period; but it is rarely possible to determine the date and location of
the prototypes or the degree to which the Roman painter adapted them to
contemporary taste and to the decorative context.

Echoes of panel-painting in other media vary in value. A small group of
polychrome vases manufactured in Centuripae in Sicily during the third and early
second centuries carries figures in naturalistic colours, but compositions are simple
and backgrounds a uniform reddish pink. More important, as we have seen, are
floor mosaics. From the pebbled pavements of Pella, dated round the turn of the
fourth and third centuries, through to the tessera *emblēmata* (inserts) of Delos and
other cities in the second century, we have an impressive sequence of mosaic
pictures in which pictorial devices such as modelling in light and shade were
freely exploited. The early examples are subject to certain conventions which
were probably rare in painting, notably an undifferentiated blue-black background (paralleled, however, in the frieze of newly excavated tomb at Vergina—
above, p. 293); and the placing of these pictures at the centre of a floor, framed
by bands of abstract pattern, scrollwork, or simply a patchwork of stone frag-

ments set in mortar, produces a totally different aesthetic effect from that of a painting hung on a wall; but many of the later examples, such as the little New Comedy tableaux of Dioscurides of Samos from the so-called Villa of Cicero at Pompeii, achieve a remarkable fidelity to the brushwork of the painter. Particularly famous in antiquity was a pavement by a certain 'Sosos' at Pergamum in which an *emblēma* representing doves perched on the edge of a bowl was set in a surround decorated to suggest litter from the dining-table. This 'Unswept Saloon' demonstrates that mosaic pictures were usually intended to be viewed by diners reclining on couches placed on the more plainly decorated outer edges of the floor. The transference of pictorial emphasis from vertical to horizontal surfaces is also partly explained by the contemporary vogue for masonry-style wall-decorations in which there was little room for representational art. But the idea of decorating a pavement with refuse reflects a more general aspect of Hellenistic times: a tendency towards the 'trivialization' of art. It is the same spirit which produces sleeping hermaphrodites, drunken fauns, and playful centaurs in sculpture, and which concentrates upon technical tricks and virtuosity at the expense of depth of meaning.

Other art forms may be briefly mentioned: ceramics (often decorated in relief), glassware (including *millefiori* and vessels with gilded ornament, both produced in the factories of Alexandria), gold and silver plate, gem engraving, and jewel-

RECONSTRUCTED WALL-DECORATION FROM THE HOUSE OF THE DOLPHINS AT DELOS (late second century BC). This type of decoration, used in the more important rooms of Hellenistic houses, is sometimes referred to as the 'Masonry Style', because of its use of plaster raised in relief to imitate ashlar masonry. The blocks were brightly coloured and sometimes, as here, a figured frieze was included.

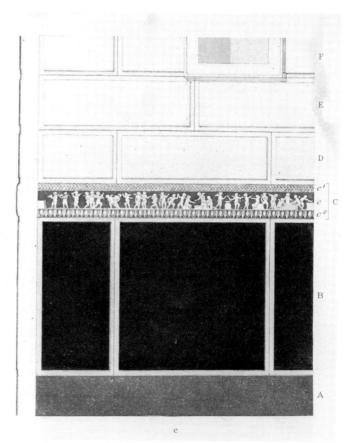

lery. The importance of these last three arts is attested by the fact that famous artists were engaged in them: Alexander, for example, issued a patent for royal portraits to Pyrgoteles the gem-cutter just as he did to Lysippus for portraits in bronze and to Apelles for those in painting; and Pliny seems to place all three artists on a par. Alexander's conquests opened up new resources of gold and introduced the Greeks to new kinds of precious stone, such as garnets, with the result that work in costly materials enjoyed something of a new lease of life. In gold jewellery the new technique of inset gems was added to the long established ones such as filigree and granulation. Alongside the surviving items, which are often of great beauty, we hear from ancient writers of much more ambitious products of the luxury arts. The most lavish and brilliant of all was Alexander's funeral carriage, elaborately decorated with gold and studded with jewels. It took nearly two years to construct.

The Transition to Roman Art

The transition from Hellenistic to Roman art was, of course, a gradual one, and we must distinguish between East and West. While the old styles and traditions remained firmly rooted in the eastern half of the Mediterranean, new aims and ideals, and above all a new patronage, sprang into existence in Italy.

Southern Italy and Sicily were always part of the Hellenistic world; and central Italy, by osmosis, acquired its own provincial-Hellenistic culture. Rome itself, as it gradually absorbed the Greek world, could hardly remain immune. In fact a passion for Greek art, along with Greek literature, swept the Roman nobility: already the capture of Tarentum and Syracuse in the third century brought works of art and artists pouring into the new metropolis, and in the second century, with Roman arms established east of the Adriatic, the tide grew to a flood. It became regular practice for Roman generals and provincial governors to bring back statues, paintings, and reliefs to decorate their Italian villas; and Greek artists found themselves working full-time to satisfy the demand.

In architecture the meeting of Greece and Italy produced a vigorous new tradition. Among its products were new types of building: the well-to-do Roman town-house combining Italic *atrium* with Hellenistic peristyle (below, pp. 718 ff.); the aisled basilica, an administrative building evidently descended from the Greek *stoa*; and the Roman temple. The latter inherited Italian features, notably a high podium and a strong frontal emphasis (much more pronounced than in the east); there was normally no access save by a monumental stairway leading up to the façade. But the decorative detail, and especially the use of Corinthian columns, was imported from the Greek world; and, once the Italian quarries at Luni had been opened in the third quarter of the last century BC, marble became the standard building material, as it had been (where possible) in Greek temples. The last step of significance in the evolution of the temple was the creation of the fully fledged Corinthian entablature, complete with modillions on the underside of the cornice; this had happened by the time of the Second Triumvirate and should perhaps be credited to the unknown architect of the temple of Venus Genetrix in Julius Caesar's Forum.

But more important than purely formal changes was the emergence in Italy of a new technique: concrete construction. This began to appear in the late third century and perhaps resulted from experimentation with *pisé* (rammed clay) building of the type previously used in Punic Africa; at all events it rapidly developed once architects discovered the remarkable cohesive strength and hydraulic properties of mortar made with the central-Italian volcanic earth known as 'pulvis puteolanus' (pozzolana). Concrete replaced ashlar as the logical medium for vault-construction. Not only did it enable buildings to be put up more economically, since materials were cheaper and the bulk of the work could be carried out by mass unskilled labour (readily available in the form of slaves and prisoners of war), but the results were also stronger and more adaptable: a well-built concrete vault, once set, is monolithic and can be used to roof much larger spaces than any form of stone construction. The new technique ultimately enabled the Romans to develop their great imperial edifices of mass circulation: the amphitheatres and public baths.

In the early stages concrete was used for types of building which had no tradition of columnar or trabeated construction, notably market- and store-buildings. The Porticus Aemilia, a huge warehouse in Rome's dockland, constructed in 193 BC and rebuilt or restored in 174, provides a precocious example, 487 m. long, 60 m. wide, and divided by 294 pillars into a grid of 350 vaulted bays. Its walls were faced with carefully fitted pieces of rubble (*opus incertum*), a style which remained in vogue throughout the second century. To the latter years of the century belongs the first great monument in the new technique, the sanctuary

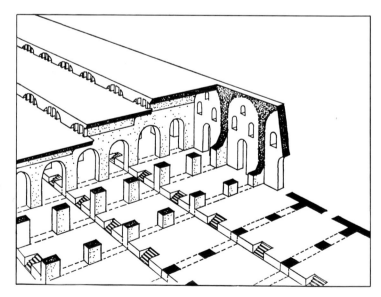

PORTICUS AEMILIA IN ROME (193 BC). The reconstruction shows how the gigantic warehouse consisted of a series of vaulted bays connected by transversal archways. It is the earliest surviving large-scale example of concrete vaulted architecture in the Roman world. The new technique provided greater floor-space, allowed better illumination, and reduced the risk of fire.

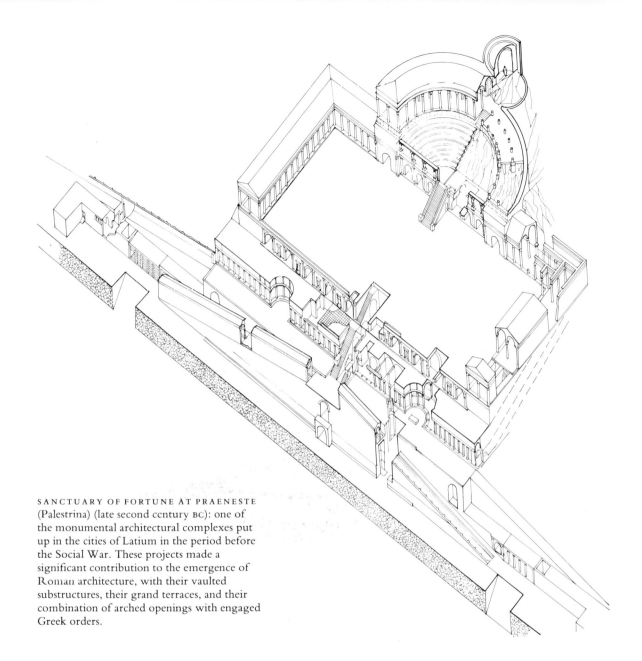

SANCTUARY OF FORTUNE AT PRAENESTE
(Palestrina) (late second century BC): one of
the monumental architectural complexes put
up in the cities of Latium in the period before
the Social War. These projects made a
significant contribution to the emergence of
Roman architecture, with their vaulted
substructures, their grand terraces, and their
combination of arched openings with engaged
Greek orders.

of Fortune at Praeneste (Palestrina). Here we find basically Hellenistic elements, such as an axial layout, open terraces, and arcaded retaining walls, employed on an unprecedented scale, thanks to the use of concrete. At the same time traditional Greek colonnades were incorporated in façades to support the front half of a longitudinal vault, or engaged in wall-schemes as a purely decorative framing for arched openings. The latter device, which was picked up by Sullan architects a few decades later, was destined to become a great favourite on Roman exteriors and serves almost as an epitome of the fusion of Italian techniques and the Hellenistic formal vocabulary.

THE BORGHESE CRATER (late second century BC): a fine example of the grand marble garden-ornaments produced by Neo-Attic workshops for the wealthy villa-owners of Roman Italy. Over five feet high, it is decorated with reliefs of Dionysus and his maenads and satyrs in a conventional classicizing style. Further, almost identical objects were found in a ship-load of *objets d'art* wrecked off the Tunisian coast soon after 100 BC.

On certain types of building concrete had a profound generative or regenerative effect. In domestic architecture it lent itself to the high-rise tenement blocks with which Roman speculators sought to capitalize on an urban population explosion in the late second and first centuries: the eventual conversion of rubble wall-facing into standardized pyramidal blocks laid in regular diagonal courses (*opus reticulatum*) was part of the same trend, for its purpose was to streamline the building process. Concrete vaults were also readily adopted in the architecture of baths, being both damp-resistant and fire-proof. Most important, concrete determined the transformation of the theatre from its Greek form, set in a hillside, to the complete structural independence of the Roman version. This process was gradual, and we know many examples of intermediate phases, with auditoria constructed wholly or partly on artificial mounds, or supported by substructures which were filled with earth; but by 55 BC the mature type, in which the substructures formed a network of passages to facilitate the circulation of the audience, was embodied in the first stone theatre in Rome, that of Pompey (above, p. 473).

If contact between the Italian and Hellenistic traditions spawned a golden age in architecture, the situation is less clear-cut in sculpture. Much of the effort of sculptors from the mid second century onwards was devoted to producing

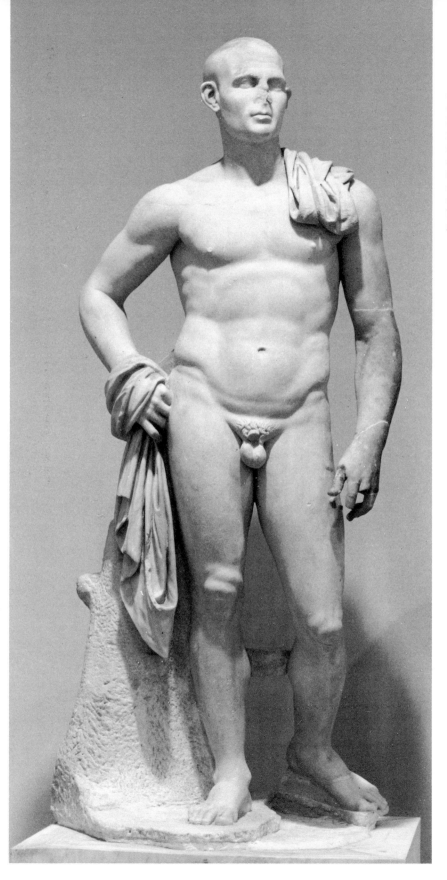

'PSEUDO-ATHLETE': statue of an Italian merchant or official from the House of the Diadumenus on Delos (early first century BC). A good example of the unfortunate effects which could result from the practice of adding contemporary portrait heads to mechanically reproduced bodies based on classical athlete statues.

classicizing work for the Roman art market. In Athens the so-called Neo-Attic school developed a popular line in marble garden ornaments (great fountain-basins and craters, candelabra, and the like) decorated with reliefs of elegant nymphs, satyrs, and maenads, beautifully carved, but devoid of all feeling. In southern Italy the school of Pasiteles concentrated upon eclectic statuary in the Classical manner, often amalgamating a Polyclitan or Praxitelean pose with an early Classical head: surviving works include stylistically improbable pairs of figures engaged in conspiratorial conversation. Along with these pastiches went the production of more or less mechanical replicas of famous statues. The earliest specimens, including a fine copy of Polyclitus' Diadumenus found on Delos, date from about 100 BC and are thought to be the result of improvements in the pointing technique; they represent the beginnings of a major industry, a vivid testimony of which are the plaster casts of parts of famous Greek statues excavated in the 1950s at Baiae near Naples. Not all such copies were intended for collectors. An important aspect of the industry was the reproduction of statue-bodies to carry contemporary portrait heads, a practice which did not always yield harmonious results.

This sort of arid Classicism continued well into the Imperial period and often found new roles for itself, particularly in the manufacture of pairs of statues in mirror image for the decoration of the niches which were a popular feature in Roman architecture. Alongside it another current, associated as far as we know primarily with Rhodian sculptors, created baroque masterpieces in the style of the Great Altar at Pergamum. The *Laocoon* and the Homeric compositions in Tiberius' grotto at Sperlonga are the main survivors of this mode, designed largely for the private delectation of emperors (below, pp. 666, 783).

More original work was produced when Greek artists were asked to tackle unfamiliar themes. A good example is the census relief from the so-called Altar of Domitius Ahenobarbus, a statue base probably made for the temple of

A ROMAN MILITARY CENSUS: detail of a relief from the so-called Altar of Domitius Ahenobarbus (actually the base of a statue-group from a temple). This earliest known example of the representation of a Roman religious ceremony in sculpture poses serious problems of dating and attribution; but the most likely date-range is between *c.*120 and *c.*50 BC.

Neptune in Rome and datable some time between the late second and mid first centuries. Three faces of the base were decorated with conventionally florid Neo-Attic reliefs, now in Munich, showing the marine *cortège* of Poseidon and Amphitrite; but the fourth side (in Paris) carries a specifically Roman subject, the taking of a census and the associated ritual sacrifice of a pig, a sheep, and a bull (*suovetaurilia*), all rendered in a harder, more matter-of-fact style. Despite uncertainties in scale and a lack of fluency in composition, this scene takes its individual figure-types from the Hellenistic repertory and is unquestionably the work of a Greek artist, probably the same man as carved the other three panels. There he was reproducing a well-tried theme; here he was tackling one for which a new iconography must be created. For all its stumblings, his effort is an important pointer towards the future: the commemoration of Roman ceremonies and events, enhanced by attendant divinities (here Mars) and personifications, and rendered in a broadly Classical style, was to be one of the mainsprings of Imperial relief sculpture, brought to maturity in the finest state monument of the Augustan age, the Ara Pacis (below, pp. 776 f.).

Another unfamiliar kind of commission was the Roman-style portrait. The Romans, under the influence of their native tradition, preferred portraits which concentrated on the face at the expense of the body and put a premium on maturity and experience rather than good looks; and, since Greek sculptors always responded well to the challenge of depicting foreign physiognomies, the outcome was the marvellous series of expressive portrait heads and busts which is perhaps the highest achievement of Late Republican sculpture. These shrewd, uncompromising faces, with their close-cropped hair, firm-set mouths, and deeply creviced cheeks, are more reminiscent of modern American financiers than of the philosophers and statesmen of the Hellenistic world; they provide a fine insight into the qualities of ruthlessness and hard-headedness which carried Roman rule to all corners of the Mediterranean. At times, as in the coin portraits of C. Antius Restio, the no-holds-barred, warts-and-wrinkles approach is carried almost to the point of caricature, and it has been attractively argued that such ruthless realism was in some measure inspired by the Greek artists' dislike of their Roman patrons. (For Republican portraits see above, pp 455, 465, 468.)

Finally painting. While the Greek tradition of panel pictures continued in both East and West (Caesar paid huge sums for two mythological paintings by Timomachus of Byzantium), a significant new development was the appearance of illusionistic murals in Italy. Inspired partly by Hellenistic stage-painting and partly by actual architecture, both past and present, wall-painters soon after 100 BC broke away from the stucco work of the so-called First Style (the Italian version of the Hellenistic fashion of masonry-style wall-decoration) to evolve a purely pictorial style which dissolved the wall into an illusion of three-dimensional space. Invariably this space was defined by an environment of simulated architecture. In the finest decorations the Italian villa-owner gave his rooms an exotic, quasi-palatial splendour, with schemes of marble columns tricked out with gilded

CORNER OF A PAINTED BEDROOM IN A VILLA AT BOSCOREALE, near Pompeii (mid first century BC), a classic example of the Second Style of wall-decoration, in which the painter used architectural forms to open up illusions of space beyond the wall. Passages in Vitruvius suggest that painted stage-sets were a source of inspiration.

ornament, glimpses of colonnaded courts receding in both linear and aerial perspective, and grand historical or religious figure-compositions set out on a podium or within a portico. Later, in the 40s and 30s, the architecture tended to become a framework for a central picture, conceived like a window opening upon another world, and occupied by sacred landscapes or mythological figure-scenes. The pictorial emphasis which in the Hellenistic world had been largely confined to the floor now returned to the wall, leaving pavements decorated simply with abstract patterns in various mosaic or mosaic-related techniques. The importance of these developments has often been underestimated, because much of our evidence comes from the bourgeois houses of small towns such as Pompeii; but remains of frescoes from imperial residences in Rome and elsewhere during the Augustan period, combined with information in the literary sources, especially Pliny, confirm that there was a clear shift in prestige from panels to murals in the late Republic and early Empire. The imitation architecture of this Second Style therefore marks the beginning of a new chapter in ancient painting, a chapter which was to see such masterpieces as the garden paintings from Livia's villa at Primaporta and the magical landscapes of the Villa of Agrippa Postumus at Boscotrecase (below, pp. 778 f.).

Further Reading

There is a shortage of good books in English dealing specifically with the art of this period, and in particular of books which effectively study the transition from Hellenistic to Roman art. A partial exception, though highly personal in approach, is T. B. L. Webster, *Hellenistic Art* (London, 1967); while good overviews of architecture and sculpture are given respectively by D. S. Robertson, *A Handbook of Greek and Roman Architecture* (2nd edn., Cambridge, 1943) and A. W. Lawrence, *Greek and Roman Sculpture* (London, 1972).

From the Greek end see the general works on Greek art and architecture cited in the bibliography to Chapter 11. Specifically on the Hellenistic period, J. Charbonneaux, R. Martin, and F. Villard, *Hellenistic Art* (London and New York, 1973) provides a broad survey in which the section on architecture is better than those on sculpture and painting. C. M. Havelock, *Hellenistic Art* (London, 1971) is more detailed on individual works but adopts heretical views on dating from Rhys Carpenter. On Hellenistic sculpture the standard book is M. Bieber, *The Sculpture of the Hellenistic Age* (2nd edn., New York, 1961), but the author tends to be too dogmatic about dating and provenance; otherwise there are only monographs on specific works such as E. Schmidt, *The Great Altar of Pergamon* (London, 1965). On the luxury arts an excellent study is H. Hoffman and P. F. Davidson, *Greek Gold: Jewelry from the Age of Alexander* (New York, 1966).

For the Roman Republic see the opening chapters of the general works cited in the bibliography to Chapter 31; the only book in English which concentrates on the period before Augustus is A. Boethius, *Etruscan and Early Roman Architecture* (Harmondsworth, 1978). G. M. A. Richter, *Ancient Italy* (Ann Arbor, 1955) deals with art in Italy in general, studying the impact on it of Hellenistic art and carrying the 'Greco-Roman' tradition through into imperial times. The Etruscan background can best be studied in O. J. Brendel, *Etruscan Art* (Harmondsworth, 1978).

ROME

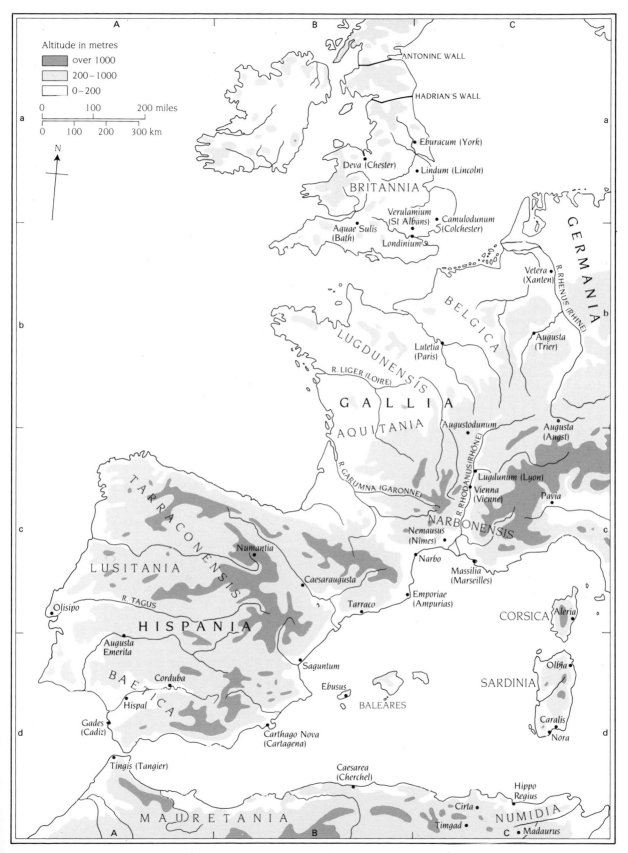

MAP 9. THE ROMAN EMPIRE (WESTERN PROVINCES)

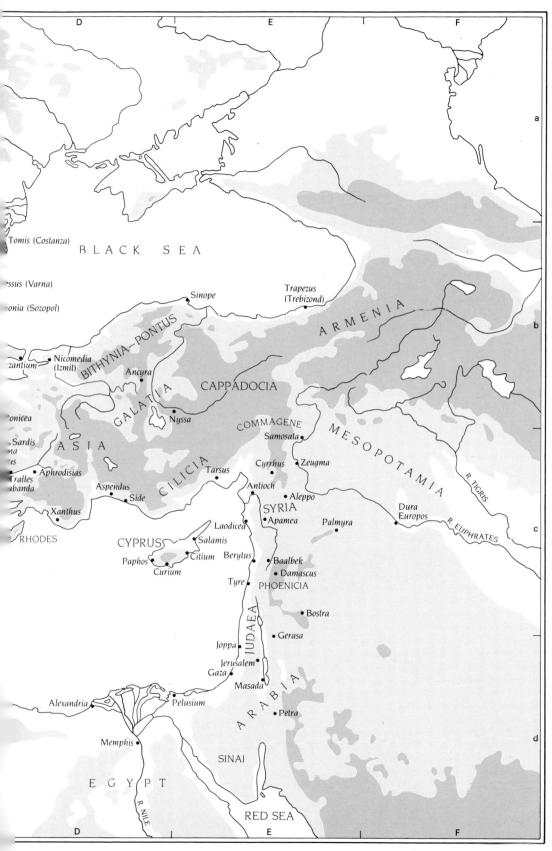

MAP 9. THE ROMAN EMPIRE (CENTRAL AND EASTERN PROVINCES)

22

The Founding of the Empire

❧❧❧

DAVID STOCKTON

THE future Emperor Augustus was born at Rome in September 63 BC. His father, Gaius Octavius, held a praetorship two years later, but any hopes there may have been of a consulship died with him in 58 BC. The Octavii of Velitrae were well-to-do, but hitherto of only equestrian standing, and Octavius' wife Atia came of no higher than modest senatorial stock on her father's side; it is not surprising that a story later spread that the destined ruler of the world had been fathered on her by the god Apollo. Yet the boy's 'bourgeois' pedigree was singularly appropriate for one who was to engineer and secure the victory of the non-political classes of Italy. And Atia's mother was sister to Gaius Julius Caesar, who himself had no son and whose only daughter Julia died without surviving issue in 54. Julius early discerned his great-nephew's precocious promise, and after his death in 44 BC his will disclosed that the young Octavius was to be his adopted son and so keep alive the name of the noble and patrician Julii Caesares. Marcus Antonius sneered that his challenger was 'a mere boy, owing everything to a name', but he was only half right: the magic of the name of Caesar was a necessary, but not a sufficient, cause of the success of Gaius Julius Caesar Octavianus, who at the tender age of eighteen at once plunged head first into the maelstrom of intrigue and war that swirled all over the Mediterranean world.

By 30 BC, still little over thirty years old, Octavian had eliminated the last and most formidable of his rivals and, like his adoptive father before him, bestrode that world 'like a Colossus'. But this new Colossus did not have feet of clay. Julius had survived barely six months after his return to Rome from his final victory in Spain before he lay murdered beneath the statue of his great opponent Pompey. His assassins (they preferred the name of 'liberators') were an ill-assorted collection of ex-Pompeians, 'Republicans', and prominent adherents of the dictator himself, united by a shared fear or abhorrence of Julius' openly despotic authority. The new Caesar, in stark contrast, survived his own final victory at Actium by nearly half a century, and when he died in his bed in his seventy-sixth year he bequeathed to Rome and Italy and the Empire not civil war and insecurity, but that stable and durable system of government that we call the 'Principate'.

The Second Triumvirate

'If Caesar, for all his genius, could not find a way out, who is going to find one now?' The bleak pessimism of Julius Caesar's old friend Gaius Matius proved amply justified, for it was to be over thirteen years before the Roman world was delivered from disruption and uncertainty, pillage and slaughter, near-anarchy and the ever-present threat of disintegration, years in which the rule of law was set aside and justice was merely 'the interest of the stronger'.

Caesar's assassins, as Cicero saw at once, had been ingenuous in their hope that with his death 'normality' would return. Marcus Antonius soon gained control of the situation in Italy. Cicero's own cynically clever attempt to use Octavian against Antony and so divide the Caesarians against themselves back-fired, and by the autumn of 43 Antony and Octavian and Marcus Aemilius Lepidus with his Gallic legions had reached the sensible conclusion that they must all hang together or all hang separately. The 'Second Triumvirate' which resulted was a three-man legal dictatorship for five years; and Cicero's head was one of the earliest to roll when the first proscription since Sulla's day issued the death-warrants of some 300 senators and 2,000 knights, as the new masters of Rome sought security and a war-chest. Leaving Lepidus to hold Italy, Antony and Octavian moved to crush the only challenge to their dominance, and in October 42 the last 'republican' leaders, Brutus and Cassius, perished in defeat at Philippi in Macedonia.

While Antony left to set the East to rights, Octavian was saddled with the unenviable task of finding land in Italy on which to settle about 100,000 discharged triumviral soldiers. Virgil's First *Eclogue* (below, pp. 617 f.) affords a glimpse of the misery of the dispossessed, driven from their holdings to penury and bitter exile. Antony's wife Fulvia and his brother Lucius (consul 41 BC) tried to exploit Octavian's unpopularity, but were briskly driven from Rome and starved into surrender at Perugia. When Antony himself returned, a fresh civil war threatened, but the legions had had enough of fighting each other, and the diplomacy of Maecenas and Asinius Pollio patched together the so-called 'Treaty of Brundisium' in October 40 BC. Lepidus was fobbed off with Africa, and Antony, before returning to the East, was married to Octavian's sister Octavia. The feeling of relief produced by this reconciliation of the dynasts and the widespread longing for a settled peace are perhaps mirrored in Virgil's Fourth *Eclogue* (below, pp. 619 f.) with its vision of the new Age of Gold that seemed about to dawn.

Such hopes quickly died. Pompey's son Sextus won naval dominance in the western and central Mediterranean, and his threat to the corn-routes compelled concessions—a five-year proconsular command in Corsica, Sardinia, Sicily, and Greece. But once Marcus Agrippa had secured Gaul for Octavian, Sextus' days were numbered. After yet another open clash between Antony and Octavian had been narrowly averted, Octavian and Agrippa (who had built and trained a fleet out of nothing) and Lepidus from Africa regained Sicily and destroyed Sextus and his huge navy off Naulochus in north-west Sicily (September 36 BC). A year earlier the tenure of the triumvirs had been retrospectively renewed for a further five years, but the three were now quickly reduced to two: Lepidus, with twenty-two legions at his back in Sicily, threw down the gauntlet in a bid for a larger share of the spoils, but his troops were not ready to shed more blood for him and preferred Octavian. Though his life was spared, Lepidus was stripped of his triumviral powers. The stage was now set for the final and decisive clash between the master of the West and the master of the East.

From 41 BC onwards Antony had had plenty of work to do. The northern marches of Macedonia had first to be secured against invaders; thereafter the Parthians never ceased to threaten Asia Minor and the Levant, where Rome's subjects were bled white by his heavy financial demands. He became increasingly dependent on the wealth of Egypt and on its Queen Cleopatra. In 37 he packed a pregnant Octavia off back to Italy, and shortly afterwards publicly acknowledged his twin children by Cleopatra, who was herself dreaming of recreating the great empire of her Ptolemaic ancestors. In the autumn of 34 he provocatively proclaimed Cleopatra's son Caesarion to be the legitimate issue of Julius Caesar, and much of the East was parcelled out to Caesarion and his mother, 'King of Kings' and 'Queen of Kings', and to his own two children by Cleopatra.

That gave Octavian a chance too good to miss: Antony could now be caricatured as a renegade apostate from the great traditions of Rome, the creature of an Egyptian she-devil. The Triumvirate was not renewed when it expired at the

GOLD COIN (*AUREUS*) ISSUED BY MARK ANTONY JUST BEFORE THE BATTLE OF ACTIUM (32–31 BC). The so-called 'legionary issue' stresses Antony's naval and military might, with a galley on the obverse, and a legionary 'eagle' (*aquila*) between two standards on the reverse. Different dies name the different military units for which the coins were intended.

end of 33; Antony retained the title and claimed the powers, but Octavian eschewed both, posing as no more than the universally desiderated champion of the ordered West. Antony was enormously powerful in ships and men and money, for he 'held the East in fee': his splendid general Ventidius Bassus had driven the Parthians back over the Euphrates in 39, and in 34 Armenia briefly became a province of Rome. But he could not invade Italy as the consort and champion of the 'scarlet woman'. He planned to lure Octavian to defeat in north-west Greece, but, outguessed and outmanoeuvred by Agrippa, he was beaten at sea off Actium in September 31, and escaped to Egypt with Cleopatra, leaving his massive, but leaderless, forces to surrender. By the summer of 30 Octavian was in Egypt, closing in for the kill. Antony took his own life, falsely believing Cleopatra to be dead, and died in her arms: she herself was taken prisoner, but preferred the deifying bite of an asp to the humiliation of being led in a Roman triumph. Two decades of civil war had at last come to an end. It remained to be seen if the new Caesar could find that way out which had eluded the old.

The Augustan Constitution

For three years or so after Actium Octavian's rule was essentially of a personal and irregular nature. He took care not to formalize his ascendancy and used this breathing space to tidy up loose ends in readiness for his first constitutional settlement in 28/7 BC, when he surrendered his supremacy and formally restored the government to Senate and People. As he himself expressed it later in his *Res Gestae* (34), the autobiographical inscription which he directed to be erected outside his mausoleum in the Campus Martius where the citizens could read and admire what their great leader had done for the Roman commons:

In my sixth and seventh consulships [28/7 BC], after I had stamped out the civil wars, and at a time when by universal consent I was in absolute control of everything, I transferred the *res publica* from my own charge ('ex mea potestate') to the discretion of the Senate and People of Rome. For this service I was given the name 'Augustus' by a decree of the Senate.

The Augustan Age had begun, and the quintessential character of the Augustan Principate was determined. The *princeps*, the 'first man' of the Roman Commonwealth, was to have no institutionalized authoritarian power, no perpetual dictatorship such as Julius Caesar had had himself voted early in 44, or anything like it. From Senate and People he accepted the charge of Gaul, Spain, Syria, and Egypt, where the great bulk of the legions was stationed and which he could govern in absence through successive deputies chosen by, and immediately subordinate to, himself. At Rome his overt authority rested on his repeated tenure of one of the two annual consulships, while his enormous personal wealth, patronage, influence, prestige, and diplomatic and political skills could be counted

WALL OF THE TEMPLE OF ROME AND AUGUSTUS AT ANKARA, showing the *Res Gestae*. Augustus' propagandist account of his achievements was inscribed on bronze tablets and set up outside his Mausoleum in Rome after his death. The original is lost, but the text was replicated on public monuments in the provinces; the copy at Ankara is the best preserved.

on to plug any gaps and to oil the wheels of government, and friends and confidants—most notably Agrippa and Maecenas—shared the burden of administration and policy-making.

Some four years later, in 23, after recovering from a near-fatal illness, Augustus resigned his consulship. (He was consul twice later, in 5 and in 2 BC, but on both occasions for only part of the year.) In its place he was voted tribunician power for life, and his command (*imperium*) as proconsul and governor of the 'imperial' provinces was specifically declared superior (*maius*) to that of any governor of a non-imperial or 'public' province. These changes and the reasons behind them have occasioned much argument: they were probably influenced both by the

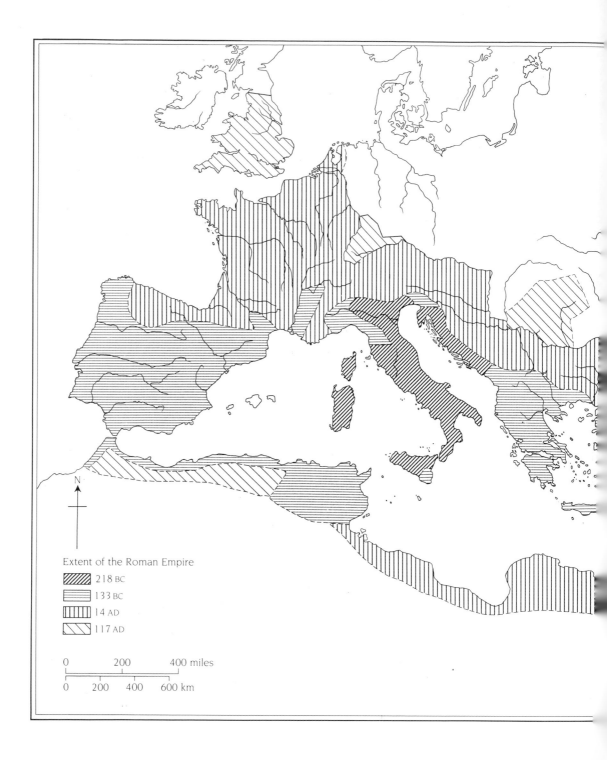

Extent of the Roman Empire

▨	218 BC
▤	133 BC
▥	14 AD
▧	117 AD

N

0	200	400 miles

0	200	400	600 km

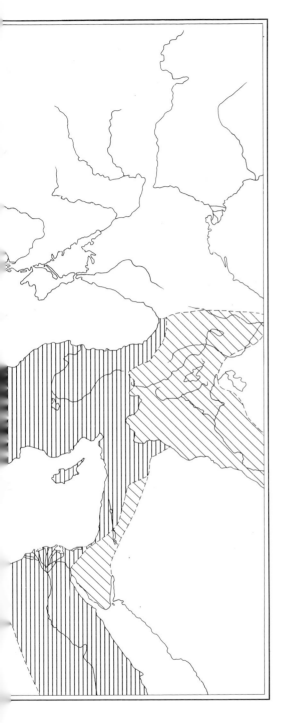

MAP 10. THE GROWTH OF
ROMAN RULE

practical experience of the working of the earlier settlement and by certain dimly detectable, but elusive, stirrings in a section of the ruling aristocracy and even among his own leading supporters. Some have judged the revisions of 23 as constituting a tactical withdrawal by Augustus, to be balanced by a new advance in 19 with the grant to him in that year of the consular power for life. (His provinces were always voted him for set periods and renewed at ten- or five-year intervals.) Others see the grant in 19 as one merely of outward trappings and appearances rather than of any substance of power. In the long-term perspective it hardly matters which view one takes. Augustus had consular *imperium* from 28/7 BC until the day he died, either as consul or as proconsul. After 23 his *imperium* was not only explicitly superior to that of any other pro-magistrate, but also exercisable within Rome itself; and in that year he had received, not only a life tenure of the tribunician power with its wide discretion to veto the administrative and legislative acts of others, succour aggrieved and injured citizens, and initiate legislation in the tribal assembly, but also a consular priority in convening the Senate and ordering its agenda. Moreover, we later find him conducting censuses and revising the Senate-roll and appointing commissioners and superintendents of several new metropolitan departments. Given all that, his pre-eminent and wide-ranging powers at and in, as well as outside, Rome were and are plain for all to see, whether we choose to attribute them to a general 'consular power' for life or alternatively to piecemeal enactments empowering Augustus to use his *imperium* in particular areas and to the gradual establishment of accepted conventions.

It is plain that the *ciuilis princeps* Augustus understood the great importance of preserving and respecting outward forms, whether we regard this as evidence of craft and duplicity or of tact and diplomacy. To have 'restored the Republic' in any literal sense would have been misguided, if not impossible, and as damaging to the loyalties and interests of the mass of the inhabitants of Italy and the Empire as to any personal ambition of Augustus himself. To have established an overt autocracy would have been to fly in the face of five centuries of history and discard much that was of immense psychological significance and solid practical value. Augustus chose a middle way, preferring (one of his own favourite maxims) 'to make haste slowly'. He appreciated, consciously or instinctively, that to close the wide rift which had opened up between loyalty to the state and loyalty to the government must call not just for skill, but for a great deal of patience.

'Res publica' connoted constitutional government, the operation of recognized rules, as opposed to what the Romans called 'regnum', absolute and arbitrary domination. In that sense, the claim that Augustus 'restored the *res publica*' was not altogether hollow. By defining his formal powers, he necessarily delimited them, making it clear in which areas he would exercise direct and open authority and in virtue of what precedents and conventions; simultaneously, he advertised in which areas he did not seek to exercise open authority. There were going to be rules, and the rules themselves were not new. Stable government and long-term policies demanded that he free himself effectively from those two fetters with which the Republican nobility had sought to restrain overgreat ambition: collegiality and limitation of tenure of powers. In practice, Augustus had no colleagues with equal power save for Agrippa and Tiberius, whom he himself chose to be his destined successors; and all his formal powers were his for life, although some—his provinces, for example—were renewed periodically, while others—like his influence over elections and his control of public finance—burgeoned gradually with the development of convention and interpretation. Augustus had come to power young, and time was on his side. Even in 23 BC, nobody much under sixty had been even a freshman member of the pre-Caesarian Senate; by AD 14 a man had to be over sixty even to have been born before Caesar crossed the Rubicon.

None of the foregoing is to be taken to imply that the sheer power of Augustus—his immense patronage, his 'party' following, his stupendous wealth, his control of the army—was not the ultimate guarantee of the stability of his new order. Had any rival been able to use the army against him, his formal prerogatives would have been of little or no avail. But in civilized societies rule is more than the possession of the biggest club to hit people on the head with. We do not take it amiss that modern governments can count on the loyalty and obedience of their military and police forces: it would be a sorry state of affairs if they could not. What worries us is the spectacle of a government which uses army and police to dominate a populace which otherwise would not tolerate it. There is no evidence at all that that was true of Augustus' government; quite the contrary, since we have good reason to believe that, apart from a very few ambitious men whose notions of what constituted 'liberty' were anything but egalitarian or democratic, the mass of the inhabitants of Italy and the Empire welcomed the peace and stability, material prosperity, and increased administrative efficiency which came with the Principate. Augustus took the army out of politics; but we may legitimately question whether his security and that of his regime would have been very long lived had he not also done much to remedy actual or potential social and economic distress and disaffection. For all its ambiguities, Augustus devised a system far more acceptable than the autocracies and anarchies which were the only practical alternatives. It was his achievement that what the Elder Pliny was to call 'the immense majesty of the Roman peace' gave to the Roman world a freedom from war and the fear of war unmatched in its duration, and that freedom under the law, one of the ideals of classical Greece and republican Rome, was still an ideal of the Principate; it grew gradually more remote, but survived to be transmitted to modern Europe. Thus, when the Emperor Claudius wanted to marry his own niece, he did not assume that he was above the law, but had the law changed so that any man could do the same: the distinction may appear slight, but on reflection can be seen to be of profound significance.

It was once accepted that one could talk of a 'dyarchy', a system in which power and executive responsibility were shared between two parties, *princeps* and Senate. That is now frowned upon, but it was certainly long accepted as the principle behind Augustus' new order. In his 'programme speech' to the Senate on his accession in AD 54, the young Nero declared his intention of abandoning the centralizing practices of his predecessor Claudius and returning to the true Augustan pattern:

he would not set himself up to be the judge in every case or issue, for a powerful few to grow fat behind the closed doors of one man's home at the expense of prosecutors and defendants alike; nothing in his household would be bought by money or open to intrigue; his private self and his public self would be kept quite separate from each other. The Senate would keep its traditional prerogatives, Italy and the public provinces should take their stand before the tribunals of the consuls, who would bring their business before the Senate for a hearing; he, the Emperor, would answer for the armies entrusted to his care. (Tacitus, *Annals* 13.4)

And earlier Augustus' immediate successor, Tiberius, had been quite explicit about the Senate's role:

I say now what I have said often before on other occasions, conscript fathers: a good and healthful *princeps*, whom you have invested with such great discretionary power, ought to be the servant of the Senate, and often of the whole citizen body, sometimes even of individuals. Nor do I regret having said this; I have found you, and I still find you, good and fair and kind masters. (Suetonius, *Tiberius* 29)

It is indicative of a very important change in attitude that, while both Augustus and Tiberius are on record as having steadfastly refused to allow themselves to be addressed as 'dominus' ('master'), by Trajan's day at latest 'dominus' had become the customary form of addressing the *princeps*, as can be seen from Pliny's letters to that Emperor.

Between appearance and reality there was, however, a great gulf set. Although Augustus owed his formal powers to the granting of Senate and People, powers theoretically and constitutionally revocable by their grantors, Senate and People had in fact simply 'rubber-stamped' Augustus' own wishes, public opposition to which would have been, to say the least, ill-advised. It was only in the most trivial sense that Senate or People had invested Tiberius with 'such great discretionary power': his adoptive father had ensured that there could be no genuine alternative. Gaius (Caligula), Claudius, and Nero—all three total strangers to the long and distinguished record of public service and high responsibilities of which Tiberius could be proud on his accession—owed their elevation to factors over which the Senate had no control, and were duly voted *en bloc* the ever-growing powers and prerogatives which went with the office of *princeps*. Thus it is no surprise to find the Senate, during the confused power struggle that followed Nero's demise, tamely decreeing 'all the customary prerogatives of the *princeps*' to each usurper in turn, nor Vespasian preferring to date his reign from the day six months earlier when he had been saluted as 'imperator' by the legions at Alexandria.

The Emperor and the Senate

The organization of Rome's military forces under the Principate and their deployment, the growth and structure of an 'imperial secretariat' of equestrian officials and slave and freedman servants of the imperial household, the administration of the provinces and the consolidation and extension of Rome's imperial domains, and the spread of the rights and opportunities of Roman citizenship beyond the limits of Italy itself, all fall to be treated in Chapter 22. Here it must suffice to stress that in all these areas Augustus laid the solid foundations on which his successors were to build. But in the end all roads led to Rome, where by the time of Augustus' death new attitudes and expectations had become established. Ever since 5 BC, when Augustus was again consul after a gap of almost twenty years, with the names of a Caesar and a Sulla adding lustre to the date, there had been four consuls in nearly every year, holding office as successive pairs, a scheme regularly followed thereafter. This can be taken to mark the definitive 'arrival', a generation after Actium, of the 'new Italians' and the steepening decline of the old republican nobility. By now the overriding influence of the *princeps* on the choice of the highest magistrates was accepted, and in practice inevitable. It was from among ex-praetors and ex-consuls that he was constrained to select his provincial governors and legionary legates, senatorial curators and prefects, so that no *princeps* could fail to be vitally concerned about the stocking of the pool in which he must fish. Direct appointment to public magistracies was neither politic nor necessary: lip-service could be paid to constitutional forms while indirect methods and the *princeps*'s public and private support did their work— though in the less deftly sure hands of a Tiberius the legerdemain lacked conviction. Tiberius indeed effectively transferred elections to the Senate in AD 15, leaving to the popular assemblies a mere ceremonial role. But those assemblies had by then lost any effective role even in legislation, which became in practice the field of senatorial decrees and imperial edicts, rescripts, and constitutions. The free inhabitants of Rome and its immediate environs had long ceased to constitute a representative cross-section of Rome's widely scattered citizens; and among the consequences of this eclipse was a diminution of extravagant electoral expenditure and a decline in the influence of the political element among the *equites*. The latter also suffered from judicial changes, for before Augustus died cases of political importance had come regularly to be heard by the Senate sitting as a high court, instead of by the mixed courts of the late Republic and of the first part of his reign, while by Claudius' time the supreme and independent jurisdiction of the *princeps* had come to be exercised frequently.

The *de facto* subordination of the Senate itself was exposed in its helpless nakedness when an ageing Tiberius removed himself from Rome to Campania and then to Capri for the second half of his reign and ruled the world through his letters and the agents of his will. In the early books of his *Annals* Tacitus often underlines and castigates the servility, and even sycophancy, of the members of the Senate. Lacking as they did the hereditary self-contained power-bases of later European nobles or any formidable 'constituencies', hopelessly outgunned by the power and patronage of the Emperors themselves, and acutely aware that any 'dyarchy' was no more than a convenient fiction, they chose the line of least resistance. Yet what other possible counterweight could men see to the potential or actual misuse or abuse of the imperial prerogatives? The Senate enjoyed an important place in the constitution, and had gained a new role as a high court of justice; it handled much business of a routine nature from Italy and the public provinces; it numbered in its ranks nearly all the highest officers of state, as well as their recent predecessors and expected successors, not to speak of the great 'friends' (*amici principis*) who had the ear and the confidence of the Emperor; it had behind it half a millennium of independent history as Rome's great council of state and of imperial success. It is then not hard to appreciate that it remained a focus of opposition dreams, even when criticism of a *princeps* had to be whispered 'at private parties and in intimate gatherings' (Tacitus, *Annals* 3. 54), or the repository of the hopes of independents like Thrasea Paetus in the early years of Nero, until men finally reconciled themselves to the 'futility of long speeches in the Senate, when the best men were quick to reach agreement elsewhere, and of endless haranguing of public meetings, when the final decisions were taken not by the ignorant multitude but by one man' (Tacitus, *Dialogus* 41). For all that, the Empire relied chiefly on senators to run it, and so no Emperor could be really secure unless his rule was founded on their consent or acquiescence. The Senate never lost its *esprit de corps*, and there was hostility to Emperors who were thought to abuse their great powers. As Tacitus expressed what was surely his own philosophy,

There can be great men even under bad emperors, and duty and discretion, if coupled with energy of character and a career of action, will bring a man to no less glorious summits than are attained by perilous paths and ostentatious deaths, with no advantage to the Commonwealth. (*Agricola* 42)

It may be that the weakness of the Senate went beyond what Augustus had desired. On more than one occasion, he tried to reduce its size to a really effective level, but in the end retired baffled from the task. He was probably well aware of the danger of distancing himself too far from average upper-class opinion. In the late Republic, the leading politicians had relied on informal 'cabinets' of friends and associates for discussion of policy and practicalities, and thus the constantly changing mosaic of politics had ensured a variety of experience and involvement not automatically guaranteed by the Augustan system. At some time before 4 BC Augustus had instituted a committee (*consilium semenstre*) made up of the consuls in office plus one each of the other magistrates and fifteen other senators selected by lot, serving for periods of six months, to help the *princeps* to prepare business for the Senate. Its random membership and relative informality should have made it a useful sounding-board; but its nature and composition changed significantly in the last year of his life, and it came to an end with Tiberius' withdrawal from Rome in AD 26. Of course, Augustus had always had an intimate circle of 'friends' and supporters (most of them senators, but including also *equites* such as Maecenas and Sallustius Crispus) whose advice and judgement and experience he valued—and needed, for 'no man is an island, entire of itself'—and with whom he could discuss in confidence the most sensitive and important issues and options; and this less institutionalized body continued under his successors. Outside Italy Tiberius was ready to devolve wide areas of delegated discretion and initiative for very long periods: the outstanding example was Poppaeus Sabinus who was left as virtual viceroy of the Balkans from AD 11 until his death in 35. But Tiberius was exceptional, and Poppaeus surely sometimes came back to Italy for leave and consultations.

The Emperor and the Gods

When M. Aemilius Lepidus, the erstwhile triumviral colleague of Octavian and Antony, long retired from public life, finally died in 12 BC, Augustus was elected to succeed him as Rome's Chief Pontiff (*pontifex maximus*), an office which now took its place among the imperial prerogatives. His election was the occasion for a massive demonstration of popular support, and this formal position as 'head of the national church' sat well with his programme of regeneration of traditional religion and morality. Already the very name 'Augustus' with its 'by the grace of God' overtones had marked him out as somewhat larger than life-size; and in 2 BC he was formally accorded the title of 'Father of the Fatherland' (*pater patriae*). Official deification had to await his death, but from very early days he had advertised that he was 'divi filius', the son of the deified Julius Caesar. For Virgil's Tityrus (*Eclogues* 1. 7–8), 'He will always be a god, often will a tender lamb from my flock be sacrificed at his altar'; and for Horace (*Odes* 3. 5. 2–4), 'Augustus will be held to be a god here on earth with the addition to the empire of Britain and Persia.' The cult of his guardian spirit, his *genius* or *numen,* became established in many western municipalities, temples were set up in most provinces to 'Rome and Augustus', and oaths were regularly taken in his name. At Rome itself the splendid Altar of Augustan Peace (well worth seeing in its modern reconstructed form) portrayed the 'royal family' in simple and awesome majesty (below, pp. 544, 776 f.). Nevertheless, there was a line which could not be overstepped, and the living Augustus was never formally and explicitly a god in Italy and the West. Things were different elsewhere: in Egypt he was as divine as the Pharaohs had been, and an inscription (*ILS* 8781) from Gangra in Paphlagonia preserves an oath of total and unreflecting devotion and loyalty to Augustus and his descendants which was taken in 3 BC 'at the altars of Augustus in the temples of Augustus' by all the inhabitants of the region (including resident Roman citizens), an oath in which Augustus is named along with 'all the gods and goddesses' as a guarantor of the oath and of the dreadful penalties for betraying it.

RELIEF OF THE IMPERIAL FAMILY on the Ara Pacis Augustae (Altar of Augustan Peace), Rome (13–9 BC). This detail is thought to show Agrippa (with head veiled in the customary Roman manner for the priest about to sacrifice), his son L. Caesar and his wife Julia, Iullus Antonius (the son of Mark Antony), and Augustus' nieces, the two Antonias, with their respective families. (Cf. below, pp. 776 f.)

By and large, Augustus' policy was followed by his Julio-Claudian successors, although neither Tiberius nor Gaius nor Nero was posthumously deified. Tiberius indeed seems to have entertained a sceptic's distaste for such matters; but a temple to the living god Claudius was early established at Camulodunum in the new province of Britain (he had to wait for Vespasian's accession for a temple at Rome itself), and Gaius notoriously came to have exaggerated notions of personal divinity. Vespasian could take it all in his common-sense stride: as he lay dying, he blandly observed, 'My goodness, I think I am turning into a god!' He was right, as usual, and like subsequent Emperors whose memory was not officially damned he duly became 'divus'.

Augustus took pains to restore the gods, and especially the old deities of Rome and Italy, to their pre-eminent place in public life. Many decayed or dilapidated temples and shrines were rebuilt, many traditional rites and ceremonies renewed or reinvigorated. He aimed to restore public confidence in divine providence, duty to fatherland, and a secure sense of continuity and order and permanence. Yet here too the might and majesty of the *princeps* and his family were kept well in evidence. New temples of the Deified Julius, Mars the Avenger, Venus the Progenitress of the Julian line, and his own special patron Apollo enriched the capital; a temple and altar of Vesta, goddess of the sacred hearth of the

TEMPLE OF MARS ULTOR, vowed after the defeat of Brutus and Cassius at Philippi in 42 BC, but constructed mainly in the last decade of the century as the dominant feature in the new Augustan Forum (dedicated in 2 BC). The temple and forum are strongly influenced by the architecture of classical Athens.

commonwealth, actually formed part of his home on the Palatine; on his return to Rome from Greece and Asia in 19 BC an altar was dedicated to Fortune the Home-Bringer; vows were regularly offered to heaven for his safety, each new year and the various anniversaries of his birth and achievements were marked by solemn public prayers for his well-being and that of his family; throughout Rome his personal household tutelary spirit (*Lar*) was venerated in the various 'parish chapels' alongside the public *Lares Compitales*. The pomp and circumstance of the great priestly colleges (of all of which he was himself a member) were refurbished, and comparable institutions created and consolidated at lower levels of society. The glittering high-point was the magnificent celebration of the Secular Games in the summer of 17 BC, the tenth anniversary of the new order, a massive public thanksgiving for the past and present grandeur of Rome.

Domestic Policy

Hand in hand with this religious renaissance went a determination to restore that high moral seriousness and restraint which had, in pious memory or myth, assured the greatness of the old *res publica*. Sallust had not been the only man to incriminate and castigate, albeit over-ingenuously, the sad and steep decline from such sober standards as the root cause of the many and grave ills that had beset Rome in the febrile brilliance of the last generations of the Republic. However much we must allow for some measure of hypocrisy in this area, Augustus set a public example in the simplicity of his personal life-style, the modesty of his house on the Palatine and its furnishings (the austerity of which later astonished Suetonius) in contrast with the splendour of the public buildings with which he beautified Rome (below, pp. 771 f.), and in his dress and table—a legacy, perhaps, of his paternal ancestors and their solid municipal tradition at Velitrae. Legislation was passed to visit severe penalties on adultery, agents and accessories as well as the guilty parties themselves. Marriage and the procreation of children to restock the human wealth of Italy were encouraged by a blend of 'stick and carrot',

THE 'TABLINUM' IN THE SO-CALLED HOUSE OF LIVIA on the Palatine in Rome. Painted about 30 BC in the late Second Style, this house almost certainly formed part of the properties owned by Augustus, properties whose modesty (by the standards of later Emperors) was commented upon by Suetonius.

penalties for the celibate and rewards for the philoprogenitive. Measures were taken to restrict ostentatious private extravagance and to check licence at public shows. Historic noble names, some half-buried in the mists of time, adorned the consulship (though the consulship was not itself normally a preliminary to a great military command, for Augustus prudently reserved such appointments in the provinces under his direct command to close relatives or 'new men' in whose competence and loyalty he could trust). The public dignity and display of the senatorial and equestrian orders were actively promoted. The older and more respectable guilds were encouraged, and Rome itself was organized in fourteen 'regions', subdivided in turn into 'districts' (*uici*) with their own local officers (*uicomagistri*). The realization and exaltation of a united Italy was nurtured with an ever-increasing number of Italians entering the Senate and other levels of government service, civil and military, and a continuing move towards a greater uniformity in municipal institutions. New building and traffic regulations, a new Board of Public Works, the creation of a Metropolitan Police Force and Fire Brigade, a Water Board to ensure the needs of a city now approaching a million inhabitants, a Tiber Conservancy Board to dredge and embank the river, and proper provision and supervision of the corn supply are only the most noticeable of the benefits which could come from a stable and effective government. Much of this spirit and achievement of regeneration and progress is reflected in the poetry of the period as well as in public architecture, statuary, and inscriptions. Cicero had ruefully observed how most men at all levels of society cared little about fighting despotism and valued above all else peace and stability in their lives; it is not surprising then to read in Tacitus (*Annals* 1. 2) how Augustus contrived to seduce all and sundry with the sweet lure of tranquil security, and lead them to prefer the present and visible prosperity and security to the uncertain dangers of the old Republic, while the provinces too, where the power-struggle of the great at Rome and the greed of governors had destroyed any confidence in the institutions of the Republic, were no less ready to accept the tangible benefits of the new order.

The Problem of the Succession

A major question for Augustus to answer was how to provide for the continuity of his new order; for, as the event showed, he was concerned to do so, whether from altruistic motives or out of a sense of pride in his achievement or following the instinctive dynastic principles of a Roman noble. A formal hereditary succession was impossible, but it was not hard to associate a destined successor as a virtual vice-gerent and 'heir-presumptive' by having him voted the requisite offices and appointments, powers and dignities. His earliest choice seems to have lighted on M. Claudius Marcellus, only son of his sister Octavia, who was married in 25 BC to his only child, his daughter Julia, and in 24 marked out for more rapid acceleration up the ladder of office than Augustus' stepson Tiberius, who had been born in the same year (42 BC) as Marcellus. The obvious favour shown to his nephew/son-in-law may have occasioned some serious reactions, especially from his old and indispensable friend and general, M. Vipsanius Agrippa; but Marcellus' premature death in 23 removed that piece from the board. The immensely capable Agrippa now emerged as the obvious candidate; Augustus had handed him his personal signet-ring during his own grave illness in 23, and two years later he was married to the widowed Julia, who bore him three sons (Gaius and Lucius Caesar and Agrippa Postumus) and two daughters (Julia and Agrippina). Entrusted in the same year with overall control of the eastern half of the Empire, he moved subsequently to Gaul and then to Spain, where he finally subdued the Cantabri. In 18 BC came the grant of tribunician power for five years, followed by a renewal for a further five years in 13, and his *imperium* was made either superior (*maius*) like that of Augustus himself or at least equipotent (*aequum*) with that of all other provincial governors in whichever part of the Empire his public duties might require him to be.

Agrippa's death in 12 BC came as a surprise: he was only fifty, and had been expected to outlive his exact coeval Augustus by some years, for his robust health contrasted with Augustus' somewhat delicate physique. His sons by Julia, Gaius and Lucius, born in 20 and 17, had been adopted by their grandfather in the latter year, but were still only children. So Augustus had to turn to his thirty-year-old stepson Tiberius, requiring him to put away his wife Vipsania (daughter of Agrippa by an earlier marriage) and marry the widowed Julia. In 6 BC Tiberius in turn was granted tribunician power. But his marriage to the wayward and imperious Julia was singularly loveless, and the one child of their union, a boy, died in infancy; on top of that, it was clear that Tiberius was cast as a stop-gap until Gaius and Lucius Caesar should reach maturity. Whether through pride or apprehension or calculation, Tiberius withdrew from public life to Rhodes— a potentially risky move, but he probably counted on his formidable mother Livia, Augustus' wife, to keep him from serious harm. Ill luck continued to dog Augustus: Lucius died at Marseilles in AD 2; and Gaius, consul for the whole year in AD 1 at the age of nineteen and then sent on an important mission to the East with experienced advisers to guide his early steps in high responsibility, fell fatally ill in Lycia on his way home in February AD 4. Two years before that, Tiberius had returned to Italy, though not to public life. Now Augustus had to turn to him again: there was no alternative, and he was himself already in his middle sixties. Tiberius became Augustus' adopted son, and received the tribunician power for ten years and an *imperium* matching that of the *princeps* himself, both grants being subsequently renewed in AD 13.

Julia meanwhile had finally tried her father's patience too far and too often with her scandalous liaisons, and probably constituted a focus of attention for men with aspirations to become the ward and guardian of her young sons: expelled to the tiny island of Pandateria in 2 BC, she was allowed to return five years later only to the very tip of Italy at Rhegium, where she remained until her death in the early months of Tiberius' principate in an exile voluntarily shared by her mother, Augustus' first wife Scribonia. Still Augustus refused to relax his determination to secure the eventual succession of his own blood-line. Tiberius, who had a sixteen-year-old son, Drusus, by his first marriage, was required to adopt his eighteen-year-old nephew. Germanicus was the elder son of Tiberius' dead brother Drusus and Antonia Minor, younger daughter of Augustus' sister Octavia; and Germanicus' children by his wife Agrippina were Augustus' great-grandchildren, since Agrippina was the daughter of Julia.

Tiberius

Some ancient writers were apparently puzzled by a certain vagueness about the precise moment of Tiberius' assumption of the office of *princeps* in AD 14. In part that was due to the uniqueness of the occasion: no precedents existed, there was no time-honoured sequence of a 'The King is dead—long live the King' kind. Further, unlike his successors in the purple, Tiberius already shared the central powers of his adoptive father: ever since AD 4 he had been his 'partner in the *imperium* and the tribunician power'; these prerogatives were his by law and in his own right and not held by delegation, so that there could be no question of their lapsing with Augustus' death, though in theory they could have been revoked by Senate and People—but not in the teeth of a veto from Tiberius himself.

The next *princeps*, Gaius, came naked to empire, so that, as Dio (59. 3) observed, 'he had to be voted in a single day all the prerogatives which Augustus over so long a span of time had been voted gradually and piecemeal, some of which indeed Tiberius had declined to accept at all'; such too was the position of Claudius, Nero, and the four Emperors of 68/9. Hence later writers, puzzled by the absence of such an enabling grant for Tiberius, may have been left floundering or guessing, ascribing delay to a supposed concern about disaffection in the Rhine and Danube legions or wariness about what Germanicus might do—although such threats, had they been real, should have called for speed rather than indecision. Apart from that, the 'accession debate' (Tacitus, *Annals* 1. 11–13) was badly mismanaged, with Tiberius clumsily or deviously rehearsing or inviting other options (when in practice all that was needed was an expression of his readiness to take over the role of Augustus), and in the end not so much saying 'yes' as ceasing to say 'no'.

Tiberius had had an outstandingly successful military and administrative career from his early twenties, in the East, Germany, and the Balkans, interrupted only during the years of his retirement. He thus came to the task of government in his mid-fifties with excellent and unrivalled credentials. But his character was dour and introspective, poisoned by unhappy private experience, with more than a touch of melancholia and insecurity. Above all, he lacked the consummate political adroitness of Augustus, his self-confidence and prestige as the restorer of

RECONSTRUCTION OF THE VILLA JOVIS ON CAPRI, viewed from the north-east. According to Tacitus, Tiberius owned twelve villas on the island; the so-called Villa Jovis, perched on the cliffs of the eastern promontory, over

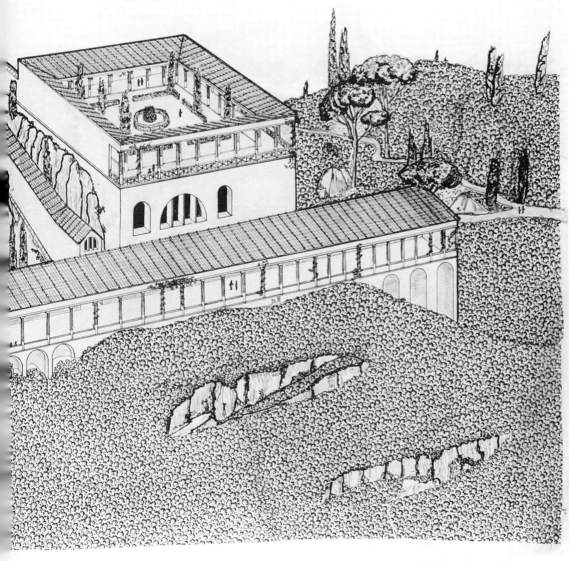

1,000 feet (334 m) above sea-level, is the best preserved. The remote situation suited Tiberius's need for security and privacy and led to the growth of scurrilous reports of his activities there.

peace and security to a world shattered by civil war, his genial tact which had moved him to ask on his death-bed 'if everybody had enjoyed the play'. Men could never be quite sure what was going on in Tiberius' mind. This led to the view, particularly prevalent in Tacitus' *Annals* (below, p. 648), that he was a hypocrite, a master of dissimulation, a view sometimes ludicrous in its strained invention or innuendo. In fact, the true dissimulation stemmed not from the man, but from the system which he inherited, the product of the great illusionist Augustus; it was only underlined by his successor's maladroitness. Criticism, flinching from finding fatal flaws in the system itself, or seeing no practical alternative to it, turned instead on the failings of individual emperors once they were safely dead and adulation must be transferred to the new from the old master. Tacitus gave grudgingly good marks to the early years of Tiberius' rule; but the curse of premature mortality fell heavy on him as it had on Augustus, and by AD 23 first his adopted son Germanicus and then his true son Drusus were in their graves, leaving him with no younger shoulders to lean on as he approached old age. He came to rely heavily on his praetorian prefect L. Aelius Sejanus, especially after his withdrawal from Rome in 26. Sejanus used his chance and the vague, but deadly, charge of treason (*maiestas*) to pick off enemies and rivals, mostly adherents of Germanicus' strong-minded and ambitious widow Agrippina, sister of the dead Gaius and Lucius Caesar and grand-daughter of Augustus himself: she and the sons whom she fought to protect and advance were deported or imprisoned. Sejanus himself aspired to the hand of Claudia Livilla, Germanicus' sister and widow of Tiberius' son Drusus, in the hope no doubt of ruling as regent and guardian of Drusus' son Tiberius Gemellus (born AD 19) once the boy's grandfather was gone. Tiberius was too wary to allow that; but by AD 31 Sejanus had reached the consulship and had thoughts of the tribunician power, which Drusus had held for the year before his death. With the *princeps* now in his seventies and no 'heir apparent' in sight, more and more men must have looked to his great minister as the star to steer by. Then came swift and utter ruin: Antonia, the widow of Tiberius' brother Drusus, penetrated the fence which Sejanus had woven around the Emperor on his remote island retreat and alerted him to much of which he had been ignorant; Sejanus was out-guiled, arrested, and executed, and there followed a blood-bath of his supporters and associates, including his children.

The final years were years of gloom, intrigue, and uncertainty, over which loomed the cynical and suspicious shadow of a lonely old man encompassed by astrologers (and, so scabrous gossip would have it, the instruments of nameless sexual perversions) on the island of Capri. If we shift our sights from Rome, it is true, the Empire seems to have been well governed, prosperous, and (apart from a quickly suppressed revolt in Gaul occasioned by the greed of Roman financiers) secure; the Treasury was healthy, and Italy flourishing. But that something went wrong under Tiberius there is no doubt. The Augustan pattern was marred, above all, by Tiberius' neglect or refusal to imitate his predecessor in persisting in the search for a tried and trusted successor who could be trained for empire and give a secure sense of continuity and direction to men with longer horizons than the failing *princeps*. To have died leaving it virtually certain that Gaius must succeed is the blackest of all indictments, whether we seek an explanation in embittered cynicism, suspicious insecurity, or a lingering and mis-judged 'constitutionalism' which saw it as the Senate's part to decide what must follow.

Gaius (Caligula)

Gaius was the son of Germanicus, and the great-grandson of both Augustus and Mark Antony: his nickname 'Caligula' he owed to the little soldiers' boots he wore as a child with his parents in the cantonments of the Rhine, 'Bootikins', an ironically innocent name. Just under twenty-five on his accession in AD 37, he lost little time in making away with the young Tiberius Gemellus, voiding the will in which Tiberius had named Gemellus as his coheir, and executing Macro, Sejanus' supplanter as praetorian prefect, who had been prompt in supporting Gaius' own accession. His brief reign has an air of melodramatic unreality: mental and emotional instability, vicious cruelty, incest, ridiculous indecision and way-wardness as exemplified in the farce of his projected invasion of Britain, fantasies of divinity which *inter alia* bred unrest among the Jews. Within less than four years it was all over, and he and his fourth wife and his young daughter all lay dead in his palace. The murder was not part of a plan to seize power for a successor, and the Senate seemed to have a fleeting chance to reassert its authority. 'But while they deliberated, the praetorian guards had resolved.' In January 41 Tiberius Claudius Nero Germanicus, Gaius' uncle and the brother of Germanicus, became the penultimate Julio-Claudian Emperor.

Claudius

Modern assessments of Claudius' principate vary widely. For some he was a strong ruler with a clear sense of direction, who had spent his long years of obscurity studying Roman history and reaching his own conclusions about the correct blending of tradition and innovation, concealing behind his unprepos-sessing physical exterior and manners an incisive and inventive intelligence; for them, his chief freedman secretaries, Pallas, Callistus, Narcissus, and the rest were the servants of the policies of a *princeps* who saw that the time was ripe for a forward development. But other scholars see him as a weak-willed, absent-minded, erratic, and malleable man, suddenly and quite unexpectedly bundled on to the throne at the age of fifty, totally devoid of any experience of the corridors of power and hence swiftly becoming the pliant tool of far more adroit and experienced manoeuverers within the imperial household—in Dio's classic formulation, 'dominated by his slaves and his wives' (60-2); for them the increased centralization which marked his reign was the consequence not of his deliberate decision, but of his own ineffectual weakness and the ambitions of his ministers. It is impossible to be sure how much truth there is in these two contrasting pictures (and neither is likely to be completely false) since the overt facts can often be interpreted to suit either. But there is probably more truth in the less favourable portrait, which was certainly that recognized by many contemporaries, criticized in Nero's accession speech to the Senate, and caricatured by Seneca (below, pp. 663 f.) in his *Apocolocyntosis*. There can be no doubt that his freedmen achieved a far greater public prominence and influence than those of his predecessors and successors (there is, incidentally, no sound basis for the view that Claudius 'created' or even first organized an imperial bureaucracy), or that his wives exerted a potent influence; Messallina's public 'wedding' to the consul-designate Silius while her husband Claudius was out of Rome was so bizarre an affair that Tacitus felt compelled to reassure his readers twice in a single paragraph (*Annals* 11. 27) that his account was history and not a farcical fairy-tale; and Augustus' private correspondence shows that that shrewd and close observer, while recognizing some faint redeeming qualities in his young kinsman, had seen him as generally incoherent, absent-minded, easily influenced, and far from circumspect in his choice of models (Suetonius, *Claudius*, 4).

Not that Claudius' reign was a failure: whatever view we take, his chief advisers were clever and able men who had risen high in the imperial household by their own talents and energies. The invasion and conquest of southern Britain was a copy-book exercise, superbly well executed, commanded by generals of ability and dash; although the conquest made little economic or strategic sense, it was a resounding and valuable political success. Something was done to repair the damage Gaius had done to the susceptibilities of the Jews; the barbaric and potentially dangerous cult of Druidism was firmly repressed; citizenship was conceded widely, if not always wisely, with the Emperor's personal advocacy of the importance of this large-minded approach, though in a speech remarkable for its banality and irrelevance; public finances were buoyant; and Mauretania and Thrace were brought from indirect to direct rule. But the judicial carnage among senators and *equites* was heavy (quite a number of them had been implicated in Scribonianus' abortive revolt in Dalmatia a few months after Claudius' accession); and for all his good intentions, which need not be denied, it seems that only too often Claudius' left hand did not know what his right hand was doing. Thus it was all very well for him to adjure senators not to behave like 'yes-men'; but Tacitus (*Annals* 11. 23-5) makes it clear, for instance, that the possible admission of some leading men from Gaul to the senatorial order had been discussed and already decided on in the Palace before Claudius brought it to the Senate, where the *princeps*'s somewhat incoherent speech was promptly followed by the automatic assent of his docile audience.

Nero

Claudius' death in October 54 was quite possibly due to poisoning by his second consort, his niece the younger Agrippina, whose son by her earlier marriage to Domitius Ahenobarbus (consul AD 32) now came to the Principate one month short of his seventeenth birthday. Like Gaius before him, Nero (or his mother—some of the imperial females were more ruthless than their kinsmen) lost no time in dispatching Britannicus (four years younger and Claudius' son by his earlier marriage to Messallina). For some time, however, all seemed fair. Nero's old tutor Seneca, and Agrippina's sometime favourite Burrus, sole praetorian prefect since 51, got the better of the Empress Dowager in the struggle to dominate the adolescent *princeps*, and presided over a period of stability and sound administration—although Thrasea Paetus, as already noted, stoutly deplored their neglect to exploit the chance to recruit the Senate's influence and authority. The first serious storm signal was hoisted when in 59 Nero grew impatient of his mother's insistent meddling and had her murdered. Three years later Burrus died, and was replaced by a pair of praetorian prefects, one of them the infamous Tigellinus, who secured a maleficent influence over the Emperor he was in the end to abandon. At this point Seneca retired, and soon Octavia, Claudius' daughter and Nero's wife, was ousted by the scheming Poppaea and later murdered. Nero was free to indulge his artistic and aesthetic pretensions, surrounded by a claque of corrupt and greedy advisers and toadies, some base-born, like the Sicilian Tigellinus, many others Greek or Levantine freedmen. His extravagance and their unscrupulous venality—not to mention the expense of warfare in Britain, where Boudicca's uprising was sparked off by Roman avarice and greed, and later in Asia Minor, where an ill-thought-out and mismanaged forward move in Armenia ended in a thinly disguised surrender of actual Roman sovereignty and the collapse of Augustus' 'diplomatic solution'—led to depreciation of the coinage and the quasi-judicial fleecing of rich victims. The Great Fire of AD 64 gave Nero the opportunity to start building his grotesquely expensive 'Golden House' (below, pp. 784 ff.) on the ruins of much of the capital: rumours that he had started the fire himself 'to clear the site' and had celebrated the occasion with poetry and song induced him to make the newly spreading Christian community of Rome, no longer seen as merely a dissident sect within Judaism, the innocent scapegoats.

Understandably, men steeled themselves to the perils of conspiring to remove a ruler who had strayed so far from the Augustan path. But in 65 a plot to replace him with the noble and popular Calpurnius Piso was uncovered, and Piso and the others involved or implicated (they included Seneca himself and his nephew, the poet Lucan) were executed. A legacy of suspicion and apprehension led to further deaths, most notably those of Gaius Petronius, 'the arbiter of elegance', and the prominent Stoics, Thrasea Paetus and Barea Soranus. When in the next year the great general Corbulo, mirror of Rome's ancient military virtues and victories, was ordered to take his own life, who could feel safe? An increasingly insecure Nero had committed the cardinal sin of unsettling his own ruling class and army commanders.

The Year of the Four Emperors

It was a descendant of an enfranchised princely house of Aquitania, Julius Vindex, the legate of Gallia Lugdunensis, whose inhabitants had, like those of Spain, suffered heavily from Nero's recent exactions, who raised the standard of rebellion in March 68 against an Emperor who had suddenly and sulkily to be summoned back to Rome from an 'artistic tour' of Greece. Vindex had appealed for support to other legates, without much response; but in Spain the seventy-one-year-old Servius Sulpicius Galba, the sole direct descendant of a Republican noble house—apart from Nero himself—holding high office, agreed to accept the headship of the movement and styled himself 'Legate of the Senate and People'. In Africa Clodius Macer threw off his allegiance. Even so, had the legions and their commanders been firmly and competently handled, Vindex and Galba must have been overwhelmed. A mysterious collision, perhaps unintended by their commanders, at Besançon between Vindex's ill-trained Gallic levies and the crack legions from Upper Germany saw the insurgents scattered like chaff: Vindex took his own life, and Galba meditated imitating him when he heard the appalling news. But Nero's house of cards was tumbling down, and few retained any confidence in him. Verginius Rufus marched his legions back to Germany, waiting on events; Tigellinus turned his coat and suborned the praetorian guard. Before other help could arrive, Nero panicked and ran, and committed suicide. On 9 June 68 the Julio-Claudian line died with him.

Against all the odds, Galba had succeeded. But his power-base was perilously narrow: he had not won a war, he had marched through an open and undefended gate. His urgent need was to consolidate his position; but a combination of short-sighted ineptness and stiff-necked disciplinarianism and parsimony served him ill. His choice of a lightweight young noble, Piso, as his successor added nothing but the empty lustre of an historic name, and antagonized the energetic and ambitious Marcus Salvius Otho. The victorious German legions were neglected and unrewarded, the Gallic tribes opposed to Vindex alienated, the praetorians denied their expected donative. Throughout the Empire those who had remained loyal to Nero urgently needed a reassurance which they did not receive. Aulus Vitellius, sent by Galba to take command in Upper Germany, was saluted as Emperor by his troops on 2 January 69, and the legions of Lower Germany promptly followed suit. At Rome and on the Danube, Otho's intrigues bore fruit, and he was himself hailed as Emperor a fortnight later. Galba and Piso were murdered, and with them died the last pretensions of the old nobility. The advance elements of Vitellius' forces under Caecina and Valens won a bloody victory over Otho's army at Bedriacum near Cremona, and Otho took his own life on 16 April. But 'the long year' was far from over.

Over a century earlier, the refugees from Pompey's beaten army at Pharsalus had included a centurion or re-enlisted veteran called Titus Flavius Petro, who made his way back home to Sabine Reate where he spent the rest of his life in the humble calling of a collector of moneys due to bankers and auctioneers. His son spent most of his life as an agent of the customs-farmers of the province of Asia, and later became a money-lender in a small way in Switzerland. Of his two sons, the elder, Flavius Sabinus, reached the consulship and the command in Moesia before becoming Prefect of the City in the latter years of Nero; the younger, Flavius Vespasianus, after brilliantly commanding the left wing of the Claudian invasion of Britain, was also a consul and a governor of Africa before Nero appointed him in 67 to a special command to suppress the Jewish rebellion. Both brothers may stand as exceptional examples of the sort of opportunities which were opened to able, ambitious, but sensible 'new men' under the new system. Cut off by space and time from the rapidly changing pattern of events to their west, Vespasian and Gaius Licinius Mucianus, the legate of Syria, composed earlier disagreements and along with Tiberius Julius Alexander, an apostate Jew who was currently Prefect of Egypt, put together a powerful coalition of military, logistic, and financial strength and high experience, which also offered a second chance to all those who had 'backed a wrong horse' previously. Mucianus set off through Asia Minor and the Balkans, while Vespasian headed for Alexandria, where he was saluted as Emperor on 1 July.

Events now moved far more quickly than anyone could have expected. The southward march of the Vitellian army from Germany to north Italy had savagely scarred the regions which it traversed, and Vitellius himself behaved more like a conqueror than a saviour. He also made the mistake of humiliating Otho's troops, but not disbanding them. The bulk of the powerful Danubian armies had not arrived in time to make their weight felt decisively at Bedriacum. The meteoric Marcus Antonius Primus now took a hand, and what an Aquitanian Roman had begun a Roman from Toulouse finished. Something of a rapscallion, he had been exiled under Nero for his part in a scandalous testamentary fraud, but recalled by Galba and given the command of one of the Pannonian legions. War, confusion, and intrigue were his true *métier*; he had little difficulty in getting the disgruntled Danubian troops to declare for Vespasian, and he used them with a speed and *élan* worthy of Julius Caesar himself. Scorning caution and delay, which could also have strengthened the enemy, he declined to await the arrival of the eastern armies and drove at full speed into Italy, catching his opponents off guard and crushing Vitellius' army, itself demoralized by the recent dismissal of its general Caecina on suspicion of treachery, in a second battle at Bedriacum in October. Vitellius fell back on Rome, where Vespasian's brother Sabinus all but persuaded him to abdicate, but was himself killed when rampaging German auxiliaries overran the Capitol. After a furious resistance and some murderous street-fighting, Primus stormed to victory. Vitellius was hunted down and butchered, and a few days later Mucianus at last reached Rome, cut Primus down to

VESPASIAN (AD 69-79), the first Roman Emperor not to have emerged from the old urban aristocracy. Born in AD 9 to an equestrian family in the central Italian town of Reate, he enjoyed a distinguished military career before his victory in the civil wars of 68-9. His portraits stress qualities of hard-headedness and experience in place of the hellenizing idealism of the Julio-Claudians.

size, and established a provisional government for the sixty-year-old Vespasian, whose two grown sons Titus and Domitian offered a prospect of continuity which the childless Mucianus could not match. 'The long year' ended at last in December 69. The task of rebuilding the shattered Empire was now in the hands of a hard-headed, down-to-earth, experienced, and immensely capable man who was to prove himself the first truly worthy successor to Augustus and who was, like Augustus, *princeps* by his own making and on his own merits.

Further Reading

I

Tacitus (*Annals* and *Histories*) and Suetonius (*Lives* of the individual Emperors) provide the most complete coverage, see ch. 25. The standard edition and commentary on Tacitus' *Annals* is that of H. Furneaux in two volumes (second editions respectively 1896 and 1907); *Histories* 1 and 2, and 4 and 5 are equipped with a *Historical Commentary* by G. E. F. Chilver (Oxford, 1979, 1985);

book 3 with one by K. Wellesley (Sydney, 1973). Other important sources are Cassius Dio's *Roman History* and the works of Velleius Paterculus and Seneca, Strabo and Pliny the Elder. All of these are available in the Loeb Classical Library. Augustus' own *Res Gestae Divi Augusti* can be consulted in the excellent edition, with translation and commentary, by P. A. Brunt and J. M. Moore (1967). A selection of the most important epigraphical evidence is to be found (untranslated) in Ehrenberg and Jones, *Documents Illustrating the Reigns of Augustus and Tiberius* (2nd edn. repr. with addenda, Oxford, 1976) and E. M. Smallwood, *Documents Illustrating the Principates of Gaius, Claudius and Nero* (Cambridge, 1967).

II

Pre-eminent place must be given to the two great works of Sir Ronald Syme: *The Roman Revolution* (Oxford, 1939) and *Tacitus* (2 vols., Oxford 1958); and mention should also be made of his *History in Ovid* (Oxford, 1978). The *Cambridge Ancient History* devotes the whole of its tenth volume (1934) to this period (44 BC–AD 70). The later chapters of H. H. Scullard, *From the Gracchi to Nero* (5th edn., 1982) constitute the best and most reliable concise treatment of the years down to AD 68. On a slightly larger scale, A. Garzetti, *From Tiberius to the Antonines* trans. J. R. Foster (London, 1974), is to be commended. T. Rice Holmes, *The Architect of the Roman Empire* (vol. I, Oxford, 1928; vol. II, 1931) covers the reign of Augustus in detail and with full citation of evidence; more recent studies in *Caesar Augustus* (Oxford, 1984) ed. F. Millar and E. Segal. For Tiberius, see R. Seager, *Tiberius* (London, 1972) and B. M. Levick, *Tiberius the Politician* (London, 1976); for Gaius, J. P. V. D. Balsdon, *The Emperor Gaius (Caligula)* (Oxford, 1934); for Claudius, A. Momigliano, *Claudius, The Emperor and His Achievement*, tr. W. D. Hogarth (repr. Cambridge, 1961) and V. M. Scramuzza, *The Emperor Claudius* (Cambridge, Mass., 1940); for Nero, B. W. Henderson, *The Life and Principate of the Emperor Nero* (London, 1903), B. H. Warmington, *Nero, Reality and Legend* (London, 1969), and Miriam Griffin *Nero: the End of a Dynasty* (London, 1984). Finally, K. Wellesley, *The Long Year A.D. 69* (London, 1975) takes us through to the accession of Vespasian.

H. M. Pelham, *Essays on Roman History* (1911), remains excellent reading, especially his chapter on 'The Domestic Policy of Augustus'; so too do chapters x and xi by H. M. Last in vol. XI of *The Cambridge Ancient History*. On public and private law, see H. F. Jolowicz and B. Nicholas, *Historical Introduction to the Study of Roman Law* (3rd edn. Cambridge, 1972); on emperor-worship, L. R. Taylor, *The Divinity of the Roman Emperor* (Middletown, 1931); on the Greek cities, A. H. M. Jones, *The Cities of the Eastern Roman Provinces* (Oxford, 1937, revd. 1971) and *The Greek City* (Oxford, 1940); on the municipalization of Italy and the spread of citizenship outside Italy, A. N. Sherwin White, *The Roman Citizenship* (2nd edn., Oxford, 1973); on economic matters in general, vols. ii–v of Tenney Frank, *An Economic Survey of Ancient Rome* (Baltimore, 1933–40).

The modern scholarly literature is enormous in its extent, and archaeology keeps uncovering new material, including inscriptions. References to such specialized work can be found in most of the books that have been mentioned. In particular, the detailed bibliographies for each chapter in H. H. Scullard's latest (paperback) edition of *From the Gracchi to Nero* (London, 1982) are comprehensive.

23

The Arts of Government

❧

NICHOLAS PURCELL

The Principate from Nero to Gallienus

IN AD 193 the military and political crisis of AD 69 was repeated; the commanders of provincial armies contended for the position of *princeps*. The balance of power of the armies had shifted east from the Rhine, but in almost every respect the conflicts were very similar. The crisis of 193 exchanged Commodus, the last of the Antonines in a succession of adoption and blood which had been continuous since the accession of Nerva in 96, for Septimius Severus, nominal heir to that tradition and founder of a similar sequence of succession which lasted until 235. Many have seen this disturbance as the harbinger of the chaos of the middle of the third century. Nothing could be further from the truth. In its resemblance to the turmoil of 69 the war of 193 is one of our most striking indications of the stability of the high principate.

In this period, to a large extent an 'age without history' in the normal sense, the narrative of events (accessions, usurpations, battles, deaths) actually obscures the tendencies and evolutions on which the historian, whose job it is to explain, must concentrate. And stability and peace challenge explanation much more than destruction and disaster. This stability had been created above all by the Flavian Emperors Vespasian and Domitian (69–79 and 81–96). Three achievements in particular may be emphasized, though we should be wary of asserting that they were brought about by design or policy rather than by accidental development. First, the revenues of Empire were organized to a high enough specification for expenditure over several years to be planned ahead; this had never before been the case. In the process some degree of administrative organization had to be fostered (but it is argued in this chapter that this should not be mistaken for a bureaucracy). Second, the last client kingdoms were subjected to the process of provincialization which had been emerging for sixty years, and at last the Empire became a tessellation of provincial units within clearly demarcated boundaries. The armies were now permanently fixed on similarly clear frontiers which divided an increasingly self-conscious empire from the non-provinces beyond. Third, the Flavian Emperors, largely disembarrassed of the remnants of the republican high aristocracy by the political chaos of Nero's reign, and of municipal Italian origins themselves, regularized the recruitment and replacement of the upper classes at Rome and advanced the process by which, through an ever more refined set of public positions in the gift of the Emperor, the élites of the cities of the Empire increasingly came to feel part of the establishment. This was the process, recognized by Tacitus in its early stages in one of the most perceptive and sophisticated historical discussions in Latin (*Annals* 3.55), that completed the transformation of the conqueror of the world into its capital. The Flavian Emperors came from the municipal élites of rural Italy. While they lacked the luxurious sophistication and amoral superiority of the ancient aristocracy which supplied and continued to flourish under the Julii and Claudii, they failed also to maintain the ceremonious constitutionalism which had characterized the wiser of their predecessors. Their impatience with the forms of Roman political life rapidly led them into autocratic manners which in the end brought down their dynasty with the assassination of Domitian.

But it was too late to return to before the Civil War. The safely respectable senator Nerva was replaced, perhaps not wholly voluntarily, by Trajan, a second-generation senator whose origin was from the Italian diaspora in the provinces. Recruitment to the Roman governing class was becoming wider all the time. Men like Trajan, native Latin speakers of Italian stock who spent all their formative years in Roman public life, were less surprising newcomers than the increasingly numerous magnates from the cities of the Hellenic East, often the descendants of the client kings through whom that area had been ruled a century before. Greek and Latin mixed on more equal terms than ever before; the new cosmopolitanism was expressed by Trajan's successor Hadrian in the style of his personal appearance and the assiduity with which he travelled in every part of the Empire. The new cultural homogeneity found one of its most splendid expressions in the lavish beautification, from Vespasian to Antoninus Pius, of the world's capital in a cosmopolitan architectural style, though the advancement of so many provincials gave a boost to competitive display in cities all over the Empire. The result—'the glitter of our age' (*nitor saeculi*), as Pliny calls it—was the imperial architecture which forms such an important part of our picture of the ancient world (below, pp. 786 ff.) The political life of the time involved the intrigues of the court and the struggle for personal advancement among the Emperor's entourage more than it had done before, for the Augustan ideal of the Principate had finally ended, and with it had come the age in which we may first legitimately call the *princeps* Emperor. Paradoxically it was now that relations between *princeps* and Senate became most amicable; even the fluctuation in popularity of Emperors, the variations in their adherence to the increasingly clear rules for respecting senatorial autonomy, became an endlessly repeated pattern. With the concerns of the Emperor increasingly related to the provinces, it mattered much less whether he was 'good' like Pius (138-61) or 'bad' like Commodus

HADRIAN (AD 117–38). Great nephew and adopted successor of Trajan, he hailed, like his predecessor, from Spain and brought a new cosmopolitan outlook to his office: more than half his reign was spent on tours of the provinces. His revival of the fashion for wearing a beard broke with a tradition of clean-shaven chins stretching back to Hellenistic times.

(180–93): except, perhaps, that Commodus' murder precipitated the crisis referred to at the beginning of this account.

The concern of the Emperors for the provinces is a reflection of the new homogeneity of the Empire, not a sign of crisis. Disorders there were, Jewish revolt under Hadrian, and plague under Marcus Aurelius, but these did not do serious damage to the inert and enormously stable fabric of Empire. The imperial élites had the prosperity which comes from peace and an ever more sophisticated economy, and opportunities of upward social mobility to invest their wealth in. In foreign affairs, too, despite the hardening of the frontiers with the great defence works of Domitian and Hadrian, the Empire was not really more defensive in the second century than in the first. The clashes were all in similar places, victories came no less easily, defeats were no more common. We see a repeating pattern of warfare, against Parthia under Trajan, Verus, and Severus; on the Danube under Nero, Domitian, Trajan, and Marcus; on the margin of the Sahara under

Tiberius, Claudius, Domitian, and Pius. Of real extensions of Empire there was only the conquest of gold-rich and fertile Dacia beyond the Danube under Trajan. The conquest of Parthia directly afterwards proved unassimilable—a significant fact. The task which Severus won for himself in 193 was no harder than that of Vespasian. Severus died at York in 211. That his family was of African background only makes it typical of the homogeneous world of that age. His power passed to men of Syrian connections, no more exotic than he, despite the colourful anecdotes attached to the name of Heliogabalus. If the emperor's power during the succession of these individuals seems less effective and his position less secure, that is not the decadence of personalities or the feebleness of characters. At last the Roman world was reaping the whirlwind which sprang from the never resolved impracticalities of the fortuitous system by which it held together.

The disasters of the third century were the product of a set of coincidences.

BUST OF COMMODUS IN THE GUISE OF HERCULES. The foppish face of the last Antonine Emperor (AD 180–92) contrasts bizarrely with the muscular torso, knotted club, and lion's head helmet of the great Greek hero; but Commodus was merely reviving a Hellenistic tradition of equating rulers with Heracles.

The homogeneous Empire was an ephemeral creation. The provinces, having been raised to a similar high level of importance and prosperity, began to drift apart and to behave independently. Their armies, recruited locally to an ever greater extent, became loyal to the regions, not to Rome. The soldiers became distanced socially and culturally from the new élite of the Graeco-Roman Empire. Chronic political instability cut short the reign of Emperor after Emperor. And all this at a time when the pressures of available manpower beyond the Empire, prevented by hard frontiers from entering the Empire unobtrusively to fill the vacancies of its perpetually falling population, posed a military threat which had not been seen for generations, and when the weak Parthian state had evolved into the ferociously effective Sassanian power in the East. The cumbersome and inefficient system of the high Empire could not cope. In the crisis economic disaster overtook most of the Empire (though many areas, including most of Italy, escaped physical devastation). But it is essential to realize that this catastrophe was sudden. The first and second centuries with their many problems and lackadaisical amateur government had been no golden age; but it was not the troubles of that age which multiplied into the chaos of the third century. The disasters were new.

The Arts of Government

'And it came to pass in those days, that there went out a decree from Caesar Augustus, that all the world should be enrolled to be taxed' (Luke 2: 1). The evangelist wants to emphasize the centrality in world history of the coming of the Messiah, and accordingly links the birth of Christ to the moment when the power of Rome seemed at its most universal. For him, as often for us, the power of Rome is most potently expressed by reference to its administrative activity. St Luke, however, was wrong. We know now that no such decree commanded a universal registration of the Roman world, at this time or any other; he exaggerated Roman omnipotence on the basis of the experience of a single province. It remains extremely easy for us too to misunderstand the scope, practice, and effects of Rome's governmental procedures. We mistake patterns of decision-making for policies and take hierarchical sequences of posts for career-structures. When we find the taking of minutes or the accumulation of archives, we immediately see a bureaucracy. Virtuosity in the public service is confused with professionalism. Recent work has been able to show well how far Rome's administration failed, or could be corrupted or subverted, or simply had no effect but oppression on thousands of provincials. There have been fewer examinations of the way in which the arts of government at which the Romans thought themselves that they excelled actually worked—imposing civilization and peace, leniency to the defeated, and war to the last with the proud (Virgil, *Aeneid* 6. 852–3). The analogies which spring most readily to our minds often mislead. Either, beguiled by the delightful portrayal of Roman administration in

Evelyn Waugh's *Helena*, we see Imperium as Raj, or we transpose to Rome with W.H. Auden the perpetual movement of memos in the offices of White-hall:

> Caesar's double-bed is warm
> As an unimportant clerk
> Writes 'I do not like my work'
> On a pink official form.

These images of government will fit neither the headquarters of the governor nor the imperial Palatine. What follows is an outline alternative.

Roman theories of government were not elaborate; the practice too was simple. Two broad categories cover almost all the activities of Roman rule: settling disputes between communities or individuals, and assembling men, goods, or money—jurisdiction and exaction. Antiquity recognized three main types of authority: magistrate, soldier, and master of a household; and all governmental activity in the Roman Empire can be linked with one of these. The first, deriving from the Greek city, covers both the immemorial officers of the city-state which Rome had been and the magistrates of the hundreds of essentially self-governing cities which made up nearly all the Roman Empire. In a *polis* magistrates ran the military; at Rome the usual citizen militia became under the Empire a permanent, institutionally separate army, whose officers played an ever greater part in government culminating in the militarization of the third century. Finally, in a slave-owning society the type of authority exercised within the household was naturally recognizably different, and also came to be of considerable importance in government. These three administrative approaches will be examined individually. But it was always through activities which we would hesitate to call governmental that Roman rule was most effectively maintained: through the involvement of the upper classes in public religion, spectacles, impressive patronage of architecture, philosophy, literature, painting; and in civil benefactions all over the Empire. The civilizing and beneficial effects of this should be remembered as we move on to find the actual administrative and executive structure of the Empire erratic and illiberal.

The City Magistrate at Home and Abroad

Rome had from the earliest times enjoyed very close contacts with the Greek world, and had, like most ancient cities, a tripartite political structure of magistrates, council (the Senate), and popular assembly. The importance of the last for our purpose is that its early power produced the uniquely Roman and constitutionally vital concept of *imperium*. The Roman people conferred upon its chosen magistrates the right to command it and the sanctions against disobedience—ever more strictly circumscribed—of corporal and capital punishment of its members. On this depended the powers of the magistrates, and therefore of the Emperor and of provincial governors under the principate. *Provinciae*, which were at first simply the military spheres of command of consuls or praetors, changed greatly towards the late Republic. Not only had access to, and tenure of, the commands been progressively regularized, but proconsuls and propraetors, encouraged no doubt by the opportunities for reasonable or unreasonable profit, found themselves deeply involved in diplomacy, in the settling of disputes, the managing of their province's finances, and the giving of justice. They often spent more time on what came to be a regular assize-tour of their province than on military matters. When Augustus, needing to take over practically all the armies of the Empire, left the provinces of senatorial governors almost without legions, there was no governmental difficulty. Some provinces came to be governed not by men who might command Roman soldiers, but by freedmen and by equestrians whose title, *procurator*, was drawn not from public law, but from the language of the household. Finally, from the Flavian period, governors who found themselves overburdened by military duties began to be assisted by special deputies who would see to the jurisdiction of the governor and were called *iuridici*. The subordination of the governors of the provinces to the Emperor—although in the case of the proconsular provinces some still showed signs of their old independence in the Julio-Claudian period—eventually also brought about the establishment of a fixed hierarchy of provinces and exact definition of their boundaries, so that the Antonines ruled an Empire which was a tessellation of exactly fitting administrative units which, it is interesting to note, showed a tendency to divide and subdivide in the second and third centuries. This exactly bounded Empire was, however, a recent creation, and until the Flavian period much remained vague about the boundaries of Empire and provinces alike. But despite the changes of the early Empire, in the second century there was still much in the government of the provinces that would have been familiar in the age of Scipio Aemilianus: proconsuls and propraetors, assisted by quaestors and assistants such as scribes and messengers drawn from public panels, and delegating their *imperium* to deputies called, if senators, *legati*, and if equestrians, *praefecti*, still ruled much of the Empire. And this includes the legates and prefects appointed by the Emperor as proconsul of his enormous province. To that extent the Roman Empire was run by the magistrates of a city-state.

This is why Rome long retained the habit of dealing with her subjects with the respect deserved by the free, and why Roman rule so long remained indirect. To the end of antiquity most of the cities of the Empire and their territories were ruled by local magistrates many of whose domestic executive actions were taken as if they were independent; indeed they often needed to be reminded that there were limits to the licence they were allowed. Similarly Rome also long tolerated local kings and dynasts, and the survival of these dependent kingdoms and free cities contributed much to the fuzzy informality of the power structure of the Empire before the age of the Antonines. Even in the third century, tens of thousands of Rome's subjects would have contact with superior executive autho-

INSCRIPTION IN HONOUR OF C. MINICIUS ITALUS at Aquileia (AD 105), the record of a distinguished equestrian career in the imperial service. From prefect of various cohorts of cavalry, Italus advanced to the rank of military tribune with the Sixth Legion, then served as a procurator in various provinces, as the Prefect of the corn supply, and ultimately as the Prefect of Egypt.

rity only through whatever magistrates had authority in their own city. It was in Italy that the autonomy of the cities was first seriously weakened; there, already before the end of the Republic, regulations define the limits of city magistrates' competence. More significant is the interference in the financial affairs of cities which becomes widespread during the second century AD. Governors in the provinces or the Senate or the Emperor had always been able to intervene in some such matters, but their competence was of course severely restricted by their limited time and knowledge. In the appointment from Rome from the end of the first century AD of senatorial or equestrian state guardians (*curatores rei publicae*) or accountants (*logistai*) in the cities we find a momentous departure from the traditional *laissez-faire* attitude to government which had hitherto prevailed. In Italy the change can be linked with other administrative policies, such as the setting up of charitable foundations for poor children or the centralizing of many local administrative functions on regions based on the great Italian highways, developments which confirm that a new attitude to government was being born. Because of the crisis of the third century and the different direction taken by the administration of the late Empire as a result of the reforms of the age of Diocletian (284–305), this attitude never evolved fully; but combined

HELP FOR NEEDY CHILDREN. This relief on Trajan's Arch at Beneventum (AD 114) commemorates the Emperor's scheme for the upkeep of the children of the poor. Trajan stands to the left of the dispensing table at the centre; parents and children queue up or depart at the right; Beneventum and three other city-goddesses who have benefited from the scheme attend in the background.

THE VIA APPIA ANTICA, near Albano Laziale, south of Rome: the first of the great highways by which the Romans secured their military and administrative grip on Italy, and the precursor of the network which was later built throughout the Empire. Initiated by Appius Claudius Caecus in 312 BC, it linked Rome with the port of Brundisium (Brindisi) in south-eastern Italy.

with the final stage in the evolution of the provinces and the maturing of the office of provincial governor, it forms one of the hallmarks of the Antonine Empire. Of this world of diminishing autonomy and growing governmental solicitude the experience of the Younger Pliny in Bithynia is not untypical. But a reading of his correspondence with Trajan, which forms our best evidence for this acme of Roman administrative excellence, leaves an abiding impression of how arbitrary, haphazard, and superficial Roman government was even then.

Without direct rule, how did Rome maintain order? The answers are social and cultural rather than administrative. It was, for example, by her open policies of corporate status and individual citizenship that she succeeded where imperial Athens had failed. The Romans remembered without shame how the nucleus of Romulus' city had been collected from nationless vagabonds and runaways who had seized their womenfolk by main force. Historically, the Romans' power in Italy had been consolidated through the slow evolution of a sophisticated hierarchy of partly citizen status which they had been prepared to extend to whole communities. From the last century of the Republic this policy was followed elsewhere too, and with the enfranchisement of non-Roman troops, the personal gift of Roman citizenship to Rome's supporters in foreign cities, the founding of Roman towns in the provinces, and the grant of privileges or citizenship to foreign communities, a highly successful means of incorporating the most influential members of the subject peoples in the Roman system was evolved. The citizenship carried various privileges, often, as St Paul found, of considerable personal use; but most importantly it gave provincials access to public appointments. The subject was involved in government, and stability resulted. The wooing of the provincial élites was one of Rome's most successful tools.

At Rome itself, the growth of the Empire had brought about indirectly an ever growing population of slaves, freedmen, foreigners, and Italians, the ambitious, the curious, the needy, and the desperate. Quite apart from the very serious problem of keeping the peace, the nourishment of scores of thousands of people and the keeping of the city wholesome and habitable posed very serious difficulties. Fortunately proceeds of empire could be devoted to the building projects, above all the aqueducts, which alone made it possible for so large a population to survive. But such projects needed organization as well as capital. In the (usual) absence of the consuls and often of the praetors, the management of Rome, the *cura Urbis*, devolved on other magistrates. Their principal resource for the job was a distinctive Roman procedure for the letting of contracts, *locatio*. This needs some stressing because it always remained one of the main governmental activities of Roman administrators, and because it was through this that so much of the civil engineering which is so eloquent a testimony of Roman rule was carried on. It was also for a very long period the principal mode, through tax-farming, of collecting public revenues, that basic activity of ancient governments. Moreover it was unique to Rome in its developed form, and appeared to Polybius (6. 117) one of the most striking and effective aspects of Roman state activity,

ARCHES OF THE AQUA JULIA IN ROME, one of the aqueducts on which the city's water-supply depended. Built by Agrippa in 33 BC to supplement the Aqua Claudia (312 BC), the Anio Vetus (272 BC), the Aqua Marcia (144–140 BC), and the Aqua Tepula (125 BC), it brought water from the Alban Hills south-east of Rome and was part of a major enlargement and modernization of water services under Augustus.

embracing all activities from the contract for feeding the sacred geese of Juno (always let first) to the taxes of the provinces or the resurfacing of main roads. Polybius saw this practice as a democratic aspect of Roman public life, no doubt because it involved in state business some prominent plebeians. For our purposes it is doubly important. First it encouraged the formation of semi-public corporate organizations, *collegia* and *societates*, the spirit of which contributed to Roman notions of how to form administrative institutions—and indeed it is from this world that the important late-Roman official title *magister* derives. Second, and even more importantly, we see again here the unwillingness of Roman magistrates to undertake themselves the direct overseeing of the activities which they sponsored. The wish to limit the public sphere and privatize official actions is again apparent.

There were occasional administrative improvements at Rome during the

Republic; but simple coercion by their attendants, and jurisdiction thus enforced, remained the magistrates' only executive agencies. By contrast, under Augustus and his immediate successors a still further worsening of the city's problems prompted a connected series of institutional innovations. Some of the new expedients were of the highest importance to the government of the Principate; moreover, the exercise of institutional change itself acted as a precedent for the later proliferation of new posts and offices. The Augustan administrative revolution consisted in the creation of boards of senior magistrates in departments (*curae*) responsible for the management of the aqueducts, the roads of the city, the banks of the Tiber, and so on; in the systematization of responsibility by means of artificial compartments, such as the fourteen regions of Rome or the eleven of Italy; and in the appointment of senior assistants responsible to the *princeps* who would control military or paramilitary bodies permanently stationed in Rome or very near by, for political and civil security. The creation of the *curae* did away with the ancient principle of annual tenure, and provided something of a permanent staff in place of sole reliance on contract labour. The formal systems of administrative units diminished competitiveness between patrons and helped ensure uniformity, stability, and comparison of results of administrative activity. And in the creation of the much more powerful posts of prefect of the praetorian guard, prefect of the city, and prefect of the fire-brigade, Augustus equipped future *principes* with three great ministers, as well as judges whose courts would acquire an importance which helped to centralize large areas of Italy on Rome and relieve other magistrates of much of their jurisdiction. We happen to know that already by the reign of Nero the prefect of the city had acquired jurisdiction comparable to that of the urban praetor. This centralization of Italian administration in turn provided an example for the management of the provinces; it is significant that the *curatores* of Rome lent their name to the functionaries described above whose financial supervision came to infringe the cities' autonomy.

This Augustan administrative revolution, for which Greek theoretical and practical precedents are perhaps to be sought, was, however, unique. Moreover, the senatorial *curae* were in part created not for administrative excellence but to subordinate these potentially prestigious activities of great senators to Augustus' regime, and they flourished as status symbols for the successful senator, to be held often by corrupt, lazy, or incompetent men. Above all, despite all the innovation, and all the extra posts and increase in personnel, the main activities remained the letting of contracts, the giving of permissions, and the business of arbitration—new posts, more subtle hierarchies, but the same old jobs.

The Army

The second general group of associations which political authority had for the governed is connected with war. Even when mercenary troops had been

CAMP-BUILDING: relief on Trajan's Column in Rome (dedicated in AD 113). The sculptured narrative of the emperor's Dacian campaigns shows the army in all its varied activities, including not only actual engagements with the enemy but also marching, sacrificing, entrenching, and listening to imperial addresses.

important, fighting had, in the classical *polis* and its heirs, remained to a large extent the preserve of a citizen militia. Until the second century BC this had been true of Rome too. It followed that a city's magistracies were often very closely associated with military command, from which derived the vital Roman concept of *imperium*, which underlay the whole governmental activity of the Empire and actually gave it its very name.

As the Hellenistic cities came increasingly to group themselves in leagues or to submit to the control of their foreign affairs by the kings and eventually by Rome, military titles such as *stratēgos*, 'army-leader', often lost their military connotations. So at Rome the praetors first, and with the Empire the consuls, came to acquire what we would call civilian functions. From the middle Republic the praetors were mainly concerned with jurisdiction, though it is interesting to observe that the regular Greek term for praetor (the Greek equivalents of Latin constitutional terms are often very revealing) is in fact *stratēgos*. Lower down the social scale the post of superintendent of engineers (*praefectus fabrum*) was practically non-military by the Julio-Claudian age, and even some types of military tribune were military only in name. It is only in the third century that the process is reversed, and military titles spread in areas of government with no necessary connection with war; the eventual militarization of the Empire brings to an end the processes described here (though, significantly, military titles such as *praepositus* and *optio* spread earlier among the servants of the Emperor). But throughout the Emperor was called by the honorific military title *imperator*, first as an informal description, then as a name, finally as a formal title, and took on himself many of the military functions once carried out by the republican magistrates. Although we usually refer to him by his senatorial style of *princeps*, it was as *imperator* (*autocrator*, 'the ruler answerable to none' in Greek) that he was perceived by the Empire. And the Emperor's military power pervaded the government of the Empire.

In the ancient world, to question the rightness of a standing army was unthinkable; and peace was the product of victory won by the soldier. But there is no easy way to translate 'civilian' into Greek or Latin, and this is because the legacy of the citizen army ensured an intermingling of the apparatus of warfare with the activities of peace. The distinction between soldier and civilian, so clear to our minds, and in our times possessing a moral as well as a practical flavour, did not exist before the triumph of the military, which began in the Severan period.

Augustus established the military system which lasted until the third century. The army was composed of two parts (and there was also a considerable fleet). The senior part was a citizen army of some thirty legions (about 165,000 men), each commanded by a senator of middling status, and subject to the more senior senatorial governors of the imperial and senatorial provinces. Gradually these legions became a permanent feature of the frontier areas in which they were established. They recruited mostly from those areas. Although some legions changed their bases, such moves were not overall very frequent. Rather more numerous were the auxiliary troops who from the reign of Claudius regularly received the citizenship on discharge. Rome had always relied on the military help of non-Romans, and the employment and incorporation of the auxiliaries became one of the most important ways in which the Empire acquired a cultural homogeneity. The regiments of auxiliaries, much smaller than legions, were commanded by citizens of equestrian rank, usually from the élites of Italy or the provinces and using these jobs to win further status and opportunities for themselves. The whole system was financed from a military treasury established by Augustus, one of the first and most fundamental steps towards financial planning taken by the Romans.

It follows that before the third century the military commanders provided from the Empire's élites were not what we would call professionals. The effectiveness and expertise of the army rested with the senior and junior centurions who often rose from the ranks and would serve as long as any ordinary soldier. It was, as far as we know, very unusual for such an officer to receive equestrian rank, and still rarer to proceed to equestrian military office. And equestrian commands, although important in the promotion game of the upper classes, were usually short and variegated, including horse and foot and in a whole range of different places. So too even with senators, whose military service as junior officer, legionary legate, or governor of a garrisoned province would usually occupy only a short period of their whole career, take place in many different areas, and give them little opportunity to become professional. This is true of almost all the military commanders we know, and it is clear that it became standard practice for the Emperor to ensure that no senator acquired too much familiarity with armies and warfare. This practice of drawing the high military command from essentially unmilitary personnel helped integrate the army into the more peaceful activities of the Empire.

The legionary army always remained part of the citizen body of Rome. Its communities, especially in non-citizen areas, enjoyed privileges like other citizen settlements, and expected the facilities—aqueducts, amphitheatres, baths and so on—of any classical city. The *castellum* (fort) was originally an ordinary member of the sequence of possible settlement-institutions which ranged from village to city. The *colonia*, originally in the late Republic a town of discharged citizen veterans which was autonomous but expected to defend itself and the interests of Rome in case of trouble, and which came to be the coveted highest status

LEGIONARY AMPHITHEATRE AT VINDONISSA (Windisch, in Switzerland). Vindonissa was the fortress of the Thirteenth Legion from about AD 16, and was subsequently occupied by the Twenty-first and Eleventh Legions before being evacuated about 100. The amphitheatre was used both for military drill and to provide the entertainments to which the legionary soldiers were accustomed at home.

attainable by a provincial city, helped to blur the distinction between camp and town still further. Outside fortresses, moreover, people congregated to form whole settlements dependent on the presence of the army, which often became independent. When not on active duty—which was more often than not, as in all armies—soldiers cultivated the land, engaged in trade, and generally lived their lives like ordinary citizens. This close contact between soldiers and other citizens and non-citizens was still further fostered by the direct involvement of soldiers in the day-to-day administration of the Empire.

A study of a system of government must not only concern itself with top level decision-making and the bureaucracy which may give it stability and effectiveness; it must also give some account of the actual execution of the directives which emanate from these two sources. Who, we must ask, actually put into effect the decisions of the Roman government? The Roman magistrates had immediate agents in their staff of strong-arm men, errand-runners, and announcers. But these were few, and it is only in the command of real soldiers, given to him by his *imperium*, that the executive power of the Roman official eventually lay.

The army was not exclusively deployed in the remoter or more barbarous provinces. True, in the mid second century Britain had three, the Rhine four, and the Danube ten of Rome's twenty-eight legions; but most of these were placed, even in this period when the frontiers were hardening, so that they commanded large areas of province as well as foreign soil; and before the Flavian period even more legionary bases were within the Empire. Detachments from these legions or auxiliary troops were anyway widely dispersed through the provinces, especially in their capitals. In the East the nine legions (above all in Egypt) were positioned even more clearly with control of the local populace in mind; and settled Africa and Spain both retained a legion each. Besides these, in coastal or riverine cities there were large naval bases. Rome had its own huge, complex garrison. Wherever the Emperor was there was a large body of troops. There were always soldiers moving from one detachment to another, above all on the great roads connecting frontier areas—living off the land by permission, by the generosity of local magnates, or by extortion, with their privileges (only military courts tried soldiers) and the needs of imperial security to justify even their crimes. 'Your teeth are shattered?', asks Juvenal, 'Face hectically inflamed, with great black welts? You know the doctor wasn't too optimistic about the eye that was left. But it's not a bit of good your running to the courts about it. If you've been beaten up by a soldier, better keep it to yourself' (16. 10 ff.). The government of the Roman Empire was what we would call military rule.

It would have been hard, indeed, for the Roman Empire to be run on any other system. Even the civil services of modern states, like the British, have often developed from military models, retaining, for example, the concept of leave. There were few possible structures of authority available that could cope with the scale involved in Roman administration: the city-state had already proved an inadequate institution for world government, and the authority of the patriarchal family was too limited. Participatory institutions there were, like the cartels which undertook the public contracts described above or collegiate organizations of city populations, worshippers, artisans, and so on; and all these bodies played a part in imperial rule, since through representatives they could deal with the rulers of the state, make petitions, and receive replies; through their privileges and corporate influence security might be maintained in sensitive areas like the larger cities of the Empire. But none of these offered the convenient, disciplined, extensive structure of the army, and so the army came to have the public image we have just seen in Juvenal. Using its own courts, answerable only to itself, privileged and greedy, it became a tyrannical force because it was omnipresent in government.

Soldiers were involved in public building; they surveyed land; they manned the customs posts at provincial boundaries; and their value to the collection of other taxes is sufficiently demonstrated by the fact that they were from time to time forbidden to take part in it. During the second century a secret service of government spies, the so-called 'grain militia' (*frumentarii*) came into being, the predecessors of the sinisterly bland *agentes in rebus* of the later Empire. Examples could easily be multiplied, but it is enough to end by referring to the vivid testimony of two papyrus lists of soldiers' duties, in one happy case referring not to atypical Egypt, but to the Danube. From Moesia we hear of soldiers with corn-shipments, on mine duty, requisitioning horses, running prisons; and from Egypt of harbour-dredging work, duty at the mint, at the paper factory (so essential to Egyptian administration), and on general river-guard duty, a police activity further illuminated by the countryside surveillance attested in a new document of this kind. Altogether there were few places in the Empire where it will have been odd to meet a soldier. 'To the soldier, at his demand—500 drachmae' is a typical note in the pathetic list of protection payments made by a wretched Egyptian subject of this government. In this at least the Egyptians were by no means unusual.

Administration Household-Style

Most governmental actions were undertaken by a very few people in every ancient state. Ancient government was top-heavy, in that a great deal of what seems to us mundane work was done by the men with most authority; there was relatively little delegation or selection of business. In the Roman Empire in the second century AD only some hundred or so men actually held *imperium* by direct grant or delegation at any one time: on them in thory fell the whole burden of government. Indeed some senators did feel that their dignity should be reflected in their agenda, and that they should not debate trivial or demeaning subjects, but others considered that an exhaustive concern for every corner of the *res publica* had been the great ideal of the statesmen of old. 'How every single thing mattered to our ancestors!', exclaims the Elder Pliny admiringly of a censorial regulation about laundrymen passed in 220 BC (*NH* 35. 197). The evidence suggests that the opinion of Pliny prevailed: even if an issue came to the attention of the authorities, it was only at the top that any consideration of it could take place. Hence the hours that the Emperors, their high officials, and the provincial governors spent in routine jurisdiction; the inscriptions recording minor local administrative decisions often taken at a very high, even at an imperial level; the small issues discussed in the surviving letters between the relatively few executives of the Roman Empire; hence too, no doubt, the hundreds, thousands of matters as important as those that did receive attention, that simply went by default. There was a great reluctance to multiply positions of authority or to complicate the business of government. There was little forward planning; new administrative measures (sometimes) followed only on acute crisis. So it was naturally to dependents that over-pressed office-holders looked for their assistants; some of these might be equestrians or free plebeian clients, but the total obedience of the unfree offered much more extensive possibilities in a slave-owning society. It is with the role of authority conferred within the household, but applied to public life, that we are here concerned.

The Emperor was the most hard-pressed administrator of all; Fergus Millar has demonstrated conclusively how his detailed concern for specific matters and his virtually undivided responsibility for all the business for which he could find time left no time for the creation of what we would call policy. His it was to begin to deal, rather, with all the appeals, petitions, embassies which reached him from below. Because it was only as judge that he was expected to act, whole areas of government—education, the economy, welfare, administration—only impinged on him accidentally, and were treated unsystematically. Nevertheless the volume of material reaching him required some management, and so it was that in the imperial household we have our clearest example of an administrator's personal dependents gaining responsibility for public affairs and enormous political power.

So great were the fortunes of some late-republican senators that the slaves or freedmen on whom they relied might find themselves in control of sums of money or tracts of land comparable in size to objects of the state's administration. This was naturally most true of Augustus, whose personal property and wealth was truly imperial in scale. The private estate of the Julio-Claudians was settled by the falling in of the shares allotted by Augustus to his family, above all to Livia and Antonia the younger, and by the policy of accumulating goods by inheritance and confiscation. Thanks to the ravages in the Roman upper class of Caligula, Nero, Domitian, Commodus, and Septimius Severus, this imperial *patrimonium* gave the Emperor control over a substantial proportion of the real estate of the Empire by means of direct ownership, not simply constitutionally sanctioned political control. Ownership entailed a different style of administration, and one which evolved very fast.

There were other ingredients as well. In Egypt royal land was a phenomenon which survived from the time of the Pharaohs. As their successors, the Emperors enjoyed in this province at least the experience of the direct management of a large proportion of the soil. Although Egypt was a very special case in this, as in so many ways, it provided a precedent, if not a model, for the running on behalf of the Emperors of other formerly royal lands, especially in the eastern part of the Empire, where royal lands had previously become public land of the Roman People. It would be very interesting to know how such tracts had been administered in the last years of the Republic. A good example is Galatia, where the extensive estates of the last king, Amyntas, became under Augustus an imperial property of a sufficient scale to make an impact on the organization of the province. The potential power of the supervisors of these estates is clearest in the case of geographically circumscribed areas like the Gallipoli peninsula (the Thracian Chersonese) which formed a single imperial property. In places like this the agent of the emperor had to exercise functions not unlike those of a provincial governor, and we hear of the punishment of one such in Judaea in the reign of Tiberius who took it on himself to give orders to Roman soldiers as if he held *imperium* (Tacitus, *Annals* 4.15). As we shall see, such licence was soon to be regularized. It was in Africa that the imperial estates reached their greatest extent, and epigraphic evidence from the second century, especially the *Lex Manciana*, reveals a good deal about their scale and management. But every province had them; they included mines, quarries, forests, as well as agricultural land; and Emperors were not slow to add to them. Septimius Severus, in particular, vastly increased the imperial holdings in the provinces, and the substitution of imperial for private markings on oil-jars from southern Spain eloquently reveals how sudden, complete, and economically important such a step could be. The inhabitants of these estates, through the hierarchy of procurators and bailiffs which separated them from the Emperor, had very much the same opportunities—or lack of them—for appeal and petition as ordinary provincials did through the governor.

It was natural that the administrators of imperial property should derive their titles from republican practice. But *procurator* remained a term of private law, and it will have sounded very strange to Roman ears to call the governors of public provinces by it. This practice, introduced for small equestrian provinces by Claudius, is a striking departure from the scrupulously traditionalistic tact of the Augustan constitutional changes. These governors had previously quite correctly been called *praefecti*. At times, too, other officials with the innovative title appear in other departments of the government as assistants to senators in their public capacities—in the various concerns of the urban administration of Rome, for example, and as financial assistants of the legates of the provinces to which the *princeps* as proconsul had to delegate governors (the 'imperial' provinces).

The change is of great importance because it made it possible for there to grow up from these domestic origins over the following two centuries what we may call a procuratorial service, in which there was available to men of equestrian rank a series of important governmental posts in the provinces and in the city of Rome, in charge of a great variety of imperial concerns, from the control of whole provinces to the running of mines, and as the assistants of senatorial functionaries. In the end there were, at any one time, some 170 of these posts, and it is here that Rome's administrative excellence, that elusive beast, used to be located. It is clear, however, that these posts did not constitute a hierarchical sequence linked by a regular promotion pattern, and that the holders of them needed no more expertise, knowledge, devotion, professionalism, or talent than their senatorial colleagues. Jurisdiction and financial watchfulness was what was expected of them too, not a serious businesslike approach different in kind from what was expected of a noble magistrate. A procurator of an Alpine district describes his job as 'the supervision of the law and the carrying out of the interests of the emperors' (*CIL* XII. 103). These posts were much less important as means of increasing the efficiency of imperial rule than as a way of incorporating in the life of government the upper classes of the provinces. Through these posts social advancement was obtained, and this secured the loyalty of the powerful men of the Empire. This cannot be overstressed: it was the ability to incorporate, not administrative excellence, that was Rome's greatest Art of Government.

Who the equestrian procurators were, and where they came from, therefore mattered. What they did mattered less. Recognition of this has sent the hunt for the supposed Roman bureaucracy into other fields. 'The description "imperial civil service" better fits the freedmen and slaves of Caesar', says a recent scholar. Here again the republican senator's dependence on his slaves and freedmen sets the precedent. The *familia* of Augustus and his successors acquired enormous power. Under Claudius and Nero in particular their influence with the *princeps* became notorious. The principal freedmen used titles derived from their principal occupations—secretary for letters, or for accounts, and the like—which became so closely associated with the Emperor that it was considered treasonable for others to use them in their households. In reaction to the hostility shown to these men, the posts they had held gradually became the preserve of men of equestrian status; but the household—the *familia Caesaris*—remained highly influential. Two flattering poems of Statius (*Silvae* 3. 3 and 5. 1) give us an idea of their possible concerns, and we get further information from some 4,000 inscriptions, mostly recording simply the title of the slave or freedmen. These titles, intricate, technical, and specific, seem to give support to the bureaucratic view. But the hostility to the freedmen raises a doubt; it seems that the Emperor was not free to delegate important matters to his freedmen without infringing public opinion. It therefore seems appropriate to look more critically at what the *familia Caesaris* actually did. It is clear that they acquired a mastery of technical information. Augustus left a list of 'names of freedmen and slaves from whom accounts could be obtained'. Some freedmen are praised by courtiers like Statius for this. Another is described on his epitaph as 'occupied throughout his life with the utmost attention to the

interests of the imperial palace' (at Formiae: *ILS* 1583). But this devotion to duty
does not entail administrative professionalism, and the importance and quantity
and nature of business handled by a freedman administrator need have been no
different from that dealt with by a senator or equestrian in public office. The
administrative jobs which they did were, however mundane, like those of their
superiors, generally to be described under the heading *litterae*. Their copying,
writing, recording, and transmitting of information was important: as an expert
on the subject says, 'the *tabellarii* (secretaries) were without doubt a necessary cog
in the administrative machine, but most of the others in the jungle that was the
Palace service seem to have been somewhat less than indispensable to the efficient
running of the Roman Empire.' But in that case we are entitled to ask where the
machine of which the *tabellarii* were a cog actually was. The freedmen did not
constitute an administrative cadre; they were not dogsbodies doing the 'real'
work of running the Empire. The specific titles that they enjoyed, great and
humble alike, mislead; they reflect only the aspect of household life which gave
them status, proximity to the Emperor. Hence, for example, the moral indignation of Epictetus (1.17. 18–19) at the high authority of the man who empties the
Emperor's chamber-pot. Epictetus, freedman of a freedman of the Emperor and
famous—if unconventional—philosopher (below, pp. 708 ff.), embodies an important truth about this milieu. The successful retinue of the Emperor were, or
aspired to be, part of the ordinary upper-class world of Rome, taking part in its
literary and intellectual culture. The inscriptions show us imperial freedmen in
all sorts of activities quite unconnected with the Palace. Like any influential
Roman, they devoted themselves to government only in an amateur and part-
time way, and when they reached, like Pallas and Narcissus, the councils of state,
it was as the friends, advisers, and confidants of the Emperor, not as expert
bureaucrats. It is because of their *personal* power that by the late Empire the
imperial domestics like the Grand Chamberlain have acquired the legitimate
public functions which make the court of that period begin to seem medieval.

Government and Litterae

The search for bureaucracy in the Roman world is vain. We should now look
a little more closely at the concern with jurisdiction and exaction which Roman
administrators really did have. Then, in conclusion, we can consider in general
terms the nature of the governmental process and attempt to discover what really
held the empire together.

Because Roman officials spent so much time in jurisdiction it was natural that
Roman law should become more complicated and more sophisticated. The
natural rule that jurisdiction gravitates to the highest available authority operated
to increase the workload of governors, the great prefects at Rome, and the
Emperor himself, and to hasten the adoption of Roman law. Even in the reign
of Augustus, Strabo can already write that Crete, despite its own venerable legal

THE BASILICA JULIA IN ROME, begun by Caesar in 54 BC and completed by Augustus. One of the great judicial buildings of the capital, it housed the civil court of the *centumviri* and was divided by wooden screens so that four cases could be heard simultaneously; but for cases of exceptional importance the whole hall was employed. Only the foundations remain.

tradition, had come, like all the provinces, to use the laws of Rome (10.4.22). And the bitterest realism about conditions in the Roman Empire cannot overlook the advantages of the existence of a legal framework to imperial rule, which the Hellenistic kingdoms had lacked, and which offered the Empire's subjects at least the theoretical possibility of redress and restrained the arbitrariness of Rome's rule. Law too grew at Rome with the problems first of city and then of Empire, and legal expertise came to provide an entry to the governing class. Professional legal practice was eventually one of the activities which gave many provincials a place in government, and Roman law was one of the most tenacious legacies of imperial rule—its greatest codification was the product of the eastern Empire under Justinian. There is not space here to recount the gradual evolution of Roman law, but the long accumulation of legal interpretations and precedents in the annual edicts of the praetors, which, when codified by Hadrian, formed the foundation of the legal system, and the role of the Emperor as a source of law and patron of the great jurists of the late second and early third centuries need stressing. For our purposes, however, two connected things are important. First, at Rome there was no question of the separation of judiciary and legislature which is so important a liberal principle to modern political thinkers. The law at Rome was on the whole the creation of judges, not lawgivers. The second point follows from this: legal measures show the same variety, casualness, and lack of generality which we find in Roman administrative decisions, and indeed it is difficult to separate the two. There is no proper ancient equivalent of statute law. The result was that the law was not always sufficiently universal, and the under-privileged might well not reap its benefits. Jewish nationalist writers, for example, compare the hypocrisy of Rome to the ambiguous associations of the unclean pig: 'Just as a pig lies down and sticks out its trotters as though to say "I am clean" [because they are cloven], so the evil empire robs and oppresses while pretending to execute justice.'

For the burdens of Roman rule on the Empire were heavy and hated, and much of Roman government was devoted to ensuring their efficacy. The collection of tribute, direct and indirect tax, rents, levies in kind, recruits, protection money, requisitioning, and so on in total amounted to a very heavy oppression, even if the amount of tax formally due was not by comparative standards very high. Roman officials from the highest to the most menial were involved with these matters, and finance was a serious administrative concern. Augustus' great catalogue of his achievements is called in full *Res Gestae et Impensae* ('His Deeds and Expenditure'). And this is undoubtedly the view that most provincials had of the way the Empire worked. A prophecy of Rome's fall concentrated on both the exactions of the ruling power and the—less often discussed but equally odi-ous—drain of manpower to Italy via the slave trade: 'the wealth that Rome has received from tributary Asia threefold shall Asia receive again from Rome, which will pay in full the price of its insolent pride. And for each of those who labour in the land of the Italians twenty Italians shall toil in Asia as needy slaves', (*Oracula Sibyllina* 3. 350 f.). Given this hostility to the harsh realities of the Empire, and given the amateur nature of Roman government, how was stability achieved?

Communications have been described as the nervous system of the body politic. Compared with what had gone before and what followed the rule of Rome, the frequency of movement and the security of roads and harbours was most impressive (though banditry never completely disappeared even from Italy). The imperial posting system, a creation of Augustus refined over the following centuries, became so huge, authoritative, and elaborate that it represented one of the heaviest burdens on the provincials whose food, animals, and dwellings were constantly being requisitioned for passing officials, as inscriptions from a wide range of places and times bear eloquent witness. But there can be no doubt that the roads and harbours of the Empire were one of the most necessary organs of Roman rule.

The transmission, retrieval, and storage of information is a still more basic

c. 1000 FEET (300 M.)

AERIAL VIEW OF THE PORT AT CARTHAGE, one of the major harbours of the Roman Mediterranean. The two artificial basins visible in the photograph go back to the Punic period; the rectangular one was designed for commercial shipping and the circular one for warships. At the centre of the circular port is an island on which recent excavations have revealed Punic ship-sheds. These were replaced by a monumental precinct in Roman times.

ingredient of the stability, durability, and effectiveness of government. Max
Weber called documents the bureaucrat's tools of production. The Roman
Empire has won a reputation for bureaucratic sophistication. So what of its
documents? Before the nineteenth century, it is interesting to note, this aspect of
Roman imperial rule did not strike students of the period. It was the discovery
of the *papyri* of Egypt which contributed to the view that Rome too had been
a bureaucracy like those burgeoning in the excavators' homelands. Since then the
spectacular complexity of the administration of Egypt has been further revealed,
and evidence from other dry regions—Dura Europus on the Euphrates is a notable
example—has shown that the volume of administrative paperwork in other eastern provinces was likewise very great. The figures can be astonishing. A third-
century regional administrator's office in Egypt consumed 434 rolls of papyrus in
a particular period of about a month. The archives of the fortress at Dura Europus
occupied more than ten rooms. It is easy incautiously to assert that this society
can truly be called bureaucratic'. But two problems must be faced. First, is the

DOCUMENT FROM THE ARCHIVE AT DURA-EUROPUS (first half of third century AD). The numerous
papyri from the archive include legal documents and contracts, a calendar of military festivals, records of
the purchase of horses, lists of soldiers, and so forth. This particular document is a letter of one Marius
Maximus concerning the reception and entertainment of a Parthian envoy.

practice of either Egypt or Mesopotamia, where the accumulation of documents was an extremely ancient aspect of government, typical of the eastern Empire in general, and is the East typical of the Empire as a whole? Papyrus archives naturally would not survive elsewhere, but the absence of the potsherds which were also extensively used at the lowest level of the Egyptian administration, is a better testimony to the singularity of the Egyptian system, since pottery is virtually indestructible. But the second question is more important: how far is this accumulation of mounds of paper by dozens of officials evidence for a bureaucratic administration of the kind found in modern states? To answer that question it will be necessary to discover why records were accumulated and how they were then deployed. Are our ancient administrative documents from working bureaux, lumber rooms, or something in between?

Even the ability to write documents such as the papyri which survive was not common in antiquity. We even hear in Egypt of illiterate scribes. Not so absurd: to be a scribe was a significant status, worth aspiring to through fraud. Of Pharaonic Egypt we know that scribes were men of very great importance in the state, and the pairing of Scribe with Pharisee is a still more familiar example of the way in which the skills conferred status. In China the skills of scholar and scribe, regulated by an amazing system of public examinations, defined the governmental class. In neither Greece nor Rome does the scribe have this status. At Rome the scribes played a role of their own in the political and social life of the city. The Emperor's service employed numerous clerks and secretaries. But it was not the handlers of documents, the men with the skills, who rose high. It was much more the *cubicularii*, the personal servants, the confidants of the Emperor or of powerful men. And they rose not through skill, dedication, or inside information, but through the patronage which came from social contacts. None of this speaks of a bureaucracy.

The scribe of ancient Egypt is portrayed cross-legged, his writing equipment on his lap, ready to move wherever he may be required. The classical scribe likewise was always mobile: there were clerks, but no offices. No ancient office building and no ancient desk will ever be discovered. Strikingly, when ancient administrative departments acquired a metaphorical name, it was not that of an unportable item of furniture, but the scribe's portable roll-satchel, the *scrinium*. Administration revolved around people, not around places or buildings, and not, despite those mountains of papyrus, around documents.

The documents were stored in archive rooms, some of which are known archaeologically. But although papers were kept, there were no filing cabinets, card indexes, reference numbers, registration forms. Collections of documents were made by pasting them together in chronological or—by no means as often as convenience would dictate—in alphabetical order. The codex, the presentation of documents as a book, was occasionally used, but the cartulary, a choice of really important documents for frequent reference, was unknown. Papers were preserved in archives, but it was well known that in most conditions papyrus did not keep well. Why did these things not matter? Because retrieval of documents from the archive was not a particularly urgent consideration in its formation. The tax assessment notice, the letter from the commanding officer, the tax receipt, the birth registration were used only once, in the process of checking a particular tax collection, or implementing a decision. Access to the document *might* be required a second time, but probably only a tiny fraction of all documents was ever looked at twice. The consultation of a document was a serious matter: 'for which reason, pious and benevolent Caesar, order that I be given a copy from your *commentarii* as your father intended' says a petitioner to Hadrian (*ILS* 338). Administrative processes were a favour, a privilege, a wonder, which is why on documents like this, where only what does credit to the purchaser of the inscription appears, what seem to us to be banal details of this kind are recorded in full. So this one actually preserves Hadrian's orders to his secretaries: 'Stasimus, Dapenis, publish the decision or opinion from the recorded version (*edite ex forma*)'. Authentication was a serious problem, never entirely solved, which helped prevent reliance on documentary authority. The *sardonychus* or imperial signet-ring gave its name to a Palatine department (see, e.g., *ILS* 1677), but there were often rumours that it had fallen into unauthorized hands. The Emperors used codes, but only rather simple ones. One of the principal reasons for the abuse of the public post system was that there was no reliable way of ensuring that only a limited number of people possessed authentic licences to demand hospitality and service. Distribution was another problem. It is very hard for us to imagine how difficult, despite the efficiency of communications, the systematic exchange of documentary information was. A letter of Trajan to Pliny making an important administrative point need never have been known in next door Asia, let alone Germania Inferior. This is perhaps one reason why Pliny's heirs

DOCUMENTS AND WRITING EQUIPMENT. From left to right an eraser, a four-leaved tablet, a double inkwell with a pen leaning against it, and a scroll. Wooden tablets coated with wax, in which writing was inscribed with a metal stylus, were used for a variety of documents, from official and business records to private letters; scrolls of parchment or papyrus, with writing in ink in the modern manner, were the standard vehicles for longer texts.

actually published his correspondence. This difficulty no doubt helped to discourage the formation of any monolithic imperial administrative structure.

Documents, once stored, were of surprisingly little use. Governmental acts could not afford to depend on such an unreliable basis. The archives represented continuity and stability, and were not for regular use. The truth appears well from the story of the disastrous fire of AD 192 at Rome, when the central imperial archives of the Palatine were completely destroyed (Dio 73. 24). There is no hint that Roman government was disrupted; but the event was taken as a token that the authority of Rome, embodied in these documents, would weaken. The omen is not so far removed from the association of Rome's universal rule with a census registration at the beginning of the Gospel of St Luke.

Another famous fire, this time not accidental, destroyed 3,000 inscribed tablets on the Capitoline during the Civil War of AD 69. Vespasian, by contrast with the events just described, saw to it that new texts were inscribed whenever another version of one of the perished documents could be discovered. State documents, we must not forget, included texts on stone and bronze and wood, and in the arts of government these were perhaps more important than the ones which were stacked in dusty muniment rooms. The ancient world was a uniquely epigraphic culture—otherwise our view of it, and especially of its institutions, would be very different. In classical Greece Athens had been exceptional in the extent to which it encouraged the publication on stone of official texts. During the Hellenistic period this important governmental act became a universal practice which was naturally enough adopted by Rome. The inscribing of a decision made it seem more permanent; it gained from the association of other venerable and welcome enactments inscribed nearby, and from the religious, political or sentimental tone of the place in which it was set up. To give only one example: the patents of citizenship of discharged auxiliary soldiers were at first tacked in hundreds to the Temple of the Good Faith of the Roman People to its Friends, high on the Capitol in the very heart of the Empire, powerfully expressing the relationship of Rome to its loyal subjects. A collection of privileges, honours, even historical or—in at least one case—philosophical texts could be a source of pride even to those who could not read them. For although there are pieces of evidence that the inscription was a source of information to the public—it was a tyrant's trick to hang savage edicts out of clear sight—it is revealing that published Roman laws sometimes contained the provision that the text was to be read aloud at regular intervals. Similarly we may assume that it was the moment when herald, ambassador, or magistrate first read the Emperor's letter to the city that it had its effect: the inscribing was a symbol of the city's gratitude and appreciation, and of the measure's permanence.

Depositing a document in an archive was not so different an act. The record depository might be in a significant temple (at Rome death registrations were kept in the grove of the goddess of funerals). The main Roman archive was part of a prestigious complex of buildings on the sacred Capitoline hill, high above

CITIZENSHIP DIPLOMA OF GEMELLUS. Dated 17 July 122, the two bronze tablets, wired together through holes at the adjacent corners, are a personal certificate of the privileges granted to a veteran on his discharge. The front (left) concludes with the words 'certified copy taken from the bronze plaque posted at Rome on the wall behind the temple of the Deified Augustus near (the statue of) Minerva'.

the Forum. The close connection between the perishable documents and the public inscription, and the purpose of preserving the text, is excellently shown by an epigraphic version from an Italian town, page by page with chapter headings, of a section of the town-council minutes relevant to the honorific purpose at hand (*ILS* 5918ᵃ). It emerges that the minutes themselves were less practical in purpose than a part itself of civic ceremony; it seems that a new roll would be formally started each year on Augustus' official birthday. The keeping of such records had very little to do with future practical utility.

If record keeping in antiquity is understood in this way, it begins to become clear that we should not be surprised at finding no serious bureaucracy and no administrative art as such in the ancient world. Those involved in government needed no special training. It is true that, for example, shorthands were developed, but it is revealing that they are associated at Rome with the names of two men of high culture, Cicero's amanuensis Tiro and Horace's patron Maecenas. But importantly, although so many papyri concern counting and taxation, the ancient world had no systematic knowledge of accounting, and no concept of numeracy. Book-keeping, hindered by the number systems of Greek and Latin, always remained primitive. It is very strange, when the marginal subsistence of the ancient poor is considered, how low a standard of accuracy is found in papyrus and epigraphical calculations. What was required of an administrator was (after loyalty and probity) *litterae*, the whole world of ancient literary culture. The Younger Pliny (*Ep.* 1. 10. 9) is most revealing on the subject. As prefect of the Roman treasury he has to spend his time at the most banal and routine administrative business; his work is 'extremely uncultured'—but the word he uses to describe it is *litterae*, none the less.

That administration was *litterae* is an observation which will enable us to end on a rather more positive note: up to now we have been necessarily preoccupied, sadly, with abandoning Auden's image of the bored clerk's 'pink official form'. It has been stressed that ancient government was concerned with warfare, jurisdiction, and the management of private property. What kept alive this ideology was the aristocratic literary culture for which ancient civilization has always been most famous. The leader of men, the just judge, and the fair master had been ideals since Homer. For Herodotus the origin of the power of the Median—and hence the Persian—kingship was simply the impartiality and importance to society of the judgements of Deioces. There was no distinction between the Arts of Government and the other *technai, artes*, with which ancient élites concerned themselves. The art of rhetoric above all united what we see as these two distinct worlds. Eloquence is one of the main requirements of the ancient administrator. The Roman Emperor himself always expressed himself in the literary forms of letters or speeches, and spent most of his day listening to similar products of ancient literary culture. The generalizations and principles expressed in Roman governmental pronouncements are not a coherent ideology, and still less an indication of imperial policies, but simply commonplaces of moral or political thought deployed appropriately in a literary composition. It was not easy to aspire to participation in this sort of exercise. In fact, in its formal intellectual demands, membership of the Roman administrative élite was not after all so very different from the system which evolved in China.

Vitruvius, the architect in the public service, expressly praises his parents for the general philological and technical/artistic education which has made him what he is (6, pr. 4). Philostratus sneers at the lack of success of an imperial freedman whose inadequate literary attainments let him down, 'Celer, a writer of technical works and a good enough secretary of the emperor, but lacking in polish' (*VS* 1. 22). For slaves and freedmen, equestrians and senators alike, culture was the sign of and often the way to social success, and at no level of the Roman administration do we find functionaries who are carrying out some sort of 'serious' administrative activity while their seniors indulge in cultural pursuits.

I have also emphasized the importance of Rome's inclusion of the élites of the Empire, above all of Greece, in her government. This too would not have been possible had Greek and Latin speakers not already come to share a common cultural heritage. It is therefore no coincidence that the age of the greatest governmental complexity of the ancient world and that flowering of culture which we call the Second Sophistic came together. The aristocratic ideals which underlay ancient government also required conspicuous expenditure on the part of rulers. Much that is familiar about the Roman world from Gibbon's portrait of the Antonine golden age derives from this. The enormous tomb which Claudius'

freedman Pallas built for himself, the vast scale of the military engineering of
Hadrian's Wall, and the great building projects of the Emperor at Rome and the
urban upper classes in the hundreds of cities of the Empire are all themselves part
of the great Art by which the Empire was maintained. The reciprocal relations
of benefaction, competition, and prestige among those who controlled the resources of the ancient world are found throughout antiquity, from the aristocracies of the archaic Greek cities to the Roman Emperors. In these relations were
included the whole range of ancient cultural activities, from architecture and
utilitarian building to the patronage of literature, music, and painting—and also
to the entertainments of the circus and the amphitheatre and the religious festivals
which were the setting of almost all these forms of display. This characteristic
aspect of ancient society produced a type of bond between the élite and the peoples
of the cities which was unique—a major source of the stability and continuity
which we associate with the Greek and Roman world.

Unfortunately ancient culture had never rid itself of its uneasy companion,
warfare. In the end this aspect came to be dominant. There came a time when
scribes were soldiers, bishops were soldiers, local governors were soldiers, the

PHILIP THE ARAB (AD 244–9), one of a
new breed of soldier Emperors who came
to the fore in the third century. Their
portraits express a new spirit of
uncompromising ruthlessness appropriate to
an age of civil wars, assassinations, and
virtual anarchy. The board-like band across
the chest belongs to a third-century style of
wearing the toga.

Emperor was a soldier. At that point the end of the ancient world was in sight. It is therefore again no coincidence that the first great crisis of Roman rule and the cultural desert of the third century came together, even if it would be too simple to say that either brought about the other.

Further Reading

Fundamental is F. Millar, *The Emperor in the Roman World* (London, 1977), not only for the role of the Emperor but for very many aspects of Roman government. For the city-state M. I. Finley, *Politics in the Ancient World* (Cambridge, 1983) is suggestive and interesting though unreliable on Rome itself; on citizenship A. N. Sherwin-White, *The Roman Citizenship*[2] (Oxford, 1973) remains basic. For the Greek world A. H. M. Jones, *The Greek City* (Oxford 1940), and for Italy W. Eck, *Die staatliche Organisation Italiens* (Munich, 1979). On town statuses F. Abbott and A. C. Johnson, *Municipal Administration in the Roman Empire* (Princeton, 1926) is still very useful. On the definition of provinces and *imperium*, A. Lintott, *Greece & Rome* 28 (1981), 53 f. For governors' assizes, G. Burton, *JRS* 65 (1975), 926.

For the military angle R. MacMullen, *Soldier and Civilian in the later Roman Empire* (Harvard, 1963), is crucial; and see now L. Keppie, *The Making of the Roman Army* (London, 1984), and J. B. Campbell, *The Emperor and the Roman Army* (Oxford, 1984); on the Emperor's military planning F. Millar, *Britannia* 13 (1982), 1 f. For *praefecti fabrum* B. Dobson, *Britain and Rome* ed. B. Dobson and M. G. Jarrett (Kendal, 1966) pp. 61 f. Amateur commanders: J. B. Campbell, *JRS* 65 (1975), 11 f.

For slaves in the public service L. Halkin, *Les ésclaves publics chez les romains* (Liége, 1897); for the *apparitores* N. Purcell, *PBSR* 51 (1983), 125 f. On the imperial household A. M. Duff, *Freedmen in the Early Roman Empire* (Oxford, 1926); P. R. C. Weaver, *Familia Caesaris* (Cambridge, 1972). The quotation about the imperial civil service is from P. A. Brunt, *JRS* 65 (1975), 124 f., which establishes that the administrators of Roman Egypt had no particular qualifications for the job. On equestrian procurators H. G. Pflaum, *Les procurateurs équestres* (Paris, 1972) presents the results of a monumental survey. For reasons for promotion see R. P. Saller, *Personal Patronage under the Early Empire* (Cambridge, 1982), chs. 2–3, making a very strong case against promotion for merit. For status, not administrative function, as the way to understand the *familia Caesaris* G. Burton, *JRS* 67 (1977), 162 f. The quotation about the *tabellarii* is from Weaver, cit.

On law, J. Crook, *Law and Life of Rome* (London, 1967); A. N. Sherwin-White, *Roman Society and Law in the New Testament* (Oxford, 1963). For a detailed survey of imperial finance, P. A. Brunt, *JRS* 71 (1981), 161 f. The remark about the pig is quoted from N. de Lange, 'Jewish Attitudes to the Roman Empire', in P. Garnsey and C. Whittaker, edd. *Imperialism in the Ancient World* (Cambridge, 1978), p. 255. For the miseries of ancient provincial subjects R. MacMullen, *Roman Social Relations* (Yale, 1974). On benefaction and dependence, P. Veyne, *Bread and Games* (English edn. of *Le Pain et le cirque* (Paris, 1976), in preparation).

Roman Egypt: a useful brief survey N. Lewis, *Life in Roman Egypt* (Oxford, 1983). On documents and records E. Posner, *Archives in the Ancient World* (Cambridge, Mass., 1972). For Rome's fostering of the élites of the empire G. E. M. de Ste. Croix, *The Class Struggle in the Ancient Greek World* (London, 1981), who (p. 503) likens the behaviour of the rulers of the Empire to that of vampire bats.

24

Augustan Poetry and Society

❧❧

R. O. A. M. LYNE

THIS is perhaps the most eventful period of Roman history, witness to civil wars, revolution, and, eventually, an imposed peace: Republic becomes Empire. Meanwhile, Latin literature produces its greatest works; Italy produces poets destined to achieve immortality. The present chapter offers a sketch of this extraordinary time. First, three divisions within the period must be identified.

Dates and Divisions

The triumviral period begins in 43 BC, when the Roman world was put into the hands of Octavian, Antony, and Lepidus 'for the purposes of setting the state in order'. Antony was defeated at the battle of Actium in 31 BC, but the first Augustan period may be said to begin in the year 27 BC when Octavian's imperial role is effectively, but discreetly, defined and he himself assumes the name Augustus. Another change is then discernible about 20 BC: Augustus exercises his monarchical power more assertively, and this has a large effect upon literature.

The works that will be considered below may now be assigned to these three divisions, though some of the assignations are approximate and some insecure. Into the first, the triumviral period, fall the *Eclogues* and most of the *Georgics* of Virgil, the *Epodes* and *Satires* of Horace; Propertius' Book 1 is published at the beginning of the first Augustan period, but much of it may have been composed earlier. Propertius' Book 2, Tibullus' Books 1 and 2, Horace's *Odes* 1–3, and Virgil's *Aeneid* are all substantially works of this first Augustan period (though the *Aeneid* is unfinished at Virgil's death in 19 BC); at the end of it we can place Horace's *Epistles* 1 and 2.1, and Propertius 3, and we can detect signs of the atmosphere of the second Augustan period in those works. To this second Augustan period we may then assign Propertius 4, and Horace's *Odes* 4, *Epistle* 2.2 (the *Epistle to Augustus*), and *Ars Poetica*. Ovid's *Amores* straddle the two Augustan periods, while the remainder of his works all belong to the second.

The Role of Poets

Our period sees the culmination of a process of change in the status of poets and poetry, a change of fundamental importance. Traditionally—let us say in the second century BC—poets, unlike historians, had been of low social status (foreigners or freedmen for example) and their works and profession were positively revered only in one particular respect, their power to confer lasting fame. Drama was of course valued as entertainment, and dramatists unlike other poets were directly paid; but in general philistinism towards poetry was endemic. Aristocrats with aesthetic taste and education like Scipio Aemilianus were exceptions. Even by the time of Cicero things have not much changed: Cicero has to tread cautiously in his defence of the poet Archias, presupposing philistinism in his audience. Nor is Cicero himself boundlessly aesthetic. Given a second life, he said, he would still not bother to read the Greek lyric poets.

When upper-class Romans do start to turn their hands to poetry, one gets the impression of amateurs, more or less condescending. Q. Lutatius Catulus and others toss off epigrams at the end of the second century, showing an acquaintance with Greek precedents, probably from anthologies; but Catulus at least, consul in 102 BC with C. Marius, had better things to do with his serious time. The satirist Lucilius is a much more significant figure (his literary *floruit* can be put in the 130s BC). He is rich and of high rank, great enough to be friend and foe of the greatest men of his generation—great enough also to utter his sometimes scarifying opinions on these great men, as well as on more humble figures, in his able and fluent verse. His development of the genre of satire is important in the history of Latin literature; so is his assertively autobiographical standpoint; so in particular is the importance he accords to the business of writing. Nevertheless I do not think we have in Lucilius an instance of an aristocrat seriously adopting the profession of poet. It was what he said that mattered to him; and, clothing his thoughts in a racy patchwork of Greek tags and often colloquial Latin and disposing all that in a range of metres, he found an eye-catching and ear-catching way of saying what he wanted to say. It was the message that mattered for him; he was a commentator on the contemporary scene rather than an artist—although as an artist he was, incidentally, pretty good.

In the shift in attitude towards poets and poetry it is the so-called Neoteric movement in the late Republic that is crucial: the group of poets comprising Catullus, Calvus, Cinna, and others. These are men of the provincial or Roman upper classes who take the profession of poetry with utmost seriousness. They at least think that it well befits an upper-class Roman simply to be a poet. Catullus, of course, we know most about. After a brief brush with active life he devoted his whole energies to poetry—and love. Symptomatic of his poetical professionalism is his interest in and knowledge of the professional poet and scholar of Alexandria, Callimachus (above, pp. 361 ff.). Catullus is probably best known for his love poetry and for his lampoons and invectives; but arguably most indicative of him as an artist and certainly as a Neotcric are his intricate and highly wrought longer poems, such as 64 (the *Peleus and Thetis*), 68, and his translation of Callimachus, 66. But these poems are also indicative of something which went hand in glove, perhaps inevitably, with this new interest in the business of poetry: aestheticism, an interest in technique for technique's sake. This tendency was probably more pronounced in Cinna. His 'miniature epic' *Zmyrna* took nine years to write and attracted a scholarly commentary in the next generation.

Our period sees the final shift in attitude towards poetry and poets. Not only can poetry now appear a reputable full-time occupation for Romans of good class. Poets relinquish aestheticism, engage themselves with society, discover or profess commitment—or have to defend non-commitment. In short, the classical Greek view of poetry is again in play: it is the work of important people and may serve the citizens of the state in a moral and educative fashion. Virgil and his poetry will be glanced at below and discussed in another chapter. Of the elegiac poets (the term refers to their metre, cf. above p. 100, and does not have the mournful overtones of the English 'elegy'), Tibullus is a knight, well off in Horace's eyes, though less so in his own; Ovid and Propertius were knights (*equites*), and Propertius had relations of senatorial rank and friends of consular standing. The attitude of these poets towards society will be discussed below. Horace is less grand than Propertius or Tibullus: he is the son of a freedman, but a freedman with enough cash to put him through the equivalent of a university education at Athens. Eventually Horace gained the status of a kind of poet laureate. He not only performs, with some intermission, the function of moral and educative poet; he expresses it in theory.

Given that poets were traditionally of low social status, and given that no system of royalties or the like existed in the Roman world (except for dramatists), how did poets live? The answer basically is: patronage. Poets attached themselves to, or were collected by, wealthy Roman aristocrats. The great epic poet Ennius, for example (above, pp. 450 ff.), was patronized by, among others, M. Fulvius Nobilior, and a catalogue of other poets could be adduced who wrote epics celebrating aristocratic generals and thereby gained their sustenance. Poets fitted into the general Roman client-patron system whereby great men were attended, cultivated, and in humble matters assisted by the humble, and in return bestowed their bounty and their protection. But even in early days there was a difference between poet-clients and ordinary clients. For what the patron got from the poet was something that was rather more estimable than that which other clients could offer: the perpetuation of their fame and glory. More than that: *memoria sempiterna*, 'being remembered for ever', was the way in which many Romans, including Cicero, viewed how they might 'live' after death; so what a poet might offer was in effect a chance of immortality. This is the keynote of Cicero's defence of Archias, mentioned above: Archias had provided immortality for

Marius and Lucullus and, through them, for the Roman People. This aspect of the poet's function in Rome is a vital one, continuing into our period.

As the status of poet changes, so does the nature of patronage. Catullus, whose family is friendly with Julius Caesar and soon to become senatorial, has no economic need of a patron and does not have one. His circle is a coterie, a grouping of equals, and his address to Cornelius Nepos in his first poem is to be construed as a friendly or polite gesture, no more. Similarly Propertius, in his first book. But patronage does persist, even among the socially enhanced poets of the Augustan period.

The circle of the great orator, soldier, and statesman, M. Valerius Messalla, consul with Octavian in 31 BC, is indicative, exhibiting both continuity and change. There are in fact points of resemblance between his circle and a coterie such as that of Catullus. Pliny tells us that Messalla interested himself in the writing of erotic versicles, and we can observe him surrounded by other love poets and poetasters (coterie fashion), who include his aristocratic niece Sulpicia. On the other hand, if the author of the *Panegyricus Messallae* in the Tibullan corpus belongs to the circle and is talking of our Messalla (as is likely), then here is continuity in the role of poet as client: the client-poet immortalizes the great man. But it is the relation of the elegist Tibullus to Messalla that is most interesting.

Although Tibullus is vastly the social inferior of the noble Messalla, he is a knight, he does reflect the change in status of poets—and yet his relationship to Messalla resembles the old one of client and patron. He writes poems that, while not being technically panegyrics, devote themselves to the celebration of Messalla and his family (1.7 and 2.5), and scatters his other poems with laudatory allusions. Patronage survives the changes in status of poets and poetry. The phenomenon is of course observable in the circle of Maecenas, and elsewhere. So we ask ourselves: To what extent is this literary patronage like the old kind? What are both parties now getting out of it?

Some basic points can be inferred—Ovid, who was patronized early in his career by Messalla, is informative. These upper-class poets were not dependent economically in the way that their predecessors had been (though more on this anon). What they obtained was the encouragement of a great man usually himself a littérateur, the cachet of being associated with a well-known group of poets, access to such like-minded people (they would meet and some would even live in the great man's house), and perhaps above all publicity. Although at this time literature is intensely literate, written ultimately to be read and propagated in texts, an initial and important mode of communication is oral: various kinds of readings—private readings among the poets, semi-public and public recitations (formal public *recitationes* were instituted in Rome by Asinius Pollio. This was the scene in which a poet might make his name, and the chance to recite to an audience organized by a great patron was crucially important to a rising poet. Horace deplored both the institution of recitation and the fact that fame accrued thereby; but deploring it did not remove it, and even Horace himself recited. As for the patron, he had the natural satisfactions that such patronage brings, and he had, too, his chance of a piece of immortality. And in the circle of Maecenas something else was happening.

In the first Augustan period, Maecenas is the Augustan patron, mediating between poets and *princeps*. We can identify very important points of difference between his circle and, say, Messalla's. First, Augustus naturally wanted his heroic deeds enshrined in an epic—his piece of immortality. The trouble was that Maecenas' poets—Virgil, Horace, and subsequently Propertius—had to a varying extent scruples, moral and literary. The accommodating Tibullus could include celebrations of Messalla and his military exploits amongst his elegies in praise of love and peace. Not so Propertius. Besides, he was not an epic poet. Nor was Horace. Neither, to begin with, was Virgil. This presented a problem. These men were not old-style client-poets to be booted into an uncongenial genre. But Augustus was, to put it mildly, powerful. How does one deal with, on the one hand, upper-class poets with scruples and, on the other, an Emperor who wants an epic? The answer is that one is diplomatic, one mediates, one explains; and it is greatly to Maecenas' credit that his poets had the freedom, for a time, to decline impositions or fulfil them in their own individual way (as will be illustrated below).

Besides the moral and artistic sensitivity of his poets, Maecenas' circle was different from others in other and crucial respects. First and simply, the scale of what was on offer. These poets were not humble paupers, but Horace at least needed a living, and all had lost property in the land confiscations of the triumviral period. What Maecenas and Augustus bestowed on Horace and Virgil was vast (particularly, it seems, in Virgil's case), enabling them to live in very comfortable leisure in town or country. A certain moral pressure must therefore have been felt by these morally sensitive artists. Secondly, the task towards which they were being pressured was not just to immortalize the heroic deeds of the greatest general. It was something unique to the circle of Maecenas, reflecting the unique nature of his and later Augustus' patronage. Augustus and the state were effectively synonymous. To be in his patronage, directly or indirectly, was to be in the patronage of government, and there was a pressure to publicize the government's policies and to burnish its image. This task could be seen as invidious, but it could also be seen as a challenging responsibility; and with varying degrees of enthusiasm and directness, these scrupulous poets tackled it.

The nature of patronage in the imperial circle changes with the second Augustan period. Indeed this change may be seen to be part-cause of the second period arising. The sophisticated Maecenas, for reasons that cannot be defined with certainty, fades in importance, and the poets come under the direct patronage of the emperor. His hand was heavier, and it was becoming increasingly so. Political life around 20 BC reveals a more confidently autocratic ruler (witness, for instance, the marriage laws of 18 BC), and poetry, lacking the mediation of Maecenas, must also respond to his touch. A fourth book of *Odes* is elicited

AGRICULTURAL SCENES, mosaic at Cherchel (Algeria). Early third century AD. The upper scenes show ploughing and sowing; the lower the tending of vineyards in the winter. Such operations are referred to in Virgil's *Georgics*, the first in Book 1 (on the cultivation of crops), the second in Book 2 (on fruit-growing).

from an unwilling Horace, for example, containing what he had largely avoided in recent years: panegyric. The 'educator of citizens' becomes the court poet—but he has ways of striking back.

Virgil

Against this background I shall now outline the careers of the individual poets. Virgil's place in the picture must be adumbrated, but with all brevity since a separate chapter (Ch. 25) is devoted to him. His *Eclogues*, written in the triumviral period, show him ambivalent between the aestheticism of the Neoterics and an emerging sense of commitment. Elegant imitations of Theocritean pastoral glance at the miseries caused by land confiscations. While writing the *Eclogues* Virgil is not in the patronage of Maecenas. While writing the *Georgics* he is; and the *Georgics*, instigated or at least encouraged by Maecenas, show that Maecenas was not immediately concerned to elicit material that directly or crudely served Octavian. But the poem is to a great degree a moral didactic, hence of potential if rather indefinite use to a ruler; and it shows Virgil's strengthening sense of his committed poetic role.

It also demonstrates an attitude towards country life, an attitude which can be paralleled. Unlike Catullus and, say, Propertius, Virgil loves and esteems rustic life. But whereas the dominating reality of contemporary agriculture was large slave-run estates, Virgil esteems the small independent farmer—and exploits his way of life as a metaphor for morality. The simple point I want to stress is that in spite of the prevalence of great ranches, such small farmers were still around. Evidence testifies to their minority existence; and the policy of settling soldiers on confiscated property might, if it was successful (as it probably was not), have increased their numbers. So Virgil's affectionate view of the country is we might say old-fashioned, blinkered, even slightly romantic; but it is not a mere fiction or poetic convention.

I said above that no immediate pressure was being exerted by Maecenas for a poem directly to serve Octavian. But both he and Virgil would know that the great man would want his exploits celebrated in epic, and that is what Virgil seems to promise at the beginning of *Georgics* III. In fact, in the sophisticated atmosphere of the first Augustan period, he developed an indirect, mythical mode whose fruit was the *Aeneid*—and the Emperor was, perhaps rather surprisingly, well pleased.

Horace

In the triumviral period Horace writes his *Epodes*, in Archilochian *iambi*, and his *Satires*, his development of Lucilius' genre. We can still discern vestiges of republican libertarianism and non-alignment in them. *Epodes* 7 and 16 consider with neutral despair the imminence of civil war. Other *Epodes* are vicious attacks, in Archilochian vein. Some *Satires* too attack personages, but in general Horace's *Satires* are more general and genial than those of Lucilius, and neither *Epodes* nor *Satires* assail men of eminence. Horace had not the protection of rank; and besides, the triumviral period was a despotic one, with the added complication that one could not be sure which despot would come out on top.

This is, however, also the period in which Maecenas gathers Horace into his circle, and Horace is induced to commit himself enthusiastically to Octavian. *Epode* 9 is a celebration of the victory of Actium, and *Epode* 1, addressed to

REMAINS OF HORACE'S VILLA AT LICENZA in the hills 40 km east of Rome. The identification of the site as the Sabine farm bestowed on the poet by Maecenas in 33 BC was made as early as the eighteenth century and is supported not only by topographical indications in Horace's own writings but also by the styles of construction and decoration, characteristic of the early Augustan period.

Maecenas, is the effusive poem of a man who definitely sees himself in a patron-ized position; it reminds one of Tibullus talking to Messalla. *Satire* 2.6 records with gratitude the gift of the famous Sabine estate, and *Satire* 1.1 is also addressed to Maecenas.

On the other hand, Horace is careful about himself and his image in his patronized position. In *Satire* 1.9, and in 1.6, the poem in which he describes his acceptance into Maecenas' circle, he is careful to define that acceptance as an honourable process, based on merit, and the circle as one of like-minded men free from the debasing procedures which characterized many client–patron groupings. Indeed he terms himself the 'friend' (*amicus*) of Maecenas. Although the language of *amicitia* was conventionally used between clients and patrons, and it would be quite clear who was the grand *amicus* and who was not, there is much evidence that Horace genuinely was friendly in the full sense of the word with Maecenas and even with Augustus. Indeed, he was familiar enough with Maecenas to allude in *Epode* 14 to an erotic liaison on the great man's part with an actor, Bathyllus.

In *Odes* 1–3, belonging to the first Augustan period, Horace assumes the role of a Roman Alcaeus. It was the usefulness of the image rather than the material of Alcaeus' texts that suggested this choice. Horace presents the image of Alcaeus, with discreet distortion, as follows (*Odes* 1.32). Alcaeus was an intensely committed citizen-poet, *engagé*, patriotically writing about the burning issues of his time; he also knew, however, that there was a place on the margins of life for leisure, for love and wine, and for poetry of leisure, poetry of love and wine; and he wrote such leisure poetry, as well as *engagé* poetry, knowing it to be leisure poetry, marginal poetry. Thus the image, and it was indeed useful to Horace. Committed at this time to his belief in the social and educative role of the poet and yet at the same time a delighted and delightful poet of love and wine, he could thus, as a Roman Alcaeus, justify his production. Like Alcaeus, he was the committed public poet, but he knew nevertheless that it could be appropriate to relax and not unseemly to write poetry for such occasions. It was vital, simply, to keep a sense of proportion, and not to let the life and literature of leisure usurp the position of the serious business of life. That was the mistake of the Elegists. Tibullus is read a lesson in this connection in the *Ode* immediately following the presentation of the Alcaean image.

Horace makes a couple of false starts in his public poetry: *Odes* 1.2 and 12 border on unpalatable panegyric, and 1.2 imputes divinity to an Augustus anxious to avoid such adoration. But during this period he evolved a satisfying and sophisticated method of public poetry, an 'indirect' method which bears comparison with Virgil's procedure in the *Aeneid*. Horace's method is a process of *association* and *substitution*. A good example is *Odes* 3.5, in which the sequence of thought is this: Augustus will be considered analogous to a god (that sort of expression was seemly) when he has conquered Britain and Parthia; mention of Parthia brings to mind Crassus' defeat at the hands of the Parthians in 53 BC and the shocking fact that Roman prisoners were now living among the Parthians as Parthians; this disgrace is, Horace implies, what Augustus will avenge. Then Horace is prompted to recall an event, almost a myth, from Roman history, the story of Regulus, a story which also involved a hated enemy, Roman prisoners, and a great Roman general; and the telling of this story occupies the rest of the *Ode*.

Now in fact the parallels between the two episodes are slight, extending not much beyond the broad features just mentioned. But by means of a glossing formula of transition and by the mere fact of juxtaposition, Horace manages to associate the two generals (Augustus and Regulus), to assimilate Augustus' imminent honourable action in the matter of Parthians and prisoners to Regulus' action in the matter of prisoners and Carthaginians. Indirectly, therefore, he presents Augustus as a new Regulus: Stoic, honourable—and republican, a useful suggestion. By this process of association he avoids the invidiousness of direct and implausible praise. By the process of substitution—eleven of the fourteen stanzas of the *Ode* are devoted to the associated figure of Regulus, who is thus substituted for the contemporary figure Augustus—he gives himself artistic and indeed moral liberty. In both artistic and moral terms it is hard to sing stirringly about the impending expedition of a contemporary general; much easier to evoke the heroic action of a quasi-mythical figure. Similarly in 3.4 Horace discreetly associates Augustus' victory at Actium with Jupiter's victory over the Giants, a traditional paradigm of the victory of civilized force over barbarism; and he then devotes his lyrical attention to this, the substituted story. What poet could not write epically about such a story? What poet, on the other hand, would not find difficulties in lauding a contemporary battle like Actium? Horace himself had, back in *Odes* 1.37.

That is Horace in public vein. Here is a taste of Horace as poet of love. The first three stanzas of the famous Pyrrha *Ode* (1.5) run thus:

> quis multa gracilis te puer in rosa
> perfusus liquidis urget odoribus,
>   grato, Pyrrha, sub antro?
>   cui flauam religas comam,
>
> simplex munditiis? heu quotiens fidem
> mutatosque deos flebit et aspera
>   nigris aequora uentis
>   emirabitur insolens,
>
> qui nunc te fruitur credulus aurea,
> qui semper uacuam semper amabilem
>   sperat nescius aurae
>   fallacis. miseri, quibus
>
> intemptata nites! ...

What slim boy, Pyrrha, drenched in liquid scents presses you in an abundance of roses under some pleasing grotto? For whom are you binding back your blonde hair in simple elegance? Alas, how often will he bewail fidelity and the gods changed, and wonder amazed at the sea made harsh by dark winds, he who now trustfully enjoys golden you, he who expects you always available, always lovable—ignorant of the deceiving breeze. Wretched are they for whom you shine untried ...!

That carries a typical Horatian message which Horace, unlike the gullible youth in the poem, knows only too well. Love, the occupation of leisure, is a fleeting, evanescent, untrustworthy thing, though it can be none the less painful for that.

Odes 3.28 gives a taste of Horace as poet of wine as well as love. It too carries a typical Horatian message: Horace announces that it is a holiday, the *Neptunalia*, and therefore leisure time. What is he to do? Answer: drink good wine, make music—and love. So, in Horace's view, leisure pursuits, love and wine, should not usurp the position of serious business; but it is equally his view, embodied in this *Ode*, that leisure is not leisure without them.

It will be noted that the girls in Horace's poetry of love and wine have Greek names. If we investigate these names, if we investigate other details in the poems, we find that this leisure poetry reflects—with discretion, stylization, romance—a real society: the Roman *demi-monde*, the *symposion* scene, where girls of probably slave or freedwoman class entertained with music and sex. This fact is important in two respects. It shows that Horace's erotic and sympotic poetry is not mere fancy and convention. And it also shows that Horace as a rule enjoyed, or liked to be seen to be enjoying, his erotic pleasures with women, or boys, of the lower classes employed for that purpose. That was considered correct at Rome. To attempt an erotic liaison with an upper-class *uirgo* was or should be an impossibility, and to have affairs with married ladies was in the Augustan age to become literally criminal. That point was not always well taken.

Many of Horace's *Odes* in Books 1–3 are concerned neither with affairs of state nor merely with leisure and pleasure, but with ethics on a private scale: how a man in his private capacity should conduct his life. After the production of *Odes* 1–3 Horace returns to the hexameter metre of his *Satires* and, in the late twenties BC, writes *Epistles* (Book 1) which are devoted to such ethical exploration and instruction. In his introductory *Epistle* to Maecenas he explains that, for this new production, he is giving up verse 'and other such frivolities'. The statement lacks neither ambiguity nor disingenuousness: for a start, Horace is at that very moment technically writing verse. It is nevertheless true that he does temporarily relinquish his role as public poet and the more overtly poetical mode of lyric.

BREASTPLATE OF THE STATUE OF AUGUSTUS FROM PRIMA PORTA (early first century AD). The imagery of the reliefs is closely related to that of Horace's *Carmen saeculare*, composed for the Secular Games of 17 BC. At the centre is depicted the recovery of the standards captured by the Parthians at the battle of Carrhae, and at the lower left and right are Apollo and Diana, the deities addressed by Horace in his hymn.

Why? Some reasons are stated, some may be inferred. Horace's dislike of the business of being a professional poet (recitations and so on) is affirmed in *Epistle* 1. 19 and reaffirmed in the *Epistle to Florus* (2. 2) of 19 BC. He also attests lack of public acclaim for *Odes* 1-3, due to his unwillingness to participate in such business; that too may have been discouraging. Then again, the question of private ethics had always been a preoccupation of his, in *Satires* as well as in *Odes*. There is perhaps one more factor: something to do with the role of public poet, the poet as immortalizer, the poet as educator. Horace may have experienced lack of confidence in the role, or perhaps disenchantment with it, as the Maecenas era drew to its close; whatever it was, the cap was no longer fitting. In Book 3 Horace had been the 'priest of the Muses', addressing future generations in public and edifying tones. In the *Epistle to Florus*, this same man turns to discuss the various reasons for writing poetry—the reasons that might induce him to turn professional again—and does not mention poetry's grand functions, its functions to immortalize and in particular to edify. The silence seems to me significant: for some reason, Horace was unhappy about the poet in this sort of role.

Not for long, or he was not allowed to be for long. The second Augustan period is upon us. For the Secular Games of the year 17 BC, the games to mark the New Age, Horace writes the public hymn, the *Carmen saeculare*. Next he is induced under the direct patronage of Augustus to compose a fourth book of *Odes* containing, as I have said, courtly poems directly panegyrical of the Emperor and his family. On the other hand—a gesture of conscious or unconscious self-assertion—the book contains some of Horace's finest poetry of love and wine. The very first poem movingly evokes Horace in love, in love again at fifty, in love with a boy called Ligurinus. Note that name. For once the love-object in a Horatian homosexual love poem does not have a Greek name; so he is neither cloaked in disguise nor assigned to an acceptably lowly class. Ligurinus is a real Roman *cognomen*. The poem is assertively personal—and very beautiful. Another beautiful poem of love and wine, also affectingly personal, is poem 11; and, satisfyingly, it is built round the birthday of the once great figure of Maecenas.

I do not think that Horace took up his public pen again totally willingly in this second Augustan period; but perhaps he was not totally unwilling. The reasons for his retirement are not, as I have said, perspicuous, and his description of poetry as frivolity was disingenuous. Certainly he came to be proud of the *Carmen saeculare*. And his *Epistle to Augustus* (2. 1, of 12 BC) asserts once more the educative function of the poet and the power of poetry to immortalize. An interesting, incidental fact: in this epistle Horace implicitly argues for classic status to be accorded the Augustan poets: Virgil, the now lost Varius, and presumably himself. Over the love elegists a significant veil of silence is drawn: Ovid was, for example, by now the rage, but there is not a word on him. Finally, the *Ars Poetica* of the last years of his life shows him seriously occupied with poetry as a serious business, both entertaining and educative.

Propertius

Propertius is socially grander than Virgil and Horace, and strikes a provocatively unconventional stance in life and literature (these two facts will not be unconnected). He seems never to have been so devoted or complete a member of Maecenas' circle as Virgil and Horace were.

Pragmatic Roman attitudes held that a man should do something serious with his life: conventionally, in the upper classes, he should advance it either in political or in economic terms. That was one position that Propertius confronted. But our period also sees, as I have said, poets regaining their classical status as civically committed, useful to the state, estimable creatures. Propertius confronts that idea too. He professes himself unemployed and unemployable in any conventional sense outside poetry, and 'useful' as a poet in ways which the conventional would regard as worse than useless. Whereas, therefore, Catullus the man had been prepared simply to *be* at leisure, Propertius declares it assertively, makes a manifesto of it; whereas Catullus the poet had occupied a position of unconcerned aestheticism, Propertius, in the new climate of artistic commitment, makes an aggressive statement of what in effect was non-commitment. I look at these points separately.

In a sequence of poems in Book 1 (1, 6, 14), Propertius declares his position on life and love. In contradistinction to Tullus, his addressee, Propertius cannot, he says, engage upon an active career. He must devote himself to love, and neither military/political nor economic advancement can distract him. He represents his love as something without sense, mad even; a disease, degradation. He takes upon himself all the condemnatory terms that Roman society customarily assigned to a hopelessly lost romantic lover. He even accepts for himself a title that society was not accustomed to fling around; he is the slave of his mistress. And yet he insists: this is for me. His position remains much the same in Book 2, and in some poems of Book 3. The commitment to love may be taken seriously; the self-condemnation less so. Later Romantics were to find that a willing espousal of wrong could be satisfyingly provocative. Propertius presents a programme of life designed to provoke—and to provoke not only stern moralists, but discreet proponents of acceptable *amour* such as Horace. Here was exactly what Horace decried: love, which should be the occupation of leisure, usurping the serious business of life, indeed becoming coterminous with life.

Before we consider Propertius' views on poetry we must consider the woman of whom he writes. Who is Cynthia? She is quite fully sketched: among other things she is described as a woman of fine artistic accomplishments, but fond too of the lower sympotic pleasures. Her exact social status is hard to pin down: she sounds like a high-class courtesan, but she may have been perhaps a divorcée or a widow of dubious morals. The point to be stressed about her is that she is sexually independent, or relatively so. Unlike the bought objects of Horace's erotic world she can and does dominate; she can dominate the besotted Propertius simply by the power of being able to say 'No'. She is an important figure. Without such a figure, the Propertian type of 'life of love' could not exist.

How does Propertius view his role as poet? In Book 1 (poems 7-9) he phrases it with a provocativeness to match the provocativeness of his programme for life. He bases himself on his premiss that love equals life. That allows him to describe the traditionally grand genre of epic as useless. Meanwhile, he claims, his elegy can perform the vital task of winning round a recalcitrant or errant mistress; and, because of the knowledge and experience it contains, it can benefit others. In other words, within the 'life of love' (the only life for Propertius), elegy is useful and indeed educational, in contrast to epic's uselessness. We should mark what Propertius is doing here. He is managing to assign to his poetry the traditionally esteemed functions of usefulness and edification, while denying them to their traditional recipient, epic. It is a neat turnabout; non-commitment is nicely phrased as commitment. In Book 3 we find him similarly misassigning, misusing (some would say) a grand view of poetry's function, the grand idea that poetry can immortalize. Poem 2 boasts the power of Propertian elegy to immortalize a *girl*. Horace would certainly be among those who would call this a misuse; and, a nice touch, Horace's own language of immortality is imported to phrase that misuse.

Such statements as these are designed to provoke rather than to offer serious information on the nature of Propertius' poetry. His love poems tend, particularly in Book 1, to be either dramatic, a 'staged' interaction between himself and Cynthia or another character, or rhetorical, speeches of indignation, pain, joy, and so on, to various addressees. They all frequently exploit mythological comparisons, the resonance of the mythical world. And their achievement is to offer insight into the personalities of Cynthia and Propertius, insight into their feelings and relationship, insight into love.

For example, poem 2 of Book 1 is a speech to Cynthia dissuading her from meretricious behaviour, in particular the use of cosmetics, and Propertius' mode of tackling the topic reveals much about his own personality, about Cynthia's personality, and about how the two interrelate. Poem 16 shrilly enquires of Cynthia why she cannot display the devotion of Calypso, Hypsipyle, and other romantic figures from myth—and exposes thereby a tension that pervades Propertius' life and fuels much of his love poetry. For Cynthia of course is not a romantic figure from myth. But that is something that the romantic Propertius finds so hard to accept. For a sample of a rhetorical poem the reader is referred to 2.8. There Propertius justifies the grief he is exhibiting at the loss of Cynthia by an appeal to the vast grief displayed by Achilles on the loss of Briseis.

In Book 1, much of which may have been composed in the triumviral period, Propertius is non-aligned and non-attached. He includes a bitter poem (21) on the Perusine war of 41 BC, bitter at the expense of the victor Octavian. This sort of independence of spirit is something he never loses.

Independence of spirit notwithstanding, the quality and popularity of Book 1 attracted the attention of Maecenas; and Maecenas suggested, inevitably, that Propertius might be well employed in putting Augustus' deeds into epic. The opening poem of Book 2 (first Augustan period) is a response to Maecenas' approach. It contains several interesting features. First, to decline the proposition of epic, Propertius employs a device which had been invented by Virgil and was used by other poets, including Horace. It is basically to say 'I would if I could', and to explain the inability by appeal to poetic powers or lack of them, or to poetic alignment. Propertius, like Virgil, claims an alignment with Callimachus and, as everyone knew, Callimachean aesthetics excluded epic. It is, however, clear that Propertius neither phrases his Callimacheanism seriously nor indeed (unlike Virgil) was seriously Callimachean; nor did he intend to be taken very seriously. He is simply declining a suggested imposition with grace and wit. And a bit of sting. When Propertius lists the heroic deeds of Augustus that he would have celebrated, had he been able, Maecenas must have felt relief that he did not. The list contains the ugliest episodes of the Civil War, including Perusia; and these, in the Augustan age, were best forgotten or reinterpreted.

Propertius declines the task of epic; but we must hereafter regard him as associated with the imperial circle—although this does not mean that his independence is snuffed. Poem 2.1 ends with the sort of praise for Maecenas that suggests the patronized: 'you whose favour all our young men covet and who are my true glory in life and will be when I die'; but the conclusion of the poem also insists on Propertius' role as a love poet—until he dies. Poem 2.7 rejoices in the abandonment of Augustus' first attempt at legislation to coerce Romans into marriage; and in 2.16, while making his characteristic noises about how shocking and degraded he is, Propertius associates himself with the shocking, degraded, romantic and magnetic figure of Mark Antony. Poem 2.34 celebrates the imminence of Virgil's *Aeneid* and, in the last couplet, celebrates Propertius himself as poet of Cynthia.

Book 3, written in the late twenties BC, opens with poems (1 and 3) that are a flamboyant assertion of Propertius' role as love poet and Callimachean. Not only flamboyant, pretentious: but one of the things Propertius is doing here is parodying Horace's just published and pretentious claims to be a Roman Alcaeus. Yet the book exhibits less interest in love poetry and, on the face of it, more concern with public issues. One scents the approach of the second Augustan period. But what Propertius gives with one hand, he takes with another—by irony and other methods. For example, poem 4 celebrates Augustus' expected Parthian victory. Propertius represents himself as the loyal observer of the triumph, reproducing an idea used by Horace and Cornelius Gallus. But he adds the slightly insolent touch that he will observe from the vantage point of his mistress's bosom; and he pairs the poem with one reminding us that Love is a god of peace.

In Book 4, which dates from the second Augustan period, we see the signs of Augustus' direct patronage. While Horace was induced to write a fourth book

ACHILLES SURRENDERS BRISEIS to the emissaries of Agamemnon: Pompeian painting (between AD 62 and 79) from the House of the Tragic Poet, probably based on a Greek masterpiece of the late fourth century BC. Achilles' loss of his favourite mistress provoked the bitter quarrel which is the subject of Homer's *Iliad* and provided Propertius with a model for an elegy on his loss of Cynthia.

of *Odes*, the 'Callimachean' Propertius felt it prudent or compulsory to produce something rather more genuinely Callimachean—and patriotic. Poems on the causes or origins of institutions had absorbed Callimachus, and Propertius in his fourth book produces poems on the causes and origins of Roman institutions: he now styles himself the 'Roman Callimachus' explicitly, and with some justification. The time was of course no longer propitious for oppositional tactics of the type seen in Book 3; yet Propertius still preserves his integrity and sense of humour. For example, one 'origin' leads into a narrative of the battle of Actium, and it is told, not parodically (as some think), but exactly as a Roman Callimachus should tell it; the exotic, rococo result would have caused Propertius much pleasure and the Emperor no pain. It is perhaps one of his best compositions. In another fine poem the moral story of Tarpeia is given an erotic motive—again pleasure for Propertius and not much pain for the emperor. In fact Book 4 contains much very good writing. Pressure, if it is not completely totalitarian, can inspire artists to creative ingenuity.

The final poem of the book is notable. It is a funeral elegy for a Roman lady, celebrating indirectly many of the moral virtues that Augustus was trying to inculcate. It should, we might think, bore, cloy, or irritate. It does not. In fact it is moving, and, for the reader of the entire Propertian collection, moving in a particular way. The dead lady speaks in the poem, and affirms how faithful, loving, and loyal she had been to her husband throughout her life—precisely the devotion that Propertius had sought and failed to find in Cynthia. Propertius' monument to an impeccable Roman lady is also therefore, by contrast, a monument to his own failure and sorrow: a pathetic irony. The poem provides a suggestive and moving end to the Propertian corpus.

Tibullus

I have touched upon Tibullus as the quasi-panegyrist of Messalla and his family. Beyond this, he hardly interests himself in national affairs, nor feels the need to explain his non-attention—a fact interesting in itself: imperial influence need not extend beyond the imperial circle. Nor is Tibullus interested in describing his role as poet, or his place in literary history. In discursive, associative elegies addressed mostly to the reader he writes of the country and his life of love.

Tibullus displays the same blinkered and slightly romantic love of the country as Virgil. But the feeling is none the less genuine, and a poem such as 2. 1, a celebration of an annual rural festival, largely depends upon it. So indeed does much of Tibullus' poetry. Tibullus would in fact like to live in the country—so he says.

The first forty-four lines of the first poem of the first book are devoted to an expression of this wish. Exactly what the wish comprised should be identified. To begin with it sounds as if Tibullus actually wants to be a small-holding and labouring farmer ('Let me as a farmer set vines in the early season'). This is revealed to be a humorously intended feint. What he actually wants to do is to dabble with work, to be a dilettante, to live a life of, in fact, leisure in rural simplicity on his own estate. He sketches this estate for us in the first poem and subsequently. It has been reduced in size, perhaps in confiscations, but it is still sufficient, with slaves to run it. Tibullus therefore, like Propertius, wants—shocking fact—a life committed to leisure, a 'life of inaction', *uita iners*, as he actually terms it; and, like Propertius, he scorns military and mercantile activity. But unlike the urban and urbane Propertius he wants to spend his life of leisure in the country. This dissimilarity between them is one among many that Tibullus wishes us to discern.

Forty-four lines express this Tibullan wish. What, we might ask, of love? Where is its place? And why, we might also ask, does Tibullus not just up and go to his estate, instead of moaning elegiacally in Rome? The basic reason is—love.

Here is how the expression of Tibullus' rural dream continues:

> parua seges satis est, satis est requiescere lecto
> si licet et solito membra leuare toro.
> quam iuuat immites uentos audire cubantem
> *et dominam tenero continuisse sinu*
>
> (I. 1. 43-6)

A small crop is enough, it is enough if it is possible to rest in a bed and lighten the limbs on a familiar couch. How pleasant it is lying there to listen to wild winds, and *to hold my mistress in tender embrace.*

By 'mistress', *domina*, Tibullus means the woman to whom he as lover is slave (as Propertius was to Cynthia), and he has in mind the one he calls Delia. The exact social status of Delia can, like Cynthia's, be argued about. But she is not dissimilar to Cynthia, probably a freedwoman, and presented to us as highly materialistic and of course essentially urban. And yet we now learn that she is part of Tibullus' vision of rural life, indeed as poem 2 reveals to us, an essential part of his vision of rural life: he would wish to rough it in the country, he says, *provided* that Delia is there. Here is the reason why the rural wish cannot be realized: it proves to contain an incompatible element—Delia: 'But I am held a prisoner ... and take my post as keeper at her door' (cf. 1. 55-6). In the first place this fact is offered as a reason why Tibullus cannot go on campaign with Messalla. But clearly a man bound to an urban mistress's door cannot simultaneously be a man of country pursuits on his rural estate.

Delia precludes Tibullus' wish being realized. So we have discovered. We have also discovered a source of tension that pervades Tibullus's life and fuels his poetry, and makes him a romantic visionary to be compared (and contrasted) with Propertius. Propertius tried to see in Cynthia a mythical figure, an attempt doomed to fail in the face of reality. Tibullus tried to see in Delia a figure compatible with his rural aspirations, an attempt also doomed to fail in the face of reality. And he, like Propertius, had moments when he knew the truth only too well. Poem 5 provides the fullest description of Tibullus' rural and erotic vision: life in the country, with Delia taking a wifely part in the harvest, and so on. But the description concludes: 'haec mihi fingebam'—it was all a dream. Tibullus has been quoting his former vision with bitter irony, in a present mood of cruel self-knowledge.

Tibullus, we have sensed, is concerned to be different from Propertius in the way he provokes conventional sensibility. He is also concerned to be even more provoking. Take the question of 'servility': Propertius professes his slavery as an unwilling burden, and has in mind psychological bondage. Tibullus talks actually of the physical humiliations meted out to slaves, and seems masochistically willing to accept them at the hands of his mistress. Tibullus, too, moves on to a different and worse mistress: Nemesis, harder, more rapacious, and more mercenary than Delia.

We might have thought that esteem for the country and love of his own estate were constants in Tibullus' life. Not so. Through Nemesis Tibullus shows us that love can make the romantic abjure not only society's values but his own. In 2.3 a rival has taken Nemesis off to a country villa, at harvest time. Tibullus' response is to curse the country's fruitfulness, to curse what he has hitherto supremely valued. There are other instances like this—and Nemesis causes Tibullus to perform abrupt about-turns on other cherished points as well: for example, he will reverse his declared views on mercenariness in love, if that is what she wants. The most poignant reversal, however, comes in 2.4. Should Nemesis want it, he would even sell off the beloved family estate. Delia had rendered the rural aspiration unrealizable, by being part of it. Nemesis can make him simply and completely abandon it. Such can be the destructive power of romantic love. So Tibullus suggests.

Tibullus produces yet a third lover to whom he is exclusively devoted, a boy, Marathus; and for this boy he demonstrates as intense and abject a love as he and Propertius had for their mistresses. This is a remarkable fact. Of course, homosexual love is often enough professed, by Horace and Catullus among others. But among the love poets it is normally considered a slight business, a sideline, not a thing to engage emotions and passions. What we are observing is Tibullus once more upping the stakes in the game of provocation. Not only does he profess devoted love for three lovers. He exhibits himself as the abject romantic lover of a mere boy.

In fact the affair with Marathus presents Tibullus at perhaps his most abject—and amusing. The relationship is triangular: Tibullus loves Marathus, while Marathus loves a girl, Pholoe; and, to ingratiate himself, Tibullus gives the boy servile and humiliating assistance in his affair with the girl.

We need not doubt the real base of Tibullan poetry in Tibullan experience. But it is also clear that this experience is organized and orchestrated to interest and provoke, in particular in comparison with Propertius (Propertius, similarly, had presented his experience with an eye on Catullus): to interest and provoke—and, sometimes, to amuse. The word crept into the previous paragraph, and humour is perhaps quite pervasive in Tibullus. The kind and degree of Tibullus' humiliations, of his masochistic assertions, all neatly narrated, preclude total earnestness. There is hyperbole here, consideration for humorous effect. And it is all 'neatly narrated': Tibullus' grovelling words to his lovers, and indeed his prayers to be a rustic, are dressed in the urbanest of styles. That suggests a certain Tibullan distance from the Tibullan story, a wink in our direction.

Ovid

It has often been said that Ovid was anti-Augustan. The label is not exactly appropriate. Ovid was indeed irreverent towards Augustus' state, laws, image. But he was irreverent towards any solemn and sitting target.

Ovid came from an old equestrian family, and began a public career, but he soon abandoned it for poetry. He was assisted in his youth by Messalla, and his later books bow in the direction of Augustus and his house. But the evidence suggests that he never maintained a position with a literary circle, even to the extent that Propertius did. He had no need to: his work was instantly popular, and he had no economic problems. And his exuberant spirit was probably best served by such non-involvement.

His first poems, the elegiac *Amores*, were published in two editions: the first was begun about 25 BC and issued over the next ten years or so; the second and smaller edition (the one which we possess) was published about the turn of the millennium.

Ovid's irreverence is instantly visible in these poems, its potential catholicity already guessable. The most obvious targets here are, not conventional moralists, but the romantic elegists, the old protesters themselves. Ovid presents himself in the first book as a lover and poet in the tradition of Propertius and Tibullus, in devoted thraldom to one mistress, whom he calls Corinna. But what he actually gives us is parody. For example, Propertius and Tibullus had expressed their dissociation from public life, from war and the life of action ('soldiering'), by projecting themselves as 'soldiers' of love. Ovid gets hold of this expressive idea and probes it for ingenious and funny effects. How can a lover be represented as a soldier in detail? Poem 1.9, comparing lover and soldier, shows us. A sample:

> Tacticians recommend the night attack,
> use of the spearhead, catching the foe asleep . . .
> Lovers use them too—to exploit a sleeping husband,
> thrusting hard while the enemy snores.

This is a ludicrous, parodic exploitation of an elegiac motif. Other elegiac motifs (the slavery of the lover, the divinity of the beloved, and so on) are similarly treated. So is the Propertian use of myth: Propertius had evoked a romantic ideal of devotion by means of resonating myths; Ovid deploys resonating myths to depict beautiful legs.

In Books 2 and 3 of the *Amores* Ovid drops his mask and displays himself as a cheerfully promiscuous lover. Love is, or should be, simply fun—a game; and the books contain racy lectures and dramatic episodes illustrating it. In this we must observe, besides his dissimilarity to the romantic elegists, his similarity to Horace. Horace considered that love should be a game, even if it could turn out bitter-sweet. So Ovid is similar to Horace—but dissimilar too. Ovid took the game so to speak earnestly, committed time and trouble to it. He did not have things in perspective, Alcaeus-fashion. He even devoted a didactic treatise to the game of love, purporting to teach one how to play it—indulging an interest in the incongruous mixture of solemn didactic form and frivolous content that he displays in other works. This treatise was the 'Art of Love' (*Ars Amatoria*), first published about 9 BC and reissued about the time of the second edition of the *Amores*, not an auspicious time.

Such a didactic obviously affronts Horatian standards. And consistently and obviously, it affronts (once more) elegiac romanticism. And Ovid turns the knife. The cynical instructions of the *Ars* are repeatedly couched in terms that recall agonized elegiac devotion. For instance, the powerless elegist was forced to utter 'you are my only love'; Ovid instructs his pupils on how to *choose* someone to whom to say 'you are my only love'. But, in affronting the old protesters, the *Ars* also affronted Augustus, a very solemn target. So, probably, had the *Amores*.

The social status of Corinna and the other women in the *Amores* is as usual hard to pin down, but what seems clear is that she, and others, are described in a way that suggests they are legally married. The *Amores* therefore explicitly suggests adultery. Adultery, too, is obviously in mind in the *Ars*, despite an unconvincing statement to the contrary at the beginning of the poem and plangent protestations from exile. For exiled is what Ovid eventually was, and the *Ars* was adduced as part cause. His exile is hardly surprising. He writes in explicitly adulterous terms, in the second Augustan period, after Augustus' laws had made adultery criminal; he produces a second edition of *Ars*, and *Amores*, at about the time when Augustus' own daughter was banished for adultery (2 BC), and when the inefficacy of the laws was only too apparent. We can see that Ovid's adulterous line fits into a pattern of catholic and non-malicious irreverence—it is not 'anti-Augustan'. But to a gloomy and disappointed Augustus it might have appeared otherwise. It is perhaps a wonder that he took so long to react, but finally he did. In AD 8 Augustus' grand-daughter was also banished for

EROTIC SCENE on a Roman pottery lamp from the Naples area. Cheerful eroticism of a type which Ovid would have approved was a favourite theme of the Roman decorative arts in imperial times, appearing in media as different as relief-decorated ceramics and domestic wall-painting.

PHAEDRA AND HIPPOLYTUS: detail of a carved sarcophagus (late second century AD). The youthful Hippolytus (centre) is shunning the advances of his stepmother, conveyed by the old nurse beside him. At the left sits the love-struck Phaedra herself, with two Erotes (Cupids) in attendance; at the right a groom or companion holds Hippolytus' horse. The fourth of Ovid's *Heroides* is an imaginary love-letter in which Phaedra declares her passion.

adultery, and Ovid, guilty of perpetrating some 'mistake' as well as his poem ('carmen et error'), was banished too, to Tomis, from whence he dispatched bookloads of not wholly laudable laments.

In between the *Amores* and the *Ars* come the *Heroides*, Ovid's first experiment with mythical narrative. This is safer fare, nevertheless congenial to read. Ovid's basic idea was to invent letters (in elegiacs) from mythical heroines to their lovers: Ariadne to Theseus, Phaedra to Hippolytus, Dido to Aeneas, Penelope to Odysseus, and so on. The examples cited show the wide range of situations that he dealt with, providing himself with wide scope for his rhetorical ingenuity and facile emotive ability. Nor is the irreverent spirit suppressed. Ovid takes pains to translate Virgil's Dido into a much more easily sympathetic figure, and one indeed who spots that Aeneas is vulnerable in the matter of his first wife's death.

At approximately this time Ovid composed his now lost tragedy *Medea*. His first extant attempt to compose on a larger and more ambitious scale is the *Fasti*. This work can reasonably be dated to the years AD 1–4; it is also reasonable to see in it an effort to balance the recently republished erotic works with something less *risqué*. The *Fasti*, also in elegiacs, aimed to go through the Roman calendar offering 'causes' for events and nomenclature in the Roman year. Thus Ovid, who had light-heartedly adopted a Callimachean stance in the *Amores*, felt as Propertius had done before him that it might be prudent to attempt something at once seriously Callimachean and patriotic: the calendar offered ample pegs on which to hang praise of Rome and praise of Augustus. Irrepressible irreverence periodically mars or improves the poem, depending on one's point of view. It was never finished. Disinclination seems to have moved Ovid to abandon it, after six, instead of twelve, books. There were external factors to support or cause disinclination. The year AD 4 saw the adoption of Tiberius and therefore another set of laudatory allusions to include; and, on the calendar, the month of August loomed, a daunting prospect for a subject of Augustus. Ovid gave up.

But he did not give up poetry, nor even Callimachean poetry. Subsequent to the *Fasti* is the *Metamorphoses*, Ovid's great hexameter poem in fifteen books. Here he assembles dozens of attractive stories from myth, stories which end in the metamorphosis of characters into animals, plants, and other forms. The stories are linked together with ingenious transitions, so ingenious that progress can seem bewildering. The opening of the poem seems sequential (from the creation of the world, through Jupiter's punishment of sinful man, to Deucalion and Pyrrha), but soon we find ourselves conducted through the stories of Daphne, Io, Phaethon, and so on—all the way through to the metamorphosis of Julius Caesar into a god in Book 15.

What is this poem? By a judicious choice of words at the beginning Ovid surprisingly advertises it as something that Callimachus eschewed: a traditional epic. We expect, therefore, an epic in which the plot is serious and a single, unified, action unfolds objectively, an epic in which the consequences of actions follow; hence, a moral poem. It very soon transpires that the *Metamorphoses* is nothing of the sort. The advertisement was a spoof. The action of the poem is neither single nor serious, but a mass of disparate stories ingeniously, artificially linked and subjectively told—told with Ovidian wit, humour, and grotesqueness. And the consequences of actions do not follow. They end in the fantasy of metamorphosis. The poem is a gloriously amoral Callimachean collection got up in epic dress, an affront to the traditional epic genre.

As always, Ovid affronts. Here, in particular, there is irreverence towards Virgil's genre—and Virgil's material: in various ways the material of the *Aeneid* gets mauled. Another sitting and solemn target. There is, too, irreverence towards the house of Augustus, despite overt but unconvincing flattery. Jupiter compared to Augustus in one context is, within a few hundred lines, chasing a girl in another. Nor does the company in which Julius Caesar's 'metamorphosis' finds itself dignify it. And there is irreverence, in a sense, towards life: it is simply the material for amusing, amoral literature.

There is a great risk of assessing Ovid too negatively: he is, we say, parodic, irreverent, unserious, unAugustan, amoral, even immoral, merely rhetorical or ingenious. This can, and should be, rephrased. Ovid is funny. His immorality serves humour, and his parodies are the sort which direct laughter on to themselves, not the parodied original (see the example quoted above, p. 611). Ovid is a poet of 'art for art's sake': Ovid reveres technique, reveres art; and amorality is indispensable to the construction of a self-contained artistic experience. Un-Augustan? In a sense Ovid is the Augustan poet *par excellence*, particularly of the second period. Augustus' actions and legislations were designed to stem a tide, to combat a prevailing spirit. Ovid represents that spirit, pleasure-loving, sophisticated, and, it must be admitted, cynical. Horace, twenty-two years older than Ovid and belonging to a different generation, may draw a veil of silence over him. But Ovid's contemporaries did not. They praised him to the skies. For them he was the true Augustan poet.

Further Reading

The Loeb Classical Library provides texts with facing translations of all the poets discussed in this chapter. The following translations may also be recommended: Niall Rudd, *Horace, Satires and Epistles* (revd. edn. 1979); W. G. Shepherd, *Horace's Odes and Epodes* (1983); Guy Lee, *Tibullus: Elegies* (2nd edn. 1982), and *Ovid's Amores* (2nd edn. 1968); Rolfe Humphries, *Ovid, The Art of Love* (1957), *The Metamorphoses* (1955).

Indispensable to a full understanding of Horace is E. Fraenkel's *Horace* (Oxford, 1957), but David West's *Reading Horace* (Edinburgh, 1967) is perhaps the best introduction; comparably useful are Margaret Hubbard's *Propertius* (London, 1974) and L. P. Wilkinson's *Ovid Recalled* (Cambridge, 1955), abridged as *Ovid Surveyed* (Cambridge, 1962). Tibullus lacks any balanced introductory book; there is Francis Cairns' *Tibullus* (Cambridge, 1979) and David F. Bright's *Haec Mihi Fingebam, Tibullus in his World* (Leiden, 1978), but both these are idiosyncratic and the initiate is better served by the introduction to Guy Lee's translation.

The following books treat the period and its poetry (or aspects thereof) more generally: R. O. A. M. Lyne, *The Latin Love Poets from Catullus to Horace* (Oxford, 1980); K. Quinn, *Latin Explorations* (2nd edn. London, 1969); L. P. Wilkinson, *Golden Latin Artistry* (Cambridge, 1963); G. Williams, *Tradition and Originality in Roman Poetry* (Oxford, 1968), abridged as *The Nature of Roman Poetry* (Oxford, 1970). C. O. Brink, *Horace on Poetry*, vol. iii (Cambridge, 1982), pp. 523 ff., offers a masterly overview of the period, and vital illumination of the social background is provided by Jasper Griffin's forthcoming book *Latin Poetry and Roman Life*.

25
Virgil

✢❦✢

JASPER GRIFFIN

Preamble

PUBLIUS VERGILIUS MARO, in English normally called Virgil, was a celebrated figure in his own lifetime, and soon after his death a number of writers
tried to satisfy the popular curiosity about the life of the greatest of Roman
poets. We are consequently much better informed about him than about most
poets in antiquity. Like most Roman writers, he was not born in Rome. He came
into the world in 70 BC, near Mantua, in what was still called Cisalpine Gaul.
Although thoroughly Romanized—we recall that Catullus came from Verona,
and Livy from Padua (Patavium)—the area did not receive the Roman citizenship
till 49, and it became officially part of Italy only in 42. Virgil's family seems to
have been respectable though by no means prominent. The ultimate origin of
the names 'Vergilius' and 'Maro' was probably Etruscan, but only the credulous
will try to explain the poet's art or his character by invoking Etruscan ancestry.

It is worth looking at the period through which Virgil lived. Born in the year
in which Pompey and Crassus forced their way into the consulship, he was seven
when Catiline fell fighting at the head of a revolutionary army opposing the
Roman legions. The gathering disorder of the 50s led to civil war; the assassination of Caesar to another, followed by proscriptions, by wars in Italy, and the
eventual victory of Octavian, after a third civil war, in 31. As late as 19, the year
of Virgil's death, there were serious riots in Rome. Of the fifty-one years of the
poet's life, sixteen were years of civil war; the proscriptions which followed the
battle of Philippi are said to have caused the deaths of at least 150 senators and
2,000 *equites*; considerable areas of Italy were devastated by fighting, by famine,
and by the forcible expropriation of land. It was a terrible period, in which even
the survival of Rome seemed to be in doubt, and that fact is of central importance
for Virgil's poetry.

The Eclogues

His first published work was a collection of ten bucolic *Eclogues*, which proclaim themselves as in the tradition of Theocritus (above, pp. 356 ff.), but which

also echo and evoke many other poets, both Greek and Latin. The influence of Callimachus, for instance, is clear at the opening of the Sixth *Eclogue*, that of Lucretius in the middle of the same poem, that of Catullus in the Fourth. There were allusions to the work of other poets, contemporary or in the last generation, which we are not now in a position to recognize. Virgil is thus, at his first appearance, a learned poet. That was always to be his manner, and in antiquity some critics made names for themselves by sniping at the poet for his 'thefts', meaning plagiarism.

It is quite wrong to imagine that Virgil lacked originality, or that his poems are no more than imitations or distillations of the work of his predecessors. If we read the first five lines of the First *Eclogue* we find a good example of the creative reworking of a model. The countryman Meliboeus speaks to a friend who is singing of love, stretched out in the shade of a tree:

> Tityre, tu patulae recubans sub tegmine fagi
> siluestrem tenui Musam meditaris auena;
> nos patriae finis et dulcia linquimus arua:
> nos patriam fugimus; tu, Tityre, lentus in umbra
> formosam resonare doces Amaryllida siluas.

> Beneath a shady beech you may rehearse
> At ease, my Tityrus, your simple verse;
> I'm forced to leave my country and to roam,
> My Tityrus, from country and from home:
> You here can fill, at leisure in the shade,
> With Amaryllis' name the wooded glade.

At once we see that we both are, and are not, in the world of Theocritus. The Greek poet is the source of the names, and of the pastoral world of love and song; the languorously beautiful hexameters, with their melodious vowels and artfully simple repetitions, also owe a lot to Theocritus' inspiration. But the world of reality, of politics and suffering, has invaded the pastoral Arcadia in which nothing but love and song could happen. Why is Meliboeus not able to stretch out and sing? Because, it soon emerges, Rome has burst into his world. After the defeat of Brutus and Cassius in 42, the Caesarian party had to take care of the soldiers in the enormous armies which now looked to them for their reward. What the soldiers wanted was land, and that could only be found by ejecting its present owners. A recent calculation estimates that a quarter of the land of Italy changed hands in the proscriptions and evictions. Meliboeus, despite his pretty Greek name, is sufficiently Italian and contemporary to be among the ejected victims:

> A godless soldier has my cherished fields,
> A savage has my land: such profit yields
> Our civil war. For them we worked our land!
> Ay, plant your pears—to fill another's hand.

Tityrus has miraculously escaped the general disaster, thanks to a 'wonderful young man' in Rome, who secured him his land. For that, Tityrus had to go to Rome:

> Urbem quam dicunt Romam, Meliboee, putaui
> stultus ego huic nostrae similem, quo saepe solemus
> pastores ouium teneros depellere fetus . . .

> I used to think the city men call Rome
> Was like our market-town, to which we come
> On market days, and drive our kids to sell.
> O foolishness . . .

The lines, standing on the very first page of Virgil's published work, have a prophetic ring. The poet, like his rustic speaker, will discover Rome; and will find that Rome is something very different from the innocent joys and sorrows of country life. The imperial city, with its fabulous wealth and power, can at will reward or destroy. That will be a central problem for the *Aeneid*.

The *Eclogues* form a unified work of art, with a structure of its own. The number of poems is itself not a random one: the first book of Tibullus contains ten poems, so does the first book of *Satires* of Horace. A poet was expected to organize his work into a pleasing shape. The First *Eclogue*, as we have seen, is in the form of a dialogue: so are all the odd-numbered *Eclogues*. The even-numbered ones, on the other hand, are monologues. The fifth poem ends with a little recapitulation, the speaker presenting his friend with the pipes on which, he says, he played the second and third poems. That marks the half-way point, and a little break, comparable to that after the third of Horace's six Roman odes (*Odes* 3.1-6); as in that cycle of poems, the second half begins with a fresh scene of invocation, in this case not of the Muse but of Apollo. Another structure, also meant to be felt, centres on the Fifth *Eclogue* (allusion to the death and deification of Caesar), which is immediately framed by the two most ambitious and least simply pastoral poems, (iv and vi), and at furthest remove framed by two poems on the evictions (i and ix). The last poem, in this structure, stands rather outside the rest; it is explicitly introduced as 'my last pastoral song'.

As we have seen, the Ninth *Eclogue* returns to the theme of the evictions. Menalcas, a singer and translator of Theocritus, has been turned out of his property near Mantua. So far from saving his land by means of his song, he was lucky to escape with his life. Ever since antiquity people have tried to make the two *Eclogues* on the evictions into an autobiographical account by the poet of his own ejection and restoration to his Mantuan property. But it is surely clear that Virgil did not mean to produce such an account. Tityrus, restored by a super-human young man (who in real life could only be the nineteen- or twenty-year old Octavian) is elderly and a slave, in neither respect like Virgil; and he is balanced by Meliboeus, for whom no providential saviour averts disaster. And in the Ninth *Eclogue* Menalcas too, it seems, finds no remedy. The two poems would add up to a very odd way of saying 'Thank you' to Octavian. What Virgil has done, rather, is to show us scenes from the evictions, what is going on in the Italian countryside, filtered through the poetic medium provided by Theocritus. If we are to guess what happened to Virgil himself, it may seem likely that he lost his family land near Mantua, and was given by his patrons a property near Naples. That is where we find him living later on, one of a group of friends of the Epicurean philosopher Siro.

One point is a vital one for understanding Virgil. Already in the *Eclogues* he is working towards the special way of writing, which in the *Aeneid* he has perfected: a manner which allows the reader to see through the poetical surface to events and personalities of a different kind, which are never made fully explicit. So in the Fifth *Eclogue* two herdsmen sing of the death and deification of Daphnis, another name from Theocritus. Cruelly cut off and lamented by his mother, Daphnis becomes a god, a patron of peace, hailed as a divinity by all nature and by the country people. Daphnis was young, beautiful, a herdsman—a far cry from the middle-aged dictator Caesar. But so soon after the assassination and elevation to godhood of the most celebrated man in the world—descended from the goddess Venus—those spectacular events could not have been wholly out of the mind of Virgil's readers.

The Fourth *Eclogue* prophesies the return of the Golden Age. The poem is addressed to Asinius Pollio, an early patron of the poet, as a compliment to his entry on the consulship in 40 BC. Its exalted language draws on a wide variety of sources: oracles, Greek versions of Jewish prophecies, Etruscan techniques of divination, Platonic myths, Homer, Catullus. In Pollio's consulship the 'mighty months' will begin to roll: a child will be born, whose birth will be marked by miraculous signs, and whose growing up will be accompanied by the gradual blossoming of the age of Apollo. The earth will produce all good things everywhere, without the need of agriculture; lions shall be harmless; venomous serpents shall cease to exist. War, too, shall cease, and the divine child shall rule the world. Many modern scholars think that this poem was written to celebrate the pact agreed at Brundisium in October 40 (above, p. 532), which included a marriage between Antony and Octavian's sister Octavia, and which averted the danger of war between the two men: the child of the poem will be the expected son of the new marriage. But a poem to honour a man's consulship should be ready for presentation on 1 January, not ten months later; and the striking parallels with Isaiah and other similar works show that this really is a Messianic poem. Such works are produced, not when successful political arrangements seem to have secured peace on earth, but when the earthly scene is so dark and hopeless that the mind turns away in despair to another order of thought. The Fourth *Eclogue* was for centuries believed to be a prophecy of the coming of Christ. The modern mind is unhappy with such notions; but perhaps that view comes closer to the real nature of the poem than it does to pin it to a specific political happening. Again Virgil is being deliberately evasive as to his exact meaning, and the sugges-

RELIEF OF MOTHER EARTH ON THE ARA PACIS (13–9 BC). The fruitfulness of the earth, portrayed in typical Hellenistic style with children in her arms, and fruit, flowers, and livestock all about her, is symbolic of the new Golden Age which Augustus sought to inaugurate and which recalls passages in the Augustan poets, such as the fourth *Eclogue* of Virgil. (Cf. below, pp. 776 f.)

tiveness of the poem is more effective than clarity would have been. And after all the treaty of Brundisium did not in the end mean lasting peace; while Octavia bore Antony two daughters, but no son. Virgil would have been surprisingly credulous if he had not thought of such possibilities.

The *Eclogues* can be ranged between two poles: some are fairly close to Theocritus (2, 3, and 7) others are further distanced but still Theocritean (8 and 9); at the other extreme some have very little contact with Theocritus at all (4 and 6). They all have in common a highly polished technique, in which Virgil shows that he has learnt everything that Theocritus, Callimachus, and Catullus had to teach him. The choice of words is punctilious, the sound of the verse is melodious, and there is a pervasive atmosphere of an exquisite and faintly melancholy beauty. The paintings of Claude Lorraine are perhaps the best analogy in another art; and he of course was much influenced by Virgil. It is a small but significant part of this that the first and last poems of the collections, and others in between, end with the coming of evening and the shadows lengthening from the hills.

Despite much scholarly endeavour, agreement is not possible on the order in which the *Eclogues* were composed. Their style does not enable us to extract many dates from the poems, which no doubt were polished to fit the positions they occupy in the final published collection. It is likely that the book of ten *Eclogues* was published about 38 BC; recent attempts to put the completion as late as 35 are not convincing. The poems seem to have been an immediate success. We are told that they were acted on the stage, and that the shy and evasive poet, on his rare appearances in Rome, was pointed at in the street. In the spring of 38, already an established writer, he introduced Horace to Maecenas, whose name does not appear in the *Eclogues*, but to whom Virgil was to dedicate his next work, the *Georgics*.

In the *Eclogues* Virgil addressed several great men: Asinius Pollio chiefly, but also Alfenus Varus. They both seem to be in the position of actual or potential patrons. In this respect Virgil resembles Horace rather than Catullus and (in his First Book) Propertius, who have no patrons but only friends. The poet Cornelius Gallus, who is praised in the Sixth *Eclogue*, also receives the supreme compliment of being the subject of the Tenth. In that poem Virgil presents the elegiac love poet as a pastoral lover in Arcadia, his amorous complaints transposed into Virgil's own metre, and the lover himself recalling Theocritus' Daphnis. The

PASTORAL LANDSCAPE BY CLAUDE LORRAINE (1645). The great seventeenth-century landscape painter was much influenced by Virgil, and this scene, with its group of shepherds (one playing the flute) and its grazing cattle and goats, perfectly catches the mood of the *Eclogues*.

procedure seems strange to us in poetry, but it would surprise us less in music: Virgil has written a variation in his own style on a theme by Gallus.

The Georgics

All that is in the past, once we turn to the *Georgics*. Lesser patrons must give way to Maecenas, friends are no longer named, and Octavian—never named and barely hinted at in the *Eclogues*—is now in the centre of the poet's view. Ancient scholars claimed to know the contents of Virgil's will, and they report that he left the very large sum of 10,000,000 sesterces, with substantial legacies to Maecenas and Augustus. No doubt they were the source of the poet's wealth. But it would be wrong to think of the relationship as primarily a financial one. In the second half of the 30s the relative position of Octavian and Antony gradually changed. The ruthless young heir of Caesar, who 'kills and keeps his temper' (a phrase which Dryden put into the mouth of Antony in *All for Love*), was cleverly transforming himself into the defender of western values against an Antony dead to decent feeling and going native in the East. The war of propaganda was lost by Antony before the battle of Actium. Maecenas, personally a luxurious, even a decadent figure, wrote verse himself, as such men usually do, in the manner of the poets of his own youth; he was of great value as an intermediary between Octavian and the poets. An artist must be flattered when the holders of power express interest in his work, and much more when the master of the world (as Octavian was after 31) is anxious to recruit his support for a programme of reform and restoration, which is to replace civil wars and disasters with peace and the good life. In their different ways Virgil, Horace, and Propertius all responded, more or less, to that most seductive appeal.

Virgil refers to the *Georgics* as 'your exacting command, Maecenas' ('tua, Maecenas, haud mollia iussa', 3.41). The phrase is hard to interpret. Obviously Maecenas did not 'command' the poet to write a poem in four books on agriculture, and Virgil also says of his writing:

> Sed me Parnasi deserta per ardua dulcis
> raptat amor; iuuat ire iugis, qua nulla priorum
> Castaliam molli deuertitur orbita cliuo. (3.291)

> But over high Parnassus' lonely crest
> Poetic rapture bears me: sweet to pass
> Where never wheel has marked the tender grass.

He wanted to produce the poem, and he felt confident that Maecenas would welcome it. For the poet it offered the challenge of a work on a large scale, some 2,000 lines in four roughly equal books, far exceeding the length not only of the *Eclogues* but also of anything ever attempted by Horace, Propertius, or Tibullus. In a period deeply marked by the Callimachean rejection of the long poem (above, p. 361), that was a striking departure. The subject-matter was challenging, too. For Catullus and his friends, the word 'rustic' had stood for all that was uncouth, ill bred, boring—both in manners and in poetry. Could the homespun rustic verse of Hesiod (above, pp. 88 ff.) be transformed into a Latin poem which would satisfy the aesthetic demands of Virgil and his audience? He was not aiming to translate Hesiod, nor simply to paraphrase him and dress him up in more elegant poetic form. Hesiod had made his practical instructions on sowing and reaping part of a moral picture of life, with hard work and traditional piety. Virgil, too, will produce a vision of a way of life, based on work, and embodying the old virtues which made Rome great: piety, tenacity, patriotism, genuineness. It must combine exact vision and description of detail, without the golden haze of beautiful generality which so often marks the *Eclogues*, and also a grand style, elevated but not hollow, for moral and poetical set-pieces. As for Maecenas and Octavian, they would have preferred an epic on Octavian's war-like feats: in the prologue to *Georgic* 3 Virgil promises that 'soon' he will write it. But the *Georgics* not only praised Octavian in glittering eulogy, but also endorsed a view of Italian and Roman life which was, in general terms, highly acceptable to him. The age of civil war must be over, and Octavian must heal a world turned upside down (1. 500). Then the vices of ambition and greed must be rooted out in favour of modesty and hard work (2. 165 ff., 458 ff.). On all that, Virgil's poem and Octavian's policy were agreed. Of course, neither of them will have expected that educated readers of the *Georgics* would rush out to buy small farms and start ploughing with their own hands.

The *Georgics* were completed in 29 BC, and some passages were clearly written after the Battle of Actium. Virgil had been at work on the poem for seven years or so, a length of time which implies constant revision and slow progress. For facts he had prose works on agriculture at his disposal. Especially valuable was Varro's *De re rustica*, a systematic treatise packed with information, far more exhaustive and practically useful than the *Georgics*. Varro's work could also give the poet other hints, as the First Book opens with the characters looking at a map of Italy (cf. *Georg.* 2. 135 ff.), and ends with the random murder of one of them in the street, a vivid instance of the violence and lawlessness which Virgil laments in his poem.

The first book of the *Georgics* has some close echoes of Hesiod, to establish the colouring of the whole. 'Nudus ara, sere nudus' ('Strip to plough and strip to sow', 1. 299) which was found very comical in antiquity, is an exact translation of a quaint Hesiodic line. Hesiod told how Zeus made life hard for men as a piece of vengeance, and laughed aloud as he did so (above, p. 96); Virgil prefers to tell how Jupiter made life hard for man's ultimate good, 'ut uarias usus meditando extunderet artes' ('that need and thought should useful arts devise', 1. 133). Virgil's Jupiter is more benevolent than Hesiod's Zeus. But even in this book there is far less of Hesiod than there is of Theocritus in the *Eclogues*. Lucretius, the great Latin poet of the last generation, is far more pervasive.

Virgil is careful to be selective. What appears to start out as a list of the necessary equipment (1. 160 ff.) actually includes only half a dozen tools, and those are mostly chosen for having a connection in Greek poetry which ennobles them: not 'a cart', but 'the slow rolling waggon of the Mother of Eleusis' (because in the great Eleusinian procession (above, pp. 268 f.) waggons were used); not 'a winnowing fan', but 'the mystic fan of Iacchus' (a minor Eleusinian deity). Virgil is anxious to avoid being dragged down from the high style by his humble subject matter. He also embellishes his material by many stylistic devices. When, for example, he is explaining that it is important to rotate crops, as some plants exhaust the soil, he creates out of this unpromising idea an exquisitely shaped couplet:

> urit enim campum lini seges, urit auenae,
> urunt Lethaeo perfusa papauera somno.
>
> (1. 77–8)

> Flax burns, and oats will burn, the fertile ground:
> No less burn heavy poppies, slumber-drowned.

The repetition of the verb, the shaping of the sentence, the unusual rhythm of the last line which goes with the drowsy poppies, all work together to impose a formal unity and beauty.

He also varies the work with great skill. The passages on actual rustic work alternate with all kinds of more obviously 'poetical' passages—on the zones of the globe, on storms, on winter in the Scythian snows, on the glories of Italy. Some of them are both lengthy and highly ambitious in style, the poet trying his wings for his future epic. The most spectacular come at crucial points in the structure of the whole. Book 1 opens with an elaborate invocation of the gods, including a startlingly fulsome address to Octavian. Book 3 opens with a long passage on the epic which Virgil will write in the future. By designed contrast, the second and fourth books have very short introductions, and each has a long poetic excursus at the end. Book 2 closes with an emotional passage extolling the life of the farmer ('O all too happy, if they knew their luck!'), contrasting rustic innocence with the vicious luxury of the city, and extolling the lot of the poet who (like Virgil) knows the rustic gods. Book 4 ends with the epyllion of Aristaeus, to which we shall return. Other set pieces are darker in tone. At the end of Book 1, an account of the weather signs which the farmer needs to know runs into an emotional treatment of the fearsome portents which marked the divine anger at the assassination of Julius Caesar, the guilt of Rome which is punished by civil war, and a fervent prayer for the survival and success of Octavian, the only hope of the world. Book 3 closes with a grisly account of the ravages of plague among cattle, arising from some apparently simple instructions for preserving the health of one's animals. The four books thus end with alternating passages of gloom and hope, a structure which has often been compared to that of a great work of music.

It would be wrong, though, to think of the *Georgics* as consisting of unpoetical instruction, enlivened by purple patches of poetry. Virgil has shot through the instructions with all sorts of devices of variety. The tone is constantly changing, from mock-solemnity and humour to pathos and indignation. Vivid pictures—of clouds, snakes, birds, horses—are enlivened by echoes of military language, or Ennius, or Hellenistic verse. The poet constantly looks at events from the standpoint of the animals he describes. An example in Book 3: Virgil follows his sources in advising that bulls and stallions should be kept from dissipating their energies by sexual indulgence:

> The female saps their vigour as they gaze;
> The bulls look on her and forget to graze,
> So sweet are her enticements: in her sight
> The haughty rivals for her favour fight.
>
> (3. 215-18)

The passage goes on to develop the battle of the bulls, the chagrin of the loser 'in distant exile, groaning for the shame of defeat and the loss of his love', his practising, and his eventual thunderous return.

In the fourth book the bees are handled in much the same way. Varro's work shows that bee-keeping was only one branch of specialized farming, listing it along with the raising of chickens, pigeons, peacocks, dormice, hares, deer, edible snails, and fancy fish. Virgil ignores all but the bees: for they are an image of human life, orderly and public-spirited. They are treated with a mixture of sympathy, admiration, and irony. The book ends with a great surprise, the epyllion of Aristaeus. The poet tells that, if one's bees die, a new swarm will be forthcoming from the correct treatment of the corpse of an ox. This fantastic procedure was discovered by the legendary hero Aristaeus, whose bees all died to punish him (as he discovers) for causing the death of Orpheus' wife Eurydice. The story of Orpheus' descent to the Underworld to fetch her back, his fatal turning to look at her, his second and final loss, and his death, is told in Virgil's most magical verse. It seems to have been Virgil who first said that Orpheus failed to revive his wife. Why he ended the *Georgics* with this tale, narrated at a length of nearly 250 verses, is not easy to say. A possible reason is that he wanted to give another side of the vision of the virtuous, patriotic bees, 'little Romans' ('paruos Quirites') as he calls them: these impersonal creatures, sexless and free from passion, who kill themselves with work and gladly die for the community, can be brought back from death: 'the race is immortal', as the poet says. But something is irreparably lost: the beautiful Eurydice and her lover, the musician Orpheus. Irreplaceable individuals, passionate and creative, they are the prey of death. Such an interpretation would be in line with an important strand in the *Aeneid*, with its bitter awareness of the conflict between fate's impersonal purposes and the passions of the human heart.

The Aeneid

Virgil was still working on his epic when in 19 BC he died. We are credibly told that at the last he asked his friends to burn his unfinished poem. Antiquity did not share our romantic interest in fragmentary and suggestive works of art, and ancient writers, like ancient artists, aimed to offer the public works as perfect as they could make them. An obvious mark of its unfinished state is the presence, unevenly distributed through the poem, of metrically incomplete lines: lines, that is, to which the poet intended to return. Some of them are very effective, and romantic readers have been tempted to think that Virgil would have left them; but that is an idea which would not have occurred to him, any more than it occurred to any of his imitators in antiquity to include incomplete lines in their poems. He did not, however, intend to carry the story further forward than the point it reaches at the end of Book 12.

Maecenas tried to induce each of the poets to produce an epic on Augustus: none of them complied. That fact alone shows that the pressure was civilized. We are not in the world of Stalin and the Writers' Union. Virgil was unlike Horace and Propertius in that from the beginning he did talk in terms of writing a martial epic 'one day' (*Eclogues* 4.54; 8.6-10), whereas they always made it clear that they could not, or would not. In the introduction to the third book of the *Georgics* he seemed to undertake that he would write it 'soon'. But in the event he produced something quite different: a mythical epic on the ultimate origins of Rome. Augustus, we know, followed its progress with impatience, begging to be shown portions of it. He accepted, that is, that the *Aeneid* really was the fulfilment of his own wish; and he was right.

Virgil had come to see that it was not possible to write an epic of which Augustus should be the central figure, and which should satisfy the highest artistic demands. The framework of an epic must be the Homeric poems, and that entailed both the constant presence of the gods as characters, and also hand-to-hand fighting among heroic warriors. But to intrude divine councils and interventions into very recent history would be a jarring fault of taste, constantly risking bathos and absurdity; so, too, would the representation of Augustus mowing down thousands with his own strong right arm. Again, the plain fact was that the battle of Actium was unsatisfactory as a theme for verse. Not only did Augustan propaganda insist that it be represented not as a civil war but as a war with the Queen of Egypt, which was universally known to be untrue; there also apparently was hardly any fighting, some contingents changing sides at the last moment, and Cleopatra suddenly sailing away in flight. Nor, finally, could Virgil have found a central role for his great talent for pathos. If Augustus were the hero, there could be little sympathy for the defeated, and no ambiguity about his triumph. Cleopatra could not be treated as sympathetically as Dido. And Virgil was to succeed in making a natural flair for the pathos of loss and defeat into a central feature, not only of the decoration of the *Aeneid*, but also of its interpretation of imperialism and of history.

The chief difficulty about the creation of the *Aeneid* was that of writing a poem which at one level should be a mythical epic about the distant past, yet which should also be about the present and the future. The difficulty was so great that Virgil said in a letter that he must have been mad to attempt it. The poem was to be all-embracing, drawing upon both *Iliad* and *Odyssey*, Attic tragedy, Hellenistic poetry, and Latin predecessors, especially Naevius and Ennius; it was to be permeated by philosophical ideas from the Greek thinkers; it must be strongly marked by Roman history and characteristically Roman values; and Virgil was anxious also to include not only Rome but also Italy, with its geography, its peoples, and its virtues. Roman history must be presented as a crescendo leading up to Augustus, a thousand years in the future. Finally, the whole poem must be written in a style grand yet flexible, showing its author's familiarity with all preceding literature.

Romans believed that their city was founded in the eighth century BC, Romulus being the actual founder, but some places in Latium had for centuries believed that their origins went back to Troy: after the sack of the city, fleeing Trojans came to the West. Such beliefs were indeed widespread all over the Mediterranean, as non-Greek peoples became sophisticated enough to wish to attach themselves somehow to the great cycles of Greek legend. (In the Middle Ages this continued to be true: Britons descended from the Trojan Brut, for example.) Some aristocratic families at Rome claimed to have migrated there from other Latin cities, and to trace their ancestry back to Troy, among them the Julii. Now, the story of Romulus was not very suitable for an epic, and it had no direct link with Augustus. Aeneas, who actually is a character in the *Iliad*, was a much better hero; and through the Julii he was Augustus' ancestor. A great drawback, however, was that Aeneas could not found Rome, as scholars put the fall of Troy 400 years earlier, in the twelfth century BC. Aeneas can only found Lavinium, from which in time Rome will derive. Virgil turns this difficulty to account brilliantly in Book 8, when Aeneas is entertained by an ally on the very site which will be that of Rome. The hero is shown the Capitol and all the places which will become opulent and celebrated, now green hills and trees. The touching scene is programmatic: Aeneas must live for a future he will not live to see.

The epic starts with Aeneas and his Trojans on their sea-journey to the West. The poet opens with a weighty introduction:

> Arms and the man I sing, who, forced by Fate
> And haughty Juno's unrelenting hate,
> Expelled and exiled, left the Trojan shore.
> Long labours, both on land and sea, he bore . . .
> (trans. Dryden).

THE BUILDING OF LAVINIUM, depicted in a painted frieze from a Roman tomb on the Esquiline (mid first century BC). The frieze showed episodes from the foundation legend of Rome and is of exceptional interest as testimony of the stock of stories available when Virgil came to compose his *Aeneid*. The city goddess is seated at the centre.

A mighty warrior with a destined mission, the hero is persecuted by a hostile goddess: and more than that, he is 'famous for his *pietas*', and even that quality—in English 'sense of duty', 'devotion'—does not protect him. Virgil goes on to remonstrate, shocked by the theology of his own story:

> O Muse! tell why the queen of heaven began
> To persecute so brave, so just a man:
> What grievance must his suffering assuage?
> Can heavenly spirits feel such human rage?

The hostility of Juno arises, we learn, from personal pique: Ganymede, Jupiter's paramour, and Paris, who judged the beauty contest of the goddesses and gave the prize to Venus over Juno, were Trojans. But also she favours Carthage, and hopes to frustrate the plan of Jupiter and Fate to confer dominion on Rome.

Aeneas had long been famous for his 'piety', and he was often depicted in the act of carrying his old father on his shoulders out of burning Troy. Virgil makes him also carry the Trojan *penates*, resident gods who are to take up their new home in Italy. *Pius* is his regular epithet in the poem (Virgil suggests but does not copy the Homeric use of 'formulaic' epithets: above, pp. 66 ff.), meaning that he above all men identifies his will with the plans of Fate. His sufferings in the poem, in which he is ship-wrecked, forced to fight a hateful war with the people of Italy, and to abandon the woman he loves, are thus clearly unjust. We hear him complain to his mother, the goddess Venus, when she has appeared to him in disguise: the episode will illustrate the way in which Virgil uses and transforms Homeric material. Asked who he is, Aeneas replies bitterly 'Sum pius Aeneas' ('I am the dutiful Aeneas') and goes on to complain that in obedient pursuit of his destiny he has seen his ships wrecked and himself cast up on an unknown African shore. His mother sharply rebukes him for his complaints. As she turns away and leaves him she allows him to recognize her, too late, and he pursues her with reproaches: why will she never stay with him? The scene, occurring in Book 1, is programmatic. It is based on several Homeric motifs: the scene in *Odyssey* 9 when Odysseus identifies himself to the listening Phaeacians ('I am Odysseus, famous everywhere for my clever tricks'); the relationship between Achilles and his goddess mother Thetis; and several scenes where gods

AENEAS AND ANCHISES: carved gemstone of the Roman imperial period. The motif of the Trojan hero carrying his father on his shoulder and leading his son Ascanius (Iulus) by the hand became a popular subject in art after the publication of Virgil's *Aeneid*, in which the dramatic episode of Aeneas' escape from Troy is described in Book 2. The composition seems to have been used for a famous statue-group in Augustus' Forum.

allow their identity to be realized only as they turn away. But Odysseus' boast is a proud and justifiably confident one, and Thetis is a different sort of mother from Venus—she truly understands her son, comes when he calls, and never deceives him. Virgil has created from these Homeric hints a scene of great poignancy, which shows us the whole position of Aeneas. He is struggling to carry out the apparently arbitrary orders of heaven; and he is lonely. That combination is an explosive one, and we are meant to understand how it follows that the next thing that happens to Aeneas is that he falls in love.

He has been driven ashore at Carthage, where Dido, a glamorous and heroic widowed queen, is founding her new city. Aeneas' wife disappeared in the confusion at the fall of Troy. Humanly, the two seem made for each other, even without the interference of the meddling goddesses. Juno hopes that Aeneas will

THE STORY OF DIDO AND AENEAS:
fourth-century AD mosaic found at Low Ham
in Somerset. The events are related counter-
clockwise from the bottom right, beginning
with the arrival of Aeneas' ships on the
African coast. At the top Venus supervises the
meeting of Aeneas and the Carthaginian
queen, at the left they go hunting, and at the
bottom they embrace while sheltering from
the storm described in Virgil's *Aeneid* 4. In the
central octagon Venus is flanked by Cupids
with lowered and raised torches, symbolizing
respectively the death of Dido and the
continuing life of Aeneas.

DIDO AND AENEAS IN THE CAVE:
illustration from a manuscript of Virgil in the
Vatican Library (*c.*AD 500). The immense
importance and popularity of the *Aeneid* in
imperial times is attested by the flourishing
manuscript tradition as well as by the frequent
echoes in the visual arts. The cave, which had
to be omitted in the Low Ham mosaic, can be
portrayed without difficulty in the
polychrome painting.

stay in Carthage and not found Rome; Venus, that Dido will be nice to her son. Together they push Dido to fall in love with Aeneas. Like Odysseus (*Odyssey* 9–12) he tells the story of his adventures, starting with Troy's fall (*Aen.* 2–3). Odysseus' audience listened with pleasure to the narration of exciting tales; Virgil adds the emotional point that, like Desdemona, Dido comes to love Aeneas as he tells her of the dangers he has passed. Juno is an unscrupulous enemy of the Trojans and anxious to frustrate the will of Jupiter and Fate, and we now see that Venus is essentially no different. She is on the right side because it happens that Aeneas is her son, but not for the right reason; and at Carthage she gets him into a terrible difficulty.

The fourth book of the *Aeneid* is the tragedy of Dido. Virgil is here strongly influenced by Euripides' Medea and by other unhappy heroines, including the Medea of Apollonius of Rhodes (above, p. 359). Dido is overwhelmed by her love, and Aeneas (we infer) drifts into a passionate affair with her. He is seen by disapproving neighbours and gods dressed up in Carthaginian crimson and gold, Dido's gift, actually helping to found Carthage (4.259). Dido, indeed, claims that they are married; though Aeneas is able to say, when the gods push him into leaving, that he never went through a regular marriage ceremony with her. Virgil was in a tight corner here. Aeneas cannot abandon a wife, but Dido cannot be allowed to carry on light-heartedly with a lover. The poet has dealt with the difficulty by constructing a situation which both is and is not a marriage. Out on a boar-hunt, Dido and Aeneas are driven by a storm to take shelter together in a cave. Juno, goddess of marriage, is present as *pronuba* (matron of honour); the nymphs raise a cry; lightning flashes, and the sky was 'conscious witness to their union' ('conscius aether conubiis'). In a sense, that is a marriage; in another important sense it is not. But we are meant to think, when Aeneas advances that plea to her, that he has sailed very close to the wind. The book is dominated by a series of passionate speeches by Dido, of reproach, entreaty, bitterness, curses. The hero speaks only once, pleading the imperative instructions of Jupiter. There is nothing else he can say. He is right to go, but he does not cut a good figure. As he sails hastily away, Dido invokes eternal enmity between Carthage and Rome, and kills herself.

Aeneas finally lands in Italy in Book 6, and is immediately told to visit the Underworld. The sombre splendours of this book lead him through the stages of his past life, meeting his own dead, as well as the traditional inhabitants of the lower world. He is not spared a terrible encounter with Dido, who in death refuses to forgive him or to speak to him, and at last turns away to the company of her first husband, 'who answered her cares and matched her love'. A last bitter twist of the knife: even Dido is better off than the isolated Aeneas. This is the only happy marriage we ever see in the *Aeneid*; and it is among the dead. Aeneas is left in no doubt that he destroyed Dido, and he can only say that he did not intend it.

In the second half of the poem he will find himself destroying other things, too. Juno stirs up a fearful war with a coalition of Italian peoples, and Books 9 to 12 are full of epic fighting. Aeneas finds an unexpected ally, an aged Greek king named Euander, who entrusts his son Pallas to the hero, to learn from him to be a warrior. Pallas is killed, and Aeneas feels bitterly responsible. He himself is forced to kill the attractive young Etruscan prince Lausus, who persists in attacking him to rescue his own father: Aeneas weeps over Lausus' body. He tries repeatedly to make peace with King Latinus and his recalcitrant people, but they break the truce and force him into battle. His fighting rage is at last aroused, and he slaughters great numbers of the Italians; yet these are peoples who are to live together in peace, and the war is horrible, a kind of civil war. The poem ends with another masterly transformation of a Homeric scene. The Italian champion Turnus finally comes face to face with Aeneas, in a duel deliberately reminiscent of the duel between Achilles and Hector. Turnus is wounded, he falls; he admits defeat and begs for his life. Aeneas is about to spare him, his fighting rage is subsiding—and then he sees round Turnus' waist the belt which he stripped from the body of Pallas when he slew him. Inflamed with anger, Aeneas avenges the death of his young friend by killing Turnus, and the epic ends with the lines

> A deadly chill his loosening limbs invades:
> His soul lamenting passes to the shades.

Such an ending reminds us that in the *Iliad* Hector was killed in Book 22, and that two books followed in which Achilles came to terms, first with the other Achaeans, and then with his enemy Priam. Here there is no such healing process of reconciliation, and the work ends with the act of killing—an act which could easily have been made less disturbing. Turnus is a killer, and his death is just; but Aeneas would have liked to spare him, if he could. That is Virgil's deepest reflection on the nature of imperialism: that it is a hard and lonely destiny, in which the conqueror repeatedly finds himself destroying what he would prefer to spare. By his victory Aeneas wins the hand of the young princess Lavinia, an *ingénue* who had been betrothed to Turnus, and who never speaks in the poem. Unlike Odysseus' wife Penelope, and unlike the Dido he has been forced to leave and to destroy, this young girl will not be a wife to console the loneliness of the battered hero—who in any case will live for only three years.

It would be superficial to regard the *Aeneid* as anti-imperialist or anti-Augustan. The message of the poem is that the domination of Rome over the world is willed by heaven, and that it will impose peace and civilization (*mos, ius*). Virgil devises a series of forward perspectives through history, to make this vision real. In Book 1 Jupiter reveals to Venus the plans of Fate: a Roman Empire without limits in time or space, and Augustus as its climax, a future god. In Book 6 Aeneas' dead father shows him the spirits of the unborn Romans of the future, who will conquer the world and, renouncing to the Greeks the fine arts, practise the arts of rule, putting down the proud and sparing the conquered. At the end of Book 8 Aeneas is brought a marvellous shield, the work of Vulcan, on which

WOUNDED AENEAS: painting from the House of Siricus at Pompeii (between AD 62 and 79), closely based on a passage in Latin poetry (Virgil, *Aeneid*, 12. 383–416). All the main motifs (Aeneas leaning on a tall spear, his son weeping beside him, the doctor trying to operate with a forceps, Venus descending with a sprig of healing dittany) occur in Virgil's description of this episode in the final battle between Aeneas and Turnus.

are depicted the wars of Rome, with the battle of Actium in the centre (brilliantly represented as a tableau, not a narrative). And in Book 12 Juno at last abandons her hostility to Rome, and she and Jupiter agree that the Italians, far from being simply defeated by the Trojans, shall contribute the native Italian toughness and valour to form the unique essence of Rome—'Italian hardihood shall make Rome great':

Sit Romana potens Itala uirtute propago.

Other poets might have produced fine poetry on the greatness of conquest and dominion. The supremacy of the *Aeneid*, and its continuing importance when the Roman Empire has turned out after all to be less than eternal, depends on two things. One is the haunting beauty of Virgil's verse, never equalled in Latin literature; the other is his ability to present at the same time, with justice but also with passion, both the achievement of Empire and also its inevitable human cost. The exquisite balance comes out clearly when Aeneas is brought the shield, glittering with the representation of Rome's martial history, culminating in the figure of Augustus receiving tribute from a conquered world. Aeneas marvels at the wonderful work, but of course he cannot really understand it, as these events have not yet happened; but he must bear the weight of them:

> These figures, on the shield divinely wrought,
> By Vulcan laboured, and by Venus brought,
> With joy and wonder fill the hero's thought.
> Unknown the names, he yet admires the grace;
> His shoulder bears the fame and fortune of his race.
>   (trans. Dryden, adapted).

Such was Virgil's fame that a number of spurious poems were ascribed to him. At least one, the *Culex*, was a deliberate fake, widely accepted as Virgilian within eighty years of the poet's death. Others make no pretence of Virgilian authorship,

DETAIL OF A MOSAIC PAVEMENT (fourth century AD) in the villa at Lullingstone, Kent. The scene of Europa and the bull is accompanied by an inscription in faultless Latin elegiacs which presupposes a knowledge, even here in the remote province of Britain, of Virgil's *Aeneid*: 'If jealous Juno had seen the swimming of the bull, more justly would she have repaired to the halls of Aeolus.' This alludes to Juno's mission to the god of the winds in *Aeneid* 1.

and it seems that the attribution was simply the result of an insatiable desire in the reading public for more poems by Rome's greatest writer. Several are quite interesting in their own right, notably the *Copa*, a short hedonistic piece about the charms of a dancer at a country inn, and the *Ciris*, a self-consciously decadent epyllion about a girl betraying her country for love. The only members of the collection with any chance of being by Virgil are one or two of the very short pieces collectively known as the *Catalepton* ('In the Slender Style'). Certainty about them will never be reached.

Further Reading

The standard text of Virgil is the Oxford Classical Text of R. A. B. Mynors. Dryden's translation is splendid in rhetoric and verse, though it is often rather far from the Latin, and his rhyming couplets inevitably impose a different movement on Virgil's hexameters. C. Day Lewis translated all of Virgil into readable modern verse (Oxford, paperback, 1966). There are good versions of the *Eclogues* by Guy Lee (Liverpool, 1980); of the *Georgics* by L. P. Wilkinson (Harmondsworth, 1982) and Robert Wells (Manchester, 1982); and of the *Aeneid* by Robert Fitzgerald (London, 1984).

Virgil is the subject of an immense modern literature, much of it speculative and idiosyncratic. J. Griffin's *Virgil* (Oxford 1986, in the Past Masters seris) deals particularly with the poet's ideas. The *Cambridge History of Classical Literature* ii (1982), 297–369 gives a generally reliable account of the poet and his works (but it is not, as is there stated, certain that the *Eclogues* were published in 35 BC). The poet's early life is well treated in the second chapter of L. P. Wilkinson, *The Georgics of Virgil* (Cambridge, 1969: paperback); the historical and political background in R. Syme's classic *The Roman Revolution* (Oxford, 1939: paperback).

The Introduction to Robert Coleman's edition of the *Eclogues* (Cambridge, 1977) is very helpful. L. P. Wilkinson's book on the *Georgics* is the best on that poem. A useful approach to the *Aeneid*: W. A. Camps, *An Introduction to Virgil's Aeneid* (Oxford, 1969: paperback). W. Y. Sellar, *Virgil* (Oxford, 1877) is a good example of solid Victorian criticism; Brooks Otis, *Virgil: A Study in Civilized Poetry* (Oxford, 1963) is more subjective. A good collection of papers: *Virgil, a Collection of Critical Essays*, edited by S. Commager (Eaglewood Cliffs, NJ, 1966; paperback). T. S. Eliot's essay 'What is a Classic?' appears in his book *On Poets and Poetry* (London, 1951). Gordon Williams, *Tradition and Originality in Roman Poetry* (Oxford, 1968) illuminates many passages in Virgil, and in other authors.

Important commentaries have appeared recently: on *Aeneid* 1, 2, 4, and 6 by R. G. Austin; on 3 and 5 by R. D. Williams; on 7 and 8 by C. J. Fordyce (all Oxford University Press); also on 8 by K. W. Gransden (Cambridge, 1976). R. D. Williams has published a shorter commentary on the whole of the *Aeneid* (London, 2 vols., 1972).

Two classic works of German scholarship: R. Heinze, *Virgils epische Technik* (3rd edn., 1914), repr. 1957), and E. Norden's Commentary on *Aeneid* 6 (Stuttgart, 1927, repr. 1957).

26

Roman Historians

❧

ANDREW LINTOTT

Origins

A small proportion of the works of the Roman historians has survived the hiatus in culture and learning that followed the decline of the western half of the Roman Empire. We have only about a half of Tacitus' major works, for example, thanks to precisely two manuscripts, and only thirty-five of the 142 books of Livy. Such is the fate of the acknowledged masters; our information about the pioneers and many other later historians is confined to brief comments and quotations. Greek historians by contrast fared much better as a result of Byzantine scholarship.

Generalization from this limited evidence is made easier by the homogeneity of what survives. A Roman historian was first and foremost a historian of Rome, 'rerum Romanarum auctor'. Like Thucydides or Xenophon, he dealt primarily with public affairs at home and abroad: 'vast wars, the sack of cities, the defeat and capture of kings, or in domestic history conflicts between consuls and tribunes, legislation about land and grain-distribution, the struggles of the aristocracy and plebs'—such in Tacitus' view was the subject-matter of the historians of the Republic. The basic aims of the historians were simple: to preserve the memory of Rome itself and to transmit to future generations the exploits and characters of her famous men. To quote Tacitus again, 'I think it a particular function of annals, that virtues should not be passed over in silence, while those responsible for wrong actions and words should be threatened with disgrace in the eyes of posterity.' This history was not purely secular, however; it also concerned Rome's relations with the gods who watched over her growth and prosperity, as revealed in the portents by which the gods communicated with mortals, and the cult practices which were the human response to them. Ideally the historian of public affairs was a man who had participated in them. With the occasional exception, notably Livy, Roman historians were senators or had held important positions in public life. Sallust claims that he was diverted from historiography by political ambitions but, when these failed and he was no longer committed to a particular faction, he readily devoted his retirement to history rather than to a life of leisure or the 'servile activities of agriculture and hunting'.

The most inspiring topic for a Roman historian was Rome's phenomenal rise to dominance over the Mediterranean during the Republican period. Yet it was only when they were approaching the zenith of this achievement that the Romans developed both the will and the ability to chronicle it properly. The first Roman historians, Q. Fabius Pictor and L. Cincius Alimentus, held public office during the second Punic War (Cincius was captured by Hannibal) and probably wrote their histories immediately afterwards, in the first decade of the second century BC. They wrote in Greek—Fabius has recently been discovered among a group of Greek historians commemorated by texts painted on wall-plaster at Taormina in Sicily. Fabius and Cincius did not merely write about their own lifetime, but tried to reconstruct Roman history from its origins. We must therefore briefly consider what sort of historical material survived from the past and how it affected the subsequent composition of histories.

The Romans maintained records of the consuls of every year (*fasti consulares*), which, as transmitted to us, stretched back to the founding of the Republic about 500 BC. These probably derive from the yearly registers said to have been kept by the chief priests, *pontifices maximi*, containing the magistrates and notable events of each year. Questions, which cannot be discussed here, inevitably arise about the genuineness of these early records and the extent to which, even if basically genuine, they were corrupted later; what is certain is that at best they were a bare factual account of wars, triumphs, portents (e.g. eclipses), and food-shortages. There was also a great stock of stories about Rome from its mythical origins onwards, some written down by Greeks like Timaeus (below, p. 639), others deriving from native traditions. By far the most significant of these were the family traditions preserved by the noble families. These had their particular origin in funerals, whose contribution to Roman self-consciousness of their military prowess was noted by the Greek historian Polybius. The dead noble was carried to the rostra in the forum amid mourners wearing the clothes and death-masks of his ancestors, and there his son or a close relative pronounced an encomium (*laudatio funebris*), which began with the dead man himself and then embraced the exploits of the other dead ancestors included in the gathering. These orations were preserved for future exploitation, but both Cicero and Livy complain of their corruption of history by the invention of achievements and improper genealogical claims.

As far as we can judge, the earliest histories were far from a mere chronicle. Their writers probably had two major purposes, corresponding to their two different readerships. Now that Rome had become the dominant power in the Mediterranean, the Roman version of recent conflicts was a useful adjunct to foreign policy. So was publicity about the nature and antiquity of the city. About this time a friend of Rome in Chios set up an inscription showing the genealogy of Romulus and Remus—interestingly, it was Fabius Pictor who first seems to

STATUE OF A ROMAN WITH THE BUSTS OF HIS ANCESTORS (late first century BC). The practice of mourners in funeral processions wearing masks to personate dead ancestors, as recorded by Polybius, tended to give way during the late Republic to the carrying of portrait-busts, presumably in a light material such as wax or terracotta.

have reconciled the Greek view that Aeneas had founded Rome with the Roman view that it was Romulus. At home the historians not only followed the poets in glorifying Roman virtues, but educated in another way by establishing the 'truth' about the Roman constitution and mores, so as to preserve these from erosion in a time of increasing foreign influence and one when many new families were reaching high office. Roman historiography was thus at the start essentially conservative in outlook.

Other senators followed Fabius and Cincius, the most noteworthy among them being the ex-consul and censor M. Porcius Cato from the town of Tusculum in Latium. Cato wrote his *Origines* in Latin. As the work's title suggests, he was concerned with the early history, not only of Rome, but of other Italian cities; but he then moved swiftly on to discuss the Punic Wars and his own lifetime (234–149 BC), enlivening the narrative with digressions on marvels, as Herodotus had done, and also versions of his own speeches. From Cato's time onwards Romans usually wrote their history in Latin, but they were still subject to Greek influences, of which three may be distinguished.

Polybius

The first of these, antiquarianism, was apparent in Roman historiography from the beginning. The obvious Greek example for the Romans was Timaeus of Tauromenium (Taormina), a Sicilian writer of the early third century BC, who in the course of his histories of Sicily and the western Mediterranean had become in effect the first historian of Rome. Secondly there was the 'tragic' approach associated with certain Hellenistic writers, whose chief features were pathos, sensationalism, and the cult of the bizarre. The third influence was Polybius of Megalopolis, a Greek taken to Italy as a political detainee in 168 BC, who became a close friend of Roman aristocrats there and set himself to describe how 'almost the whole inhabited world had come under the sole rule of the Romans within fifty-three years'. He aimed to write 'pragmatic' history, a political and military history, which would be of practical value for the serious reader, both because it explained the links of cause and motivation between events and because it judged critically the behaviour of men under stress as examples for future conduct. Because the whole history of the Mediterranean had become united through Roman power, he believed it was possible to write a universal history which was at the same time coherent and had explanatory value. Polybius' work was thus the culmination of Hellenistic historiography, in that politico-military history, traditionally focused on the city-state, was given the breadth of a universal chronicle. His narrative, chronologically based on Olympiads and their constituent years, dealt successively with the different regions of the world known to the Greeks, cross-cutting in order to keep parallel stories in step with one another and stressing their interrelation and convergence. At the same time he transformed Greek historiography because his central theme was the rise of an alien empire.

Like Thucydides (above, pp. 193 f.), he is a historian's historian, self-conscious about the principles and methodology of his craft, but more ready to discuss openly problems such as the selection of material, composition of speeches, portrayal of character, and explanation of causes. His approach is in essence a reaffirmation of Thucydides' first priority, the search for the truth from the most authentic evidence possible—autopsy, the questioning of eyewitnesses, and the sifting of their accounts. However, he extended his researches to the past, especially the generation before his own, and he made critical use of other men's writings. Yet he also stresses the historian's personal contribution to history and, while in abhorring the fabulous and over-emotional he distances himself from both the antiquarians and the 'tragic' writers, he shares the latter's preoccupation with making an impression on his readers. He reconciles these beliefs by a theory centring on the Greek term *emphasis*, which covers the authoritative impression given by a writer, the vivid significance of the events he recounts, and the powerful impression left in the reader's mind. He believes that it is the truth of events which influences a reader more than rhetorical devices. Yet this requires the historian as a medium, selecting and presenting events with appropriate comment on motive, cause, and outcome. On the other hand, the historian's ability derives from his own political and military experience either in the events themselves or other events like them. So the good historian is writing out of his own experience, whatever he relates, and the resulting authenticity and explanatory power makes the impact on the reader, without which history is useless for the man seeking instruction.

The instruction Polybius gives is often explicit. He discusses technicalities such as the computation of the size of cities and the use of fire-signals; he moralizes on the fortitude of Regulus in disaster, the foolish presumption of the Aetolians, the arrogance of Philip V of Macedon; he illustrates the dangers of using mercenaries. One book is devoted to the relative merits of the Roman, Carthaginian, and Spartan constitutions. Individual political decisions are analysed directly: he claims to have avoided fiction in speeches, but to have selected from the available material the central arguments, on whose background and outcome he adds his own comments. His treatment of the causes of war is perhaps not quite sophisticated enough. Although he carefully distinguishes the preliminary acts of a war and the pretexts alleged by the combatants from the causes proper, he finds the latter only in the mental disposition of the aggressor and the circumstances which had so disposed him. No allowance is made for occasions when there is no long-term resolve to fight, but the diplomatic interaction of the two parties drives one or both of them over the brink, nor is enough weight given to complicity in the state attacked, for example Rome in the Second Punic War, when it acquiesces in, and plans for, the attack threatening it. Like Thucydides, Polybius refused to attribute to chance what can be rationally explained. However, he shared the fascination of his Hellenistic and classical predecessors for the paradoxes of fortune (*tychē*), that is, rapid changes in human circumstances, whose particular components can be rationally explained, but whose cumulative effect is unpredictable and awe-inspiring. Most strikingly, he states that the rise of Rome to world-domination was directed by *tychē*, though he argues elsewhere that chance played no part in Roman success, but it was to be expected in the light of their power, political stability, and enterprise. This apparent inconsistency can be explained. Polybius seems to have regarded Rome as the worthy victor in a contest which had, as it were, been promoted by *tychē* through the coincidence in time of several great and ambitious powers. But it was chance that the conflict in the West between Rome and Carthage, which had a causal nexus of its own, coincided in time with the expansion of Philip V and Antiochus III, and so political processes throughout the Mediterranean became enmeshed with each other.

The Late Republic

Roman historians did not share Polybius' interest in theory, nor did they match his universality in treating events. Nevertheless, he had put Rome firmly in the centre of world history, and the practical educational aim he ascribed to history would have ensured its respectability in Roman eyes. Furthermore, his desire that politicians and generals should write history, not men sitting in libraries, was in accordance with existing Roman tradition. How did Roman writing develop under these Hellenistic influences? In the late second century a distinction was drawn between *annales*, in the strict sense of a chronicle of events year by year, and *historiae*, which involved causal analysis. In due course the term 'historiae' was to be used by Sallust and Tacitus for works about their own lifetime, while 'annales' tended to mean ancient history. Cato had been the pioneer in turning history into a political weapon; by 100 BC politicians were writing memoirs to set the record right about themselves. This trend led in time to Caesar's commentaries and Augustus' autobiography and *Res Gestae*. Biography developed also: C. Gracchus wrote about his elder brother and in the late Republic great men—Caesar, Pompey, Cato, and Cicero, for example—were commemorated by their admirers. However, side by side with contemporary history antiquarian history flourished as never before. The material in the earlier annals was expanded by material culled from a variety of documents, whether genuine or forged, and supplemented by frequently stereotyped inventions, such as led Livy to wonder how the Volscians and Aequians had enough men to be slaughtered so often by the Romans.

No one could now complain of a shortage of Roman history, but in the view of Cicero's contemporaries what existed was not readable. Cicero's friends pestered him for a history—'a work in itself most suited to an orator'—and when he died, Cornelius Nepos (himself a writer of chronicles and short biographies) lamented that the chance of casting the rough and shapeless mass of material into a worthy literary form was lost. Cicero himself argued that Roman histories could not be compared with Greek because they lacked *ornatus*, attractive presentation. This comprised variations in colour and tone, good word-order, and an easy flowing style, in which ideally the rhythm of the sentences reproduced the rhythm of events. However, more than language was involved in Cicero's view: histories required proper chronological disposition and geographical descriptions, interpretations of policy and motive, and judgements on the execution of these policies. Although the fragments known to us of early annalists show spectacular language and a vigorous narrative skill, they lack the smoothness to beguile a reader over long periods. More important, they may not have given enough space to interpretation.

Julius Caesar

Caesar's commentaries on his Gallic and Civil Wars are the first good evidence we have of the progress of Roman historiography. Although they are memoirs with a political purpose, they share many of the characteristics of less committed histories: indeed tendentiousness and self-glorification are not vices unique to autobiography. Stylistically, Caesar seems to have improved on his predecessors. The narrative flows clearly and smoothly, but there is little variety of tone nor a great range of vocabulary, and the style generally resembles that of the official letters we find in Cicero's correspondence. Cicero praised their naked and austere beauty, precisely because they were stripped of verbal ornament. In organization and interpretation of his material Caesar meets Cicero's requirements more closely. Indeed the themes of Caesar's *Gallic War* are typical of mature Roman history. Caesar tells us of the expansion of Roman power in a successful war, enlivening the story with digressions on geography and the characteristics of foreign races, and explains its significance by comments in the first person and by speeches in which both he and his opponents justify their conduct. The whole work is a testimony to Roman virtue, not only that of Caesar himself, but of his troops, whose abilities are rarely portrayed so effectively elsewhere. There is a political message too. Although Caesar was radical and violent in his own political career, when discussing the Gallic communities he exalts established power and conservatism. Danger comes from ambitious men who solicit help from the plebs by largesse and aim at revolution. In spite of the irony which the reader can find in these remarks, Caesar would have written them quite sincerely: Rome had traditionally sought aid from the 'establishments' among her allies when securing her empire. The *Civil War* could not so easily be given a Roman interpretation. Yet once again Caesar's soldiers are heroes, and Caesar defends his own conduct according to traditional values: when his dignity was threatened and he was deserted by former friends, he took up arms in defence of the liberty of the Roman people against the machinations of a few powerful men.

Sallust

C. Sallustius Crispus (born 86 BC), a partisan of Caesar's who took to history about the time of the latter's murder, was more innovative stylistically and developed a terse epigrammatic style, which owed much to the short simple sentences and ponderous vocabulary of the early annalists, in particular Cato, but had greater variety of language and tone. Unfortunately his major work, the *Histories*, which dealt with late Republican history down to 67 BC, only survives

VICTORIES WITH A SHIELD: relief from a triumphal monument in Rome (early first century BC). This and other reliefs in the same hard grey stone, all showing trophies and armour, have been attributed to the base of a statue-group of 91 BC depicting Sulla's capture of Jugurtha, the North African king whose conflict with Rome forms the subject of Sallust's *Jugurthine War*.

in fragments and we have to base our judgement of him mainly on the monographs *Catiline* and *Jugurtha*. In these Sallust makes plain his preoccupation with the portrayal of virtue; in fact he alludes to the importance of the death-masks of the nobility as inspiration for later generations, thus recalling the influence of Roman funerals on historical writing. However, to throw virtue into relief he gives as much emphasis to vice, and he does not limit himself to the character of individuals, but portrays the *mores* of whole sections of society. Patriotically he gives Roman military glory its due, but contrasts this with the moral corruption which in his view attended the expansion of the Roman Empire. It was above all the aristocracy itself which through greed and ambition was not only self-destructive, but created injustice for the poor or encouraged corruption in them also. Rome was only saved by the outstanding virtue of a few of her leaders. Sallust also highlights conflicts between the nobility and the plebs, which had begun in the early Republic before corruption had set in, but returned in earnest in the late Republic after a brief period of harmony during Rome's most critical wars. He shows sympathy with plebeian sufferings (he had himself been tribune of the plebs and taken a popular stance at that time). Yet when writing of the late Republic, in a passage influenced by Thucydides, he denounces both those who claimed to defend the status quo of senatorial dominance and those who championed plebeian rights, for seeking in reality their own power. For Sallust vice and decadence were as important subjects as virtues and victories, and it was vice which gave him the greatest opportunities for extended portrayal of character, for example those of Catiline and Jugurtha themselves, and minor characters like Sempronia, the educated society woman in Sallust's *Catiline*. However, the analysis of the causes of decadence is comparatively superficial. Roman political organization and the Roman economy are but briefly mentioned. For Sallust the fundamental causes were prosperity and the lack of foreign enemies: these gave rein to a sort of original sin, which only the hardships of foreign wars could hold in check. This notion was not discovered by Sallust: it goes back to the politics and historiography of the second century BC. But Sallust transmitted it in a most memorable form.

Livy

T. Livius is the first annalistic writer whose work survives in any quantity, and it is through him and the elements of earlier writings discernible in his history that we are able to form judgements on the annals of the Republic. Moreover, his history was the last great annalistic history of the Republic written in Latin. Livy was born at Patavium (Padua) in 59 BC and wrote from about the age of thirty onwards after twenty years of civil war and the conversion of the Republic into a form of monarchy. A man of industry and learning rather than political or intellectual distinction, he came nearest to fulfilling the expectation which Cicero's friends had of Cicero—the production of a readable history of Rome. His resources in language and deployment of his material were everything

THE BATTLE OF PYDNA: detail of the sculptured frieze on the monument set up by Aemilius Paullus at Delphi in honour of his victory in 167 BC (above, p. 418). Besides accurately reproducing the army of the combatants (note the characteristic Macedonian round shield with embossed ornament) the artist corroborates Livy's account of the part played by a runaway pack horse in precipitating an engagement.

that Cicero himself could have wished. Avoiding Sallustian abruptness, he yet contrived a swift and varied narrative built from a rich vocabulary and an immense flexibility of construction. His approach to his subject was conservative, as had probably been traditional among annalists: in wars he was patriotic, in politics he supported senatorial authority against the demagoguery of tribunes. Although he shows some sympathy with the *plebs* in his account of their struggle with the patricians, he shows an immense fascination with aristocratic hardliners who resisted inflexibly any concession to the *plebs* or deviation from tradition. It is likely that he retained this attitude in his lost books on the fall of the Republic and saw a reason for that fall in the failure of such men. One supreme example would have been Cato Uticensis, who opposed Caesar and had already been highlighted for selfless devotion to the Republic in Sallust's *Catiline*. Although Livy wrote in the aftermath of political failure and civil conflict, it was also a period when Roman imperial power was at its height. Faced by this discrepancy and by the coincidence of prosperity with the moral turpitude exemplified by the shedding of Roman blood, Livy, like Sallust, argued that Rome had succumbed to the weight of her own success.

As an interpreter of history in detail, Livy was unoriginal or simply defective in his treatment of causes. However, he substituted for explanation a vivid human sympathy shown in his portrayal of emotions both in the speeches he composed and in the narrative. This is essentially an imaginative skill. There was no evidence about the feelings of the people of Veii, when the Romans drove them from their city and razed it to the ground, or about what the Roman soldiers felt when sent under the yoke by the Samnites (both these episodes took place in the fourth century BC); there was probably little more about the Romans' reaction to their defeat by Hannibal at Trasimene in 217. Yet these are some of the most memorable passages in what survives of Livy. It was the 'tragic' approach to history that influenced him much more than the 'pragmatic' approach of Polybius. Livy carried his history down to 9 BC—a mammoth work never to be emulated, not least because in the meantime the Republic became a dead subject.

The Early Empire

The Principate of Augustus and his successors brought changes in political life and in literary style. Both the People and the Senate gradually lost the power to make effective political decisions on matters of importance: policies were formed by the Emperor and his intimates *in camera*; promotions ultimately depended on imperial favour. So secrecy led to ignorance of the *arcana* of the Empire among contemporaries and later historians and, to compensate, fed rumour and suspicion, while the court atmosphere encouraged intrigue and backbiting. Meanwhile the luxuriant oratory of men such as Cicero was abandoned in favour of a style pointed and abrupt, like Sallust's, but more striking in its phraseology, especially apt for lampoon and denunciation.

Some historians who chronicled the transition from republic to monarchy maintained their independence from the new regime. One, Cremutius Cordus, had his books burnt under Tiberius and later reproduced under Gaius in a censored edition. In general, however, history, as Tacitus pointed out, was corrupted in two ways, by flattery of the present emperor and detraction of his predecessors. The former was stimulated by the requirement to deliver formal panegyrics of the Emperor in the consul's oration of thanks, instituted in Augustus' time (Pliny's *Panegyric* of AD 100 is the first surviving example). By contrast, Seneca's *Ludus* or *Apocolocyntosis* about the death and deification of the Emperor Claudius is a remarkable specimen of licensed defamation. Equally detrimental to the historian was the lack of traditional material. After Augustus' time most emperors did not seek major new conquests; at home there was no room for the great political conflicts of the Republic. The rivalries of the aristocracy centred on trials for treason, as they jockeyed for position in the Emperor's favour or the esteem of their equals. Important developments in the early Principate—changes in administration at home and abroad, the spread of citizenship and Graeco-Roman culture, the growth of cities—were not the stuff which had interested historians in the past and did not lend themselves to pathos or sensationalism. Yet Rome's greatest historian worked in what he himself believed was a narrow and inglorious field.

Tacitus

C. Cornelius Tacitus was born in the middle of the first century AD and reached senatorial rank and high office under the Flavian dynasty. He wrote mainly under the Emperor Trajan, in what was held to be an unexampled era of security and prosperity after the murder of the last Flavian Emperor, the 'tyrannical' Domitian. One early work was a written version of a funeral panegyric about his father-in-law Agricola. Both here and in his two major historical works—the *Historiae*, dealing with the Flavian period (AD 69–96), and the *Annales* on the Julio-Claudian dynasty from AD 14 to AD 68—he proclaims his traditional concern with virtue and vice. 'The age was not so barren of virtues that it did not produce some fine examples of conduct.' These were not quite those of republican annals. 'Mothers accompanied their children into exile, wives followed their husbands ... loyal slaves even gave insulting answers to their torturers.' Nevertheless,

INSCRIBED LEAD WATER-PIPE FROM THE FORTRESS AT CHESTER, one of the only two documents from Britain which name Agricola. The longest-serving and most successful of Britain's governors (AD 78–84), Cn. Julius Agricola was also the father-in-law of the historian Tacitus, who commemorated him in a famous, if somewhat rose-tinted, biography. The imperial titulature dates the pipe to 79.

Tacitus' work is full of miniatures of the *Agricola* type—obituary notices of those who prospered under the regime or fell foul of it through treason trials. 'Let us make this concession to the reputation of famous men that, just as in their funeral rites they are kept apart from mass burials, so they may each have their own notice in the records of deaths.'

He aimed not only to give moral edification by parading virtue and vice, but to give practical instruction. This justified his attention to intrigue and treason trials. Under the Republic, he explains, when power was at one time with the *plebs*, at another with the Senate, one had to discover how to manage the masses and equally how to influence the nobles who dominated the Senate. By the same token under an autocracy it was helpful to understand how an Emperor's mind worked. It was for success in this respect that Tacitus was so admired by men like Machiavelli and Guicciardini in the Renaissance. Although he gave their due to those who were destroyed by Emperors, he reserved his greatest admiration for those, like himself and his father-in-law Agricola, who survived. 'Let all those, whose habit is to admire acts of civil disobedience, realize that great men can exist under bad emperors, and that compliance and an unassuming demeanour, if backed by energy and hard work, can attain a pitch of glory, which the majority reach through an ostentatious and untimely death.' He had no illusions about the leading victims of the Julio-Claudians, pointing out how they tried to maintain status by self-display and extravagant spending, and contrasting them with the modest and parsimonious new men brought into the senate.

As a historian of the Empire he is most interesting for his ability to put the case for the opposition, not only denouncing the corruption of Roman rule (part of a Roman orator's stock-in-trade in so far as he had to appear for Rome's subjects in extortion cases), but also highlighting courageous independence and resistance to the blandishments of Roman civilization. 'If you wish to rule everyone, does it follow that everyone should accept slavery?', asks the captured British leader Caratacus. A feature of that slavery was 'the amenities that make vice agreeable—porticoes, baths, and sumptuous banquets'. On the other hand he could contrast the peace and justice that Roman rule brought with the insecurity of tribal rivalries. Most revealing, however, is the comment attributed to a Roman commander rejecting a plea from a German tribe to be allowed to settle in Roman territory. 'Men must obey their betters: the gods they invoked had empowered the Romans to decide what to give and what to take away, and to tolerate no judges but themselves.'

Tacitus lamented the lack of military material available to him. Yet, though he can give an exciting and not inaccurate account of a campaign (like Livy, he is especially effective in portraying the feelings of the men involved), his style leads to an irritating vagueness about detail. This style, however, was admirably suited to the portrayal of imperial politics. Two chief features were irony, used to contrast the appearances of public life with the underlying realities of power, and a deliberate cultivation of ambiguity. Tacitus delights in the deflating post-

ROMAN BATHS AT WROXETER (ancient Viriconium) near Shrewsbury (second century AD). Thermal baths were one of the amenities that, according to Tacitus, made 'vice agreeable' to the natives of Britain. Here the pillars of the underfloor heating of the warm room (*tepidarium*) have been partially restored in the foreground.

script. He also has an elaborate technique of providing alternative explanations—some his own, some ascribed to others—which do not clarify, but increase the uncertainty over the motivation of those he describes. His classic achievement was his portrayal of Tiberius. His sources reported an Emperor who, in spite of great talents and a concern for the well-being of the Empire, ended his life with an intermittent grasp over his administration and abominated by his people. Tacitus seized on Tiberius' well-known hypocrisy as the answer to the enigma, and saw his life as the gradual peeling of skins of plausibility from a bitter and malevolent inner self. Tiberius was presented as a man of acute intelligence warped by his early life and love of domination. Guicciardini wrote, 'Cornelius Tacitus teaches very well every man who lives under a tyrant the way to live and manage his affairs prudently, just as he equally teaches tyrants the ways to found their tyranny.'

In spite of the supposedly happy era in which he wrote, Tacitus' attitude to history was pessimistic. The doom of the Republic was inevitable; the miseries under Tiberius were ascribed to divine wrath. Tacitus seems to have had genuine doubts about the free will of men, which should have subverted his endeavours to give them advice. Did the friendship or enmity of the Emperor depend on predestination and one's lot at birth or was policy of some avail? For Tacitus the world was either a realm of pure chance unmitigated by divine providence or else determined in its destiny, whether by rational chains of cause and effect, as the Stoics believed, or by the planets. Though not always complimentary to individual astrologers, Tacitus was respectful to the science itself, as were many of his contemporaries, including the Flavian Emperors. As for the old gods of Rome, Tacitus said little of religious ceremonies and his treatment of portents was equivocal. The disasters which befell the Roman people were proof that the gods had no care for their tranquillity, only for their punishment. In AD 69 there

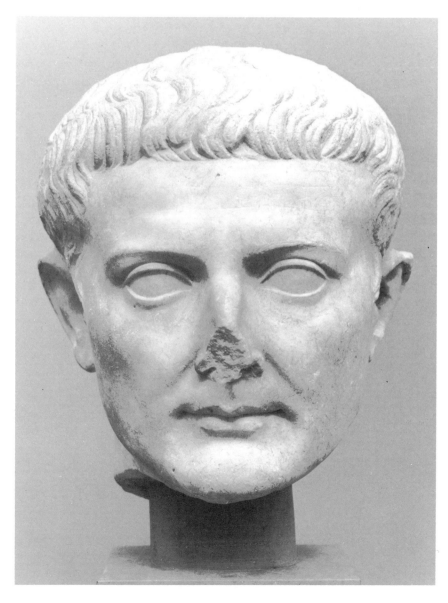

HEAD OF TIBERIUS, second of the Roman Emperors (AD 14–37). The portrait conveys something of the character painted by Tacitus in his *Annals*: a man of ability but of an underlying viciousness whose true nature was only revealed as the layers of hypocrisy were gradually cast off. Modern historians take a more charitable view, attributing Tiberius' failure to indecisiveness, reserve, and mistrust.

were 'monstrous animal births and numerous other signs and wonders of the kind that in primitive centuries were noted in peacetime, but now are only heard of when men are afraid.' It is hard to deduce a consistent religious or philosophical view from his work. However, this did not affect his moral purpose. Destiny might provide an explanation for human conduct, but not an excuse.

Suetonius

Tacitus' achievement was to adapt traditional principles to the history of the early principate and create a historical style which reflected the period. For over two centuries no one writing in Latin tried to match his achievement. Already in his lifetime literary fashion was turning from history to biography, where special attention could be given to psychology and personal relations, the subjects that had fascinated Tacitus himself. Moreover, from the point of view of the Roman upper class the lives of the Emperors were the main thread of history. Monographs might be written on their achievements, especially their campaigns. Fuller biographies would spice their official career with succulent details of their private life and judgements on their character. Tacitus' younger contemporary, C. Suetonius Tranquillus, is the most effective exponent of this literary genre known to us and he was followed by other writers, whose work was the basis for the creation in the late empire of the *Historia Augusta*, a collection of imperial biographies whose authorship and reliability are much disputed.

The core of Suetonius' work is the raw material of a Roman epitaph or funeral oration—the public record of an Emperor, his exploits at home and abroad, and the moral qualities revealed by these. Set against the official career is his private life. The domestic virtues of an Emperor had become a topic for panegyric by the time of the Younger Pliny. But there was much more scope there for detraction. Certainly, an Emperor was criticized for military failure, the waste of public money, and brutality towards the rest of the upper class (Suetonius did not on the whole judge the administrative reforms he recorded). Yet public faults could best be exploited as the result of the personal inadequacies of the Emperor, and his vices were revealed in his home, especially in his dining-room and bedroom. So we find in Suetonius catalogues of achievements placed side by side with scandalous descriptions of the Emperor's more intimate life, both copiously illustrated by anecdotes. In spite of the fact that these two elements are rarely well fused, an effective, though not necessarily accurate, character portrait often results.

Suetonius may be compared with a Greek contemporary of Tacitus, Plutarch of Chaeronea, the greatest biographer of antiquity (below, pp. 667 ff.). Most of Plutarch's biographies took the form of parallel lives, in which an eminent Greek was compared with an eminent Roman of the Republic. These were intended as character portraits (Plutarch specifically compares his work to both sculpture and painting), in which small faults were to be toned down without being completely omitted, in order that the requirements of truth should be fulfilled but the reader should not be distracted from the general outline of the man. To this end Plutarch did not simply recount the lives of his subjects from birth to death, but included general descriptions of their behaviour in certain contexts (it is here especially that, like Suetonius, he introduces anecdotes). The men are described and compared in terms of ethical concepts derived from Platonic and Aristotelian philosophy. Men should be brave, but not rash; modest, and not insolent in success; moderate and scrupulous in their use of wealth; and they should control the passions of their subordinates while not being themselves swept away by passion. The biographies seek to show the relative success or failure of great men in living up to such precepts. Compared with this, Roman biography is ethically crude. The values of the Roman historians had arisen not so much from a view of the good man, but from a view of the success of Rome, and utility to Rome was a narrow foundation on which to base judgements on personality.

Why did the flow of Roman history dry up after Tacitus? It is significant that the next great history of Rome was written in Greek by a Roman senator of Greek origins, Cassius Dio from Bithynia. This was a universal history of Rome up to the time of writing (the early third century AD), which was intended to emulate Thucydides' work in its explanations and political generalizations. By contrast, Roman explanations of their political history (in spite of Polybius' example) had rarely gone beyond the simplistic in political terms. Thus, once the history of a period had been eloquently written by a Livy or Tacitus there was little call to rewrite it. Since the Empire and the Principate were consolidated and apparently unlikely to change, the lives of the Emperors might be written as a series of appendices to a story already well told. Later, in the fourth century, a Syrian from Antioch, Ammianus Marcellinus, tried to make a new start by writing in Latin on the period from the end of Tacitus' work to his own day. The usual material is to be found there—wars, geographic and ethnographic descriptions, trials, seditions in Rome and other cities, and, not least, digressions on morals. Yet, in spite of the vivid and sensational presentation, little is said to explain the crises of the fourth century and the changes in society. This is perhaps one reason why the Roman upper class had abandoned writing history in the traditional fashion. They could find nothing new to say within the old framework.

Further Reading

English translations exist of most surviving historical works mentioned in this chapter; there is, however, no translation of the fragments of Roman historians. Apart from the translations facing texts in the Loeb Classical Library, the most complete range is now in the Penguin Classics. Especially good are those of Tacitus' *Annals* (M. Grant) and *Histories* (K. Wellesley), Sallust, Caesar (S. A. Handford), and Polybius (I. Scott-Kilvert), although this contains little of Polybius dealing with events after the Second Punic War. The best translation of Polybius is by E. S. Shuckburgh (2 vols., 1889/1962). Major translations of Tacitus include those of A. J. Church and J. Brodribb (London, 1882) and W. Fyfe (Oxford, 1912).

A general survey is provided by M. L. W. Laistner, *The Greater Roman Historians* (California, 1963). There are also useful collections of essays, *Latin Historians* and *Latin Biography* (ed. T. A. Dorey, London, 1966 and 1967), which contain chapters on Polybius and Plutarch respectively as well as on writers in Latin. A. Momigliano, *Essays in Ancient and Modern Historiography* (Oxford, 1977), especially chs. 4, 5, and 7, is important for both the historians themselves and their place in the development of historiography.

On *Early Historians* see E. Badian's chapter in *Latin Historians* (above) and Momigliano (above); for a more controversial study of early Roman records B. W. Frier, *Libri Annales Pontificum Maximorum. The Origins of the Annalistic Tradition* (Rome, 1979).

Polybius has been studied above all by F. W. Walbank. See his *Polybius* (California, 1972); also the introduction to *A Historical Commentary on Polybius*, vol. i. (Oxford, 1957). For Polybius' views of the historian's function see K. Sacks, *Polybius and the Writing of History* (California, 1981).

The best introduction to *Sallust* is D. C. Earl, *The Political Thought of Sallust* (Cambridge, 1961; Amsterdam, 1966). R. Syme, *Sallust* (Oxford, 1964), is a more detailed and wide-ranging investigation.

Caesar has been treated by F. E. Adcock, *Caesar as a Man of Letters* (Cambridge, 1956). P. G. Walsh, *Livy* (Cambridge, 1961), provides a concise and valuable general study of that author. Also useful is the introduction in R. M. Ogilvie, *A Commentary on Livy I–V* (Oxford, 1965).

R. Syme, *Tacitus* (2 vols., Oxford, 1958), is the major work in English on that historian. R. Martin, *Tacitus* (London, 1981), is a simpler work full of good sense. The introduction in H. Furneaux, *The Annals of Tacitus*, vol. i (Oxford, 1884), is also useful. B. Walker, *The Annals of Tacitus* (Cambridge, 1952, 1960), seeks to distinguish the factual and non-factual elements in the work. See also the collection of essays in *Tacitus*, ed. T. A. Dorey (London, 1969), and K. C. Schellhase, *Tacitus in Renaissance Political Thought* (Chicago, 1976).

On biography see A. Wallace-Hadrill, *Suetonius* (London, 1983); D. A. Russell, *Plutarch* (London, 1972); C. P. Jones, *Plutarch and Rome* (Oxford, 1971).

Other developments in imperial history and biography are most easily appreciated from reading *Latin Historians* and *Latin Biography* (above).

27

The Arts of Prose
The Early Empire

❧

DONALD RUSSELL

Two Languages, One Literature

THE first two centuries of the Christian era produced an extensive and important prose literature, both in Greek and in Latin. Though the greatest genius, Tacitus, was a Roman whose ways of thinking seem peculiarly difficult to express in Greek, the two languages were in many respects vehicles of a single literature, and the Greek contribution is arguably the more significant of the two.

Not that Greek and Latin were at all on an equal footing. Native Greek speakers seldom troubled to learn Latin, except for the purposes of official life, and they seem to have found its nuances hard to grasp. 'Longinus' (*On Sublimity* 12.4) wisely asks indulgence for trying to judge Cicero; Plutarch (*Demosthenes* 3) disclaims the ability to do so, and clearly had a struggle with his Latin. It was natural that there should be a steady demand for Greek books giving information on Roman subjects: Dionysius of Halicarnassus' *Roman Antiquities*, Plutarch's Roman *Lives*, Appian's *Wars of the Romans* catered for the need, which increased as the period advanced and more and more Greek speakers sought positions of influence in imperial administration and politics. Thus by the end of the second century Latin historiography has dried up, but Herodian and the much more competent Cassius Dio attest the vigour of Greek. Latin speakers, on the other hand, if they were destined for official position or literary education (and the two were always closely linked), learned Greek from childhood, and often preferred it, especially for philosophical or scientific purposes, to their native tongue. It is in no way surprising that the Emperor Marcus Aurelius wrote *To Himself* in Greek, nor that Pliny's friend Corellius Rufus announced his resolution to take his own life with the Greek word *Kekrika*, 'I have decided'. At the same time, there is an extensive literature conveying Greek learning and philosophy to a Latin public, pursuing the Ciceronian and Augustan ideal of making Latin literature a complete and self-contained expression of Graeco-Roman culture. Celsus' encyclopedia, Quintus Curtius' *Alexander*, Pliny's *Natural History* are examples of this.

But what was common to the two languages is more important than this difference. Both were self-consciously literary languages, diverging considerably from the spoken tongue. The difference was sharper in Greek. From the Augustan period onwards—indeed earlier—teachers of Greek grammar and rhetoric inculcated an ever closer approach to the precise linguistic and grammatical forms attested by the Attic classics of the fifth and fourth centuries BC, especially Thucydides, Xenophon, and the orators. This movement reached a high point in the middle of the second century, when the marvellous archaizing pastiches produced by great 'sophists' won the applause of packed theatres and the admiring patronage of Emperors. In Latin, the chronological perspectives were different. Latin literature had only recently reached what was quickly recognized as its classical maturity. Prose style had continued to develop naturally after Cicero, partly in reaction against the norms of sentence structure and decorum which he had tried to establish. This reaction lasted about a century, until Quintilian tried to reverse it. It was not till the Antonine period (AD 97–180) that the trickle of prose archaizers (*antiquarii*) became a flood, and something rather like Greek 'Atticism' developed. Before this happened, there had been much enrichment and experimentation; but the sources of this, it is important to notice, lay much more in poetry and in the devices of older Greek rhetoric than in the resources of everyday Latin speech. These remained largely untapped, though educated speech is clearly echoed in parts of Seneca, and Petronius (below, pp. 689 ff.) went so far as to make some of the characters in his comic novel speak the incorrect language of the uneducated: a unique experiment, so far as we know, whether in Latin or in Greek.

The salient point is that almost all the works of significance, in both languages, are written in what Eduard Norden, the scholar who has contributed most to our understanding of these matters, called *Kunstprosa*, 'prose of art' or 'formal prose', the product of assiduous teaching and imitation. The main mark of *Kunstprosa*, both in Greek and in Latin, is its dependence on deliberate choice made in advance by the writer for the particular task before him. He has to determine what is the appropriate stylistic level (*genus dicendi* or—in Greek—*charaktēr*) for the job; a common classification distinguished 'grand', 'middle', and 'delicate' styles, but this was by no means the only categorization that was possible. In any case, there was a choice to be made in vocabulary, and this was very much determined by literary precedent and association; there was also a choice of sentence-structure, between the long and elaborately organized 'periodic' sentence and a more simple pattern; and, most striking to the modern reader, there was the choice of rhythm. Some regularity in the quantitative pattern of sentence endings (*clausulae* in Latin) is to be seen in classical Greek prose; but it seems to have been the Hellenistic rhetors and their Roman pupils who systematized and enforced practices which had become second nature to writers of our period. Most Roman historians and

VITRUVIUS AND POMPEII: Vitruvius' prose treatise on architecture (*c*.28–23 BC) has proved an important manual for modern students. He describes one of the favourite techniques for good-quality domestic architecture (*opus reticulatum*) as 'charming' but he comments also on the danger of cracks along the joints. The technique, illustrated here at Pompeii, is essentially a wall of mortared rubble, but with an attractive surface provided by a network of little pyramidal blocks set point inwards. On Vitruvius see also p. 772.

some Greek sophists do, it is true, break all known rules; but this is itself an act of choice, dictated by the genre. Tacitus has regular Ciceronian 'clausulation' in his *Dialogue*, but not in his historical works. Quintilian (9. 15. 18) rationalizes this traditional preference—probably based on observation of Thucydides—by alleging that the speed of historical narrative makes the pauses marked by rhythmical *clausulae* inappropriate, because they slow the whole movement down.

Kunstprosa had already had a long history. Developed by the fifth- and fourth-century Greek sophists and orators, partly to give prose something of the dignity and affective power of poetry, but partly also to provide an unambiguous and elegant written language (*graphikē lexis*: Aristotle was the most important theorist who discussed this), it existed, in our period, in many different forms, and was a versatile and many-sided instrument. It was the vehicle, not only of the higher ranges of literature—history, oratory, *belles-lettres*—but of a great deal of technical and didactic writing. Dionysius' *The Arrangement of Words*, 'Longi-nus' *On Sublimity*, and Onasander's *The General*, are good Greek examples, all of the first century; Celsus' encyclopedia (of which the medical books alone survive), Columella's treatise on farming, and Quintilian's manual of oratory are Latin ones of the same epoch. There are, however, works from which the signs of formality are absent, and which seem much less 'literary': Vitruvius' *Architecture* in Latin and Arrian's *Discourses of Epictetus* in Greek are notable instances.

This lack of formality was itself often deliberate. Arrian wrote his *Expedition of Alexander* in Xenophon's Attic dialect, and his book on India in Herodotus' Ionic; so it was with the same deliberate selection of medium that he set down the discussions of the slave-philosopher Epictetus in the first-century technical language in which such things were actually expressed.

Critics and Rhetoric: The Sense of Decline

A literature with such exacting formal standards and so closely linked with education was bound to be self-conscious and self-critical. It is no wonder that this was the great age of literary criticism, though not, strictly speaking, of literary theory. In particular, the progress and decline of letters were anxiously monitored. Some saw improvement, more saw decline. This was a conventional pessimism, a literary application of the idea, which is as old as Homer and Hesiod, that men are 'not what they were'. Often a convenient mode of polemic, it is not therefore necessarily insincere.

Dionysius of Halicarnassus arrived in Rome very soon after Octavian's victory at Actium (31 BC). He settled there for a career which included rhetorical teaching, literary criticism, and the composition of an elaborate history of early Rome. In the preface to his series of studies on the Attic orators, he sets out the achievement of his age as he sees it. There have been great changes. The 'old philosophic rhetoric'—which embraces the Attic orators down to Demosthenes—was displaced 'after the death of Alexander the Macedonian' by an 'ill-bred' substitute, a new immigrant from some Asiatic hell-hole; but this vulgar and abandoned upstart has miraculously been put in her place by a revival of classical standards, the result of the good taste of the educated Roman governing class. This is a polemical picture, but it makes important points. The new mandarin prose is the expression of a rhetoric which is not just a bag of tricks, a technique of fallacious advocacy and intellectual blackmail, but 'philosophical rhetoric' (*philosophos rhētorikē*), a proper moral and social formation for an age of good government. Essentially, this was the ideal of Isocrates, 350 years earlier, restated for a larger world.

The three stages of development presupposed by Dionysius' account—acme of perfection, degeneration, and revival—are a familiar pattern in Greek theoretical accounts of literary and artistic history. It was at first not easy for the Romans to adapt this scheme to the circumstances of their own development. When Horace, Dionysius' contemporary, glories in the Augustan poetic achievement, his pride is in the techniques that have superseded the immaturity and imperfections of the past, not in the displacement of a corrupt or degenerate fashion. But it is not long before the pattern appears. In oratory, the Ciceronian age was seen to be the acme, corresponding to the period of Demosthenes. Everything that followed was a decline. The Elder Seneca, writing under Tiberius or Caligula, is an early witness to the discussion of corruption and decline which is prominent in first-century speculation. He gave weight to three causes of deterioration: a political cause, the loss of republican liberty; a moral cause, the idleness and indiscipline of sensation-seeking youth; and finally the mere malevolence of the natural order which lets nothing stay at the peak of its development. His son, the philosopher Seneca, urged the moralists' view. Style, he thought, reflects a way of life, both in the individual and in the society: 'Where you see *oratio corrupta* give pleasure, you may be sure that morals also have strayed from the right path' (*Epistles* 114. 11). He wrote this in AD 62. A generation later, he himself is pilloried in the Roman replay of a sort of Dionysian classicism, initiated by the great teacher Quintilian (*c.*AD 35-100), in whose eyes the very charm of Seneca's faults makes him a particularly pernicious model. From Quintilian's point of view, this is not unjust. Seneca's short sentences, unselective vocabulary, and jaunty fluency make him the type of a Latinity radically opposed to Ciceronian dignity and decorum. But Seneca too, we must not forget, writes *Kunstprosa*; in no writer is the beat of the *clausulae* more insistent.

Quintilian's important *Institutio Oratoria*, in twelve books, describes the education and training of the orator in greater detail than any other ancient work. It insists on morality as the basis of oratory, and it is especially interesting on education. He also wrote a book, now lost, on the causes of 'corruption' in style, doubtless a statement of his programme. Tacitus' *Dialogue on Orators*, the dramatic date of which is AD 73 though it was probably written nearly thirty years later, is concerned to state both 'conservative' and 'modernist' points of view. Another statement of the problem is in Greek, in the last chapter of 'Longinus', *On Sublimity* (*Peri hypsous*). This little book is a detailed discussion of the means by which grand, solemn, and emotionally powerful effects may be obtained in literature. It is the most stimulating of ancient critical works, as well as one of the most influential. Some uncertainty about its date must be admitted. It is transmitted as the work of a famous third-century scholar and statesman; but this attribution is widely disbelieved, and with reason, for the links with first-century speculation and interests are unmistakable. 'Longinus' represents 'a philosopher' as advocating the view that the inferiority of contemporary oratory is due to loss of liberty and of 'democracy', but he himself, though rhetorician by trade and not philosopher, very pointedly takes the more moral line: it is the war of the passions and the corruption of the heart that inhibit the creation of great thoughts. It is difficult to cash these statements in terms of a specific historical situation. In a Greek context, *On Sublimity*, taken as a whole, makes sense as a reaction against Hellenistic extravagance and frivolity. Indeed, it seems a more sophisticated and profound reaction than Dionysius' frigid classical revival, because 'Longinus' puts the primary emphasis on the importance of emotional impact in oratory and in literature generally, and the thrust of his argument is to show how this is involved with high thinking and moral ideals. He thus makes a contrast between classical Greek literature, in which all the worth-while models are to be found, and the rhetors and sophists of his own degenerate day, whose only chance of salvation lies in a supreme moral and imaginative effort.

In the closing chapter, however, the perspective seems rather to be Roman. The 'philosopher's' view that high oratory has been destroyed by loss of freedom seems to reflect the transition from Republic to Principate. The author's 'reply' to this then takes the debate away from political revolutions to personal ethics, but makes the point, clearly directed against his imagined opponent, that 'people like us' are perhaps better under control, lest our greed ruin the world. The combination of Greek and Roman perspectives is confusing, but typical of this bilingual culture.

The Uses of Formal Prose

The carefully fostered, and minutely monitored, arts of prose were used in this period for a wide range of purposes.

First, and most importantly, for history, as the preceding chapter has explained.

Secondly, for oratory. This was of course the original primary function; but critics such as 'Longinus' were clearly right in their perception that the age no longer offered political rewards for the orator. The great trials and debates in which Cicero's contemporaries had re-enacted the dramas of the Demosthenic age were in the past; imperial *causes célèbres* were less earth-shaking. First-century Roman oratory anyway is lost to us; we do not know how significant or innovative it was, and the classicizing revival at the end of the century caused a change of taste which consigned it to oblivion. We do, however, have two important dated works from the second century: Pliny's *Panegyricus* (102) and Apuleius' *Apologia* (157/8: below, pp. 692 ff.) The 'panegyric', spoken by Pliny as consul in the Senate before Trajan, shows what Quintilian's Ciceronianism, with a strong element of 'silver' ingenuity and point, could achieve in the 'epideictic' or ceremonial mode. The 'apology', in which Apuleius defends himself on a charge of using magic to secure the affections of a wealthy widow, shows forensic oratory turning into pure literature, a vehicle for verbal virtuosity, frivolous erudition, and emotive rhetoric. Pliny is of course inspired by the values of Roman public life, and Apuleius is steeped in old Latin learning; but they both exemplify here a Greek phenomenon, the use of rhetoric for entertainment, the typical activity of the 'sophists' of the age.

The history of oratory throughout this period is in fact much more a Greek than a Latin theme. Dio Chrysostom—that is, 'the golden-mouthed'—a leading citizen of Prusa in Bithynia, orator and moralist, harangued the citizens of Rhodes and Alexandria, calming passions and rebuking folly, around the end of the first century AD. Polemo of Laodicea, Favorinus of Arles, Herodes Atticus, and many others went on embassies, pleaded cases, taught pupils, and entertained multitudes with their ingenious historical or grimly comic fantasies, all in the Greek of Demosthenes or some other early classic. This period, with its celebrated travelling virtuoso orators, is often called the 'Second Sophistic': the great speakers were idolized like pop-stars. In the sight of posterity it has often seemed a vanity; in its time, it was a literary and social movement of great influence and significance.

A third use of *Kunstprosa* breaks new ground. This is the age in which what may be called the 'essay' flourished as a recognizable, though unnamed, literary form. Very many of the works of Seneca, Dio, Lucian, and Plutarch are best so described. They are short discourses, often dealing with ethical questions, but sometimes with literature or education or some antiquarian matter. They are, as a rule, very personal in tone, in the sense that the *persona* of the writer is prominent, though they admit also much allusive learning and literary elaboration. In style, they tend to the less periodic. Several traditions went to the making of this class of writing. One was that of the philosophical dialogue, not in the form Plato generally preferred, but in that used by Aristotle, with long speeches instead of sharp question and answer. The dialogue continued to be written throughout our period—Cicero, Tacitus, and Plutarch were notable practitioners—but its techniques and even its name (*dialogus*) were also applied to works in which the element of conversation was not present. Another ancestor was the less polished popular sermon or moral address—'diatribe' is the modern scholars' word—which seems to have flourished in Hellenistic times, and is especially associated with the Cynics. Bion of Borysthenes, acknowledged by Horace as an exemplar for his satire, certainly contributed to the technique of imagery and anecdote which Seneca and Plutarch deployed with such lavishness and enthusiasm. Though these urbane essays were, for the most part, philosophical in tone and content, this does not mean that they did not sometimes come within the province of the rhetorician. Philosophical *theses*—'on providence', 'on marriage', and the like—were an established part of the elementary rhetorical curriculum. Moreover, the popularity of the casual-sounding address led the teachers of rhetoric to lay down precepts for it much as they did for formal speeches; they called it *lalia*, 'chat', and prescribed simple style, an anecdote or simile to capture attention at the start, and studied concealment of rhetorical and logical structure.

Barely separable from the 'essay' is the letter (the fourth use), for the 'essay' is often cast in epistolary form. The letter was, however, a recognized genre, for which we have intelligent and careful instructions in the treatise of Demetrius *On Style*, probably to be dated around the beginning of our period. Artemon, who had published the letters of Aristotle, had said that the letter was 'one side of a dialogue'. Demetrius (223 ff.) disagrees: the dialogue-writer imitates an extempore speech, the letter is 'sent as a gift' and one must pay the recipient the compliment of care and art. The central consideration is that a letter is 'the image of one's mind'; more than any other kind of writing, it presents its author's personality. So it must not be too technical—'a treatise with an address at the top'—nor periodic in style like a forensic speech. In a word, it is 'a brief expression of affection, an exposition of a simple theme in simple words'.

RECONSTRUCTION MODEL OF PLINY THE YOUNGER'S LAURENTINE VILLA, based upon the detailed description in one of his letters. C. Plinius Caecilius Secundus (*c.*AD 61–*c.*112) was one of the most important prose-writers of the Trajanic period, being a master both of the literary epistle and of the art of rhetoric. Like his uncle and adoptive father (the Elder Pliny), he enjoyed a distinguished career in public service.

The letter is a particularly important form in our period. Seneca used it for what is by common consent his best work, the *Epistulae morales*, written in retirement to his friend Lucilius. Epicurus' letters were an influence here; so were Cicero's letters to Atticus. Roman gentlemen recognized the letter as a form ideally suited to the amateur, an apt expression of the friendships and common interests of their class. Statius (*Silvae* 1.3. 104) imagines his friend Vopiscus, in his country retreat at Tibur, writing epic or lyric or satire—or else a letter, as highly polished as any of these. He does not make it clear whether the letter is prose or verse; it may, we must remember, be the latter, in the model of Horace's or Ovid's 'epistles'. The Younger Pliny's stylish collection of letters is one of the most elegant and informative witnesses to the culture and education of the time. It is interesting, and perhaps surprising, that we have so little comparable Greek material. We have, it is true, a mass of Greek letters dating from this period; but these are fictions, purporting to be written by imaginary characters or historical figures. They are little more than rhetorical exercises, though occasionally (as in the *Letters of Crates* and *Chion of Heraclea*) we find sets of letters composed to form something like epistolary romance.

This may remind us that the last of the areas in which *Kunstprosa* was employed is pure fiction. This was a late development, despite the partial classical model of Xenophon's *Cyropaedia*. Origins and influences are hotly debated; whether the characteristic content is of 'oriental' origin and whether the stories were used as a vehicle for religious teaching, specifically that of the mystery religions, are questions which have been repeatedly raised and variously answered over the past century. What seems certain is that the novel, not being a part of the high classical tradition, originally had a different audience in view from history or philosophy. It gradually makes its way into more sophisticated circles, sometimes viewed patronizingly and parodied, sometimes taking its place as a serious successor to epic and drama. The surviving Greek novels are surprisingly similar in plot, and it is a plot which has the suggestiveness of myth. Two lovers undergo long travels, dangers, and separations, their chastity is sorely tried, but they are ultimately united and live happily ever after. Such is the framework of the novels of Chariton, Longus, Achilles Tatius, Xenophon of Ephesus, and Heliodorus. Their tones and settings of course differ: love, magic, violence, humour, the curiosities of distant countries and remote historical times, the rhetoric of trials and debates, are standard ingredients, present in varied degree. Most charming to modern readers is the pastoral romance of Longus, *Daphnis and Chloe*; most divergent from the common pattern are the two Latin examples, Petronius' *Satyrica* and Apuleius' *Metamorphoses*. The novel is, in many ways, the most intriguing literary achievement of the period; it looks forward to mediaeval romance, and it is one of the roots of modern prose fiction. But it is an escapist form; set in the past or at the ends of the earth, its fictions generally portray the human condition with the minimum of reference to the social and political structures within which its readers lived.

Seneca: Father and Son

The remains of this literature fill many volumes. Many of the Greek authors—Plutarch, Lucian, Aristides—were morally and stylistically ideal texts for Byzantine education, and their survival was assured. The Latins were less lucky. Though Pliny's *Natural History* and Seneca were much read in the medieval West, Tacitus survived by a singular accident, and much important historical writing has been lost. But, in both languages, there is a lot to read; and we must confine ourselves here to a brief indication of the qualities of some of the principal figures.

Given the association between education and power, literary success and political activity, it is no wonder that families figure largely in the story. A good example is the family of the Annaei, from Corduba in Spain, who held a high place in both literary and public life for three generations. L. Annaeus Seneca, 'the Elder', was born around the middle of the first century BC, studied at Rome in the triumviral and early Augustan period, and then divided his time between Rome and his native place. Like many writers of the time (Livy, Caecilius of

Caleacte, Dionysius) he was both historian and rhetorician, though he was not a professional teacher of rhetoric. Late in life, he compiled for his three sons a collection of the brilliant rhetorical strokes he remembered from the 'declaimers' of his youth. His enthusiastic anthology has much charm. The prefaces and character sketches especially display an attractive shrewdness. I cite as a specimen a piece from the 'deliberative exercises' (*Suasoriae* 2. 17), in which he speaks of a connection of his own who made a fool of himself by his handling of the hackneyed theme of the Three Hundred Spartans at Thermopylae:

There was a person called Seneca—his name may have reached your ears—of a confused and disorderly cast of mind, who wanted to speak in the big style. In the end, this weakness obsessed him and made him ridiculous. He wouldn't have slaves unless they were big, or silver vessels unless they were big. Believe me, I'm not joking. His madness led him ultimately to wear shoes that were too big for him, to eat no figs except *mariscae* [these had a poor flavour, despite their size], and to have a mistress of vast proportions. He was nicknamed Seneca Grandio. Well, when I was a young man, he gave a version of this exercise. He posed the objection: 'All who had been sent from Greece ran away.' To answer it, he raised his hands, and stood on tip-toe (he used to do this, to seem bigger) and cried: 'I rejoice, I rejoice!' We wondered what piece of luck had come his way. 'Xerxes will be entirely mine', he cried.

L. ANNAEUS SENECA the Younger (*c.*4 BC–AD 65). Born at Corduba in Spain, he uneasily combined the roles of a wealthy money-lender, imperial tutor and minister, and Stoic philosopher. His fame as a philosopher accounts for this portrait-bust being set back to back with one of Socrates.

PONT DU GARD, near Nîmes (late first century BC). This gigantic aqueduct bridge bears witness to the engineering skills of the Romans and to their ability to endow functional architecture with nobility of form.

DETAIL OF THE CANOPUS in Hadrian's Villa at Tivoli (between AD 124 and 133). As often with Roman villas, parts of the emperor's country retreat were named after famous sites and monuments of the East, in this case a suburb of Alexandria.

HEAD OF AUTUMN: detail of a mosaic at Cirencester, Gloucestershire (late second century AD). The Four Seasons were a popular subject in mosaic pavements and painted ceilings, since one could be placed at each corner. Here Autumn is characterized by the grapes in her hair and a pruning knife above her shoulder.

That is to say, speaking in the role of a Spartan at Thermopylae, he welcomed the absence of reinforcements, on the ground that he would be able to fight Xerxes and his million men single-handed. Of the three sons to whom Seneca's anthology is addressed, one (Mela) was the father of the poet Lucan, one (Novatus) was adopted by Junius Gallio and appears in history as the proconsul of Achaea at the time of St Paul's stay in Corinth (Acts 18: 12), and the middle son, another L. Annaeus Seneca, became without question the leading literary figure of his generation, as well as a man of great wealth and influence, especially in the early years of Nero, whose tutor he was.

Growing up in the early years of Tiberius (*Epist.* 108. 22), the younger Seneca was much attracted by philosophy, especially the more ascetic kind. He became a vegetarian, influenced by Pythagorean ideas, and only desisted in deference to his father, who feared that such eccentricity would earn a black mark from people who mattered: it was one of the times when 'foreign superstitions' were under governmental attack. Seneca was in any case no rebel. His ambitions soared high. He was prominent enough to be exiled for a court intrigue under Claudius, but was recalled, and was continuously in a position of influence from about AD 49 to AD 62. He then fell from grace, and spent the last three years of his life in study and writing: a retirement not unlike Cicero's, and perhaps modelled on it. His tragedies are discussed in Chapter 28. His surviving prose works (some interesting pieces are only known indirectly) include 'consolations'—notably that to his mother Helvia on his own exile—and a number of 'essays' on moral themes, some short, some (*On Anger, On Benefits, On Clemency*) elaborate treatises in several books. In his retirement he embarked on grander schemes: *Natural Questions*, a rhetorically elaborate account of current theories about winds, earthquakes, lightning, and similar phenomena; and a comprehensive study of ethics from the Stoic point of view, never executed, but reflected in many of the *Moral Letters*, which he addressed to his friend Lucilius and which are his most popular and readable work. When Macaulay said that reading Seneca was like dining on nothing but anchovy sauce, he expressed something of the pleasure in witty detail and the dissatisfaction with the whole that most readers experience; it is the smaller scale and more intimate tone of the *Letters* that saves them from the worst effects of Seneca's incontinent ingenuity. So repetitive a writer seems made for the anthologist; and I cite two passages from which his manner may perhaps be judged.

In the first (*Tranquillity of Mind* 12–13) he adapts a theme from the end of the third book of Lucretius, on restlessness of soul; Stoic though he is, he has no compunction about using the common stock of philosophic moralizing, even if it is of Epicurean origin. What he implies about taste in scenery in this passage is of interest; so is his incidental attack at the end on the cruel fashion for gladiatorial shows.

Some things give the body pleasure and pain at once, like turning over before one side is tired, or tossing in one position after another. Thus Achilles in Homer, now on his face, now on his back, makes himself comfortable in different ways. This is what sick people do, who cannot endure anything long and use change as medicine. Hence futile travels and coastal excursions. The inconsistency that hates whatever is at hand experiments with the sea one moment, with the country the next. 'Let's go to Campania.' Pretty scenery is a bore. 'Let's go to a wild place, let's head for the mountains of Bruttium (the Abruzzi) and Lucania.' But in the wilderness some softer charms are wanted, something to relieve an eye sated with the grimness of a savage land. 'Let's make for Tarentum, the harbour everyone admires, the mild winter resort, the countryside that kept even its ancient population in affluence.' 'Now back to town!' It is too long since he heard the applause and the uproar. Now he wants the pleasure of human blood!

Secondly, one of the shorter *Letters* (60). The theme is the vanity of human desire and the narrowness of our real needs. The technique is very characteristic: exclamations, rhetorical questions, allusion to a classic (here Sallust), examples from the animal kingdom, personification of Nature, and a striking epigram at the end.

I've a grievance, I'm taking you to court, I'm angry. Do you still wish for what your nurse and your tutor and your mother wished for on your behalf? Don't you understand how much harm they wished for? How true it is that our friends' prayers are our enemies! All the more so if they have been fulfilled. I no longer find it surprising if all our troubles stay with us from childhood; we grew up amid our parents' curses. Perhaps one day the gods may hear a disinterested prayer from us! How long shall we go on asking them for something, as though we could not yet feed ourselves? How long shall we go on filling the territories of vast cities with our crops? How long shall a whole nation harvest them for us? How long will all those ships from many a sea supply the service of one man's table? The bull contents himself with a few acres' pasture; a single forest feeds many elephants; does one man need earth and sea to nourish him? Has Nature, having given us so modest a physique, then endowed us with a belly so insatiable that we surpass the greed of the hugest and hungriest of beasts? Indeed not. How small a quantity it is that is given to Nature! She is cheaply dismissed; it is not our belly's hunger that costs dear, but our pride. So let us count 'the belly's obedient servants', as Sallust calls them, as beasts, not men—and some not even live beasts, but dead creatures! A man who is of use to many is alive. A man who uses himself is alive. But for those who hide away in torpor, home is no better than a tomb. You might as well inscribe on marble at their door 'They predeceased their death.'

Pliny: Uncle and Nephew

The Annaei suggest a comparison with a rather later literary family, the Plinii. The earlier man of note is C. Plinius Secundus, 'the Elder Pliny', born about AD 23. He had a distinguished military and administrative career as an *eques*, serving in Germany under Claudius and Nero, but then retiring to a more private life until his friendship with Titus and Mucianus assured a succession of procuratorships under Vespasian. He died, as commander of the fleet at Misenum, in the eruption of Vesuvius in AD 79. He was curious to observe it, and went too far.

Pliny was not only an active official but a tireless student and writer. He wrote a history of the German wars in which he had served, a narrative history of Rome from AD 47 to AD 70, and a life of one of his commanding officers, the literary man Pomponius Secundus. All this is lost. What survives is a *Natural History*, in thirty-seven books, an encyclopedia of knowledge of the universe, the earth, man, animals, and plants, with large sections also on medicines and on the visual arts. It was a prime source of belief about the universe in the Latin Middle Ages and later, 'an immense register', as Edward Gibbon put it, of 'the discoveries, the arts, and the errors of mankind'.

Pliny's stylistic ambitions were not matched by competence or taste. He does not appear to have mastered either the periodic elegance in which, for example, Columella and Celsus wrote successfully on technical themes, or the staccato Senecan lucidity, which Seneca himself had used impressively for science. But he aims high; and, though a torment to translators, he has often tempted them, not only for his content but for a certain richness of language, especially in his many moralizing digressions and exclamations. His summary of Augustus' career (7.147 ff.) reveals a talent for satire, and the syntax of Mr. Jingle:

In Divine Augustus ... if all things were judged carefully many volumes of human destiny might be found; defeat in his uncle's time for the Mastership of the Horse; preference given to Lepidus over his candidature; unpopularity from the proscriptions; participation in the triumvirate with the most evil men—and in no equal share at that, but dominated by Antony; illness at Philippi, flight, three days' hiding in the marsh, ill and (according to Agrippa and Maecenas) swollen with subcutaneous water; Sicilian shipwreck; another concealment, this time in a cave; plea for death made to Proculeius in the rout at sea, with the enemy fleet hard upon him; anxiety in the Perugian war; mutinies; dangerous illnesses; suspicion of Marcellus' intentions; shocking exile of Agrippa; all the plots against his life; accusations about his children's deaths; mourning whose sadness was not due simply to bereavement; daughter's adultery and the disclosure of her plans for parricide; his stepson Nero's rude withdrawal from court; adultery again, in his granddaughter; then a combination of evils—lack of revenue, rebellion in Illyricum, call-up of slaves, shortage of recruits, plague in Rome, famine in Italy, determination to die, four days without food, when much of death entered his body; on top of this, disaster of Varus, foul insults to dignity, Postumus Agrippa adopted, rejected, and then missed, suspicion of Fabius and his betrayal of secrets, apprehensions concerning his wife and Tiberius. This was his last anxiety. In short, this god who perhaps not only achieved heaven, but deserved it, died leaving his enemy's son as his heir.

Pliny's nephew, 'the Younger Pliny', could never have written this. A studious youth, who wrote a Greek tragedy at fourteen, he describes himself, at the age of about eighteen, quietly reading Livy during the great eruption that killed his uncle. The boy was a pupil of Quintilian and of a noted Greek rhetor Nicetes Sacerdos. He went on to have a distinguished senatorial career, culminating in a consulship under Trajan in AD 100, the honorific and important *cura* of the Tiber river-works and urban drainage system, and finally the governorship of Bithynia. His most famous work, his *Letters*, to some extent reflects his public life, especially

STATUE-GROUP OF LAOCÖON AND HIS SONS (*c.* AD 10–30), one of the few works of art described in Pliny the Elder's *Natural History* to have survived. It was discovered in 1506 near the Golden House of Nero, where Pliny appears to have seen it. He describes it as 'a work superior to all paintings and sculptures.'

his and others' advocacy in the courts. But it is more a demonstration of what should be a cultured man's interests and values than an image of an individual achievement or personality. The letters have great elegance and finish. There are certain links with Greek rhetoric. In the formal descriptions (*ecphrases*), the reports of wonders of nature, and the technique of anecdote, we recognize the skills of Greek sophists such as Lucian. The general effect however is essentially Roman. Pliny depicts, no doubt in an idealized form, the style of public duty and literary taste that his generation felt to be its own. Literary prestige is important to him. He writes to Tacitus (7.20) that he has read and commented on his book—it is probably a part of the *Histories*, just possibly the *Dialogue*—and hopes for the like service in return, such being the traditional function of Roman 'friendship' (*amicitia*) when the parties are men of letters. He is pleased with the thought:

How it delights me that, if posterity cares at all, it will always be told in what harmony, sincerity and loyalty you and I lived! It will be a rare and notable thing that two men, near equals in age and position, and of some repute in letters—for I must needs speak sparingly of you when I am also speaking of myself!—encouraged each other's studies.

Plutarch

Among Pliny's contemporaries, and sharing some of his acquaintance, was the most important Greek writer of the age. L. Mestrius Plutarchus—to give him his names as a Roman citizen (he was in fact of equestrian status)—was from mainland Greece. His was the leading family of the historic, but decayed, town of Chaeronea in Boeotia. The past of his native district was particularly real to him: he defends the ancient Thebans against Herodotus' innuendos and accusations, and he sets up Epaminondas as an ideal of the philosopher statesman. But it was not enough to record the past, for there was a present revival to be fostered. Plutarch chose to teach his pupils philosophy at Chaeronea, he served the city whenever he could, and he worked hard for the restoration of the oracle and shrine at neighbouring Delphi, which enjoyed imperial patronage under Domitian and his successors. But for books and learned conversation—other than what he could gather around him at home—Plutarch had to visit Athens, where he learned his Platonist philosophy and enjoyed the company of the wise and the rich. Towards the end of his life, under Trajan and Hadrian, a happy age for many literary men, he received signal honours, notably the insignia of a consul (*ornamenta consularia*, a great distinction for an *eques*) and a post as procurator of Greece, nominally in charge of all imperial properties in the province. In later times it was well if a philosopher or scholar could claim descent from him; some did so even in the fourth century. This reputation was built on two foundations: personal charm and wisdom, and an immense activity of writing. Plutarch was not the man to command audiences like the great histrionic sophists of the age, nor did he wield any real political influence. His massive but superficial learning and his generous and unpedantic style served to project a conspicuously—some would say self-righteously—humane personality. We possess about half of what he wrote. He was popular in Byzantine times, but this was all that the thirteenth-century scholars managed to collect. All the same, it fills a dozen volumes. It falls into two parts: the great unified effort of the *Parallel Lives* and the seventy or so surviving miscellaneous works—mainly 'essays' and dialogues—which are usually called the *Moralia*.

The *Parallel Lives* were dedicated to Q. Sosius Senecio, an acquaintance of Pliny, and a great man—four times consul—of Trajan's reign. The plan was open-ended. Each book contained the lives of a Greek and a Roman whose careers had something in common: wisdom as lawgivers, courage, perseverance, eloquence, a period of exile, or a great fortune. Formal comparisons usually followed. The result was a presentation of classical history that, more than any other, created the Renaissance image of antiquity. Plutarch's purposes were confessedly moral. He sought to expound the virtues and vices of his great men and show how they responded to the challenges of fortune. He was not concerned with them as historical forces, only as men of certain qualities who were placed under the stress of great events and decisions. Whether it is Theseus or Pericles, Coriolanus or Caesar, the problem is seen in the same light, and (sources allowing) the biography follows more or less the same pattern: origin and childhood, introduction into public life, the career and its points of crisis, the death and posthumous reputation. It has often been pointed out that this partly echoes a well-attested rhetorical scheme for 'encomium'—origin, nature, character, actions and virtues, accomplishments, comparison with others—and this is of course true. But the distance between Plutarch's attitudes and that of a rhetorical encomiast can hardly be exaggerated. 'Rhetors', said Cicero, 'are allowed to tell lies in history, so as to be in a position to say something clever.' This is what Plutarch never does. His respect for evidence should not be questioned, though his interpretation of it, and his view of what biographical evidence is, may excite surprise. We should not expect in him any recognition of the difference between a primary and a secondary source; and we must be willing to accept 'probability'—meaning accord with what one expects of a certain kind of person in certain kinds of circumstances—as a criterion for judging between alternative accounts of the facts. What makes the *Lives* live, however, is not their moral preoccupations, nor yet their evident concern to demonstrate the political as well as the intellectual greatness of classical Greece; it is above all Plutarch's narrative gift, his willingness to listen to his sources and his skill in choosing the telling detail. No one forgets the death of Cato at Utica, or the love of Antony and Cleopatra; and it is from Plutarch that these episodes came into the consciousness of the modern world.

Some of the *Moralia* provoke comparison with Seneca. Both men wrote on Tranquillity and on Anger, though with different philosophical outlooks and with different expectations of their readership: Plutarch is far richer in learned allusion

PAINTING OF ANTONY AND CLEOPATRA by Sir Lawrence Alma-Tadema (1885): a late-Victorian romantic view of the affair which Plutarch immortalized in his *Life* of Antony. Plutarch's influence on the Renaissance was considerable, and North's translation of the *Parallel Lives* (1579) inspired Shakespeare's play, which set the tone for the modern conception of the fatal lovers.

and quotation, and is naturally critical of Stoic views. 'Essays' such as these, and the pieces on Curiosity, Talkativeness, and False Shame have been to many the most attractive of Plutarch's works. Through the translations of Amyot and Philemon Holland they have made a strong impact on the French and English essayists, from Montaigne to Emerson. But Plutarch himself would presumably have laid the weight elsewhere, on his more substantial philosophical exegesis (below, pp. 704 f.) and controversy, and especially on a group of dialogues which he wrote, it seems, towards the end of his life. Four of these have their setting in contemporary Delphi, and explore the antiquities of the oracle and the theory of prophecy. The most elaborate of them—'On those whom God is slow to punish'—rehearses views on the nature of evil, and concludes with a myth in the Platonic manner on the fate of the soul after death. Plutarch's revival of this theme—he used it twice besides in the works we have, and notably also in the lost *On the Soul*—is remarkable. His 'Underworld' has a stellar setting, and his descriptions are full of colour, light, and vividly imagined horror.

Philosophy and myth are not, however, the only elements in his dialogues:

there is also a dramatic dimension. Thus he wrote *The Divine Sign of Socrates* with the liberation of Thebes from Spartan occupation in 379 BC as background (above, p. 148). The adventure story, told again in the life of Pelopidas, is punctuated by discussions on prophecy and the most splendid of the myths. In the *Eroticus*, again, he weaves a contemporary intrigue—a widow has enticed a younger man to marry her—into a discourse on homosexual and heterosexual love, Platonic in detail but very un-Platonic in conclusions. For all their dependence on tradition—not only Plato's *Symposium*, *Critias*, and *Phaedrus*, but a Hellenistic inheritance, now only dimly discernible—Plutarch's dialogues are works of powerful originality. More than any of the other authors we have here selected for consideration, he is a witness to the deepening religious and theological consciousness of the age. In *The Decline of the Oracles*, he portrays a Spartan called Cleombrotus, freshly arrived in Delphi from the desert shores of the Red Sea. This personage advances views on 'demons' which there is good reason to think Plutarch does not take seriously; but the description of Cleombrotus' mission in life passes well for Plutarch's own:

Fond of seeing and learning, having adequate means and not thinking it worth while to acquire more, he employed his leisure for such travels, and assembled information (*historia*) to be the material of what he himself called 'philosophy with theology as its goal'.

Not that Plutarch would wish to seek out holy men in the desert. He stayed at home, and they came to him.

Lucian

The second great Greek writer of the period was born in Plutarch's latter years, around the beginning of the reign of Hadrian.

Lucian is in many ways Plutarch's antithesis. He came, not from the old heartland of Greece, but—much more typically of the period—from the more recently Hellenized East. His home was Samosata on the Euphrates, capital of the defunct kingdom of Commagene, one of whose princes—Philopappus—had been a friend of Plutarch's at Athens. His education would be quite different from Plutarch's, and this indeed is evident from their writing. Plutarch's Greek, allusive and classicizing as it is, is a link in a continuous tradition, passing through Hellenistic writing back to classical times. Lucian's—he claims it was his second language, Syriac being the first—is pure imitation (*mimēsis*) of the classical models, fascinatingly flexible, but clearly an artificial creation. There are other contrasts too. Plutarch takes religious belief, especially men's hopes and fears for what follows death, with great and humane seriousness. For Lucian all this is mockery. The judgement of the dead, the ferryman of the souls, 'and all the Vain, Infernal Trumpery', are for him simply the setting for a rather simple form of satire; visions, ghosts, magic are the contemptible inventions of charlatans whom it is the honest man's business to expose. Again: what Plutarch tells us of his life is evidently true. We believe in his regard for his father and his grandfather, his affectionate marriage, and his sorrow at his little daughter's death. Lucian, by contrast, gives us a stylized picture which it is foolish to treat as autobiography. We are not bound to believe in the family council that apprenticed him to his sculptor uncle, or his vision of Education (*Paideia*), or his abandonment of Rhetoric for Dialogue at the age of forty. We recall that Socrates too started as a sculptor, and Ovid's vision of Elegy and Tragedy (*Amores* 3. 1) is all too similar to Lucian's. A good deal of what Lucian says about himself is no more to be trusted than the voyage to the moon that he recounts so persuasively in the first person in *True Stories*.

Even his claim to have been the first to adapt the philosophical dialogue to comic purposes is hard to sustain. To go no further back, there is something of this in Plutarch—notably in *Gryllus*, where one of Circe's new pigs converses with Odysseus—and the evidence of Varro and Horace suggests the Hellenistic model of an earlier Syrian Greek, Menippus of Gadara, held by some to be a main source of Lucian's ideas. That Menippus' writings were a significant model is doubtful. More important than any such borrowing is Lucian's relentless exploitation of the limited range of classical texts that everybody knew, and his ingenuity in using the same motifs again and again. He does indeed have his originality, and it may well be that the 'miniature dialogue', in which he excelled, is one place where we should look for it. It was in this form that he composed his dialogues of the dead, of the gods, of the nymphs and deities of the sea, and of the educated prostitutes (*hetairai*) of comedy. Like the epigram, the letter, and the apophthegm—all of which flourished in this period—the miniature dialogue is directed at a readership which finds long texts trying. It has a clear connection with the elementary rhetorical exercises of narrative, anecdote, and description, and indeed with the even more elementary game of paraphrase. Yet in Lucian's hands it has real charm. We enjoy Doris' suggestion that Polyphemus really only likes Galatea because her complexion reminds him of the milk and cream cheese in which his riches lie. We admire the *ecphrasis* of Europa and the bull as seen with the eyes of Zephyrus, the West Wind, or Zeus' pleased revelation to Ganymede of who he really is. We relish the mild salaciousness of the conversations between the innocent young prostitute and her hopeful and ambitious mother— so long, that is, as we suspend any social feelings towards the widow whose only resource is to employ her daughter in this way. Lucian is sometimes regarded almost as a socialist before his time. This is to take him much too seriously. To see virtue in the poor and wickedness in the wealthy is a standard rhetorical pose of the age. And Lucian's consistent aim is to entertain.

Many of Lucian's dialogues are enlargements of the techniques of the 'miniatures'; but we also have—among nearly eighty books which seem to be genuine— not only purely rhetorical pieces ('talks', declamations, pastiches of Herodotus), but some works with a more serious link with the intellectual life of the time. These last include a 'life' of the Cynic Demonax, and devastating, though largely fictitious, accounts of two famous religious charlatans, Alexander of Abonu-teichus, an inventor of Mystery Rites, and the cynic Peregrinus Proteus, who spectacularly burnt himself to death at Olympia in 167. But it is perhaps *True Stories*, an ancestor of science fiction, that best conveys the elegance of his imagination, the Lucianic blend of satire and fantasy that appeals to educated children of all ages. The following episode needs no explanation; its techniques of surprise are easily seen (1. 30–1).

Often, it seems, a change for the better heralds trouble. We had just two days' fair weather sailing. As the third day broke, we suddenly glimpsed against the sunrise a multitude of monsters and whales, the biggest of all being about 200 miles long. It was approaching with its mouth open, stirring up the sea, the foam breaking around it. It was displaying teeth taller than a human penis, sharp as rocks and white as ivory. We embraced one another and spoke our last farewells. Then we waited. It was upon us now, and it swallowed us up, ship and all. However, it failed to break the ship in pieces; she slid down through the gaps in the teeth into the interior. When we were inside, all was dark at first, and we could see nothing. After a while, however, the monster opened its mouth and we had sight of a high, broad area, large enough to accommodate a city of 10,000 people. In the middle, there were little fishes and many other animals, all chopped up, with ships' sails, anchors, human bones, cargoes, and, among all this, land and hills—formed, I imagine, out of the silt that had settled down. There was a wood and trees of all kinds, with vegetables growing, and they had the look of being cultivated. The circuit of the land area was 30 miles. Sea birds—gulls and halcyons—could be seen nesting in the trees.

Aelius Aristides

Neither Plutarch nor Lucian figures among the second-century 'sophists' whose lives Philostratus wrote, though both were on the fringe of the grand 'sophistic' world—Lucian indeed more closely involved. Aelius Aristides, Lucian's near contemporary, may stand as the typical Antonine sophist, wealthy, much travelled, flamboyant, egocentric. He has had little favour in modern times. Unravel his complexities—his style aimed especially at the density of thought of his models, Demosthenes and the speeches in Thucydides—and the labour seems wasted, so little is there left to grip the mind. We admire, but hardly wish to read twice, the subtle reconstructions of the political situations of 413 and 370 BC which underlie his 'Sicilian' and 'Leuctrian' declamations. It is no wonder that no complete translation of Aristides in any modern language has been attempted till recently; the magnificent scholarship of Willem Canter's Latin (1566) lay long unstudied and unappreciated. But it is all a little unjust. There are at least three claims that Aristides has on our attention. One—perhaps the best known—arises from his encomium of Rome, delivered in the summer of 144, a fine, flattering statement of the achievement of the Antonine Empire, from a grateful subject's point of view. A second rests on his achievement in extending the range of prose

COSMOLOGICAL MOSAIC AT MÉRIDA (EMERITA) IN SPAIN (mid second century AD). The imagery of the pavement has been compared with that of Aelius Aristides' encomium of Rome, delivered in 144, in which Rome is likened to a sea into which all rivers flow and the Roman Empire is equated with the inhabited world. In the mosaic personifications of the winds, seasons, rivers etc. frame a symbolic representation of the Mediterranean, and the central position was perhaps occupied by a seated figure (now missing) of Rome.

oratory to include the hymn, hitherto the prerogative of poets. He is proud of this, and not unjustly. His prose hymns to Sarapis, Athena, and Dionysus have many splendours; the hymn 'to the Aegean Sea', with its colourful vision of sea and islands, is perhaps the most attractive of all. Thirdly, Aristides is the author of a singular spiritual autobiography (*Hieroi Logoi*), the day-by-day record of the interventions of the god Asclepius in his life, as adviser and healer. Hypochondriacs are not attractive people; but the completeness of Aristides' record, his naïve vanity and credulity, and the vividness of his language (for once not elaborate, indeed hardly *Kunstprosa* at all) combine to produce a text which has claimed deserved attention from historians, psychologists, and students of the religious mind. Asclepius guided him in strange ways; here he is on a short, but stormy, voyage from Clazomenae to Phocaea, along the coast of Asia Minor (2. 12–14):

An easterly breeze got up, and, as we proceeded, a brisk east wind, which broke out in the end into a fearful gale. Up went the ship at the prow, and down at the stern. She nearly foundered. She was awash everywhere. Then she headed out to sea. Sweating and shouting from the sailors, screams from all on board—some of my friends were with me—but all I said was 'O Asclepius!' After many hazards, driven out to sea time and again when we were on the point of making port, and causing the people watching great anxiety, we finally reached land—safe and happy, but only just! When night came, the god commanded me to purge myself, and told me how. The purging was as complete as if I had taken hellebore, as those who had had experience of that drug told me. *Everything* was moved by the waves! The god now told me the whole truth, namely that I was destined to be shipwrecked and this was why these things had happened, and now, both for safety and to fulfil my destiny, I must get into a boat in the harbour and contrive that it should capsize and sink; someone would then rescue me and bring me ashore. I was of course happy to do this. Everyone was amazed at the ingenious fake shipwreck, coming on top of the real danger. We knew that it was Asclepius who had saved us from the sea. The purging was an additional blessing.

Conclusion

We began this survey by emphasizing that the prose literature of the period was one of highly professional art. Both in Latin and in Greek, the reading public expected accuracy, elegance, and virtuosity in a very elaborate verbal game. We conclude by making the complementary observation, to which the intimate detail of our last extract from Aristides particularly lends colour, that it was also a literature of personal statement. The letter, the essay, the speech that confesses a personality are, for the first time, leading literary forms. What unites these two features—which may at first sight seem ill matched—is the nature of the society on which the literature is based. This was a governing class of diverse origins but homogeneous education, for whom distinction in their studies both lent respectability to worldly success and often led to it. The members of this élite, whether in Syria or in Spain, were of personal interest to themselves and to one another. Their feelings, their moral problems, even their illnesses were fit matter for writing. They shared a common range of cultural reference, and a common interest in the classical past.

It is hard to point to a prose genius, though common consent would except Tacitus. The Christian writers to come have a better claim. But the high level of skill, the charm and interest of the persons concerned, and the massive information they communicate about so many aspects of ancient life, in their own and earlier days, deserve appreciative readers and careful students. Seneca and Pliny,

Plutarch and Lucian, and many others, are articulate witnesses to a state of civilization which has many affinities with our own. They look inwards upon themselves and backwards to the past, and in their two literary languages they have a superb instrument to express these two great concerns.

Further Reading

GENERAL

Besides the standard histories of literature etc. the following works are particularly useful for the whole period: E. Norden, *Die antike Kunstprosa* (3rd edn. Leipzig, 1915, repr. 1958); A. D. Leeman, *Orationis Ratio* (Amsterdam, 1963), on Latin prose; B. P. Reardon, *Courants Littéraires grecs des IIe et IIIe siècles* (Paris, 1971); G. Kennedy, *The Art of Rhetoric in the Roman World* (Princeton, 1972). Two older books may be added: J. P. Mahaffy, *The Silver Age of the Greek World* (Chicago–London, 1906); S. Dill, *Roman Society from Nero to M. Aurelius* (London, 1904). Both are still worth reading.

AUTHORS

Texts and translations of most of the works mentioned are available in the Loeb Classical Library (LCL). This, like the bilingual French Budé series, is of varying quality, but is particularly useful for late Greek authors, and contains some recent editions of great value, e.g. Seneca the Elder (M. Winterbottom), Pliny's Letters (B. Radice), Herodian (C. R. Whittaker). Authors *not* available in Loeb are asterisked in the following list. When an author is not mentioned, it may be assumed (i) that there is a Loeb; (ii) that there is no outstanding special study in English.
*Aristides: A. Boulanger, *Aelius Aristide* (Paris, 1923). Good discussions of the 'diary' of his illnesses in E. R. Dodds, *Pagan and Christian in an Age of Anxiety* (Cambridge, 1965); and in A. J. Festugière, *Personal Religion among the Greeks* (Berkeley and Los Angeles, 1954), LCL has a selection only; the most recent translation of the 'diary' is C. A. Behr, *Aelius Aristides and The Sacred Tales* (Amsterdam, 1968), which also contains a discussion of Aristides' career.
Arrian: P. A. Stadter, *Arrian of Nicomedeia* (Chapel Hill, 1980).
M. Aurelius: Good study by A. S. L. Farquharson, whose text, translation, and commentary are standard: *The Meditations of the Emperor Marcus Antoninus* (Oxford, 1944; reissued 1968).
Demetrius: Tr. G. M. A. Grube, *A Greek Critic* (Toronto, 1961). Also (part) by D. C. Innes in *Ancient Literary Criticism*, ed. D. A. Russell and M. Winterbottom (Oxford, 1972), where translations of other critical texts of the period (e.g. 'Longinus', Tacitus, extracts from Dionysius and Plutarch) may be found.
Dio Chrysostom: C. P. Jones, *The Roman World of Dio Chrysostom* (Cambridge, Mass., 1978).
Dio Cassius: F. Millar, *A Study of Cassius Dio* (Oxford, 1974).
Dionysius of Halicarnassus: S. F. Bonner, *The Literary Treatises of Dionysius of Halicarnassus* (Cambridge, 1939). LCL edn. of critical works not yet complete; Budé (G. Aujac) supplies the gap, also edns. of some treatises by W. Rhys Roberts (Cambridge, 1901; London–Edinburgh, 1910).
*Greek novelists: A collected volume of translations (ed. B. P. Reardon) is promised. Meanwhile, Xenophon of Ephesus, Chariton, and Heliodorus are *not* in LCL, but Budé has a good edn. of the last. General study: B. E. Perry, *The Ancient Romances* (Berkeley, 1967); but E. Rohde, *Der griechische Roman* Leipzig, 1876 3rd. edn. 1914) remains a classic. See also G. Anderson, *Eros Sophistes* (*American Classical Studies* 9, 1982).
Greek letter-writing: Few of the 'epistolographi' are available in English: R. Hercher's edn. (Paris, 1873) remains standard. But note esp. I. Düring, *Chion of Heraclea* (Göteborg, 1951) which has a translation of this 'epistolary romance' and a useful introduction.

'Longinus': Ed. with commentary, D. A. Russell (Oxford, 1964; repr. 1982). For translation see under Demetrius.

Lucian: J. Bompaire, *Lucien écrivain* (Paris, 1958); G. Anderson, *Lucian: Theme and Variation*, and *Studies in Lucian's Comic Fiction*, *Mnemosyne*, suppls. 41 and 43 (1976); Penguin selection, tr. P. Turner. Complete Eng. tr. by H. W. and F. G. Fowler.

Philostratus: Abridged translation of *Life of Apollonius*—part novel, part pagan hagiography—by G. W. Bowersock (Penguin).

Pliny (the Younger): Comm. A. N. Sherwin White (2nd edn. London, 1969).

Plutarch: C. P. Jones, *Plutarch and Rome* (Oxford, 1971); D. A. Russell, *Plutarch* (London, 1972); A. G. Wardman, *Plutarch's Lives* (London, 1974). Penguin translation of many Lives. Elizabethan translation of Lives (Sir T. North) and 'Morals' (Philemon Holland), both important for English literature.

Quintilian: G. Kennedy, *Quintilian* (New York, 1969).

Seneca (the Elder): Recent studies by L. A. Sussman: *The Elder Seneca*, *Mnemosyne*, suppl. 51 (1978) and J. Fairweather (Cambridge, 1981).

Seneca (the Younger): M. T. Griffin, *Seneca: A Philosopher in Politics* (Oxford, 1976); A. L. Motto, *Seneca* (New York, 1973); also a collection of essays in *Seneca*, ed. C. D. N. Costa (London–Boston, 1974).

28

Silver Latin Poetry and the Latin Novel

⚘

RICHARD JENKYNS

The Silver Age: Problems and Solutions

THE word 'silver', applied to those Latin poets who wrote after the death of Augustus, is a modern label. Like all such labels, it can easily be misleading; time flows on continuously, and any attempt to divide the past into ages or periods is bound to be a more or less artificial attempt to impose simple patterns upon a complex and unceasing flux. None the less, the phrase 'silver age' has its uses. We customarily think of the Augustan age as a time of dazzling poetic achievement, but it is often forgotten that this achievement belongs largely to the first half of Augustus' long reign. During his last twenty-five years and more there was no major poet still active except Ovid; and there is evidence in his later work that Ovid saw himself as a lone survivor, the last of a line. The quarter century following Ovid's death is one of the most barren for poetry in Latin literary history; it is not unrealistic to think in terms of one chapter closing and another beginning.

The term 'silver age' is of course designed to contrast with the 'golden age' which preceded it. This implied contrast contains, once again, a truth and a danger. We should not let ourselves be trapped by a mechanical view of the rise and fall of cultures into supposing that the silver age was a second-rate period which necessarily produced second-rate literature; it includes, at the lowest estimate, at least one poet of genius and several distinctive talents of a lesser order, and it also gave birth to a great historian and by far the best prose fiction to come out of the ancient world. On the other hand, it is indeed true that the poets who came after the Augustans were faced with a peculiar difficulty and a peculiar challenge; and to understand what these were we must first recall the situation of their predecessors.

From the start the Latin poets wrote in the consciousness that the Greek achievement loomed large behind them; the shadow of a mighty past falls dark across their verses. The Greeks seemed to have mastered every field of literature; how could Latin poets hope to produce anything that would not seem a pale and lifeless imitation? That was their dilemma, and a number rose to the challenge by openly acknowledging their debt to Greece, sometimes boldly, sometimes with a studied modesty. The aim was to point the reader's attention to the Greek models, in order to draw out the no less significant divergences from those models; imitation could thus become a kind of originality. The supreme example of this technique is the *Aeneid*.

The silver poets inherited this situation, but with a new difficulty. There was now a mighty body of Latin classics as well. Virgil, Horace, and Ovid, in their different ways, had brought the various genres which they had attempted to such a pitch of perfection that it must have seemed impossible for their successors to develop them further. How could one now write an epic poem which would not read like a pastiche of Virgil, or lyric poetry which would not seem a mere shadow of Horace? It is interesting to find Velleius Paterculus, who wrote second-rate history during the reign of Augustus' successor Tiberius, observing that the highest achievements in any particular genre of literature all occur within a relatively brief period of time; he concludes that genius, despairing of surpassing what has already been perfected or seeking for new territory to conquer, passes on to new fields of endeavour. These remarks are significant precisely because Velleius was himself no genius: he reflects the attitudes of a more or less conventional literary gentleman. We find much talk of decline in the writers of the first century AD. Some of them assert that there has indeed been a decline, others indignantly deny it. Naturally there was no general agreement; what matters is that the state of contemporary literature was an issue that was in the air as never before.

It is intriguing, too, to find Statius, near the end of the century, concluding his epic *Thebaid* by insisting that his work is far inferior to the immortal *Aeneid*. What Statius is doing is dramatizing his dilemma and at the same time playing an elegant literary game by adapting a traditional motif to new circumstances. The theme of self-deprecating homage to a great predecessor had been heard often—Horace, for example, with nicely calculated humility contrasts himself with the torrential genius of Pindar—but never before in epic, where a pose of confidence was expected. Statius, however, who begins his poem by asking what story he shall take for his subject, concludes it on a note of self-doubt. More than ever, poetry has become reflective upon its own nature; the Augustan self-consciousness has been given a new twist.

Manilius' *Astronomica*, begun in the last years of Augustus and continued under Tiberius, illustrates the possibilities and the pitfalls. This is a didactic poem on the theory of astrology, conceived on a heroic scale. Lucretius' *De rerum natura* is the obvious exemplar, and its influence is patent throughout. Like Lucretius, Manilius speaks of struggling with the intractability of his subject-matter; the difficulty of putting arithmetic into verse is at once his problem and his delight.

HYLAS SEIZED BY WATER-NYMPHS: painting by William Etty (1833). This romantic episode from the voyage of the Argonauts was described by several Hellenistic and Roman poets, including Valerius Flaccus, who introduced one or two new elements into the story (e.g. the idea that Hylas came to the spring in pursuit of a deer, not in search of water).

But whereas Lucretius' wrestle with the complexities of Epicurean physics is inspired by deep moral seriousness and driven forward by a formidable intellectual energy, the *Astronomica* seems to be at heart a literary exercise. The game of putting sums into polished hexameters is essentially pointless and quickly becomes tedious. In other parts of the work Manilius reveals himself as a poet of considerable talent, with a gift for the sonorous line and the piquant phrase; but his gifts have not found an adequate object.

The epic poet had two types of model before him, the mythological (such as the *Aeneid*) and the historical, such as Ennius' *Annales*. Silius Italicus (*c.* 26–101) got the worst of both worlds by trying to combine the two: his *Punica*, which is (alas) the longest of classical Latin poems, relates Hannibal's invasion of Italy, but with the full mythological apparatus of divine interventions, a descent to the underworld, and so on. The result is painfully incongruous. The *Argonautica* of Valerius Flaccus (died *c.* 92) and the *Thebaid* of Statius (*c.* 45–96), both mythological epics, are better; but though both poets had talent, neither found a way of imparting genuine freshness and life to his subject. Few are those who have read to the end of either work for pleasure. Of Statius' other verse there survives the *Achilleid*, a fragment of an uncompleted epic, and the *Silvae*, a collection of mostly occasional poems, of which the shortest (5. 4), nineteen lines addressed by the insomniac poet to the god of sleep, is deservedly well known.

But, as Martial unkindly observed (10. 4), there was not much life left in the old mythology now: 'You who read of Oedipus and of Thyestes in the dark, of Colchian women and Scyllas, of what are you reading but monsters? ... Why does the empty nonsense of a wretched sheet please you? Read this, of which life can say, "It is mine." You will not find Centaurs, Gorgons, or Harpies here; my page smells of man.' (Oedipus appears in Statius' *Thebaid*; Seneca had composed a *Thyestes*.) The one man who found a way to reinvigorate the epic genre was Lucan. He went to history for his theme, but to history told in a wholly new way.

SILVER DISH FROM KAISERAUGST (fourth century AD) depicting scenes from the early life of Achilles, the subject of Statius' *Achilleid*. On the rim (anti-clockwise) the dipping of the child Achilles in the River Styx to confer immortality on him, his education by the centaur Chiron, and his concealment, disguised as a woman, among the daughters of King Lycomedes on Skyros. In the central tondo his exposure by the ruses of Greek warriors.

Lucan

Lucan (39–65) is one of the most remarkable figures in Latin literature. He was compelled by Nero to take his own life at the age of twenty-six; by this time he had already composed numerous works, all of which have perished except for the ten books of his uncompleted epic on the civil war between Caesar and Pompey, known as the *Bellum civile* or *Pharsalia*.

Conventionally, the epic poet announces the heroic character of his theme in the first line, and even with the first word. Thus Virgil opens the *Aeneid* with the word 'arma' ('arms'), and Lucan, in apparently similar vein, begins 'bella', ('wars'). But then immediately he twists the theme in a new direction:

> Bella per Emathios plus quam ciuilia campos
> iusque datum sceleri canimus . . .

Of wars more than civil on the plains of Thessaly I sing, of legality granted to crime . . .

This will prove to be a heroic poem without a hero, for Caesar is portrayed as a villain, and though Pompey is more sympathetic, he is, as Cato is made to say, far inferior to earlier Romans in his respect for the bounds of law. (Cato himself, though the pattern of republican propriety, is of secondary importance only.) The staple of epic warfare had been the *aristeia*, in which an individual hero showed his prowess in a series of duels, each vividly described. Lucan allows none of his characters so much honour. There is not a single *aristeia* in his account of the battle of Pharsalus, and only one individual death is described; the rest is a senseless welter of mass slaughter. The gods, too, hitherto essential in epic, are given no place at all in the poem, but instead we see a world plunging to disaster, and at the climax of the action Lucan shouts out (7.446 f.), 'The world is swept along by blind chance; we lie when we say that Jupiter reigns.'

In the same spirit, there is not the usual appeal to the Muse for aid and inspiration at the beginning of the work. After announcing his theme, Lucan turns instead to address the citizens of Rome with sorrow and indignation (1.8): 'Quis furor, o ciues, quae tanta licentia ferri?' ('What was this madness, citizens, what was this great orgy of slaughter?') For this is to be not just a historical, but also a political, poem. Homer and Virgil had been remarkable for the breadth of their sympathies: both Greeks and Trojans in the *Iliad*, both Trojans and Italians in the *Aeneid* excite our admiration and compassion. Lucan deliberately does away with this, admitting that his approach is partisan and his purpose to get his readers to favour one side against the other (7.207–13).

In keeping with this outlook is the poet's declamatory method. The epic poet had traditionally kept his own personality out of his work, preserving an Olympian objectivity, but Lucan constantly involves himself with his characters, haranguing and mocking them, For example, Book 7 begins with one of Lucan's most moving passages: Pompey on the night before his defeat dreams of the triumphs of his earlier life. At first the scene is described without the author intruding his presence, but at line 24 he addresses the guards of the camp, urging them not to sound the reveille and disturb their general's slumbers. At line 29 he speaks to Pompey himself and continues addressing him until line 42. In line 43 he addresses the whole Roman nation; in line 44 he is back with Pompey again. He is like an advocate in court, turning to the gentlemen of the jury and then back to the witness in the box. Constantly we are aware of the poet's personal voice, harsh, passionate, and sarcastic.

On every page of the *Bellum civile* we find epigram, paradox, and bitter wit. Lucan carried to its extreme the fondness of the silver age for what Romans called the 'sententia', the pithy or pointed saying. The first line of the poem, besides asserting the work's epic character, announces this other element also, for it contains the poem's first epigram. The war is 'more than civil' because it is a conflict not just between fellow citizens but between members of the same family, Pompey having previously been Caesar's son-in-law. Lucan remodels epic to give it a sardonic and even a satiric tone.

The blend of political passion and rhetorical conceits is the essence of the *Pharsalia*. In the first book the character of Caesar is sketched in sharp terse phrases which recall Sallust. Cato's summing up of Pompey's career shows a historical sense, setting the great man in the context of his time and balancing virtues against faults with a dignified restraint:

> 'ciuis obit', inquit, 'multum maioribus impar
> nosse modum iuris, sed in hoc tamen utilis aeuo,
> cui non ulla fuit iusti reuerentia; salua
> libertate potens, et solus plebe parata
> priuatus seruire sibi, rectorque senatus,
> sed regnantis, erat.'

> (9. 190–5)

'A citizen has died', he said, 'far inferior to our ancestors in recognizing the limits of legality, but valuable in this present age, which has had no reverence for justice. He was powerful, and yet preserved liberty; he alone stayed a private citizen when the people were ready to be his slaves; he was ruler of the Senate, but of a Senate which kept the sovereignty.'

The last five words show how the *sententia* could be directed to the service of a political and historical theme: the difference between autocracy and dictatorship is put with admirable concision. Sometimes, too, the *sententia* displays a psychological acuity, as when the boy king of Egypt takes a child's delight at 'being grown up' and ordering the death of Pompey:

> adsensere omnes sceleri. laetatur honore
> rex puer insueto, quod iam sibi tanta iubere
> permittant famuli.

> (8. 536–8)

All voted for the crime. The boy king delights in the unaccustomed honour—that now his slaves should allow him to issue such important orders.

Unfortunately, though, an account of Lucan that dwelt only upon his virtues would be seriously misleading, for his faults are very gross. The promise of historical and political seriousness which the poem appears to make is for the most part unfulfilled; Caesar soon turns into a mere pantomime villain, a preposterous ranter hardly worth the compliment of our hatred. The rhetoric is often absurd, and the ceaseless search for paradox produces results that are often tedious and far-fetched; worst of all, the poem lacks variety of style and theme, and the unchanging note of sardonic bleakness becomes wearisome. The way in which Lucan allowed a taste for rhetorical smartness to run away with him can be seen (for example) in the speech of Pothinus at the court of Ptolemy (8. 484–535): for a line or two it looks as though this may be a powerful if cynical defence of expediency against absolute morality, but Pothinus quickly becomes a cardboard monster mouthing clever epigrams of the kind that would persuade nobody. Lucan is, apart from Ovid, the one major Latin poet surviving who composed with speed and fluency, and he has all the faults of the man who never blots a line. His early death leaves us with one of the most intriguing 'ifs' of Latin literary history: had he survived, would he have developed into a great master, or was he by nature one of those highly talented men who are for ever revealing unexpected shallows?

Tragedy

Quintilian (above, p. 657), while admiring Lucan's passion and epigrammatic brilliance, judged him more suitable for orators than poets to imitate. The influence of rhetoric has been commonly blamed for the vices of silver Latin poetry, and the charge has force; but it is wrong to regard rhetoric as the necessary enemy of poetry, and it should be clear that Lucan's virtues are as much the product of his rhetorical cast of thought as are his faults. In Juvenal rhetoric becomes an essential element of great poetry—as it does in the *Aeneid*, for that matter. If, on the other hand, we want to see what happens when the rhetorical manner is used in the absence of imagination, we may turn to the tragedies of Seneca. Ten plays have come down to us under his name, of which one is certainly and another probably spurious. The loss of all other Roman tragedies and the influence which Seneca's are supposed to have had on renaissance drama—an influence, however, which was probably much smaller than has usually been thought—have ensured for them a greater attention than their literary quality alone would deserve.

Like other Latin poets, Seneca develops a Greek genre in a new direction: he turns Attic tragedy towards the gruesome, the sensational, and the extreme. The Hippolytus of Euripides is chaste, pure, puritan; Seneca's Hippolytus is a neurotic with an exaggerated aversion from city life. Euripides' *Medea* ends sensationally enough, but Seneca has a still more sensational, though much coarser, *coup de théâtre* in store for us: Medea, aloft, prepares to ascend into the skies in her chariot,

THE DEATH OF ASTYANAX:
terracotta relief of the late first century
BC or the early first century AD. In
front of a typical theatrical backdrop
(*scaenae frons*) tragic actors perform a
scene from a Roman drama, probably
the *Astyanax* of Accius (second
century BC). The same scene, in which
Odysseus demands the surrender of
the child Astyanax from its mother
Andromache, recurs in the *Troades* of
Seneca (lines 707–813).

and tosses down to Jason the bodies of their dead children; he closes the play by
railing at her, 'Go through the lofty regions of high heaven, and bear witness
where you ride that there are no gods' (testare nullos esse, qua veheris, deos'—
there is a savage punch in the very last word of all). Euripides' Theseus beholds
the mangled body of his dying son Hippolytus; Seneca's Theseus tries to re-
assemble the corpse's scattered pieces, while the chorus add helpful advice, as
though he were doing a jigsaw puzzle. In more talented hands such bizarreries
might have a grotesque kind of power, and some critics have claimed to find
unappreciated merits in these plays; but when we contemplate the amount of
feeble rant that fills play after play, we may conclude that they have let faith
triumph over plausibility.

Epigram and Satire

'I have not drenched my lips in the nag's spring,' declared Persius (34–62), in
disrespectful allusion to the fountain Hippocrene, that classic symbol of poetic
inspiration. Vitality came more easily to those poets who did not burden themselves with the pretensions of the more exalted genres. Persius himself, who
wrote six satires before his early death, is a curious and intriguing figure. He
describes himself as 'iunctura callidus acri' (5. 14 'clever at the pungent combining
of words'): his blend of a compressed, clotted style, thick with literary allusion,

and a contorted moral seriousness makes difficult reading. He was much admired and imitated by the satirists of the English renaissance, and the reader of Donne's satires may catch something of his odd, pungent flavour.

Martial (*c*.40–101), as we have seen (above, p. 680), also took trouble to set himself at a distance from the grander poets; but he is, by contrast, easy and undemanding. Active mainly in the reign of Domitian, he is the father of the epigram in the modern sense of the term: the short poem, sometimes very short, with a witty point or a twist in the tail. For example:

> Hesterno fetere mero qui credit Acerram,
>   fallitur: in lucem semper Acerra bibit.
>
> (1. 28)

He who thinks Acerra reeks of yesterday's wine is wrong: Acerra always drinks till dawn.

Sometimes the wit has a touch of Ovid's or (to look forward) of Herrick's charm:

> Intactas quare mittis mihi, Polla, coronas?
>   a te uexatas malo tenere rosas.
>
> (11. 89)

Why, Polla, do you send me chaplets that you have not touched? I had rather hold roses that your hands had disturbed.

And sometimes he achieves pathos, still without losing his epigrammatic pointedness, as in his poem on the death of Erotion in childhood, which ends thus:

> mollia non rigidus caespes tegat ossa nec illi,
>   terra, grauis fueris: non fuit illa tibi.
>
> (5. 34. 9 f.)

Let the turf be not hard that covers her soft bones; earth, be not heavy upon her; she was not heavy upon you.

On the other hand, a high proportion of his epigrams is obscene; and he cheerfully allows that his object is to titillate his readers.

We have seen that silver epic was most successful when, with Lucan, it shaded into satire; the finest fusion of rhetorical magnificence and epigrammatic harshness comes, however, in Juvenal, the greatest poet of the silver age. Little is known about his life: a fair hypothesis is that he was born around 65 or a little later and died around 130. His style is dense, muscular, declamatory. He seems to have composed slowly and laboriously, since he has left us just fifteen satires and a fragment of a sixteenth, probably unfinished.

Since Juvenal's is the Latin poetry most like satire in the modern sense, it should be stressed that he departed decisively from the traditions of Roman *satura*. Lucilius and Horace had adopted a rapid, discursive, informal manner; they offered, or purported to offer, a view of the poet off duty, with the quirks of his personality freely on display. Juvenal, by contrast, reveals very little of himself. His voice is exceedingly distinctive, but we learn next to nothing of the man behind it. The combination of impersonality and distinctive timbre recalls Lucretius; and it is again Lucretius whom of all Roman poets he most resembles in his blend of satiric sharpness with the grand manner. Many details of style and allusion show that the poet who most influenced him, surprising as it may at first seem, was Virgil, echoes of whom he sometimes uses to point an ironic contrast between the imaginary worlds of heroic or pastoral poetry and the ugly realities of the present time. Though he pays lip-service to the memories of Lucilius and Horace in his first satire, they seem to have made no substantial impression on his verse.

Much ink has been spilled on the question whether Juvenal was a genuine moralist or an opportunist who did not care what his target was, provided he could make a poem out of it; but the whole debate is to some extent misconceived. Though in a few of his later (and generally weaker) satires he assumes a high moral tone, he is for the most part concerned to excoriate human behaviour not for being wicked but for being sordid, vulgar, or disgusting. He is above all a social observer, who combines exactness of observation with imagination. We do not turn to him for wisdom, and he did not intend that we should.

In his first satire Juvenal presents himself as almost overwhelmed by the chaos of his own impressions; and the sixth, a diatribe against the female sex almost 700 lines long, is (by design, we may suppose) a vast ramshackle edifice in which women are assailed for every vice from promiscuity to artiness, and even for being tediously virtuous. But he also liked to organize his satires along a particular line of argument illustrated by a mass of examples, a technique borrowed from the declaimers. Thus Satire 8 opens with the words 'What is the use of family trees?', and the entire poem argues the vanity of noble birth. Even the sixth satire is strung along a thread of this kind, however loosely: the poet purports to be giving an acquaintance the reasons for not marrying. This technique is seen at its most impressive in the tenth satire. 'What should a man pray for?' is the theme, and Juvenal passes one by one over the traditional objects of human aspiration— power, fame, conquest, long life, beauty—exposing the vanity of each by a succession of illustrations from history, mythology, and Roman life: Sejanus, Cicero, Hannibal, Alexander, Priam are all paraded before the reader's eyes.

Juvenal's favourite line of attack is to display things exactly as they are: to refuse to be deceived, as he sees it, by ideas and abstractions. What is military glory, with its processions of captured weaponry and triumphal arches, if you simply *look* at it? Juvenal gives us the answer (10. 133–6): 'The spoils of war, a corslet fastened to a stump as a trophy, a cheek-piece hanging from a broken helmet, a yoke shorn of its pole, the flagstaff of a captured trireme and a sad prisoner at the top of an arch . . .' Broken objects and wretched humanity—that is all there is to see, if one looks with Juvenal's dispassion.

In similar spirit, the first question that he asks about Hannibal is how much does his dust now weigh; the solid, physical world is what concerns him. And Hannibal's ambition—to ride in triumph through Rome—is viewed with the same harsh literalism: he wanted to plant his standard in the Subura, a shabby and crowded part of the city. The Carthaginian general had lost an eye, and he rode upon an elephant (a 'Gaetulian beast'). Juvenal puts these facts together, considers the picture that they make (notice the words 'facies' and 'tabella') and ends up with a vision both strange and ludricous:

> o qualis facies et quali digna tabella
> cum Gaetula ducem portaret belua luscum.
>
> (157 f.)

What a sight it was, what a picture it would make, when the Gaetulian monster carried the one-eyed commander.

And the great man is finally dispatched in some famous lines:

> finem animae, quae res humanas miscuit olim,
> non gladii, non saxa dabunt nec tela, sed ille
> Cannarum uindex et tanti sanguinis ultor
> anulus. i, demens, et saeuas curre per Alpes
> ut pueris placeas et declamatio fias.
>
> (163-7)

Not swords, not stones or spears shall put an end to the life of this man who once threw human affairs into confusion, but that punisher for Cannae and avenger for so much blood, a little ring. Go, madman, run over the savage Alps, to become the schoolboys' favourite and become a subject for declamation.

This is magnificent rhetoric. The epigrammatic *sententia* which concludes the passage has an irony that embraces not just the boys in school but, more subtly, the poet as well: for what is he doing himself with Hannibal if not declaiming about him? The little word 'anulus', thin and scornful in its isolation at the beginning of a new line, contrasts admirably with the slow massive rhythm of the line before. But characteristically, the metrical technique serves a visual purpose as well: it is a *little* ring in which Hannibal kept poison ('anulus' is a diminutive, a fact which in the context is felt), and we are made to see how small an object has put an end to so great a life.

Juvenal is, indeed, a masterly observer, with a brilliant eye for the telling detail: a woman's ear-lobes pulled downwards by the weight of the pearls worn on them (6.458 f.), the wife whose infidelity is betrayed to her husband by her glowing ears (11.189), the soldiers' 'brawny calves drawn up to big benches' when their civilian victim appears before the military court (16.14). Often this vividness is enhanced by a touch of fantasy, and inanimate things are 'brought to life'. The windows seem to be watching the man rash enough to walk through Rome by night (3.275); roast boar, piping hot, seems to be foaming like the living boar of Meleager (5.115 f.); the figure on an equestrian statue seems to be in the act of aiming his lance (7.128); a purse crammed with money 'swells with

PORTRAIT OF A WOMAN from Roman Egypt (first half of second century AD). Juvenal's denunciation of women in his sixth satire includes scathing references to female self-adornment, such as the wearing of emerald necklaces, heavy pearl ear-rings, and make-up.

its mouth stuffed full' just like a greedy human being (14. 138). Some of his grimmest inventions are poetically suggestive, as in this picture of one of the emperor Domitian's councillors (4. 109 f.): 'saevior illo/Pompeius tenui iugulos aperire susurro' ('Pompeius, more savage than he [Crispinus] at slitting throats with his thin whisper'). The sinister sound of the verse matches the sinister compression of phrase which assimilates the thin sound of the informer's whisper to the thin edge of the razor cutting through flesh. Juvenal has often enough been praised as a satirist; he deserves to be more widely known for his powers of poetic imagination.

His contemporary Tacitus remarks (*Ann.* 4. 32), 'nobis in arto et inglorius labor' ('Mine is a narrow and inglorious task'). We catch a similarly self-contemptuous note in the poet; we are often reminded of Juvenal's claim that 'indignatio' inspired his verse, less often of the context in which that claim was made:

> si natura negat, facit indignatio uersum
> qualemcumque potest, quales ego uel Cluuienus.
>
> (1. 79 f.)

If nature denies, scorn makes such verses as it can—such as I write or Cluvienus.

In other words, the kind of verse that scorn produces is poor stuff. Yet both the poet and the historian, we may feel, protest too much. Tacitus would not really prefer, as he pretends, to be relating the glorious deeds of the Roman republic: the very bleakness and narrowness of his subject have a poetic grandeur of a novel kind. The same moral may be applied to Juvenal: his bitter, grating voice and narrowness of theme are not at odds with the splendour of his rhetoric but are the very essence of that splendour. The kind of sardonic grandeur that was achieved fitfully by Lucan was attained with full assurance by Juvenal. Political circumstances made men sour; literary circumstances demanded a new kind of poetry. Juvenal was the one poet, as Tacitus was the one historian, who found a theme and tone which answered to both the social and literary conditions of his age.

The Novel

Prose fiction was conventionally regarded as a very low form of art. Not one of the literary critics of antiquity thought it worth his consideration. Tacitus treated the life and death of Petronius in his *Annals* without deigning to mention that the man had written a novel; such things were below the dignity of history. We have seen that the poets who continued to work in the traditional or 'classic' genres were always liable to fall under the curse of academic art and become competent but lifeless. Perhaps we should not be surprised to find in the novel, the most despised of all genres, unfettered by literary convention, unencumbered by the legacy of great predecessors, a new sparkle and vitality. An ancestry can, it is true, be found for the Roman novel; in 'Milesian tales', stories of erotic or supernatural adventure; in Menippean satire, a genre which mixed prose and verse, as does Petronius; and, in the case of Apuleius at least, the Greek love romance. But all that we know about these often obscure ancestors suggests that our two surviving specimens of Roman novel-writing went far beyond them; they are gloriously original and uninhibited works, as unlike anything else in antiquity as they are unlike each other.

Petronius' date and identity have been disputed. Most scholars, though not all, believe him to be identical with Nero's 'arbiter elegantiae', compelled by the Emperor to take his own life in AD 66, and that is the assumption made here. Only one episode of the *Satyrica* (to give what is commonly called the *Satyricon* its correct title) has come down to us entire: this is what has become known as the *Cena Trimalchionis*, "Trimalchio's dinner-party'. The rest of the *Satyrica* survives in very patchy fragments only. If it was written on the same scale as the *Cena*, it must have been an enormous work, far longer than any other novel of antiquity; but it is possible that the dinner party was a centre-piece, like the tale of Cupid and Psyche in Apuleius' *Golden Ass*, developed in far more detail than any other part of the story.

Since so much is lost, any account of the work as a whole has to be somewhat vague. The story is narrated by one Encolpius, thief, pervert, parasite, and man of the world. The novel charts his wanderings, along with his faithless catamite, the boy Giton, and his rival Ascyltus (all three names have sexual connotations): we find them by the Bay of Naples, on shipboard, and at Croton in the far south of Italy. A recurrent theme appears to be the hero's persecution at the hands of Priapus, the god of sexual potency. It has been suggested that the whole work is a kind of burlesque epic, with Encolpius as a disreputable Ulysses or Aeneas, and the ithyphallic Priapus taking the role of the more dignified gods Neptune or Juno.

Encolpius himself, cultivated and depraved, is scarcely a character in the modern sense but a pair of hard clever eyes through which we view an extraordinary comic world. Part of the *Satyrica*'s fascination lies in its combination of low life with literary wit and social satire, all set out with a cold brilliant detachment. Some of the scenes are obscene, even monstrously obscene. There are grotesque inventions, as when Eumolpus, turning metaphor into actuality, decrees that his legatees must first eat the flesh of his corpse; but we also meet the rhetorician Agamemnon, who elicits from Encolpius a fruity declamation against declamation, while Eumolpus, for his part, is depicted as an obsessed versifier. Several times incidents are compared to scenes from mime, and there is something of the quality of pantomime, too, when members of the cast step out of character for the better entertainment of the audience. Encolpius, by turns rogue and literary gentleman, cynical and soft-hearted, is a protean figure who adapts to whatever role is suggested by the convenience of the moment; the blundering Eumolpus is allowed to tell the story of the widow of Ephesus in dashing style; Trimalchio's foolish astrology has a sharp edge to it (39): anyone born under the sign of the ram, he remarks, has a 'a hard head, a brazen forehead, sharp horns. Many professors are born under this sign . . .'

In the conversation of the guests at Trimalchio's dinner, Petronius deploys a racy colloquial Latin to brilliant effect. The talk is fast and varied: dour, gossipy, and sentimental. We even catch a foretaste of Sam Weller. '"Oro te," inquit Echion centonarius, "melius loquere. 'Modo sic, modo sic' inquit rusticus; uarium porcum perdiderat"' (45) ('"Please, please," said Echion the rag-merchant, "don't talk so gloomily. 'There's light patches and there's dark patches', as the yokel said when he'd lost his spotted pig"').

Trimalchio himself is one of those characters, like Shylock, who ought to be a monster but turns out oddly endearing; whether Petronius designed this effect is perhaps an open question. His behaviour is self-contradictory, in this case not because the author has no consistent view of his character but because it is in the nature of that character to be a mass of inconsistencies. A former slave who has attained enormous, even preposterous riches (he contemplates buying property in Sicily so that he will be able to travel all the way to Africa on his own land (48)), he is anxious to play a part, but unable to decide what part to choose. At one moment he tyrannizes over his slaves, at another he apes the philosophers, declaring that slaves are human beings and have drunk the same milk as other men. He observes sagely that one should talk culture at dinner, and treats his guests to an outrageously confused account of the Trojan War; but he cannot forgo the rival pleasures of inverted snobbery: the epitaph he has composed for himself declares (71), 'Virtuous, brave and true, he began humbly, left 30,000,000 sesterces, and never listened to a philosopher.' He has a skeleton brought in to remind him of his mortality (34)—a gesture which would be more impressive were the skeleton not made of silver. He is superstitious and sentimental, his puns are childishly awful, and his attempts to be stylish are disastrously vulgar (he uses

SILVER BEAKER WITH SKELETONS of Greek poets and philosophers (first half of first century AD). Several works of art in late Hellenistic and Roman times betray a morbid fascination with death, foretokening the medieval 'dances of death'. Compare Trimalchio's silver skeleton: 'So shall we all be, when the Underworld has claimed us; then let us live while all is well.'

a silver chamber-pot in public, and then wipes his hands on a slave's head). Some of his remarks are what Englishmen call Irish: he has cups depicting 'Cassandra's dead children' so skilfully engraved 'that you would think they were alive' (52); he has told his slaves that he means to free them in his will 'so that my household may love me now just as though I were dead' (71). Constantly he craves affection: 'No one in my house loves me more,' he says, as he feeds his dog (64). At the end of the feast, now thoroughly drunk, he decides to rehearse his funeral. Trumpeters are summoned, his shroud fetched, and lying on a heap of cushions he announces (78), 'Pretend I'm dead. Say something nice.' This is childish behaviour, certainly; perhaps childlike also. The scene seems an extravagant flourish on Petronius' part to mark the climax of Trimalchio's feast, so it is sobering to learn from Seneca's letters of a certain Pacuvius who behaved in just such a fashion. It is Petronius' strength that he is a fantasist who does not lose touch with reality.

Apuleius was born at Madaurus in the province of Africa around 123 and was active in the second half of the century. Several works from his hand survive, including the *Apologia*, his self-defence on a charge of gaining his wife's love by the use of magic (below, p. 767); but his fame rests above all on his novel the *Metamorphoses*, also known as *The Golden Ass*. This is based on a Greek tale, *Lucius, or The Ass*, possibly written by Lucian, of which an abridged version is still extant. Comparison with the Greek story serves to demonstrate how brilliantly Apuleius enlarged and adapted his model. *The Golden Ass* is in eleven books and is told in the first person. After nearly three books of amorous and humorous incidents the narrator, as a consequence of an experiment with magic which goes wrong, finds himself transformed into a donkey; and the rest of the work consists of a series of picaresque adventures which befall the hero in his animal form, interrupted by a large number of other tales recounted by various of the characters who figure in the main narrative. The longest of these, the tale of Cupid and Psyche, occupies about a fifth of the entire work.

Finally, after a vision of the goddess Isis, the narrator Lucius is restored to his human shape. The last scenes of the novel provide one of the most remarkable accounts of religious experience to come down from classical paganism. It has often been thought that we see here the influence of Christian spirituality; on this supposition Apuleius was fighting Christianity but doing his best to steal the rival religion's clothes. The last book also presents the interpreter of Apuleius with his most teasing problem; no entirely satisfactory explanation has yet been given, and perhaps none is possible. How are we to reconcile the tone of the conclusion, with Lucius as an adept of the goddess, vowed to celibacy and simplicity of life, with the huge gusto with which the rest of the story is told? Lucius repeatedly tells us that he is 'curiosus' ('inquisitive'), or 'sititor ... nouitatis', ('a thirster after novelty'); for this inquisitiveness he is punished and ultimately redeemed, but until the last book the whole atmosphere and style of the narrative encourages us to rejoice and share in this thirst for adventure and experience. The work begins,

THE WORSHIP OF ISIS: painting from Herculaneum (mid first century AD). Lucius' conversion to the Egyptian religion which enjoyed such success in late-Hellenistic and early-imperial times forms a rather uneasy conclusion to Apuleius's rumbustious novel *The Golden Ass*.

indeed, with an explosion of zest and hilarity: the narrator presents himself in ingratiating and persistent tones, almost as though he were a huckster pressing dirty postcards on a passer-by:

At ego tibi sermone isto Milesio uarias fabulas conseram auresque tuas beniuolas lepido susurro permulceam—modo si papyrum Aegyptiam argutia Nilotici calami inscriptam non spreueris inspicere—figuras fortunasque hominum in alias imagines conuersas in se rursum mutuo nexu refectas ut mireris.

Now then, I would like to stitch together a variety of stories in this Milesian tale and soothe your kindly ears with an elegant whisper—so long as you do not scorn to examine this Egyptian manuscript written with the neatness of a pen of the Nile—so that you may marvel at men's forms and fortunes changed into new shapes and then one with the other restored to themselves again.

Suddenly there is an interruption from the audience: 'exordior. "quis ille?" paucis accipe' ('I'll begin. "Who's this fellow?" I'll tell you briefly'). In elaborate and eccentric language the narrator explains that he is a Greek who learnt Latin at Rome in his adolescence. 'Lector intende; laetaberis', he concludes ('Reader, attend; you will be entertained'). All this passes in a very few sentences; everything speaks of briskness, energy, entertainment. And entertainment indeed is what we get, though often of a grotesque sort. Sex and magic, comedy and horror, elegant romance and coarse bawdy are blended into an intoxicating mixture: men are soused in urine or spattered with excrement; cuckoldry, castration, copulation are recurrent themes; the entire work is drenched in blood, torture, and hideous death.

The cement that holds this strange diversity together is provided by Apuleius' idiosyncratic style; it is his style, again, which prevents the work turning, as the Greek romances sometimes do, into mere vulgar titillation, by giving to the whole the gloss of an elaborate sophistication. The vocabulary is a weird blend of archaism, poeticisms, colloquialism, and neologism, elements which are curiously reminiscent of the babu English spoken in the last century by Indians who had educated themselves from a mixture of Shakespeare, newspapers, and modern slang imperfectly understood. That analogy is not as far-fetched as it may at first appear, for the narrator reveals that he is a Greek and apologizes for his imperfect command of the Latin language. 'Fabulam Graecanicam incipimus,' he explains ('I am beginning a Grecian tale'); characteristically he replaces the ordinary word for Greek, 'Graecus', with an uncommon form.

But of course the claim to imperfect Latin is all a feint; he is a stylistic virtuoso, a 'circus rider' by his own confession. With much adroitness he arranges his bizarre vocabulary into lilting mesmeric rhythms which sometimes have an almost incantatory effect. He loves assonances like 'sauia suauia' ('sweet kisses' 6.8) or, more elaborately, 'sordis infimae infamis homo' ('a notorious fellow of extreme squalor', 1.21). In place of the periodic structures and careful variations traditional in Latin art prose, he favours loose series of echoing phrases which on

NILE BOAT-TRIP: mosaic panel from Tivoli (second century AD). General Nilotic subjects were popular in the Roman decorative arts. Here some unusual features, such as the water pouring from a hole in the boat, suggest that a specific story was being illustrated, perhaps an episode from romantic fiction.

ARRETINE BOWL MADE BY M. PERENNIUS TIGRANUS (late first century BC). Relief-moulded pottery superseded painted ceramics as the favourite fine tableware of the Mediterranean from the third century BC onwards. This fine example, from Arretium (Arezzo), is decorated with scenes of lovemaking in an elegant classical style.

DECORATED GLASSWARE FROM THE RHINELAND (third century AD). The so-called 'snake-thread' glass, pioneered in the eastern Mediterranean during the late second century AD, later became a popular line in the Rhenish workshops. The jug is decorated with swan-like forms, the cup (in the shape of a gladiator's helmet) with a bird pecking cherries.

occasion even fall into the pattern of rhyming verse. Psyche's prayer to Ceres, for example, is a kind of coloratura aria (part of it is arranged here so as to bring out the rhyming effect):

Per ego te frugiferam tuam dexteram istam deprecor, per laetificas messium caeremonias, per tacita secreta cistarum et per famulorum tuorum draconum pinnata curricula et glebae Siculae sulcamina
    et currum rapacem
    et terram tenacem
    et inluminarum Proserpinae nuptiarum demeacula
    et luminosarum filiae inuentionum remeacula
et cetera quae silentio tegit Eleusinis Atticae sacrarium, miserandae Psyches animae supplicis tuae subsiste. (6. 2)

I beseech you, by your right hand that bears the fruits of the earth, by your joyful ceremonies of harvest, by the unspoken secrets of your baskets, by the winged cars of the dragons your servants, by the furrows of the Sicilian soil, by the chariot that seized your daughter and the earth that held her, by the descent of Proserpine to a wedding unlighted by torches, by her ascent when she was found by the light of torches, by all else that the shrine of Eleusis in the land of Athens shrouds in silence, help the pitiable soul of Psyche, your suppliant.

Apuleius' rococo glitter is at its most dazzling in the story of Cupid and Psyche. On one level this is a fairy story, rich in folk-tale motifs, and opening with a disarming simplicity (4. 28): 'In a certain country there lived a king and queen' (it comes as small surprise that Psyche is the youngest and fairest of their three daughters, more lovely than Venus herself). On another level the tale hints at quasi-Platonic allegory: the marriage of Psyche, the soul, with Cupido, fleshly desire. On a third level the story is a comedy in the Ovidian manner, with Olympian goddesses constrained by the laws and etiquette of contemporary Rome; and on yet a fourth level it is the *ne plus ultra* of bejewelled preciosity. One of the virtues of Apuleius' high fantastical style is that it enables him to drift among these different levels of discourse.

Outside the story of Psyche, too, it enables him to create an atmosphere of his own, and to produce effects unlike anything else in Latin literature. His is a fantasy world, and yet it gives a curiously convincing picture of life under the Roman empire. The scene in which Lucius falls for the slave-girl Fotis when he sees her stirring the porridge in a seductive manner is at once erotic and absurd (2. 7). Lucius asks a cackling crone for directions to Milo's house; she answers with a terrible joke, but Lucius continues straight-faced with an elaborate gravity (1. 21): '"Remoto" inquam "ioco, parens optima, dic oro et cuiatis sit et quibus deuersetur aedibus"' ('"Jesting aside, my good woman," I answered, "tell me, pray, what manner of man he is and in what abode he lodges"'). Set against the comedy are glossy set-piece descriptions: the statues in Byrrhaena's house, so lifelike that they seem to be in motion (2. 4); the beauty of a head of hair,

CUPID AND PSYCHE: marble statue-group from the House of Cupid and Psyche at Ostia, copied from a second-century BC original. The fairy tale of Cupid and Psyche is the most famous of the stories embedded in *The Golden Ass*. The two lovers are eventually united after various trials and tribulations occasioned by the jealousy of Venus and Psyche's sisters.

glittering gold in the light, with shadows the colour of honey (2.9); the sheen of Cupid's dewy wings, with tender little downy feathers dancing tremulously at their edges as he sleeps (5.22). Many of Apuleius' stories are told with an outrageous insouciance, with loose ends left hanging all over the place. One might expect the result to be a disordered ragbag, but the combination of mannerism and panache holds the work together. Apuleius is a curious figure with whom to end the account of a period; but it is stimulating to know that in the second half of the second century AD Latin literature could still throw up a writer so full of vitality and imagination.

Further Reading

Petronius has been translated by W. Arrowsmith (Ann Arbor, 1962); there are translations in the Penguin Classics series of Persius (together with Horace's *Satires* and *Epistles*) by N. Rudd; Petronius (together with Seneca's satire *Apocolocyntosis*) by J. P. Sullivan; selected epigrams of Martial by J. Michie; Juvenal by P. Green; and Apuleius, *The Golden Ass* by R. Graves. Marlowe translated Lucan's first book. Dryden's rendering of Persius and five satires of Juvenal (*The Poems of John Dryden*, ed. J. Kinsley (Oxford, 1958), vol. 2) are a part of English literature; his version of Juvenal gives a better idea of the grand declamatory manner than is possible in a modern idiom. Compare too Samuel Johnson's 'imitations' of *Satires* 3 and 10, 'London' and 'The Vanity of Human Wishes'. Walter Pater incorporated a translation of Apuleius' story of Cupid and Psyche into ch. 5 of his *Marius the Epicurean*; it conveys something of Apuleius' elegance, though not of his verve. The Loeb Classical Library contains none of Apuleius' works except *The Golden Ass*, but otherwise includes all the works discussed in this chapter.

G. Williams, *Change and decline: Roman literature in the early empire* (Berkeley, 1978) surveys the whole period. On individual poets see M. P. O. Morford, *The Poet Lucan: Studies in Rhetorical Epic* (Oxford, 1967); F. M. Ahl, *Lucan: An Introduction* (Ithaca, 1976); J. C. Bramble, *Persius and the Programmatic Satire: A Study in Form and Imagery* (Cambridge, 1974); D. Vessey, *Statius and the Thebaid* (Cambridge, 1973); G. Highet, *Juvenal the Satirist* (Oxford, 1954); R. G. M. Nisbet, 'Persius' and H. A. Mason, 'Is Juvenal a classic?', in *Critical Essays on Roman Literature: Satire*, ed. J. P. Sullivan (London, 1963); R. Jenkyns, *Three Classical Poets: Sappho, Catullus and Juvenal* (London, 1982), part 3 'Juvenal the poet'. On satire generally see M. Coffey, *Roman Satire* (London, 1976).

On the Latin novel: B. E. Perry, *The Ancient Romances: A Literary-Historical Account of their Origins* (Berkeley, 1967); P. G. Walsh, *The Roman Novel* (Cambridge, 1970); J. P. Sullivan, *The Satyricon of Petronius: A Literary Study* (London, 1968); J. Tatum, *Apuleius and The Golden Ass* (Ithaca, 1979).

29

Later Philosophy

❧❧

ANTHONY MEREDITH

General Tendencies

THE period with which this section is concerned is bracketed by the lives of the two most interesting and important figures of later philosophy, Posidonius of Apamea in Syria (d. 51 BC) and Plotinus, an Egyptian by birth, who died in Rome in 270 AD. The former of these two was one of the most widely travelled and deeply learned men of his age, who interested himself in a whole range of subjects including rhetoric, geography, and recent history, taking over in the latter field where Polybius had left off. He was also a philosopher and represents a tendency present in a good deal of the philosophy of the period, to harmonize the apparently conflicting views held by the main schools of the age. So, though he was himself a Stoic, he seems to have been willing to depart from the traditional views of his school in two important matters, theology and anthropology. Unlike such Stoics as Zeno and Chrysippus, he seems to have admitted the existence of a god who was in some sense transcendent, and also to have accepted the existence in man of the irrational appetites as being truly human. In both of these areas he departs from the monism and the intellectualism of the Stoic school as it is represented both in the founders of the fourth century and the later Stoics, Epictetus and Marcus Aurelius in the second century AD. Plotinus, too, though an immeasurably greater philosopher, indeed arguably the greatest since Aristotle and for a long time to come, was also prepared, as his biographer and pupil Porphyry tells us in his *Life*, to use the teachings of both Aristotle and the Stoics in addition to his master Plato.

In between these two towering figures crowd a host of lesser men whose main claim to fame is that they help to explain the genesis of Plotinus, but who also shed light both on the history of their respective schools and on the early growth of Christian reflection and doctrine. There are, however, certain overall features which can be found to a greater or lesser extent in all the writers of the period.

(a) The first two centuries after Christ were intensely conservative and traditional in their interests, and although it is doubtless true that under cover of a devotion to the past they intruded their own particular concerns, it cannot be

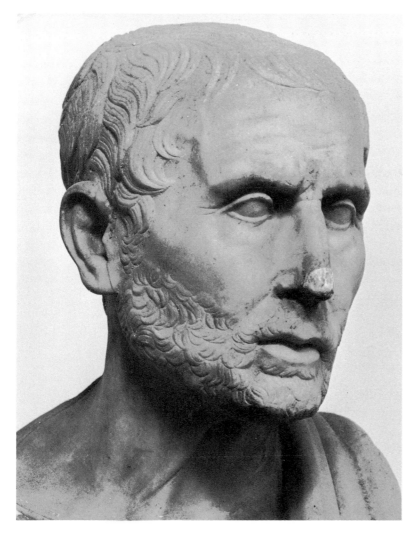

POSIDONIUS OF APAMEA (*c.*135–50 BC), the last of the great polymaths of the Hellenistic age; he wrote on geography, astronomy, and history, as well as philosophy. His ideas influenced several Roman writers, including Sallust, Caesar, Tacitus, and especially Cicero, who studied under Posidonius in Rhodes in 78.

denied that in all branches of their literary activity the writers of the age looked back to the great masterpieces of the golden age of Athens for their inspiration both in point of content and of style. It was their preoccupation with style that led many of the writers of the Second Sophistic to devote a good deal of attention to Plato, and it was perhaps for that reason that the philosophical renaissance of the age owes more to him than to Aristotle. As to content, most of the writers of the age can in general be classed as Platonists. The interest in the more dogmatic side of Plato can be dated to the earlier part of the first century BC and is connected with the figure of Antiochus of Ascalon, the first systematically to break away from the scepticism which had dominated the school since the days of Carneades (d. *c.*129/8 BC). The devotion to Plato shows itself in a number of ways, but above all in the constant use of quotation from him and in the general adherence to the main lines of his philosophy, the belief in the transcendence of God and in the immortality of the soul. So often were some of the commonplaces of Plato repeated by the writers of the period, above all by Plutarch, Maximus, and Albinus, that it has been thought by some scholars that they possessed a Platonic anthology, now lost, from which these excerpts were taken. It does not seem necessary to postulate such a book, but it still remains true that certain phrases, such as that from Plato's *Timaeus* 28 b 'To discover the maker and father of the universe is indeed a hard task, and having found him it would be impossible to tell everyone about him', recur with remarkable frequency in all the writers of the period, whether pagan or Christian.

(b) Alongside the intense traditionalism of the period may be found a strong tendency to amalgamate the central tenets of differing philosophical schemes, with the result of forming a united philosophical front. All the main schools must have had substantial followings over the period. Mention has already been made of Platonists and Stoics. But there was also a flowering of Pythagoreanism, again beginning at the opening of the first century BC with the figure of Nigidius Figulus (praetor in 58 BC). He was followed by men like the wandering preacher Apollonius of Tyana, whose biography, written by Philostratus for the Empress Julia Domna at the opening of the third century AD, came to be thought of as a rival to the Gospels. Another interesting Pythagorean of a slightly later date and more immediately philosophical interests was Numenius of Apamea, who made the interesting claim that Plato derived his doctrines from Pythagoras. He is therefore a witness to the belief that not only were Plato's doctrines derived, but also that underneath certain verbal differences all philosophers were saying the same thing. This mixture of appeal to antiquity, together with a desire to water down important divergences in favour of a common front, is characteristic of nearly all the writers of the age and is a mark of their learning, sterility, and general timidity.

(c) Most of the authors with whom we shall be concerned exemplify the revival in classical Greek style, known as the Second Sophistic Movement, of which Philostratus writes in his *Lives of the Sophists*. Marcus Aurelius wrote in Greek, and the 'cultured commonplaces' of Maximus were intended to help young men to develop the power of speaking elegantly in public on general themes. Again the interest of all the writers of the age, with the solitary exception of Plotinus, was practical. In Plutarch the moral and practical interest predominates, and in one of his *Discourses* Epictetus asks: 'But what is philosophy? Does it not mean making preparation to meet the things that come upon us?' It was for their lack of interest in giving practical help to the state that the Platonist philosopher Celsus was critical of Christians. Such a criticism would have sounded oddly from Plotinus, with his resolute and consistent exaltation of contemplation over action and his lack of interest in either the theory or the practice of politics. Finally, Plotinus differs from all his immediate predecessors in the systematic rigour that he brings to philosophy. Neither Plutarch nor Epictetus has

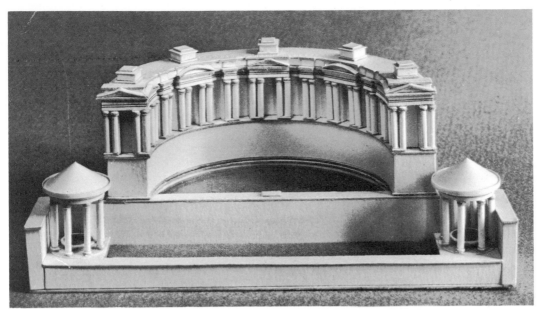

THE NYMPHAEUM OF HERODES ATTICUS AT OLYMPIA (reconstruction model). The immensely wealthy Athenian sophist (*c.*AD 101–77) was not only a much admired literary stylist but also a Roman senator and consul, a friend and tutor of Emperors, and a liberal patron of the arts. Among the buildings which he sponsored were concert halls in Athens and Corinth and fountain-buildings in Corinth and (here) Olympia.

any interest in speculation as such; for them philosophy subserves the life of action.

(d) The second-century sceptical writer Lucian (above, pp. 670 ff.), makes it clear that there was a good deal of religiosity in evidence in these years, and several of his essays are designed to poke fun at the various quacks and charlatans who thrived on some such atmosphere. *Essay* 42 deals with the false prophet Alexander of Abonuteichus who played grossly on the credulity of the period, and no. 55, 'On the death of Peregrinus', is an amusing account of a man who passed through Cynicism and Christianity to end up an Indian mystic. Lucian is hardly more merciful on grammatical pedants (*Essay* 41) or on philosophers (*Essay* 70, 'Hermotimus', a sustained attack on all philosophical schools). It was an era in which there appears to have been an abnormal flowering of many forms of occult piety, philosophical syncretism, and genuine religion. This sort of evidence has led E.R. Dodds to label it 'an age of anxiety', and to suggest that what led men and women to seek peace and revelation in all manner of mysteries was a sense of misery, a *fin de siècle* feeling, which encouraged such strange and unwonted outbursts. It is an attractive hypothesis, though it is hard to see why the age of the Antonines (97–180 AD) should be thought of as especially wretched. The historian Gibbon would hardly have subscribed to such a view. It is certainly true that many of the writers of the period seem to be very self-obsessed; some of them indeed like Herodes Atticus seem to have been pathological cases. It is also true that the age saw the rapid expansion of Christianity, but it would be hardly fair to label all Christians as either pathological introverts or seekers after secret and mystical revelation.

Platonism

It is possible to discern at least two widely different strands in the writings of Plato, the dogmatic and the critical: the Plato, in other words, who is responsible both for the theory of forms and the immortality of the soul on the one hand, and on the other the Plato who, in the tradition of his master Socrates, subjected all propositions to the sharpest criticism. Not long after his death in 347 the Academy which he had founded came under the influence of those who belonged for one reason or another to the second, sceptical stream. Partly in opposi-

PLATO'S ACADEMY: mosaic panel found near Pompeii (late second or first century BC). According to a recent theory, the figure at the left is Heraclides Ponticus; the figure pointing to the globe would be Plato himself; and the whole scene would represent a discussion on astronomy. Platonic philosophy continued to exercise influence, in modified form, on the thinkers of Roman times.

tion to Stoic dogmatism, partly under the influence of Pyrrho, the leaders of the school, above all Arcesilaus (316/15–242/1) and Carneades, denied the possibility of any formal knowledge of anything. The last undisputed head of the Academy was Philo of Larissa (160/59–80), after whom, under the influence of his pupil Antiochus of Ascalon, the school lost its nerve and lapsed into dogmatism—a characteristic which it retained throughout the rest of its history right down to the closing of the Athenian Academy in 529 AD by order of the Emperor Justinian.

Of Antiochus we know very little, and that little is derived almost wholly from Cicero. He was born somewhere between 130 and 120 BC, and his death is put in 68. Our sources clearly regard him as a breakaway from the true Academy, largely if not entirely because he rejected the sceptical attitude to truth, which had been received 'doctrine' since the days of Arcesilaus, if not before. In another respect also he heralds a new age. He believed that there was fundamental agreement between the Old Academy of Plato and the Lyceum of Aristotle. Again this was a revolutionary step; and as we shall see, some Platonists, who might have been happy to admit the possibility of knowledge, regarded the proposed alliance between Plato and Aristotle with some distaste. The best known of the 'opposition' were Plutarch and Atticus. But beyond the fact that in these two respects Antiochus betrayed his immediate predecessors it is hard to be at all clear precisely what he taught.

Ironically enough, the clearest and most copious witness to the views of the Middle Platonists, as they are now called, is the Alexandrian Jewish writer Philo (*c*.25 BC–*c*.45 AD). From his lengthy allegorical commentary on the first five books of the Bible it is possible to extract a system which closely resembles the sort of picture which emerges from Plutarch and Albinus. It must, however, be remembered that, useful though he is for our purposes, Philo was a Jew and was thoroughly influenced by biblical ideas and images. Even so, in the first book of his commentary he provides us with a structured hierarchy of reality, beginning with the supreme God and ending with matter, like that which characterizes Middle Platonism. The question which the structure seeks to answer is 'How is it possible to derive the multiplicity which we see from the absolute unity which we believe to lie at the summit of the world?' The Bible, in common with all the great transcendental philosophers of classical antiquity, had assumed that above all there was a single indivisible self-sufficient principle; and although they might call it (him) sometimes God, sometimes Monad (Pythagorean), sometimes Absolute Beauty or the Idea of the Good (Plato's *Phaedrus* and *Republic*), sometimes the Unmoved Mover or Self-thinking Thought (Aristotle's *Metaphysics*), they were all agreed that it was single. The derivation of or relation to the One of the All was the problem. The theory of forms and the account of the making of the world in the *Timaeus* represent attempts at a solution. But Plato, Aristotle, and arguably the account of creation in the first chapter of Genesis, all tend to assume the eternity of matter as the condition of the possibility of the making of the world. Philo was perhaps the first to take the bold and interesting step of trying to present a picture of the making of the world which took into account all these insights. For him the maker of the world is the only one who is eternal in both senses of the word. That is, he held that God is both without beginning and without end (=durationally eternal) and also absolutely timeless. 'For God is the maker of time also, for he is the father of time's father. ... Thus time stands to God in the relation of a grandson. ... To the elder son, the intelligible universe, He assigned the place of the first-born.' This passage gives us in a nutshell the Philonic system. Beneath the first God and Father of all, who is incomprehensible and eternal, there comes a second God or Logos, who is described sometimes as the mind of God, sometimes as the place of the ideas or the intelligible world, sometimes as the first-born, sometimes as the agent in creation. Beneath him is the world of sense, created through the agency and on the model of the Logos. This last is less perfect and more multiple than is the world of forms.

It is clear what Philo is aiming at:

(a) He has replaced the confusing picture of three independent principles in the *Timaeus* with a neatly ordered pattern.
(b) He has achieved this by welding together rather disparate elements which he assumes enjoy a basic coherence.

Above all, the second principle draws together into one the creative word of Psalm 33:6, the Stoic Logos (though it is raised above and not identical with the material universe), the Platonic world of forms, and the Aristotelian self-thinking thought. On occasion he even calls the Logos 'God' and distinguishes him from the first God by the simple device of dropping the definite article. This distinction within the realms of the divine, which suggests the possibility of introducing degrees within the concept of God, was subsequently employed with considerable fruit and frequency by most of the later Middle Platonists and some of the Neoplatonist writers, notably by Albinus, Numenius, Plotinus, and the Christian Origen.

Plutarch was by birth a Greek and came from Chaeronea in Boeotia. He studied philosophy in Athens and at a later date went to Rome, where he taught for a period, and then returned home. He spent the last thirty years of his life a priest at Delphi. He died *c.*120 AD at about the age of seventy-five. Opinions about his philosophical seriousness vary from the declared and consistent, if not always orthodox Platonism attributed to him by Donald Russell, to the dismissive 'tea-table transcendentalist' of E.R. Dodds. A good example of this alleged incoherence is in his attitude to Stoicism. On the one hand he was sharply critical of much that the Stoics stood for. This is clear from two books of his *Moralia*, *Stoic Self-contradictions* and *On Common Conceptions*. So, for example, in the former book he argues that the Stoics believed that 'whatever is, is right', while believing at the same time that God chastises the wicked. On the other hand

Plutarch owes a good deal of his belief in a benign providence to the Stoics, and to them also he, indirectly, owes his conviction that it is possible to know.

Plutarch's own attitude to the possibility of accounting for the existence of evil in a divinely ordered universe is not without its difficulties. His explanation of the origin of evil is not quite the same as Plato's, though he adduces passages in *The Laws* and *Timaeus* in defence of his own account. In his treatise *On Isis and Osiris*, an allegorical discussion of the Egyptian pantheon, he argues that there are two independent and eternal principles: Osiris, the principle of good, and Typhon, the principle of evil. This assertion of the existence of an eternal evil principle may be attributed to the influence of Xenocrates and could owe something to Iranian dualism, the eternal struggle between good (Ahura-Mazda), and evil (Ahriman); but it is at variance with the general tendency of Plato to deny to evil any place among the forms, and it is in clear conflict with the optimism of the Stoics and of Plotinus. In another treatise, *On the Obsolescence of Oracles*, Plutarch produces a slightly different explanation, attributing evil to the demons that exist between the divine world and that of the visible universe. Here we can see clear echoes of Plato's *Symposium*, with again the significant difference that Plato's demons are good or neutral, Plutarch's are evil.

In one final respect Plutarch's Platonism was modified by his Pythagorean teacher Ammonius, whose interpretation of the mysterious E at Delphi is related for us by Plutarch in his treatise of that name. According to Ammonius the purpose of the inscription is to identify the supreme principle of the universe with the utter simplicity of oneness that stands at the summit of the Pythagorean system. He concludes as follows: 'Under these conditions, therefore, we ought, as we pay Him reverence, to greet him and to address Him with the words, "Thou art"; or even . . . as did some of the men of old "Thou art One".' This Pythagorean influence enables Plutarch to go beyond the other Middle Platonists; and in his insistence on the unity and simplicity of the supreme principle he closely approximates to the One of Plotinus.

Of all the Middle Platonist writers known to us the most characteristic and the most easily available is Albinus, sometimes called Alcinous. Of his life next to nothing is known, except that he lived in the middle of the second century AD and that he wrote two *Introductions* to the philosophy of Plato, both of which survive. His particular interest for us is that, unlike Philo and Plutarch, he seems to have been untouched by non-Hellenic influences. His work is decidedly eclectic in tone and marks a deliberate attempt to schematize his inherited Platonism on hierarchical principles. At the summit of the pyramid is the first God or Mind, ineffable, perfect, eternal, father of all. He fills the whole universe with himself because of his will. Beneath him comes second Mind: Mind, that is, in its active and passive side. After him comes the third principle, Soul. It should be noted that for Albinus the supreme God is both ineffable and personal and shares certain features in common with the first Mind of Aristotle, though differing from Aristotle in attributing to him both ineffability and personal involvement in the universe. Again, exalted though the God of Albinus is, he is not so utterly simple as the Pythagorean Monad of Philo and Plutarch, or the One of Plotinus. It is not surprising, therefore, to to discover that he makes no use in his writings of the passage in *Republic* 509 b, on the source and nature of Being, of which later Platonists made so much.

From what has been said it is clear that Albinus, in common with Celsus and Maximus of Tyre, but unlike Plutarch and Atticus, believed in the fundamental harmony between Plato and Aristotle. This is clear not only from the willingness to treat the ideas of Plato as thoughts in the mind of Aristotle's god, but also from the extensive use made of Aristotle's logical works. On one further point of major importance the Aristotelianizing Platonists were at one. They all thought that the account of creation contained in Plato's *Timaeus* demanded an allegorical rather than a literal interpretation. The natural sense of Plato is that the making of the world took place in time. For Albinus such a suggestion implied some sort of change in God and must therefore be ruled out. It is of interest to note that on the three occasions when Plotinus discusses the problem of the making of the visible world he sides with Albinus. The same may also be said for the great Christian theologian Origen (185–254), who perhaps owed his views to Aristotelian influence.

The Middle Platonists hardly form a clear, organized body of thought. There is very little evidence that they exercised any influence on each other. It has indeed been suggested that Plotinus read Philo, but that is hardly likely. What unites them, rather, is the possession of certain common concerns and a general, if ill-defined, allegiance to Plato. The Bible, Pythagoras, and Aristotle were all thought of in their differing ways as being somehow in accord with Plato. The common concern that unites them is the desire on the part of all to interpret Plato in such a way as to overcome the crucial difficulty in his system; that of bridging the gulf created by the theory of forms between ultimate, static, reality and the changing unstable world of matter and sense. Connected with this is the effort towards transcendence manifested in differing ways by all the main authors: the incomprehensible God of Philo, the simple/complex Mind of Albinus, and the Monad of Plutarch.

Plotinus (204/5–270), the founder of Neoplatonism, is known to us both from the biography written by his devoted, but possibly not altogether comprehending pupil, Porphyry, and from the collections of his writings, organized topically into six volumes, *Enneads*, by the same pupil. He was by birth and early training an Egyptian and claimed to have learnt most of his philosophy from Ammonius Saccas. The content of this teaching is beyond recovery, since Ammonius left no writings behind him and speculation about him has yielded no certain results. In 244 Plotinus left Egypt for Rome, where he spent the rest of his life. His teaching was conducted by means of seminars, to which he attracted some of the influential men of his day. An index of the power of his views and personality is the fact that one of his auditors, a senator, Rogatianus, was persuaded to abandon his life of public service. This incident highlights the fact that politics was the only branch of ancient philosophy in which Plotinus showed no interest. Indeed at times he displays a positive antipathy towards it.

Plotinus thought of himself as a Platonist, and in much of his teaching Platonic influence is evident. Like Plato he believed in the superiority of intellect to sense and of the spiritual world to the material. In this area he consciously rejected precisely those philosophies which he thought undermined the basis of Platonic intellectualism, above all Scepticism, Stoicism, and Gnosticism, (a body of esoteric doctrines which denied the reality of the flesh and the physical world). Against the first of these he insisted that we can know, and that our knowledge is neither derived from nor reducible to sense impressions, but comes on the contrary from a direct, ever present awareness of spiritual reality, which is always available to us if only we concentrate our minds upon it. Against the Stoics Plotinus argued that 'reality' is not primarily material but spiritual, and that the existence of matter results from the absence of form and spirit; in other words, that it is a negative rather than a positive thing. However, we are not to suppose that his critique of Stoicism made Plotinus into a despiser of the visible order. His third main opponents were the Gnostics, whose devaluation of matter made it necessary for them to believe in the need to escape from this world. He also objected to their tendency to underrate the importance of choice and mind in their effort towards salvation. One of his grandest *Enneads*, 2.9, is directed against the Gnostics and has been described as a 'noble apology for Hellenism' in its insistence on the goodness and beauty of the visible order and its vindication of the centrality of freedom and reason in the good life. In his reactions to Stoicism and Gnosticism we can see Plotinus delicately or precariously balanced between two conflicting world views, tending respectively to the deification and vilification of the world we see.

Apart from the evident Platonism of the *Enneads* and the no less evident willingness to incorporate into this general system elements drawn from Aristotle and the Stoa, two other features need mention. The most widely known and distinctive of these is the One, the supreme principle which stands at the climax of the ladder of reality. The One is impersonal and beyond the reach of predication and of any direct knowledge, yet it is at the same time the source of all reality and all value. It combines the One of Plato's *Parmenides* and the Good of the *Republic*. It is from the One as the infinite and generous source of life and value that all else comes. In making this step Plotinus goes beyond both Plato and his own immediate predecessors. For them, absolute reality is both limited and static. For Plotinus, on the other hand, the One, and even more the second substance, the Mind, is boiling with life. On one occasion he writes that being is 'not a corpse, and not not-life and not not-thinking.'

The second feature of importance in Plotinus' system is that it is experienced rather than argued for. It was his own acute awareness of the One gained as the fruit of intense concentration that helped him to formulate the system above outlined. His biographer tells us two important things about him. He was strongly opposed to all forms of ritualistic religion and observed on one occasion that 'the gods must come to me, not I to the gods'. Towards the end of his biography Porphyry also says that during the time during which he knew him Plotinus experienced ecstasy. This state, which is described in great detail at the end of the last *Ennead*, entailed for him 'a simplification and surrender of the self, an aspiration towards contact, which is at once a stillness and a mental effort of adaptation'. Union of this type is experienced only briefly and is the climax of a process of moral purification, introversion and contemplation of 'the vision that makes happy'. The culminating state of union, in which any awareness of distinction is for the time abolished, seems to have led Plotinus to postulate the One at the summit of the hierarchy of reality, as the only possible explanation for the variety we normally experience and for the state of exalted unification which he underwent on at least four occasions.

It is hard to exaggerate the importance of Plotinus. His system was the outcome both of the philosophical syncretism that preceded him and of his own personal mystical experience. He is also significant because of his attempt to break down the layered vision of his immediate predecessors in favour of a dynamic, spiritual monism, in which as Dean Inge notes 'there are no straight lines drawn across the map of the universe'. The tensions in his own vision result almost entirely from his effort to break through the more static, dualistic presuppositions of his ancestors. Finally, it would be unfitting not to mention the extraordinary influence he exercised directly or indirectly on later Platonists, like Porphyry and Proclus, and on Christian writers of the stature of Denis the Areopagite and St Augustine.

Stoicism

Epictetus (*c*.55–135 AD) was a rough contemporary of Plutarch, but whereas Plutarch was a Boeotian aristocrat, Epictetus was by birth a slave. He belonged to Epaphroditus, the freedman and secretary of Nero, who later served Domitian until his murder in 95 AD. Epictetus was allowed to attend the lectures of the celebrated Stoic Musonius Rufus, and in 89, together with all other philosophers, he was banished from Rome and took up residence at Nicopolis in Epirus. There he spent the rest of his life expounding the precepts of Chrysippus (above, Ch. 15) and making his own comments on them. These comments were collected and organized by one of his hearers, Flavius Arrian, consul for 130, into eight books, four of which still survive. His work has a wider appeal than that of his predecessors; it was addressed to the humble and the poor rather than to the few and the self-reliant, and the main tenet of his teaching was the need to cultivate inner peace as the way to true freedom.

'With Posidonius the Stoa opened itself to Platonic influence.' The principal question to be asked about the philosophy of Epictetus is whether he continued in the direction mapped out by Posidonius, or whether he reverted to the pure doctrine of Zeno, Cleanthes, and Chrysippus, the founders of the school. On this central point opinions differ. Some scholars believe that in Seneca, Epictetus, and Marcus Aurelius, the Platonizing of the Stoa continues. Others, however, take the opposite line, at least for the central figure, and see in him a reversion to origins.

It cannot be doubted that a good deal of the language of Epictetus' *Discourses*, if taken literally, suggests a departure from the monistic position of Chrysippus. In some places, for example, God is described, not as a world process, as nature, but rather as the Other or Another. On the same point it is worth noting also that on many occasions reference is made to 'the God', 'the gods', and to 'Zeus'. It is not clear how far the use of such religious language implies belief in a god, or gods, existing separately from nature. Another arguably Platonizing element is the treatment of the soul. In *Discourse* 1.9.11 Epictetus speaks about our natural kinship to the gods, which we will be able to realize once we have dispensed with the fetters that bind us; that is, the body and its possessions. Such language is more akin to the 'body a prison' idea of Plato's *Phaedo* than to the doctrines of most of the Stoics, who denied such an opposition of soul and body. Again, therefore, the question must be asked: does such language express a profound metaphysical dualism, or has it some other function? In making a decision about the best method of understanding Epictetus' position three points should be noticed. First of all he was not primarily interested in the construction of an ontology but rather had an ethical concern, to which his metaphysical beliefs, if he had any, were not of the first importance. Then also, despite the appearance of transcendental, dualist language, such talk accounts for only a relatively small part of the actual usage of the *Discourses*. The old Stoic identification of 'God' and 'Nature' continues to be used (cf. fr. 1). Finally, it would be unfair to suggest that the existence of dualist language is restricted to Epictetus and the later Stoics. It also occurs in the *Hymn to Zeus* written by the unquestionably 'orthodox' Cleanthes somewhere towards the beginning of the third century BC. As Bonhoeffer notes, the Stoic school from its beginning had employed a dualist language alongside its basic monism. It seems therefore on the whole preferable to see in Epictetus, though arguably not in Seneca and Marcus Aurelius, a return to pure Stoicism, after the brief flirtation with Platonism evident in the Middle Stoicism of writers like Posidonius, Panaetius, the Pseudo-Aristotle, and the Book of Wisdom. If the above analysis is correct, it means that we see in Epictetus, and perhaps also in Cleanthes before him, a very interesting juxtaposition of two ways of talking, a metaphysical monism alongside a religious dualism.

The main concern of Epictetus is ethical. Like all the great moral philosophers of classical antiquity, he is concerned to ensure the happiness of those whom he addresses. But, unlike Aristotle, and to some extent unlike Plato, he subordinates philosophy to the cure of the soul. 'Men,' he writes, 'the lecture room of the philosopher is a hospital' (*Diss.* 3.23.30). Happiness is made to consist in peace of mind, a quality which is always within our power, and therefore must in no sense be made to depend upon things outside our control. Dependence upon external things, whether they be material possessions, the affection and esteem of others, even good health, necessarily impedes our own peace, because any of these things may be taken from us. Such a system, if it is to succeed, clearly relies on the power to make the fundamental distinction between what does and what does not lie within our power. In the first chapter of his *Encheiridion* or *Handbook* he writes as follows: 'Some things are under our control, while others are not under our control. Under our control are conception, choice, desire, aversion, and in a word, everything that is our doing; not under our control are our body, our property, reputation, office, and, in a word, everything that is not our doing.' This is all clear enough, though it might be objected that the clarity with which the distinction is made is a little deceptive. It is an often expressed corollary of this that the way to happiness is not straining after the impossible, but cutting down desires, not allowing yourself to be disturbed at all by the things that you cannot remedy, and even when you can remedy evil, not impairing your own peace of mind in the process. At *Diss.* 4. 4. 33 he writes:

And how shall I free myself?—Have you not heard many times that you ought to eradicate desire utterly; direct your aversion to things that lie within the sphere of the moral purpose, and these only; that you ought to give up everything, your body, your property, your reputation, your books, turmoil, office, freedom from office? For if once you swerve aside from your course, you are a slave, you are a subject.

It follows from all this that the root of our malaise is failure to make the correct judgements about what is and what is not in our power, and that the remedy for such errors is the formation of correct judgements and the control of the impressions that come into the mind. The aim of life and the way to happiness is for me to adapt myself to the particular expression of nature that is to be found in me. Once I have discovered that, I shall be in a position to live my life and adapt my moral purpose accordingly.

The system as outlined above clearly aims to offer the maximum of happiness, and at the same time it is highly intellectualist, in the best traditions of the primitive Stoa. Unlike Aristotle, and also unlike the Middle Stoics, Epictetus is not prepared to allow the emotions any part to play in the picture of man or in the end of the moral life. Again, an ethical system that consists largely in discovering where nature calls and following there, can hardly be prescriptive. In other words if 'whatever is, is right', there is little if any room left for any attempts to bring about the improvement of the world. By concentrating his efforts on the purification of the moral purpose—a central and new idea in him— Epictetus hardly preached a revolutionary system. Epictetus' ethics can be summed up not unfairly in the celebrated life formula 'Endure and Renounce'. Their restraint may echo his early life as a slave, where freedom of movement would have been greatly restricted; and it may be true that, as his translator

BRONZE STATUE OF MARCUS AURELIUS ON HORSEBACK. The Roman Emperor (AD 161–80) was inspired by Stoic philosophy and wrote the *Meditations*, a collection of personal thoughts which has achieved great success since the sixteenth century; it was his tragedy to have been committed, during his reign, to a career of almost continuous warfare.

observes, 'they hardly provide a sufficient programme for a highly organized society making towards a goal of general improvement.' Nevertheless there is something inexpressibly noble in the character they reveal and the programme they outline. In an age where the little man must have been made increasingly aware of his impotence in the face of a crushing imperial machine, Epictetus' invitation to win peace of soul, and with it happiness, by adapting oneself to one's circumstances and restricting one's desires within the bounds of the possible, must have sounded both wise and attractive. Conformity of such a sort reaches religious proportions when 'nature' becomes the same as 'God'.

Marcus Aurelius, born in 121 AD, was adopted by the Emperor Antoninus Pius in 138 and himself became Emperor in 161. A good deal of his time in power was spent pacifying the northern and eastern frontiers of the Empire, and the twelve books of *Meditations* are almost certainly the result of his private self-communing during his campaigns. Book 2 was probably written 'among the Quadi on the Gran' and Book 3 at Carnuntum, now Haimburg, in Austria. This will give a date of somewhere between 171 and 173. Unlike the *Discourses* of Epictetus, they were not intended for an audience; but like them they are not composed in an orderly, schematic fashion. There seems to have been no idea in the mind of Marcus of future publication, and in that respect they differ from the *Letters* of Pliny or of Gregory of Nazianzus, which though perhaps initially meant for the immediate addressee, seem almost always, perhaps as a result of later revision, to have a wider audience in view. Marcus' *Meditations*, however, passed unnoticed until 350, and then they drop out of notice for 550 years. It was, in fact, only with their printing in 1558 that their popularity as a work of comfort and instruction began.

He presents the same sort of problems of classification as did his master Epictetus. He too uses from time to time dualistic language about the relation of body and soul, and personal transcendent language about the divine. *Meditation* 5.27 is a good example of this practice. 'Walk with the Gods. And he does walk with the Gods who lets them see his soul invariably satisfied with his lot and carrying out the will of that "genius", a particle of himself, which Zeus has given to every man as his captain and guide.' On the other hand *Med.* 4.23 seems to hold up as an ideal conformity with the Universe, which is taken as the equivalent of Nature and the city of Zeus. Such language is more monist in tone. In another traditionally Stoic passage Marcus writes 'For there is but one Universe, made up of all things and one God immanent in all things, and one substance and one law, one Reason common to all created intelligences, and one Truth.' There is also an unresolved ambiguity in his mind on the question of personal survival, an ambiguity which seems to distinguish him from Epictetus. Thus he can write 'What then remains [*sc.* of us] after death? To wait with a good grace for the end, whether it be extinction or translation.' One point, particularly connected with his moral advice, seems to distinguish him from his master, and to argue at the same time in favour of a slightly greater influence of Platonism. Marcus was

AERIAL VIEW OF CARNUNTUM, where Marcus Aurelius wrote part of his *Meditations*. Occupying an important strategic position on the Danube frontier, Carnuntum was permanently garrisoned from the time of Tiberius, and was Marcus' headquarters from AD 172 to 174 during the Marcomannic wars. In the left foreground the excavations of part of the civil settlement near the modern town of Petronell; the site of the legionary fortress is in the distance (under the light-coloured field next to the modern highway).

a great advocate of introversion. 'Look within. Within is the fountain of Good, ready always to well forth if you are prepared to dig deep enough.' Introversion of this sort, and the reflexion it implies, would appear to rule out a purely materialistic concept of the soul, and this point, together with the distinct possibility of the existence of life after death, seems to tip the scales in favour of seeing in Marcus a Platonizing Stoic.

Despite the tendency to adopt certain Platonic ways of thinking on occasion, it remains true that in the basic drive of his system Marcus keeps to the fundamental Stoic tenet that the way to well-being in this life is through obedience to nature and the suppression or mastery of passion. We ought to follow the god or the gods and live in agreement with nature. He uses the classic Stoic formula of 'life in accord with nature' only once; but the idea is always there in the background. On the whole Marcus prefers the more to the less personal expressions. He has less to say about curbing desire than does Epictetus, but being a person in supreme authority he had less obvious need to free himself from unsatisfiable wishes than his master. Among the precepts which he records there is one which expresses in a paradoxical way the ideal of the Stoic sage: 'At the same time to be utterly impervious to all passions and full of natural affection.' Noble though such an ideal undoubtedly is, it may be doubted whether it is at all attainable.

Stoicism, much more than Platonism, was devoted to helping men to live at peace with themselves and with the world, and was always in danger of toppling over into conformity, comfortable or otherwise. In accepting nature, or what happens, as the ultimate criterion of right and wrong, the Stoics were incapable on their own principles of criticizing society, and found some measure of peace in adapting themselves to its vagaries. This inevitably led them to pursue a sort of inner tranquillity through introversion, which represents at the same time a withdrawal from the external world and the assumption of an inner reality that lay beyond the reach of external tyranny. But in seeking such a peace it may be doubted if they remained true to the very principles of anti-dualism from which they began.

Scepticism

Despite Antiochus' abandonment of the sceptical position of the New Academy in favour of a Stoic belief in the possibility of certainty in perception and knowledge, it must not be supposed that the anti-dogmatic habit died at once to be resurrected only with the sixteenth century. Almost at the same time as the Academy abandoned the scepticism common to it since the days of Arcesilaus and Carneades, there arose at some time between 100 and 40 BC a champion of the ancient and true sceptic tradition—Aenesidemus of Alexandria. Little is known about his life except that he denounced, not surprisingly, Antiochus and, surprisingly, Arcesilaus and Carneades, because, he argued, they taught that scepticism was a dogma, whereas they should have said that it was a possibility, not a certainty.

The final flowering of Scepticism as a system took place in the second century and is available to us through the writings of Sextus Empiricus (d. *c.*200 AD). In the course of fourteen books he expounded the principles of Scepticism, and then took issue with all brands of dogmatists and instructors. His work and that of those he represents has been described somewhat eulogistically as the 'antecedent of freedom of conscience, rational criticism, and the absolute right of scientific thought'.

As in the other systems here described, the central aim was one of offering the maximum of happiness. It must be admitted at the outset that their conception of happiness is decidedly negative and owes a good deal to Epicureanism—a philosophy by no means dead, at least to judge from the massive inscription put up at the close of the second century AD by Diogenes of Oenoanda in his native city to instruct his fellow citizens in the Epicurean system. The aim of life is *ataraxia* or freedom from disturbance. The way to this state of mind is through

PART OF THE INSCRIPTION OF DIOGENES OF OENOANDA (second century AD). Over 200 fragments of this amazing philosophical text have now been discovered. It is thought originally to have been about 100 m long. This particular fragment sheds interesting light on Epicurean attitudes to the gods: they should not be portrayed as forbidding or vengeful, and should not be feared, but should be reverenced and accorded the traditional cult-practices.

suspension of judgement, which is arrived at by a realization that certainty is impossible and no argument incontrovertible. The main interest of the whole system is the way in which they thought this state of realization was to be achieved. It was supposed to happen through the ten celebrated 'tropes' of Aenesidemus. The aim of the tropes is to challenge the value, and even more the bare possibility, of going beyond the appearances and arriving at what Stoics and Platonists alike would have termed knowledge. Antisceptic though he was, Plotinus thought it necessary to refute their objections to the possibility of knowledge. In fact *Ennead* 5.5.1 can be read as accepting their critique of Stoic sensualism, before he propounds his own theory. The principal type of argument proposed by Aenesidemus and Sextus is that, because the way in which objects appear to us differs from person to person, it is impossible to make absolute claims about the nature of the thing in itself. The first trope argues that, as the same object produces differing impressions on different living creatures, no valid inference about the actual object may be drawn from the report of our senses, and therefore that the only proper and possible attitude towards them is one of suspension of judgement, *epochē*. In his treatise *On the Drunkenness of Noah* Philo writes: 'These and similar phenomena are clear proofs of the impossibility of apprehension'. There is a certain rigour evident in the arguments of the Sceptics, which is in striking contrast to the somewhat incoherent dogmatism of the founders of Middle Platonism, notably Antiochus of Ascalon. As far as we know, no refutation was provided of the arguments of Sextus and Aenesidemus; nevertheless the school did not last. Perhaps it was thought of as too uncompromisingly destructive for an age which needed the support of a metaphysical or religious vision.

Further Reading

One of the best introductions to the thought and atmosphere of the whole period is *Conversion* by A. D. Nock (Oxford, 1933), a study in the Old and the New in Religion from Alexander the Great to Augustine of Hippo. To this should be added *Pagan and Christian in an Age of Anxiety* by E. R. Dodds (Cambridge, 1965), which offers an explanation of the success of Christianity in psychological categories. The chapters on philosophy by Nock and F. H. Sandbach in Vols. x and xi of the *Cambridge Ancient History* are also useful.

For more specifically philosophical treatment the last volume of Zeller's *History of Philosophy*, entitled *Stoics, Epicureans and Sceptics* (London, 1892), is still probably the most thorough and helpful treatment, though he does not deal with Plotinus. A good, though rather general, survey of the whole classical period of philosophy is also to be found in Vol. i of *A History of Philosophy, Greece and Rome* (London, 1946) by F. C. Copleston. The most easily accessible account of Plotinus and of his immediate predecessors and followers, and also of Philo and of the main Christian philosophers of the first three centuries AD, is to be found in *The Cambridge History of Late Greek and Early Medieval Philosophy* (Cambridge, 1967) ed. A. H. Armstrong. More detailed accounts of imperial philosophy can be had in *Stoic Philosophy* by R. M. Rist (Cambridge, 1969) and in *The Middle Platonists, a Study in Platonism, 80 BC–AD 220* by J. Dillon (London, 1977), and *Neoplatonism* by R. T. Wallis (London, 1972).

Most of the authors of the period can be read in the Loeb Classical Library, which are often furnished with useful introductions and, in the case of Plutarch and Plotinus, with helpful analyses of the contents of the various treatises. The Stoics are represented by the *Discourses* of Epictetus (London, 1925) with an introduction and translation by W. A. Oldfather, and by the *Meditations* of Marcus Aurelius Antoninus (London, 1916), edited, translated, and introduced by C. R. Haines. The appendix contains the speeches and sayings of Marcus and a useful note on his attitude to Christians, in which Haines challenges the popular view that Marcus was hostile to them. Later Platonism is best illustrated by the *Moralia* of Plutarch, especially in Vol. v (London, 1936), translated by F. C. Babbit, which contains *Isis and Osiris* and *The E at Delphi*. Neoplatonism is represented by the *Enneads* of Plotinus (1966), not yet all available, with translation and useful synopses of the complex argument by A. H. Armstrong. A good impression of the mind of Plotinus is available from *Ennead* 1. 6 On Beauty and 2. 9 Against the Gnostics.

30

The Arts of Living

❦

ROGER LING

Introduction

THE object of the present chapter is to review those aspects of Roman art and architecture which impinge upon life, and conversely those aspects of life which encroach upon the realms of art. Thus, while Chapter 32 will deal with High Art and 'art for art's sake', we shall here concentrate on topics such as houses and gardens in so far as they affect and reflect life-style, on fittings, furnishings, and interior decoration as documents of contemporary taste and attitudes, on eating and drinking, on personal effects and ornaments, and on household implements and utensils. The field is vast and varied, and generalization is inevitable. It is inevitable, above all, that much of the material discussed will relate to Roman Italy and to the first and early second centuries AD, for which we have an unparalleled abundance of evidence, both literary and archaeological. The literary evidence is provided by social poets such as Persius, Statius, Martial, and Juvenal, by novelists (Petronius), by encyclopedists (the Elder Pliny), and by letter-writers (Pliny the Younger and, for an earlier period, Cicero). The archaeological evidence comes chiefly from the remarkable remains of two 'provincial' towns, Pompeii and Herculaneum, buried by the eruption of Mount Vesuvius in AD 79. There is, of course, much evidence from other archaeological sites, for example second- and third-century Ostia; but none of these supplies the same *embarras de richesse* as Pompeii, still less the same precision of dating.

Houses and Villas

The traditional middle- and upper-class town-house of republican and early-imperial Italy was the *domus*, a spreading mansion focused on two inner light-sources, the *atrium* at the front and a colonnaded garden or peristyle at the rear. The *atrium*, the social and religious centre of the house, was the first open space to confront the visitor as he entered from the street, and it was fittingly endowed in most cases with majestic height, and sometimes with lofty columns framing the shallow rectangular catchwater basin (*impluuium*) in the centre of the floor.

Light flooded through a central opening in the roof (*compluuium*) and was diffused to the chambers round the *atrium*—bedrooms, offices, store-rooms, small dining-rooms, often a pair of broad and deep recesses (*alae*) used to display masks or busts of the family's ancestors. At the back, separable from the *atrium* by a curtain or wooden partition, was the main reception room, the *tablinum*. The second light-source, the peristyle, generally lay behind this. Often of great size, it was surrounded by further rooms, including open-fronted *exedrae* and banqueting-halls (*oeci*).

The first important characteristic to observe in this kind of house is its privacy. The ground floor at least was entirely inward-looking; apart from a few slit

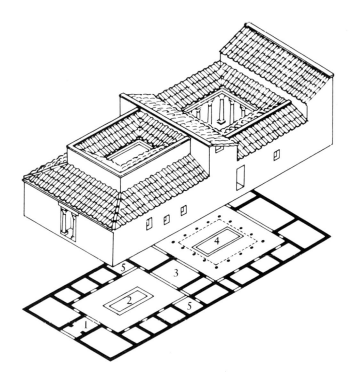

ISOMETRIC DIAGRAM OF A POMPEIAN HOUSE. The tendency to an axial layout with a sequence of roofed and unroofed elements is clearly emphasised: the entrance passage (1) leads to the front hall or *atrium* (2), behind which the reception room or *tablinum* (3) opens on to the colonnaded garden or peristyle (4). The recesses (*alae*) for the display of family portraits are at the back corners of the *atrium* (5).

windows at a high level, its exterior walls presented a blind face to the surrounding world—as much to insure against burglary, one imagines, as to shut out the noise and bustle of the streets. Another characteristic is a tendency to axial planning. Even if it could not always be achieved in practice, the implicit ideal of the *domus* was a vista running from the front door through the centre of the *atrium* and the *tablinum* into the peristyle, often focusing on an architectural feature of some form at the rear. In the House of the Faun, a grand double-*atrium* survivor of Pompeii's palmiest days, larger even than the royal palace at Pergamum, the main vista through the western *atrium* culminated in the columnar *exedra* paved with the Alexander mosaic (plate facing p. 438). In other Pompeian houses a more ostentatious later generation installed a brightly coloured mosaic

THE INTERIOR OF THE HOUSE OF THE TRAGIC POET AT POMPEII: imaginative reconstruction drawing by William Gell (1832), looking from the *atrium* through to the peristyle. At the rear a mosaic
fountain-niche forms the focus of an axial vista from the street door. Gell's drawing, together with the other
illustrations in his *Pompeiana*, helped to inspire Lytton's description of the house of Glaucus in *The Last Days
of Pompeii* (1834).

fountain-niche at the back of the garden, strategically placed to catch the eye of
callers at the street-door. A further notable feature of the house was its strong
contrasts of light and shade. In the bright Mediterranean summer the aesthetic
effect of the vista would have been conditioned by the alternation of deep shadow
and dazzling sunlight, and even in the darker days of winter the rhythm of light
and shade would have been a potent visual factor.

This last point leads naturally to the consideration of lighting, heating, and
related amenities. In summer the cool, lofty rooms and the shady garden porticoes
of the *domus* provided welcome relief from the heat and glare; but in winter the
same rooms could be uncomfortably cold and dark. Although the chill of mosaic
and mortar pavements could doubtless be alleviated with the aid of woven rugs,
there was no entirely satisfactory way of heating living-rooms and bedrooms in
early-imperial times. The underfloor heating systems which were employed in
bath-suites were rarely introduced for other kinds of room, except (later) in the
colder climes of the northern provinces. Generally householders had to rely on
charcoal braziers, a source of heat which would have been unpleasantly smoky,
especially in those chambers which were less well ventilated. At the same time
the rarity of window glass, not widely available before the first century AD,
created a lighting problem, since openings created to admit light would let out
the heat. This is one reason why the older parts of houses had few and small

windows. By the time of Seneca the darkness of old-style bathrooms was a matter for comment, but even now the problem of lighting must have remained in many rooms, whether in baths or elsewhere, if the owner could not afford the luxury of window glass and was obliged to employ shutters or hangings to retain the heat. The candelabra and oil lamps used in antiquity would have provided, at best, an inefficient light and would have contributed to the fumes emitted by braziers. Under the circumstances it was often felt appropriate to decorate the walls of badly illuminated rooms with light colour schemes; but there are just as many examples where the heavy polychromy of the murals increased the gloom.

Generally speaking, however, amenities improved as time went on. The increasing use of window glass led to a better lit and more efficiently heated style of housing; the gradual introduction of more durable and fire-resistant building materials, notably (from Augustan times onwards) brick-faced concrete, brought new standards of stability and safety; and the steady expansion of aqueduct schemes provided running water to cities which had previously relied on wells and rainwater cisterns. Even now, however, running water reached very few private houses. In Pompeii, while well-to-do proprietors such as the Vettii and D. Octavius Quartio could service elaborate garden fountains and water-plays which looked forward across the centuries to the aquatic showpieces of Renaissance Italy, the vast majority of householders, including even the family which lived in the imposing House of the Menander, had to use rainwater or fill their pitchers at the streetside fountains.

The improvements in amenities were accompanied by general changes in the style of urban housing. The *domus*, laid out chiefly on one floor, was prodigal of space and belonged primarily to those periods and those cities in which there was plenty of room for expansion. But right from the first it was not the only, or even the predominant, mode of dwelling. In second-century BC Pompeii, a remarkably prosperous town, there were innumerable small 'lower-class' houses and shops, many of which consisted of only a couple of rooms or a single room containing a mezzanine storey; and in contemporary Rome population pressures were already promoting the development of 'high-rise' apartment blocks. We have a fascinating report in Livy of an ox which, as early as 218, climbed to the third storey of a house near the Roman cattle-market, whence it fell to its death; and in 191 two oxen in another quarter of Rome went up the stairs right to the roof (they survived the climb but were immolated for their efforts). By the late first century BC the architectural writer Vitruvius was able to refer to tower blocks with fine views, and Augustus was obliged, for safety reasons, to limit their height to 70 feet. An echo of this development is discernible at Pompeii, where upper storeys were added piecemeal to many of the older houses, and new blocks such as the Forum Baths, built soon after 80 BC, were provided from the start with upstairs flats accessible directly from the street. By AD 79 Herculaneum had at least two new-style shop-and-apartment blocks, one of which has survived to a height of three storeys. Pressure on space and the growth of the small

THE HOUSE OF DIANA AT OSTIA, a fine example of brick-faced tenement architecture of the mid second century AD. It rose at least four floors, with separate small apartments grouped round a central light-well. The broad shop-openings, the small windows lighting mezzanine floors above them, and the shallow balcony carried on arched corbels, are all characteristic of this building type.

commercial classes also led to the break-up of the old mansions, many of which, like the Victorian houses of modern Britain, came to be divided into independent rented units.

The housing of a major commercial city of the high imperial age is best studied at Ostia, largely rebuilt according to new building standards during the second and early third centuries AD. Here, although some single-storey *domus* still survived and new kinds of courtyard houses, complete with resplendent marble veneer, were added at a later date, the characteristic type of accommodation was the *insula*, or apartment block, three, four, or five storeys high. Unlike the *domus*, this faced outwards, with large windows often opening on to shallow balconies (not always accessible, however, and designed more to shelter the windows beneath than to provide extra space for the tenants). Its great virtue was its flexibility, both in plan and, as a consequence, in the life-style that it offered. It could take the form of a long narrow block, one living-unit in depth; of a rather deeper block, with two sets of living-units arranged back to back; or, where a building plot was particularly deep or neighbouring buildings obstructed the light, of a four-sided block round a central court. Within these basic formulae the variations were legion. A favourite treatment of the street front, foreshadowing the architecture of medieval and Renaissance Italy, was a succession of barrel-vaulted shops interspersed with stairways leading straight from the street

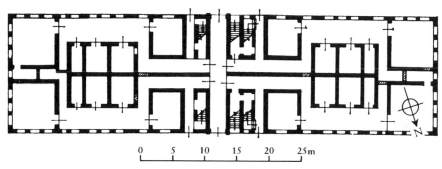

GARDEN HOUSES AT OSTIA (AD 117–38): one of a pair of identical blocks at least three, and probably four, storeys high. These symmetrically planned groups of maisonettes surrounded by open space must have presented a remarkably modern appearance.

to the upper storeys. The ground floor of the *insula* might, alternatively, be divided into two or four more or less identical self-contained flats, entered either directly from the exterior or from an internal dividing corridor. Sometimes, as in the House of the Muses and the House of the Painted Vaults, the whole, or a large part, of the ground floor constituted a single living-unit. In such cases the occupant was perhaps also the owner of the block, and the other occupants his tenants; at the very least he was himself a superior tenant, able to afford space and amenities denied to his upstairs neighbours, many of whom may have had very small apartments and even single rooms.

We know less about the quality of life in the Ostian *insulae* than we do for the houses of Pompeii, because so few of the furnishings and fittings survive. Doubtless standards of comfort were a great deal higher than in Late-Republican Rome; and doubtless Juvenal's accounts of tumbling tenements and the constant danger of incineration in the Rome of his own day were somewhat exaggerated. But conditions in these multiple dwellings could not have been ideal. Even if water could be piped to the ground floor, upstairs tenants would still have been obliged to draw water from the public fountains or cisterns. Very few flats would have had private lavatories: the cry of 'gardyloo' was perhaps as familiar in the streets of Ostia as it was in eighteenth-century Edinburgh. Moreover there was enough timber in the upper floors and internal fittings to make the risk of fire a real one, especially since no truly safe means of heating and cooking were available. Lighting also remained a problem, as at Pompeii, for those tenants who could not afford window glass; many windows were filled with barely translucent panes of selenite or simply had wooden shutters.

Country residences, like town dwellings, ranged over the whole gamut of possibilities, from simple huts and cottages through small working farms to grand villas in which the management of an estate, though generally an important factor, was strictly segregated from a luxurious quarter in which the owner could maintain a life-style appropriate to his taste and station. This last type is well represented in the archaeological record, both in the countryside devastated by the eruption of Vesuvius, and in other parts of Italy and the Empire. We also see it portrayed in Pompeian paintings and read about it in the letters of Cicero and Pliny. Generalizations are difficult, but recurrent features included peristyle gardens, grand colonnaded façades, and (on sloping ground) a podium which Vitruvius calls the *basis uillae*, often containing an underground corridor (*cryptoporticus*). In the grandest examples, including the Villa of the Papyri at Herculaneum and the recently excavated villa at Oplontis, west of Pompeii, both of which have been attractively ascribed to leading families of the Roman nobility, no check was imposed upon the spatial extent of the buildings. At the same time such

PAINTING OF A SEASIDE VILLA of the early-imperial age. Unlike the town-houses of Pompeii and Herculaneum, which turned away from the surrounding streets to focus upon internal gardens and light-wells, the luxury coastal and lakeside villas of the nobility faced outwards over the water. Behind them were wooded parks containing shrines and gazebos.

villas, unlike the aristocratic town-houses, were outward-looking; their colonnaded façades and terraces addressed themselves to a landscape or overlooked a
garden. In the coolness and shelter of the portico the owner could stroll and
philosophize, like the Younger Pliny, about the delights of nature, far from the
toils of the city. A favourite form, especially renowned in the Bay of Naples and
reflected in numerous murals, was the maritime villa, built along the sea-front or
even terraced out into the sea; Pliny, for example, could dine in his Laurentine
villa with 'a view from the front and sides, as it were, of three different seas'
(above, p. 660). In vain did Horace inveigh against the villa-builders of fashionable Baiae, whose concrete piers seemed almost to remodel the coast-line.

Interior Decoration

Interior decoration was an essential ingredient of the Roman life-style and can
hardly be considered apart from domestic architecture. Its strictly art-historical
aspects are dealt with elsewhere (Chapter 32); here we must examine its function
and its meaning to the householder.

At the most mundane level a fine mosaic pavement or a set of painted murals
were designed to beautify a room. The finest decorations were generally reserved
for the main dining- and reception-rooms, but other areas of the house which
were likely to be seen by visitors—the *atrium*, the peristyle, the baths, certain
bedrooms—could also receive special treatment. Only in the more prosperous
houses, however, was the majority of rooms elaborately decorated. Even in
Pompeii the painted walls which conform to the four well-known styles were
outnumbered by those with simple striped and panelled schemes and by walls
with plain plaster, and the mosaic pavements were concentrated in a few particularly opulent dwellings, while the majority of floors were of mortar with
perhaps at the most a sprinkling of inset tesserae or marble fragments. In less
prosperous cities or societies, for instance in certain parts of Roman Britain, the
house- or villa-owner concentrated most of his resources upon adorning one
room: the central dining-room of the Lullingstone villa, with its Bellerophon
and Europa mosaics, is a case in point (above, p. 660).

At a more ambitious level the proprietor used decorations to transform and
enhance his environment. This is particularly true of the Pompeian styles of
wall-painting, in which the imitation veneering of the First Style echoed the real
veneers of Hellenistic palaces. The porphyry columns and exotic architecture of
the Second Style (above, pp. 522, 546) also evoked the grandeur of a court,
though probably transmitted through the medium of stage-painting, and the
baroque extravagances of the Fourth Style (below, p. 784) may have owed
something to the theatre but were probably more a form of escapism into a
world of pure imagination. The perspective forms of both styles also, of course,
seemed to enlarge the physical space within a room; and in some instances, by
offering a glimpse of sky above the painted architecture, or by opening a window

through it on to a mythical world, the decoration seemed to break right through the bounds of the wall. The ultimate expression of this is provided by those paintings, such as the garden murals from Primaporta, which turned the room into an open-sided pavilion set in a magic forest. The aesthetic value of such paintings in rooms which were often cramped and badly lit is easily appreciated.

Another role of interior decoration was to turn parts of the house into picture-galleries (*pinacothecae*). In Hellenistic times, copies of well-known paintings were carried out in mosaic to embellish the central fields of pavements, and the same tradition continued in certain cities of the east, such as Syrian Antioch, through the imperial age. But in the Roman west these copies were incorporated as painted panels within wall-decorations. Well-off Pompeians, such as the brothers Vettii and the owner of the House of the Tragic Poet, collected reproductions of Greek old masters in much the same way as more recent generations have collected copies of the Laughing Cavalier or the Mona Lisa. This was one means whereby the *nouveaux riches* could make a display of their culture. Truly cultured householders, like the owners of the villa at Boscotrecase just north of

THE PENTHEUS ROOM IN THE HOUSE OF THE VETTII at Pompeii (between AD 62 and 79): one of the finest surviving examples of a domestic 'picture-gallery', with copies of well-known Greek paintings set at the centre of each wall-decoration: the Punishment of Dirce, the Death of Pentheus, and the infant Heracles strangling the snakes sent by Hera, perhaps the famous work by Zeuxis of Heraclea (*c.*400 BC).

Pompeii, preferred original paintings in which the stories of Alexandrian and Ovidian elegy and the bucolic world of Theocritus' *Idylls* could be evoked in an altogether more subtle and mysterious manner (above, p. 357).

Whether there are deeper meanings to be discerned in ancient wall-decorations is a question which has recently roused controversy. The Swiss scholar Karl Schefold argues from the Pompeian evidence, not only that painters or their patrons chose subjects which were relevant to the type of room being decorated, but also that the subjects within a decoration were normally linked in a consistent programme embodying deeply-felt moral or religious ideas. Thus one decoration will present a hymn to the great deities of love and fertility, Aphrodite and Dionysus; another will contrast the exploits of a divinely favoured hero with the sufferings of an offender against the gods. Landscape paintings are invariably sacred, still lifes are offerings to the gods, and so forth. The same idea is explored by Mary Lee Thompson, though with a more pragmatic approach: for her most of the programmes are on a relatively superficial plane, dealing with a particular hero such as Achilles, a particular locale such as Thebes, and particular conceptual combinations such as love and water. There is doubtless some truth in all this, for a strong religious element appears in many Roman murals (compare the cult-objects and sacrificants lurking in the painted architecture), and in some cases a thematic link between balancing paintings is unmistakable. The left *ala* of the House of the Menander at Pompeii contains a Trojan cycle in which paintings of the wooden horse and of the death of Laocoon, both allusions to warnings unheeded by the Trojans, are combined, as in a Greek tragedy, with the ruinous sequel: Priam watching griefstricken while Menelaus seizes Helen and Ajax assaults Cassandra. That the Romans often looked for thematic associations is illustrated by a picture gallery described by Petronius, fictional but perhaps based on fact, in which the story of Ganymede is grouped with those of Hylas and Hyacinthus, all three illustrating the love of immortals for beautiful youths and the resulting 'apotheosis' of the loved ones. But to try to apply such rules universally, and above all to look for recondite religious and ethical interpretations, is to expect too grave and profound an outlook in the ancient householder, whereas Pompeian painting contains much that is clearly humorous and much that appeals directly to the senses. It also leads very quickly to inconsistencies: to fit his theories Schefold has to argue that Medea is now contrasted with Penelope as a paradigm of false love, now compared with her as a beatified heroine.

The other main art form found in private houses is sculpture. Here we must distinguish between the religious statuettes of the household shrine (the *Lares*, the *genius* of the paterfamilias, and the protecting deities of the household) and works which were more purely decorative or ostentatious. The latter can again be divided. On the one hand there were small figurines designed to be kept on shelves or sideboards in private parts of the house, for example the terracottas including a gladiator, a porter, Venus arranging her hair, and two slaves carrying a litter, all less than 16 cm. high, found in the family quarters of the House of M.

Lucretius at Pompeii, or the even smaller bronze figurines (a seated philosopher, an old man milking a goat, and an ape brandishing arms) from the ruins of the upper storey of the House of the Marbles, also at Pompeii. On the other hand there were the statues, statuettes, and reliefs which were displayed in gardens and other open parts of the house. These raise the same programmatic questions as wall-paintings and merit closer attention.

In most cases domestic sculptural displays were somewhat arbitrarily compiled and arranged. The need to 'shop around' for available pieces presented a totally different situation from that involved in commissioning a mural decoration and naturally led to heterogeneous collections. The great and wealthy imported works from Greece, but not always with great discrimination, as we can judge from Cicero's requests to Atticus to supply him with sculptures for his villa at Tusculum: 'anything you consider suitable for the palaestra and gymnasium ... reliefs to be set in the plaster of the *atriolum* and a couple of figured well-heads'. Apparently almost any pieces would do so long as they were Greek. Even the sculptures of Hadrian's Villa at Tivoli seem to have been employed in a rather haphazard way. The statues round the Canopus ('Egyptian pool') included a splendid crocodile and much other appropriately Egyptian or egyptianizing material, but there were also very different items, for example copies of Classical Greek wounded Amazons, figures of Hermes and Ares, a statue group showing Scylla and her victims, and replicas of the Erechtheum caryatids. Since Hadrian and his successors were presumably better able than most patrons to get what they wanted, this heterogeneous assortment could hardly have been dictated solely by market forces.

The private collection about whose arrangement we know most is that of the Villa of the Papyri at Herculaneum, from which no fewer than eighty-seven sculptures were recovered and all their find-spots recorded. The late-republican or early-Augustan aristocrat who formed the collection, perhaps L. Calpurnius Piso Pontifex, the consul of 15 BC, was clearly a man of culture rather than of great artistic sensibility: his penchant for busts of Attic orators, Stoic and Epicurean philosophers, and early-Hellenistic dynasts evinces an interest in humanistic studies, but the artistic quality of the collection was variable, ranging from excellent copies of Greek masterpieces to second-rate pastiches and decorative hackwork. Such programmatic arrangements as can be discerned were superficial and not consistently carried through (despite the efforts of modern commentators to argue otherwise). For example, in the large peristyle two figures of runners, a statuette of the seated Hermes, and busts of various philosophers evoked the idea of a gymnasium, but interspersed with them were Hellenistic *condottieri*, animal figures, and drunken satyrs—strange bedfellows indeed. Hermes actually sat back to back with one of the inebriates. Indeed this latter grouping illustrates the point that compositional balance, well exemplified by the favourite Roman device of pairing statues in mirror image, was more important to the householder than thematic correspondence.

THE GARDEN OF THE HOUSE OF M. LUCRETIUS at Pompeii, an excellent example of the use made by the early-imperial *bourgeoisie* of decorative statuary. At the rear, standing in a niche, a Silenus poured water from a wine-skin down the steps into the central pool; all around, scattered in the shrubbery, were animals, birds, and satyrs; in the foreground a young satyr inspected the foot of a Pan, and cupids rode dolphins.

The average Pompeian householder of the years before 79 did not lay claim to the literary culture of Piso: he preferred to concentrate on decorative subjects. Admittedly he might display a portrait herm of an ancestor in his *atrium* as a kind of guarantee of a respectable pedigree, but the bulk of his collection consisted of Bacchic figures, *putti*, herms, and animals, with perhaps the odd decorative statuette of a divinity such as Venus, Apollo, or Diana thrown in for good measure. Some of the items were inherited or bought from older collections, where no doubt they had been used in different roles; many, especially the marbles, were churned out by contemporary local workshops. A large number of them were designed or adapted to serve as fountain-pourers, in which capacity they could be set along the margins of the *impluuium* in the *atrium*, between the columns of the peristyle, or actually in the garden, where they discharged their water into ponds or marble basins. A good example is the satyr squeezing water from a wine-skin down the steps of a *nymphaeum* in the House of M. Lucretius. In addition to figures in the round, many collectors had reliefs, whether set in walls, displayed on top of pillars, or hanging in the form of shields between the columns of porticoes. Whatever the theme or function of the individual works, the householder's chief goals were to accumulate as many exhibits as possible and to place them so as to be visible from certain crucial vantage-points: thus the

IMPLUVIUM AND CARTIBULUM in the House of the Wooden Partition at Herculaneum. The *impluvium* in the foreground is the basin which collected rainwater from the opening in the roof of the *atrium* and channelled it into an underground cistern. Behind it, the *cartibulum* was a marble table for the display of utensils and serving-ware.

BRONZE LAMP-STAND from the Villa of Diomedes at Pompeii (before AD 79): a particularly ornate example in which the lamps are suspended from spiralling branches and the base is decorated with a figurine of a satyr riding a panther. As so frequently in Roman furnishings, the feet are in the form of animal paws.

garden statuary of M. Lucretius is disposed for the benefit of visitors in the *tablinum* and the adjacent dining-room. Bronzes in particular, being more expensive and more highly prized, were flaunted in prominent positions.

If we combine the Pompeian material with evidence from elsewhere, we get a reasonable idea of decorative furnishings in use in imperial times. Tables in both bronze and marble, round or rectangular, were regularly supported by elaborate legs compounded of lions' paws, volutes, griffins' foreparts, and the like. Small bronze tripod stands, complete with raised rims to prevent things from rolling off, had deers' legs or (less tastefully) legs formed by ithyphallic satyrs. Couches were mainly of wood, which with one or two exceptions has perished, leaving only the bronze fittings: elegant lathe-turned legs, headboard ornaments with cast appliqués in the form of busts or horses' heads, and railings

WOODEN CUPBOARD-SHRINE in the House of the Wooden Shrine at Herculaneum. The shrine, in the form of a little temple with finely carved Corinthian colonnettes at the corners, contains statuettes of the household gods, the Lares and Penates. Below is a cupboard containing glassware and ornaments. The lighter coloured parts of the woodwork are modern restorations.

with silver inlay. Sometimes such fittings were in other materials, such as silver, tortoise-shell, or ivory, and a couch with reliefs of bone has recently been partially restored with the aid of remnants in the Fitzwilliam Museum, Cambridge. Bronze lamp-standards came in many more or less ornate types, among which the simplest consisted of a slender fluted column resting on three animal-paws and surmounted by some form of calyx, while more complicated versions had four or more arms, either in the form of volutes or shaped like tree branches, from which lamps were suspended. An especially ornate example from the Villa of Diomedes at Pompeii had a platform at the base, decorated with a figurine of a satyr on a prancing panther. Household chairs and stools, which were mainly of wood, have not survived, but interesting representations of armchairs in basket-work are known from later imperial times. Also of wood were cupboards and cabinets: examples from Pompeii and Herculaneum reveal that they were usually simple affairs divided by shelves into compartments and closed at the front by twin doors; but occasionally an architectural touch was bestowed by the addition of a gabled top or of flanking colonnettes. Even the family strongbox, a stout chest of wood or iron (or both) kept in the *atrium*, could be decorated with bronze plaques carrying figural and vegetal ornament.

Gardens

Ornamental gardening was not invented by the Romans: shrubs and trees had been used by the Greeks to beautify temple precincts and *gymnasia*, and a late-Hellenistic landscaped park has recently been identified outside Rhodes. But it was only in the Roman period that pleasure gardens became a major facet of the arts of living.

The term used by the Elder Pliny for ornamental gardening is *opus topiarium*, whose derivation from the Greek word *topia* (landscapes) reveals both the Greek origins of the art and one of its main themes. The original aim of the gardener was, in fact, to create attractive natural settings: in a famous passage Pliny seems to list varieties of landscape gardens as 'groves, woods, hills, fish-pools, canals, rivers, coasts'. But the artificial element soon came to play a predominant role, and we find increasing evidence for the use of statuary and garden furniture, the introduction of formal layouts and the shaping of trees, and the combination of plants with water displays.

The association of statuary and landscape began with works such as the Victory of Samothrace (above, p. 504), set on a ship in a rock-filled pool, and continued with the sculpture-grottoes of the Rhodian park, a theme later carried to extremes of grandiloquence by Rhodian artists working in the service of the emperor Tiberius at Sperlonga and on Capri. But the combination of statues with foliage soon became equally fashionable. When the word *topiaria* first appears in Latin literature, in a letter of Cicero dated to 54 BC, it is in connection with the growing of ornamental ivy as a backdrop to Greek statuary in one of his brother's villas at Arpinum. Such effects were doubtless employed by many of Cicero's illustrious contemporaries in the parks which they created in the area of Rome itself and round their luxury villas in the country; it was for Italian garden settings that the sculptured marble bowls and candelabra produced in Neo-Attic workshops were primarily designed.

Formal planning and topiary in the modern sense probably began in the time of Augustus. This is when, according to Pliny, one C. Matius invented *nemora tonsilia* ('barbered groves'). As the desire to impose formal shapes almost certainly went hand in hand with the desire to create formal plans, we can assume that the same period saw the first symmetrically planned gardens, especially as the improvements in the water-supply of Rome and other parts of Italy undertaken by Agrippa and his successors would have favoured the cultivation of low, ornamental plants. The first formal gardens in wall-painting belong to the first half of the first century AD, laid out in plots framed by hedges or trellis fences: an example in the *tablinum* of the House of M. Lucretius Fronto at Pompeii shows an enclosed flower-bed on either side of a focal tree, reflecting the symmetry of the villa-façade which overlooks it (plate facing p. 471). Little archaeological evidence of formal gardens is known, though one fine specimen has been reconstructed in the villa at Fishbourne, with a central path bordered by hedges fashioned into a series of alternating rectangular and semicircular recesses. But that such gardens existed on a grander scale in Rome and its surroundings is demonstrated by examples represented on the Severan marble plan of the city (for example, in Vespasian's Temple of Peace) and by parts of a plaque now in Urbino preserving the plan of a funerary park. The further development of

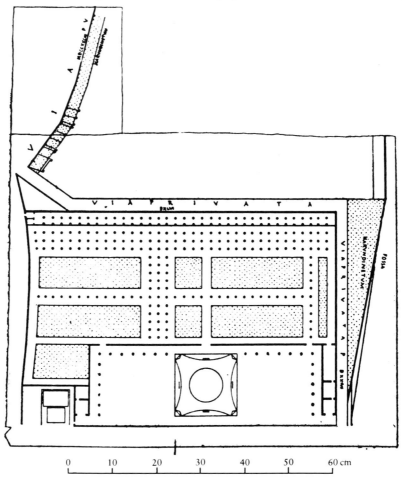

PLAN OF A FUNERARY GARDEN IN ROME: engraving on marble (third or fourth century AD). The actual mausoleum, evidently a three-storeyed affair with a square podium supporting a concave-sided structure crowned by a small rotunda, is shown at the bottom; behind it lies the garden, a formal arrangement of lines of trees (indicated by small circles) and rectangular parterres.

MOSAIC FOUNTAIN NICHE in the House of the Bear at Pompeii. Such niches were a favourite feature of Pompeian gardens once running water had been laid on during the first century AD. The decoration includes an incrustation of pumice and lines of shells, recalling the origin of the niches in the form of natural grottoes sacred to the nymphs or Muses. The mosaic is composed largely of brightly coloured glass tesserae, rare in floor-decoration.

topiary, as distinct from formal plans, apparently knew no bounds. By the time that the *Natural History* was published Pliny could report not only that cypresses were clipped to form hedges but also that they were shaped into elaborate tableaux portraying 'hunt scenes, fleets of ships, and other images'; and in his nephew's villa at Tifernum in Tuscany there were box trees cut into the shapes of wild animals and into numerous other forms, including the letters of Pliny's and his gardeners' names. It was the description of the gardens at Tifernum that inspired the box parterres and labyrinths of the sixteenth and seventeenth centuries.

The same improvements in water-supply which favoured diversification in types of planting also ushered in the age of the garden fountain. Already in the wall-paintings from Boscoreale, dated around 40-30 BC, we see a depiction of a piano-shaped marble fountain at the mouth of a vine-draped grotto; while Propertius, writing in the 20s, reveals that a fountain decorated with a sleeping

CANAL IN THE GARDEN OF D. OCTAVIUS QUARTIO at Pompeii (between AD 62 and 79). In imitation of the canals of villa-parks, this wealthy householder laid out a series of elaborate waterways and fountains, spanned by pavilions and pergolas. In the middle pavilion is a statue of the sleeping Ariadne, derived from a well-known Hellenistic type.

Silenus played among the plane trees of Pompey's porticoes in Rome. The importance of water displays in Pompeian house-gardens has already been mentioned. In addition to statuettes pouring water into basins, many peristyles enclosed large ornamental pools fed by jets of water or fountain-niches at the rear, while other gardens, foreshadowing a vogue of the third and fourth centuries AD, had whole walls enlivened by a façade of niches and pavilions (*aediculae*) from which water flowed. Two large gardens in the east of the city, those of D. Octavius Quartio and Julia Felix, contained central canals with bridges at intervals, sculptures along the edges, and open pergolas bestriding them. On either side ran pathways overhung by climbing plants. A generation later the Younger Pliny took great pride in a fountain which played within a vine-arbour in his Tuscan villa and whose marble basin he and his guests used as a kind of supper table, resting larger dishes on the rim and allowing small dishes of hors d'oeuvres to float in the water.

The trees and plants cultivated in ornamental gardens put the accent on greenery rather than floral displays. Besides the box and cypress trees favoured by topiarists, the ancient sources mention plane trees, laurel, myrtle, hound's tongue, acanthus, maidenhair, butcher's broom (whose evergreen foliage, we are told, was sometimes used in wreaths to make up for a lack of flowers), and a shrub called 'Jupiter's beard' which had silvery leaves and could be trimmed into a round shape. Our picture is supplemented by the shrubberies represented in garden paintings; among the items identified by modern botanists are such flowering plants as poppies, oleanders, lilies, and viburnum. Roses, one of the few flowers attested in Pliny's garden at Tifernum, are shown next to fountain-basins in a mural in the House of the Floral Chambers at Pompeii.

An idea of the overall appearance of small private gardens in the early Imperial age is obtainable at Pompeii, where the recent work of Wilhelmina Jashemski, involving excavation, the study of carbonized plant-material, and pollen analysis, has opened a whole new perspective on the subject. A surprisingly large proportion of peristyle-gardens has turned out to contain fruit- and nut-trees, not to mention vines, all grown for food rather than for fancy; but purely ornamental gardens laid out to formal designs certainly existed in the better appointed houses. The more pretentious examples, combining shrubs, fountains, decorative statuettes, and often frescoes on the enclosing walls, reflect the aspiration of the wealthy middle class to import the villa life of Roman aristocrats into their urban homes. Thus the huge wall-paintings of wild animals which overlook many late-Pompeian gardens evoke the game- or safari-parks (*paradeisoi*) of the nobility, a theme which is also echoed by statuettes of dogs attacking wild boar amid the actual plants and fountains. Some details, such as marble ducks and ibises at the waterside, a bronze fisherman dangling his rod in a fountain, and a sleeping marble pixie amazingly akin to a modern garden gnome, are almost kitsch. The palm for vulgarity should perhaps be awarded to L. Ceius Secundus for commissioning a painting of a nymph who appears to empty her bowl of water into a real gutter in the pavement.

Eating and Drinking

Closely linked with the garden were the delights of dining. The U-shaped masonry dining areas (*triclinia*) found in Pompeian gardens, often accompanied by clam or snail shells and the bones of meat-animals, confirm that the modern Mediterranean practice of eating out of doors on hot summer evenings goes back

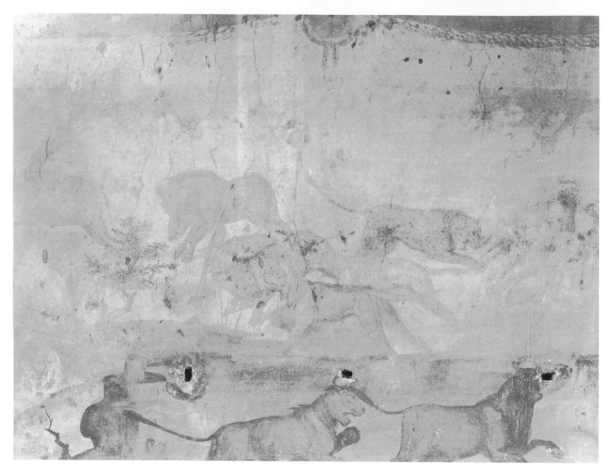

WILD ANIMALS PAINTED IN THE GARDEN OF THE HOUSE OF THE CEII AT POMPEII (between AD 62 and 79).
Such paintings were inspired by the safari parks of Hellenistic monarchs and of the republican nobles who imitated them;
they introduced an incongruous element of grandeur and exoticism to the cramped internal garden of a small town-
house.

SLEEPING PIXIE: marble
statuette of a small boy
wearing a hooded cloak, from
the House of the Small
Fountain at Pompeii (before
AD 79). Round him lie three
baskets, one of which serves as
his pillow; they have been
identified as the apparatus of a
fisherman. Such genre subjects
were much in fashion as
garden-ornaments in the
imperial age.

to antiquity. Sheltered by an awning or by a vine-arbour and cushioned by mattresses and pillows, the diners would recline on their elbows in the Greek manner, picking titbits from a central table or, like Pliny's guests, from floating dishes in the form of little boats and water-birds; as night drew on, lamps would be lit in surrounding candelabra, some of them, as in the House of the Ephebe, suspended from the hands of bronze statues.

The banquets described by Martial, Pliny, Petronius, and others should not mislead us; the diet of the vast mass of the people was always frugal, and even the great men of affairs ate little before evening. But when occasion demanded meals could be splendid and cooking carried to the realms of fine art. A cookery book ascribed to the early-imperial gastronome M. Gavius Apicius gives some fascinating glimpses of Roman haute cuisine: for example, 'Sucking pig à la Frontinus: fillet, brown, and dress; put in a casserole of fish-sauce and wine, wrap in a bouquet of leeks and dill, pour off the juice when half-cooked. When cooked, remove and dry, sprinkle with pepper and serve.' Apicius was famous for his sauces and dressings, and gave his name to various cakes; he is also said by

GARDEN DINING AREA IN THE HOUSE OF THE EPHEBE AT POMPEII (between AD 62 and 79). The masonry couches formed a ∏-shaped *triclinium*, on which diners reclined round a low central table, shaded by a vine-covered pergola. In the background water played from a small fountain shrine; in the foreground a cylindrical pedestal supported the bronze statue of a youth who held candelabra to light the evening banquets.

Pliny to have invented dishes of flamingos' tongues and mullets' livers, and to have pioneered a form of pâté de foie gras. It was one of the arts of the Roman chef to disguise dishes so that no one could divine their ingredients. This was taken to extremes at the feast described by Petronius, where a dish of pork was dressed up by Trimalchio's cook to look like a fattened goose garnished with fish and different kinds of birds ('If you want it, he'll make you a fish out of a sow's womb, a wood-pigeon out of bacon, and a turtle-dove out of a ham', brags the host), and the guests were treated to a whole sequence of unnerving surprises: peahens' eggs containing beccaficos rolled in spiced egg-yolk, a wild boar containing live thrushes, a pig full of sausages and black puddings, cakes and fruit filled with liquid saffron, thrushes made of pastry and stuffed with raisins and nuts, quinces decorated with thorns to look like sea-urchins. Each dish emerged in artistic form or with some histrionic display; the wild boar, for example, arrived with an escort of hunting dogs, and a boiled calf was sliced with a sword by a slave impersonating the frenzied Ajax. Such excesses, though inflated by the writer's fertile imagination, were certainly based upon the pageantry of real banquets. So too were some of the entertainments devised for Trimalchio's guests. The gold hoop laden with gifts which was let down from the ceiling recalls the revolving dome of Nero's Golden House which showered flowers on the diners below. The musicians, singers, acrobats, and dancing girls echo the performances provided at banquets such as the one that seduced a potential guest of Pliny: invited to a homely supper with a poetry recitation and a performance on the lyre, this philistine preferred the gourmet dishes and Spanish dancing-girls of another host.

The delights of more modest dinner-tables are celebrated by the succulent fruits, game-birds, and sea foods represented in Pompeian still-life paintings. These *xenia* ('guest-gifts'), named, according to Vitruvius, after the provisions Greek hosts supplied to visitors on self-catering holidays, call to mind menus described by Martial and Juvenal. Martial, for instance, offers a dinner in which the hors d'oeuvres are listed as mallows, lettuces, leeks, mint, rocket, sliced eggs and anchovies, and sows' udders in tunny sauce; the main course was a kid and cutlets with haricot beans and tender green-sprouts, with the addition of a chicken and the residue of a ham which had already served three suppers; and the dessert consisted of ripe fruit and a vintage Nomentan wine. Wine was, of course, the essential concomitant of good eating, and no meal was complete without a jar of a fine vintage—preferably the 'immortal Falernian', the Château Lafite of Roman Italy.

To serve a sumptuous repast the host needed the best silver and tableware. Discoveries of silver hoards hidden by their owners in Pompeii and nearby Boscoreale at the time of the eruption of Vesuvius reveal both the quality of the plate in domestic use during the early imperial period and also the zeal with which it was prized and protected. The superb beakers, cups, bowls, and dishes decorated with repoussé reliefs of plant arabesques or mythological scenes, together with the simpler, but still elegant, spoons and ladles, lend significance to Petron-

STILL-LIFE PAINTINGS OF
FOOD, from Herculaneum.
According to Vitruvius, such
paintings were called *xenia*
('guest-gifts') after the gifts of
poultry, eggs, vegetables, fruit,
and the like, provided by hosts
for their guests. One panel shows
a hare and a plucked game-bird;
the other a brace of partridges
and a pair of eels.

ius' gibes at the extravagance and tastelessness of his millionaire freedman Trimalchio, who used a chamber-pot of silver and gave orders for a silver dish which had been dropped during his banquet to be swept away like broken pottery. The quality of silverware was maintained during the later Empire. It is to this period that we must ascribe such masterpieces as the octagonal dish from Kaiseraugst in Switzerland, adorned with scenes from the life of Achilles.

If an owner could not afford silverware, the next-best thing was bronze or glass. Both these materials were in much wider use in the home than is generally realized, since the process of recycling has militated against the survival of specimens in domestic contexts. The excavations at Pompeii and Herculaneum have again done much to set the record straight; among the finds are numerous graceful bronze jugs and wine-jars with appliqué reliefs at the base of the handles, and a rich, but barely known, series of glass vessels of all types: bottles, phials, cups, beakers, plates, jugs and the like, translucent or coloured, blown or cast, plain or decorated. Deluxe items of glassware are the so-called 'cameo-glass' vessels, of which the most famous are the Blue Vase from Pompeii and the mysterious Portland Vase, decorated with figures in white relief on a blue-black ground. During the second, third, and fourth centuries the use of glass became more widespread, largely replacing bronzeware (the snobbish Trimalchio makes excuses for using glassware rather than antique Corinthian bronze), and the later imperial period saw the production of further expensive lines, such as various

EMBOSSED SILVER WINE-CUP from the Hildesheim hoard (first century AD). The finely worked Bacchic reliefs, including theatrical masks, Bacchic wands (*thyrsi*) and masks of Silenus, are wholly appropriate to the function of the vessel. Roman silver plate frequently found its way, through trade or plunder, to sites such as Hildesheim which lay beyond the imperial frontiers.

kinds of figured cut glass and the cage-cups with openwork decoration manufactured probably in Italy and the Rhineland.

Lack of space precludes a full examination of the domestic equipment of Roman times. Fine pottery, notably the red-gloss ware from Arretium (Arezzo) and (later) Gaul, imitated the embossed reliefs and even some of the subjects of figured metalware; but the careful moulded decoration of the first and second centuries tended to die away in many areas, to be replaced by simpler techniques including rouletting and relief motifs in applied clay. By the fourth century pottery was to a large extent overtaken by glass as the usual form of fine tableware. Other artistic products in domestic use included carved bone or ivory handles for knives and the ubiquitous bronze or terracotta lamps, with their simple figure-reliefs and distinctive wick-holding nozzles. Less artistic, but unambiguously geared to the pleasures of the table, was the extraordinary series of objects known as *gliraria*—large terracotta jars used to rear dormice, a delicacy which particularly appealed to the Roman palate. Surviving examples from Pompeii are provided with regular holes to admit air and with a spiral ramp round the interior wall to enable the animals to reach a pair of feeding trays near the rim.

Dress and Personal Effects

Dress is the aspect of the arts of living about which we are perhaps least well informed. We know from Roman writers that the ceremonial toga, a semicircular white woollen wrap between 5 and 6 m. in diameter, had to be donned with great art and no little difficulty, a circumstance which encouraged many men to view with relief those 'off-duty' occasions when they could wear the simple *tunica*. Portrait statues give us some idea of what the toga looked like, with its distinctive curving hem; and from the same source we get representations of the long dress, or *stola*, of the Roman matron. Other works of art illustrate further garments, such as the *pallium*, a version of the heavy Greek cloak; the *lacerna*, a short cape fastened at the neck with a brooch; and the *paenula*, a kind of hooded poncho. To the late-imperial period belong depictions of the long-sleeved tunic or dalmatic. But for all this comparative wealth of illustrative material there is little to convey the rich colours and embroideries, still less the fine fabrics (muslins and silks), worn especially by society ladies. The fragments of surviving textiles from Egypt, though instructive on the range of possible weaves, patterns, and colours, are mostly late in date (fourth or fifth centuries), while the pieces from other parts of the Roman world are rarely well preserved or of any artistic pretensions. Nor is there much information in the Latin authors beyond vague indications of cut or colour, for example the green tunic and red belt of Trimalchio's flunkey, the red tunic, yellow belt, and gilded slippers of his wife, and the close-fitting *lacerna* and well-tailored red, green, and purple cloaks given by Statius' friend Atedius Melior to his young favourite Glaucias.

FEMALE HAIR-STYLE OF THE TRAJANIC PERIOD (AD 98–117). The honeycomb quiff of the preceding (Flavian) period now gave way to superposed rows of tightly spiralling curls, with a great interwoven chignon like a bird's nest at the back. The most prominent patron of the new fashion was Trajan's sister Marciana.

We may know little of fine clothing, but fashionable hairstyles are well known from the sculptured portraits of Emperors and their womenfolk. These varied considerably over the years. In the first century the studied disorder of Augustus' hair gave way to the carefully styled waves and sideburns of Nero; and in the second century Trajan's 'Beatle' cut was replaced by the neat Hellenic beard and carefully cultivated coiffure of Hadrian, a fashion carried to extremes in the full beards and tightly crisped locks of his Antonine successors. The imperial ladies were not surprisingly even more fashion-conscious. Although Livia and the Julio-Claudian princesses favoured classicizing styles with gently waving hair running from a central parting to loose ringlets over the ears and a chignon at the nape of the neck, the *grandes dames* of Flavian and Trajanic times piled up elaborate edifices of spiral curls or interwoven plaits on wire frames. In the most extravagant examples these scaffoldings, like the *onkoi* of heroines in Greek tragedy, doubled the height of the head, and it must have been a great relief to all and sundry when the trend-setters of the second century reverted to simpler styles reminiscent of the Julio-Claudian period, albeit with a more deliberate crimping of the waves.

Beautification of the female did not, of course, stop with the hair. References in the Latin poets to tooth polish, painted cheeks, pencilled eyebrows, and eye-shadow have a familiar ring; and the wearing of excessive jewellery was a practice which legislators had long since given up trying to curb, though moralists still condemned it. Pliny rails against women who wore pearls on their fingers, on their ear-rings, and on their slippers, and reports with disapproval how Caligula's first Empress, Lollia Paulina, turned up to a feast wearing emeralds and pearls on her head, hair, ears, neck, and fingers. Similarly in Petronius' novel it is a mark of Trimalchio's lack of decorum that he flaunts his wife's gold jewellery—anklets, bracelets, and a gold hairnet. 'She must have six and a half pounds weight on her', he declares.

Numerous items of personal gold jewellery have survived. At Pompeii some of the objects, such as rings and bracelets in the form of snakes, continue the Hellenistic tradition, but new types also appear—ear-rings decorated with pendant clubs, hemispheres, or clusters of plasmas, and necklaces with crescent or wheel-shaped pendants. Generally speaking the use of inset stones remained popular in Roman times, but in place of a single species we find a profusion of colours and materials combined, for example sapphires, garnets, and crystals alternating in a single necklace. At the same time the fine techniques of filigree and granulation declined in favour, giving way to plain surfaces of gold or to a new openwork (*interrasile*) style of ornament. Finger rings were widely worn, both by women, as tokens of engagement, and by men, as signets. A popular device was an engraved portrait of the Emperor, and imperial gold coins or medallions were frequently set as bezels in rings; they also appeared as pendants on necklaces and as ornaments on brooches. Among the various types of brooches the most successful was the crossbow, widely worn in the fourth century. All this jewellery retains the technical quality of its Greek forerunners, but there is a certain reduction in artistic sensitivity in favour of bolder and showier effects.

This last comment, applicable also to other personal ornaments and effects, from combs and hairpins to toilet-boxes and mirrors, sums up what is a general characteristic of many of the arts of living discussed above. There is in them a certain lack of restraint, even a certain vulgarity—a love of immediate and over-elaborate effects which places imperial taste in the same bracket as that of the Victorian period. Like Victorian taste, it was the product of the fruits of world empire, for example of the free availability of exotic materials and commodities, from precious stones and metals to coloured marbles, tropical beasts,

CARVED-IVORY TOILET BOX (third century AD). The wall is carved with Dionysiac reliefs: a reclining maenad (one of Dionysus' female followers) and two running Cupids, one of whom (here) carries a purse. The knob on the lid is in the form of a pine-cone.

and (in the case of nineteenth-century England) American and oriental timbers. And, like Victorian taste, it was the prelude to an age of chaos and uncertainty, an age in which life and art suffered an almost total divorce.

Further Reading

For the ancient authors who give us information on this subject (Cicero in his letters, Petronius, Statius, Ovid, Martial, Juvenal, the Younger Pliny) see the translations etc. cited in the bibliographies of Chapters 19, 24, 27 and 28.

Pompeii and Herculaneum. The best book is T. Kraus and L. von Matt, *Pompeii and Herculaneum: the Living Cities of the Dead* (New York, 1975). Also valuable, though difficult to obtain, are the various editions of the exhibition catalogue *Pompeii 79* (London, 1976; Boston, 1978) edited by J. B. Ward-Perkins and A. Claridge. Brief popular surveys are M. Grant, *Cities of Vesuvius: Pompeii and Herculaneum* (London, 1971); A. De Franciscis, *The Buried Cities: Pompeii and Herculaneum* (London, 1978); R. Seaford, *Pompeii* (London, 1978); and J. J. Deiss, *Herculaneum: A City Returns to the Sun* (London, 1968). Still an important synopsis, though excluding the twentieth-century discoveries, is A. Mau, *Pompeii, its Life and Art* (transl. F. W. Kelsey, 2nd edn., New York, 1902).

Ostia. R. Meiggs, *Roman Ostia*, 2nd edn. (Oxford, 1973) includes much relevant material on housing. See further A. Boethius, *The Golden House of Nero* (Ann Arbor, 1955).

Many of the aspects covered in the present chapter are dealt with in the stimulating, but somewhat too gloomy, survey of J. Carcopino, *Daily Life in Ancient Rome* (New Haven, 1940). On domestic architecture the only general book is A. G. McKay, *Houses, Villas and Palaces in the Roman World* (London, 1975), which is confused and frequently at fault; much better are the relevant sections in J. B. Ward-Perkins, *Roman Imperial Architecture* (Harmondsworth, 1981). On gardens the fundamental work is now W. F. Jashemski, *The Gardens of Pompeii, Herculaneum and the Villas Destroyed by Vesuvius* (New York, 1979).

Decorative and luxury arts. See the general works cited in the bibliography of Chapter 32, especially M. Henig (ed.), *A Handbook of Roman Art* (Oxford, 1983). On specific themes the following are all useful studies: R. J. Charleston, *Roman Pottery* (London, 1955); R. A. Higgins, *Greek and Roman Jewellery* (London, 1966); G. M. A. Richter, *The Furniture of the Greeks, Etruscans and Romans* (London, 1966); D. E. Strong, *Greek and Roman Gold and Silver Plate* (London, 1966). The techniques of artists and craftsmen are examined in D. Strong and D. Brown (eds.), *Roman Crafts* (London, 1976).

31

Roman Life and Society

❧❧

JOHN MATTHEWS

Distances and Diversity

IN the year AD 333 a Christian pilgrim set out from his home city of Bordeaux for the Holy Land. Measuring the early stages of his journey by the 'leagues' still at this late date in use in south-western Gaul, he travelled by land across the Alps and north Italy, through the Balkans to Constantinople, and from there through Anatolia and Syria until, 170 days and 3,300 Roman miles (about 3,100 modern miles) after his departure, he came to Jerusalem. The pilgrim's journey is not merely testimony to the long-distance travel possible, and frequently undertaken, in all periods of the Roman Empire; it is also a challenge to the imagination. How did the pilgrim react to the different landscapes through which he travelled, the languages he heard spoken, the cities, towns, and way-stations in which he lodged as he passed from Bordeaux, penetrated by the Atlantic tides, to the edge of the Judaean wilderness? The modern historian, influenced perhaps by the Mediterranean perspective of his ancient informants and by his own knowledge of the future, tends to see the history of the Roman Empire in terms of the relationship between East and West, Greek and Latin; but a journey not much shorter than that of the Bordeaux pilgrim could be made from north to south, beginning at the militarized frontier region of Hadrian's Wall and passing through Celtic Britain and Gaul through Romanized north Africa to the edge of the Sahara. Such a journey might take in the capital of the Empire and, in southern Italy and Sicily, enclaves of Greek speech in the west surviving from the colonial period. The traveller would find diversities of dress no less striking than those of climate and geography, from the wool-clad, hooded countrymen of the cool northern provinces, as we see them on grave reliefs and wall-paintings, to the bright oriental silks of a family from Edessa, shown with its Syriac names on a mosaic pavement from that city. The jurist Ulpian pronounced that it did not matter in what language certain legal documents were framed, citing Punic and Celtic as examples of languages that might be used, and in another he considered the legal status of statements made in Punic or Syriac 'or any other language' in reply to questions asked in Latin. If modern scholars are hesitant as

TRAVELLERS: detail of a funerary relief from Arlon (Orolaunum) in Belgium (third century AD). The two figures, well wrapped in woollen cloaks against the cool northern climes, are seated in a wagon. The Roman peace (and the road system) facilitated long-distance journeys, but communications were still painfully slow by modern standards.

to the actual extent of the franchise of Celtic and Punic by the time of these pronouncements in the early third century, no such uncertainty attends Syriac (better called Aramaic), a language spoken in its various dialects by Levantine easterners for centuries before its rise to become a great literary language. The same is true of Egyptian demotic, a spoken language for long before it acquired a script and, as Coptic, became a language of the written word. Celtic leaves no indigenous literature from ancient (as opposed to medieval) times, nor at any time does the language which modern scholars sometimes, though misleadingly, call 'Berber'—an indigenous African language commemorated on hundreds of inscriptions from one end of Roman north Africa to the other, and by a distinctive nomenclature attested as late as the fourth century.

A single city could present an extraordinary cultural diversity between the town and the surrounding country, and even within the town itself. Paul and Barnabas, performing a cure at Lystra in Lycaonia (Asia Minor), were hailed as Zeus and Hermes by the local people shouting 'in the Lycaonian language' (Acts 14: 8 ff.). The priest of Zeus was all for making a sacrifice, as he brought oxen and garlands to the gates of the town from his temple outside the walls, but was dissuaded, and the evangelists' visit was terminated when hostile Jews from the cities of Pisidian Antioch and Iconium provoked the evidently volatile crowd into pelting them with stones. Despite this misadventure, the journeys of St Paul generally show him exploiting the modest social prestige of a man who had inherited the Roman citizenship from his father in the days when, as Tacitus remarked of a Gallic Roman citizen of the same period, that honour was given only rarely and in recognition of merit. A Jew from Tarsus, he no doubt belonged at Jerusalem to that community of Jews from Greek cities who stirred up hostility to Stephen (Acts 6: 9 ff.). Then, after his conversion and decision to turn to the Gentiles—that is, to the non-Jewish Greek communities of the East—he travelled from city to city, attracted particularly to centres where Greek culture, philosophical learning, and Roman officials were to be found; finally using his status as a citizen to appeal to the Roman Emperor, he went to Rome and for a time lived there, among many thousands of Graeco-Orientals who had settled there before him. Jesus of Nazareth, in contrast with this picture of physical and cultural mobility, pursued his mission in the villages and townships of local communities, eventually meeting his death during his single known visit to Jerusalem as an adult, exchanged by an indifferent Pilate for a popular bandit chief and executed by a penalty reserved for slaves, brigands, and aliens of the lowest social status. The contrast between the social milieux of Acts and of the Gospels leaps to the eye at every turn.

It was precisely the achievement of the Roman Empire to have assimilated in one political and administrative system the immense diversities of the Mediterranean, and much of the northern European, worlds. The Bordeaux pilgrim undertook his journey to the Holy Land to see for himself the historical location of a religion that was within a few years of the conversion of Constantine (AD 312) to provide a coherent ideology for the entire Roman Empire. His near-contemporary, Eusebius of Caesarea, saw in the *pax Augusta* the providential dispensation of God to facilitate the expansion of Christianity through the Roman world.

For the power of the Romans [he wrote] came to its zenith at precisely the moment of Jesus' unexpected sojourn among men, at the time when Augustus first acquired power over all nations, defeating Cleopatra and putting an end to the succession of the Ptolemies. ... From then also the Jewish nation has been subject to the Romans, that of the Syrians likewise, the Cappadocians and Macedonians, Bithynians and Greeks; to put it briefly, all the nations which now fall under the Roman Empire. (*Demonstratio Evangelica* 3. 7. 30 ff.)

With what difficulty, remarked Eusebius, would the disciples otherwise have travelled to foreign lands, 'the various nations being at war with one another, their diversities of government preventing relations between them'.

Eusebius' conception, for all its grandeur, fails even to mention the western and northern regions of the Roman Empire. It is not just that, by his time, the

Empire was divided into largely self-contained administrative and political units. The reserved attitude of Greeks towards the West, the Latin language, and its literature, though modified when, in the fourth century, a Latin-speaking imperial court governed from Constantinople, is a fundamental aspect of ancient cultural history. Not that they otherwise allowed themselves to be inhibited, for in the republican and early-imperial age the intellectual and human current from east to west massively exceeded that in the reverse direction. In the three centuries before Eusebius' time, Greeks by the myriad had gone to the west to seek their fortune as artists, writers, teachers, and exponents of the other diverse skills mentioned by Juvenal: 'grammarian, orator, geometer, painter, wrestling-master, prophet, tightrope walker, medical man, wizard—he can do anything, your penniless Greek ...' (*Satires* 3. 76–8). It was of course precisely his 'penniless' state that the humble Greek wished to remedy in going to Rome, and he had many examples, at the highest levels of distinction, to spur him on; Tiberius' astrologer, the famous mathematician Thrasyllus, Claudius' doctor Xenophon of Cos and his librarian Ti. Claudius Balbillus of Alexandria, not to mention the cohorts of literary men and scientists found at Rome under Augustus. In these professions, as Virgil had conceded in a famous passage (*Aeneid* 6. 847 ff.), Greeks were allowed the supremacy.

Juvenal's attitude to Greeks is usually linked with his notorious allusion to the Orontes pouring into the Tiber, bringing its hordes of Greco-Syrian rhetoricians, musicians, religious fanatics, and prostitutes, but he goes on in later lines to mention also towns and islands of old Greece and Asia Minor, his examples (Sicyon, Amydon, Andros, Samos, Tralles, Alabanda) being chosen, no doubt, for their adaptability to hexameter verse and their ability to suggest the sound of Greek speech, but truly identifying the ancient homelands and colonial area as well as the Hellenized Orient as the origins of the Greeks who made their presence felt in imperial Rome. From the greater cities of Asia Minor, notably metropolitan centres such as Ephesus, Sardis, and Mytilene, had come ambitious dynasts (hardly 'penniless' Greeks) of the first and second centuries, to hold senatorial office, the consulship and provincial governorships (thereby refuting the second part of Virgil's prophecy, reserving for Romans the arts of government and administration). The historian Cassius Dio came from Nicaea in Bithynia. The son of a senator who had himself become consul and governed the province of Lycia–Pamphylia, Dio was twice consul and in the later 220s, as an old man, rather surprisingly made governor of Pannonia, a Danubian military province for whose inhabitants and culture he had little understanding or sympathy. A barbarous race, he thought them, their life enhanced by no liberal arts or any of the things that make an honourable life worth while. They produced only a little poor wine, drank beer, and lived in extreme cold. Dio wrote this (he claims) from personal observation of conditions among them, having been their governor, but his attitude is in reality as prejudiced as that of Juvenal towards Greeks, and with as little excuse. It betrays the depth of a Mediterranean man's, and a Greek civilian's, incomprehension of those non-Mediterranean military provinces of the Empire which, as events would quickly show, were crucial to its survival.

The limits to the cultural unity achieved, or attempted, by the Roman government in its diverse regions and between its social classes, were then palpable—no less so, perhaps, than those between the Empire at its fringes and the barbarian world beyond; for the frontiers, generally based on rivers, which promote cultural exchange, rather than on mountain ranges, which prevent it, were far from impervious to the influence of foreign cultures. Yet the degree of uniformity of language and culture achieved within the empire, and the physical resources which made this uniformity possible, were extraordinarily impressive. Tacitus wrote of the Roman Empire as encircled by rivers and seas, every part—armies, provinces, navies—joined together as one system, and he was right. It was a rhetorical theme, sustained to the end of the Roman Empire, that Rome the city (*urbs*) had made the world (*orbis*) its own; conversely, that in Rome the city the entire world possessed a symbol of its identity. A commonplace sentiment perhaps, but a real one, and one with practical (if sometimes unexpected) consequences. It was not permissible, for example, for a man exiled from his own city to reside in Rome, for this was the 'common homeland' of all citizens. It is conventional to point to the sheer distances that were involved in travel between provinces, and between Rome and the frontiers, to the constant dangers of sea journeys and the inevitable slowness (given the nature of the available technology) of transport by land. But this is a relative matter; journeys like that of the Bordeaux pilgrim were undertaken, made possible by roads driven through provinces, over passes, across wide rivers. The bridge built by Trajan across the Danube at Drobeta was dismantled by Hadrian to prevent easy access to the Empire for hostile intruders; its piles were left in place and seemed to Dio, who had seen them, to show that there was nothing that could not be accomplished by human ingenuity. Its designer, Apollodorus of Damascus (below, pp. 791 f.) who was responsible also for the Forum of Trajan, with its column and library, was an architect of genius who would have been perfectly at ease in the company of Leonardo or Brunelleschi. He was certainly aware of his own abilities; indeed, his contemptuous opinion of the architectural efforts of Hadrian, a gifted amateur, was believed to have led to his exile and execution by that jealous man when he became Emperor.

The roads built by the Romans, originally for military purposes but in the nature of things quickly acquiring economic uses, linked together distant regions by direct routes that were not matched until modern times, for it is not every society that has a frequent use for long-distance travel. Aerial views of the Roman roads of Britain often show vividly the contrast between their direct, purposeful routes, professionally surveyed for long-distance communications, and the local lanes and field-boundaries of medieval and early modern England which adjoin them, betraying the lines of an altogether more local economy. The maintenance

BRIDGE ACROSS THE DANUBE, shown in a detail of the reliefs from Trajan's column (AD 113). Constructed by the greatest engineer and architect of the day, Apollodorus of Damascus, the bridge consisted of a timber superstructure carried on stone piers; the roadway is shown in bird's eye view at the top between a pair of railings. In the foreground the emperor conducts a sacrifice.

of the roads, once built, fell as a corvée on the local communities through whose territories they passed, and these communities naturally undertook the construction of subsidiary roads, way-stations, and bridges. Of the latter, the most 'stupendous' (Gibbon's word), and certainly from a historical point of view one of the most interesting, is the bridge over the river Tagus at Alcantara in western Spain, standing high over the river to accommodate winter spate and built, as an inscription shows, by the co-operative efforts of eleven Lusitanian communities. The name of its builder, C. Julius Lacer, appears in another inscription attached to the shrine of Trajan at the bridge; his achievement, he there declared with a totally justified pride, would 'last for ever through the ages'.

Along the roads of the Empire and across the pacified seas, the Emperor sent his emissaries, confident that, whatever diversities of culture and language they traversed, they would be understood by those to whom they were sent. In turn, and perhaps still more to the point, provincial communities could dispatch envoys to the Roman government with a similar confidence that, within the normal limits of human will and energy and with only a small allowance for misadventure, they would reach their destination; knowing too that within the mode of communication established by Greco-Roman culture and maintained by the educated élite, their petitions would be understood. Such embassies, undertaken by leading citizens on behalf of their communities, are among the best-attested civic functions of Roman society. They reveal vividly the sheer physical movement required of subject as well as of Emperor in the administration of the Empire and show how this too was, from the point of view of the communities themselves, an expression of their social structure; for the ambassadors, filling their role as a social duty and deploying in its service the classical education which marked them out as members of the élite of their cities, returned (if successful) as the benefactors and patrons of their cities, leaving an enhanced prestige for their sons to inherit and, in their turn, surpass.

As all this implies, the comprehension of the Roman Empire as a rational social organization involves a marked simplification of its actual nature—a simplification in which the emperors themselves and the leaders of local communities concurred, for it reinforced their power over outsiders and the less favoured classes. Celtic might still be spoken in Gaul and Britain, Aramaic in the Levant, demotic in Egypt, Libyan in large areas of north Africa, and who knows what in the remoter parts of Asia Minor; but all could be reached in one of two major languages. However diverse the physical nature of the communities of the Empire, they could be defined in terms of one civic status or another (*colonia, municipium, uicus, castellum*) and their inhabitants' status described in terms of Roman law, even if the actual law to which they were subject in minor matters was based on local practice and custom, administered by local magistrates. On major matters and before the Roman governor, no such concessions were envisaged. Pliny the Younger, encountering Christians in a town of Pontus, consulted Trajan on certain matters of legal procedure and social status, and on the question of anonymous denunciations posted in public places. In cases of admitted Christians of low social status, he had no hesitation in ordering immediate execution and was apparently prepared to treat 'pertinacious obstinacy' as a punishable offence. Pliny noted to Trajan that before his intervention the 'contagion' of Christianity had attacked not only the cities, but also the villages and the countryside of the province (it is the only reference to the countryside in his whole correspondence from Bithynia-Pontus); now, however, the temples were full of pious worshippers and sacrificial meat was again on sale in the markets. One wonders for how long *that* revival lasted, once Pliny had departed.

Town and Country

It is a natural instinct, encouraged somewhat by our sources, the products of city men, to see the Roman Empire as a vast confederation of city-states. If there is an over-simplification here it relates to the degree of uniformity to be found in the cities and in their economic functions, and in the different rates at which cities in fact developed. Tacitus in one passage shows himself aware of a process of urbanization which had in his own day become established in Numidia but had not yet begun in the time of Tiberius. The process is documented for just that region by the archaeology and epigraphy of cities such as Madaurus, Cuicul (Djemila), Milevis, and Sitifis, native settlements which progressed from municipal to colonial status at the turn of the first and second centuries. In Britain the governor Agricola encouraged the use of the toga, the building of houses and public amenities, and the use of the Latin language, and put his name to the forum building at Verulamium (St Albans) at a time when the settlement, though already a *municipium*, still consisted largely of wooden-framed structures and generally lacked properly made-up streets. Again according to Tacitus, the tribe of the Frisii in the Low Countries, having rebelled under Tiberius because of oppression in respect of their taxes, paid in elk-skins, were in the time of Claudius settled by the military governor and given 'senate, magistrates, and laws'. Presumably what is meant is some sort of civic foundation with a charter; but we are left to imagine for ourselves what this new civic community actually looked like.

Everywhere in the West arose new cities. In central Gaul the Celtic *oppidum* of Bibracte (Mont Beuvray), inconveniently located in the hills of the Morvan, gave way to Augustodunum (Autun), a city of immense circuit built on an accessible site by the river Arroux. By the time of Tiberius the sons of the Gallic nobility were already receiving there an education in liberal studies—to pave their way (which, for reasons too complex to describe here, they never really took) into the high aristocracy of the empire. Bibracte declined, not through coercion—for archaeology shows that the site was still inhabited after the foundation of Autun, and declined progressively—but through sheer inconvenience and the attractions of the new city. In similar fashion, the native settlement of the Magdalensberg in Noricum gave way to the new town and provincial capital of Virunum (just to the north of Klagenfurt). In the East little new city foundation was called for, nor did the activities of Hellenistic kings leave much room for it. With certain exceptions such as colonial foundations in areas of uncertain tranquillity like southern Asia Minor, the main influence in the East was the steadily increasing prosperity made possible by the *pax Augusta* rather than any particular intervention of the Roman power. The caravan cities of Palmyra, Gerasa, Bostra, and Damascus gained new prosperity as more settled Roman relations with the East encouraged economic activity and Roman control of the area became more definite. The spectacular urbanization of Palmyra, though its origins were in the Hellenistic period, was essentially a product of the Roman Empire, beginning in

AERIAL VIEW OF CUICUL (Djemila, in Algeria): a fine example of urbanisation in Numidia during the first and second centuries AD. In this photograph, taken from the west, the initial colony of AD 96-7 is in the foreground, occupying a rocky spur between two wadis; the more irregular second-century suburb lies outside the south gate, at the right.

the time of Tiberius and ending only with the collapse of the Palmyrene empire in the later third century.

It was above all in the West that living conditions were transformed, by the growth of cities and the development of those resources most conducive to public health, economic development, and organized leisure. Rome itself saw an immense change, achieved by huge capital outlay on the part of Augustus and his successors, which not only altered the appearance of the city, as Augustus rightly claimed for his own achievement, from one of brick to one of marble, but raised the quality and reliability of its food and water supplies to unheard-of levels. The gang of slave maintenance-workers assembled by Agrippa for the upkeep of the aqueducts was on his death inherited by Augustus and transferred by him to public ownership (that is, to the domain of the *curator aquarum*). We should not forget that in the cities of the Empire most men lived, not in palaces or the town houses of Pompeii and Herculaneum, with their gardens, fountains, statuary, and frescoed rooms, but in the plain tenement blocks best known to us from the remains of Ostia (above, pp. 722 f.). After the fire of Rome in 64, remedies were undertaken which have much to say about the general conditions of life in first-century Rome and, no doubt, in other large cities also. Limits were fixed to the permitted height of residential buildings, which must possess their own walls and not adjoin others directly; a proportion of the construction must be of fireproof stone, without timber frames; financial incentives were offered for early completion of building works; unauthorized tapping of the water system was prevented by government inspectors, to ensure an adequate flow to the public supply, and householders were required to keep fire-fighting equipment in an easily accessible place. All agreed that the new city was more gracious than the old; some claimed (it being impossible to please everyone) that it was less healthy than the old city, whose narrow streets and high buildings had provided shade and coolness which the new open spaces did not allow. A more pertinent complaint might have concerned the area of the city taken up by Nero's dream, the 'Golden House' (below, pp. 784 ff.), with lawns, lakes, and rustic landscapes devised by its builders, as Tacitus said, to make good by art the deficiencies of nature.

Although the city was the fundamental unit of ancient social and administrative life, many were those who lived outside its range, in different ways; in tribal reservations which, at least in certain parts of north Africa, persisted to the late Empire and beyond; in townships (*uici*) and the great villas which in the northern provinces were quite as important a facet of the economic and social process of Romanization as were the cities. In mountain areas, such as exist in north Africa

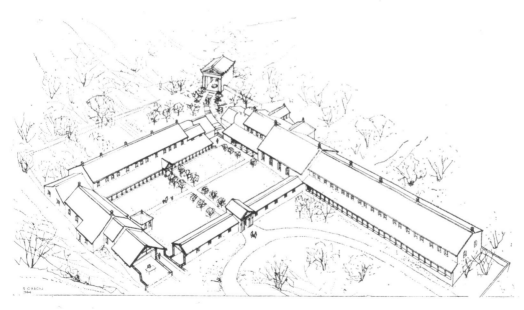

VILLA AT CHEDWORTH (Gloucestershire): reconstruction drawing of the buildings about AD 300. This well-preserved example of a comfortable farm-house in the northernmost of Rome's provinces has a secluded inner courtyard surrounded by the best-appointed domestic accommodation and an outer yard opening to the estate. The owner's wealth was probably based upon stock-breeding and wool-production.

(the Kabylie and Aurès) and Isauria in southern Asia Minor, lived enclaves of mountain folk hardly touched by Roman civilization but a threat to it if economic conditions turned against them, for then they would descend on the agricultural territories of Roman cities. On the desert fringes to the south and to the east transhumant peoples, and in the north barbarians, moved in and out of Roman territory in a way that paid little regard to the formal barriers of the frontier systems.

In taking the cities and their articulate classes (and therefore most of the surviving evidence) as the basis for the analysis of Roman society, we risk ignoring the great majority of the population on whose labours the prosperity of the cities depended but who do not make a proportionate impact on the surviving source material: the rural peasantry. That the cities in fact depended on the economic exploitation of the peasantry is axiomatic. But it would be a mistake to assume from this that the cities and the countryside were in consequence divided by an overt mutual enmity. The city, as a market, centre of distribution, source of occasional delights and pleasures and, not least, home of the major gods, was a real and active presence in the life of the peasantry, even if a relatively small part of their physical existence was spent there. In the fourth century John Chrysostom remarked on the Syriac peasantry flooding into Antioch on Christian feast days, 'divided from us in language but at one in faith'; it is one of the few literary acknowledgments we possess of the peasantry or, as in this case, of its non-classical language, but the situation it evokes is evidently common and immemorial. By the same token the local aristocracies, in whose hands lay the conduct of civic politics and the provision of public services, were the owners of the land and spent much time on their farms and country estates—a pattern of life illustrated by Apuleius for second-century Oea (in Tripolitania) as much as by the historian Ammianus Marcellinus for fourth-century Leptis Magna and Nisibis (in Mesopotamia). Among true 'city-dwellers' we should count professional men such as teachers and doctors, craftsmen, fortune-tellers and magicians, traders, merchants, and so on. For the activities of many of these professions, the value system of Greek and Roman society, rooted in the attitudes of landed amateurism, was reluctant to assign proper respect. At all levels of society, provincial and metropolitan, it was the landed interest that was most closely connected with the tenure of political office. The senatorial class of the early Empire was composed of landed magnates who came to politics with a census qualification that ensured they were men of substantial private means, and they embarked on careers that did not in general (though exceptions could always be made) require a specifically military, financial, or other expertise so much as all-round literary culture and general experience. In the domain of local politics trade secured no foothold even at Arles or Lyon, where it was a prominent and profitable activity; only at Ostia, an exceptional case because of its restricted territory and the overwhelming dominance of trade in the economy, did the trading interest make much impact on the conduct of its civic and political life.

APPLE SELLERS: funerary relief from Arlon (second century AD). The produce of the farms and smallholdings would be brought, as in medieval and modern times, to the market-towns for sale; here we see a fruit-stall with a customer (or the farmer himself?) standing at the right.

SHOP-KEEPER AND LADY WITH A DOG: reconstructed funerary monument from Lillebonne (second century AD). The shopkeeper is shown standing behind his counter with glass flagons and boxes on the shelves above him and tools hanging on the wall behind him. The lady (his wife?) holds her pet dog in her left hand and offers it a titbit with her right.

A man who turned his back on politics to pursue commercial interests might be spoken of as following a life of *quies*, that is, the freedom to make money without the constraints and inhibitions imposed by the political life and its values. The two brothers, Seneca and Mela, were prominent respectively in the senatorial and equestrian orders of later Julio-Claudian Rome, the latter expressing what Tacitus called a 'perverse ambition' in choosing to enrich himself by holding imperial procuratorships. Possibly the brothers were even cleverer than Tacitus acknowledged, in vesting their interests equally in the two great enterprises, politics and commerce. Cassius Dio alleged that among the causes of the revolt of Boudicca was Seneca's calling-in of loans of 40,000,000 sesterces he had made to the Britons, with an eye to the high interest rates he might extract. If true, or even plausible, it is an intriguing suggestion, not only of a senator indulging in speculative finance, but also, we may suspect, of the high costs to the leading men of the new province of their own Romanization. Buildings to construct and furnish, mosaicists to commission, statuary and luxury goods to import from all over (the early palace at Fishbourne gives an indication); there was a lot to pay for and not much money yet in the province.

The importance of trade, manufacture, and commerce in the actual conditions of life in the Roman provinces is as obvious as that of agriculture, which provided their economic base and of which they were very often the direct expression. So much is clear from many sources: from one of the most important inscriptions of any period of Roman history, the Edict of Maximum Prices by Diocletian in AD 301; from the patterns of ostentatious expenditure manifest in the great consuming cities of the Empire; from the incidence of discovered shipwrecks, rising to a peak in the late-republican and early-imperial periods; not least, from the illustration on large numbers of grave reliefs, especially from the western provinces, of a wide variety of trading, commercial, and generally professional enterprises, in which those commemorated evidently took pride and found respect (they would not otherwise have been shown on their tombstones). Viewed in another perspective, there are the various trades and occupations, more than a hundred of them, named on the inscriptions of a small town in south-east Asia Minor; and no less than 250 in the slice of life represented by a fourth-century manual of astrology. Why should we ever wish to apply to such modestly successful *petits bourgeois* a social attitude to trade, commerce, and manual labour formulated by the philosophers, and repeated by the rhetoricians, of a different social class—men freed by position, unearned income, and the labour of others from the need to contemplate the normal facts of economic life?

Yet it remains true that it was in the hands of the traditional aristocratic, rather than of the trading or commercial, interest that the physical maintenance and political conduct of the cities of the Roman Empire rested and also, therefore, much of what appears to us as its achievement. By generosity and munificence, these local aristocracies built their cities, sustained their physical amenities, patronized their literary culture by supporting municipal chairs of grammar and rhetoric, and provided their entertainments. They constructed aqueducts, porticoes, temples, theatres, built and provided the heating for public baths, kept the streets clean and lit at night. They maintained peace in the surrounding countryside, provided distributions of oil, grain, and cash and, at a personal expense recorded on many a commemorative inscription, employed professional gladiators and charioteers, acrobats and jugglers, singers and musicians, and imported exotic beasts to be hunted down in public shows for the general enjoyment. In return they were acclaimed by grateful multitudes as 'benefactors', 'providers', and 'patrons' of their cities in demonstrations of goodwill which ensured the continued influence of their families.

There was also the pressing need to channel into legitimate forms of expression the social tensions which, left unchannelled, could have destroyed civic life. Life in the ancient world did not possess the measured regularities of modern times— office hours and working weeks, factory shifts and teaching days, time-tabled

INTERIOR OF THE *FRIGIDARIUM* (COLD ROOM) IN THE NORTH BATHS IN PARIS (last quarter of second or first quarter of third century AD). This well-preserved example of a public bath-building now forms part of the Cluny Museum. The original fabric, courses of small blocks punctuated by bands of brickwork, is clearly distinguishable from later alterations.

SCENES OF BEAST HUNTS (*VENATIONES*) IN THE AMPHITHEATRE: mosaic from Smirat in Tunisia (mid third century AD). Four huntsmen named Spittara, Bullarius, Hilarinus, and Mamertinus have been pitted against four leopards named Victor, Crispinus, Romanus, and Luxurius; in the centre a herald holds a tray with four money-bags, and a pair of inscriptions record the munificence of one Magerius who has put up the money to pay the performers.

transport, deep-frozen food stocks, and regulated prices; not to mention the instant communication of verbal and visual information (what did the Emperor even look like?), and a mode of political organization designed to promote class and economic interests by systematic process of election, discussion, and legislation. Ancient social life was more discontinuous, the role of government more passive and intermittent. Through provincial councils focused on the imperial cult, cities could periodically exchange views and explore their common interests, if necessary send an embassy to press their case before the Emperor; but for most of the time they lived separate lives, as often inclined to seize advantage over their neighbours as to co-operate with them. Disputes about provincial primacy, as between Ephesus and Smyrna, Nicaea and Nicomedia, or local economic rivalries, as between Lyon and Vienne, could impinge on the imperial administration because they led to disorder. They might occasionally affect the course of a civil war or campaign for the imperial throne by a pretender, a situation in which a mistaken judgement might lead a city into the need to make an expensive apology (or worse), but in which a correct one could enhance the status of a community and enrich those leading members who had guided its choice.

Even the financial situation of the landowning politicians contributed to the

AERIAL VIEW OF THE AMPHITHEATRE AT ARLES (last quarter of first century AD). The elliptical auditorium was developed in central Italy about 100 BC as the home *par excellence* of the immensely popular beast-hunts and gladiatorial games; and the Colosseum in Rome (inaugurated in AD 80) inspired a rash of stone versions in northern Italy and the western provinces. That at Arles is still used for bull-fights, the modern equivalents of *venationes*.

relative abruptness of civic life. It was in fact the fundamental cause of it, as the landowners drew incomes in cash rentals and the sale of market produce, in a society with few banking facilities, low liquidity ('I am totally involved in farming', said the Younger Pliny in explanation of his inability at short notice to raise 3,000,000 sesterces to purchase another estate), few possibilities for alternative investment, and a consequent need to dispose of their surpluses in whatever ways would give them satisfaction, add lustre to their material wealth, and increase their prestige.

The explosions of colour, pageantry, and popular demonstrations that mark ancient games and entertainments, not to mention their ritualized violence, reflect this discontinuous pattern of life, much as the disorder and rioting in the cities often reflect the abruptness of the economic conditions that framed it. It was not easy to be a recluse in an ancient town. Public life was conducted in specific locations, much of it out of doors in a particular area of the city (the *agora*, flanked by public buildings, temples, and the senate-house), and the leaders of the society would be known by personal appearance to the population; if things went wrong it would be known who was to blame. Famine, which could be sudden and extremely local in its incidence, could turn the affection of the people for its leaders into aggression, when mobs demonstrated in the streets and the landowning politicians fled for safety to their well-provided country estates. At such moments the upper classes show themselves in one of the more self-interested of their many roles, as they hoard grain supplies to secure high prices in times of shortage, by physical obstruction and specious argument resisting governors' attempts to bring down the price. For the historian of the city of Rome above all, social unrest and violence are to the end a central theme, their causes impressively consistent; partisanship over performers and factions in the public games and races provided by the Emperors and (in the late Empire) the resident aristocracy of Rome, and food shortages, especially of corn and wine. A new factor may be mentioned here, though it is beyond the scope of this survey; rioting and

CIRCUS GAMES, shown on a funerary relief of the second century AD. At the left are portraits of the deceased couple, while in the centre a charioteer drives his team past the triple turning-posts (*metae*) and the central obelisk of the Circus Maximus. Rivalry between the four colours of the circus (red, white, blue, and green) frequently led to violent disturbances, which increasingly took a political form.

violence (on one notorious occasion resulting in 137 dead on the floor of a Christian basilica) over rival claims for the bishopric of the city. We might take these as the remote descendants of the late-republican battles between Clodius and Milo and the demonstrations in favour of rival triumvirs—just as the ritualized acclamations of the late Empire in circus and theatre descend from the political demonstrations so frequently mentioned in the *Lives* of Suetonius and described, with dubious political theory but fascinating examples, in the later chapters of the *Pro Sestio* of Cicero. At Alexandria, a city well known for its civic disturbances, riots in the fourth century between Christians and pagans, and between rivals for the bishopric, appear as the natural successors to the rioting of the early Empire between the Greek and Jewish communities.

Social Organization

The inequalities of wealth, social standing, and privilege between what a modern government might have called the 'socio-economic categories' of the Roman world were immense. They embraced not only the physical conditions of life and the opportunities open to individuals for their self-betterment, but areas in which modern citizens, in theory at least, are equal: as in the differing legal penalties thought appropriate for different classes of men. Those described as 'more honourable' (*honestiores*) were in the course of the second century made exempt from such punishments as flogging, burning alive, exposure to wild beasts, and condemnation to the mines and quarries, penalties regularly imposed, by the most summary of legal procedures, on members of the lower classes. *Honestiores*, to be broadly identified with the order of local councillors of the cities of the Empire, might legally be executed only by the sword, and were able to claim rights of appeal to the jurisdiction of higher courts; in these respects they had inherited some of the privileges enjoyed by Roman citizens in the first century, before that class had become too extensive to make them worth while.

Had a programme of social reform ever been devised by the Roman government (which in fact never saw any need for such a thing), it would no doubt have identified a free urban citizenry consisting of the craftsmen, traders, and professional men whose activities were indicated earlier. Since it was usual for a craftsman to market his own products in a shop attached to the premises, there would be no need to separate sharply the means of production and of exchange, though it might be necessary to distinguish those people who, like porters, teachers, entertainers, and prostitutes, provided a service for a fee, and whose only asset might lie in physical strength or adroitness, intelligence, and the possession of an acquired skill. There were also the free labourers, whose numbers, for long underestimated, are in more recent study attaining their correct proportions; builders and manual workers, who ignored the contempt of Cicero for such occupations and worked for hire for any employer who would pay them. 'You must let me feed my people', said the Emperor Vespasian to an inventor who offered him a labour-saving device for the transport of building materials. We should no doubt consider separately the skilled workers, such as bakers, whose services to the community merited, and attracted, special attention. They and analogous workers, such as masons, silversmiths, wool-workers, undertakers (to select just four examples) belonged to trade associations, or *collegia*, which possessed social, religious, and sometimes quasi-political functions, as well as providing an organization for the businesses with which they were concerned. The city of Ephesus offers cases of silversmiths organizing demonstrations in the theatre against the preachings of St Paul in order not to lose their trade in the manufacture and sale of images of Ephesian Artemis and, in the second century, of the guild of bakers withholding their labour in pursuit of some aim of their own and being called to order by the proconsul. Considerations of public order prevented Trajan from agreeing to the formation of a fire brigade at Nicomedia, against the clearly implied advice of Pliny as governor of the province. Apart from the active political role implied by such episodes, the trade guilds were active in the ceremonial and pageantry of their cities. When Constantine entered Autun in 311, he was received by the usual crowds, and by the 'statues of the gods, music, and the emblems of the collegia'; the emblems were evidently not devised for this particular occasion, but indicate the regular part played by the trade guilds in their cities' public lives.

The countryside would be seen (from the socio-economic point of view here imagined) in far simpler terms, the more so because some of its most prominent figures, the local gentry, would already have been classified as urban dwellers, with the consequent over-simplification of their actual way of life mentioned earlier, and because the cities, the economic focus of the surrounding countryside, were also the centres for its administration. Yet here again we should not underestimate the diversity in the conditions of life found in the countryside. The peasants themselves might own their land or rent it from local or absentee landlords; in the fourth century Libanius (an influential professor of rhetoric at Antioch) draws the distinction for Syria between villages under 'one master' and those owned by 'many masters', that is by free peasant proprietors. Some were lessees of public land taken under long leases with preferential terms to encourage the planting of uncultivated or unsurveyed land, some were tenants of temple lands or of the Emperor. Such farmers, like the tenants of absentee landlords other than the Emperor, would normally be supervised (in some cases, which are documented for this reason, oppressed) by a land agent or bailiff or, in the case of imperial estates, the procurator of the province. As in the towns, so too in the country there would be a numerous free labour force, sometimes recruited as need arose from the surplus labour of nearby towns or from those local peasants who happened at a given time to be underemployed, sometimes migrant from region to region; and there were pastoralists following the seasons between upland and valley, desert and steppe. This is the context of a famous episode of republican history, the *calles siluaeque*, the 'tracks and forests' offered as a prospective command to the consuls of 59 in order to curb the ambitions of Julius Caesar. *Calles* are the droveways, in Italian *tratturi*, of transhumant shepherds, as described in an informative inscription of the time of Marcus Aurelius, from Saepinum in old Samnite country.

The women of the community would generally be seen in terms of the socio-economic categories assigned to the men. Their rights at law were however much more extensive than one might have expected, the institution of 'guardianship' of adult women, though it was not abolished, having by the late second century become a formality. It is already clear in the late Republic that women of senatorial status could in practice manage their own business and financial affairs, and with the early and almost universal acceptance of a form of marriage in which the woman retained her own legal identity rather than passing into the control of her husband, women had rights to own, inherit, and dispose of property which in modern Britain were not matched until the Married Women's Property Act of 1870. The marriage of Pudentilla of Tripolitanian Oea to the young philosopher Apuleius (above, pp. 692 ff.) in the mid second century was the occasion of a provincial *cause célèbre* from which Apuleius, accused before the proconsul by her first husband's relatives of having bewitched her by magic arts, was no doubt glad to escape. Pudentilla had for her part gone against their expressed wishes in choosing to marry Apuleius, which she was perfectly able to do. The real issue was that of the property, and Pudentilla's 'guardian' had to certify in court that a farm whose purchase he had formally authorized had been acquired not for Apuleius but for herself.

At less opulent social levels women are found frequently, in evidence that seriously under-represents their actual numbers, sharing in their husbands' work and its organization, particularly in the finer crafts and luxury trades such as silver-working and perfumery; and there were of course those service occupations in which opportunities to make a living, and even to achieve a certain scandalous distinction, conflicted with a social disapproval that was itself, as we should expect, shaped by that essential tool of a dominant class, moral hypocrisy. An early-fourth-century law on adultery took it for granted that the mistress of a tavern need not have sexual relations with the male clientele, while the serving-maids would normally be expected to, and so, unlike their mistress, were exempt from accusation as being 'unworthy of the cognizance of the laws'; and the same assumption was applied to women of the stage, whose immorality was held, again in Christian legislation of the fourth century, to preclude their returning to their profession after baptism. The social role of the woman was dominant, above all, in the home and in the day-to-day upbringing of children. The most intimate, if not the most endearing portrayal of this relationship, as of many other aspects of provincial family life, is Augustine's description of his mother Monica in the *Confessions*. It was not exclusively as an expression of personal affection, but of the normal patterns of family life in ancient cities, that Augustine's relations with his mother were so intense, and with his father so formal and distant by comparison.

A distinction in Roman society instantly recognizable through fundamental legal and social distinctions was that between slave and free. It is a truism hardly worth asserting, that Roman society was in some sense dependent on slave labour. But in what sense? One of the most important facets of the social and economic history of the Empire as opposed to the Republic is the declining rate of slave importation, the servile population being now to a far greater extent (one would not say entirely, in view of the evidence for the continuance of the slave trade under the Empire) maintained by reproduction among those who were already of this status, through what were in effect recognized as slave marriages. The effect of this is that the function of slavery in the Empire evolved within a wider social and economic pattern and was not imposed upon it. In whatever occupational milieu we find ourselves—among shopkeepers, building workers, members of *collegia*—we encounter a mixed population of slave, freed-man, and free citizen. By a *senatusconsultum* of AD 52—introduced to the Senate by Claudius as the idea of his freedman Pallas—free women who entered into permanent relationships with slaves were themselves reduced to that status *if the master was unaware of the relationship*, or to that of freedwoman if he was aware and had given his consent. Though sometimes viewed as a socially oppressive measure, the *senatusconsultum* is more interesting to the historian for the situations it entitles him to visualize, of stable marital relationships freely undertaken between men and women of different legal status, but similar occupational groups, living (no doubt) in similar social conditions and in situations where the master might not know what was going on. The woman might find her legal status affected, but her marriage took her into the social network and protection afforded by the house to which her husband belonged; and in those frequent cases where the slave husband worked independently of his master, or under only indirect supervision, she might find her way of life little changed. Tacitus wrote of the disorder arising in Rome during the Civil War of AD 68 as affecting in opposite ways the stable part of the people connected with the great houses, and the spectacle-loving mob and the worst of the slave population. The first group, including by implication the 'better sort' of the slave population, welcomed the end of the reign of Nero and the prospect of better things to come; the second, used to Nero's extravagances, regretted his end, and, fearing the worst and fed on rumour, aggravated the general instability.

The social relations, expressed through various forms of munificence, between the great houses of Rome (and so, on a lesser scale, in all cities of the Empire) and their dependants, and between the Emperor and his special clients, the people of Rome, provided a common interest for sectors of society that ought, on any rational calculation of economic advantage and disadvantage, to have been irrev-ocably opposed to each other. Yet this was only the tangible expression of the more extensive moral and legal relations between 'client' and 'patron' upon which ancient society was built. The failure of societies in which such inequalities are rampant, extreme, and blatant to the eye, to articulate their differences in terms of class conflict is a tribute (if that is the word) to the strength and flexibility of the relations between classes which can be summed up in the word 'paternalism': the art of extending social benefits and alleviating the effects of misfortune while enhancing the prestige and moral worth of the giver of the benefits, and thereby reinforcing rather than undermining the existing social structure. There were of course other means of 'alleviating the effects of misfortune', and it would be hard in conclusion to imagine a more vivid expression of the sheer variety of social relations and vicissitudes of human experience of which the historian must take account, than some questions envisaged on a late-third- or early-fourth-century papyrus as appropriate for putting to an oracle (the numbers are given on the papyrus):

72. Shall I get my pay? ... 74. Shall I be sold up? ... 78. Am I to get leave? 79. Shall I get the money? ... 82. Is my property to be proscribed? ... 85. Am I to be sold as a slave? 86. Shall I go into exile? 87. Shall I go on an embassy? 88. Am I to become a town councillor? 89. Is my escape cut off? 90. Shall I be separated from my wife? 91. Am I under a spell? ... (*Oxyrhynchus Papyri*, No. 1477)

Further Reading

The literary sources mentioned are available in the Loeb Classical Library, and in most cases also in Penguin Classics, especially Tacitus, *Annals* (by Michael Grant, 1956) and *Histories* (by Kenneth Wellesley, 1964; all dates are those of first publication); Suetonius, *Lives of the Caesars* (by Robert Graves, 1957); Pliny the Younger, *Letters* (by Betty Radice, 1963). See also Lucian, *Satirical Sketches* (by Paul Turner, 1961) and Apuleius, *The Golden Ass* (by Robert Graves, 1950); the last two are extremely rewarding from a historical point of view, though their literary complexity makes them difficult to use. Particularly recommended is the splendid collection of source-materials, documentary and epigraphic as well as literary, by Naphtali Lewis and Meyer Reinhold, *Roman Civilization, Sourcebook II; the Empire* (paperback, New York, 1966). This collection contains hundreds of well-chosen passages, and responds equally well to browsing or to systematic reading; a real education in Roman history.

Fundamental both to the interpretation of Roman society and to the appreciation of the actual conditions of life in it is M. I. Rostovtzeff's *Social and Economic History of the Roman Empire* (2nd edn. by P. M. Fraser, Oxford, 1957); to be read (for it is a controversial work) with Arnaldo Momigliano's appreciation in his *Studies in Historiography* (London, 1966), pp. 91–104. Fergus Millar, *The Roman Empire and its Neighbours* (2nd edn., London, 1981) shares some of Rostovtzeff's emphasis on the provincial diversities of the Empire. G. E. M. de Ste. Croix's marvellously fertile *The Class Struggle in the Ancient Greek World* (London, 1981) in fact contains much directly on and relevant to the Roman imperial period. In Tim Cornell and John Matthews' *Atlas of the Roman World* (Oxford 1982) are brief illustrated accounts of some of the issues mentioned above (for instance public shows, manufacture and trade, technology) and of the provinces of the Empire and the city of Rome. There is still much of interest in Ludwig Friedlander's old *Roman Life and Manners under the Early Empire*, especially in the Supplementary Volume with various excursuses (English tr. London, 1910).

On the conditions of travel in the Roman empire, see Lionel Casson's two books, *Ships and Seamanship in the Ancient World* (Princeton, 1971) and *Travel in the Ancient World* (London, 1974), with E. D. Hunt's fine *Holy Land Pilgrimage in the Later Roman Empire* (Oxford, 1982). On the role of Greeks in Roman Society, G. W. Bowersock, *Augustus and the Greek World* (Oxford,

1965) and *Greek Sophists in the Roman Empire* (Oxford, 1969) are both excellent books, concise, lively and well documented.

The economic functioning of the cities of the Empire is much discussed; see especially Chapters I and II of A. H. M. Jones, *The Roman Economy: Studies in Ancient Economic and Administrative History* (ed. P. A. Brunt, Oxford, 1974); R. Duncan-Jones, *The Economy of the Roman Empire: Quantitative Studies* (Cambridge, 1974) includes particularly full discussions of levels of civic munificence, and Philip Abrams and E. A. Wrigley (edd.), *Towns in Societies: Essays in Economic History and Historical Sociology* (Cambridge, 1978) contains a particularly good discussion by Keith Hopkins on the roles of trade and agriculture in the economic development of classical cities. The subject of Bruce W. Frier, *Landlords and Tenants in Imperial Rome* (Princeton, 1980) is urban leasehold law but he has much to say about the physical conditions of life, especially at Ostia; on which see Russell Meiggs, *Roman Ostia* (2nd edn., Oxford, 1973). Among the many interesting articles reprinted from the journal *Past and Present* in M. I. Finley (ed.) *Studies in Ancient Society* (London and Boston, 1974) is P. A. Brunt's splendid 'The Roman Mob' (pp. 74–102).

The debate about trade and labour and social attitudes towards them, reopened by Finley in *The Ancient Economy* (London, 1973), has been vigorously pursued; see, for instance, the collections of studies edited by Peter Garnsey, Keith Hopkins and C. R. Whittaker, *Trade in the Ancient Economy* (London, 1983), by Garnsey and Whittaker, *Trade and Famine in Classical Antiquity* (Cambridge, Philological Society, Suppl. Vol. 8, 1983) and by Garnsey, *Non-slave Labour in the Greco-Roman World* (ibid. 6, 1980); and John d'Arms, *Commerce and Social Standing in Ancient Rome* (Cambridge, Mass., and London, 1981). On the techniques of farming, K. D. White, *Roman Farming* (London, 1970).

On the role of law in social life, see J. A. Crook, *Law and Life of Rome* (London, 1967), and on the penal system of the Empire Peter Garnsey, *Social Status and Legal Privilege in the Roman Empire* (Oxford, 1970) and more generally A. N. Sherwin-White, *The Roman Citizenship* (2nd edn., Oxford, 1973). On slavery and social relations there are articles of interest in M. I. Finley (ed.) *Slavery in Classical Antiquity* (Cambridge, 1960); and see from a very different historical tradition Joseph Vogt, *Ancient Slavery and the Ideal of Man* (transl. Thomas Wiedemann, Oxford, 1974).

Social relations in general are discussed in two most illuminating books, written with characteristic zest and an eye for detail, by Ramsay MacMullen, *Enemies of the Roman Order; Treason, Unrest and Alienation in the Empire* (Cambridge, Mass., and London, 1967) and *Roman Social Relations, 56 B.C. to A.D. 284* (New Haven, Conn., and London 1974). Zvi Yavetz, *Plebs and Princeps* (Oxford, 1969) discusses the relations between the Emperor and People of Rome in the context of developments from the late Republic, and has most interesting material on modes of popular expression. Keith Hopkins, *Sociological Studies in Roman History*, I: *Conquerors and Slaves*, and II: *Death and Renewal* (Cambridge, 1978 and 1983) offers a radical approach to the evidential problems inherent in the writing of ancient social and economic history. Still more intractable are those relating to religious history, on which a stimulating introduction for the imperial age is E. R. Dodds, *Pagan and Christian in an Age of Anxiety* (Cambridge, 1965).

32

Roman Art and Architecture

❧✣❧

R. J. A. WILSON

The Augustan Principate

WHEN C. Octavius (soon to take the title Augustus) emerged triumphant from the battle of Actium in 31 BC, he lost little time in embarking on a building programme the like of which Rome had never seen before. The reign of Augustus was an age of enormous architectural and artistic fervour, in which cautious conservatism was combined with revolutionary new ideas. The establishment of the Principate created for the first time a stability which enabled a long-term, coherent planning programme to be worked out for the monuments of the capital. The Emperor, with his family and associates, provided a motivated patronage which drew architects, sculptors, and painters to the capital, a patronage which was vital for creating the right conditions for works of art and buildings on the grand scale; and with that imperial patronage came the centralized control of state funds. Such conditions had of course existed before in the ancient world—in Periclean Athens, for example, and especially in the Hellenistic kingdoms such as Pergamum—but for Rome they were essentially new. Augustus was also not slow to realize the political overtones of a lavish architectural and sculptural programme: Caesar had already shown the way with his great vision of a monumental reorganization of the heart of Rome, and some of his projects were duly completed by Augustus. Caesar's adoptive son launched a building programme on an even more ambitious scale which, by his death in AD 14, had totally transformed the physical appearance of the capital. Mobilizing the building industry was one way of stimulating the economy; building theatres and amphitheatres, baths and basilicae, *fora* and temples, curried favour with a restless populace; and in the show-pieces of the Augustan programme the potential for using monuments as vehicles of elaborate propaganda was exploited to the full.

Some idea of the scale of the new building programme can be judged from Augustus' astonishing claim that he built or restored no less than eighty-two temples in one year alone, quite apart from other types of building; add to that the projects sponsored by other energetic builders in his family, and one can gain some impression of the building fever that gripped Augustan Rome. Many of the new structures were essentially conservative, repeating the formulae already tried and tested in the late Republic. The theatre of Marcellus, for example, begun by Caesar but not finished until *c.*13–11 BC, with its seats raised on concrete substructures and with an outer façade of superimposed arcades (each row framed by a continuous colonnade of engaged columns, a formula which much influenced architects from the sixteenth century onwards), was essentially the type of building already established at Rome by the earlier theatre of Pompey (55 BC). Many of the temples, too, continued to use traditional materials, either travertine (a hard white limestone quarried near Tivoli) or one of the variety of local volcanic stones liberally covered with stucco. Such conservatism in the Augustan building programme would have delighted the contemporary architect, Vitruvius, whose ten books *On Architecture*, written between about 28 and 23 BC, enjoyed enormous fame from the Renaissance onwards, especially as a source-book for the Classical Greek orders. Conscious, but disapproving, of the radical changes going on around him, Vitruvius issues strictures against the haste and the boldness of the new generation of architects, while lavishing undiluted praise on the use of ashlar, on the materials of local quarries, even on the usefulness of mud-brick. Vitruvius was no progressive; his writings are more important for the light they shed on Greek and Roman Republican architectural practice than as a commentary on his own age.

For the materials on which Vitruvius pinned his faith were not to be those of the future. The Augustan age was an age of experiment, in using new materials and in exploring fresh uses for old. The quality of concrete, for example, was constantly being improved, and innovatory architects were trying out a new method of roofing, the hemispherical dome in concrete, which was to play such a vital part in the Roman architectural revolution of the next 150 years: the earliest surviving example, probably Augustan, is the so-called 'Temple of Mercury' at Baiae. Another arrival of lasting significance was kiln-fired brick, not a newly-invented material as such, but employed now for the first time as a continuous facing for concrete. In Rome it appears to have been used only modestly until after Augustus' death; real confidence in handling the new material was gained elsewhere, especially in Italian cities such as Turin. With brickwork, as with the dome, the significant developments were yet to come, but Augustan architects deserve credit for pointing the way forward.

A more immediate impact on the architectural scene was made by marble. Augustus boasted, according to Suetonius, 'that he found Rome a city of (mud-)brick and left it a city of marble'; and it is clear from the sheer number of marble-faced buildings which sprang up in the capital that this was no idle boast. Caesar had probably been the first to realize the potential of the rich Carrara marble quarries near Luna in north Italy, but their full-scale exploitation began only with Augustus' reign. Dead-white, crystalline, and clean-breaking (and therefore excellent for crisp carving and cutting), this handsome material

INTERIOR OF THE SO-CALLED 'TEMPLE OF MERCURY' AT BAIAE, actually a circular bathing hall in a thermal complex (late first century BC or early first century AD). The building is notable for its hemispherical concrete dome, the earliest large-scale example in Roman architecture. Owing to the sinking of the earth-level in the region, the hall is now half submerged in water.

won immediate and widespread popularity. Alongside Luna appeared an increasing range of polychrome marbles from abroad: yellow African marble, salmon-pink marble from Chios, and greeny-blue *cipollino* from Euboea, as well as Phrygian marble from Asia Minor. Marble had come to stay; and although the Augustan use of polychromatic effects, both for columns and in paving and wall veneers, remained restrained by comparison with later fashions, the new material gave a welcome touch of elegance and sophistication, as well as a splash of colour, which the architecture of the capital had hitherto lacked.

But the exploitation of marble brought with it a problem, lack of Roman expertise in handling it. That is why an army of Greek craftsmen were drafted into the capital: their role in shaping the distinctive creations of the Augustan programme is hard to overestimate. A new, precise language of architectural ornament, based on that of classical Greece, but with fresh variations and combinations, set the tone for the rest of the Empire and in turn was a source of inspiration for generations of Renaissance and Neo-classical architects. Even the

PORTA PALATINA AT TURIN, one of the monumental gateways of the Augustan colony founded *c*.25 BC, and an early instance of brickwork on the grand scale. In form it belongs to a familiar North Italian and Gaulish type of the early-imperial period, with projecting towers at the sides and an arcaded corridor above. Originally there would have been a rectangular inner courtyard.

one original Roman contribution to the classical orders, the Composite, with its blending of the volutes of Ionic with the acanthus leaves of Corinthian, makes its first known appearance in Augustan Rome and is hardly to be dissociated from the creative genius of Greek craftsmen in the capital.

The marriage of Greek skills and traditions with Roman taste and demands is nowhere more clearly documented than in the two monuments which mark the culmination of the Augustan programme, the Ara Pacis Augustae (dedicated in 9 BC), and the Forum of Augustus (2 BC). The forum in concept and planning is quintessentially Roman: the great Italic-style temple of Luna marble on a lofty podium dominates an open space flanked by porticoes, a formal, axial layout following the strict principles already established in Republican architecture. Roman too is the use of the forum as a portrait gallery of the great trail-blazers of Roman history, including Augustus himself, identified as just another hero in a long line of Republicans. As an ingenious and disingenuous piece of imperial propaganda and as a blueprint for architectural planning, the forum of Augustus was unmistakably Roman; yet its detail was no less unmistakably Greek: the

COMPOSITE CAPITAL re-used in the Church of Santa Costanza in Rome. Dated on stylistic grounds to the early Augustan period (*c*.40–20 BC), this is one of the earliest examples of the new hybrid order which combines Ionic volutes with Corinthian acanthus leaves. The first examples in position on a dated building are those of the Arch of Titus (soon after AD 81).

CARYATID ORDER OF THE FORUM OF AUGUSTUS (end of first century BC). The upper storey of the colonnade enclosing the new forum was articulated with a series of carved female figures copied directly from the Caryatid porch of the Erechtheum in Athens (above, p. 125)—a vivid illustration of the classical Greek element in Augustan architectural decoration.

textbook Corinthian capitals, the zoomorphic pilaster capitals with figures of Pegasus at the corners, most obviously of all the line of Caryatids above the colonnades, are closely matched in the Classical or late-Hellenistic architecture of Attica.

The Altar of Augustan Peace is an even more eloquent witness of the cultural interchange of Greece and Rome. The altar itself, set on a stepped platform, was surrounded on all sides by lofty screen walls broken by entrances on the west and east. Mythological panels flanked each entrance—Mother Earth (above, p. 620) with children on her lap and personifications of Ocean and Water at her side, a scene carved fully in the Hellenistic tradition and exuding the blessings of tranquillity and renewed fertility that accompanied the Augustan peace; Aeneas sacrificing at the spot where he first set foot on Italian soil. Just around the corner, near the head of the procession on the south side, is Augustus in the same act of solemn sacrifice: the propaganda message is being hammered home, that Augustus is the new Aeneas, the bringer of hope and the architect of a Rome reborn. The rest of the south side shows members of his family (above, p. 544), while magistrates and their families fill up the north side; it is a commemoration in marble of an actual procession and sacrifice that took place in 13 BC in thanksgiving for the Emperor's safe return after a provincial tour. The idea of historical relief sculpture to record a specific event had been tentatively explored during the late Republic, but it was to find full expression only during the Empire. As an exercise in political propaganda, the Ara Pacis succeeds brilliantly in presenting some of the essential values that Augustus stood for: *grauitas* witnessed by the solemnity of the occasion; *humanitas* witnessed by such touches as a tired child pulling at his father's toga and by the overall flavour of a 'family occasion'; above all *pax*, peace both in Italy and in the world at large. As a sculptural monument, too, the friezes of the Ara Pacis are superlative, a tribute to the skills of the Greek sculptors who worked on them. The influence, above all, of Athens is paramount: in the overall form of the altar, a copy on a more monumental scale of the Altar of Pity in the Athenian *agora* (*c.* 420); in the processional friezes which inevitably recall those of the Parthenon; in the quiet solemnity reminiscent, perhaps, of Attic grave reliefs of the Classical age; and in the superbly disciplined yet exuberant floral scroll occupying the lower half of the screen wall, which, while at present most closely paralleled in Hellenistic Asia Minor, may well have been derived from now lost Attic models. The Ara Pacis epitomizes the Roman genius for borrowing freely from the Greek repertoire, but moulding it and adapting it into something new and distinctively Roman.

Another vital element of the new Roman propaganda machine was image-building; and Greek sculptors played a key role in fashioning a series of portrait-types of Augustus which were copied in vast numbers so that all corners of the Empire could be systematically bombarded with the image of the *princeps*. The types now created for Augustus and his family were not the ruthlessly realistic portraits of the late Republic, but a delicate blend of realism and statesmanly ideal. The mood might vary from the grim determination of the Capitoline Octavian, fashioned at a time before the total consolidation of his position, through the sober *auctoritas* of Augustus as *pontifex maximus*, carved some thirty years later yet with hardly a hint of ageing, to the supremely self-confident Primaporta Augustus, where the Emperor with expansive gesture harangues an unseen populace; but the overriding impression of a determined, efficient, authoritative leader is common to all.

In private life Augustus is reputed to have been a man of simple tastes who chose to dwell in a modest house unostentatiously adorned; certainly the property excavated on the Palatine and identified as his shows no greater luxury than comparable patrician residences of its day. In the fresco paintings of this and other properties of the imperial family, the overbearing architectural schemes which characterize the full-blown Second Style give way instead to decoration with a lighter touch, which favours architecture of less substantial form and an increasing emphasis on large central mythological 'panel' pictures as the focal point of each wall. The logical culmination of this trend was to deny altogether the illusion of depth and to emphasize instead the solidity of the wall. The new scheme of decor

PAINTED WALL-DECORATION IN THE VILLA OF AGRIPPA POSTUMUS AT BOSCOTRECASE (*c*.10 BC). A fine example of the early Third Style: above a black socle (not shown) the wall is predominantly red, with divisions effected by delicate bands of polychrome ornament. The central panel contains a superb landscape painting of the sacro-idyllic type.

which thus emerged (the so-called Third Style) depended for its effect on intricate and often fanciful decorative detail, especially floral and abstract designs, usually interspersed with figured tableaux which varied a good deal in size and number, while architectural elements, if they survived at all, now became flimsy and unreal. The new decorative scheme can be seen fully developed at another imperial property, the country house at Boscotrecase near Pompeii. The elegance and restraint of the frescoes here, in stark contrast to the excesses of the Second Style at its most extravagant, mark the culmination of a quiet but decisive revolution in artistic taste, achieved through the skill of court painters, but dictated, no doubt, by the personal preferences of the imperial family itself.

The individual ingredients of the new style of painting reflect the eclecticism of Augustan art as a whole. One ingredient was unashamedly classicizing: the wall schemes adopted by Augustan decorators, with their mythological panel pictures, large and small, were ideal vehicles for the widespread copying of Classical and Hellenistic Old Masters, and in this they set the tone for Roman

DETAIL OF A STUCCO VAULT-DECORATION from a suburban villa in the grounds of the Villa Farnesina, Rome. This landscape corresponds to the sacro-idyllic paintings of the same period, with both sacred and domestic buildings and both worshippers (bottom centre) and genre figures (bottom right). Certain elements, such as the house and tree at the left, suggest Egyptian influence.

wall painting for the next century. Another ingredient was the Egyptianizing element. This, like copying, was not entirely new, but it received an undoubted boost after the annexation of Egypt in 30 BC, when the curiosity value of things Egyptian ran high in Italy for a time. Some of the recurrent decorative features in Third Style compositions, such as sphinxes, ibises, cult objects, and figures of Isis, as well as vignettes of Nilotic scenes, were directly derived from the Egyptian repertoire. More controversial is the source of another popular ingredient in Augustan and later painting, the dreamy landscapes loosely referred to as 'sacro-idyllic' because they usually centre around a fanciful 'votive' column or flimsy shrine, with a variety of figures in attendance. Though they are often claimed as the products of Alexandrian mannerism, inspired by the bucolic poetry of Theocritus, no Hellenistic precedents in painting are so far known, and while some elements may well have had Hellenistic forerunners, the idea of peopling these artificial settings with shepherds, flocks, and dogs appears to begin only with the striking sacro-idyllic pictures from Boscotrecase; they may, therefore, be essentially an Augustan creation. Here the name of Studius is possibly relevant. He was the first, so Pliny tells us, who went in for the 'very charming paintings' of landscape gardens and the like filled with people engaged in the tasks of everyday life. This sounds like the sort of thing which crops up in several Augustan residences: tiny figures, depicted impressionistically in flat monochrome, walking and fishing and chatting and going about their daily business, in a setting of bridges, porticoes, and topsy-turvy pavilions. Certainly Studius did not invent landscape as such, nor can his name be associated with another masterpiece of Augustan painting, the 'garden of Livia' from her villa at Primaporta: here are no human figures, and so far from being impressionistic, the fruit and flowers of this wilderness of a paradise garden are executed with a loving care for naturalistic detail. Judgement must be suspended on this unique painting as to whether it, too, owes all or something to Hellenistic predecessors, or whether it is rather an exuberant product of the Augustan genius for originality.

The principal advances of Augustan art and architecture were worked out, of course, mainly in the capital; but the Augustan age saw in addition an enormous outpouring of building energy elsewhere in Italy and the Empire, especially in the western provinces. In many cases, indeed, we have to turn to these areas for preserved examples of buildings which are only fragmentary, or have vanished altogether, in Rome itself. One such is the triumphal arch, a characteristic monument of imperial propaganda of which several early examples still stand in north Italy and southern Gaul. Commemorative arches of a sort had been known in Republican Rome, but the developed form, articulated with columns, architrave, and attic bearing an inscription, is essentially an Augustan creation. Many of the buildings newly erected in the provinces at this time were based directly on metropolitan blueprints or from models elsewhere in Italy. Indeed in some instances (as at the famous Maison Carrée in Nîmes of AD 2–3) the presence of stonemasons and sculptors who had actually worked on the Augustan building programme in Rome can be argued. One of the most familiar of all Roman monuments, the stately Pont du Gard aqueduct near Nîmes, a harmonious structure which vividly demonstrates that the aesthetics of appearance need not be divorced from practical function, is also an Augustan monument, erected in the last quarter of the first century BC (plate facing p. 662). In the East, where urbanization was already deep-rooted, the impact of Augustus was less dramatic; but in the West—above all in his creation of a road system and in his establishment or refounding of innumerable, carefully chosen towns in Yugoslavia, Gaul, the Iberian peninsula, and along the north-African littoral—Augustus left a decisive and enduring stamp on the map of western Europe.

The Julio-Claudians: Tiberius to Nero (AD 14–68)

Augustus died on 19 August AD 14, and within a month he had been deified. Among the trappings of the official state cult of *diuus Augustus* was a newly

THE GEMMA AUGUSTEA, one of the finest examples of the large sardonyx cameos carved with propagandist reliefs by artists of the imperial court. According to the most likely interpretation, the upper register shows the deified Augustus and Tiberius descending from his triumphal chariot, while in the lower register Roman soldiers erect a trophy of victory, with barbarian prisoners in attendance, for Tiberius' German campaigns of AD 10–11.

created iconographical language for depicting the deceased Emperor in the company of gods. An eloquent early expression can be seen in the cameo known as the Gemma Augustea, a frank glorification of the dead Augustus, half draped, as befits his divine status, and surrounded by personifications of Rome, *Oikoumenē* (the inhabited world), Ocean, and Earth. Yet the new language rarely lost an opportunity to speak clearly also about the living, emphasizing the 'continuity factor' between the old regime and the new. On the Gemma Augustea, for example, Augustus looks across to his chosen successor Tiberius stepping from the chariot of victory, while the lower register alludes to Augustus' German wars, in which the prime architect of victory was none other than Tiberius. Some scholars claim that this and similar scenes were intended for private circulation during Augustus' lifetime; but that the man who himself shunned personal worship was instrumental in creating the new idiom seems unlikely. These scenes stand at the beginning of a long line of historical reliefs which use elaborate allegorical paraphrase to convey a political message.

Few monumental reliefs of Julio-Claudian date from Rome survive; those that do display a rather dry style entirely in the Augustan classicizing mould. The grand processional reliefs in the Villa Medici, for example, thought by some to be part of an Ara Pietatis ('Altar of Piety') of *c.* AD 22–45, are conceived and executed very much in the manner of the Ara Pacis; only in one major respect do they break fresh ground, in their detailed rendering of architectural setting, though the problem of providing this without sacrificing the prominence of the human figures has yet to be solved. A roughly contemporary relief showing a procession of city magistrates also marks an advance in its hesitant adoption of a slightly aerial perspective rather than a horizontal one: the heads of the second row are raised slightly above those in the foreground. Neither architectural setting nor vertical perspective was entirely new to the sculptural arts, but for the state reliefs of the capital they were a fresh departure, much exploited in the years to come.

Sculpture in the round was long to be dominated by the influence of Greek works and of the 'neo-Attic' school. Much of this was dreary and repetitive copying of the established Classical and Hellenistic masterpieces, in constant demand for decorating the town and country houses of the rich, as well as public *fora*, gardens, and bath-buildings; what little originality existed was usually limited to feeble pastiches. Not all of this sculpture, however, lacked vitality:

RELIEF FROM THE ARA PIETATIS IN ROME (dedicated by Claudius in AD 43 in belated thanks for the recovery of the Dowager Empress Livia from a serious illness twenty-one years earlier). A sacrifice takes place in front of the Temple of Magna Mater, one of the first instances in Roman sculpture of a precisely rendered architectural setting.

HEAD OF ODYSSEUS FROM SPERLONGA. The hundreds of fragments of baroque sculptural compositions from a grotto identified as that where Tiberius narrowly escaped death in a rock-fall in AD 26 have been reconstructed to form four main groups showing adventures of the Greek hero Odysseus; this head from the Blinding of Polyphemus is a good sample of their emotional, chiaroscuro style.

witness, for example, the outstanding work produced by the Rhodians Hagesander, Athanadorus, and Polydorus. One, the Laocoon (above, p. 666), found in the Golden House of Nero, exerted a powerful influence on Michelangelo and his contemporaries; the other, a series of dramatic larger-than-life groups including the Blinding of Polyphemus and Odysseus' ship passing Scylla, adorned a grotto in Tiberius' villa at Sperlonga. None of this sculpture was probably wholly original, being best regarded as adaptations and reworkings from Hellenistic models; but nor is it derivative hack-work: it testifies to the continuing vibrancy, intensity, and superb technical quality of Hellenistic baroque at its best, well into the early years of Empire.

Magnificent sculpture of this sort was to play an increasingly important part in grandiose interior decoration; the more generous the setting, the more colossal the sculpture to suit it. Nor are other indications lacking of a growing luxury in

Julio-Claudian interior decor: an expanding range of polychrome marbles for floor slabs and wall veneer, abandoning the comparative restraint of Augustan taste; wall mosaic using glass tesserae of dazzling colours, which was soon employed to good effect in sparkling fountains at Pompeii and elsewhere; mosaic work, too, to cover the soaring surfaces of concrete vaults, a medium with a long future down into Byzantine and early medieval times. Wall-painting, too, shared in the increasing desire for elaboration. One has only to compare some examples of the late Third Style, as in the House of Lucretius Fronto at Pompeii (*c.* 34–45), with the early-Augustan versions of the same style (as at Boscotrecase) to appreciate just how significant a shift in taste had taken place: there is still the horizontal wall division into three, still the prominent mythological panel in the centre, but the restraint and elegant simplicity of an earlier generation has been replaced by a riot of contrasting sweeps of colour, and by a wide range of intricate, often fussy detail; while the virtuoso pavilions in the top register with their shifting planes look forward to the even more elaborate developments of the Fourth Style.

The transition to the fully developed Fourth Style seems to belong to the 50s; certainly its use on the grand scale is brilliantly seen a decade later in the frescoes of the Domus Aurea, the Golden House of Nero (AD 64–8), inspired creations of the court painter Fabullus. It is a style marked above all by the 'opening up' of the wall to provide once more an architectural vista, usually to each side of a central panel (more rarely in an 'all-over' composition). No longer, however, in

WALL-DECORATION IN THE GOLDEN HOUSE OF NERO, recorded in an eighteenth-century engraving. Above a dado veneered with coloured marbles rose a painted scheme of flimsy fantasy architecture in the manner of the Fourth Style; figures and vases were set within the pavilions as if in a real environment. The colour scheme (despite the effect of the engraving) was mainly yellow on a dark-red background.

the Fourth Style are the architectural forms grounded in reality. In the Golden House they form a scintillating essay in airy and insubstantial fantasy, creating a whimsical framework around full-length figures, mythological panels, landscapes, and patches of 'solid' wall in a dazzling *tour de force*. Enlivened too by dainty arabesques, the whole series of frescoes is executed with a light touch; while some of the vignettes, displaying deft and rapid brushwork, are masterpieces of the Roman impressionistic manner. Many of these features recur in varying degrees of elaboration in countless examples of Fourth Style paintings at Pompeii and Herculaneum; and another aspect of the frescoes of the Golden House, the use of

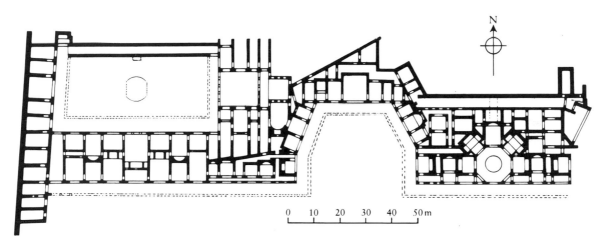

NERO'S GOLDEN HOUSE (AD 64–8): the Emperor's fabulous urban villa contained mechanical wonders and decorations 'all smeared with gold and picked out with jewels'; but more significant was its experimentation with new shapes and volumes within the basically rectangular plan. The novelty of the experiments is indicated by the presence of awkward, redundant triangular spaces between the main groups of rooms.

white as the background colour, was also to be of lasting influence, for it gained increasingly in favour, especially from the mid second century onwards. Even today, ravaged by the passage of time, the decoration of the Golden House makes a stunning impact on the visitor, just as it did nearly five centuries ago when Raphael and Giovanni di Udine, according to Vasari, 'were both seized with astonishment at the freshness, beauty, and excellent manner of these works.'

The Golden House of Nero was indeed no ordinary building. In the history of architecture, too, it represents a watershed, for the octagonal room in the east wing is roofed by the first surviving dome in the capital. This major achievement provided a novel flexibility in interior planning which at once opened up exciting possibilities for the future. The octagonal plan in itself (as also the five-sided court immediately to the west) is symptomatic of an impatience with the traditional rectangular room shapes which had long dictated architectural planning. Now, with concrete roofing a flexible tool in the hands of confident architects, the exploitation of circular, ovoid, and apsidal shapes in conjunction with stock rectangular ones created a variety in interior design that had not been possible before. In time, when the exterior shell was stripped away, the juxtaposition of widely differing room shapes with their medley of domes, semi-domes, barrel-vaults, and cross-vaults, often produced a positively ugly exterior. But the new Roman architecture is not an architecture of the exterior: rather it derives its dramatic impact from the interplay of light and space in the interior, so that the void becomes every bit as important as the solid envelope that encloses it. The dome of the Domus Aurea is but a small beginning, but it heralds the dawn of a new architectural approach which had a decisive influence on European architecture down to the present century.

The Golden House and its attendant pleasure park were created by an act of opportunism and imperial greed after the great fire of AD 64 had devastated the heart of Rome. That fire also presented Nero's city planners with a golden opportunity for revitalizing the domestic housing of the urban poor by replacing the sprawling tenement dwellings of the past with the tight, rational planning of the multi-storey rectangular apartment block (above, pp. 722 f.). It was a severely functional architecture, its sober façades rarely relieved by decorative detail; but it also has an uncompromisingly modern look, for the formula was repeated countless times in the urban housing of Renaissance and modern Rome. The material which made all this possible was brick-faced concrete, a winning combination which was strong, light and, as far as possible, fireproof. Having served its apprenticeship under the Julio-Claudians, brickwork was poised to sweep all before it and to take over as the principal facing material for major construction work in central Italy down to the very end of antiquity.

The Flavians, Nerva, and Trajan (AD 69–117)

In the autumn of 69 Vespasian established himself as sole master of the Roman world. A man of plebeian stock, he was a down-to-earth realist with the common touch, and it is probably not accidental that the best-known portrait of him, in Copenhagen, strips away the idealizing varnish and reveals a tough, experienced, ageing man, his leathery skin creased by long years of military campaigning. It is a frank portrayal in the Late Republican vein, shunning the blend of idealism and realism normally adopted in imperial portraits of the time (above, p. 558).

Vespasian's name is indissolubly linked with the most celebrated of all Roman buildings, the Colosseum, the amphitheatre he provided for the entertainment and gratification of the Roman people. Only in its enormous size, however, which called for great architectural ingenuity to ensure efficient crowd control, does it break fresh ground; in other respects it is essentially conservative. Two other Flavian buildings are more important as trend-setters in the brick-faced concrete style. One is the public baths of Titus, which stands at or near the head of a distinguished line of imperial bath-buildings, each rationally and symmetrically arranged around its central short axis. The other is the imperial palace built

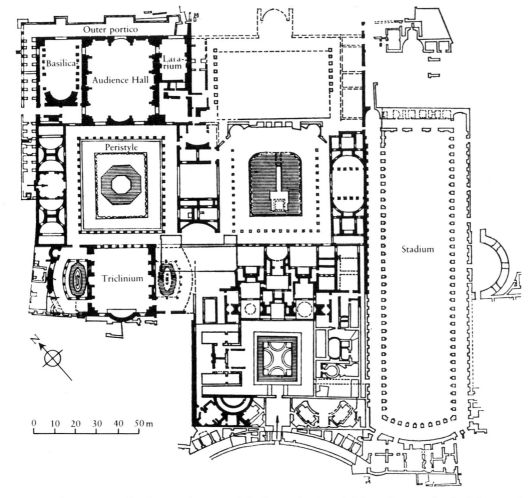

Outer portico

Basilica

Audience Hall

Lararium

Peristyle

Triclinium

Stadium

0 10 20 30 40 50 m

DOMITIAN'S PALACE (the Domus Augustana) in Rome (AD 81–92). The palace consisted of three main blocks: at the left the official palace including the state rooms; in the centre the Emperor's private residence; at the right the so-called Stadium, a sunken garden in the form of a hippodrome. The detailed planning shows a new facility in the integration of curvilinear and rectilinear shapes.

by Domitian on the Palatine hill in the 80s and early 90s, a building which later spawned numerous provincial imitations. Within its tight rectilinear exterior, the Palatine palace enunciates many of the distinctive tenets of the new architectural thinking: confident handling of enormous masses of brick-faced concrete, grouped in split-level arrangement to take maximum advantage of a complex site; a continuing interest in the dome—three examples in all, each resting on walls which open out into alternating apses and rectangular recesses, now fully integrated with the maze of rooms beyond; and a delight in the curvilinear at the expense of the rectangular. All created novel visual and spatial effects, replacing the expected with the unexpected at every turn. But Domitian's palace was designed not just to surprise, but to impress. 'The edifice is august, immense, splendid,' wrote Statius, 'an edifice to stupefy the neighbouring abode of Jupiter the Thunderer'; and awe, even intimidation, was the keynote of such halls as the palace vestibule (down in the forum) with walls 98 feet high, the vast audience chamber, the dining-room only slightly smaller, and the 'basilica' in the north-west corner where the Emperor sat in judgement. This, with its apse and double row of columns, probably derives from the palaces of Hellenistic kings, but the distinctive plan was later to have a decisive influence on the layout of the early Christian church. Ablaze with brilliant polychrome marble, adorned, too, with enormous statues, these grandiose state apartments, among the largest interiors yet created by Roman architects, were designed to overwhelm, to make the visitor feel he was in the presence of a very god. Domitian paid the price of an assassin's dagger for such overt assumption of divine honours, and his immediate successors played down this inflated image of the imperial personage, even though they continued to live amid the splendour of his palace.

Domitian's conviction of his own divine status is further emphasized by one of the reliefs from the Papal Chancellery, where he sets out for war in the exclusive company of deities. There can be no doubt that this relief was carved in the Emperor's lifetime, as his head was later reshaped with the features of his successor Nerva. No earlier relief indisputably shows a living Emperor in such divine company; but the almost contemporary relief from the Arch of Titus, erected by Domitian in his brother's memory, is an equally frank glorification of the Emperor, showing him accompanied by Rome and other personifications rather than by ordinary mortals. From now on this elaborate allegorical short-hand became a fully fledged part of the grand tradition of historical relief sculpture,

RELIEF OF DOMITIAN'S DEPARTURE FROM ROME (*PROFECTIO*). Between AD 81 and 96. The Emperor is seen off on a military campaign by an assortment of deities and personifications, including Mars, Minerva (or the Goddess Roma), Virtus (Courage), the Roman Senate, and the Genius (Spirit) of the Roman People. The mixing of historical event and allegory is typical of Roman state relief.

CAPTURED SPOILS FROM JERUSALEM, relief panel in the passageway of the Arch of Titus (soon after AD 81). The two reliefs in the arch, which represent the Emperor Titus' triumphal procession after the defeat of the Jewish Revolt in AD 70, have an unprecedented effect of bustle and movement and of being excerpts from a much larger action.

and by the time of Trajan a generation later the conventions are fully established, without hubristic overtones.

The Chancellery reliefs, competently carved but overall rather dull, are still firmly shaped by the mould of Augustan classicism. By contrast the lively reliefs on the Arch of Titus are brim-full of the excitement of a triumph in progress, especially in the procession of the spoils, where the participants spring along past the spectator, placards waving, and wheel round through an archway into the distance. There is a new interest in the handling of depth here, with the figures carved in higher or lower relief according to their distance from the spectator; but the illusion of life and movement owes more, perhaps, to the Hellenistic tradition than to any immediately preceding Roman work, even though the subject matter is an entirely Roman one.

Nowhere, however, is a sense of life and movement more dramatically conveyed than on the stupendous 700-foot frieze of Trajan's Column in Rome. Dedicated in AD 113, and designed to commemorate the Dacian Wars of 101-2 and 105-6, it undoubtedly represents the very apogee of continuous narrative sculpture in the ancient world. The problem of receding space was not tackled

TRAJAN ADDRESSING HIS TROOPS (*ADLOCUTIO*). This relief from Trajan's column (dedicated in AD 113) demonstrates the concern of the artist to fill the whole height of the frieze which spiralled up the column's shaft, partly by the use of landscape elements (the tree at the left) and partly by a distribution of figures at different levels.

in any consistent fashion; rather the designer's first priority was to present an almost uninterrupted flow of action-packed scenes. The constant switching between horizontal and bird's eye perspective, the frequent placing of figures 'above' and 'below' one another without perspective diminution, the incongruities of scale for some figures in relation to buildings, tend not to detract from the whole but to lend to it increased variety and vitality; the action relentlessly unfolds from bottom to top, never flagging despite its enormous length. Here, then, is a veritable textbook of the Roman army at work—gathering stores, preparing for the march, foraging for supplies, building camps, engaging the Dacian foe—delineated with supreme attention to detail. When Trajan appears it is always as the calm, authoritative commander-in-chief addressing his troops, consulting his generals, performing sacrifices, receiving envoys: for on the column there is nothing of the majestic tone of the 'grand style' reliefs with their episodic treatment and full use of allegorical paraphrase; indeed personifications are entirely absent except when required for occasional scene-setting. The overall organization of the frieze called for imagination and dexterity of the highest order;

and no less remarkable is the execution in very low relief of some 2,500 figures by a group of sculptors who (as on the Parthenon frieze) reached a uniformly high level of craftsmanship. The modelling of the figures is still firmly rooted in the Classical tradition, and some of the battle scenes can be traced back to late-Hellenistic groups, while other set-pieces are derived from the established repertoire of imperial iconography. But the overall effect is totally novel, a fully fledged product of pure Roman art, un-Greek in conception and execution. Most original of all is the use of a 100-foot column as a vehicle for propaganda sculpture, a bold stroke which marks the Column of Trajan with a touch of genius.

That touch of genius may well have been furnished by Apollodorus of Damascus, the architect of the forum in which the column stands. A man of forceful character, later to fall out with the Emperor Hadrian (who had strong, if idiosyncratic, architectural ideas of his own), Apollodorus was a first-rate structural engineer whose achievements included a half-mile-long bridge over the fast-flowing Danube, an amazing technical feat justly admired in antiquity. His forum too won high renown, not least for its impressive scale and the riot of gilded statues and polychrome marbles; but with the exception of the column and the integration of a basilica on the transverse axis (a novelty for the capital), the forum as a whole was closely linked with the past, consciously imitating the Forum of Augustus; and the relief sculpture, too, harks back to an Augustan dignity and simplicity of line. By contrast the friezes on a contemporary monument (the rebuilt temple in the Forum of Caesar) favour instead an ornate, highly decorative style with deep undercutting (intended to provide strong shadows and hence a powerful 'black and white' effect), a style with a longer future ahead of it in later Roman sculpture than restrained and sober classicism.

While Apollodorus' forum, however, looks decisively to the past, the accompanying market and shopping precinct terraced into the Quirinal hill looks no less emphatically to the future. Here is a complex where Apollodorus' mastery of the contemporary architectural idiom is displayed to the full: some 170 shops, offices, and storehouses, in brick-faced concrete up to four storeys high, brilliantly arranged on no less than six levels in an immensely complicated and irregular site. The jewel of the whole complex is a covered market-hall, roofed by one of the earliest large-scale examples of groined cross-vaulting to survive. This simple idea—a barrel-vault on the long axis intersected at right angles by a series of lesser barrel-vaults—marks an enormous architectural stride forward: for now the weight of the roof can be borne by great piers at intervals instead of by the entire length of the side walls, and windows can be opened up to the very crown of the vault, thus creating an imaginative, well-lit interior instead of the cavernous gloom of the usual barrel-vaulted hall. The first tentative steps in this direction were taken in the reign of Nero, but it needed the architectural ingenuity of a master-builder of Apollodorus' calibre to bring the idea to full fruition. Henceforth the cross-vault was to play a major role in Roman architecture, not

COVERED HALL IN TRAJAN'S MARKETS in Rome (c.AD 100-12). The central space is flanked on each side by six shops (*tabernae*) of the standard Roman form, with a wide door, a barrel-vaulted interior and a window to light a mezzanine storey. Above these ran galleries with further shops set back behind them; and between them rose the piers of a series of cross-vaults which spanned the central hall.

least in the central halls of imperial bath-buildings with their impressive vistas opening off in all directions; and it is hardly surprising that the baths of Trajan, the first mature example of the axial type, three times the size of Titus' baths, were also the creation of Apollodorus himself.

Hadrian and the Antonines (AD 117-193)

It is tempting to link Apollodorus' name also with Hadrian's temple to all the gods, the Pantheon, the construction of which was already in full swing within a year or so of Trajan's death; but no ancient authority does so, and the creator of what is unquestionably one of the great architectural masterpieces of all time remains anonymous. Characteristically it is not the exterior which wins admiration. The façade with its conventional portico and gable was very much run-of-the-mill for the temples of its time, and the radical conjunction of a rectangular porch with massive circular *cella* is positively disharmonious. Yet this incongruity is quite forgotten once one steps inside the enormous rotunda: for the impact of the interior, as any visitor to the Pantheon knows, is breathtaking. The eye is drawn up, immediately and irresistibly, to the superb lines of its coffered concrete dome, at 148 feet in diameter the largest man-made dome in the world until modern times. Sheer size is one element in the building's appeal: surprise is another. For the Pantheon is designed not along the lines of a conventional temple building dominated by a longitudinal, horizontal axis, but around a vertical axis, an invisible line joining the centre of the floor with the opening in the summit of the dome. Nothing is allowed to distract from this vertical aspect of the building, so that the articulation of niches and *aediculae* in the cylindrical drum wall is deliberately restless. Even the impact of the apse opposite the door is muted, no longer fulfilling its usual role as the focal point of a temple building. Yet despite this apparent complexity the essential geometry of the Pantheon is based on a simple, harmonious formula: the diameter of the whole building is identical to its height. Size, surprise, simplicity—these are three keynotes of this extraordinary temple. It is a building which embodies all the principal characteristics that define the specifically Roman contribution to architecture since Augustus: controlled use of polychrome marbles for columns, floor paving, and wall veneer, from Africa, Egypt, and Asia Minor; mastery of the properties of brick-faced concrete in its 20-foot-thick walls, constructed with numerous relieving arches and recesses to lessen the chances of settlement; mastery, too, in the pouring of some 5,000 tons of concrete for the soaring dome, with carefully graded ingredients ranging from strong basalt near its spring-line to light pumice at its summit. Above all the Pantheon is a supremely eloquent essay in the creation of interior space, and in the lighting of that space, through a single, bold opening at the very crown of the dome. More than any other Roman building it has inspired countless imitations and adaptations, starting in Hadrian's own reign with the Temple of Asclepius at Pergamum, and continuing on well into the present century.

The other architectural *tour de force* of Hadrian's reign is the sprawling stately home constructed by the Emperor near Tivoli over an enormous tract of rolling countryside. The whole bears the unmistakable stamp of the personality of its self-indulgent owner, who had at his disposal both the technical resources and the bottomless purse necessary to create the succession of luxurious living quarters, baths, pavilions, banquet halls, libraries, and grandiose ornamental pools. Throughout the villa the variety of room shapes and the ingenuity shown in their interrelationship betoken a lively interest in the architecture of interiors; while in the central court of the pavilion in the Piazza d'Oro, or in the villa-in-miniature on its artificial island (where Hadrian could retreat when in reclusive mood), a delight in the curvilinear is carried to baroque extremes. Roofing, too,

INTERIOR OF THE PANTHEON (*c.*AD 118–28). The great Hadrianic rotunda dedicated to the planetary gods is a fine example of the new interest in interior space and surface ornament which developed in imperial architecture. The diameter of the dome (42.50 m) was greater than that of St Peter's and remained unsurpassed till the present century.

DOMED HALL IN THE GARDENS OF SALLUST, ROME (engraving by Piranesi): a fine example of the ambitious vaulting techniques explored in Hadrianic times, especially in the emperor's villa at Tivoli. The dome consists of eight sectors alternately flat and concave. Hadrian may have had a personal interest in designing such domes: Trajan's architect Apollodorus is said to have told him in a famous exchange of words, 'Go and draw your pumpkins.'

was the subject of fresh experiment: the dome in the vestibule of the Piazza d'Oro was no longer provided with an outer masonry skin to cloak its inner form (a frank admission that it was interior effect, not exterior appearance, which really mattered in Roman architecture); while the Serapeum has a spectacular example of the new 'pumpkin' dome, composed of distinct radiating segments alternately concave and flattened. Hadrian himself had a personal interest, possibly even a creative role, in this fresh variation of the dome, and an even more ambitious example occurs in another of his palaces, in the Gardens of Sallust at Rome.

While the architecture of Hadrian's villa was uncompromisingly Roman, the sculptural detail was no less uncompromisingly Greek. Hadrian was by far the most philhellenic of all Roman Emperors, and the enthusiasm which earned him the nickname of 'Greekling' carried him on occasion a little too far: his attempt to implant a temple of entirely Greek form, the Temple of Venus and Rome, in the very heart of the capital was widely regarded as an aesthetic failure. Sculpture, however, was a different matter; and such was the influence wielded by artistic patronage that the personal predilections of the Emperor could and did leave a decisive mark on the sculpture of the age. When Hadrian opted for a 'Classical revival' he stopped dead in its tracks for a generation the development of an authentically Roman sculptural style, such as was beginning to emerge on Trajan's Column. Instead he welcomed to Rome Greek sculptors and craftsmen on a scale not seen since Augustus' day, and evidence of their work can be detected in the embellishment of all the major projects associated with Hadrian. That evidence points to Asia Minor as the homeland of these gifted men, for the architectural ornament in Rome can sometimes be matched, detail for detail, with work at Pergamum, Ephesus, and elsewhere. Much of it was carved in the fine white marble (with a pronounced blue streak) from the quarries of Proconnesus near Istanbul, a material which arrived in Rome for the first time with these Asiatic craftsmen. Also carved by them on Italian soil was a wide range of sculpture both in relief and in the round, much of it with life and spontaneity suggestive of genuine creativity. Certainly it was to sculptors from the Greek world that Hadrian turned to perpetuate the melancholy beauty, diffident manner, and lithe and sensuous frame of his boyfriend Antinous, deified after drowning in the Nile in October 130. In original creations such as this Greek artists made a more important contribution to Hadrianic sculpture than did routine copies of Caryatids and other fifth-century Attic masterpieces which line the Canopus pool at the Tivoli villa, copies mechanically reproduced in Italian workshops long accustomed to demands of this kind.

The introduction of fresh currents from Greek lands into the mainstream of art and architecture was also symptomatic of an increasing cosmopolitanism in Rome and the Roman world under Hadrian and the Antonines. The second and third quarters of the second century were a particularly glorious age for the provincial cities of the Roman Empire, as self-confidence increased, living standards rose, and horizons widened. One graphic witness of the new outlook is provided by the rush to construct or refurbish in marble, which resulted in an astonishing boom in the export of coloured marbles. Its beginning can be dated to the early years of Hadrian's reign, and by the middle of the century nearly all new public buildings in major provincial cities were being constructed with marble columns and architraves and marble veneers. In some cases there is evidence that the imported materials were carved on arrival by craftsmen from the country of source; a process also documented later in the second century (as well as in the third) for the elaborate marble relief sarcophagi from Greece and Asia Minor, which were shipped in a roughed-out state and only worked in detail once they had reached their destination. This is no longer a Rome-centred world

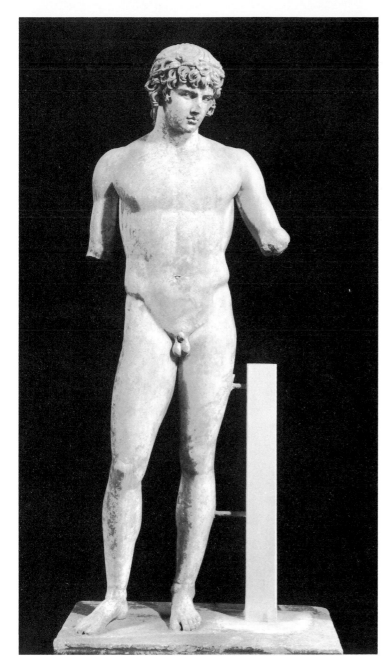

STATUE OF ANTINOUS in the museum at Delphi. The young Bithynian, Hadrian's boy-friend, drowned in mysterious circumstances in the River Nile in 130, was commemorated by numerous statues, based on a type which was the last great original creation in the classicizing style. It combined a body of mid-fifth-century form with a head which conveys a new emotional intensity.

in which a metropolitan building type or decorative motif could be transmitted without substantial transmutation to a provincial centre: instead we are presented with an infinitely more complex and sophisticated organization which took architects, sculptors, and even jobbing masons far from their homes, with the resulting diffusion of fresh ideas and techniques into a common pool. Rome was no longer the only or even the dominant force in shaping provincial art and architecture: other vital creative centres had their part to play, leading to the emergence of an art which was no longer always individualistic along narrow provincial lines, but was common to widely separated parts of the entire Roman Empire.

That Asia Minor was among the most important of those creative centres has already been made clear. While art and architecture in the region generally retained its conservative, late-Hellenistic flavour during the first century, sparks of originality were also there: the recently discovered Sebasteion reliefs from Aphrodisias for example, dating to the fifties, glorify members of the imperial house in an individual style untramelled by the dictates of Italian state sculpture. But it was in architecture that the sparks of creativity really flew: and in such marble extravaganzas as the fountain building at Miletus (*c.* 100) or the library of Celsus at Ephesus (*c.* 117-20) we are treated to a controlled display of traditional, classical architectural elements presented in new guise: simple two-columnar *aediculae* are combined in straddle formation to achieve novel visual effects,

CLAUDIUS OVERWHELMING BRITANNIA: relief from the Sebasteion (building of the imperial cult) at Aphrodisias in Caria (AD 54-68). The vigorous style owes a good deal to Classical and Hellenistic models, as does the heroic nudity of the Emperor. Other reliefs from the building celebrate the victories of Augustus and the remaining Julio-Claudians, concluding with Nero.

FOUNTAIN-BUILDING AT MILETUS (beginning of second century AD). The reconstruction reveals a number of features characteristic of Roman 'baroque' architecture: the elaborate play of advancing and receding entablatures, the sideways misplacement of pavilions so that those of the upper storeys straddle the spaces between those below, and the enlivenment of the whole façade with statue-niches. Such features were especially common in the eastern provinces.

heightened by baroque detail such as segmental and volute pediments. The notion of such elaborate columnar screens won widespread popularity, especially in theatre back-drops the length and breadth of the empire; while the language of baroque architecture finally became common currency during the second century in the architectural repertoire of the East, although it only occurred spasmodically in Italy or the West until Renaissance architects discovered it in the late fifteenth century. It is possibly also to the Hellenistic East that we must look for the origins of another highly influential idea, that of springing arches direct from columns, a device with a long and distinguished role to play from the early fourth century onwards in the architecture of the Christian church.

In fresco painting all the indications point to a decline after the end of the first century. There are some exceptions, but the monotonous frescoes from Ostia show that in general Hadrianic and Antonine interior decorators were content with repeating hackneyed decorative schemes which echo the Third and Fourth Styles of the previous century with increasing simplification and hardly a hint of originality—broad splashes of colour, especially red and yellow and white, but fewer and fewer mythological panels, which were gradually replaced completely by individual figures or motifs floating free in the centre of each zone. Ceiling decoration, by contrast, reached new heights of inspiration during the Antonine period: the strikingly detailed stuccoes from the Tombs of the 'Valerii', the

PAINTED MARINE DECORATION from one of a pair of rooms excavated in the vicinity of the docks on the Tiber in Rome (*c*.AD 131). Painted *aquaria* appeared in the vaults of bath-suites of the first century, where fish were reflected in the water of a pool and appeared to be swimming among the bathers; but the combination of such marine creatures with mythological or idyllic scenes (the rowing boat) is a trend of the second and later centuries.

Pancratii, and the Nasonii at Rome, all *c*. 160, represent the very apogee of the Roman stucco-worker's craft. But it too seems to have declined thereafter, and by the early third century we have instances of walls and ceiling in the same room being painted with identical, humdrum, compartmentalized schemes, as in some of the early catacombs. Only in the occasional 'all-over' figured composition does second-century wall painting show signs of a different approach, as in a lively Hadrianic fishing scene from near the Porto Flumentano in Rome, but this appears to have become widespread only from early in the third century.

While painting was apparently in the doldrums, second-century mosaic work took on a new lease of life. The richly coloured, intricately figured panels of Hellenistic origin had continued to be made in Italy throughout the first century, and spasmodically even later, but they had been joined by modest black-and-white figural mosaics in a silhouette style from the Augustan period onwards. From about AD 110 fresh life was injected into this style, with ambitious and enormously successful wall-to-wall compositions, depending for their effect not on spatial depth or naturalistic detail but on superb draughtsmanship. Outstanding Hadrianic examples include lively marine tableaux in the Baths of Neptune, and animal scenes in the Baths of the Seven Sages at Ostia; but the black-and-white style flourished throughout the Italian peninsula (and occasionally elsewhere) well into the third century. Purely ornamental mosaics in black and white, also widespread in Italy, became increasingly ornate, and both complicated curvilinear patterns and delicate floral arabesques enter the repertoire now. Ornamental designs were carried further in the experiments in polychromy that followed, both in Italy and the western provinces, from the mid second century; while the floral arabesque was adopted in polychromy by African workshops, which were already preparing the way for the enormous outburst of creativity that mosaicists there were to display during the third and fourth century. That story, however, lies outside our scope; but in the prelude to the full flowering of mosaic in late antiquity, the second-century mosaicists of Italy had a vital role to play.

In state sculpture too, the second century represents a crucial transition, heralding the emergence of a late antique style which breaks free from the shackles of the Classical heritage. We have seen how the personal tastes of Hadrian left a distinctive mark on the sculpture of a generation; and an entirely classicizing spirit, technically excellent but frigid and dull, can be seen on 'official' relief sculpture from his reign, such as two panels from a demolished triumphal arch (*c.* 136–8). The subject of one depicting the apotheosis of his wife Sabina, borne to heaven by a winged female figure and watched by Campus Martius and an impassive Hadrian, is taken up again on the monumental base for Antoninus' Column, dedicated posthumously in 161. Here it is the deceased Emperor as well as his consort who are conveyed aloft on an even more preposterous winged figure, probably a personification of the Golden Age, with Campus Martius and Roma in attendance below. Again we are dealing with sculpture which shows consummate naturalistic handling of its material; yet the overall impression is static, pompous, even comic. The same serene and rather lifeless quality also pervades some of the reliefs dedicated by Marcus Aurelius, probably on an arch of 175–6; these display in addition an increasing simplification of composition and the beginning of a more frontal emphasis for the Emperor, a pose that was to become *de rigueur* by the fourth century. All these state reliefs, however, despite high technical skill, mark the very end of the road for the Classical tradition: sculptors now found themselves in a cul-de-sac, anxious for an avenue

BLACK-AND-WHITE MOSAIC in the Baths of Neptune at Ostia (*c*.AD 140). While second-century mosaicists in parts of northern Italy and the north-western provinces were moving towards a polychrome 'carpet' type of pavement decoration, the artists of central and southern Italy preferred a highly effective style of all-over figured pavements with black silhouettes on a white ground. Here the god Neptune is surrounded by sea-creatures in a grand marine *cortège*.

of escape from what was becoming routine and devoid of challenge. The earliest sign of the search for a new sculptural language comes on the Antonine Column base of 161, in two panels showing scenes of a funeral procession, each with ten footsoldiers of the Praetorian guard encircled by seventeen horsemen. The combination of horizontal and bird's eye perspective in a single scene is not in itself new, but on this scale it is novel, on a neutral background stripped of all setting; and the handling of the individual figures, with their large heads and dumpy bodies, also represents a new departure. The trend towards a fresh simplicity and abstraction of form is further developed on the Column of Aurelius, commemorating the Marcomannic Wars of 172–5 but not finished until 193. Inevitably compared unfavourably with the Column of Trajan, it lacks the involved action, the variety, the attention to detail of its forerunner. But its designer and sculptors were not seeking to make a duplicate of Trajan's Column. They intended to convey an impression of war rather than a detailed commentary on it, by presenting fewer episodes carved boldly and clearly; and instead of careful modelling we find rather flat surfaces, with grooved lines for drapery, and deep undercutting around the figures, designed to enhance the 'black-and-white' effect of the whole. A yet further stage in the development of what might be termed impressionistic sculpture can be seen on the Arch of Septimius Severus in the Roman Forum (AD 203). It is easy to dismiss the groups of ill-proportioned two-dimensional figures with their heavily drilled hair and clothing as naive and degenerate products, representative of sculpture in decline; but as the figures of the Seasons or the Victory spandrels on the same Arch—or indeed the magnificent contemporary figured sarcophagi commissioned by private patrons—amply demonstrate, the sculptors of the period had not forgotten how to carve naturalistically; they were merely searching for a new and different means of expression. In this they paved the way for the transition to late antiquity, and ultimately, through Byzantium, to the cathedral sculpture of medieval Europe.

CAVALRY PARADE on the base of the column of Antoninus Pius (*c*.AD 161). This relief marks a sharp break with the classical style of previous state sculptures, dispensing with conventional visual perspective and with indications of setting. The foot-soldiers are supposed to be standing in the middle, with the cavalry passing in front of and behind them.

ADLOCUTIO OF MARCUS AURELIUS. This scene from Marcus's column (AD 180–95) can be compared with the same subject on the column of Trajan three quarters of a century earlier. The elimination of landscape, the more repetitive poses of the figures, the tendency to arrange figures in two distinct tiers, the reliance on drill-grooves to model drapery, the stumpy proportions of the figures, and above all the frontality of the imperial group, all foretoken the end of classical art.

Further Reading

An excellent collection of source material in translation with brief linking commentary can be found in J. J. Pollitt, *Art of Rome* (Englewood Cliffs, NJ, 1966, reissued Cambridge, 1983). There is no up-to-date translation and commentary on Vitruvius, but M. H. Morgan's translation (1914; repr. New York, 1960) remains serviceable; for a brief discussion, A. McKay, *Vitruvius, Architect and Engineer* (London, 1978). For Rome there is a collection of ancient sources in translation in D. R. Dudley, *Urbs Roma* (London, 1967), and the reference work of S. B. Platner and T. Ashby, *Topographical Dictionary of Ancient Rome* (Oxford, 1929) and the photographic archive of E. Nash, *Pictorial Dictionary of Ancient Rome* (2 vols., 2nd. edn., London and New York, 1968) remain fundamental.

The best short introduction in English to Roman art is that of J. M. C. Toynbee, *Art of the Romans* (London and New York, 1965); the most balanced longer account that of D. E. Strong, *Roman Art* (Harmondsworth, 1976, reissued in integrated format 1980), but the latter was published posthumously and shows signs of being unfinished. Neither deals with architecture. M. Henig (ed.), *Handbook of Roman Art* (Oxford, 1983), is a well illustrated up-to-date account for the general reader with essays of uneven quality from several hands. The most lavishly illustrated single-volume treatment of Roman art, with copious colour and black-and-white photographs, is B. Andreae's *The Art of Rome* (New York, 1977; London, 1978), and there are also excellent illustrations in R. Bianchi Bandinelli's *Rome, The Centre of Power* and *Rome, The Late Empire* (London and New York, 1970 and 1971). Sir Mortimer Wheeler's *Roman Art and Architecture* (London and New York, 1964) has a lively if slightly idiosyncratic text and deals mainly with architecture, thematically by building type; the chapters on painting, sculpture, and the minor arts are very sketchy. Somewhat idiosyncratic, too, is the arrangement of material adopted by R. Brilliant, *Roman Art* (London, 1974). More balanced, well-illustrated accounts include G. M. A. Hanfmann, *Roman Art* (London and New York, 1964) and H. Kähler, *Rome and Her Empire* (London and New York, 1963), but both are now slightly out of date. O. Brendel, *Prolegomena to the Study of Roman Art* (New Haven and London, 1979), is especially useful on the different attitudes to Roman art from the eighteenth century onwards.

On Roman architecture, J. B. Ward-Perkins's *Roman Imperial Architecture* (Harmondsworth, 1981) is magisterial and will long remain the standard work; this is a revised version of part of A. Boethius and J. B. Ward-Perkins, *Etruscan and Roman Architecture* (Harmondsworth, 1970) now reissued as two separate books. J. B. Ward-Perkins's *Roman Architecture* (New York, 1977) is a briefer, but no less lucid, account from the same hand. F. Sear, *Roman Architecture* (London, 1982), largely rehearses the same ground as Ward-Perkins with few fresh insights. Briefer essays include F. E. Brown, *Roman Architecture* (New York, 1961), and G. Picard, *Living Architecture: Roman* (London and New York, 1966); more specialized are W. L. MacDonald, *The Architecture of the Roman Empire* I (New Haven and London, 2nd edn., 1982), a detailed study of five buildings in Rome from Nero to Hadrian (especially good on vaulting), and the collection of essays on various topics by A. Boethius, *The Golden House of Nero* (Ann Arbor, 1960). MacDonald's essay on *The Pantheon* (Harmondsworth, 1976) provides not only a lucid analysis of that singular building but also an account of its many imitators down to the present century. On baroque there is M. Lyttelton, *Baroque Architecture in Classical Antiquity* (London and Ithaca, NY, 1974).

On painting there is no adequate monograph in English; G.-Charles Picard's *Roman Painting* (London and Greenwich, Conn., 1970) is superficial and, despite its title, does not deal exclusively with painting. Better concise accounts of the Pompeian material can be found in the books cited in the Bibliography of Chapter 30. W. Dorigo's *Late Roman Painting* (London and New York 1971) deals with the post-Pompeian material and includes mosaic; although well illustrated, the discussion is verbose and, at times, wayward. On mosaics, K. M. D. Dunbabin's *Mosaics Of Roman North Africa* (Oxford, 1978) includes survey chapters on more general aspects of the medium and ranges outside Africa; while on the Italian black-and-white school, there is now J. R. Clarke, *Roman Black and White Figural Mosaics* (New York 1978).

On sculpture, D. E. Strong, *Roman Imperial Sculpture* (London, 1961), remains the best introduction; A. W. Lawrence, *Greek and Roman Sculpture* (London and New York, 1972), is a fuller but more austere account. Notable essays on specific works include J. M. C. Toynbee's study of the Ara Pacis in *Proceedings of the British Academy* 39 (1953), 67–95, and her *The Flavian Reliefs from the Palazzo della Cancelleria in Rome* (Oxford, 1957). Trajan's Column has received monograph treatment in English from L. Rossi, *Trajan's Column and the Dacian Wars* (London and Ithaca, NY, 1971, with poor photographs), while I. A. Richmond's classic 1935 treatment is now available in his *Trajan's Army on Trajan's Column* (London 1982). The reliefs on the Antonine column base are fully discussed by L. Vogel, *The Column of Antoninus Pius* (Cambridge, Mass., 1973).

Envoi: On Taking Leave of Antiquity

HENRY CHADWICK

T H E ancient classical world is a large entity to take leave of. How did it all end? Or should one ask how it survived so long? What principally distinguishes 'ancient' history from that which we label medieval or modern? One obvious difference is that the available sources, though massive enough, are on a far smaller scale, so that the writing of ancient history is a distinct operation from writing modern history where the quantity of documents overwhelms the student. But that is of the accidents rather than the substance of what makes ancient classical studies a special and unique discipline. The rock whence western civilization is hewn is the old Mediterranean world, beginning with high achievements at the eastern end in the Nile valley, in the Assyrian and Persian worlds, in Judaea, but then seeing the centre of gravity move westwards: first to the Greeks, with a high peak of excellence in the fifth and fourth centuries BC, then to the Romans, whose power ultimately yields to the energy of the despised, crude, bibulous barbarians of the north and north-west.

Yet even the barbarian invasions of the fifth century AD fail to mark a decisive ending to the structures and values of classical Greece and Rome. If by 'the end of the ancient world' we mean the loss of a uniquely privileged position for Greek and Latin classics in western education and culture, then the shift cannot be described as decisive until the twentieth century, an age in which powerful forces are inimical to the very notion of a 'classic' of the past providing a model or criterion of judgment over the present. Even as the twentieth century draws to a close, the continued centrality of Rome and of the old Mediterranean world retains at least one living and undiminished symbol in the Papacy, presiding over a community of more than 700 million people, most of whom do not live in Europe. Until very recent times the renewal of high culture in the West has been linked with some direct contact with the prime sources of this culture in antiquity: in Greek philosophy, in Roman law and administration, in the universalism stemming from biblical monotheism.

That is not to say that these three main sources are, or were at the time felt to be, wholly harmonious and co-operative friends. The Romans, from Cicero to Pope Gregory the Great, regarded the Greeks as too clever to be honest. The Greeks, as is clear from Plutarch, admired the Romans, but did not greatly appreciate being conquered by them and would have preferred their own incompetent government to Roman efficiency and justice. Christian monotheism represented a disruptive challenge to immemorial local cults and social customs throughout the Empire, and was met by vigorous resistance in the form of philosophic criticism and state harassment.

It is astonishing that the Roman Empire survived the crisis of the third century AD. Already by 200 a serious trade recession had begun to hit the Mediterranean world, and people spoke anxiously of a falling birth-rate. In the middle years of the century the legions suffered fearful defeats from Persians, Goths, and other Germanic tribes; and the ferocity of internal civil wars brought the enterprise of imperial government to the verge of disintegration. This was averted by the new deal imposed first by Diocletian (Emperor 284–306, died 316 at Split), then by Constantine the Great (Emperor 306–37). From about 250 there was drastic inflation, which Diocletian vainly tried to check by fixing prices (which drove goods off the market altogether), and which Constantine fuelled when gold from pagan temple treasuries was allowed to flood the market. The repulse of the barbarians was achieved at the price of almost total concentration of power in the Emperor's hands and the decline in political significance of the old Senate, though senators remained in possession of their great estates and served in high offices of state. A rigid caste system enforced order. The graded rank of officials in the bureaucracy was marked by insignia in their clothing, particularly shoes and girdles, and by special titles—in descending order *illustris, spectabilis, clarissimus, perfectissimus*, inferior officials in the secretariat being *deuotus* or *modestus*, and so on.

Diocletian divided the old provinces into two, thereby multiplying the costs of the civil service. Late Roman society felt the hand of bureaucracy heavy upon it, especially when even good bureaucrats, who felt themselves underpaid, took for granted a substantial tip from any whose interests they served. The worst officials expected 'protection money'. In the case of high officers of state whose support was indispensable in an important matter, a *douceur* would be substantial; we hear of petitioners landing themselves in huge debts at crushing interest rates, and perhaps even then not getting what they sought.

Usury was frowned on by Christian moralists. But the effect of making it difficult to obtain redress from a defaulter through the lawcourts must be to push interest rates higher, since the lender then spreads the risk over fewer customers. In practice loans continued with little restriction and became a target for sharp criticism when people of little means took out loans on the security of their

CONSTANTINE THE GREAT: fragments of the gigantic statue from the Basilica of Constantine, Rome (c. AD 313). The full-size column and doorway at the right of the picture give an idea of the scale of the statue, which showed the Emperor seated with his right hand gripping a sceptre or spear and his left hand holding symbols of power and victory.

houses or small holdings and ended by being evicted. Towards the end of the fourth century a series of infectious urban riots occurred which Jerome ascribed to the rage at wholesale evictions resulting from exorbitant interest rates. In the late Empire there was a constant tendency for land and property to be concentrated in fewer hands. Under pressure the weak sold to the strong, who competed with each other in the size of their estates.

There seems to have been no time in antiquity when corruption was excluded from the lawcourts and the tax system. Cyprian, bishop of Carthage (martyred 258), trenchantly described the system in which a man who had bought office felt justified in recouping his outlay and gathering more for the day when he fell from favour. The Emperors realized what inefficiency resulted from corruption and made intermittent attempts to stop it. One Christian preacher of about 370, probably at Edessa, illustrates the awesomeness of the last judgement by painting a word-picture of a provincial governor handing in his seals of office, standing trembling, white with fear, in the anteroom of the palace awaiting an interview with the Emperor. To check corruption Diocletian created an inspectorate, but they became merely a secret police, using power for their own advantage and at least as corrupt as anyone else.

The administration separated the Latin and Greek halves of the Empire, with two praetorian prefects in each half at the head of the civil services. They were responsible for justice and taxation, but not for the army. Under them were deputies (*uicarii*) administering groups of provinces called dioceses, and provincial governors. At court lay the central officers of State, the most influential being the Master of the Offices, responsible for intelligence services, the government postal service (not available to private individuals), arsenals, coastguards, keeping the Emperor informed, and seeing that his wishes were carried out. The civil service was organized in departments called 'cabinets' (*scrinia*). Other major officers were the Treasurer; the administrator of the Privy Purse; and, especially powerful, the Quaestor of the Palace, responsible for justice. Diocletian copied the Persian court, enhancing his authority by the mystery of elaborate ceremonial, with veils separating the anterooms from the audience chamber, and a series of silentiaries to guard the way. The number of veils to be passed was an index of the dignity of an official's place in the bureaucracy. Eunuchs became important as major-domos, not only in rich households, but also at court. In the office of High Chamberlain they would exercise an influence resented by high officers of state.

Diocletian's division of the Empire into two halves was reversed by Constantine, who by 324 had disposed of superfluous colleagues and made himself sole Emperor. But the division was later restored, and from 395 the western and eastern empires were in effect administered increasingly independently. People talked of 'both governments', recognizing the Empire to be a duality in more than language. In 476 the barbarian army commander Odovacer sent the Emperor Romulus Augustulus into pleasant retirement and assumed the insignia of regal office. The Ostrogothic king Theoderic, educated at Byzantium, was sent to remove Odovacer in 493, but he too found that his status in relation to the east-Roman Emperor Anastasius (491–518) was uneasy. There was regret at the ending of the line of Roman emperors in the West, even though they had long been controlled by barbarian generals. Anastasius, Justin (518–27), and Justinian (527–65) aspired to restore Roman control. Two decades of desolating war were the price that Italy paid for having the Goths (whose administration under Theoderic (493–526) was pre-eminent) turned out by Justinian's armies under Belisarius and Narses. Soon the Goths were succeeded by the Lombards; and in the generations after Justinian's death Slavs and Avars poured into the Balkan peninsula (the Avars leaving a lasting mark in the name Navarino). The Emperor Heraclius exhausted the Empire's military strength in beating back the Persians and left the Jordan desert frontier defenceless against the Arabs. The Arabs had long been restless and marauding in Palestine and Egypt, but were now inspired by Islam and dreams of world conquest.

But until the Arab invasions of the seventh century the peoples of the

Mediterranean world still felt themselves to be inhabiting a Roman world. The Vandals at Carthage were a nuisance for a hundred years of piracy, but Justinian's wars ended that. In the barbarian kingdoms of the West the Germanic tribes lived according to their own tribal law, while Romans continued under Roman law. The great aristocratic families served under the barbarian military authorities (the elevation of dukes above counts being one permanent consequence), and provided a civil service and lawcourts. Self-consciously they tried to educate their new masters, whom they found hard-drinking and malodorous. The Visigoths in southern Gaul and the Burgundians early in the sixth century produced legal codes, in the one case juxtaposing, in the other amalgamating, Germanic and Roman enactments. Thanks to the value placed on Roman imperial edicts in the Germanic kingdoms, there survives the law-code of the Emperor Theodosius II, published in the East on 15 February 438 and then also accepted in the West. The Theodosian Code was transmitted with a supplement of additional edicts or 'novels' for the years 438-58.

The 'end of the western Empire' in 476 was an event that no one at the time much noticed. There was no sudden collapse of Roman resistance against external barbarians. The barbarians had long been providing the army, and all that had happened was that the man with the real power assumed the ceremonial insignia as well. But the landed aristocrats of Italy and the Byzantine Emperors soon realized that the Gothic kingdom of Theoderic was much less Roman than they liked. We hear complaints of the appalling Gothic taste in music, of trousers and hair-grease. In the West the Church increasingly came to be the vehicle of Roman culture and civic values. It is characteristic, for example, that the clergy did not adopt barbarian dress at the time when their congregations were doing so, but continued to wear the 'Sunday best' of old Roman aristocrats—which we today think of as ecclesiastical vestments. It mattered little or nothing that Rome as a city had long given place to Milan and then Ravenna as the western Emperor's residence. Ravenna had the merit of being surrounded by marshes on the landward side, with a good port at Classis. Behind its walls Emperors felt safe. From there Theoderic administered Italy, and his palace chapel is now Sant' Apollinare Nuovo. There too in Justinian's time the exquisite church of San Vitale was erected and adorned with incomparable mosaic, including portraits of Justinian and Theodora.

The barbarian domination made people assertive about *Romanitas*. In Theoderic's Italy Boethius and Cassiodorus set about preserving ancient culture and philosophy. Boethius declared his 'fear that many things which are now known soon will not be'. At Constantinople Priscian wrote a Latin grammar which long educated the medieval West. Justinian's loudest assertion of Roman values was his code of laws superseding the Theodosian Code. All imperial edicts not included were declared invalid. In the Theodosian Code some edicts ('laws of citations') prescribed the legal authorities which could be cited as argument in court: Papinian, Paulus, Ulpian, Modestinus, Gaius, a majority among them

MOSAIC OF JUSTINIAN WITH GUARDS, OFFICIALS, AND CLERICS, in the church of San Vitale at Ravenna (*c.*AD 547). The Emperor, who briefly reunited Italy to the Eastern Empire, is shown wearing a halo and carrying a gold vessel at the consecration of the church; the Archbishop Maximian stands at his side.

being decisive. Under the great quaestor Tribonian, Justinian instructed his law commission of professional jurists to make a digest of the classical authorities, and this huge book remains the main source for our knowledge of classical Roman law. The way in which Tribonian's commissioners went about the task of compiling the *Digest* has given modern legal historians an unrivalled problem in detection and decoding, to which the utmost ingenuity has been applied. Justinian also put his name to a textbook of law, *Institutiones* or elementary instructions, designed to ensure that even students at law-school had a guidebook sealed with imperial authority. Both *Digest* and *Code* are Latin texts, though produced in the Greek East. The corpus of civil law had a third part, mainly in Greek, consisting of Justinian's further edicts or 'novels' promulgated subsequently to the *Code*, which appeared in 534 with a pompous fanfare of an introduction.

Historians of the law and of architecture cannot say an *envoi* to Justinian without a salute of deep admiration for his extraordinary achievements. The *Code* and *Digest*, Sancta Sophia at Istanbul, and San Vitale at Ravenna are enough to put the person responsible among the greater giants of western civilization. But one cannot help feeling about him as the Anglican John Bramhall in 1658 felt about Henry VIII—that great good can come of the deeds of dreadful men. In

INTERIOR OF THE CATHEDRAL OF ST SOPHIA, ISTANBUL (AD 532–7), the crowning architectural achievement of Justinian's reign. The most lavish of all Byzantine churches, it incorporated materials from all over the Mediterranean and outdid the buildings of pagan Rome in the daring of its structure: the first dome collapsed in 558 and had to be replaced.

the Church, especially in the West, many found the Emperor hard to bear. He loved to issue elaborate edicts on orthodox dogma, and then to summon large synods to ratify what he had prescribed. The horribly maltreated Pope Vigilius experienced Justinian as a disaster. Pagan intellectuals, not accustomed to agreeing with the Pope, found reason to dislike the Emperor very much. In 529 the Platonic Academy at Athens was led by the militantly anti-Christian Neoplatonist Damascius. Justinian closed the place down and confiscated the endowments, leaving Damascius, with Simplicius and other philosophers, to emigrate to the Persian Empire in a hope for liberty which was sadly unrealized. They all soon returned. At Alexandria the Neoplatonic school kept a much lower profile, writing commentaries on Aristotelian logic. Justinian did not interfere there at all. Moreover, among the Alexandrian exegetes of Aristotle was the Christian John Philoponus, with an intelligence that anticipated many of Galileo's discoveries. The most significant evidence of the way Justinian was regarded is the attitude of the principal chronicler of his military and architectural glories, Procopius of Palestinian Caesarea, an eloquent writer with a sardonic pen who served under Belisarius. How intense was his hatred of Justinian and Theodora stands out from every line of his *Anecdota* or 'Secret History', a portrait of a Stalin-like tyrant married to a grimly penitent harlot. Procopius thought the apotheosis of arbitrary autocracy unspeakable and appalling.

The imperial absolutism of Diocletian, Constantine, and their successors had long been presupposed by the Roman legal system. In the second century AD the jurist Gaius says explicitly that imperial decrees have the full force of law without needing further legitimation from the Senate. The supreme sovereignty of the Emperor was enhanced by the confusions and contradictions of edicts, of which the fourth-century historian Ammianus Marcellinus complains. Fourth-century Emperors were surrounded by lawyers, both civil and ecclesiastical, assuring them that their will was the sole source of valid law, and that they stood above it in the sense of not being bound by the enactments of their predecessors.

When those enactments were so full of contradictions, autocracy was no doubt a necessary doctrine. Naturally the Emperor was expected to preserve law and order and to defend the frontier. Tyrannical government made men remember old Stoic vindications of the right to tyrannicide. Christian writers like Ambrose of Milan, on the other hand, could appeal to the Emperor's status above the law to justify the Emperor Gratian (376–83) in suspending pagan cult at the Altar of Victory. If the Emperor Julian (355–63) chose to sit among the senators and spoke of himself as the enforcer of laws by which he felt himself bound, this was a criticism of his predecessor Constantius II, whose language and actions were at times absolutist, dangerously fortified by the belief that he was called to represent divine monarchy on earth, rather than a restatement of an older and more collegial political theory. In practice Julian's reversion to polytheism imposed on him a necessity to assert his unique position as the embodiment of public law and as principal exponent of a philosophical theology designed to vindicate pagan cults. Many students have been struck by the resemblance in political theory and practice between Julian and Justinian, both Emperors regarding religious dissent as a treason to society and the Empire. Paradoxical though it may seem, the 'democratic' ideal of populist participation came to our modern world more from Christian beliefs in the share of all the faithful in the society of the people of God than from Aristotle, the Stoics, or the Greek experience generally. Likewise surprising is the recognition that the Anglo-Saxon tradition of the common law owes more to the operations of ecclesiastical canon law than to classical Roman law.

The ancient political ideal was certainly very slow to die. When early in the fifth century Augustine of Hippo came to describe his ideal society, he did so in anachronistic terms of the classical city-state, with an autonomy that no city of the Empire had enjoyed for some centuries past—an antiquarianism which emerges again in his description of Roman religion on the basis of Varro's work, in tactful silence about the contemporary scene. Augustine's attitude to imperial power was considerably indebted to the sombre pages of Sallust, and he writes with a hot and cold ambivalence about Rome's domination of the Mediterranean world: a manifestation of cupidity and lust to dominate on the one hand, yet, on the other, a beneficent force for centralized order and peace, without which human society would degenerate into jungle warfare. Augustine was well informed about Roman law, whose maxims and principles he cited with admiration. Friends to whom he turned for advice when questions of arbitration in civil cases were referred to him for judgement, included jurisconsults. He was aware that good Emperors can enact laws with unfortunate and unfair consequences, that bad Emperors may enact legislation that has a wholly beneficent effect, and that the problems of social justice are anything but simple.

Like his elder contemporary Jerome, Augustine was master of the classical literary tradition. Both men's writings abound in echoes and allusions to Cicero and Seneca, or the poets Virgil, Horace, Juvenal, and Tibullus. Terence was especially familiar. Though Augustine came from a small provincial town where a single schoolmaster taught all subjects to every child, the ancient educational system was not ineffective for him. He tells of one lifelong friend named Simplicius who 'knew Virgil backwards'; cite a line and he could tell you the preceding line, and he knew by heart several of Cicero's orations. A century later Boethius' prose and verse in the *Consolation of Philosophy*, written without access to a library in prison at Pavia, abounds in reminiscences of classical texts in which his mind was soaked. At one time in his youth Augustine taught grammar, and even wrote a textbook on the subject, together with other guides to the liberal arts of rhetoric, dialectic, geometry, and music (rhythm and metre, not pitch, on which he never wrote—Boethius was to take it up later). His writings show a sustained interest in grammar and diction. He could not but be acutely aware of the gulf between Ciceronian usage and the colloquial Latin of the Hippo waterfront.

Language

Before Diocletian introduced elaborate court ceremonial on the Persian model, Emperors were already being addressed as abstractions such as 'Your Majesty'. Powerful bureaucrats would be addressed as 'Your Excellency' or 'Your Eminence'. A tendency to verbal inflation went hand in hand with the debauch of the currency in the third century. Style became elaborate and formal. It was an indication of a person's importance if he was addressed in the third person rather than the second (a feature still apparent in Italian and German and in English etiquette for formal invitations). In the letters of Cyprian of Carthage, a man of upper-class origin, we see the use of similar courtesies entering ecclesiastical forms of address—'Your Holiness', or 'Your Beatitude'. By the fifth century the epithet 'venerabilis' is used for either Popes or Emperors. An Emperor is often 'serenissimus' or 'christianissimus', while a bishop is 'religiosissimus' and/or 'reverentissimus'. The plural form of self-designation and of address is adopted by Emperors and by Popes, who speak of themselves as 'we' and of their correspondent as 'you' (plural). Government chancellery formulas speak not of 'him', but of 'the aforesaid' or 'the above-mentioned', 'suprascriptus', 'memoratus', and so on. Instead of saying 'this', they write 'the present', 'praesens'. These and similar pedantries of formal style, familiar still in the formula books of European and American administrators, were established in this age.

The barbarian invasions of the fifth century had moments of tense military crisis, especially with the Vandals crossing the Rhine in 406, and later with the arrival of Attila, but for the most part the infiltration of the Germanic tribes was fairly gradual. Through service in the army a Vandal, Stilicho, could attain the summit of effective power. Such men learnt to speak and write fluent Latin; and in the West Latin remained a principal medium of communication among all well-educated men until the end of the medieval period, only gradually yielding to the vernacular. It required the zealous advocacy of Thomas More and William Tyndale (highly educated men who did not otherwise agree about much) to persuade English people that their language could be a proper medium for discussing serious subjects.

But at the everyday level Latin was by 700 in process of undergoing transformation into Romance. The travel diary of the pilgrim lady Egeria who in 384 journeyed from Spain to the Holy Land and ascended Sinai, or the sixth-century Rule of St Benedict, illustrates a colloquial idiom indifferent to the forms and syntax of Cicero. In the Carolingian renaissance after Alcuin had sent men back to school to learn formal Latin again, the rough colloquialisms of Benedict seemed vulgar and distressing to monks of high culture, so that a version of the Rule in correct Latinity had to be provided, saying, for instance, 'ausculta', not 'obsculta', for 'listen'. By Benedict's time plural nouns of the first declension use the accusative form for the subject of the sentence. Verbal forms have long become largely periphrastic; in fact, the auxiliary verb 'to be' mainly drops out of use, so that in some writers one meets long sentences with chains of participles and apparently no main verb. The spoken language in Italy was on the way to becoming Italian: one Roman inscription of the seventh century has 'essere abetis' for 'eritis'. The French definite article, in the forms *lo, la, lis*, is first attested in eighth-century Gaul. A council of bishops at Tours in 813 ruled that sermons be not in Latin but in 'rustica Romana lingua' so that everyone can understand. (The rest of the service evidently remained in Latin.) In sixth-century Merovingian Gaul the Latinity of Gregory of Tours, historian of the Franks, feels like a conscious act of resistance to demotic speech. Naturally, to admit the rustic Frankish form of pidgin Latin to the pulpit was to make possible a more rigorous purity of Latin for the educated élite in the government and the Church. From Alcuin on, a correct Latin was the preserve of this élite. To know it well, to be able to decorate a letter with a tag from Horace's *Ars Poetica* or the *Aeneid*, was to be elevated above the common herd and to have access to positions of considerable emolument.

Pronunciation of Latin varied regionally. When Augustine moved from Carthage to Milan, his African vowels brought comment from his Italian hearers. Africans made no distinction, as Italians still did, between long and short vowels. He astringently remarks that whether the third syllable of *ignoscere* is long or short is a matter of sublime indifference to a man crying to God for pardon. But only the educated in North Africa knew anyway, because the pronunciation would have been identical without regard to the quantity. In Gaul, on the other hand, there came to be a habit of making *c* before *i* or *e* to sound *ts*. But among the northern barbarians in Britain the older hard *k* sound was kept for *c*. In the tenth century Abbo of Fleury (no mean logician) came to England to live for two years at Ramsey Abbey, and was pained by what seemed to him sad evidence of the uncivilized ways of the English who, though hospitable, were so uncultured as to pronounce *ce* and *ci* as *ke* and *ki*. It would have provoked incredulous astonishment to inform him that the crude barbarians of the north had preserved a more original usage than his own. It is likely that both Bede and Alcuin were accustomed to use the hard *k*, which was usual in the Irish schools, the isolation of which after the barbarian invasions produced deep conservatism.

In Augustine's mercantile congregation at Hippo (mainly sailors, dockers, and farm workers—very unlike Carthage, where he could address people who knew what a Stoic or Epicurean was), popular speech said 'dolus' for 'pain' when a grammarian would have prescribed 'dolor'. Having an identical pronunciation for both ōs, mouth and ŏs, bone, the people had replaced the latter by ossum. Although by training and every acquired reflex Augustine was acutely conscious of grammatical correctitude, he also knew, and liked to quote Horace to reinforce the point, that what is correct usage is determined by custom, the *consuetudo loquendi* which has a way of defying both logicians and grammarians with indifferent serenity. He reserved special scorn for people more offended by a linguistic vulgarism than by a fundamental breach of ethical principle. He admired the spontaneous vigour of popular Latin. While the Latinity of the *Confessions* is highly elaborate rhyming prose, never more sophisticated in rhetorical skill than when denouncing the meretricious arts of rhetoric, his sermons are in a direct style using short sentences and everyday idioms, usually with some apology and occasionally a swipe at scornful secular grammarians who did not know what was important in human life. In both Jerome and Augustine we find classical literature regarded as essentially secular. In Jerome's famous nightmare he dreamt of being arraigned before the Judgement Seat on a charge of being a Ciceronian, not a Christian. His promise of reform was ineffective. Augustine could also express reserve ('a certain Cicero', he wrote in the *Confessions*), but the Virgil who had first inflamed his heart as a schoolboy remained a lifelong love, together with Plotinus. He thought it very possible that the fourth *Eclogue* was a prophecy of Christ, the poet being inspired without being aware of the fact, and hoped the great sages and poets of the classical world had not only a providential role in the preparation for the gospel, but also a place in God's kingdom.

Augustine knew how to write moving Latin prose, whether simple or sophisticated. In the later Roman Empire there was a strong taste for a rococo style with out-of-the-way words and neologisms to challenge the reader's erudition and flatter his ingenuity in discovering the author's meaning. At its worst it became a tendency to say nothing as elaborately as possible. Literary allusions could provide a kind of esoteric code in letters between cultivated friends conscious of living in an increasingly unappreciative world. The Latinity of the pagan Martianus Capella, writing in Vandal Carthage about 470, or Ennodius, bishop of Pavia (*d.* 521), is not intended to communicate in the most direct terms with the ordinary reader. In Capella the technique is used as a mask for his essentially pagan sympathies. This mannerist style long continued. In the seventh century the Italian Jonas, educated in the Irish monastery at Bobbio, composed a *Life* of his hero St Columban. His Latin style is full of poetic reminiscences and neologisms of the most *outré* kind, extravagant etymologies in which he takes special pleasure, and an impressive sprinkling of Greek words. All this is mingled with richly demotic usages—*pluriores* for *plures*, present participles used with passive force, confusions between similar-sounding words, and malapropisms such as *limes* for *limen*.

Nevertheless Jonas shows that classical literature was still being taught in schools. Augustine shows that the level of culture varied very much from place to place. At Carthage there were those who had read the *Aeneid* and could pick up an allusion. At Hippo no one except the bishop had read Virgil. His Hippo congregation knew the story of Dido, or ('a specially popular theme') the Judgement of Paris, from attending the local theatre, not from reading any books.

In the writing of Latin prose an awareness of the old rhythmic *cursus* was not lost. Schools continued to teach the rules. In Monte Cassino during the eleventh century proper prose rhythm even became something of an obsession. The replacement of quantity by accent, first seen coming in the third century, had decisive consequences for the writing, of verse. Monastic and episcopal schools transmitted Latin through the most precarious age of the barbarian kingdoms, until they in turn gave ground to the newly founded universities. Medieval universities were directed towards vocational training in theology, law, medicine, and the *artes*. In them the study of classical Latin did not necessarily prosper better than it had done in the older episcopal schools. Until the twelfth century what was known in the Latin West about Plato came indirectly through Apuleius, Calcidius, Macrobius, Martianus Capella, and Boethius, who had also provided translations of Aristotle's *Organon* (only his versions of the *Categories* and *Interpretation*, and of Porphyry's *Isagoge* being generally known). The schoolmen's fascination with logic, stimulated further by contact with Muslim writers such as Avicenna and Averroes, also led them to coin neologisms of a repellent kind to meet their needs when negotiating a hesitant way over the *pons asinorum*.

The Renaissance reacted against the Schoolmen and their continual moulding of Latin to contemporary needs. Lorenzo Valla treats Boethius with a patronizing mixture of admiration and distaste—the last man to write decent Latin, but sadly tolerant of barbarisms. The Renaissance enthusiastically demanded classical Latin in its purity and beauty. Thereby, paradoxically, it reduced Latin to the status of a dead language. Once the churches of the Reformation required the vernacular, there was a further dethronement of the language from any ordinary employment. In the twentieth century even the Roman Catholic Church capitulated, and the Latin mass went the way of the steam engine.

The Greek language did not have so many problems to contend with, but underwent nevertheless a comparable development. The conquests of Alexander the Great might have made *koinē* Greek the normal means of communication in government administration and trade, but it was not used everywhere in the same way. The language of the Alexandrian waterfront or Syrian bazaars was very different from anything known to Aeschylus or Thucydides. One has only to pick up St Mark's Gospel to see that; he writes the demotic language of the streets. Pronunciation too varied in different regions. Lucian of Samosata was strongly conscious of his tell-tale accent; anyone could deduce he came from Syria. The educational system prescribed certain texts as pre-eminently suitable for educational purposes. The main corpus of classical Greek literature familiar to us today is the selection made by some anonymous schoolmasters, perhaps at Alexandria or Pergamum or Athens in the third century BC. The vast amount that is lost to us is what they omitted from their selection as unfitted for ordinary level work. The tension between poetry and philosophy, which surfaces in Plato's *Republic* and to which Plutarch devoted a tract, long continued into the Roman period.

The supreme model in poetry always remained Homer. Even in eleventh-century Byzantium, according to the express testimony of Michael of Ephesus, schoolboys learnt each day between thirty and fifty lines of Homer by heart. An elementary school course normally included the first book of the *Iliad* and one play each of Sophocles, Euripides, and Aristophanes, with a few bits of Pindar and Theocritus thrown in. Byzantine schoolmasters of the twelfth century are found still debating the question keenly discussed a millennium earlier (for instance, by Dio Chrysostom) whether the superhuman elements in Homer's poetry required disbelief in the historicity of Odysseus and even of the Trojan War—a debate which Origen in 248 invokes as analogous to the debate about the miraculous element in the gospel narrative. A Homeric allusion always added a touch of class to the prose of any Byzantine author other than the most radically world-rejecting monk. In the fifth century Theodoret, bishop of Cyrrhus in Syria, who wrote a *Life* of the contemporary pillar saint Simeon Stylites, also composed urbane letters decorated with Homeric echoes to officers of the imperial consistory. Michael Psellos tells in his *Chronicle* how when the Emperor Constantine IX first introduced his mistress at court, one courtier quoted just two words from the Trojan elders' awe at the beauty of Helen. Everyone got the allusion except the lady, whose inferior education was revealed by the need to explain the highly sophisticated reference to her.

High style in the Byzantine world was necessarily marked by a self-conscious archaism. The demotic usages of the streets and farmyards were not appropriate for anyone with pretensions to be read in polite society. But the presence of the demotic element exerted a mounting pressure. Early in the seventh century a Cilician monk named John Moschos, intimate confidant of Sophronius the sophist, author of *Anacreontica*, and then first patriarch of Jerusalem under the Arab occupation, compiled an anthology of unusual, sometimes macabre stories about monastic heroes, entitled *Leimonarion*, the spiritual 'Meadow'. The work is fascinating not only for its folklore elements (one story reappears in the *Thousand and One Nights*), but also for the colloquial diction and syntax. Words and phrases characteristic of modern demotic Greek can go back a long way: *nero* for cold water appears in the apophthegms of the Desert Fathers of the fourth century. The eleventh-century epic *Digenes Akritas* ('the Borderer') used popular idioms, and regularly said *na* for *hina*. Beneath the surface veneer of high Byzantine style there was a popular speech uninfluenced by upper-class archaizing. Gradually poets and then prose writers came to have the confidence to use the demotic idiom. The twentieth-century tensions between demotic and *katharevousa* are in part a distant legacy of the divergence between the self-conscious correctness of the city of Constantinople with its literary élite and the everyday language of colloquial usage. Even in the second century AD the grammarian Phrynichus was warning aspiring writers against admitting barbarous or uneducated words into their prose. A number of the usages which he specifically vetoes appear in the New Testament as ordinary unselfconscious speech. Throughout the history of the language, the conservative preservation of a pure and more archaizing or classical Greek is connected with the acknowledgement that in the classical age lie the supreme achievements of all Greek literature, history, and philosophy. To make the demotic language standard usage is obviously to weaken a link that gives wide access to that classical world, though at the same time it may prevent contemporary Greeks from thinking that they have inherited with their mother's milk a capacity to understand Aeschylus or Lycophron. In the continuous development of the Greek language since antiquity, an élite has always existed which wished to recite Homer and to write prose in the manner of Thucydides. Such a manner can be achieved only by some degree of affectation, and sophisticated Byzantine prose of the late-medieval period can be uncommonly difficult to interpret. It must have been found so at the time. Some neo-Latin writers of the Renaissance offer obvious parallels.

Philosophy and Religion

The Christian mission in the Graeco-Roman world, initially led by a Christian Jew from Tarsus whose followers were at times baffled by the profundity and dynamism of his understanding of Christ and the Church, met with a success sufficient to provoke government persecution and philosophical criticism. To their persecutors the Christians replied when in co-operative mood that an ethic which demanded stable family life and honesty in trade deserved encouragement, and that, provided one had no part in polytheistic cult which they thought honouring evil spirits, one could render to both God and Caesar whatever was their due. Indeed they recognized a religious obligation to pay taxes. They further claimed that the intellectual tradition of the classical past was not alien to them. They soon found ways to make it their own. Stoic ethics required attitudes to slavery or wealth that they found congenial. 'Seneca saepe noster' ('Seneca is often one of us'), said Tertullian. Platonic metaphysics affirmed divine transcendence, the freedom of the will, the immortality of the soul, and that virtue is necessary and sufficient for happiness. In Justin, Clement of Alexandria, and Origen, Platonism and Christian thought come to keep house together.

The marriage went with allegorical or symbolist exegesis of parts of the Pentateuch, already worked out in detail by the Jew Philo of Alexandria. This principle was soon extended to any part of the authoritative corpus of biblical writings accepted for reading in church lectionaries (this acceptance being a criterion of 'canonicity'). How deeply the first Christians pondered the complex relation between faith and history is apparent in St John's Gospel, where it is a general rule of interpretation that if anything can have two or more levels of meaning, it does: the history is a sacramental vehicle of spiritual truth. The Christians were not the first to discern a pattern in history that discloses the nature and meaning of human existence (Thucydides had already travelled that way); but symbolist writing in literature has its principal springs in the New Testament.

The dialogues of Plato that fascinated the Neoplatonists were *Timaeus*, *Parmenides* and *Republic*. The *Timaeus* set out Plato's cosmogony and therefore a doctrine of the relation between the Creator and the cosmos. The *Parmenides* dealt with dialectical problems about being, identity, and difference. These two dialogues and the Neoplatonic commentaries on them were read by Christians with obvious sympathy.

The marriage of Platonism and Christianity, however, had its tiffs. The pagan Platonists were not in the least grateful for the hand of intellectual sympathy which the Christians stretched out towards them, and asked awkward questions about the compatibility of the notion of incarnation with divine immutability, which Plato had argued to be necessary to the concept of perfection. From the Christian side there was fierce criticism of the Platonic axiom of the eternity of the world, the belief that the soul possesses an eternity and immortality independent of the Creator, and, above all, the fatalism inherent in the notion of reincarnation.

Clement of Alexandria speaks of the Church as a river emerging from the confluence of Biblical faith with Greek philosophy. Apocalyptic hope, passing from late Judaism into early Christian preaching, is that element in Christianity which to a Platonist critic (Celsus) seemed most bizarre. Yet from apocalyptic the Christians brought to the western world the sense that the historical process is moving to a divine event—whether near or far off they disputed. In Romans 8 Paul sees the sufferings of this life as the birth-pangs preceding a new age.

Apocalyptic language implies a negative view of much of the world's way of going about its business. Neoplatonic ethics also encouraged world rejection and withdrawal. 'Plotinus always seemed ashamed of being in the body.' Before Plotinus' time Clement and Origen were articulating an ascetic ladder of the soul's ascent from passion and pleasure to a training and discipline of the character whose final goal is expressed in mystical terms of the vision of God granted to the pure in heart.

An accurate delineation of the distinctive features of early Christian ethics in comparison with the philosophical ethics of antiquity is intricate, certainly not susceptible of simplistic formulas. When the pagan Celsus dismisses Christian ethical teaching as having 'nothing new', Origen in reply is delighted to concede; for the gospel is a gift of the Creator for the realization of those duties or goods which the informed conscience recognizes, imprinted by the creative reason, the light that lightens every man coming into the world. The early Christians had not read Kant (though John Chrysostom anticipates verbatim Kant's dictum that God is discerned through the moral law within and the starry heavens above). They did not think moral reasoning a special way of exercising rational judgment separate from other deployments of the reason. They did not talk about the moral imperative as command coming from an alien force outside the soul and asking for blind obedience. The doctrine of man made in God's image, fused with Platonic language about the soul's 'affinity' with God, helped them to say that the soul naturally recognizes how right and rational it is to be good and just. The imperatives in the conscience are signposts to what the source of all goodness is like. But the Christians dissented deeply from the Socratic principle that none errs knowingly or deliberately, and saw human nature as a noble ruin whose self-inflicted misery called for a restoration transcending human powers. The stress on redemption and grace went with an insistence on obedience and humility of which Christ is model. But the main shift in ethical concern resulting from conversion to Christianity comes to lie in an intense interest in motive as the source of value. Augustine was especially fascinated by the fact that circumstances and motives are primary in evaluating the moral significance of an act.

The most striking manifestation of Christian detachment from the secular appears in the monastic movement of the fourth century. In a sermon of the mid third century Origen observed that renunciation of the world is not achieved by physically moving oneself out into the desert, a remark which suggests that already somebody thought otherwise. The complex motives that drove men and women to become hermits or, more commonly, to join communities of ascetics living under obedience are only partly visible to us. The fourth-century Church experienced the movement as a shock to its sytem. Many bishops opposed the weakening of urban or village congregations which resulted from the exodus of the most dedicated members into special separate communities owing an allegiance to their abbot and often showing a cool reserve to the ordinary life of the Church. The earliest document yet found to mention a monk is a papyrus from the Fayum of 6 June 324. Athanasius of Alexandria portrayed the hermit Antony in a *Life* which owed something to Pythagorean hagiography about their founder. In the Nile valley from about 320 the Copt Pachomius was establishing large communities of monks under virtually military discipline, some of which were embarrassingly successful in agriculture. In Asia Minor in the 360s and 370s Basil of Caesarea composed rules for communities under rule with a common habit and dedicated to the service of the outside community.

The monks enraged writers such as Libanius or the Alexandrian schoolmaster Palladas, whose embittered epigrams won a place in the *Palatine Anthology*, or in the West the poet Rutilius Namatianus. The Platonic Christian, Synesius of Cyrene, disliked their rejection of culture, and much misgiving was provoked by the readiness of some monks to form bands for the dismantling of pagan shrines. Augustine begs his people to win the minds and hearts of their pagan neighbours, not to infuriate them by insulting matters they held dear, even if obviously corrupt and superstitious.

The Church and the End of the Ancient World

The change of religion had some social consequences which affected the world from which the Church wished to be detached and independent. The capture of society, in principle largely achieved by 400 (though pockets of pagan resistance long continued), also affected the Church itself. Could the Church be respectable in class terms without losing its sense of obligation to and identification with the poor? The first charge on the local church chest was the maintenance of those whose names stood in the 'register of the poor' (the phrase is first attested in 422, but the thing is much earlier). Augustine knew that the alms of the faithful were inadequate to the problem of destitution, and longed for the imperial government to provide subsistence benefit, financed by redistributive taxation that, he felt sure, good men would be happy to pay. Rich benefactors usually preferred to see their money put into buildings or mosaic and marble decoration in basilicas. Then there were questions about compromise with the political and social system. Gregory of Nyssa boldly attacked the institution of slavery. Augustine thought the domination of man over his neighbour an inherent wrong, but saw no way of ending it and concluded that, since the ordering of society prevented the misery of anarchic disintegration, slavery was both a consequence of the fall of man and at the same time a wrong that providence prevented from being wholly harmful. Slaves were not a very large proportion of the ancient labour force, since the cost of a slave to his owner exceeded that of employing free wage-labourers. Slaves in a good household with a reasonable master enjoyed a security and standard of living that seldom came the way of free wage-labourers. But not all slaves had good masters, and in special cases bishops used the church chest to pay the costs of emancipation. Refusal on moral grounds to own slaves became a rule for monasteries.

The ancient Church deeply disapproved of capital punishment and judicial torture. A Roman church-order of about 200 forbids a Christian magistrate to order an execution on pain of excommunication. No Christian layman could tolerably bring a charge against anyone if the penalty might be execution or a beating with lead-weighted leather thongs. There was a tendency, first apparent in the fifth century, to modify rigorism against capital punishment in all circumstances; Pope Innocent I (405) ruled against excommunicating magistrates who imposed it, which was not to say that such penalties were welcome. Torture forced so many innocent people to confess to crimes they had not committed that the Christian hatred of it commanded wide assent. Nevertheless, by what were deemed necessities of state it continued. In the Merovingian period conciliar canons had to be content with forbidding clergy to be present in the torture chamber. The Bulgar king was probably little moved when in 866 Pope Nicolas I told him that torture is contrary to both divine and human law. The military impact of Islam first made some Christians argue the controversial thesis that one could resort to violence to withstand the infidel. Even after that had been admitted and implemented in the Crusades, in the west it was not effectively until the age of the papal monarchy that torture and execution began to be deployed against heretics, and there were those at the time who noted the break with immemorial tradition. Although Augustine justified coercion against the Donatist schismatics of north Africa, seeing how successful the policy was, nevertheless he laid down strict limits to the penalties that might be imposed, and refused all resort to force. The pain of his legacy arose from his need to reason out a theoretical justification of the coercion, and this survived the particular situation and his mitigating hand.

People bequeathed estates to churches and monasteries, and landownership brought responsibilities for the work-force and for correct financial trusteeship which were a source of anxiety to bishops and abbots, but nevertheless gave them powers of patronage. As the barbarian kingdoms took control in the West, aristocratic and cultured Romans, such as Sidonius Apollinaris in Gaul, found a bishopric a vantage-point for preserving independence and for protecting the secular interests of church members before an unsympathetic government. A bishop was not expected to confine himself to preaching good expository sermons. He had to be a community leader. In Syria Theodoret of Cyrrhus built porticos, baths, two bridges, and an aqueduct for his little town. Christianity never shrugged off its origins as an urban religion moving from the town out into the surrounding countryside which was slow to be converted and tenacious of old peasant superstitions. The Church was joined by many women and manual workers, but never had a proletarian ethos. From the start (as I Corinthians shows) it contained a proportion of well educated people, capable of private Bible study at home. In a society where rhetoric was a part of the school curriculum eloquent sermons were appreciated, but it was often observed that sincerity and personal passion in the preacher mattered more than a fine turn of phrase. The bishops, based in the city, became identified with the city community in a way which, after the barbarian invasions, became socially important. Even by the third century bishops signed their names appending an adjectival form of the name of their town.

Among bishops the level of education varied by extremes. They were elected by their congregations subject to the veto of the consecrating bishops of the province under the metropolitan; they were local people, not brought in from outside or overseas, and closely reflected the style of their laity. Illiterate bishops—a favourite butt for the mockery of the half-educated, as Augustine once observed—were rare. By the mid fifth century a bishopric could be the destiny of a voluntarily retired praetorian prefect or a forcibly retired emperor. When Cyrus of Panopolis, a pagan poet who rose to be city prefect of Constantinople, fell foul of the chamberlain Chrysaphius, he saved himself by baptism and a Phrygian bishopric where the enraged population had lynched his four predecessors. Although individual bishops were occasionally unpopular, we hear more of the respect and affection in which their people held them. Like a rich patron, a bishop was expected to intercede with magistrates or tax authorities on behalf of his people and even to get employment for them. Augustine liked to quote a wise man's aphorism, that he had too much regard for his own reputation to vouch for other people's. He feared the dangers of his social role. When an acquaintance was elected to a bishopric, he wrote to warn him of the trappings of office, the raised throne with embroidered cloth, and the choir of nuns singing to welcome him; 'the honour of this world is passing away.'

The storms of the fifth-century invasions made all honour in this world seem infinitely precarious. The establishment of the barbarian kingdoms formalized a take-over which had long been reality. Even before Constantine's time Germanic tribes were providing some of the best soldiers for the legions. Julian's hymn of hate against Constantine includes the charge that he elevated barbarians to great offices of state. To the distress of the Roman aristocrats, Julian himself found it necessary to put a barbarian general into the prestigious post of consul. At the beginning of the fifth century the Vandal Stilicho held all real power in the West. Long before 476 collaboration had gone so far that resistance was no option. When the Goths poured into the Balkan peninsula to escape the Huns in 375, and shattered the imperial army of Valens at Adrianople (378), Ambrose of Milan saw the fulfilment of biblical prophecies of Gog and Magog coming from the north to ravage the city of God. Augustine would not accept this exegesis: 'the city of God has as much room for Goths as for Romans.'

The question has been repeatedly asked. Did Rome's conversion to Christianity directly cause or indirectly contribute to the end of the ancient world? Is there truth (even if now to be drastically reformulated in secular terms) in the contention of those whom Augustine sought to refute in the *City of God*, who thought Alaric's capture of Rome in 410 a consequence of Rome's abandonment of the old gods, the closing of the temples in 391, and the prohibition of pagan sacrifices?

In 412 the proconsul of Africa, Volusianus, later a Christian, but at that time still pagan, asked a friend of Augustine if the ethic of the Sermon on the Mount would bring the collapse of the Empire. Was war justifiable in self-defence or to recover stolen property? Augustine thought so, for it was in the cause of justice, and 'those who desire peace must first love justice.' Yet the wars of the Empire must be so conducted that afterwards the vanquished can enjoy justice and peace. Likewise mercy to prisoners of war is a fundamental principle. (The redemption of prisoners of war was a ground on which bishops thought it right to sell church plate given by wealthy benefactors.) There is no evidence that the Church denounced or discouraged the defence of the Empire against Attila. At this period we meet the first evidence for military chaplains attached to units of the Roman army. Augustine observed that Christ did not ask the centurion in the gospel to find a new career. But he might have felt strong misgivings had he seen the order of service prescribed for Toledo cathedral about 500 'when the Visigothic king goes forth to war'.

A more plausible answer than pacifism (or what Gibbon memorably called the Christian preaching of patience and pusillanimity) is that the Church provided an alternative society with a rival career structure and different loyalties. Warnings in ascetic texts betray awareness that bishoprics could be sought for reasons not exclusively religious. The Church competed for the available talent. It drew into its power structure men ambitious, not necessarily for themselves, but for the cause they served, who might well have been useful soldiers or administrators or traders or manufacturers increasing the material wealth of society instead of channelling it into poor relief or noble basilicas like the Ravenna churches. Even this answer to the question evidently rests on a concealed value judgement. In the second century Celsus thought the Church had too few educated people ready to accept public office. Was it that in the fourth and fifth century it employed too many?

The evidence of the time shows that the churches of late antiquity were desperately understaffed. Successive north-African councils deplored the shortage of clergy. Those whom they did have seem from Augustine's correspondence to be altogether unremarkable. There are obvious exceptions. Ambrose left a provincial governorship to become bishop at Milan, where his sermons instructed Valentinian II in his duties. He served as special envoy in matters of state. In that age bishops were often so used; there was an assumption that as negotiators they might be successful because they had divine aid. The millionaire Paulinus sold most of his estates to retire to Nola to write religious verse in honour of St Felix. His renunciation was not well regarded by all Christians; when he asked for a papal audience to tell the glad tidings, he was abruptly refused.

One could move from high positions in the world to become a bishop, but it was not socially proper to move in the reverse direction. In late antiquity bishops did not, like their successors in the late Middle Ages or the Renaissance, combine spiritual office with major secular administration. It was thought highly unusual when Cyrus, the patriarch who surrendered Alexandria to the Arab invaders in 641, combined his patriarchate with the post of prefect of Egypt. He wore one shoe with the insignia of the patriarch, the other with those of the prefect—the ancient equivalent of wearing two hats.

There is one unquestionable respect in which conversion to Christianity brought to the administration of the Empire complexities it would prefer to have done without. The Christians tended to quarrel about ever more refined points of dogma and to take their disagreements to the crucial point of suspending eucharistic communion. That meant a denial that those with whom one refused to hold communion were part of the commonwealth of God; they were to be held as strangers and outsiders. From 311 until the coming of Islam at the end of the seventh century the great Church of north Africa was split between two rival groups, whose theological disagreement was enforced by rancour, by prohibitions on mixed marriages, and by one side wholly rejecting the validity of orders and sacraments on the other side. In the East also there were successive splinter-groups, some only small but others very substantial. The followers of Nestorius flourished outside the Empire in Persia and across central Asia into China. At the opposite end of the theological spectrum the Monophysites, unable to accept the decisions of the fourth General Council at Chalcedon (451), set up a rival hierarchy against those in communion with the Orthodox patriarchates. The government harassed them in Egypt and Syria, and as a result, when these provinces first met the force of the Arab invaders from 634, the capacity of the Byzantine army and administration to resist was weakened by the deep alienation of many of its Monophysite citizens, who soon found their new rulers, though not always tolerant, at least much easier to live with than the Constantinople straitjacket. In Egypt the scale of apostasy to Islam so saddened one seventh-century monk on Sinai that in despair he took his life, and in the circumstances even suicide incurred no censure.

The Arab conquest of Syria, Egypt, north Africa, and then southern Spain and Sicily, ended the unity of the old Roman world as no other factor did. The Mediterranean was no longer a Roman lake.

Further Reading

The classic study of the 'end of the ancient world' remains Edward Gibbon's *Decline and Fall of the Roman Empire* (1776-88, best read in J. B. Bury's edn., London 1909-14); it is good until the sixth century, though Gibbon lacked a sense of history as process and had a complex personal attitude to sex and to Christianity. (Richard Porson's judgement stands: 'Mr Gibbon's humanity never slumbers unless when women are ravished or the Christians persecuted.') See also the early volumes of the *Cambridge Medieval History*. On the fourth century: N. H. Baynes, *Constantine the Great and the Christian Church* (2nd edn. London 1973); D. Bowder, *The Age of Constantine and Julian* (London, 1978); T. D. Barnes, *Constantine and Eusebius* (Cambridge, Mass., 1981). On Julian: specialized studies by R. Browning: *The Emperor Julian* (London, 1975); G. W. Bowersock, *Julian the Apostate* (London, 1978); and P. Athanassiadi-Fowden, *Julian and Hellenism* (Oxford, 1981), which supplement the symposium edited by A. Momigliano, *The Conflict Between Paganism and Christianity in the Fourth Century* (Oxford, 1963). On social and economic history, especially the bureaucracy, see A. H. M. Jones, *The Later Roman Empire* (Oxford, 1964). On the barbarians, see J. B. Bury, *The Invasion of Europe by the Barbarians* (London, 1928); J. M. Wallace-Hadrill, *The Barbarian West* (3rd edn. London, 1967); *The Frankish Church* (Oxford, 1983); E. A. Thompson, *The Visigoths in the Time of Ulfila* (Oxford, 1966); *The Goths in Spain* (Oxford, 1969). C. E. Stevens, *Sidonius Apollinaris and his Age* (Oxford, 1933). On Spain, H. Chadwick, *Priscillian of Avila* (Oxford, 1976).

Of Augustine there is a striking portrait by Peter Brown: *Augustine of Hippo* (London, 1967). For his ideas see John Burnaby, *Amor Dei* (London, 1938 and repr.); É. Gilson, *The Christian Philosophy of St. Augustine* (ET London, 1961); H. A. Deane, *The Political and Social Ideas of St Augustine* (New York-London, 1963). On the sixth century: R. Browning, *Justinian and Theodora* (London, 1971); A. M. Honoré, *Tribonian* (paperback, London, 1981). Averil Cameron, *Agathias* (Oxford, 1970); H. Chadwick, *Boethius; The Consolations of Music, Logic, Theology, and Philosophy* (Oxford, 1981); M. Gibson (ed.), *Boethius* (Oxford, 1981).

On the development of the languages: E. Löfstedt, *Late Latin* (ET Oslo, 1959); R. Browning, *Medieval and Modern Greek* (2nd edn. Cambridge, 1983).

Monks: Owen Chadwick, *John Cassian* (2nd edn. Cambridge, 1968); D. J. Chitty, *The Desert a City* (London, 1966); P. Rousseau, *Ascetics, Authority and the Church* (Oxford, 1978). On the Church in ancient society: H. Chadwick, *The Early Church* (Harmondsworth, 1967); *History and Thought of the Early Church* (London, Variorum, 1982).

TABLES OF EVENTS

TABLES OF EVENTS

Before about 600 BC most dates are approximate

THE MEDITERRANEAN WORLD

The Age of Palace Cultures

3000	Beginnings of Minoan culture in Crete
2200–1450	Middle Minoan palace culture in Crete
2100	Probable arrival of Mycenaean Greeks in Greece
1600–1200	Development of a Mycenaean palace culture in Greece, initially dependent on Cretan models
1450	Mycenaeans take over the Cretan palace settlements and dominate the Aegean area; palace settlements develop at Mycenae, Tiryns, Thebes, Pylos, Cnossus, and elsewhere; this culture is the historical reality behind the Greek heroic myths

The Dark Age and the Period of Migrations

Between 1250 and 1150 there was a breakdown of settled conditions in the eastern Mediterranean and Asia Minor.

1220	The destruction of Troy VIIa may be the historical event behind the legend of the Trojan War, and perhaps the last major enterprise of the Mycenaean Greeks
1200	Widespread destruction of Mycenaean sites in Greece
1184	Traditional date for the destruction of Troy worked out by later Greek writers
1150	Final destruction of the citadel of Mycenae
1100–1000	Invasion of the Dorian Greeks into mainland Greece (in myth 'the return of the sons of Heracles') usually placed in this period
1050–950	Migration of Ionian and other Greeks from the mainland to the Aegean islands and the coast of Asia Minor
1050	Beginnings of widespread use of iron in Greece, and the renewal of contacts with Cyprus

THE NEAR EAST

2700–2200	Old Kingdom in Egypt
2700–2000	Sumerian period in Mesopotamia
2130–1800	Middle Kingdom in Egypt
2000–1700	Old Babylonian period in Mesopotamia
1575–1100	New Kingdom in Egypt
1460–1200	Hittite Empire dominates central Anatolia
1400	Beginning of Assyrian domination of central Mesopotamia
1230	First settlement of the Israelites in Canaan
1200	Hittite Empire destroyed by peoples from south Russia, who include the Phrygians. The 'peoples of the sea' (perhaps marauders and refugees) repulsed from Egypt
1100	End of the New Kingdom in Egypt and of the centralized Pharaonic state

1000–960	David King of Israel
960–931	Solomon King of Israel
910	Beginning of the expansion of Assyria, opposed by Urartu and later by the city and tribal cultures of Syria and Palestine
1000–750	Age of Phoenician prosperity and expansion overseas
814	Traditional date of foundation of Carthage
744–612	Assyrian Empire at its height

1050–900	Proto-geometric pottery
975	Hero's tomb at Lefkandi

The Age of Euboean Expansion

In the period from 825 to 730 the Euboean cities of Chalcis and Eretria are the leading settlements in Greece, responsible for overseas foundations for trade and the early developments of the colonizing movement. The leading artistic centre in Greece until about 730 is Athens.

875–750	Geometric pottery
800	Foundation of Eretria and gradual decline of Lefkandi
	Euboeans and Cypriots establish a trading post at Al Mina on the mouth of the Orontes river (north Syria) on an important route for eastern exports to the Greek world
776	First Olympic Games: the four-year cycle of games became later the basis for dating historical events in the Greek world
775	Euboeans establish a trading post on the Bay of Naples (Pithecusae, Ischia); beginning of contact with Etruria and the west
753	Traditional date of the foundation of Rome
750–700	Greek alphabet created on Phoenician models and rapidly diffused in varying forms throughout the Greek world
	New heavy ('hoplite') armour development in the Greek world
735	Foundation of the first Sicilian colony, Naxos
734–680	Lelantine War between Chalcis and Eretria, involving much of the Greek world, and resulting in the end of Euboean influence

THE GREEK WORLD

The Orientalizing Period

From about 730 Corinth emerges as the most advanced city in Greece, both culturally and politically; but other cities also become important, notably her neighbours around the Isthmus (Sicyon, Megara), Aegina, Samos, Miletus, Athens, and Sparta. Eastern influences begin to affect Greek art and life.

POLITICAL EVENTS	CULTURAL DEVELOPMENTS	THE NEAR EAST
	750–700 Homer and Hesiod	
733 Foundation of Corcyra and Syracuse by Corinth	725 First stone temple of Artemis Orthia at Sparta	
730–710 Spartan conquest of Messenia	720–690 Early Proto-Corinthian pottery	720 Sargon of Assyria conquers Cilicia and Syria; fall of Israel (722)
720 Sybaris (south Italy) founded; Colonization of Chalcidice (north Greece) by Chalcis and Eretria; Greeks begin to move into the area of the Hellespont	720 Orsippus of Megara runs naked to win an Olympic victory; nudity becomes the rule in sport	
700–650 Diffusion of hoplite tactics		700 Cimmerian invasion from south Russia into Asia Minor; destruction of Phrygian kingdom of Midas Median monarchy founded
		696 Sack of Tarsus by Assyrians
683 Athenian archon list begins	690–650 Middle Proto-Corinthian pottery	687 Kingdom of Lydia founded by Gyges (687–652)
675 ?Lycurgan reforms at Sparta	675–640 Archilochus of Paros active as poet	
670 Zaleucus of Locri, earliest lawgiver in western colonies		670 Assyrian power begins to decline
668 Argive defeat of Sparta at battle of Hysiae		
664 Greeks begin to penetrate Egypt as mercenaries and traders		664 Foundation of Saite dynasty in Egypt under Psammetichus I (664–610)
657–625 Tyranny at Corinth under Cypselus	655 Chigi vase	

650–620	Sparta fights second Messenian War
650	Tyranny of Orthagoras at Sicyon
	Foundation of Thasos
	Beginnings of Greek settlement in the Black Sea
640	Tyranny of Theagenes at Megara
632	Attempted tyranny at Athens by Cylon
630	Foundation of Cyrene in north Africa

650	Terpander of Lesbos, Callinus of Ephesus, Semonides of Amorgos, Tyrtaeus of Sparta active as poets
650–630	Late Proto-Corinthian pottery

650	Rise of Media under Phraates (650–625?)
626	Independence of Babylon from Assyria under Nabopolassar
625	Naucratis established as main Greek trading post in Egypt
	Coinage invented in Lydia
612–09	Fall of Nineveh: division of Assyrian Empire between Babylon and Media
591	Expedition of Psammetichus II of Egypt to Nubia: Greek mercenaries write their names at Abu Simbel
587	Capture of Jerusalem by Nebuchadrezzar of Babylon; exile of Jews

The Early Archaic Age

This period sees the rise to dominance first of Sparta and then of Athens in mainland Greece.

625–585	Periander tyrant of Corinth
625–600	Thrasybulus tyrant of Miletus
621	Draco promulgates Athens' first written laws
620–570	Period of tyrannies at Mytilene
600–570	Cleisthenes tyrant of Sicyon
600	Smyrna destroyed by Lydians
	Foundation of Massilia by Phocaeans
	Athens wins Salamis from Megara
595–586	First Sacred War for control of Delphi
594	Solon, archon at Athens, promulgates new law-code, and institutes social and political reforms
583	End of Corinthian tyranny

630	Mimnermus of Colophon and Alcman of Sparta active as poets
625–595	Early Corinthian pottery
	First marble *kouroi*
610	Attic black-figure pottery begins
610–575	Alcaeus and Sappho active as poets on Lesbos
600	Temple of Hera, Olympia
600–560	Solon active as poet
585	Thales of Miletus predicts eclipse of sun
582–573	Establishment of cycles of games (Pythia 582, Isthmia 581, Nemea 573)
580	Temple of Artemis at Corcyra; first major temple of Athena at Athens

THE NEAR EAST (cont.)

570–526	Amasis Pharaoh of Egypt
560–546	Croesus king of Lydia
559–530	Cyrus founds Persian Empire
550	Cyrus conquers Media
550–480	Lives of Buddha and Confucius
545	Persian capture of Sardis; end of Lydian Empire
539	Persian capture of Babylon; return of Jews from exile
530	Death of Cyrus; accession of Cambyses (530–522)
525	Death of Amasis of Egypt; Persians conquer Egypt and north Africa

THE GREEK WORLD (cont.)

POLITICAL EVENTS

560	War between Sparta and Tegea, ending in alliance; First tyranny of Pisistratus at Athens (560–556)
556	Chilon ephor at Sparta; End of tyranny at Sicyon

The Late Archaic Age: the Conflict with Persia

546 was 'the year the Mede came' (Xenophanes): the arrival of the Persians on the Mediterranean shore was a turning-point, and the conflict with Persia dominates the next fifty years.

546	Sparta defeats Argos at the battle of the champions; Pisistratus establishes his tyranny at Athens with the battle of Pallene
545	Conquest of Ionian Greeks by the Persians
540	Battle of Alalia; Carthaginians and Etruscans check Greek expansion in the western Mediterranean
535	Polycrates tyrant of Samos
528	Death of Pisistratus; Athens ruled by Hippias
525–3	Spartan expedition to Samos; fall of Polycrates

CULTURAL DEVELOPMENTS

570–550	Anaximander of Miletus active as philosopher
566	Reorganization of Panathenaic festival at Athens
560	Sicyonian treasury at Delphi; Stesichorus of Himera active as poet
548	Temple of Delphi burned
570–475	Lifetime of Xenophanes of Colophon (philosopher and poet)
550	Anaximenes of Miletus active as philosopher
540	Theognis of Megara, Hipponax of Ephesus, and Ibycus of Rhegium active as poets
535–490	Anacreon of Teos active as poet
535	Attic red-figure pottery begins
534	First tragedy performed at City Dionysia in Athens
530	Pythagoras active in south Italy as philosopher
525	Siphnian treasury at Delphi

524	Etruscans defeated at Cumae			521	Darius seizes power in Persia
520–490	Cleomenes king of Sparta	520–468	Simonides of Ceos active as poet	520–519	Darius recaptures Babylon
519	Alliance of Athens and Plataea			518	Darius' Behistun inscription
514	Harmodius and Aristogeiton murder Hipparchus at Athens			514	Darius' Scythian expedition
				512	Darius conquers Thrace
510	Expulsion of Hippias from Athens	510–490	Temples at Agrigentum (Sicily) built	509	[Traditional date of foundation of Roman Republic]
508	Reforms of Cleisthenes at Athens				
506	Abortive Spartan invasion of Attica; Athens defeats Chalcis and Boeotians				
505	Tyranny begins at Gela	500	Alcmaeon of Croton (doctor), Hecataeus of Miletus (historian), and Heraclitus of Ephesus (philosopher) active		
499	Ionian Revolt				
498	Athenians and Eretrians help to burn Sardis	498	Earliest surviving poem of Pindar (*Pythian* 10)		
494	Battle of Lade; sack of Miletus and end of Ionian revolt; Spartans defeat Argos at battle of Sepeia				
493	Themistocles archon at Athens; establishment of port of Piraeus				
491	Gelon becomes tyrant of Gela				
490	First Persian expedition to mainland Greece	490	Statues on the temple of Aphaea at Aegina		
	Death of Cleomenes of Sparta		Parmenides of Elea active as philosopher		
	Destruction of Eretria				
	Battle of Marathon				
487–483	Ostracisms at Athens	487	First comedy performed at City Dionysia at Athens	487–485	Revolt of Egypt
	War between Athens and Aegina				
485	Gelon becomes tyrant of Syracuse	485–450	Bacchylides of Ceos active as poet	486	Death of Darius; accession of Xerxes
482	Discovery of silver at Laurium in Attica, spent on the fleet of Athens	484	First victory of Aeschylus		
480	Great Persian Expedition by land to Greece; battles of Artemisium, Thermopylae, and Salamis; Athens sacked by the Persians; Carthaginians invade Sicily and are defeated at the battle of Himera				
479	Battles of Plataea and Mycale				

THE GREEK WORLD

POLITICAL EVENTS	CULTURAL DEVELOPMENTS

The Classical Age: The Fifth Century

In this period Athens developed her empire out of the league against Persia, and expanded it to cover the Aegean area; conflict between her and Sparta began in 461, and culminated in the Second Peloponnesian War (431–404), in which Athens was finally defeated and lost her empire. Economic activity became centred on the Piraeus; and culturally this was the golden, Periclean age of Athens, as the imperial city became 'the education of Greece' (Pericles), and evolved the most extreme democratic government the world has known.

	POLITICAL EVENTS		CULTURAL DEVELOPMENTS
478	Foundation of Delian League against Persia with Athens as leader	478	The Charioteer at Delphi cast
	Refortification of the city of Athens		
477–67	Death of Gelon tyrant of Syracuse; Hiero succeeds him	476	Pindar's First *Olympian Ode* and Bacchylides' Fifth *Ode* for victory of Hieron at Olympia
	Naval campaigns of Cimon, culminating in the battle of Eurymedon (467), which effectively removes the Persian threat	472	*Persae* of Aeschylus
474	Syracusans defeat Etruscans at battle of Cumae	470	Pindar's First *Pythian Ode*
471	Ostracism of Themistocles, and subsequent flight to Persia	470–430	Career of sculptor Myron
466	Death of Hiero and end of tyranny at Syracuse	468	First victory of Sophocles over Aeschylus
465	Revolt of Thasos from Delian League	467	*Seven Against Thebes* of Aeschylus
464	Murder of Xerxes; Artaxerxes I succeeds as King of Persia		
	Earthquake at Sparta and revolt of Spartan helots		
462–454	Revolt against Persians in Egypt, supported by Athens	462	Anaxagoras of Clazomenae (philosopher) arrives in Athens
461	Cimon ostracized; radical reforms at Athens under Ephialtes; murder of Ephialtes. Pericles' supremacy begins (461–429)	460–420	Career of sculptors Polyclitus and Phidias
461–451	War between Athens and Sparta: First Peloponnesian War		
458	Building of Long Walls from Athens to Piraeus; battle of Tanagra; Athens conquers Boeotia	458	*Oresteia* of Aeschylus
		456	Death of Aeschylus
			Completion of Temple of Zeus at Olympia
454	Treasury of the Delian League moved to Athens	455	First production by Euripides
451	Five year-truce between Athens and Sparta		
	Thirty Years Peace between Sparta and Argos		
	Pericles' law defining citizenship		

Year	Political and military events	Year	Cultural events
450	Cimon's return from exile and death on campaign against Persia in Cyprus	450	Zeno of Elea and Empedocles of Acragas active as philosophers
449	Revolt against Persia in Syria		
447	'Peace of Callias' ends hostilities between Athens and Persia Loss of Athenian land empire in Boeotia at battle of Coronea	447	Building of the Parthenon begins
446	Revolt of Euboea	446	Pindar's last ode (*Pythian* 8)
445	Thirty Years Peace between Athens and Sparta [Ezra and Nehemiah active rebuilding walls of Jerusalem]	445–426	Herodotus of Halicarnassus active
443	Athenian foundation of Thurii in south Italy Ostracism of Thucydides son of Melesias, Pericles' last opponent	442–438	Parthenon frieze
440	Revolt of Samos from Athenian Empire	440	Leucippus invents atomic theory Temple of Poseidon at Sunium
		438	*Alcestis* of Euripides Statue of Athena dedicated in Parthenon
437	Athenian foundation of Amphipolis	437–432	Work on Propylaea of Acropolis and Parthenon pediments
		436	Birth of Isocrates (educator)
435	War between Corinth and Corcyra over Epidamnus	435	Work begins on Erechtheum
433	Athenian alliance with Corcyra		
432	Revolt of Potidaea from Athens		
431	Start of Second Peloponnesian War	431	Thucydides begins his history *Medea* of Euripides
430	Plague at Athens	430	Democritus of Abdera (atomic theorist), Meton of Athens (astronomer), Hippocrates of Cos (doctor), Socrates, and Protagoras of Abdera (philosophers) active Phidias' statue of Zeus at Olympia
429	Death of Pericles Siege of Plataea		
428	Revolt of Mytilene	428	*Hippolytus* of Euripides Birth of Plato
427	Capture of Plataea by Spartans and Mytilene by Athenians First expedition of Athenians to Sicily	427	Embassy of Gorgias of Leontini to Athens begins the formal art of rhetoric
425	Fortification of Pylos and capture of Sphacteria by Athenians Cleon dominant at Athens	425	*Acharnians* of Aristophanes Hellanicus of Lesbos (historian) active
424	Boeotians defeat Athenians at battle of Delium Peace conference of Sicilians at Gela Death of Artaxerxes; accession of Darius II in Persia	424	*Knights* of Aristophanes Thucydides the historian exiled from Athens
423	Armistice between Athens and Sparta for a year	423	*Clouds* of Aristophanes

THE GREEK WORLD (*cont.*)

POLITICAL EVENTS		CULTURAL DEVELOPMENTS	
422	Brasidas and Cleon killed in north Greece	422	*Wasps* of Aristophanes
421	Peace of Nicias between Athens and Sparta	421	*Peace* of Aristophanes
418	Spartan defeat of Athenian–Argive coalition at battle of Mantinea; Thirty Years Peace between Sparta and Argos	420–400	Temple of Apollo at Bassae built Hippias of Elis (antiquarian and polymath) active
416	Athenians attack Melos and enslave its inhabitants		
415	Athenian expedition to Sicily; affairs of the Mutilation of the Hermae and Profanation of the Mysteries; Alcibiades exiled	415	*Trojan Women* of Euripides
413	Sparta renews the war and establishes a permanent fort in Attica at Decelea	414	*Birds* of Aristophanes
	Athenian expedition destroyed in Sicily		
412	Revolt of Athenian allies; Persia enters the war	412	*Helen* of Euripides
411	Oligarchic revolutions at Athens	411	*Lysistrata* and *Thesmophoriazusae* of Aristophanes
410	Battle of Cyzicus; democracy restored at Athens		
409	Carthaginian expedition to Sicily; destruction of Selinus and Himera	409	*Philoctetes* of Sophocles
		408	*Orestes* of Euripides
407–406	Alcibiades' return from exile		
406	Athenian defeat at Notium and victory at Arginusae	406	Deaths of Euripides and Sophocles
405	Battle of Aegospotami; siege of Athens	405	*Frogs* of Aristophanes
	Dionysius becomes tyrant of Syracuse; peace between Syracuse and Carthage		*Bacchae* of Euripides performed
404	Capitulation of Athens; installation of regime of the Thirty		
	Democratic exiles seize Phyle		
	Death of Darius II; accession of Artaxerxes II in Persia		
403	Fall of the Thirty; restoration of democracy at Athens		

The Classical Age: The Fourth Century

Politically, the fourth century saw a series of attempts to establish dominance by Sparta, Athens, and Thebes, with Persia holding the balance of power, helping Athens at first, but ending as guarantor of a Spartan-imposed peace. In the 370s Thessaly became important, and from the 350s onwards Macedon under Philip began to expand; in 338 Macedonian overlordship was finally established. In Sicily the Deinomenid dynasty controlled Syracuse and led the struggle against Carthage, until Timoleon created a Greek revival in the late 340s. Athens remained the dominant intellectual centre; with the schools of Plato, Isocrates, and Aristotle, philosophy, rhetoric, and prose in general become the main forms of literature.

401	Expedition of Cyrus and 10,000 Greek mercenaries against the Persian king; battle of Cunaxa (subject of Xenophon's *Anabasis*)
398	Agesilaus succeeds as king of Sparta
396–394	Campaigns of Agesilaus to free the Greeks of Asia Minor from Persia
395–386	Corinthian War: Sparta against Corinth, Thebes, Argos, and Athens backed by Persia
395–393	Athens rebuilds her Long Walls
394	Persian fleet under an Athenian defeats the Spartans at Cnidus
387	Dionysius I captures Rhegium
387	Gauls sack Rome
386	Peace of Antalcidas or King's Peace imposes Persian-backed control by Sparta on Greece
382	Spartan troops seize Theban citadel
379	Liberation of Thebes
378	Alliance between Athens and Thebes; Foundation of Second Athenian Confederacy
377–353	Mausolus dynast of Caria
375–370	Rise of Thessaly under Jason
371–362	Domination of Thebes under Pelopidas and Epaminondas
371	Thebes destroys Spartan power at battle of Leuctra
369	Foundation of Megalopolis and liberation of Messenia
367	Death of Dionysius I; Dionysius II becomes tyrant of Syracuse
366–360	Satraps' Revolt from Persian king
365	Athens expels Samians and colonizes Samos
364	Thebes destroys Orchomenus; death of Pelopidas
362	Thebes defeats Sparta at battle of Mantinea; death of Epaminondas
360	Death of Agesilaus
359	Philip II becomes king of Macedon

410–387	Careers of Andocides and Lysias as speech-writers
401	*Oedipus Coloneus* of Sophocles produced posthumously
400–360	Antisthenes (cynic), Aristippus of Cyrene (hedonist) and Euclides of Megara, pupils of Socrates, active
399	Trial and execution of Socrates for corrupting the youth of Athens
397–338	Isocrates (educator and writer) active
396–347	Plato (philosopher) active
395	Thucydides' *History* published; Antimachus, epic poet, active
392–388	Last plays of Aristophanes
390–354	Xenophon (historian and essayist) active
387	Plato founds the Academy
384	Aristotle and Demosthenes born
373	Earthquake destroys temple at Delphi
370–330	Praxiteles and Scopas (sculptors) active
367	Plato visits Syracuse to educate Dionysius II; Aristotle joins the Academy
361	Second visit of Plato to Sicily
360–315	Lysippus (sculptor) active
360–323	Diogenes (cynic philosopher) active

THE GREEK WORLD (*cont.*)

POLITICAL EVENTS

357	War between Athens and Philip; Philip captures Amphipolis
357–355	Social War between Athens and members of her confederacy
356–354	Dion, uncle of Dionysius and pupil of Plato, controls Syracuse
356–352	Phocians seize Delphi and provoke Sacred War, bringing Philip into central Greece against them
356	Birth of Alexander the Great
348	Philip seizes Olynthus
346	Philip and Athens make peace (Peace of Philocrates) Second tyranny of Dionysius II
344–338	Timoleon arrives in Sicily, ends the tyrannies, and defeats the Carthaginians at Crimisus (341); revival of Greek Sicily
338	Philip defeats Athens and Thebes at Chaeronea; end of Greek independence Murder of Artaxerxes III
337	Philip founds Corinthian League of Greek states, which declares war on Persia
336	Death of Philip

CULTURAL DEVELOPMENTS

358–330	Theatre of Epidaurus built
355	Literary and political careers of the orators Demosthenes (died 322) and Aeschines (left Athens 330) begin
353	Death of Mausolus; Mausoleum begun
350–320	Apelles (painter) and Theopompus (historian) active
350–300	Stilpo (philosopher) active at Megara
347	Death of Plato; Speusippus becomes head of the Academy
343–342	Aristotle in Macedonia as tutor to Alexander
342	Menander born
341	End of *History* of Ephorus
339	Xenocrates becomes head of the Academy
338	Death of Isocrates
338–334	Lycurgus in charge of finances of Athens, inaugurates major public building programme

ROME

Early Rome

The dates and the reality of events in early Roman history are quite uncertain. Rome began as a community on the fringes of Etruscan culture; under the later kings she was in effect an Etruscan city dominating Latium. The establishment of the republic caused a decline in her power as she fought for survival against the Etruscans and sought to re-establish her dominance in Latium. The fifth century was a period of acute social tension. The destruction of Veii ended the Etruscan threat, and the sack of Rome by the Gauls proved only a temporary setback. By 338 Rome had incorporated Latium and moved into Campania.

753	Traditional date for foundation of Rome
753–509	Period of kings
616–579	Tarquinius Priscus
579–34	Servius Tullius; military reforms and creation of *comitia centuriata*; treaty with the Latins and foundation of Temple of Diana on the Aventine
534–09	Tarquinius Superbus; draining of Roman forum suggests creation of an urban centre
509	Foundation of the Republic; first treaty with Carthage; foundation of Temple of Jupiter on the Capitoline
496	Latins defeated at battle of Lake Regillus; treaty with Latins

ROME (*cont.*)

494–440	Struggle of the Orders
450	Publication of Laws of Twelve Tables
405–396	Siege and capture of Veii
390	Sack of Rome by the Gauls
366	First plebeian consuls
340	Latin War; Latin League dissolved
338	Campania incorporated into the Roman state

THE HELLENISTIC WORLD

POLITICAL EVENTS	CULTURAL DEVELOPMENTS

Alexander the Great

War against Persia had long seemed a means of recreating Greek unity, and events since 400 had shown both the wealth and the military weakness of the Great King. Alexander took up Philip's plan to invade the Persian Empire; within twelve years he had conquered as far as the steppes of Russia, Afghanistan, and the Punjab. These conquests created the Hellenistic world.

	POLITICAL EVENTS		CULTURAL DEVELOPMENTS
336	Accession of Alexander		
335	Alexander sacks Thebes. Accession of Darius III of Persia	335	Aristotle begins teaching at Athens and founds the Lyceum (Peripatetic school)
334	Alexander crosses into Asia. Battle of Granicus; conquest of Asia Minor		
333	Defeat of Darius at battle of Issus		
332	Sieges of Tyre and Gaza. Alexander enters Egypt. Foundation of Alexandria		
331	Alexander defeats Darius at battle of Gaugamela, takes Mesopotamia, and enters Babylon, Persepolis, and Pasargadae		
330	Burning of palace of Persepolis. Darius murdered by his supporters	330	Aeschines and Demosthenes defend their political careers in the two opposed speeches *Against Ctesiphon* and *On the Crown*
330–328	Alexander campaigns in Bactria and Sogdiana		
327	Marriage of Alexander and Roxane. Alexander enters India	327	Callisthenes (historian of Alexander and nephew of Aristotle) executed by Alexander. The philosophers Pyrrho (sceptic) and Anaxarchus, accompanying Alexander, meet Brahmins
326	Alexander crosses the Indus and wins battle of Hydaspes. Conquest of Punjab. Alexander sails down the Indus to the Indian Ocean		

325	Alexander returns through Baluchistan, suffering great hardships in the desert
324	Alexander at Susa
323	Death of Alexander, aged thirty-two

Age of the Successors

The struggles of the generals who divided Alexander's empire centred on the attempts of first Perdiccas and then Antigonus the One-Eyed to maintain the empire's unity. By 306 the family of Alexander had been eliminated, and the contenders felt sure enough to claim the title of king in their own areas; by 276 the three great powers of the Hellenistic world, Macedon, Egypt, and the Seleucid Empire were firmly established.

323–320	Perdiccas tries to maintain unity through his regency, but is killed in Egypt
323–322	Athens and her allies attempt to free themselves from Macedon in the Lamian War
320–301	Antigonus the One-Eyed aims at universal empire
317–289	Agathocles tyrant of Syracuse
317	Philip III half-wit half-brother of Alexander murdered
315	Olympias mother of Alexander murdered
315–311	Coalition of satraps against Antigonus
312	Seleucus captures Babylon; beginning of Seleucid era

326–324	Voyages of Nearchus, admiral of Alexander, down the Jhelum and back to Mesopotamia through the Persian Gulf

325–300	Pytheas of Massilia circumnavigates Britain
322	Deaths of Aristotle and Demosthenes; Theophrastus becomes head of Lyceum
321–289	Career of Menander (poet of New Comedy)
320–05	Hecataeus of Abdera writes first Hellenistic cultural history of Egypt
317–07	Demetrius of Phaleron (Peripatetic philosopher) is Macedonian governor of Athens
317	*Dyscolus* of Menander performed; End of Attic gravestone series
314	Polemo becomes head of Academy on death of Xenocrates

The Colonization and Conquest of Italy

The period from 334 to 264 saw the gradual expansion of Rome to control by colonization, conquest, and alliance of all Italy south of the Po valley.

327–304	Second Samnite War against Samnites in the central Apennines

THE HELLENISTIC WORLD (*cont.*)

POLITICAL EVENTS	CULTURAL DEVELOPMENTS
311 Peace between the successors recognizes in effect the division between Antigonus (Asia), Macedon/Greece (Cassander), Thrace (Lysimachus), Egypt (Ptolemy), and by omission the eastern satrapies (Seleucus)	310 Clearchus of Soli (Peripatetic philosopher) visits Aï Khanoum in Afghanistan(?)
311–306 War between Agathocles and Carthage; invasion of Africa	310 Zeno of Citium establishes the Stoic school in *Stoa Poikilē* at Athens
310 Murder of Alexander IV, son of Alexander the Great and last member of the dynasty	309 Philitas of Cos (scholar and founder of Alexandrian poetry) appointed tutor to future Ptolemy II
307 Demetrius the Besieger, son of Antigonus, 'liberates' Athens	307–306 Exile and recall of Theophrastus from Athens
306–304 Antigonus, Ptolemy, and Seleucus call themselves kings	307 Epicurus establishes his philosophical school at Athens
305–304 Siege of Rhodes by Demetrius	302–290 Megasthenes (author on India) at court of Chandragupta
303 Seleucus cedes Indian territories to Chandragupta founder of Mauryan dynasty for 500 war elephants	300 Ptolemy I founds Museum of Alexandria on advice of Demetrius of Phaleron; Zenodotus royal tutor and first head of the library
301 Destruction of power of Antigonus and Demetrius at battle of Ipsus; Antigonus killed	Euhemerus writes his utopian romance
	Euclid (mathematician) active
297 Death of Cassander ruler of Macedon	295 Tyche of Antioch; Colossus of Rhodes
297–272 Career of Pyrrhus of Epirus	

ROME (*cont.*)

310	Roman advance into Etruria
298–290	Third Samnite War

285	Demetrius the Besieger captured by Seleucus, dies of drink in 283
283	Ptolemy I Soter dies; Ptolemy II Philadelphus succeeds
281	Lysimachus killed
	Seleucus assassinated; his son Antiochus I succeeds
	Foundation of Achaean League
279	Invasion of Macedon and Greece by Gauls
276	Antigonus Gonatas, son of Demetrius, defeats the Gauls and becomes king of Macedon, founding the Macedonian dynasty

290	Berossus (Babylonian priest) writes history of Babylonia
287	Theophrastus dies; Strato head of Lyceum
280	Duris of Samos (leading exponent of 'tragic history') active
	Bion of Borysthenes (satirist) active
276	Death of Polemo, head of the Academy

280–275	Pyrrhus of Epirus crosses into south Italy to help the Greek cities against Rome, and is defeated by the Romans
	Earliest Roman coinage
272	Surrender of Tarentum; alliance with Greek cities in south Italy
272–215	Hiero, lieutenant of Pyrrhus, elected general and then king (270) at Syracuse; Syracusan age of prosperity and building

The Balance of Power

The third century saw the creation of an uneasy balance of power between the great kingdoms, with conflict confined to disputed areas: the Ptolemies and the Seleucids fought over Syria and Palestine, while the Greek cities of the Aegean area sought to manipulate the great powers in order to achieve independence. This was the great age of Hellenistic culture: philosophy was centred on Athens, while the patronage of Ptolemy II created Alexandrian literature and science. From the 230s there are signs of the re-emergence of non-Greek forces on the political scene.

274–271	First Syrian War between Ptolemy II and Antiochus I
271	Death of Epicurus
270–242	Arcesilaus converts the Academy to scepticism
270	Callimachus, Theocritus, Lycophron (or a century later), Aratus, and Posidippus active as poets
	Manetho (historian and Egyptian priest) lays foundations of Egyptian history

THE HELLENISTIC WORLD (*cont.*)

POLITICAL EVENTS	CULTURAL DEVELOPMENTS
	Ctesibius of Alexandria (engineer) and Herophilus of Chalcedon (doctor) active
	Aristarchus of Samos proposes heliocentric theory of universe
267–262 Chremonidean War: Ptolemy unsuccessfully supports Greek independence from Macedon. Antigonus Gonatas enters Athens	269 Death of Strato, last head of Lyceum
	265–235 Archive of Zeno illuminates economic life of Egypt
263–241 Eumenes ruler of Pergamum founds independent power and begins building programme	262 Cleanthes succeeds Zeno as head of Stoics
261 Antiochus II succeeds to Seleucid kingdom	
260–253 Second Syrian War between Ptolemy II and Antiochus II	260 Hieronymus of Cardia (historian of the Successors) dies aged 104; Timaeus of Tauromenium (historian of the west) dies aged ninety-six

ROME (*cont.*)

The First Punic War

Rome begins to emerge on the western Mediterranean scene with her expansion into Sicily, Corsica, and Sardinia, and her response to the Carthaginian expansion in Spain

264   First gladiatorial show at Rome
Roman army enters Sicily to help Mamertines against Carthage: First Punic War begins

263   Hiero of Syracuse becomes ally of Rome

256–255 Expedition of M. Regulus to Africa ends in disaster

255–249 Series of Roman naval disasters

247 Hamilcar Barca begins Carthaginian offensive in Sicily

241 Roman victory off Aegates Islands; end of First Punic War

240–207 Livius Andronicus (earliest Roman poet and playwright) active

Apollonius of Rhodes writes *Argonautica* (epic)

Herodas (author of mimes) active

Erasistratus of Ceos (doctor) understands action of heart and distinguishes motor and sensory nerves

260–212 Archimedes (mathematician and inventor) active

256 Asoka, king of Mauryans (269–232), proclaims his Buddhist mission to the Greek world

250 Ariston of Chios (Stoic philosopher) active at Athens

246 Eratosthenes becomes head of Library at Alexandria; literary scholar and pioneer of scientific geography, he calculates the circumference of the earth correctly

251–213 Career of Aratus of Sicyon statesman and general of Achaean League

246 Ptolemy III succeeds to kingdom of Egypt
Seleucus II succeeds to Seleucid kingdom

246–241 Third Syrian War between Ptolemy III and Seleucus II

244–241 Agis IV attempts to reform Sparta and is executed

239 Demetrius II succeeds Antigonus Gonatas as king of Macedon
War between Macedon and the Achaean and Aetolian Leagues

239–130 Independent Greek kingdom established in Bactria

238 Emergence of Parthia

238–227 War of Attalus of Pergamum against Galatians; he becomes master of Asia Minor and takes royal title

THE HELLENISTIC WORLD (cont.)

POLITICAL EVENTS		CULTURAL DEVELOPMENTS
235–222	Cleomenes III king of Sparta; he reforms Spartan state in 227	
	235	Apollonius of Perge (mathematician) active
	232	Chrysippus succeeds Cleanthes as head of Stoics
223	Antiochus III succeeds to Seleucid kingdom	
	225	Eratosthenes of Cyrene (polymath) and Ariston of Ceos (Peripatetic philosopher) active
221	Philip V succeeds to kingdom of Macedon; Ptolemy IV succeeds to kingdom of Egypt	
219–217	Fourth Syrian War between Ptolemy IV and Antiochus III; Egypt is saved from conquest by Egyptian native troops at battle of Raphia	

ROME (cont.)

237	Roman occupation of Corsica and Sardinia; Hamilcar begins Carthaginian expansion in Spain, followed by Hasdrubal
236	Naevius' first play produced
228	Rome establishes protectorate over the Illyrian coast
227	Sicily and Sardinia are made provinces
221	Hannibal, aged twenty-five, takes command of Carthaginian forces in Spain; Rome allies with Saguntum in Spain
219	Siege and capture of Saguntum by Hannibal

ROME

The Conquest of the Mediterranean

'There can surely be no-one so petty or so apathetic in his outlook that he has no desire to discover by what means and under what system of government the Romans succeeded in less than fifty-three years (220–167) in bringing under their rule almost the whole of the inhabited world, an achievement which is without parallel in human history' (Polybius). About 200 Rome began to develop a culture of its own, heavily dependent on Greek models.

THE EAST	THE WEST	CULTURAL DEVELOPMENTS
	218–201 Second Punic War	
	Hannibal invades Italy	
	217 Hannibal defeats Romans at Lake Trasimene	
	216 Hannibal defeats Romans at Cannae	
215 Philip V of Macedon allies with Carthage	215 Hannibal in south Italy	
	Roman victories in Spain	
214–205 First Macedonian War between Rome and Philip	Carthage allies with Syracuse	
	213 Romans besiege Syracuse	
212–205 Antiochus III campaigns in the east in an unsuccessful attempt to reconquer Parthia and Bactria	212 Romans besiege Capua	
211 Roman alliance with Aetolian League	211 Hannibal marches on Rome	
	Capua and Syracuse fall	
	Roman defeats in Spain	
209 Attalus I of Pergamum allies with Rome against Philip	211–206 Scipio Africanus defeats Hasdrubal in Spain	
206–185 Revolt and independence of Upper Egypt	Spain divided into two provinces	204–169 Ennius active at Rome as poet and teacher
204 Ptolemy V succeeds in Egypt	204 Scipio invades Africa	Plautus' *Miles Gloriosus* performed
203–200 Philip and Antiochus make a secret alliance against Egypt; fifth Syrian War: Antiochus seizes Syria	203 Hannibal recalled from Italy	204 Career of Plautus 204–184
	202 Scipio defeats Hannibal at battle of Zama	202 Fabius Pictor writes first prose history of Rome in Greek
	Carthage becomes a dependent of Rome	

ROME (*cont.*)

THE EAST	THE WEST	CULTURAL DEVELOPMENTS
200–197 Second Macedonian War between Rome and Philip	202–191 Roman conquest of Cisalpine Gaul	200 onwards Greek art begins to become known to the Romans
196 Rome declares the freedom of the Greeks at the Isthmus of Corinth	197–133 Wars in Spain	200 Aristophanes of Byzantium (scholar) becomes head of Library at Alexandria
196–179 Philip rebuilds the power of Macedon		
194 Romans evacuate Greece		
192–188 Syrian War between Rome and Antiochus		186 Senatorial edict against Bacchic rites
187 Antiochus III dies		184 Censorship of the Elder Cato
		179 Basilica Aemilia and Aemilian Bridge built at Rome
179 Philip V dies and is succeeded by his son Perseus		
175 Antiochus IV Epiphanes succeeds to Seleucid empire		
171–167 Third Macedonian War		
170–168 Sixth Syrian War		
167 Battle of Pydna ends kingdom of Macedon; Rome divides territory into four republics	167 Direct taxation of Roman citizens abolished	167 Polybius the historian arrives in Rome
Rome orders Antiochus IV out of Egypt		
Rome declares Delos a free port		
Desecration of Temple at Jerusalem brings to a head Jewish resistance against Antiochus' policy of hellenizing the Jews; Maccabean Revolt		166–159 Plays of Terence produced Great Altar of Zeus and Athena built at Pergamum
164 Death of Antiochus IV; book of Daniel composed		

AT HOME

148	Fourth Macedonian War and war against Achaean League Corinth is sacked and Macedonia becomes a Roman province
149–146	Third Carthaginian War: Carthage, destroyed by Romans; Africa becomes a province

The Late Republic

The history of this period is the history of Rome *domi militiaeque*, at home and abroad. Rome exploited ruthlessly her control of the Mediterranean world; her generals led her citizens to ever richer conquests. But at home the strains of empire began to destroy republican government. Culturally Rome became the centre of patronage, and Latin literature flourished.

136–132	First Sicilian Slave War
133	Tribunate of Tiberius Gracchus

ABROAD

142	Independence of the Jews
141	Parthians attack Babylon
137	Roman army defeated at Numantia in Spain
133	Attalus III of Pergamum bequeaths his kingdom to Rome; it becomes the province of Asia (129)

CULTURAL DEVELOPMENTS

155	Carneades (head of the Academy) comes to Rome on an embassy and introduces the Romans to philosophy
150	Agatharchides of Cnidus (Ptolemaic geographer) flourished
149	Publication of Cato's *Origines* or history of Rome
145	Aristarchus (scholar and head of the Library) and other intellectuals flee from Alexandria on accession of Ptolemy VIII
144	Panaetius (Stoic philosopher c.185–109) arrives in Rome
135	Nicander (medical poet) active
133	Calpurnius Piso (Roman historian) consul; his work covered Roman history down to 146
	Lucilius (Roman satirist) active

ROME (cont.)

AT HOME	ABROAD	CULTURAL DEVELOPMENTS
125　M. Fulvius Flaccus proposes enfranchising the Latins	130　Antiochus VII dies fighting the Parthians	
123–122　Tribunates of C. Gracchus		
121　First use of *senatusconsultum ultimum* to authorize massacre of Gracchan supporters	121　Gallia Narbonensis becomes a Roman province	120–110　Temple of Fortuna at Praeneste built
		Circular temple in Forum Boarium, Rome
	118–117　Roman campaigns in Dalmatia	118　Polybius dies soon after this
	114–110　Series of Roman defeats	
107–100　C. Marius consul six times; he reforms the army	112–106　War against Jugurtha of Mauretania ended by Marius	106　Cicero born
104–102　Second Sicilian Slave War	102–101　Marius defeats the Teutones and Cimbri	
100　Caesar born		100　Philo of Larissa becomes head of the Academy
		99　Lucretius born
		95　Meleager of Gadara (poet and collector of earliest epigrams in the Greek Anthology) active
91–88　Attempted reforms of M. Livius Drusus lead to Social War between Rome and her Italian allies. Rome defeats the allies by force and offers of citizenship		
88　L. Sulla marches on Rome	88–85　Mithridates VI of Pontus massacres Roman citizens in Asia and seeks to free the Greeks from Rome	88–68　Antiochus of Ascalon becomes head of the Academy at Athens; Philo of Larissa leaves for Rome
87　Marius seizes Rome, but dies in 86	86　Sulla in the East captures Athens and Greece	87–51　Posidonius (philosopher, historian, and polymath) active in Rhodes and at Rome
83–82　Sulla returns to Italy; civil war	83–82　Second Mithridatic War	84　Catullus born

Date	Event	Date	Event
81	Cicero's earliest extant speech	82–80	Sulla appointed dictator of Rome; Sullan reforms. He resigns in 80 and dies in 78
78	Sisenna (Roman historian) praetor. The Tabularium (record house) on the Capitoline built	80–72	Sertorius, Marian supporter, controls Spain
75–35	Philodemus (poet and Epicurean philosopher) active at Rome Aenesidemus (Sceptic philosopher) active	73–71	Slave Revolt of Spartacus
		74–63	Third Mithridatic War
70	Cicero's *Verrine Orations* delivered Virgil born Valerius Antias (Roman historian) active	70	Consulate of Crassus and Pompey Trial of Verres
68	Cicero's correspondence begins	66–63	Pompey defeats Mithridates and reorganizes the East. End of Seleucid monarchy (64) and of independent kingdom of Judaea; provinces of Bithynia, Cilicia, Syria, Crete organized, and client kings established elsewhere
65	Horace born		
63	Cicero's *Catilinarian Orations* delivered Augustus born	63	Consulate of Cicero Catilinarian conspiracy Caesar elected *pontifex maximus*
		62	Pompey returns to Italy and disbands his army
		61	Trial and acquittal of P. Clodius on religious charge
62	Cicero's *pro Archia* delivered	60	'First triumvirate' formed between Pompey, Crassus, and Caesar
		59	Consulate of Caesar; legislation in favour of the triumvirs; Pompey marries Caesar's daughter, Julia
60–30	Diodorus of Sicily compiles his *Historical Library*	58–57	Cicero's exile and return
		56	Agreement between triumvirs renewed at Luca
59–54	Catullus' poems to Lesbia		
58–52	Caesar writes his account of the *Gallic Wars*	58–49	Caesar campaigns in Gaul
55	Death of Lucretius; his poem published posthumously Theatre of Pompey completed	55–54	Caesar's invasions of Britain
		55–53	Crassus in the East, killed by Parthians at battle of Carrhae (53); his army destroyed
		54	Julia dies; the link between Caesar and Pompey is severed

ROME *(cont.)*

AT HOME	ABROAD	CULTURAL DEVELOPMENTS	
52	Clodius murdered by Milo in gang warfare		54	Cicero's *pro Caelio* delivered Catullus dies
		51	Parthian invasion of Syria	52	Cicero's *pro Milone* written
				51	Cicero writes his *de Republica*
				50	Andronicus of Rhodes discovers and begins editing the lost works of Aristotle; foundation of our modern knowledge of Aristotle
49	Civil War: Caesar crosses the Rubicon and Pompey leaves for East			49–27	M. Terentius Varro (antiquarian) active
48	Caesar defeats Pompey at battle of Pharsalus Pompey murdered in Egypt	47–45	Caesar campaigns against Republicans in the East, Africa, and Spain		
47–44	Dictatorship of Caesar			46	Forum of Caesar begun in Rome Cicero's *pro Marcello* delivered
45	Caesar returns from Spain			45–44	Cicero's main philosophical works published
44	(15 March) Caesar is murdered			44	Cicero's *de Officiis* written

THE ROMAN EMPIRE

POLITICAL EVENTS

CULTURAL DEVELOPMENTS

The Second Triumvirate and the Age of Augustus

Caesar's heirs struggled for control of the Roman world; the final victory of his nephew Octavian (later Augustus) saw the establishment of monarchy under the guise of a 'restored Republic'. His long reign was marked by consolidation and reform in every sphere of politics and culture. The great age of Latin poetry began with the Triumvirate and continued into the Augustan age.

POLITICAL EVENTS		CULTURAL DEVELOPMENTS	
44	M. Antonius, surviving consul, controls Rome	44	Cicero attacks Antony in his *Philippics*
		44–AD 21	Strabo (geographer and historian) active

43	Murder of Cicero
	Birth of Ovid
40	Didymus (last great Alexandrian literary scholar) active
	Virgil's Fourth *Eclogue*
38	*Eclogues* of Virgil published
37–30	Horace's *Satires* written
30	Horace's *Epodes* published
29	Virgil's *Georgics* and Propertius' *Elegies* I completed
28–23	Vitruvius *On Architecture* written
	Mausoleum of Augustus begun
26–16	Propertius' *Elegies* 2–4 written
25	Ovid begins writing *Amores*
24–23	Publication of Horace *Odes* 1–3
23	Effective end of Maecenas' patronage of poetry
20	Building of Temple of Mars the Avenger begun
	Horace's *Epistles* I published
19	Tibullus (elegiac poet) and Virgil die
17	Horace writes *carmen saeculare* for performance at Secular Games
13–11	Theatre of Marcellus
12	Horace *Epistles* 2.1 to Augustus published
9	First edition of Ovid's *Art of Love*
	End of Livy's history of Rome
	Dedication of Ara Pacis Augustae
8	Death of Maecenas and Horace
2	Second edition of Ovid's *Art of Love*
	Forum of Augustus dedicated

43	Octavian seizes the consulate
	Second triumvirate of Antony, Lepidus, and Octavian formed; their opponents murdered in the proscriptions
42	Republicans defeated at battle of Philippi; Brutus and Cassius commit suicide
	Cisalpine Gaul incorporated into Italy
41–32	Antony in the East
40	Antony marries Octavia; pact of Brundisium
37	Renewal of Triumvirate
36–35	Campaigns against Sextus Pompeius, son of Pompey
32	Final breach between Antony and Octavian
31	Octavian defeats Antony at battle of Actium
30	Antony and Cleopatra commit suicide
	Annexation of Egypt by Rome
27	'The Republic restored': the first constitutional settlement. Octavian given the name *Augustus*
27–19	Agrippa completes conquest of north-west Spain
23	Conspiracy against Augustus and second constitutional settlement
20	Settlement with Parthia: Parthians return Roman standards
19	Constitutional readjustment of Augustus' powers
18	Augustan marriage and social reforms
12	Death of M. Agrippa, heir apparent
	Augustus becomes *pontifex maximus* on death of Lepidus the triumvir
12–9	Tiberius campaigns in Pannonia
6–AD 2	Tiberius in retirement on Rhodes
2	Scandal of the elder Julia

THE ROMAN EMPIRE (*cont.*)

POLITICAL EVENTS

AD 2–4	Lucius and Caius Caesar die
	Final dynastic settlement: Tiberius is given tribunician power and adopts his nephew Germanicus
8	Scandal of the younger Julia
6–9	Pannonian Revolt
9	Disaster in Germany: Rhine becomes Roman frontier

The Julio-Claudian Dynasty

Despite the excesses of individual Emperors in Rome, the imperial governmental system was consolidated under a dynasty which claimed hereditary descent from Augustus.

TIBERIUS (14–37)

19	Death of Germanicus
23	Death of Drusus, Emperor's son
26	Tiberius retires to Capri
31	Sejanus, praetorian prefect and effective ruler of Rome, executed

GAIUS (CALIGULA) (37–41)

CLAUDIUS (41–54)

43	Invasion of Britain under Aulus Plautius

NERO (54–68)

54–62	Burrus and Seneca control the young Emperor
58–62	Conquest and loss of Armenia
59	Murder of Agrippina on Nero's orders
61	Revolt of Iceni in Britain under Boudicca
62	Death of Burrus and end of Seneca's influence
64	Fire in Rome for nine days; persecution of Christians
65	Pisonian Conspiracy against Nero
66–73	Jewish Revolt

CULTURAL DEVELOPMENTS

AD 1–4	Ovid's *Fasti* written
3	Maison Carrée at Nîmes built
8	Ovid banished to the Black Sea
	Manilius (astronomical poet) and Velleius Paterculus (historian) active
	Philo (Jewish writer) active
	Death of Elder Seneca (writer on oratory)
49	Seneca (philosopher and tragedian) made tutor to future Emperor Nero
54	Seneca's *Apocolocyntosis* published; Lucan (epic poet) and Persius (satirist) active
64–8	Building of Nero's Golden House
65	Suicides of Seneca and Lucan
66	Suicide of Petronius (author of *Satyrica*)
67	Josephus, rebel leader in Judaea and future author, deserts to the Romans

The Flavian Dynasty

With the Flavian dynasty power shifted to the bourgeoisie of Italy; luxury became unfashionable at Rome as the Emperor displayed 'old-fashioned standards'. Literature gives way to government as the art of Rome.

69   The Year of the Four Emperors: Galba, Otho, Vitellius, and Vespasian struggle for power

VESPASIAN (69–79)

70   Destruction of Temple at Jerusalem

74   Frontinus (administrator and technical writer) consul

TITUS (79–81)

79   Eruption of Vesuvius; destruction of Pompeii and Herculaneum

79   Death of Elder Pliny (administrator, naturalist, and encyclopedist) investigating eruption

80   Fire at Rome: destruction of Capitoline Temple

80   Inauguration of Colosseum

DOMITIAN (81–96)

78–85   Campaigns of Agricola in Britain

86–92   Domitian's wars against Dacians

Domitian's palace on Palatine hill built

Status, Silius Italicus, Martial (poets), and Quintilian (writer on rhetoric) active

The Age of the Antonines

'If a man were called to fix the period in the history of the world, during which the human race was most happy and prosperous, he would, without hesitation, name that which elapsed from the death of Domitian to the accession of Commodus' (Edward Gibbon). Culturally the Greek world began to revive as city life prospered.

NERVA (96–8)

TRAJAN (98–117)

97   Tacitus consul

101–6   Trajan conquers Dacia (modern Rumania)

100–11   Dio Chrysostom (Greek orator), Epictetus (moralist), and Plutarch (essayist and biographer) active in Greek literature

100–11   Pliny the Younger (orator and letter-writer) consul and governor of Bithynia

Tacitus writes *Histories* and *Annals*

114–17   Trajan's Parthian War: Armenia and Mesopotamia annexed

112–13   Forum of Trajan and Trajan's Column dedicated

115–17   Jewish Revolt

THE ROMAN EMPIRE (*cont.*)

POLITICAL EVENTS		CULTURAL DEVELOPMENTS	
HADRIAN (117–38)			Appian (historian), Lucian (satirist), and Ptolemy (astronomer) active in Greek literature; Suetonius (biographer) and Juvenal (poet) in Latin
132–5	Bar Kochba's revolt leads to final dispersal of Jews		The Pantheon (Rome), Hadrian's Villa (Tivoli), and Hadrian's Wall (Britain) built
ANTONINUS PIUS (138–61)			
		143	Pausanias writes his description of Greece
			Herodes Atticus (Greek orator) and Fronto (Latin orator) consuls
		144	Speech of Aelius Aristides (Greek orator) in praise of Rome
		148	900th anniversary of founding of Rome
			Apuleius (Latin writer) and Galen (doctor) active
MARCUS AURELIUS (161–80)			
162–6	Parthian Wars of L. Verus		
165–7	Plague spreads through the Roman Empire	165	Apuleius (Latin writer) and Galen (doctor) active
168–75	German Wars of Marcus		Justin (Christian apologist) martyred
		174–80	*Meditations* of Marcus Aurelius
COMMODUS (180–92)			
193	With the murder of Commodus four Emperors contend for power.	193	Column of Marcus Aurelius completed

The Severan Dynasty

'Our history and the affairs of the Romans descend from an age of gold to one of iron and rust' (Cassius Dio, contemporary historian). The causes of the decline and subsequent transformation of the Roman world are complex. Militarization of the Empire and a shift of power from centre to outlying frontiers as barbarian pressure increased, brought strains which began to emerge under the Severans.

SEPTIMIUS SEVERUS (193–211)

Philostratus (literary biographer), Herodian (historian), Marius Maximus (biographer), Sextus Empiricus (sceptic philosopher), Alexander of Aphrodisias (commentator on Aristotle), Tertullian and Clement of Alexandria (Christian writers) active

208–11 Severus campaigns in Britain and dies at York

Severus lavishly rebuilds his home town of Leptis Magna and builds the Arch of Septimius Severus in the Roman Forum

CARACALLA (212–17)

212 The *constitutio Antoniniana* grants citizenship to all inhabitants of the Empire

216 Baths of Caracalla completed

200–54 Origen (Christian philosopher) active

ELAGABALUS (218–22)

SEVERUS ALEXANDER (222–35)

223 Murder of Ulpian, praetorian prefect and jurist, by his troops

226 Ardashir the Sassanian, crowned King of Kings in Iran, inaugurates 400 years of intermittent war with the Roman Empire

229 Cassius Dio (historian) consul for the second time with the Emperor

THE ROMAN EMPIRE (*cont.*)

The Late Empire

Fifty years of military anarchy (235–84, with nearly twenty Emperors) were ended by Diocletian's reforms and the establishment of the Tetrarchy. But intractable problems of frontier defence, heavy taxation, inflation, and excessive bureaucracy remained, and were not affected by Constantine's conversion to Christianity. The Late Empire was a new world in which from time to time Emperors such as Julian, or literary figures, sought to recapture the values of a lost society. Only a few leading events are mentioned in this brief list.

POLITICAL EVENTS		CULTURAL DEVELOPMENTS	
		249–51	Decius' persecution of the Christians
		258	Martyrdom of Cyprian
		270	Death of Plotinus (Neoplatonist philosopher)
267	Heruli invade Greece	271	Aurelian Walls of Rome built
		303–5	Great Persecution
284–306	Diocletian re-establishes central power and founds the Tetrarchy		
306–37	Career of Constantine the Great	307–12	Basilica of Maxentius in Rome, completed by Constantine
312	Constantine wins battle of Milvian Bridge under the sign of the Cross: Christianity declared official state religion	313–22	First Christian basilica built in Rome
360–3	Julian the Apostate Emperor		
378–95	Theodosius the Great Emperor		
395	Division of the Empire between the sons of Theodosius		
410	Sack of Rome by Alaric the Visigoth		
	Rome formally renounces Britain	430	Death of Saint Augustine
439	Vandals conquer Carthage and Africa		
476	End of Roman Empire in the West		
527–65	Justinian, eastern emperor, seeks to reconquer Italy and Africa		The *Digest* of Roman Law is compiled
		529	Justinian orders the closure of the Academy at Athens
633–55	Arab conquest of Syria, Egypt, and the Sassanid Empire		
1453	Conquest of Constantinople by the Turks and end of the Eastern Roman Empire		

LIST OF ILLUSTRATIONS

ENDPAPERS

Front Battle between Macedonians and Persians: details of Alexander Sarcophagus. Marble, *c.* 325–300 B C. Ht. of frieze 69 cm. Istanbul Archaeological Museum. (Hirmer Photoarchiv).

Back Roman soldiers in front of a fort: Trajan's Column, Rome (A D 113). Marble (cast). Ht. of frieze approx. 1.25 m. (Photo German Archaeological Institute, Rome).

COLOUR PLATES

BLACK-AND-WHITE ILLUSTRATIONS

INDEX

Set and printed in Great Britain by
Butler & Tanner Ltd.
Frome, Somerset